EJ Hanson
Horticulture

Physiology of
Woody Plants

Physiology of Woody Plants

Paul J. Kramer

Department of Botany
Duke University
Durham, North Carolina

Theodore T. Kozlowski

Department of Forestry
University of Wisconsin
Madison, Wisconsin

ACADEMIC PRESS, INC.

(Harcourt Brace Jovanovich, Publishers)

Orlando   San Diego   San Francisco   New York
London   Toronto   Montreal   Sydney   Tokyo

ACADEMIC PRESS, INC.
Orlando, Florida 32887

United Kingdom Edition published by
ACADEMIC PRESS, INC. (LONDON) LTD.
24/28 Oval Road, London NW1 7DX

Library of Congress Cataloging in Publication Data

Kramer, Paul Jackson, Date
    Physiology of woody plants.

    Based in part on the author's Physiology of
trees published by McGraw–Hill, 1960.
    Bibliography: p.
    1. Woody plants––Physiology. 2. Trees––
Physiology. I. Kozlowski, Theodore Thomas,
Date joint author. II. Title.
QK711.2.K72   582'.15'041   78–27356
ISBN 0–12–425050–5

PRINTED IN THE UNITED STATES OF AMERICA

84 85 86 87   9 8 7 6 5 4 3

Contents

5 PHOTOSYNTHESIS

6 ENZYMES, ENERGETICS, AND RESPIRATION

7 CARBOHYDRATES

8 LIPIDS, TERPENES, AND RELATED SUBSTANCES

NITROGEN METABOLISM AND NUTRITION

 MINERAL NUTRITION AND SALT ABSORPTION

 TRANSLOCATION

 THE IMPORTANCE OF WATER AND THE PROCESS OF TRANSPIRATION

 ABSORPTION OF WATER, ASCENT OF SAP, AND WATER BALANCE

Contents

Preface

This book was written for use as a text by students and teachers and as a reference by investigators and others who desire a better understanding of how trees grow. It should be useful to a wide range of people, including arborists, foresters, horticulturists, plant physiologists, ecologists, and even those who merely wish to know more about trees. It is difficult to write for such a varied audience because of the wide differences in their knowledge and interests. However, it must be assumed that users will have some knowledge of elementary botany and physiology. Nevertheless, we realize that some readers may find parts of the book too technical, while others may find the same sections too elementary. We started with the assumption that it is necessary to understand how trees grow in order to grow trees efficiently. Therefore, we remind those practical people who find some sections rather technical and theoretical that it is necessary to introduce some biochemistry in order to understand physiological processes, such as photosynthesis and respiration, which play essential roles in tree growth. On the other hand, those who find some sections rather elementary are reminded that this book was written primarily for foresters and horticulturists rather than for specialists in plant physiology. This volume is intended to explain how physiological processes are involved in growth of woody plants and how they are affected by the environment, in addition to explaining the mechanisms of the processes themselves.

The viewpoint of this book is somewhat different from that in most textbooks of plant physiology because it places strong emphasis on tree structure and on the interactions of trees and stands of trees with their environment. Considerable attention is devoted to environmental physiology, that is, to the effects of environmental factors on physiological processes. Thus our approach is more ecological than biochemical, although it is made clear that environmental factors operate at the cellular and molecular level. For example, light and temperature affect photosynthesis at the cellular level by affecting guard cell behavior and at the molecular level through effects on the biochemical and biophysical processes occurring in the chloroplasts. There also are repeated references to the internal control systems that regulate and coordinate growth of various tissues and organs and rates of various processes, producing the harmonious combination of structure and function necessary for a plant to thrive.

We emphasize the close interrelationship between structure and function because it is impossible to understand the processes of a plant without understanding its structure. Furthermore, the structure of a tree comes into existence as the result of a complex series of physiological processes that are too often hidden behind the term "growth." We have therefore given considerable attention to structure and the processes by which the various tissues and organs of trees are produced. Vegetative and sexual reproduction are discussed in detail, both because they are important and because they illustrate interesting and important physiological processes.

This book represents a revision, expansion, and updating of two earlier books, "Physiology of Trees" and the two-volume "Growth and Development of Woody Plants." In this volume attention is given to the physiology of ornamental woody plants as well as forest and orchard trees. Readers should understand that the same general physiological processes operate in all kinds of woody and herbaceous plants.

A list of general references has been placed at the end of each chapter and papers cited in the text are listed in the Bibliography at the end of the book. We have attempted to present significant reference material from the world literature so as to make the work authoritative and well documented. Many references refer to recent work but some refer to older work, either because they are interesting historically or because they provide data not available from more recent work. The number of research publications has increased tremendously in the two decades since "Physiology of Trees" was written. It therefore was possible to cite only a fraction of the relevant literature, and we have omitted many important papers. In spite of the great increase in research and publication there is a lack of definitive information on many important topics and much uncertainty about some. Contrasting views have sometimes been presented and in many instances we have given our personal interpretations of the available information. We caution readers that as new information is acquired some conclusions will need to be revised, and we hope that readers will be ready to modify their views when changes become necessary.

In the text, common names are generally used for well-known species and Latin names for less common ones. A list of scientific names and common names of species, when available, is given following the text. Names of North American forest trees are based on E. L. Little's "Check List of Native and Naturalized Trees of the United States," Agriculture Handbook No. 41, U.S. Forest Service, Washington, D.C. (1953). Names of other species are from various sources.

We express our appreciation for the contributions of the many people who assisted directly and indirectly in the preparation of this book. Much information and stimulation came from our graduate students and from foresters, plant physiologists, and horticulturists all over the world with whom we have worked and discussed problems. We also express our appreciation to the Atomic Energy Commission, the National Science Foundation, the Fulbright Commission, the Food and Agriculture Organization of the United Nations, the U.S. Department of Agriculture, the International Society of Arboriculture, the Wisconsin Department of Natural Resources, the School of Natural Resources and Graduate School of the University of Wisconsin, and the Department of Botany of Duke University, as well as other agencies that financed our research and travel. The senior author also wishes to acknowledge the role of the late C. F. Korstian who first directed his attention to the need for research in the field of tree physiology.

The entire manuscript was read by Henry Hellmers and various chapters were read by R. S. Alberte, R. H. Burris, D. I. Dickmann, J. P. Helgeson, W. Lopushinsky, P. E. Marshall, A. W. Naylor, S. G. Pallardy, R. P. Pharis, C. W. Ralston, J. N. Siedow, E. L. Stone, and B. R. Strain. Their helpful suggestions are greatly appreciated. However, the text has gone through various revisions since they read it, and they should not be held responsible for any errors that may occur. Others who assisted in preparation of the manuscript include J. Buriel, K. Henning, R. C. Koeppen, T. L. Noland, and M. Peet. S. G. Pallardy assisted in preparation of the Index.

Paul J. Kramer
Theodore T. Kozlowski

1

The Role of Plant Physiology

INTRODUCTION

This book describes how trees grow, in contrast to books on silviculture and horticulture which describe how to grow trees. It deals with the physiology of woody plants of all sizes. However, because of their large size, long life, and low ratio of photosynthetic to nonphotosynthetic tissue, trees present special problems and will be used most frequently as examples. Nevertheless, the basic physiological processes are similar in all seed plants so what is said about trees applies to shrubs if adjustments are made for differences in size and length of life.

Trees have different meanings for different people. For our ancestors they were a source of fuel and shelter and sometimes an object of worship. To the home owner they are a source of pleasant shade in the summer, but in the autumn a nuisance which shed leaves on the lawn. Wood was once the chief source of fuel and, as other fuels become scarcer, trees may again become an important renewable source of fuel. To the arborist trees are ornamental objects in the landscape; to conservationists and sportsmen they protect watersheds and game and provide recreation; to the foresters they are a source

1

of timber and pulpwood; and to horticulturists they are a means of producing fruit. To physiologists, however, trees are complex biochemical factories which grow from seeds and literally build themselves. Physiologists are therefore interested in the numerous metabolic processes that collectively produce what we term "growth."

The magnitude of the synthetic process occurring in trees is emphasized by the fact that a hectare (2.47 acres) of temperate zone forest produces about 20 metric tons of dry matter annually, and a hectare of tropical rain forest as much as 100 tons. Readers are warned that these numbers refer to gross, not net, productivity; the latter being much lower, as will be seen in Table 6.1 and in Kira (1975). All of this material is produced from relatively simple raw materials: water, carbon dioxide, and a few kilograms of nitrogen and mineral salts. Thus the success of trees and other green plants depends on their efficiency in manufacturing carbohydrates, nitrogen-containing compounds, and lipids and converting them into new plant tissue. However, growth involves much more than a series of synthetic processes. There must be absorption of sufficient water and mineral nutrients, translocation of organic and inorganic substances to growing regions, and control systems which correlate the numerous processes. This book attempts to explain how these processes occur, how they are affected by the environment and by cultural practices, and how all of these interacting factors affect the quantity and quality of growth.

Plant physiologists are primarily interested in learning how trees grow, while arborists, foresters, and horticulturists are interested primarily in how to grow trees efficiently. The two objectives are more closely related than generally supposed because in order to grow trees efficiently one must understand the basic physiological processes which control growth and how they are affected by environmental factors and cultural processes. Thus basic physiological research can contribute to silvicultural and horticultural research and vice versa. The greatest overall progress will occur when physiologists learn more about how trees grow while foresters and horticulturalists learn more about the physiology of trees, and the two groups cooperate to solve the problems of growing trees as efficiently as possible.

THE ROLE OF PLANT PHYSIOLOGY

The general role of plant physiology is to explain how plants grow and respond to environmental factors and cultural treatments in terms of their physiological processes and conditions. Study of processes such as photosynthesis, translocation, assimilation, respiration, and transpiration may seem far removed from the practice of forestry or horticulture. However, growth is the result of the interaction of physiological processes, and in order to understand why trees grow differently in various environments and with different cultural treatments it is necessary to understand the nature of these physiological processes and how they are affected by the environment.

Nearly everyone knows that the growth of trees, like that of all other organisms, is controlled by their inherited genetic potentialities and their environment, but too little consideration is given to the means by which this control is exerted. To say that shade or drought reduces growth, or that a new combination of genes is responsible for rapid growth of a hybrid, does not really explain how the observed effects are brought about. We need a better understanding of how various causes produce their respective effects. The following diagram shows how heredity and environment interact through the internal physiological processes and conditions of trees to control the quantity and quality of growth. It also shows the relationships among several fields of science which are involved in the study of these phenomena.

Hereditary Potentialities
 The field of genetics
 Selection and breeding programs
 Potential rate of growth, size and longevity of
  trees
 Type of xylem, depth and extent of root systems

Environmental Factors
 The field of ecology, soil science, climatology,
  meteorology, etc.
 Radiation, temperature, minerals, competition,
  pests, silvicultural practices, etc.

Physiological Processes and Conditions
 The field of plant physiology
 Photosynthesis, carbohydrate and nitrogen
  metabolism
 Respiration, translocation
 Plant water balance and its effects on growth and
  metabolism,
 Growth regulators, etc.

Quantity and Quality of Growth
 The field of arboriculture, forestry, and
  horticulture
 Amount and quality of wood, fruit, or seed
  produced
 Vegetative versus reproductive growth
  Root versus shoot growth

Klebs's Concept

This scheme sometimes is called Klebs's concept because the German plant physiologist Klebs (1913, 1914) was one of the first to point out that environmental factors can affect plant processes only by changing internal processes and conditions. Lundegardh (1931) also made important contributions to this viewpoint. Klebs's concept emphasizes the basic biological principle that the only way in which heredity or environment can affect the growth of an organism is by affecting its internal processes and conditions. The physiological processes of a tree constitute the machinery through which heredity and environment operate to control growth. Therefore, in order to understand why trees are affected by any particular factor or treatment, we must learn how that factor or treatment affects their physiological processes.

Applications of Klebs's Concept

The application of this concept can be illustrated by some specific examples. For instance, if a hybrid grows faster than its parents in the same environment it is because a new combination of genes has produced a more efficient balance of physiological processes, resulting in more food being converted into plant tissue. This may result from increased efficiency of structures or processes, or both. The rate of photosynthesis per unit of leaf area might be increased by increased chlorophyll content, or by structural changes which increase the intake of carbon dioxide or by better exposure of leaves to light. A more extensive root system or a thicker layer of cutin might result in maintenance of a higher level of turgidity in the tree, which in turn would be favorable for photosynthesis and also for cell enlargement.

If a certain slash pine produces more gum than its neighbors in the same environment, this probably is caused by a different genetic constitution resulting in higher rates of those processes which cause food to be converted into gum. Another possibility is that structural differences increase the rate of gum flow. If one species exhibits greater cold or drought resistance or greater shade tolerance than another, it is because its genetic constitution produces differences in structures and or processes which result in more resistance to unfavorable environmental conditions.

Even though a change in rate of growth can be attributed to some structural modification, basically it is dependent on a change in processes. Structures are the products of biochemical processes included in the complex of physiological processes involved in growth, and changes in structure result from changes in processes. Thus processes control structure even though they also are modified by changes in structure.

Unfavorable environmental conditions reduce tree growth because they interfere with various essential physiological processes. For example, water deficits reduce growth because they cause closure of stomata, reduction in photosynthesis, loss of turgidity, cessation of cell enlargement, and other unfavorable conditions within the tree. A deficiency of nitrogen reduces growth because nitrogen is an essential constituent of the proteins required for formation of new protoplasm, enzymes, and other essential substances. Phosphorus, potassium, calcium, sulfur, and other mineral elements are essential because they function as constituents of various structures of essential compounds such as coenzymes, in buffer systems, and in other biochemical systems essential for proper functioning of various physiological processes.

Attacks by insects and fungi reduce tree growth or cause death only when the injury severely interferes with one or more physiological processes. Defoliation of a tree does not reduce growth directly, but does so indirectly by reducing the amount of photosynthesis and synthesis of growth regulators in the crown. If the phloem is attacked, injury to the tree results from decreased translocation of food and growth regulators to the roots, and damage to the root system is harmful to the tree because it reduces the absorption of water and nutrients from the soil. Pathologists and entomologists sometimes have been too much concerned with the description and classification of the causal organisms and have tended to overlook the fact that they were really dealing with physiological problems. Resistance to attacks of insects and fungi is largely biochemical in nature, and injury is the result of disturbance of biochemical and physiological processes. Just as the control of human diseases has progressed enormously through the use of biochemical and physiological approaches, so will the control of tree diseases become more successful as entomologists and pathologists become more aware of the physiological aspects of the problem, instead of merely describing organisms and applying sprays.

We repeat for the sake of emphasis that the only way in which genetic differences, environmental factors, cultural practices, and diseases and insects can affect tree growth is by affecting their internal physiological processes and conditions. The operations of arborists, foresters, and horticulturists should be aimed at producing the most favorable genotypes and environments possible for the operation of the physiological machinery which really controls growth. To do this effectively and efficiently they must understand the nature of the principal physiological processes, their roles in growth, and their reactions to various environmental factors.

THE SCOPE OF TREE PHYSIOLOGY

As Huber (1937) stated, trees have always been regarded by nonbotanists as representing the apex of development in the plant kingdom. Because of their size and beauty they have often been credited with a special personality and have even been worshipped. The peculiar characteristics of trees are a matter of degree rather than of kind, however. They go through the same stages of growth and carry on the same processes as other seed plants, but their larger size, slower maturity, and longer life accentuate certain problems as compared with smaller plants having a shorter life span. The most obvious difference between trees and herbaceous plants is the greater distance over which water, minerals, and food must be translocated and the larger percentage of nonphotosynthetic tissue in trees. Also, because of their longer life span, they usually are exposed to greater variations and extremes of temperature and other climatic and soil conditions than annuals or biennials. Thus, just as trees are notable for their large size, they are also notable for their special physiological problems.

Some Important Physiological Processes and Conditions

The successful growth of trees depends on the interaction of a large number of processes and conditions. Some of the more important physiological processes and the chapters in which they are discussed are listed below:

Photosynthesis: the synthesis of carbohydrates from carbon dioxide and water, by which the chlorophyllous tissue of trees provides the basic food materials for other processes (see Chapter 5)

Nitrogen metabolism: the incorporation of inorganic nitrogen into organic compounds, making possible the synthesis of proteins and protoplasm itself (see Chapter 9)

Lipid or fat metabolism: synthesis of lipids and related compounds (see Chapter 8)

Respiration: the oxidation of food in living cells, releasing the energy used in assimilation, mineral absorption, and other energy-using processes (see Chapter 6)

Assimilation: the conversion of food into new protoplasm, cell walls, and other substances; a basic process in growth (see Chapter 6)

Accumulation of food: the storage of food in seeds and in the parenchyma cells of the wood and bark (see Chapter 7)

Accumulation of salt: the concentration of salt in cells and tissues by an active transport mechanism dependent on the expenditure of metabolic energy (see Chapter 10)

Absorption: the intake of water and minerals from the soil and oxygen and carbon dioxide from the air (see Chapters 5, 10, and 13)

Translocation: the movement of water, minerals, foods, and hormones from place to place in trees (see Chapter 11)

Transpiration: the loss of water in the form of vapor (see Chapter 12)

Growth: permanent increase in size, resulting from the interaction of the various processes listed above (see Chapter 3)

Reproduction: production of cones or flowers, and fruits and seeds; this also results from the interaction of a number of physiological processes

Vegetative reproduction: plays an important role in some species (see Chapter 4)

Growth regulation: the complex interaction of hormones and nutritional balance (see Chapters 15 and 16).

Some of the important physiological conditions affecting growth are as follows:

Amount and efficiency of chlorophyll (see Chapter 5)

Kinds and amounts of carbohydrates present and their interconversion, for example, change of starch to sugar and the reverse (see Chapter 7)

Kinds and amounts of nitrogen compounds and the ratio of carbohydrates to nitrogen (see Chapter 9)

Kinds and amounts of other constituents, such as fats (see Chapters 6 and 8)

Protoplasmic characteristics: cold and drought resistance probably are at least partly dependent on special characteristics of protoplasm (see Chapter 16)

Osmotic pressure of cell sap: increased osmotic pressure is often associated with exposure to drought and cold (see Chapter 14)

Turgidity of cells: loss of turgidity causes cessation of growth and affects rates of various physiological processes (see Chapters 13 and 16)

To physiologists belongs the task of measuring these conditions and processes, studying their mechanisms, observing their reaction to various environmental conditions, and identifying their role in tree growth. The more physiologists can learn about the mechanisms of the principal physiological processes, the better they can assist foresters and horticulturists in solving their practical problems. If we knew enough about the physiological requirements of trees, we could predict how a particular species would behave in a particular soil or climatic condition, or how it would react to a particular treatment.

Complexity of Physiological Processes

A physiological process such as photosynthesis, respiration, or transpiration actually is an aggregation of chemical and physical processes. In order to understand the mechanism of a physiological process it is necessary to resolve it into its physical and chemical components, and plant physiology depends more and more on the methods of biochemistry in its efforts to accomplish this. The biochemical approach has been very fruitful, as shown by the progress made toward a better understanding of such complicated processes as photosynthesis and respiration.

The primary objective of this book is to explain how trees grow, and our approach is more ecological than biochemical, giving more attention to the manner in which processes are affected by environmental factors than to detailed discussions of physiological processes. However, we will discuss briefly how environmental factors operate at the cellular and molecular level. Factors such as temperature, water, and light affect physiological processes directly, in straightforward ways which are easily explained, and indirectly by circuitous control systems which are more difficult to explain.

For example, decreasing temperature reduces the rate of respiration by slowing molecular motion, which reduces the rate of chemical reactions. It also decreases the permeability of membranes and increases the viscosity of protoplasm, thereby decreasing the rate at which reactants move to reaction sites on membranes. Furthermore, low temperature produces complex, indirect effects such as the breaking of dormancy and "bolting" or premature flowering which presumably are caused by changes in concentration of growth-regulating hormones. This must involve the activation and/or inactivation of genes which control the synthesis of specific enzyme proteins. Water stress reduces cell enlargement and stomatal opening directly by reduction in cell turgor, but it also has important indirect effects on enzyme-mediated processes such as protein synthesis. Light has a specific direct effect on photosynthesis but it also has important indirect effects on growth and flowering (photomorphogenesis) through gene regulation of enzymatically controlled synthesis of growth regulators. Mineral nutrients likewise have direct effects as constituents of important cell components and indirect effects as coenzymes. Many of these effects will be discussed in more detail in later chapters.

Processes Controlling Various Stages of Growth

It has been recognized ever since the time of Sachs that different physiological processes are most important at various stages of growth. For example, conditions often are so favorable for seed germination under pine stands that numerous pine seedlings appear, but conditions are unfavorable for seedling establishment and they die within a year or two. Climatic and soil conditions in a region may be favorable for vegetative growth but so unfavorable for reproduction that, although trees of a certain species thrive when planted, they are unable to reproduce themselves. In Table 1.1 are indicated the principal processes which seem to dominate each stage of growth and the environmental factors which are most important. We lack a full understanding of these processes, and it is probable that our ideas about the role of some of them will be revised after future study.

TABLE 1.1   Important Processes and Environmental Factors at Various Stages of Growth

Stage	Processes and conditions	Most important environmental factors
Seed germination	Absorption of water Digestion Respiration Assimilation	Temperature Water Oxygen
Seedling establishment	Photosynthesis Assimilation Internal water balance	Light Water Temperature Nutrients
Vegetative growth	Photosynthesis Respiration Assimilation Translocation Internal water balance	Light Water Temperature Nutrients
Reproduction	Photosynthesis C/N balance Readiness to flower Initiation of flower primordia Accumulation of food	Light Nutrients Temperature
Senescence	Unknown (possibly water and hormonal relations, translocation, and balance between photosynthesis and respiration)	Water Nutrients Insects and diseases

PROBLEMS AND PROSPECTS

Differing Problems of Foresters, Horticulturists, and Arborists

Trees are grown for quite different reasons by foresters, horticulturists, and arborists, and the kinds of physiological problems which are of greatest importance in each field vary accordingly. Foresters are concerned chiefly with producing the maximum amount of wood per unit of land area and they must deal with trees growing in stands and with factors affecting competition among the trees in a stand. Horticulturists are concerned chiefly with the production of fruit, hence they wish to get trees to flower and fruit at the earliest possible age. Because of the high value of orchard trees, horticulturists, like arborists, can often afford to deal with problems of individual trees and they are greatly concerned with the control of insect and fungus pests. Arborists are most concerned with growing individual trees and shrubs of good form and appearance which must create aesthetically pleasing effects regardless of soil and other environmental conditions. As a result, arborists often have problems caused by poor drainage, inadequate aeration, soil filling or root damage resulting from construction, gas leaks, air pollution, and other environmental injuries. Although the primary objectives of arborists, foresters, and horticulturists are different, attainment of them has a common requirement, a good understanding of tree physiology.

Physiology in Relation to Present and Future Problems

Important changes are occurring in silvicultural and horticultural methods which have already produced some problems, and on the basis of our knowledge of tree physiology it can be predicted that more will develop. Increased exploitation of tropical forests is disclosing problems not encountered in the temperate zones (Johnson, 1976) and increasing interest in wood quality requires a better understanding of the factors controlling wood density and other properties. The use of shorter rotations will emphasize the need to obtain more rapid growth (Brown, 1976) and also will probably produce mineral nutrition problems, as will more complete utilization of trees (see Chapter 10). Most silvicultural and horticultural treatments such as thinning, pruning, and fertilization are successful only to the extent to which they improve the physiological functioning of trees.

Some procedures which are economically desirable may be physiologically undesirable. For example, it has been suggested that if deciduous fruit trees in the Central Valley of California were chemically defoliated in the autumn, pruning could be started sooner. However, if late season photosynthesis contributes significantly to the carbohydrate reserves of these trees, premature defoliation would be very undesirable. It often is convenient to lift seedlings from the nursery and package them far in advance of planting time, but this can be injurious if their carbohydrate reserves are depleted while in storage. Also, the largest seedlings are not necessarily those most likely to show best survival when outplanted and we need to learn more about how to produce physiologically successful seedlings. To do this requires additional information on food accumulation and on seasonal variation in the ability of seedlings to produce new roots. The increasing production of seedlings in containers also will increase interest in the physiology of seedling production. Tree improvement and breeding programs have created a need for methods for inducing earlier flowering, more abundant seed production, and more successful rooting of cuttings (see Chapter 4). This creates contradictory demands because early physiological maturity is desired for flowering and seed production, but maintenance of the juvenile condition is desired to facilitate rooting of cuttings. The possibility of using cell and tissue culture methods to reproduce desirable genotypes is just beginning to be investigated.

Horticulturists have made more progress than foresters in understanding the physiology of trees, especially in the field of mineral nutrition. However, numerous problems remain, such as shortening the time required to bring fruit trees into bearing, the elimination of biennial bearing in some varieties, and the elimination of excessive fruit drop. An old problem which is becoming more serious as new land becomes less available is the difficulty of replanting old orchards, the "replant" problem. This is likely to become more important in forestry with use of shorter rotations (see Chapter 17). There also is increasing use of dwarf trees, often planted in hedges, to reduce the labor costs of pruning, spraying, and fruit picking. This new approach has created a strong interest in dwarfing rootstocks and probably will be accompanied by development of new physiological problems.

Arborists also are interested in small, compact trees for small city lots and both arborists and horticulturists are concerned with the problem of aging because of the short life of some important fruit and ornamental trees. Unfortunately, practically nothing is known about the biochemistry or physiology of aging or why bristlecone pine and Sequoia trees live to an age of 3,000 or 4,000 years while peach trees and some other kinds of trees live only a few decades.

We also need to consider the effects of small but measurable changes in such environmental factors as the CO_2 concentration of the atmosphere and temperature. The CO_2 concentration is increasing steadily and may reach 400 ppm by the year 2000, which could produce a significant increase in temperature, the so-called greenhouse effect (Baes *et al.*, 1977). On the other hand, temperatures in the northern hemisphere have been decreasing for several decades and the direction of the long-term trend is uncertain. It would be desirable to learn what the effect of increasing CO_2 and small decreases or increases in temperature will be on important tree species. Various species may react differently and knowledge of this will be useful in planning future plantings, especially where temperature already is a limiting factor. Air pollution also will continue to be a serious problem in some areas and we need to know more about why some species are injured more than others.

Trees once were the chief source of fuel and they still are an important source of chemicals. Concern about future sources of energy is stimulating renewed interest in forests as renewable sources of fuel and of chemicals now produced from coal and oil. According to Smith and Johnson (1977), forests are a more efficient source than annual crops in terms of the energy harvested per unit of energy invested. As the energy cost of planting and harvesting is much greater than the cost of growing tree crops, an increase in length of the rotation might increase the efficiency of energy use. This might require reconsideration of the current trend toward shorter rotations and even of what is the best type of tree.

More Productive Use of Physiology

Foresters and horticulturists sometimes complain that physiological research largely explains already known behavior and contributes little to improving the production of wood and fruit. It is true that the contributions of physiology have been more explanatory than predictive. For example, research on root physiology explained why cold or wet soil damages roots and reduces water and mineral absorption, research on plant water relations explained why droughts reduce growth, and research on cold resistance explained why some species can survive in lower temperatures than others. We now need to use physiological information more effectively in breeding and selecting plants that grow more successfully when subjected to various environmental stresses.

To do this we must determine which stresses are most limiting in various situations and through what physiological processes they are operating to limit growth and yield. Selection usually is for such general characteristics as cold or drought resistance, or simply for yield as measured by diameter and height growth or weight of fruit produced. Many physiological processes contribute to yield, and physiologists must determine which processes are most likely to be limiting in a particular environment. Is it water stress? If so, is it operating chiefly through stomatal closure, decreasing uptake of CO_2 and reducing photosynthesis or in part by decreasing leaf area, or by damage to the chloroplasts. Can water stress be avoided or postponed by selection for deeper root systems, better stomatal and cuticular control of transpiration, or some other factor? After physiologists have determined what physiological processes are limiting growth in particular environments, plant breeders can work more effectively toward producing plants tolerant of these limitations.

The slow progress being made in solving problems of tree growth results less from lack of information than from failure to use existing information (Minckler, 1976). Failure to make effective use of existing information results in part from lack of imagination and in part from lack of exchange of ideas between field and laboratory workers. There is too much compartmentation, some bureaucratic and some merely mental, between workers in various fields of forestry and horticulture. Efficient solution of problems in forestry and horticulture requires cooperative research by various kinds of scientists who are willing to combine their different skills and knowledge.

The prospects for productive research in tree physiology seem increasingly good both because there is a better understanding of the role of physiology and because of improvements in equipment and techniques. Among the important technological improvements are the introduction of chromatography, tracers labeled with radioactive isotopes, infrared gas analyzers, diffusion porometers, and methods for measuring water potential. The use of controlled environment chambers to analyze the effect of environmental factors and the use of computers to model growth and predict effects of environmental factors and silvicultural treatments are particularly important developments.

We hope that readers will be challenged to contribute to filling some of the gaps in our knowledge that are indicated in the following chapters.

GENERAL REFERENCES

Bidwell, R. G. S. (1974). "Plant Physiology." Macmillan, New York.

Bonner, J., and Varner, J. E., eds. (1976). "Plant Biochemistry," 3rd ed. Academic Press, New York.

Büsgen, M., and Münch, E. (1931). "The Structure and Life of Forest Trees," 3rd ed. Wiley, New York.

Cannell, M. G. R., and Last, F. T., eds. (1976). "Tree Physiology and Yield Improvement." Academic Press, New York.

Kozlowski, T. T. (1971). "Growth and Development of Trees," 2 vols. Academic Press, New York.

Larcher, W. (1975). "Physiological Plant Ecology." Springer-Verlag, Berlin and New York.

Leopold, A. C., and Kriedemann, P. E. (1975). "Plant Growth and Development," 2nd ed. McGraw-Hill, New York.

Lundegardh, H. (1931). "Environment and Plant Development." Arnold, London.

Lyr, H., Polster, H., and Fielder, H. J. (1967). "Gehölzphysiologie." Fischer, Jena.

Miksche, J. P., ed. (1976). "Modern Methods in Forest Genetics." Springer-Verlag, Berlin and New York.

Salisbury, F. B., and Ross, C. W. (1978). "Plant Physiology." 2nd ed. Wadsworth, Belmont, California.

Zimmermann, M. H., and Brown, C. L. (1971). "Trees. Structure and Function." Springer-Verlag, Berlin and New York.

$\mathbb{2}$

Structure

INTRODUCTION

Knowledge of variations in the form and structure of woody plants is as essential to the understanding of physiological processes as is a knowledge of chemistry. For example, crown characteristics have important implications in many physiological processes that influence growth and various expressions of growth such as shoot growth, apical dominance, cambial growth, root growth, and competition among woody plants.

It is necessary to know something about leaf structure in order to understand how photosynthesis and transpiration are affected by various environmental factors. Information on stem structure is basic to understanding ascent of sap, translocation of food, and cambial growth; and a knowledge of root structure is important for an appreciation of the mechanisms of absorption of water and salts. Because every physiological process is more or less affected by the structure of the tissues and organs in which it

13

occurs, a knowledge of anatomy is essential to an understanding of growth processes in woody plants.

A tree may be regarded as consisting of six organs. Three of these—leaves, stems, and roots—are vegetative structures, while the other three—flowers, fruits, and seeds—are reproductive structures. Each of these organs is composed of a number of tissues. Xylem and phloem tissues are particularly important because they form continuous conducting systems for water, salts, and food between the tips of the deepest roots and the uppermost leaves in the top of the crown. This chapter will discuss the gross morphology and anatomy of leaves, stems, and roots as a basis for later discussion of physiological processes.

LEAVES

The leaves of woody plants play a paramount role in photosynthesis, the process by which practically all energy enters our biosphere. A knowledge of leaf structure is central to understanding the photosynthetic process as well as the process of transpirational water loss from leaves. A relatively large leaf area is necessary for the photosynthesis needed to support good growth.

Structure of Angiosperm Leaves

The typical foliage leaf of angiosperms is composed mainly of primary tissues. The blade or lamina, usually broad and flat and supported by a petiole, contains ground tissues, or mesophyll, enclosed by an upper and lower epidermis. Mesophyll is composed of varying amounts of palisade tissue and spongy parenchyma. The columnar, regularly shaped palisade cells below the upper epidermis (and sometimes above the lower epidermis) are easily distinguished from the irregularly shaped spongy parenchyma cells adjacent to the lower epidermis (Fig. 2.1). There may be only a single

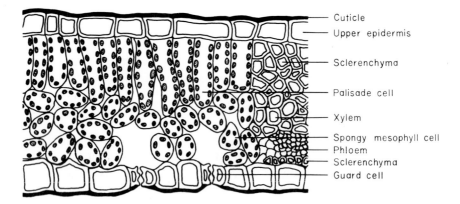

Cuticle
Upper epidermis
Sclerenchyma
Palisade cell
Xylem
Spongy mesophyll cell
Phloem
Sclerenchyma
Guard cell

Fig. 2.1. Transection of a portion of a leaf blade from a broad-leaved tree.

Fig. 2.2. Net venation of leaf of sweet birch. Photo courtesy of D. H. Franck.

layer of palisade cells perpendicularly arranged to the upper epidermis, or there may be as many as three layers (see Fig. 12.10). When more than one layer is present, the cells of the outermost layer are longest, and those of the innermost layer may grade in size to resemble the spongy parenchyma cells. When the difference between palisade and spongy cells is very distinct, most of the chloroplasts are localized in the palisade tissues.

Food, water, and minerals are supplied to and removed from the leaves through veins which thoroughly penetrate the mesophyll tissues (Fig. 2.2). Venation may be netted as in dicotyledons or parallel as in monocotyledons. In parallel venation the veins are connected laterally by numerous small bundles. The vascular bundles of major veins are imbedded in parenchyma tissues and isolated from the mesophyll. In contrast, the minor veins usually are located in the upper part of the spongy parenchyma, and divide the mesophyll into small sections called areoles.

Stomata

The mesophyll tissue has abundant intercellular spaces connected to the outer atmosphere by numerous openings (stomata) in the epidermis, each surrounded by two specialized guard cells (Figs. 2.1 and 2.3). Stomata play an essential role in the physiology of plants because they are the passages through which most water is lost as vapor from leaves and through which most of the carbon dioxide used in photosynthesis enters leaves.

In most broad-leaved trees, stomata occur only on the lower surface of the leaf, but in some woody plants, poplars for example, they occur on both leaf surfaces. When stomata are present on both leaf surfaces they usually are more numerous on the lower surface (Table 2.1).

Of particular physiological importance are the wide variations that occur among species and genetic materials in stomatal size and frequency. For example, stomatal size (guard cell length) varied among 38 species of trees from 17 to 56 μm and stomatal frequency from approximately 100 to 600 stomata/mm^2 of leaf surface (Table 2.2). Generally a species with few stomata per unit of leaf surface tends to have large

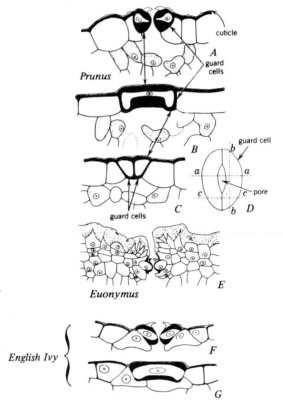

Fig. 2.3.   Stomata of woody angiosperms. A–C: stomata and associated cells from peach leaf sectioned along planes indicated in D by the broken lines, aa, bb, and cc. E–G: stomata of Euonymus and English ivy cut along the plane aa. G: one guard cell of English ivy cut along the plane bb. From Esau (1965).

stomata. For example, sugar maple and silver maple have many small stomata, whereas white ash and white birch have fewer but larger stomata. Oak species are an exception, having both large and numerous stomata. Stomatal size and frequency vary greatly within a genus, as in *Crataegus, Fraxinus,* and *Quercus* (Davies *et al.,* 1973). As may be seen in Table 2.1, differences were found in stomatal size and distribution among species and clones of poplars.

Leaf Waxes

In leaves of many plants, both angiosperms and gymnosperms, the loss of water by cuticular transpiration is decreased by waxy coatings (see Fig. 8.3). The cuticle is considered to be the noncellular membrane that lies over the epidermal cells. It often extends into stomatal openings as a thin lining of the subsurface cavities. The cuticle, a layer of cross-linked hydroxy fatty acids, usually is bounded by a layer of wax (see Chapter 8). The amount of surface wax varies greatly among species and in some may

TABLE 2.1   Variations in Stomatal Distribution (Number of Stomata per cm^2) on Lower and Upper Leaf Surfaces of *Populus* Species[a]

Clone	Lower surface	Upper surface
Populus maximowiczii × *P. nigra*	45,351 ± 1,003	4,216 ± 155
Populus maximowiczii	33,521 ± 868	7,730 ± 242
Populus trichocarpa	23,378 ± 581	5,013 ± 193
Populus deltoides	22,628 ± 408	18,693 ± 575
Populus nigra	20,450 ± 434	5,762 ± 313

[a] From Siwecki and Kozlowski (1973).

TABLE 2.2   Variations in Average Length and Frequency of Stomata of Woody Angiosperms[a]

Species	Stomatal length (μm)	Stomatal frequency (number/mm^2)
Acer saccharinum	17.3	418.8
Acer saccharum	19.3	463.4
Acer negundo	21.6	233.9
Betula nigra	39.4	281.3
Betula papyrifera	33.2	172.3
Catalpa bignonioides	23.2	328.6
Crataegus sp. I.	22.3	399.1
Crataegus sp. II.	37.4	221.4
Fraxinus americana	24.8	257.1
Fraxinus pennsylvanica	29.3	161.6
Ginkgo biloba	56.3	102.7
Gleditsia triacanthos	36.1	156.3
Hamamelis mollis	25.3	161.6
Juglans nigra	25.7	342.0
Malus sp.	23.8	219.5
Populus deltoides	30.4	163.4
Prunus serotina	30.5	306.3
Prunus virginiana	27.1	244.6
Quercus rubra	26.7	532.1
Quercus macrocarpa	24.0	575.9
Quercus palustris	30.9	530.4
Rhus typhina	19.4	633.9
Robinia pseudoacacia	17.6	282.1
Salix fragilis	25.5	215.2
Tilia americana	27.2	278.8
Ulmus americana	26.3	440.2
Vitis vinifera	29.7	120.5

[a] From Davies *et al.* (1973).

represent up to 15% of leaf dry weight. In a number of species the stomatal pores are occluded by deposits of wax which reduce the cross-sectional area available for diffusion of water and carbon dioxide (Kozlowski *et al.*, 1974; Davies and Kozlowski, 1974a).

Structure of Gymnosperm Leaves

Except for a few genera such as *Larix* and some species of *Taxodium* the leaves of gymnosperms are evergreen. Most gymnosperm leaves are linear or lanceolate and bifacially flattened but other shapes also occur. For example, the leaves of *Podocarpus*, spruce, and occasionally larch are tetragonal in cross section. Scalelike leaves are characteristic of *Sequoia*, *Cupressus*, *Chamaecyparis*, *Thuja*, and *Libocedrus*. Broad, ovate, and flat leaves are found in *Araucaria*.

In *Abies*, *Pseudotsuga*, *Dacrydium*, *Sequoia*, *Taxus*, *Torreya*, *Ginkgo*, *Araucaria*, and *Podocarpus*, the leaf mesophyll is differentiated into palisade cells and spongy parenchyma (Fig. 2.4). The leaves of the last two genera have palisade parenchyma on both sides (Esau, 1965). In pines the mesophyll is not differentiated into palisade cells and spongy prenchyma (Fig. 2.5).

Pine needles, which are borne in fascicles, are hemispherical (two-needled species) or triangular (three-needled species). Those of the single-needle pinyon pine are circular in cross section. Sometimes the number of needles per fascicle varies from the typical condition. This often is a response to unusual nutritional conditions, injury, or abnormal development.

In pines the deeply sunken stomata are arranged in rows (Fig. 2.6). Below the epidermis and surrounding the mesophyll is a thick-walled hypodermal layer. Parenchyma cells of the mesophyll are deeply infolded. The one or two vascular bundles per needle are surrounded by transfusion tissue consisting of dead tracheids and living parenchyma cells. Two to several resin ducts also occur in pine needles. The cells of the endodermis, which surrounds the transfusion tissue, are rather thick walled. The epidermis of pine needles has a heavy cuticle and considerable wax is often present in stomatal antechambers (Fig. 2.7).

STEMS

Stems of woody plants support the crown, conduct water and minerals upward from the roots, and conduct foods and hormones from points where they are manufactured to those where they are used in growth or stored for future use.

As may be seen in Figs. 2.8 and 2.9, a mature stem of a temperate zone tree typically consists of a tapering column of wood (xylem) composed of a series of layers or annual increments, added one above the other, like a series of overlapping cones, and enclosed in a covering of bark. At the apex of the stem and each of its branches is a terminal growing point where increase in length occurs. Between the bark and wood of

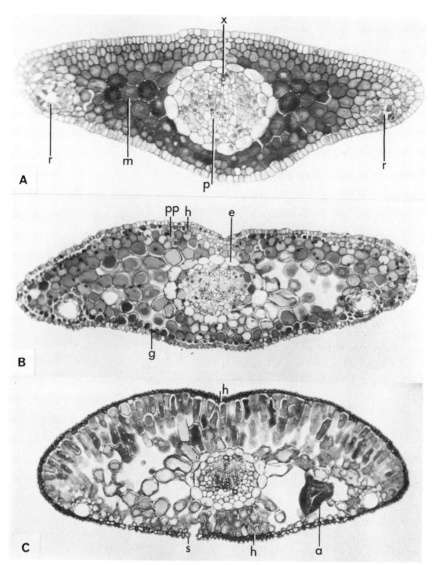

Fig. 2.4. Transections of Douglas-fir needle at various stages of development. A: needle 2 mm long at first stages of differentiation of phloem (p), xylem (x), mesophyll (m), and resin ducts (r). B: leaf which is nearly fully elongated, showing later stages of differentiation of spongy mesophyll, resin ducts, vascular tissue endodermis (e), and hypodermis (h). Note undifferentiated isodiametric palisade parenchyma (pp), differentiating guard cells (g), and large air space in the lamina. C: mature needle with fully differentiated tissues. Note thick cuticle, scattered hypodermis (h), subsidiary cells (s), definite palisade parenchyma, and large air spaces in spongy mesophyll with the large astrosclereid (a). From Owens (1968).

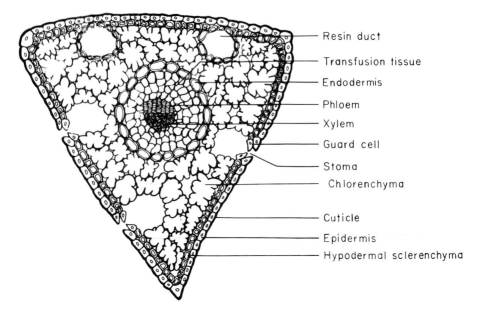

Resin duct

Transfusion tissue

Endodermis

Phloem

Xylem

Guard cell

Stoma

Chlorenchyma

Cuticle

Epidermis

Hypodermal sclerenchyma

Fig. 2.5. Transection of secondary needle of eastern white pine.

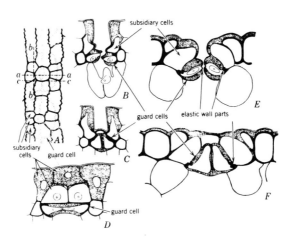

Fig. 2.6. Stomata of gymnosperms. A: surface view of epidermis with sunken stomata of *Pinus merkusii*. B–D: stomata of pines; E and F: stomata of *Sequoia*. The broken lines in A indicate the planes along which the sections were made in B–F: aa, B, E; bb, D; cc, C, F. From Esau (1965).

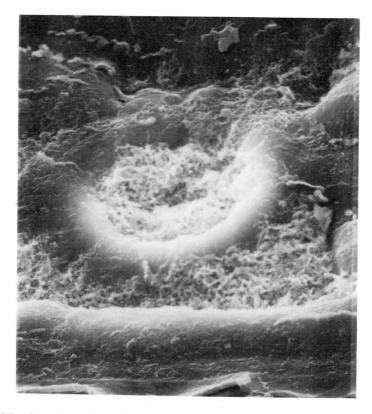

Fig. 2.7. Scanning electron micrograph of surface of red pine needle showing occlusion of antestomatal chamber by waxes (× 1,900). From Davies *et al.* (1974).

the stem, branches, and major roots is the vascular cambium (hereafter called cambium), a thin, sheathing lateral meristem.

Sapwood and Heartwood

Young xylem or sapwood conducts sap (primarily water), strengthens the stem, and to some extent serves as a storage reservoir for food. The living parenchyma cells in the sapwood, which are very important because they store food reserves, consist of transversely oriented ray cells and, in many species of woody plants, of vertically oriented axial parenchyma cells as well. On the average only about 10% of the cells in the sapwood are alive. As the xylem ages all the living cells die and the walls usually become darker, producing a central cylinder of dark-colored dead tissue, called heartwood, which provides mechanical support and is no longer involved in physiological processes. This is demonstrated by the fact that old trees from which the heartwood has been destroyed by decay can survive for many years, supported by a thin shell of

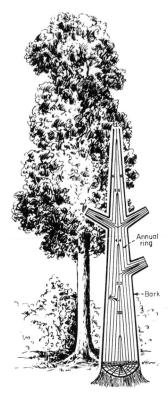

Fig. 2.8. Diagrammatic median longitudinal section of a tree showing pattern of annual xylem increments in the stem and major branches.

sapwood. A great variety of compounds, including oils, gums, resins, and tannins, are deposited in cells as heartwood is formed (see Chapter 16). In trees with dark heartwood a number of phenolic compounds that are highly toxic to fungi are deposited. These include terpenoids, tropolenes, flavonoids, and stilbenes. Once the heartwood begins to form it continues to increase in diameter throughout the life of a tree. The width of the sapwood band varies greatly among species (see Table 2.3), being relatively wide in stems of young trees and narrow in old trees.

Xylem Increments and Annual Rings

In trees of the temperate zone the annual rings of wood (xylem) stand out prominently in stem and branch cross sections because the xylem formed early in the season is composed of cells of larger diameter than that formed later. Wood formed early in the growing season also is less dense than that formed later. Because of the uniformity of composition of gymnosperm xylem, changes in cell wall thickness are closely correlated with changes in density. In angiosperms, however, the density of wood

Outer bark
Inner bark
Cambium
Sapwood
Heartwood

Fig. 2.9. Generalized structure of a tree stem showing orientation of major tissues including outer bark, inner bark, cambium, sapwood, and heartwood. Photo courtesy of St. Regis Paper Co.

TABLE 2.3 Variations in Thickness of Sapwood among Angiosperms[a]

Genus/species	Number of xylem rings in sapwood
Catalpa speciosa	1–2
Robinia pseudoacacia	2–3
Juglans cinerea	5–6
Maclura pomifera	5–10
Sassafras officinale	7–8
Aesculus glabra	10–12
Juglans nigra	10–20
Prunus serotina	10–12
Gleditsia triacanthos	10–12

[a] From Sargent (1926).

depends not only on cell wall thickness but also on the proportion of various cell types present. This proportion is relatively constant within a species and even within many genera, although it varies within a season. However, the arrangement of cells and proportions of different cell types vary greatly among different genera of angiosperms.

Because of the consistent periclinal (tangential) divisions of the cambial cells (see Chapter 3) the young, undifferentiated xylem and phloem cells are regularly aligned in radial rows. In gymnosperms such a regular radial arrangement is generally maintained throughout differentiation of tracheids. In contrast, in angiosperms the early radial alignment of cambial derivatives in the xylem is obscured as some cells, such as vessel members, enlarge greatly and distort the position of rays and adjacent cells. Hence, it is not uncommon for a narrow ray to be bent around a large vessel. However, rays that are many cells wide generally are not affected by the enlarging vessel elements.

As may be seen in Fig. 2.10, angiosperms are classified as ring porous or diffuse porous. In ring-porous trees, such as oaks, ashes, and elms, the diameters of xylem vessels formed early in the growing season are much larger than those formed later. In diffuse-porous trees, such as poplars, maples, and birches, the vessels generally are of small diameter and those formed early in the growing season are of approximately the same diameter as those formed later.

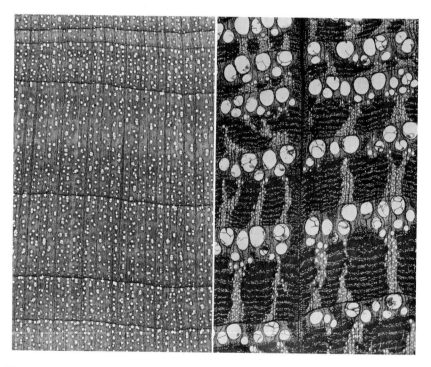

Fig. 2.10. Stem transections showing variation in vessel diameters and distribution within annual growth increments of a diffuse-porous species, silver maple (*left*) and a ring-porous species, white oak (*right*) (× 50). Photo courtesy of U.S. Forest Service.

Considerable variation exists in the outer boundaries of annual xylem growth increments. In areas of high rainfall and cold winters the boundaries between annual xylem increments as seen in cross sections of stems or branches are well defined in comparison to those in species growing in hot, arid regions. In the juvenile core of the stem of a normal tree, the transition from one year's xylem increment to another is gradual nearest the pith and becomes increasingly abrupt in the older wood. In old trees the lines of demarcation between xylem increments generally are very sharp. The width of annual rings is often materially reduced by drought and this fact has been used extensively to study climatic conditions in the past and even to date ancient structures built by man (Fritts, 1976).

Earlywood and Latewood

The wood of low density usually (but not always) produced early in the season will be called "earlywood." The part of the annual xylem increment which usually is produced late in the growing season and is of higher density than wood produced early in the season will be called "latewood." There is much interest in earlywood–latewood relations of trees because they affect wood quality. This is discussed further in Chapter 16.

Earlywood and latewood have been used in the literature as synonyms for "springwood" and "summerwood," but the latter terms are really misnomers because either type of wood may be produced in more than one season in the same year. Chalk (1937) suggested that the terms springwood and summerwood be abandoned but their wide usage has persisted despite their shortcomings. Glock *et al.* (1960) also objected to the terms earlywood and latewood because the latewood sometimes is found at the beginning of a growth layer or as fragments within an annual increment. They preferred to use the terms "lightwood" and "densewood," thereby emphasizing the structure of the tissues rather than the time when tissues form or their relative position within a growth layer or increment.

The boundary between the earlywood and latewood of the same ring can be very sharp or gradual. The boundary is sharp in hard pines, Douglas-fir, larch, and juniper. Ladefoged (1952) found an abrupt earlywood–latewood transition in ring-porous angiosperms and a gradual one in diffuse-porous species. Various arbitrary methods of clearly characterizing both earlywood and latewood have been advanced. One of the most popular standards for gymnosperms is that of Mork (1928) who considered a latewood tracheid to be one in which the width of the common wall between the two neighboring tracheids multiplied by 2 was equal to, or greater than, the width of the lumen. When the value was less than the width of the lumen the xylem was considered to be earlywood. All measurements were made in the radial direction. Mork's definition originally was applied to spruce xylem but has been adopted widely for general use with gymnosperm woods. This definition is not useful for angiosperm woods and, as emphasized by Doley (1974), there often are serious problems in distinguishing between earlywood and latewood in angiosperms.

Within an annual xylem increment the width of the earlywood band generally decreases and the width of the latewood band increases toward the base of the tree. In gymnosperms the earlywood tracheids are wider toward the stem base than at the top within the same xylem increment. The transition between the last earlywood tracheids and first-formed latewood tracheids of the annual increment also is sharper in the lower stem than in the upper stem. This is partly due to the larger diameter of earlywood cells and the thicker walls of the latewood cells present in the lower stem. The very thick walls of latewood cells in the lower stem also contribute to the sharp transition. The narrow diameter earlywood cells in the upper stem contribute to making the earlywood–latewood transition less distinct than it is in the lower stem (Fig. 2.11).

Some tracheids fit the usual definition of latewood because of a decrease in their radial diameter, without appreciable change in wall thickness. Other tracheids, how-

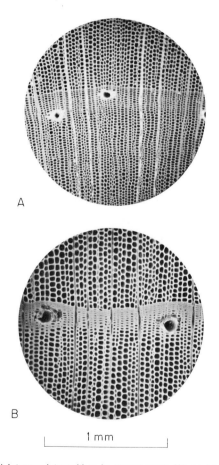

Fig. 2.11. Earlywood–latewood transition in upper stem (A) and lower stem (B) of 10-year-old loblolly pine tree. The transition is sharper in the lower stem because of larger diameter earlywood cells and thicker walled latewood cells in the lower stem than in the upper stem. Photo courtesy of U.S. Forest Service.

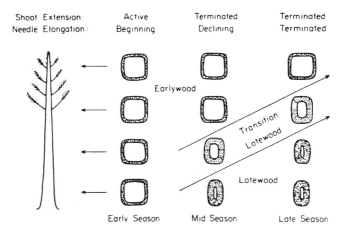

Fig. 2.12. Seasonal variation in formation of earlywood, transition latewood, and latewood at different stem heights of a red pine tree. From Larson (1969b).

ever, become latewood because of an increase in wall thickness without change in diameter. Both dimensions show continuous change from the top of the stem toward the base until the latewood forms. In upper parts of stems "transition latewood" often forms which cannot be conveniently classified as either true earlywood or latewood (Fig. 2.12).

Growth Rings in Tropical Trees

Cambial growth of tropical species is very diverse and appears to be strongly determined by heredity. In many species xylem increment may continue to be added during most or all of the year. Hence, many tropical trees, especially the diffuse-porous species, lack growth rings or have very indistinct ones. Other species produce distinct growth rings, often more than one each year. In subtropical southern Florida, some species which are more or less evergreen, such as *Swietenia mahogani,* have growth rings, while others that are briefly deciduous, such as *Ficus* spp., lack growth rings (Tomlinson and Craighead, 1972). Growth rings may or may not be correlated with periods of shoot growth. For example, in rubber tree saplings, shoot growth occurred in flushes at 42-day intervals, each flush being associated with an increment of xylem leading to a distinct growth ring. By comparison, some tropical pines produce as many as five shoot growth flushes in a year but form only one ring (Tomlinson and Gill, 1973).

The specific anatomical features that delineate growth rings in tropical woods vary greatly among species. In *Acacia catechu,* for example, growth rings are outlined by narrow bands of marginal parenchyma, and sometimes by thick-walled fibers in the outer latewood. The growth rings of *Bombax malabaricum* are identified by radially compressed fibers and parenchyma cells in the outer latewood. The xylem increments of *Shorea robusta* have many irregularly shaped parenchyma bands which sometimes are mistaken for annual rings. These do not always encircle the tree and form more than once a year. When they do form annually they are not produced during the same month each year (Chowdhury, 1939).

Phloem Increments

The annual sheaths of mature phloem are much thinner than the increments of xylem because less phloem than xylem is produced annually. The total thickness of phloem is limited because the old phloem tissues often are crushed, and eventually the external nonfunctional phloem tissues are shed.

In many woody plants the phloem is divided by various structural features into distinguishable growth increments. However, these are not as clearly defined as annual xylem increments. Often the structural differences of early and late phloem are rendered indistinguishable by collapse of sieve tubes and growth of parenchyma cells.

In some species the annual increments of phloem can be delineated because early-phloem cells expand more than those of the late phloem. In pear, tangential bands of fiber sclereids and crystal-containing cells are characteristic boundaries of annual growth of phloem (Evert, 1963). Early- and late-phloem increments sometimes are also identifiable by features of phloem parenchyma. For example, phloem parenchyma cells produced early have little tannin and they collapse when the phloem eventually becomes nonfunctional (Chapter 11). In contrast, the tannin-laden, late-phloem parenchyma cells become turgid. Hence, their appearance is useful in identifying limits of annual increments. In some species the annual increments of phloem can be identified by the number of distinct zones of various types of cells.

It is especially difficult to identify the annual increments of secondary phloem in gymnosperms. Although differences occur in diameters of early and late sieve cells, these often are obscured by pressure from expanding parenchyma cells. In cypress (*Chamaecyparis*) and white cedar the early formed fibers of an annual increment have thicker walls than the fibers formed later. According to Huber (1939) and Holdheide (1951), the early phloem of the Pinaceae is made up almost wholly of sieve elements. As sieve elements collapse they form a dark band which outlines the boundary of the annual increment. Using such criteria, Srivastava (1963) attempted to identify annual growth increments in the phloem of a variety of gymnosperms. The results were variable. Some species, including Jeffrey pine, blue spruce, Norway spruce, and European larch, had distinct growth increments. In a number of other species, however, the boundaries of growth increments were not readily discernible either because phloem parenchyma cells were scattered, or because a distinct line of crushed sieve cells could not be identified between successive bands of phloem parenchyma.

Conducting and Nonconducting Phloem

The layer of phloem that has conducting sieve tubes is exceedingly narrow. For example, the layer of conducting phloem is only about 0.2 mm wide in white ash; 0.2 to 0.3 mm in oak, beech, maple, and birch; 0.4 to 0.7 mm in walnut and elm; and 0.8 to 1.0 mm in willow and poplar (Holdheide, 1951; Zimmermann, 1961). Because of distortions of tissues in the nonconducting phloem it is only in the narrow conducting zone that important characteristics of phloem tissues can be recognized. These include shapes of various phloem elements, presence of nacreous (thickened) walls, structure of sieve plates, and variations among parenchyma cells. After sieve elements cease functioning, several important changes occur in the phloem including intensive sclerification, deposition of crystals, collapse of sieve elements, and dilation of phloem tissues resulting from enlargement and division of axial and ray parenchyma cells. The extent to which each of these changes occurs varies with species. Seasonal changes in phloem are discussed further in Chapter 12 in connection with its role in translocation.

WOOD STRUCTURE OF GYMNOSPERMS

In most gymnosperm stems the longitudinal elements of the xylem consist mainly of tracheids and a few axial parenchyma and epithelial cells (Fig. 2.13). Axial parenchyma cells occur in xylem of redwood and white cedar but not in pine. The transversely oriented elements, which are relatively few, include ray tracheids, ray parenchyma cells, and epithelial cells. Interspersed also are longitudinally and transversely oriented resin canals which are intercellular spaces of postcambial development rather than cellular elements. Resin is secreted into these canals by the adjacent epithelial

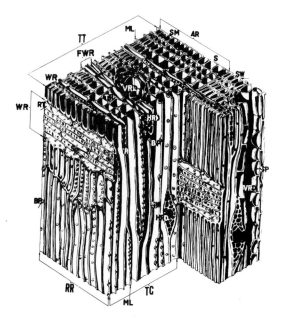

Fig. 2.13. Anatomy of gymnosperm wood. TT: transection; RR: radial section; TG: tangential section; TR: tracheids; ML: middle lamella; S: earlywood; SM or SW: latewood; AR: annual ring; WR: wood ray; RT: ray tracheid; FWR: fusiform wood ray; SP: simple pit; BP: bordered pit; HRD: horizontal resin duct; VRD: vertical resin duct. Photo courtesy of U.S. Forest Service.

cells. Resin canals are a normal feature of pine, spruce, larch, and Douglas-fir. In addition, traumatic resin canals caused by wounding may occur together with normal resin canals, or they may be found in woods lacking normal resin canals such as *Cedrus,* hemlock, and true firs. Commercial production of resin is discussed in Chapter 8.

Longitudinal Elements

As much as 90% of the wood or xylem of gymnosperms is made up of vertically stacked, overlapping tracheids, arranged in rather uniform radial rows. These four-to-six-sided, thick-walled, tapering cells often are as much as 100 times longer than wide. They may vary in length from about 3 to 7 mm, but in most temperate zone gymnosperms they average 3 to 5 mm in length. Those formed early in the growing season are larger in cross section and have thinner walls than those formed later. The transition from large, earlywood cells to small, latewood cells may be gradual as in sugar pine, or it may be abrupt as in loblolly pine or longleaf pine (Fig. 2.14).

Walls of longitudinal tracheids have various types of pits that facilitate transfer of materials between adjacent cells (Figs. 2.15 to 2.17). Large bordered pits develop between adjacent longitudinal tracheids, smaller bordered pits between longitudinal tracheids and ray tracheids, and half-bordered pits between tracheids and ray parenchyma cells. Pits on tracheid walls occur predominantly on radial surfaces and tend to be concentrated near the ends of tracheids.

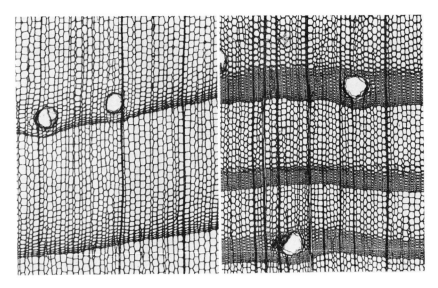

Fig. 2.14. Variations in transition from earlywood to latewood in gymnosperms. Gradual transition of sugar pine (*left*) and abrupt transition in longleaf pine (*right*) (× 27.5). Photo courtesy of U.S. Forest Service.

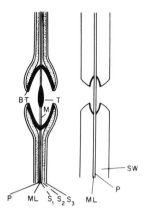

Fig. 2.15. Pit of gymnosperm wood (*left*) and angiosperm wood (*right*). In the gymnosperm wood, ML: middle lamella; P: primary wall; S_1: outside layer of secondary wall; S_2: middle layer of secondary wall; S_3: inner layer of secondary wall; M: pit membrane; T: torus; and BT: initial border thickening. In the angiosperm wood, ML: middle lamella; P: primary wall; and SW: secondary wall. From Wardrop (1962).

Bordered pit pairs have a common membrane of primary walls and a lamella. In such a pit pair the secondary wall of each adjacent cell arches over the pit cavity. In many gymnosperms the pit membrane consists of a disc-shaped or convex, lens-shaped thickening called the torus, surrounded by a thin margin, the margo (Fig. 2.15). Appreciable differences in membrane structure occur. For example, in earlywood of pine the torus is flat and disc-shaped, whereas in latewood it is convex-lens shaped. In *Thuja, Gnetum, Cycas,* and *Welwitschia* the pit membrane lacks a torus (Bauch *et al.,* 1972). The membranes of bordered pits are made up of cellulose strands that radiate from the torus to the margin of the pit cavity. Liquid moves readily through the pores in the margo of the pit membrane when the torus is in a medial position. However, when a pit is aspirated (the torus is pushed against the pit border) (Fig. 2.16) or when pit membranes become encrusted with amorphous substances, the flow of liquid through the pit is restricted (see Chapter 16).

Perforations in the membranes of bordered pits of gymnosperm xylem vary from less than 1 nm* to several nm in the same pit. Pit diameter also varies greatly among species. The bordered pits of gymnosperms are more numerous and much larger in earlywood than in latewood of the same annual ring (Fig. 2.17). There appears to be much more resistance to water transport in latewood than in earlywood (Kozlowski *et al.,* 1966).

When present in gymnosperms axial parenchyma occurs as long strands. Axial parenchyma is relatively abundant in redwood and bald cypress, sparse in larch and Douglas-fir, and absent in pines.

*1 nm or nanometer $= 10^{-9}$ m, 10^{-6} mm, or 10^{-3} μm.

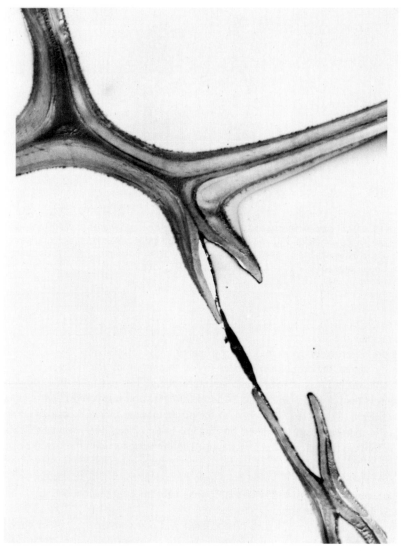

Fig. 2.16. Aspirated bordered pit of redwood. Photo courtesy of U.S. Forest Service.

Transverse Elements

Wood rays comprise the major transversely oriented elements of wood. These ribbon-shaped aggregates of cells radiate in a stem cross section like wheel spokes. As mentioned previously, the rays play a very important physiological role in radial translocation of water, minerals, and organic compounds.

Two types of rays occur in gymnosperms: (1) narrow rays, usually one cell wide

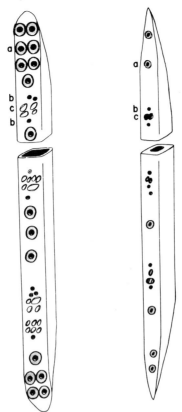

Fig. 2.17. Earlywood and latewood tracheids of pine. a: intertracheid bordered pits; b: bordered pits to ray tracheids, c: pinoid pits to ray parenchyma. Photo courtesy of U.S. Forest Service.

(uniseriate), although some species have biseriate rays; and (2) wide fusiform rays when transverse resin canals are present.

In the majority of gymnosperms the narrow rays are only about 10 to 15 cells high, but in some species, such as bald cypress, they may be up to 60 cells high.

Individual rays of gymnosperms are composed of ray parenchyma cells or of both ray parenchyma cells and ray tracheids, or solely of ray tracheids. Ray tracheids always occur in pine, spruce, larch, and Douglas-fir and are less commonly found in true firs, bald cypress, redwood, cedar, incense cedar, and junipers. When the prosenchymatous ray tracheids are present, they may occur in rows at ray margins or among layers of ray parenchyma cells.

Ray parenchyma cells have thin walls and living protoplasts when they are located in the portion of the ray that is in the sapwood. Ray tracheids have thick lignified walls. The ray tracheids of hard pines are described as dentate because of the presence of toothlike projections on their inner walls.

Fusiform rays, which may be found in pine, spruce, Douglas-fir, and larch, consist of marginal ray tracheids, ray parenchyma cells, and epithelial cells around a horizontally oriented resin canal. Fusiform rays are proportionally few in number and do not exceed 5% of the total number of rays present.

WOOD STRUCTURE OF ANGIOSPERMS

Angiosperm wood consists of longitudinal prosenchymatous (elongated cells with tapering ends) components (vessels, tracheids, and fibers) and parenchymatous components such as axial (longitudinal) parenchyma and epithelial cells (Fig. 2.18). As a rule, angiosperms lack transversely oriented prosenchymatous cells. Their transverse elements include ray parenchyma and, infrequently, epithelial cells. Although longitudinal or transverse resin canals occur normally in various tropical angiosperms, they are conspicuously absent in virtually all temperate-zone species.

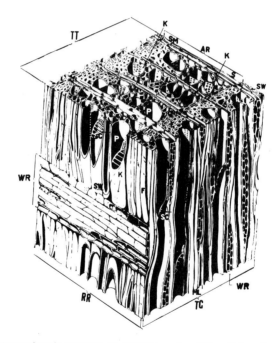

Fig. 2.18. Anatomy of angiosperm wood. TT: transection; RR: radial section; TG: tangential section; P: vessel; SC: perforation plate at end of vessel; F: fibers; K: pit; WR: wood ray; AR: annual ring; S: earlywood; SM or SW: latewood; ML: middle lamella. Photo courtesy of U.S. Forest Service.

Longitudinal Elements

There are more cell types in the xylem of angiosperms than in that of gymnosperms. Most conspicuous are the vessels, which are the chief water-conducting components. Because of the absence of end walls in vessels of angiosperms there is much less resistance to upward water flow than there is in the tracheids of gymnosperms with end walls present. Vessels are made up of vessel members, single cells from which end walls have disintegrated, which are superimposed one above another to create a tubular structure that may vary in length from a few centimeters to several meters.

In cross section most vessels are oval in shape but in woods of the more primitive species the vessels tend to be angular. Vessel arrangement is variable but fixed for species and therefore very useful in wood identification. For example, vessels may be solitary or arranged in various groups. They occur in holly in chains and in elm and hackberry as groups in the latewood in concentric wavy bands.

Tracheids are individual cells and they are smaller in diameter than vessels. Two types of tracheids occur in angiosperms, vascular tracheids and vasicentric tracheids. Vascular tracheids are imperforate cells resembling small vessel members in form and position. Vasicentric tracheids are short, irregularly formed tracheids in the immediate proximity of vessels and do not form part of the definite axial rows.

The bulk of the xylem of angiosperms usually consists of fibers. These somewhat resemble tracheids but have thicker walls, fewer pits, and smaller lumens. Xylem elements of angiosperms lack the orderly radial alignment characteristic of gymnosperm tracheids. The seemingly random distribution of elements in angiosperms results from extensive diameter growth of vessel members after they are cut off by the cambium. This forces other cells out of orderly alignment and causes narrow rays to bend around large vessels. This random arrangement is also partly caused by a lesser tendency for division of cambial initials opposite rapidly expanding vessels than of initials in a region where no large earlywood vessels form (Panshin *et al.,* 1966).

In angiosperms liquids move vertically through the perforated vessels. Lateral movement of liquids occurs through bordered and half-bordered pits. Pits of angiosperms may connect fibers to fibers, vessels to fibers, fibers to ray cells, and vessels to ray cells. The membrane of bordered pit pairs of angiosperms is the primary lamella of adjacent cells. There are no openings in this membrane, which is made up of randomly arranged microfibrils rather than centrally radiating ones as in gymnosperms (Coté, 1963).

The amount of axial parenchyma in wood of most angiosperms is considerably greater than in gymnosperms. In some tropical trees as much as half of the wood volume may consist of axial parenchyma. However, in most temperate zone trees axial parenchyma makes up less than 50% of the wood volume, and in some only a few percent. In poplar the amount of axial parenchyma is negligible. Patterns of arrangement of axial parenchyma vary greatly among species and are of considerable value in wood identification.

Transverse Elements

Width, height, and spacing of rays are much more variable in angiosperms than in gymnosperms. Usually rays are two to many cells wide and in oaks they may be up to 30 cells wide. Some species of angiosperms have rays of two size classes, with the smaller rays being only one cell wide. A few genera of woody plants (alder, bluebeech, hazel) have "aggregate" rays consisting of groups of narrow, closely spaced rays with intervening tracheary tissue. These aggregates often appear to be a single, very wide ray. Ray height is also extremely variable in angiosperms. The shortest rays are only a few microns high and the tallest ones may exceed 5 cm in height.

Rays of angiosperms are made up exclusively of parenchyma cells. Ray cells are variously classified. They may be radially oriented (procumbent) or vertically oriented (upright). Rays are classified as homocellular when comprised of parenchyma cells of similar size and shape, and heterocellular when cell size and shape are dissimilar. The structure and size of pits in ray parenchyma cells, which may be simple to bordered, are used as diagnostic features in wood identification.

Differences in ray structure of angiosperms account for variations in the figure or grain of wood. For example, more ray tissue is exposed on quarter-sawn lumber (produced by cutting the wide faces in a radial longitudinal plane of a log) than on flat-sawn lumber (produced by cutting the wide face tangentially to the annual rings) (Fig. 2.19). In quarter-sawn boards ray patterns vary from an inconspicuous figure in maple, with small rays, to the lustrous grain of oak, with conspicuously large rays.

BARK

The bark is a much more complex tissue system than the wood. In a mature tree the bark includes all tissues outside the cambium, including the inner living phloem and dead outer tissue (rhytidome). More specifically, in tissues that have gone into secondary thickening, bark tissues include primary and secondary phloem, cortex, and periderm. However, in stems not yet undergoing secondary thickening, only the primary phloem and cortex are included in the bark. The phloem plays an essential role in translocation while the periderm reduces water loss and provides protection from mechanical injury.

In early times the phloem fiber of some trees, known as bast fiber, was used for cordage and matting. The name "basswood," often used for linden, refers to the fact that its bark was a good source of bast fiber. In the Pacific Islands the inner bark of *Broussonetia papyrifera* was used extensively to make tapa cloth, and linen, hemp, and jute are prepared from phloem fibers.

The cambium-produced secondary phloem is comprised of vertically and transversely oriented systems of cells. In gymnosperms the secondary phloem is relatively simple, consisting only of vertically oriented sieve cells, parenchyma cells, and, often, fibers. The transversely oriented, generally uniseriate rays contain only parenchyma or parenchyma and albuminous cells. Vertical parenchyma often contains resins, crystals, and tannins.

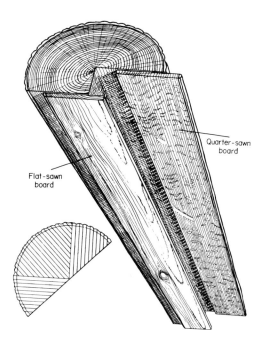

Quarter-sawn board

Flat-sawn board

Fig. 2.19. Variations in figure of quarter-sawn and flat-sawn lumber. For explanation, see text. Photo courtesy of U.S. Forest Service.

The secondary phloem of angiosperms is much more complicated and variable among species than the phloem of gymnosperms. Angiosperm phloem consists of vertically oriented sieve tubes, usually with companion cells, parenchyma cells, and fibers. The rays may be uniseriate, biseriate, or multiseriate. The axial and transverse system may also have sclereids, laticifers, secretory elements, idioblasts, and crystals.

Bark Formation

Although most increase in diameter growth of woody plants is traceable to activity of the vascular cambium, a small amount is the result of meristematic activity of another lateral meristem, the phellogen or cork cambium, located outside the vascular cambium. By periclinal division the phellogen, which consists of only one type of initial, produces phellem (cork) cells to the outside and phelloderm cells to the inside (Fig. 2.20). The three layers (phellem, phellogen, and phelloderm) together constitute a periderm, a protective secondary tissue which in most species replaces the epidermis early in the life of a seedling.

The suberized dead cork cells are arranged in radial rows, and lack intercellular spaces. Because of its cell structure cork has many valuable properties such as resistance to liquid penetration, resilience, compressibility, buoyancy, low thermal conductivity, and chemical inertness. Two common types of cork occur, and both may be present in the same tree. In one type the cells are hollow, thin-walled, and wide in a

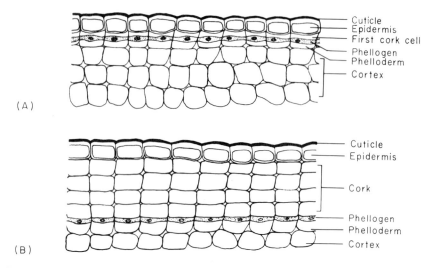

Fig. 2.20. Transection of stem portion showing origin of phellogen (A) and development of tissues by division of phellogen cells (B).

radial direction. In the other type the cells are thick-walled and flattened radially. In true firs, Douglas-fir, poplar, willow, and elm the cork is composed predominantly of thin-walled cells. In birch, beech, and redgum, however, most of the cork cells are thick walled. In some species of birch the occurrence of both thin- and thick-walled cork cells results in peeling of bark in thin sheets as separation occurs between the two layers. Unlike cork cells, the phelloderm cells, which resemble cortical parenchyma cells, remain alive and their walls are unsuberized. Sometimes they carry on photosynthesis and store starch. More cork than phelloderm cells usually are formed, but the amount of cork formed varies greatly with species. Some species lose external cork by cracking and peeling, so the cork layer on a tree remains about the same thickness. Other species, such as cork oak, build up thick cork layers but form very few phelloderm cells.

Periderm Formation

The epidermis of the stem ruptures and is sloughed off as trees begin to increase in diameter by cambial growth during the first year. Before the epidermis is lost, however, most trees form a cylindrical periderm at various depths in the cortex, outside the vascular cambium, that is relatively constant for a species. In stems of most genera of trees the first periderm arises in the cortex just beneath the epidermis. Examples are basswood, catalpa, ash, oak, poplar, walnut, and elm. There are exceptions, however, and in pear stems epidermal and subepidermal cells give rise to the first periderm. In black locust, honey locust, and species of pine and larch the first phellogen forms in the second or third cortical layer of the stem. Particularly deep initiation of first periderms is characteristic of arborvitae, barberry, and grape stems. In these genera the first phellogen is initiated near the phloem or even in the phloem parenchyma.

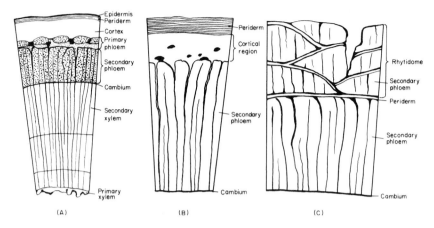

Fig. 2.21. Variation in periderm formation. (A) young stem; (B) mature bark of species which does not form rhytidome; (C) mature bark of species which forms abundant rhytidome. Photo courtesy of U.S. Forest Service.

In some trees, such as birch, fir, blue beech, and beech, the first periderm persists and remains active for many years. In the majority of tree species, however, the first periderm is replaced within a few years, or even in the first year, by periderms that form successively deeper in the cortex (Fig. 2.21). In those species in which the first periderm characteristically is initiated in very deep tissues, as in grape, the subsequently formed periderms are complete cylinders like the first periderm. By comparison, in species in which the first periderm is a superficial encircling layer, the second and subsequent periderms arise as arcs or lunes that curve toward the outside of the plant axis (Fig. 2.22). The successive periderms are active for varying lengths of time. In some species, such as beech, they function for life, or for many years, as in true firs and birch. In grape and some other species they originate annually, or seasonally, as in black locust (Srivastava, 1964). The timing and development of periderms also vary with environmental conditions and cultural practices especially water supply, light intensity, photoperiod, temperature, and herbicides (Borger and Kozlowski 1972,a,b,c,d,e,f,g). Tissues outside the periderm soon perish as they are isolated from food and water by the impermeable layers of cork in the periderm.

Development of Bark Characteristics

Bark patterns vary among species from smooth to rough (Fig. 2.23) depending on the manner in which bark is formed and shed. Specifically the appearance of bark depends on the radial position of the first periderm, patterns of formation of subsequent periderms, and composition and arrangement of phloem cells (Borger, 1973).

In smooth-barked trees the first periderm persists for a long time, as in some birches, or even for the life of the tree, as in trembling aspen and beech. In smooth-barked species the periderm increases in circumference by anticlinal division of cells and expansion of phellogen cells. Increase in the circumference of phloem involves

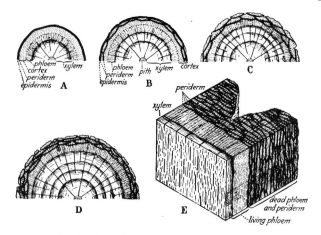

Fig. 2.22. Diagrams showing formation of successive periderm layers in bark of a typical woody stem. A: 1-year-old twig in which the first periderm forms a complete cylinder inside of an epidermis. B: 2-year-old twig in which the epidermis and first periderm have been ruptured and new arc-shaped layers have formed deeper in the cortex. C: 3-year-old stem, in which the outer tissues have weathered away and periderm has begun to develop in the secondary phloem. This process continues in D, a 4-year-old stem. E: outer part of a mature tree stem, showing a narrow band of living phloem and the deeply fissured outer bark made up of dead phloem and periderm layers. Considerable tissue has weathered away from the outside of the bark. From Eames and MacDaniels (1947). Copyright 1947; used with permission of McGraw-Hill Book Company.

Fig. 2.23. Variations in bark patterns: (A) sycamore; (B) mangrove; (C) shagbark hickory; (D) sequoia; (E) ponderosa pine; (F) white birch. Photo courtesy of St. Regis Paper Co.

formation of dilation tissue by anticlinal division and tangential expansion of phloem ray cells. Tissues of smooth barks usually are shed slowly and the rate of shedding is correlated with the rate of cork formation.

In cork oak the first periderm which develops in the epidermis consists of an abundance of cork cells and relatively few phelloderm cells. When the first layer of cork is harvested at an age of 12–15 years the phellogen dies but a new phellogen forms deeper in the cortex and produces cork faster than the original phellogen. After the second and subsequent harvests of cork, usually at 9–10-year intervals, other phellogens develop to continue the process of cork formation throughout the life of the tree.

In species that develop scaly barks the first periderm may persist in a superficial position for a very long time. However, small additional periderms eventually form in patches below the first periderm, and they continue to form throughout the life of the tree. Hence a thick outer bark is produced that consists of alternating layers of periderms and tissues cut off by them in the form of flakes, as in Scotch pine, or in sheets, as in sycamore maple. In shagbark hickory periderms arise in long vertical strips, hence bark tissues are cut off in vertical, platelike strips, reflecting the orientation of periderms, and a banded interlocking arrangement of numerous fibers in the phloem.

In species with furrowed barks the phloem contains abundant sclerenchyma tissue, especially fibers. Usually arcs of periderm arise in the outer phloem and the cells outside of the periderms die but do not separate because of the interlocking system of fibers. This results in very deep, furrowed, loose, and fibrous bark, as in *Sequoia sempervirens*. The furrowed barks of willow, oak, elm, ash, and walnut owe their individuality of pattern to various proportions of cork cells and sclerified tissues. The soft bark of American elm contains large amounts of cork cells and little sclerified tissue, whereas the hard barks of oak and ash contain many sclerified cells and relatively little cork. The "stringy" barks of several species of *Eucalyptus* owe their patterns of shedding to a cohesive but loose fibrous rhytidome. The groups of eucalypts known as "ironbarks" contain large amounts of a hard, resinous substance, called kino, which prevents rupture of the rhytidome (Borger, 1973).

In species with "ring barks" (as in grape, clematis, honeysuckle, and species of Cupressaceae) the first periderm is initiated in very deep tissues. The second and subsequent tissues are concentric cylinders. This results in shedding of hollow cylinders of loose bark. Separation occurs through thin-walled cork cells but the rhytidome remains attached, giving the outer bark a characteristic shaggy appearance. For more details on bark formation the reader is referred to Borger (1973).

ROOTS

The roots are important for anchorage, absorption of water and minerals from the soil, and for storage of reserve foods. Root systems of trees consist of a framework of relatively large perennial roots and many smaller, short-lived branch roots. Variations in the distribution and extent of roots are important because trees able to produce deeply penetrating and branching root systems absorb water and minerals from a larger soil mass than trees with more restricted roots (Kozlowski, 1972b). Rooting depth varies greatly among species and often shows little relation to the size of the plant above ground. The effective rooting depth of tea bushes, for example, often is greater than that of the tall, overtopping trees.

Roots often penetrate more deeply into the soil than is generally realized. Roots of mesquite and some other trees and shrubs of dry habitats penetrate 6 to 10 m and apple trees in a well aerated loess soil in Nebraska penetrated over 10 m. Plants of dry habitats often have a high root/shoot ratio. According to Fernandez and Caldwell (1975) the root/shoot ratio of shrubs in the cool semi-desert of Utah may be as high as 9:1 in contrast to 1:5 in an apple tree or a young loblolly pine stand. However, Barbour (1973) claims that the root/shoot ratio of desert plants usually is less than one and this is supported by data for chapparal shrubs (Kummerow, *et al.* 1977).

Caldwell (1976) suggests that the growth of roots is inefficient in terms of material and energy expended. The death of large numbers of small absorbing roots, the loss of efficiency as absorbing surfaces, and the necessity of continually producing new roots

Fig. 2.24. Root system of 16-year-old Cox's Orange Pippin apple tree on Malling II rootstock. From Rogers and Head (1969).

often result in one-half or more of the food produced by some plants being used in root growth. The reasons for this seemingly inefficient behavior deserve further study.

Tree roots often spread laterally as far as or well beyond the width of the crown (Fig. 2.24). However, the extent of lateral spread of roots varies markedly with site and especially with soil type. For example, roots of fruit trees growing on sand extended laterally about three times as far as the crown; on loam about twice as far; and on clay about one and one-half times as far (Rogers and Booth, 1959, 1960).

Forest trees tend to develop a high concentration of roots in the surface soil, perhaps because it is well aerated, contains a higher concentration of minerals than deeper soil horizons, and is well watered by summer showers. This is especially true in tropical forests, but also is common in the temperate zone. In the heavy clay soils of the North Carolina piedmont, Coile (1937b) found 90% of the small roots under oak and pine stands in the upper 12 cm of soil. In Texas more than half the root growth of 2-year-old loblolly pines was in the upper 7.5 cm and over 70% of the root weight was in the upper 15 cm (Bilan, 1960). On the other hand, roots penetrate to great depths in well-aerated soils. In deep loam soil in California orchards Proebsting (1943) found the greatest concentration of roots of fruit trees at 0.5 to 1.5 m, with some penetrating to 5 m. Wiggans (1936) found roots of apple trees penetrating over 10 m into a well-aerated loess soil in Nebraska.

Classification of Roots

Root systems of most tree seedlings are strongly fixed by heredity and have been classified in one of two general types, those with taproots that grow rapidly downward and penetrate deeply and those with slowly growing, shallow primary roots and extensive, rapidly growing lateral roots. However, classifying root systems of adult trees of some species often is complicated because site and soil conditions may modify root growth so much that species characteristics are obscured. For example, species of *Eucalyptus* in dry areas develop a long taproot with few, poorly developed laterals. On good sites, however, they form a shallow, fibrous root system (Zimmer and Grose, 1958). Red maple develops shallow, lateral roots in swamps and deep taproots in upland soils. By comparison, the root system of sycamore maple, consisting of a taproot with evenly spaced short laterals, is not altered substantially under a variety of environmental conditions (Majid, 1954).

Despite the plasticity of roots of some species, various systems of root nomenclature have evolved. One system, which is used in Europe for the different parts of a root system, is shown in Fig. 2.25.

Heterorhizic Roots

Most pines have a "heterorhizic" root system made up of long and short roots (Wilcox, 1964). The long roots consist of the main root and fast-growing laterals of the first and second order which account for the overall development of the root system. Long roots are considered permanent and they increase in diameter by cambial growth. The ephemeral and slow-growing short roots that occur along the long roots have an apical meristem but not a true rootcap. Short roots lack secondary growth and most

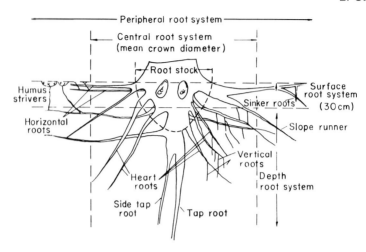

Fig. 2.25. Schematic representation of a root system of a mature tree. From Lyr and Hoffman (1967).

disappear during their first or second year. They commonly are converted to mycorrhizae. The long roots of pines, which are important in developing the framework of the root system, have been further subdivided into ''pioneer'' and ''mother'' roots by Noelle (1910) and Aldrich-Blake (1930). Wilcox (1964) added a third category of ''subordinate mother roots'' for red pine. Pioneer roots, the largest diameter members of the pine root system, were so named by Noelle (1910) because they accounted for rapid extension of the root system. Pioneer roots are never abundant and generally can be found only during the late spring and late summer when root growth is most active (Wilcox, 1964). Mother roots, so named because of their profuse branching, are smaller in diameter and shorter in length than pioneer roots. The subordinate mother roots of red pine that were described by Wilcox (1964) are finer and of smaller diameter than mother roots. They are comparable to second-order laterals of 2-year-old seedlings (Table 2.4).

As Wilcox (1962b) emphasized, forestry literature in the past tended to oversimplify in implying that both long and short roots are present in tree root systems, probably because of the association of short roots with mycorrhizae. Although short roots occur throughout the Pinaceae and in a few other gymnosperms and in the Betulaceae and Fagaceae, they are absent in many woody plants. Incense cedar, for example, like other trees in the Cupressaceae, does not develop a heterorhizic root system.

The system of classification based on long and short roots is not always useful because short roots eventually may be converted into long roots, or into thickened anchor roots capable of absorbing water at or near the tips (Leshem, 1965).

Woody and Nonwoody Roots

Clowes (1950) and Lyford and Wilson (1964) considered the classification of roots as long or short to be inadequate for certain angiosperms. Lyford and Wilson (1964)

TABLE 2.4 Classification, Distribution, and Diameters of Roots of 2-Year-Old Nursery Seedlings and Adult Red Pine Trees[a]

		Diameter (mm)			
		Mature trees		Seedlings	
Class of roots	Number of roots	Average	Range	Average	Range
Pioneer	10	1.66	(1.32–1.81)		
Mother	26	0.85	(0.74–1.21)		
Subordinate mother	37	0.54	(0.36–0.71)		
Short roots	207	0.42	(0.23–0.50)	0.34	(0.26–0.41)
Primary				1.03	
First-order laterals				0.99	
Second-order laterals				0.55	

[a] From Wilcox (1964).

prefer to classify red maple roots as woody or nonwoody. They consider a mature root system to be a framework of permanent woody roots bearing many fans of relatively short-lived, nonwoody roots. The woody roots extend from the stem base in essentially straight lines, tapering rapidly near the stem to ropelike structures, with relatively small diameters (up to 2.5 cm) and great length (up to 25 m). At approximately 1- to 5-m intervals, lateral woody roots branch off the main root. The first nonwoody roots

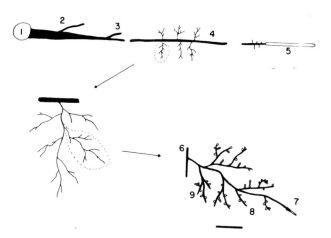

Fig. 2.26. Relationships of woody and nonwoody roots in red maple. 1: stem; 2: adventitious roots in zone of rapid taper; 3: lateral root; 4: nonwoody root fans; 5: tip of woody root and first-order, nonwoody roots; 6: second- and higher order nonwoody root emerging from first-order nonwoody roots; 7: uninfected tip of second-order nonwoody root with root hairs; 8: third-order nonwoody root with bead-shaped mycorrhizae; 9: fourth-order nonwoody root with mycorrhizae. From Lyford and Wilson (1964).

TABLE 2.5   Characteristics of Red Maple Roots[a]

Root type	Approximate tip diameter (mm)	Approximate final length	Frequency of laterals per cm of length	Frequency of mycorrhizae
Woody	2.0	10–25 m	0.3–1	None
Nonwoody				
First order	0.5–1.0	20–40 cm	2–3	None
Second order	0.5–1.0	10–15 cm	3–10	Low
Third order	0.3–0.5	1–2 cm	3–10	High
Higher than third order and mycorrhizae	0.2–0.3	1–10 mm	—	Almost all

[a] From Lyford and Wilson (1964).

emerge at right angles to a woody root at intervals of 1 to 3 cm behind its root tip. The first-order woody roots and those of higher order originating from them comprise a complex pinnate "root fan" about 20 to 40 cm long (Fig. 2.26). Such short-lived root fans become less frequent on old and thick roots. As shown in Table 2.5, diameters of tips and length of nonwoody roots decrease in successively higher orders, but distribution of mycorrhizae and lateral roots increases.

Suberized and Unsuberized Roots

Individual roots of trees may continue to grow for several weeks and produce lateral roots or they may stop growing after only a few weeks. The outer cortical tissues of roots remain unsuberized and white for a short time, which in apple may vary from 1 to 4 weeks during the summer and up to 3 months in the winter (Head, 1966b). The cortical tissues then turn brown and degenerate. The remaining central cylinder may or may not undergo secondary thickening. The onset of browning of cortical tissues is associated with suberization. Structural changes during secondary growth of a woody root are shown in Figs. 3.30, 13.1, and 13.2.

As root systems age an increasing proportion of the total surface becomes suberized. Only the most recently formed roots are unsuberized and their total surface area is exceedingly small in comparison to the surface of the total root system. Kramer and Bullock (1966) followed seasonal changes in proportions of growing and suberized roots in loblolly pine and yellow poplar trees growing in North Carolina. The surface area of growing, unsuberized roots under a loblolly pine stand usually amounted to less than 1% of the total root surface area (Table 2.6). It exceeded 1% at only one sampling time following a heavy rainfall in July. Most of the unsuberized root surface consisted of mycorrhizae, and the surface provided by growing tips plus mycorrhizal roots never exceeded 7% during the growing season. Thus from 93–99% of the root surface was suberized. This situation suggests that considerable absorption of water and minerals must occur through suberized roots (see Chapters 10 and 13).

TABLE 2.6 Seasonal Variation in Percentage of Surface Area in Unsuberized and Suberized Roots under a 34-Year-Old Loblolly Pine Stand in North Carolina[a]

Date	Growing tips (%)	Mycorrhizal (%)	Total unsuberized (%)	Total suberized (%)
March				
1	0.06	0.53	0.59	99.41
8	0.15	1.20	1.35	98.65
15	0.13	1.18	1.31	98.69
22	0.13	1.64	1.77	98.69
29	0.13	2.06	2.39	97.61
April				
8	0.43	2.27	2.70	97.30
13	0.39	5.09	5.48	94.52
22	0.53	2.77	3.30	96.70
30	0.34	5.30	5.64	94.36
May				
9	0.72	5.76	6.48	93.52
31	0.30	3.95	4.25	95.75
June				
7	0.25	6.06	5.31	93.69
17	0.48	3.05	3.53	96.47
24	0.38	3.00	3.38	96.62
July				
1	0.22	3.00	3.22	96.78
15	0.54	2.38	2.92	97.08
29	1.36	2.81	4.17	95.83
November				
11	0.61	2.84	3.55	95.83

[a] From Kramer and Bullock (1966).

Specialized Roots

Many woody plants have specialized or morphologically modified root systems which often have important physiological implications in growth. These include mycorrhizal roots, grafted roots, aerial roots, nodulated roots, and buttressed roots.

Mycorrhizal Roots. The root systems of most woody plants are greatly modified by the presence of mycorrhizae (Fig. 2.27). These structures, formed by invasion of young roots by fungal hyphae, are symbiotic associations between nonpathogenic or weakly pathogenic fungi and living cells of roots.

Most mycorrhizae fall into two broad groups—the ectotrophic forms which exist both inside and outside the root, and the endotrophic forms which exist entirely within the host cells. These associations always form in the cortical cells of the host roots and do not extend into the endodermis or stele.

Ectotrophic mycorrhizae occur in many economically important trees. They are common in the Pinaceae, Salicaceae, Betulaceae, Fagaceae, Juglandaceae, Caesal-

Fig. 2.27. Variations in mycorrhizae on Douglas-fir roots. A: mycorrhizal cluster; B: grey, pinnate mycorrhiza; C: orange mycorrhiza; D: yellow mycorrhiza showing rhizomorphs of fungus symbiont. Photo courtesy of U.S. Forest Service.

pinoideae, and Tiliaceae. Important genera having ectotrophic mycorrhizae include *Pinus, Picea, Abies, Pseudotsuga, Cedrus,* and *Larix* among the gymnosperms, and *Quercus, Castanea, Fagus, Nothofagus, Betula, Alnus, Salix, Carya,* and *Populus* among the angiosperms (Meyer, 1966). Although endotrophic mycorrhizae are widely distributed in the plant kingdom, they are found only in tree species of the genera *Liriodendron, Acer, Liquidambar,* and various members of the Ericaceae.

In ectotrophic mycorrhizae the fungus produces a weft of hyphae on the root surface and the mycelia may form either thin, loosely woven tissue, tightly woven masses, or compacted pseudoparenchymatous structures. The fungus penetrates the cortex, forcing its way between the cortical cells without actually entering individual cells of the host. In root transections the cortical cells appear to be separated by a fungal net, called the Hartig net (Marks and Kozlowski, 1973).

Variations in structure of mycorrhizal and uninfected roots of *Eucalyptus* are shown in Fig. 2.28. Quantitative differences in structure include: (1) lack of production of root

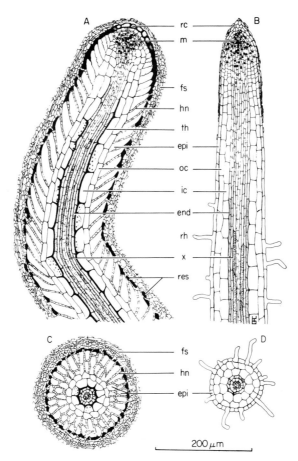

Fig. 2.28. Anatomy of mycorrhizal and uninfected roots of Eucalyptus. A,B: median longitudinal sections of mycorrhizal and uninfected root, respectively; C,D: transverse sections through fully differentiated region of mycorrhiza and uninfected root, respectively. rc: rootcap; m: meristematic region; fs: fungal sheath or mantle; hn: Hartig net; th: thickened walls of inner cortex; epi: epidermis; oc: outer cortex; ic: inner cortex; end: endodermis (shaded to indicate extent of tannin impregnation); rh: root hair; x: lignified protoxylem; rs: collapsed residues of cap cells. From Chilvers and Pryor (1965).

hairs by mycorrhizae and some root hairs in uninfected fine roots; (2) limited rootcap tissue in mycorrhizae (rarely more than two cell layers between the apex and fungal sheath) and extensive rootcap tissue in uninfected roots; and (3) occurrence of differentiation much closer to the apex in mycorrhizal than in uninfected roots. The morphology of mycorrhizal rootlets is similar to that which might occur from slow growth as a result of unfavorable environmental conditions. Among qualitative differences abscribed to fungal infection are thickening of the inner cortex and radial elongation of epidermal cells.

In endotrophic mycorrhizae the fungus lives intracellularly and does not have any communication with the surface of the soil. These associations cause less change in host morphology than is caused by the ectotrophic forms.

Mycorrhizae play an important role in tree physiology by increasing the absorption of minerals, especially phosphorus. Although trees can be grown successfully without mycorrhizae under certain conditions, such as very high soil fertility, they usually grow much better with mycorrhizae. In fact, on most sites mycorrhizal fungi appear to be required for tree survival.

There is much evidence indicating that trees and mycorrhizal fungi exist symbiotically. The relationship appears to be one in which the tree supplies carbohydrates and other metabolites beneficial to the fungus and in turn the fungus benefits the tree by increasing the availability of nitrogen, phosphorus, and other nutrients (Harley, 1969; Harley and Lewis, 1969). There is also some evidence that mycorrhizal fungi may protect the host tree from disease by utilizing excess carbohydrates, acting as a physical barrier, secreting fungistatic substances, and favoring protective organisms of the rhizosphere (Zak, 1964; Marx, 1969). The physiological importance of mycorrhizae in mineral uptake is discussed further in Chapter 10.

Grafted Roots.   There is considerable interest in root grafting because water, metabolites, and various toxic substances are transported from one plant to another through root grafts (see Chapter 11). Natural grafts between roots are common. They have been observed in more than 150 species of woody plants and doubtless occur in other species (Graham and Bormann, 1966). Kozlowski and Cooley (1961) found extensive within-species root grafting in both angiosperms and gymnosperms (Fig. 2.29). Roots were fused in both saplings and old trees but the grafts were more plentiful among the older trees. Often a community of trees was organically united by a complicated system of many within-species grafts. The main requirements for grafting appeared to be compatibility and growth pressure. Feeder roots did not graft readily. The angle of approach did not seem important because roots grafted at many different angles. Grafting was common over or adjacent to stones, suggesting that growth pressure of one root on another lodged against a stone promoted grafting. The presence of stones was not necessary, however, because many grafts occurred in the absence of stones. In addition to true grafts, many cases of abrasion and callus development were observed where roots crossed, suggesting that fusions eventually would occur as a result of growth pressure at these points of contact.

Plantations generally do not show root grafting until some critical age is reached, because the wide spacing among trees in early years precludes frequent root contacts.

Fig. 2.29. Root grafts in closely grown balsam fir trees. From Kozlowski and Cooley (1961).

The proportion of root-grafted Norway spruce trees in a plantation increased from 3–5% at the time of the first thinnings to 25–35% by the time the trees were 40 to 60 years old (Holmsgaard and Scharff, 1963). Schultz and Woods (1967) reported that 5–25% of trees in loblolly pine stands 25 to 85 years old were connected by root grafts. However, in nurseries root grafting often occurs among the closely grown seedlings at an early age (Kozlowski, 1971b). Eis (1972) considered that compatibility, tree proximity, shallow and stony soils, and concentration of roots were the most important factors influencing root grafting.

True root grafts involve vascular connections that are brought about by union of cambium, phloem, and xylem of previously unconnected roots. Stone and Stone (1975b) observed water flow through root grafts, and the survival of girdled trees for a decade or more indicates the existence of functioning phloem connections (Stone, 1974). The most usual types of root fusions appear to be self-grafts among roots of the same tree or roots of different trees of the same species. Interspecies grafts among related species occur much less commonly (Kozlowski, 1963).

Eis (1972) described the process of root grafting in conifers. After firm physical contact was established between roots of compatible trees, cambium cells of the ray region enlarged rapidly, producing mounds of callus tissues. Cell division began just before latewood formation began. The callus mounds usually grew simultaneously and, on young roots, opposite each other. In young small roots these mounds broke through the bark during the second growing season and the two cambia united almost immediately. Grafting of older roots with thick bark was much slower and sometimes required as much as 4 years. On large roots, with extensive areas of contact, the callus mounds did not always grow directly opposite each other. In such cases the callus of a root did not penetrate the bark of the other root and fusion did not occur. The heavy bark of large roots was a very strong barrier to grafting.

Aerial Roots. Although most roots are subterranean they are not exclusively so. Often roots appear above ground when seeds germinate in an above-ground medium that later erodes away or decays to expose the roots. Kozlowski and Cooley (1961)

Fig. 2.30. Fused mass of horizontal aerial roots of yellow birch. From Kozlowski and Cooley (1961).

observed many exposed roots of yellow birch. These resulted when seeds germinated on old stumps or felled logs and sent roots downward. After the stumps or logs decayed the roots were exposed (Fig. 2.30). Normal subterranean roots of old trees also may be exposed by soil erosion, road cuts, or other construction.

Aerial roots are a conspicuous feature of many tropical woody plants. Such roots vary widely in form and the original aerial roots of some tree ferns arise from an aerial stem and remain imbedded in other tissues. In many lianas roots arise from aerial organs and become exposed "clasping" roots. *Ficus* spp. produces free-hanging aerial roots that originate in the branches and undergo secondary thickening before they reach the soil (Fig. 2.31).

A number of species produce "stilt" roots which emerge from the main stem of the tree, bend downward, and enter the soil. Stilt roots often branch above ground and give rise to secondary and tertiary roots below ground. The mangroves (*Rhizophora*) are perhaps the best examples of trees that produce stilt roots (see Fig. 2.32), but such roots also form on a number of trees found in freshwater swamps and rain forests. Other genera that form stilt roots include *Pandanus, Clusia, Tovomita, Elaeocarpus, Xylopia, Dillenia, Eugenia,* and *Musanga.* Another mangrove, *Avicennia nitida,* pro-

Fig. 2.31. Aerial roots of India rubber tree. (*Ficus elastica*). Photo courtesy of U.S. Forest Service.

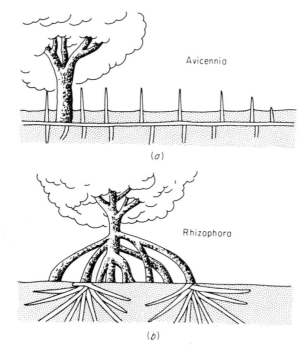

Avicennia

(*a*)

Rhizophora

(*b*)

Fig. 2.32. (a) Vertical branches of roots extending into the air found in *Avicennia*. (b) Stilt or prop roots of *Rhizophora*. From Scholander *et al.* (1955).

duces air roots that are vertical branches of horizontal roots (Fig. 2.32; see also Chapter 6). *Armoora, Caropa,* and *Heritiera* have similar air roots (Groom and Wilson, 1925).

Some species have vertical "knee" roots (Fig. 2.33). The origin of these varies somewhat among species. Roots of baldcypress develop vertical knees because of active, localized cambial activity that adds thick layers of wood on the upper surfaces of roots. In *Bruguiera* and *Ceriops* the knees arise from upward growth of a horizontal root until it emerges from the soil. In *Avicennia marina* the knees arise as lateral branches of horizontal roots, which, after growing upward for some time turn downward, reenter the soil and then grow horizontally (McCusker, 1971). The knee roots of *Mitragyna stipulosa* develop either by accelerated local cambial activity as vertical protuberances of horizontal roots or by arching roots above the surface (McCarthy, 1962).

Cypress knees do not develop in deep water or when the period of flooding is very short (Kurz and Demaree, 1934; Penfound, 1934). In areas which are flooded periodically they grow to a height approximating the high water level. Apparently cypress knees develop as a result of localized cambial activity in regions which are better aerated than the remainder of the root (Whitford, 1956). The role of cypress knees and other pneumatophores in respiration is discussed in Chapter 6.

Buttressed Roots.   A few species of temperate zone woody plants that grow in swamps, such as tupelo gum and many species of tropical trees produce buttresses at the stem base. Whereas the buttresses of tupelo-gum are narrow, basal stem swellings, the conspicuous buttresses of tropical trees vary from flattened plates to wide flutings (Figs. 2.34 and 2.35). Their size increases with tree age and, in some mature trees, they may extend upward along the stem and outward from the base for nearly 10 m. Most buttressed tropical trees have three or four buttresses but they may have as many

Fig. 2.33. Abundant development of "knees" in a dense stand of baldcypress growing in South Carolina. Photo courtesy of U.S. Forest Service.

Fig. 2.34. Buttressing in *Pterygota horsefieldii* in Sarawak. Photo courtesy of P. Ashton.

Fig. 2.35. Stages in development of buttresses caused initially by excessive cambial growth on the upper surfaces of horizontal roots. Photo courtesy of Kepong Forest Research Institute, Malaysia.

Fig. 2.36. Root nodules of *Alnus glutinosa*. From Becking (1972).

as 10. The formation of buttresses is an inherited trait. It occurs commonly in tropical rain forest trees in the Dipterocarpaceae, Leguminosae, and Sterculiaceae. The expression of buttressing in species having an inherent potential for it is regulated by environment. Buttressing is most prevalent at low altitudes and in areas of high rainfall. Soil depth appears to be very important in regulating buttress development (Richards, 1966) as it is more pronounced on shallow soil. Smith (1972) suggested that buttressing provides better support to a tree than a cylindrical base containing the same volume of wood.

Buttresses generally form only in trees with superficial root systems and well-developed, horizontal lateral roots. In young trees cambial growth of roots is normal and lateral roots are concentric in cross section. After a few years, however, cambial growth along the upper sides of lateral roots and the stem above them accelerates greatly to produce very excessive thickening, leading to the formation of conspicuous buttresses.

The lower stems of buttressed trees are very eccentric and stem transections often are stellate. The central stems of buttressed trees taper downward from the level to which buttresses ascend, and they taper upward from this height. Downward tapering of lower stems does not occur in young trees but develops progressively during buttress formation. Hence, formation of buttresses appears to involve a control mechanism that allows for preferential mobilization of metabolites by the buttressing sites.

Nodulated Roots.   Roots of many species form tubercles or nodules (Fig. 2.36) which are of much interest to plant physiologists because the nodules are important in nitrogen fixation. Root nodules form on roots of many leguminous woody plants and of many nonleguminous genera as well. Important nodulated nonlegumes include such gymnosperm genera as *Agathis, Araucaria, Libocedrus, Phyllocladus, Dacrydium,* and *Sciadopitys*. Important genera of nodulated nonleguminous angiosperms include *Alnus, Casuarina, Coriaria, Eleagnus, Hippophaë, Shepherdia, Comptonia (Myrica), Ceanothus,* and *Purshia*. Root nodules of nonlegumes are perennial and increase in size annually, sometimes becoming as large as tennis balls.

Nodule formation in legumes results from penetration of roots by *Rhizobium* bacteria through root hairs or injuries along the roots. Two forms of nodules have been described, the most common type resulting from infection of cortical parenchyma cells (Allen and Allen, 1958).

In nodules of leguminous woody plants the endophytes involved in nitrogen fixation are bacteria of the genus *Rhizobium*. In nodules of nonlegumes the endophytes of most species are Actinomycetes. In a few species, however, the endophyte appears to be a species of *Rhizobium* (Becking, 1975). Nitrogen fixation is discussed in more detail in Chapter 9.

GENERAL REFERENCES

Esau, K. (1965). "Plant Anatomy." Wiley, New York.

Esau, K. (1977). "Anatomy of Seed Plants." Wiley, New York.

Fahn, A. (1974). "Plant Anatomy." Pergamon, Oxford.

Jane, F. W. (1970). "The Structure of Wood." Black, London.

Harlow, W. M. (1970). "Inside Wood-Masterpiece of Nature." Am. For. Assoc., Washington, D.C.

Marks, G. C., and Kozlowski, T. T., eds. (1973). "Ectomycorrhizae." Academic Press, New York.

Panshin, A. J., De Zeeuw, C. G., and Brown, H. P. (1966). "Textbook of Wood Technology," Vol. I. McGraw-Hill, New York.

Torrey, J. G., and Clarkson, D. T., eds. (1975). "The Development and Function of Roots." Academic Press, New York.

3

Vegetative Growth

INTRODUCTION

Growth of woody plants has been characterized from quantitative, anatomical, morphogenetic, and physiological viewpoints. Quantitative investigators often use classical growth analysis techniques that emphasize growth rates rather than final measurements of size or yield. Early increase in size or dry weight of plants, organs, or tissues is approximately linear. Eventually, however, various internal growth-controlling mechanisms induce departure from a linear relationship so that over a long period growth can best be characterized by a sigmoid curve. Seasonal and lifetime growth of shoots, roots, and reproductive structures generally conform to such a pattern (Evans, 1972).

Plants grow in height and diameter through the activity of meristematic tissues which comprise a very small fraction of the total mass. The various parts of plants grow at different rates and often at different times of the year. For example, woody plants of the temperate zone fluctuate from a state of endogenously controlled, deep-seated winter dormancy to meristematic activity during the growing season. But even during the frost-free season periods of growth lapse into periods of inactivity or quiescence followed by recurrence of growth. Although many tropical trees have been reported to grow more or less continuously throughout the year, closer examination shows that their growth often occurs in cycles.

This chapter will discuss the nature and periodicity of shoot growth, cambial growth, and root growth of trees of the temperate zone and tropics. This will be done as an aid to subsequent discussion of growth as the end result of a series of coordinated physiological processes that involve synthesis of foods, their conversion to soluble forms, and their translocation, partitioning, and assimilation into new tissues. Reproductive growth will be discussed in Chapter 4. Control of both vegetative and reproductive growth will be discussed in Chapters 16 and 17.

SHOOT GROWTH

Growing shoots, which usually consist of a stem portion plus leaves, consist of nodes and internodes. Nodes are parts of stems at which leaves are attached. Often the term node is also used to refer to the region of stem where long shoots or branch whorls are attached. Internodes are lengths of stem between two successive nodes.

Shoots elongate as the result of bud opening and expansion at the many growing points (apical meristems) distributed over the stem, branches, and twigs. Bud opening may involve leaf enlargement, meristem activity in the internodes between leaves, or faster growth of bud scales on inner than on outer surfaces (Fig. 3.1). During shoot expansion the duration of expansion of internodes and of leaves often varies appreciably, depending at least in part on cell turgor and supply of food growth regulators.

The apex of a growing shoot is a harmoniously developing continuum consisting of an apical meristem and associated subapical and maturing regions. The overall growth of a shoot involves division of cells of the apical meristem and their subsequent

Fig. 3.1. Hickory buds in various stages of opening. Photo courtesy of U.S. Forest Service.

elongation, differentiation, and maturation. These phases are not sharply delimited and occur sequentially at varying distances from the tips of stems and branches. Almost all shoot extension is the result of internode elongation.

Bud Characteristics

A mature bud is an embryonic shoot, or part of a shoot, bearing at the tip the apical meristem from which it originated. Most lateral buds are initiated in leaf axils and arise in relatively superficial tissues. The initiation of buds involves cell division in cell layers in the leaf axil to form a bud protrusion as well as organization of the apical meristem.

Usually buds are classified as to location, contents, or activity (e.g., terminal, lateral, axillary, dormant, adventitious, flower, or mixed buds). Each of these may be further classified as active or dormant. Vegetative buds vary greatly in maturity. They may consist of little more than an apical meristem. More commonly, however, they contain a small mass of meristematic tissue, nodes, internodes, and small rudimentary leaves, with buds in their axils, all enclosed in bud scales. Flower buds contain embryonic flowers and most also have rudimentary leaves. Mixed buds contain both flowers and leaves.

During formation of vegetative buds leaf primordia appear in upward succession. Hence, the largest and oldest leaf primordia are located at the bud base and the smaller rudimentary leaves occur toward the growing point (Fig. 3.2). The leaves form as a

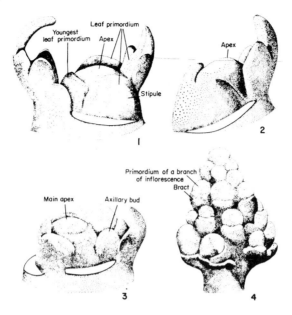

Fig. 3.2. Vegetative shoot apex of grape. From Fahn (1967).

result of divisions in subsurface cells of apical meristems. When leaves are first formed they occur close together and nodes and internodes are indistinguishable. Subsequently, as meristematic activity occurs between leaf insertions, internodes become recognizable as a result of intercalary growth (Esau, 1965).

Dormant and Adventitious Buds

Only part of the buds produce shoots, the rest remaining dormant, sometimes throughout the life of a woody plant. Dormant buds, originally developed in leaf axils, are subsequently connected to the pith by a bud trace. Branching of dormant buds occurs rather commonly (Fig. 3.3). Buds that form irregularly on older portions of a plant and not at the stem tips or in the leaf axils are called adventitious buds. These form on parts of the root or stem which have no connection to apical meristems. They may originate from either deep or peripheral tissues. For example, adventitious buds may arise from callus tissue around wounds, in the cambium, or from mature tissues in the endodermis or pericyclic region (MacDaniels, 1953). Unlike dormant buds, adventitious buds do not have a bud trace all the way to the pith.

Many branches produced following pruning, stump sprouts originating from root collars and the lower stem, epicormic branches of angiosperms, and sprouts of gymnosperms following fire or injury arise from dormant rather than from adventitious buds. Root sprouts (''root suckers'') arise from adventitious buds. Reproduction by root suckers is well known in trembling aspen and bigtooth aspen but it also occurs in sweetgum, beech, ailanthus, black locust, lilac, black tupelo, and sassafras.

Fig. 3.3. Cross section of shortleaf pine stem showing branching of dormant buds. From Little and Somes (1956).

Leaf Growth

Trees bear several types of leaves including cotyledons, foliage leaves, and cataphylls. Cotyledons or "seed leaves" are developed in the seed and contain or have access to stored foods (see Chapter 14). They generally differ in size and shape from the first foliage leaves (Fig. 3.4). Cataphylls or "lower leaves," which usually are involved in storage, protection, or both, are represented by bud scales.

Fig. 3.4. One-week-old box elder seedling showing variations in size and shape of the elongated, entire cotyledons below the serrated first foliage leaves. Photo courtesy of U.S. Forest Service.

Origin and Development of Leaves

Cell division predominates during the early stages of development of leaf primordia. Subsequently, a leaf achieves its final shape and size by both cell division and expansion, with the latter predominating. Ultimate leaf size depends on the number of cells in the primordia, the rate and duration of cell division, and sizes of mature cells, but cell number appears to be most important (Humphries and Wheeler, 1963).

Angiosperms

Leaves of angiosperms form only on shoot apices. The apex swells to form a leaf primordium consisting at first of uniform meristematic cells. Shortly thereafter cell division stops in the area of attachment and the leaf base is differentiated. The upper part of the primordium continues to divide and forms the blade. The petiole forms later from an intermediate meristematic zone. The various leaf parts, such as petiole, blade, sheath, and stipule are initiated soon after the primordium has formed.

Growth of the leaf is at first localized at the tip but this continues for a short time only and is followed by intercalary growth (through activity of a meristem inserted between more or less differentiated tissue regions), which accounts for most of the increase in leaf length. The flattened form of the blade is initiated from meristems located along the two margins of the leaf axis.

The epidermal tissue from which stomata originate is differentiated early. Hence, most stomata are found on leaves in young buds but differentiation may also occur late in leaf development. Formation of the vascular system also begins early during blade formation.

Variations in duration of cell division and expansion in the epidermis and mesophyll layers result in palisade and spongy mesophyll. The epidermal cells keep expanding longer than palisade cells, causing intercellular spaces to form.

Gymnosperms

Three distinct types of foliar appendages form sequentially in gymnosperm seedlings. First are the cotyledons which are present in the embryo, then the primary needles of a young seedling, and finally the secondary needles which form the permanent complement of leaves. Leaf growth in gymnosperms starts with foliar primordia located on the flanks of apical meristems. Both apical growth and intercalary rib meristem activity form the leaf axis, but apical growth is of short duration. The narrow leaf blade is initiated by marginal growth.

Seasonal Leaf Growth Characteristics

Several patterns of seasonal production of foliage leaves have been shown. Trees of some species achieve maximum leaf area early in the season and do not produce any more leaves during the year, whereas others add new leaves, either by continuous production and expansion of new leaf primordia, or by several intermittent "flushes" of growth involving recurrent formation and opening of buds during the growing season followed by expansion of their contents.

The duration of expansion of individual leaves varies greatly among species, type of shoot, its location on the tree, and environmental conditions, especially temperature and water supply. In apple the time required for expansion of leaves from dormant spur buds varied from 2 days for basal spur leaves to 15 days for other leaves (MacDaniels and Cowart, 1940). The early leaves of white birch and trembling aspen, that were contained in the winter bud, expanded within 2 weeks after buds opened (Kozlowski and Clausen, 1966). By comparison, individual leaves of grape expanded and matured in about 40 days (Mounts, 1932).

The rather rapid expansion of individual leaves of many deciduous angiosperms contrasts with the relatively slow expansion of many gymnosperm leaves. For example, elongation of Scotch pine needles in England continued until early August (Rutter, 1957). In the United States, internode elongation of eastern white pine and red pine is completed early in the growing season. However, the needles elongate throughout much of the summer. In some gymnosperms the needles often increase in length for more than 1 year, as in alpine fir (Stover, 1944), and longleaf pine (Lodewick, 1931). Leaves of evergreen angiosperms generally expand slowly. For example, citrus leaves expanded for 130 days (Scott *et al.,* 1948). Even after leaves of evergreens are fully expanded in area they may continue to thicken and increase in dry weight. Leaves of deciduous trees may also continue to thicken and increase in dry weight during much of the growing season, as shown in Fig. 13.22.

Leaf Area Index

Leaf surfaces are often expressed as leaf area index (LAI), the ratio of leaf area surface of a plant or stand to ground surface area. Inasmuch as the units used for leaf area and ground area are usually the same (m^2), the LAI is a dimensionless measure of the amount of leaf cover. LAI varies with plant size, age, spacing, and various factors influencing leaf size.

Many communities of deciduous woody plants have LAIs of 3 to 6; broad-leaved evergreens up to 8. Most gymnosperms have considerably higher indices than angiosperms (often up to 16). Communities of desert plants have lower values and some fast-growing angiosperms may have much higher values than those given above. For example, some hybrid poplars grown under intensive culture developed unusually high LAIs of 16 to 45, depending on spacing (Isebrands *et al.,* 1977).

Net productivity of forests is greatest when leaves are so arranged that photosynthetically active radiation is absorbed as completely as possible. This usually is the case when the LAI is approximately 4 (Fig. 3.5). If the LAI is less than 4 the light available to individual plants is high, and consequently photosynthetic efficiency is high. Nevertheless the yield per unit of ground area is low in such an open stand.

Maximum gross productivity usually occurs at LAI values in the range of 8 to 10. When trees are very closely spaced the leaves overlap extensively and light intensities in shaded areas are not adequate to maintain a positive CO_2 balance. Hence, net photosynthesis and yield are reduced because of high respiratory losses required to maintain a large volume of leaf and supporting tissues (Fig. 3.5).

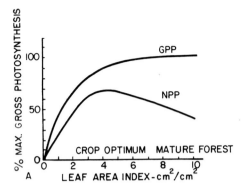

Fig. 3.5. Productivity model for forest showing relations between gross primary production (GPP) and net primary production (NPP) and leaf area index. From Odum (1971).

SHOOT TYPES AND GROWTH PATTERNS

Shoots generally are classified on the basis of location, development, or type of bud from which they are derived. Shoots are classified with respect to their location as terminal leaders, laterals, or basal shoots. Coppice shoots are those that arise from dormant buds near the base of a woody plant. As mentioned, root suckers arise from adventitious buds on roots. Other important types of shoots are determinate and indeterminate shoots, epicormic shoots, preformed and heterophyllus shoots, recurrently flushing shoots, long and short shoots, and abnormal late-season shoots. Some of the more important shoot types and their growth patterns will be discussed briefly.

Determinate and Indeterminate Shoots

In some woody plants such as pine, spruce, oak, and hickory shoot growth results from expansion of terminal buds on the main axis and its branches. After the terminal shoots elongate, there is a period of inactivity until new terminal buds form and expand. In such determinate (monopodial) species only one bud may expand on a shoot each year, or two or more may form sequentially and expand in the same year. In indeterminate (sympodial) trees the shoots do not expand from true terminal buds but arise from secondary axes. Sympodial growth often results when a reproductive structure occurs at the end of a branch or when a shoot tip aborts. In indeterminate species the subtending bud, which often is mistaken for a terminal bud, can be identified as a lateral bud by the scar resulting from abortion of the shoot tip (Fig. 3.6). Shoot tip abortion occurs commonly in such genera as *Betula, Carpinus, Catalpa, Corylus, Diospyros, Gleditsia, Platanus, Robinia, Salix, Tilia,* and *Ulmus.*

Epicormic Shoots

Dormant buds on the main stem or branches of trees often are stimulated by sudden exposure to light to produce epicormic shoots (also called water sprouts). There is

Fig. 3.6. Aborting shoot tip of American elm showing abscission site *(arrow)*. From Millington (1963).

much concern about epicormic shoots because they produce knots that greatly reduce the grade of lumber. Epicormic shoots occur much more commonly in angiosperms than in gymnosperms. Their production also varies greatly among species, age of trees, and degree of exposure.

Inasmuch as species vary widely in the abundance of dormant buds produced, the tendency for epicormic sprouting often can be predicted. For example, oaks tend to produce many epicormic shoots and ashes produce few (Table 3.1). Within a species more epicormic shoots are produced by young and small trees than by old and large trees. Suppressed trees tend to have more epicormic shoots than dominant trees of the same species (Bachelard, 1969b). Formation of epicormic shoots is also influenced by the severity of thinning of forest stands. For example, white oak trees in heavily thinned stands produced more than 35 epicormic shoots; in moderately thinned stands 21; and in unthinned stands 7 epicormic shoots, respectively (Ward, 1966). Blum (1963) noted that the tendency to produce epicormic shoots was greater in border trees than in those growing within forest stands.

Preformed and Heterophyllous Shoots

Shoots may be formed by "fixed growth," "free growth," or a combination of both. Fixed growth involves the elongation of preformed stem units after a rest period. For example, winter buds of adult trees of many species of angiosperms and gymnosperms contain primordia of all the leaves that will expand during the following growing season. In such species shoot formation involves differentiation in the bud during the first year (n) and extension of the preformed parts into a shoot during the second

TABLE 3.1 Variations among Species in Production of Epicormic Shoots[a]

Number of epicormic shoots	Species
Very many	White oak
	Red oak
Many	Basswood
	Black cherry
	Chestnut oak
Few	Beech
	Hickory
	Yellow poplar
	Red maple
	Sugar maple
	Sweet birch
Very few	White ash

[a] From Smith (1966) and Trimble and Seegrist (1973).

year $(n + 1)$ (Kozlowski, 1964a). Examples of species exhibiting this pattern are some northern pines (such as red pine and eastern white pine), as well as spruce, hemlock, and beech. In such plants the growth of their predetermined (fixed) shoots is completed in a relatively short period, often one-half or less of the frost-free season (Kozlowski and Ward, 1961). Western hemlock, for example, expands its preformed shoots in approximately 7 weeks (Owens and Molder, 1973).

The time of formation of leaves in "fixed" buds is quite variable. In many species all the leaves of buds that open in the spring are formed by late autumn of the previous year (n). In some species, however, all leaves may be formed by midsummer of year n and in still others only shortly before bud opening in year $n + 1$. Fast-growing provenances of some trees predetermine more leaves than slow-growing provenances, primarily because they continue accumulating leaf primordia in their buds later into the autumn of year n (Pollard, 1973; Cannell and Willett, 1975).

In contrast to fixed growth, free growth involves the elongation of a shoot by simultaneous initiation and elongation of new stem units (Pollard and Logan, 1974). In adult trees of certain species some of the shoots are fully preformed in the bud (fixed) and other shoots are not. The preformed shoots produce early leaves only and generally expand into short shoots. Internodes of short shoots are only 1 to 2 mm long in ginkgo and those of striped maple are 1 to 2 cm long. The shoots which are not fully preformed in the winter bud are long shoots, called heterophyllous shoots, which produce two sets of leaves: (1) early leaves which are relatively well developed in the winter bud; and (2) late leaves which expand from primordia present in the winter bud or, more commonly, from leaf primordia which continue to form and grow during year $n + 1$ while the shoot is elongating (Figs. 3.7 and 3.8). Such free growth resembles that shown by a

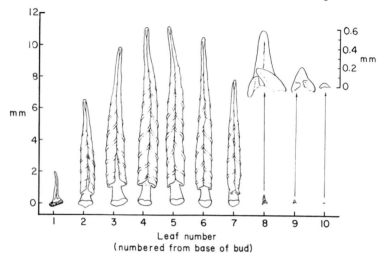

Fig. 3.7. Contents of a winter bud of *Populus trichocarpa*. The first leaf has aborted. The three leaf primordia (8 to 10) are shown in an enlarged scale at the upper right. From Critchfield (1960).

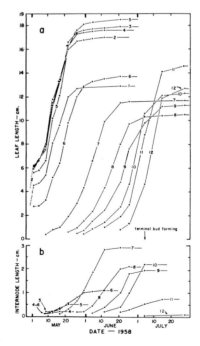

Fig. 3.8. Development of a heterophyllous shoot of *Populus trichocarpa*. a: Growth in length of early leaves (1 to 6) and late leaves (7 to 12). b: growth of internodes (4 to 12). The numbers of the various internodes are the same as the leaf numbers at the upper end. From Critchfield (1960).

number of herbaceous plants. By the end of the growing season the heterophyllous long shoots typically have more leaves than were present in the winter bud. The two sets of leaves often are distinguishable since they may differ in size, lobing, venation, toothing, thickness, and stomatal development. Early leaves generally are larger than late leaves (Fig. 3.9). Examples of woody plants exhibiting free growth are poplars, apple, white birch, yellow birch, redgum, woodbine, several species of *Acer* and *Eucalyptus,* ginkgo, larch, and some tropical pines.

Some species that have been rather hastily classified as having only preformed shoots in the winter bud (exhibiting fixed growth only) often show considerable free growth as well as fixed growth when they are in the seedling stage. For example, free growth of black spruce shoots occurred only in the early years of seedling develop-

Fig. 3.9. Leaf dimormophism in black poplar. A: early stage (5 weeks after bud opening) in development of heterophyllous shoots. The six early leaves have almost completed expanding and the first late leaf is beginning rapid growth. B: a short shoot collected on same date as A. Three early leaves are mature and the terminal bud is beginning to form. C: later stage in development of a heterophyllous shoot. The six early leaves are fully expanded and the first one or two late leaves nearly so. D: early and late leaves. E: leaves 1 and 7 of an adventitious shoot. From Critchfield (1960).

ment, but was an important factor accounting for differences in growth of various provenances (Pollard and Logan, 1976).

In species that are often classified as heterophyllous, the tendency for free growth and production of long shoots diminishes with increasing tree age. For example, whereas a 15-year-old ginkgo tree had only long shoots, a 100-year-old tree had about as many short shoots as long shoots (Gunckel *et al.*, 1949). By the time trembling aspen trees were 6 years old, long shoots made up only 13% of the canopy and there were no long shoots at all in 52-year-old trees (Pollard, 1970). Kozlowski and Clausen (1966) found that all shoots of adult trembling aspen trees were predetermined and all leaves were present at bud break. In both striped maple and red maple, short shoots greatly outnumbered long shoots after the first few years of growth, with long shoots comprising only 4–5% of the annual shoots of adult trees (Wilson, 1966; Critchfield, 1971).

Considerable caution is advised in rigidly classifying patterns of shoot development for groups of woody plants that have a large number of species and occupy extensive ranges. For example, shoot development in *Pinus,* with more than 100 species distributed from the tropics to the arctic, is very diverse. The range of variation in shoot development within the genus is from entirely fixed growth of some species, as in northern pines, to entirely free growth in certain others, such as some tropical pines (Lanner, 1976) (also see Section on ''Foxtail Pines''). Shoot organization and growth patterns are also diverse in the genus *Acer.* Some species of the genus have fully preformed shoots in the winter bud and other species have some of their shoots organized into long shoots which exhibit free growth and produce both early and late leaves (heterophyllous species). The majority of the species of *Acer* belong to the heterophyllous group and include *A. rubrum, A. saccharinum, A. spicatum, A. pseudoplatanus, A. tataricum, A. ginnala, A. caudatum, A. campestre, A. monospessulanum,* and *A. orientale. Acer* species in which the shoots are mostly fully

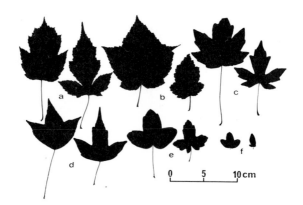

Fig. 3.10. Variations in shape and size of early and late leaves of several heterophyllous species of *Acer.* a: *A. tataricum;* b: *A. rufinerve;* c: *A. campestre* var. *leiocarpum;* d: *A. buergerianum;* e: *A. monspessulanum;* f: *A. orientale.* From Critchfield (1971).

preformed in the bud include *Acer saccharum* and *Acer platanoides*. In most heterophyllous species of *Acer,* the early and late leaves are distinctly different in size and shape (Fig. 3.10). In *Acer saccharinum,* however, the late leaves of long shoots differ only slightly from the early leaves at the base of the same shoot (Critchfield, 1971).

Recurrently Flushing Shoots

Shoot growth of some temperate-zone pines such as loblolly and Monterey, most tropical pines, and many tropical and subtropical angiosperms occurs in a series of waves or "flushes" during the growing season. Such growth involves elongation of more than one terminal bud per shoot each year. After the first bud with its fixed complement of leaves expands into a shoot, a second bud forms rapidly at the apex of the same shoot and this bud also expands shortly thereafter, thereby cumulatively extending the shoot. The second growth phase may be followed by additional waves of growth from even more buds formed and expanded sequentially at the tip of the same shoot axis. In southern pines of the United States, such as loblolly and longleaf pines, the first seasonal growth flush is usually the longest (Fig. 3.11). The number of successive buds which form and expand on the same shoot varies with individual trees, species, shoot location on the stem, and climatic conditions. The terminal leader and upper-whorl shoots usually produce more buds and show more growth flushes than do lower branches. The terminal leader of an average adult loblolly pine tree does not

Fig. 3.11. One year's stem elongation in the recurrently flushing shortleaf pine. From Tepper (1963).

elongate more than two or three times annually, but as many as seven successive elongations have been recorded in one summer for terminal leaders of some trees (Wakeley and Marrero, 1958).

The periods of inactivity between growth flushes may be long or short. Recurrently flushing shortleaf and pitch pine trees in New Jersey had distinct periods of growth inactivity between flushes (Tepper, 1963), whereas in Louisiana the successively formed buds of young loblolly pine trees formed rapidly and expanded, so the shoots elongated almost continuously (Eggler, 1961). Seasonal continuity of shoot expansion in longleaf pine has also been reported (Allen and Scarbrough, 1969).

Seasonal Duration of Shoot Growth

Seasonal duration of shoot growth varies greatly among species. Shoots of some species may fully elongate in a few weeks but others may elongate over a period of several months (Fig. 3.12). The duration of shoot growth varies with the timing of development of shoot components in the bud. Species that have only fully preformed, unexpanded shoots in winter buds (fixed growth) elongate their shoots very rapidly. For example, the fixed shoots of some oaks may expand in only 2 to 3 weeks (Kozlowski, 1964a). In Wisconsin, elongation of red pine shoots usually is completed by the beginning of July (Kozlowski and Ward, 1961). In Connecticut shoot expansion of sugar maple and beech trees lasted about 60 days, and 90% of annual shoot growth was completed in a 4-week period (Kienholz, 1941).

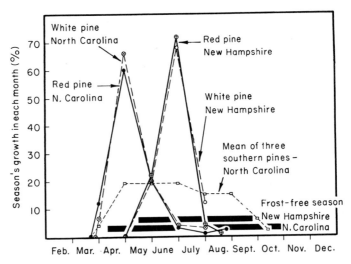

Fig. 3.12. Variations in seasonal height growth patterns of northern pines (red and eastern white pines) in North Carolina and New Hampshire and of three southern pines (loblolly, shortleaf, and slash pines) in North Carolina. The two northern pines have preformed shoots (fixed growth) and exhibit only one annual growth flush whereas the southern pines grow in recurrent flushes. From Kramer (1943).

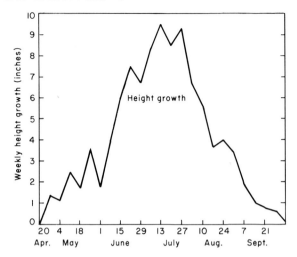

Fig. 3.13. Seasonal height growth in young trees of the heterophyllous eastern cottonwood. From Minckler and Woerheide (1968).

Shoots of heterophyllous species, which are not fully preformed in the winter bud, expand over a much longer time than preformed shoots. For example, shoots of young eastern cottonwood trees continued to elongate from late April until late September (Fig. 3.13). Somewhat similarly, the shoots of apple trees, which exhibited free growth, elongated from late May into September (Mochizuki and Hanada, 1957).

In recurrently flushing species the shoots usually elongate for a very long time in a series of waves. For example, in North Carolina loblolly, shortleaf, and slash pine made 15–20% of their seasonal height growth in each month from April to August. By comparison, red pine and eastern white pine, which have preformed shoots and do not show recurrent flushes of growth, expanded their shoots rapidly and made more of their growth in April than in all other months combined (see Fig. 3.12).

Abnormal Late-Season Shoots

Some trees produce an abnormal late-season burst of shoot growth from opening of recently formed buds which are not expected to open until the following year. The two main types of late-season shoots are (1) lammas shoots which result from elongation of a terminal bud and (2) proleptic shoots occurring from expansion of lateral buds at the base of the terminal bud (Fig. 3.14). Lammas and proleptic shoots may be found alone or in combination. Such late-season shoots may be shorter or longer than the early shoots of the first growth flush. Abnormal late-season shoots have been reported for many gymnosperms and angiosperms. They occur in *Quercus, Fagus, Carya, Alnus, Ulmus, Pinus, Pseudotsuga,* and other genera.

Lammas and proleptic shoots often are stimulated to form by abundant late-season rainfall. There also is strong genetic control of these late-season shoots. Rudolph

Fig. 3.14. Normal and abnormal late-season shoots of jack pine. A: normal shoot and winter bud. B: proleptic shoots; three lateral buds at the base of the terminal bud cluster lost dormancy and expanded after completion of normal seasonal growth. From Rudolph (1964). C: typical lammas shoot; all but the upper part of the lammas shoot is bare of needles.

(1964) demonstrated that the tendency for production of abnormal late-season shoots in jack pine was higher for southern seed sources than for northern ones.

Both lammas and proleptic shoots often suffer winter injury because such shoots do not always harden adequately to cold. Lammas and proleptic shoots also may cause poor stem form. Stem forking is caused by proleptic shoots if a lammas shoot does not form, and also if a lammas shoot forms but then fails to survive the winter. In one study Jump (1938) found stem forking as a result of late-season shoots in 63–94% of red pine trees sampled. If both lammas and proleptic shoots form on a branch there often is competition for apical dominance among them.

Within-Tree Variations in Shoot Growth

Growth of shoots on a given tree often is quite variable. For example, both the rate and amount of growth of stump sprouts often greatly exceed growth of shoots of nonsprout origin. In red maple leaf and internode growth of stump sprouts of trees that had been cut in the winter were much greater than growth of long shoots of control (uncut) trees (Table 3.2). However, the amount by which growth of sprouts exceeded that on nonsprout shoots depended on the time when the sprouting trees were cut (Wilson, 1968).

Apical Dominance

In most gymnosperms the terminal leader elongates more than the lateral branches below it. This produces a more or less conical tree form, often described as having excurrent branching. For example, the terminal leader of red pine trees grew more each

TABLE 3.2 Growth during 1967 of Leaves and Internodes of Long Shoots of Uncut Trees and Stump Sprouts of Red Maple Trees Cut at Different Times of Year[a]

Time of cutting	Leaf pairs produced per week	Leaf length (mm)		Internode length (mm)		Maximum height growth (mm/week)
		Maximum	Maximum elongation per week	Maximum	Maximum elongation per week	
Uncut tree	1.0–1.3	87–116	20–30	78–86	25–40	79–126
Autumn 1966	1.3–2.3	180–208	44–66	107–183	50–88	202–306
May 31, 1967	1.0–1.6	c				87–141
June 14, 1967	0.8–1.5					70–133
June 30, 1967	1.0–1.3					114–170
July 28, 1967	1.0–1.5					10–86
August 24, 1967	1.0[b]					3

[a] From Wilson (1968a).

[b] Only one stump sprouted; the one bud produced one leaf pair.

[c] For stumps cut May 31 to August 24 data were taken only on the rate of leaf pair production and rate of height growth.

year than any of the branches, and annual branch elongation was greatest in the uppermost whorl and decreased in lower whorls (Table 3.3). Furthermore, shoots coming off a main branch elongated less than the main whorl branch itself. Thus a strong pattern of correlative growth inhibition was evident in which the amount of annual shoot elongation decreased progressively downward and inward in the tree. Fraser (1962) also described strong apical dominance in white spruce. The four side branches in the uppermost two whorls averaged about two-thirds as much elongation as the terminal leader. Branches of lower whorls grew much less than those of upper whorls.

A few gymnosperms lack strong apical dominance. For example, second-order branches of *Araucaria excelsa* apparently lack the inherent capacity to assume apical dominance and removal of the apical shoot is not followed by formation of a new leader by one of the lateral branches as occurs in pine and spruce. Rooted cuttings of this species may grow horizontally for many years. Although many pines exhibit strong apical dominance for a long time, some species, such as *Pinus pinea,* often lose apical dominance rather early in life (Fig. 3.15).

Variations in shoot growth within the same tree are much more orderly in gymnosperms as a group than in angiosperms. In some angiosperms many lateral shoots expand at approximately the same rate, producing numerous branches and a rounded crown. These trees are said to have decurrent or deliquescent branching. This growth habit is particularly marked in the elm, which generally loses its terminal buds, resulting in branching and rebranching from lateral buds until the main stem loses its identity in the broadly spreading top. The rate and seasonal duration of growth of shoots of fruit trees are quite variable. Some shoots grow all season; others expand early and stop

TABLE 3.3 Variations in Shoot Elongation on Different Locations of Stems of 6-Year-Old Conifers[a,b]

Conifer	Primary axis (terminal leader)	Secondary axis whorl number				Tertiary axis whorl number					Quaternary axis whorl number	
		1 (Terminal)	2	3	4	2	3 Upper set	3 Lower set	4 Upper set	4 Lower set	3	4
Red pine	57.7 ± 6.2	34.6 ± 7.7	32.5 ± 4.9	27.7 ± 5.4	15.4 ± 8.0	17.1 ± 5.8	15.3 ± 5.4	13.7 ± 4.5	11.5 ± 4.9	8.1 ± 4.8	6.2 ± 2.7	4.7 ± 2.5
Eastern white pine	44.3 ± 7.6	25.5 ± 8.2	24.8 ± 7.0	19.1 ± 4.1	14.1 ± 2.2	12.3 ± 5.1	10.5 ± 3.4	9.5 ± 3.4	7.8 ± 8.4	7.3 ± 3.7	4.3 ± 0.6	3.0 ± 0.5
White spruce	33.5 ± 5.7	19.8 ± 4.1	17.4 ± 3.5	15.3 ± 2.8	11.8 ± 3.0							
Black spruce	23.8 ± 6.4	17.3 ± 3.5	16.5 ± 2.5	14.1 ± 3.3	10.0 ± 3.2							

[a] From Kozlowski and Ward (1961).
[b] All measurements are in centimeters.

Fig 3.15. Ten-year-old *Pinus pinea* tree showing lack of apical dominance. Photo courtesy of A. de Phillipis.

elongating; others have two rapid growth flushes with an intervening period of slow growth; and still others flush recurrently with negligible periods of inactivity between the waves of growth (Glock *et al.*, 1964). Control of apical dominance and tree form is discussed further in Chapter 16.

The occurrence of apical dominance is very important to foresters. When apical dominance is destroyed by invasion of the terminal leader of eastern white pine by the white pine weevil *(Pissodes strobi),* one of the lateral shoots of the first whorl eventually assumes dominance while other shoots in the same whorl are suppressed. However, because of competition among branches, considerable time elapses before one of the whorl shoots establishes dominance and others are suppressed. Meanwhile the tree is degraded as a potential log because of the fork that develops in the stem as a result of the injury to the terminal leader.

Loss of apical dominance in branches often is fostered by Christmas tree growers. Many conifers have long internodes in the main stem and branches and these give the tree a spindly appearance. By "shearing" or cutting back current shoots or by debudding shoots, Christmas tree growers inhibit shoot elongation and stimulate expansion of dormant buds as well as formation and expansion of new buds. Thus new lateral shoots form along branches and produce bushy, high-quality Christmas trees.

Long and Short Shoots

Several genera of gymnosperms, such as *Larix, Ginkgo,* and *Cercidiphyllum,* and some angiosperms, such as *Betula,* produce both long shoots with long internodes and short shoots (sometimes also called spur shoots) which lack appreciable internodes and have leaves crowded together at the stem tip (Fig. 3.16).

In short shoots of tamarack all needles appear at bud break. These expand rapidly and eventually are slightly longer than the early needles of long shoots. There is essentially no internode elongation. On long shoots both early and late needles are

Fig. 3.16. Branches of tamarack bearing both long and short shoots.

produced. All of the early needles appear at bud break. Late needles are produced continuously during much of the summer (Clausen and Kozlowski, 1967b). On long shoots of tamarack all the basal needles and about one-half of the stem needles were preformed in the bud. There were no marked morphological differences between the preformed needles and those formed by free growth after buds opened (Clausen and Kozlowski, 1970).

Maximum Height

Species vary greatly in the height attained by mature trees. Among the tallest trees are species of *Sequoia* and *Eucalyptus*. Less tall, but still exceeding 65 m in height are Douglas-fir, noble fir, sugar pine, and western white pine. Other tall trees of the United States include white fir, ponderosa pine, and Sitka spruce.

Maximum height of a species usually is related more to its longevity than to annual rate of shoot growth, type of shoot produced, or seasonal duration of shoot elongation. Bigtooth aspen and trembling aspen often grow rapidly but never achieve great height because they are short lived. By comparison, some relatively slow growing but long-lived trees such as white oak often are more than 30 m tall.

The relatively long-lived sugar pine, with preformed shoots in the winter bud, is taller at maturity than Monterey pine which has recurrently flushing shoots. Although the rate of height growth of the recurrently flushing loblolly pine and shortleaf pine is greater for about 70 years than that of western white pine, the latter attains greater height at maturity. This is because western white pine continues to increase in height at a relatively fast rate for well over 100 years. Great height of some species, such as Douglas-fir and Sitka spruce, is attributable to fast growth of young trees and its continuation for many years in these long-lived species.

SHOOT GROWTH IN THE TROPICS

Shoot growth of tropical woody plants is very diverse. In general it is intermittent, with shoots expanding in one to several growth flushes during the year. Examples are cacao, coffee, olive, citrus, rubber, tea, mango, and many species of forest trees. The intervals between growth flushes vary among species, cultivars, climatic regimes, individual trees within species, and even branches of a given tree. Classification of growth patterns of many species is difficult because they vary widely in different regions. For example, species of *Thespasia* and *Duabanga* are considered "evergrowing" in Singapore but "deciduous" in India (Koriba, 1958).

Whereas shoots of *Acrocarpus fraxinifolius, Chlorophora excelsa,* and *Schizolobium excelsum* tend to flush only once or twice annually, those of cacao may flush as many as five times. The interval between shoot growth flushes of mango sometimes exceeds 12 months but it may be only a few days in tea.

In tropical climates characterized by wet and dry seasons flushing is seasonal. In Bahia, Brazil, for example, the major flush of shoot growth of cacao occurs in September and October and two or three minor flushes occur between November and April. In citrus there usually are two major flushes of shoot growth and from one to three minor ones, depending on location and climatic conditions.

Young trees of a given species usually flush more often than old trees. For example, young trees of *Litchi chinensis* and cacao exhibited more shoot growth flushes than old trees (Huxley and Van Eck, 1974). Young mango trees tend to flush more or less continuously, whereas old trees tend to have much longer periods of inactivity between flushes. In Nigeria leaves were produced by *Bombax* seedlings for 8 months of the year but only for 1 to 3 months in old trees (Njoku, 1963, 1964).

Both internode elongation and leaf expansion of many tropical trees can be very rapid. Bamboo may grow up to 1 m/day. Examples of rapid height growth were given by Longman and Jenik (1974): *Terminalia superba,* 2.8 m/year; *Musanga cecropiodes,* 3.8 m/year; *Ochroma lagopus,* 5.5 m/year. Such high rates of growth are often determined for open grown trees or at the forest border. Within the forest community the rates tend to be much lower and they often decline rapidly with increasing age of trees. Tropical woody plants exhibit several patterns of leaf initiation in relation to leaf expansion. For example, in *Oreopanax* most leaf primordia are formed very shortly before leaves expand (Borchert, 1969). By comparison, leaf primordia of tea are produced more or less continuously but leaves expand during intermittent growth flushes. Still another pattern occurs in *Rhizophora,* with production of leaf primordia and leaf expansion well synchronized, but with the rate of leaf initiation varying according to season (Tomlinson and Gill, 1973).

Leaf shedding tends to occur more or less continuously in tropical forests. However, there are mild peaks of leaf abscission and these vary among species and with distribution of rainfall. Leaf shedding of many rain forest species is easily induced by even mild water stress. Longman and Jenik (1974) recognized the following four patterns of leaf retention and shedding in tropical forest trees (Fig. 3.17), but they pointed out that sharp lines could not be drawn among these classes.

1. Periodic Growth, Deciduous Type. Leaf shedding occurs well before bud opening. The life span of leaves is about 4 to 11 months. The entire tree or branch is leafless for several weeks to months. Leaf shedding and bud opening do not appear to be related. An example is *Terminalia ivorensis.*

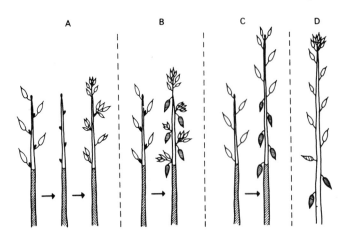

Fig. 3.17. Patterns of leaf abscission and retention in tropical forest trees. A: periodic growth, deciduous type; B: periodic growth, leaf exchanging type; C: periodic growth, evergreen type; D: continuous growth, evergreen type. From Longman and Jenik (1974).

2. Periodic Growth, Leaf Exchanging Type. Leaf shedding is related to bud opening. The life span of leaves often is about 6 to 12 months. The new leaves emerge approximately when the old ones are shed. In *Terminalia catappa* this occurs twice a year; in *Dillenia indica, Entandophragma angolense,* and *Ficus variegata* once a year.

3. Periodic Growth, Evergreen Type. Leaf shedding occurs long after bud opening. The life span of leaves is 7 to 14 months. The branch or tree is definitely evergreen. Examples are *Celtis mildbraedii* and *Mangifera indica.*

4. Continuous Growth, Evergreen Type. Leaf initiation and loss occur continuously. No dormant buds are formed. The life span of leaves is variable but may be up to 14 months. Leaf production and shedding are irregular and vary with environmental factors. Examples are *Trema guineensis, Dillenia suffruticosa,* and young seedlings of many other species.

Shoot growth of pines in the tropics may be similar to their growth in the temperate zone, or it may be quite different. Normal growth is by typical recurrent flushing with the axis elongating by extension of a succession of buds formed on the terminal leader of the main stem. After a period of elongation, growth of the stem ceases briefly and a new terminal bud cluster forms. Shortly thereafter the recently formed buds expand to further lengthen the terminal leader and to produce a whorl of lateral branches. Generally from two to four such growth flushes occur annually. In contrast, some pine trees develop abnormally and grow continuously as a result of failure to set buds which would elongate to form lateral branches (Lanner, 1964, 1966a). Lloyd (1914) described such growth as "foxtailing" because the upper part of the abnormally elongating shoot had a conical or "foxtail" appearance (Fig. 3.18).

This striking form of exaggerated apical dominance often produces trees with up to 6 m, and occasionally up to 13 m, of branchless stem. This environmental response is a problem of variable degree wherever pines are grown in the tropics. Among pines

Fig. 3.18. Five-year-old normal branched trees and branchless foxtail forms of *Pinus caribaea* var. *hondurensis* in Malaysia. From Kozlowski and Greathouse (1970).

reported to show foxtailing growth are *Pinus canariensis, P. caribaea, P. cembroides, P. echinata, P. elliottii, P. kesiya (insularis), P. merkusii, P. oocarpa, P. palustris, P. radiata, P. taeda,* and *P. tropicalis.*

Foxtailing is a good example of free growth. Near the tip of a foxtail shoot the unexpanded needles are tightly packed and enclosed in unbroken sheaths. Below these the needles penetrate their sheaths and increase in length, giving the upper part of the continuously expanding shoot a conical appearance. New needle primordia are more or less constantly formed at the apex and are subsequently expanded, resulting in a progression of needle sizes and stages of development (Fig. 3.19).

Needle retention appears to be increased during periods of foxtailing. As observed in Malaysia, the branchless stem portions retain needles during several growth periods, but lose these needles soon after the tree reverts to a normal growth pattern.

Various degrees of foxtailing were observed in large Malaysian plantations of *P. caribaea* var. *hondurensis* trees up to 15 years of age (Fig. 3.20). For example: (1) in some trees continuous growth of the terminal leader occurred without pause after field planting, resulting in a single stem with no side branches; (2) foxtailing began at the time of field planting and ceased after a few years, thereafter a normal pattern of shoot growth occurred; (3) trees grew normally for a while and then foxtailed; (4) foxtailing began at the time of field planting, ceased after a few years, and subsequently resumed in the terminal leaders. Thus, conversions from continuous shoot elongation to a recurrently flushing pattern, and the reverse, were observed (Kozlowski and Greathouse, 1970). Foxtailing pines and recurrently flushing pines together provide

Fig. 3.19. Branch of foxtail shoot of *Pinus caribaea* var. *hondurensis* showing active growing point and progression of needle sizes from the tip. From Kozlowski and Greathouse (1970).

Fig. 3.20. Foxtailing of both terminal leader and lateral branches of *Pinus caribaea* var. *hondurensis*. From Kozlowski and Greathouse (1970).

excellent experimental materials for studies of hormonal relations controlling shoot growth. Apical dominance is discussed further in Chapter 16.

Although most reports of foxtailing refer to the phenomenon as a characteristic of the terminal leader, lateral shoots may also show the foxtailing trait (see Fig. 3.20). Such laterals either gradually or abruptly become vertically oriented. The apical parts of foxtailed branches are morphologically similar to those of foxtailed terminal leaders. Alternation of normal and foxtail growth sometimes produces individual trees of grotesque form.

Most foresters consider foxtailing to be an undesirable trait because it is associated with wind breakage, reduction in diameter growth, absence of latewood formation, presence of compression wood, and restricted seed production.

CAMBIAL GROWTH

Increase in the diameter of trees occurs primarily from meristematic activity in the vascular cambium, a cylindrical lateral meristem located between the xylem and phloem of the stem, branches, and roots. The cambium is composed of elongated spindle-shaped cells, called fusiform initials, and short ray initials. The latter have often been described as isodiametric cells. However, Wodzicki and Brown (1973a) showed that in the Pinaceae the ray initials often vary in dimensions and consist of two types: (1) marginal ray initials with radial diameters equal to or smaller than their axial

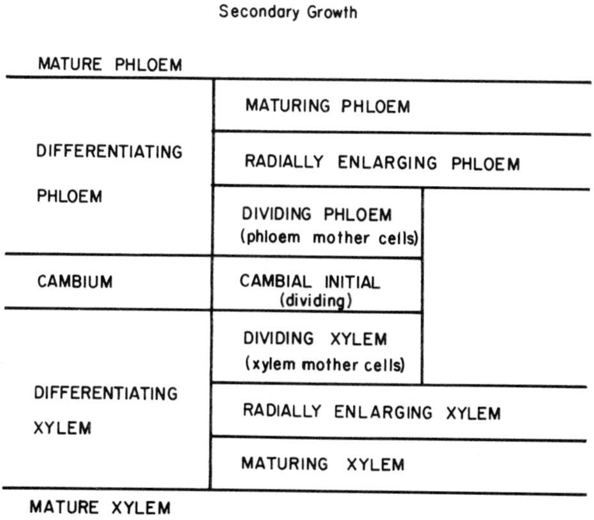

Secondary Growth

MATURE PHLOEM		
DIFFERENTIATING PHLOEM	MATURING PHLOEM	
	RADIALLY ENLARGING PHLOEM	
	DIVIDING PHLOEM (phloem mother cells)	
CAMBIUM	CAMBIAL INITIAL (dividing)	
DIFFERENTIATING XYLEM	DIVIDING XYLEM (xylem mother cells)	
	RADIALLY ENLARGING XYLEM	
	MATURING XYLEM	
MATURE XYLEM		

Fig. 3.21. Terminology for describing cell types and tissues associated with cambial growth. From Wilson *et al.* (1966).

length, and (2) radially elongated initials of the ray interior. Both fusiform initials and ray initials often are radially offset from neighboring cells and from each other.

Cambia are commonly classified as storied (stratified) and nonstoried (nonstratified). In stored cambia (e.g., black locust) the fusiform initials appear in horizontal tiers in tangential view. Nonstoried cambia (e.g., gymnosperms, poplars) have fusiform initials with overlapping ends. In European ash, the cambium is intermediate between the two types, having localized storied areas as well as nonstoried areas (Krawczyszyn, 1977).

Over the years there has been spirited controversy about whether the term cambium should refer exclusively to a single layer of cambial initials or whether it should encompass both the cambial initials and their recent meristematic derivatives, the xylem mother cells and phloem mother cells. One problem is the difficulty of identifying the single (uniseriate) layer of initials. While recognizing the existence of such a layer it often is useful to use the term "cambial zone" to refer to the entire zone of dividing cells (the uniseriate layer plus the xylem and phloem mother cells). A useful terminology for the various cell types and tissues involved in cambial activity is given in Fig. 3.21.

The cambial zone in dormant trees may vary from 1 to 10 cells wide, but in growing trees the width is extremely variable. Bannan (1962) found the cambial zone to be 6 to 8 cells wide in slow-growing trees and 12 to 40 cells wide in fast-growing trees.

Cell Division in the Cambium

Two types of cell division occur in the cambium: additive and multiplicative. Additive division involves periclinal (tangential) division of fusiform initials to produce xylem and phloem mother cells which in turn produce xylem and phloem cells. Multiplicative division involves anticlinal divisions of fusiform initials which provide for circumferential expansion of the cambium.

Production of Xylem and Phloem

Following winter dormancy the cambium of temperate zone trees is reactivated to produce xylem inwardly and phloem outwardly. This reactivation appears to be caused by apically produced hormones moving downward in the stem (see Chapter 16). New annual increments of xylem and phloem are thus inserted between old layers of these tissues, causing the stem, branches, and major roots to increase in thickness.

Most investigators agree that cambial reactivation occurs in two stages which involve change in appearance of the cambium (change in color, translucence, slight swelling) (Evert, 1960, 1963; Deshpande, 1967), followed by mitotic activity that produces cambial derivatives. As the second phase begins, the first few cell divisions may be scattered and discontinuous at different stem levels in large trees having buds on many lateral branches. Nevertheless, once seasonal cambial growth starts, the cambial growth wave is propagated downward beginning at the bases of buds (Wilcox, 1962a; Tepper and Hollis, 1967).

Time of Initiation of Xylem and Phloem

Many early investigators reported that annual xylem production preceded phloem production. However, as Evert (1963) emphasized, differentiating sieve elements were not adequately investigated in early studies. Furthermore, the same criteria of cell development were not applied to different sides of the cambium. For example, differentiation of phloemward cells that had overwintered in the cambial zone usually was interpreted as maturation of phloem mother cells left over from the previous season. New phloem production was not considered to begin until new phloem mother cells were derived from cambial initials. In contrast, differentiation of overwintering xylem mother cells was accepted as evidence of cambial activity and xylem production. Hence, the criteria on which the widely held view that xylem formation preceded phloem formation was founded are questionable.

In several ring-porous angiosperms phloem differentiation throughout much of the plant axis begins slightly earlier or about the same time as xylem differentiation. For example, in black locust phloem differentiation began about a week before xylem differentiation (Derr and Evert, 1967). In a wide variety of diffuse-porous angiosperms and in gymnosperms, phloem differentiation occurs first, sometimes preceding xylem differentiation by several weeks (Fig. 3.22). For example, in pear phloem differentiation preceded xylem differentiation by 8 weeks (Evert, 1960) and in trembling aspen, jack pine, red pine, and eastern white pine by as much as 6 weeks (Davies and Evert, 1965; Evert, 1963; Alfieri and Evert, 1968). In tamarack, balsam fir, and black spruce much of the phloem increment was produced before new xylem differentiation even began (Alfieri and Evert, 1973).

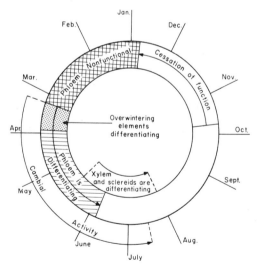

Fig. 3.22. Seasonal changes in cambial activity of pear trees. From Evert (1960). Originally published by the University of California Press; reprinted by permission of the Regents of the University of California.

Amounts of Xylem and Phloem Produced

The order of formation of cambial derivatives appears to have no direct relation to the amount of tissue produced annually on opposite sides of the cambium. By the end of the growing season the number of xylem cells cut off by the cambium greatly exceeds the number of phloem cells produced. This is so even in species in which initiation of phloem production greatly precedes initiation of xylem formation. For example, as many as 100 rows of tracheids and only 10 or 12 rows of phloem elements were produced in a radial file each season by Douglas-fir (Grillos and Smith, 1959). In white fir xylem and phloem cells were produced in a ratio of 14 to 1 (Wilson, 1963).

In at least some species, the xylem increment is more sensitive than the phloem increment to environmental stress. As conditions for growth become unfavorable, the xylem–phloem ratio often declines. In northern white cedar the xylem–phloem ratio varied from 15 to 1 to 2 to 1, with decreasing tree vigor (Bannan, 1955). In pecan seasonal increment of small, 2-year-old, fruit-bearing branches had a xylem–phloem ratio of less than 3, but in rapidly growing branches the ratio often exceeded 5 (Artschwager, 1950). Bannan (1955) found the annual phloem increment to be about the same in fast-growing northern white cedar trees as in slow-growing ones. In pear the uniform phloem increment, together with greater variability in xylem production, suggested that phloem production had precedence over xylem development (Evert, 1960). These relations apparently do not hold for certain subtropical species which lack recognizable annual growth rings in the phloem. In *Eucalyptus camaldulensis,* for example, the ratio of xylem to phloem changed only in a narrow range under different environmental conditions. A similar xylem–phlem ratio, about 4 to 1, was found for both fast-growing and slow-growing trees. The ratio also was rather independent of the width of the cambial zone (Waisel *et al.,* 1966).

Differentiation

After xylem and phloem daughter cells are cut off by the cambium they differentiate in an ordered sequence of events that include cell enlargement, secondary wall formation, lignification, and loss of protoplasts (Fig. 3.23). These events do not occur stepwise, but rather as overlapping phases. For example, secondary wall formation often begins before growth of the primary wall ends. During cell differentiation most cambial derivatives are altered morphologically and chemically into specialized elements of various tissue systems.

Cambial derivatives that are cut off on the inner side of the cambium to produce xylem may differentiate into one of four types of elements: vessel members, fibers, tracheids, or parenchyma cells. Vessel members, tracheids, fiber tracheids, and libriform fibers develop secondary walls and the end walls of vessels become perforated, but the derivatives of ray initials change little during differentiation. However, the ray tracheids of gymnosperms are greatly altered as they develop secondary walls and lose their protoplasts. Changes in cell size also vary appreciably among different types of cambial derivatives.

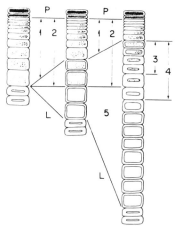

Early season   Mid-season   Late season

Fig. 3.23. Variations in radial files of tracheids of red pine at different times during the growing season. 1: Primary wall zone; 2: cytoplasm zone; 3: flattened latewood cells; 4: Mork latewood cells; 5: mature earlywood; P: phloem; L: latewood of the preceding year. From Whitmore and Zahner (1966).

Full differentiation of individual cambial derivatives generally occurs over a few to several weeks. The time required for differentiation varies with species, cell type, and the time during the growing season when a given type of element is produced. For example, radial expansion of earlywood tracheids of Monterey pine required about 3 weeks; that of latewood tracheids took half as long. On the other hand, secondary wall formation took much longer as the season progressed; 3 to 4 weeks for wall thickening in the spring; 8 to 10 weeks in the autumn (Skene, 1969).

As mentioned, the rate of differentiation varies with types of cambial derivatives. In ring-porous angiosperms differentiation of vessels usually precedes that of other elements (Evert and Kozlowski, 1967; Zasada and Zahner, 1969).

Increase in Cell Size

As water is absorbed by vacuoles of cambial derivatives turgor increases, causing cell expansion (Fig. 3.24). The cambial derivatives that develop into vessel members expand rapidly radially and tangentially but do not elongate appreciably. Tracheids and fibers undergo some radial expansion and elongate to varying degrees among different plant groups. In angiosperms the tracheids and fibers elongate greatly, whereas gymnosperm tracheids elongate very little. According to Bailey (1920), cambial derivatives of angiosperms elongated up to 500%, but gymnosperm tracheids by only 20%. However, cambial initials are much longer in gymnosperms than in angiosperms. Hence, despite relatively limited elongation of cambial derivatives of gymnosperms, they still are longer than those of angiosperms when both are fully developed.

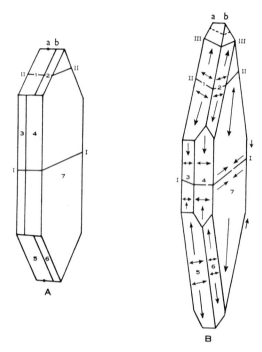

Fig. 3.24. Changes in form of a gymnosperm tracheid during differentiation. A: cambial initial; B: mature tracheid. As the tracheid increases in volume it elongates and the ends become more acute. The radial walls widen and tangential walls narrow. Corresponding parts are shown by Arabic and Roman numerals and by the letters a and b. The length of the cell is reduced approximately 50 times. From Wardrop (1954).

Growth in length of cambial derivatives is restricted to cell tips or at least to the apical zone. The increase in length involves intrusive growth and, when elongation of particular cells occurs, intercellular adjustments are necessary within a vertically static tissue. According to Wenham and Cusick (1975) an elongating cambial derivative secretes an enzyme that weakens the middle lamella between it and the cells adjacent to it. Where this occurs, these cells, during their turgor expansion, round off from each other at the corners. The tip of the elongating cell fills this space as it is created.

Cell Wall Thickening

The walls of most mature xylem cells consist of a thin primary wall and a thick secondary wall. The primary wall forms at cell division in the cambium and encloses the protoplast during surface growth of the cell. The secondary wall forms after completion of surface growth.

The primary wall is not lamellated and tends to have loosely packed microfibrils. The secondary wall, is deposited in three layers (designated S_1, S_2, and S_3) on the

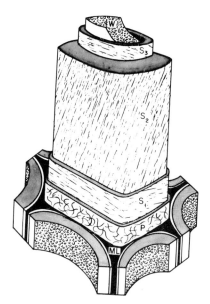

Fig. 3.25. Diagram of cell wall organization of a mature tracheid. ML: middle lamella; P: primary wall; S_1, S_2, and S_3: secondary walls; W: warty layer. From Coté (1967), "Wood Ultrastructure," Washington University Press, Seattle, Washington.

primary wall (Fig. 3.25), and is made up of a fibrillar component, cellulose, as well as encrusting substances, primarily lignin, but also hemicellulose, pectin, and small amounts of protein. The cellulose microfibrils are laid down by apposition, whereas lignin and other encrusting substances are deposited by intussusception within the cellulose framework (Torrey *et al.*, 1971). The amount of lignification varies among plant groups and species, cells, and different parts of the same cell. Mature gymnosperm tracheids and angiosperm vessels are heavily lignified but fiber tracheids and libriform fibers of angiosperms show little deposition of lignin.

Unlike most xylem cells that develop thick cell walls, most phloem cells remain soft-walled and eventually collapse or become greatly distorted. Phloem fibers, however, develop secondary walls.

Loss of Protoplasts

Final stages of maturation of xylem cells such as vessel elements and tracheids involve breakdown and autolysis of protoplasts. All of the important organelles are present during secondary wall formation, but in the final stages of maturation the vacuolar membranes, cytoplasmic organelles, cytoplasm, and plasmalemma undergo autolysis, and the nucleus disintegrates, thus terminating the life of tracheid protoplasts. Lysis of protoplasts of differentiating xylem elements occurs rather rapidly. For example, in eastern hemlock tracheids it occurs in approximately 4 days (Skene, 1972); in Scotch pine tracheids in 2 to 5 days (Wodzicki and Brown, 1973b).

Expansion of the Cambium

As a tree grows it becomes necessary for the cambial sheath to increase in area. This is accomplished by adding new cambial cells in two ways: (1) by increasing the length of the cambial sheath through addition of new cells from the procambium behind the root and stem tips, and (2) by increasing the circumference of the cambial sheath by anticlinal division of fusiform cambial cells, either by longitudinal division (in angiosperms with storied cambia) or by pseudotransverse division (in angiosperms with nonstoried cambia and in gymnosperms). In addition a small percentage of fusiform cambial cells divide anticlinally to produce segments off the sides of the initials (Fig. 3. 26).

In pseudotransverse division the cell wall laid down near the center of the dividing fusiform initial may vary from short and almost transverse to elongate and inclined. Usually the partition averages about 15% of the length of the dividing cell but sometimes it may approximate one-third to one-half of the length of the original cell (Bannan, 1964). After pseudotransverse division occurs, each of the two new daughter initials is slightly longer than one-half the length of the former initial. The cells then elongate during several periclinal divisions until the original length is attained, and then another pseudotransverse division may occur.

During pseudotransverse division there is an overproduction and loss of fusiform initials, resulting in only a small increase in number of cells. Cell size and degree of contact with vascular rays appear to be major factors in survival of fusiform initials during intracambial competition. The longer sister initial of a pseudotransverse division is more likely to survive than is the shorter initial (Bannan, 1957; Evert, 1961). The surviving long initials have most ray contacts. The newly formed short initials that

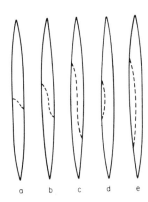

a   b   c   d   e

Fig. 3.26. Tangential view of fusiform initials cells showing various types of anticlinical division involved in multiplication of cambial cells. Pseudotransverse division (a–c); lateral division (d, e). From Bannan (1967).

have few ray contacts either lose their capacity for periclinal division and mature or they are reduced in size and converted to ray initials.

Tip growth of fusiform cambial cells involves intrusion of some cells among others. In some species much greater elongation of fusiform initials occurs consistently at one end, but this is not true for other species. In Pinaceae, for example, the direction of growth of fusiform initials after pseudotransverse division was primarily upward (Bannan, 1968). In northern white cedar it was primarily downward (Bannan, 1960), and in pear there was no polarity in direction of cell elongation (Evert, 1961).

The rate and distribution of pseudotransverse divisions of cambial initials change with age of trees. In rapidly growing young trees pseudotransverse divisions occur frequently throughout the growing season and the rate of survival of new initials is very high. Under these conditions both the new fusiform initials and cambial derivatives are short. As trees age, however, pseudotransverse divisions occur less often and are confined to the latter part of the growing season, by which time most of the annual ring has formed. Furthermore, the rate of survival of newly formed initials declines in older trees. Since the surviving initials have more space into which to expand, longer fusiform initials and cambial derivatives are gradually produced until a maximum size characteristic for a species is reached.

Variations in Growth Increments

Cambial activity is not continuous in space or in time. It may be general over a tree at certain times and at other times, as during droughts, it may be localized. Hence, trees produce a sheath of xylem that varies in thickness at different stem and branch heights and, at a given stem height, it often varies in thickness on different sides of the tree.

Sometimes trees that form complete xylem increments in the upper stem do not form any annual xylem rings in the lower stem. Such "missing rings" are especially characteristic of very suppressed or old trees. Also, as branches undergo successive suppression by new branches above, those in the lower stem fail to produce xylem at the point of juncture with the main stem (see Chapter 17).

Sometimes more than one growth ring is produced in the same year (Fig. 3.27). Such "false" or "multiple" rings often occur when cambial activity stops during an environmental stress, such as drought, and then resumes. When this happens, alternations of earlywood and latewood are repeated. False rings also result from injuries by insects, fungi, or fire.

Sometimes the cambium is dead or dormant on one side of a tree, leading to production of partial or discontinuous rings that do not complete the stem circumference. Discontinuous rings may be found in overmature trees, heavily defoliated trees, suppressed trees, senescing branches, and stems of trees with one-sided crowns. In the last group, the ring discontinuities generally occur on the stem radius below the underdeveloped crown. Discontinuous rings are common in roots, which often are eccentric in cross section.

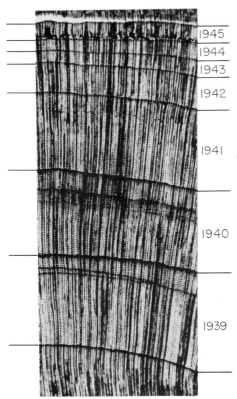

Fig. 3.27. Multiple rings formed during 1939 and 1940 in a branch of Arizona cypress. From Glock *et al.* (1960).

Seasonal Duration of Cambial Growth

The time during which the cambium is active varies with climate, species, crown class, and different parts of stems and branches. In a given region seasonal cambial growth of evergreens as a group usually continues for a longer time than it does in deciduous trees (Winget and Kozlowski, 1965b). The cambium of a suppressed tree may produce xylem for only a fraction of the time during which the cambium of an adjacent dominant tree of the same species remains active (Kozlowski and Peterson, 1962). In the same tree seasonal cambial growth begins at about the same time that shoot activity begins, but cambial growth often continues for a long time after shoot elongation ceases. Seasonal cambial growth continues for a longer time in the upper stem than in the lower stem. It should be remembered that cambial growth is very responsive to environmental stresses. Hence, it often stops during droughts and resumes after a rain. The control of cambial growth is discussed in more detail in Chapters 16 and 17.

Anomalous Cambial Growth

Most information on cambial growth characteristics has been obtained from studies of temperate zone trees. Secondary growth of such species is considered to be normal. In a number of species of tropical trees and lianas, cambial growth often deviates from the normal pattern. For example, Obaton (1960) reported anomalous cambial growth in 108 species of woody lianas in 21 families of plants in western Africa. Anomalous or atypical cambial growth may be found in some plants in which the cambium is in normal position. In other plants the cambium is atypically located. Often anomalous cambial growth is the result of unequal activity of various cambial segments, changes in amounts and position of xylem and phloem, or production and activity of successive cambia. The various forms of anomalous cambial growth are difficult to classify into distinct groups because of their diversity and intergrading with normal forms of cambial growth.

In some families of angiosperms (e.g., Amaranthaceae, Chenopodiaceae, Menispermaceae, and Nyctaginaceae) and certain gymnosperms (lianas of the genus *Gnetum* and *Welwitschia* and members of the Cycadales) a series of successive functional cambia form. Usually the normal cambium functions for a while and then dies. New cambia then form sequentially toward the outer stem surface. Each successive cambium functions in a normal manner but only for a limited time. Thus the wood is comprised of alternating bands of xylem and phloem. An example of a species forming successive external cambia is *Avicennia resinifera*. In this species, the first of the supernumerary cambia arises by division of the inner cells of the cortex and subsequent cambia arise within derivatives of the preceding cambium. In transection, the mature stem of *Avicennia* consists of a series of units, each of which is produced by a single cambium. Each unit consists, from the inside out, of sequential bands of parenchyma, secondary xylem, secondary phloem, and sclereids (Studholme and Philipson, 1966).

Bougainvillea also forms successive cambia, each of which originates among derivatives of the preceding cambium (Fig. 3.28). Each cambium is bidirectional and produces xylem inward and phloem outward. Vascular tissues are produced in the following order: (1) conjunctive tissues and xylem fibers, (2) phloem, (3) more xylem with vessels and more phloem. The phloem and xylem differentiate from radially seriated derivatives. However, radial seriation may be obscured by divisions among phloem initials and growth adjustments in differentiating xylem.

In some woody plants strands of secondary phloem are found within the secondary xylem. The origin of such "included phloem" varies. In *Combretum,* for example, a portion of the cambium may cut off derivatives inwardly which differentiate as phloem. In *Strychnos* strips of the cambium stop growing. As the cambium at the sides moves outward, the gap gradually heals over, leaving a strand of included phloem in the xylem. In some species certain portions of the cambial cylinder produce more xylem than phloem and other portions cut off more phloem than xylem. In some desert shrubs, such as *Peganum harmala, Zygophyllum dumosum,* and *Zilla spinosa,* marked discontinuities in cambial activity around the axis result in formation of ridged stems which often split (Ginzburg, 1963). An interesting type of anomalous cambial growth

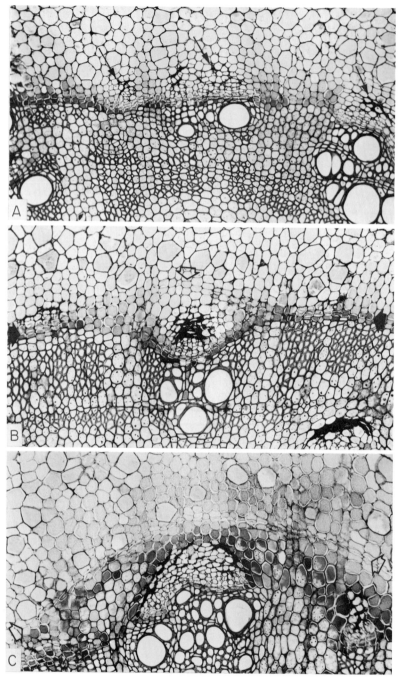

Fig. 3.28. A: anomalous cambial growth of *Bougainvillea* as seen in transections of roots. B: the cambium forms a continuous layer outside the xylem; phloem at arrows. C: a new cambium has originated outside the phloem of the oldest bundle and is continuous with the old cambium (solid arrows). The new cambium (open arrows) is in a slightly later stage of development than in B. From Esau and Cheadle (1969).

occurs in the Bignoniaceae. After a cambial cylinder forms at the end of primary growth, four strips of cambium stop producing xylem but continue to produce phloem cells. Hence two cambial types occurs, one with bidirectional activity and the other with unidirectional activity.

Wounding and Wound Healing

Tree wounds are invasion routes for pathogenic organisms. Wounds result from broken branches, tops, or roots and by exposure of xylem as a result of mechanical wounds, animal wounds, fire wounds, etc. The severity of the wound and vigor of the host influence the rate and effectiveness of plant response to wounding. Wounds that break the bark and only slightly injure the cambium generally heal rapidly.

Shigo (1975) considers decay processes in trees following wounding to occur in three sequential stages. Stage I includes all processes associated with response of the host to wounding. This involves some discoloration of the xylem as a result of chemical processes (see Kozlowski, 1971a, pp. 146–154). After wounding, reserve materials in storage cells are depleted, phenolic and quinoic compounds accumulate, and patterns of enzyme activity are altered (Sharon, 1974). Stage II includes events that occur when microorganisms overcome chemical protection barriers and invade the xylem areas. Ray parenchyma cells are invaded first. Pioneer invaders usually (but not always) are bacteria and nonhymenomycetous fungi. Wood discoloration is intensified because of interactions between living xylem cells and the invading microrganisms. As tissues die and discolor, minerals accumulate and moisture increases. In some species changes occur without a color change and "wetwood" forms in association with bacteria. In Stage III microorganisms, especially Hymenomycetes, invade and degrade cell wall substances. By this time all xylem cells are dead. After invasion by pioneer decay microorganisms, many other microorganisms follow and compete for the remainder of the tissues. These organisms include Phycomycetes, Actinomycetes, and nematodes. Whether the processes continue through all three stages depends greatly on host vigor and severity of wounding. When wounds are small and trees vigorous the processes generally do not proceed beyond Stage I.

Host Response to Wounding

The living sapwood shows a dynamic response to wounding and discolored wood containing various extractives forms around the area containing microorganisms. Such "protection wood" resists invasion by microorganisms.

When chemical protective barriers are overcome by microorganisms, the host tree often responds by compartmentalizing the wounded tissues. Barriers to invasion include plugging of vessels in some species, formation of tyloses in others, and production of thick-walled xylem and ray cells by the cambium. These changes create a barrier wall that separates the wounded tissues from those formed after wounding. Invading microorganisms then spread along the path of least resistance, vertically through the compartmentalized tissues. If a tree is wounded again, another barrier wall forms and surrounds the inner compartments.

The physiology and biochemistry of the reactions to wounding and infection are complex and poorly understood. As just mentioned, there are extensive changes in protein metabolism, increases in the number of mitochondria and in respiration, increases in enzymes, especially polyphenoloxidases and peroxidases, and in ethylene production in both the injured tissue and in adjacent uninjured tissue. There also often are changes in concentration of growth regulators (Dekhuijzen, 1976). This indicates that a substance or substances must move out of the injured tissue and affect genes controlling specific enzymes in adjacent cells. Some investigators attribute these effects to ethylene produced in injured tissue, but the evidence for ethylene as a general agent is not convincing. It is more likely that there are specific substances, sometimes called wound hormones, which affect the metabolism of the adjacent tissue and produce the changes in metabolism which result in compartmentalization and callus formation associated with healing of wounds. Some aspects of this complicated problem are discussed by Uritani (1976).

Wound Healing

Healing involves closure of a wound as well as walling off of infected and invaded tissues associated with the wound. Many large wounds on old trees never close; yet they heal from the inside.

Cambial Growth in Wound Closure

Healing of deep stem wounds involves the sequential production of callus tissue and formation of a new vascular cambium by conversion of callus cells to cambial cells. A phellogen is also regenerated during the wound healing process. Abundant callus formation usually is associated with healing of longitudinal frost cracks in tree stems. Such wounds may recurrently open and close in response to sudden temperature decreases and increases. During the rehealing phase, vertically oriented protrusions of abundant callus tissue, the so-called "frost ribs," often develop along the edges of the wound.

Although the origin of callus may vary considerably among species, in most woody plants the vascular rays make the major and sometimes the only contribution to callus formation. Occasionally other components of the cambial zone contribute to production of callus tissue. Thus, wound callus may be produced by parenchyma of xylem rays and phloem rays, undifferentiated xylem cells, and cortical tissues.

The amount of callus formed during healing of stem wounds may vary with the size of the wound. Callus formation in shallow wounds sometimes is restricted or absent. The amount and rate of callus production following wounding also differ among species of plants. For example, callus was produced earlier and much more abundantly by injured *Populus* and *Acer* stems than by those of *Pyrus* (Soe, 1959). Formation of a new vascular cambium was independent of the amount or rate of callus production. Formation of a phellogen preceded regeneration of the vascular cambium. The new phellogen became active as soon as the callus pad was well developed.

Initiation of new cambium in wounded trees often has been associated with the original cambium at the edges of a wound as in *Hibiscus* (Sharples and Gunnery, 1933) and *Populus* (Soe, 1959). In some species, however, regeneration of a new cambium does not depend on the position or presence of an existing cambium at the sides of the wound. For example, in wounded *Trema orientalis* stems, a new vascular cambium was differentiated in the middle of the callus (Noel, 1968).

The early activity of a newly regenerated cambium may be normal or abnormal. In *Hibiscus* the new cambium produces normally distributed tissues (Sharples and Gunnery, 1933). This contrasts with very abnormal distribution of vascular tissue which forms during healing of stem wounds in *Trema orientalis* (Noel, 1968), *Populus, Acer, Malus,* or *Pyrus* (Soe, 1959). In *Populus,* new xylem and phloem elements were cut off soon after the vascular cambium formed (about 9 days after wounding) but the first-formed derivatives were abnormal and distorted. Normal production of xylem and phloem was first observed at about 20 days after wounding.

Factors Affecting Wound Closure

The rate of closure of wounds is positively correlated with the rate of cambial growth. Wounds heal most rapidly in vigorous trees. Since cambial growth of trees in the north temperate zone occurs primarily during May, June, and July, wounds made prior to May heal rapidly; those made after July heal little. Wound shape has little effect on the rate of healing.

A number of wound dressings have been used on the wounds over the years. These include asphalt-type materials, shellac, house paints, and petrolatum. Their usefulness has been widely debated. Neely (1970) concluded that wound dressings had no significant effect on increasing the rate of wound healing. In fact, a petrolatum dressing reduced the rate of healing. Shigo and Wilson (1977) found no significant effect of several wound dressings on the rate of wound closure, vertical extensions of discolored and decayed wood, or presence of decay fungi. In addition, the dressings did not prevent infection by decay fungi. Shigo and Wilson (1977) acknowledged that wound dressings have a strong psychological appeal but their usefulness in accelerating wound healing has not been demonstrated.

Perhaps the best ways of dealing with tree wounds are to concentrate on prevention of wounding; removing injured branches, bark, and wood to produce as clean a wound as possible; stimulating cambial growth by fertilizing and irrigating trees; and removing less valuable trees that may be crowding the injured tree.

ROOT GROWTH

The seed contains a radicle or root meristem in the embryo from which the first tap root develops. The first root branches and elongates to produce a ramified root system, or it may die back. Whereas lateral shoots on stems originate from peripheral tissues, lateral roots arise from the deep-seated outer layer of the stele known as the pericycle (Fig. 3.29). During initiation of lateral roots, several pericyclic cells become meristematic and divide periclinally to produce cells that then divide, both periclinally and anticlinally, to form a protruding lateral primordium which grows out through the

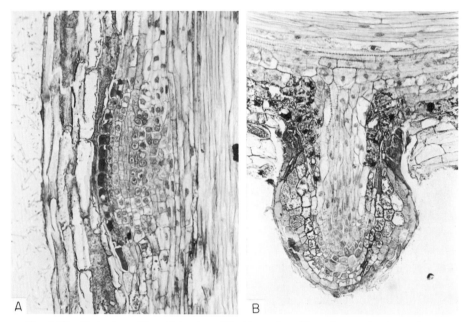

Fig. 3.29.   Early stage (A) and late stage (B) of formation of lateral roots of red pine. Photo courtesy of H. E. Wilcox.

endodermis, cortex, and epidermis. Before a lateral root breaks through the surface tissues of the main root, it develops a well-defined apical meristem and rootcap. Both digestion of surrounding tissue and mechanical pressure appear to be involved in the outgrowth of lateral roots through the cortex. Initiation of lateral roots appears to be regulated by synergistic effects of several hormonal growth regulators (Torrey, 1976).

The extent of branching and rebranching of both woody and nonwoody long roots is truly remarkable. Lyford (1975) calculated that a mature red oak tree had a minimum of 500 million live root tips. Rapid proliferation of roots has also been shown in very young woody plants. Kozlowski and Scholtes (1948) found wide differences among species in root branching (Table 3.4). Whereas a greenhouse-grown 6-month-old flowering dogwood seedling had over 2,600 roots with a total length of 5,144 cm, a loblolly pine seedling of the same age had only 760 roots with a total length of 387 cm. In both species the growth potential of individual roots of higher orders declined progressively. Kolesnikov (1966) reported that apple seedlings produced about 40,000 roots with a total length of 230 m in a single growing season, distributed in seven orders of branching.

Three types of lateral root branches may form on woody long roots. The new branch may be a long root that eventually undergoes secondary thickening and becomes a part of the permanent woody root system. The second and most common type of branch roots are short roots. The third type develops when a short root lateral is converted to a long root. Branches of long roots usually are replacement roots following injury to a

TABLE 3.4 Variation in Development of Roots of Flowering Dogwood and Loblolly Pine Seedlings[a,b]

	Flowering dogwood		Loblolly pine	
Order	Number of roots	Total length (cm)	Number of roots	Total length (cm)
First	1	44.1	1	32.2
Second	93	859.7	71	187.5
Third	1035	2714.4	496	146.1
Fourth	1336	1357.0	199	21.1
Fifth	191	168.1	0	0.0
Sixth	1	0.6	0	0.0
Total No.	2657	5143.9	767	387.0
Length (m)		51.4		3.87

[a] From Kozlowski and Scholtes (1948).
[b] Seedlings were 6 months old and grown in the absence of competition.

long root tip (Wilson, 1975). Injury also commonly occurs on nonwoody laterals and is followed by formation of replacement roots and forking.

Longevity of Roots

Root systems of woody plants consist of the relatively long-lived large perennial roots and many short-lived small roots. Unfavorable environmental conditions, attacks by insects, fungi, and other organisms, and advancing tree age also are responsible for root mortality (Kozlowski, 1971b). In healthy trees many of the small roots die shortly after they form. In apple trees, for example, small lateral roots live only about a week (Childers and White, 1942). According to Kolesnikov (1966), the tips of main roots of seedlings of orchard trees die by the time the seedlings are 2 months old. Species appear to vary, however, in longevity of their small roots. In Norway spruce most absorbing rootlets usually lived for 3 to 4 years, only about 10% dying during the first year and 20% living for more than 4 years (Orlov, 1960). Head (1966a) noted that black currant roots lived for more than a year. However, many of the smaller so-called "feeder roots" of fruit and forest trees live less than a year. Death of small roots generally varies with order of branching. For example, in red pine there is more mortality in second-order lateral roots than in primary roots (Wilcox, 1968).

In the temperate zone the greatest mortality of small roots occurs during the cold months. In *Juglans regia* more than 90% of the absorbing roots were lost during the winter (Bode, 1959). According to Voronkov (1956) the dry weight of active roots of tea plants was about 12% lower in February than in the previous December. By early April, however, growth of new roots had more than made up for the winter loss.

Root Elongation

Tips of roots may be pointed in long roots and rounded in short roots. A longitudinal section of the end of a young root typically has four cell regions of different character. At the tip is the protective cellular mass comprising the rootcap. Behind it is the growing point, a meristematic region of small, thin-walled, cubical cells with dense cytoplasm. Mitotic figures often can be seen in this growing point, which usually is about 1 mm long. As the number of cells increases, some are added to the rootcap and others to the region of elongation located above the meristematic zone. In this region the cells produced in the growing point rapidly increase in size, primarily in a longitudinal direction. Above the region of elongation is a zone of differentiation and maturation. Eventually the newly formed cells at the base of the region of elongation lose their capacity for further expansion and become differentiated into the epidermis, cortex, and stele.

Considerable variation may be found among species and different roots in the delineation of root zones. The rootcap, for example, does not occur in mycorrhizal roots of pines. The zone of differentiation often is difficult to measure because various types of cells are differentiated at various distances from the root tip. Furthermore, the distance from the apex at which cells differentiate is a function of the rate of root growth. Wilcox (1954) found that various elements of roots of noble fir matured closer to the apical initials in slow-growing than in fast-growing roots, and this is generally true.

Growing root tips are pushed out through the soil by the elongating cells and often follow an irregular course as they bend to pass around obstacles. Nevertheless, the long horizontal roots of red maple radiate outward as much as 25 m from the base of a tree in a remarkably straight line. When deflected laterally by a barrier they curve back toward the original direction after passing it (Lyford and Wilson, 1964; Wilson, 1967). According to Head (1965) spiral growth is common in roots, but spiraling is sometimes confused with twisting. Wilson (1964) reported that a maple root was twisted more than four times in a distance of 22 m. J. E. Stone and Stone (1975b) reported some twisting in roots of red pine, but no spiraling.

When seasonal root elongation ceases, roots often turn brown in a process called metacutization. This involves lignification and suberization of cell walls of the cortex and dormant rootcap. Many roots retain a white root tip even though a metacutization layer is present. Presence or absence of a white root tip depends on how many layers of dead cells are cut off outside the metacutization layer.

Root Hairs

The absorbing surface of roots of many species of woody plants is greatly increased by development of root hairs. These tubular outgrowths usually arise as protrusions from the external, lateral walls of epidermal cells, although in a few species they originate from cortical cells one or two layers beneath the epidermis. In conifers the root hairs of short roots arise from a surface layer of cells, whereas those of long roots arise from the second or third layer of cortical cells. The root hairs originate from the surface layer only where persistent root cap layers are absent (Bogar and Smith, 1965). Root hairs usually form in the area just behind the zone of most active meristematic tissue and they decrease in length toward the apex. They generally form after the rate of elongation of epidermal cells declines.

The highly vacuolated and thin-walled root hairs vary in life span. Most of them live only a few hours, days, or weeks and are eliminated by changes of secondary thickening, including suberization and lignification. The zone of root hairs migrates because, as old root hairs die, new ones form regularly behind the growing point of an elongating root. Some trees, including honey locust, Kentucky coffee tree, and Valencia orange may retain suberized or lignified root hairs for months or years (MacDougal, 1921; Hayward and Long, 1942). Such persistent root hairs appear to be relatively inefficient in absorption.

Both hereditary differences among species and environmental factors influence the abundance of root hairs. Kozlowski and Scholtes (1948) found that roots of the average 7-week-old black locust seedling grown in the greenhouse developed over 11,000 root hairs (520/cm^2) whereas those of loblolly pine of the same age had less than 600 root hairs (217/cm^2) (Table 3.5). Differences in root hair production of sycamore maple and red oak were reported by Richardson (1953a). Sycamore maple had a normal pattern of root hair development, with the root hair zone located just behind the growing tip and extending for 2 to 3 mm. By comparison, red oak had root hairs only on roots of the lowest order of branching and these were produced only after root growth stopped.

At times, many trees, such as avocado and pecan, lack root hairs. They also are absent on roots of some gymnosperms and on mycorrhizal roots. In general root hair formation is stimulated by environmental factors that decrease mycorrhizal develop-

TABLE 3.5 Development of Roots and Root Hairs of 7-Week-Old Black Locust and Loblolly Pine Seedlings[a]

	Root length (cm)	Root surface area (cm^2)	Root hairs (no.)	Root hair surface area (cm^2)
Black locust				
Primary	16.20	3.45	1,166	3.63
Secondary	115.62	15.72	8,321	25.22
Tertiary	30.60	3.12	2,081	5.18
Total	162.42	22.28	11,568	34.03
			520 root hairs/cm^2	
Loblolly pine				
Primary	6.45	2.73	215	2.80
Secondary	5.93	0.97	371	2.08
Total	12.38	2.70	586	2.87
			217 root hairs/cm^2	

[a] From Kozlowski and Scholtes (1948).

ment and accelerate root elongation (Sutton, 1969; Marks and Kozlowski, 1973). However, mycorrhizal development and root hair occurrence do not wholly exclude one another. Wide variations have been found in control by mycorrhizae of root hair development, from no suppression to total elimination of root hairs (Laing, 1932). In Douglas-fir, root hairs were absent from mycorrhizal roots, but in long lateral roots, root hairs and a Hartig net were not incompatible (Bogar and Smith, 1965).

Rate of Root Growth

The rate of root elongation of woody plants varies among species, genetic materials, tree age, season, site, and environmental conditions. Roots may elongate from a fraction of a millimeter to well over 25 mm a day during the period of most active growth. Long roots of apple at East Malling grew 4–6 cm/week; those of cherry 7–8 cm/week (Head, 1973). According to Hoffman (1966), a few roots of black locust and a species of poplar had exceptionally high growth rates of about 5 cm/day. Head (1965) and Lyr and Hoffman (1967) found root elongation to be consistently greater during the night than during the day. Reed (1939) observed root growth rates of southern pines in a plantation of 2 to over 3 mm/day when they were growing most rapidly. Barney (1951) reported an average daily growth rate for loblolly pine roots on seedlings in a greenhouse of 5.2 mm/day at a soil temperature of 25°C, but only 0.17 mm at 5°C.

Seasonal Variations

The annual growth of roots involves two components: (1) elongation of existing roots, and (2) initiation of new laterals and their subsequent elongation.

In the temperate zone root elongation usually begins earlier in the spring and continues later in the autumn than shoot elongation in the same tree (Fig. 3.30). The time interval between the cessation of shoot elongation and of root elongation varies greatly among species. Root elongation may continue for many weeks in species whose shoots are fully preformed in the winter bud and expand rapidly. However, in heterophyllous and recurrently flushing species, with shoots expanding for many weeks, root elongation may continue for only a slightly longer time than does shoot extension. In southern pines root elongation occurs every month in the year (Kramer, 1969, pp. 127–129). However, in the winter it is limited by low temperature; in the summer by dry soil.

The rate of root growth may be expected to vary greatly during the growing season. As may be seen in Fig. 3.30 maximum root growth, including number of growing roots and their rate of elongation, occurred in early summer, but in some species considerable late-season root growth occurred. Root growth of young mugo pine trees in southern Ontario continued from April to late November. During the summer daily root elongation averaged about 6.5 mm but during the autumn it was 2.9 mm (Mason *et al.*, 1970).

Many investigators have reported seasonal root growth of both forest and orchard trees to occur in two or more surges which often appeared to be responses to environmental changes. This is discussed further in Chapter 17.

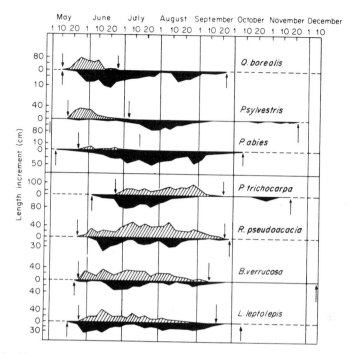

Fig. 3.30. Variations in seasonal shoot and root growth characteristics of eight species of forest trees. Shading indicates shoot growth and solid black represents root growth. Seasonal initiation and termination of growth are described by arrows. From Lyr and Hoffmann (1967).

Cambial Growth in Roots

Primary growth of some roots is followed by secondary growth involving formation of secondary vascular tissues by the cambium and of periderm by a phellogen. Secondary thickening may start during the first or second year. Stages in formation of the cambium and secondary growth of a woody root are shown in Fig. 3.31. At first some parenchyma and pericycle cells become meristematic and form a wavy cambial band on the inner edges of the phloem strands and outside the xylem. Eventually the cambium produces xylem in a complete cylinder. Shortly after the cambium forms, some of the pericycle cells divide to form the phellogen (cork cambium) which cuts off phelloderm tissue to the inside and cork to the outside. After cork formation begins, the cortex with its endodermis is shed and the tissue arrangement thereafter is similar to that in the stem.

The root cambium produces xylem first in roots located near the soil surface and later in those in deeper soil layers. The downward migration of the cambial growth wave often is slower than in the stem. In orange trees, cambial activity occurred in the

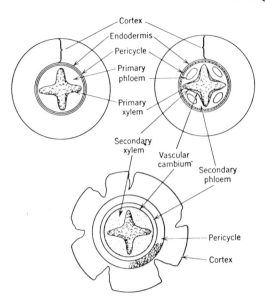

Fig. 3.31. Secondary growth of a woody root, showing development of vascular cambium and production of secondary xylem and phloem. Enlargement by addition of secondary tissue crushes the primary phloem and endodermis and splits off the cortex. After Esau (1965).

stem and branches in April and spread to the main root within two weeks. Subsequently the spread of cambial growth into the root system was slow and xylem production did not begin in lateral roots until late July, and in some small roots not until late September (Cameron and Schroeder, 1945).

Cambial growth is much more irregular in roots than in stems. It varies markedly along the length of the root and around its circumference. Maximum xylem production consistently occurs near the soil line. Hence, annual xylem increments taper rapidly below the soil line and gradually beyond to the root tip (Fig. 3.32). However, there may be departures from this pattern. For example, Head (1968) found that thickening of apple roots was irregular along the length of the root. Sometimes appreciable thickening began first in more distal parts of the roots and in some years there was no cambial growth at all. Young roots generally are circular in transection, but as they age xylem deposition around a root becomes more uneven. Hence old roots tend to be very eccentric in cross section (Fig. 3.33). False and double xylem rings abound in roots. The horizontal roots of many tropical species show much greater xylem production along the upper side than the lower one, leading to formation of buttresses. One explanation attributes the formation of cypress knees to very rapid cambial activity on the upper surface of roots.

There is great variability in xylem production in different roots of the same tree. Usually there is greater growth eccentricity in the lateral horizontal roots than in vertical or oblique roots in the central portion of a root system.

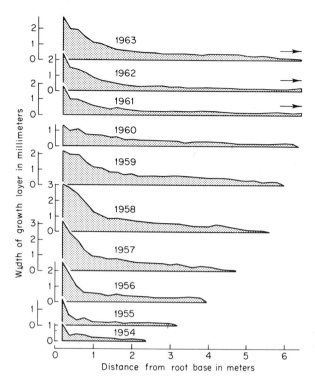

Fig. 3.32. Annual xylem production along a main lateral root of red pine. From Fayle (1968).

Fig. 3.33. Cross section of a horizontal root of arborvitae showing marked eccentricity of cambial growth. Photo courtesy of U.S. Forest Service.

MEASUREMENT AND ANALYSIS OF GROWTH

Measurement of tree growth can be made by various methods, depending on the objectives of the investigator. Most important to foresters is measurement of the annual increment of wood produced by a stand of trees. This is calculated from measurements of bole diameter and height and is modified somewhat by the amount of bole taper. It usually is expressed as volume per unit of land area, but for some purposes is better expressed as weight per unit of land area. Tree height often is used as an indicator of site quality expressed as site index, usually defined as the height of the average dominant trees at the age of 50 years. For slow-growing trees 100 years sometimes is used as the base.

Physiologists are interested in more detailed studies of the seasonal course of diameter and height growth and how growth is affected by environmental and cultural factors. They also are interested in the partitioning of growth among the different parts of a plant. Such studies require more frequent and more precise measurements than are necessary for estimating the annual increment of wood.

Height Growth

It is very difficult to obtain precise measurement of tall trees. Generally heights of tall trees are measured indirectly with various hypsometers, all of which are based on the principle of the relation of the sides of similar triangles, or on the relation between the sides and trigonometric functions of the angles of right triangles (Husch *et al.*, 1972). A surveyor's transit also can be used to measure tree height rather precisely (Worrall, 1973).

Height growth of young trees can be measured with meter sticks or graduated poles. Jointed poles are sometimes used to measure trees 10 or 15 m in height (Liming, 1946). Various kinds of growth gauges, rules, and meter sticks have been used to measure height growth of seedlings. Cremer (1976) used a growth recorder, adapted from a hygrothermograph, to continuously record diurnal changes in height growth of seedlings.

Cambial Growth

Much attention has been given to the measurement of cambial growth because of its obvious contribution to tree volume, its sensitivity to various internal and environmental factors, and the ease with which it is measured. For measuring cambial growth various kinds of dendrometers, calipers, and tapes have been used. There are two basic kinds of dendrometers: those that measure changes in stem circumference by means of a band and those that measure changes of a single stem radius by gauging the distance between a fixed plane anchored in the wood of a tree and a point on the surface of the bark. In the latter group are dial gauge dendrometers, micrometer caliper dendrometers, and recording dendrometers (usually called dendrographs). Various kinds of optical dendrometers have been used to measure diameters in upper parts of stems of standing trees (Grosenbaugh, 1963).

Tree ring bands such as that shown in Fig. 3.34 measure changes in circumference, but they cannot differentiate between expansion of bark and wood or between changes caused by growth and changes caused by variations in water content. Dial gauge dendrometers such as that shown in Figure 3.35 detect the beginning of cambial growth and periodic shrinkage more accurately than tree rings (Bormann and Kozlowski, 1962). Dendrographs such as that shown in Figure 3.36 or electrically operated dendrographs (Phipps and Gilbert, 1960) measure and record growth over periods of time. Figure 3.37 shows an example of continued radial growth superimposed on almost daily stem shrinkage caused by water stress, except on March 13, which was a rainy day.

Unfortunately, measurements made at a single height or at a single position in the circumference of a tree bole do not accurately measure growth of the entire bole. As pointed out earlier in this chapter, there often is little cambial activity in the lower part of the bole of suppressed trees, but considerable activity in the upper part. Also, cambial activity differs on different sides of a tree and several dendrometers must be installed around the stem circumference to obtain an accurate record of radial growth.

Stem diameters and volume of wood in individual trees sometimes are estimated from crown diameters. Methods of determining crown diameters from aerial photographs and in the field are discussed by Spurr (1960) and Husch *et al.* (1972).

Fig. 3.34. A tree ring band for measuring changes in circumference of tree trunks (Liming, 1957). Photograph courtesy of U.S. Forest Service.

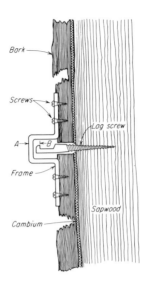

Fig 3.35. A dendrometer for measuring radial growth of tree trunks. The distance A–B is measured periodically with a micrometer caliper. After Byram and Doolittle (1950).

Most dendrometers were designed for use with large trees. For measuring diameter growth of seedlings, micrometer calipers have often been used. Splinter (1970) adapted a recording micrometer for continuous measurements. Kozlowski (1967b) obtained continuous measurements of diameter changes in tree seedlings by mounting a dendrograph on a supporting frame. The stem of the experimental seedling was backed against a removable steel plate. The dendrograph rod, bearing on the opposite side of the stem, continuously registered changes in stem diameter. These were transcribed to

Fig. 3.36. A dendrograph for recording radial growth of tree trunks (Fritts and Fritts, 1955). Photograph courtesy of H. C. Fritts.

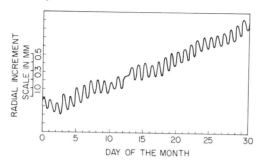

Fig. 3.37. Diurnal variations in radius superimposed on long-term radial growth of a *Pinus canariensis* tree in Australia. Note the effect of a rain on March 13. After Holmes and Shim (1968).

charts on a rotating drum actuated by a clock mechanism. Small changes in stem diameters of seedlings have also been measured with strain gauges and transducers (Namken *et al.*, 1969).

The problems inherent in measuring growth of trees are discussed in more detail by Kozlowski (1971b, Chapter 4), Kozlowski (1972a, Chapter 1), and Husch *et al.* (1972).

Analysis of Growth

According to Ledig (1976) a better understanding of what constitutes optimum allocation or partitioning of growth among the various organs of a plant is one of the most important tasks of plant physiology. This requires a much more intensive analysis of plant growth than is provided by measuring diameter and height. Information concerning the partitioning of growth among the roots, stem, branches, and leaves is necessary to an understanding of how various environmental and cultural practices affect growth.

Dry matter production depends basically on the amount of photosynthetic surface and the rate of carbon fixation (photosynthesis) per unit of leaf surface. Leaf area is expressed for crops and stands of trees as leaf area index, the leaf area per unit of land surface, and weight increase per unit of leaf surface or mass as net assimilation rate (NAR). Physiologists are therefore interested in learning whether various factors affect growth chiefly by affecting the rate of photosynthesis per unit of leaf area, the leaf area itself, or the distribution of photosynthate among roots, stem, branches, and leaves. It was claimed by Watson (1952) and others in England that most of the variation of yield of agricultural crops is related to differences in rate of increase in leaf area rather than differences in net assimilation rate. There is considerable evidence that biomass production of forests is also positively correlated with leaf biomass or leaf area index up to some optimum. Beyond this there may be a decrease in net assimilation rate because of increasing shading of lower leaves, as pointed out earlier in this chapter. Length of life of leaves also is important and retention of a large leaf surface able to carry on photosynthesis until late in the autumn is likely to increase dry matter production (Zavitkovski *et al.*, 1974). One effect of nitrogen fertilization is to delay senescence of leaves and prolong photosynthetic activity.

Problems in Studying Partitioning of Photosynthate

Study of the partitioning of dry matter or biomass among the various parts of plants is more difficult in trees than in herbaceous plants because their large size restricts the amount of sampling. Estimates of dry matter production from nondestructive measurements such as CO_2 uptake are unreliable (Helms, 1976). Sometimes the proportions of dry matter in leaves, branches, bole, and roots are measured on a tree of average size and the results are extrapolated to all the trees of a stand. This is only reliable if the trees are of uniform size, because the proportions of total biomass in the various components vary with tree age and size, as shown in Table 3.6.

A more acceptable method is to harvest and measure the components of several trees of various sizes and relate the weights of the components to some easily measured dimension such as bole diameter by regression analysis. The problems of sampling are discussed by several authors in the book edited by Reid and Fechner (1974).

Relative Growth Rates

Another problem is how to compare the growth of plants of different sizes. It was established long ago that plant growth follows the compound interest law, the amount of growth made in a unit of time depending on the amount of material or size of plant at the beginning of the period. Thus seedlings developing from large seeds are likely to increase in size more rapidly than those of the same species developing from small seeds, and large seedlings would be expected to grow more rapidly than small ones. This fact led to development of the concept of relative growth rate (RGR) or measurement of increase in dry weight per unit of time per unit of growing material, often in

TABLE 3.6 Approximate Ratio of Leaf to Branch and Stem Weight at Various Ages for Birch and Loblolly Pine [a]

	Ratios			
	Birch		Loblolly pine	
Approximate age of stand	Leaves: branches	Leaves: stems	Leaves: branches	Leaves: stems
5	1:1	1:1	1:1	1:10
25	1:6	1:20	1:2	1:20
45	1:12	1:50	1:6	1:50
55	1:12	1:55	1:8	1:70

[a] From data of Switzer *et al.* (1968).

grams per gram dry weight per week. This permits comparison of the effects of various factors in the environment on rate of growth independently of the size of the plants which are being compared.

The equation for calculating mean relative growth rate is:

$$RGR = \frac{\ln W_2 - \ln W_1}{t_2 - t_1}$$

W_1 and W_2 are the dry weights at the beginning and end of the sampling period, t_1 and t_2 are the dates of sampling, and ln is the natural logarithm of the numbers.

As growth depends on the rate of photosynthesis and the area or weight of photosynthetic tissue the relationship can be shown as follows:

$$RGR = NAR \times LAR$$

In this expression NAR (net assimilation rate) is dry weight increment per unit of leaf area and LAR (leaf area ratio) is the ratio of leaf area to total dry weight, all for the specified time interval $t_2 - t_1$, which usually is 1 or 2 weeks.

The development and application of these concepts are discussed by Kvet *et al.* (1971), by Ledig, in Reid and Fechner (1974), and in Cannell and Last (1976). They also are discussed in more detail in a book by Evans (1972). The important contribution is that they provide a means for comparing growth of plants of different sizes and ontogenetic development and for studying the relative importance of leaf area and rate of photosynthesis per unit of leaf area. Following the analogy to return on capital suggested by the compound interest law, the photosynthetic capital is the leaf area and the more photosynthate converted into leaf area the more rapid the growth. As Ledig (1976) states, this can lead to the rather ridiculous conclusion that the most efficient plant in terms of dry matter production would consist entirely of leaves. Actually, stems and branches are necessary for elevating leaves to a position where they are well exposed to the light and roots are necessary to supply water, mineral nutrients, and growth regulators. Thus an efficient tree or other plant represents an optimum compromise in allocation of photosynthate to leaf growth and to the structures which support the leaves.

Trees are at a disadvantage, compared with annual plants, because an ever-increasing fraction of their total dry weight exists as wood which is photosynthetically nonproductive. This is shown in Table 3.6. Thus the relative growth rate tends to decrease with increasing age and is generally lower for woody perennial plants than for herbaceous annuals.

From an economic standpoint, efficient growth is that which produces the maximum yield of the desired product. This may be wood, fruit, seeds, or even flowers, and thus there has been selection by plant breeders to convert the largest possible fraction of photosynthate into the desired economic product. For foresters the desired product usually is wood. The wood-producing capacity of a tree depends on the interaction of three major components. One is the rate of photosynthesis per unit of leaf area or mass or per unit of chlorophyll. A second component is related to structure, duration, exposure, and area of canopy (Farmer, 1976). A third component in yield is related to differences in distribution and partitioning of photosynthate among the various organs of trees, resulting in different ratios of dry matter in the crown, bole, and roots. A major contribution of plant physiology is to learn how these components of wood production can be manipulated to produce efficient yields of wood. In contrast to foresters, horticulturists desire the largest possible yield of fruit. This has caused a trend toward dwarf trees which convert a larger fraction of photosynthate into fruit because their leaves support a smaller fraction of nonphotosynthetic tissue than the leaves of large trees.

GENERAL REFERENCES

Alvim, P. de T., and Kozlowski, T. T., eds. (1977). "Ecophysiology of Tropical Crops." Academic Press, New York.

Cannell, M. G. R., and Last, F. T., eds. (1976). "Tree Physiology and Yield Improvement." Academic Press, New York.

Clowes, F. (1961). "Apical Meristems." Blackwell, Oxford.

Esau, K. (1977). "Anatomy of Seed Plants." Wiley, New York.

Evans, G. C. (1972). "The Quantitative Analysis of Plant Growth." Univ. of California Press, Berkeley.

Hallé, F., Oldeman, R. A. A., and Tomlinson, P. B., eds. (1978). "Tropical Trees and Forests: An Architectural Analysis." Springer-Verlag, Berlin and New York.

Kozlowski, T. T. (1964). Shoot growth in woody plants. *Bot. Rev.* **30,** 335–392.

Leopold, A. C., and Kriedemann, P. E. (1975). "Plant Growth and Development." McGraw-Hill, New York.

Longman, K. A., and Jenik, J. J. (1974). "Tropical Forest and Its Environment." Longmans, Green, New York.

Marks, G. C., and Kozlowski, T. T., eds. (1973). "Ectomycorrhizae." Academic Press, New York.

Philipson, W. R., Ward, J. M., and Butterfield, B. C. (1971). "The Vascular Cambium: Its Development and Activity." Chapman & Hall, London.

Richards, P. W. (1966). "Tropical Rain Forest." Cambridge Univ. Press, London and New York.

Romberger, J. A. (1963). Meristems, growth and development in woody plants. *U.S., Dept. Agric., Tech. Bull.* **1293.**

Tomlinson, P. B., and Zimmermann, M. H., eds. (1978). "Tropical Trees as Living Systems." Cambridge Univ. Press, London and New York.

Torrey, J. G., and Clarkson, D. T., eds. (1975). "The Development and Function of Roots." Academic Press, New York.

Zimmermann, M. H., and Brown, C. L. (1971). "Trees, Structure and Function." Springer-Verlag, Berlin and New York.

Reproductive Growth

INTRODUCTION

One of the more important concerns in forestry and horticulture is production of adequate amounts of high-quality planting stock. Most woody plants reproduce in nature by seeds, but vegetative propagation also occurs by means of stump sprouts, root suckers, and layering.

Often it is better to propagate woody plants vegetatively by the rooting of cuttings, grafting, layering, or by the use of tissue cultures than by sexual propagation. It has been known for centuries that fruit trees do not grow true to type from seed but must be propagated vegetatively. It is now known that most trees are highly heterozygous, because the embryo in a seed receives different sets of chromosomes from the pistillate and pollen parents, hence, it differs genetically from both parents. Even if an embryo is produced as a result of self-pollination, it will not be identical to the parent on which the seed is borne because of the high degree of heterozygosity and the random manner in which chromosomes separate during reduction division and recombine during the union of egg and sperm. By comparison, vegetatively propagated plants contain only the genetic information of the parent plant.

There are other reasons for propagating woody plants vegetatively in addition to ensuring that the offspring will resemble the parent. For example, by budding or grafting, a tree top with certain desirable characteristics can be combined with a root system of another type which grows more vigorously or is more resistant to disease, as when *Vinifera* varieties of grapes are grafted on American varieties of rootstocks which are resistant to phylloxera. Another example of vegetative propagation to produce a desired type of growth is the production of dwarf apple trees by grafting them on rootstocks known to cause dwarfing, such as Malling IX (M9), and dwarf pears by grafting on quince rootstocks (see Chapter 17). Asexual propagation is required to grow cultivars that do not produce viable seeds, such as some grapes, figs, oranges, and bananas. Furthermore, vegetative propagation is more reliable than sexual reproduction for plants whose seeds germinate slowly or poorly, or plants that have a long juvenile stage during which they do not produce flowers, fruits, and seeds and sometimes also have other undesirable characteristics, such as thorniness.

One of the most important and least understood problems in both horticulture and forestry involves the irregular and unpredictable production of flowers, fruits, and seeds. Fruit and seed crops vary not only among species, but also among trees of the same species and from year to year in the same tree. As Matthews (1963) emphasized, the success of geneticists and tree breeders in introducing superior varieties and improved cultivars of orchard and forest trees requires reliable reproduction at an early age. Accomplishment of this depends on better understanding the internal processes in reproductive growth. These include initiation of flower primordia, flowering, pollination (transfer of pollen from anther to stigma), fertilization (fusion of male and female gametes), growth and differentiation of the embryo, growth of the fruit and seed to maturity, and ripening of fruits and cones. In order to have a good fruit or seed crop, each of these sequential reproductive phases must be successful. Unfortunately blocks to one or more of these phases often occur and prevent completion of reproductive growth.

PERIODICITY OF REPRODUCTIVE GROWTH

Many botanists define a flower as "a determinate sporogenous shoot bearing carpels" (Hillman, 1963), thereby restricting the term to angiosperms. However, this volume will use the term more broadly, in line with common usage of foresters and horticulturists, and consider a flower to be "a determinate sporogenous shoot" (Jackson and Sweet, 1972), making it possible to treat the young cones or strobili of gymnosperms as flowers also.

Temperate Zone Trees

Woody plants pass through a juvenile stage during which they do not flower. Once they pass beyond the juvenile stage and achieve the capacity for flowering they usually retain it thereafter as a seasonal phenomenon. The length of the juvenile period may vary greatly among species (Table 4.1). Some varieties of apple, like Wealthy, may flower when 3 to 4 years old and others, like Northern Spy, often do not do so until 15 to 20 years old. Time of first flowering often varies greatly within a genus as well as

TABLE 4.1 Variation in Length of Juvenile Period in Trees as Determined by Time to First Flowering

Species	Juvenile period (years)	Reference
Pinus sylvestris	5–10	Wareing (1959)
Larix decidua	10–15	Wareing (1959)
Pseudotsuga menziesii	15–20	Wareing (1959)
Picea abies	20–25	Wareing (1959)
Abies alba	25–30	Wareing (1959)
Betula pubescens	5–10	Wareing (1959)
Fraxinus excelsior	15–20	Wareing (1959)
Acer pseudoplatanus	15–20	Wareing (1959)
Quercus robur	25–30	Wareing (1959)
Fagus sylvatica	30–40	Wareing (1959)
Tea (*Camellia thea*)	5	Bubrjak (1961)
Apple (*Malus*)	7.5	Visser (1964)
Pear (*Pyrus*)	10	Visser (1964)
Tangerine (*Citrus reticulata*)	5–7	Furr *et al.* (1947)
Sweet orange (*Citrus sinensis*)	6–7	Furr *et al.* (1947)
Grapefruit	7–8	Furr *et al.* (1947)
Tangelo (*Citrus paradisi* × *C. reticulata*)	5–8	Furr *et al.* (1947)

between genera. Jack pine may produce cones in the third year and lodgepole pine in 5 to 6 years. Slash pine, however, seldom bears cones until 10 years of age or older, and does not bear them in large numbers until it is about 20 years old.

The duration of the nonflowering juvenile stage is greatly modified by environmental factors that influence growth rate. Vigorous trees reach the flowering stage before suppressed ones of the same species. Occasional precocious flowering in some species does not necessarily mean that the adult stage has been reached. Citrus, for example, may flower as a very young seedling and then grow only vegetatively for several years until it completes its juvenile growth phase. Subsequently it flowers regularly as an adult plant.

Even after the adult stage has been reached, woody plants do not flower every year because physiological conditions and environmental factors can control the initiation of flower primordia. Open-grown trees and well-illuminated ones in forest borders often flower for the first time at an earlier age and produce more seeds than those in closed stands and dense shade (see Chapter 17). Woody plants growing in the warm part of a species range flower earlier than those in the cooler part. For example, flowering dogwood blooms in Jacksonville, Florida in mid-February; in St. Louis, Missouri in early April; and in Columbus, Ohio in early May (Wyman, 1950). The effect of environment on flowering is emphasized by Tydeman's (1964) observation that over a 43-year period the date of full bloom of Cox's Orange Pippin apple trees in England varied from April 15 to May 23rd, depending on temperature.

An example of periodicity in reproductive growth is the well-known biennial bearing of fruit trees. In some varieties of apple, a heavy flower and fruit crop is produced one year and little or none the following year. The tendency for biennial bearing is much greater in York Imperial and Golden Delicious varieties than in Rome Beauty or Jonathan. The alternate-year bearing is a physiological characteristic of individual trees as well as parts of trees. Some trees in an orchard flower and fruit heavily one year while neighboring trees bear lightly. In the following year the order is reversed with the previously heavy-bearing trees having a light crop and those that previously had a light crop bearing abundantly. Furthermore, in the same year one branch may produce a large flower and fruit crop, while other branches do not. The next year, the reverse occurs, with the previously fruiting branch remaining vegetative. The biennial bearing sequence of trees can be reversed by early destruction of reproductive structures. When early frost destroys a fruit crop, the normally bearing year becomes a vegetative one. The subsequent year becomes one of heavy fruiting and the biennial habit is continued (Davis, 1957).

In contrast to the more or less predictable pattern of reproductive growth in orchard trees, the pattern of flowering and fruiting in forest trees is very irregular and unpredictable. The amount of seed produced by forest trees varies greatly among species and from year to year. Generally flowering and fruiting are much more regular in plantations than in natural forest stands.

Some species such as tupelo gum and southern magnolia tend to produce good seed crops annually; others such as beech have good seed crops at intervals of several years. Some species, including sugar maple, have good seed crops at fairly regular intervals while black walnut and yellow poplar produce good seed crops irregularly. Between good seed years, seed crops are often light or sometimes total failures. Wide variations often occur in seed production among different species of the same genus. For example, *Populus trichocarpa*, *P. balsamifera*, and *P. deltoides* generally produce good seed crops annually, whereas *P. grandidentata* and *P. tremuloides* tend to bear abundantly only once every 4 to 5 years. Irregular bearing also is discussed in Chapter 16.

Seed production by different species of forest trees in the same stand can vary greatly. Western hemlock is a very prolific seed producer, whereas the associated species, grand fir and western white pine, produce small seed crops.

Tropical Trees

Tropical forests are never without flowers because of the large numbers of species they contain and variations among species in time of flowering. Although some tropical trees flower continuously throughout the year, most have a distinct flowering season or flower irregularly (Longman and Jenik, 1974).

Some tropical trees are easily classified on the basis of their flowering periodicity. However, rigid classification is difficult for many other species because their flowering patterns vary greatly with environment, especially with seasonal distribution of rainfall and photoperiodic regimes. An example is cacao, which flowers throughout the year in Costa Rica where rainfall is nonseasonal and there is little temperature change. However, in the states of Bahia and Espirito Santo, Brazil, which have distinct rainy seasons, flowering of cacao is essentially confined to the wet months of October to June.

Some idea of variation among flowering periodicity in the tropics may be gained from Alvim's (1964) classification which listed tropical woody plants in four broad groups:

1. *Everflowering Species*. These produce flowers continuously throughout the year. Examples include *Hibiscus* spp., *Ficus* spp., and *Carica papaya* as well as *Trema guineensis* in Ghana and *Dillenia suffruticosa* in Malaysia.

2. *Nonseasonal Flowering Species*. These species exhibit variation in flowering periodicity from plant to plant and branch to branch. They become seasonal flowering species at some distance from the equator. Examples include *Spathodea campanulata*, *Michelia champaca*, *Cassia fistula*, *Cassia splendens*, and *Lagerstroemia flos-reginae*.

3. *Gregarious Flowering Species*. These flower at indefinite times of the year, with practically every specimen of the species in flower at the same time over a wide area. In gregarious species flower buds form regularly but remain closed for long periods (weeks or months) and are stimulated to open by marked environmental changes. They flower almost invariably when rain follows a period of drought. Examples are *Coffea* spp. (Rees, 1964a), *Clerodondron incisum* (Rees, 1964b), *Pterocarpus indicus* (Holttum, 1953), *Tabebuia serratifolia* (Schulz, 1960). *Bambusa*, *Strobilanthes*, *Hopea*, and *Schornia* flower gregariously at very long intervals. *Bambusa* for exam-

ple, first flowers in 7 to 13 years in southern Brazil and up to 30 years elsewhere (Walter, 1962; Alvim, 1964).

   4. *Seasonal Flowering Species*. These flower seasonally in areas with alternating rainy and dry seasons or seasonal variations in day length. They often become everflowering or nonseasonal in certain areas. Examples of seasonal flowering species are *Monodora tenuifolia* and *Bosqueia angolensis* in Nigeria (Njoku, 1963). In the seasonal climate of Trinidad about one-half of the deciduous trees flower during the rainy season and one-half during the dry season (Beard, 1946).

SEXUAL REPRODUCTION IN ANGIOSPERMS

Floral Structure and Arrangement

   Typical complete flowers of angiosperms bear four types of organs on their receptacles (Fig. 4.1). The lowermost of these are the sepals which together make up the

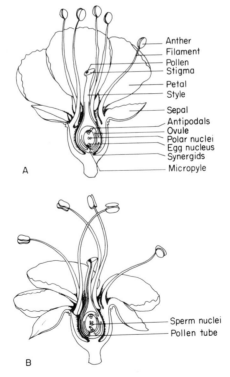

Fig. 4.1. Typical flower before and after fertilization. A: flower before fertilization; B: flower shortly after union of sperm nucleus and egg nucleus. Some petals have fallen and stamens are withered. (From "The Ripening of Fruit," J. B. Biale. Copyright © 1954 by Scientific American, Inc. All rights reserved.)

calyx. Above the sepals are the petals, collectively called the corolla. The sepals and petals together comprise the perianth. Inside the perianth are the pollen-producing stamens, collectively called the androecium, and the carpels which comprise the gynoecium. A flower may have one to several carpels. These usually consist of a lower, fertile part, the ovary, and an upper sterile part, the style. At the top of the style is the stigma on which the pollen grains land prior to fertilization of immature seeds or ovules. The ovule is important in reproduction because it is the site of megaspore formation and development of the female gametophyte called the embryo sac.

Floral Modifications

Woody plants show many examples of floral modifications and often lack some of the parts of the complete flower. For example, flowers of poplars and black walnut lack a corolla and those of willows lack both calyx and corolla (Fig. 4.2). Another floral modification involves fusion of floral parts. In grape and rhododendron, for example, carpels are fused; in catalpa petals are fused; and in viburnum sepals are fused. Fusion of parts of the perianth or carpels may date from the time of their origin or may have occurred at a later stage of evolutionary development.

Some flowers have nectaries. These are surface areas of organs which secrete a sugary liquid, called nectar, which attracts bees and other insects. Eames (1961) distinguished between two general types of nectaries: (1) localized areas which secrete nectar and (2) nectar-secreting organs which have been transformed from their original form and function. Nectaries may develop on both reproductive and vegetative tissues. Floral nectaries may occur close to the base of perianth parts as in hibiscus, as a shallow or concave ring between the stamens and base of the ovary (*Cercis siliquas-*

Fig. 4.2. A: pistillate and staminate flowers of willow; B: pistillate and staminate flowers of red oak. Photo courtesy of W. M. Harlow.

trum, Robinia, Prunus, Rubus), between the stamens and styles when an inferior ovary is present (*Eucalyptus*), or as a distinct ring around the base of the ovary (*Citrus*). Extrafloral nectaries often occur on the teeth of the leaves (Fahn, 1967).

Nectaries may excrete nectar in several ways including: (1) diffusion through thin-walled epidermal cells, (2) diffusion from thin-walled epidermal papillae, (3) excretion from the tips of hairs, (4) excretion through stomata specially modified for this function, and (5) excretion as a result of rupture of the cuticle caused by swelling of the outer wall (Fahn, 1967). In magnolia the entire flower has been termed a nectary because nectar diffuses through petal cuticle and is excreted through stomatal pores on petal bases and carpel surfaces (Eames, 1961).

Whereas flowers of many fruit trees are very showy those of most forest trees are very inconspicuous. Flowers of angiosperms are borne individually or more commonly, in groups on various types of inflorescences. Flowers of apple trees are pro-

Fig. 4.3. Flowers of woody angiosperms. A: flowers of pear; B: flowers of black locust; C: staminate and pistillate flowers of black maple; D: flowers of basswood; E: pistillate flowers of eastern cottonwood; F: staminate flowers of eastern cottonwood.

duced in clusters of three to seven, usually five. As in apple, the pear flower bud opens into a terminal cluster of about five flowers. In olive the flowers are borne in paniculate inflorescences, each consisting of about 15 flowers. The inflorescenses appear on shoots 1 or sometimes 2 years old. The flowers are either perfect, with functioning stamens and pistils, or staminate, with the pistil aborted.

In magnolia and yellow-poplar the flowers occur singly in leaf axils. In black cherry and striped maple they are borne in racemes; in poplars, birches, and alders in catkins; in buckeye in panicles; and in elder and viburnum in cymes.

Most forest trees are monoecious, with staminate and pistillate flowers on the same plant as in birch and alder. Others, such as persimmon, poplar, and willow, are dioecious and bear staminate and pistillate flowers on separate plants. It should be obvious that a staminate tree will not produce seed. If ornamental dioecious shrubs or trees such as holly are grown for their berries, care must be taken to plant some staminate trees along with the pistillate trees to insure pollination and production of berries. A few genera, such as *Aesculus*, have perfect flowers, bearing both stamens and pistils as well as both staminate and pistillate flowers. Still another combination occurs in *Rhamnus* and *Fraxinus* which have perfect flowers as well as either staminate or pistillate flowers. Some examples of flowers of woody angiosperms are shown in Fig. 4.3.

Floral Initiation and Development

In many angiosperm trees of the temperate zone flower primordia form rather early in the season preceding the spring in which the flowers open. Although the specific time of induction varies among species, for a large number of woody plants of the temperate zone it takes place between early May and late July (Matthews, 1963). For example, after completion of vegetative growth in late June, nearly all of the buds of mature sycamore maple trees are vegetative and later the apex of most of these buds passes through a transitional stage into a floral one. By cell division and enlargement the floral apex forms an inflorescence that remains undeveloped throughout the winter. Rapid development is resumed in the spring and trees bloom in late May and early June (Anderson and Guard, 1964).

The time of floral initiation is influenced by weather, site conditions, and management practices. Therefore, the period of floral initiation changes somewhat from year to year and it varies in different parts of the natural range of a species. The degree of structural differentiation of flowers during the first season varies greatly among species.

Some variations in time of flower initiation have been observed for different shoot locations. In apple, for example, flowers are initiated later in terminal buds of shoots than of spurs. They also are initiated later in terminal buds of spurs on 2-year-old shoots than on 3-year-old shoots. Within a flower cluster the central flower forms after the lateral flowers but it develops faster (Zeller, 1955).

A flower develops from an apical meristem, with floral parts arising at the receptacle tip as rounded protuberances of meristematic activity. Usually, development is acropetal with sepals appearing first, followed in order by petals, stamens, and carpels. Early stages of development of floral appendages resemble those of leaf formation at the stem tip. The floral parts arise by periclinal divisions in subsurface layers of apical meristems. These divisions are followed by others which include anticlinal divisions. Growth in length and width of floral parts follows as a result of apical and marginal growth (Esau, 1965).

Production and Shedding of Pollen

A good flowering year sometimes fails to result in a large crop of seed or fruit because conditions are unfavorable for pollination. Enormous amounts of pollen are produced by trees, particularly those that are wind pollinated. According to Faegri and Iversen (1975), a single anther of wind-pollinated birch may produce 10,000 pollen grains while an anther of the insect-pollinated maple produces only 1,000 grains. Pollen grains of birches, poplars, oaks, ashes, elms, hickories, sycamores, and conifers are dispersed by wind; those of basswood, maples, willows, and most fruit trees are dispersed by insects, chiefly bees. A larger proportion of the pollen will be wasted when distributed randomly by wind than when distributed more systematically by insects moving from flower to flower. Pollination by bees is largely an incidental by-product of their nectar collecting, but in a few cases there is a highly specialized relationship between the insects and the plants they pollinate. An example is the complex process of pollination of figs by Chalcid wasps (Galil and Neeman, 1977).

Effects of Climatic Conditions on Pollen Dispersal

Daily fluctuations in temperature and humidity have important effects on pollen release and dispersal. Sarvas (1962) reported that in Finland the most pollen is shed on the warmest day of the season. In general most pollen was released near midday and almost none at night. However, on the few nights when the relative humidity was low there was abundant release of pollen. Low humidity causes desiccation of the anther cells and promotes anther opening, while rain often stops anther opening and pollen dispersal. Cold, rainy weather at the time of pollination also reduces insect activity and sometimes results in a poor set of fruit. Weather is particularly important because pollen shedding generally is completed in a short period of time, often only 1 to a few days (Sharp and Chisman, 1961).

Pollen Dispersion Distance

The pollen of most tree species is dispersed over greater areas than the seed. Forest geneticists are particularly interested in the implications of pollen dispersion distances on trees in seed orchards, controlled pollinations, and development of local races. Wright (1953) has emphasized the importance of pollen dispersion distance in forest genetics and forest regeneration. For example, in cutting a forest if male and female white ash trees are left 90 m apart only about 1% of the ovules will be fertilized, but if they are only 60 m apart 15% will be fertilized. The width of isolation strips around seed orchards also depends on the pollen dispersion distance. Wright (1976) discusses pollen dispersion in relation to forest genetics.

There is considerable variation among species in respect to the distance over which pollen is dispersed and some difference in opinion concerning the importance of long-range dispersal (Wright, 1952, 1962). Wright (1953) presented evidence that most airborne pollen falls rather close to the source tree and most cross pollination occurs in adjacent trees, as indicated by the fact that most natural hybrids occur near their parents. Where pollen dispersion distances are relatively short, most seed on open pollinated species results from pollination by nearby trees. As a result, trees growing within 100 m of one another are more similar genetically than those growing several kilometers apart (Wright, 1976). Nevertheless, considerable long-range dispersal of pollen occurs, especially among conifers. For example, Sarvas (1955b) observed a greater rain of pollen on a ship 20 km off the coast of Finland than in the forest along the shore. Likewise, Andersson (1963) found that during a year of abundant pollen production a layer of spruce pollen about 1 cm deep was deposited on some rocky islands located 4 to 8 km from the nearest forest. Lanner (1966b) suggested that pollen can be lifted upward and carried for great distances in the air, possibly eventually to be washed out of the air by rain.

In general pollen grains of spruce, Douglas-fir, pines, and ash have more rapid rates of fall and shorter dispersion distances than pollen grains of poplar, elm, walnut, and hazel (see Table 4.2). There seems to be no marked difference in dispersion distance between insect and wind dispersed pollen. Also there is no clear correlation between pollen size and dispersion distance (Wright, 1953).

Tree Pollen and Hayfever

Broadleaved trees are a major cause of early spring hayfever, which coincides with the periods of pollen shedding of oaks, elms, poplars, birches, maples, walnut, and willow. Several species of willows often grow together and pollen shedding of these as a group often lasts for several weeks. Similarly, several species of birch grow together.

TABLE 4.2 Relative Dispersion Distances of Pollen Grains of Forest Trees[a,b]

Pinus cembroides var. *edulis*
Pseudotsuga menziesii
Cedrus spp.
Picea excelsa
Fraxinus spp.
Coryllus avellana
Juglans regia
Ulmus americana
Populus deltoides
Populus nigra var. *italica*

[a] Species are listed in order of increasing dispersion distance.
[b] From Wright (1952).

Although each species sheds pollen for less than a week, their pollen shedding times overlap. Thus, as a group they shed pollen for 3 to 4 weeks. In contrast, species of elm usually grow singly and shed pollen for a brief period. Hence the severe hayfever they induce lasts for only a short time. Although gymnosperms produce very large amounts of pollen they are not an important factor in inducing hayfever.

Woody plants are unimportant in causing early and mid-summer hayfever. Early summer hayfever is caused primarily by grass pollen. Still later in the season, hayfever is caused largely by pollen of ragweeds and cockleburs.

Pollen Preservation

Collection and preservation of pollen often are essential for the breeding of woody plants. In temperate regions the flowering period of many species of woody plants is so short that pollen must be collected rapidly. Pollen can be stored best if kept cool and dry. Wright (1976) recommends short-term storage of pollen in cotton-stoppered vials kept in desiccators at 25% or lower relative humidity and a temperature of 3°-4°C, or −10°−−20°C if a deep freeze is available.

It is best to use fresh pollen in breeding work. However, pollen of grape, pine, and spruce can be stored for as much as 1 year at −18°C at very low relative humidity. The long-term storage life of pollen can be increased by pretreatment. For example, pollen of Douglas-fir was successfully stored for 2 years at −18°C if it was given the following successive pretreatments: (1) air dried to 8% moisture content for 4 hr, (2) stored at 0°C for 30 days, (3) placed in a vacuum at −77°C for 1 hr, and (4) sealed in airtight vials (Livingston and Ching, 1967).

Fertilization

A requirement for pollination is receptivity of the stigma when viable pollen reaches it. Such synchronization occurs within and among monoecious flowers on the same plant. In other cases, however, pollen shedding and stigma receptivity are not synchronized. For example, in individual plants of certain monecious species, such as sugar maple, pollen is released before the time of stigma receptivity; on other plants, pollen is released after the period of stigma receptivity has passed (Gabriel, 1968). Similar differences may be found in some dioecious species among plants with unisexual flowers. Such differences in timing prevent self pollination. This is a valuable characteristic because progeny produced by cross pollination generally are more vigorous than those resulting from self pollination.

The essentials of the ovule inside the ovary are the outer integuments, the micropylar opening opposite the stalk end, and the embryo sac which occupies most of the ovule. Before fertilization the embryo sac generally contains eight nuclei. The three located at the micropylar end consist of the egg nucleus and two synergids. Two polar nuclei are located in the central part of the embryo sac, and the three nuclei at the end opposite the micropyle are the antipodals (see Fig. 4.1).

When viable pollen grains reach a receptive stigma they imbibe water and germinate, producing pollen tubes. After the pollen tube penetrates the stigmatic surface, it grows between cells of the style by secreting enzymes that soften the pectins of the middle lamella. A number of additional enzymes, which are secreted by pollen as it grows, promote changes in the metabolism of tissues of the style and probably produce substrates for pollen growth (Stanley, 1964).

Pollen tubes grow at various rates through the style and into the ovary which contains the ovules. Although many pollen tubes may reach the ovary, only one enters the ovule. The tube nucleus and generative nucleus of the pollen grain enter the pollen tube when it is formed. The generative nucleus undergoes an early mitotic division to produce two sperms. When the ovule is reached, the pollen tube enters the embryo sac and discharges its two sperms. One of these fuses with the egg and the other with the two polar nuclei to form an endosperm nucleus. After fertilization is completed and a zygote formed, the remaining nuclei of the embryo sac, consisting of two synergids and three antipodals, usually degenerate.

Because pollen tubes grow very rapidly (sometimes several mm/hr) the time span between pollination and fertilization usually is rather short. According to Maheshwari (1950), in most angiosperms only 24 to 48 hr elapse between pollination and fertilization. However, this interval varies widely among woody species, and may be 12 to 14 hr in *Coffea arabica* (Mendes, 1941), 3 to 4 months in *Corylus avellana* (Hagerup, 1942), and 12 to 14 months in certain oaks (Bagda, 1948, 1952). Pollination and fertilization in gymnosperms will be discussed later in this chapter.

Postfertilization Development

After fertilization there is intense activity, characterized by rapid growth of the endosperm and translocation of food into the enlarging ovule. Normal growth and differentiation of the embryo depend on the endosperm. As the embryo increases in size it draws on the contents of endosperm cells and in some species may consume nearly the whole endosperm. The mature endosperm is rich in carbohydrates, fats, proteins, and growth hormones.

Several lines of evidence emphasize the importance of the endosperm as a nurse tissue for growth of the embryo. At the time of fertilization the embryo sac lacks an appreciable amount of food. As the endosperm grows, however, it accumulates enough food to supply the developing embryo. The zygote usually does not divide until after considerable endosperm growth takes place. Furthermore, the embryo develops normally only when the endosperm is organized. Should endosperm abortion occur, growth of the embryo is subsequently inhibited (Maheshwari and Rangaswamy, 1965).

Polyembryony

Multiple embryos sometimes develop in the seeds of angiosperm trees. Polyembryony has been classified as either false or true. False polyembryony involves fusion of two or more nucelli or development of two or more embryo sacs within the same nucellus. In true polyembryony the additional embryos arise in the embryo sac either by cleavage of the zygote or from the synergids and antipodal cells. Adventive embryos also are an example of true polyembryony. The adventive embryos arise from tissues outside the embryo sac (e.g., cells of the nucellus or integuments). Ultimately they enter the embryo sac where they grow to maturity. Adventive embryos differ from sexual embryos in having a lateral position, irregular shape, and lack of suspensor. They also are genetically different, the adventive embryos containing only genes from the maternal plant. In several species polyembryony has been linked to genetic causes and appears to be caused by hybridization (Maheshwari and Sachar, 1963).

Polyembryony has been of particular practical importance in propagating certain species of trees. For example, adventive embryos, which inherit characters of the maternal parent, have been used to provide genetically uniform seedlings of mango and citrus. In citrus they have been used as orchard stock on which grafts from other types have been made. In addition, citrus clones which have deteriorated after repeated vegetative reproduction have been restored to original seedling vigor with nucellar embryos (Maheshwari and Sachar, 1963). Such vegetative invigoration, or "neophysis," may be traceable to hormonal influences of the embryo sac. Hofmeyer and Oberholzer (1948) raised better citrus seedlings from adventive embryos than from cuttings. The difference was attributed to infection of cuttings with virus diseases which were absent in nucellar embryos.

Apomixis

Although seeds usually arise from sexual reproduction, in a few species of woody plants an asexual method occurs. Plants in which embryos arise without fertilization of the ovule are called apomicts. The many species of hawthorns and blackberries in the eastern United States are apomictic derivatives. Apomixis is presumed to be present but not yet demonstrated in forest trees. Apomixis is of great interest to geneticists because all seedlings produced by this process have the same genetic constitution.

Parthenocarpy

Ordinarily the development of mature fruits requires fertilization of the egg. In a few species, however, fruits are set and mature without seed development and without fertilization of an egg. Such fruits, called parthenocarpic fruits, are well known in some figs, pears, apples, peach, cherry, plum, and citrus. Parthenocarpy also occurs in several genera of forest trees including maple, elm, ash, birch, and yellow-poplar.

Some types of parthenocarpy require pollination and others do not. For example, fruit development in citrus and banana may occur without pollination. In other species of fruit trees, such as cherry and peach, seedlessness may occur because the embryo aborts before the fruit matures. In some species pollination stimulates fruit development, but fruits mature without the pollen tube reaching the ovule.

The physiology of parthenocarpy is not well understood. Fruits with many ovules often are parthenocarpic, suggesting that ovules are a source of chemicals that promote fruit set and development. The fact that ovules are sites of auxin synthesis and that spraying of plants or treating of pistils with synthetic auxin causes fruit set in some species suggests that auxins are important in fruit set. However, as such treatments have not been effective in causing setting of parthenocarpic fruits in most deciduous orchard trees (except fig, pear, and some varieties of apple) an additional factor seems to be important for fruit set. Chemical induction of parthenocarpy is most successful with species that naturally produce parthenocarpic fruits. In olive, avocado, and mango, auxin applications can cause initial fruit set, but pollination is necessary for continued fruit development. Setting of fruits with auxins often causes developing embryos, which may have been fertilized, to abort. The role of growth regulators in both vegetative and reproductive growth is discussed further in Chapters 15 and 16.

Growth of Fruits

The period from anthesis to fruit ripening varies from about 3 weeks in strawberry to 60 weeks in Valencia orange. However, in fruits of many species this interval is about 15 weeks. Various kinds of fruits grow at different rates and reach different sizes at maturity. For example, olives and currants grow very slowly (about 0.01–0.02 cm^3/day) (Bollard, 1970). It should be remembered, however, that growth rates of fruits vary greatly among seasons, environmental conditions, cultural practices, and different fruits in the same crop.

Growth of fruits involves various degrees of cell division and cell expansion. During anthesis there is little cell division, but after the fruit is set it becomes an active carbohydrate sink, and many of its tissues become meristematic. In some fruits (e.g., currants, blackberries) cell division (except in the embryo and endosperm) is completed by the time of pollination; in others (e.g., apple, citrus), cell division occurs for a short time after pollination; and in still others cell division occurs for a long time after pollination. In avocado, cell division continues throughout the life of the fruit. However, in most species increase in cell size makes the greatest contribution to total fruit expansion. In grape the increase in cell number accounts for a doubling of fruit size whereas increase in cell volume accounts for a 300-fold size increase (Coombe, 1976).

Growth Curves

Growth curves of fruits fall into two general types. The first of these is a simple sigmoid type in which there is initially an exponential increase in size followed by slowing down of growth in a sigmoid fashion (Fig. 4.4). This type of curve is characteristic of apple, pear, orange, date, banana, avocado, strawberry, mango, and lemon. The precise shape of the growth curve often differs somewhat with variety. The growth curve for development of Early Harvest apple fruits resembles a straight line, whereas that for each successively later ripening variety flattens as the season progresses. The rate of fruit growth also is a varietal characteristic, with early-ripening varieties growing faster than late-ripening ones (Tukey and Young, 1942).

The second type of growth curve, characteristic of stone fruits (fig, cherry, peach, apricot, plum, and olive), as well as some non-stone fruits (such as grape and currant), is a double sigmoid type that depicts growth occurring in three stages (Fig. 4.5). In stone fruits during Stage I the ovary, nucellus, and integuments of the seed grow

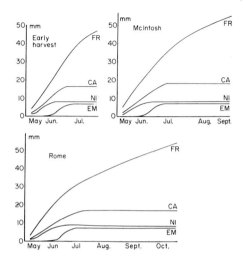

Fig. 4.4. Increase in length of the embryo (EM), nucellus and integuments (NI), carpel (CA), and whole fruit (FR) of Early Harvest, McIntosh, and Rome apples from full bloom to fruit ripening. From Tukey and Young (1942), University of Chicago Press.

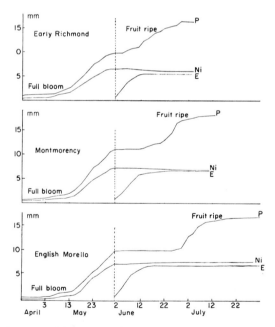

Fig. 4.5. Growth curves of the pericarp (P), nucellus and integuments (Ni), and embryo (E) of three varieties of cherry ripening at different seasons. The time of rapid increase of embryo growth and related inhibition of growth of the nucellus and integuments and pericarp were similar for all varieties. Periods of rapid embryo increase also were similar but rates of pericarp development were not. From Tukey (1935).

TABLE 4.3   Duration of Stages of Fruit Development in Cherry[a]

Variety	Stage I (days)	Stage II (days)	Stage III (days)	Full bloom to ripening (days)
Early Richmond	22	5	14	41
Montmorency	22	12	23	57
English Morello	21	28	17	66

[a] From Tukey (1935).

rapidly, but the embryo and endosperm grow little. During Stage II the embryo and endosperm grow rapidly, but the ovary does not increase much in size. Sclerification of the pit also begins and, by the end of Stage II, the embryo achieves full size and the amount of endosperm material increases greatly. Finally, in Stage III a new surge of ovary growth begins and continues to fruit ripening. The duration of the three growth stages is quite variable. Stage II may last only a few days in early-ripening varieties and about 1 month in late-ripening ones (Table 4.3).

According to Chalmers and van den Ende (1977) seeds and pericarps compete strongly for nutrients and the seed is the weaker competitor because of its position in the translocation system. Nevertheless, they conclude that the seed controls fruit growth because it provides the signal which brings about the translocation of food to the developing fruit. The actual stimulation of translocation is said by Chalmers and van den Ende (1977) to be caused by ethylene produced by the pericarp.

Neither of the two major types of growth curves is restricted to a particular morphological type of fruit. For example, growth of certain berries, pomes, simple fruits, and accessory fruits can be characterized by one or the other type of growth curve. The development of fleshy fruits was reviewed by Coombe (1976) and fruit growth was treated in detail in the monograph edited by Holme (1970–1971).

Ripening of Fruits

Ripening of fruits is correlated with a number of changes in metabolism that are driven by respiratory energy. Changes associated with fruit ripening include loss of chlorophyll, unmasking other pigments, softening of the flesh, development of odor and flavor, and decrease in dry weight. These changes are paralleled by chemical alterations such as production of ethylene, hydrolysis of insoluble pectins, conversion of starch to sugar in some fruits, and disappearance of tannins in others. Several of these changes are general and occur in many fruits. Although most fruits ripen on the tree, a few, such as avocado, will not do so. Ripening of normally tree-ripened fruits can often be accelerated by picking.

Changes associated with fruit ripening are linked to the climacteric increase in respiration in many species. For example, the drop in respiration following the climacteric peak is rather sharp and terminates in physiological breakdown or fungal invasion.

Biale (1960) considered the climacteric to be a critical stage identifying the end of fruit development and maturation and the beginning of senescence. A number of changes associated with ripeness occur at or shortly after the climacteric. For example, fruits change color (green to yellow in some varieties of apple, pear, banana, and papaya; green to red in plums and mangos; green to dark brown in some varieties of avocado). Changes in color may result from disappearance of chlorophyll (banana) or formation of carotenoids (orange). Also, the flesh may soften. In pear, "eating ripeness" occurs at the climacteric peak. In apples, bananas, and avocados the highest state of edibility occurs shortly after the climacteric peak. Further discussion of the respiration of fruits can be found in Chapter 6.

Flavor

Development of fruit flavor is influenced by both physical changes during development and chemical constituents. As mentioned, transformation of insoluble to soluble pectins occurs in cell walls of ripening fruits. Rupture of some of the cells follows and juices are released into spaces between cells, and thereby the taste of fruits is enhanced.

Flavor of fruits is determined by a balance between sugars, acids, and astringent components. Sucrose, glucose, and fructose are the major sugars present in varying proportions in different fruits. In apples all three sugars are present; in peaches and apricots sucrose predominates; in cherry, glucose and fructose make up the bulk of the sugars present. Important edible fruits, including grape, banana, orange, and apple have 9 to 20% sugar. Grapes often have much higher concentrations. In contrast to seeds, fleshy fruits do not accumulate large amounts of starch or storage proteins.

Organic acids increase in amount and affect flavor of growing fruits. The organic acids probably are translocated into the fruits from the leaves as inferred from decreases in acid content of fruits following reduction of leaf area and higher acid contents in the center than in the periphery of grapes and apples (Nitsch, 1953). The concentration of organic acids in fruits is relatively high, often amounting to 1–2% of fresh weight in apples and pears and up to 4% in black currants. The most important organic acids of fruits are malic in pome fruits, citric in citrus, tartaric in grapes, and isocitric in blackberries. Many other fruits contain mixtures of these acids (Nitsch, 1953). Flavor is also associated with aroma provided by such constituents as amyl esters of formic, acetic, caproic, and caprylic acids (Chandler, 1957).

Softening of Fruits

Softening of fruits is related to changes in pectic compounds and hydrolysis of starch or fats. During fruit development, insoluble protopectin is laid down in primary cell walls and accumulates to high concentrations in some fruits, such as apple, pear, and citrus. Changes from insoluble pectins (protopectin and calcium pectate), to soluble compounds such as pectin, pectic acid, and pectinic acid are closely related to ripening. Changes in pectic compounds during ripening probably are due to the activity of the enzyme protopectinase. Between the green and ripe stages, soluble pectins in peaches may increase by a factor of 2, in apple by 12, and in pear by 20. In overripe fruits, pectic substances tend to disappear and fruits soften greatly. In ripening citrus fruits, similar but smaller changes in pectic compounds occur. In final stages of fruit senescence, protoplasts may disintegrate and cell walls collapse. The actual breakdown of fruits appears to be linked to disorganization and loss of control over enzymatic processes rather than to depletion of foods.

Abscission of Reproductive Structures

Reproductive structures abscise by a process that is basically similar to leaf abscission. Floral structures abscise as parts of flowers, entire flowers, or inflorescences. Shedding of petals usually results from softening of the middle lamella (Esau, 1965). The investigations of Lott and Simons (1964, 1966, 1968a,b) showed the same general patterns of development of floral cup and style abscission zones in a number of species of *Prunus*. However, important differences also were found among species in rates of development of abscission zones, with those of *P. cerasus* and *P. avium* developing more rapidly than those of *P. persica* and *P. armeniaca* (Table 4.4).

Abscission of fruits sometimes occurs prematurely shortly after pollination and fruit set or during growth of the young embryo. Premature abscission of immature fruits is an especially serious problem with apples, pears, oranges and grapefruits. In apple, three normal periods of fruit drop occur. These include (1) "early drop" between the time of initial ovary enlargement and beginning of endosperm development; (2) "June drop" of young fruits, and (3) the preharvest drop.

Premature abscission of fruits of wind-pollinated species of forest trees also is well known. For example, most of the potential acorn crop of white oak often abscises prematurely (Table 4.5). Williamson (1966) found that from early May to mid-July, the period of pollination, ovule development, and fertilization, almost 90% of white oak acorns were shed prematurely.

The location of the abscission layers of fruits varies with species. Pome fruits abscise at the base of the pedicel. The fruitlets of plum abscise with attached stems in

TABLE 4.4 Variations in Rate of Development of Floral Tube and Style Abscission in Various Species of *Prunus* [a]

Species	Cultivars	Days from anthesis to:		
		Petal fall	Floral tube abscission zone evident	Style abscission
P. avium	"Starking Hardy Giant"	3–4	5–6	3–4
P. avium	"Stark Gold"	3–4	5–6	5–6
P. cerasus	Montmorency	3–4	5–6	5–6
P. armeniaca	Wilson Delicious	3–5	6–8	18–20
P. persica	12 cultivars	3–6	7–10	20–24

[a] From Lott and Simons (1968a).

TABLE 4.5   Percentage of Abscission of White Oak Acorns at Various Development Stages[a]

	1962		1963	
Development stage	Starting date	Percent abscissions	Starting date	Percent abscissions
Pollination	April 30	55.6	April 24	28.4
Ovule development	May 17	10.6	May 20	37.9
Fertilization	June 4	15.8	June 6	18.1
Embryo development	July 6	16.7	July 3	10.5
Maturation	Sept. 19	1.3	Sept. 20	5.1
		100.00		100.00

[a] From Williamson (1966).

the first two of the three seasonal waves of fruit drop, and without stems in the third drop. Two abscission zones occur in sweet cherry, with fruits separating either between the pedicel and peduncle or between the peduncle and spur. In plum, mango, avocado, and orange, the separation of fruits at maturity occurs at the base of the fruit (Stösser *et al.*, 1969). After fruits of many tropical species form their stalks, they separate from them by a second abscission layer. The shedding of fruits together with their stalks also is common in temperate zone forest trees such as willow, poplar, basswood, black locust, and elm.

Abscission of buds, flowers, or fruits of Washington navel oranges in California occurred from February to July (Erickson and Brannaman, 1960). Almost half of the buds dropped before they opened. Abscission of open flowers amounted to 16.7% of all flower buds initiated. Abscission of small fruits continued throughout and following the flowering period. Small fruits abscised either at the base of the ovary or at the base of the pedicel, abscission at the base of the pedicel occurring about 10 times as commonly as at the base of the ovary. Most abscission occurred when fruits were very small. Only 0.2% of the buds formed finally produced fruits (Table 4.6).

SEXUAL REPRODUCTION IN GYMNOSPERMS

The calyx, corolla, stamens and pistil are absent in gymnosperms. The flowers consist of pollen cones and seed cones (staminate and ovulate strobili) which in most species are produced on the same tree (Fig. 4.6).

The pollen cones are often bright yellow, purple, or red when mature and consist of an axis bearing a series of spirally arranged scales. Each of the scales bears two pollen sacs on the undersurface. The sometimes colorful seed cones, which are larger and more persistent than the pollen cones, consist of an axis bearing ovulate scales, each of which is borne in the axis of a bract. Two ovules appear as protuberances on the upper side of a scale. At the end of the ovule near the cone axis is an opening, the micropyle, through which pollen grains may enter.

TABLE 4.6 Numbers of Reproductive Structures (Buds, Flowers, and Fruits) Abscised per Tree from Washington Navel Orange at Riverside, California[a]

Diameter of ovary (mm)	Buds	Flowers	Fruits With pedicel	Without pedicel	Total
1 or less	59,635	674	1,002	12	61,323
2	22,790	14,939	13,953	344	52,026
3	10,804	15,295	25,043	541	51,683
4	3,114	2,321	13,469	589	19,493
5		6	3,853	460	4,319
6			2,399	634	3,033
7		-	1,250	643	1,893
8			586	450	1,036
9			417	663	1,080
10			179	462	641
11			77	357	434
12			37	275	312
13			20	194	214
14			7	137	144
15			7	118	125
16			3	79	82
17			2	71	73
18			2	55	57
19			2	40	42
20				32	32
21 or more				232	232
Total	96,343	33,235	62,308	6,388	198,274
Average no. of mature fruits per tree					419
Total flower buds per tree					198,693
Percent	48.5	16.7	31.4	3.2	Crop = 0.2

[a] From Erickson and Brannaman (1960).

Seeds of gymnosperms generally require a long time (1 to 3 years) to develop. The life cycle is one year in cycads, *Ginkgo, Ephedra, Gnetum*, and most members of the Cupressacae and Taxodiaceae; 1 or 2 years in *Podocarpus,* depending on species; and 2 years in *Caphalotaxus* and *Torreya*. Cone initiation in *Pinus* occurs in autumn or early winter, pollination in spring, fertilization a year later, and the seed cone matures and sheds seeds during the next autumn. Hence the life of a seed cone of pine extends over three growing seasons (Kozlowski, 1971b; Singh and Johri, 1972).

Cone Initiation and Development

Two distinct patterns of cone initiation occur in conifers. Cone buds of cedar, hemlock, larch, and spruce are normally formed by transition of vegetative shoots into reproductive ones. This transition may require from 2 weeks in red pine (Duff and

Fig. 4.6. Flowering in gymnosperms. A: pollen and seed cones of Douglas-fir; B: pollen and seed cones of Carolina hemlock; C: pollen cones of slash pine shortly before shedding pollen; D: seed cone of baldcypress; E: receptive seed cone of noble fir; F: pollen cones of noble fir, showing swollen pollen sacs about one day before shedding. Photo courtesy of U.S. Forest Service.

Nolan, 1958) to 11 weeks in Douglas-fir (Owens, 1969). Pines, true firs, Douglas-fir, and spruce initiate new axillary shoots that develop into cone buds rather than first functioning as vegetative shoots (Allen and Owens, 1972).

The time of cone initiation varies among species, and within a species in different environments, but cones normally are initiated in the season before pollination occurs. The precise time varies from early spring for Douglas-fir to early summer for western red cedar to autumn for certain pines. After initiation, cone development requires many months in all species. The order of morphological changes is similar in different environmental regimes, but the time of occurrence of developmental events varies

TABLE 4.7 Variation in Time of Initiation of Pollen Cones and Seed Cones

Species	Time of initiation		Source
	Pollen cone	Seed cone	
Alaska Cedar	Mid-June–early July	Late June–mid-July	Owens and Molder (1974)
Cryptomeria (Sugi)	Late June–late Sept.	Mid-July–mid-Sept.	Hashizume (1962)
Slash pine	Late June–July	Late August	Mergen and Koerting (1957)
Western red cedar	Early June	July	Owens and Pharis (1971)
Western hemlock	June	July	Owens and Molder (1974)

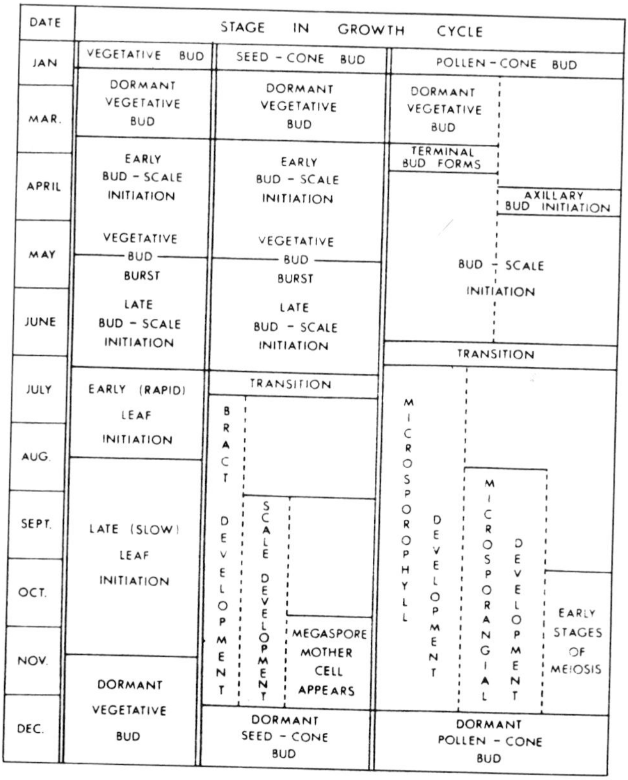

Fig. 4.7. Phenology of vegetative, seed cone, and pollen cone bud development in western hemlock growing near Victoria, British Columbia. From Owens and Molder (1974).

appreciably. As may be seen in Table 4.7 and Fig. 4.7, pollen cones and seed cones are differentiated at different times of the year and at different rates, with pollen cones usually forming first and differentiating faster. In pine, Douglas-fir, and western red cedar, seed cones are most abundant in the upper crown, pollen cones in the lower crown (Kozlowski, 1971b; Owens and Pharis, 1971; Allen and Owens, 1972). In firs the seed cones are always concentrated on the uppermost branches, pollen cones in the upper half of the crown (Matthews, 1970; Krugman et al., 1974).

Pollination and Fertilization

The amount of pollen produced varies among species and years, and within a species, and it differs among stands, individual trees, and parts of trees (Sarvas, 1962). The time of pollen shedding also is variable from year to year. In Finland shedding of Scotch pine pollen occurred during a 5- to 10-day period. An individual stand shed its pollen in 2 or 3 days less than this; an individual tree in even less time. Shedding of pollen occurred for a longer time in Scotch pine than in Norway spruce or European silver birch (Sarvas, 1955a,b, 1962). During a year of a large crop most pollen was shed during the middle of the flowering period. However, during years of light crops, a peak period of pollen production could not be identified.

The period of pollen receptivity of female flowers usually does not exceed a few days to a week. An exception is Douglas-fir, with an unusually long receptive period of 20 days. Appreciable variation sometimes occurs in receptivity of flowers in different locations in the same tree. Since duration of the receptive period is influenced by prevailing environmental factors, especially temperature, humidity, and wind, it may be expected to vary from year to year.

Cross pollination occurs commonly in gymnosperms because the female flowers are concentrated in upper branches and male flowers in lower ones. The wind-transported pollen grains drift between the cone scales and contact the ovules. Most gymnosperms exude a sugary "pollination drop" at the micropyle, but *Abies, Cedrus, Larix, Pseudotsuga*, and *Tsuga* are exceptions. This fluid fills the micropylar canal during the receptive period. The pollination drop is secreted in the morning and disappears during the day. Exudation occurs for a few days or until the ovule is pollinated (Doyle, 1945; McWilliam, 1958). Pollen grains become incorporated in the fluid and, as the drop is withdrawn, pollen is sucked into the micropyle to contact the nucellus.

The pollen grains germinate to form a number of pollen tubes that grow downward into the nucellus. As each pollen tube elongates, its generative cell divides to form a stalk cell and a body cell. The latter subsequently divides to form two sperm cells. The larger of these fuses with the egg nucleus within an archegonium and fertilization is completed. The other sperm cell disintegrates.

The time span between pollination and fertilization is extremely variable among gymnosperm genera. Pollen grains stay dormant on the nucellus for a few days in spruce, about 3 weeks in Douglas-fir, and 9 months in *Cedrus*. In pines, fertilization occurs approximately 13 months after pollination (Konar and Oberoi, 1969).

Polyembryony

The presence of more than one embryo is a common feature of embryogeny of the Pinaceae. Two types of polyembryony occur in gymnosperms: (1) simple polyembryony, in which additional embryos result from fertilization of several archegonia in a gametophyte; and (2) cleavage polyembryony, in which several embryos arise from the splitting of embryonal cells of a single zygote. In cleavage polyembryony it sometimes can be determined at a very early stage of development which of the embryos will be successful (determinate cleavage polyembryony). At other times it is difficult to predict early which embryo will be successful (indeterminate cleavage polyembryony). All genera of Pinaceae exhibit simple polyembryony and cleavage polyembryony occurs in *Pinus, Cedrus, Tsuga, Taxodium, Cryptomeria, Cunninghamia, Sequoia,* and *Podocarpus.*

Even though multiple fertilization takes place in the female gametophyte of *Pinus* most mature seeds of this genus have only a single embryo. Occasionally, however, *Pinus* has more than one embryo per seed. The occurrence of multiple embryos appears to be higher in pines with large seeds than in those with small ones. Berlyn (1962) found four embryos per mature seed in approximately one-third of the seeds of sugar pine and Swiss stone pine examined and in a few seeds of eastern white pine. In another study Berlyn (1967) found eight embryos present in one sugar pine seed.

Parthenocarpy

Development of unpollinated cones with fully formed but usually empty seeds is termed parthenocarpy and occurs in a number of genera of gymnosperms. Parthenocarpy is common in *Abies, Juniperus, Larix, Picea, Taxus,* and *Thuja* and has also been reported in *Chamaecyparis, Cryptomeria, Pseudotsuga,* and *Tsuga* (Orr-Ewing, 1957), but it rarely occurs in *Pinus*. For example, only 0.4% of Scotch pine cones had completely aborted ovules (Sarvas, 1962) and only 1 out of 76 developing cones of red pine had no developing ovules (Dickmann and Kozlowski, 1971).

Duration and Timing of Cone Development

Some idea of the similarities and differences in cone development of different gymnosperm genera in the temperate zone may be gained by comparing the timing of the significant events in reproductive growth of red pine and Douglas-fir.

In central Wisconsin the cone primordia of red pine are differentiated one season but the conelets are not externally visible until late May or early June of the following year. Pollination occurs in early June. The cones begin to enlarge after pollination and the scales close. By late July the cones have lengthened to 10–12 mm and little additional increase in length occurs during the rest of the first year (Lyons, 1956). Meanwhile, the pollen grains have germinated but the pollen tubes stop growing and are quiescent during late summer and winter. Megaspores form approximately 3 weeks after emergence of the seed cone. Successive cell and nuclear divisions of one of the megaspores result in an enlarged megagametophyte. A period of winter dormancy follows.

The cones resume growing early in the spring of the second season and attain their final length by early July. Growth of the megagametophyte also resumes in early spring, but the pollen tube does not grow until around mid-June of the second year when fertilization occurs. Embryo development then follows rapidly and seeds ripen by early September in Wisconsin (Dickmann and Kozlowski, 1969a).

Important events in growth of Douglas-fir cones throughout their 17-month developmental cycle at Corvallis, Oregon, were studied by Owens and Smith (1964, 1965). Initiation of lateral vegetative, pollen cone, and seed cone primordia occurred during the second week of April. The reproductive tissues were formed about 1 month before vegetative buds opened and at the same time as the current season's seed cones opened. Cataphylls were initiated from early April to mid-July and bract initiation was continued from mid-July to early October. Scales were initiated early in September and continued until the cone became dormant early in November. Growth was resumed early the following March and the cone buds burst approximately a month later. The cones achieved maximum size early in July. Maturation occurred in July and August and it generally was completed in September. The timing and duration of significant events are summarized in Table 4.8.

Increase in Size and Dry Weight of Cones and Seeds

In pines which ripen cones over a 2-year period, most increase in size and dry weight of cones occurs during the second year of their development (Fig. 4.8). For example, when growth of first-year conelets of red pine in Wisconsin ended they were only about one-fortieth the weight, one-thirtieth the volume, and one-third the length of mature cones at the end of their second year of development (Dickmann and Kozlowski, 1969a).

Seasonal patterns of increase in dry weight and size of first- and second-year cones of red pine in Wisconsin are shown in Figs. 4.9 and 4.10. The dry weight of first-year cones increased at a steady rate until late September, by which time the average cone weighed slightly less than 0.2 g. Patterns of dry weight increment were similar during each of three successive growing seasons. The length and width of first-year cones increased until mid-July and changed little thereafter. At the end of the first season, an average cone was 8 mm in diameter and 14–15 mm long.

During the second year of development, red pine cones resumed growing in mid-April. Dry weight increased slowly during May but rapidly during early June and continued at a high rate until early August, when maximum dry weight was recorded. Dry weight of the average second-year cone increased from less than 0.2 g in April to nearly 8 g in August. Most increase in size of second-year cones occurred in June. The second-year cones reached maximum size about 1 month before maximum dry weight increase was recorded.

Seasonal changes in dry and fresh weight and moisture content of fertilized ovules or seeds of red pine are shown in Fig. 4.11. Dry weight of seeds increased rapidly from

TABLE 4.8 Timing of Events in Development of Buds and Seed Cones (Ovulate Strobili) of Douglas-Fir near Corvallis, Oregon [a]

Event	Date	Elapsed time from bud initiation (months)
All buds		
Lateral bud primordia initiated	Early April	Ovulate buds burst
Zonation becomes apparent	Mid-May	1.5
Cataphyll initiation complete, apical enlargement occurs, leaf, bract, or microsporophyll initiation begins	Mid-July	3.5
Ovulate Strobilus		
Beginning of scale initiation	Early Sept.	5
All bracts initiated	Early Oct.	6
All scales initiated and ovulate buds become dormant	Early Nov.	7
Ovulate buds resume growth	Early March	11
Ovulate buds burst and pollination occurs	Early April	12
Fertilization	Early June	14
Elongation of strobilus complete	Early July	15
Maturation complete, strobilus opens, seeds released	Early Sept.	17

[a] From Owens and Smith (1965).

Fig. 4.8. Cones of slash pine in three stages of development (from left to right): 2 years, 1 year, and 1 month. Photo courtesy of U.S. Forest Service.

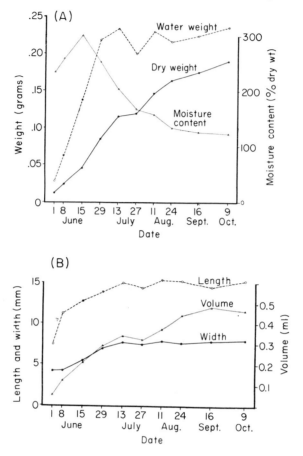

Fig. 4.9. Seasonal changes in dry weight, weight of water (per conelet), and percent moisture of first-year conelets of red pine (A). Seasonal changes in length, width, and volume of first-year conelets (B). From Dickmann and Kozlowski (1969b).

June until late August when it ceased. Moisture content (as percentage of dry weight) decreased sharply from a late June average of nearly 600% to 50% in late August. Subsequently, moisture content of seeds decreased gradually to 17% by early October.

Changes in diameter and length of seed cones of Douglas-fir (which require 1 year for maturation) are shown in Fig. 4.12. Length of cones increased rapidly to a maximum by June 1. Diameters of cones increased from 6 mm (excluding bracts) on April 24 to 24 mm on June 1, when maximum diameter was approached. Dry weight changes of cones followed a typical sigmoid pattern (Fig. 4.13) but the scales stopped gaining dry weight in July, whereas seeds increased in dry weight until September. From early June to August dry weight of cones increased, moisture content rapidly decreased, and weight of fertilized seeds increased as the seed enlarged.

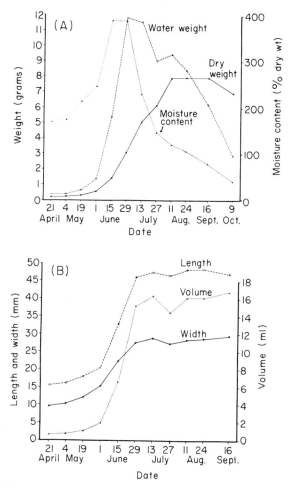

Fig. 4.10. Seasonal changes in dry weight, weight of water (per strobilus), and percent moisture of second-year cones of red pine (A). Seasonal changes in length, width, and volume of second-year cones (B). From Dickmann and Kozlowski (1969b).

Physiology of Cone Development

This section will consider some aspects of carbohydrate, mineral, and water relations during growth and development of cones. The role of hormonal growth regulators in the control of reproductive growth will be discussed in Chapter 16.

Carbohydrates

The rapidly developing cones of gymnosperms require large amounts of carbohydrates. The contribution of photosynthesis by green cones to their own growth appears to be inadequate to provide carbohydrates in needed amounts (Dickmann and Koz-

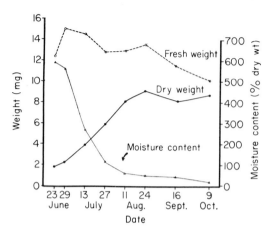

Fig. 4.11. Changes in fresh weight, dry weight, and percentage moisture of developing red pine seeds from just after fertilization to maturity. From Dickmann and Kozlowski (1969b).

lowski, 1970b). However, ample evidence is available of diversion of carbohydrates into growing cones. Dickmann and Kozlowski (1968, 1970a) reported a preferential mobilization of currently produced carbohydrates by reproductive tissues of red pine. A changing seasonal pattern in the source of current photosynthate for cone development was also shown. The 1-year-old needles were the major source of current photosynthate for cone development early in the season. In June the 2- and 3-year-old needles also contributed some current photosynthate for cone development, but after late June their contribution was slight. The supply of carbohydrates from old needles

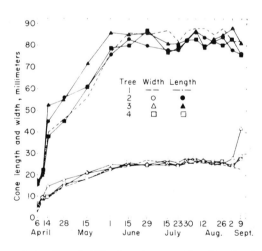

Fig. 4.12. Changes in length and width of seed cones of four Douglas-fir trees near Corvallis, Oregon. From Ching and Ching (1962).

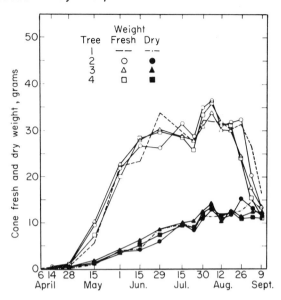

Fig. 4.13. Changes in fresh and dry weight of seed cones of four Douglas-fir trees near Corvallis, Oregon. From Ching and Ching (1962).

declined late in the season as cones mobilized increasingly more carbohydrates from needles produced during the current year.

Dickmann and Kozlowski (1969b) studied changes in reserve and structural carbo-hydrates during development of first-year and second-year red pine cones in Wisconsin. Major changes in composition occurred only during the last 3 months of development. The major components of cones during the first year and the early part of the second year included both reserve carbohydrates and products of current photosynthesis. During this period, reserves increased at a rate which paralleled the overall weight increase of young cones and comprised about one-half their dry weight. Carbohydrates accumulated at a rate commensurate with their incorporation into storage and structural materials or losses in respiration. For these reasons, reserves remained rather stable during the first season and during April and May of the second season of cone development (Figs. 4.14 and 4.15).

During the latter part of the second season of cone development there was a shift from high levels of reserves and low levels of structural materials, especially cellulose, to a reversal in their relative proportions (Fig. 4.15). The amount of extractable reserves increased rapidly from early May until the end of June. Subsequently, reserves increased gradually until early August, although their concentrations decreased sharply after mid-June. At the same time, a sharp increase in cellulose was recorded and continued until August. The data showed that large amounts of reserve carbohydrates were converted to cellulosic secondary cell wall components from mid-June to September. Whereas starch was abundant in scales and pith of cones in late June, it had

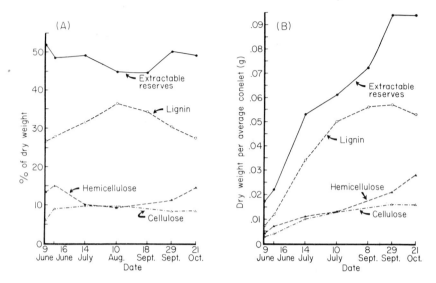

Fig. 4.14. Seasonal changes in extractable reserves, lignin, hemicellulose, and cellulose of first-year conelets of red pine. Data are given in concentration (percent of dry weight) (A) and in weight per conelet (B). From Dickmann and Kozlowski (1969b).

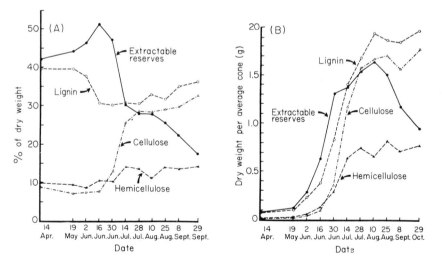

Fig. 4.15. Seasonal changes in extractable reserves, lignin, hemicellulose, and cellulose of second-year cones of red pine. Data are given in concentrations (percent of dry weight) (A) and in weight per cone (B). From Dickmann and Kozlowski (1969b).

virtually disappeared by early September, further indicating conversion of reserves to structural materials.

Mineral Relations

Dickmann and Kozlowski (1969c) also studied mineral relations of first- and second-year seed cones and developing seeds of red pine. During the first year the major macronutrients moved steadily into developing cones. The rate and magnitude of accumulation were in the following order: N > K > P > Ca > Mg. However, the concentration of N decreased, whereas that of the other macronutrients was rather stable. Micronutrients also moved into conelets during the first year (Fig. 4.16).

The seasonal pattern of uptake and accumulation of nutrients during the second year of cone development differed from the first-year pattern. During the period of rapid growth of cones following fertilization, uptake of macro- and micronutrients continued. However, translocation of Mn into cones stopped abruptly in mid-June when the cones reached their maximum size. Beginning in mid-July, N, P, and K began moving out of maturing cones. Other macro- and micronutrients continued to accumulate in cones during the entire second year of growth (Fig. 4.17).

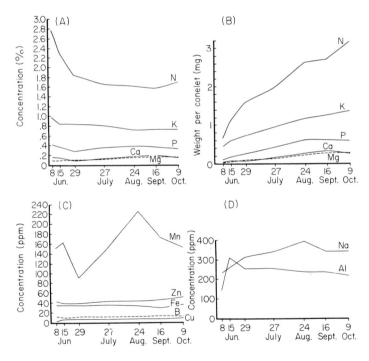

Fig. 4.16. Seasonal changes in macro- and micronutrients of first-year cones of red pine. (A): changes in concentration of macronutrients. (B): changes in weight of macronutrients per cone. (C): changes in concentration of micronutrients. (D): changes in concentration of Na and Al. From Dickmann and Kozlowski (1969c).

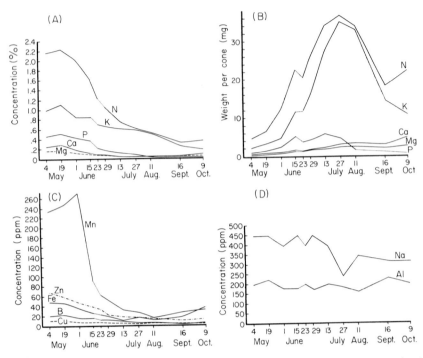

Fig. 4.17. Seasonal changes in macro- and micronutrients of second-year cones of red pine. (A): changes in concentration of macronutrients. (B): changes in weight of macronutrients per cone. (C): changes in concentration of micronutrients. (D): changes in concentration of Na and Al. From Dickmann and Kozlowski (1969c).

At the same time that mature cones were beginning to senesce, N, P, K, Mg, Mn, Zn, and Fe were rapidly mobilized by developing seeds. Nitrogen accumulated in high concentrations. Senescing cone tissue apparently supplied much of the N, P, and K that was translocated into seeds. Calcium was present in low concentrations in seeds, whereas Na accumulated in large amounts. Aluminum did not move into seeds after fertilization occurred (Fig. 4.18).

Water Relations

Seasonal patterns of hydration are different in first-year cones than in second-year cones. In first-year cones of red pine there was a period of rapid hydration which lasted until mid-June. Thereafter, the weight of water in cones remained stable, but percent moisture content decreased, primarily because of increasing dry weight (Dickmann and Kozlowski, 1969a).

Water moved into second-year cones until late June, but percent moisture reached a maximum during mid-June. Maximum water content was recorded at about the time the cones achieved maximum size, but were still increasing in dry weight. Thereafter, the cones dehydrated and shrank rapidly until they matured (Fig. 4.19). Thus, stabiliza-

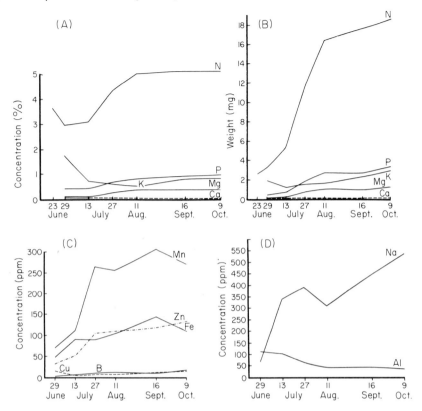

Fig. 4.18. Seasonal changes in macro- and micronutrients of developing seeds of red pine. (A): changes in concentration of macronutrients. (B): changes in weight of macronutrients in seeds per cone. (C): changes in concentration of micronutrients. (D): changes in concentration of Na and Al. From Dickmann and Kozlowski (1969c).

tion in dry weight, accompanied by continued dehydration, characterized the stage immediately prior to cone maturity.

Opening of cones apparently is caused by drying rather than by growth. Willis (1917) noted that Douglas-fir cones did not begin to open until at least 20% of their water was lost. All cones were fully opened by the time they lost about one-half of their water. Harlow *et al.* (1964) demonstrated that the opening of cone scales was related to greater shrinkage of ventral tissues than dorsal ones. They found that the dorsal zone of scales of pine cones consists principally of wood fibers and the ventral zone is made up of a band of short, rectangular, thick-walled cells. The dorsal fibrous tissues show little variation in lengthwise dimensions as they dry. In contrast, the ventral tissues shrink longitudinally by 10–13% depending on species.

During certain stages of cone development, the decrease in moisture content can be attributed primarily to rapid increase in dry weight rather than to translocation of water from the cone. For example, whole cones, scales, and seeds of white spruce and

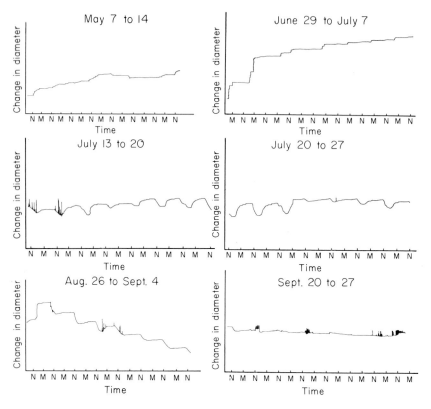

Fig. 4.19. Diameter changes in second-year red pine cones. N = noon; M = midnight. From Dickmann and Kozlowski (1969a).

tamarack achieved their highest percentage moisture content, approximately 400%, in late May or early June (Clausen and Kozlowski, 1965a). They then showed an overall seasonal decrease until reaching their lowest values, less than 50%, in September. An initial increase in percentage of moisture between late May and early June was the result of an increase in actual moisture content which exceeded the dry weight increase. From early June to late July, percentage of moisture decreased markedly even though actual weight of water per cone remained the same or even increased. The decrease in percentage of moisture was traceable to a proportionally greater increase in dry weight. After the beginning of August, by which time the increase in dry weight was completed, the decrease in percent moisture resulted primarily from dehydration. Hence, percent moisture of developing cones and seeds may change because of water translocation into or out of tissues, changes in dry weight, or both.

Diurnal Shrinkage and Expansion of Cones

Superimposed on dimensional-growth changes of cones are reversible size changes which reflect changes in hydration. During a mid-period of development, cones often

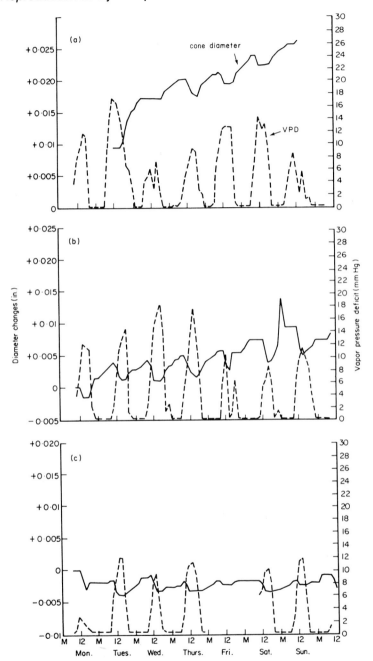

Fig. 4.20. Diurnal variations in diameters of jack pine cones and changes in vapor pressure deficit (VPD) at various times during the growing season. (a): July 10–17; (b): July 12–24; (c): July 24–31. From Chaney and Kozlowski (1969c).

shrink during the day and expand at night (Dickmann and Kozlowski, 1969a; Chaney and Kozlowski, 1969c). The amount of diurnal shrinkage and expansion of cones varies with the stage of cone development. Chaney and Kozlowski (1969c) showed that white spruce and jack pine cones made intermittent stepwise increases in diameter early in their development. Cones expanded during the evening and night, while the vapor pressure deficit of the air was decreasing or low, and did not change in diameter during the daytime when the vapor pressure deficit was high. In the mid-stage of cone development, reversible diurnal expansion and contraction of cones occurred; these fluctuations were inversely correlated with vapor pressure deficits (Fig. 4.20). Maturing cones decreased in diameter in a stepwise pattern.

ASEXUAL REPRODUCTION

This section will briefly discuss asexual reproduction of woody plants by sprouting, rooting of cuttings, layering, grafting, and the use of cell and tissue cultures.

Sprouting

Sprouting is a typical response to sudden death of parent tree tops as a result of fire or cutting or to disease and physiological disorders. The capacity of woody plants to produce sprouts is of tremendous importance to their survival.

Sprouts originating from root collars and the lower part of the stem usually arise from dormant buds (see Chapter 3). Such "stump sprouts" (Fig. 4.21) represent the most important type of vegetative reproduction of hardwood forest stands. For example, many of the New England hardwood forests and most of the oak forests of Pennsylvania originate from stump sprouts. "Stool sprouts" develop from adventitious buds which arise from between the bark and wood of stumps. Ordinarily, stool shoots are short-lived and of no real importance in vegetative propagation.

Capacity for sprouting is common in angiosperms and rare in gymnosperms. There is also considerable variation among species of angiosperms. For example, Little (1938) observed that white and post oaks produced more but shorter sprouts per stump than did black and scarlet oaks. Chestnut oak stumps gave rise to nearly as many stems as did those of white oak, yet the sprouts were more vigorous at the end of the first season than were those in the black oak group. Before the fourteenth year, vigor, as measured by height, was greatest for scarlet oak followed by black oak. Persistence of sprouts ran in the following order: post oak, white oak, chestnut oak, black oak, scarlet oak. Stump sprouting also varies with the season of cutting and often is correlated with amounts of available carbohydrate reserves (see Chapter 7).

All angiosperms do not sprout equally throughout their ranges. For example, sugar maple, beech, and hophornbeam sprout vigorously in the northern but not in the southern part of their ranges. Many oaks, however, sprout vigorously throughout a greater part of their range (Braun, 1950).

Fig. 4.21. Stump sprout of black cherry. Photo courtesy of U.S. Forest Service.

Although regeneration by sprouts is relatively unimportant in gymnosperms, a few species sprout prolifically, especially after fire. Gymnosperms with good sprouting ability include redwood, pitch pine, shortleaf pine, pond pine, and baldcypress. According to Cheyney (1942), only three American gymnosperms, shortleaf pine, baldcypress, and redwood, produce sprouts that grow to merchantable size.

Sprouting in gymnosperms following fire or mutilation of seedlings often has been attributed to adventitious buds. However, E. L. Stone and Stone (1954) found that several species of pines had small buds in the axils of primary needles just above the cotyledons. At that location the needles were closely spaced, and the buds generally appeared clustered after the stem thickened. These buds often produced basal or root collar sprouts. When a stem was sectioned the bud steles were traced back to an origin in the first-year stem. Hence, the sprouts arose from dormant buds rather than from adventitious buds (see Chapter 3).

Following disturbances of hardwood forest stands by heavy cutting or fire, some species of trees regenerate largely by root suckers which originate from adventitious buds on roots of the residual and cut trees. Reproduction by root suckers is best known

Fig. 4.22. A stand of root sprouts from a 40-year-old sweetgum tree. From Kormanik and Brown (1967).

in aspens but it also occurs in other species such as sweetgum, beech, ailanthus, black locust, lilac, black tupelo, and sassafras (Fig. 4.22). The importance of opening of aspen stands to production of root suckers was emphasized by Stoeckeler and Mason (1956). They counted more than 1,100 aspen sprouts per hectare on open sites following heavy cutting and as few as 150 sprouts per hectare on undisturbed sites.

Stem Cuttings

Rooting stem cuttings is one of the best methods of asexually propagating woody plants. This involves placing of stem pieces with one or more buds under conditions that favor formation of adventitious roots. The term "adventitious" applies to roots and their branches which do not originate at the root pole of the embryo. The adventitious roots may arise from new "induced" primordia or from preformed primordia which developed during branch or stem formation. Adventitious roots may form on twigs, branches, leaves, aerial stems, underground stems, and old roots.

Induced Primordia

Haissig (1974) summarized the work of several investigators who showed that induced root primordia may be initiated in many different tissues. Buds, epidermis, cortex, pericycle, phloem, cambium, xylem, and pith parenchyma all contain cells capable of initiating root primordia. The cambium, phloem, and pericycle have been shown to be the most frequent origins of induced root primordia; the cortex, pith, and xylem are less important. Callus formation at the base of cuttings appears to be required for rooting of some species (Satoo, 1956b; Heaman and Owens, 1972), but not others (Kozlowski, 1971b). Cuttings of species difficult to root initiate most root primordia in basal callus tissue.

The time of initiation of induced root primordia varies greatly among species. Whereas it begins within a few days in easily rooted cuttings, it may take months or may not occur at all in difficult-to-root woody cuttings. The time of formation and origin of adventitious roots may be different in the juvenile and adult stage of the same species. Adventitious roots in the internodes of cuttings of juvenile phase plants in English ivy originated in phloem ray parenchyma above the basal cuts in 6 to 10 days. The roots emerged in 1.5 to 2 weeks after the cuttings were made (Girouard, 1967a,b). In cuttings of the adult phase, adventitious roots were initiated in 2 to 4 weeks in phloem ray parenchyma of internodes and in callus near the basal end of cuttings. The roots emerged at the end of 3 to 5 weeks (Girouard, 1967a,b).

Preformed Primordia

There is less variation in the rate of initiation of preformed primordia than of induced primordia. Preformed primordia initiate most often in nodes from cambial cells or ray parenchyma cells recently cut off from the cambium. In some trees, such as poplars, preformed primordia are initiated in longitudinal files between nodes (Shapiro, 1958). According to Carlson (1938, 1950) preformed root primordia are differentiated during the first year and develop slowly. Differentiation generally requires at least 2 to 3 years, but sometimes may not be completed for many years. As a stem increases in diameter, the root primordia increase in length, perpendicularly to the stem axis, in an amount equal to that of cambial growth. Some of the preformed root primordia do not develop. However, under favorable environmental conditions even the youngest and least differentiated preformed primordia can develop into roots (Haissig, 1974).

Leaf Cuttings

Some plants, such as certain rhododendrons, are more easily propagated by leaf cuttings with their accompanying basal buds than by stem cuttings. Needle fascicles of some pines also root more easily than stem cuttings. However, in most cases buds and shoots do not form. In jack pine, but not some other pines, this problem can be overcome by using fascicles with preformed buds (Wright, 1976).

Root Cuttings

Certain species of woody plants that reproduce naturally by root suckers can be propagated better by planting root segments than stem cuttings. Propagation by root cuttings is most successful if the root pieces are taken from young stock plants in late winter or early spring before shoot growth begins. The proximal end (that nearest the crown) of the root piece should be oriented upward or horizontally in the planted cutting, never downward.

Control of Rooting of Cuttings

Many factors have been shown to affect rooting of cuttings. These include plant species (Table 4.9), age of the tree from which cuttings are taken, position of the cutting on the tree, the time of year when cuttings are taken, sex of the parent tree, nutrient status of the cutting, and environmental conditions under which cuttings are rooted.

One of the most consistent characteristics of juvenile woody plants is the relative ease of rooting of their cuttings when compared with cuttings from old trees of the same species. This is true of most species and constitutes one of the most serious problems facing plant breeders because, when a woody plant has reached an age at which it has clearly demonstrated certain desirable characteristics, it may no longer be possible to propagate it by cuttings.

There often is considerable seasonal variation in rootability of a given species. Cuttings of some woody plants, such as holly, can be successfully rooted when taken over a period of weeks or months but in other species, including beech and lilac, the time limits are shorter. In most cases it is best to make cuttings in the spring before the beginning of shoot growth or shortly thereafter. Cuttings taken later root poorly and do not make appreciable top growth during the same season. For detailed information on techniques of rooting stem cuttings of woody plants, the reader is referred to Hartmann and Kester (1975) and Wright (1976). Internal factors controlling rooting of cuttings are discussed in Chapter 16 of this volume.

Layering

Layering refers to the formation of roots on attached branches, where they come into contact with a moist medium. The rooted stem can then be detached as a means of propagation. Natural layering occurs commonly in raspberries, blackberries, currants, gooseberries, and in some species of forest trees when the lowest branches touch the soil. For example, black spruce and northern white-cedar in peat swamps reproduce by layering. According to Lutz (1939), layering occurs in *Tsuga, Picea, Abies, Chamaecyparis*, and *Taxus*, but only rarely in *Pinus*. Little (1944) described an interesting case of natural layering that was promoted by a heavy snowfall that bent branches to the ground. He observed that red maple, flowering dogwood, *Viburnum pubescens*, and *Clethra alnifolia* layered readily.

Several modifications of artificial layering methods have been used to good advantage by plant propagators. For example, many clones whose cuttings are difficult to root can be propagated by layering. The method is largely confined to species that layer naturally or cannot be propagated by other methods. Layering is commonly used to

TABLE 4.9 Variations in Rooting Capacity of Forest Trees[a]

Very easy to root	Easy to root	Moderately difficult to root	Difficult to root	Very difficult to root
Willows	Monterey pine	Aspens	Most eucalyptus	Most oaks
Non-aspen poplars	Cryptomeria	Red maple	Pines	Beeches
	Yews	Some birches	Spruces	Chestnuts
	Junipers	Some hemlocks	Larches	Ashes
			Birches	Walnuts
			Maples	
			Black locust	

[a] From Wright (1976).

propagate apple rootstocks, filbert, and muscadine grape. Probably the most useful artificial layering methods are simple layering and trench layering. In simple (common) layering a branch is bent to the ground and a portion of it is covered with soil before growth starts. Several centimeters of the tip are left exposed so as to form leaves. Sometimes the part of the stem that is to be covered with soil is first notched and treated with a root-inducing hormone. In trench layering roots develop on shoots that arise from the buried part. Air layering involves wounding of a tree branch,

Fig. 4.23 Air layer process for obtaining rooted branches of pine. Photo courtesy of U.S. Forest Service.

applying a growth-regulating compound to the wound, and covering the wound with moist sphagnum followed by wrapping with waterproof paper or plastic (Fig. 4.23). After aerial roots form around the wound, the rooted portion of the plant is severed and replanted. For an excellent discussion of details of layering methods the reader is referred to Hartmann and Kester (1975).

Grafting

Various grafting techniques have been used for a very long time to propagate woody plants. For example, Hartmann and Kester (1975) mentioned that grafting was used by the Chinese as early as 1,000 BC, that Aristotle (384–322 BC) wrote extensively about grafting, and that grafting was particularly popular during the days of the Roman Empire.

In grafting, the cambium of an excised branch (scion) is placed in contact with the cambium of a rooted plant (stock) in order to bring about a cambial union between the two. Sometimes a piece of stem (interstock) is inserted by means of two graft unions between the stock and scion.

Before differentiation of connecting vascular tissues occurs, wound callus tissues, which are formed by both the stock and scion, form and fill the voids between them. The stock and scion may produce about the same amounts of callus tissue, or one member of the union may produce considerably more than the other. In pine grafts, for example, the stock produces most of the wound callus tissue (Mergen, 1955). In Douglas-fir grafts the production of callus by the scion exceeded that by the stock for the first 7 days. Within 10 days, however, most callus was being contributed by the stock (Copes, 1969).

As the cells damaged in the grafting operation turn brown and die, the callus cells produced by the stock and scion are separated by a brown boundary line of dead cells, called the isolation layer. In some genera, for example *Citrus*, wound gum may develop along the isolation layer. Uninjured cells soon enlarge on both sides of the isolation layer and subsequently divide profusely to produce callus tissue. Within a few weeks, isolated tracheary elements begin to differentiate in the callus and across the isolation layer, and shortly thereafter the isolation layer breaks down and is resorbed. Eventually vascular cambium is formed through the intermingled callus of the stock and scion. The new cambium usually forms first where existing cambia of the stock and scion are in contact with callus tissue. Subsequently, cell division occurs in the callus to form a cambium and extend it until it meets other newly formed, converging cambial cells. When xylem and phloem are produced by the new cambium, vascular continuity is established between the stock and scion of compatible combinations. In bud grafts the converging cambium differentiates in the callus mass, usually beginning at the edge of the bark flap, following the line of the original wound surface until it finally joins with the cambium of the bud. Shortly thereafter, rapid growth occurs in the cambium of the bud shield and the bud is gradually lifted out of the bark slit. As normal vascular tissues are formed from the joined cambium in compatible combinations, the graft union increases in strength (Mosse, 1962).

Incompatibility of Graft Unions

Successful grafting depends not only on contact between cambia and other meristematic tissues, but also on compatibility between members of the graft union. Incompatibility in graft unions occurs commonly (Fig. 4.24) and has plagued plant propagators for centuries. Incompatibility may refer to failure of grafted partners to unite in a mechanically strong union, poor vigor, or premature death, where failure is caused by differences between the stock and scion. The severity of the symptoms of incompatibility may range from rapid and complete failure of stock and scion to graft or sudden collapse in the first year to vigorous growth in the first year and a subsequent slow decline. Sometimes symptoms of incompatibility are delayed for many years. For example, when varieties of pear are grafted to quince, incompatibility may be greatly delayed (Garner, 1967).

Causes of incompatibility in graft unions have been studied much more extensively in orchard trees than in forest trees. Herrero (1956) placed graft incompatibilities into four categories: (1) graft combinations where the bud failed to grow out; (2) graft combinations where incompatibility was due to virus infection; (3) graft combinations with mechanically weak unions, in which the cause of death of trees usually was breakage, and poor vigor or growth, if demonstrated, was due to mechanical obstruction at the union; (4) and graft combinations where poor growth was not directly due to abnormal union but was associated with abnormal starch distribution.

Mosse (1962) classified graft incompatibilities of fruit trees in two groups, translocation and localized incompatibility. Neither type is confined to a particular species

Fig. 4.24. Incompatibility of graft unions. A: 6-year-old trees of Oullins gage on common mussel broken smoothly at the union; E: apricot (var. Croughton) on plum root stock (Brampton); C: planed surface of a stem section of Williams Bon Chretien (pear) on Quince A, showing different rates of oxidation in pear and quince, and a strongly oxidized parenchyma layer between them. Photos courtesy of East Malling Research Station.

and both can occur in the same graft combination. Translocation incompatibility is associated with (1) accumulation of starch above the union and absence below it; (2) phloem degeneration; (3) different behavior of reciprocal grafts; (4) normal vascular continuity at the union, although there might be marked overgrowth of the scion; and (5) early effects on growth. Localized incompatibility is associated with (1) breaks in cambial vascular continuity, (2) similar behavior of reciprocal combinations, and (3) gradual starvation of the root system with slow development of external symptoms.

Copes (1970) found two major internal symptoms of incompatibility after grafting of Douglas-fir trees: (1) initiation and penetration of suberin zones in bark areas of the unions (Fig. 4.25), and (2) initiation and development of wound xylem areas (Fig. 4.26). The suberin zones, which were initiated in cortex cells of the union and became visible during the summer of the year of grafting, intensified with age. The wound xylem areas formed only in union zones where suberin had previously developed into the inner phloem or the cambium. The wounds developed at the beginning of the second and subsequent years. Wound xylem areas resulted from natural regrafting of stock and scion tissues at the beginning of each growing season.

Early detection of incompatible stock–scion combinations is difficult because external symptoms of incompatibility such as chlorosis and leaf shedding may not be

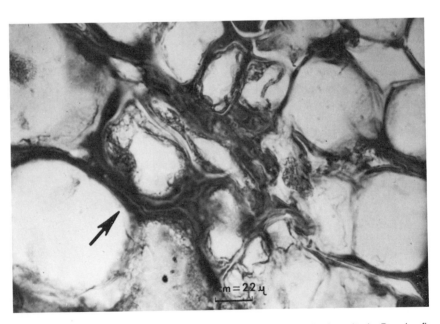

Fig. 4.25. Incompatibility of graft union as indicated by suberin deposits in Douglas-fir within cortex areas where stock and scion cells merge. Suberin deposits (indicated by arrow) were located on the outer cell walls, middle lamellae, and intercellular spaces. Photo courtesy of U.S. Forest Service.

Fig. 4.26. Incompatibility of graft unions as indicated by wound xylem areas (arrows) formed in all union areas at the beginning of the second year's growth and in subsequent years. Photo courtesy of U.S. Forest Service.

apparent until many years after grafting. A delay in the initiation of root growth is an early indication of incompatibility, but the usefulness of this response is limited under field conditions. However, Copes (1969) found that delay in development of vegetative buds of Douglas-fir clones at the beginning of the second year of growth was a good index for detecting incompatible graft unions.

It is widely accepted that grafts within species are more likely to be successful than those between species, genera, or families. Hence, close genetic relationships between stock and scion increase the likelihood of compatible unions. In Douglas-fir the incidence of incompatibility was nearly twice as great when grafted on unrelated stocks as when grafted on related stocks (Copes, 1973). Copes (1974) found that graft rejection in Douglas-fir was controlled primarily by additive genes. He showed that increase in compatibility can be made through careful parental selection and cross breeding among the best parents. Sweet and Thulin (1973) reported that graft incompatibility suddenly appeared and caused serious losses in a 14-year-old seed orchard of Monterey pine. They suggested that this might force them to switch from grafting to rooting cuttings in their tree improvement program.

Readers are referred to Hartmann and Kester (1975) and Wright (1976) for more detailed discussions of the grafting methods used with fruit and forest trees and ornamental woody plants.

Cell and Tissue Culture

In recent years there has been a surge of interest in reproducing woody plants by using unorganized systems such as callus or cell suspension cultures. Such cultures, which can be started from any cells that have potential for division, are grown in a defined medium under aseptic conditions. Single or mass callus cells may then be induced to divide and differentiate leaves, stems, roots, or whole plants (Fig. 4.27).

Culturing of Vegetative Tissues

Callus production, cell cultures, and protoplast fusion provide important possibilities for the improvement of woody plants. Callus cells may proliferate from parental cells in the cambium, cortex, or pith regions of stem sections. In culture the callus cells are mainly parenchymatous. Callus can be subcultured and maintained indefinitely on a nutrient medium balanced for each species. Good results have been obtained with callus from seedlings, root sprouts, 1-year-old angiosperm branches, and 1-year-old gymnosperm branches (Winton and Huhtinen, 1976).

Cheng and Voqui (1977) produced Douglas-fir plantlets in tissue culture under defined conditions from cotyledon explants obtained from 2- to 4-week-old seedlings. They cut cotyledons into segments and caused them to develop callus. Then bud growth was stimulated followed by treatment with NAA (naphthaleneacetic acid) to induce root production. The seedlings were transplanted to soil and 90% survived.

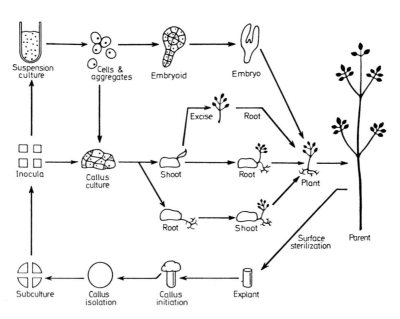

Fig. 4.27. Regeneration of woody plants from callus or suspension cultures. From Winton and Huhtinen (1976).

Fusion of protoplasts has been used for nonsexual hybridization between species. Protoplasts can be prepared from leaf mesophyll, meristems, microspores, and megagametophytes. Usually a combination of pectinase and cellulase enzymes is used to remove cell walls. Without cell walls protoplasts may fuse to form new cells as in fusion of sex cells during fertilization.

Culturing of Gametophytic Cells and Tissues

Many plant breeding problems might be solved with cultures from gametophytic or reproductive parts of woody plants. The two primary sources of haploid cells are reproductive tissues (microspores) in anthers and nutritive cells in the megagametophytes of gymnosperms. The two main advantages of culturing haploid gametophytic cells are that: (1) haploid cells can be used for producing protoplasts so the fused hybrid cells will have the diploid conditions of somatic cells; and (2) plants grown from haploid cells might be induced to double their one set of chromosomes, thereby producing diploid plants with homozygous alleles at each gene locus. That would assure valuable traits in self-fertile plants that would be expressed in following generations.

Unsolved Problems

The major difficulty with tissue cultures has been inducing an unorganized system to become an organized one, that is, to induce differentiation and formation of organs. Treatments for inducing differentiation seem to be very specific for given plant material. Progress in reproducing woody plants by tissue culture has been much slower than with herbaceous plants. In a number of herbaceous species many genetically identical plants can be obtained in a few weeks. By comparison, plantlets of relatively few woody angiosperms and some difficult-to-propagate conifers have been obtained. The major reason for limited success with forest trees appears to be a lack of effort (Durzan and Campbell, 1974).

Despite the difficulties encountered, the potential for tree improvement by use of cell and tissue culture is very great indeed. The prospects of developing screening methods to identify superior genotypes from gametic cells of selected plants are particularly promising. Haploid plantlets produced in tissue culture can be used for screening for inherent vigor, disease and pest resistance, drought resistance, frost resistance, and other desirable characteristics. For example, Berbee *et al*. (1976) produced virus-free poplars from infected poplar clones by a technique involving differentiation of plantlets from callus. The growth rates of different clones can be rapidly screened under a wide range of environmental conditions. When adequate screening techniques are developed it should be possible to rapidly select a wide range of desirable genotypes for establishing plantations. Another benefit of culturing haploid cells may be the development of homozygous diploid lines of plants that will breed true from seed when self-pollinated. Such homozygous lines would be useful in breeding programs to obtain hybrid vigor (Brown, 1976).

For good discussions of techniques and potential of tissue culture the reader is referred to the books by Street (1973) and Kruse and Patterson (1973).

GENERAL REFERENCES

Biale, J. B. (1950). Postharvest physiology and biochemistry of fruits. *Annu. Rev. Plant Physiol.* **1**, 183–206.

Coombe, B. G. (1976). The development of fleshy fruits. *Annu. Rev. Plant Physiol.* **27**, 507–528.

Durzan, D. J., and Campbell, R. A. (1974). Prospects for the mass production of improved stock of forest trees by cell and tissue culture. *Can. J. For. Res.* **4**, 151–174.

Esau, K. (1977). "Anatomy of Seed Plants," pp. 375–473. Wiley, New York.

Faegri, K., and Iverson, J. (1975). "Textbook of Pollen Analysis." Hafner, New York.

Garner, R. J. (1967). "The Grafter's Handbook." Faber & Faber, London.

Hansen, E. (1966). Postharvest physiology of fruits. *Annu. Rev. Plant Physiol.* **17**, 459–480.

Hartman, H. T., and Kester, D. E. (1975). "Plant Propagation: Principles and Practices." Prentice-Hall, Englewood Cliffs, New Jersey.

Hulme, A. C., ed. (1970, 1971). "The Biochemistry of Fruits and Their Products," Vols. 1 and 2. Academic Press, New York.

Jackson, D. I., and Sweet, G. B. (1972). Flower determination in temperate woody plants. *Hortic. Abstr.* **42**, 9–24.

Kozlowski, T. T., ed. (1971). "Growth and Development of Trees," Vol. 2. Academic Press, New York.

Kozlowski, T. T., ed. (1972). "Seed Biology," Vol. 2. Academic Press, New York.

Kozlowski, T. T., ed. (1973). "Shedding of Plant Parts." Academic Press, New York.

Kruse, P. F. Jr., and Patterson, M. K., eds. (1973). "Tissue Culture: Methods and Applications." Academic Press, New York.

Longman, K. A., and Jenik, J. (1974). "Tropical Forest and its Environment." Longmans, Green, New York.

Murashige, T. (1974). Plant propagation through tissue cultures. *Annu. Rev. Plant Physiol.* **25**, 135–166.

Richards, P. W. (1966). "Tropical Rain Forest." Cambridge Univ. Press, London and New York.

Tomlinson, P. B., and Zimmermann, M. H., eds. (1978). "Tropical Trees as Living Systems." Cambridge Univ. Press, London and New York.

Wright, J. W. (1976). "Introduction to Forest Genetics." Academic Press, New York.

Photosynthesis

5

INTRODUCTION

Photosynthesis is the process by which light energy is trapped and used to synthesize reduced carbon compounds from carbon dioxide and water. The process occurs only in illuminated green tissue, because chlorophyll plays an essential role in the conversion

163

of light energy to chemical energy. The term "photosynthesis" was proposed by Charles Reid Barnes of the University of Chicago early in this century. In Europe this process is often termed "assimilation" or "carbon assimilation," but most American plant physiologists prefer to use the term assimilation in reference to the production of new tissue from carbohydrates and nitrogen compounds (see Chapter 6).

The importance of photosynthesis cannot be overemphasized, because all the energy in our food is directly or indirectly stored by the process of photosynthesis and most of the energy used to operate our factories comes from fossil fuels where it was stored by photosynthesis in the distant past. Lieth (1972, 1975) estimated that land plants produce 100×10^9 metric tons of dry matter per year, of which over two-thirds is produced by trees. The total energy stored in plants each year by photosynthesis is about 100 times greater than that in all the coal mined in the world during a year. Although forests occupy only one-third of the earth's land surface, they produce about two-thirds of the dry matter while cultivated land occupies about 9% and produces only 9% of the dry matter (Lieth, 1975).

Until coal came into general use most of the heat energy used by man came from the combustion of wood. Today we are concerned more with the use of wood as a building material and as a source of paper than with its use as fuel, although interest in the latter is again increasing. Regardless of how it is used, we must remember that the energy and dry matter found in wood is stored there by the process of photosynthesis. Efficient forest management therefore should be directed toward improving the amount of photosynthesis per unit of land area and the efficiency with which the products of photosynthesis are converted into plant material.

THE CHLOROPLAST PIGMENTS

Chlorophyll deserves special attention because it is the light-absorbing pigment in the photosynthetic process and incidentally because it produces the dominant color of the earth's land surface. Occasionally the yellow carotenoid pigments are apparent, as in certain ornamental trees and shrubs, or when they are unmasked because conditions become unfavorable for chlorophyll synthesis or maintenance. Leaves of a few varieties of trees such as copper beech and Japanese maple are red or purple because of the presence of anthocyanin pigments which occur in the cell sap rather than in the plastids. Many other trees develop anthocyanins in the autumn, but the development of autumn coloration of leaves will be discussed in Chapter 7.

Chlorophyll and carotenoids occur in many tissues in addition to leaf blades, including petioles, buds, cotyledons, cortical parenchyma of young twigs, and the phelloderm of older stems of some species. Chloroplasts usually are rare in epidermal cells, except for the guard cells. They occasionally develop in roots exposed to light and are common in flower parts, young fruits, and sometimes even in the embryos of seeds. However, most of the chlorophyll and carotenoid pigments are concentrated in the chloroplasts of leaf mesophyll cells.

Chloroplasts are ovoid, disk- or saucer-shaped bodies, about 5 μm in diameter and 2 or 3 μm in thickness, which are enclosed in differentially permeable membranes. The internal structure of chloroplasts is rather complex, consisting of a colorless, proteinaceous matrix, the stroma, in which are embedded numerous more or less cylindrical bodies called grana. These consist of stacks of disk-shaped membranous structures called lamellae or small thylakoids on which the chlorophyll is bound. The grana are connected to one another by unstacked, intergrana thylakoids. This complex system of membranes plays an essential role in the separation of electric charges, electron transport, and photophosphorylation. The pigments and the enzymes involved in the photo-

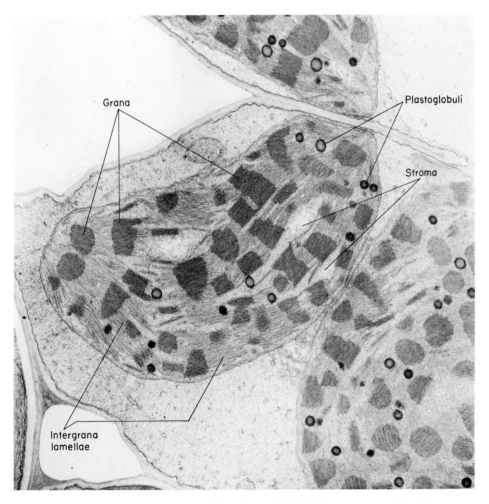

Fig. 5.1. Electron micrograph of a chloroplast ($\times$ 24,750). Photo courtesy of R. F. Evert.

chemical phase of photosynthesis are associated with the membrane system while those involved in carbon fixation occur in the stroma. An electron micrograph of a chloroplast is shown in Fig. 5.1.

In addition to chlorophyll and carotenoid pigments, chloroplasts contain membranous proteins, lipids (including triglycerides, phospholipids, sulfolipids, and galactolipids), enzymes, starch, soluble carbohydrates, amino acids, RNA, DNA, and inorganic elements. Some writers regard chloroplasts as practically autonomous structures, both physiologically and genetically (Park, 1976). More details and additional references on chloroplast structure and composition can be found in Govindjee (1975) and Park (1976).

Chlorophylls

Although several kinds of chlorophyll occur in the plant kingdom, chlorophylls *a* and *b* are the only important ones in woody plants. Chlorophyll *a* has the formula $C_{55}H_{72}O_5N_4Mg$; the formula of chlorophyll *b* is $C_{55}H_{70}O_6N_4Mg$. The structural formula of chlorophyll *a* is shown in Fig. 5.2. It has a structure consisting of four cyclized pyrrole rings with side chains, which are coordinated with magnesium in the center. Chlorophyll is fluorescent, absorbing certain wavelengths of visible light, primarily in the red and blue part of the spectrum, and reradiating longer wavelength red light.

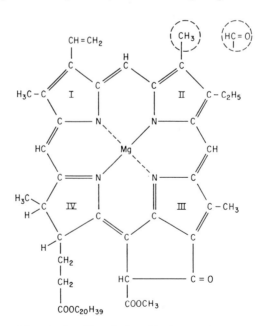

Fig. 5.2. Structural formula for chlorophyll *a*. The formula for chlorophyll *b* is the same except that an HC=O group occurs in place of the CH_3 group enclosed in a dashed circle in pyrrole ring II. Another arrangement of double bonds is possible, and an alternative linkage of magnesium is indicated by the dashed lines.

Carotenoids

The yellow or orange color sometimes observed in variegated leaves or those kept in darkness is caused by carotenes and xanthophylls, two groups of fat-soluble pigments which also occur in chloroplasts. More than 60 different carotenoids occur in plants. Carotenes are hydrocarbons with the empirical formula $C_{40}H_{56}$, composed of eight isoprene units (see Chapter 8). There are several isomers, of which β-carotene, the precursor of Vitamin A, is most abundant and may make up as much as 0.1% of the leaf dry weight. The red pigment, lycopene, found in ripe tomatoes, rose fruits, and other plant parts, is also an isomer of carotene.

Most xanthophylls have the formula $C_{40}H_{56}O_2$, and are yellowish to brownish in color. Xanthophylls can be separated physically from carotenes because they are more soluble in alcohol and much less soluble in petroleum ether. The most abundant leaf xanthophyll is lutein which sometimes occurs in higher concentrations than β-carotene.

The carotenoids, unlike chlorophyll, are formed to some extent in darkness; hence seedlings grown in darkness usually are yellow in color. As carotenoids are also more resistant than chlorophyll to destruction under unfavorable conditions, leaves kept in darkness for several days or subjected to water stress usually become yellow because destruction of the chlorophyll exposes the yellow carotenoid pigments. The more rapid destruction of chlorophyll than of carotenoids also brings about the yellow coloration of leaves of some species in the autumn (see Chapter 7). Carotenoids function as accessory pigments in photosynthesis and may also protect chlorophyll from irreversible photooxidation. They also are the source of most of the yellow and red pigmentation found in animals.

Relative Amounts of Leaf Pigments

The amounts and proportions of pigments vary with species, environment, and leaf age. Generally there is about three times as much chlorophyll as carotenoid. The amount of total chlorophyll varies widely among species, some having two or three times as much, per unit of leaf dry weight, as others. Chlorophyll a is usually two to three times as abundant as chlorophyll b, and carotenes exceed xanthophylls by a similar amount. The ratio of chlorophyll a to b often changes appreciably in the same plant. For example, in the autumn and in leaves subjected to water stress chlorophyll a is destroyed more rapidly than chlorophyll b.

The chloroplast pigments can be extracted fairly easily by solvents such as acetone and methyl alcohol, and the various pigments in the extract can then be separated by differential solubility or by chromatographic methods (Strain and Svec, 1966).

The Photosynthetic Unit

The chlorophyll molecules are organized within the chloroplasts in photosynthetic units, each consisting of several hundred molecules. According to Alberte *et al.* (1976), the photosynthetic units of conifers and deciduous trees are fewer in number but considerably larger than those found in herbaceous plants. The photosynthetic units of shade needles of pine also are larger than those of sun needles. The chlorophylls are organized in several kinds of complexes, each having its distinct protein moiety and spectral properties (Thornber, 1975; Thornber *et al.*, 1977). One, known as the P700 chlorophyll *a*–protein complex, also contains β-carotene and is associated with Photosystem I. Another known as the light-harvesting, chlorophyll *a/b*–protein complex, contains chlorophylls *a* and *b* and traces of carotenoids. It is principally associated

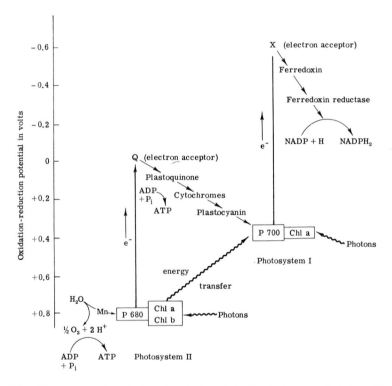

Fig. 5.3. Diagram showing electron flow in the photochemical stage of photosynthesis. Light energy trapped by the pigments of Photosystem II causes photolysis of water, release of O_2 and H^+, and excitation of electrons to a high energy level where they are accepted by an unidentified acceptor, Q. Electrons then move down through a series of electron carriers, including plastoquinone, cytochromes, and plastocyanin to the chlorophyll of Photosystem I. Some energy is used to produce ATP (adenosine triphosphate), possibly at two different sites, by noncyclic photophosphorylation. The pigments of Photosystem I also absorb light energy and the resulting excited electrons move to acceptor X and thence to ferredoxin. NADP is reduced to $NADPH_2$ by H^+ released by the photolysis of water. There also sometimes is direct "spillover" of energy from system II to system I. Photosystem II absorbs light principally at wavelengths below about 680 nm, while Photosystem I is operative principally at longer wavelengths. The important products of the photochemical stage are ATP, $NADPH_2$, and O_2.

with Photosystem II. The two photosystems carry on noncyclic photophosphorylation and produce the reducing power ($NADPH_2$) and ATP required for CO_2 fixation. The interaction of these two systems is shown in Fig. 5.3. According to Alberte *et al.* (1976), the chlorophyll *a/b* ratio and other characteristics of the pigments are similar in the coniferous and deciduous tree species and the herbaceous species studied. However, it is suggested that the fewer photosynthetic units in the chloroplasts of trees may be at least a partial explanation of the fact that the rate of photosynthesis of leaves of woody plants is typically lower than the rate of leaves of herbaceous plants (Larcher, 1975).

FACTORS AFFECTING CHLOROPHYLL FORMATION

Failure to develop or maintain chlorophyll results in such obvious yellowing or chlorosis that it has been studied extensively and found to depend on a number of internal and environmental factors.

Internal Factors

The most important factor is the genetic potential of the plant, because occasionally mutations result in complete loss of the ability to form chlorophyll and short-lived albino seedlings result. More often the process is only partly disturbed, resulting in lack of chlorophyll in certain areas of leaves (variegated leaves) or a uniformly low chlorophyll content which causes leaves to assume the yellowish hue of the *aurea* varieties often used as ornamental trees and shrubs. Occasionally bud mutations result in albino or variegated branches on otherwise normal trees and shrubs. Many genes are involved in chlorophyll synthesis and its assembly into photosynthetic units, and abnormalities in chlorophyll formation are fairly common. Chloroplast development is dependent on both nuclear and chloroplast DNA, as well as on both cytoplasmic and chloroplast ribosomes.

An adequate supply of carbohydrates seems essential for chlorophyll formation, and leaves deficient in soluble carbohydrates may fail to become green even if all other conditions are favorable. If such leaves are floated on a sugar solution, they usually begin to form chlorophyll. Viruses often interfere with chlorophyll formation, causing "yellows" characterized by uniform chlorosis or bronzing of leaf blades as well as vein clearing (Berg, 1964). The mottled leaves of some ornamental plants are the result of virus infection.

Environmental Factors

The major environmental factors affecting chlorophyll formation and maintenance are light, temperature, minerals, water and oxygen, but chlorophyll formation is very sensitive to almost any factor which disturbs metabolic processes.

Light

In general light is essential for the formation of chlorophyll although some conifer seedlings and a few other plant species develop chlorophyll in darkness. Relatively low light intensities are effective in initiating or promoting chlorophyll formation. Dark-grown, yellow seedlings contain protochlorophyll, the precursor of chlorophyll *a* but its reduction to chlorophyll *a* requires light.

Very bright light causes a net decomposition of chlorophyll, hence chlorophyll is always simultaneously being synthesized and destroyed. In bright light equilibrium is established at a lower concentration than in light of low intensity and shade leaves usually have a higher concentration of chlorophyll than sun leaves. There also is a higher proportion of chlorophyll *a* to *b* in sun than in shade leaves.

Temperature

Synthesis of chlorophyll apparently occurs over a wide range of temperatures. Evergreens of the temperate zone must synthesize chlorophyll from temperatures near freezing up to the highest temperatures of mid-summer. Many conifers become some-what chlorotic during the winter, presumably because destruction exceeds synthesis of chlorophyll at very low temperatures. For example, Perry and Baldwin (1966) found that the first winter frost caused various degrees of breakdown of chloroplasts of several species of evergreen trees in the southeastern United States and Senser *et al.* (1975) observed it in Germany.

Minerals

One of the most common causes of chlorosis is a deficiency of one of the essential elements. Nitrogen deficiency is a common cause of chlorosis in woody plants, especially in the older leaves. Iron deficiency is another common cause of chlorosis, especially in the younger leaves. Apparently an adequate supply of iron is essential for chlorophyll synthesis even though it is not a chlorophyll constituent, iron being a cofactor for a chlorophyll precursor. Magnesium is a constituent of chlorophyll, hence a deficiency of it naturally causes chlorosis. In fact, a deficiency of most of the major elements and several of the minor ones results in chlorosis. This suggests that almost any disturbance of normal metabolism is likely to interfere with synthesis of chlorophyll. Chlorosis caused by mineral deficiency is discussed in more detail in Chapter 10.

Water

Moderate water stress slows chlorophyll formation (Bourque and Naylor, 1971; Alberte *et al.,* 1975) and severe dehydration of plant tissues not only interferes with chlorophyll formation but also causes destruction of that already present. As a result leaves of plants subjected to drought tend to turn yellow. The light-harvesting chlorophyll *a/b* protein is most severely affected by water stress (Alberte *et al.,* 1977). Unfortunately, leaves on trees and shrubs may also turn yellow when the soil around their roots is saturated with water. As discussed in Chapters 16 and 17 the effects of both drought and poor soil aeration probably are partly indirect, chlorophyll formation being hindered by the general disturbance of metabolism.

Oxygen

Seedlings will not develop chlorophyll in the absence of oxygen even when illuminated. This indicates that aerobic respiration is necessary for some processes for the production of intermediate compounds or for the supply of metabolic energy necessary for chlorophyll synthesis.

THE PHOTOSYNTHETIC MECHANISM

In simple terms photosynthesis consists of the reduction of atmospheric CO_2 to carbohydrate by use of light energy, with an associated release of oxygen from water. This reaction can be summarized by the following generalized equation:

$$CO_2 + 2H_2O \xrightarrow[\text{chlorophyll}]{\text{light}} (CH_2O) + O_2 + H_2O$$

Like many other physiological processes, photosynthesis consists of a number of sequential steps. Because of their complexities, a thorough discussion of these lies beyond the scope of this book and the reader is referred to books such as those by Zelitch (1971), Whittingham (1974), Govindjee (1975), and Gregory (1977) for more details. However, the enormous importance of photosynthesis requires that the main features of the mechanism of the process be discussed briefly. Some knowledge of the nature of the process is necessary in order to understand how it is affected by various environmental factors.

Photosynthesis can be broken down into the following sequential events: (1) trapping of light energy by chloroplasts; pigments other than chlorophyll (e.g., carotenoids) play an accessory role in photosynthesis by transferring energy to chlorophyll a; (2) splitting of water and release of high-energy electrons and O_2; (3) electron transfer leading to generation of chemical energy in the form of ATP and reducing power as $NADPH_2$; and (4) terminal steps involving expenditure of energy of ATP and the reducing power of $NADPH_2$ to fix CO_2 molecules in phosphoglyceric acid and reduce it to phosphoglyceraldehyde, and finally convert this compound into more complex carbohydrates, such as sucrose, starch, cellulose, and hemicellulose.

Discussions of photosynthesis naturally place primary emphasis on carbohydrates as the principal product. However, large quantities of the primary products are immediately converted into other compounds in addition to glucose, such as lipids, organic acids, and amino acids, which are equally important in plant metabolism. Some of the pathways followed in these conversions are indicated in Fig. 6.20.

Light and Dark Reactions

Photosynthesis includes a photochemical phase requiring a light as well as a dark phase. During the light phase $NADPH_2$, ATP, and O_2 are generated, but the reduction of CO_2 occurs in the dark phase. Although the dark reactions do not require light they do not occur to any great extent without it because they depend on $NADPH_2$ and ATP, both of which are products of the light reaction.

The photochemical phase occurs very rapidly (in 0.00001 sec) and at least the primary photochemistry is independent of temperature, although electron transport is temperature dependent. The dark stage occurs more slowly, requiring about 0.04 sec at 25°C, and is slowed down by low temperatures. Obviously the rate of photosynthesis will be limited by the reaction which is occurring most slowly, hence in bright light the chemical or dark stage is likely to be the limiting one and the process is sensitive to temperature, but at low light intensities the photochemical stage is more likely to be limiting. Under normal light conditions CO_2 concentration is more often a limiting factor than temperature, except possibly for evergreen plants in the winter.

The photochemical phase of photosynthesis actually consists of two light reactions, termed Photosystems I and II, which are joined together by electron carriers. The systems operate through different pigments. The redox active chlorophyll in the reaction center of Photosystem I is a species of chlorophyll *a*. Because its absorption peak is at 700 nm it is known as P700. Additional pigments of Photosystem I, including other forms of chlorophyll *a* and carotenoids, also participate in the transfer of light energy to the active centers of P700. The pigments of Photosystem II include an active species of chlorophyll *a* with an absorption maximum at about 680 nm, some additional chlorophyll *a,* chlorophyll *b,* and carotenoids.

The postulated linkage of Photosystems I and II is shown in Fig. 5.3. The operation of each system involves absorption of one quantum of light energy by each reaction center, which is then said to be in an ''excited'' state. In Photosystem I the ''excited'' reaction center gives up an electron to an electron acceptor and the electron then moves down the energy scale to ferredoxin and is involved in the reduction of NADPH to $NADPH_2$.

In Photosystem II the energy absorbed is used to bring about the excitation of electrons and the photolysis of water. The photolysis of water yields H^+ electrons (e^-), and O_2. This reaction can be summarized as follows:

$$2H_2O \longrightarrow 4e^- + 4H^+ + O_2$$

The excited electrons move to an acceptor (Q in Fig. 5.2) and then through a series of electron carriers, including plastoquinone, cytochromes, and plastocyanin, to the active chlorophyll (P700) of Photosystem I. Some of the energy is drained off to produce ATP by noncyclic photophosphorylation, possibly at two different sites. Cyclic photophosphorylation has been demonstrated in laboratory preparations and in algal cells. The NADP is reduced to $NADPH_2$ by electrons released during the photolysis of water.

Not all the steps in this system are fully explained and there may be changes and additions to it as more information is acquired. However, the important results of the photochemical stage are the production of ATP and $NADPH_2$ needed for the reduction of CO_2, and the liberation of O_2 into the air. Production of ATP and $NADPH_2$ occurs in or on the thylakoids; reduction of CO_2 to carbohydrate occurs in the stroma.

Carbon Fixation Pathways

The actual fixing of carbon from CO_2 in stable compounds involves a complicated sequence of events which can occur in the absence of light, but is dependent on a supply of ATP and $NADPH_2$ produced by the photochemical stage. Information concerning the compounds formed in carbon fixation was obtained by supplying radioactive CO_2 to unicellular algae for shorter and shorter periods of time, then killing the cells and analyzing them. Within a minute after $^{14}CO_2$ was supplied the "tracer" carbon was found in sugars, sugar phosphates, organic acids, and other compounds. The sequence of the most important events is shown in Fig. 5.4. This cycle is usually termed the Calvin–Benson cycle because Calvin and his colleagues worked out most of its details. The important features can be summarized as follows, after Govindjee (1975): (1) carboxylation of a 5-carbon (C_5) sugar phosphate (ribulose 1,5-bisphosphate) with production of two molecules of phosphoglyceric acid (C_3); (2) conversion of phosphoglyceric acid to triose phosphate (C_3) with the aid of $NADPH_2$ and ATP generated in photochemical reactions; (3) interconversion of sugars. For six molecules of CO_2, one molecule of hexose is formed and six molecules of ribulose 1,5-bisphosphate are regenerated and continue the cycle. Also, in the conversion of ribulose monophosphate to ribulose 1,5-bisphosphate an ATP molecule is needed. For each glucose molecule the net reaction can be summarized as follows:

$$6 \ CO_2 + 12 \ NADPH_2 + 18 \ ATP \rightarrow C_6H_{12}O_6 + 12 \ NADP + 18 \ ADP + 18 \ P_i + 6 \ H_2O$$

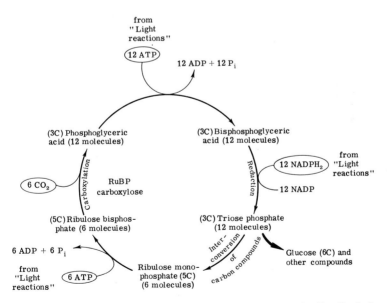

Fig. 5.4. The path of carbon fixation by the C_3 or Calvin–Benson cycle. After Govindjee and Govindjee (1975). (For other compounds formed from the primary products of photosynthesis refer to Fig. 6.20.)

Most crop and nearly all woody plants are termed C_3 plants because after CO_2 combines with the five-carbon sugar, ribulose bisphosphate in the carbon cycle, it is converted to two molecules of the three-carbon compound, phosphoglyceric acid (see Fig. 5.4). Ribulose bisphosphate carboxylase (RuBP carboxylase) is the carboxylating enzyme. This enzyme also functions as an oxygenase. As a result O_2 is a competitive inhibitor of CO_2 fixation. However, in some species of plants such as maize and sugar cane the first detectable products of photosynthesis are four-carbon compounds, chiefly aspartic, malic, and oxaloacetic acids. In this system, known as the Hatch–Slack pathway, phosphoenolpyruvic acid (C_3) is the CO_2 acceptor and phosphoenolpyruvate carboxylase (PEP carboxylase) is the carboxylating enzyme. This enzyme has a very high affinity for CO_2 and is not inhibited by O_2, as is the RuBP carboxylase of the Calvin–Benson cycle. In typical C_4 plants the initial fixation of carbon in C_4 organic acids occurs in the mesophyll cells, but the acids are then transported into the large-bundle sheath cells characteristic of C_4 plants where decarboxylation occurs, releasing CO_2 which is used in the Calvin cycle and pyruvic acid which reenters the Hatch–Slack system, as shown in Fig. 5.5. This transport process concentrates CO_2 where RuBP carboxylase can easily fix it into phosphoglyceric acid. It should be emphasized that the Hatch–Slack carbon pathway is not an alternative to the Calvin–Benson cycle, but an added system which increases its efficiency under some circumstances (Moore, 1974). Only the Calvin cycle is truly autocatalytic in the sense that it can generate more CO_2 acceptor than was originally present and therefore produces a net increase in fixed carbon (Kelly *et al.*, 1976).

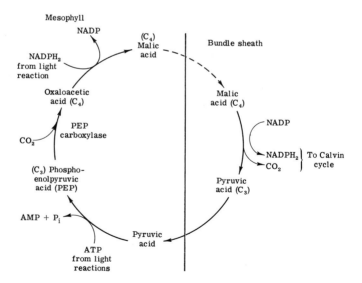

Fig. 5.5. The C_4 or Hatch–Slack pathway for carbon fixation. From Govindjee and Govindjee (1975).

In addition to the difference in the first product of photosynthesis and a higher CO_2 compensation point, C_3 plants are light saturated at a lower intensity than C_4 plants and their rate of photosynthesis is increased if the oxygen concentration is lowered. Furthermore, they lack the large-bundle sheath cells characteristic of leaves of C_4 plants where CO_2 can be concentrated. The high CO_2 compensation point of C_3 plants is at least partly attributable to the fact that the carboxylase activity of RuBP carboxylase is competitively inhibited by oxygen. This also accounts for the observation that a decrease in O_2 concentration results in a large increase in CO_2 fixation in C_3 plants. Increasing the CO_2 concentration reduces the oxygenase activity of RuBP carboxylase, which is favorable to increased net CO_2 fixation.

An important characteristic of plants having the C_4 pathway is the very low rate of photorespiration as compared with C_3 plants. Photorespiration refers to light-dependent production of CO_2 by photosynthetic tissue and is in no way related to the basic respiration discussed in Chapter 6 which involves a cytochrome system. The substrate is a recent product of photosynthesis, probably glyoxylic acid derived from ribulose bisphosphate by the oxygenase activity of RuBP carboxylase. The measurable rate appears to be negligible in C_4 plants, probably because the CO_2 released by photorespiration is nearly all recycled by the more efficient combination of carboxylases in the combined Hatch–Slack and Calvin cycles than in the Calvin cycle alone. The fact that photorespiration occurs in all green plants suggests that it has some essential function, but its exact role is uncertain. It has been suggested that it contributes to the synthesis of amino acids and perhaps to ATP synthesis in mitochondria, but these may be merely minor alternative metabolic pathways.

Because of the large loss of carbohydrate in photorespiration, up to one-half of the carbon fixed in photosynthesis, there has been discussion of the possibility of increasing net photosynthesis and crop yields by finding a genetic or chemical means of decreasing photorespiration (Zelitch, 1971; Oliver and Zelitch, 1977b). However, all important woody species, except possibly some mangroves and a few others, use the C_3 carbon pathway and carry on photorespiration, yet they are very successful in nature. Servaites and Ogren (1977) suggest that inhibition of photorespiration is not accompanied by increased photosynthesis, but, on the contrary, reduces it. While the C_4 carbon pathway is more efficient in terms of carbon balance than the C_3 pathway alone at the level of individual leaves, it seems to provide little advantage at the level of plant stands (Gifford, 1974). Furthermore, there is some question as to whether growth of plants in favorable environments is often limited by the potential rate of photosynthesis per unit of leaf area. This question is discussed further at the end of this chapter.

Another variation of carbon fixation, known as the crassulacean acid metabolism (CAM) is found in many succulents and a few other plants that are able to fix large quantities of CO_2 in darkness. CAM carboxylation reactions lead to the formation of oxaloacetic and malic acids in the dark through the activity of phosphoenolpyruvic carboxylase. In the light malic acid is decarboxylated, yielding pyruvic acid and CO_2 which is used in photosynthesis by way of the Calvin–Benson cycle. In such plants the acidity becomes very high at night, but decreases during the day while the sugar content increases. In many succulents the stomata are open at night, permitting the entrance of CO_2, but they are mostly closed during the day, preventing the loss of water. This is a very efficient arrangement for plants growing in dry habitats, but is not known to occur in woody plants.

As mentioned earlier, there is much interest in finding methods of increasing the efficiency of photosynthesis. Some of the possibilities were discussed by Bassham (1977) and Radmer and Kok (1977), but the prospects for a significant improvement do not seem promising. Natural selection, operating for millenia, has produced a compromise in photosynthetic biochemistry and biophysics which will be very difficult to improve for field conditions.

Carbon Dioxide Uptake by Photosynthetic Tissues

The entrance of CO_2 occurs mostly through the stomata, although a small amount presumably diffuses through the cuticle and epidermal cells. Inward diffusion of CO_2 obeys the same laws which govern outward diffusion of water vapor and can be represented by the following equation:

$$CO_2 \text{ flux} = \frac{C_{air} - C_m}{r_{air} + r_{leaf}}$$

The term $C_{air} - C_m$ represents the difference between the concentration of CO_2 in the outside air and that of the chloroplasts in the mesophyll cells, and r_{air} and r_{leaf} are the resistances to diffusion in the outside air and in the leaf. The term r_{leaf} contains two components, r_s or stomatal resistance, and r_m or mesophyll resistance which is relatively large for the water phase in mesophyll cells. The air resistance varies from about 0.5 sec/cm in moving air to 2 or 3 sec/cm in quiet air, while stomatal resistance varies from 1 to 7 sec/cm with open stomata to 50 to 150 sec/cm when they are closed. The mesophyll resistance is negligible for water vapor, but about 6 to 10 sec/cm for CO_2.

Thus, partial closure of stomata increases the resistance to water movement much more than the resistance to CO_2 movement and should reduce transpiration more than it reduces photosynthesis. This theory forms the basis for use of metabolic antitranspirants which cause closure of stomata to reduce transpiration (see Chapter 13). The physical processes involved in CO_2 uptake are discussed by Nobel (1974) and Zelitch (1971, Chapter 7).

Tissues Carrying on Photosynthesis

Although most photosynthesis occurs in foliage leaves, some takes place in other green tissues, including cotyledons (see Chapter 15), buds, stems, flowers, and fruits. In the vast majority of species the photosynthetic contributions of tissues other than cotyledons and foliage leaves are relatively unimportant. For example, photosynthesis by green fruits of locust, lemon, orange, avocado, grape, and plum generally is too low to contribute appreciably to their own growth. Photosynthesis of rapidly expanding green cones of red pine is not adequate to balance their high respiratory evolution of CO_2, and most of the carbohydrates needed for the growth of cones are mobilized from other sources (Dickmann and Kozlowski, 1970b). By comparison, the photosynthetic contribution of the green fruits of coffee is appreciable and may account for up to one-third of their own dry weight increment (Cannell, 1975).

Bark photosynthesis of most species is low, amounting to only 5% of the total in eastern cottonwood (Schaedle, 1975), but photosynthesis of branches and bark is an important adaptation of certain arid-zone species. A number of desert shrubs which shed their leaves during the dry season have persistent, photosynthetically active stems and branches. For example, palo verde is leafless during most of the year and its green branches may produce up to 40% of the total annual photosynthate (Adams and Strain, 1969).

VARIATIONS IN RATES OF PHOTOSYNTHESIS

The rate of photosynthesis of woody plants varies widely and is influenced by interactions of many external and plant factors, and such interactions vary with time and species. Measurement techniques also have sometimes been unsatisfactory, a topic discussed later. Avery (1977) examined 49 papers which reported widely different rates of photosynthesis in apple. Among the reasons he gave for the variations among experimenters were: too low rates of air flow, excessive leaf temperatures, water stress, use of trees grown in greenhouses which have leaves differing in structure and photosynthetic capacity from those of outdoor trees, and failure to take into account the presence of fruit, which may increase the rate 45–60% above the rate for comparable trees without fruit.

It is often difficult to make meaningful quantitative comparisons of photosynthesis of morphologically dissimilar plants. Rates of photosynthesis of different sized plants generally are expressed as amount of CO_2 absorbed per unit of leaf dry weight, leaf surface, or stomata-bearing leaf surface. In some species with thin cuticles, appreciable CO_2 uptake occurs directly through the leaf surface which has no stomata. In other species the leaf surface lacking stomata is relatively impermeable to CO_2. Kozlowski (1949) found higher rates of CO_2 uptake in oak than in pine seedlings on both a leaf area and a leaf dry weight basis, but the magnitude of the difference varied with the physiological unit on which photosynthesis was based. Tranquillini (1962) noted that apparent photosynthesis of European larch was about twice that of Swiss stone pine on a leaf dry weight basis, but their rates varied little on a leaf area basis. For further discussion of some of the problems involved in comparing photosynthesis of different species the reader is referred to Decker (1955a) and Zelawski and Walker (1976).

Photosynthetic capacities sometimes are estimated from net dry weight increment. Such data are especially meaningful because the increment represents an average net increase over a considerable time in an environment which includes the usual periodic environmental stresses. In contrast, short-time measurements of CO_2 uptake usually are made in a controlled rather than a fluctuating environment. This may be favorable to all or only some of the species compared. A number of angiosperm species are as efficient in conducting photosynthesis at low light intensities as they are at high ones, whereas many gymnosperms are much more efficient at high intensities. Comparisons of these two groups at low or at high light intensities often give different impressions of photosynthetic capacity in terms of food accumulation (Kramer and Kozlowski, 1960). Furthermore, gymnosperms often accumulate some dry weight during the dormant season whereas deciduous angiosperms lose some through respiration. Therefore, a gymnosperm with a slightly lower rate of photosynthesis than a deciduous angiosperm during the growing season might accumulate as much or more total dry matter over a year because of the much longer duration of photosynthetic activity (Sweet and Wareing, 1968).

Species and Genetic Variations

Photosynthetic capacity often varies appreciably among species as well as among varieties, clones, and provenances of the same species. Such variations usually are related to basic differences in metabolism or in leaf anatomy. In addition both species and varieties of a species differ appreciably in crown development, and greater leaf production or a longer growing season often compensates for a low rate of photosynthesis per unit of leaf area or dry weight. For example, Sweet and Wareing (1968) reported that although larch seedlings initially produced dry matter more rapidly than pine seedlings, after larch lost its leaves photosynthesis continued in the pine seedlings and they increased 25% in dry weight, almost catching up with the larch.

Species Variations

Several investigators have reported variations in photosynthetic capacity of different species. A few examples will be given. In forest trees particularly high rates of photosynthesis have been observed for several angiosperms including poplar, apple, ash, and eucalyptus, and for such gymnosperms as Douglas-fir, larch, and metasequoia (Larcher, 1969). Kramer and Decker (1944) found that CO_2 absorption was much higher per unit of leaf area in red and white oak than in flowering dogwood or loblolly pine. Polster (1955) observed high rates of photosynthesis in Douglas-fir, intermediate rates in white pine, and low rates in Norway spruce. Weide (1962) noted that metasequoia, with very high photosynthesis and low respiration rates, was more efficient than beech, oak, pine, spruce, or larch. The rate of photosynthesis often varies appreciably among species in the same genus. For example, *Eucalyptus globulus* had much higher rates than *E. marginata*.

Variations have also been reported in orchard trees. The carbon dioxide uptake per unit of leaf surface of pear and apple leaves was at least three times that of leaves of evergreen perennials such as citrus (Avery, 1977; Heinicke, 1966; Kriedemann, 1968b; Kriedemann and Canterford, 1971). In another study, photosynthesis varied in the following order: apple > pear > cherry > plum. Apple leaves not only had the highest rates but they also maintained photosynthesis longer into the autumn. Plum was the first to stop absorbing CO_2 (Friedrich and Schmidt, 1959; Friedrich, 1962).

Genetic Variations

There are many examples of genetic variations in rates of photosynthesis and only a few examples will be given.

Polster and Weise (1962) found large differences in the photosynthetic capacities of two clones of European larch. Krueger and Ferrell (1965) noted that Douglas-fir seedlings from a Vancouver Island source had higher rates of photosynthesis than seedlings from a Montana source at certain temperatures, but the variations among seedlings from the same source were sometimes greater than the differences between seedlings from the two sources. Luukkanen and Kozlowski (1972) reported large differences among poplar clones in rates of photosynthesis, photorespiration, and dark respiration per unit of leaf surface area, and in CO_2 compensation points. Representatives of the *Aigeiros* section had lower rates of photosynthesis and higher compensation points than members of the *Tacamahaca* section.

Differences in photosynthetic capacity among genetic materials may be the result of anatomical or biochemical differences, or both. Often variations in stomatal characteristics account for variations in CO_2 uptake. Bjurman (1959) demonstrated higher photosynthetic capacity for diploid currant plants than for tetraploids. Since the diploids had approximately 45% more stomata per unit of leaf area and a slightly lower chlorophyll content than the tetraploids, he attributed the differences in photosynthesis primarily to greater resistance to diffusion of CO_2 into the leaf mesophyll of the tetraploids.

Variations in photosynthesis per plant of different genetic materials sometimes are more a result of differences in leaf development than of differences in photosynthetic efficiency of individual leaves. For example, Huber and Polster (1955) found some differences in rates of photosynthesis per unit of leaf area in poplar clones, but clonal differences in total leaf volume caused much of the difference in rates of photosynthesis per plant. McGregor *et al.* (1961) found that loblolly pine seedlings from Georgia showed higher photosynthesis than Florida seedlings, but the differences in rates per seedling were caused by variations in amounts of foliage rather than in higher rates per unit of foliage. Similarly, Gatherum (1964) found that the greater leaf volume of a Scotch pine seed source from west-central Germany compared with one from east-central Turkey accounted for differences in photosynthesis.

Much interest has been shown by forest geneticists in using rates of photosynthesis as indices of growth potential of trees. However, both high and low and even negative correlations between photosynthetic capacity and growth of trees have been demonstrated. Positive correlations between photosynthetic rates and growth were reported by Huber and Polster (1955) for poplar, Gatherum *et al.* (1967) for aspen–poplar hybrid clones, and Campbell and Rediske (1966) for Douglas-fir seedlings. However, rates of photosynthesis and dry weight increment of seedlings were not well correlated in lodgepole pine (Sweet and Wareing, 1968). Brix (1967) found a close relationship between rates of photosynthesis and growth of Douglas-fir seedlings under one set of growing conditions, but a poor relationship under another set. Emmingham and Waring (1977) found a high correlation between their index of potential photosynthesis and wood production of Douglas-fir in western Oregon, but a much lower correlation in the central Cascade Mountains.

Some investigators have even found inverse relationships between photosynthesis and growth potential. For example, Gordon and Gatherum (1968) found that rates of photosynthesis and growth of Scotch pine seedlings were related to seed source. However, the seedlings that grew most had the lowest rate of photosynthesis on a leaf dry weight basis. In the fast-growing seedlings a smaller proportion of total needle weight was photosynthetically active. This was due either to (1) more mutual shading of needles in the fast growing plants, or, more likely, to (2) anatomical or biochemical differences in needles among the seed sources. This problem is discussed at the end of this chapter in the section on Growth Rate.

As emphasized by Ledig (1969), short-time measurements of photosynthetic capacity are not always reliable for estimating growth potential because, in addition to photosynthetic rates alone, at least three other important physiological considerations determine growth potential. These include the duration of growth or the seasonal pattern of photosynthesis, the relation of photosynthesis to respiration, and the distribution of photosynthate within the tree. Helms (1964, 1976) also discussed the difficulties in relating growth and rates of photosynthesis.

The lack of positive relationships between photosynthesis and growth often is due to the sampling inadequacy of short-time measurements of photosynthesis. A plant with a high rate of photosynthesis at one stage of its seasonal cycle may have a low rate at another stage. Zelawski and Goral (1966) found that a highland ecotype of Scotch pine had higher rates of photosynthesis than two lowland ecotypes from April to August. Thereafter the rate of the highland ecotype declined rapidly and, during autumn, was lower than that of either lowland ecotype. Thus, prediction of dry matter increment from measurements of photosynthesis should be based on both rates and rate-duration aspects of photosynthesis. This view was supported by Logan (1971) who found that, because jack pine provenances differed in their seasonal pattern of photosynthesis, their ranking changed with time. One provenance had one of the highest photosynthetic rates in July and one of the lowest rates in November. An important finding of this study was that provenances with very high rates in October and November also had the highest growth rates.

Diurnal Variations

In the early morning of a bright, clear, warm day, photosynthesis is low because of low light intensity and low temperature, despite a high leaf moisture content and high carbon dioxide concentration in the intercellular spaces of leaves. As light intensity increases and the air warms up, stomata open and net photosynthesis begins to increase rapidly and may reach a maximum before or near noon. Often the maximum is followed by a midday decrease which may be slight or severe. This midday slump often is followed by another increase in photosynthesis in the later afternoon, and then a final subsidence, which generally follows the late afternoon and early evening decrease in light intensity and temperature (Fig. 5.6). Because of variations in environmental conditions from day to day, and within the same day, the diurnal pattern often deviates considerably from the pattern described above as can be seen by comparing Figs. 5.6 and 5.7.

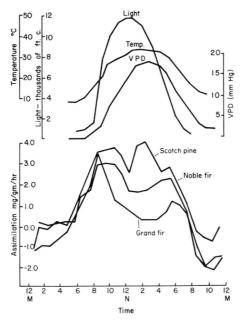

Fig. 5.6. Diurnal variation in photosynthesis of Scotch pine, noble fir, and grand fir on a clear day during the summer. VPD = vapor pressure deficit. From Hodges (1967).

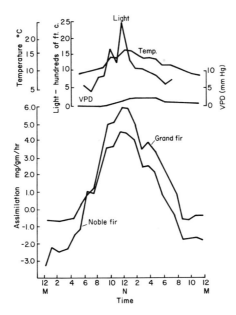

Fig. 5.7. Diurnal variation in photosynthesis of grand fir and noble fir on overcast day during the summer. VPD = vapor pressure deficit. From Hodges (1967).

In general, except for the midday decreases, most diurnal changes in photosynthesis are fairly well correlated with changes in light intensity. For example, in an open area the peak rates of photosynthesis of three species of angiosperms occurred at midday and corresponded to peak rates of total solar radiation. Under a forest canopy the rate of photosynthesis fluctuated considerably during the day, with highest rates occurring in sun flecks. The daily pattern of photosynthesis of gymnosperms was very different on cloudy and on sunny days. Under fully exposed conditions the typical pattern on overcast or cloudy days was one in which the rate of net photosynthesis increased to a maximum about noon, then either decreased or remained more or less constant for an hour or two and finally decreased. By comparison, on bright sunny days, photosynthesis normally increased rapidly, reached a peak between 9 and 12 AM, then decreased until late afternoon when it increased again and reached a second but much lower peak (Hodges, 1967).

Causes of Diurnal Variations in Photosynthesis

Control of daily photosynthesis by various external and internal factors appears to be complicated. Light, temperature, water availability, CO_2 content of the air, and various interactions among them appear to be the major external factors involved. Internal control of CO_2 uptake has been variously attributed to water stress, stomatal closure, excessive respiration, accumulation of photosynthetic end products, and photooxidation of enzymes (Kozlowski and Keller, 1966). There often is a shifting in the importance of factors controlling CO_2 absorption (Kozlowski, 1949). For example, in the morning when cells are turgid the increasing rate of photosynthesis is correlated with warming of the air and increasing light intensity. However, a midday decrease at the highest light intensities often occurs, especially on hot days, because of excessive water loss followed by stomatal closure. For example, in *Rhagodia baccata,* an Australian shrub, daily photosynthesis was closely related to stomatal aperture. Midday stomatal closure and inhibition of photosynthesis occurred rapidly when leaves dehydrated. Later in the afternoon turgor was regained, stomata opened, and photosynthesis increased again. The correlation between rates of photosynthesis and degree of stomatal opening was very high (Hellmuth, 1968).

Seasonal Variations

It is important to distinguish between seasonal variations in the photosynthetic capacity of trees caused by leaf development and metabolic state and actual rates in the field which are determined by both photosynthetic capacity and superimposed environmental conditions. This distinction is important because studies of seasonal variations of photosynthesis often have involved periodically bringing plants into the laboratory from the out-of-doors and measuring photosynthesis under standard and favorable environmental conditions. Actual rates of photosynthesis in the field show much greater fluctuations from day to day, because of changing environmental conditions, than do rates measured under standard conditions.

Seasonal changes in photosynthetic capacity are more gradual in gymnosperms than in deciduous angiosperms (Saeki and Nomoto, 1958). As temperature increases in the spring and night frosts become less frequent, the photosynthetic capacity of gymnosperms increases gradually. The rate also declines gradually in the autumn (Pisek and Winkler, 1958). In deciduous angiosperms photosynthesis accelerates rapidly in the spring as trees refoliate, remains high during the summer, declines rapidly in late summer as leaves senesce, and finally subsides to zero as they abscise. The seasonal capacity for photosynthesis in angiosperms varies among species which have different patterns of leaf development. Species with shoots fully preformed in the winter bud achieve maximum leaf area early in the season, whereas heterophyllous and recurrently flushing species continue to add foliage during the season, either gradually or in flushes (see Chapter 3). Hence seasonal photosynthetic capacity may be expected to change as leaf surface area changes. In gymnosperms photosynthetic capacity also changes as new foliage is added, and gymnosperms retain their capacity for appreciable photosynthesis longer into the autumn than angiosperms. In areas with warm winters photosynthesis in evergreen gymnosperms may occur during every month of the year. In fact, Fry and Phillips (1977) found no decrease in photosynthesis of several species of conifers in the mild winter weather of southwestern England where temperatures seldom remained below freezing more than a few hours. Tranquillini (1959) found that young Swiss stone pine plants at the alpine timber line absorbed small amounts of CO_2 as soon as snow disappeared. With increasing temperatures, high rates of photosynthesis were recorded by late May. Thereafter the daily rate was influenced by temperature changes and soil drying.

Total photosynthesis of a tree and its seasonal pattern often vary appreciably from year to year because of differences in amounts of leaf area and in climatic variations. For example, the rate of photosynthesis of Douglas-fir trees was more than twice as high during 1962 as in 1961. The higher rate in 1962 reflected cooler and moister conditions during the growing season (Helms, 1964). Such differences may be reflected in the width of annual rings.

Some idea of the seasonal trend and day-to-day fluctuations in photosynthesis of an 8-year-old McIntosh apple tree in the field may be gained from the study of Heinicke and Childers (1937). Leaf development was rapid from May 20 to June 10, after which leaves were added slowly. Leaves began to fall in mid-October, and 90% had fallen by November 17, when measurable photosynthesis was still occurring (Fig. 5.8).

When the experiment started in mid-May, respiration exceeded photosynthesis. Respiration was high because of rapid metabolism associated with the production of new shoots, expanding foliage, and maturing of flower parts. Shortly after bloom, photosynthesis began to exceed respiration. Apparent photosynthesis then increased rapidly from mid-May through June. By June 25 the highest rates were recorded even though the tree had not yet produced its maximum leaf area. During the rest of the summer there was considerable fluctuation in photosynthesis from day to day. Although the highest rate occurred in late June, more total photosynthesis occurred during the months of July, August, and early September than in June because of the smaller

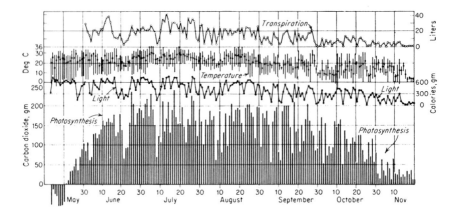

Fig. 5.8. Seasonal course of photosynthesis and transpiration of an 8-year-old McIntosh apple tree at Ithaca, New York. Variations in photosynthesis were correlated with variations in light intensity during most of the season. During the early part of May the tree was starting growth and released more CO_2 in respiration than it used in photosynthesis. From Heinicke and Childers (1937).

amount of foliage in June. A gradual decline in photosynthesis began in mid-September and continued during October. By early November photosynthesis had dropped to a very low ebb, but the few leaves left on the tree in November were surprisingly efficient during the short periods of high light intensity. Figure 5.8 also shows a strong correlation between photosynthesis and light for the entire tree, with high rates of photosynthesis occurring on the sunniest days. The general slow decline at the end of the season reflects the decrease in light intensity, in addition to the decreasing photoperiod, temperature, and leaf area.

Seasonal changes in photosynthetic capacity of loblolly pine and eastern white pine seedlings in North Carolina were studied by McGregor and Kramer (1963). The seedlings were kept out-of-doors but brought into the laboratory where measurements of CO_2 uptake were made periodically at 25°C and 43,000 lux of light. Beginning in February the rate of photosynthesis per seedling for both species increased slowly until April, then accelerated rapidly and subsequently declined during the autumn and winter (Fig. 5.9). The maximum rate for loblolly pine was reached in mid-September, after which the autumn decline was rapid. The maximum rate for white pine occurred between July 15 and September 15, and the autumn decline was more gradual. The higher and later peak of photosynthesis of loblolly pine was, to a large degree, due to the fact that the seedlings made three flushes of shoot growth, adding new needles until late summer. The white pine seedlings, however, made only one flush of shoot growth which occurred early in the season.

Some of the increase in the rate of photosynthesis after April 9 for each species was attributed to increasing photosynthetic surface. However, the significant increase from

February 14 to April 9 could not be explained on this basis because no new foliage had expanded by April 9, but must have resulted from recovery of photosynthetic capacity by needles already present. Similarly, the decrease after the midseason maximum in both species was not caused by loss of needles but rather from a decreased photosynthetic capacity of existing needles. This conclusion also is supported by the observation by

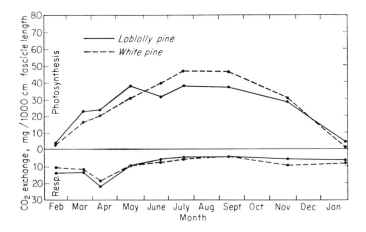

Fig. 5.9. Seasonal changes in net photosynthesis and respiration per unit of leaf surface of loblolly and white pine seedlings. The seedlings were kept out-of-doors, but photosynthesis was measured indoors at 25° C and a light intensity of 43,000 lux. From McGregor and Kramer (1963).

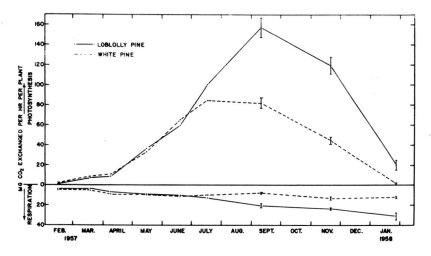

Fig. 5.10. Seasonal changes in net photosynthesis and respiration per plant of loblolly and white pine seedlings. From McGregor and Kramer (1963).

Strain *et al.* (1976) of change in photosynthetic capacity during the life of loblolly pine needles.

Seasonal rates of photosynthesis per unit of foliage were considerably different from those expressed as rates per seedling (Fig. 5.10). In loblolly pine the rate of photosynthesis per unit of fascicle length increased markedly from February to March even though no new needles were added during this period. The needles attained maximum rates per unit of fascicle length in May, 4 months before the maximum rate per seedling was recorded. This high rate continued until September, and then the rate per unit of needle length and the rate per seedling began to decrease. The needles of white pine also showed a marked increase in photosynthesis from February to March, but did not reach a maximum until July. The high rate continued through September, decreased somewhat in November, and reached a minimum in January.

Winter Photosynthesis in Evergreens

In regions with mild winters evergreens can carry on appreciable photosynthesis throughout the year, but where winters are severe photosynthesis may be negligible for weeks or months.

Net CO_2 absorption or dry weight increase during the winter has been confirmed for shortleaf and loblolly pines in the southern United States (Hepting, 1945; Strain, 1975); Monterey and Scotch pines in Aberystwyth, Wales (Pollard and Wareing, 1968); and broad-leaved evergreens in northern Italy (Larcher, 1961). Douglas-fir trees accumulated considerable photosynthate in the mild winter climate of the coastal region of the northwestern United States. During a dry year the net gain of photosynthate during the winter approximated one-fourth of the total for the whole year (Helms, 1964). Along the coastal area of Norway, pines and spruces decreased in dry weight for short periods during the winter but they showed a net increase for the entire winter, indicating an excess of photosynthesis over respiration (Hagem, 1962). Dry weight of Sitka spruce seedlings in southern Scotland doubled between late September and mid-April. Most of the increase took place during late March and April but some occurred in mid-winter (Bradbury and Malcolm, 1978).

In regions with cold winters, measurable rates of photosynthesis in evergreens have been recorded down to or even slightly below freezing. For example, near Munich some CO_2 uptake by Norway spruce occurred on days when air temperature was slightly below freezing (Parker, 1953).

In the valley at Innsbruck, Austria, photosynthesis of Norway spruce continued during a mild winter until severe frosts occurred. However, at the tree line on nearby Mt. Patscherkofel, freezing weather in November ($-10°$ to $-15°C$) caused photosynthesis to cease (Pisek and Tranquillini, 1954; Winkler, 1957). Pisek and Winkler (1958) showed that the rate of net photosynthesis of Norway spruce and Swiss stone pine was appreciable until late in autumn. Thereafter, variations of a few degrees below and above freezing caused CO_2 uptake to fluctuate. As soon as the temperature dropped below $-4°$ to $-5°C$, net photosynthesis stopped, and if freezes recurred for several nights thereafter, photosynthesis was inhibited during the day, even when the temperature rose above freezing. After a freeze of $-6°$ to $-8°C$, net photosynthesis ceased and several mild days in succession were required for restoration of photo-synthetic capacity. Complete recovery of photosynthesis did not occur before the temperature increased in the spring. This was especially true for portions of the crown in which chlorophyll breakdown had occurred during the winter. When temperatures fluctuated in the spring, the rate of photosynthesis did also. Hence, the photosynthetic apparatus remained functional only as long as winter was without severe freezes or prolonged moderate freezes. At timberline, temperatures were so low for 4 to 5 months that photosynthesis was essentially eliminated.

Measurement of Photosynthesis

Discussion of rates of photosynthesis should be accompanied by reference to some of the problems involved in measuring the process. Over long periods of time the best measure of net photosynthesis is the increase in dry matter of a tree or stand of trees. Thus the forester measures yield in volume of timber or pulpwood, the ecologist in weight of dry matter produced per unit of land surface. However, these methods are not usable for the short-term measurements needed in research, which are generally based on measurements of CO_2 uptake. Great improvements have been made in methods of measuring CO_2 absorption since the 1930's when Heinicke and other investigators collected CO_2 in alkali-filled absorption towers and laboriously titrated the alkali. Later titration was supplanted by conductometric determination of the change in concentra-tion of the alkali. Since World War II infrared gas analyzers have come into almost universal use, although short-term pulse labeling with $^{14}CO_2$ is used as a field method to measure CO_2 uptake by individual leaves (McWilliam *et al.,* 1973). Measurements of CO_2 uptake are being made with enclosures ranging from large, air-conditioned chambers enclosing a part of a stand of plants to small cuvettes clamped over a portion of a leaf for as short a time as 1 min (see Jarvis *et al.,* in Sestak *et al.,* 1971). Thus the technology of photosynthesis measurements is well developed. Readers are referred to Sestak *et al.* (1971) for much useful information on methodological problems. Strain (1975) and Zelawski and Walker (1976) also discussed some of the problems and cited the literature on measurements of CO_2 uptake.

The reliability of measurements of photosynthesis can be reduced by a variety of easily made errors. These include failure to move air through enclosures rapidly enough to prevent excessive depletion of CO_2, overheating in cuvettes, failure to maintain a constant vapor pressure deficit in the cuvette, development of unobserved and unmeasured water deficits, failure to take into account the past history of the plant material such as comparisons between field- and greenhouse grown plants, and failure to take into account the present physiological condition of the material. For example, Avery (1977) states that apple trees bearing fruit will have a rate of photosynthesis about 50% greater than comparable trees bearing no fruit. In general many mea-surements under a range of carefully described conditions are necessary to evaluate the CO_2 uptake of plants of any species.

It is difficult to compare measurements of photosynthesis made by various workers because rates are reported on such diverse bases as fresh weight, dry weight, leaf area, stomated leaf area, leaf volume, and chlorophyll content. The most satisfactory base probably is leaf area, but it must be stated whether this refers to one surface, or both. Leaf area can also be misleading because thick leaves have more chloroplasts per unit of surface than thin leaves and they therefore usually have a higher rate of CO_2 uptake per unit of surface, regardless of what caused the difference in thickness (Nobel, 1976; Patterson *et al.*, 1977). There also may be differences in size and number of photosynthetic units. Such differences may be important in explaining differences in CO_2 uptake between sun and shade leaves, those grown in growth chambers and those grown out-of-doors, and those from mineral-deficient and nondeficient plants.

Light Measurements

One of the troublesome problems in studies of photosynthesis is proper measurement of radiation, both in terms of units in which it is measured and where it is measured. Light intensity decreases rapidly within the crown of a tree and within the canopy of a closed stand and no single measurement can accurately describe the light conditions within a canopy. As mentioned earlier, individual leaves are light saturated at much lower intensities than stands of plants. Also, many measurements of light saturation values are misleading because they fail to take into account leaf exposure and self shading, age of leaves, and conditions to which leaves were exposed before the measurements were made.

There also has been an unfortunate amount of uncertainty concerning the most suitable units to use in measuring the radiation. It has been measured as illuminance in terms of foot candles or lux; as photosynthetically active radiation (PAR), which is the radiation between 400 and 700 nm, often expressed in $\mu E/cm^2/sec$; or as total energy in units such as W/m^2, mW/cm^2, or langleys/min (see Downs and Hellmers, 1975, Chapter 2). Physical scientists have generally favored measurement of total energy, but this ignores the fact that such measurements include a large amount of energy useless in photosynthesis and can be very misleading with respect to physiological processes, especially when comparing sunlight and incandescent and fluorescent lamps. For example, in a controlled environment chamber where the wattage input ratio in fluorescent to incandescent lamps is 2.5:1 the ratio of illuminance in lux from the two sources is 9.4:1; the ratio of PAR in $\mu E/m^2/sec$ is nearly 7:1; and the ratio of total energy in W/cm^2 from the two sources is 0.56:1 (Downs and Hellmers, 1975). It seems that in studies of photosynthesis measurement of light energy in the PAR range in $\mu E\ m^2/sec$ or similar units is most satisfactory.

FACTORS AFFECTING PHOTOSYNTHESIS

Large variations in photosynthesis are to be expected because the rate is influenced by a complex of environmental and plant factors, which often are interacting. Some factors, such as light and CO_2, influence photosynthesis directly, and others (e.g., water and minerals) often exert indirect effects. During a typical day first one and later another factor may be limiting. For example, photosynthesis in the morning often is correlated with light intensity, but later in the day it is controlled by leaf water stress as it affects stomatal aperture and absorption of CO_2. There also are seasonal shifts from one controlling factor to another, temperature being limiting during winter and spring and stomatal resistance, carbon dioxide and light during the summer. For example, in western Oregon summer droughts inhibit photosynthesis during the growing season, but this is compensated by mild winters which permit photosynthesis during the dormant season.

Environmental Factors

The principal environmental factors that influence photosynthesis of trees are light, temperature, CO_2 concentration in the air, water, soil fertility, atmospheric pollutants and applied chemicals, insects, and diseases. Photosynthesis of trees is therefore responsive to sivicultural treatments such as thinning of stands, pruning, irrigation, and addition of fertilizers.

Light Intensity

In darkness there is no photosynthesis; therefore carbon dioxide produced in respiration is released from leaves. With increasing light intensity a compensation point is reached at which photosynthetic uptake of carbon dioxide and its release in respiration are equal, and there is no net gas exchange between the leaves and atmosphere. This light compensation point varies with species and genetic materials, leaf type (shade leaves have lower light compensation points than sun leaves), leaf age (young leaves have higher light compensation points than old leaves), CO_2 concentration in the air, and temperature. Since respiration increases more rapidly than photosynthesis with rising temperature, the light compensation point also increases, and reaches very high values above 35°C (Larcher, 1969).

With additional light intensity above the compensation point, photosynthesis increases and is proportional to light intensity until light saturation occurs, after which the rate of photosynthesis becomes more or less constant. In some species very high light intensities may even cause a decline in photosynthesis. For example, when Kozlowski (1957) exposed tree seedlings to a high light intensity throughout the day, photosynthesis was high for an hour or two, then decreased during the rest of the day.

It is often stated that most plants are light saturated for photosynthesis at one-fourth to one-half of full sunlight. This is true of individual leaves and sometimes even of seedlings, but it is not true of large trees or shrubs, or of stands of plants. Individual leaves of Golden Delicious apples are saturated at 21,000 to 43,000 lux (Barden, 1971), and pears at about 53,000 lux (Kriedemann and Canterford, 1971). However, the leaves in the interior of an apple tree are never saturated, and the photosynthesis of an entire tree is closely related to light intensity, as shown in Fig. 5.8 from Heinicke and Childers (1937). Kriedemann (1968b) found that photosynthesis of orange and lemon leaves was light saturated at one-fourth to one-fifth of full sun, but the light intensity in the interior of a tree crown is much lower than this, as shown in Larcher (1975, p. 14).

Kramer and Decker (1944) compared photosynthesis of red and white oak, flowering dogwood, and loblolly pine seedlings at light intensities varying from 3,200 to 108,000 lux. All four species showed rapid increase in photosynthesis with increase in light intensity at the lower intensities. Photosynthesis of loblolly pine increased with incresed light intensity up to the equivalent of full sun, but the three broad-leaved species achieved maximum photosynthesis at one-third or less of full light, and any further increase in light intensity produced no further increase in photosynthesis (Fig. 5.11). Other broad-leaved forest tree seedlings, such as red maple and bur oak, reached maximum rates of photosynthesis at relatively low light intensities (Kozlowski, 1949). Ronco (1970) noted that photosynthesis of lodgepole pine did not become light saturated even at 129,000 lux, whereas saturation of Engelmann spruce occurred at 54,000 lux. However, no measurements were made on entire trees, nor was light intensity measured in the interior of a canopy or a stand.

The response of photosynthesis of some trees to light intensity varies with the types of foliar appendages present. Loblolly pine seedlings with foliage composed of primary needles, alone or mixed with developing secondary needles, reached maximum photosynthesis at relatively low light intensity. This response was different from that of older seedlings, which achieved maximum photosynthesis only at light intensities corresponding to full sun (Bormann, 1956). Apparently the radial arrangement of primary

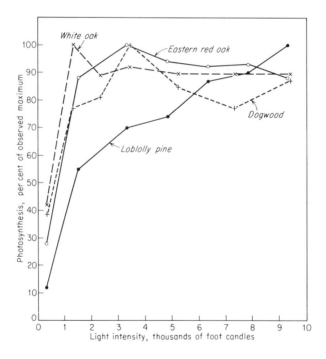

Fig. 5.11. Effects of light intensity on photosynthesis of loblolly pine and broad-leaved seedlings. Measurements were made at 30° C. From Kramer and Decker (1944).

needles gives much better exposure and less self-shading than the clusters of needles found on older seedlings.

Effect of Mutual Shading of Leaves

Because light intensity varies greatly in different parts of tree crowns, photosynthesis within the crown may be expected to decrease rapidly with increasing depth of foliage. However, the rate of decrease of light intensity from the exterior of the crown inward varies greatly among species and depends on the shape of the crown and density of foliage. In some trees, such as cypress, the crown is so dense that essentially no light reaches the interior and leaves do not form in the heavily shaded portions. In trees with more open crowns leafy branches extend to the crown interior which is penetrated by diffuse light (Fig. 5.12). Light intensity in the interior crowns of citrus trees often was less than 2% of the light intensity outside the crowns (Monselise, 1951). The crowns of Red Delicious apple trees had two distinct light zones, a high light intensity of between 65,000 and 118,000 lux in direct sun and a low light intensity zone of 4,300 to 7,500 lux in shade. The shade from even a single leaf reduced light intensity by this amount. Rates of photosynthesis varied greatly in the two light zones. Average net assimilation rate (NAR) was 26.2 mg CO_2 dm^2/hr in the high-light-intensity zone and 7.4 mg CO_2/hr in the low-intensity zone. Photosynthesis and light intensity within the high-light-intensity zone were not well correlated, indicating that photosynthesis reached a maximum value below 65,000 lux (Heinicke, 1966). Similarly, in Bancroft and Jonathan apple trees, photosynthesis was three to four times higher in the outer than in the inner crown, reflecting differences in mutual shading of leaves (Mika and Antoszewski, 1972) (Fig. 5.13).

Photosynthetic efficiency also varies greatly with crown height, largely as a result of differences in amounts of foliage and shading. The inefficient lower branches, with

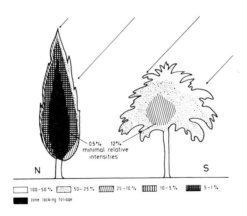

Fig. 5.12. Variation in light intensity within the dense crown of a cypress tree (*left*) and the open crown of an olive tree (*right*). Light intensity, measured at noon in midsummer, is given as a percentage of light in the open air. From Larcher (1975).

relatively few and heavily shaded leaves, often do not contribute any carbohydrates for growth of the main stem. In a 38-year-old Douglas-fir tree with 18 whorls of branches, maximum photosynthesis occurred in current-year needles around whorl 7 from the top in the zone between full light and full shade. The rate then decreased progressively toward the base (Fig. 5.14). Photosynthesis was consistently higher on the south side than on other sides of the same branch whorl. Despite diurnal and seasonal variations in photosynthesis at all crown heights, the crown surface could be stratified into zones of photosynthetic efficiency (Fig. 5.15). The relationship between zones was rather constant during the spring and summer even though absolute rates varied significantly (Woodman, 1971).

The kinds and arrangements of leaves vary considerably among species, with correspondingly variable effects on mutual shading. The leaves of vines on walls usually form a mosaic in which each has the maximum exposure to light and the same situation often exists with leaves on the surface of a tree crown. This seems to be produced by bending of the petioles in response to a phototropic stimulus. However, the needles of pines occur in fascicles, causing considerable mutual shading. When the needles of loblolly pine are spread out flat and fully exposed to light in a cuvette they are light-saturated at approximately the same intensity as leaves of deciduous tree seedlings (Fig. 5.16). However, seedlings require an intensity three times greater for saturation because of mutual shading (Kramer and Clark, 1947). Bormann's (1956) observation that the radially arranged primary needles of pine seedlings are better exposed than the secondary needles was mentioned earlier.

Adaptation to Light Intensity

Plants of some species such as eastern and western hemlock, beech, maple, and dogwood are notably tolerant of shade and thrive in an understory while others such as aspen, yellow poplar, the birches, and many pines are intolerant of shade and thrive only in the sun. Much of the difference in shade tolerance is related to differences in the ability of the photosynthetic apparatus to adapt to low light intensity. For example, the rate of photosynthesis of the shade-grown leaves of the tolerant European beech is four to five times greater than that of sun-grown leaves when measured at very low light intensities, and the rate of photosynthesis of shade-grown sugar maple leaves also is relatively high (Logan and Krotkov, 1969). In contrast, Kozlowski (1949) found no evidence of adaptation in shade-grown leaves of loblolly pine and overcup oak. However, measurements on several conifers indicated that photosynthesis is higher for sun than for shade needles, whether calculated on the basis of needle weight, volume, or surface area. Among the species studied were *Cryptomeria japonica* and *Chamaecyparis obtusa* (Takahara, 1954), red pine (Bourdeau and Laverick, 1958), balsam fir and white spruce (Clark, 1961), and Engelmann spruce (Ronco, 1970). Lewandowska and Jarvis (1977) reported that the photosynthetic capacity was lower in shaded shoots from the lower than for exposed shoots from the upper part of the canopy in a stand of Sitka spruce.

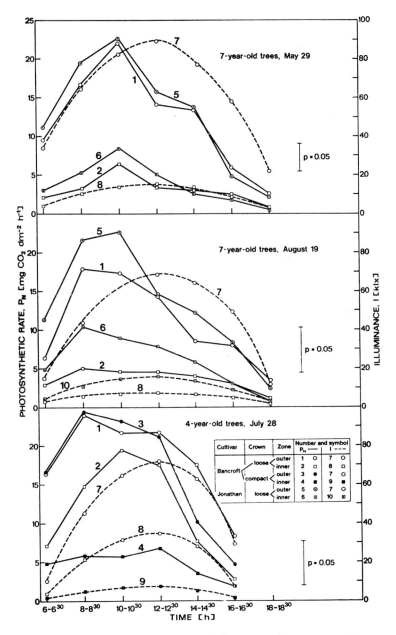

Fig. 5.13. Diurnal variations in photosynthesis in the outer and inner crown of Bancroft and Jonathan apple trees on three different days. From Mika and Antoszewski (1972).

Generally there are important differences in leaf morphology and the photosynthetic machinery between sun and shade leaves. Sun leaves are generally smaller and thicker and have a greater volume and more chlorophyll per unit of leaf area than shade-grown leaves. They also usually have a lower stomatal and mesophyll resistance to CO_2 diffusion (Boardman, 1977). As a result, sun leaves have a higher rate of photosynthesis per unit of leaf area and are light saturated at a higher intensity than shade leaves. Nobel (1976) attributed the higher rate of photosynthesis of the small, thick, sun leaves of the desert shrub, *Hyptis emoryi,* to the fact that they contain more mesophyll tissue, more chlorophyll, and have a greater ratio of internal to external surface than shade

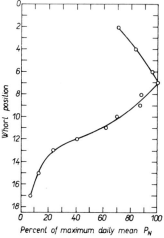

Fig. 5.14. Variations in photosynthesis in different parts of the crown of a 38-year-old Douglas-fir tree. From Woodman (1971).

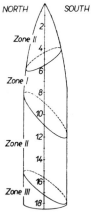

Fig. 5.15. Zones of relative photosynthetic efficiency on the north and south sides of a 38-year-old Douglas-fir tree. From Woodman (1971).

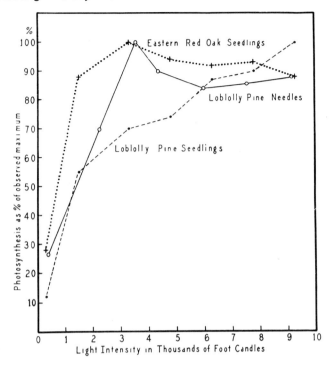

Fig. 5.16. Rates of photosynthesis of individual loblolly pine needles, entire loblolly pine seedlings, and eastern red oak seedlings at seven light intensities. From Kramer and Clark (1947).

leaves. In several experiments the differences in photosynthesis between sun and shade leaves, when expressed on a leaf area basis, decreased or disappeared when calculated on a specific leaf-weight or leaf-volume basis (Patterson *et al.*, 1977).

At the biochemical level the thicker, sun-grown leaves contain more carboxylating enzyme and more electron carrier per unit of leaf surface than shade leaves. According to Alberte *et al.* (1976), shade-grown leaves contain larger photosynthetic units which have a higher proportion of light-harvesting chlorophyll *a/b*–protein than sun leaves. This increases the efficiency of light utilization at low intensities, but decreases it at high intensities because it decreases the intensity at which light saturation occurs. It appears that adaptations which favor high efficiency under one extreme of light intensity are unfavorable to efficiency under the other extreme (Boardman, 1977).

Another problem concerns the extent to which adaptation can occur in leaves which have developed in one light intensity and then are exposed to another, as, for example, when a dense stand of trees is severely thinned. In such instances significant changes in morphology or anatomy are impossible, yet experiments on herbaceous plants indicate that, after a week's exposure, leaves of maize and *Amaranthus* plants transferred from sun to shade or vice versa had rates of photosynthesis comparable to those kept continuously under that light intensity. This was attributed largely to changes in concentration of carboxylation enzymes (RuBP carboxylase in C_3 plants, PEP carboxylase in C_4 plants). Patterson (1975a) also observed adaptation to increased light by leaves of oriental bittersweet. The whole field of photosynthesis in sun and shade leaves was reviewed by Boardman (1977).

Temperature

The effects of temperature on photosynthesis often are as important and complex as the effects of light. Pearcy (1977) follows earlier workers in suggesting that the temperature dependence of CO_2 uptake results from several temperature-dependent, rate-limiting steps which operate alone or in combination. There may be three major components: (1) an exponentially increasing process which is dominant at low temperatures; (2) an antagonistic process, or processes, which gradually increases with temperature (probably dark respiration); and (3) inactivation of the CO_2 fixation process at high temperatures. Thus, in addition to direct effects on the synthesis and activity of the carboxylating and possibly other enzymes, there are indirect effects through changing rates of dark respiration and changing stomatal conductance for CO_2. High temperature often increases transpiration, causing water deficits which close stomata and reduce the supply of CO_2 to the chloroplasts.

Photosynthesis of woody plants occurs over a wide temperature range from near freezing to over 40°C, with the specific range depending on plant age and origin, and season. In most temperate zone species the rate of photosynthesis increases from near freezing until it attains a maximum between 15° and 25°C. In tropical species the minimum temperature for photosynthesis generally is several degrees above freezing and the optimum well above 25°C (Fig. 5.17). The effect of temperature on photosyn-

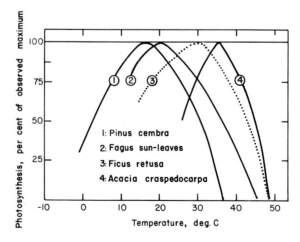

Fig. 5.17. Effect of temperature on photosynthesis of temperate and tropical trees. Adapted from Larcher (1969).

thesis generally is modified by light intensity, CO_2 availability, water supply, and preconditioning effects of environmental factors.

Trees often show a photosynthetic adaptation to the temperature regime in which they are grown. For example, balsam fir seedlings showed a clinal pattern of adaptation in their temperature optimum for photosynthesis with respect to an elevational gradient, the change in temperature, optimum for photosynthesis being 2.7°C for each 300 m of elevation (Fryer and Ledig, 1972).

Soil temperatures as well as air temperatures affect photosynthesis, the rate of CO_2 uptake decreasing at low temperatures (see Table 5.1). The effects are largely due to decreased absorption of water at low temperature which often leads to stomatal closure (Babalola *et al.*, 1968).

TABLE 5.1 Effect of Soil Temperature and Soil Water Potential on Net Photosynthesis of *Pinus radiata* Seedlings[a]

Soil temperature (°C)	Soil water potential (bars)	Net CO_2 uptake (10^{-5} cm^3 cm^{-2} sec^{-1})
10.0	−0.35	2.90
15.6	−0.35	3.46
21.1	−0.35	4.06
26.7	−0.35	4.28
10.0	−2.50	1.66
15.6	−2.50	1.99
21.1	−2.50	2.23
26.7	−2.50	2.36

[a] From Babalola *et al.*, 1968.

With increasing CO_2 supply and high light intensity, net photosynthesis usually increases with rising temperature up to some critical temperature above which it begins to decline rapidly. This often is because respiration continues to increase above a critical high temperature, at which photosynthesis begins to decrease (Fig. 5.18). In the alpine species, Swiss stone pine, net photosynthesis of seedlings increased steadily to a maximum at 10° to 15°C and decreased thereafter with rising temperatures. At approximately 35°C, CO_2 was given off by the leaves, indicating that respiration was exceeding photosynthesis (Tranquillini, 1955). In contrast, maximum photosynthesis of the desert shrub, *Hyptis emoryi,* occurs at about 30° (Nobel, 1976).

Sometimes the decline in net photosynthesis at high temperature involves an effect on photosynthesis rather than on respiration because the photosynthetic inhibition is too large (Decker, 1944; Pearcy, 1977) to be explained by increasing dark respiration alone. Increased photorespiration may also be important at high temperatures. Temperature optima for photosynthesis are generally higher in tropical than in temperate species except for some desert plants which grow at very high temperatures. Such observations suggest that photosynthesis is partly limited by enzyme inactivation at very high temperatures (Wareing *et al.*, 1968). Armond *et al.* (1978) attribute the

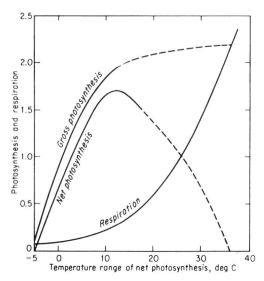

Fig. 5.18. Effects of temperature on photosynthesis, respiration, and net or apparent photosynthesis of Swiss stone pine seedlings. Solid parts of lines are from actual measurements; broken parts are estimated. From Tranquillini (1955).

acclimation of the photosynthetic apparatus to high temperature observed in some plants to greater heat stability of thylakoid membranes produced at high temperatures.

Preconditioning Effects of Temperature

Subjecting plants to either a high or low temperature affects the subsequent rate of photosynthesis at another temperature (Pearcy, 1977).

Although subfreezing temperatures injure the photosynthetic mechanism, the damage generally is reversible with time at temperatures above freezing. When Douglas-fir and ponderosa pine seedlings were subjected to subfreezing temperatures ($-2°$ to $-12°C$) for varying numbers of nights, photosynthesis on the following day was depressed by an amount which varied with the number of nights at a given subfreezing temperature and with the coldness of the night. Recovery of photosynthesis generally occurred for most plants at 3°C, but the time of recovery depended on species and on the subfreezing pretreatment (Fig. 5.19). After a single night at $-4°C$, photosynthesis of ponderosa pine recovered completely within 6 days whereas in Douglas-fir it recovered only partially in 60 days. After exposure to $-6°$ or $-8°C$, photosynthesis of pine recovered only partly and, after $-10°C$ treatment, neither species showed photosynthetic recovery when returned to 3°C. When recovery from subfreezing treatments did occur, plants that were warmed slowly subsequently carried on photosynthesis at higher rates than plants that were warmed rapidly (Pharis et al., 1970a).

The inhibitory effect of high-temperature preconditioning on photosynthesis may last for many days, with the aftereffect much greater on photosynthesis than on respiration. For example, when European silver fir and sycamore maple leaves were exposed

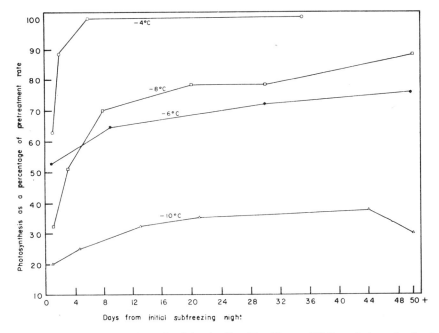

Fig. 5.19. Effect of a single 16-hr night of −4°, −6°, −8°, or −10° C on photosynthesis of ponderosa pine seedlings. The plants were maintained and photosynthesis was measured at 3° C. The chilling treatment is shown on the individual curves. From Pharis *et al.* (1970a).

to nearly lethal heat for 60 min., CO_2 uptake at moderate temperatures was inhibited for many days whereas respiration rates were not appreciably altered (Larcher, 1969).

Species often vary in their photosynthetic responses to heat preconditioning. For example, the inhibitory aftereffect on photosynthesis at 20°C occurred in European silver fir after heating at 38°C, in sycamore maple after heating at 42°C. At increasing temperature stress the amount of photosynthetic inhibition was greater in maple than in fir. Photosynthesis recovered in both species from exposure to heat as long as there was no killing of tissue. The rate of recovery depended on the preconditioning temperature, and was slower after preconditioning at higher temperatures. If, as soon as photo-synthetic capacity at 20°C was restored after one period of heat stress, plants were exposed to a second period of heat stress, photosynthesis was less sensitive. Hence, the first heat treatment appeared to induce heat resistance (Bauer, 1972). Preconditioning effects should be considered in planning or evaluating measurements of photosynthesis. The effects of the growing temperature on photosynthesis of loblolly pine were studied by Strain *et al.* (1976) and the effects on northern red oak by Chabot and Lewis (1976).

Carbon Dioxide

Photosynthesis of trees well exposed to light is limited chiefly by the low carbon dioxide concentration of the air which is increasing about 1 ppm/year. In 1976 the concentration was about 330 ppm or 0.033% by volume, significantly higher than the concentration of 300 ppm given in textbooks a few decades ago. Apparently the production of carbon dioxide by burning of fossil fuels exceeds the rate at which it can be removed by plants and absorbed by the ocean, and the concentration probably will continue to increase as long as we continue to burn large quantities of gas, oil, and coal (Baes, *et al.,* 1977). This presumably will cause an increase in the rate of photosynthesis, as indicated by experiments with enhanced carbon dioxide concentration (Green and Wright, 1977).

Locally the carbon dioxide concentration may rise far above the world wide average of 330 ppm because of industrial activity, or it may fall below it because of removal by photosynthesis. In the absence of wind there usually are diurnal fluctuations in the carbon dioxide content of the air in and over vegetation, with a minimum in the afternoon (Koch, 1963). The carbon dioxide concentration near the soil surface often is high because of release by decay, and the concentration in the plant canopy is sometimes measurably decreased by use in photosynthesis. By midday, carbon dioxide concentrations in forest stands may decrease by one-fourth or more (Huber, 1958; Miller and Rüsch, 1960), presumably because of removal of carbon dioxide by photosynthesis. Böhning (1949) found an afternoon decrease in photosynthesis of apple trees under constant illumination which was caused by low carbon dioxide content in the air during the middle of the day. When he substituted tanks of compressed air in which carbon dioxide concentration was nearly constant, instead of subjecting leaves to the usual fluctuations in atmospheric carbon dioxide of outdoor air, no cyclic variation in photosynthesis occurred. However, it should be remembered that a limitation of carbon dioxide availability is often compounded by midday stomatal closure under conditions of high transpiration and leaf water stress.

Increased photosynthesis may occur on foggy days if light is not limiting because the carbon dioxide content of the air may be higher on such days than on clear days (Wilson, 1948). In addition, fog often is considered to favor plant growth through its favorable effect on maintaining leaves in a turgid condition. Fog probably produces more uniform illumination within plant canopies.

It often has been supposed that, because volume percentage concentration of carbon dioxide in air is similar at different altitudes, carbon dioxide has no influence in determining altitudinal species distribution. However, as Decker (1947) pointed out, diffusion of carbon dioxide into a leaf is a function of carbon dioxide pressure rather than of concentration, and the pressure of carbon dioxide in air varies directly with total atmospheric pressure. Normal pressure of atmospheric carbon dioxide is approximately 0.228 mm of mercury at sea level and only 0.130 mm of mercury at an altitude of 4,500 m. This altitudinal gradient in carbon dioxide may well be one of the complex of factors which govern altitudinal zonation of species.

There is much interest in accelerating photosynthesis and growth of plants by use of controlled CO_2-enriched atmospheres (Wittwer and Robb, 1964). In one experiment growth was essentially doubled in young eastern white pine seedlings maintained for 4 months in an atmosphere in which the normal CO_2 content was enriched to 1,000 ppm (Funsch *et al.,* 1970).

Regardless of the external concentration, the availability of carbon dioxide to the photosynthetic tissue is strongly limited by the resistances in its inward diffusion path. These resistances are similar to those affecting the outward diffusion of water, including boundary layer or air, cuticular, stomatal, and mesophyll resistances. The boundary layer resistance of most conifer needles is small, although it may be increased toward the base of pine needles in tight fascicles. The resistance increases with leaf size and decreases with wind speed. Typical values for a leaf 1 cm wide are 1.0 and 0.10 sec/cm at wind speeds of 10 cm/sec and 10 m/sec, but for a leaf 10 cm wide they are 3.0 and 0.3 sec/cm (Slatyer, 1967). The cuticular surfaces of most leaves are relatively impermeable to carbon dioxide, hence the stomatal resistance becomes a dominant factor. This is discussed later in the chapter and we will merely mention that photosynthesis is often limited by stomatal closure caused by leaf water deficits. The mesophyll resistance includes rate limitations imposed by diffusion of carbon dioxide into cells and the biochemical process of carbon fixation. The mesophyll resistance therefore tends to be rather high as compared to the resistance of open stomata (Table 5.2).

Water Supply

Availability of water is an important factor in photosynthesis because the rate is reduced by a water deficit in leaves. Either a deficiency or excess of soil moisture can cause leaf water deficits.

Water deficits can inhibit photosynthesis by reducing leaf area, closing stomata, and decreasing hydration of protoplasm. According to some investigators, the most serious

TABLE 5.2 Resistances to Movement of Water Vapor and CO_2[a]

Species	Net photosynthesis (mg CO_2 dm²/hr)	Transfer resistances (sec cm⁻¹)				
		Water vapor			CO_2	
		r_a[b]	r_s[c]	r_c[d]	r_s[c]	r_m[e]
Populus tremula[f]	12.2	0.57	2.33	—	3.96	8.2
Betula verrucosa[f]	14.0	0.67	1.36	56	2.31	6.3
Quercus robur[f]	7.5	0.88	7.5	150	12.8	10.6
Acer platanoides[f]	8.8	0.69	4.7	85	8.0	7.3
Helianthus annuus[g]	35.7	0.55	0.38	—	0.65	2.4

[a] From Holmgren *et al.* (1965).
[b] r_a = boundary layer resistance.
[c] r_s = stomatal resistance.
[d] r_c = cuticular resistance.
[e] r_m = mesophyll resistance.
[f] Experiments performed at 22°C at light intensities of 10 or 11 × 10⁴ ergs cm⁻² sec⁻¹.
[g] Experiments performed at 22°C at light intensities of 18 × 10⁴ ergs cm⁻² sec⁻¹.

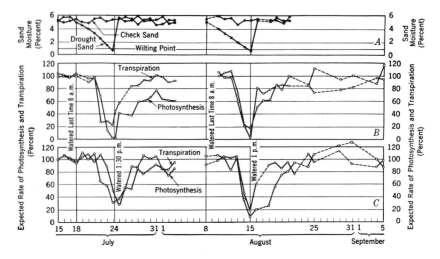

Fig. 5.20. Effect of decreasing soil moisture on photosynthesis and transpiration of pecan seedlings growing in sand. A: moisture content of sand; B: rates of photosynthesis and transpiration during the afternoon, expressed as percentages of the rate expected with well-watered plants; C: similar rates during the morning. Effects of dry soil were greater in the afternoon because more rapid transpiration caused a larger water deficit in leaves in the afternoon. From Kramer (1949); after Loustalot (1945).

effect of drought is the reduction of the photosynthetic surface due to a decline in leaf expansion and premature leaf senescence, with a resultant decrease in dry weight increment. However, reduction of the photosynthesis rate per unit of leaf surface also is important. The large decline in photosynthesis per unit of leaf area in plants undergoing water stress usually is associated with stomatal closure. This is shown by reduction of both transpiration and photosynthesis by similar amounts (Fig. 5.20). Other effects of water stress on photosynthesis are discussed by Boyer (1976a,b).

Soil Moisture and Photosynthesis

There has been considerable debate over the years about the effect of soil moisture supply on photosynthesis. Some investigators found significant inhibition of photosynthesis when irrigated soil dried only slightly, but others reported that photosynthesis was not appreciably inhibited until much or most of the available soil water was depleted. For example, photosynthesis of loblolly pine and white oak decreased long before the permanent wilting percentage was approached (Fig. 5.21), and photosynthesis of Japanese red pine was inhibited by a slight decrease in soil moisture below field capacity (Negisi and Satoo, 1954b). However, apparent photosynthesis of apple trees did not decrease until more than 60% of the available soil water had been removed (Allmendinger *et al.*, 1943).

Some of the disagreement about photosynthetic responses to moisture supply stems from the fact that investigators often assumed that plant water deficits increase in proportion to soil water deficits. However, trees growing in dry soil may not develop

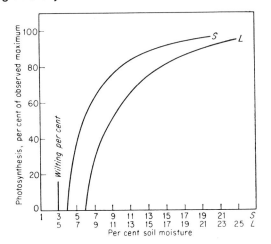

Fig. 5.21. Net photosynthesis of sweetgum (S) and loblolly pine (L) with high light intensity and decreasing soil moisture content. Sweetgum data from Bormann (1953); loblolly pine data from Kozlowski (1949).

high internal water deficits when atmospheric conditions are conducive to low transpiration. Conversely, during periods of high temperature and low relative humidity, even trees in moist soil may develop high leaf water stresses. Water stress in plants depends on relative rates of absorption and transpiration, and not on absorption alone (see Chapter 13). Hence, although mild leaf water deficits often decrease the rates of photosynthesis, a small decrease in soil moisture content does not always do so.

The importance of variations in air humidity on photosynthesis is shown in Fig. 5.22. At very low humidity the temperature optimum for photosynthesis of citrus was lower than at high humidity. Although photosynthesis of plants in low humidity declined rapidly, at temperatures above 15°C the rate of plants in high humidity showed no serious decline up to a temperature of 25°C (Kriedemann, 1968b). These observa-

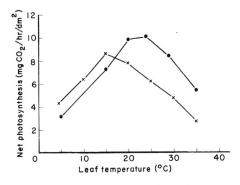

Fig. 5.22. Variations in photosynthesis of an orange leaf in humid (●) and dry (x) air over a range of leaf temperatures. From Kriedemann (1968b).

tions emphasize the importance of relating photosynthesis responses to internal water deficits in plants rather than to soil moisture content.

Plant Water Deficits and Photosynthesis

In many mesic species of the temperate zone the rate of photosynthesis begins to decrease when leaves are only slightly dehydrated, e.g., when leaf water potential (see Chapter 12) decreases to minus a few bars, and it stops or becomes negligible at zero turgor. There is some variation, however, among species and genotypes in the critical leaf water deficit at which photosynthetic inhibition begins. For example, Al-'Ani *et al.* (1972) reported differences between coastal and inland populations of *Simmondsia chinensis* and also between plants grown in the field and in the greenhouse.

The rate of photosynthesis of loblolly pine seedlings declined when water potential dropped below −4 bars, and when it reached −11 bars photosynthesis was negligible. The rate of recovery of CO_2 uptake from water stress was greatly influenced by the root system. Probably a decrease in water-absorbing or conducting capacity of the root system during wilting resulted in a slow rate of recovery from water stress in the leaves following rewatering of the soil (Brix, 1962). Photosynthesis of grape was very sensitive to leaf dehydration, with the rate declining at leaf water potentials below −5 bars and falling to zero at about −12 to −15 bars (Kriedemann and Smart, 1971). In 23-year-old Douglas-fir trees net photosynthesis began to decline when shoot water potential decreased to about −10 bars (Brix, 1972) (Fig. 5.23), in loblolly pine at −5 or −6 bars (Brix, 1962).

As mentioned by Boyer (1976a) and others, there is some uncertainty as to how much of the reduction in photosynthesis of stressed plants is caused by stomatal closure and how much by decrease in photosynthetic capacity. Brix (1962) found that photosynthesis and transpiration decreased to the same extent in loblolly pine as water stress increased, suggesting that both were reduced by stomatal closure. Beadle and Jarvis

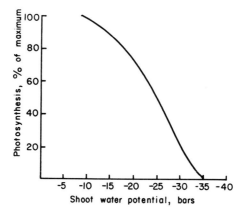

Fig. 5.23. Effect of shoot water potential on photosynthesis of Douglas-fir trees. From Brix (1972).

(1977) observed a rapid decrease in CO_2 uptake and stomatal conductance in Sitka spruce seedlings at a shoot water stress below -12 bars, and CO_2 uptake ceased at -23 or -24 bars. However, the decline in CO_2 uptake was greater than the decline in stomatal conductance, leading to the conclusion that there was an increase in mesophyll resistance. There was little decrease in carboxylase activity or the activity of Photosystems I or II, but this may have been related to the methods used to measure activity. There was a decrease in content of chlorophyll *a,* but not of chlorophyll *b.*

Apparently, some plants that are adapted to growth in arid regions can maintain measurable photosynthesis at very low plant water potentials. For example, water potentials at dawn of plants of creosote bush growing in Palm Desert, California, ranged from -24.5 bars in February to -52.4 bars in September. Net photosynthesis was strongly correlated with dawn water potential (Fig. 5.24), decreasing from 75 mg CO_2/day/g dry weight of leaf tissue in Feburary to 9 mg in September (Oechel *et al.,* 1972). Nevertheless, positive net photosynthesis occurred throughout the year, and Strain (1975) mentioned other examples in desert plants. On the other hand, when the stomata of oil palms are closed for long periods by water stress, a serious deficit in carbohydrates often develops.

Work reported by Mooney *et al.* (1977) indicates that the photosynthetic apparatus of creosote bush and probably other drought tolerant plants is capable of considerable

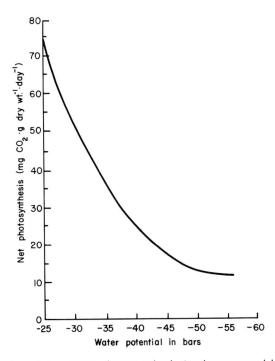

Fig. 5.24. Net daily photosynthesis of creosote bush at various seasonal dawn water potentials. From Oechel *et al.* (1972).

adaptation to water stress. Photosynthesis of plants grown in humid air and moist soil was strongly inhibited at a plant water potential of −20 bars, but photosynthesis of plants grown under severe stress in Death Valley was only slightly inhibited at −29 bars. Most of the inhibition in well watered plants was caused by nonstomatal factors, but no inhibition attributable to nonstomatal factors was found in creosote bush grown under stress. The mechanism by which adaptation to water stress occurs has not been identified, but it probably involves changes in membrane structure, as suggested for heat adaptation.

When plants undergoing drought are rewatered, photosynthesis may or may not return to normal, depending on the species, severity and duration of the drought, and dryness of the air. Photosynthesis of Japanese red pine plants which had undergone drought recovered to the rate of control plants 1 day after watering (Negisi and Satoo, 1954a). By comparison, photosynthesis of Douglas-fir seedlings subjected to drought did not recover to predrought values after watering (Fig. 5.25) (Zavitkovski and Ferrell, 1970). More time usually is required for stressed plants to recover their photosynthetic capacity after rewatering than for recovery of transpiration rate. This indicates that considerable time is required for protoplasm to regain full photosynthetic efficiency after it is rehydrated. The failure of water-stressed plants to recover full photosynthetic capacity after irrigation may also indicate some permanent damage, including injury to chloroplasts, leaf abscission, damage to stomata, and death of root tips. Often a period of drought results in damage to stomata which inhibits their capacity to open despite recovery of leaf turgor (Kozlowski, 1972b). Brix (1962) noted that photosynthesis of loblolly pine seedlings was reduced for a period of several weeks when the root tips had been injured by drought, even if internal water balance had been restored.

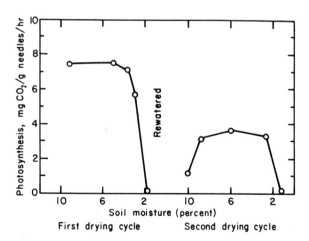

Fig. 5.25. Effect of two soil drying cycles on net photosynthesis of Douglas-fir seedlings. From Zavitkovski and Ferrell (1970).

Excess Soil Moisture

In flooded soils the excess gravitational water displaces air from the pore space and the resulting poor aeration impedes water uptake by roots, causing drying of leaves (see Chapter 13) which reduces photosynthesis. Childers and White (1942) found, for example, that leaves of flooded apple trees contained less water than those of control trees which were in unflooded soils, and photosynthesis was reduced by flooding, usually within 2 to 7 days. Loustalot (1945) also reported that a few days of root submersion caused substantial reduction in photosynthesis of pecan leaves. The amount of reduction was greater in the afternoon than in the morning, suggesting that it was caused by a water deficit. Photosynthesis of flooded trees in sand was reduced to as low as 11% of normal, whereas in leaves of trees in a heavier soil it ceased. When excess water was removed, photosynthesis increased but did not return to normal for several days.

Soil Fertility

Deficiencies of essential nutrients have both direct and indirect effects on photosynthesis. It is reduced directly by the depressed synthesis of chlorophyll which often accompanies mineral deficiencies, but it is also reduced by decreased leaf area, possibly by changes in leaf structure, and even by decreased stomatal activity. Effects on enzymes and internal processes in general also doubtless occur, as indicated by the fact that photosynthesis sometimes is reduced by deficiencies although no visible symptoms, such as chlorosis or necrosis, occur.

Macronutrients

Complete NPK fertilizer increased photosynthesis materially in grape leaves (Kodenko and Erygina, 1953) and leaves of poplar hybrids (Neuwirth and Fritzsche, 1964). Fertilizer effects were most pronounced when other factors such as light and temperature were most favorable for photosynthesis.

Nitrogen influences photosynthesis by affecting chlorophyll and protein synthesis, leaf size, and stomatal responses. Since chlorophyll content is more or less proportional to nitrogen supply over a wide range, a deficiency of nitrogen inhibits photosynthesis. Heinicke (1934) found that apple leaves with high nitrogen contents had high rates of CO_2 uptake, and Childers and Cowart (1935) demonstrated that photosynthesis of apple leaves was inhibited more by deficiency of nitrogen than by deficiency of other macronutrients. The rate of photosynthesis of nitrogen-deficient leaves was only 37% of controls; leaves low in phosphorus or potassium had rates about 91% of controls. However, nitrogen-deficient leaves had more stomata per unit of leaf area. Neuwirth and Fritzsche (1964) also found that nitrogen deficiency depressed CO_2 uptake of poplar more than phosphorus or potassium deficiency.

Keller and Koch (1962a) found CO_2 uptake of nitrogen-deficient (1.8% nitrogen) and high-nitrogen (3.4% nitrogen) leaves of poplar was about the same at light intensities up to 5,000 lux. However, nitrogen-deficient leaves reached light saturation at

20,000 lux and at 40,000 lux the rate of net photosynthesis of nitrogen deficient leaves was only 60% of that of high-nitrogen leaves. Leaf size and chlorophyll content also were well correlated with nitrogen content. Similarly nitrogen, chlorophyll content, and photosynthetic rate were well correlated in pine and spruce seedlings grown in various nutrient solutions (Keller and Wehrmann, 1963). On the other hand, Brix (1971) found that the effect of nitrogen on photosynthesis of Douglas-fir was partly produced by increasing the leaf area and only partly by increasing the rate.

Photosynthetic responses to nitrogen fertilizers sometimes vary with the form in which nitrogen is supplied. For example, the rate of photosynthesis of young Scotch pine seedlings was increased more by nitrogen fertilizers supplied as ammonium chloride than by nitrate or ammonium nitrate (Lotocki and Zelawski, 1973; Zajaczkowska, 1974).

Phosphorus deficiency may impede photosynthesis by disturbing the energy transfer of the ADP–ATP (adenosine diphosphate–adenosine triphosphate) system, but the depressing effect appears to be relatively weak (Childers and Cowart, 1935; Neuwirth and Fritzsche, 1964). Addition of phosphorus fertilizer to apple trees led to the formation of large leaves containing a high percentage of palisade tissue. The number of stomata per unit of leaf area was decreased, but their control was more efficient (Reinken, 1963). Because mineral nutrition affects leaf structure, the basis used to express the rate of photosynthesis is important, as pointed out on p. 187.

A shortage of potassium, like that of phosphorus, may impede photosynthetic energy transfer and increase respiration (Pirson, 1958), thus lowering the rate of net photosynthesis. Potassium ion flux is also related to stomatal response (see Chapter 13).

Although magnesium is known to be a constituent of the chlorophyll molecule and to act as an activator of many enzyme systems, neither photosynthesis nor growth of poplar was significantly affected by moderate Mg deficiency (Neuwirth and Fritzsche, 1964).

Micronutrients

Iron deficiency inhibits photosynthesis by inducing chlorosis and affecting enzymatic activity. Iron occurs in ferredoxin and in the cytochromes which are essential components of the electron transport systems in both photosynthesis and respiration. Chlorophyll contents of fertilized leaves of poplar were highly correlated with iron contents. Photosynthesis was consistently higher in fertilized than in unfertilized plants over a range of light intensities (Table 5.3). In iron-deficient plants, CO_2 absorption was decreased per unit of leaf area and total CO_2 uptake was also decreased because of reduced leaf size (Keller and Koch, 1962b, 1964).

As manganese is essential for the release of oxygen and may also serve as an activator of other enzyme systems, it can influence photosynthesis if present in too small or excessive amounts. However, Reuther and Burrows (1942) suggested that manganese deficiency reduced CO_2 uptake by tung more by decreasing leaf area than by diminishing efficiency of photosynthesis per unit of leaf area. Partially chlorotic

TABLE 5.3 Effect of Fertilizing *Populus euramericana marilandica* Plants with Iron Chelate on Photosynthesis[a,b]

Light intensity (lux)	Photosynthesis (mg CO_2 dm²/hr)		Increase (%)
	Control	Fertilized	
500	0.96	1.26	31
2,500	1.98	2.94	48
5,000	3.60	5.03	40
10,000	5.86	9.34	59
20,000	7.92	13.57	71
40,000	10.09	14.72	45.9

[a] From Keller and Koch (1964).
[b] The potted plants were watered in late June with 500 ml of 0.2% solution of the iron chelate. Photosynthesis was measured in late August and early September.

leaves were not strikingly less efficient than leaves which had resumed a normal green color after an application of manganese sulfate.

Severe deficiencies of copper and zinc reduced photosynthesis of tung leaves by 30% and 55%, respectively, without producing visible symptoms such as chlorosis or necrosis (Loustalot *et al.,* 1945). Copper occurs in plastocyanin and plastoquinone and zinc and copper are also cofactors for enzymes involved in NO_3 reduction.

Air Pollutants and Applied Chemicals

Atmospheric pollutants and various chemicals used to control fungus diseases, noxious insects, competing weeds, and transpiration, often appreciably inhibit photosynthesis. The effects of these compounds on photosynthesis are exerted by: (1) clogging stomata and impeding CO_2 uptake, (2) altering optical properties of leaves by changing reflectance and decreasing light penetration, (3) altering the heat balance of leaves, (4) altering leaf metabolism, (5) causing changes in leaf anatomy, or (6) various combinations of these. In addition, photosynthesis is reduced by chemicals when they cause lesions, chlorosis, browning of leaves, or leaf fall.

Air Pollutants

The effect of air pollutants is becoming increasingly important on forest trees and orchards near large industrial plants as well as on shade and ornamental trees in cities (see Chapter 17). A number of air pollutants inhibit photosynthesis both directly and indirectly (Mudd and Kozlowski, 1975). Pollutants often act synergistically and even tolerable levels of a single pollutant will injure plants when present with another pollutant which also is present in small amounts. The most important air pollutants with respect to photosynthesis are sulfur oxides, ozone, fluorides, peroxyacyl nitrates, oxides of nitrogen, and particulates. A few examples of effects of air pollutants on photosynthesis follow.

Sulfur Dioxide.   Fumigation of spruce twigs with 1 ppm of SO_2 caused a decrease in photosynthesis after several hours. If fumigation was interrupted, photosynthesis recovered, but when fumigation was resumed, CO_2 uptake dropped to an even lower level (Börtitz, 1964). Fumigation of pine seedlings with 1 ppm of SO_2 also caused a decline in photosynthesis. As long as visible symptoms of injury to leaves were not apparent, photosynthesis recovered quickly (Vogl, 1964). Photosynthesis was depressed without visible needle injury in Norway spruce and mugo pine exposed to 1-hr fumigations of 10 or 20 ppm SO_2, but when obviously acute injury occurred, photosynthesis dropped to a very low rate or stopped (Vogl *et al.*, 1964). Short-term fumigation of white ash seedlings and quaking aspen root sprouts with 1 ppm SO_2 or higher for 2 hr reduced photosynthesis, but not respiration, of both species (Jensen and Kozlowski, 1974). Injury from SO_2 is common in forests many kilometers down wind from power plants burning large quantities of coal high in sulfur.

Ozone.   The ozone concentration of the air tends to rise above normal each sunny day in urban areas because of photooxidation of substances in auto exhaust gases and volatile industrial wastes. The ozone concentration in Los Angeles, California, and other urban areas is said to rise above 0.10 ppm, and widespread damage to both herbaceous and woody vegetation occurs. In fact, it is reported that most of the ponderosa pine in southern California is slowly dying from ozone injury.

Fumigation of 3-year-old ponderosa pine seedlings with 0.15, 0.3, or 0.45 ppm of ozone for 30 days reduced apparent photosynthesis by 10, 70, and 85% (Miller *et al.*, 1969). Exposure of slash, pond, eastern white, and loblolly pine seedlings to 0.05 to 0.16 ppm of ozone for several weeks reduced photosynthesis and increased respiration. The rate of photosynthesis was reduced by concentrations too low to cause visible injury to the needles (Barnes, 1972). In other experiments, branches of 5-year-old eastern white pine exposed to consecutive doses of 0.5 to 0.8 ppm for 4 hr and 0.80 to 0.90 ppm for 3 hr showed a small reduction in photosynthesis, and a second exposure to 0.90 to 1.00 ppm for 5 and 3 hr reduced photosynthesis by about 80% (Botkin *et al.*, 1971). There was considerable variation in sensitivity among individual white pine saplings. Above the threshold of 0.5 ppm for reduction in photosynthesis trees were divided into three classes of ozone sensitivity. In sensitive trees a treatment with 0.90 to 1.00 ppm for 10 hr stopped net photosynthesis; in intermediate trees this concentration reduced it by about half; and in resistant trees it was not affected (Botkin *et al.*, 1972).

Fluorides.   Injury to plants from fluorides is common in the vicinity of ore smelting, aluminum, and fertilizer plants, and brick and ceramic factories. Plants are very susceptible to fluorine, and photosynthesis of fruit trees is reduced by a few hours' exposure to concentrations of 0.02 to 0.05 ppm. The reduction in photosynthesis is related to reduced synthesis of chlorophyll, reduction in the Hill reaction, and damage to leaf tissue.

Particulates. Substances such as cement kiln dusts, some fluorides, soot, magnesium oxide, iron oxide, foundry dusts, and sulfuric acid aerosols may impede photosynthesis by occluding stomatal pores (Czaja, 1966), causing shading of leaves, or affecting leaf metabolism. Clean leaves of *Ulmus pumila* and *Tilia cordata* increased in dry weight over a period of 6 days as much as 40% more than leaves that were covered with soot (Ersov, 1957). Dustlike fluoride compounds (NaF, CaF_2, and cryolite) drastically inhibited photosynthesis of Scotch pine and European silver birch, often without visible injury (Keller, 1973).

Nuclear Radiation. Fallout from nuclear explosions and wastes of nuclear reactors emit ionizing radiation which has important inhibitory effects on photosynthesis. Woody plants are particularly sensitive.

Chronic radiation often does not inhibit photosynthesis for a long time after initial exposure, whereas acute radiation does so immediately. Photosynthesis of pitch pine trees exposed to chronic radiation decreased during the winter and recovered during the spring. However, the inhibitory effect was not apparent until after at least 1 month's exposure to 1,300 roentgens/day or after 5 months of exposure to 30 roentgens/day (Bourdeau and Woodwell, 1964). By comparison, acute exposure of loblolly pine trees to as little as 1,250 roentgens administered at 8,000 roentgens/hr rapidly decreased CO_2 uptake. After 21 days the degree of depression was proportional to the radiation exposures, with the highest exposure (total of 13,200 roentgens) reducing the rate of photosynthesis by 80% (Hadley and Woodwell, 1966). Miller (1965) found that water stress during irradiation increased the severity of injury of loblolly pine.

The use of radioisotopes in physiological research subjects plants to a potential internal chronic source of radiation, which at critical dosages may be toxic to plants. This was demonstrated by Ursino (1973) who exposed white pine seedlings for 1 hr to various activities of $^{14}CO_2$. At 2.5 months after treatment, seedlings which incorporated 110 microcuries of $^{14}CO_2$ or more had proportionally lower photosynthetic rates and shorter needles than the control plants.

Applied Chemicals

In the past large quantities of fungicides and insecticides have been applied to trees with little regard to their physiological effects, so long as obvious injury did not result. In recent years it has become evident that undetected physiological effects are being produced by some pesticides.

Insecticides. A number of insecticides reduce photosynthetic efficiency. The reduction usually is greater when the lower leaf surface is sprayed than when the upper surface is sprayed. The inhibition of photosynthesis may be produced by clogging of stomata, metabolic disturbances, or both.

Oil-based insecticides, in particular, depress photosynthesis for a very long time. For example, photosynthesis of citrus was inhibited by petroleum oil sprays for at least 2 months after application (Wedding *et al.*, 1952). However, some insecticides that are not based on oil sprays such as metasystox (0.1%), parathion (0.02%), and DDT (0.02%) inhibited photosynthesis of grape for only a day or two (Bosian *et al.*, 1960).

Whereas the systemically acting dimethoate caused a slight reduction of photosynthesis for 2–4 days in poplar, lindane reduced photosynthesis by as much as 60% within 1 hr, but the inhibition lasted for only 1 day (Keller, 1964). The phosphate insecticides Diazinon, Guthion, and Ethion reduced photosynthesis in the foliage of Red Delicious apple. Maximum inhibition occurred immediately after treatment and decreased with time, but was still significant after 14 days (Westwood *et al.*, 1960). Ayers and Barden (1975) found that 10 out of 33 insecticides tested reduced photosynthesis of young apple trees, two increased photosynthesis, and 21 had no significant effects.

Fungicides.   Some fungicides inhibit photosynthesis by reducing the light intensity reaching the leaf, plugging stomata, or affecting metabolism. Normal doses of fungicide sprays can reduce the light intensity reaching grape leaves by 200 to 500 lux, whereas 1.5% lime-sulfur or abnormally heavy doses of other fungicides can reduce light intensity by 1000 lux (Bosian *et al.*, 1960). The effects of Bordeaux mixture have been reported to be primarily physiological rather than mechanical, with the soluble-copper fraction responsible for the reduction in photosynthesis (Southwick and Childers, 1941).

Sulfur fungicides markedly inhibit photosynthesis. Spraying Baldwin apple trees with lime-sulfur reduced photosynthesis by about one-half during the first 5 days after application. This represented a reduction in production of dry matter equivalent to that in a half-bushel of apples (Heinicke, 1937a). Hyre (1939) found that each of 22 sulfur fungicides decreased photosynthesis of McIntosh and Baldwin apple trees (Fig. 5.26). Bordeaux mixture caused only slight reduction, wettable sulfurs were next in order, and lime-sulfur solution reduced photosynthesis more than the wettable sulfurs. Mixtures of sulfur fungicides had the most inhibitory effect. Nevertheless, in general the beneficial effects outweigh the losses which may occur if fungicides are not applied.

Not all fungicides decrease photosynthesis. The organic fungicides, Ziram, Zineb, Captan, and Phaltan increased photosynthesis of poplar slightly whereas the inorganic copper oxychloride decreased it (Barner, 1961).

Herbicides.   Many herbicides inhibit photosynthesis of woody plants, often by inhibiting the Hill reaction (Ashton and Crafts, 1973). The effects vary greatly among species and varieties of plants, the chemical and dosage used, time of application, age of plant, season, stage of plant growth, soil type, weather, and other factors (Kozlowski, 1971a). Seedlings in the cotyledon stage are particularly susceptible to herbicides (see Chapter 14). The inhibitory effects often vary greatly even among structurally related chemicals. For example, photosynthesis of recently germinated seedlings was depressed by several triazine herbicides, but much more by simazine and atrazine than by propazine or ipazine (Sasaki and Kozlowski, 1968b).

The manner of herbicide application is important since the effect of photosynthesis depends on how much herbicide is absorbed by plants. Actual toxicity of herbicides to plants cannot be determined by applying them to the soil because they often are lost to a variable degree by evaporation, leaching, microbial or chemical decomposition, and irreversible adsorption on the soil. The inhibitory effects of commercial formulations of herbicides on photosynthesis may be exerted by active or by inert ingredients as well as by synergistic effects of both (Sasaki and Kozlowski, 1968b,c).

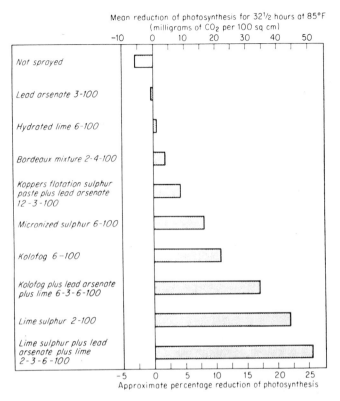

Fig. 5.26. Effect of various spray materials on net photosynthesis of Baldwin and McIntosh apple leaves. Negative values indicate increased photosynthesis. From Hyre (1939).

Frölich (1961) found that a 3% spray of 2,4,5-T depressed photosynthesis of spruce and birch trees completely within 30 min and caused a steep increase in respiration which lasted for several days or until the plants died. Wedding *et al.* (1954) concluded that inhibition of photosynthesis of orange trees by 2,4,-D was related to the concentration of undissociated 2,4,-D acid molecules.

Antitranspirants. There are many examples of beneficial use of antitranspirants. For example, film-type antitranspirants improved water balance in transplanted citrus trees, increased fruit production in established olive and peach trees, and reduced transpiration of ornamental plants (Davenport *et al.*, 1971). However, it should be remembered that film-type antitranspirants are more permeable to water vapor than to CO_2, hence complete coverage of leaves with an antitranspirant film will reduce CO_2 uptake more than transpirational water loss. The effects of antitranspirants on photosynthesis vary with the compounds and dosage used, plant species, manner of application, and environmental conditions.

Davies and Kozlowski (1975b) found that a number of film-type antitranspirants greatly reduced photosynthesis of white ash and red pine seedlings for a very long time.

There was considerable variation in the duration of the inhibitory effect as various compounds wore off or cracked, but several reduced CO_2 uptake for at least 32 days (the duration of the experiment). Often by the time the direct physical effects of a compound wore off, physiological toxicity became apparent. Photosynthetic inhibition was much greater when antitranspirants were applied as leaf dips than as sprays, indicating less effective leaf coverage with the sprays. Leaf structure, and especially the degree of occlusion of stomata with cuticular waxes in certain species, affected the efficiency of antitranspirants. For example, both photosynthesis and transpiration were decreased more by film antitranspirants in sugar maple with small stomata, occluded with cuticular waxes than in white ash with large stomata, not occluded with cuticular waxes (Lee and Kozlowski, 1974; Davies and Kozlowski, 1975b). Antitranspirants reduced photosynthesis in red pine by as much as 90% by combining with waxes in stomatal pores to form impermeable plugs. Stomatal plugging in both angiosperms and gymnosperms eventually was followed by altered metabolism, chlorosis, browning of leaves, and reduced leaf growth. Phytotoxicity sometimes was apparent early and sometimes late after treatment. Olofinboba *et al.* (1974) found that several film-type antitranspirants not only reduced photosynthesis of 3-year-old red pine plants in a forest nursery but also reduced the rates of conversion of photosynthates into ethanol-insoluble components after treated seedlings were exposed to $^{14}CO_2$.

Experiments with metabolic antitranspirants were variable. Whereas atrazine, phenylmercuric acetate, and succinic acids were phytotoxic (Kozlowski and Clausen, 1970; Waisel *et al.*, 1969), abscisic acid (ABA), was not. ABA quickly decreased photosynthesis by causing stomatal closure. However, recovery of turgor was accompanied by eventual reopening of the stomata and CO_2 uptake of treated plants then exceeded that of control plants (Davies and Kozlowski, 1975a).

Diseases

In diseased trees photosynthesis is inhibited as a result of loss of photosynthetic tissue, damaged chloroplasts, inhibited chlorophyll synthesis, altered metabolism, or combinations of these. Disease symptoms such as reduced leaf growth, necrotic lesions, leaf spots, and defoliation all decrease carbohydrate synthesis by reducing the leaf surface as well as the efficiency of the remaining photosynthetic tissue. Photosynthesis of pecan leaves with downy spot disease was reduced more than would have been expected from reduction in photosynthetic tissue alone (Loustalot and Hamilton, 1941). Virus diseases often induce chlorosis and cause breakdown of chloroplasts. Decker and Tio (1958) found the rate of photosynthesis of papaya leaves showing symptoms of mosaic disease, caused by a virus, was only 36% of the rate of healthy leaves. Some virus diseases such as phony peach disease inhibit photosynthesis without directly affecting the chlorophyll content.

Some diseases reduce photosynthesis largely through disturbed water relations. For example, root diseases cause reduced absorption of water, leading to stomatal closure and decrease in absorption of CO_2 by leaves.

In trees infected by vascular pathogens, chlorophyll reduction, leaf desiccation, leaf abscission, and stomatal closure variously contribute to inhibition of photosynthesis. The rate of photosynthesis often decreases before wilting occurs. Photosynthesis was depressed early in American elm seedlings inoculated with the Dutch elm disease pathogen (*Ceratocystis ulmi*) or subjected to drought (Roberts, 1972). The rate of photosynthesis of banana fluctuated markedly for about 6 days after inoculation with *Pseudomonas solanacearum* and the rate became negligible when wilting finally occurred. Similar fluctuations occurred in uninoculated plants from which water was withheld. Photosynthesis of diseased plants could be readily restored to normal when plant water stress was alleviated by saturating the air over the leaves. These observations indicated that leaves of infected plants had normal photosynthetic capacity but that the rate of photosynthesis decreased largely because of high stomatal resistance resulting from decreased water supply (Beckman *et al.*, 1962). Other examples of effects of diseases on photosynthesis and respiration are given by Daly (1976).

Plant Factors

Among the important plant factors which influence photosynthesis are age and structure of leaves; size, number, and response of stomata; chlorophyll content; internal water deficits; and carbohydrate utilization and accumulation.

The rate of photosynthesis is low in very young leaves, increases with increasing leaf age up to some critical level of maturity (usually full leaf expansion) and then declines with age. In grape, for example, peak photosynthesis was reached when the leaves became fully expanded and then declined gradually (Fig. 5.27). In date palm

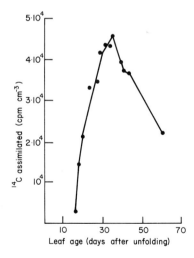

Fig. 5.27. Effect of leaf age on photosynthesis ($^{14}CO_2$ assimilated) of grape leaves. From Kriedemann *et al.* (1970).

and citrus, the rate of photosynthesis increased during the first year to full leaf expansion, then declined progressively during the next 3 years (Nixon and Wedding, 1956; Rhoads and Wedding, 1953). In general the changes in rates of photosynthesis in leaves of gymnosperms are similar to those of evergreen angiosperms. The rates of pine needles generally increase until full size is attained and then decrease. In needles 1-year old or older, the rate of photosynthesis decreases progressively with needle age (Fig. 5.28).

Changes in rate of photosynthesis with leaf age are associated with anatomical and physiological alterations. Increases during leaf expansion are related to development of internal leaf structure and stomata, synthesis of chlorophyll, decrease in diffusion resistance, increase in rate of photosynthetic phosphorylation, increase in protein synthesis, increase in RuBP carboxylase activity, and an abrupt decrease in mitochondrial respiration. The gradual decrease in photosynthesis after leaf expansion is completed is correlated with increase in diffusion resistance, decrease in the synthetic activity of the phosphorylation system of chloroplasts, in protein, RNA and DNA, and in RuBP carboxylase activity. Furthermore, relatively high levels of photorespiration develop and a marked decrease in mitochondrial respiration occurs (Dickmann *et al.*, 1975).

Variations in photosynthetic capacity of leaves of different ages in gymnosperms have important implications in source–sink relations of growing tissues. For example, in one experiment the rapidly expanding needles of red pine had high carbohydrate requirements and could not supply enough photosynthate for their own growth. Early in the season they obtained large amounts of photosynthate from the 1-year-old needles which had higher rates of photosynthesis than the 2- or 3-year-old needles. The supply of current photosynthate to new shoots, chiefly from old needles, decreased later in the season after the new needles achieved maximum expansion. By that time the new needles had the highest rates of photosynthesis and replaced the old needles as major

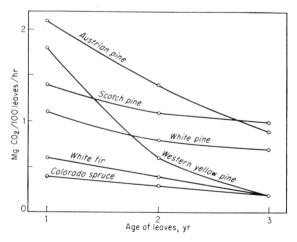

Fig. 5.28. Effect of age of gymnosperm needles on net photosynthesis. From Freeland (1952).

exporters of carbohydrates (Dickmann and Kozlowski, 1968). Shortly after buds opened, the new needles of balsam fir released more CO_2 in respiration than they absorbed in photosynthesis. By mid-June the new needles neither absorbed nor released CO_2, but it was not until late August that photosynthesis of the new needles was as high as that of the 1-year-old needles (Clark, 1961).

Stomatal Characteristics

The resistance offered by stomata to CO_2 uptake by leaves often provides a major limitation for photosynthesis. Therefore, variations in stomatal size, stomatal frequency, or control of stomatal aperture may account for differences in stomatal diffusion resistance and hence in photosynthesis (Siwecki and Kozlowski, 1973).

The importance of stomatal control is shown by the simultaneous reduction in stomatal aperture and in photosynthesis during developing droughts, and by midday dips in photosynthesis during periods of temporary stomatal closure. Kriedemann (1971) found that leaf resistance (a measure of stomatal aperture) and rates of CO_2 uptake by citrus leaves were closely related in plants in drying soil (Fig. 5.29). Large differences in rates of photosynthesis among species have also been shown to be related to variations in stomatal resistance to CO_2 diffusion (Holmgren *et al.*, 1965). Simultaneous reduction of rates of transpiration and photosynthesis with increasing water stress also indicates that photosynthesis is inhibited by diffusional resistance to CO_2 uptake, largely as a result of stomatal closure (Brix, 1962).

During development of water stress caused by drought, photosynthesis is first reduced by stomatal closure and direct inhibitory effects on the photosynthetic apparatus do not occur until dehydration is much more severe. Troughton and Slatyer (1969)

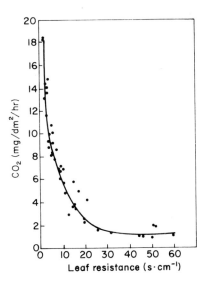

Fig. 5.29. Effect of leaf diffusion resistance (stomatal aperture) on photosynthesis of orange leaves. From Kriedemann (1971).

found that although photosynthesis of cotton was depressed by mild water stress, no direct effects were exerted on the photosynthetic mechanism until plants were desiccated beyond the permanent wilting percentage. On the other hand, Mooney *et al.* (1977) found that at a water stress of -27 bars only 25% of the reduction in photosynthesis of creosote bush could be attributed to stomatal closure.

Chlorophyll Content

Photosynthetic capacity of leaves with an abnormally light green color usually is lower than in leaves with a healthy, dark-green color. The importance of chlorophyll content to photosynthesis is emphasized by declines in both chlorophyll and photosynthesis in mineral-deficient leaves and in senescing leaves. Under controlled conditions a high correlation has often been shown between the chlorophyll content of leaves and CO_2 uptake (Fig. 5.30). In the field, however, the rate of photosynthesis may not vary much over a considerable range of leaf color and it appears that chlorophyll content often is less important than other factors in controlling the rate of photosynthesis (Anderson, 1967). The organization of the chlorophyll in terms of number and size of photosynthetic units may be as important as the amount (Alberte *et al.*, 1976). Nevertheless, severe chlorosis from whatever cause invariably is correlated with reduced photosynthesis.

The winter decline in photosynthesis is often associated with disorganization of chloroplasts and breakdown of chlorophyll. However, there seems to be considerable variation among trees, even those of the same species, with respect to the extent of disorganization of the photosynthetic apparatus during the winter. Both the chlorophyll content and the rate of photosynthesis decreased in seedlings of Swiss stone pine during

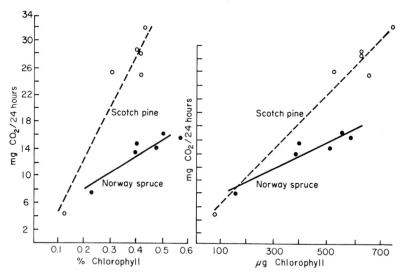

Fig. 5.30. Relation between chlorophyll content and photosynthesis in Scotch pine and Norway spruce. From Keller and Wehrmann (1963).

the winter and increased in the spring in an alpine habitat (Tranquillini, 1957). In the southeastern United States pines become chlorotic during the winter and Perry and Baldwin (1966) observed extensive chloroplast disorganization in loblolly pine which disappeared after a week or more of warm weather in early spring. Senser *et al.* (1975) also observed disorganization of chloroplasts during the winter in Norway spruce at Munich, Germany. However, it was not observed in conifers in the milder climate of southwestern England (Fry and Phillips, 1977) nor in white pine or rhododendron in New England (Parker and Philpott, 1963).

Growth Rate

The relationship between growth and photosynthesis is complex. It was stated at the beginning of this chapter that forest management should be directed toward increasing the amount of photosynthesis per unit of land area, because in general the rate of plant growth is dependent on the supply of photosynthate. However, it cannot be assumed that an increase in the rate of photosynthesis will automatically result in increased growth. It often is assumed that plants with a high rate of photosynthesis per unit of leaf area will produce more dry matter and grow more rapidly than plants with a low rate. This is sometimes true, but not always (Carter, 1972). For example, Ledig and Perry (1967) measured the rate of photosynthesis of 18 families of loblolly pine and found that, although the most rapidly growing family had the highest rate, the correlation between CO_2 uptake and growth was slightly negative for all 18 families combined. Carter mentioned several other investigators who found little or no correlation between CO_2 uptake per unit of leaf area and growth. Helms (1976) also discussed the difficulties in relating growth to rate of photosynthesis. These difficulties likewise exist in herbaceous plants (Evans, 1975b). Part of the poor correlation may occur because photosynthesis usually is measured only a few times during the growing season and dry matter production (growth) is a product of rate, leaf area, and duration, and all three vary during the growing season.

Went (1958) suggested that under some conditions the rate of growth may directly affect the rate of photosynthesis by affecting the rate at which photosynthate is translocated out of leaf cells, and there is considerable evidence to support this view. Thus we may ask to what extent the rate of photosynthesis controls the rate of growth and to what extent the rate of growth controls the rate of photosynthesis. There is evidence that both situations occur, the latter being most frequent under conditions favorable for photosynthesis. It has been demonstrated for a number of woody and herbaceous species that even under optimum conditions the rate of photosynthesis usually is well below the maximum possible rate and this is generally attributed to a less than maximum demand for the products (Neales and Incoll, 1968; Evans, 1975a). It therefore appears that the photosynthetic machinery of plants often runs considerably below its maximum capacity.

The rate of photosynthesis has been altered experimentally by changing the ratio of carbohydrate sinks to carbohydrate sources. If a portion of the leaf area of an apple tree is removed, the translocation pattern of carbohydrates is altered and photosynthesis increases in residual leaves as they supply a larger carbohydrate sink (Maggs, 1965).

Partial defoliation of Monterey pine was followed by marked increase in photosynthesis of residual leaves, even at saturating light intensities (Sweet and Wareing, 1966; Wareing et al., 1968). The rate of photosynthesis also has been increased by removing part of the root system. This stimulates production of many new roots which increase the demand for photosynthetic products. Removal of half the root system of young apple trees increased net assimilation by 17% (Maggs, 1964a). Decrease in number of sinks by deblossoming or defruiting also tends to decrease photosynthesis in apple (Maggs, 1963) and fruiting often is accompanied by an increase in rate of photosynthesis (Lenz, 1977). Preventing rapid withdrawal of photosynthetic products from leaves likewise is followed by a decrease in photosynthesis. Substantial reduction of net photosynthesis occurred in pecan leaflets within 1 to 2 days after branches were ringed, thereby preventing outward translocation of carbohydrates. Reduced photosynthesis was still evident 50 days after the branches were girdled. Respiration of leaves was also increased by ringing of branches, so that the observed reductions in apparent photosynthesis probably reflected not only inhibition of photosynthesis but also increased respiration (Loustalot, 1943).

Wareing et al. (1968) studied the mechanism involving changes in photosynthetic activity of leaves as source–sink relations were altered. When trees were partially defoliated, the remaining leaves became greener and larger. Furthermore, the total protein content increased (Table 5.4), as did the level of carboxylating enzymes. They concluded that increased photosynthesis after partial defoliation resulted from an increase in amount of carboxylating enzymes. This was attributed to increased protein synthesis caused by an increased supply of cytokinins to the remaining leaves from the roots. This conclusion was supported by the observation that removal of part of the roots prevented an increase in photosynthesis of the remaining leaves after partial defoliation. Their conclusion is based on the assumption that photosynthesis is commonly limited by the supply of RuBP carboxylase, an assumption questioned by some investigators.

The results of these and other experiments indicate that there are rather complex interactions between growth and photosynthesis and that the rate of photosynthesis can be increased or decreased by altering the rate of growth. The effect on photosynthesis might be brought about either by a change in source–sink relationships with respect to carbohydrates, or by hormone interactions, or by both. Thorne and Koller (1974)

TABLE 5.4 Effect of Partial Defoliation on Leaf Protein Content of *Salix viminalis*

| Treatment | Protein content (mg/g fresh weight) | | | |
| | Days after treatment | | | |
	0	5	10	15
Control	0.49	0.55	0.72	0.88
Partial defoliation	0.49	0.75	0.98	1.15

suggest that the role of carbohydrate as a regulator of photosynthesis is less important than the role of hormones, a view supported by Wareing *et al.* (1968). Perhaps hormones act partly through enzyme synthesis and membrane permeability and partly through effects on translocation. Readers are referred to Wareing and Patrick (1975) and Evans (1975a,b) for additional material on this interesting problem. Obviously, more research is needed on the relationship between growth and photosynthesis in an attempt to find methods by which plants can be caused to more fully utilize their photosynthetic capacity. Perhaps improvement in partitioning and translocation of carbohydrates to growing regions will prove to be more beneficial than increase in rate of photosynthesis. For example, it might be advantageous from the standpoint of timber production to promote rapid leaf growth early in the season but thereafter to divert the maximum amount of carbohydrate to wood production.

GENERAL REFERENCES

Bonner, J., and Varner, J. E., eds. (1976). "Plant Biochemistry," 3rd ed. Academic Press, New York.

Burris, R. H., and Black, C. C., eds. (1976). "CO₂ Metabolism and Plant Productivity." Univ. Park Press, Baltimore, Maryland.

Cannell, M. G. R., and Last, F. T., eds. (1976). "Tree Physiology and Yield Improvement." Academic Press, New York.

Cooper, J. P., ed. (1975). "Photosynthesis and Productivity in Different Environments." Cambridge Univ. Press, London and New York.

Govindjee, ed. (1975). "Bioenergetics of Photosynthesis." Academic Press. New York.

Gregory, R. P. F. (1977). "Biochemistry of Photosynthesis." Wiley, New York.

Hatch, M. D., Osmond, C. B., and Slatyer, R. O. (1971). "Photosynthesis and Photorespiration." Wiley (Interscience), New York.

Larcher, W. (1975). "Physiological Plant Ecology." Springer-Verlag, Berlin and New York.

Marcelle, R., ed. (1975)."Environmental and Biological Control of Photosynthesis." W. Junk, The Hague.

Schaedle, M. (1975). Tree photosynthesis. *Annu. Rev. Plant Physiol.* **26,** 101–115.

Thornber, J. P. (1975). Chlorophyll-proteins: Light-harvesting and reaction center components of plants. *Annu. Rev. Plant Physiol.* **26,** 127–158.

Whittingham, C. P. (1974). "The Mechanism of Photosynthesis." Am. Elsevier, New York.

Zelitch, C. P. (1974). "Photosynthesis, Photorespiration, and Plant Productivity." Academic Press, New York.

6

Enzymes, Energetics, and Respiration

INTRODUCTION

Among the important processes occurring in living organisms are the release by the process of respiration of chemical energy stored in foods and its use to transform carbohydrates, fats, and proteins into new protoplasm and new tissue (assimilation). An understanding of how these complex processes occur requires at least an elementary knowledge of enzyme activity and energy transfer. We will first discuss enzymes and energy transfer in general terms and then discuss the biochemistry and ecology of respiration in more detail.

ENZYMES AND ENERGETICS

Enzymes

One of the most important characteristics of living cells is the high rate at which chemical reactions occur within them at temperatures of 5° to 40°C. The same reactions occur very slowly if at all in the laboratory at those temperatures. For example, wood, coal, and other fuels do not burn until they have been heated to a critical temperature, after which they burn spontaneously. Even glucose must be heated to a high temperature to burn (oxidize) in air, but it is readily oxidized at 5° to 10°C in living cells. This is because most chemical reactions, even those which release energy, do not occur spontaneously, but require the addition of a certain amount of energy, the energy of activation, to start them. Enzymes are organic catalysts which lower the energy of activation to a point where reactions can occur at ordinary temperatures. This usually is accomplished by momentarily binding substrate molecules on the surface of the enzyme molecules and thereby increasing the probability of a reaction occurring. Most enzymes are very specific and catalyze only one reaction or one type of reaction. This is because enzymes are basically protein molecules with specific structural configurations which only permit combination with substrate molecules having a certain molecular structure. While the substrate molecules are temporarily bound on the surfaces of the enzyme there is rearrangement of atoms and chemical bonds, resulting in production of different molecules, often with a different free energy. Many enzymes catalyze reversible reactions which proceed one way or the other, depending on the concentration of reactants, pH, and other factors. Enzymes sometimes exist in several molecular forms which act on the same substrate. These are known as isozymes (Scandalios, 1974).

There are hundreds of different enzymes in living cells, many of them carefully compartmented in various organelles. For example, the enzymes involved in the Krebs cycle occur in mitochondria, enzymes involved in electron transport occur in both mitochondria and chloroplasts, while those involved in glycolysis and the pentose shunt occur principally in the cytoplasm. Some extracellular enzymes even occur on the external surfaces of cells or diffuse out into the surrounding medium.

The basic structure of an enzyme is a protein molecule and enzymes differ because of differences in the sequence of amino acids in their proteins. Some enzymes such as urease and papain consist only of protein molecules, but many require that a nonprotein constituent, often termed a cofactor or coenzyme, be closely associated with or bound to the protein molecule. Cofactors that are integral parts of the enzyme, such as the copper in tyrosinase and ascorbic acid oxidase and the iron in catalase, are known as prosthetic groups. Many enzymes are active only in the presence of ions such as Mg^{2+}, Mn^{2+}, Ca^{2+}, and K^+. These ions are known as metal activators and the most important function of the micronutrient elements in plants and animals is as prosthetic groups or metal activators of enzymes. Some enzymes are active only in the presence of complex organic molecules which, if tightly bound, are termed prosthetic groups but, if loosely bound, are termed cofactors or coenzymes.

Several vitamins, especially those of the B complex, play important roles as enzyme cofactors. Some examples follow. Pyridine nucleotides are of great importance as cofactors of enzymes involved in metabolic energy transfers. NAD (nicotinamide adenine dinucleotide) and NADP (nicotinamide adenine dinucleotide phosphate) are essential coenzymes of the enzymes involved in oxidation–reduction systems of living cells, both in respiration and in photosynthesis. In their reduced form, $NADH_2$ or $NADPH_2$, they are high-energy compounds which supply reducing power in such processes as electron transport and the reduction of carbon in the process of photosynthesis. Two other important enzymes involved in oxidation–reduction reactions are the flavin nucleotides FMN (flavin mononucleotide) and FAD (flavin adenine dinucleotide), which are derived from one of the B_2 vitamins, riboflavin.

Thiamine pyrophosphate is derived from vitamin B_1 (thiamine) and serves as a coenzyme for various decarboxylases, oxidases, and transketolases. Pyridoxal, pyridoxine, and pyridoxamine constitute the vitamin B_6 complex, from which is derived pyridoxal phosphate, an important enzyme in reactions in amino acid synthesis. Another vitamin, pantothenic acid, is a precursor of coenzyme A, which plays an important role in metabolism (see Figs. 6.1 and 6.20). Thus several vitamins are essential because of their roles as coenzymes in important metabolic reactions.

The complement of enzymes produced in a plant is determined primarily by its genotype, and occasionally metabolic disorders are caused by gene mutations which eliminate specific enzymes. Some genetic control also exists outside the nucleus, especially in the chloroplasts. Among the most conspicuous mutations in plants are those which produce defects in chlorophyll development, but many others occur. These often result in the death of seedlings and go unnoticed. Study of mutations provides much information about the role of enzymes in metabolism. The regulation of enzyme activity is complex and not fully understood, but it involves feedback by accumulation of end products, activation by metabolites, and energy charge regulation. Examples of various types of regulation are given in Chapter 10 of Bonner and Varner.

In addition to genetic controls, enzyme activity is affected by such factors as temperature; hydrogen ion concentration; concentration of enzyme, substrate, and end products; hydration; and various growth regulators. In microorganisms, formation of enzymes is often induced by the presence of substrate and some examples of enzyme induction occur in seed plants. For instance, formation of nitrate reductase seems to be induced by the presence of nitrate. Various substances also inhibit enzyme action and much has been learned about metabolic processes by the careful use of selective inhibitors. There are two general classes of inhibitors, competitive and noncompetitive. Competitive inhibitors are compounds so similar in structure to the substrate molecule that they partially replace it in reaction sites on the enzyme and interfere with normal enzyme action. An example is the blocking of the conversion of succinic acid to fumaric acid by the addition of malonic acid, which resembles succinic acid in structure. Noncompetitive inhibitors such as fluoride, cyanide, azide, copper, and mercury form permanent combinations with enzyme molecules, rendering them inactive.

Enzyme Classification

Enzymes are classified on the basis of the reactions they catalyze. The following major types are recognized:

1. Oxidoreductases: catalyze oxidation–reduction reactions (e.g., oxidases, dehydrogenases)
2. Transferases: catalyze transfer of a chemical group from a donor compound to an acceptor compound (e.g., transaminase)
3. Hydrolases: catalyze hydrolytic cleavage of C-O, C-N, C-C, and some other bonds (e.g., sucrase)
4. Lyases: catalyze removal of chemical groups from substrates by nonhydrolytic means. These enzymes cleave C–C, C–O, C–N, and other bonds by elimination, leaving double bonds or adding groups to double bonds (e.g., decarboxylases)
5. Isomerases: catalyze conversion of a compound into some of its isomers (e.g., triose phosphate isomerase)
6. Ligases (synthetases): catalyze linking together of two molecules together with hydrolysis of a pyrophosphate bond in ATP (e.g., thiokinases)

Energetics

The existence of living organisms depends on a continuous supply of energy for use in synthesis of new protoplasm, maintenance of the structure of organelles and membranes, active transport of ions and molecules across membranes, and in mechanical activity such as cytoplasmic streaming. In motile organisms much energy is used for locomotion, and in warm-blooded organisms for maintenance of the body temperature. The immediate source of this energy is food, that is, carbohydrates, fats, and proteins accumulated in the organisms, but the ultimate source varies. Autotrophic organisms manufacture their own food, either by photosynthesis (as described in Chapter 5) or by chemosynthesis. Examples of chemosynthesis are found in bacteria which obtain energy to synthesize carbohydrates by oxidizing NH_3 to NO_2, NO_2 to NO_3, H_2S to SO_4, or ferrous iron to ferric iron. Heterotrophic organisms, which include animals and nongreen plants, are dependent on green plants for the food which supplies their energy. It may be said that the success of plants depends on their ability to acquire, store, and release energy as needed. The acquisition and storage of energy in green plants by the process of photosynthesis were discussed in Chapter 5 and we are now concened with how energy is stored and released in other tissues.

A brief discussion of the energetics of oxidation–reduction reactions is needed at this point. A compound is said to be oxidized if it loses electrons or hydrogen atoms and it is reduced if it gains electrons or hydrogen atoms. Obviously, when one substance is reduced another is oxidized. In the following equation compound A is oxidized and compound B is reduced

$$AH_2 + B \xrightarrow{\text{dehydrogenase}} A + BH_2$$

The oxidation of glucose can be summarized as follows.

$$C_6H_{12}O_6 + 6O_2 \longrightarrow 6\ CO_2 + 6H_2O + 686{,}000\ cal$$

The carbon in the glucose is oxidized to CO_2 by splitting off hydrogen and combining it with oxygen to form water, and during the rearrangement of atomic bonds a large amount of energy is released. If this process occurs as ordinary combustion in the laboratory the energy is released as heat, but in living cells about two-thirds of the energy is captured and stored in ATP from which it can later be released to do chemical work. In living cells this process requires about 25 enzymes and numerous steps, as shown in Figs. 6.1 and 6.2. The reverse is the reduction of the carbon in CO_2 to glucose. This requires the input of in excess of 686,000 cal/mole of light energy which is used to split H_2O and release H^+. The H^+ combines with NADP to produce the reducing compound $NADPH_2$, which ultimately supplies the hydrogen required to reduce the carbon. Light energy also is used to produce ATP which supplies the energy for other steps in the carbon cycle. Thus, in summary, as described in Chapter 5, carbon is reduced, $NADPH_2$ is oxidized, and energy is stored in the products of photosynthesis:

$$CO_2 + 2NADPH_2 \longrightarrow CH_2O + 2NADP + H_2O$$

However, this also occurs in many steps and requires nearly 20 enzymes (see Figs. 5.2 and 5.3).

Thus reduction is accompanied by an increase in free energy, oxidation by the release of free energy. For example, the reduced forms of NAD and NADP, $NADH_2$ and $NADPH_2$, have much higher free energies than the oxidized forms and, because they can supply hydrogen atoms, they are said to have reducing power. The same is true of FMN and FAD and their reduced forms, $FMNH_2$ and $FADH_2$. An example of the role of NAD is the conversion of malic acid to oxaloacetic acid, in which malic acid loses two hydrogen atoms and NAD is reduced to $NADH_2$.

$$\begin{array}{c}CH_2{-}COOH \\ | \\ HO{-}CH{-}COOH\end{array} + NAD \xrightarrow[\text{dehydrogenase}]{\text{malic}} \begin{array}{c}CH_2{-}COOH \\ | \\ O{=}C{-}COOH\end{array} + NADH_2$$

Oxidation and reduction of cytochrome oxidase is accomplished by change in valence of the iron which shifts from Fe^{3+} (oxidized) to Fe^{2+} (reduced). The role of ATP as a medium for energy transfer is discussed later.

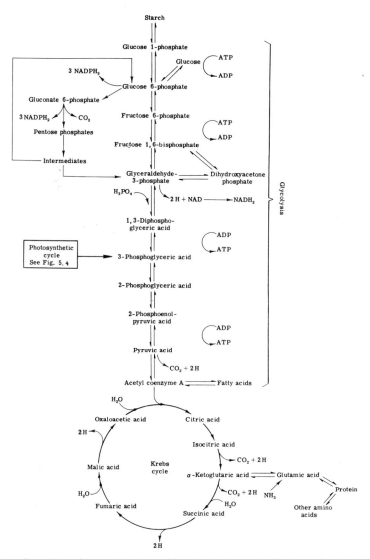

Fig. 6.1. An outline of the principal steps in glycolysis and the Krebs cycle. Each pair of hydrogens released yields 3 ATP and a molecule of water when it passes through the terminal electron transport system shown in Fig. 6.2. Figure 6.20 shows the relationship between various products of these reactions and other important compounds found in plants. The processes in the linear portion called glycolysis occur in the cytoplasm, but those of the Krebs cycle occur in the mitochondria.

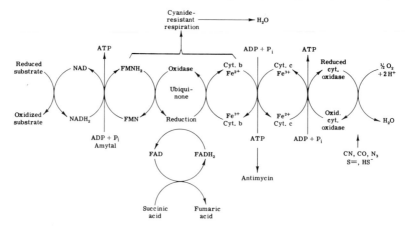

Fig. 6.2. Diagram of the mitochondrial electron transport system. Ubiquinone is also known as CoQ. P_i refers to inorganic phosphorus, in contrast to phosphorylation in glycolysis where most of the phosphorus for formation of ATP comes from the substrate. The alternate oxidase system indicates that in some tissue possessing cyanide-resistant respiration the usual cytochrome system is bypassed. The site of action of several common inhibitors is indicated. Amytal is a strong inhibitor in both plant and animal tissue, rotenone only in animals. From Ikuma (1972).

RESPIRATION

This section describes the process of respiration at the cellular level, discusses its occurrence in various tissues and organs, and deals with some of the factors which affect respiration rate. Respiration not only releases the energy required for maintenance of the structural integrity of the existing protoplasm, but also that required for synthesis of the numerous compounds required for the production of new protoplasm and plant structure (assimilation). The quantity of energy required for the synthesis of various compounds is indicated by the data for O_2 consumption and CO_2 production in Table 6.3. That portion of the carbohydrates produced by photosynthesis which is not oxidized in respiration or used in assimilation is accumulated in fruits, seeds, and vegetative structures, chiefly as starch, protein, or lipids. Assimilation is discussed at the end of this chapter and accumulation of carbohydrates in Chapter 7.

Respiration can be defined as the oxidation of food (substrate) in living cells, bringing about the release of energy. The energy released is that stored as chemical energy in the substrate molecules. Part of the energy released is used to maintain the structure of protoplasm (maintenance respiration), some is used in synthetic processes (growth respiration), some is used in transport of materials, some is used in mechanical processes such as protoplasmic streaming, some occurs as electrical energy, and some is dissipated as heat.

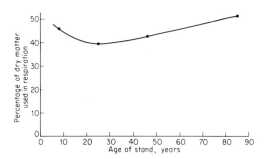

Fig. 6.3. The percentage of food produced which is used in respiration by stands of beech trees of various ages. From Möller *et al.* (1954a,b).

General Characteristics

Respiration occurs continuously in all living cells of plants, but the rate is extremely low in physiologically inactive structures such as dormant seeds. It is most rapid in meristematic regions such as cambia, root and stem tips, and very young tissue. It also is sometimes rapid in maturing fruit, where much of the energy is released as heat which seems to serve no useful purpose. The storage life of fruits and seeds can be prolonged significantly by storing them under environmental conditions which keep the rate of respiration low. On the other hand, reduction of the respiration rate in growing tissues by low temperature or low oxygen concentration is undesirable because it reduces the rate of growth.

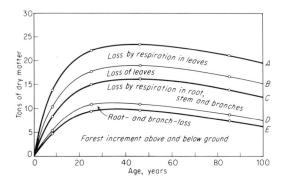

Fig. 6.4. The amounts of dry matter used in various processes by stands of European beech of various ages growing on good sites in Denmark. The ordinate represents metric tons of dry matter per hectare per year. The upper heavy curve (A) indicates total or gross production by photosynthesis. The middle heavy curve (C) indicates net photosynthesis, and the lower heavy curve (E) indicates the amount of dry matter added in growth each year. The area between curves A and B represents loss of dry matter by leaf respiration, that between B and C loss by leaf fall. The area between curves C and D represents loss of dry matter by respiration in roots, stems, and branches, and the area between D and E represents dry matter lost by death of roots and branches. From Möller *et al.* (1954).

TABLE 6.1   Productivity and Loss of Dry Matter in Various Organs of
Two Types of Forests in Tons per Hectare per Year and as Percentage of
That Produced in Photosynthesis[a]

	Tropical rain forest		Danish beech forest	
Increase in biomass				
Leaves	0.03		0.00	
Stems	2.90		5.3	
Roots	0.20		1.6	
Total	3.13[b]	2%[c]	6.9	35%[c]
Loss by death and decay				
Leaves	12.0		2.7	
Stems	13.3		1.0	
Roots	0.2		0.2	
Total	25.5	20%	3.9	20%
Used in respiration				
Leaves	60.1		4.6	
Stems	32.9		3.5	
Roots	5.9		0.7	
Total	98.9[d]	78%	8.8	45%

[a] From Larcher (1975).
[b] According to Sanchez (1973) the regrowth of forest in Guatemala amounts
to about 10 ton/ha/year during the first decade after cutting, considerably
more than the amount shown above for an older tropical rain forest.
[c] Percentage of photosynthesis.
[d] Recent work indicates that this should be 55 tons or 65% of total photosynthesis (Kira, 1975).

Although some minimal rate of respiration is essential for survival, and a higher rate
is necessary for growth, the rate often rises far above the essential level. This results in
the unproductive consumption of food which might have been used in assimilation to
produce new tissue or accumulated in storage organs. A large fraction of the food
produced by trees is used in respiration by the nonphotosynthetic tissue (Figs. 6.3 and
6.4 and Table 6.1). Polster (1950) suggested that the productivity of forests might be
increased more by treatments which reduce respiration, such as the removal of parasitic
branches, than by treatments to increase photosynthesis.

Cellular Respiration

The usual substrate for respiration is glucose and its complete oxidation under ideal
conditions can be shown by the following equation:

$$C_6H_{12}O_6 + 6O_2 \longrightarrow 6CO_2 + 6H_2O + 686{,}000 \text{ cal/mole}$$

The process is much more complex and occurs in many more steps than is indicated by
this summary equation, which does not explain how the oxygen is used, how the

carbon dioxide and water are formed, or how energy is released in usable form. We will now attempt to explain how all of this occurs.

Biological Oxidations

As mentioned earlier, oxidations usually involve the removal of hydrogen atoms or the transfer of electrons from substrates to an acceptor. In cells hydrogen atoms (proton plus an electron) are split off from the substrate by enzymes known as dehydrogenases and transferred to an acceptor or oxidizing agent. In cells this acceptor usually is NAD (nicotinamide adenine dinucleotide) or NADP (nicotinamide adenine dinucleotide phosphate) which become $NADH_2$ or $NADPH_2$ when reduced. The hydrogens are then transferred from the reduced NAD or NADP through a series of acceptors in a terminal oxidase system containing cytochromes and combined with oxygen to form water (see Fig. 6.2). At the same time energy is released and part of it is used to form the high-energy compound ATP (adenosine triphosphate) by attaching a phosphate to ADP (adenosine diphosphate).

ATP

As ATP is the most important high-energy compound in plants, it deserves description. Adenosine is formed from the purine, adenine, and a sugar called ribose. When a phosphate group is added to adenosine by an ordinary ester bond, AMP (adenosine monophosphate) results. If a second phosphate is added by a pyrophosphate bond, ADP results, and addition of a third phosphate group by another pyrophosphate bond produces ATP. This is termed a high-energy compound because, when the terminal pyrophosphate bond is broken by hydrolysis at pH 7.0 and 25°C, nearly 7,300 cal/mole of energy are released, in contrast to only about 2,200 cal/mole when the ester bond of AMP is broken. It should be emphasized that the high energy is *not* in the bond, but refers to the difference in energy content between the original compound and its products. Energy is released because after the terminal phosphate is split off there is a new arrangement of electrons with a much lower total energy than existed in ATP. The actual amount of energy released by the reaction ATP $\rightarrow$ ADP + Pi varies somewhat with the pH and other factors, but is often given as 7,300 or 7,600 cal/mole, though under the conditions existing in cells it may approach 12,000 cal/mole.

Metabolically active tissue contains large amounts of adenosine phosphates. For example, Ching and Ching (1972) reported that embryos in germinating seedlings of ponderosa pine contained 80 times as much adenosine phosphate as those of nongerminating seeds. The ratio of ATP and ADP to total adenosine phosphate is called the adenylate energy charge and it is considerably higher in growing tissue than in nongrowing tissue. Some data are given in Fig. 14.8 and Table 14.4.

Other High-Energy Compounds

There are other phosphate compounds such as phosphoenolpyruvate, 1,3-diphosphoglycerate, and acetyl phosphate which have even higher standard free energies of hydrolysis than ATP. Acetyl coenzyme A possesses a high free energy and the pyridine nucleotides in their reduced forms ($NADH_2$ and $NADPH_2$) also have high free energies. However, ATP occupies a unique position because it is intermediate in the free energy scale and can transfer phosphate groups from compounds with a high free energy to those with a lower free energy such as glucose and glycerol, resulting in glucose-6-phosphate and glycerol-3-phosphate. Thus ATP and ADP are involved in nearly all enzymatic phosphate transfer reactions in cells and thereby control the energy flow (Lehninger, 1971).

Glycolysis and the Krebs Cycle

The oxidation of glucose occurs in a series of steps which fall into two groups, a linear sequence of transformations called glycolysis, by which glucose is converted to pyruvic acid, followed by the Krebs or tricarboxylic acid cycle in which pyruvic acid is oxidized to carbon dioxide and water. These steps were shown in an abbreviated form in Fig. 6.1. Glycolysis occurs in the cytoplasm, but the reactions of the Krebs cycle and oxidative phosphorylation occur in the mitochondria. The role of mitochondria in plant respiration is discussed by W. D. Bonner (1973).

In the complete aerobic oxidation of a mole of glucose 38 moles of high-energy ATP are formed. A total of 10 moles are formed during glycolysis, but 2 moles are used to phosphorylate hexose sugar, leaving a net gain of 8. Three high-energy phosphate bonds are formed for each of the five pairs of hydrogen atoms released per molecule of pyruvic acid oxidized in the Krebs cycle, resulting in a total of 30 moles for the 2 moles of pyruvic acid formed from each mole of glucose. If the energy stored during formation of the terminal pyrophosphate bonds in a mole of ATP is taken as 7,300 calories, 277,400 calories (38 $\times$ 7300) are stored in ATP, or 40% of the total energy stored in glucose. If the free energy is taken as 12,000 cal/mole, which is nearer to the value in cells, 66% is stored. The remainder of the energy is dissipated as heat. Glycolysis and the Krebs cycle can be summarized as follows:

$$\text{Glucose} \qquad\qquad\qquad \text{Pyruvic acid}$$
$$\text{Glycolysis: } C_6H_{12}O_6 + O_2 + 8ADP + 8P_i \rightarrow 2CH_3COCOOH + 2H_2O + 8ATP + 58{,}400 \text{ cal}$$

$$\text{Pyruvic acid}$$
$$\text{Krebs cycle: } 2CH_3COCOOH + 5O_2 + 30ADP + 30P_i \rightarrow 6CO_2 + 4H_2O + 30ATP + 219{,}000 \text{ cal}$$

Thus each mole of glucose yields 2 moles of pyruvic acid, 2 moles of water, and 8 moles of ATP, and each mole of pyruvic acid which goes through the Krebs cycle yields 3 moles of carbon dioxide, 2 moles of water, and 15 moles of ATP, or a total of 6 moles of carbon dioxide, 6 moles of water, and 38 moles of ATP for the entire process. The water is formed by combination of the hydrogen split off by dehydrogenase enzymes, with oxygen in a complex terminal electron transport system.

The steps in the complex series of transformations were shown in Fig. 6.1, beginning with the phosphorylation of glucose by transfer of phosphate from ATP, producing glucose-6-phosphate and ADP. Food stored as starch can be converted to glucose-1-phosphate by phosphorylase and then to glucose-6-phosphate. Another rearrangement and addition of a second phosphate produces fructose-1,6-bisphosphate, and later transformations result in the production of ATP and $NADH_2$, which, when oxidized through the cytochrome system, yields 3 ATP. The end product of glycolysis is pyruvic acid. Under aerobic conditions a molecule of carbon dioxide and two hydrogen atoms are split off from the pyruvic acid, and acetyl coenzyme A is formed. It combines with oxaloacetic acid in the Krebs cycle to form the six-carbon atom citric acid. Citric acid is successively converted to five- and four-carbon atom acids as carbon dioxide molecules and hydrogen atoms are split off, and the cycle finally returns to oxaloacetic acid, as was shown in Fig. 6.1. Carbon atoms are split off by decarboxylases in the formation of acetyl coenzyme A, α-ketoglutaric acid, and succinic acid, producing three molecules of carbon dioxide per molecule of pyruvic acid oxidized. Pairs of hydrogen atoms are split off by dehydrogenases in the formation of acetyl coenzyme A, and α-ketoglutaric, succinic, fumaric, and oxaloacetic acids. These hydrogen atoms are passed through a series of acceptors in a terminal electron transport system (see Fig. 6.2) and combined with oxygen to form water, and 3 moles of ATP are formed for each 2 moles of hydrogen split off. Although five pairs of hydrogen atoms are split off per molecule of pyruvic acid oxidized, three molecules of water are used in the cycle, so there is a net release of 2 moles of water per mole of pyruvic acid.

Electron Transfer and Oxidative Phosphorylation

The conversion of the hydrogen to water is a complex process and very important because it is accompanied by the production of ATP. It is called oxidative phosphorylation. The general scheme was shown in Fig. 6.2, although some details are not yet explained.

In this scheme, NAD accepts hydrogen split off in the Krebs cycle and is reduced to $NADH_2$. The hydrogen is transferred to FMN (flavin mononucleotide) and the $FMNH_2$ then transfers its hydrogen and corresponding electrons to ubiquinone and then to cytochrome. There may be three to seven cytochromes in this system and the final one transfers two H^+ and two electrons to an atom of oxygen, producing water. According to current views, during this process an electron transport system pumps protons across the membrane on which the enzymes are bound, producing a gradient in H^+ concentration which provides the energy for ATP formation. This scheme, known as the Mitchell chemiosmotic theory is discussed in more detail by Hinkle and McCarty (1978). One ATP is produced for each pair of hydrogens. The sequence of events was shown in Fig. 6.2. Thus the oxygen is reduced to produce water in the final stage of respiration, and a major part of the ATP is produced. In contrast to this oxidative phosphorylation, the production of ATP in glycolysis is termed substrate-level phosphorylation because the phosphate added to ADP to form ATP comes chiefly from the substrate, rather than from inorganic phosphate as in oxidative phosphorylation and the photophosphorylation associated with photosynthesis.

It should now be obvious that the Krebs cycle has two important functions. One is the production of intermediate compounds important in the synthesis of such substances as amino and fatty acids. The other is the formation of large quantities of ATP which provides energy for various synthetic processes.

The numerous enzymes involved in the Krebs cycle and oxidative phosphorylation occur in the mitochondria, while those involved in glycolysis occur in the cytoplasm.

Other Oxidases

There are a number of other oxidase systems in plants in addition to the cytochromes. Catalase, an iron-containing enzyme, is very abundant. It splits hydrogen peroxide into water and molecular oxygen while peroxidase transfers hydrogen from a donor to peroxide, producing two molecules of water. $NADH_2$ and $NADPH_2$ are also oxidized by peroxidase and this may have a control effect on cell metabolism. Peroxidase and phenol oxidase may be involved in the synthesis of lignin. The phenol oxidases are copper-containing enzymes which are responsible for the darkening of cut surfaces of plant tissue such as apple or potato. They apparently are carefully isolated or compartmented in intact tissue, but are released and cause discoloration when cells are damaged. They also are a nuisance to laboratory workers in the separation of plant enzymes and mitochondria. Another important oxidase system, glycolic acid oxidase, occurs in stems and leaves, but not in roots, and converts glycolic acid to glyoxylic acid, an important reaction in photorespiration. These are termed soluble oxidases because they occur in the cytoplasm, in contrast to the cytochromes which occur on membranes within the mitochondria.

The Pentose Shunt

An alternate pathway found in plants for the oxidation of glucose is the pentose shunt, or hexose monophosphate pathway. Glucose-6-phosphate is oxidized to gluconate-6-phosphate and NADP is reduced to $NADPH_2$. This is followed by another transformation, yielding the pentose sugar ribulose-5-bisphosphate, carbon dioxide, and another $NADPH_2$. Thus the pentose shunt produces considerable reducing power in the form of $NADPH_2$, which is used in reactions such as fatty acid synthesis. The pentose sugar undergoes a series of transformations similar to those in the Calvin–Benson cycle and produces compounds needed for the synthesis of nucleic acids, adenine and pyridine nucleotides, and other substances. Further rearrangements of the pentose sugar lead to glyceraldehyde-3-phosphate and pyruvic acid or back to glucose-6-phosphate. Although this pathway yields less ATP than glycolysis and the Krebs cycle it is important because it produces reducing power and substances needed for other synthetic processes. According to some workers it is a major path for hexose metabolism in germinating seeds.

Acetyl Coenzyme A

This compound is formed from pyruvic acid and coenzyme A and the acetyl group has a standard free energy slightly higher than that of ATP. Acetyl coenzyme A is a key compound in metabolism because carbohydrates, fatty acids, and amino acids all yield it as a major degradation product which enters the Krebs cycle. Most of the carbon atoms of these compounds finally enter the respiratory cycle by way of acetyl coenzyme A. For example, in the oxidation of fatty acids successive pairs of carbon atoms are split off and transferred through acetyl coenzyme A to the Krebs cycle. It also is in the synthetic pathway for fatty acids. Its central position is shown in Figs. 6.1 and 6.20.

Anaerobic Respiration

In the absence of oxygen the terminal electron transport system cannot operate, oxidative phosphorylation does not occur, and the only energy released is that made available during glycolysis. The general situation is shown in the following diagram:

Glucose → Intermediate Compounds → Pyruvic Acid

- Aerobic → $CO_2 + H_2O$, 686,000 cal
- Anaerobic → Organic acids, Aldehydes, Alcohols, CO_2, 15,200 cal

Thus anaerobic respiration is very inefficient and does not supply enough energy to support rapid growth. Furthermore, the accumulation of incompletely oxidized compounds, such as alcohols and aldehydes, often is injurious. The relationship of anaerobic respiration to flooding injury of root systems and to fruit and vegetable storage will be discussed later.

Respiratory Quotient

The nature of the substrate markedly affects the ratio of CO_2 produced to O_2 used, the respiratory quotient or RQ. This is illustrated by the following summary equations.

The complete oxidation of carbohydrate has an RQ of 1.

$$C_6H_{12}O_6 + 6O_2 \longrightarrow 6CO_2 + 6H_2O \quad \frac{6CO_2}{6O_2} = 1.0$$

The complete oxidation of highly reduced compounds such as proteins and fats gives an RQ considerably less than 1. For example, oxidation of tripalmitin, a common fat, gives an RQ of 0.7.

$$C_{51}H_{98}O_6 + 72.5\,O_2 \longrightarrow 51CO_2 + 49H_2O \quad \frac{51CO_2}{72.5O_2} = 0.7$$

In plants such as the succulents which oxidize organic acids the RQ may be considerably more than 1. For oxalic acid it would be 4 and for malic acid 1.33.

$$C_4H_6O_5 + 3O_2 \longrightarrow 4CO_2 + 3H_2O \quad \frac{4CO_2}{3O_2} = 1.33$$

If sugars are converted to organic acids, oxygen may be used without the production of CO_2.

Because several different substrates may be oxidized at once and several reactions may be occurring simultaneously in plant tissue, the respiratory quotient is not necessarily a good indicator of the predominant type of reaction.

Photorespiration

For many years plant physiologists debated whether respiration of photosynthetic tissue in the light is the same, greater than, or less than in darkness (Zelitch, 1971). Finally, experiments by Decker (1955, 1959), Decker and Wien (1958), and many later investigators showed that CO_2 production of plants having the C_3 carbon pathway is much higher in the light than in darkness. The process of photorespiration is not fully understood, but it is quite different from dark respiration because it responds differently to inhibitors and oxygen. It is closely related to photosynthesis, seeming to depend on a recent product of photosynthesis as a substrate, possibly glyoxylic acid derived from glycolic acid formed from ribulose bisphosphate. Three-carbon plants use 20 to 50% of the CO_2 fixed by photosynthesis in photorespiration. There is therefore considerable interest in the possibility of increasing yields of crop plants by reducing the amount of photorespiration, either through breeding or by some biochemical means (Oliver and Zelitch, 1977b; Servaites and Ogren, 1977). The role of photorespiration in relation to growth is discussed further in Chapter 5.

RESPIRATION OF PLANTS AND PLANT PARTS

The Amount of Food Used in Respiration

The total amount of food used in respiration by plants is of interest because it affects the amount available for use in the assimilation processes associated with growth and the amount accumulated in fruits and seeds. Practically all of the food is manufactured in the leaves, but it is consumed by respiration in every living cell, and the total amount used by leaves, twigs, and the living tissue of boles and roots is a considerable fraction of the product of photosynthesis.

Entire Trees

Several measurements of the food budget (sometimes termed the carbon budget) of trees have been made. Heinicke and Childers (1937) enclosed 8-year-old apple trees in small greenhouses and measured carbon dioxide uptake, the amount of tissue added during the year, and rates of respiration. From these data they estimated that about one-third of the photosynthate produced by the trees was used in respiration. Kinerson (1975) estimated that 58% of the photosynthate produced by 14-year-old loblolly pine trees is used in respiration, and Larcher (1975, p. 73) states that forests in the humid tropics may use over 70% of the products of photosynthesis in respiration, as was shown in Table 6.1. However, in a footnote to a more recent paper, Kira (1975) states that respiration of the tropical rain forest was overestimated and should be about 55 tons/ha or 65% of the total product of photosynthesis.

Möller and his colleagues (1954) made an intensive study of the amounts of food used in various processes by stands of beech growing on good sites in Denmark. As was shown in Fig. 6.3, the proportion of food used in respiration increased from 40% of that produced by photosynthesis in 25-year-old trees to about 50% in 85-year-old trees. This occurs because the ratio of respiring tissue to photosynthesizing tissue increases with age. According to the data shown in Fig. 6.4, the annual dry matter increment of a beech stand decreases with increasing age, partly because of increased loss of roots, branches, and twigs and partly because of a small decrease in photosynthesis and increase in respiration. It appears that, in general, as trees grow older the ratio of photosynthetic tissue to respiring tissue decreases, providing less food for growth and slowing the rate. As loblolly pine trees grow older the ratio of foliage to stem weight decreases from 1:2 at 10 years to 1:6 at 50 years (Switzer *et al.*, 1968). Other data on leaf to stem and branch ratio are given in Table 3.6. One reason for the slow growth of overstocked stands may be the excessive use of food in respiration because many small stems have more cambial surface carrying on respiration than a few large stems with the same basal area. For example, 100 trees only 5 cm in diameter have the same basal area as one tree 50 cm in diameter, but 10 times as much circumference and 10 times as much cambial surface.

Trees growing in the open with large crowns would be expected to have a higher ratio of leaf area to woody tissue and hence a higher ratio of photosynthetic surface to respiring tissue than trees growing in closed stands, and should therefore grow more rapidly. Although this is generally true the larger, lower branches often contribute little or nothing to bole growth and may even be parasitic. It has been demonstrated that the branches can be removed from the lower two-thirds of the length of the bole of loblolly pine trees without serious reduction in growth (Fig. 6.5). Apparently most of the

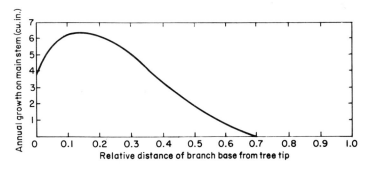

Fig. 6.5. The volume of main stem growth contributed by branches at various heights on a loblolly pine 30 years old and 15 m in height. A live crown ratio of 0.4 produces the maximum volume of clear bole, but a live crown ratio of only 0.3 produces 89% as much clear bole. From Labyak and Schumacher (1954).

carbohydrate manufactured by leaves on the lower branches is used in them by growth and respiration and does not reach the trunk.

Respiration of Various Parts of Trees

The rates of respiration of various parts of a tree differ widely, largely because of differences in proportions of physiologically active tissue.

Leaves

Although the leaves constitute the smallest part of the mass of a tree, they have the highest rate of respiration of any part of a tree because they contain a larger percentage of living material than the woody parts. They account for 50% of the total respiration in a 60-year-old beech forest, 60% in a tropical rain forest (Larcher, 1975), and 32% in a young loblolly pine stand (Kinerson et al., 1977). The daytime respiration rate of leaves of lemon and orange trees was 15 to 20% of the rate of photosynthesis. If these rates were maintained during the entire 24 hr they would use 30 to 40% of all the carbohydrates manufactured (Wedding et al., 1952). However, the lower temperature at night should reduce the night rate materially below the day rate. The leaves of a tropical rain forest were estimated to use 47% of the total photosynthate, those of a beech forest 28%, and those of a young loblolly pine stand 32%. In contrast, Heinicke and Childers (1937) estimated that leaves of an isolated 8-year-old apple tree used less than 10% of the total photosynthate in respiration. This low percentage may be related to the better exposure of the relatively large crown of a single apple tree resulting in a higher rate of photosynthesis than for trees in closed stands. The high percentage of photosynthate used in leaf respiration in the tropical rain forest probably is related to the fact that it had a leaf area index of 11.4 or twice that of the beech forest, many of the leaves are shaded and have a low rate of photosynthesis, and high night temperatures cause high rates of respiration.

Buds

Although buds constitute a very small part of the mass of a tree, during the growing season they are organs of high physiological activity. There naturally is a well-defined seasonal cycle in activity, as shown in Fig. 6.6, where it can be seen that the rate of respiration suddenly increased about fivefold when dormant buds began to grow, then decreased abruptly in August when stem elongation ceased. In this instance, twig respiration remained high long after the buds became dormant and did not reach a minimum until January.

It has been shown by several investigators that bud scales hinder the entrance of oxygen, and respiration of intact Norway maple buds measured in terms of oxygen uptake is only about half as great as that of buds from which the scales have been removed. There also was evidence of anaerobic respiration, and Pollock (1953) thought this might cause accumulation of inhibitors and cause dormancy or prolong it. The effect of the removal of the scales on respiration of white pine buds is shown in Fig. 6.7.

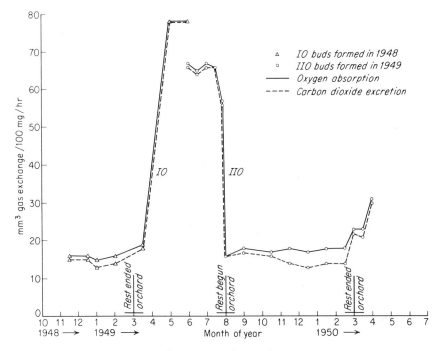

Fig. 6.6. Seasonal course of respiration of buds of pear trees. From Thom (1951).

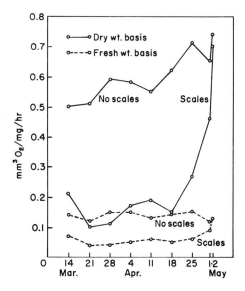

Fig. 6.7. The effect of the removal of bud scales on the respiration of buds of white pine at various stages in development, calculated on dry and fresh weight basis. From Kozlowski and Gentile (1958).

Stems

In boles and large branches most of the respiration occurs in the new phloem and xylem adjacent to the cambium. One of the few studies of respiration in tree trunks was that by Goodwin and Goddard (1940). They found respiration to be highest in the cambial region of red maple, but in black ash it was highest in the newly differentiating xylem just within the cambium (Fig. 6.8). Although living ray and axial parenchyma cells absorb oxygen, their number is so small that the total rate of respiration is low. In Goodwin and Goddard's experiments the heartwood absorbed a small amount of oxygen, but this probably resulted from oxidation of organic compounds in dead tissue rather than from respiration because boiled blocks of heartwood absorbed nearly as much oxygen as unboiled wood.

Möller (1946) also found the lowest rate of respiration in the oldest parts of tree trunks, but he reported that respiration was concentrated near the cambium to a greater extent in oak than in beech. In beech there was a very gradual decrease in respiration from the cambium inward. As mentioned earlier, because stem respiration is concentrated in the cambial region it would be expected that a forest stand consisting of a small number of trees of large diameter would have a more efficient ratio of photosynthesis to respiration than a stand of the same basal area composed of more trees of smaller diameter.

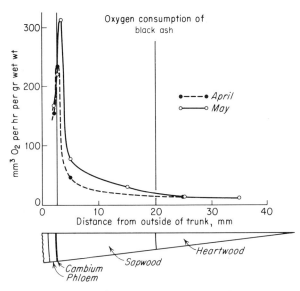

Fig. 6.8. Rates of respiration of various parts of a trunk of a black ash tree before and after bud opening, measured as oxygen uptake. From Goodwin and Goddard (1940).

Seasonal Variations in Respiration

There are marked seasonal variations in rate of respiration which are related to temperature and physiological activity. The seasonal course of respiration for the various components of a young loblolly pine is shown in Fig. 6.9. The increases and decreases follow the curve for temperature and the temperature coefficient was calculated to be 2.9. However, the relationship involves the effects of warming and cooling on the growth cycle as well as the direct effects on the rate of respiration. Figure 6.10 shows that stem respiration is increased more by high temperature after cambial activity begins than while it is inactive. Johansson (1933) observed strong seasonal cycles in respiration of trunks and branches of conifers and hardwoods in Denmark. Maximum respiration occurred at the time of most rapid growth and the rates for hardwoods declined more rapidly in late summer than the rates for conifers. There are diurnal variations in respiration rates in tree trunks and the rate is said to be higher on the sunny side than on the shaded side of tree trunks (Geurten, 1950).

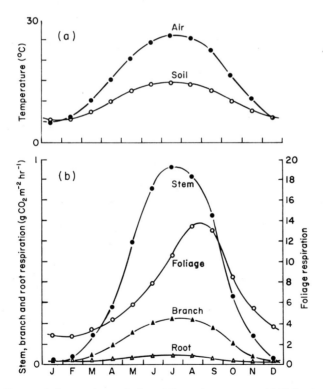

Fig. 6.9. Seasonal changes in respiration of the various organs of loblolly pine trees in a 14-year-old plantation. Note that the scale for foliage is 20 times that for the other organs, and the rates are per square meter of soil surface. From Kinerson (1975).

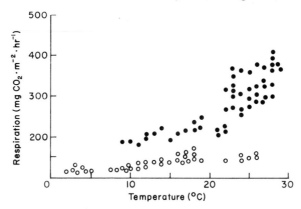

Fig. 6.10. Respiration of tree trunks at various temperatures before (open circles) and after (closed circles) the initiation of cambial activity. The average Q_{10} was calculated to be 2.9. From Kinerson (1975).

Gases in Tree Trunks

Carbon dioxide is produced by the living cells in the wood and accumulates in vessels and tracheids because the cambial region is relatively impermeable to the diffusion of gases. As a result, considerable gas accumulates in the xylem, especially in the large vessels of the earlywood, where the water columns tend to rupture when rapid transpiration causes high tension to develop in the sap. MacDougal and Working (1933) claimed that in willow water occupies the latewood and gas the earlywood of several annual rings, resulting in concentric cylinders of water-filled tissue separated by cylinders of gas-filled tissue. In pine and redwood most of the space in the bole except for the outer three or four annual rings is said to be occupied by gas.

The cylinder of cambium and sapwood is so impermeable to gas that the concentration of O_2 usually is much lower and the concentration of CO_2 much higher in the heartwood than in the outside air, at least during the growing season, as shown in Fig. 6.11. There also are large seasonal changes in composition, related to variations in metabolism, CO_2 being higher and O_2 lower during the growing season than in the winter (Fig. 6.12).

Chase (1934) reported that more CO_2 accumulates in the stems of rapidly growing trees such as cottonwood than in stems of more slowly growing species such as bur and red oak. It seems reasonable to speculate that the O_2 deficiency in the older wood has an important role in bringing about the development of heartwood.

Gas rarely accumulates in the bark because its intercellular spaces usually are connected with the outside air by lenticels. Also, the distance over which gas must diffuse to reach the cambium is quite short so the cambium is unlikely to be subjected to an oxygen deficiency.

Abnormally high gas pressures have been reported in tree stems of a number of species. Occasionally, the pressure is high enough to blow cores out of increment borers and the gas is sometimes combustible. Gas pressures also are reported in trees

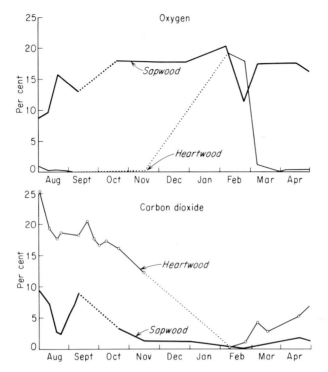

Fig. 6.11. Seasonal change in concentrations of oxygen and carbon dioxide in the heartwood and sapwood of a poplar bole. Dotted lines indicate periods when samples could not be obtained. From Chase (1934).

suffering from a disease known as "wet wood." Such pressures apparently are caused by gas produced by organisms which are decaying the wood and have nothing to do with normal respiration. However, their occurrence is evidence that the outer wood is relatively impermeable to gas, even under pressure.

Roots and Pneumatophores

The respiration of roots and other underground structures is of particular interest because they are often subjected to low concentrations of O_2. Respiration of roots and soil organisms tends to reduce the O_2 and increase the CO_2 content and flooding aggravates this situation.

Roots

The meristematic regions of roots have high rates of respiration and small roots contain large numbers of living cells. As a result they are often injured by inadequate aeration. It is well known that alcohol, lactic acid, and other incompletely oxidized substances accumulate in roots of flooded plants (Crawford, 1967; Hook and Brown,

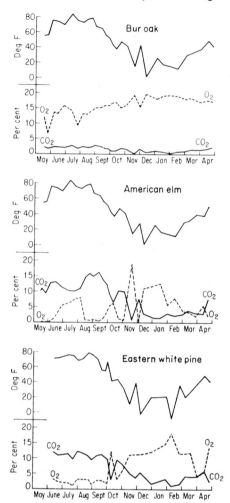

Fig. 6.12. Seasonal variation in the gas concentration in boles of three tree species. From Chase (1934).

1973). Species such as cypress, tupelo gum, willow, and mangrove, which normally grow in wet soil, are much more tolerant of inadequate aeration and flooding than species such as dogwood, tulip poplar, and sweet gum, which ordinarily grow in well-drained soil. In effect, distribution of many species is restricted by their high O_2 requirement which excludes them from areas where the soil is often saturated. There probably are two reasons why plants of some species tolerate flooding. Either their stem and root structure permits diffusion of O_2 from the shoots to the roots or the roots tolerate anaerobic respiration. Both kinds of adaptations occur in roots of some woody species, such as sweet gum (Hook and Brown, 1973). Filling with soil over the roots of trees is a common cause of death and the effects of filling on the composition of the soil gas is shown in Fig. 6.13. Toxic substances such as sulfides, methane, ferrous iron,

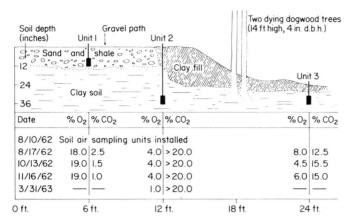

Fig. 6.13. Change in oxygen and carbon dioxide concentrations beneath soil fills of sand and clay. From Yelenosky (1964).

and other reduced compounds also accumulate in poorly aerated soil. Kawase (1974, 1976) reported that ethylene accumulates in the roots of flooded plants and diffuses upward to the shoots, where it induces the epinasty and chlorosis characteristic of flooded plants. Sanderson and Armstrong (1978) concluded that anoxia is more damaging than accumulation of toxic substances and attributed the lower flooding tolerance of Sitka spruce than of lodgepole pine to the lower internal supply of oxygen from its shoots to its roots.

According to the data summarized by Larcher (1975, p. 72) about 8% of the total respiration of a beech forest and 6% of the respiration of a tropical rain forest occur in the roots. Kinerson's (1975) data indicate that only about 3% of the respiration of a 14-year-old loblolly pine stand occurs in the roots although they contain 18 to 20% of the dry matter. Perhaps the rate of root respiration is depressed by the low oxygen concentration of the soil.

Pneumatophores

Trees of swamp habitats or those subject to tidal flooding, such as mangroves, often have specialized root systems, called "pneumatophores," which are involved in gas exchange. Mangroves of the type represented by *Avicennia nitida* may produce thousands of air roots or pneumatophores which protrude from the mud around the base of the tree (see Fig. 2.32). Scholander *et al.* (1955) reported that air is sucked in through lenticels of vertical pneumatophores in *Avicennia* when the tide falls and is forced out when the tide rises. The stilt roots of *Rhizophora mangle* have lenticels on the surface which are connected by air spaces to roots buried in the mud (see Fig. 2.32). Plugging the lenticels with grease caused the O_2 content of the roots buried in mud to decrease, indicating that the stilt roots serve as aerating mechanisms for the submerged roots (Scholander *et al.*, 1955).

Roots of cypress trees growing in frequently flooded soil develop conical, vertical growths or "knees" (see Fig. 2.33) because of active, localized cambial activity which adds thick layers of wood on upper surfaces of roots. Although many claims have been made that cypress knees, like other pneumatophores, serve as aerating organs which supply O_2 to submerged roots, the evidence that they play such a role is not convincing. If O_2 transfer commonly occurs through the knees to the root system, then when knees are detached the amount of O_2 they absorb should be immediately reduced. Kramer *et al.* (1952) found, however, that respiration in detached knees was higher than in attached knees for 2 days but then decreased with time. Because of the large amount of active cambial tissue in knees, it appears that most of the oxygen may be utilized locally and that cypress knees are not important as aerating organs. The growth of pneumatophores is discussed in Chapter 2.

Respiration of Fruits

The respiration of fruits is scientifically interesting because of the climacteric change during maturation. It also is of practical importance because the storage life of fruits depends on the control of respiration.

Respiration of Growing Fruits

The respiration of developing fruits varies considerably with the course of development. Krotkov's (1941) study of apple indicates that respiration is most rapid immediately after fruits are set and decreases rapidly during the early summer and slowly during the late summer, with a rise called the "climacteric" just after picking. These

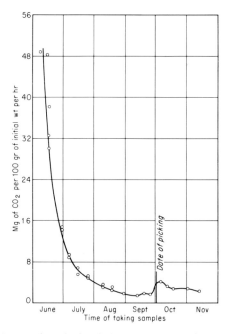

Fig. 6.14. Change in rate of respiration during development of an apple fruit. From Krotkov (1941).

data are shown in Fig. 6.14. According to Biale (1950) the climacteric phase sometimes occurs in apples while still on the trees, but never in attached avocado fruit. Apple epidermis is covered by a relatively impermeable layer of cutin which hinders gas exchange, and respiration of the internal tissues of large fruits probably is commonly limited by low O_2. Anaerobic respiration sometimes results in discoloration of the internal tissue of fruits especially apples, and also of lettuce and cabbage if stored or shipped with inadequate aeration. Fruit growth is discussed in more detail in Chapter 4.

Respiration of Harvested Fruits

Much attention has been given to the biochemistry and physiology of harvested fruit in attempts to find ways of prolonging its life in storage. The final stage of ripening of many or perhaps most fruits is characterized by a complex group of changes. This period of intense enzyme activity and increased respiration is called the climacteric. It finally terminates in the softening and deterioration of fruits, which then become increasingly susceptible to destruction by microorganisms. The rapid deterioration of fruits during senescence suggests that control over enzyme activity is lost, perhaps

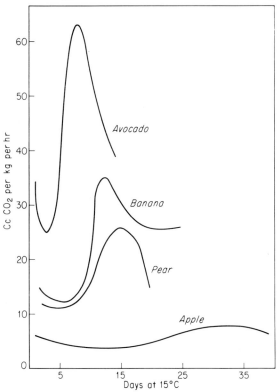

Fig. 6.15. Climacteric rise in respiration of different kinds of fruit. From Biale (1950). Reproduced with permission from the *Annual Review of Plant Physiology*, Vol. 1. © 1950 by Annual Reviews Inc.

because compartmentation is breaking down, releasing enzymes which are normally compartmented. At one time the increase in respiration was supposed to supply energy needed for ripening, but this is questionable (Sacher, 1973), and it is more probable that the increase in respiration results chiefly from biochemical changes incident to ripening which provide increased amounts of respiratory substrate. Respiration in fruits apparently occurs both by the Krebs cycle and through the pentose shunt. The complex interaction of factors which controls fruit ripening was reviewed by Coombe (1976). The climacteric burst of CO_2 production is shown by many kinds of fruit, but not usually by citrus. It occurs in avocados after they are picked, but not if they are left on the trees. Differences in the magnitude of CO_2 production during the climacteric rise are seen in Fig. 6.15. Incidentally, climacteric respiration is not inhibited by cyanide, but the cyanide resistant pathway is not essential for ripening (Theologis and Laties, 1978).

As stored fruits ripen, ethylene is evolved which in turn promotes ripening of other fruits stored in the same room; other volatile substances are produced which affect taste and odor. During senescence the mechanism controlling aerobic respiration breaks down, enzyme activity causes solubilization of cell wall pectins, cells begin to separate, and softening and physical breakdown occur. These changes also produce conditions favorable for invasion by fungi and bacteria.

Fruit Storage

Successful storage of fruits and vegetables is closely related to control of respiration, and storage at low temperatures is the simplest method of reducing the rate of respiration. However, storage of apples, pears, and other fruits and certain vegetables in refrigerated spaces sometimes is accompanied by pitting, internal browning, and other evidences of physiological breakdown (see Chapter 17). Cooling does not reduce the rates of all processes to the same degree, and injury may occur from accumulation of products of anaerobic respiration, phenol oxidase activity, and other abnormal physiological processes. Storage life in refrigeration of many plant materials can be greatly increased by lowering the O_2 concentration to 2 or 3% and increasing the CO_2 concentration to 2 to 6% or even to 20% or more in some instances. The high concentration of CO_2 not only inhibits anaerobic respiration, but also reduces ethylene injury and sometimes increases shelf life when fruit is removed from cold storage. Readers are referred to Dewey (1977) for more specific recommendations concerning the best temperatures and gas concentrations for storage of various materials. Accumulation of ethylene increases the rate of deterioration and is sometimes removed by absorption in $KMnO_4$.

Respiration of Seeds

Seeds show large changes in respiration during their ontogeny. Rates are high in the early stages of development but decrease during maturation and seeds which become dry when mature have very low rates. The respiration rate must be extremely low in seeds which remain viable in dry storage for a century or longer, *Cassia*, for example.

The low rate of respiration may result from the low water content in which case it increases immediately when water is supplied. In some instances respiration and germination are inhibited by seed coats impermeable to H_2O and O_2, and in some instances the physiological immaturity of the embryo prevents germination. This is discussed in Chapter 14, and the development, storage, and germination of seeds are discussed in detail in the three volumes of *"Seed Biology"* edited by Kozlowski (1972c).

Germination is always accompanied by a large increase in rate of respiration, at least partly because hydrolytic processes make more sugar available as a substrate. The oxidation of food in respiration causes a measurable decrease in the dry weight of germinating seeds, in spite of the increase in fresh weight caused by development of the seedling. Increase in dry weight cannot occur until the leaves expand to the point where the weight of dry matter produced by photosynthesis exceeds that destroyed by respiration. Seed germination is discussed in Chapter 14.

FACTORS AFFECTING RESPIRATION

In simplest terms the success of trees and other plants depends on the relative rates of respiration and photosynthesis. The rate of respiration is influenced by several internal and environmental factors which often interact. Among the important internal factors are age and physiological condition of tissues, amount of oxidizable substrate, and hydration. Environmental factors include soil and air temperature; gaseous composition of the soil; available soil moisture; light; injury and mechanical disturbances; and chemicals such as herbicides, fungicides, insecticides, and fertilizers.

Age and Physiological Condition of Tissues

Young tissues with a large proportion of protoplasm to cell wall material and few dead cells have a higher respiration rate than mature tissue which contains less physiologically active material. For example, respiration of small twigs is more rapid per unit of dry weight than respiration of branches, and respiration of young leaves is more rapid than respiration of older leaves. It was mentioned earlier that respiration of buds increases severalfold when growth begins and decreases equally rapidly when growth ceases. Figure 6.10 showed the large increase in stem respiration after cambial activity begins.

Available Substrate

The law of mass action applies to respiration, hence an increase in the amount of oxidizable substrate usually results in a higher rate of respiration. This is very noticeable in ripening fruits in which the conversion of starch to sugar is accompanied by an increase in the rate of respiration. The high carbohydrate concentration of the youngest sapwood may be a factor in its high rate of respiration (see Fig. 6.8).

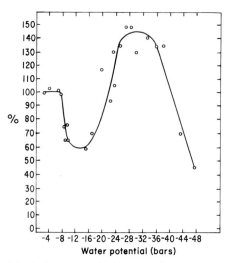

Fig. 6.16. Effects of dehydration on respiration rate of loblolly pine. Water stress is expressed as leaf water potential, rate of respiration as percentage of rate when soil was at field capacity. From Brix (1962).

Hydration

Within limits the rate of respiration is correlated with the water content. This is particularly conspicuous for dry seeds, where the rate of respiration decreases as the seeds mature and become dry, but increases immediately when the seeds are wetted. In general, respiration is somewhat reduced by water stress, as reported by Kozlowski and Gentile (1958) for eastern white pine buds, but a few exceptions are reported. Parker (1952) reported that if conifer twigs and needles are severely dehydrated there is a temporary increase in respiration followed by a decrease. Brix (1962) reported a similar phenomenon in loblolly pine, shown in Fig. 6.16. Bunce and Miller (1976) reported that water stress increased respiration in the light for several woody species from dry habitats, but decreased it in species from moist habitats.

Soil Moisture

There may be unfavorable effects from either a deficit or an excess of soil water. The effects of excesses have already been discussed under root respiration. Shoots suffer long before roots from a deficiency of soil water. According to Schneider and Childers (1941), when soil moisture dropped much below field capacity respiration of apple leaves increased, although photosynthesis and transpiration decreased. The highest respiration occurred when transpiration and photosynthesis were lowest and the leaves were beginning to wilt. It is possible that the increase in respiration occurred because dehydration favored conversion of starch to sugar, providing more substrate, but this is conjecture. When the soil was rewatered to field capacity, respiration decreased to normal. Flooding apple trees also caused leaf water deficits and increased respiration (Childers and White, 1942).

Soil and Air Temperatures

The rate of respiration is greatly influenced by temperature and therefore varies with changes in soil and air temperatures, as was indicated in Figs. 6.9 and 6.10. The effects of temperature on processes often are indicated by their Q_{10} which refers to the ratio of the rate at temperature T to the rate at temperature T-10°. If the rate doubles the Q_{10} is 2. Kinerson (1975) calculated the Q_{10} for the stems of loblolly pine trees to be 2.9. Foote and Schaedle (1976) found measurable respiration in stems of trembling aspen at $-11°C$, the lowest temperature used, but no photosynthesis below $-3°C$. These results are similar to those reported for conifers, in which output of CO_2 began when the stems were warmed to about 3°C, possibly because the cortical cells thawed at this temperature. The seasonal course of respiration and photosynthesis for aspen twigs is shown in Fig. 6.17.

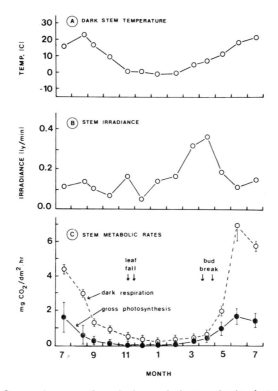

Fig. 6.17. Seasonal course of respiration and photosynthesis of stems of *Populus tremuloides*. Individual measurements indicated that respiration occurred down to $-11°C$, the lowest temperature during the study. No measurable photosynthesis occurred below $-3°C$. From Foot and Schaedle (1976).

An injurious increase in respiration may occur at high temperatures because the optimum temperature for photosynthesis usually is lower than the optimum for respiration. For example, increasing the temperature of red and white pine from 20° to 40°C greatly decreased the net photosynthesis and reduced the ability of trees of these species to accumulate carbohydrates (Decker, 1944).

Low temperature increases the storage life of fruits and vegetables because it reduces the rates of respiration and other physiological processes. As mentioned earlier in the section on Fruit Storage, the effectiveness of low temperature for storage of some fruits and vegetables can be increased by use of an atmosphere low in oxygen and high in carbon dioxide.

Composition of the Atmosphere

There is no significant variation in the O_2 concentration of the atmosphere, but O_2 concentration often becomes a limiting factor in tree stems and in the interior of buds, fruits, and seeds. The inner phloem is probably well supplied with O_2 by inward diffusion through lenticels and cracks in the outer bark. However, diffusion of O_2 is drastically reduced in solution, and respiration of tissues within the cambium must often be reduced by low O_2 concentration. Experiments by Pollock (1953) showed that a higher than normal concentration did not increase respiration of dormant buds, but did increase it in growing buds (Fig. 6.18).

Effects of inadequate soil aeration were discussed in the section on Root Respiration. Respiration of roots and soil organisms tends to reduce the O_2 and increase the CO_2 concentration, and the deviation from normal usually increases with depth and is greater in the summer than in the winter. Flooding of the soil in the winter therefore is

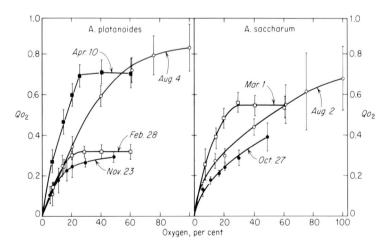

Fig. 6.18. Effects of season and external oxygen concentration on oxygen uptake by maple buds at 25°C. Oxygen uptake (Q O_2) is expressed in microliters of oxygen per milligram dry weight per hour. From Pollock (1953).

less injurious than flooding in the summer. Leyton and Rousseau (1958) found that respiration of excised root tips of several coniferous species was reduced in 5% O_2 to about one-half of the rate in 20% O_2, but root growth was reduced to 20% of the control rate. Coniferous roots died in 2 days in an unaerated medium, but willow roots lived and made 50% of the normal rate of growth. Leyton and Rousseau suggested that willow roots obtain O_2 from the shoots, a suggestion made long ago by Cannon (1932) and more recently with respect to tupelo-gum by Hook and Brown (1973).

Filling in with soil over established root systems often injures or kills trees and shrubs by reducing the O_2 supply to the roots (see Fig. 6.13). Arborists sometimes install wells, tile, and gravel fills to increase gas exchange. Some species are more tolerant than others of filling, presumably because their roots are more tolerant of a reduced oxygen concentration.

Inadequate aeration of roots produces a series of metabolic disturbances and root growth and mineral and water absorption are usually reduced. Decreased water absorption often produces water stress in the shoots which reduces photosynthesis and increases respiration. Decreased nitrification reduces the nitrogen supply and the overall effect is to reduce growth and vigor or even to cause death.

Injuries and Mechanical Stimuli

Handling, rubbing, and bending leaves often cause large increases in rate of respiration, as shown in Fig. 6.19. This suggests that care should be taken to avoid rough handling of plant tissue before measuring respiration and perhaps some other processes. Wounding, such as slicing fruits or cutting out a block of bark or wood, usually

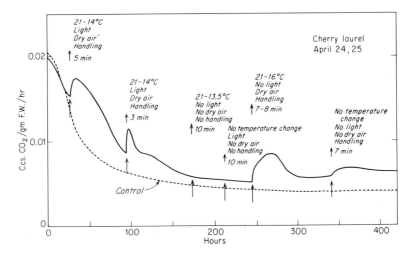

Fig. 6.19. Effects of mechanical disturbance on respiration of cherry laurel leaves. The controls were disturbed as little as possible, the other group was subjected to some handling during measurements. From Godwin (1935).

is accompanied by an increase in respiration which may be explained in several ways. Removal of a piece of tissue increases the supply of O_2 to the exposed surfaces. It also disrupts the compartmentation which normally exists in cells and releases both enzymes and substrates. For example, the browning of cut surfaces of plant tissue results from the oxidation of phenolic compounds exposed to the action of phenol oxidases released by cell damage. Attacks by fungi sometimes cause an increase in rate of respiration, but little is known about the mechanism (see Daley, 1976).

Chemicals

Respiration is sensitive to a variety of chemicals which inhibit various stages of the overall process. For example, fluoride blocks the conversion of phosphoglyceric acid to phosphoenolpyruvic acid, and specific steps in the Krebs cycle are blocked by fluoroacetate and malonate. Antimycin A blocks between cytochromes b and c, and inhibitors such as cyanide, azide, and carbon monoxide block the final stage in electron transport (see Fig. 6.2). In some plant tissues there is a considerable fraction of respiration which is resistant to cyanide and other terminal inhibitors, indicating that there must be an alternate pathway for electron transport which bypasses the cytochromes or at least cytochrome oxidase (see Fig. 6.2). Cyanide-resistant respiration also increases in some storage tissues when incubated aerobically. This is discussed by Ikuma (1972). No data on cyanide-resistant respiration in woody tissues are available. Solomis (1977) recently reviewed this topic.

In general the respiratory pathway is similar in plant and animal tissue and both generally respond to the same inhibitors, but there are some differences. For example, rotenone is a powerful inhibitor of electron transport in animal mitochondria, but relatively ineffective in plants. The limited data available indicate no differences between woody and herbaceous species in their reaction to respiratory inhibitors (Barnes, 1958). There may be some differences in respiratory pathways in seedlings and older tissue which cause differences in reaction to inhibitors, but little information is available on this point.

Some herbicides greatly increase the rate of respiration and it is affected by various insecticides, fungicides, and other chemicals. Air pollutants such as SO_2 and the constituents of smog also affect respiration. This is discussed in Chapter 17.

ASSIMILATION

The term ''assimilation'' as used here refers to the conversion of food, that is, carbohydrates, fats, and proteins, into new tissue. Not only does this require large amounts of energy supplied by respiration, but it also uses materials synthesized in various parts of the respiratory cycle. Reference to Fig. 6.20 indicates that nucleic acids and nucleotides, amino acids, fatty acids, and other substances important in the metabolism of plants originate in different parts of the respiratory cycle. Many of the metabolic pathways in the synthesis and degradation of these substances pass through

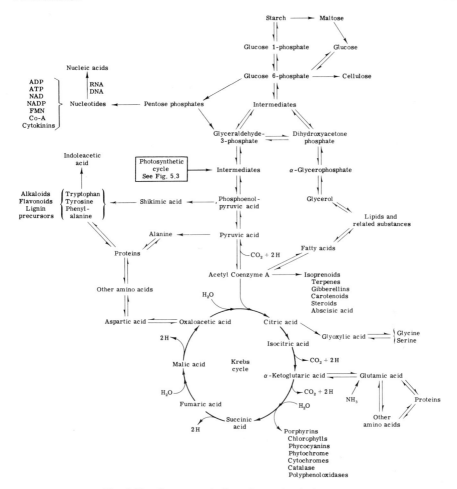

Fig. 6.20. Some metabolic pathways in plants.

acetyl coenzyme A, which is the crossroads for a variety of important metabolic reactions.

Assimilation is an integral part of growth and it therefore is most conspicuous in meristematic regions such as the cambia and root and stem tips. The simple carbohydrates translocated to these meristematic regions are converted into cellulose, pectic compounds, and lignin in the cell walls and the amino acids and amides into the protein framework and enzymes of new protoplasm. The existing protoplasm not only produces new protoplasm and new cell walls, but a wide variety of other substances such as organic nitrogen compounds; chlorophyll, the carotenoids and other pigments; lipids and isoprene derivatives such as essential oils, oleoresins, and rubber; sterols; tannins; alkaloids; hormones; and numerous other compounds. Most of these play important roles in plant metabolism, but some, such as the alkaloids and rubber, seem to have no

TABLE 6.2 Chemical Composition of Shoots of Loblolly Pine as Percentages of Oven Dry Weight[a]

Constituents	Percent of dry weight
Nitrogenous compounds	8.4
Amino acids	(7.2)
Protein	(90.7)
Nucleic acids	(2.1)
Carbohydrates	38.0
Reducing sugars	(5.1)
Sucrose	(8.2)
Cellulose	(56.0)
Hemicelluloses	(25.7)
Pectin	(5.0)
Lipids	5.3
Fatty acids and resin acids	(74.8)
Glycerols	(6.0)
Unsaponifiable	(19.2)
Lignin	23.3
Organic acids	3.5
Shikimic	(48.7)
Quinic	(51.3)
Phenolics	20.0
Minerals	1.5

[a] From Chung and Barnes (1977). Numbers in parentheses are subfraction percentages of major fractions.

known essential functions in plants. The origin of some of these compounds is shown in Fig. 6.20.

Table 6.2 shows the approximate chemical composition of the shoots (needles and adjacent twig) of loblolly pine, expressed as percentage of total dry weight. The composition is about what might be expected, except for the high percentage of phenolics which is surprising in view of the high energy requirement for their synthesis and the uncertainty concerning their usefulness. The relative amounts of substrate used and CO_2 produced per gram of each of the major constituents is shown in Table 6.3. The amounts of substrate required and CO_2 released increase with the degree to which a compound is reduced, because more energy is required to produce highly reduced compounds such as lipids and phenolics. For example, synthesis of 1 g of carbohydrate requires about 1.2 g of glucose and 0.11 g of O_2 with 0.149 g of CO_2 being released, but synthesis of 1 g of highly reduced lipid requires 3.0 g of glucose and 0.3 g of O_2 with 1.5 g of CO_2 being released. Synthesis of lignin also is expensive in terms of the amount of carbohydrate used.

The course of assimilation and the kinds of substances produced are controlled by the enzymes present. These in turn are controlled by heredity, although the amounts and kinds of enzymes present may be modified by the environment. Various plant

TABLE 6.3 Amounts of Substrate Used and CO_2 Produced during Synthesis of the Principal Constituents of the Shoots of Loblolly Pine[a,b]

	Substrate used		By-products	
Constituents	Glucose	O_2	CO_2	H_2O
Nitrogenous compounds	1.58	0.28	0.40	0.65
Carbohydrates	1.18	0.11	0.13	0.16
Lipids	3.02	0.30	1.50	0.82
Lignin	1.90	0.04	0.27	0.66
Organic acids	1.48	0.35	0.48	0.35
Phenolics	1.92	0.37	0.56	0.73

[a] Amounts are in grams per gram of constituent.
[b] From Chung and Barnes (1977).

families produce characteristic chemical compounds. For example, each species of pine produces its own characteristic oleoresins, and there are sometimes differences among geographic races (Mirov, 1954; Zobel, 1951). Various attempts have been made to correlate plant classification with chemical composition (Gibbs, 1958, 1974; Fairbrothers, *et al.*, 1975, for example). Use of chemical tests to identify cultivars is discussed briefly in Chapter 8.

GENERAL REFERENCES

Becker, W. M. (1977). "Energy and the Living Cell." Lippincott, Philadelphia, Pennsylvania.
Beevers, H. (1961). "Respiratory Metabolism in Plants." Harper, New York.
Bonner, W. D., Jr. (1973). Mitochondria and plant respiration. *Phytochemistry* **3**, 221–261.
Forward, D. F. (1965). The respiration of bulky organs. *Plant Physiol.* **4**, 311–378.
Ikuma, H. (1972). Electron transport in plant respiration. *Annu. Rev. Plant Physiol.* **23**, 419–436.
Lehninger, A. L. (1971). "Bioenergetics." Benjamin, Menlo Park, California.
Yemm, E. W. (1965). The respiration of plants, and their organs. *Plant Physiol.* **4**, 231–310.

7

Carbohydrates

INTRODUCTION

Carbohydrates are of special importance because they are direct products of photosynthesis and are, therefore, the primary energy storage compounds and the basic organic substances from which most other organic compounds found in plants are synthesized. Carbohydrates also are the chief constituents of cell walls; they are the starting point for the synthesis of fats and proteins; large amounts are oxidized in respiration (see Chapter 6); another fraction is accumulated as reserve foods; and still another fraction is variously lost from plants. Soluble carbohydrates increase the osmotic pressure of the cell sap, and such carbohydrates as the pentosans, pectic compounds, gums, and mucilages increase the water-holding capacity of tissues. Quantitatively, carbohydrates are the most important constituents of woody plants, comprising about three-fourths of their dry weight. This chapter deals with the kinds of carbohydrates found in woody plants, their uses, accumulation, and losses.

258

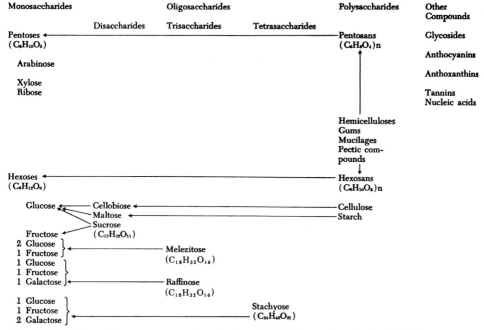

Fig. 7.1. Relationships among some important carbohydrates and products of their hydrolysis.

KINDS OF CARBOHYDRATES

Carbohydrates are made up of carbon, hydrogen, and oxygen in accordance with or approximating the empirical formula $(CH_2O)n$. Many carbohydrates also contain other elements such as phosphorus or nitrogen. The carbohydrates can be classified in three main groups: monosaccharides, oligosaccharides, and polysaccharides. Fig. 7.1 shows the classification of the more important carbohydrates.

Monosaccharides

The monosaccharides include simple sugars and their derivatives. They are the basic carbohydrate units from which more complex compounds are formed. Monosaccharides consist of carbon atoms to which are attached hydrogen atoms, a hydroxyl group, and either an aldehyde $(-\overset{\text{O}}{\overset{\|}{C}}-H)$ or ketone $(-\overset{}{\underset{\text{O}}{\overset{\|}{C}}}-R)$ group. The number of carbon atoms in monosaccharides varies from three to eight, but the most common number is five (e.g., pentoses, $C_5H_{10}O_5$) or six (e.g., hexoses, $C_6H_{12}O_6$). Monosaccharides do not yield smaller molecular weight sugars on hydrolysis.

Many simple sugars occur in woody plants, usually in very small amounts, probably because of their rapid incorporation into polysaccharides. Exceptions are the six-carbon sugars, glucose and fructose. Glucose is present in large amounts, especially in certain fruits, and probably occurs in every living cell. Fructose is also common and abundant, although it usually occurs in lower concentrations than glucose. Glucose and fructose not only occur in living cells but also in the xylem sap of certain trees such as maples and birches (see Chapter 11). Derivatives of glucose and fructose which have been phosphorylated, i.e., have had phosphate groups attached to them, form the starting point for many metabolic transformations of carbohydrates (see Fig. 6.20). Some of the hexose sugars occur chiefly in their condensed forms, for example, galactose and mannose as galactans and mannans.

Although only traces of pentose sugars are found free in plants, their condensation products, the pentosans, are important constituents of cell walls. The pentose sugars, arabinose and xylose, rarely occur free but are often present as parts of cell wall polymers, the arabans and xylans. Ribose, another pentose sugar, also occurs in a combined form as a constituent of such nucleotide coenzymes as ATP, NAD, NADP, FAD, and coenzyme A. Ribose also is found as a part of ribonucleic acid (RNA). Deoxyribose occurs as part of the nucleotides comprising deoxyribonucleic acid (DNA).

Many of the monosaccharides are found in the Calvin–Benson dark cycle of photosynthesis and in the pentose shunt of respiration. Glucose is the principal compound produced in the former and serves the latter. The pentose, ribulose 1–5 bisphosphate (RuBP), produces the binding site for CO_2 in photosynthesis. Both cycles, but especially the pentose shunt, are the source of pentose and many other monosaccharides found as parts of the more complex molecules present in plants.

Oligosaccharides

The oligosaccharides consist of linkages of two or more molecules of monosaccharides. The major oligosaccharides include disaccharides (e.g., sucrose, maltose), trisaccharides (e.g., raffinose, melezitose), and tetrasaccharides (e.g., stachyose). The disaccharide sucrose is considered the most important oligosaccharide in plants because of its high concentration in cells, its wide distribution, and its metabolic importance. Together with starch, sucrose is a major reserve carbohydrate. In many plants sucrose represents over 95% of the dry weight of translocated material in the sieve tubes of the phloem. Maltose also is common, but it usually occurs in lower concentrations than sucrose.

Sugars other than sucrose and maltose often are found in variable amounts. For example, small amounts of the higher oligosaccharides of the raffinose family (raffinose, stachyose, and verbascose) are found in sieve tubes of certain plants. These sugars are all related and consist of sucrose with variable numbers of galactose units attached (Fig. 7.2). Whereas sugars of the raffinose family are relatively unimportant in most plants, they are of considerable importance in a few families of plants, including the Bignoniaceae, Celastraceae, Combretaceae, Myrtaceae, Oleaceae, and Verbenaceae (Zimmermann, 1957).

The types of carbohydrates often vary in different tissues. For example, Dietrichs and Schaich (1965) reported that the carbohydrates in beech included sucrose, glucose,

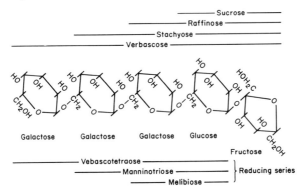

Fig. 7.2. The raffinose family of oligosaccharides. From Zimmermann and Brown (1971).

fructose, maltose (or cellobiose), raffinose, stachyose, and five unidentified ketoses. Sucrose, glucose, and fructose were the main sugars throughout the tree. Raffinose and sometimes stachyose occurred in the buds and young leaves. Phloem sap contained mostly sucrose, with some raffinose and traces of fructose.

Polysaccharides

The most important polysaccharides in trees are cellulose and starch. Cellulose is the most abundant organic compound. Of some 30 billion tons of carbon that are converted into organic compounds by plants, about one-third is transformed into cellulose (Albersheim, 1965). Cellulose is the chief constituent of the cell walls which form the framework of woody plants. Each cellulose molecule consists of at least 3,000 glucose residues linked together by oxygen bridges between the 1 and 4 carbon atoms of adjacent molecules to form long, straight, unbranched chains (Fig. 7.3). The chains are packed together into micelles, which in turn are organized into microfibrils. The spaces in pure cellulose walls, such as those of cotton fibers, are occupied by water but become partly filled with lignin in woody tissue and with pectin compounds, cutin, or suberin if these substances are present. Among the notable characteristics of cellulose are its insolubility in water and organic solvents as well as its high resistance to both chemical and enzymatic degradation. The breakdown of cellulose to glucose requires two enzymes: (1) cellulase, which catalyzes the formation of cellobiose; and (2) cellobiase, which carries the digestion further to glucose.

Starch is the most abundant reserve carbohydrate in woody plants. Starch grains cannot pass from cell to cell; hence starch must have been synthesized in those tissues where it is found. It is formed by the condensation of hundreds of glucose molecules into long, spiraled chains. As in cellulose the glucose residues are linked together by oxygen bridges between the 1 and 4 carbon atoms, but starch has an α linkage while cellulose has a β linkage. Unlike cellulose, starch is readily degraded enzymatically and is thus available in metabolic processes. Starch consists of two components which differ in some physical properties. The most abundant component of most starch is amylopectin, which consists of very long molecules with numerous branched side

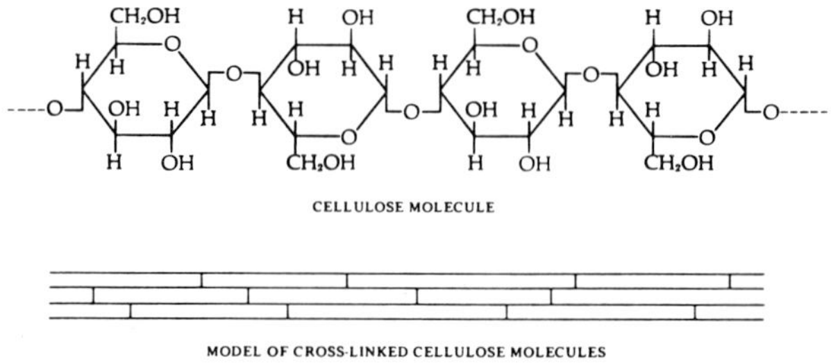

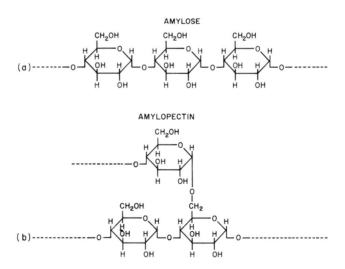

Fig. 7.3. Structure of cellulose, consisting of alternating α and β glucose units. The OH groups which project from both sides of the chain form hydrogen bonds with neighboring OH groups, resulting in bundles of cross-linked parallel chains.

chains. The other component is amylose, which consists of unbranched chains containing 300 to 1,000 residues (Fig. 7.4). Amylose gives a deeper blue color with iodine and is more water soluble and more viscous than amylopectin. Starch accumulates in definite grains formed of many layers which give them a laminated appearance. Starch grains often occur in living cells (axial and ray parenchyma) of the sapwood of woody plants. They also occur in the living phloem cells of the inner bark. The amount of starch in the woody structure of trees varies seasonally, as will become apparent later. Starch grains also occur in large numbers in the living cells of almost all leaves.

Hemicelluloses comprise a somewhat poorly defined group of polysaccharides that occur in all woody tissues. They include arabans, xylans, galactans, and mannans.

Fig. 7.4. Structure of starch: (a) Amylose; (b) amylopectin.

Unlike cellulose, hemicelluloses are soluble in dilute acids and alkalies and they are sometimes digested and used as reserve foods. Hemicelluloses occur in some seeds, including those of persimmon and certain palms, and they are digested and used during germination. There is some debate concerning the extent to which the hemicelluloses found in cell walls of the woody structure are used as reserve food.

Pectin compounds are hydrophilic substances that occur in the middle lamella and in the primary walls of cells, especially in fruits, but are not present in woody tissues in large amounts. Gums and mucilages are compound carbohydrates that somewhat resemble pectic compounds. Spruce gum is a well known example. Examples of mucilages are the slimy substance from the inner bark of slippery elm and the sticky substances found in the seed pods of the carob and honey locust. The well-known gum arabic, also known as gum acacia, comes from the African acacia, and most readers are familiar with the gum that exudes from wounds in the stems of cherry, peach, and plum trees.

In prunes, peaches, citrus, and some other trees, excessive gum formation as a result of wounding is called gummosis. It is caused by hydrolysis of cell wall constituents. This gum is quite different chemically from the resin released by wounded conifers.

CARBOHYDRATE TRANSFORMATIONS

Many of the carbohydrates found in plants are continually undergoing conversion from one form to another or are being transformed into compounds used in respiration or synthesis of fats, proteins, and other noncarbohydrates (see Fig. 6.20).

Starch–sucrose conversions in both vegetative and reproductive tissues occur commonly. In developing seeds, for example, there is a period during which sugars, principally sucrose, are converted to starch. In a number of ripening fruits starches are converted to sugars. When plants are exposed to $^{14}CO_2$, radioactive carbon is rapidly incorporated into a wide variety of carbohydrates, organic acids, and other compounds. A few examples will be given.

After a 1-min exposure of grand fir shoots to $^{14}CO_2$, about 50% of the label was in sugars and starch and 30 to 40% in phosphoglyceric acid (PGA) (Miliszewski and Levanty, 1972). When Shiroya *et al.* (1962a) exposed eastern white pine seedlings to $^{14}CO_2$ for 8 hr, about 98% of the ethanol-soluble ^{14}C was in the sugar fraction and the remaining 2% was equally divided between amino acids and organic acids. Sucrose formed about 75% of the sugar fraction, and glucose and fructose comprised an additional 20%. Only small amounts of raffinose were found. At various times during the year Nelson (1964) exposed 3-year-old eastern white pine seedlings to $^{14}CO_2$ for 1 hr followed by 8 hrs of assimilation in air. The bulk of ^{14}C recovered from roots was in sugars. Sucrose was the main sugar recovered at all seasons, accounting for 79% of the sugars in April, 89% in May, 94% in July, 86% in August, and 88% in October. Raffinose accounted for up to 16% of the sugars in April and up to 6% in October, with none detected in July. Glucose and fructose were present in small amounts throughout the year, usually from 2 to 5% each. Trip *et al.* (1963) illuminated detached leaves from 20 species of plants in $^{14}CO_2$ and found radioactive carbon in the following compounds: mannitol in four species, verbascose in three, stachyose in nine, raffinose in 16, melibiose in two, maltose in 15, sucrose in 20, galactose in eight, glucose in 17, and fructose in 12.

Phosphorylation

The first step in many carbohydrate transformations is phosphorylation, a process in which monosaccharide sugars react with ATP (adenosine triphosphate) to form phosphate esters, while ATP is converted to ADP (adenosine disphosphate). A sugar, for example, may be converted to another sugar by the following general scheme.

$$\text{Sugar A} + \text{ATP} \xrightarrow{\text{Enzyme A}} \text{Sugar A-phosphate} + \text{ADP}$$

$$\text{Sugar A-phosphate} \xrightarrow{\text{Enzyme B}} \text{Sugar B-phosphate}$$

A specific example is the conversion of glucose to glucose-6-phosphate and then to fructose-6-phosphate:

Glucose	Glucose-6-phosphate	Fructose-6-phosphate

Phosphorylated monosaccharides are among the primary products of photosynthesis. They are directly involved in chemical reactions or converted to translocated and accumulated forms. Starches accumulate whenever a high level of sugars occurs and are transformed to sugars when sugar concentrations are low. At low temperatures the equilibrium is shifted in favor of sugars.

Phosphate esters are particularly important since they are intermediate in the synthesis and degradation of starch and sucrose. They also are substrates in glycolysis, the fermentation of sugars, photosynthetic CO_2 fixation, and in a number of oxidative processes. In addition, phosphate esters are constituents of nucleic acids and coenzymes.

The important carbohydrate transformations are not limited to the sugars. For example, sugars may be converted to alcohols, as in the formation of sorbitol and mannitol from glucose and mannose.

Sucrose

The formation of sucrose from glucose and fructose may take place when one of the sugar units occurs as a sugar–nucleotide complex. For example, glucose in the form of uridine diphosphoglucose (UDPG) may react with fructose to form sucrose.

$$\text{UDP-D-glucose} + \text{D-fructose} \rightleftarrows \text{sucrose} + \text{UDP}$$

UDPG may also react with fructose-6-phosphate to form sucrose phosphate which in turn is hydrolyzed by a phosphatase, resulting in formation of free sucrose (Hassid, 1969).

$$\text{UDP-D-glucose} + \text{D-fructose-6-phosphate} \rightleftarrows \text{sucrose phosphate} + \text{UDP}$$

Sucrose yields glucose and fructose when hydrolyzed. The reaction is catalyzed by sucrase and is not reversible.

$$\text{C}_{12}\,\text{H}_{22}\,\text{O}_{11} + \text{H}_2\text{O} \xrightarrow{\text{sucrase}} \text{C}_6\,\text{H}_{12}\,\text{O}_6 + \text{C}_6\,\text{H}_{12}\,\text{O}_6$$

| Sucrose | | Glucose | Fructose |

Starch

The synthesis of starch occurs in several ways. Perhaps the most important are the following: (1) phosphorylase reaction, which involves the joining together of glucose-1-phosphate units until a starch molecule is formed according to the following scheme (Meyer *et al.*, 1973).

$$\text{Glucose-1-phosphate} + \text{glucose chain } (n \text{ units}) \xrightarrow[\rightleftarrows]{\text{Phosphorylase}} \text{glucose chain } (n + 1 \text{ units}) + \text{phosphate}$$

(2) Uridine diphosphate glucose (UDPG) pathway:

$$\text{Glucose-1-phosphate} + \text{UTP} \xrightarrow{\text{pyrophosphorylase}} \text{UDPG} + \text{pyrophosphate}$$
$$\text{UDPG} + \text{glucose chain } (n \text{ units}) \xrightarrow{\text{transglucosylase}} \text{UDP} + \text{glucose chain } (n + 1 \text{ units})$$

(3) adenosine diphosphate glucose (ADPG) pathway:

$$\text{Glucose-1-phosphate} + \text{ATP} \xrightarrow{\text{pyrophosphorylase}} \text{ADPG} + \text{pyrophosphate}$$
$$\text{ADPG} + \text{glucose chain } (n \text{ units}) \xrightarrow{\text{transglucosylase}} \text{ADP} + \text{glucose chain } (n + 1 \text{ units})$$

Starch is degraded to sugar by two separate reactions involving phosphorylases or hydrolases. The reaction involving phosphorylase predominates in tissues that do not have a major food storage role.

Hydrolases are found in highest concentrations in tissues having a major food storage function. The hydrolase reaction involves starch digestion by means of the breaking of bonds together with the incorporation of water. The maltase reaction involves hydrolysis of starch to glucose via intermediate products.

$$Starch \rightarrow Dextrins \rightarrow Maltose \rightarrow Glucose$$

Starch is degraded to maltose by α-amylase and β-amylase, both of which act on amylose and amylopectin. The final conversion of maltose to glucose is accomplished by the enzyme maltase.

USES OF CARBOHYDRATES

The carbohydrates formed by photosynthesis have several possible roles. A very large fraction is used in growth, being translocated to the stem and root tips, the cambium, and reproductive structures, where it is converted into new protoplasm, cell walls, and other products of metabolism. Another fraction is accumulated as reserve food and eventually is used in growth. A considerable amount of carbohydrate is oxidized in respiration, releasing the energy needed in the synthetic processes associated with growth (see Chapter 6). Carbohydrates may be translocated to neighboring plants through root grafts and sometimes to hemi- and holoparasites (see Chapter 11). Some carbohydrates are lost by leaching and volatilization from leaves and by exudation from roots. According to Tukey (1970), as much as 800 kg of carbohydrates per hectare may be lost annually by leaching from leaves of apple trees. By comparison, carbohydrate losses in root exudation are small. Some carbohydrates are diverted to symbionts, such as mycorrhizae and nitrogen-fixing bacteria. Mycorrhizae absorb sucrose, glucose, and fructose from the host plant and convert these to carbohydrate forms such as mannitol, trehalose, and glycogen that cannot be reabsorbed by the host (Harley, 1969). Harley (1971) estimated that up to 10% of the annual potential wood production in a spruce forest was diverted to production of fruiting bodies of mycorrhizal fungi. It should be remembered, however, that the benefits derived by mycorrhizal woody plants in enhanced nutrient uptake also are high (Marks and Kozlowski, 1973).

The proportions of the carbohydrate pool that are used in various ways differ greatly among species and different conditions. Heinicke (1937b) estimated that about 35% of the total carbohydrate supply goes into fruits, 45% into vegetative growth, and 18% into respiration. By comparison, Larcher (1975) estimated that about 35% of the photosynthate of beech trees in Denmark is used in growth, 45% in respiration, and 20% is lost by shedding of leaves, twigs, and other plant parts. As was pointed out in Chapter 6, a higher proportion of the photosynthate is lost in respiration by tropical trees than by those of the temperate zone.

The relative proportions of carbohydrates used in growth of the crown, stem, and root system varies with plant age. In old trees more of the dry weight is in the main stem and proportionally less in the crown and root system. Roots of young Scotch pine trees accounted for almost one-half the total weight of the plant, but in old trees the proportion was much lower (Ovington, 1957).

Growth

Both reserve and currently produced carbohydrates are used in growth. When growth begins in the spring, carbohydrate reserves in both roots and shoots are depleted (Priestley, 1962a,b) by translocation to growing tissues. The various carbohydrate sinks generally first deplete the carbohydrate reserves that are close to the site of utilization. Because various parts of trees grow at different rates and at different times of the year, the utilization of carbohydrates is extremely variable over the tree axis (Kozlowski and Keller, 1966). For example, shoot expansion of most species utilizes carbohydrates for a shorter part of the year than does cambial growth in the same tree (see Chapter 3), and seasonal duration of root elongation is greater than that of either cambial growth or shoot expansion. Hence, it depletes carbohydrates for a very long time. The rate and duration of carbohydrate depletion by cambial growth along the stem, branches, and major roots also vary considerably.

The percentage of the total available carbohydrate supply that is diverted for producing new tissues varies with species and from year to year. The large annual variations in the amount of food used in vegetative growth of trees of a given species often are related to the irregularity of reproductive growth.

During years of heavy fruiting or seed production, a very large percentage of the carbohydrate supply is diverted from vegetative to reproductive growth (Fig. 7.5). In trees such as peach in which fruit production is not strongly biennial, the relative allocation of photosynthate to vegetative and reproductive growth changes progressively with tree age. Vegetative growth of peach trees up to the first year of fruit production (6 years) was rapid (Chalmers and van den Ende, 1975). Thereafter, vegetative growth declined at an accelerating rate, and fruit production increased. The diver-

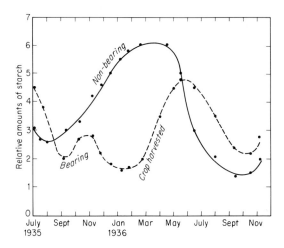

Fig. 7.5. Effect of bearing fruit on the starch content of evergreen avocado trees. From Cameron and Borst (1938).

sion of photosynthate to fruit growth was largely from the roots and main stem, leaf and shoot growth being little reduced. Hence, a strong competitive source–sink relationship developed as soon as the trees began to produce fruit and intensified thereafter. Source–sink relations are discussed in more detail in Chapter 11.

ACCUMULATION OF CARBOHYDRATES

The topic of food accumulation rarely receives much space in textbooks of plant physiology. This is unfortunate because accumulation of a reserve of food materials each growing season is essential for survival of perennial plants in regions with winters too cold for photosynthesis. This is particularly true in deciduous woody plants, where maintenance of life during the winter and resumption of growth in the spring depend on food accumulated during the previous growing season. Although starch is the main storage product in woody plants, other substances also are stored. These include fats, nitrogen compounds, sucrose, raffinose, fructosans, and hemicelluloses. This section will discuss the forms, places, and times of carbohydrate accumulation and utilization. The accumulation and use of reserve fats and proteins will be discussed in Chapters 8 and 9.

The carbohydrate economy of a woody plant can be expressed as follows:

Income = carbohydrates manufactured by photosynthesis
Expenditures = carbohydrates used in assimilation and respiration
Balance = carbohydrates accumulated

Carbohydrate Distribution

Carbohydrate reserves are accumulated largely in parenchyma cells and death of cells is accompanied by incorporation or withdrawal of reserves (Ziegler, 1964). Many studies have been made of the accumulation of starch and sugars in different tissues and organs. As might be expected, there are marked variations in the amounts of carbohydrates in various parts of woody plants and there are also large seasonal variations in amounts and kinds of carbohydrates present. There also are differences between deciduous and evergreen species and between temperate and tropical species in seasonal variations in carbohydrate accumulation.

It is important to distinguish between the total amount and concentration of carbohydrates in different parts of plants. Carbohydrate distribution often is expressed in percent of dry weight in various tissues. This may be misleading because high concentrations of carbohydrates often occur in tissues that comprise a low proportion of the total dry weight of a plant. For example, in both young and old trees the concentration of carbohydrates usually is higher in the roots than in the tops. Nevertheless, in adult trees the above-ground parts are the primary carbohydrate reservoir because the stem, branches, and leaves make up more of the total dry weight of a tree than do the roots. The apple trees studied by Murneek (1933, 1942) had a higher carbohydrate concentration in the roots than in the stems, yet the above-ground parts, which were about three

TABLE 7.1 Distribution of Starch and Sugars in Grimes Apple Trees in Mid-October[a]

	Dry weight (lb)	Starch and sugar	Percent of oven-dry weight	Starch (lb)	Percent of oven-dry weight	Sugar (lb)	Percent of oven-dry weight
Leaves	32.82	3.09	9.41	0.92	2.80	2.17	6.61
Spurs	6.33	0.69	10.90	0.37	5.85	0.32	5.05
Wood aged:							
1 year	5.94	0.65	10.94	0.35	5.89	0.30	5.05
2 years	7.12	0.73	10.25	0.45	6.32	0.28	3.93
3 years	8.74	0.85	9.73	0.51	5.84	0.34	3.89
4–6 years	46.27	2.48	5.36	1.32	2.85	1.16	2.51
7–10 years	124.00	7.20	5.81	4.46	3.60	2.74	2.21
11–18 years	101.20	5.95	5.88	4.01	3.96	1.94	1.92
Main stem	68.19	7.57	11.10	6.14	9.00	1.43	2.10
Total above ground	400.61	29.21	7.29[b]	18.53	4.63[b]	10.68	2.67[b]
Root stump	62.80	9.94	15.83	6.91	11.00	3.03	4.83
Roots aged:							
18-14 years	46.90	8.22	17.53	6.34	13.52	1.88	4.01
13-7 years	22.52	5.52	24.51	3.97	17.63	1.55	6.88
6-1 years	5.40	1.10	20.37	0.86	15.93	0.24	4.44
Total in soil	137.62	24.78	18.01[b]	18.08	13.14[b]	6.70	4.87[b]
Total for tree	538.23	53.99	10.03[b]	36.61	6.75[b]	17.38	3.23[b]

[a] Adapted from Murneek (1942).
[b] Mean.

times as heavy as the roots, contained more total carbohydrates (Table 7.1). The proportional distribution of carbohydrates above and below ground is also a function of tree age because root–shoot ratios decrease progressively with increasing age. In 1-year-old apple trees carbohydrate reserves were about equally distributed above and below ground (Priestley, 1962b).

The leaves usually contain a high concentration of carbohydrates, but this is a relatively small proportion of the total amount in a woody plant. Foliage of shortleaf pine contained 16.6% carbohydrates, a concentration about seven times as high as in the stem wood (Hepting, 1945). Carbohydrates (starch plus sugar) of apple leaves amounted to 9%, a much higher value than that reported for other tissues. However, the total amount of carbohydrates in the leaves was only about 5% of the carbohydrate reserve of the whole tree (Murneek, 1942).

In stems, branches, and roots, the axial (longitudinal) and ray parenchyma cells as well as pith cells comprise the major accumulation sites of starch. In dealing quantitatively with food reserves in stems of woody plants it is desirable to distinguish between sapwood and heartwood because the latter contains no living cells and ordinarily accumulates no food.

In the bark, starch is deposited in parenchyma and albuminous cells which are distributed in a variety of patterns. The concentration of carbohydrates in the bark often is very high but in many species the total amount in the bark is less than in the wood. In mature beech trees in winter the inner living phloem of branches, main stems, and roots often has two to three times as high a concentration of carbohydrate reserves as the wood. Nevertheless, the total amount is greater in the wood than in the bark (Gäumann, 1935). Wenger (1953a) also found a higher concentration of carbohydrates in stem bark than in stem wood of sweetgum but the wood had much more total carbohydrate. In shortleaf pine root bark had a much higher concentration of carbohydrates than the root wood (Hepting, 1945).

Role of Rays in Storage and Translocation of Carbohydrates

Ray parenchyma cells serve an important function in storing reserve materials (Fig. 7.6). Both the amount and type of reserves in rays vary with distance from the cambium. Starch grains are abundant in ray cells near the cambium and they decrease

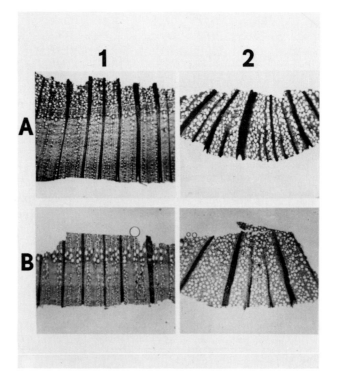

Fig. 7.6. Cross sections of wedges of root tissues stained with I₂KI, showing the number and width of rays and large amounts of starch stored in the ray tissues. A: red oak; B: white oak. 1: at root collar, 2: 1.05 m from root collar. From Wargo (1976).

toward the inner sapwood. Ray cells in the heartwood contain negligible amounts of starch or none at all. In contrast to the pattern of radial distribution of starch in xylem ray cells, the fat content of ray cells in the inner sapwood is higher than in ray cells near the cambium.

Evidence that rays function in lateral translocation comes from various sources. Radioactive sucrose applied to the cambial region moves along rays to the inner sapwood and survival of fusiform cambial initials depends on contact with ray cells. When Ziegler (1965) exposed leaves of woody plants to radioactive sulfur, radioactivity was subsequently found in the phloem and xylem rays, further emphasizing the important role of ray cells in lateral transport.

The amount of carbohydrate reserves in ray cells varies seasonally. Murmanis and Evert (1967) found that small starch grains appeared in phloem ray cells of eastern white pine in March in central Wisconsin. The amount of starch then increased during the growing season to a maximum in early autumn. Thereafter it declined and by January was absent, but reappeared in early spring.

In addition to transporting carbohydrates from the phloem into the xylem, the rays also release sugars to vessels from specialized ray cells, called "contact cells," that are connected to vessel elements by large pits. Sauter (1972) found that starch began to disappear from xylem parenchyma cells in the spring at the same time that sugars appeared in the vessel sap of sugar maple. These changes coincided with bud swelling. The rate of release of sugar into vessels is many times faster than can be accounted for by diffusion. The release of sugar by contact cells into vessels depends on metabolic cellular activity and is temperature dependent. The respiratory inhibitor PCMB (*p*-chloromercuribenzoate) drastically decreases the release of sugars from parenchyma cells into vessels. Since PCMB inhibits most of the dehydrogenases essential for respiration, it appears that respiratory activity is required for release of sucrose into vessels (Sauter *et al.*, 1973).

Uses of Reserve Carbohydrates

The most obvious use of reserve carbohydrates is in maintaining respiration and growth at times when food is not supplied directly from photosynthesis. All metabolic activity at night depends on food accumulated during the day, and respiration and other processes are maintained in deciduous trees during the winter by the use of reserve foods. In young apple trees less than one-fourth of the carbohydrate reserves was used in growth of new tissues in the spring and much of the remainder was used in respiration (Hansen and Grauslund, 1973).

In addition to their role in maintaining respiration, reserve carbohydrates are important for early season growth. This is emphasized by the occurrence of root growth of many species of deciduous trees before their leaves unfold. Production of stump sprouts and shoot suckers also depends on mobilization of carbohydrate reserves. Clark and Liming (1953) found that practically all sprouting of oaks took place during the first and second season after girdling, before exhaustion of reserve carbohydrates. Sprouting was delayed to the second year for trees girdled late in the season. Tew

(1970) observed that the length of time during which root suckers were produced by aspen was related to the amount of carbohydrate reserves, and Schier and Zasada (1973) found positive correlations between the weight of aspen suckers and the amount of carbohydrate reserves. These observations indicate that sprouting decreases as carbohydrate reserves are exhausted. In contrast, Wenger (1953a) reported a second minimum in sprouting of sweetgum in late summer when carbohydrate content of roots was relatively high. He concluded that growth regulators were more important than food reserves.

Sprouting is least abundant from stumps cut in early summer when trees have just fully leafed out and carbohydrate reserves are low, compared to abundant sprouting from stumps of trees that are cut during the dormant season. As shown in Fig. 7.7, when oak trees were girdled in June in Missouri fewer trees sprouted and there was higher mortality of stump sprouts, fewer sprouts per tree, and smaller sprout clumps than when trees were girdled during any other month.

Because of the lack of photosynthesizing leaves at the time when buds of temperate zone deciduous trees begin to expand and increase in dry weight, initial phases of shoot

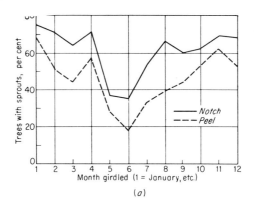

(a)

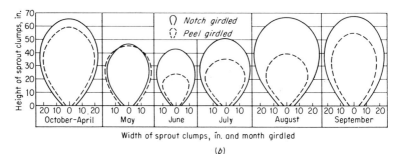

(b)

Fig. 7.7. Effect of season of girdling on number and size of sprouts produced by blackjack oak trees. Observations were made six seasons after girdling. (a) Number of trees producing sprouts after girdling in various months; (b) height and width of clumps of sprouts produced after girdling in various months. From Clark and Liming (1953).

growth depend on carbohydrate reserves. An extreme case of the importance of reserve carbohydrates to shoot growth was cited by Schimper (1903). He reported that a bud of a species of *Brownia* in the tropics had expanded for several days at a rate of 2.6 cm/day while the leaves were still rolled and photosynthetically inactive, emphasizing that this growing shoot was supported by carbohydrate reserves translocated from other parts of the tree. Another example of the importance of reserves is shown by the emergence of a second crop of leaves from dormant buds of temperate zone trees in the spring when the first set of young leaves is killed by an early frost. The importance of reserves in deciduous trees is further emphasized by rapid depletion of reserve carbohydrates as buds open and shoots expand (Kozlowski and Keller, 1966) and by mobilization of ^{14}C-labeled reserves (Hansen, 1967a,b,c; Quinlan, 1969). Hansen (1971) estimated that one-half to two-thirds of the carbohydrate requirements for growth of flowers and shoots of apple trees very early in the growing season were supplied from reserves rather than from current photosynthate. This applied only to the period of development of the first five to six leaves, after which growth of fruits and shoots was attributed to utilization of products of current photosynthesis.

Unlike deciduous trees, evergreen trees already have a functioning photosynthetic system when annual shoot growth begins. For example, pines use currently produced carbohydrates from the old needles during very early phases of shoot expansion (Dickmann and Kozlowski, 1968). Evergreens cannot withstand defoliation as well as many deciduous trees. Such observations have led to questioning the importance of reserve carbohydrates in shoot growth of evergreens. However, there is considerable evidence that reserve carbohydrates do play an important role in growth of evergreens. For example, root growth that begins early in the growing season utilizes considerable reserve carbohydrates. In addition the accumulation and utilization of reserves in growth of above-ground tissues is an important feature of growth.

A portion of the late season photosynthate of temperate zone evergreens is stored and used in growth during the following growing season. When needles of red pine seedlings were exposed to $^{14}CO_2$ in late August, after seasonal shoot growth ceased, labeled photosynthates were translocated and stored in roots, stems, and twigs. In the spring the reserve carbohydrates in the twigs were used in shoot growth (Olofinboba and Kozlowski, 1973). Additional evidence for the use of reserves in shoot growth of gymnosperms comes from observations of rapid depletion of carbohydrates from twigs during shoot expansion. For example, from April to early June, when new shoots of Douglas-fir were expanding rapidly, the amount of carbohydrates in 1-year-old shoots decreased rapidly. Both the concentration and amount of carbohydrates in the new expanding shoots increased from the time of bud opening to mid-June (Fig. 7.8). When old needles of red pine were exposed to $^{14}CO_2$ late in the growing season, some of the ^{14}C was fixed in reserves. During the next growing season a portion of the ^{14}C was mobilized by the shoots and used in their growth (Gordon and Larson, 1970). Schier (1970) reported that a large proportion of the ^{14}C photosynthate fixed in the autumn by 2-year-old red pine needles was used in growth of tissues the following spring. Significant decreases in the dry weight of old needles of red pine and balsam fir as new shoots begin to expand also suggested translocation of carbohydrates from the old needles to

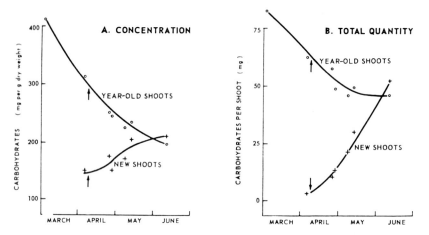

Fig. 7.8. Changes in carbohydrate contents of 1-year-old and new shoots of Douglas-fir. From Krueger (1967).

supplement the use of current photosynthate during early season growth (Clausen and Kozlowski, 1967a, 1970; Loach and Little, 1972). In young yew plants a large proportion of the carbohydrates used in shoot growth was from that stored in the old needles (Splittstoesser and Meyer, 1971).

SEASONAL CYCLES IN CARBOHYDRATE CONTENT

Woody plants accumulate carbohydrate reserves during periods of excess production and deplete them whenever the rate of utilization exceeds the rate of current production. In particular, reserve carbohydrates are depleted from twigs, stems, and roots during periods of most rapid growth in a pattern that varies with species growth characteristics.

Seasonal carbohydrate cycles are particularly well defined in many deciduous trees of the temperate zone. Total carbohydrate contents of stems and branches reach a maximum in the autumn about the time of leaf fall, begin to decrease in late winter, and decrease rapidly in early spring when carbohydrates are being depleted by accelerated respiration and used in growth of new tissues (Figs. 7.9 and 7.10).

Two seasonal maxima of starch have been found in many species, one in the spring and the other in late summer or early autumn. Following the spring maximum, the starch content drops as a result of utilization of reserves by shoot and cambial growth. The winter decline in starch content reflects its conversion to sucrose at low temperatures, as shown in Fig. 7.11 for black locust.

Annual carbohydrate cycles of recurrently flushing species are characterized by depletion of carbohydrates with each growth flush, followed by carbohydrate replacement. For example, orange trees in California showed a reduction in carbohydrates in

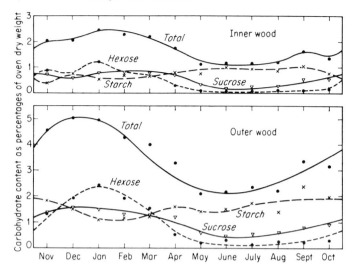

Fig. 7.9. Seasonal changes in hexose sugars, sucrose, starch, and total carbohydrates of inner and outer wood (outer sapwood) of sugar maple in northern Vermont. From Jones and Bradlee (1933).

stems, twigs, and small branches shortly after the beginning of shoot growth, starch being depleted in the phloem and, in some instances, in the outer xylem of adjacent branches (Cameron and Schroeder, 1945). In Florida, sugar content fluctuated in expanded Valencia orange leaves. The largest decline occurred immediately following the beginning of the spring growth flush. Starch, which was present in smaller amounts, was almost totally exhausted during growth flushes, but carbohydrates reaccumulated between periods of growth (Smith *et al.*, 1952). Similarly, in Arizona a rapid decrease in carbohydrates in old leaves of Valencia orange in March was correlated with development of large numbers of leaves and blossoms. The decrease was entirely in reducing and nonreducing sugars. After the spring growth flush, all carbohydrate fractions increased (Hilgeman *et al.*, 1967). Sharples and Burkhart (1954) also showed that rapid utilization and redeposition of starch were correlated with shoot growth cycles of grapefruit trees. Stored starch was rapidly converted into readily usable soluble carbohydrates during spring growth.

Annual carbohydrate cycles of evergreen trees differ somewhat from those of deciduous trees. Evergreen species accumulate carbohydrates much later into winter (compare Figs. 7.9 and 7.12) and in general seasonal variations in carbohydrate reserves are much smaller in evergreen than in deciduous trees. In California, carbohydrate contents of branches varied much more during the year in the drought-deciduous California buckeye than in the evergreen California live oak (Mooney and Hays, 1973). In California buckeye, during the period of fruit production in the autumn the stems were leafless and the carbohydrate content decreased from 17 to 10% (Fig. 7.13). As new leaves developed in February, there was further rapid depletion of

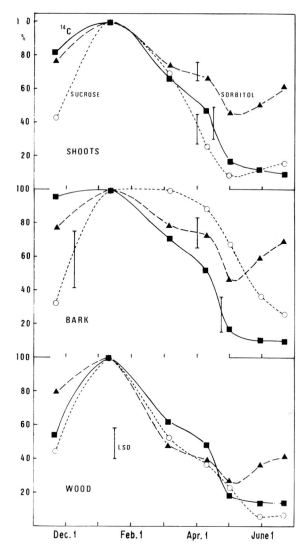

Fig. 7.10. Seasonal variations in concentrations of soluble ^{14}C (■), sorbitol (▲), and sucrose (○) of shoots and bark and wood of branches plus trunk of young apple trees. From Hansen and Grauslund (1973).

carbohydrate reserves until they dropped to the seasonal low level of 5%. During March and April, when the trees were in full leaf, carbohydrate levels of branches were restored to the highest values of the year. By comparison, carbohydrate contents of the leafy stems of California live oak were very stable, varying from about 3.5 to 5.0%.

Even trees of seasonal tropical climates show yearly cycles in carbohydrates, although they generally are more limited in range than the cycles occurring in trees of

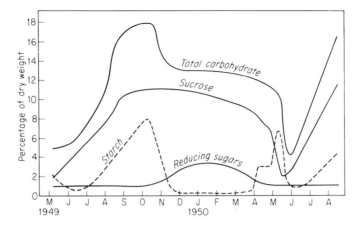

Fig. 7.11. Seasonal variations in various carbohydrate constituents of the living inner bark of black locust trees growing near Ottawa, Canada. From Siminovitch *et al.* (1953).

cooler climates. Recurrently flushing tropical trees show some carbohydrate depletion with each growth flush. For example, the carbohydrate content of twigs of cacao decreased each time a shoot growth flush occurred, but the decreases were relatively smaller than the spring decrease in deciduous trees of the temperate zone (Humphries, 1947). Similar patterns of depletion of twig carbohydrates were reported for *Antiaris africana* in Nigeria (Olofinboba, 1969). For further information on carbohydrate cycles in tropical woody plants, the reader is referred to the book by Alvim and Kozlowski (1977).

AUTUMN COLORATION

Autumn coloration will be discussed at this time because the anthocyanin pigments responsible for the pink, red, and purple colors are related to the carbohydrates and carbohydrate accumulation favors their formation. Anthocyanins are glycosides formed by reactions between various sugars and cyclic compounds called anthocyanidins. They are water soluble and usually occur in the cell sap. Anthocyanins usually are red in acid solution and may become purplish to blue as the pH is increased. The amount of anthocyanin pigments depends primarily on the possession of certain hereditary potentialities for their production, but environmental factors also have an influence.

With declining autumn temperatures the leaves of trees stop producing chlorophyll, and at the same time some species which contain large amounts of carbohydrates and the hereditary potential to do so begin to form anthocyanins in their leaves. As chlorophyll synthesis stops, the chlorophyll already present begins to disintegrate and the newly formed anthocyanins are unmasked. In those trees which do not form anthocyanin pigments, the autumn breakdown of chlorophyll unmasks the relatively

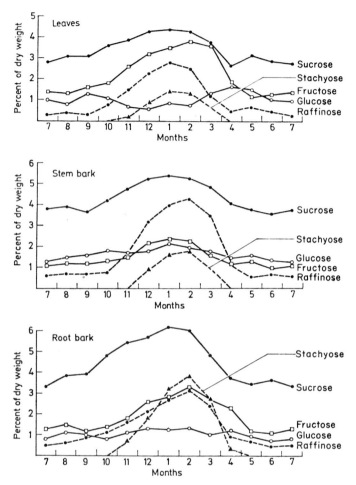

Fig. 7.12. Seasonal variations in various carbohydrates in leaves, stem bark and root bark of mugo pine in southern Germany. From Jeremias (1964).

more stable yellow to orange carotene and xanthophyll pigments, resulting in clear-yellow colored leaves, as in yellow-poplar or hickory, or there may be an admixture of red anthocyanin pigment with yellow carotene to give a bright orange color, as in some species of maple. In other species both chlorophyll and carotenoids disintegrate simultaneously and new carotenoids are synthesized. Thus, by disintegration of green pigments and the unmasking of yellow ones, the formation of red pigments, or all three, the leaves may assume various shades of yellow, orange, crimson, purple, or red.

Trees such as alders and black locust show little color change. In contrast, a large group of trees, including black walnut, catalpa, elm, hickory, basswood, and sycamore turn to a mixture of rusty green and yellow. Leaves of poplars, honey locust, ginkgo, beech, and most species of birch change to yellow of various shades. But by far the

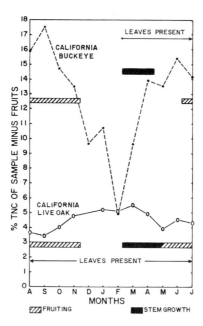

Fig. 7.13. Seasonal cycles of total nonstructural carbohydrates (TNC) in twigs of California buckeye (drought-deciduous) and California live oak (evergreen). From Mooney and Hays (1973).

most dazzling displays are seen in the reds of red and sugar maples, sassafras, sumac, white oak, scarlet oak, shadbush, and winged euonymus, which form large amounts of anthocyanin pigments. Various species and individuals of maple show much gradation from yellow to deep red.

Trees of the same species growing together often show much difference in color because of individual variation in amounts of soluble carbohydrates. Some reach their peak of color later than others. Species of oaks color late in the autumn, usually after the best maple color has developed and disappeared. The yellow-brown colors of beech and some species of oak are caused by the presence of tannins in leaves, in addition to yellow carotenoids.

Variations among species in rate of autumnal color change often reflect wide differences in rate and amount of chlorophyll breakdown. Wieckowski (1958) reported that, whereas rapid chlorophyll disintegration occurred in a species of magnolia (35 days), slow breakdown took place in white mulberry (more than 60 days). Before they abscised, leaves of sycamore maple and beech lost practically all their chlorophyll, whereas those of lilac lost only 40%. Wolf (1956) demonstrated wide variations in the chlorophyll content of leaves and in chlorophyll breakdown during the autumn (Table 7.2). Chlorophyll *a* was destroyed more rapidly than chlorophyll *b* in many species.

Goodwin (1958) followed changes in both chlorophyll and carotenoid pigments from June to November in *Prunus nigra*, English oak, and sycamore maple. In oak and maple both chlorophylls and carotenoids decreased almost to zero. In oak these were

TABLE 7.2   Chlorophyll Content of Green and Yellow Autumn Leaves of Forest Trees[a]

Species	Total chlorophyll (mg/g)		Chlorophyll A (%)		Reduction in total chlorophyll (%)
	Green leaves	Yellow leaves	Green leaves	Yellow leaves	
Liriodendron tulipifera	2.19	0.29	67.5	40.1	86.8
Populus nigra var. italica	1.79	0.27	73.6	63.4	85.2
Magnolia grandiflora	1.74	0.14	75.4	47.9	91.9
Cercis canadensis	1.55	0.12	71.8	43.0	92.2
Acer saccharum	1.38	0.19	69.4	56.5	86.5
Liquidambar styraciflua	1.23	0.05	70.1	57.4	96.2
Acer saccharinum	1.19	0.26	62.5	42.7	78.1
Juglans nigra	1.10	0.26	65.4	49.4	76.4
Celtis occidentalis	1.06	0.32	71.5	65.1	69.7
Cornus florida	0.97	0.18	64.9	53.6	81.4
Ulmus americana	0.93	0.15	70.4	57.9	83.6
Quercus macrocarpa	0.92	0.11	68.0	47.4	87.6
Fagus grandifolia	0.90	0.22	64.4	57.4	75.3
Quercus palustris	0.87	0.17	71.3	54.2	80.6
Carya sp.	0.76	0.16	70.7	67.1	78.9

[a] From Wolf (1956).

depleted simultaneously, whereas in maple the decline in chlorophyll preceded that in carotenoids. In *Prunus* the carotenoids tended to disappear first, but carotenoids and chlorophylls decreased by only about one-half. Eichenberger and Grob (1962) found that when maple leaves began to change color, a carotenoid pigment was formed that was different from carotenoids present in the summer and the total amount of carotenoids decreased.

Any factor that influences the synthesis of carbohydrates or the conversion of insoluble to soluble carbohydrates will favor anthocyanin formation and bright autumn colors. Among the most important environmental factors controlling autumn coloration are temperature, light, and water supply. The lowering of temperature above the freezing point favors anthocyanin formation. However, severe early frosts actually make red autumn colors less brilliant than they otherwise would be. Bright light also favors red colors, and anthocyanin pigments usually develop only in leaves that are exposed to the light. If one leaf is covered by another during the period when red pigments form, the lower leaf usually does not form the red pigment at all. Water supply also affects formation of anthocyanin pigments, drought favoring bright red colors. Rainy days without much light occurring near the time of peak coloration will actually decrease the intensity of fall colors. In summary, the best autumn colors occur under conditions of clear, dry, and cool but not freezing weather.

GENERAL REFERENCES

Aspinall, G. O., ed. (1973). "Carbohydrates." Butterworth, London.

Berdanier, C. D., ed. (1976). "Carbohydrate Metabolism: Regulation and Physiological Role." Halsted Press, New York.

Bonner, J., and Varner, J. E., eds. (1976). "Plant Biochemistry," 3rd ed. Academic Press, New York.

Guthrie, R. D. (1974). "Introduction to Carbohydrate Chemistry." Oxford Univ. Press (Clarendon), London and New York.

Kozlowski, T. T., and Keller, T. (1966). Food relations of woody plants. *Bot. Rev.* **32**, 294–382.

Pigman, W. W., and Horton, D., eds. (1970). "The Carbohydrates," 2nd ed., Vols. 2A and 2B. Academic Press, New York.

Priestley, C. A. (1962). Carbohydrate resources within the perennial plant. *Commonw. Bur. Hortic. Plant. Crops (G.B.), Tech. Commu.* **27.**

Zimmermann, M. H., and Brown, C. L. (1971). "Trees: Structure and Function." Springer-Verlag, Berlin and New York.

Lipids, Terpenes, and Related Substances

INTRODUCTION

The compounds dealt with in this chapter are a heterogeneous group which have little in common except their low solubility in water and high solubility in organic solvents such as acetone, benzene, and ether. Included are simple lipids, cutin, suberin, waxes, and compounds composed of substances in addition to glycerides, such as phospholipids and glycolipids. Another large group of compounds discussed in this

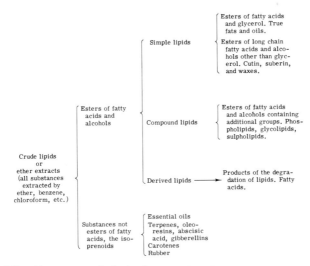

Fig. 8.1. Relationships among principal substances found in ether extracts of plant tissue.

chapter are the isoprenoids or terpenoids, which are derived from isoprene. This group includes essential oils, resins, carotenoids, and rubber. The relationships of the major groups are shown in Fig. 8.1 and the terpenoids or isoprenoids are shown in more detail in Fig. 8.6.

Plant lipids are discussed in detail by Galliard and Mercer (1975) and Hitchcock and Nichols (1971), and in books on plant biochemistry by Bonner and Varner (1976), Goodwin and Mercer (1972), and Miller (1973, Vol. II).

Lipids are important constituents of protoplasm, especially protoplasmic membranes. In the form of cutin, wax, and suberin, they form protective coverings over the outer surfaces of leaves, fruits, and stems. Internal deposits of cutin or related lipids occur in some tissues (Esau, 1965, pp. 155–157). Lipids also are important as storage forms of food, especially in seeds and fruits, and some are of great commercial value. Examples are oil from palm, olive, and tung trees. So-called "essential oils" are extracted from a variety of trees and used for flavoring. The terpenes obtained from pines are important as a source of commercial rosin and turpentine. The latex from which natural rubber is made comes chiefly from *Hevea brasiliensis*, and an isomer of rubber called gutta-percha comes from *Palaquium gutta* and other trees.

LIPIDS

The term lipid includes the simple triglycerides found in common oils and fats; various compound lipids such as phospho- and glycolipids; and other compounds such as cutin, suberin, and the waxes.

Simple Lipids

The simplest and most common lipids are the triglycerides. They are esters of glycerol and various fatty acids that form ordinary oils and fats. If the ester is a liquid at ordinary temperatures it is called an oil, but if it is a solid it is a fat. A generalized formula for an oil or fat is

$$R_1 - COOCH_2$$
$$R_2 - COOCH$$
$$R_3 - COOCH_2$$

R_1, R_2, and R_3 represent the carbon chains of the same or different fatty acids.

In simplified form, the synthesis of oils and fats involves a reaction between the three $-OH$ groups of glycerol and three molecules of fatty acid. The fatty acids linked to a given glycerol molecule often are different, producing mixed glycerides. The essential features of the reaction can be shown as follows.

$$
\begin{array}{ccc}
H_2-C-OH & C_{15}H_{31}COOH & C_{15}H_{31}COOCH_2 \\
| & & | \\
& & \text{lipase} \\
H-C-OH \quad + & C_{15}H_{31}COOH & \rightleftharpoons \quad C_{15}H_{31}COOCH + 3H_2O \\
| & & | \\
H_2-C-OH & C_{15}H_{31}COOH & C_{15}H_{31}COOCH_2 \\
\\
\text{Glycerol} & \text{Palmitic} & \text{Tripalmitin} \\
& \text{acid} &
\end{array}
$$

The actual starting points probably are α-glycerophosphate and fatty acids built up of acetate units derived from acetyl coenzyme A. The place of fat synthesis in the general metabolic scheme is shown in Fig. 6.20. Readers are referred to plant biochemistry books (see General References) for a more detailed description of the synthesis of glycerol and fatty acids and their reaction to form fats. There is some uncertainty concerning the site of fat synthesis, and mitochondria, organelles called glyoxysomes, and the endoplasmic reticulum have all been implicated in fat metabolism. In leaves, synthesis of lipids also appears to occur in chloroplasts, and over 50% of the lamellar membranes is composed of lipid material. Lipid synthesis obviously occurs in the cells where they are found because their insolubility in water makes translocation from cell to cell impossible.

Fatty Acids

The fatty acids are classified as saturated if no double bonds occur or unsaturated if double bonds occur between carbon atoms. The most important fatty acids found in woody plants are shown in Table 8.1. Palmitic acid is the most widely distributed fatty acid in woody plants, but most fatty acids in trees are unsaturated, oleic and linoleic being most common. The oils containing large amounts of unsaturated fatty acids combine with oxygen when exposed to the air and form the hard films characteristic of "drying oils," such as those obtained from tung and flax. The unusual property of cocoa butter of remaining a solid to just below body temperature, then suddenly melting, is attributed to the special arrangement of fatty acids in its triglycerides (Wolff, 1966).

The major acids found in liquid triglycerides (oils) are unsaturated, such as oleic, linoleic, and linolenic, while the major fatty acids in solid triglycerides (fats) are saturated fatty acids, such as palmitic and stearic. Taking the plant kingdom as a whole, oleic and palmitic are probably the most abundant fatty acids. The leaf tissues of most kinds of plants contain similar fatty acids, chiefly palmitic, linoleic, and linolenic, and considerable linolenic acid occurs in chloroplasts. There is much more variation among species with respect to the fatty acids found in seeds than in leaves and those in the seeds may differ from those found in the vegetative structures of the same plant. According to Hitchcock (1975) the fruit of oil palms contains chiefly palmitic, oleic, and linoleic acids, but the seed contains considerable lauric, myristic, and oleic acid in addition to palmitic acid. Animals are dependent on plants for some fatty acids, notably linoleic and linolenic.

It appears that plants growing in cool climates usually produce more unsaturated fatty acids such as linoleic and linolenic than plants growing in warm climates (Lyons, 1973). It also appears that species with a wide climatic distribution contain more unsaturated fatty acids in the cooler part of their range, although Mirov (1967) pointed out some exceptions in pines. Apparently the temperature at which a phase transition from the liquid to the solid state occurs in cell membranes is lower if unsaturated fatty acids predominate. This change in state has important effects on physiological processes. For example, resistance to chilling injury may be associated with a low phase transition temperature (McGlasson and Raison, 1973; Murata *et al.*, 1975).

Differences in root resistance to water uptake between warm and cold climate plants in cold soil might also be explained by differences in phase transition temperatures related to the kinds of fatty acids present in roots. St. John and Christiansen (1976) found that the linolenic acid content was increased in root tips of cotton germinated at low temperatures. They suggested that chilling injury of cotton seedlings may be at least partly the result of decrease in water uptake caused by lack of unsaturated fatty

TABLE 8.1 Some Important Fatty Acids Found in Plant Fats

Saturated acids		
Lauric	$C_{12}H_{24}O_2$	$CH_3(CH_2)_{10}COOH$
Myristic	$C_{14}H_{28}O_2$	$CH_3(CH_2)_{12}COOH$
Palmitic	$C_{16}H_{32}O_2$	$CH_3(CH_2)_{14}COOH$
Stearic	$C_{18}H_{36}O_2$	$CH_3(CH_2)_{16}COOH$
Unsaturated acids		
Oleic	$C_{18}H_{34}O_2$	$CH_3(CH_2)_7CH{:}CH(CH_2)_7COOH$
Linoleic	$C_{18}H_{32}O_2$	$CH_3(CH_2)_4CH{:}CHCH_2CH{:}CH(CH_2)_7COOH$
Linolenic	$C_{18}H_{30}O_2$	$CH_3CH_2CH{:}CHCH_2CH{:}CHCH_2CH{:}CH(CH_2)_7COOH$

acids in unhardened roots. Willemot (1977) also found a positive correlation between the concentration of linolenic acid and cold hardiness in roots.

Stumpf (1976) and other authors cited earlier discussed lipid metabolism in detail and we will merely point out that the long-chain fatty acids are built up from acetate units and that acetyl coenzyme A plays an important role in both the synthesis and degradation of fatty acids (see Fig. 6.20). For example, in the digestion of oil and fat the fatty acids are degraded to acetyl CoA and then can be either transferred to the Krebs Cycle and oxidized with the release of energy or enter the glyoxylate cycle and be transformed into sugar.

WAXES, CUTIN, AND SUBERIN

Cuticle

The outer surfaces of herbaceous stems, leaves, fruits, and even flower petals usually are covered by a relatively waterproof layer, the cuticle. According to Kolattukudy (1975), the cuticle is composed of wax and cutin and is anchored to the epidermal cells by a layer of pectin. The arrangement of the various constituents is shown in Fig. 8.2. The cuticle is typically quite thin on shade plants and much thicker on those exposed to bright sun. There also are said to be genetic differences in the cuticle of different plant species and varieties. In addition to reducing water loss, cutin is believed by some to provide a barrier against invasion by pathogens (Kolattukudy, 1975), although this is questioned by others (Martin, 1966).

Schönherr (1976) made extensive investigations of the permeability to water of cutin layers stripped from leaves of citrus, pear, and onion scales. He found little difference in permeability between the entire epidermis and the cuticular layer stripped off of it.

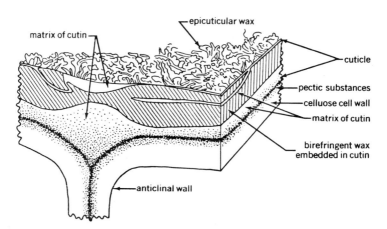

Fig. 8.2. Diagram of outer cell wall of the upper epidermis in pear leaf showing details of cuticle and wax. After Norris and Bukovac (1968).

The permeability to water is controlled by the extractable wax content of the cuticle rather than by the thickness of the matrix. Extraction of the wax with lipid solvents increased permeability of cuticular membranes 300- to 500-fold, demonstrating the role of wax in controlling permeability.

Waxes

The waxes are esters of long chain monohydric alcohols and longer-chain fatty acids than those found in simple lipids, that is, with carbon chains containing more than 20 carbon atoms. Waxes also contain alkanes with odd numbers of carbon atoms, primary alcohols, and very long-chain free fatty acids. It has been shown that wax synthesis

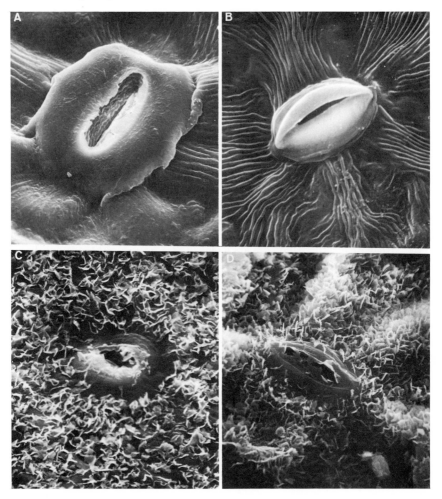

Fig. 8.3. Variations in leaf waxes of broadleaved trees. A: american elm (× 2000); B: white ash (×2000); C: sugar maple (×2000); D: redbud (×2000). Photos by W. J. Davies.

occurs in the epidermal cells of apple fruits and several kinds of leaves, and it obviously must occur near the site where it is deposited because of the difficulty of transporting such an insoluble material. Waxes probably are generally synthesized in the epidermal cells as droplets, pass out through the cell walls by thus far unidentified channels, and form layers on the outer surfaces. Some wax is pushed out through the cutin–wax layer, forming a deposit of plates and rods of wax on the cuticle and producing the "bloom" characteristic of some leaf and fruit surfaces (see Fig. 8.3). According to Chambers et al. (1976), in eucalyptus the wax molecules probably arrive at the outer surface of the cuticle by movement through lamellar channels in the cuticle, in oil solution, and are deposited in various configurations as the solvent evaporates. Apparently wax generally accumulates on the external surfaces of plants, in contrast to suberin, which accumulates in cell walls, and to cutin, which sometimes accumulates on internal as well as external surfaces. An exception is the accumulation of liquid wax in the seeds of jojoba (Simmondsia chinensis).

The amount of wax on leaf surfaces varies widely among species and with environmental conditions, ranging from traces to as much as 15% of leaf dry weight (Eglinton and Hamilton, 1967). When present as irregular masses, wax makes leaf surfaces difficult to wet and a wetting agent, or "spreader," must be added to spray materials to ensure even coverage.

Some waxes are of considerable commercial importance. Among the best known is carnauba wax, obtained from the leaves of a palm, Copernicia cerifera, found in Brazil. It contains about 80% alkyl esters of long-chain fatty acids and 10% free monohydric alcohols. Palm wax occurs on the trunk of the wax palm (Ceroxylon andicola) in layers up to 2 or 3 cm in thickness. It consists of about one-third true wax, the remainder being resin. Other commercial palm waxes are ouricuri wax, obtained from the Attalea palm (Attalea excelsa), and raffia wax obtained from the dried leaves of the Madagascar raffia palm (Raphia pedunculata) (Deuel, 1951). Eucalyptus gunni var. acervula of Tasmania, and the leaves of white sandalwood (Santalum album) also yield wax. The leaves of Myrica carolinensis supply the fragrant wax used in bayberry candles. There is some interest in a liquid wax which can be extracted from the seeds of a desert shrub, jojoba (Simmondsia chinensis), because it might serve as a substitute for sperm oil.

Cutin

Kolattukudy (1975) describes cutin as a hydroxy fatty acid polymer. Not much is known about its synthesis, but it probably is a polyester formed spontaneously from hydroxy acids. Like wax, it must be formed near the site of deposition, presumably in the epidermal cells of leaves. Cutin or a cutinlike substance also sometimes accumulates on cell surfaces exposed to intercellular spaces.

Suberin

Suberin is another component of waterproof layers in plants, chiefly the bark. In older woody stems and roots the walls of the outer layers of phloem cells that constitute the bark are impregnated with suberin and become relatively waterproof. Suberin contains very long-chain acids, alcohols, and phenolic compounds which are absent or less abundant in cutin.

INTERNAL LIPID LAYERS

Some years ago it was demonstrated that the surfaces of cell walls that are exposed to intercellular spaces are often covered with a hydrophobic lipid layer. Scott (1964) thinks the deposition of this cutin- or suberinlike layer occurs wherever cells are pulled apart during enlargement and wall surface is exposed to the air. This considerably increases the resistance to evaporation of water from mesophyll cell surfaces and lowers the vapor pressure in the intercellular spaces (Jarvis and Slatyer, 1970). Scott (1963) also claims that a cutinlike layer forms on the outer surface of young root cells, but this apparently often is covered by a layer of pectic material. The Casparian strips of endodermal cells are formed by deposition of suberin, and other examples of internal cutinization and suberization have been reported.

In this connection readers are reminded that although cutin and wax layers are relatively impermeable to water when dry, they are more permeable when moist, as is the case with roots in moist soil and in the interior of leaves. Also, when leaf surfaces are wetted, substances in solution penetrate readily through the cuticle.

COMPOUND LIPIDS

Lipids form complex compounds with phosphorus (phospholipids), carbohydrates (glycolipids), and sulfur (sulfolipids).

Phospholipids

These are esters of phosphoric acid and various alcohols including glycerol, inositol, and phytosphingosine which occur in all living cells. The glycerophosphatides are most widespread in plants. Phospholipids contain both a hydrophobic, water-insoluble portion (the fatty acid) and a hydrophilic, water-soluble portion such as glycerol, inositol, or choline. This probably is the reason for their importance in membranes.

Glycolipids

In glycolipids, a terminal hydroxy group is attached to a sugar, either galactose or glucose. Mono- and digalactosyl diglycerides are found in chloroplasts where they are esterified with linolenic and linoleic acids. The glycolipid containing glucose also contains sulfur and is called a sulfolipid. It likewise is most abundant in chloroplasts, but also occurs in nonphotosynthetic tissues.

OCCURRENCE OF LIPIDS IN WOODY PLANTS

Lipids occur in all living cells of plants and animals, but the concentration in vegetative structures of plants usually is quite low, often being less than 1% of the total dry weight. However, even in this small quantity lipids are very important because of their essential role as constituents of cell membranes. Most of the data on lipid content are based on ether extracts which contain considerable material in addition to simple lipids. For example the total ether extract from leaves usually is less than 5% of the dry weight, but this includes wax, cutin, and other substances so the content of true lipid is quite low. The lipid content of the wood also is low, rarely exceeding 2 or 3% and the concentration in the sapwood usually is lower than that of the heartwood. The concentration in the bark usually is higher than that of the wood, presumably because of the suberin which it contains.

Fischer (1891) and other early investigators attempted to classify trees as "fat" or "starch" trees on the basis of the predominant type of reserve food in their wood during the winter. Sinnott (1918) in the United States and Arrhenius (1942) in Sweden classified conifers and linden as high in lipids and ash, oak, elm, and maple as low in lipids (see Figure 8.4). Ishibe (1935), working in Japan, also concluded that there are significant differences among species in lipid content, Japanese red pine being much higher than oak. Like other investigators, Ishibe found a low lipid content in roots. According to Preston and Phillips (1911) very small amounts of lipids were found in the roots of the species they studied.

There is some evidence of seasonal variations in lipid content, there being a tendency toward accumulation in the winter or spring in some species and a decrease during the summer in all species studied (Figs. 8.4 and 8.5). At one time it was reported that considerable transformation of carbohydrates to lipids occurs during the winter in leaves of conifers (Lewis and Tuttle, 1920, 1923) but this was based on microchemical tests. Later observations by Doyle (1938) indicated that the tests used were not specific for lipids and that there is no reliable evidence that lipids accumulate in conifer leaves during the winter. The available evidence suggests that seasonal cycles in lipids are controlled more by internal metabolism than by seasonal changes in temperature.

The lipid concentration of fruits and seeds is much higher than that of vegetative structures. For example, oil accumulates in the parenchyma cells of the fruit or pericarp of avocado and olive and the seeds of oil palm. Olive fruits contain 20 to 30% oil; seeds of Brazil nut, coconut palm, pinyon pine, and pecan 60 to 75%; acorns of red and scarlet oak 20 to 30%. The oil may be stored chiefly in the endosperm, as in coconut, or in the embryo, as in acorns. In jojoba seed the wax constitutes 50 to 60% of the fresh weight of the cotyledons and it is converted to carbohydrates during germination (Moreau and Huang, 1977), as are the fats in acorns and some other fatty seeds.

Synthesis of oil and fat obviously occurs in the organs where they are stored as their insolubility in water makes translocation impossible. The kinds of oils accumulated may differ in such adjacent tissues as the fruit coat and seed of palm, or the leaves and the fruits of other species. Synthesis and accumulation of oils and fats occur very

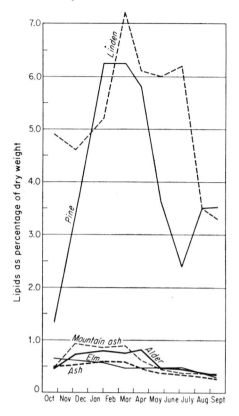

Fig. 8.4. Comparison of lipid content of wood of pine and several deciduous species in Sweden. From Arrhenius (1942).

rapidly during a short period in the development of fruits and seeds. Thor and Smith (1935) found that as late as September 1 oil formation had hardly begun in pecan but during the next 30 days 75 to 80% of the eventual oil content was laid down in the kernel. By September 19 oil constituted 70% of the dry weight of the kernels. After this there was a gradual increase until harvest, when the Burkett variety of pecan contained 74% and the Stuart variety 75% oil on a dry-weight basis. Similarly, Sell *et al.* (1948) found the oil content of tung kernels to increase from 3.88 to 58.29% over a 4-week period from mid-July to mid-August, but there was little increase thereafter. The same pattern of rapid fat formation was shown to occur in almond and walnut by Sablon (Table 8.2). Other examples of rapid accumulation are cited by Mazliak (1973).

The importance of lipids as constituents of cell membranes and as protective surface coatings has already been mentioned. Lipids also are very important forms of food storage, particularly in seeds where they often are the chief storage form, as indicated in the preceding section. As they contain much less oxygen in proportion to carbon and hydrogen than carbohydrates, they release more energy when degraded and oxidized.

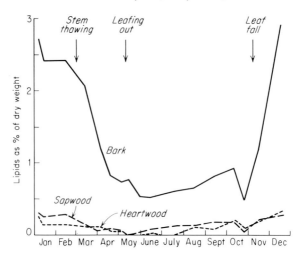

Fig. 8.5. Seasonal variation in lipid content of bark, sapwood, and heartwood of beech in Switzerland. From Gäumann (1935).

TABLE 8.2 Development of Fats in Tree Fruits and Seeds

Walnut seed[a]		Almond seed[a]	
Date	Oil, %	Date	Oil, %
July 6	3	June 9	2
Aug. 1	16	July 4	10
Aug. 15	42	Aug. 1	37
Oct. 4	62	Oct. 4	46

Black walnut kernels[b]		Tung fruit[c]	
Date	Oil, %	Date	Oil, %
June 15	3.54	July 15	3.88
July 15	13.44	Aug. 15	58.29
July 29	39.26	Sept. 15	64.18
Aug. 12	51.12	Oct. 15	63.83
Aug. 26	61.92	Nov. 15	63.19

[a] After du Sablon (1896).
[b] After M'Clenahan (1909).
[c] After Sell et al. (1948).

During seed germination the stored fat is converted to fatty acids and glycerol which are further degraded. The glycerol is converted through α-glycerol phosphate to dihydroxyacetone phosphate from which it can be broken down by glycolysis and oxidized in Krebs cycle reactions or transformed into sugar. The fatty acids are converted to acetyl coenzyme A and then can either be oxidized in the Krebs cycle, releasing ATP and NADH, or enter the glyoxylate cycle and be transformed into sugar. Moreau and Huang (1977) studied the conversion of lipids to carbohydrates during germination of jojoba seeds.

ISOPRENOIDS OR TERPENES

The terpenes or isoprenoids are of both biochemical and economic interest. They are hydrocarbons built up of varying numbers of isoprene (C_5H_8) units and include essential oils, resins, carotenoids, and rubber. The relationships are shown in Fig. 8.6. All plants can synthesize carotenoids and steroids, but the ability to synthesize the other terpenes is scattered very irregularly through the plant kingdom. The carbon atoms usually come from acetate, sometimes termed the crossroad in plant metabolism because it is the starting point for so many compounds.

Essential Oils

The essential oils are straight chain or cyclic compounds and may be mono-, sesqui-, or diterpenes. Their varying characteristics are determined by the chemical groups associated with them. Essential oils are the source of most of the odors found in the flowers, fruit, or wood of many plants. They are most common in species of the

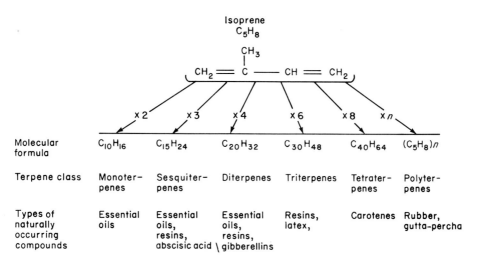

Fig. 8.6. Relationships among isoprenoid compounds. After Bonner (1950).

Pinaceae, Umbelliferae, Myrtaceae, Lauraceae, Rutaceae, Labiatae, and Compositae. All organs of plants, including the bark, wood, and leaves may contain essential oils. They often are produced in groups of glandular cells or in glandular hairs on flowers, leaves, and stems and sometimes they are secreted into specialized ducts in leaves and stems. The essential oils have no known essential functions in plant metabolism although they may be useful in attracting pollinators or repelling predators. Many are volatile and evaporate into the air, especially on warm days, producing the odors which are typical of various kinds of flowers and of coniferous forests.

Rasmussen and Went (1965) estimated that the vegetation of the world releases 438 $\times$ 10^6 tons of volatile material annually. More is released on warm sunny days than on rainy days and large amounts are released from drying vegetation. The latter is the source of the odor of recently mown grass and hay and of recently fallen autumn leaves. Photooxidation of this volatile material is believed to produce the blue haze or natural smog characteristic of the Blue Ridge Mountains of Virginia and other heavily vegetated areas. The release of volatile hydrocarbons from vegetation is an important source of air pollution. For example, it is reported that from 0.1 to 3.0% of the carbon fixed in photosynthesis by live oak leaves is lost as isoprene (Tingey and Ratsch, 1978). It apparently escapes chiefly through the stomata and the loss is greatest in bright light at high temperatures.

Essential oils are extracted commercially on a small scale by steam distillation from leaves of such conifers as pine, eastern arborvitae, black spruce, balsam fir, and eastern hemlock, and from wood of cedar, sweet birch bark, and sassafras roots and buds. Turpentine is the most important essential oil obtained from trees. The attractive odors of conifer leaves are attributed mainly to the presence of borneol and bornyl esters.

The large quantities of essential oils in the leaves of some shrubs make them very flammable and greatly increase the speed with which fire spreads. An example is chamise, an important shrub of the California chaparral (Kozlowski and Ahlgren, 1974, p. 338). Some species of sagebrush and eucalypts also are very flammable.

Resins

Resins are a heterogeneous mixture of resin acids ($C_{20}H_{30}O_2$), fatty acids, esters of these acids, sterols, alcohols, waxes, and resenes (Wise and Jahn, 1952).

Conifers and hardwoods both synthesize resins, but conifers usually produce much larger amounts. Resin yields of 0.8 to 25% have been reported for coniferous woods as compared to only 0.7 to 3% for hardwoods (Wise and Jahn, 1952). Most resin used commercially comes from trees of the families Pinaceae, Leguminosae, and Dipterocarpaceae. Copals are a group of resins extracted from forest trees of the Leguminosae and are known for their hardness and high melting point. Trees of the Dipterocarpaceae produce a resin called "dammar" in commerce. Another commercially important resin is "Kauri gum," obtained from the Kauri tree (*Agathis australis*) of New Zealand (Howes, 1949). Amber is a fossil resin.

Most resins are secreted into special ducts or canals by the layer of parenchyma cells which surrounds them. The ducts are formed schizogenously, that is, by separation of cells. The canals often are much branched, so that when one of the branches is tapped or wounded, resins will flow toward the cut area from considerable distances. Resins may also be found occasionally in cell interiors and in cell walls. They are not used as reserve foods, and their role in the metabolism of woody plants is unknown.

Haaglund (1951) distinguished between physiological and pathological resin, the former occurring normally inside the woody tissue while formation of the latter is a result of bark or wood injury. Büsgen and Münch (1931) emphasized the protective nature of resins, pointing out that the resinous wood of pine is more resistant to decay than spruce wood, which is low in resin. The presence of resin retards attack by decay-producing fungi, as evidenced by the durability of pine stumps and knots and the resinous heartwood of pine. Baltic amber is said to be the resin from species of pine which grew 40 to 50 million years ago.

There has been considerable discussion of the role of resins with respect to resistance to bark beetle attacks on coniferous trees. The copious resin flow which often accompanies borer activity is said sometimes to be lethal and to hinder further attacks, but it sometimes attracts other insects. It has been claimed that host specificity is associated with the type of resin formed by pines. According to Callaham and Smith (in Gerhold *et al.*, 1966), a given species of borer is tolerant of the terpenes produced by its host but intolerant of those produced by other species. There also is some evidence that conifers respond to fungus infection by producing terpenes which are repellent or inhibitory to bark beetles and associated fungi (Russell and Berryman, 1976). Both Vité and Wood (1961) and Lorio and Hodges (1968) claim that, when environmental conditions such as water stress cause a reduction in oleoresin exudation pressure, pine trees become much more susceptible to attack by bark beetles. The role of terpenes and other plant products as protective agents deserves further study.

An abnormal flow of resin called "resinosis" may be stimulated by wounds or attacks by fungi. Resinosis is characteristic of conifer stems attacked by white pine blister rust, larch canker, and red ring rot of spruce. Root collars of pines may show pronounced resinosis when shoestring rot caused by *Armillaria mellea* is present. A fungus disease of planted white and red pines known as "resinosis disease" is characterized by copious resin flow from the butts of trees (Boyce, 1948).

Oleoresins

The most important resins commercially are the oleoresins obtained from pines. Oleoresin is a term applied to the viscous liquid secreted by cells bordering the resin ducts of conifers. Its composition is approximately 66% resin acids, 25% turpentine (an essential oil), 7% nonvolatile neutral material, and 2% water (Wise and Jahn, 1952).

Oleoresin-yielding tissues are parenchymatous and occur in roots, leaves, stem-wood, and inner bark. Oleoresin is produced by living cells, so-called epithelial cells, which separate to form resin canals or ducts that are especially active in the outer sapwood. Scarifying the tree trunk exposes the resin canals, and oleoresin oozes out. Oleoresins are obtained commercially from pines by "chipping" or cutting through the bark and exposing the surface of the sapwood, as shown in Fig. 8.7. The amount and duration of the resin flow can be increased by spraying sulfuric acid on the wounded surfaces. Oleoresin yield varies not only among species but also among different trees of the same species. Bourdeau and Schopmeyer (1958) found the amount of flow in slash pine to be controlled by the number and size of resin ducts, resin pressure, and viscosity of the exudate. Resin pressures vary diurnally, the highest resin pressures occurring about dawn and the lowest in the afternoon when the water content of the trunk is lowest (Bourdeau and Schopmeyer, 1958). Lorio and Hodges (1968) reported that diurnal variations in oleoresin exudation pressure of loblolly pine are related to soil and atmospheric moisture conditions.

It has been demonstrated that injection of the herbicide paraquat into stems of pine trees greatly increases the production of oleoresins in a strip of wood often extending several meters above point of injection (Roberts, *et al.*, 1973; Roberts and Peters, 1977). The oleoresin is deposited in the sapwood, producing the resin-soaked wood

Fig. 8.7. Slash pine tree "chipped" to produce oleoresin. Photo courtesy of U.S. Forest Service.

known as "lightwood" which is an important source of naval stores such as rosin and turpentine. Much of this material is now obtained by steam extraction of lightwood from stumps or by "turpentining" living trees. If sufficient lightwood formation can be induced in young trees they can be cut at pulpwood size, the oleoresins extracted, and the chips used for wood pulp. The treatment is said to be effective on slash, longleaf, and loblolly pine and preliminary tests indicate that it is effective on red, ponderosa, lodgepole, limber, and Scotch pine, but not on Douglas-fir or northeastern conifers such as balsam fir, hemlock, tamarack or Norway spruce (Rowe *et al*, 1976).

Injection of paraquat causes typical wound reactions such as increased respiration and production of ethylene. It also has been demonstrated that injection of ethrel (ethephon), a commercial compound releasing ethylene, increases resin formation in conifers. This suggests that the increased resin production following wounding may be caused by ethylene released from the wounded tissue (Wolter, 1977). It is believed that the increase in oleoresins in treated tissue is caused by transformation of precursors already present in that tissue rather than by translocation of precursors from a distance.

Unfortunately, paraquat kills the cambium to a considerable height above the point of treatment, producing a strip of dead wood and bark. This limits the amount of circumference that can be treated. Treated trees also are more susceptible to attack by bark beetles and the total effect of treatment is a considerable increase in mortality. Nevertheless, there is wide interest in the possibilities of increasing the production of resin-saturated lightwood by chemical treatment because it might be possible to obtain more resin and turpentine by this method than could be obtained by conventional methods over a period of several years.

The composition of turpentine from southeastern and western pines of the United States varies considerably. Turpentine of southeastern pines is of relatively simple composition and consists essentially of two monoterpenes, α- and β-pinene. Turpentines of western pines are complex and contain, in addition to the pinenes, some aliphatic hydrocarbons, aliphatic aldehydes, Δ-3 carene, and sesquiterpenes. Turpentine of southeastern pines resembles that of European species, while that of trees growing in western areas resembles turpentine from pines of southeast Asia (Mirov, 1954). Franklin (1976) reported variations in the composition of oleoresins of slash pine from base to crown as well as among trees. He suggested that the base-to-crown variation may be controlled by growth regulators transported downward from the crown.

After the volatile turpentine has been removed from the oleoresin by distillation, the remaining substance is a hard resin, varying in color from amber to almost black, called rosin. Its chief constituent is abietic acid.

Other commercially important oleoresins are "Canada balsam" and "Oregon balsam." The former, obtained from balsam fir, is secreted in resin canals formed by the separation of cells in the bark and occurs in small blisters under the bark. Oregon balsam, obtained from Douglas-fir, is found in cavities in trees which were produced by wind shake. Venetian turpentine, used in the arts, is obtained from the European larch.

Carotenoids

The only naturally occurring tetraterpenes are the carotenoids, which have the formula $C_{40}H_{56}$. The carotenes are pure hydrocarbons which include red, orange, and yellow pigments occurring in all organs of plants. They apparently are involved in light trapping in photosynthesis and probably protect chlorophyll from photooxidation. The xanthophylls are yellow or brownish pigments which occur commonly in leaves and also in algae. They contain a small amount of oxygen and generally have the formula $C_{40}H_{56}O_2$ (see Chapter 5).

Rubber

Rubber may be described as a polyterpene composed of 500 to 5,000 isoprene units joined linearly in the following pattern.

$$-CH_2-\underset{\underset{CH_3}{\vert}}{C}=CH-CH_2-CH_2-\underset{\underset{CH_3}{\vert}}{C}=CH-CH_2-$$

It occurs in latex as more or less spherical globules 5 to 6 μm in diameter and stabilized by a thin adsorbed film of protein and phospholipid.

Rubber is formed by about 2,000 species of plants, including herbs, shrubs, trees, and vines. It is formed only in dicotyledonous angiosperms and is not synthesized by monocotyledons, gymnosperms, or lower plants. Especially well represented with rubber-producing species are the families Euphorbiaceae, Moraceae, Apocynaceae, Asclepiadaceae, and Compositae. Most rubber-producing woody plants are tropical, and guayule is said to be the only temperate zone woody plant that produces enough rubber for commercial extraction. The chief source of natural rubber is the tropical tree *Hevea brasiliensis*, which is in the family Euphorbiaceae. The *trans* isomer of rubber, gutta-percha, is obtained chiefly from *Palaquium gutta*, which belongs in the family Sapotaceae.

Rubber is occasionally found in parenchyma cells, as in guayule (*Parthenium argentatum*) where the top of the plant must be harvested to obtain the rubber. More often it occurs as suspended globules in latex, a complex liquid system containing a variety of substances in solution or suspension. Among these are terpene derivatives, sugars, starch grains, organic acids, sterols, and enzymes. The exact composition varies widely among species and even among individual plants of the same species. Starch grains occur in latex in *Euphorbia,* but not in *Hevea* latex. *Ficus* latex is high in protein, the latex of *Papaver somniferum* is high in the alkaloids of opium, and the latex of *Carica papaya* is the commercial source of the enzyme papain. The chicle used in chewing gum is obtained from latex of a tropical tree, *Achras zapota*, which grows in Mexico, Central America, and Venezuela. According to Bonner (1965), in *Hevea* rubber occurs as particles suspended in the highly specialized cytoplasm of the latex ducts that also contains nuclei, mitochondria, ribosomes, and enzymes.

Rubber does not occur in the latex of all plants and, when present, usually is found in very low concentrations. It occurs in commercially useful quantities in only a few species, notably in *Hevea brasiliensis*, where it comprises 20 to 60% of the latex on a dry-weight basis, and in guayule, where it sometimes amounts to over 10% of the dry weight of the plant. Neither latex nor rubber is used as reserve food by plants.

Latex occasionally is formed in parenchyma cells, as in guayule, but it usually is formed in latex vessels. These are ducts produced by the elongation of single cells or the union of many specialized cells to form complex systems (Esau, 1965). In woody plants, such as *Hevea brasiliensis*, the latex ducts occur in the bark as vertically oriented tubes up to several meters in length.

Rubber trees usually are tapped by cutting a spiral groove in the bark halfway or more around the stem at an angle of 25° to 30° from the horizontal (Fig. 8.8). The latex flows down the groove from the opened latex vessels and is collected at the bottom. The initial flow is caused by elastic contraction of the latex vessels, but later there is osmotic movement of water into the vessels and the viscosity and rubber concentration of the latex decrease. Flow stops after a few hours because the latex coagulates when exposed to the air and every second day a thin slice is removed from the bottom of the groove, causing renewed flow. Wounding stimulates metabolic activity in the phloem and the ribosomes, mitochondria, enzymes, and rubber particles lost in the outflow are quickly regenerated. In *Hevea* the tapping is not deep enough to injure the cambium so the bark is regenerated in a few years and the process can be started over again.

The pressure and rate of flow seem to depend at least in part on the internal water balance and vigor of the tree and therefore vary with season, site conditions, and time of day. There also are genetic differences among trees, and stems with a potential for high rubber yield are sometimes grafted onto disease-resistant root stocks. The flow usually is greater in the morning than in the afternoon and is reduced by dry weather. Efforts have been made to increase the flow by applying chemicals, and 2,4-D, 2,4,5-

Fig. 8.8. Tapping of rubber tree to produce latex. Photo courtesy of Rubber Research Institute, Malaysia.

T, and Ethrel have been used extensively. In some instances use of 2,4,5-T increased yield as much as one-third over a period of years without injury to the trees. Yokoyama *et al*. (1977) reported that application of the auxin 2-(3,4-dichlorophenoxy)-triethylamine to guayule increased rubber synthesis two- or threefold. Buttery and Boatman (1976) wrote a good summary of what is known about latex production.

Related Compounds

Several important compounds are derived from the terpenes.

Abscisic Acid.   This important plant growth regulator is derived from a sesquiterpene and is discussed in Chapter 15.

Gibberellins.   The gibberellins are another important group of plant growth regulators derived from diterpenes and are also discussed in more detail in Chapter 15.

Steroids.   The steroids or sterols are an important group of compounds, derived from isoprenoid compounds and found in both plants and animals. The triterpene squalene is a precursor of cholesterol which in turn is the precursor of other steroids. Those produced in plants are often termed phytosterols. Examples are stigmasterol and ergosterol, the precursor of vitamin D. The functions of sterols in plants are largely unknown, but they have important physiological roles in animals and certain plant sterols are used as the starting point for synthesis of synthetic animal hormones.

Terpenoid Glycosides.   Some terpenoids, especially sterols, exist as glycosides, including the saponins and cardiac glycosides such as those obtained from *Digitalis*.

Phytol.   Phytol, an alcohol which is a component of chlorophyll, is derived from a diterpene.

FUNCTIONS OF SECONDARY COMPOUNDS IN PLANTS

It has been suggested that the terpenes or isoprenoids contain more different compounds than any other group of plant products, although the alkaloids must be nearly as numerous. The carotenoids, abscisic acid, and gibberellic acid, have important physiological functions in plants and certain essential oils and oleoresins seem to be important in repelling predators or attracting pollinators. However, many of the compounds synthesized by plants, especially terpenes and alkaloids, have few known functions. It sometimes is argued that everything in an organism must have a function, but it seems improbable that every aspect of plant metabolism is equally important in the process of natural selection. It is more probable that many of these substances are merely products of synthetic processes which originated incidentally in ancient ancestors and have persisted simply because they do not have enough negative effect on survival to have been eliminated by natural selection. On the other hand, considerable attention has been given to the possible protective functions of phenolic compounds and other compounds against pathogens and insect pests (Lunderstädt, 1976; Wallace and Mansell, 1975).

The small percentage of food diverted into rubber in wild plants apparently has not reduced their competitive ability, so rubber synthesis has persisted even though the rubber appears to be useless to the plants which form it. However, man has recently released the rubber tree from natural competition and has selected strains which probably convert food into rubber at the expense of vegetative growth. It is unlikely that such plants could survive competition in nature.

Some attempts have been made to use fatty acids, essential oils, and terpenes as aids in classifying plants. However, fatty acids are not useful because the same ones occur in the seeds of unrelated plants and there also are genetic differences in fatty acids within genera and even among individuals of the same species. Hitchcock and Nichols (1971) present a brief discussion of the use of lipids in plant classification. Mirov (1961) studied differences in the terpenes for clues to the taxonomic relationships among the pines and Squillace (1971, 1976) discussed inheritance of terpenes in slash pine as well as various methods of analysis. Flake *et al.* (1969) and others used terpene composition to study population distribution of eastern redcedar and Erdtman (1973) discussed the use of secondary plant compounds in plant taxonomy.

There is increasing interest in using biochemical methods as aids to morphological descriptions in characterizing and identifying new varieties for plant patents and other purposes. Conventional descriptions are inadequate because size, form, and color vary with environmental conditions, but at least some biochemical characteristics should be relatively stable. Larsen (1969) proposed the use of isoenzymes to distinguish between cultivars and Kuhn and Fretz (1978) separated them in rose cultivars by electrophoresis. Asen (1977) reported that use of high pressure liquid chromatography permits rapid characterization of the flavonoid profile in plants. Thielges (1972) found differences in foliage polyphenols among pines from different provenances and Fretz (1977) distinguished among the many varieties of creeping junipers by measuring differences in concentrations and proportions of various terpenes by gas chromatography in plants grown under similar conditions. Much work is being done in this field and it appears that biochemical methods may provide important additions to the morphological descriptions now used for identification of cultivars and races of plants.

GENERAL REFERENCES

Bonner, J., and Varner, J. E., eds. (1976). "Plant Biochemistry," 3rd ed. Academic Press, New York.

Galliard, T., and Mercer, E. I., eds. (1975). "Recent Advances in the Chemistry and Biochemistry of Plant Lipids." Academic Press, New York.

Gibbs, R. D. (1974). "Chemotaxonomy of Flowering Plants." McGill University Press, Montreal.

Goodwin, T. W., and Mercer, E. I. (1972). "Introduction to Plant Biochemistry." Pergamon, Oxford.

Hitchcock, C., and Nichols, B. W. (1971). "Plant Lipid Biochemistry." Academic Press, New York.

Martin, J. T., and Juniper, B. E. (1970). "The Cuticle of Plants." Arnold, London.

Miller, L. P., ed. (1973). "Phytochemistry." Van Nostrand-Reinhold, Princeton, New Jersey.

Smith, P. M. (1976). "The Chemotaxonomy of Plants." Arnold, London.

Nitrogen Metabolism and Nutrition

INTRODUCTION

Compounds containing nitrogen constitute only a small proportion of the total dry weight of woody plants but they are extremely important physiologically. The nitrogen content of the foliage amounts to about 1.0 to 1.2% of the dry weight in apple and pine, while that of the wood is much lower (Tables 9.1 and 9.2). The low concentration of nitrogen compounds is in contrast to that of cellulose, which is a structural component

TABLE 9.1   Distribution of Nitrogen in Apple Trees in Mid-October[a,b]

	Oven-dry weight (kg)	Nitrogen (kg)	Nitrogen (percent dry weight)
Leaves	13.43	0.166	1.23
Spurs	2.57	0.027	1.04
Wood aged:			
1 year	4.56	0.043	0.93
2 years	5.55	0.037	0.67
3 years	5.38	0.029	0.54
4–6 years	19.88	0.070	0.35
7–10 years	65.48	0.177	0.27
11–18 years	62.93	0.102	0.16
Main stem	30.75	0.044	0.14
Total above ground	210.52	0.694	0.33
Root stump	22.75	0.059	0.26
Roots aged:			
1–6 years	2.45	0.030	1.24
7–13 years	13.30	0.080	0.60
14–18 years	20.96	0.067	0.32
Total in roots below ground	59.45	0.236	0.40
Total for tree	269.97	0.930	0.34

[a] From Murneek (1942).

[b] Average of three varieties—Grimes, Jonathan, and Delicious.

of cell walls and constitutes over one-half of the dry weight of woody plants, but is physiologically and biochemically inactive. The relatively small amounts of nitrogen-containing compounds occur in living cells where they have essential roles in biochemical and physiological processes. First in importance among these compounds are the proteins, which form the structure of protoplasm, and the enzymes, which catalyze the biochemical processes of plants. Large amounts of protein also accumulate in the seeds of some plants. Large amounts of nitrogen occur in substances such as amides, amino acids, nucleic acids, nucleotides and other nitrogenous bases, hormones, vitamins, and alkaloids (see Fig. 6.20). Most of these substances are of great physiological importance, but the alkaloids, although economically important, seem simply to be by-products of metabolism which at most provide modest protection against attacks by pests.

From the seedling stage to mature trees, nitrogen is required for growth and nitrogen deficiency is, after water stress, the most common limitation on growth. The largest amount of nitrogen is required for the production of proteins used in the formation of protoplasm for new cells. Another important use is in the formation of chlorophyll and cytochrome, and a large part of the nitrogen in leaves occurs as enzymes in the chloroplasts and mitochondria. One of the most common symptoms of nitrogen deficiency is the pale or mottled green color of leaves resulting from inadequate synthesis

TABLE 9.2 Amounts of Nitrogen in Various Parts of Trees in a 16-Year-Old Loblolly Pine Plantation[a]

Tree part	Nitrogen (kg/ha)	Percentage
Needles, current	55	17.1
Needles, total	82	25.5
Branches, living	34	10.6
Branches, dead	26	8.0
Stem wood	79	24.6
Stem bark	36	11.2
Above-ground total	257	80.0
Roots	64	19.9
Total	321	

[a] From Wells *et al.* (1975).

of chlorophyll. Lack of chlorophyll reduces photosynthesis and thus indirectly reduces growth.

The demand for nitrogen is closely related to the amount of growth. Those trees completing a large part of their annual growth early in the season use large amounts of nitrogen at that time. Although few data are available regarding the source of this nitrogen, much of it must come from reserves in the tree because the average forest soil is rather low in available nitrogen and absorption would therefore be slow. Orchardists commonly supply nitrogen to fruit trees to ensure an adequate supply during this critical period of growth. Most forests suffer from some degree of nitrogen deficiency (see Anonymous, 1968) and foresters are now finding that they can afford to apply fertilizer under at least some conditions. However, nitrogen deficiency is less serious for trees with their long growing season, in which absorption can occur over a long period of time, than for crop plants, which make most of their growth and require most of their nitrogen within a few weeks. As nitrogen is very mobile within plants it is commonly translocated from inactive to active tissues, making a deficiency somewhat less obvious than for a less mobile element.

DISTRIBUTION AND SEASONAL FLUCTUATIONS OF NITROGEN

Because of its physiological importance, numerous studies have been made of the fluctuations in the nitrogen content of various parts of trees. The amount of nitrogen present varies with the tissue, the age or stage of development, and the season. Much of the nitrogen occurs in the protoplasm and associated, physiologically active substances. Thus the highest concentrations of nitrogen are found in tissues composed chiefly of physiologically active cells, including leaves and meristematic tissues such as cambia and root and stem tips. Seeds are also often high in nitrogen, but there it occurs chiefly as reserve food and is relatively inactive physiologically. Some data on the protein content of seeds are given in Chapter 14.

Concentration in Various Tissues

Table 9.1 shows the distribution of nitrogen in various parts of an 18-year-old apple tree sampled in mid-October. The concentration in the leaves was higher than in any other part of the tree, except possibly the youngest roots, and it decreased from the youngest to the oldest wood. Of the total nitrogen in the apple tree, 75% was in the above-ground parts and nearly 20% in the leaves. Earlier in the season even more of the total nitrogen content probably was in the leaves, because the outward movement which occurs before leaf fall probably would have already started in mid-October. The concentration in the fruit spurs also was relatively high. Essentially the same situation apparently exists in broad-leaved evergreen trees, because Cameron and Compton (1945) found that nearly 50% of the total nitrogen present in bearing orange trees was in the leaves, about 10% in twigs, and 25% in the branches and trunk. Less than 20% of the total was in the roots. In another study Cameron and Appleman (1933) found that in 3.5-year-old orange trees 60% of the total nitrogen occurred in the leaves, but in 10-year-old trees the leaves contained only 40% of the total nitrogen. Although the concentration was relatively high in roots, they never contained more than 21% of the nitrogen in the trees. The distribution of nitrogen in various parts of 16-year-old loblolly pine trees was shown in Table 9.2. As in apple and orange, about 25% of the nitrogen in the trees occurs in the leaves and it appears that, in general, the concentration of nitrogen is higher in the leaves than in any other part of trees.

This high concentration of nitrogen forms the basis for the suggestion that when trees are cut the foliage ought to be saved and processed to provide a nitrogen supplement for cattle and even for human food. This apparently is being done in Russia where the product is called ''muka'' (Young, 1976). Leaf protein has been recommended for some years as a supplement to protein-deficient human diets (Pirie, 1975). The concentration of nitrogen, carbohydrates, and pigments in leaves of *Populus* are similar to those in forage crops such as alfalfa, and forest foliage seems to be a good potential source of supplementary food for livestock as well as for humans (Dickson and Larson, 1977). The nutritive value of leaves and twigs of trees and shrubs is evidenced by the success of such browsing animals as deer, giraffes, and elephants.

The nitrogen content of the heartwood usually is much lower than that of the sapwood, as shown in Fig. 9.1. This decrease in nitrogen content from sapwood to heartwood is associated with the death of parenchyma cells and the movement of their nitrogen to growing regions. The pith and adjacent annual ring contain more nitrogen than the bulk of the heartwood and sometimes more than the sapwood. Similar patterns of distribution were found in conifer and hardwood stems by Merrill and Cowling (1966), who reported that high nitrogen content favors the activity of wood-rotting fungi. Allsopp and Misra (1940) found that the newly formed xylem of ash and elm contained about 5% nitrogen, but the older sapwood contained only 1.3 and 1.7%, respectively. Considerable amounts of soluble nitrogen compounds, mostly amides and

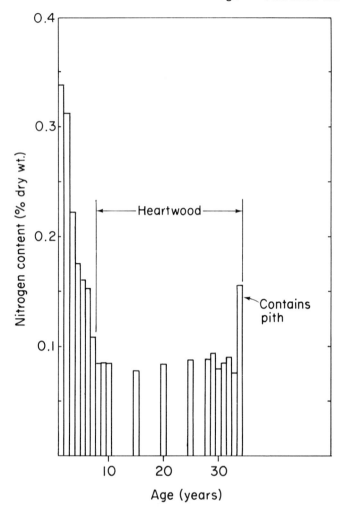

Fig. 9.1. The nitrogen content of sapwood and heartwood of red oak. The distribution patterns are similar in white ash, Sitka spruce, and white pine. From Merrill and Cowling (1966).

amino acids, also occur in the xylem sap (Bollard, 1960; Barnes, 1963a,b; also see Chapter 10).

The phloem ("bark") contains considerably more nitrogen than the wood (Figs. 9.2 and 9.3) and is an important source of nitrogen for growth. In orange trees each flush of growth is accompanied by a decrease in the nitrogen content of the adjacent branch bark (Fig. 9.2).

Seeds often contain considerable nitrogen because in some species the principal reserve food is protein. Several species of acorns averaged about 1.1%, pinyon pine

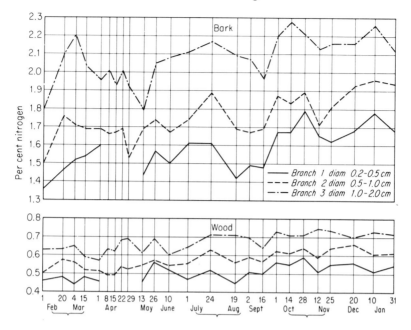

Fig. 9.2. Seasonal changes in the nitrogen content of wood and bark of branches of various sizes on Valencia orange trees, expressed as percentages of dry weight. Brackets under dates indicate periods of shoot growth. From Cameron and Appleman (1933).

2%, digger pine 5%, and longleaf pine 6% nitrogen. Data on the chemical composition of a number of tree seeds are presented in Table 14.1.

Seasonal Changes in Nitrogen Content

There is strong interest in seasonal changes in the content of nitrogen and other constituents in leaves and woody tissue of perennial plants because they provide the material required for the first flush of growth in the spring. There also is interest in learning when these materials accumulate, because this information may indicate the best time to fertilize and it aids in predicting the severity of injury resulting from defoliation by insects, pathogenic organisms, or storms. As a result, so many studies have been made of the accumulation of nitrogen and other minerals, chiefly on fruit trees and forest plantations, that only a few can be mentioned.

In both deciduous and evergreen trees the concentration of nitrogen in the woody tissue tends to increase during the autumn and winter, to decrease when growth begins, and then to increase again as growth slows and ceases. Figure 9.4 shows seasonal changes in the nitrogen content of various parts of 15-year-old Stayman Winesap apple trees over an entire year. The total amount of nitrogen in the wood decreased when growth was rapid and increased when growth ceased. Apparently much of the nitrogen in the leaves was translocated back to the spurs in the early autumn before leaf fall

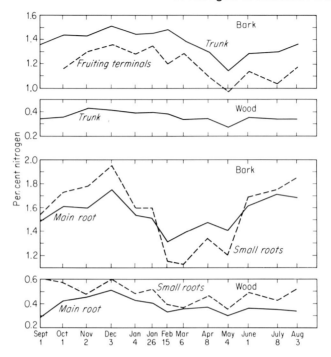

Fig. 9.3. Seasonal variations in nitrogen content of root and stem wood and bark of young Valencia orange trees. From Cameron and Appleman (1933).

occurred. Figure 9.5 shows seasonal variations in several forms of nitrogen in apple leaves. Tromp (1970) summarized considerable data on seasonal changes in total nitrogen, protein nitrogen, soluble nitrogen, and arginine in the wood and bark of young, nonbearing, well-fertilized apple trees. The amounts of all forms of nitrogen were high during the winter, decreased in the spring, and remained low until growth ceased. Accumulation occurred again during the autumn, reaching a maximum in December and January. It is possible that nitrogen accumulation actually begins in the latter part of the growing season, but if expressed on a percentage basis the increase is obscured by the increase in dry matter that normally occurs as the growing season progresses. The decrease in the nitrogen content of wood and bark in the spring is caused by transport to developing buds and new shoots. It has been shown for apples (Oland, 1963; Tromp, 1970), peaches (Taylor and May, 1967), and grapes (Possingham, 1970) that nitrogen stored in the bark and wood is more available for new growth than that supplied externally. This view is based on observations that, when growth starts, nearly as much stored nitrogen is removed from the tissues of fertilized as from those of unfertilized plants. It also is supported by other data. It was reported that the nitrogen content of the bark (living phloem) of Bartlett pear decreased when growth began, but began to increase after growth slowed down and reached a maximum in the winter (Mulay, 1931). Levi and Cowling (1968) found that as leaves

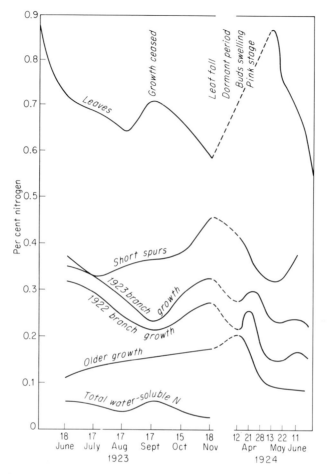

Fig. 9.4. Seasonal changes in the total nitrogen content of leaves, short spurs, and 1-year, 2-year, and older branches of apple as percentages of fresh weight. From Thomas (1927).

developed there was a marked decrease in the nitrogen content of the sapwood of southern red oak. Likewise, each flush of growth in orange trees produces a decrease in the nitrogen content of the adjacent woody tissue (see Fig. 9.2). Apparently the chief source of nitrogen is the phloem, since the wood shows smaller changes in nitrogen content than the bark. Figure 9.3 showed large seasonal fluctuations in the nitrogen content of root and shoot bark of young, nonfruiting Valencia orange trees.

The data on seasonal changes in nitrogen in conifers are somewhat limited but indicate that they are similar to those in deciduous species. Study of loblolly pine by Nelson *et al.* (1970) in the mild climate of Mississippi showed that both dry matter and nitrogen are accumulated throughout the year, although the rate becomes quite low in the autumn and winter. There was evidence of translocation of nitrogen out of the bark

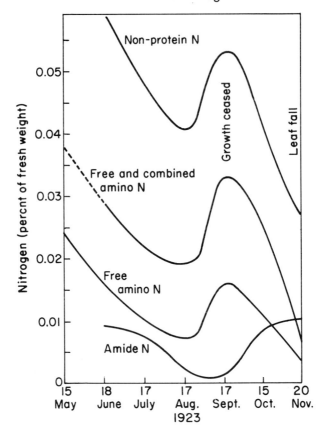

Fig. 9.5. Seasonal changes in the forms of nitrogen present in apple leaves, expressed as percentages of fresh weight. From Thomas (1927).

and wood during the period of rapid stem elongation and an increase during late summer and autumn to a winter maximum, followed by a decrease in late winter (Fig. 9.6). Translocation out of wood and bark in late winter began before stem elongation was resumed but the material presumably was used in the first flush of growth.

Durzan has published several papers reporting effects of season, time of day, light intensity, and mineral nutrition on the amount and kinds of nitrogen compounds in conifers. He concluded that more attention needs to be paid to changes in amino acids in relation to shade tolerance and other environmental factors (Durzan, 1971).

Tromp (1970) reviewed considerable research on seasonal changes in the composition of the soluble nitrogen fraction in wood and bark of fruit trees. Arginine seems to be an important constituent during the dormant season, but the arginine content in wood and bark decreases in the spring, probably because of translocation to growing shoots and incorporation into new protein and possibly because of conversion into other

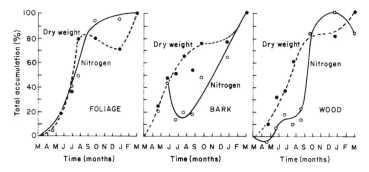

Fig. 9.6. The relative dry matter and nitrogen accumulation in foliage, bark, and wood during the fifth year of development of a loblolly pine stand. From Nelson *et al.* (1970).

compounds. It has been suggested that arginine is synthesized from amides in the autumn and winter but this has not been conclusively demonstrated. Application of nitrogenous fertilizer seems to increase arginine more than other soluble nitrogen compounds. It also is reported that the concentration of arginine is quite high in the xylem sap of apple during the autumn and winter, but decreases during the growing season when asparagine and aspartic acid are the chief organic nitrogen compounds in the sap (Bollard, 1960). The latter two compounds largely disappear during the dormant season. Table 9.3 shows changes in the composition of the xylem sap of apple

TABLE 9.3 Proportions of Various Nitrogenous Compounds Present in Apple Xylem Sap at Several Times during the Growing Season in New Zealand[a,b]

	Date					
Compound	Oct. 12	Oct. 19	Oct. 26	Nov. 29	Dec. 29	Jan. 26
Aspartic acid	12	10	22	31	58	41
Asparagine	65	59	52	65	34	48
Glutamic acid	+	+	+	1	2	3
Glutamine	20	27	24	4	6	7
Serine	+	1	+	+	+	2
Threonine	2	1	1	+	+	+
Methionine + valine	1	1	1	+	+	1
Leucine	1	1	+	+	+	+
Total nitrogen (μg/ml)	41	117	131	48	22	12
Percentage of total nitrogen contributed by aspartic acid + asparagine	77	69	74	96	92	89

[a] From Bollard (1958).

[b] Results expressed as percent *N* by each compound. + = present but less than 1%.

during the growing season. Siminovitch and Briggs (1949) found that exposure of trees to low temperatures was accompanied by an increase in water-soluble proteins. Parker (1958) reported that the total protein content of the inner bark of trees of several species increased from August to December. The concentration of several free amino acids decreased during this period, but proline increased. Changes in nitrogen supply, water stress, and other environmental factors often produce significant changes in the kinds of nitrogen compounds occurring in trees.

Autumn Movement from Leaves

It was mentioned earlier that leaves may contain over 40% of the total nitrogen content of trees. Fortunately, a considerable part of the nitrogen and other materials in the leaves usually is translocated back into the twigs and branches before leaf abscission occurs. This movement is quite important because otherwise a large fraction of the nitrogen in the plant would be lost at least temporarily by leaf fall. Oland (1963), in Norway, made a careful study of the changes in the major constituents of apple leaves during senescence and abscission. He estimated that the decreases during 3 to 4 weeks of senescence amounted to 16% of the dry matter, 52% of the nitrogen, 27% of the phosphorus, and 36% of the potassium. There was no change in magnesium content and an 18% increase in calcium during this period. Loss by leaching was regarded as negligible during the experimental period, and most of the material was transported into the perennial woody structures of the 12-year-old apple trees. The time course for

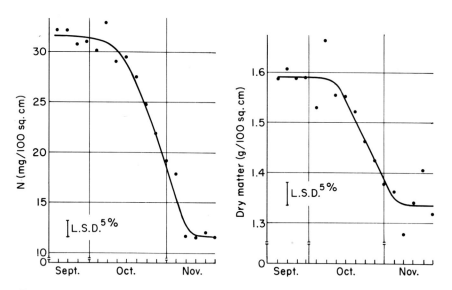

Fig. 9.7. Changes in dry matter and nitrogen content per 100 cm² of leaf blade of senescing apple leaves. From Oland (1963).

the autumn decrease in dry matter and nitrogen is shown in Fig. 9.7. Grigal *et al.* (1976) studied changes in the nitrogen content of five deciduous shrubs in Minnesota—maple, alder, shadbush, hazel, and willow—during late summer and autumn. The concentrations of nitrogen, phosphorus, and potassium in the leaves decreased in the autumn while the concentrations in the twigs and stems were increasing. In these species the calcium content of all components increased over time, but the data for magnesium content were variable. Grigal *et al.* (1976) cite considerable literature on seasonal changes in the concentrations of various components of woody plants.

The autumn movement of nitrogen out of leaves has been observed in many other deciduous species, including beech, elm, forsythia, cherry, horsechestnut, pear, plum, and yew. Reports of translocation out of leaves range from one-third to two-thirds of their nitrogen content. However, some of the measurements failed to take into account losses by leaching while the leaves were still on the trees, as shown in Fig. 9.7. Satisfactory studies require measurement of gains in the woody parts of plants as well as losses from their leaves, but this is very difficult. In contrast to the data on deciduous species, Cameron and Appleman (1933) reported no decrease in the nitrogen content of orange leaves before abscission. There seem to be few data for conifers, except the decrease in nitrogen concentration with increased age mentioned later, but Wells (1968) reported no changes in the nitrogen concentration of loblolly pine needles during the autumn and early winter in the southeastern United States.

Changes in Distribution with Age

Changes in nitrogen content associated with aging are confounded with the effects of season, especially in leaves of deciduous plants. For example, as leaves grow older the proportion of cell wall material increases and this causes an apparent decrease in nitrogen and other constituents when expressed as percentage of dry weight (Tromp, 1970). Madgwick (1970) reported that the nitrogen content of needles of Virginia pine decreased from 1.2% in first-year needles to 1.0% in third-year needles, but some of this apparent decrease possibly was caused by increase in dry weight. Penning de Vries *et al.* (1975, p. 73) assumed that 30 to 50% of the nitrogen in pine needles is moved back into the tree before needle fall occurs, but the basis for this estimate was not given. In California most of the nitrogen moves into leaves of Gambel oak and California black oak early in their development, but leaf expansion continues, resulting in a gradual decrease in nitrogen per unit of leaf area during the summer. There is a rapid decrease in nitrogen content in the autumn as senescence occurs and nitrogen compounds are translocated back to the wood before abscission occurs (Sampson and Samisch, 1935).

The decrease in nitrogen content with increasing age is particularly noticeable in the woody parts of trees. Table 9.4 shows little difference in the nitrogen concentration of new growth, leaves, or fruit of apple trees of various ages, but there is a decrease in the woody parts of older trees. In loblolly pine the nitrogen concentration of the woody parts decreases with age, but that of the current leaves of older trees remain high, as

TABLE 9.4 Effect of Age on Nitrogen Content of Leaves, New Growth, Trunks and Branches, Roots, and Fruit of Apple Trees[a]

Age (years)	Leaves		New growth		Trunks and branches		Roots		Fruit	
	Oven-dry weight (%)	Nitrogen (g)	Oven-dry weight (%)	Nitrogen (g)	Oven-dry weight (%)	Nitrogen (g)	Oven-dry weight (%)	Nitrogen (g)	Oven-dry weight (%)	Nitrogen (g)
1	1.71	0.44			0.30	0.29	0.39	0.20		
2	2.09	1.51			0.57	1.36	0.88	1.14		
5	1.76	7.84	0.89	1.93	0.48	17.20	0.64	9.85		
9	1.70	61.50	0.82	9.08	0.35	85.50	0.58	81.00	0.31	10.55
30	2.09	394.00	0.95	13.60					0.31	258.00
100	1.04	435.00	1.04	390.00	0.27	2,863.00	0.22	417.00		

[a] From Gardner et al. (1952). Copyright 1952; used with permission of McGraw-Hill Book Company.

TABLE 9.5 Changes in Percentage of Nitrogen with Increasing Age in Various Tissues of Loblolly Pine Growing on Good Sites[a]

Tree age	Current foliage	Older branches	Stem bark	Stem wood
4	1.00	0.41	0.42	0.16
8	0.95	0.24	0.24	0.06
18	1.08	0.23	0.23	0.06
30	1.22	0.22	0.19	0.04
56	1.16	0.21	0.17	0.03

[a] From Switzer *et al.* (1968).

shown in Table 9.5. Thus, conifers and hardwoods seem to show similar trends. It was mentioned earlier that sapwood contains more nitrogen than heartwood and the youngest sapwood has the highest concentration, presumably because it contains the most living parenchyma cells. In general, nitrogen appears to move out of cells as they become senescent and the nitrogen concentration of old tissue typically is lower than that of young tissue.

IMPORTANT NITROGEN COMPOUNDS

Having discussed the distribution of nitrogen in trees we will consider some of the compounds in which it occurs. Among the most important of these are amino acids, amides, nucleic acids, nucleotides and nucleosides, proteins, and the alkaloids (see Fig. 6.20). Much of our information concerning nitrogen metabolism comes from research on microorganisms. Plant proteins are often difficult to work on because, when plant tissue is macerated, oxidases and proteolytic enzymes are released and proteins often are precipitated by tannins that are abundant in some plants. Only the outlines of protein metabolism can be mentioned and readers are referred to books such as those by Bonner and Varner (1976), Goodwin and Mercer (1972), and Hewitt and Cutting (1968) for more detailed discussions.

Amino Acids

The amino acids are the basic building blocks of protoplasmic proteins. Most amino acids have the basic formula $R\text{-}CHNH_2\text{-}COOH$ and have properties of both bases and acids, because each amino acid has an amino group (NH_2) and a carboxyl group ($COOH$). In the simplest amino acid, glycine, R is represented by a hydrogen atom ($CH_2NH_2\text{-}COOH$). In others, R may be very complex and may contain additional amino or carboxyl groups. Some 20 amino acids are commonly considered to be components of plant proteins and all of them presumably occur in woody plants (Bollard, 1958).

Amino Acid Synthesis

Amino acids can be produced in several ways, including reductive amination, transamination, chemical transformation of acid amides or other nitrogen compounds, and hydrolysis of proteins by enzymes. The first two methods probably are the most important.

Nitrate Reduction

Nitrate is the most common source of nitrogen for plants, and reduction of nitrate to ammonia is an important step in nitrogen metabolism. Nitrate is absorbed readily by trees and usually is quickly reduced, although it may accumulate if the carbohydrate supply and level of metabolic activity are low. The level of nitrate reductase activity may also vary, leading to variation in the amount of nitrate present (Hewitt and Smith, 1975). A possible pathway is as follows:

$$NO_3^- \longrightarrow NO_2^- \longrightarrow N_2O_2^{2-} \longrightarrow NH_2OH \longrightarrow NH_3$$

| Nitrate | Nitrite | Hypo-nitrite | Hydroxyl-amine | Ammonia |

In another pathway preferred by some, the nitrogen is reduced more directly to ammonia (Burris, 1976). The energy for nitrate reduction is supplied by oxidation of carbohydrates, and the ammonia produced is finally combined with organic acids to form amino acids, as will be shown later. Some intermediates of the reduction process are toxic in moderate concentrations, but they ordinarily do not accumulate in sufficient quantities to cause injury.

It is generally assumed that, at least in well-fertilized crop plants, nitrate reduction occurs chiefly in the leaves (Beevers and Hageman, 1969), the nitrate being translocated from roots to leaves in the xylem sap (Shaner and Boyer, 1976). However, in the numerous species of woody plants studied, it appears that nitrate is reduced in the roots because organic forms of nitrogen predominate in the xylem sap. Bollard (1958) found traces or small amounts of nitrate in the xylem sap of only one-third of 131 woody and herbaceous species examined, but a variety of amino acids and amides were present in the sap of all species. All nitrogen in the sap of apple and several other Rosaceous fruits occurred as amino acids and amides, the most common during the growing season being asparagine, aspartic acid, and glutamine. Barnes (1963b) found 17 amino acids and ureides in the xylem sap of 60 species of North Carolina trees analyzed in June and July. Citrulline and glutamine comprised 73 to 88% of the organic nitrogen in the seven species of pine which were studied, and Bollard (1957b) found the same compounds predominating in the xylem sap of Monterey pine, sampled in New Zealand. Where large amounts of organic nitrogen occur in the xylem, it seems reasonable to assume that nitrate reduction occurs chiefly in the roots.

Reductive Amination

The ammonia resulting from nitrate reduction can react with an organic acid to produce an amino acid by reductive amination, as shown in the following reaction.

$$
\begin{array}{l}
\text{COOH} \\
| \\
\text{C}=\text{O} \\
| \\
\text{CH}_2 \\
| \\
\text{CH}_2 \\
| \\
\text{COOH}
\end{array}
\;+\;\text{NH}_3\;+\;\text{NADH}_2
\;\xrightarrow[\text{dehydrogenase}]{\text{glutamic}}\;
\begin{array}{l}
\text{COOH} \\
| \\
\text{CHNH}_2 \\
| \\
\text{CH}_2 \\
| \\
\text{CH}_2 \\
| \\
\text{COOH}
\end{array}
\;+\;\text{H}_2\text{O}\;+\;\text{NAD}
$$

α-Keto-glutaric acid   Glutamic acid

This process is catalyzed by glutamic dehydrogenase, and NAD or NADP as a coenzyme. The α-ketoglutaric acid is produced by the Krebs cycle (tricarboxylic acid cycle) as was shown in Fig. 6.20. A quantitatively less important pathway starts with pyruvic acid and yields alanine and oxaloacetic acid, which yields aspartic acid.

Transamination

Transamination involves the transfer of an amino group from one molecule to another. This is exemplified by the reaction between glutamic and oxaloacetic acid to produce α-ketoglutaric acid and aspartic acid. A transaminase enzyme is involved.

$$
\begin{array}{l}
\text{COOH} \\
| \\
\text{CHNH}_2 \\
| \\
\text{CH}_2 \\
| \\
\text{CH}_2 \\
| \\
\text{COOH}
\end{array}
\;+\;
\begin{array}{l}
\text{COOH} \\
| \\
\text{C}=\text{O} \\
| \\
\text{CH}_2 \\
| \\
\text{COOH}
\end{array}
\;\xrightarrow{\text{transaminase}}\;
\begin{array}{l}
\text{COOH} \\
| \\
\text{C}=\text{O} \\
| \\
\text{CH}_2 \\
| \\
\text{CH}_2 \\
| \\
\text{COOH}
\end{array}
\;+\;
\begin{array}{l}
\text{COOH} \\
| \\
\text{CHNH}_2 \\
| \\
\text{CH}_2 \\
| \\
\text{COOH}
\end{array}
$$

Glutamic acid   Oxalo-acetic acid α-Keto-glutaric acid   Aspartic acid

Another group of amino acids originates from shikimic acid and gives rise to tyrosine, phenylalanine, and tryptophan (see Fig. 6.20). Phenylalanine and tyrosine may be incorporated directly into protein or serve as precursors of alkaloids or components of lignin. Tryptophan also gives rise to alkaloids but is best known as the precursor of the plant hormone indoleacetic acid.

Peptides

Peptides, like proteins, consist of amino acids joined by peptide linkages, that is, by the bonding of the carboxyl group of one amino acid molecule with the amino group of another molecule. If the molecular weight of the resulting compound is less than 6000 it is arbitrarily designated a peptide. From the standpoint of human pathology some of the smaller peptides are of great interest. Penicillin is a tripeptide, pollen allergens also are peptides, and other peptides are pharmacologically active. It is predicted by Goodwin and Mercer (1972) that many other physiologically important peptides will be identified.

Amides

Among the common nitrogen compounds found in plants are the amides glutamine and asparagine. Glutamine is formed from glutamic acid by a reaction with ammonia.

$$
\begin{array}{c}
\text{COOH} \\
| \\
\text{CHNH}_2 \\
| \\
\text{CH}_2 \quad + \text{NH}_3 \ + \text{ATP} \\
| \\
\text{CH}_2 \\
| \\
\text{COOH}
\end{array}
\xrightarrow[\text{synthetase}]{\text{glutamic}}
\begin{array}{c}
\text{COOH} \\
| \\
\text{CHNH}_2 \\
| \\
\text{CH}_2 \quad + \text{ADP} \ + \text{H}_3\text{PO}_4 \\
| \\
\text{CH}_2 \\
| \\
\text{CONH}_2
\end{array}
$$

Glutamic   Glutamine
acid

It would be expected that asparagine would be formed from aspartic acid in the same manner, but this has not been demonstrated (Goodwin and Mercer, 1972, p. 227). It is supposed that synthesis of these amides prevents the accumulation of injurious concentrations of ammonia in plants. They also appear in seedlings when storage proteins are being used in growth. If severe carbohydrate deficiency develops they can be oxidized, but this may be accompanied by the release of injurious amounts of ammonia. Glutamine also is important metabolically. It appears to be the donor of the nitrogen group in the synthesis of carbamyl phosphate and it probably is the donor of nitrogen to aspartic acid in the formation of asparagine.

Nucleic Acids and Related Compounds

Substituted purine and pyrimidine bases are the constituents of many extremely important compounds. These include nucleic acids (RNA and DNA); nucleosides such as adenosine, guanosine, uridine, and cytidine; nucleotides such as AMP, ADP, and ATP; the nicotinamide nucleotides (NAD and NADP); thiamine; coenzyme A; and cytokinins (see Fig. 6.20). Nucleotides are phosphate esters of nucleosides and the nucleic acids (DNA and RNA) are high-molecular-weight polymers formed from long chains of four kinds of nucleotide units derived from adenine, guanine, thymine, and cytosine. The genetic material in the nucleus is DNA, each molecule consisting of two polynucleotide chains arranged in a double helix. Small amounts of DNA occur outside of the nucleus in mitochondria and chloroplasts.

RNA molecules consist of single strands. The sugar associated with RNA is ribose while that associated with DNA is deoxyribose. Thymine is replaced by uracil in RNA molecules. Three kinds of RNA occur in ribosomes, nuclei, and other organelles: messenger RNA (mRNA), transfer RNA (tRNA), and ribosomal RNA (rRNA). Their role in protein synthesis will be discussed later.

Proteins

Proteins are the principal organic constituents of protoplasm. They are exceedingly complex nitrogenous substances of high molecular weight which differ from one another in shape, size, surface properties, and even in function. They all, however, have in common the fact that they are built up from amino acids, are amphoteric, and have colloidal properties. An amphoteric compound acts as an acid or a base. Proteins possess basic NH_2 and acidic COOH groups and are positively charged at pH values below the critical "neutral" value, known as the isoelectric point, and negatively charged at pH values above the isoelectric point. In addition to forming the structural framework of protoplasm, proteins also occur as enzymes and reserve foods, especially in seeds.

Although the molecular weights of proteins are always high, there is considerable variation in weights of the various types. Some of the seed or storage proteins have molecular weights of 200,000 to 400,000. Amandin, a protein of almond, has a molecular weight of 329,000, and hippocastanum, a protein found in horsechestnut seed, has a molecular weight of 430,000. Some enzymes also are very large, urease having a molecular weight of 400,000 and catalase, 500,000. On the other hand, some protein molecules are quite small, with molecular weights of 10,000 to 50,000.

On a dry-weight basis, proteins usually contain 50 to 55% carbon, 6 to 7% hydrogen, 20 to 23% oxygen, and 12 to 19% nitrogen. All plant proteins contain small amounts of sulfur and some also contain phosphorus.

The classical method of classifying proteins was on the basis of solubility, but separation on this basis has become increasingly unsatisfactory and classification on a functional basis might be more useful. For instance, they might be classified as structural or protoplasmic, storage, and enzyme proteins. The structural proteins include those in protoplasm and its components, such as chloroplasts. Storage proteins are particularly abundant in seeds and are an important source of food for humans and animals as well as for germinating seedlings.

Some enzymes such as urease and papain function alone. They are simply protein molecules and their catalytic properties are determined by the arrangement of the amino acid residues of which they are composed. Others require that a cofactor or prosthetic group be associated with the protein molecule. In some instances the cofactor is a metal ion such as copper or iron. Still other enzymes require the presence of nonprotein prosthetic groups or more loosely associated cofactors such as the pyridine nucleotides, NAD and NADP.

When decomposed by acids, alkalies, or enzymes, proteins produce a mixture of amino acids, but during the course of hydrolysis several products of intermediate complexity are formed as follows:

Proteins → proteoses → peptones → polypeptides → dipeptides → amino acids

Enzymatic degradation is more specific, the enzymes usually attacking certain specific chemical bonds and splitting off specific amino acids or groups of amino acids, rather than the large, poorly defined groups or compounds split off by acid or alkali hydrolysis.

A protein molecule consists of a long chain of amino acids brought together by peptide linkages or bonds in which the carboxyl group of an amino acid unites with the amino group of another amino acid, with water being split off in the reaction. An example of a peptide linkage is the union of two molecules of glycine (CH_2NH_2COOH).

$$CH_2CO(OH + H)-N \qquad \longrightarrow \qquad CH_2CONH \qquad +\ HOH$$

CH_2COOH		CH_2COOH	
$CH_2CO(OH+H)-N$		CH_2CONH	$+\ HOH$
NH_2	H	NH_2	
Glycine	Glycine	Dipeptide	Water

Inspection of the dipeptide formed in this reaction shows a free carboxyl and a free amino group available for possible linkage to other amino acids. No matter how many additional amino acids are linked to such a dipeptide, there are always free amino and carboxyl groups in the resulting complex molecule. Thus, with the union of several hundred amino acids in peptide linkages, a protein is formed. The skeleton of a protein molecule might be pictured as follows:

In this chain, R_1, R_2, R_3, and R_4 represent residues of different amino acids. In the case of glycine (CH_2NH_2COOH) R = H; in alanine (CH_3CH-NH_2COOH) R = CH_3.

In a living plant proteins are in a dynamic state and are constantly being broken down and reformed, but the total amount of protein may remain constant over considerable periods of time, because degradation is being balanced by synthesis. Various proteins differ in stability and have their characteristic rates of turnover.

Protein synthesis occurs most energetically in cells of meristematic regions where cell division is occurring and in storage organs where protein is accumulated, as in endosperms of seeds. It takes place on ribosomes in the cytoplasm. Ribosomes are organelles composed of protein and RNA. The sequence of amino acids, and therefore the kinds of protein formed, is controlled genetically by messenger RNA from the cell nucleus. Units of messenger RNA are produced under the control of DNA strands in the nucleus and migrate to the ribosomes where they function as templates or models for the formation of protein molecules. Transfer RNA also is involved in the movement of amino acids to ribosomes. Readers are referred to biochemistry or plant physiology texts for a more complete discussion of this important but complex process.

Alkaloids

Alkaloids are a large and complex group of cyclic compounds which contain nitrogen. About 2,000 different compounds have been isolated, some of which are of pharmacological interest. These include morphine, strychnine, atropine, colchicine, ephedrine, quinine, and nicotine. They are most common in herbaceous plants, but some occur in woody plants, chiefly tropical species.

Alkaloids are commonly concentrated in particular organs such as the leaves, bark, or roots. For example, although nicotine is synthesized in the roots, 85% of that in a tobacco plant occurs in the leaves, and the cinchona alkaloids are obtained from the bark. Alkaloids also sometimes occur in wood, and the wood of some species of the families Anacardiaceae, Apocynaceae, Euphorbiaceae, Leguminosae, Rutaceae, and Rubiaceae contains so much alkaloid that it produces dermatitis (Garratt, 1922). Among alkaloids derived from trees the cinchona alkaloids are best known because of their use in the treatment of malaria. They occur in the Andean genera *Cinchona* and *Remijia* of the family Rubiaceae.

In spite of their wide occurrence in plants no essential physiological role has been found for alkaloids. However, it is possible that in some instances they discourage fungal, bacterial, or insect attacks. They appear to be by-products of nitrogen metabolism which ordinarily cause neither injury nor benefit to the plants which produce them, and the amount of nitrogen diverted into them apparently is too small to be of selective importance in competition.

Phytotoxins and Pathogenicity

Among the more exotic areas of nitrogen chemistry are the phytotoxins (Strobel, 1974) and the biochemistry of pathogenesis (Albersheim and Anderson-Prouty, 1975). A number of phytotoxins produced by fungi are derived from amino acids. Also, the specificity of host–parasite relationships is said to depend to a considerable degree on nitrogenous compounds. Albersheim and Anderson-Prouty (1975) suggest that susceptibility to attack by pathogens often depends on the fact that the plasma membranes of plant cells contain proteins which are specific receptors for antigenlike carbohydrates of the pathogen. Also the polysaccharide-degrading enzymes produced by plant pathogens play an important role in infection. This area is just beginning to be studied and doubtless will receive more attention in the future.

NITROGEN REQUIREMENTS

Numerous estimates have been made of the nitrogen requirements of forest and fruit trees. Table 9.6 shows the annual nitrogen requirements for various purposes of individual 20- and 25-year-old apple trees. Nearly one-third of the total annual requirement of the younger trees and about one-fifth of that of the older trees is used in the fruit and is removed by harvesting it. As trees grow older, proportionally less of the total nitrogen is used in fruits and a higher proportion is used in root and top growth. Five to six percent of the nitrogen is temporarily lost by the shedding of flowers and young fruits in the spring and 30 to 40% by abscission of leaves in the autumn.

It is reported that in years when a heavy fruit crop develops, little nitrogen is stored

TABLE 9.6   Estimated Annual Nitrogen Requirements of Apple Trees[a]

	20-year-old-trees[a]		25-year-old trees[b]	
	Grams	Percent of total	Grams	Percent of total
For fruit crop	180	30.53	150	21.57
Loss (temporary) from abscised blossoms and fruit	30	4.59	40	5.88
Loss (temporary) from abscised leaves	180	30.53	270	39.22
For top and root growth (maintenance)	160	26.72	230	33.33
Removed by pruning	50	7.63	230	
Total	590	100.00	690	100.00

[a] From Murneek (1942).
[b] From Magness and Regeimbal (1938).

and existing reserves are seriously or completely depleted (Murneek, 1930). This results in decreased vegetative growth and inhibition of flower bud formation during the current and even the following year. Sometimes more than 1 year is required for complete recovery. These effects are similar to the effects of heavy fruiting on carbohydrate reserves, discussed in Chapter 7.

In Europe it was estimated that deciduous forest stands use 30 to 60 kg of nitrogen per hectare and return about 80% in leaf fall. Baker (1950) estimated the uptake at 40 to 50 kg/ha, of which about 80% is returned in leaf fall. However, the data presented earlier in this chapter suggest that at least in some species one-third of the nitrogen in leaves is translocated back to the branches before leaf fall and the losses in leaf fall are much lower than 80%. Data for minerals returned to soil by leaf fall (see Table 10.7) indicate that relatively small amounts of nitrogen are temporarily lost in this way, about 19 kg/ha in New York and a little less in South Carolina.

According to Switzer et al. (1968), a 20-year-old stand of loblolly pine contains over 300 kg/ha of nitrogen and uses about 70 kg/ha annually for the production of new tissue. Of this, 38 kg comes from the soil and the remainder comes from within the tree, chiefly from the leaves. The distribution of nitrogen in young pine trees was shown in Table 9.2. The total loss in litter (leaves, twigs, branches) is estimated at 30 kg/ha/ year. Of course this loss is temporary, since most of the nitrogen is recycled; hence only about 8 kg/ha of new nitrogen are required. Recycling will be discussed later, but this much new nitrogen might be supplied in precipitation.

Bormann et al. (1977) state that a 55-year-old beech, maple, and birch forest in New England contains 351 kg/ha of nitrogen in the above-ground biomass and 180 kg/ha in the below-ground biomass. About 120 kg are used in growth, of which one-third is withdrawn from storage in the plant tissue. About 20 kg/ha of nitrogen are added to the system each year, of which about 14 kg are supplied by fixation in the soil and about 6 kg by precipitation. Very little nitrogen is lost from this forest.

These data indicate that considerably less nitrogen is required for tree growth than for cultivated crops. Corn, for example, absorbs over 175 kg/ha of nitrogen and alfalfa may use over 200 kg/ha in a growing season, most of which must be absorbed from the soil in a short time. According to Hardy and Havelka (1976), soybeans use nearly 300 kg/ha of nitrogen, of which about 25% is fixed in root nodules. Fruit trees typically have high nitrogen requirements, ranging from 60 to 175 kg/ha depending on the number and size of the trees. Forest trees obtain most of their nitrogen from the decay of litter and atmospheric fixation, but fruit trees must be fertilized.

There is evidence that tree species differ in their nitrogen requirements, because some species occur only on fertile soil while others can grow on infertile soil. After extensive studies on the mineral nutrition of 12 common deciduous species, Mitchell and Chandler (1939) divided them into three categories with respect to nitrogen requirements. Red, white, and chestnut oak, trembling aspen, and red maple are most tolerant of low nitrogen; pignut hickory, sugar maple, beech, and blackgum are intermediate; and white ash, yellow-poplar, and basswood have high nitrogen requirements. Roberds *et al.* (1976) reported considerable variation in response to nitrogen fertilization among different families of loblolly pine. More research on the nitrogen requirements of tree species and families within species would be profitable.

SOURCES OF NITROGEN

Trees can use nitrogen in the form of nitrates, nitrites, ammonium salts, and organic nitrogen compounds such as urea, but regardless of its initial form most nitrogen probably is absorbed in the form of nitrate or ammonium (Hauck, 1968). It is converted into organic compounds in the roots, chiefly amides and amino acids, which are then translocated to the shoots in the xylem sap (Barnes, 1963a,b; Bollard, 1975b; Mothes and Engelbrecht, 1952). Early pot studies indicate that loblolly pine can absorb both nitrate and ammonium nitrogen, nitrate being preferable at low pH, ammonium nitrogen at higher pH values (Addoms, 1937). According to Nemec and Kvapil (1927), European conifers absorb most of their nitrogen as ammonia, while hardwoods, especially ash, beech, and oak, obtain it chiefly as nitrate. Pharis *et al.* (1964) reported on the complex interaction between various forms of nitrogen and the calcium supply with respect to growth of loblolly pine seedlings, and Hauck (1968) discussed the soil–fertilizer interactions involving pH, water, aeration, and other elements that make it difficult to generalize concerning the best source of nitrogen.

The principal sources of the nitrogen used by forest trees are that fixed in the soil by microorganisms, that washed out of the atmosphere by rain and snow, and that released by decay of litter in the forest floor. Commercial fertilizers are the most important source of nitrogen for orchard trees and ornamental shrubs and are beginning to be used on forest trees. Some nitrogen is lost to the atmosphere during ammonification and denitrification and some is lost by leaching during heavy rainfall.

Nitrogen Fixation

Although the atmosphere consists of about 80% nitrogen, atmospheric nitrogen is very inert and this potential source can be used by trees only after it is "fixed" or combined with other elements. Nitrogen fixation by microorganisms and lightning replaces nitrogen lost from the soil by leaching, fire, and absorption by plants and prevents its ultimate exhaustion. The biological aspects of nitrogen fixation are discussed in a book edited by Quispel (1974) and are reviewed briefly by Burris (1976).

Nitrogen fixation occurs by the same process in both free living and symbiotic organisms. An enzyme complex called nitrogenase reduces N_2 through several steps by combination with hydrogen, forming NH_3 which is combined with organic acids to form amino acids (see Fig. 6.20). ATP also is required and the process can be described by the following equation:

$$N_2 + 6e^- + 6H^+ + nATP \rightarrow 2NH_3 + nADP + nP_i$$

The hemoglobin found in root nodules, the only place it occurs in the plant kingdom, seems to play an indirect role by controlling oxygen concentration. Nitrogenase can reduce various other substrates, including hydrogen. Reduction of hydrogen leads to the production of acetylene (C_2H_2), which is easily reduced to CH_4, and this reaction is widely used to measure nitrogenase activity. Free-living bacteria fix less nitrogen per unit of protoplasm than those in nodules because they use more energy in growth (Mulder, 1975).

Nonsymbiotic Nitrogen Fixation

Nitrogen fixation in the soil occurs largely as the result of activity by saprophytic bacteria of the genera *Azotobacter* and *Clostridium*. These bacteria are mostly free-living in the soil but a few species have been found which are restricted to the rhizosphere of certain plants. Some blue-green algae also fix nitrogen and are effective colonizers of raw soil and other extreme habitats. Anaerobic forms are said to be more common than aerobic forms in forest soils, probably because the high acidity common in forest soils is unfavorable for the aerobic nitrogen-fixing bacteria. According to Russell (1973, p. 353) the number of nitrogen-fixing bacteria is so low in many soils that it is doubtful that they fix a very large quantity of nitrogen. Nonsymbiotic nitrogen fixation is discussed in detail in a book edited by W. D. P. Stewart (1975).

Symbiotic Fixation by Legumes

As was mentioned in Chapter 2, bacteria of the genus *Rhizobium* penetrate the roots of many species of legumes, producing root nodules in which nitrogen fixation occurs. Symbiotic nitrogen fixation is most important in forestry where trees are closely associated with numerous wild, herbaceous legumes, as in the southeastern United States. Chapman (1935) reported increased height and diameter growth of several species of hardwoods planted beside black locust trees. He also found that total nitrogen in the soil was greatest near the black locust trees and concluded that the improved growth was the result of nitrogen fixation by the locust.

Nitrogen fixation by bacterial nodules on roots can be affected in several ways by water stress. Infection and nodule formation can be reduced and nitrogen fixation can be reduced by loss of water from nodules in drying soil. It is possible that plant water stress reduces the transport of nitrogen compounds from roots to shoots and it has been suggested that the reduced supply of carbohydrates produced by stressed shoots reduces nitrogen fixation in nodules (Sprent, 1976). At any rate there seems to be an indirect effect of water stress in the shoot in addition to the direct effects on nodules. The rate of nitrogen fixation often, but not always, is affected by the rate of photosynthesis and nodules are strong "sinks" for the products of photosynthesis (see Papers 31 and 35 in Nutman, 1976). Increasing the CO_2 concentration of the air to 800 to 1,200 ppm increased both dry weight and nitrogen fixation of soybeans (Paper 31 in Nutman, 1976).

Fixation in Nonlegumes

Nitrogen-fixing root nodules usually are identified with the family Leguminosae. However, root nodules occur on a number of nonleguminous dicotyledonous plants and have been reported on many species of trees and shrubs in various families including Betulaceae, Eleagnaceae, Myricaceae, Rhamnaceae, Casuarinaceae, Coriariaceae, Zygophyllaceae, and Rubiaceae (Allen and Allen, 1958). These observations were confirmed and extended by Bond (see Paper 32 in Nutman, 1976). All the plants in these families are adapted to growth on poor sites. Bond and his co-workers have demonstrated appreciable nitrogen fixation by several nodulated nonleguminous woody plants, including *Alnus, Myrica, Hippophaë, Shepherdia,* and *Casuarina.* This work was summarized by Bond (1967, 1976). A root system bearing nodules was shown in Fig. 2.36. Alder plants, grown from seeds in the greenhouse and caused to develop nodules by inoculation with a suspension of crushed nodules from field seedlings, showed excellent growth in a rooting medium free of combined nitrogen, indicating that fixation of elemental nitrogen is associated with the nodulated plant. In another experiment, Bond (1956) showed that field nodules of alder, like those of greenhouse-grown plants, regularly fix nitrogen; he concluded that the amount of nitrogen fixed is substantial. Bond and Gardner (1957) reported that under experimental conditions nitrogen fixation by European alder and *Myrica gale* during the first year of growth exceeded that of annual legumes and of. black locust.

Nitrogen fixation by nodulated nonlegumes appears to be of considerable ecological significance in certain areas. For example, Crocker and Major (1955) noted that at Glacier Bay, Alaska, an average of 61.6 kg/ha of nitrogen accumulated under alder thickets. This created a favorable site for Sitka spruce, which succeeded alder. There is increasing interest in the nitrogen-fixing capacity of red alder in forests of the Pacific Northwest. The value of interplanting alder in conifer plantations to improve the growth of conifers has long been recognized by Europeans and is also practiced in Japan. The beneficial effects are undoubtedly due to greater nitrogen availability.

Virtanen (1957) demonstrated that when spruce was planted beside alder, it obtained nitrogen fixed in the root nodules of the alder. He calculated that, in a grove of alders about 2.5 m high and with 10,000 trees per hectare, the leaf fall and roots remaining in the soil would add about 200 kg/ha of nitrogen. Nitrogen losses were not taken into account in his calculations. For comparison, Hardy and Havelka (1976) state that soybeans use about 300 kg/ha of nitrogen of which about 25% is fixed in root nodules. Actinomycete nodules on the roots of California chaparral also fix significant amounts of nitrogen (Kummerow *et al.*, 1978).

The nodules on nonleguminous plants appear to be composed of much-branched lateral roots, whereas those on legumes are usually developed from cortical cells (Torrey, 1976). Also, in almost all of the nonlegume or *Alnus*-type nodules nitrogen fixation is carried on by actinomycetes of the genus *Frankia*, the best-established exception being the occurrence of *Rhizobium* in root nodules of *Trema*, a woody genus of the Ulmaceae growing in New Guinea (Bond, Paper 32 in Nutman, 1976). Readers are warned that enlargements on roots can be caused by nematodes and other agents and the presence of nodules should not be assumed to indicate the presence of nitrogen-fixing organisms without careful verification. Blue-green algae are said to form symbiotic relationships with and supply nitrogen to mosses, lichens, and some seed plants, but only in the herbaceous genus *Gunnera* do they actually invade the cells (Silvester, Paper 37 in Nutman, 1976). It has been reported that some bacteria form nodules and fix nitrogen in the leaves of several kinds of plants, including species of *Psychotria, Pavetta, Ardisia,* and *Dioscorea.* However, van Hove (Paper 39 in Nutman, 1976) concluded from acetylene reduction and growth tests that if nitrogen reduction occurs in these leaf nodules it is too limited in amount to be important in the nitrogen economy of the plants. It is possible, however, that the bacteria produce growth regulators such as cytokinin or other substances which are beneficial to the plants. It is also claimed that bacteria living on leaf surfaces (the phyllosphere) can fix nitrogen (Ruinen, 1965; Jones, 1970). For example, Jones claims that bacteria living on the surfaces of Douglas-fir needles fix measurable amounts of nitrogen.

There is wide interest in finding methods for increasing the amount of nitrogen fixed by vegetation. This includes searching for methods of increasing nitrogen fixation in those plants where it already occurs and possibly inducing microbial nitrogen fixation in the rhizosphere of species other than the tropical grasses in which it has been observed. A more exotic approach involves genetic manipulation by use of recombinant DNA techniques to introduce the nitrogen-fixing gene into plant species where it does not exist. Another possibility is fusion of protoplasts to transfer the gene or genes which make legumes good hosts for *Rhizobium* to other plants. However, formidable difficulties must be solved before the desired types of plants can be produced by these techniques.

Atmospheric Nitrogen Fixation

Measurable amounts of nitrogen are returned to the soils in rain and snow. Precipitation brings down ammonia and nitrogen oxides fixed by electrical storms, released by volcanic and industrial activity, and a small amount leached from tree canopies. Baker (1950) estimated that about 5 kg/ha of nitrogen is returned from the atmosphere annually, but Larcher (1975) gives a maximum of 10 kg/ha per year. He states that this is only about one-seventh the amount fixed by microbial activity. Although the amount seems small, Wells *et al.* (1975) state that rainfall supplies nitrogen to forests in the southeastern United States at about the same rate that it is removed by conventional harvesting methods, or about 6.5 kg/ha/year for a pulpwood cutting of a 16-year-old pine stand.

Release from Litter

Some of the nitrogen absorbed by trees is returned to the soil in fallen litter. Maintenance of forest soil fertility is partly dependent on the return of nitrogen and mineral nutrients by decay of litter. Leaves and twigs which are annually added to the forest floor may add up to several thousand pounds of organic material containing approximately 1% nitrogen-containing compounds. Baker (1950) gives 3,400 kg/ha for fully stocked forests on good sites in the United States as a reasonable average annual amount of leaf and twig deposit. Wide variations occur, however, and values as low as 500 kg/ha have been measured on poor beech sites while the best European beech stands return as much as 6,700 kg/ha of leaf and twig debris.

The amount of nitrogen in litter varies greatly with species. Chandler (1941) found the nitrogen content of leaf litter of hardwoods in central New York State to vary from 0.43 to 1.04%, with an average of 0.65%, while Coile (1937a) found values ranging from 0.50% to 1.25% in conifers and hardwoods in the Piedmont of North Carolina. Hardwood leaves and litter generally have higher average nitrogen contents than do coniferous leaves. Conifer leaves which have been shed contain about 0.6 to 1.0% nitrogen, while fallen hardwood leaves generally contain from 0.8 to 2.0% nitrogen (Baker, 1950). However, values considerably lower than 0.8% have been reported for several hardwoods (Coile, 1937a; Chandler, 1941; Alway *et al.*, 1933).

With an average addition of 3,400 kg/ha of litter by forest trees and an average nitrogen content of 0.6 to 2.0%, the return of nitrogen is approximately 20 to 70 kg/ha. Larcher (1975, p. 126) reports a nitrogen loss in leaf fall of 61 kg/ha from a mixed deciduous forest in Belgium and 33 kg/ha/year for an evergreen oak forest in southern France. This is approximately 70% of the nitrogen absorbed.

The rate of decomposition of litter varies with species, nutrient conditions of the soil, aeration, moisture conditions, and temperature. In general, hardwood leaves decompose more rapidly than do coniferous leaves. Decomposition is slow in northern latitudes and most rapid in tropical areas (Lutz and Chandler, 1946). In northern forests up to 50 years may be required to release all the nitrogen from 1 year's twig and leaf litter, and serious mineral deficiencies can develop because of the slow rate of decay. The increased rate of growth following thinning of overstocked young stands is caused at least in part by the release of nitrogen and other nutrients from the decay of the slash (Tamm, 1964, pp. 148–149). In tropical forests decay is very rapid and the turnover is correspondingly rapid. In shallow, acid, infertile tropical soils it is believed that the fungal mat often found in the surface layer plays an important role in speeding up the recycling of nitrogen and other nutrients (Went and Stark, 1968).

Nitrogen Fertilization

It has long been standard practice to fertilize fruit and ornamental trees, and fertilization of forest plantations is increasing. Although benefits are obtained from phosphorus in Australia, New Zealand, and special areas such as the wet coastal plains of the southeastern United States, and fruit and ornamental trees often show deficiencies of micronutrients, forest trees generally benefit most from applications of nitrogen. A number of different kinds of nitrogen fertilizers are available and there has been considerable research on the relative merits of ammonium and nitrate nitrogen, urea, and various slow-release formulations. Hauck (1968) stated that there is no clear evidence that one form is much better than another, and the economics of first cost and cost of application may be determining factors in the choice of the form of nitrogen to be used. The response to nitrogen fertilization depends on other environmental factors such as water supply, soil aeration, and the adequacy of the supply of other mineral nutrients. For example, Wells *et al.* (1976) estimated that fertilization of pole-size stands of loblolly pine increased wood production by 14 m³/ha over a 5-year

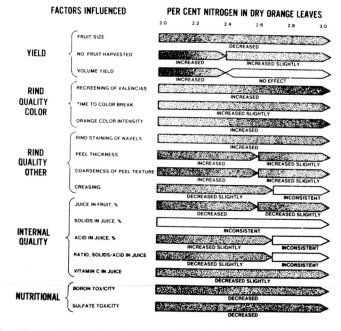

Fig. 9.8. Effects of increasing nitrogen on yield and quality of oranges. The greater the intensity of stippling the greater the effect on the factor. From Embleton *et al.* (1975).

period on a nitrogen-deficient soil, but only 2.1 m³ on a soil high in nitrogen. Considerable information on the fertilization of forest trees can be found in *Forest Fertilization: Theory and Practice* (Anonymous, 1968) and Youngberg and Davey (1970). The complex effects of nitrogen fertilization on yield and quality of oranges are shown in Fig. 9.8.

THE NITROGEN CYCLE

In general, growth of trees and other plants is limited more often by a deficient supply of nitrogen than by lack of any other substance, except water. As a result there has long been a keen interest in the rates at which nitrogen is absorbed and lost during

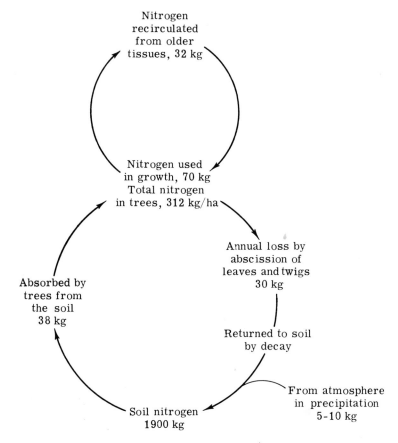

Fig. 9.9. A simplified diagram of the major components of the nitrogen cycle in a 20-year-old loblolly pine stand, based on data of Switzer *et al.* (1968).

cycling in various kinds of plant stands and ecosystems. Larcher (1975, pp. 91–100) and Curlin (in Youngberg and Davey, 1970) summarized considerable information on this subject. According to Switzer *et al.* (1968) the 20-year-old pine stand studied by them contained 2,300 kg/ha of nitrogen, including about 1900 kg/ha occurring in the surface soil, but only used 70 kg/ha/year, of which 38 kg came from the soil and the remainder from foliage and twigs before they abscised. The falling foliage and other plant parts were estimated to return about 30 kg/ha to the soil, leaving 8 kg to be supplied from other sources. This much probably could be supplied by atmospheric fixation. A simple diagram of the nitrogen cycle of this pine stand is shown in Fig. 9.9. The nitrogen budgets of an American and a European pine stand are shown in Table 9.7. Mitchell *et al.* (1975) produced a tentative nitrogen budget for a mature hardwood forest in southwestern North Carolina, which is shown in abbreviated form in Table 9.8. This system seems to contain considerably more nitrogen than either pine stand shown in Table 9.7, but it is considerably older. As in the pine stand, about 80% of the nitrogen occurs in the soil and a little more than 10% in the trees. The turnover of leaves is more rapid than for conifer foliage, but there probably is little difference between the rates of turnover of nitrogen in other parts of the system in pine and hardwood forests. According to Bormann *et al.* (1977) in a New England hardwood forest about 90% of the nitrogen is in soil organic matter, 9.5% in the vegetation, and 0.5% exists as available nitrogen in the soil. In contrast, nearly 30% of the nitrogen in the surface soil, and trees of a tropical forest ecosystem is in the trees (Sanchez, 1973).

A generalized diagram of the nitrogen cycle on a global basis is shown in Fig. 9.10. The input of nitrogen comes from fixation by symbiotic and nonsymbiotic bacteria and

TABLE 9.7   Comparison of the Distribution of Nitrogen within Plantation Ecosystems[a,b]

Ecosystem fraction	Corsican pine[c] (37 years)	Loblolly pine[d] (20 years)
Trees (crowns,	83	89
boles,	60	85
stumps, and roots)	113	138
Total trees	256	312
Ground vegetation	8	0
Forest floor	322	124
Total organic matter	586	436
Soil	1376	1900
Total ecosystem	1962	2336

[a] From Switzer *et al.* (1968).
[b] Data given in kg/ha.
[c] Corsican pine in Scotland.
[d] Loblolly pine in central Mississippi.

TABLE 9.8 Estimated Nitrogen Content of Various Components of a Mature Hardwood Forest in Southwestern North Carolina[a]

Component	Nitrogen (kg/ha)
Reproductive structures	2.7
Leaves	95.0
Stems and branches	310.0
Roots	150.0
Litter	137.0
Total N in trees	694.7
Soil organic matter	3873.0
Soil organisms	175.0
Total N in soil	86.5
Total N in system	4829.2

[a] Adapted from Mitchell *et al.* (1975).

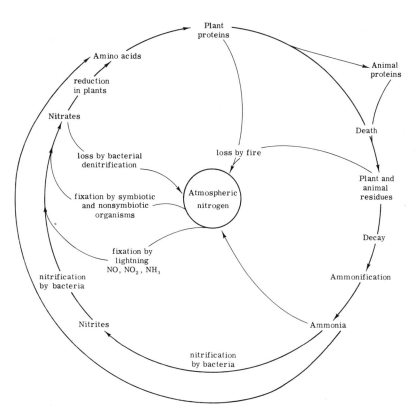

Fig. 9.10. A simple, generalized nitrogen cycle

other organisms, atmospheric fixation by lightning, that escaping from volcanoes and industrial processes, and that supplied by fertilization and the decay of plant and animal residues. The last is not really an input but the recapture of nitrogen lost during decay. Nitrogen fixation was discussed in more detail earlier in this chapter and does not require further discussion.

The losses of nitrogen are caused chiefly by the action of denitrifying bacteria which reduce nitrates to molecular nitrogen, loss of ammonia during decay of plant and animal residues, fire, and leaching. Forest fires, set either by lightning or man, have occurred from the earliest times and have had considerable effect on the types of tree stands. For example, the forests of the southeastern United States are composed chiefly of fire-resistant species. The frequency and importance of fires are well documented by various writers in *Fire and Ecosystems,* edited by Kozlowski and Ahlgren (1974). In recent years, prescribed burning has become a common silvicultural tool to control diseases, reduce hardwood reproduction, and decrease the damage from wild fires. This has produced considerable interest in the effects of fire on the mineral nutrition of trees.

Considerable nitrogen is lost when the litter and organic matter on the forest floor are burned, but other elements are released and become immediately available so that growth may actually be increased. Viro (1974, p. 39) concluded that in northern Europe the gains from increased mineralization of nitrogen after fire greatly outweigh the effect of the losses during fires. This may also be true in California chaparral where mineralization is slow and nitrate nitrogen increases in the soil after burning (Christensen, 1977). Also in the southeastern United States pine stands have been burned repeatedly over many years without significantly reducing the rate of growth. Effects of fire on site quality also are discussed in Chapter 17.

Losses of nitrogen and other nutrients by leaching are negligible in undisturbed forests (Bormann *et al.,* 1977) and ordinarily are not seriously increased by prescribed burning. If all vegetation is destroyed, as in one of the Hubbard Brook experiments (Likens *et al.,* 1970), losses may be heavy. However, there usually is rapid regrowth of vegetation after clear cutting or burning, and this recaptures most of the nutrients released by decay of slash or left in the ash after a fire.

GENERAL REFERENCES

Anonymous (1968). "Forest Fertilization: Theory and Practice," Symposium on Forest Fertilization, Gainesville, Florida, 1967. Tenn. Valley Auth., Muscle Shoals, Alabama.

Beevers, L. (1976). "Nitrogen Metabolism in Plants." Arnold, London.

Bonner, J., and Varner, J. E., eds. (1976). "Plant Biochemistry," 3rd ed. Academic Press, New York.

Burns, R. C., and Hardy, R. W. F. (1975). "Nitrogen Fixation in Bacteria and Higher Plants." Springer-Verlag, Berlin and New York.

Goodwin, T. W., and Mercer, E. I. (1972). "Introduction to Plant Biochemistry." Pergamon, Oxford.

Hewitt, E. J., and Cutting, C. V., eds. (1972). "Recent Aspects of Nitrogen Metabolism." Academic Press, New York.

Hewitt, E. J., and Smith, T. A. (1975). "Plant Mineral Nutrition." Wiley, New York.

Miller, L. P. (1973). "Phytochemistry." Van Nostrand-Reinhold, Princeton, New Jersey.

Nutman, P., ed. (1976). "Symbiotic Nitrogen Fixation in Plants." Cambridge Univ. Press, London and New York.

Pirie, N. W., ed. (1975). "Food Protein Sources." Cambridge Univ. Press, London and New York.

Quispel, A., ed. (1974). "The Biology of Nitrogen Fixation." Am. Elsevier, New York.

Stewart, W. D. P., ed. (1975). "Nitrogen Fixation by Free-Living Microorganisms." Cambridge Univ. Press, London and New York.

10

Mineral Nutrition and Salt Absorption

MINERAL NUTRITION

Mineral nutrition is an important phase of tree physiology because an adequate supply of certain mineral elements is essential for successful growth. Plants require oxygen, water, carbon dioxide, nitrogen, and about a dozen mineral elements as reagents or raw materials for various synthetic processes and for other purposes. Persons not trained in plant physiology often call mineral nutrients "plant foods" and arborists speak of "feeding" trees when they apply fertilizers. Plant physiologists frown on such undiscriminating use of the term "food" because they usually restrict it to carbohydrates, fats, and proteins which can be used directly as sources of energy when oxidized in respiration or as building materials in the formation of new tissue (see

334

Chapter 6). Minerals and carbon dioxide usually are regarded by physiologists as raw materials, reagents, or accessory substances necessary for the synthesis of foods, rather than as foods.

General Functions of Minerals

Mineral nutrients have many functions in plants. Among their more important roles are as constituents of plant tissues, catalysts in various reactions, osmotic regulators, constituents of buffer systems, and regulators of membrane permeability. Examples of minerals as constituents are calcium in cell walls, magnesium in the chlorophyll molecule, sulfur in certain proteins, and phosphorus in phospholipids and nucleoproteins. Although nitrogen is not a mineral element, it often is included with them and its importance as a constituent of protein should be noted. Several elements—including iron, copper, and zinc—although required in very small quantities are essential because they are prosthetic groups or coenzymes of certain enzyme systems. Other minerals, such as manganese and magnesium, function as activators or inhibitors of enzyme systems. Some elements, such as boron, copper, and zinc, which are required in extremely small quantities in enzyme systems, are very toxic if present in larger quantities. Toxicity of these and other ions such as silver and mercury probably is related chiefly to their injurious effects on enzyme systems.

Although much of the osmotic pressure of cell sap is attributable to soluble carbohydrates, a measurable fraction results from the presence of mineral salts, and salt often is the major source of the high osmotic pressure of halophytes. Phosphates form one of the important plant buffer systems, and elements such as calcium, magnesium, and potassium form the cations of the organic acid buffer systems. The kinds of ions present often affect the hydration of protoplasm and the permeability of cell membranes, di- and trivalent cations usually decreasing and monovalent cations increasing permeability. Certain ions tend to counterbalance the effect of others, and this is known as an antagonistic or balancing effect. For example, a low concentration of calcium is required to balance sodium and prevent the injury which occurs in a solution of sodium chloride alone.

The importance of an adequate supply of minerals for good plant growth has been appreciated in agriculture and horticulture for many years, but has been largely neglected in forestry until recently. Even now much of the research is on seedling growth in nurseries, but increasing costs of land and higher prices for timber are changing this situation. As tree improvement programs supply planting stock with a higher growth potential, it often becomes necessary to provide a more adequate supply of mineral nutrients if the growth potential of the stock is to be realized. Furthermore, shorter rotations and utilization of parts other than the boles will greatly increase the rate at which mineral nutrients are removed from the soil. For these reasons it may become as important to fertilize forest tree plantations as it now is to fertilize agricultural crops. More research on the specific mineral requirements of trees is badly needed as a basis for silvicultural management and to insure better adaptation of trees to site conditions.

The Essential Elements

More than half of the elements in the periodic table have been found in plants, and it seems probable that every element occurring in the root environment is absorbed. At least 27 elements were identified in certain samples of white pine wood (Wilcox, 1940), and others doubtless occur in small quantities. Not all the elements found in trees are essential, however. For example, Parker (1956) found platinum, tin, and silver in leaves of ponderosa pine, and considerable quantities of aluminum, silicon and sodium occur in plants, but none of these elements is regarded as essential.

A mineral element is considered essential if (1) plants cannot complete their life cycle without it, and (2) if it is part of a molecule of some essential plant constituent (Epstein, 1972). The essentiality of an element can be determined under only the most carefully controlled conditions which exclude the possibility of contamination with the element under study from the salts, the water, the containers in which the plants are grown, or even from dust in the air. The minimum amounts of various elements necessary for successful growth can be determined most readily by using soil, sand, or water cultures, or by field fertilization experiments. The adequacy of the supply of various elements in the field can also be studied by analysis of soil and plant tissues (foliar diagnosis) and by observation of the effects of supplying various elements to the soil or directly to the foliage. Methods for such studies are discussed by Epstein (1972), Gauch (1972), and Reisenauer (1976) who also cite many papers on methods and on mineral composition of plants.

The elements required in fairly large quantities usually at least 1,000 ppm, are nitrogen, phosphorus, potassium, calcium, magnesium, and sulfur; these are some-

TABLE 10.1   Relative Amounts of Various
Elements Found in Dried Leaf Tissue of a
Healthy Plant[a]

Element	Content (ppm)
Nitrogen	20,000
Potassium	15,000
Calcium	15,000
Magnesium	3,000
Phosphorus	2,500
Sulfur	2,000
Iron	100
Boron	40
Manganese	40
Zinc	40
Copper	25
Molybdenum	1

[a] From Bollard (1955).

TABLE 10.2 N, P, K, Ca, and Mg in Various Components of Trees in a 16-Year-Old Loblolly Pine Plantation[a]

Component	N	P	K	Ca	Mg
Needles, current	55	6.3	32	8	4.8
Needles, total	82	10.3	48	17	7.9
Branches, living	34	4.5	24	28	6.1
Branches, dead	26	1.5	4	30	3.0
Stem wood	79	10.7	65	74	22.7
Stem bark	36	4.2	24	38	6.5
Above ground, total	257	30.9	165	187	46.2
Roots	64	16.9	61	52	21.9
Total	321	47.8	226	239	68.1

[a] From Wells *et al.* (1975).
[b] Measurements are in kg/ha.

times called the major elements or macronutrients. Elements required in smaller quantities include iron, manganese, zinc, copper, boron, molybdenum, and chlorine. It is possible that this list will be expanded further with time. For example, some species of *Atriplex* require sodium, and selenium appears to be essential for some species of *Astragalus*. Those elements required in very small quantities often are called the minor elements or micronutrients. The relative amounts of various essential elements likely to be found in samples of leaf tissue are shown in Table 10.1, and the amounts of certain essential elements found in various parts of trees in a young stand of loblolly pine are shown in Tables 10.2 and 10.3. Other data are presented in Table 10.4 and Fig. 10.1.

Relatively little intensive research has been done on the specific mineral requirements of forest trees, but experience with fruit trees suggests that they have the same requirements as herbaceous plants, although the required quantities of some elements

TABLE 10.3 Mn, Zn, Fe, Cu, Al, and Na in Above Ground Components of Trees in a 16-Year-Old Pine Plantation[a,b]

Component	Mn	Zn	Fe	Al	Na	Cu
Needles, current	1.222	0.166	0.334	2.178	0.258	21.5
Needles, total	2.544	0.327	0.650	4.116	0.356	31.6
Branches, living	1.716	0.345	0.915	2.519	1.384	63.7
Branches, dead	—	0.289	1.281	2.902	0.314	69.5
Stem wood	8.445	1.086	1.830	1.790	3.640	275.0
Stem bark	0.951	0.336	1.126	9.705	0.590	59.4
Tree total	13.656	2.383	5.802	21.032	6.284	499.2

[a] From Wells *et al.* (1975).
[b] Measurements of Mn, Zn, Fe, Al, and Na are in kg/ha; those of Cu are in g/ha.

TABLE 10.4 Distribution of Minerals in Various Parts of Trees in Fully Stocked Stands of European Trees on Average Sites[a]

		Percentage of total amount found in:				
Species	Total use (kg/ha)	Wood	Bark	Faggots	Thin-nings	Litter
		Phosphorus				
Spruce	4.5	1	3	7	17	72
Fir	6.3	3	3	5	17	72
Pine	2.7	5	3	6	17	69
Beech	6.3	13	2	6	6	73
Oak	5.0	8	2	5	15	70
		Calcium				
Spruce	30.8	3	1	2	8	86
Fir	35.4	1	1	2	4	92
Pine	11.8	10	2	4	16	68
Beech	45.8	3	1	2	4	90
Oak	35.4	3	1	3	9	84
Percentage of total dry matter in each part		50	5	7	32	6

[a] From Baker (1950, Table 16). Copyright 1950; used with permission of McGraw-Hill Book Company.

may be lower. Generally the necessity for an element should be demonstrated for plants of several unrelated species. The fact that an element improves growth does not prove that it is essential. For example, sodium seems to improve the growth of sugar beets and several other species, but it is not considered essential for them because they will grow without it.

Functions of Various Elements

Most of the research on the roles of various elements has been done with herbaceous plants because their short life cycle permits shorter experimental periods, but some experiments have been performed on fruit trees and forest tree seedlings. The following discussion is based on the reasonable assumption that various elements perform the same functions in both herbaceous and woody species. For more details, readers are referred to Epstein (1972, Chapter 11) and Gauch (1972, Chapters 9 and 10) and the papers cited by them. Descriptions of a few specific functions of each of the essential elements follow.

Nitrogen

The essential role of nitrogen as a constituent of amino acids, the building blocks of proteins, is well known. It occurs in a variety of other compounds such as the purines and alkaloids, enzymes, growth regulators, chlorophyll, and cell membranes. Nitrogen deficiency is accompanied by failure to synthesize normal amounts of chlorophyll,

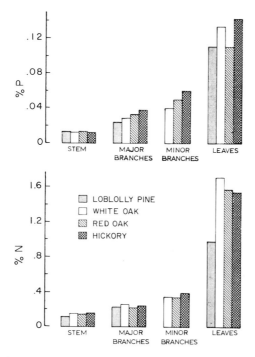

Fig. 10.1. Average concentration of nitrogen and phosphorus in various parts of trees of four species. All data for loblolly pine branches included under major branches. From Ralston and Prince (1965).

resulting in chlorosis of the older leaves and of younger foliage in cases of extreme deficiency. The role of nitrogen was discussed in more detail in Chapter 9.

Phosphorus

This element is a constituent of nucleoproteins and phospholipids, and the high-energy bonds associated with phosphate groups seem to constitute the chief medium for energy transfer in plants. Phosphorus occurs in both organic and inorganic forms and is translocated readily, probably in both forms. Deficiency often causes severe stunting of young trees in the absence of other visible symptoms.

Potassium

Although large amounts of potassium are required, it is not known to occur in organic forms. It apparently is involved in enzyme activity, and a deficiency is said to hinder the translocation of carbohydrates and nitrogen metabolism, but this may be an indirect rather than a direct effect. It is interesting to note that plant cells distinguish between potassium and sodium, and the latter cannot be completely substituted for the former. Potassium also is believed to play a role as an osmotic agent in the opening and closing of stomata. It is highly mobile in plants.

Sulfur

Sulfur is a constituent of cystine, cysteine, other amino acids, biotin and thiamin, and coenzyme A, and occurs in the sulfhydryl group. Deficiency of sulfur causes chlorosis and failure to synthesize proteins, resulting in accumulation of amino acids. Sulfur is less mobile than nitrogen, phosphorus, or potassium.

Calcium

Calcium occurs in considerable quantities in cell walls as calcium pectate and apparently influences cell wall elasticity. It is also involved in some manner in nitrogen metabolism. Calcium is an activator of several enzymes, including amylase. It is relatively immobile, and a deficiency results in serious injury to meristematic regions, especially root tips. Surplus calcium often accumulates as calcium oxalate crystals in leaves and woody tissue.

Magnesium

This element is a constituent of the chlorophyll molecule and is also involved in the action of several enzyme systems. A deficiency usually produces chlorosis. Magnesium is also involved in maintaining the integrity of ribosomes, which disintegrate in its absence. It is translocated readily in most plants.

Iron

Deficiency of iron is one of the most common and conspicuous micronutrient deficiencies of trees, occurring chiefly on alkaline and calcareous soils where the high pH prevents absorption. Much of the iron in leaves occurs in the chloroplasts, where it plays a role in the synthesis of chloroplast proteins. It also occurs in a number of respiratory enzymes such as peroxidases, catalase, ferredoxin, and cytochrome oxidase. Iron is relatively immobile, and deficiencies usually develop in new tissues because it is not translocated out of older tissue.

Manganese

This element also is essential for the synthesis of chlorophyll. Its principal function probably is the activation of enzyme systems, and it probably also affects the availability of iron. A deficiency often causes a malformation of leaves known as "frenching" and the development of chlorotic or dead areas. Manganese is relatively immobile and is toxic except in low concentrations. Manganese concentrations in tree leaves often approach toxic levels, but deficiencies occur in trees planted on calcareous soils.

Zinc

In several species of trees, zinc deficiency produces leaf malformations resembling virus diseases, possibly because it is involved in the synthesis of tryptophan, which is a precursor of indoleacetic acid. Zinc is also a constituent of carbonic anhydrase. Smith and Bayliss (1942) described well-defined symptoms of zinc deficiencies in Monterey pine in Australia, including development of a flat top, and Bollard (1955) discussed boron, manganese, and zinc deficiencies of fruit trees. In spite of widespread occurrence of zinc deficiency in orchards, it has been reported in forests only in Australia. Zinc is very toxic at relatively low concentrations and it would not be surprising if examples of injury from excess zinc are identified as forest management intensifies.

Copper

Copper also is a constituent of certain enzymes, including ascorbic acid oxidase and tyrosinase. Very small quantities are needed, and too much is toxic. Benzian and Warren (1957) demonstrated the need of copper in spruce seedlings and Smith (1943) demonstrated it in Monterey pine. A deficiency causes dieback in citrus, but it does not appear to be a serious deficiency in forest trees. Symptoms of copper deficiency are rather indefinite (Stone, 1968).

Boron

This is another element required in very small quantities, the specific requirements varying from 5-15 ppm, depending on the species. Unfortunately, the concentration for best growth closely approaches the toxic concentration in some species. Conifers probably tolerate lower concentrations of boron than angiosperms. A deficiency causes serious injury and death of apical meristems and it seems to be necessary for sugar translocation. Plants deficient in boron contain more sugars and pentosans and have lower rates of water absorption and transpiration than normal plants. Boron deficiency is common in orchard trees, and according to Stone (1968) it appears to be one of the most common micronutrient deficiencies in forest plantations all over the world.

Molybdenum

This element is required in the lowest concentration of any essential element, less than 1 ppm sufficing for most plants. Molybdenum is involved in the nitrate-reducing enzyme system and probably has other functions (H. J. Evans, 1956). Molybdenum deficiency is not common in orchard or forest trees, but it may reduce nitrogen fixation by leguminous trees and by alder.

Chlorine

It appears that chlorine is essential (Broyer *et al.*, 1954), and it may be involved in the water splitting step of photosynthesis. However, there probably is no serious chlorine deficiency in woody plants.

Other Elements

Aluminum, sodium, and silicon occur in large quantities in some plants, but although these elements sometimes increase growth, they are not usually regarded as essential (Gauch, 1972). An excess of aluminum is highly toxic and ability to tolerate high concentrations of aluminum is very important to the success of some varieties of grain on acid soils. This problem has not been studied in trees. There are numerous and complicated interactions among various elements, one element modifying the absorption and utilization of another, but readers are referred to books such as those by Epstein and Gauch and the review by Stone (1968) for discussions of these interactions. However, it should be mentioned that differences in the success of competing species may depend in part on differences in ability to tolerate abnormally high or low concentrations of specific elements.

Concentration and Distribution of Mineral Elements in Various Organs

In general, the concentration of minerals as percentage of dry weight is as follows: leaves > small branches > large branches > stems. This relationship was shown graphically in Fig. 10.1 for loblolly pine and three species of hardwoods. The relative amounts of minerals in various parts of several species of trees were shown in Tables 10.2, 10.3, and 10.4. The concentration of calcium and magnesium is sometimes higher in bark than in leaves. According to Ralston and Prince (1965) a white oak stand in the North Carolina Piedmont will contain twice as much nitrogen, phosphorus, and potassium, and 15 times as much calcium as a loblolly pine stand of equal basal area. They concluded from these data that a considerably higher level of mineral nutrition is necessary for hardwoods if they are to grow at the same rate as pines.

Although the mineral concentration of leaves is generally high compared to the woody parts it varies considerably with age and position on the tree. Some data illustrating seasonal changes in orange leaves are shown in Fig. 10.2 and seasonal changes in calcium and potassium in leaves of deciduous species are shown in Fig. 10.3. The latter figure also illustrates the effect of increase in dry weight of leaves on apparent mineral content.

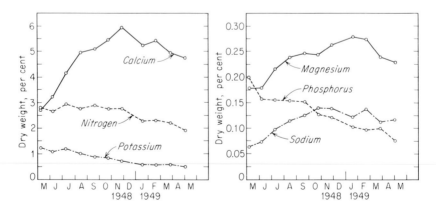

Fig. 10.2. Seasonal variations in mineral concentration in leaves of Valencia orange trees. From Jones and Parker (1951).

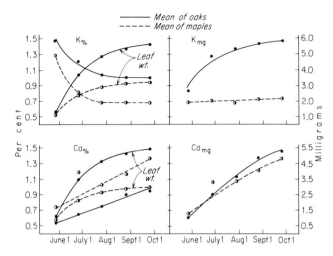

Fig. 10.3. Seasonal trends in calcium and potassium content of leaves of oaks and maples expressed as percentages of dry weight and as milligrams per leaf. The curves for leaf dry weight indicate relative changes rather than absolute weights. From Mitchell (1936).

Symptoms of Mineral Deficiencies

Mineral deficiencies cause changes in biochemical and physiological processes which often produce morphological changes or visible symptoms. Growth sometimes is depressed by deficiencies before other symptoms appear (Ingestad, 1957). Some of the more important morphological and physiological reactions to mineral deficiencies will be discussed briefly.

Visible Symptoms of Deficiencies

The most important general effect of mineral deficiencies is reduced growth, but the most conspicuous effect often is yellowing of the leaves caused by reduced chlorophyll synthesis. Leaves seem to be particularly sensitive indicators of deficiency, tending to be reduced in size, abnormal in shape or structure, or pale in color, and they sometimes even develop dead areas on the tips, the margins, or between the principal veins. In some instances leaves tend to occur in tufts or rosettes, and pine needles occasionally fail to separate properly, producing a disorder known as fused needles. A common symptom of certain types of mineral deficiency in herbaceous species is frenching, in which stem elongation is inhibited and leaf blade growth is reduced, resulting in rosettes of slender leaves which often show a network of chlorotic areas. The visible symptoms of deficiencies of various elements are so characteristic that experienced observers can identify them by appearance. Some examples are shown in Fig. 10.4, and others can be found in various papers and books, including *Forest Fertilization, Hunger Signs in Crops,* Hacskaylo *et al.* (1969) and Kozlowski (1971a, pp. 332–344).

(a)

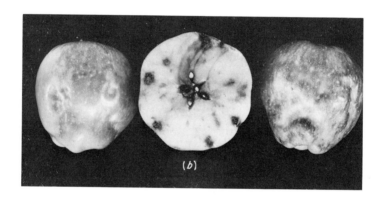

(b)

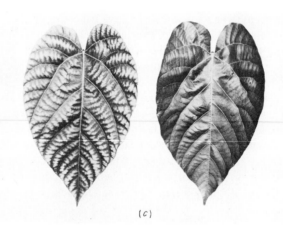

(c)

Deficiencies sometimes cause trees to produce excessive amounts of gum, resulting in so-called "gummosis." In Australia, resin exudation around buds is characteristic of a zinc-deficiency disease of Monterey pine (Kessel and Stoate, 1938). Gummy exudates also occur on the bark of fruit trees suffering from exanthema or dieback (Anderssen, 1932) caused by copper deficiency.

Severe deficiencies often cause the death of leaves, shoots, and other tissues, resulting in symptoms described as dieback. Copper deficiency has been observed to cause dieback of shoots in a variety of forest and fruit trees (Stone, 1968). Dieback of the terminal shoots of copper-deficient apple trees produces a stunted, bushy appearance. Boron deficiency is said to cause dieback and finally death of the cambium in citrus and pine, and death of phloem and physiological breakdown of fruits in other species. Deficiency of a single element sometimes produces several different symptoms. For example, boron deficiency in apple trees causes brittle, deformed leaves, phloem necrosis, lesions in bark, and injury to the fruit (Shannon, 1954).

Chlorosis

The most commonly observed symptom of a wide variety of deficiencies is chlorosis, caused by interference with chlorophyll synthesis. It varies in the pattern, the extent to which young and old leaves are involved, and the severity, according to the species, the element, and the degree of deficiency. Chlorosis most often is associated with lack of nitrogen, but it also is caused by deficiencies of iron, manganese, magnesium, potassium, and other elements. Furthermore, numerous unfavorable environmental factors other than mineral deficiency cause chlorosis, including an excess or deficiency of water, unfavorable temperatures, toxic substances such as sulfur dioxide, and an excess of minerals. Chlorosis also is caused by genetic factors, which produce plants ranging from albinos, totally devoid of chlorophyll, to various degrees of deficiency found in virescent seedlings and various types of striping or mottling of leaves.

The wide variety of factors producing chlorosis suggests that it is caused by general disturbances of metabolism as well as by the specific effects of a deficiency of a particular element. Iljin (1951) concluded that lime-induced chlorosis of several species of woody and herbaceous plants growing on calcareous soils is caused by abnormal nitrogen and organic acid metabolism. He found 5 to 15 times as much soluble nitrogen and considerably more organic acids in chlorotic than in nonchlorotic leaves and suggested that the abnormal concentration interferes with chlorophyll synthesis. This view was also held by Steinberg (1951), who found an increased concentration of amino acids and decreased protein content in tobacco plants suffering from a variety of mineral deficiencies. He demonstrated that an excess of isoleucine caused typical frenching of tobacco and that other free amino acids caused characteristic

Fig. 10.4. Examples of symptoms caused by mineral deficiencies. (a) Development of symptoms on apple leaves associated with magnesium deficiency. (b) Breakdown of tissue in apple fruits apparently caused by boron deficiency. (c) Manganese-deficient (*left*) and normal (*right*) leaves of tung. (Photographs (a) and (b) courtesy of Crops Research Division, U.S. Department of Agriculture; photograph (c) courtesy of R. D. Dickey, Florida Agricultural Experiment Station.)

chlorosis, necrosis, and abnormalities in leaf form. Steinberg suggested that probably all mineral deficiencies cause disturbance of nitrogen metabolism, and the resulting imbalance in nitrogen compounds produces such visible symptoms as chlorosis and leaf injury.

One of the most troublesome and common types of chlorosis is that found in a wide variety of fruit, shade, and forest trees growing on alkaline and calcareous soil. This usually is caused by the unavailability of iron at high pH, but is sometimes caused by manganese deficiency. The most severe lime-induced chlorosis occurs on fine textured, poorly aerated, cold soils where conditions are unfavorable for mineral uptake. Drought also can increase chlorosis caused by iron deficiency. This is common in azaleas. In leaves of angiosperms the midrib and smaller veins remain green while the interveinal areas become pale green, yellow, or even white. The youngest leaves are usually most severely affected. In conifers the young needles are pale green or yellow and if the deficiency is severe they may turn brown and fall off.

Interpretation of iron chlorosis has been confused by statements that the concentration of iron in chlorotic tissue was as high or higher than in healthy tissue. However, Stone (1968) cites research indicating that many of the high iron contents reported are caused by surface contamination with iron and are greatly reduced if the leaf surfaces are washed before analysis.

Chlorosis caused by iron deficiency can be partially or completely eliminated by reducing the soil pH, spraying the plants with a solution containing iron, or injecting iron into the trees. The soil pH can be lowered by adding sulfur or aluminum sulfate. In earlier days ferrous sulfate was often added to the soil or sprayed on iron-deficient foliage, but iron chelates are now generally used in a spray. Success has been achieved with some, but not all, species of orchard and shade trees by introducing ferric salts or solutions into holes drilled into tree trunks, or even by driving nails into the trunk, but the availability of iron chelates makes such measures unnecessary today. Stone (1968) discussed iron chlorosis in trees and Gauch (1972) also covered the topic.

Anatomical and Cytological Symptoms

Mineral deficiencies produce internal changes visible only under the microscope, as well as macroscopic external symptoms. Davis (1949) found that calcium-deficient seedlings of loblolly pine not only had smaller buds and stem tips but smaller leaves with fewer and smaller cells and less xylem and phloem, less primary and more secondary tissue in stems, and abnormally blunt root tips with fewer mitotic figures than in normal seedlings. Cell division was reduced more than cell enlargement or differentiation by calcium deficiency, resulting in the lignification of xylem very close to the meristematic region.

Noticeable changes in cell structure are often caused by mineral deficiencies. Reed and Dufrenoy (1935) found that the palisade cells of zinc-deficient citrus leaves were wider than in normal leaves, rhomboidal instead of columnar in shape, and often transversely divided. Chloroplasts were reduced in number and abnormally high in fat, while starch grains were slender and elongated. Microchemical tests indicated the presence of phytosterol or lecithin in the vacuoles of cells of zinc-deficient leaves, but not in leaves of normal plants. Reed (1938) later observed that zinc deficiency retarded differentiation in leaves, resulting in a very compact mesophyll with reduced intercellular spaces. Some effects of mineral deficiencies on fine structure of cells are shown in Hewitt and Smith (1975, Plates 72–90). Additional anatomical and cytological research would be useful in explaining effects of deficiencies at the cellular level.

Mobility of Ions in Relation to Symptoms

The location of the symptoms of deficiencies of various elements seems to be related as much to their relative mobilities as to their functions. For example, symptoms of deficiencies of nitrogen, phosphorus, potassium, and magnesium appear in the older leaves while the young leaves remain healthy, because these elements are readily translocated from old to young tissues. In contrast, symptoms of boron and calcium deficiencies appear in the growing stem tips and those of iron, manganese, and sulfur deficiency in the younger leaves, because these elements are not readily translocated from old to new tissues (Müller, 1949).

Physiological Effects of Mineral Deficiencies

The visible morphological effects or symptoms of mineral deficiencies are the results of changes in various internal biochemical and physiological processes, but it usually is difficult to determine how deficiency of a particular element produces the observed effects because of the complex interactions which exist. For example, a deficiency of nitrogen might reduce growth because of a reduced supply of nitrogen for synthesis of protoplasm, but synthesis of enzymes and chlorophyll also is reduced and the photosynthetic surface is decreased. This causes reduction in photosynthesis, which decreases the supply of carbohydrates available for growth, and this may further reduce the uptake of nitrogen and minerals. A single element often has several roles in plants, and it is difficult to determine which role or combination of roles is responsible for the visible symptoms. Manganese, for example, is an activator of certain enzyme systems, and it is necessary for chlorophyll synthesis, and a deficiency causes several physiological diseases, including frenching of tung trees.

Some interesting research has been done on the relationship between mineral deficiency and major physiological processes, including respiration, photosynthesis, nitrogen metabolism, fat synthesis, and water relations, mostly on apple (Batjer and Degman, 1940; Childers, 1937; Heinicke and Hoffman, 1933) and tung (Drosdoff *et al.,* 1947; Loustalot *et al.,* 1950). Relatively little work of this type has been done on forest trees, and further research is badly needed, especially with respect to effects of mineral deficiencies and fertilization on photosynthesis and on water relations. Some of these effects will be discussed further in the chapters dealing with various major physiological processes. Usually, nitrogen deficiency causes a marked reduction in photosynthesis (Brix, 1971), but the effects of deficiencies of other elements are not as predictable.

Mineral deficiency usually decreases both the synthesis of carbohydrates and their translocation to growing tissues. Photosynthesis is often affected differently from respiration (see Chapter 5). For example, a marked deficiency of potassium reduces photosynthesis and increases respiration, thereby decreasing the amount of carbohydrates available for growth. Translocation of carbohydrates sometimes also is inhibited. This effect is pronounced in boron-deficient trees with phloem necrosis. The decreased availability of carbohydrates results in decreased growth of tissues in one part of a tree but may result in carbohydrate accumulation in another part. Seed production sometimes is decreased because of low carbohydrate reserves. Heavy applications of nitrogen fertilizer resulted in greatly increased seed production by beech and sugar maple trees, and the percentage of sound seeds and the dry weight of the maple seed were increased (Chandler, 1938). Cone and seed production of young loblolly pine were also greatly increased by adding fertilizer (Wenger, 1953b). When trees are not mineral deficient, however, additions of large amounts of nitrogenous fertilizers may decrease fruit and seed production by stimulating vegetative growth.

Disease

The effects of fertilizers on susceptibility to disease are very difficult to predict. Foster (1968) stated that the more important root diseases will become more serious with increased fertilization. However, the symptoms of little leaf disease, which results from root injury by *Phytophthora cinnamomi,* can be controlled by heavy fertilization with nitrogen (Copeland, 1962), and fertilization reduces the severity of several other dieback diseases. According to Parker *et al.* (1947) development of Dutch elm disease is less severe in young trees on fertile soils than in trees on soils deficient in mineral nutrients. There is some evidence that fertilization reduces attacks by defoliating insects and borers, but increases injury by sucking insects. Foster (1968) reviewed the rather unsatisfactory data on the relationship between fertilization and attacks by insects and pathogenic fungi. There also are very complex effects of fertilization on soil organisms which may be helpful or harmful (Parr, 1968).

Species and Individual Differences in Response to Mineral Deficiency

It has been shown repeatedly that species differ in their ability to accumulate various elements. For example, leaves of flowering dogwood and white oak contain over twice as much calcium as leaves of post oak and loblolly pine growing in the same soil. Trifoliate orange is more susceptible to zinc and iron deficiency than some other root stocks such as rough lemon, especially in calcareous soils, apparently because of restricted translocation from roots to shoots (Kahdr *et al.,* 1965). It also is more susceptible to magnesium deficiency in the presence of high concentrations of potassium. Species differences in mineral absorption are discussed in more detail later in this chapter. Because of differences in ability to absorb and translocate minerals, trees of various species and even individuals of the same species react differently to mineral deficiencies. On flat sand plains in New York State that had been abandoned for agriculture because of low potash and general infertility, trees of red pine showed general stagnation, with little difference in deficiency symptoms among individual trees. White pine, however, showed wide variations among individual trees, dead trees occurring beside trees making considerable height growth. Norway spruce and white spruce showed even more pronounced deficiency symptoms, with many dead trees but with large cone crops on small living trees. In contrast, mugo pine showed virtually no deficiency symptoms, while Scotch pine and jack pine showed only slight chlorosis (Heiberg and White, 1951).

Hobbs (1944) found that tip chlorosis of seedlings was followed by necrosis in four species of pine seedlings grown in magnesium-deficient cultures. The severity of the symptoms varied with the species, being more severe in the more rapidly growing white and red pine than in the more slowly growing pitch and shortleaf pines. Pessin (1937) found somewhat different symptoms of magnesium deficiency in longleaf pine, which developed necrosis without prior yellowing. Stone (1953) observed that the most conspicuous symptom of magnesium deficiency in several coniferous species in New York was a bright yellow discoloration of the needles of the current year. The chlorosis appeared in the autumn and chiefly affected the upper part of the trees. Whenever severe deficiency developed, death or premature loss of needles followed the yellowing. Chlorosis was much less conspicuous on white than on red pine. Norway spruce, however, reacted by a generalized yellowing rather than the apical yellowing on new needles shown by the pines.

Worley *et al.* (1941) observed that the behavior of Siberian elm, ailanthus, and northern catalpa grown from seed in sand cultures differed when subjected to deficiencies of various elements. For example, in the absence of potassium catalpa leaves were dark green, ailanthus intermediate, and elm yellowish. It, therefore, is necessary to observe the appearance of trees of various species known to suffer from deficiencies of certain elements in order to learn their characteristic reactions or symptoms. Even then it is possible that differences in climatic conditions may modify the reactions.

Symptoms of Excess Minerals

Forest soils rarely contain an excess of mineral nutrients, but heavy fertilization of orchards and nurseries sometimes produces a concentration of salts high enough to cause injury. There also are large areas of arid land where most or all species of vegetation are excluded by high salt content. Irrigation with water containing a high concentration of salt likewise causes injury. This occurs because the osmotic pressure is increased, because of unfavorable changes in pH, because the proportions of various ions become unbalanced, or because of a combination of these factors.

Increased osmotic pressure of the soil solution reduces water absorption, increases leaf water deficits, and results in injury to tissues from desiccation on days when wind and high temperatures cause rapid transpiration. More prolonged and severe dehydration also causes stomatal closure and interferes with photosynthesis. High concentrations of salt in the soil may injure the roots by plasmolysis, especially in sandy soils (Bear, 1942), and interfere with their synthetic activities. Injury to leaves sometimes occurs from foliar application of high concentrations of liquid fertilizers, and citrus leaves have been reported to accumulate injurious concentrations of sodium from sprinkling with irrigation water high in salt.

The amount of injury caused by excessive fertilization depends on the species, the type of fertilizer used, and the time of application. Mulberry trees are said to tolerate only one-fifth as concentrated a soil solution without injury as apple trees, and different species and varieties of citrus vary in their salt tolerance (Gardner *et al.,* 1952). Baxter (1943) states that *Juniperus* and *Thuja* are unusually susceptible to injury from an excess of fertilizer.

Considerable discussion has occurred concerning the relative importance of the osmotic pressure of the soil solution versus its composition and pH as factors in causing injury from an excess of salts in soil. Investigators at the Salinity Laboratory at Riverside, California, considered the osmotic effects in reducing water absorption as most important, but some ionic effects also exist. Root growth of peaches was reduced more on Lovell than on Shalil rootstocks and was reduced more by sulfates than by chlorides at the same osmotic pressure (Hayward *et al.,* 1946). Brown *et al.* (1953) found calcium chloride to be more toxic to stone fruits than isoosmotic solutions of sodium chloride. Unpublished observations suggest that conifers are more susceptible to injury from excess salt than deciduous species.

It seems probable that good root growth can occur over a considerable pH range if all the essential mineral elements are available, although Leyton (1952) found the best growth of Sitka spruce roots between pH 4 and 5. Much of the injury in very acid soils apparently is caused by the increased solubility of aluminum, while injury at higher pH values most often results from decreased availability of elements such as iron and manganese. Howell (1932) found that ponderosa pine seedlings survived over a pH range from 2.7 to 11 but only grew well over a pH range from 3.0 to 6.0. Guest and Chapman (1944) found no direct injury to roots of sweet orange seedlings over a range from pH 4.0 to 9.0, although indirect effects were observed at both extremes. Another indirect effect of abnormal pH or chemical composition may be to increase injury from pathogenic organisms.

Excessive fertilization of orchard and ornamental trees late in the season sometimes prolongs the growing season until there is insufficient time for trees and shrubs to become cold resistant before frost. Twigs formed too late in the season are likely to be very susceptible to frost injury. Overfertilization also sometimes stimulates the production of large numbers of branches, flowers, and fruits on older trees. Pines may respond by producing clusters of cones (Boyce, 1948). Other responses to excessive fertilization include fasciation or flattening of stems (Kienholz, 1932) and internal bark necrosis (Shannon, 1954). An undesirable effect on seedlings is to stimulate excessive top growth, producing a low ratio of roots to shoots, which often results in poor survival after outplanting.

Application of excessive amounts of fertilizer is economically wasteful. It also is environmentally objectionable because the excess may be leached out in the drainage water and reach streams or underground water supplies. This is particularly important with nitrogen, which usually escapes as nitrate, but pollution can be a problem with any element applied in excess. There probably is little danger of applying excessive amounts of fertilizer to forests but citrus growers are said to often apply more than is necessary.

Field Diagnosis of Mineral Deficiencies

In agriculture, forestry, and horticulture it is very useful if mineral deficiencies can be anticipated or at least detected before they cause serious injury. Large plantations often cover several soil types, which may vary widely in fertility, and different nutritional problems may arise in different parts of the plantation. Soil analyses are often useful in predicting probable deficiencies, although there is some uncertainty about the best method for extracting firmly bound elements such as phosphorus. Foliar analysis also has proven useful after the levels required for good growth have been established (Pritchett, 1968; Wells, 1968) and is used extensively in horticultural and vegetable crop production to determine fertilizer needs. Some data on leaf concentrations of phosphorus and potassium in orange as indicators of nutrient status are shown in Table 10.5. Jones and Embleton (1969) discuss the use of foliar analysis on citrus fruits and emphasize the need to standardize methods with respect to age and location of leaves collected for testing.

Experienced observers often can determine what deficiencies exist by the appearance of the foliage. Some examples of mineral deficiencies are shown in Figures 10.4 and 10.5 and pictures of a number of deficiencies in trees are shown in the back of the monograph, *Forest Fertilization,* in *Hunger Signs in Crops* (Sprague, 1964), and in Kozlowski (1971a). As more experience accumulates, the diagnostic procedures for forest trees are reaching the level of reliability found in agriculture and horticulture. Readers interested in diagnostic procedures should consult the guide edited by Reisenauer (1976).

Remedies for Mineral Deficiencies

Improved ability to recognize mineral deficiencies and to identify their causes in forest and horticultural crops has naturally caused increased efforts to remedy them.

TABLE 10.5 Leaf Analysis Guide for Diagnosing Nutrient Status of Mature Valencia and Navel Orange Trees[a]

Element	Ranges in percent (dry matter basis)				
	Deficient	Low	Optimum	High	Excess
N	<2.2	2.2–2.3	2.4–2.6	2.7–2.8	>2.8
P	<0.09	0.09–0.11	0.12–0.16	0.17–0.29	>0.30
K	<0.40	0.40–0.69	0.70–1.09	1.10–2.00	>2.30

[a] From Embleton *et al.* (1975).

Fig. 10.5. Magnesium deficiency in peach in first two leaves. Control leaf is at far right. Photo courtesy of N. F. Childers.

These efforts take several forms, including the application of fertilizers, the selection of those strains which are most efficient in using the elements available, and occasionally the use of nitrogen-fixing species such as alder as companion or understory plants to increase the supply of nitrogen.

Fertilization

Application of fertilizers to improve the quantity and quality of growth has long been a common practice for orchards (Childers, 1966a,b) and ornamental trees and shrubs (Neely *et al.,* 1970; Pirone, 1972). Fertilization has also been a common practice in forest nurseries for many years, but until recently it was uncommon in forest management in the United States. However, in Europe it has been used much longer because the high cost of land and labor, site deterioration caused by removal of litter, and the higher prices of forest products caused European foresters to find it economically attractive before it was seriously considered in the United States (Tamm, 1968). Now, increasing land values, the higher price of forest products, and the use of planting stock selected for high potential growth rates cause fertilization to be increasingly attractive to North American foresters. As a result extensive research has been done on forest fertilization in the major forest areas of North America. Much of this work has been summarized in bibliographies and monographs such as those by White and Leaf (1957), Weiner and Mirkes (1972), *Forest Fertilization* (Anonymous, 1968), and *Tree Growth and Forest Soils,* edited by Youngberg and Davey (1970).

Fertilization of large areas of forest and even of orchards is often done by airplane or helicopter. In a few instances sewage sludge has been applied in liquid form. Sometimes urea and other nutrients are sprayed on the foliage and branches, especially on fruit and ornamental trees. Stoate (1950) stated that zinc deficiency was cured by spraying of plantations of Moneterey pine in South Australia. Foliar application of the major mineral nutrients as sprays generally is regarded as a supplement to rather than a substitute for soil applications. However, experience in California and Florida with citrus suggest that soil and foliar applications of nitrogen and potassium are often equally effective and the choice of methods should be determined by economic considerations. Nutrients sprayed on the bark are absorbed through naturally occurring cracks and splits, pruning wounds, and lenticels (Harley, 1956; Tukey *et al.*, 1952). Spraying the bark is a modern variant of the old custom of smearing manure on tree trunks. Zinc and iron deficiencies have even been cured by driving zinc-coated tacks or iron nails into the bark of the affected trees.

It should be emphasized that, in horticulture, fertilization may have complex effects on the quality as well as the quantity of the product, be it flowers, fruit, or ornamental shrubs [see *Hort. Science* **10**, 41–56 (1975)]. Abundant nitrogen increases the yield, but often decreases the color of apples and delays their maturity. Flavor and keeping quality of some deciduous fruits are also said to be affected by fertilization. The most detailed studies of the effects of fertilization on fruit quality have been made on citrus

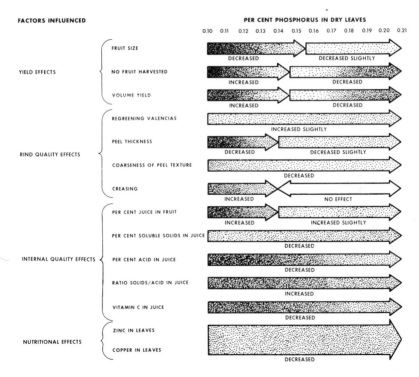

Fig. 10.6. Effects on yield and fruit quality and the Zn and Cu nutrition of change in P content of 5-to 7-month-old spring cycle orange leaves in California. The more intense the stippling the greater the effect on the factor. From Embleton *et al.* (1975).

fruit, and some relationships between phosphorus concentration in leaves and fruit quality and yield are shown in Fig. 10.6. It seems that fertilization must often involve compromises between fruit quality and yield.

Macronutrient Deficiencies

Current opinions on forest fertilization in various sections of the United States and in Europe were summarized in the monograph, *Forest Fertilization: Theory and Practice* (Anonymous, 1968). This summary indicates that nitrogen is widely deficient in forest soils and significant deficiencies of phosphorus and potassium occur in some regions. These elements are also the most important in the mineral nutrition of fruit trees. The widespread importance of phosphorus deficiency in Australia and New Zealand is well known. Pines also respond well to phosphorus in the wet coastal plain soils of the southeastern United States. It appears to make little difference in what form nitrogen or phosphorus is applied, although there may be an advantage in applying some of the nitrogen in a slowly soluble form.

Some responses to forest fertilization by several species are shown in Table 10.6.

Micronutrient Deficiencies

Most work on the fertilization of forests deals with macronutrients such as nitrogen, phosphorus, and potassium. However, deficiencies of micronutrients such as iron, zinc, copper, and boron are often found in fruit and shade trees, especially in calcareous or sandy soils, and they are beginning to be detected in forest plantations all over the world. No doubt more examples of such deficiencies will appear as exotic species are planted under soil and climatic conditions to which they are poorly adapted. Stone (1968) has an excellent review of the micronutrient problem in forest trees. Experience with citrus fruits indicates that deficiencies of manganese, zinc, and molybdenum are best remedied by foliar sprays. However, iron should not be sprayed on citrus. On calcareous soils, it should be applied to the soil as a chelate.

Understory Vegetation

In agriculture nitrogen-fixing leguminous crops are used to increase the nitrogen supply in the soil and cover crops are grown to increase the organic matter content of the soil. Alder occurs as an understory in conifer plantations in Europe and Japan and, because of the nitrogen-fixing organisms on its roots, it may provide enough nitrogen to improve the growth of conifers. Broom (*Cytisus* sp.) has been used in Great Britain to improve the growth of spruce on nitrogen-deficient soils and lupine (*Lupinus* sp.) in Germany, but the results are not very impressive. Chapman and Lane (1951) reported that black locust is a good nurse crop for hardwoods planted on abandoned fields, at least partly because nitrogen fixed in nodules in its roots becomes available to the adjacent trees. It was mentioned earlier that hardwood litter high in calcium facilitates the decay of conifer litter. As fertilizers become more expensive, increasing attention will probably be given to determining what combinations of species will be most effective in maintaining soil fertility with the minimum application of fertilizers.

TABLE 10.6 Growth of Nine Forest Species in 38 Tennessee Valley Forests as Affected by Fertilizing with 335 kg/ha of N with and without P[a,b]

	Control		Nitrogen alone			Nitrogen with phosphorus		
	Number of trees	Basal area growth/tree	Number of trees	Basal area growth/tree	Increase (%)	Number of trees	Basal area growth/tree	Increase (%)
Northern red oak	118	19.5	85	52.0	167	73	39.0	100
White oak	310	56.7	260	77.1	36	321	64.1	13
Chestnut oak	78	21.4	76	55.7	61	53	57.6	70
Southern red oak	45	49.2	68	61.3	25	55	99.4	102
Yellow-poplar	139	56.7	173	83.6	48	136	95.7	69
Black cherry	8	19.5	6	29.7	52	2	33.4	71
Hickory	149	16.7	174	60.4	261	215	45.5	172
Cucumber tree[c]	13	13.9	30	28.8	107	20	42.7	207
Dogwood	86	10.2	107	13.9	36	70	27.9	173

[a] From Jones and Curlin (1968).
[b] Growth measured in square centimeters of basal area per tree.
[c] Asheville Site No. 6.

Low vegetation sometimes competes with trees for minerals. Bollard (1957c) and others have observed that grass cover sometimes reduces the yield of apple trees. Richardson (1953b) reported that the competition for nitrogen by grass reduced growth of young trees of sycamore maple in root observation boxes, and Leyton (1954) reported that reducing the growth of heather by shading resulted in increased growth of young spruce trees.

Species and Clonal Differences

As will be mentioned later, in the section on salt absorption, there are large differences among trees within a species and among species in their ability to absorb and utilize mineral nutrients as measured by wood production. Bengtson (1968) cited several examples for macronutrients in forest trees, Ralston and Prince (1965) noted differences between pines and hardwoods, and Gerloff (1963) also cited numerous examples, chiefly among herbaceous species. Differences have also been reported among cottonwood clones, as shown in Fig. 10.7 (Jones and Curlin, 1968). Stone (1968) pointed out that horticultural research shows many differences in susceptibility to micronutrient deficiencies, some of which are clearly genetic. In pine, differences in response to fertilization occur not only with respect to wood production, but also seed production, some clones showing large increases in seed production while others show none.

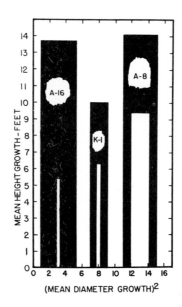

Fig. 10.7. Differences in growth response of three clones of cottonwood to fertilization with 330 kg/ha of nitrogen. The light area within each bar is the growth without fertilizer. Clone A-8 is superior with or without fertilizer, while A-16, which is below average without fertilizer, made a tremendous growth after fertilization. However, the average clone, K-1, responded poorly. Diameter shown in inches. From Jones and Curlin (1968).

It seems that more attention should be given to the selection of genotypes with favorable physiological characteristics, such as efficient utilization of mineral nutrients, as suggested by Jones and Curlin (1968) and by writers in Cannell and Last (1976).

There has been some concern lest the increase in growth which often follows fertilization be accompanied by a decrease in wood quality. Schmidtling (1973) cites work indicating that fiber length and specific gravity have sometimes been decreased. However, in his experiments Schmidtling found that mowing to reduce weed competition and fertilization over a period of 9 years greatly increased wood production of longleaf, slash, and loblolly pine without any decrease in fiber length or specific gravity. The relationship between fertilization and wood quality deserves more study.

Factors Limiting Response to Fertilization

It should be emphasized that maximum results can be obtained from fertilization only if other factors are not seriously limiting. Summer droughts can limit growth so seriously that little or no increase in growth can be obtained by applying fertilizer. Waterlogging of the soil and attacks by nematodes and pathogenic fungi can injure the

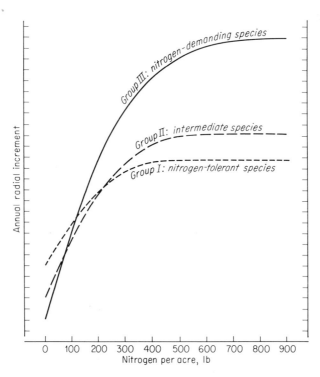

Fig. 10.8. Relative growth responses to increasing nitrogen supply of tree species with low (group I), intermediate (group II), and high (group III) nitrogen requirements. From Mitchell and Chandler (1939).

root system and reduce mineral absorption. Defoliation by insects or fungi can reduce photosynthesis until growth is limited by lack of carbohydrates rather than by lack of mineral nutrients. Competition with herbaceous vegetation can also be detrimental. Thus weather and other environmental conditions should be taken into account when interpreting the results of fertilization experiments. Obviously, good results cannot be expected where other unfavorable environmental factors are reducing the basic physiological processes to a level where they cannot respond to improved mineral nutrition.

Even under favorable conditions the law of diminishing returns operates with respect to fertilization, as shown in Fig. 10.8. Species with both low and high nitrogen requirements respond well to nitrogen at low levels, but the response decreases with increasing supply, even for species having high nitrogen requirements.

The Mineral Cycle

Mineral cycling refers to the fact that much of the minerals absorbed by vegetation eventually are returned to the soil by decay of fallen leaves and other plant tissues. This recycling of mineral nutrients is an important feature of all kinds of ecosystems, but especially so in natural forests. The mineral cycle of a forest is composed of several subcycles of various lengths. The shortest cycle is for minerals leached out of leaves by rain and from the frass of leaf-eating insects, because these may be immediately recycled. Decay of foliage and twigs releases minerals in from a few weeks or months in warm climates to a few years in cold climates, but minerals incorporated in large branches and tree trunks are not recycled for decades or even centuries, depending on the longevity of the trees and the rate of decay of the wood.

In forests of the temperate zones a large proportion of the total nitrogen and minerals in the cycle is in the soil. According to Switzer and Nelson (1972), nearly 20% of the total nitrogen and minerals in the forest floor and biomass of a 20-year-old stand of loblolly pine are cycling; about 80% of this goes into production of foliage, and 15% into stems and branches. According to Sanchez (1973), in tropical forests a much larger percentage of the total minerals that are cycling occurs in the biomass than in temperate zone forests. For example, in a forest in Ghana over 40% of the N, P, K, Ca, and Mg in the vegetation and the top 30 cm of soil occurred in the vegetation (Greenland and Kowal, 1960). The vegetation contained 30% of the N, 50% of the exchangeable Ca and Mg, 58% of the exchangeable K, and over 90% of the P. According to Bormann *et al.* (1977) in a northern hardwood forest only about 9.5% of the N is in the vegetation and about 90% is in soil organic matter.

Because of interest in the magnitude of mineral turnover, many papers have been published on the amounts of nitrogen and various mineral elements in trees and in their litter, chiefly trees of the North Temperate Zone. Baker (1950) estimated the average litter fall of forests in the United States at about 3,400 kg/ha, and Ovington (1956) gave similar values for well stocked British forests, but Bray and Gorham (1964) gave a value of 5,425 kg/ha/year for warm temperate coniferous forests. Stone (1975) pointed out the pitfalls encountered in attempting to draw conclusions concerning differences in the mineral contribution made by litter from different species. Litter production is higher in tropical forests than in temperate forests, ranging from 5 to 15 tons/ha. In general, hardwood and coniferous forests produce about the same amount of litter per unit of land area. However, hardwood litter often contains a higher concentration of minerals (Table 10.7; also Cromack and Monk, 1975) and it generally decays more rapidly; hence turnover in the mineral cycle is usually more rapid in hardwood than in coniferous forests. Recycling is very rapid in tropical forests where half of the dry matter may be mineralized in 8 to 10 weeks (Sanchez, 1973), but it is often very slow in cold, northern coniferous forests.

In addition to the minerals released by decay of litter an appreciable amount is leached from the foliage and returned to the soil in throughfall and stem flow (Patterson, 1975) and measurable amounts of nitrogen and minerals are supplied in rainfall. Some nitrogen is added by nitrification in the soil, and minerals are added by decomposition of rock. There also is some loss by leaching in the drainage water, but the amount is small in undisturbed ecosystems. For example, 9 years after fertilization of red pine with potassium, 60% of the potassium in the foliage came from the fertilizer, and after 23 years 40%. Considerable amounts of the applied potassium also remained in the litter and surface soil indicating that little is lost from this type of soil (Stone and Kszystyniak, 1977). According to Richardson and Lund (1975) losses from clear-cutting are often small, but if all vegetation is destroyed loss of minerals can be quite large (Likens *et al.*, 1970).

The amount of some elements, especially sulfur, supplied by rainfall has increased in recent years because of increasing atmospheric pollution as a result of human activities. Wells *et al.* (1975) state that harvest of wood by conventional methods in which the slash is left to decay removes nitrogen at about the same rate at which it is supplied from the atmosphere. The data of Schreiber *et al.* (1976) and others cited by them indicate that the addition of several mineral elements from the atmosphere in

TABLE 10.7   Amounts of Minerals Returned to the Soil by Leaf Fall

	Annual litter fall	Minerals returned to soil by leaf fall[a]					
		N	P	K	Ca	Mg	Total
New York:							
Hardwood[b]	3,042	17.8	3.7	15.1	73.5	98.9	121.2
Conifer[c]	2,759	25.4	2.0	7.3	29.7	5.0	70.5
South Carolina[d]:							
Hardwood	4,142	24.8			99.1	23.4	
Pine-hardwood	4,285	28.6			57.7	12.5	
Pine	3,292	14.2			19.4	6.25	

[a] Measurements given in kg/ha.
[b] From Chandler (1941).
[c] Average of seven species of conifers, from Chandler (1944).
[d] From Metz (1952).

rainfall often exceed the leaching losses in runoff (Table 10.8). The increasing acidity of the rainfall in Scandinavia, western Europe, and the northeastern United States, caused by the conversion of sulfur dioxide in the air to sulfuric acid, is of increasing concern. The resulting "acid rain" has produced undesirable changes in pH of lakes and may in the long run cause a decrease in the pH of poorly buffered soil. This problem was reviewed briefly by Dochinger and Seliga (1976).

The situation is very different in orchards and forests from which crops are harvested. Large quantities of minerals and nitrogen accumulated in fruits and seeds are removed by harvesting. According to Cromack and Monk (1975) over 10% of the nitrogen and minerals in the total litterfall of an oak stand was in the acorns. A crop of apples is said to remove over 80 kg/ha of minerals and a good crop of oranges will remove over 200 kg/ha of nitrogen and minerals (Labanauskas and Handy, 1972). For comparison, harvesting the grain from a crop of corn removes about 160 kg/ha of nitrogen and minerals, and harvesting the grain and stalks removes over 300 kg/ha (Fried and Broeshart, 1967). According to Wells *et al.* (1975) a conventional pulpwood thinning of a 16-year-old loblolly pine plantation removes about 61 tons/ha of wood, containing 54 kg of nitrogen—21% of the total in the ecosystem, and 120.5 kg of P, K, Ca, and Mg (28% of the total). However, complete harvest of the trees removed in thinning would remove a total of 74 tons/ha of the biomass and a proportionately larger amount of nitrogen and minerals. Complete harvest of all above ground parts of all trees would remove 257 kg of nitrogen and 429 kg of P, K, Ca, and Mg/ha. Harvesting of roots would remove another 64 kg of nitrogen and over 150 kg of P, K, Ca, and Mg/ha. Increasing quantities of micronutrients would also be removed by complete harvesting, but since Mn, Zn, and Cu tend to be concentrated in the wood a larger proportion of these elements than of N and P is removed by a conventional pulpwood thinning.

There is increasing discussion among foresters concerning the possibility of harvesting the entire tops of trees and even the roots. The foregoing discussion and the data in

TABLE 10.8 Average Input of Mineral Nutrients in Precipitation and Losses in Runoff from Five Pine-Forested Watersheds in Northern Mississippi for 1 Year[a]

Nutrient	Input (kg/ha)	Loss	Gain or loss
NO_3	3.12	0.32	+2.80
NH_4	5.73	3.35	+2.38
PO_4	0.07	0.04	+0.03
K	4.98	3.31	+1.67
Ca	7.72	6.21	+1.51
Mg	3.03	3.05	−0.02

[a] From Schreiber *et al.* (1976), by permission of American Society of Agronomy—Crop Science Society of America—Soil Science Society of America.

TABLE 10.9 Biomass and Nutrient Removal Rates for Clear Cut Compared with Alternative Tree Harvest Methods at Age 16[a]

Harvest method	Biomass[b]		N[c]	P[c]	K[c]	Ca[c]	Mg[c]
	Total	Annual					
Complete above-ground + roots >4 cm	185	11.6	17.6	2.3	12.6	12.8	3.6
Complete above-ground	156	9.8	16.1	1.9	10.3	11.7	2.9
Pulpwood to 8-cm top	116	7.2	6.5	0.9	5.0	6.4	1.6
Debarked pulpwood to 8-cm top	102	6.4	4.6	0.8	3.8	4.3	1.3

[a] From Wells *et al.* (1975).
[b] Measurements in tons/ha.
[c] Measurements in kg/ha/year.

Table 10.9 indicate that such procedures will greatly increase the amount of minerals removed and increase mineral nutrition problems. Boyle (1976) discussed methods of estimating the effects of harvesting whole trees on site quality and pointed out that the effects will be most serious on shallow, mineral-deficient soils. The increasing use of fast growing species with shorter rotations will doubtless create additional nutritional problems. Readers are referred to Ovington (1965), Duvingneaud and Denaeyer-DeSmet (1970), Likens *et al.* (1977), Stone (1975), Kimmins (1977), and to monographs such as *Mineral Cycling in Southeastern Ecosystems,* edited by Howell *et al.* 1975, for more details on mineral cycling.

Fire sometimes causes loss of nitrogen, but increases the availability of other elements. Some pine forests in the southeastern United States have been burned repeatedly for decades without deterioration of soil fertility or physical properties (Jorgensen and Wells, 1971). Stark (1977) concluded that prescribed burning can be practiced indefinitely in the forests of western Montana without decreasing soil fertility. Readers interested in effects of fire are referred to Kozlowski and Ahlgren (1974). Nitrogen cycling also is discussed in Chapter 9 and prescribed burning in Chapter 17.

SALT ABSORPTION

The absorption of mineral nutrients is as important to the successful growth of plants as the absorption of water but is not as well understood because it is considerably more complex. Salt absorption by intact plants involves several steps: (1) movement of ions from soil to root surfaces, (2) ion accumulation in root cells, (3) radial movement of ions from root surfaces into the xylem, and (4) their translocation from roots to shoots. Most of these steps are discussed in more detail in books by Fried and Broeshart (1967), Epstein (1972), and Gauch (1972), and more briefly in Chapter 7 of Kramer (1969). Voigt (1968) has a good discussion of the mineral absorption process as it operates in trees.

Terminology

Before discussing salt absorption, some of the terminology will be reviewed. Absorption and uptake are general terms applied to the entrance of substances into cells or tissues by any mechanism. Accumulation refers to the concentration of a specific substance within cells or tissues against a gradient in electrochemical potential or concentration, requiring the expenditure of metabolic energy. Movement of materials against gradients of concentration or electrochemical potential brought about by the expenditure of metabolic energy is called *active transport,* in contrast to passive movement by diffusion along concentration gradients or *mass flow* caused by pressure gradients, such as the flow of water into roots and upward in the xylem of transpiring plants.

Membranes

Accumulation of ions can only be detected behind relatively impermeable membranes, because substances leak out through permeable membranes by diffusion as rapidly as they are moved in by active transport. A membrane can be defined as a boundary layer which differs in permeability from the phases which it separates. Membranes which permit some substances to pass more readily than others are termed differentially permeable, or less accurately, semipermeable membranes. Cell membranes include monomolecular layers, the membranes surrounding organelles such as nuclei and plastids, and the inner and outer boundaries of the cytoplasm, the vacuolar membrane or tonoplast, and the plasmalemma. In addition, multicellular membranes such as the epidermis and endodermis and the bark play important roles in plants. Some writers have also treated the entire cortex of young roots as a multicellular membrane, but the endodermis is usually regarded as the critical membrane in roots with respect to the entrance of water and solutes because the Casparian strips on its radial walls render them relatively impermeable to water and solutes. The importance of the endodermis probably has been overemphasized, as will be shown later.

Free Space

An important concept with respect to the movement of ions into roots is that of apparent free space or outer space (Epstein, 1972, Chapter 5). This is that part of a cell or tissue into which ions or other solutes can move freely by diffusion, in contrast to those regions which are inaccessible by diffusion but in which substances can be accumulated by active transport. The weight of evidence suggests that free space consists only of the space in the walls occupied by water, although it has been claimed by some writers that it includes the cytoplasm. In young roots free space consists of the water in the walls of the epidermal and cortical parenchyma cells, and solutes can move by diffusion and mass flow along these cell walls as far as the endodermis. Of course some cations are bound on the negatively charged walls. After passing through the endodermal cells in the symplast ions eventually are freed into the xylem sap and move upward to the leaves. There they move out of the xylem of the leaf veins into the cell walls which constitute free space. From this solution solutes are selectively accumulated by the leaf cells. The existence of considerable amounts of ions in free space in leaves explains the leaching of salt by rain, and the absorption of substances applied to the surfaces of leaves. Crafts (1961) terms free space the apoplast and the nonfree space the symplast, following the terminology of Münch (1930). The symplast refers to the protoplasts of adjacent cells that are connected together by plasmodesmata.

Active Transport

Movement of ions in free space is nonselective, reversible, and independent of metabolism. However, uptake of salt by plant cells is relatively selective and nonreversible, and dependent on the metabolic activity. For example, some ions are accumulated in cells to much higher concentrations relative to the external concentration than others, and it was shown many years ago by Hoagland and other investigators that the salt content of cell sap is very different in composition from that of the medium in which the plants are growing. Thus it must be accepted that the absorption of ions by cells is largely controlled by a selective active transport mechanism. On the other hand, practically all ions found in the root medium are found in varying quantities in the tops of plants, indicating that the ion barriers in roots are leaky.

Several theories have been proposed to explain active transport across cell membranes and accumulation in vacuoles, but the most widely accepted explanation is the carrier theory. This assumes that ions form combinations with special molecules called carriers at the outer surfaces of membranes, much as enzymes form temporary combinations with substrate molecules. The resulting complex can move through membranes which the ions themselves cannot penetrate, and on the inside the ions separate from the carrier and move to the vacuole or some other part of inner space. The carrier molecule is then available to move another ion. The rate of turnover must be extremely rapid and the concentration of carrier molecules seems quite low. Thus active uptake is often limited by the availability of carriers. The exact nature of the carrier molecules is uncertain, but they may be enzymes or phosphorylated compounds. Metabolic energy is used in the synthesis of carrier molecules and perhaps in forming the union between carriers and ions, or in splitting it. Energy is also required to maintain membrane structure. Selectivity in ion transport probably is controlled by differences in ability of carriers to form combinations with various ions.

It should be mentioned that some investigators question the conventional explanation of ion uptake by carriers and deny the existence of "ion pumps" because they would require too much energy. They regard cells as ion exchange systems containing negatively charged sites on which cations are bound. The space in this system is occupied by structured water which plays a role in controlling the kinds of ions absorbed. Some opposing views on this theory were presented in *Science* **193**, 528–532 (1976). Readers are referred to a review by Nissen (1974) for an attempt to deal with the controversy concerning a dual mechanism of ion uptake and control of uptake by the plasmalemma versus the tonoplast. These controversies are of interest chiefly to specialists in the field of salt accumulation.

Absorption of Salt by Roots

The absorption of mineral nutrients through roots involves the movement of ions from soil to root surfaces, accumulation in and movement through root cells to the xylem, and release into the xylem sap where they are carried to the leaves in the transpiration stream.

Ion Movement in Soil

Movement of ions through the soil toward the roots occurs by diffusion and by mass flow of water toward the root surfaces of rapidly transpiring plants. The relative importance of diffusion and mass flow varies with the kind and concentration of ions in the soil solution, the rate at which ions are being accumulated by roots, and the rate of water flow toward the roots, which is controlled by the rate of transpiration (Barber, 1962; Olsen and Kemper, 1968). The concentration of ions in the soil solution in forest and agricultural soils usually is quite low. Some anions such as phosphorus are usually bound on soil particles and organic matter while others such as nitrate are relatively mobile. Voigt *et al.* (1964), Bray (1954), and others differentiate between the root system absorption zone, the total soil mass occupied by a root system, and the root surface absorption zone, which they took as the soil within 1 cm of a root (Fig. 10.9). Calculated in this manner, the volume of the root absorption zone is only about 10% of the total soil volume occupied by the root system of a young pine tree. They concluded that, nevertheless, the amount of available calcium and potassium in the root surface absorption zone was adequate to supply the annual requirement of the young pitch pine trees studied by them.

Roots of forest trees tend to form a dense mat in the surface soil which intercepts minerals released by decaying litter. However, that fraction of the roots that penetrate more deeply into the soil must supply a substantial amount of minerals and most of the water (Russell, 1973). The volume of soil occupied by roots is an important factor in determining the amount of minerals and water available to trees and shrubs. Root extension becomes especially important in the uptake of nutrients such as phosphorus which diffuse slowly (Newman and Andrews, 1973). The "little leaf" disease of shortleaf pine occurs where the combination of soil conditions unfavorable for root

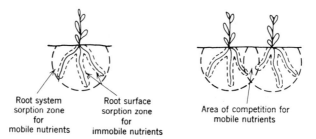

Root system   Root surface
sorption zone   sorption zone   Area of competition for
for   for   mobile nutrients
mobile nutrients   immobile nutrients

Fig. 10.9. Diagram showing that the total soil volume occupied by a root system is larger than the volume of soil in close contact with the individual roots, the rhizosphere. After Bray, 1954.

growth and damage by *Phytopthora cinnamomi* reduces the absorbing surface so much that symptoms of severe nitrogen deficiency develop (Campbell and Copeland, 1954). Fried and Broeshart (1967) have an extensive discussion of the complex relationships between soil and roots with respect to ion absorption. This is complicated by the large population of bacteria, fungi, nematodes, and protozoa often found in the rhizosphere or layer of soil surrounding roots (Russell, 1973).

Ion Movement into Roots

Radial movement of water and salt into roots is often assumed to occur across the protoplasts of the epidermal and cortical cells. However, it is now believed that much of the movement occurs in the cell walls, where the resistance to flow is much lower than across the protoplasts. Some salt is accumulated from the solution moving through the walls by the cortical parenchyma cells, and at the endodermis most of the salt probably enters the symplast by active transport. It seems probable that salt is then secreted by the xylem parenchyma cells adjoining the xylem elements into the xylem sap (Laüchli *et al.,* 1971; Anderson, 1976). Cross sections of woody roots are shown in Figs. 13.1 and 13.2. In slowly transpiring plants roots tend to function as osmometers and water moves to the stele chiefly by diffusion, but in rapidly transpiring plants it moves by mass flow, carrying salt with it at least as far as the endodermis. The effectiveness of the endodermis as an ion barrier may be overestimated. Gaps produced by developing branch roots at least temporarily allow some passage of salt by mass flow in transpiring plant (Dumbroff and Pierson, 1971). Although in young roots the endodermis appears to function as the principal ion barrier or differentially permeable membrane controlling the entrance of ions, it is absent in older roots where secondary growth causes loss of cortical parenchyma and endodermis (see Fig. 3.31). The ion barrier has not been localized in older roots but it might be the cambium. The existence of an ion barrier in older roots is indicated by the development of root pressure (O'Leary and Kramer, 1964). Root development was discussed in Chapter 3 and several stages were shown in Fig. 3.31. The transport of ions into roots and the roles of the apoplast and symplast are discussed by several authors in the volume edited by Lüttge and Pitman (1976).

The Absorbing Zone

It is generally assumed that salt absorption occurs chiefly through the region just behind the root tip. However, experiments by Wiebe and Kramer (1954), Canning and Kramer (1958), Russell and Sanderson (1967), Clarkson and Sanderson (1974), and others indicate that salt enters roots readily several centimeters behind the tips. As pointed out in Chapter 13, 95% or more of the root surface of forest trees is suberized (Kramer and Bullock, 1966). During secondary growth the epidermis, cortical parenchyma, and endodermis disappear and the outer phloem usually becomes heavily suberized. Although such roots usually are regarded as impermeable to water it has been demonstrated repeatedly that significant amounts of water and salt can enter through them (Chung and Kramer, 1975). Entry apparently occurs chiefly through lenticels, fissures between plates of bark, and openings caused by the death of small branch roots, and movement of salt probably is by both diffusion and mass flow. Some data on salt and water uptake through suberized roots are shown in Table 13.1. The ion barrier of suberized roots has never been identified, but the cambium may be a partial barrier because its thin cell walls may force most of the water and salt to cross the protoplasts on the way to the xylem. The role of suberized roots in salt and water absorption deserves further investigation.

Mycorrhizae

The effective absorbing zone of roots is modified on many woody and some herbaceous plants by the occurrence of mycorrhizae (see Figs. 2.24 and 2.25). The mycelium forms a sheath around roots (ectotrophic) or grows within the root tissue (endotrophic), and strands of hyphae grow out into the soil, greatly increasing the amount of surface in contact with soil particles. Experiments with radioactive tracers have demonstrated that ions absorbed by the hyphae are quickly transferred to the seedlings on which the fungus is growing. Bowen (1973) points out that roots of woody species do not occupy the soil as thoroughly as roots of many herbaceous species, but the mycelial strands and hyphae extending out several centimeters from mycorrhizal roots compensate for this. Also, the absorbing life of mycorrhizal roots is much longer than the life of the unsuberized region of any given nonmycorrhizal root. According to Marx (1973) mycorrhizal roots also are less subject to attack by root pathogens such as *Phytophthora, Pythium,* and *Fusarium* than nonmycorrhizal roots. Mycorrhizae are discussed in detail in the book, *Ectomycorrhizae,* edited by Marks and Kozlowski (1973) and in Kozlowski (1971a, pp. 277–305). Articles by Meyer (1974) and Harley (1970) also provide interesting information. The development of mycorrhizal roots was discussed in Chapter 2.

Movement of Ions from Roots to Shoots

After the various mineral elements enter the sap in the root xylem, they are carried to the shoots by mass flow in the transpiration stream, largely in inorganic form. As was mentioned in Chapter 9, in woody plants much or all of the nitrogen moves in the form of organic compounds, chiefly amino acids and amides. Some sulfur and phosphorus also is said to move in organic form, but most of these two elements and all of the others move as inorganic ions. Certain ions, notably zinc and iron, are sometimes precipitated in the xylem and fail to reach the shoots. A part of the salt tolerance of certain species and varieties of plants (e.g., grapes) is attributed to the unusual capacity of their root systems to retain salt, especially sodium, and prevent it from reaching the shoots (Jacoby, 1964). Seasonal changes in composition and concentration of the xylem sap are well established and an example is shown in Fig. 10.10. The highest concentration usually occurs about the time fruit trees are flowering and the lowest concentration during the dormant season. There also is a diurnal cycle in concentration, the lowest concentrations occurring about midday when rapid transpiration causes water to enter roots more rapidly than salt, diluting the xylem sap (Petritschek, 1953). As salt moves upward in the xylem some ions move radially out of the xylem sap into the phloem and are used or translocated downward to the roots. Sometimes so much

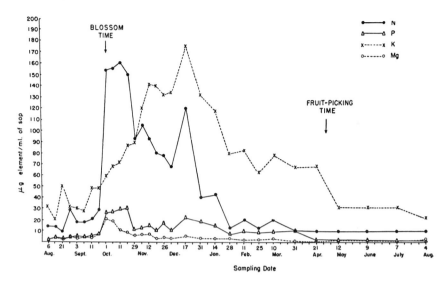

Fig. 10.10. Seasonal variations in concentrations of nitrogen, phosphorus, potassium, and magnesium in the xylem sap of apple in New Zealand. The nitrogen moves as organic nitrogen, the other elements largely or entirely in inorganic form. From Bollard (1958).

salt is removed that the concentration in the xylem sap is materially decreased (Klepper and Kaufmann, 1966).

Much, but not all, of the salt which reaches the leaves is accumulated in leaf cells by active transport. There is considerable movement of mobile elements such as nitrogen, phosphorus, and potassium from older to younger leaves, and movement out of senescing leaves was mentioned earlier. Calcium and magnesium are relatively immobile and tend to accumulate as leaves age, as shown for calcium in Fig. 10.3. When tracers such as radioactive phosphorus are supplied to leaves, they usually are soon found in the roots as well as in younger leaves, indicating that mineral nutrients are carried downward as well as upward.

Effects of Transpiration

It has already been mentioned that the flow of water toward the root surfaces of transpiring plants increases the movement of salt to the root surfaces. It may also increase the rate of movement into roots. The classical view is that all salt movement into roots occurs by active transport and is little affected by the rate of water intake. However, rapid flow of water through the root xylem tends to sweep out the salt and the decreased concentration should increase active transport. Also, as mentioned earlier, in older roots where lenticels, openings caused by death of branch roots, and other "leaks" permit some mass flow of water it is probable that an appreciable amount of salt is carried into the stele in the transpiration stream. Upward movement in the stem xylem, out into the leaf veins, and eventually into the walls of leaf cells can also be regarded as mass flow in the transpiration stream.

The relationship between salt and water absorption is discussed in more detail by Kramer (1969, pp. 244–247).

Selective Versus Nonselective Absorption

The existence of more than one path for salt movement into roots explains the somewhat contradictory fact that, although plant cells are highly selective in ion uptake, plants contain almost every element found in their root environment. This paradox results from the fact that, although a large fraction of the minerals in plants is selectively accumulated in the protoplasts of living cells, another significant fraction occurs in the free space of cell walls and dead tissue and these two fractions cannot be distinguished by chemical analysis of plant tissue.

Factors Affecting Salt Absorption

The amounts and kinds of ions absorbed by trees vary widely with species and environmental conditions, but the factors involved can only be discussed briefly.

Species Differences

There are some rather consistent differences among species with respect to salt content. For example, Coile (1937a) found the ash content of leaves of flowering dogwood, white oak, and sweetgum to be about twice as high (7.0 to 7.2%) as that of loblolly pine and shortleaf pine (3.0 to 3.5%) growing on the same soils. Coile also found that leaves of flowering dogwood, yellow-poplar, redbud, and white oak contained over 2% calcium while leaves of scarlet oak, post oak, and loblolly pine contained less than 1%. Beeson et al. (1955) found that blackgum accumulates many times as much cobalt as most other species growing on the same soil, gallberry accumulates zinc, and sweet pepperbush accumulates large amounts of both cobalt and zinc. Large differences in species with respect to mineral content have been reported by other workers.

It has been argued by foresters both in Europe and in the United States that the presence of trees with leaves high in calcium and phosphorus is desirable because they improve decomposition of litter and soil fertility, especially under stands of conifers. However, Stone (1975) questions whether growth of particular species or combinations of species can have significant effects on soil fertility within a few decades.

Some species of mangrove that grow in sea water exclude salt, but others absorb 10 to 20% of the salt and excrete it through salt glands in the leaves. Some halophytes such as *Atriplex* also are notable for the secretion of salt while other species seem to exclude it. In many instances differences in ion uptake are controlled by the roots, perhaps by their ability to bind certain ions and prevent export to the shoots. Oranges grown on trifoliate orange rootstocks are said to be more susceptible to zinc and iron deficiencies than those on other root stocks such as rough lemon. In some instances differences in ion uptake among herbaceous species and strains of species are known to be genetically controlled (Gerloff, 1963; Stone, 1968), but little information is avail-

TABLE 10.10   Exclusion of Manganese by Species of *Cornus* [a]

Species	Mn content (ppm)	Mn content of other species from the same site (ppm)	Date sampled	Soil pH
Cornus canadensis	149	936	7–12–59	4.0
Cornus racemosa	71	905	6–18–59	5.1
Cornus racemosa	28	122	7–13–60	5.8
Cornus rugosa	64	210	6–29–59	5.6
Cornus stolonifera	37	52	7–14–60	7.4

[a] From Gerloff *et al.* (1966).

able for woody plants. An example of exclusion of manganese by several species of *Cornus* is shown in Table 10.10.

Composition and Concentration of the Soil Solution

Foresters and farmers know that the growth of plants is greatly affected by the concentration of essential mineral nutrients in the soil. In addition, the presence of high concentrations of toxic elements such as lead, zinc, and copper, the soil pH, and the excess of salt found in saline soils all present problems for the growth of woody vegetation as well as herbaceous plants. Among the complex interactions among ions which affect their availability, the role of calcium is particularly important. Some kinds of plants, known as calcicoles or calciophiles, occur chiefly or exclusively on calcareous, alkaline soils and others, known as calcifuges or calciphobes, occur on noncalcareous, acid soils. In some instances there seems to be a higher calcium requirement among calcicole plants than among related species which are calcifuges (Epstein, 1972, pp. 354–359), but there are other effects such as variations in pH which are important. Plants can be grown in solution cultures over a wide pH range if precautions are taken to keep the essential elements in solution. However, in nature the pH is important because it affects the solubility of several elements. In alkaline soils iron and phosphorus deficiencies are common and in acid soils calcium and magnesium are frequently deficient and the increased solubility of aluminum, manganese, and other ions may produce concentrations toxic to plants.

The ecological importance of such specialized soil conditions as salinity, calcareous soils, and the presence of heavy metals was discussed in detail by Epstein (1972, Chapter 13). The serpentine soils found along the Pacific Coast of North America are characterized by low calcium and high magnesium concentrations and by poor growth of vegetation. It should be noted that, although some plants growing successfully on soils high in toxic elements exclude them, other plants absorb large quantities without injury. At least some plants appear to form chelating compounds which bind various elements in the cell walls and render them harmless (Antonovics *et al.*, 1971). Individual variations among plants with respect to ion uptake are discussed by Bollard and Butler (1966) and by Gerloff (1963), but most of the research has been done on herbaceous species. Halophytes are good examples of plants that grow in spite of unfavorable soil conditions, but even they do not all survive for the same reason. As mentioned previously, some species of mangroves and *Atriplex* exclude salt, but others absorb large quantities and dispose of at least part by secreting it through salt glands.

Biogeochemical Prospecting

It is clear that there are consistent differences among species in their ability to accumulate both essential elements such as calcium and potassium and nonessential elements such as selenium and silica. On the other hand, it is equally well established that the kinds and concentrations of mineral elements found in plants are influenced by the kinds and concentrations found in the soil in which they grow. This fact forms the basis for foliar analysis as an indicator of fertilizer needs. It also is the basis for biogeochemical prospecting, in which the mineral composition of plant tissue is used to indicate the presence or absence of certain mineral elements in the soil. This method seems to have been rather widely employed all over the world, using both woody and herbaceous indicator plants. Examples are described by Cannon (1960) and Epstein (1972).

Moisture Content of Soil

Abnormally low or high soil water content has such important effects on root growth that it is difficult to separate direct effects on mineral absorption from indirect effects produced by changes in the rate of root growth and differentiation. Dentrification occurs in water-saturated soils and microbial activity is reduced in dry soils. The concentration of reduced forms of such elements as iron and manganese sometimes reaches toxic levels in saturated soils. Plants in dry soil tend to be low in phosphorus and potassium because these elements tend to become fixed in the soil and because root growth is reduced and the absorbing surface is decreased. Symptoms of iron and manganese deficiency also are more common in plants growing in dry soil. Richards and Wadleigh (1952) discussed this complex problem in detail.

Root Metabolism

Mineral uptake involves active transport which depends on the expenditure of metabolic energy, hence salt absorption is affected by environmental factors such as aeration and temperature. Most of the research has been done on the roots of herbaceous plants, but the limited data available indicate that roots of woody species behave in a similar manner. The effect of oxygen on potassium uptake by mycorrhizal roots is shown in Fig. 10.11 and the effect of temperature on the movement of phosphorus is shown in Fig. 10.12. The data shown in Table 10.11 indicate that respiration inhibitors reduce phosphorus uptake to about the same extent in mycorrhizal and nonmycorrhizal roots. It has been established that deficient aeration often limits nutrient uptake by herbaceous crops and the same is doubtless true for most woody species. However, as

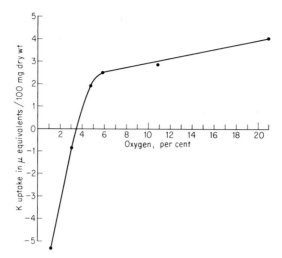

Fig. 10.11. Effect of oxygen concentration on uptake of potassium by excised mycorrhizal roots of beech. From Harley (1956).

with soil moisture, it is difficult to separate the direct effects of deficient aeration and low temperature on salt uptake from the indirect effects on root growth, which also reduce salt uptake. The complicated effects of inadequate aeration and fungal infection are exemplified in the little leaf disease of southern pines. Furthermore, the reduced shoot growth which accompanies cold or poorly aerated soil also reduces the use of salt. Since root growth and metabolism depend on a supply of carbohydrates and growth regulators from the shoots, factors that reduce photosynthesis and shoot growth are likely to reduce root growth and salt absorption even more.

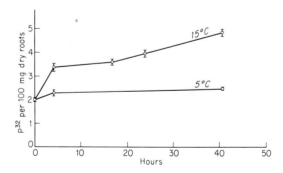

Fig. 10.12 Effect of temperature on movement of radioactive phosphorus from the fungal sheath into the core of mycorrhizal roots of beech. From Harley (1956).

TABLE 10.11   Effect of Respiration Inhibitors on Accumulation of Radioactive Phosphorus by Mycorrhizal and Nonmycorrhizal Loblolly Pine Roots[a]

	Root tips		Mycorrhizal segments	
Treatments at pH 4.7–4.8	Counts/min	Activity as % of control	Counts/min	Activity as % of control
Control	81,713		77,306	
0.025 *M* malonic acid	77,330	94.6	67,405	87.2
0.001 *M* sodium azide	308	0.4	965	1.2
0.005 *M* sodium fluoride	986	1.2	1,620	2.1

[a] From Kramer (1951).

GENERAL REFERENCES

Anderson, W. P., ed. (1973). "Ion Transport in Plants." Academic Press, New York.

Anonymous (1968). "Forest Fertilization: Theory and Practice," (1968). Symposium on Forest Fertilization, Gainesville, Florida, 1967. Tenn. Valley Auth., Muscle Shoals, Alabama.

Epstein, E. (1972). "Mineral Nutrition of Plants: Principles and Perspectives." Wiley, New York.

Gauch, H. G. (1972). "Inorganic Plant Nutrition." Dowden, Hutchinson & Ross, Inc., Stroudsburg, Pennsylvania.

Hewitt, E. J., and Smith, T. A. (1975). "Plant Mineral Nutrition." Wiley, New York.

Higinbotham, N. (1974). Conceptual developments in membrane transport. *Plant Physiol.* **54,** 454.

Likens, G. E., Bormann, F. H., Pierce, R. S., Eaton, J. S., and Johnston, N. M. (1977). "The Biogeochemistry of a Forested Ecosystem." Springer-Verlag, Berlin and New York.

Lüttge, U., and Pitman, M. G., eds. (1976). "Transport in Plants IIB," Encycl. Plant Physiol., New Ser., Vol. 2B. Springer-Verlag, Berlin and New York.

Reisenauer, H. M., ed. (1976). "Soil and Plant-Tissue Testing in California," Bull. No. 1879. Div. Agric. Sci., University of California, Davis.

Rorison, I. H., ed. (1969). "Ecological Aspects of the Mineral Nutrition of Plants." Blackwell, Oxford.

Russell, E. W. (1973). "Soil Conditions and Plant Growth," 10th ed. Longmans, Green, New York.

Sanchez, P. A. (1973). A review of soils research in tropical Latin America. *N. C., Agric. Exp. Stn., Tech. Bull.* **219.**

Torrey, J. G., and Clarkson, D. T., eds. (1975). "The Development and Functions of Roots." Academic Press, New York.

Youngberg, C. T., and Davey, C. B., eds. (1970). "Tree Growth and Forest Soils." Oregon State Univ. Press, Corvallis.

11

Translocation

INTRODUCTION

The success of plants more than a few centimeters in height depends on the movement of water, minerals, and some organic compounds from their roots to their shoots and the movement of carbohydrates and other organic compounds from their shoots to their roots. Continued growth requires that an adequate supply of water, mineral nutrients, organic nitrogen compounds, and certain growth regulators be available at the various meristematic regions. Thus the transport of these substances to the regions where they are being used as building materials and substrates for respiration is as important for growth as the synthetic processes which produce them.

In small, relatively undifferentiated organisms every cell can carry on all essential processes and no cell is far from a source of raw materials. In such low-growing plants as mosses and liverworts diffusion, perhaps aided by cytoplasmic streaming, suffices for the short-distance translocation that is necessary. However, rapid, bidirectional, long-distance translocation upward and downward is essential for the existence of large land plants such as trees because root growth depends on sugar and probably growth regulators from the leaves and the leaves depend on the roots for their supply of water, mineral nutrients, organic nitrogen compounds, and some growth regulators. As roots and leaves are often 30 to 100 m apart in trees and large quantities of materials must be moved simultaneously in opposite directions, the problem becomes complex.

The evolution of a vascular system that makes possible rapid long-distance transport was essential to the development of tall plants. Its mechanical strength also serves the equally essential purpose of supporting a large leaf area where it is well exposed to the sun. Thus development of the modern vascular system marked a change in morphology and physiology that made trees possible.

Proper partitioning of metabolites among the various organs and tissues, including root and stem tips, cambia, and developing fruits and seeds, is essential to plant development, hence consideration must also be given to the factors which control translocation. An understanding of the tissues involved and the forces affecting translocation is essential not only for an appreciation of the physiology of trees, but also for an understanding of how certain pathogens and insects, and injuries such as girdling, damage trees.

In seedlings, where transport is chiefly from cell to cell, diffusion suffices, but as they grow taller it becomes inadequate. Although diffusion of molecules is rapid over distances measured in nanometers, or even millimeters, it is very slow over distances measured in meters. For example, it was estimated that 940 days would be required for 1 mg of sucrose to diffuse 1 m in an aqueous solution through a water-filled tube with a cross section of 1 cm^2 from a 10% solution into what was initially pure water. Thus mechanisms more rapid than diffusion must be involved to move daily 150 or 200 liters of water from roots to shoots or several hundred grams of sugar out of the leaves. We will discuss the pathways and transport mechanisms for the principal substances moved and consider some factors affecting long-distance transport.

WATER TRANSPORT

Water transport is discussed in Chapter 13, but it will be discussed here as a carrier for the upward transport of solutes. On a hot sunny day, 100 to 150 liters of water may be transported through the roots and stem to the leaves of a large tree. This sap stream moves by mass flow through the xylem, the structure of which was discussed in Chapter 2. As water moves radially inward from the soil to the root xylem, it crosses a mass of living cells, probably moving chiefly in the walls (the apoplast). In leaves it moves outward from xylem in the walls of mesophyll cells. However, essentially all longitudinal movement occurs through the lumens of dead vessels and tracheids. Although water movement in the xylem is almost always upward, there are no valves or other structures to prevent downward flow, and the direction can be reversed to a limited extent under certain conditions (Daum, 1967). As pointed out in Chapter 13, the driving force usually is a gradient in water potential from soil to leaves produced by the evaporation of water. Thus the rate of water flow is controlled primarily by the rate of transpiration, although other factors are involved (Passioura, 1976).

Composition of Xylem Sap

The xylem sap of trees is a dilute solution of mineral salts and organic substances, including nitrogen compounds, carbohydrates, enzymes, and growth regulators, especially cytokinins and gibberellins (Table 11.1). The concentration and composition of the xylem sap vary diurnally and seasonally. The daily increase in rate of water flow caused by rapid midday transpiration reduces the concentration of solutes in the sap.

Carbohydrates

The carbohydrate content of xylem sap tends to be high in winter and early spring, falling to a minimum in late spring and early summer. In pear, it begins to increase in late summer, rising to a maximum in the winter (Anderssen, 1929). Sucrose, glucose, and fructose are the principal sugars in the xylem sap. The outstanding example of xylem sap high in sugar is that of sugar maple, which contains so much sucrose (1 to 7%) that it is used to make maple syrup. Birch sap contains measurable amounts of fructose and glucose. Birch and maple sap flow are discussed in Chapter 13.

Nitrogen Compounds

Most of the nitrogen used by trees is reduced to organic compounds in the roots and moved to the shoots in the xylem sap. Different nitrogen compounds are characteristic

TABLE 11.1 Concentrations of Solutes in Sap of Xylem and Phloem of Red Ash[a,b]

	Xylem sap (mg/ml)	Phloem sap (mg/ml)
Dry matter	1.4	220
Sucrose	0.128	140
Potassium	0.177	2.1
Magnesium	0.0115	0.077
Sodium	0.004	0.037
Calcium	0.018	0.049
Phosphorus	0.005	0.052
pH	4.9–5.0	7.5

[a] From von Die and Willemse (1975).
[b] Sieve tube exudate and xylem sap were collected for analysis on October 10.

of the sap of different plant families, but most of the nitrogen occurs as amino acids and amides and only traces of nitrate and ammonia nitrogen have been reported (Bollard, 1953, 1957a,b). The concentration and composition of the nitrogen compounds vary with the season. In elm sap 21 amino acids were identified, and the amino acid content was found to decrease gradually from early spring to summer (Singh and Smalley, 1969a). In apple sap aspartic acid and glutamine were most common in the summer, but in September aspartic acid decreased and arginine increased and was the dominant constituent all winter (Tromp, 1970). Glutamine was the most important amino acid in seven species of pine studied by Barnes (1963b), but other amino acids were important in other species studied. In spite of the fact that Barnes (1963a) found only 20 ppm of nitrogen in the xylem sap of pines, he estimated that, because of the high rate of transpiration, about 50 kg/ha/year of nitrogen could be transported to the crowns in the xylem sap of a pine stand. Nitrogen nutrition was discussed in more detail in Chapter 9.

Other Constituents

In addition to carbohydrates and organic nitrogen compounds, xylem sap usually contains substantial amounts of various minerals and small amounts of growth regulators, especially cytokinins and gibberellins, enzymes, and miscellaneous compounds. While minerals constitute a relatively small fraction of the solid matter in the xylem sap of trees in late winter and early spring, they are often the only important solutes in the xylem sap of herbaceous plants. Salt transport is discussed in the next section; transport of growth regulators near the end of this chapter.

MINERAL TRANSPORT

Practically all of the movement of minerals from roots to shoots occurs in the xylem sap, carried by mass flow in the transpiration stream. There is also considerable lateral movement of minerals between the xylem and phloem, and minerals diffuse out of the xylem during ascent, presumably because of their use in growing regions along the way. Figure 11.1 describes an experiment that demonstrated the occurrence of such movement. The cells of stem tips, the cambial regions, and other metabolically active regions all accumulate minerals, producing gradients which cause movement toward these regions.

Upward Movement

Data on the amounts and proportions of various minerals in the xylem sap are given in Table 11.1 and data on seasonal changes in mineral concentration of the xylem sap were shown in Fig. 10.10. The rate of transport of minerals is controlled chiefly by the rate of transpiration and is therefore much slower in bare trees than in those which have leafed out (Graham, 1957). Flow rates of injected radioisotopes of up to 60 m/hr are shown in Table 13.3. Surprisingly, not all mineral elements move upward in xylem at

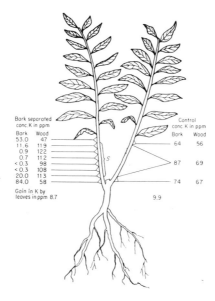

Bark separated
conc. K in ppm

Bark	Wood
53.0	47
11.6	119
0.9	122
0.7	112
<0.3	98
<0.3	108
20.0	113
84.0	58

Gain in K by
leaves in ppm 8.7

Control
conc. K in ppm

Bark	Wood
64	56
87	69
74	67

9.9

Fig. 11.1. Path of upward movement of radioactive potassium in willow. The bark of the left-hand branch was separated from the wood by a layer of paraffined paper, while the right-hand branch was left intact. Very little potassium was found in the bark where it was separated from the wood, but large amounts where it was in normal contact. This experiment indicates that upward movement occurred chiefly in the xylem but that lateral movement from wood to bark also occurs. From Stout and Hoagland (1939).

the same rate, movement of some ions apparently being slowed by adsorption on the walls of the xylem elements. Examples of slow-moving ions are calcium, iron, and zinc. Also, some kinds of plants apparently retain more of certain ions in their roots than others. For example, certain varieties of grape translocate less salt to the shoots than others when grown in concentrated solutions of sodium chloride (Ehlig, 1960). As was pointed out in Chapter 10, cells are highly selective with respect to ion accumulation and root systems are fairly selective, but at least traces of almost every ion in the root enviroment leak through the ion barriers in roots and occur in the free space or apoplast of leaves.

Recirculation of Minerals

Although xylem sap is the primary source of minerals and nitrogen for growing regions in shoots, recirculation or recycling in the phloem also plays an important role in mineral nutrition. Thus growing leaves may receive minerals via both xylem and phloem. Continual movement of minerals into leaves in the transpiration stream tends to cause accumulation of salt as the season progresses. This sometimes causes injury to leaves of plants that are too heavily fertilized or are growing in saline soil. Elements such as calcium, magnesium, and in saline soil sodium, usually accumulate as the growing season progresses, but the concentrations of such mobile elements as nitrogen, phosphorus, and potassium often decrease, when expressed as percentage of dry weight (see Fig. 10.3). There is a general tendency for the more mobile elements to move out of older tissues, which are less active metabolically, to young leaves, growing fruits, and other metabolically active regions (Williams, 1955). There also is extensive export of minerals from senescing leaves to twigs in the autumn. Figure 11.2 shows mineral cycling in trees.

Measurable amounts of salts are lost from the free space or apoplast of leaves by the leaching action of rain (see Chapter 10). Some plants lose salt through secretion from salt glands and some is lost in the guttation water forced out of hydathodes by root pressure. Experiments with radioactive tracers such as ^{32}P show that when supplied to the leaves they often move down to the roots in the phloem where some leaks out and some is transferred to the xylem and moves upward.

The mobility of various ions in the phloem varies widely. Bukovac and Wittwer (1957) classified K, Rb, Na, Mg, P, S, and Cl as highly mobile; Fe, Mn, Zn, Cu, and Mo as intermediate; and Ca, Li, Sr, Ba, and B as relatively immobile. However, the mobility of ions in the intermediate group varies with the species, the stage of growth, and the amount of the element in the plant. For example, Cu, Zn, and S are mobile only

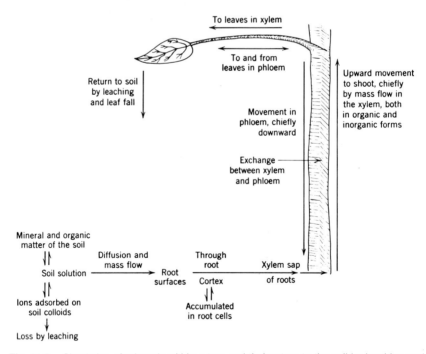

Fig. 11.2. Circulation of minerals within a tree and their return to the soil by leaching and leaf fall. From Kramer (1969). Copyright 1969; used with permission of McGraw-Hill Book Company.

when the concentration is high, and mobility is low in plants deficient in these elements (Loneragan *et al.*, 1976). The concentration of immobile elements may be adequate in old leaves, while young leaves on the same plant show symptoms of deficiency. Conversely, freely mobile elements such as N, P, and K often move out of older leaves, causing deficiency symptoms, while the young leaves show no evidence of deficiency. This situation must be taken into account when sampling leaves to test for mineral deficiencies. The recirculation of minerals was reviewed by Loneragan *et al.* (1976).

Control of Mineral Uptake

We now return to the problem of what controls the uptake of minerals, both at the plant and the tissue level. At the plant level, mineral uptake is largely controlled by the rate at which ions are transported from the soil across roots and released into the root xylem. This is affected both directly and indirectly by the rate of water movement into the root xylem. Rapid water flow moves ions in the soil toward roots and expedites their movement in free space and the symplast toward the root xylem. A rapid transpiration stream also reduces the salt concentration in the root xylem and facilitates release into the xylem sap (Sutcliffe, 1976).

At the tissue level, ion accumulation seems to be related to protein synthesis and sink strength therefore is high in growing tissue. Thus, young leaves often obtain ions from older tissue and as they grow old lose ions to young leaves and fruits and other metabolically active tissues. It is often stated that plant hormones play a role in controlling salt movement, but it is difficult to separate the effects of rapid use in growing tissues from the large amount of hormones produced in such tissues. The most likely examples of hormone effects on ion uptake are in situations such as the excretion of H^+ caused in the pulvini by auxin or the loss of K^+ from guard cells caused by abscisic acid. It also is claimed that ABA reduces ion transport into the root xylem without reducing ion uptake by the roots. This poorly understood field was reviewed by Van Steveninck (1976).

TRANSLOCATION OF ORGANIC COMPOUNDS

Serious study of the translocation of organic substances in plants began with the work of the forest botanist, Theodor Hartig. He described sieve tubes in 1837 and in 1859 discovered that sap could be obtained by puncturing them, thus providing the methodology for many later studies of translocation. A variety of organic compounds are translocated in plants, including carbohydrates, nitrogen-containing compounds, growth regulators, vitamins, viruses, and applied biocides such as herbicides, fungicides, and insecticides (Ziegler, 1975). Most of the organic compounds are translocated in the phloem, as shown by girdling experiments, analysis of phloem exudate, and experiments with radioactive tracers.

A growing plant can be regarded as an integrated system of competing food sinks with the direction of translocation and the amount of carbohydrate and nitrogen-containing compounds moved to various tissues, depending on the food requirements of the sinks and the magnitude of the various sources of supply. Thus any discussion of translocation requires consideration of the amount of growth taking place and where it is occurring.

Carbohydrates

The quantity of carbohydrates translocated exceeds that of all other solutes combined. Net carbohydrate transport is predominantly downward, but considerable upward movement also occurs. The sources of carbohydrates are pools of reserve carbohydrates and currently produced photosynthate, and the amount moved depends on the carbohydrate requirements and on the proximity of growing tissue to sources of supply. In most woody plants carbohydrates are translocated largely or entirely as sucrose, but in a few plant families raffinose, stachyose, and verbascose are important constituents of the phloem sap. The sugar alcohol, sorbitol, is found in apple and cherry, and mannitol in ash. Reducing sugars do not occur in the phloem sap. Biblical "manna" may have come from various sources, but commercial manna is obtained from phloem sap containing mannitol, obtained by wounding manna ash.

In young, temperate zone gymnosperms the roots typically are the major carbohydrate sinks before buds open (Fig. 11.3). After buds open a reversal of translocation takes place, with larger amounts of carbohydrates moving to the expanding shoots. At this time cambial growth forms a secondary carbohydrate sink. When seasonal shoot

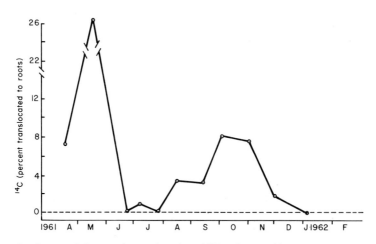

Fig. 11.3. Seasonal changes in translocation of ^{14}C to 3-year-old eastern white pine trees. From Nelson (1964).

growth is completed, cambial growth and renewed root growth commonly comprise the major carbohydrate sinks. This generalized seasonal pattern may be greatly altered during a year of heavy fruiting, when reproductive tissues monopolize the bulk of available carbohydrates (Kozlowski and Keller, 1966; Kozlowski, 1971a,b).

When both roots and shoots are growing the proportion of photosynthate retained by the shoots and translocated to the roots depends on the relative strength (growth rate) of each of these sinks and their proximity to carbohydrate sources. For example, after both fast- and slow-growing white spruce seedlings were exposed to $^{14}CO_2$, more photosynthate was retained by the shoots of the fast-growing plants (70%) than by shoots of slow-growing plants (55%), but more ^{14}C was translocated to the roots of the slow-growing plants (Ursino, 1973). The amount of photosynthate translocated to roots also varies with root development. In red pine and eastern white pine seedlings with poorly developed root systems, translocation of photosynthate was much lower than in seedlings with extensive, rapidly growing root systems (Shiroya *et al.,* 1962b).

The importance of source–sink relations in translocation has been demonstrated by experimentally altering the relative strengths of sources and sinks. For example, during the prebloom and bloom period, grape shoots were relatively independent of each other for a supply of photosynthates. However, an increase in the carbohydrate requirement of one shoot, caused by a gibberellin-induced growth stimulus, caused compensatory movement of photosynthate from an adjacent shoot. Similarly, a reduction in available photosynthate, within a shoot or part of a shoot, caused by shading or defoliation, resulted in translocation of photosynthate from adjacent leaves. Such compensatory translocation was demonstrated both within and between shoots. In contrast, removal of a sink increased the availability of carbohydrates to adjacent sinks. Although these experiments were conducted under controlled conditions they indicated that temporary shading of certain leaves, or injury to leaves by insects or diseases, exerts an effect on the pattern of translocation of photosynthetic products (Quinlan and Weaver, 1970).

Carbohydrates exported early in the growing season from leaves to roots of seedlings may later be exported upward to strong sinks such as rapidly expanding shoots. For example, in 3-year-old eastern white pine seedlings whose shoots were exposed to $^{14}CO_2$ in June, the concentration of photoassimilated ^{14}C in the roots increased from 1% after 8 hr to 10% after 1 month. During the next month, however, the concentration of ^{14}C in the roots decreased to 4%, but by October it had increased again to 14%. The decrease in ^{14}C concentration of the roots between the first and second month after photoassimilation indicated that retranslocation of ^{14}C had occurred from the roots back into the shoots (Ursino *et al.,* 1968). By comparison, in 8-year-old red pine trees reserve carbohydrates in the roots were relatively unimportant for shoot growth. When the phloem was blocked by girdling the main stem at ground level before the growing season began, preventing phloem translocation of stored carbohydrates from roots to above-ground tissues, subsequent shoot growth was only negligibly inhibited (Kozlowski and Winget, 1964a). There is considerable evidence that as trees increase in size and the translocation path from shoots to roots becomes longer, there is decreasing dependency of growing tissues in the upper crown on carbohydrate reserves in the lower stem and roots. Thus the contribution of the lower branches to the upper stem steadily decreases as trees grow larger.

Shoot Growth

Both carbohydrate reserves and current photosynthate are used in shoot growth, the proportion of each varying with species, genetic makeup, type of shoot, and shoot location on the stem.

In addition to utilizing reserve carbohydrate for early growth, growing shoots of angiosperms also use currently produced photosynthates. There is a changing seasonal pattern in the sources of currently produced carbohydrates used in shoot growth by gymnosperms. Early in May, when terminal buds of red pine shoots are opening in central Wisconsin they begin to mobilize carbohydrates, largely photosynthate from the 1-year-old needles. By June 1, when shoots are in the "candle" stage (internodes well expanded and needles along the internode relatively unexpanded), the 1-year-old needles are supplying most current photosynthate to the expanding shoots, with smaller amounts obtained from 2- and 3-year-old needles. The supply of current photosynthate from the old needles declines in mid-August. By that time the now mature, current-year needles have replaced the old needles as the primary photoassimilating tissues and exporters of carbohydrates for growth for various tissues (Dickmann and Kozlowski, 1968). Gordon and Larson (1968) found that translocation of labeled photosynthate from the old needles to expanding shoots of red pine was greatest when the new needles were elongating rapidly.

Overall, the old needles are the most important source of metabolites for shoot growth of red pine. By defoliation, phloem blockage by girdling and various combinations of these before the growing season began, Kozlowski and Winget (1964a) studied the role of reserves in branches, stems, and roots as well as that of reserves plus current photosynthate of needles on shoot growth of 8-year-old red pine trees. Defoliation and girdling, alone or in combination, reduced shoot growth. Reductions in shoot growth due to treatment were in the following decreasing order: branch girdling + needle removal > girdling at base of main stem + needle removal > needle removal > branch girdling > girdling at stem base. The contribution to shoot growth of reserves from tissues other than old leaves was in the following order: branches > main stem > roots (Table 11.2).

The direction of net translocation of carbohydrates from individual leaves on heterophyllous shoots of angiosperms varies as the shoot expands and continues to add new leaves. In general, very young leaves import carbohydrates from mature leaves below them; when leaves are partly expanded there is both import and export, but when fully expanded there is only export. As a leaf of a heterophyllous shoot expands, the pattern of carbohydrate export shifts from upward to bidirectional and finally, when it is overtopped by several well-expanded leaves, to a predominantly downward direction. Eventually, as leaves senesce, photosynthesis and export decline. Such patterns have been demonstrated in cottonwood and apple (Larson and Gordon, 1969a; Hansen, 1967a,b). Most of the carbohydrates exported upward are used to develop vascular and structural tissues of the stem (Larson and Gordon, 1969b).

TABLE 11.2 Estimates of Contributions of Various Plant Parts to Dry Weight of Shoots and to Elongation of Terminal Leaders[a]

Contributing plant parts	Dry weight of shoots (% of control)
Needles + main stem + branches + roots	100.0
Needles:	
On whole tree	87.6
Minus roots	75.8
On branches	66.7
Branches	5.7
Main stem:	
With old needles on tree	13.9
With old needles removed	4.9
Main stem + roots:	
With old needles removed	6.7
Roots:	
With old needles on tree	13.6
With old needles removed	1.8

[a] From Kozlowski and Winget (1964a).

The presence of growing fruits often modifies the pattern of carbohydrate export from leaves of heterophyllous shoots. Such fruits are powerful carbohydrate sinks and often monopolize available carbohydrates even to the extent of causing a reversal of translocation directly from wholly downward to bidirectional. When this occurs, some of the photosynthates are exported upward into fruits from leaves below and downward from leaves higher up on the branch. Both Quinlan (1965) and Hansen (1967b) showed such a translocation pattern in apple shoots.

According to Kriedemann (1969), rapidly growing orange shoots import large amounts of carbohydrates. However, once the leaves on the current growth cycle (most recent growth flush) or those on a previous growth cycle are fully expanded, they become exporters of carbohydrates, primarily to nearby growing fruits. Mature leaves at some distance away from a growing shoot export carbohydrates primarily to the roots (Kriedemann, 1969).

Cambial Growth

The cambial region is a relatively diffuse meristem and a weak carbohydrate sink and therefore does not compete well with the strong sinks of rapidly elongating shoots and roots or enlarging reproductive structures. Nevertheless, the active cambium—which sheathes the main stem, the entire branch system, and major roots—consumes large amounts of carbohydrates over the growing season. Carbohydrates are used in the production of new cambial initials and accretion of xylem and phloem. As most new cambial initials are cut off by pseudotransverse division, there is overproduction and loss of many of the new cells. The initials with the most ray contacts survive, suggesting intense competition for carbohydrates and water.

Since, in many deciduous species, cambial activity below the buds begins before the buds open, early-season cambial growth must depend on carbohydrate reserves. In particular, considerable reserve carbohydrate is used in phloem production, which begins very early in the season, and often precedes xylem production, sometimes by as much as several weeks (see Chapter 3). Such early cambial growth is accompanied by depletion of reserve carbohydrates from storage tissues such as axial and ray parenchyma cells.

In addition to reserves, currently produced photosynthate is used early in the season in cambial growth of gymnosperms. For example, in 3-, 5-, and 15-year-old red pine trees appreciable amounts of ^{14}C were concentrated in differentiating tracheids shortly after whole trees or individual branches were exposed to $^{14}CO_2$ (Larson, 1969a; Rangenekar and Forward, 1969; Rangenekar et al., 1969). When Dickmann and Kozlowski (1970a) exposed 1-year-old needles of 20-year-old red pine trees to $^{14}CO_2$ in mid-June, considerable ^{14}C was rapidly incorporated into structural compounds in the xylem, further emphasizing early utilization of currently produced carbohydrates in cambial growth.

Use of the carbohydrate pool in cambial growth is not uniform in time or space. In many temperate zone species, carbohydrates are used in cambial growth during only a few months of the year. And even during that time the use of carbohydrates is intermittent because of competition of cambial growth with stronger carbohydrate sinks and because of effects of fluctuations in climatic factors, insect attacks, diseases, etc., on the supply of photosynthate. In many tropical species carbohydrates are used in cambial growth during every month of the year, but there are seasonal variations in the rate of carbohydrate mobilization. Sometimes tropical trees that show cambial increment during each month of the year produce multiple growth rings, emphasizing the uneven utilization of carbohydrates.

Utilization of carbohydrates at different stem heights and branches also is quite variable. For example, in seedlings and in vigorous, open-grown adult trees more carbohydrates are used in cambial growth in the lower stem than in the upper stem. In suppressed trees and very old trees carbohydrate utilization in growth is largely confined to the upper stem, as often shown by missing xylem rings in the lower stem.

In gymnosperms the branch whorls of the upper crown are the primary source of current photosynthate for cambial growth. For example, in average red pine trees the branches in the upper one-third of the crown supply most of the carbohydrates used in cambial growth. Such relatively unshaded branches have a high photosynthetic capacity as well as a short translocation path to the main stem. The relative importance of carbohydrates produced by other branches will vary with growth conditions, tree age, competition, and other factors (Larson, 1969b). In open-grown trees the retention of branches in the lower stem provides an important source of carbohydrates for cambial growth in the lower stem. Under severe competition in closed stands, natural pruning of lower branches, or their lack of vigor, confines the carbohydrate source for cambial growth to branches located in the upper stem.

The carbohydrate supply for cambial growth from individual branches decreases as they become increasingly suppressed. In gymnosperms, for example, as the lower branches age and are overlaid by more and more branch whorls, they become increasingly shaded and their photosynthetic activity declines. Such lower, suppressed branches have less carbohydrates available for export and for cambial growth than do branches higher up on the stem.

As mentioned earlier, in many adult trees the suppressed lower branches do not contribute any carbohydrates for growth of the main stem. Such "negative" branches may not even translocate enough carbohydrates for xylem production along the entire branch length. For example, there often were nine to ten fewer xylem rings in the bases of lower branches of adult Douglas-fir trees than there were in the main stem at the point of intersection with the branch (Reukema, 1959). Branches of loblolly pine in the lower one-half of the crown with fewer than three branchlets, or branches in the lower one-fourth of the crown with fewer than five branchlets, did not contribute any carbohydrates for growth of the main stem (Labyak and Schumacher, 1954).

There is a changing seasonal pattern in the importance of different-aged needles as carbohydrate sources for cambial growth. In young red pine trees most of the earlywood in older stem internodes was produced while shoots were elongating and during the early stages of needle expansion, and the new needles did not contribute an appreciable amount of photosynthate for cambial growth at this time. Rather, carbohydrates exported from the old needles (mostly 1 year old) were used in earlywood production. When the new needles were almost fully expanded they began to provide large amounts of carbohydrates for xylem production. At the same time a change occurred in the direction of translocation of carbohydrates from the old needles, transport now occurring primarily to the roots and very little moving upward to the new branches. The increased carbohydrate supply following maturation of the new needles was correlated with secondary wall thickening of tracheids, indicative of latewood development. Toward the end of the growing season, the new needles supplied carbohydrates to the new buds and to cambial growth in upper stem internodes, and the old needles supplied carbohydrates for cambial growth of lower stem internodes. Late in the season, when the cambium was no longer a significant sink, all age classes of needles supplied carbohydrates to the roots, and reserve carbohydrates accumulated in parenchyma tissues throughout the tree (Gordon and Larson, 1968; Larson and Gordon, 1969a).

Reproductive Growth

As previously mentioned growing fruits are strong sinks and they use large amounts of reserve and/or currently produced carbohydrates. For example, large amounts of reserve carbohydrates were transported into expanding flowers and fruits of beech trees, mostly from the twig wood (Gäumann, 1935). Cameron and Borst (1938) found a much lower starch content throughout the summer and autumn in branches of bearing avocado trees than in nonbearing trees. Storage of starch during the autumn and early winter apparently was reduced by the requirements of the growing fruits. Preferential use of carbohydrates for reproductive growth was shown by Ryugo and Davis (1959) for five varieties of peach that fruit at different times. In each variety there was a decrease in starch content in the fruiting branches prior to the harvest of fruits and an increase after harvest.

Carbohydrate reserves are greatly affected by alternate bearing. For example, the starch concentration in leaves of mandarin orange trees that produced a small number of fruits was about twice as high as in leaves of trees with large crops (Lewis *et al.*, 1964). Young and old fruits on the same tree also compete for available carbohydrates. Leaving mature orange fruit on trees for several months before harvesting tended to accentuate alternate bearing and to decrease yield of the next crop (Jones and Cree, 1954), probably because late harvesting reduced the carbohydrates available for the subsequent crop (Jones *et al.*, 1964).

In the fifth or sixth week after full bloom, the starch content of fruit-bearing apple spurs dropped rapidly to about one-third of the amount in nonbearing spurs (Table 11.3). Such rapid depletion of reserves coincided with a large increase in the gibberellin content of developing seeds. The continuing supply of hormones from the growing seeds appeared to stimulate translocation of carbohydrates to the rapidly growing fruits (Grochowska, 1973).

In addition to mobilizing reserves, reproductive structures also use large amounts of current photosynthate. A few examples will be given for both angiosperms and gymnosperms. Mochizuki (1962) treated bearing apple trees with $^{14}CO_2$ at various times after flowering. Early in the season the bulk of the photosynthate went into vegetative tissues but late in the summer most of it was translocated into fruits. Hansen (1967a) showed that apple fruits obtained up to 90% of the ^{14}C from nearby leaves. Stone fruits are particularly strong carbohydrate sinks throughout their development. For example, peach and apricot fruits were such strong sinks that they competed successfully with nearby expanding leaves for current photosynthate. This was in contrast to the situation in citrus where young, rapidly growing vegetative tissues comprised the stronger sink (Kriedemann, 1968a,b).

TABLE 11.3 Starch Content of Fruit-Bearing and Nonbearing Spurs of the Apple Cultivar Landsberger–Reinette[a,b]

	Weeks after full bloom							
Spur[c]	−2	0	3	6	9	12	15	18
Nonbearing	3.56	1.96	2.81	4.50	4.48	4.46	4.51	4.19
Bearing	3.59	2.08	3.05	1.19	3.10	2.29	2.65	3.78
Differences	0.03	0.12	0.24	3.31	1.38	2.17	1.86	0.41
Least significant difference at 1%		0.29						

[a] From Grochowska (1973).
[b] Measurements are in mg/g fresh weight.
[c] Measured in 1969.

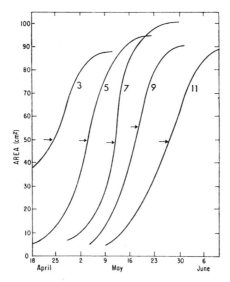

Fig. 11.4 Growth curves of five leaves of grape showing the date (indicated by arrows) on which the leaves began exporting carbohydrates. From Hale and Weaver (1962).

In rapidly growing grape shoots, carbohydrate translocation followed the pattern described for shoots exhibiting free growth, except that it was modified by development of a fruit cluster (Figs. 11.4 and 11.5). A young leaf at first imported carbohydrates from the leaves below. When it was about one-half expanded, the leaf began to export carbohydrates to the new and unexpanded leaves above it. Such strictly upward transport lasted for only 1 or 2 days. Thereafter some of the photosynthate also moved downward to the fruit. This pattern lasted for only 2 or 3 days and then translocation was entirely downward. The former function of the leaf of supplying the growth shoot tip with carbohydrates had now been assumed by young leaves closer to the shoot tip.

In early stages of development of grape shoots, when photosynthate moved into the shoot tip from the first leaf to start exporting, the flower cluster was a weak sink and it remained so until after full bloom. However, following the set of berries, about 10 days after full bloom, the berry cluster became the dominant sink. At that time the shoot tip became a somewhat weaker sink as the rate of shoot growth decreased. When fruit development started, large amounts of carbohydrates moved into the cluster from above and also from leaves below (Hale and Weaver, 1962).

In elongating fruiting pecan shoots, carbohydrate translocation from different leaves varied with differential development along the shoot axis and with varying strengths of fruit sinks (Fig. 11.6). Beginning with bud opening and continuing through leaf expansion, carbohydrates were not translocated from leaves. The immature leaves were partially self-supporting but they also depended on carbohydrates stored during the previous season. When a leaf was fully expanded it exported carbohydrates both upward and downward until the leaf above it matured (Fig. 11.6, Pattern II), after which translocation of carbohydrates from the lower leaf was only downward (Fig.

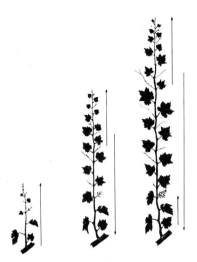

Fig. 11.5.   Three stages of development of grape shoot showing main direction of translocation of photosynthate from various leaves. From Hale and Weaver (1962).

11.6, Pattern III). This pattern was maintained as leaves higher up on the stem matured
sequentially, and eventually all the leaves were exporting carbohydrates.

During early development of the pecan shoot, a high percentage of leaves exported
carbohydrates both upward and downward, indicating that both immature leaves and
pistillate flowers were strong sinks for current photosynthate. The proportion of leaves
that exported carbohydrates in both directions decreased to a low level during fruit
enlargement. However, during rapid kernel development, carbohydrate translocation
from basal leaves again occurred in an upward as well as a downward direction. After
the fruit matured there was another shift and all leaves translocated carbohydrates only
downward. During a non- or weak-fruiting year, and after all leaves on a branch were

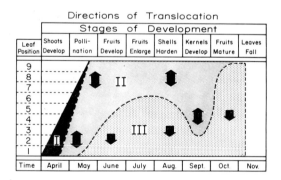

Fig. 11.6.   Direction of translocation of photosynthate from the pecan leaf at various times
during the growing season. Pattern I: assimilation but no export. Pattern II: bidirectional
translocation. Pattern III: basipetal translocation. From Davis and Sparks (1974).

Fig. 11.7. Radial section through living stump of Douglas-fir showing continued cambial growth and new tissues forming across the cut surface. The stump was connected to an adjacent tree by root grafts. Photo courtesy of U.S. Forest Service.

fully expanded, downward translocation of carbohydrates predominated (Davis and Sparks, 1974).

At certain stages of their development reproductive structures of gymnosperms are very strong carbohydrate sinks. In their first year of development the conelets of red pine grow little and consequently are relatively weak carbohydrate sinks. However, in the second year of their development the rapidly growing cones utilize more carbohydrates than the growing shoots with which they are competing. Reproductive structures (first-year conelets and second-year cones) mobilized almost three times as much carbohydrate from old needles as was mobilized by shoots (Dickmann and Kozlowski, 1970a, 1973).

There is a changing seasonal pattern in sources of carbohydrates for growth of the second-year cones. Early in the season carbohydrate reserves are important because the cones begin to increase in dry weight during mid-April in Wisconsin, when temperatures are cool and the rate of photosynthesis is low. By early May the cones are importing currently produced carbohydrates. The 1-year-old needles (those expanded during the previous growing season) are the most important source of photosynthate for early- and mid-season growth of cones, with 2- and 3-year-old needles progressively less important. Translocation of carbohydrates to cones from the currently expanding needles only becomes important late in the growing season after these needles are mature. Before that time the new needles retain most of the ^{14}C that they fix. Photosynthesis by the green cones themselves is relatively unimportant (Dickmann and Kozlowski, 1970b).

Growth Regulators

All the classes of growth regulators except ethylene are found in both xylem and phloem and apparently move long distances. Labeled growth regulators move out of leaves at the same rate as other organic compounds, and the flowering stimulus moves rapidly from leaves to stem tips. Auxin, gibberellins, ABA, and cytokinins (see Chapter 15) all move out of roots in the xylem. Thus there is no question about the occurrence of long-distance transport of growth regulators. However, the data on the physiological significance of this long-distance transport are not clear because growth regulators can be synthesized in all the organs of plants. It therefore appears possible that *in situ* synthesis might explain most of the results attributed to transport from roots or other distant tissues and further study of sources and sinks is needed in order to evaluate the importance of long-distance transport (King, 1976).

Herbicides

Individual herbicides vary greatly in their mobility in plants. Movement may occur via the symplast or apoplast. Whereas 2,4-dichlorophenoxyacetic acid and 2,4,5-trichlorophenoxyacetic acid move principally in the phloem, the triazines (e.g., simazine, atrazine, propazine) and substituted ureas move freely only in the xylem. Still other herbicides, e.g., TBA (2,3,6-trichlorobenzoic acid), picloram, and maleic hydrazide move freely in both the xylem and phloem. Herbicides of the latter group may migrate from the phloem to the xylem and recirculate in plants much like phosphorus. Translocation of herbicides is influenced by many factors, including the formulation, dosage, plant species, tissue to which applied, strength of various sinks, and environmental factors (Crafts and Crisp, 1971).

Phloem-translocated herbicides move with carbohydrates. When applied to leaves 2,4-D penetrates the cuticle, enters the symplast, finally reaches the sieve tubes, and then moves with the assimilate stream into strong sinks, often bypassing mature tissues that are exporting assimilates. Crafts and Yamaguchi (1964) demonstrated that ^{14}C-labeled 2,4-D was readily translocated out of green leaves but not from yellow ones. Depending on sink strength (growth rate of different tissues), movement at times is predominantly downward into roots, or primarily into growing shoots, flowers, or fruits. For an excellent review of translocation of a wide variety of herbicides the reader is referred to the book by Crafts and Crisp (1971).

Viruses

Virus infections are produced only by direct introduction into certain tissues, usually by insect vectors. Practically all viruses can enter parenchyma cells. Some viruses appear to be adapted to specific tissues and others, such as the mosaic viruses, may infect most living cells of a plant. Most of the more restricted viruses depend on phloem tissue for establishing infection, but some apparently move in the xylem.

Translocation of the infectious agent between parenchyma cells, or between parenchyma cells and sieve elements, apparently occurs through plasmodesmata. Transport from one sieve element to another takes place through sieve plate pores. Systemic spread of the viral agent in the phloem may come from two sources: (1) virions that passively accumulated in young sieve elements, or (2) their membrane-associated intermediates that replicated there or in parenchyma cells that are in contact with sieve elements and other tissues that sustain virus multiplication.

The infectious viral agent translocated in the phloem moves in the assimilation stream. Since the phloem is continuous throughout the plant and transport follows a source to sink pattern, virus infection can readily spread throughout the whole plant. Infections caused by phloem-limited viruses cannot pass a ringed part of the stem. In comparison, infections caused by mosaic viruses can pass such a ring by using parenchyma cells in the xylem of the ringed part of the stem. Since the infectious viral agent moving through a plant may leave some parts uninfected, it appears that the agent is transported passively. Some virus infections produce serious injury to the phloem, others do not.

The rate of spread of virus infections in different tissues varies greatly. Movement in parenchyma cells is very slow, but once the infectious agents reach the vascular tissues they move much faster. Phloem transport in leaves and stems is rapid, up to 150 cm/hr for movement of curly top virus in beet petioles (Bennett, 1956). However, movement of phloem-translocated virus infection from roots generally is very slow. Since roots are a more or less constant carbohydrate sink, outward movement through the phloem is greatest in the spring from roots that contain stored reserves. Virus infections spreading with the transpiration stream may move in the xylem at a rate of up to approximately 30 cm/min.

INTERPLANT TRANSLOCATION

Many woody plants are involved with other plants in associations that vary from parasitic to symbiotic. The capacity of disease-causing fungi to derive carbohydrates from host plants is well documented in books on plant pathology and is beyond the scope of this volume. A few other examples of plant associations that involve transfer of carbohydrates, water, minerals, and various other substances from one plant to another will be discussed briefly.

Symbiotic and Parasitic Associations

As was emphasized in Chapters 2 and 10, symbiotic relationships exist between many woody plants and mycorrhizal fungi, with the latter obtaining carbohydrates and water from the host and playing an important role in increasing mineral uptake by the host. After exposing seedlings to $^{14}CO_2$, Melin and Nilsson (1957) demonstrated that labeled photosynthetic products were rapidly translocated into associated mycorrhizal fungi. Although there is some evidence that carbohydrates can also move from mycorrhizal fungi to the host, the movement appears to be predominantly from the host to the fungi (Hacskaylo, 1973).

Several studies show that mycorrhizae increase mineral uptake and transfer minerals to the host. For example, Melin and Nilsson (1950) demonstrated that fungal hyphae absorbed radioactive phosphorus and transferred it to pine seedlings, and later they showed that fungi could transfer other substances from the medium to seedlings (Melin and Nilsson, 1955). Bowen (1973) has an excellent discussion of mineral relations of mycorrhizal associations in woody plants. Mycorrhizal roots were described in Chapter 2 and their role in mineral absorption in Chapter 10.

Some chlorophyll-containing plants, such as the mistletoes, are parasitic on woody plants for carbohydrates and water. Dwarf mistletoes (*Arceuthobium* spp.) are generally considered capable of limited photosynthesis, but Miller and Tocher (1975) showed that photosynthesis of *Arceuthobium tsugense* contributed only a fraction of the carbohydrates needed for respiration and growth. Hull and Leonard (1964a,b) demonstrated that dwarf mistletoes derive most of their carbohydrates from their host, whereas green mistletoes (*Phoradendron* spp.) synthesize most of the carbohydrates they utilize and derive only very small amounts from the host. They also showed that carbon fixed by both dwarf and green mistletoes is not translocated to the host.

Mistletoes also obtain water from the host trees, as indicated by their uptake of dye injected into the host (Tainter and French, 1973). Mark and Reid (1971) showed that the water potential gradient is favorable to dwarf mistletoe shoots even when the host is under considerable water stress.

Dwarf mistletoes are considered to be among the most damaging disease agents of forest trees of the western United States. They not only reduce growth of trees but often kill them. The mechanism of growth reduction of the host by mistletoes is not fully understood, but it apparently involves depriving the host of carbohydrates, water, and minerals. Such diversion of materials needed for growth eventually leads to crown deterioration and reduction of the photosynthetic surface to a level below that necessary to support growth of the host (Hawksworth and Wiens, 1972).

Root Grafts

As was mentioned in Chapter 2, considerable transfer of water, carbohydrates, minerals, hormones, biocides, microorganisms, and fungus spores occurs from one tree to another through root grafts. Therefore, many individual trees are not independent entities.

Living Stumps

Most stumps die within 1 or 2 years after a tree is cut. However, a community of trees may be connected so effectively through root grafts that if all but one tree are cut, the remaining root systems can survive on carbohydrates and growth regulators supplied by the crown of the remaining tree. Cambial growth often continues for a long time in stumps grafted to living trees (see Fig. 11.7). In selectively cut Douglas-fir stands, 45% of the stumps grew subsequent to felling and many were living as late as

32 years after the cutting. Sixty-five percent of the living stumps were located less than 2 m from their donor trees, but some donor trees supported living stumps almost 10 m away. Distribution of the radial increment was similar on living stumps and grafted detopped trees. Usually, up to stump height, xylem increment was irregular and widest above the main grafts. At higher stem levels xylem increment was fairly uniform around the entire circumference and gradually decreased with height (Eis, 1972).

The importance of intertree translocation of food varies with crown classes of the grafted partners. For example, Eis (1972) found four general relationships in cambial growth of stumps grafted to donor trees:

1. When a codominant tree was cut from a dominant–codominant union, cambial growth of the stump slowly declined and within 3 to 4 years was about 20–30% of its original rate. Cambial growth of the dominant donor tree increased slightly, reflecting reduction in competition.

2. When the grafted trees were of similar size and crown class (e.g., both were dominants or when a dominant tree was cut from a dominant–codominant union), cambial growth of the stump decreased rapidly. After the first year, a few years of slow cambial growth followed. Subsequently, cambial growth of the stump increased and leveled out at about 20 to 30% of the rate before cutting. Cambial growth of the donor tree subsequently increased, presumably because of reduced competition.

3. When a dominant tree was cut from a dominant–suppressed or dominant–intermediate union, the stump lived for only a few years. Cambial growth of the suppressed donor tree decreased while the stump was still living and increased slowly after its death.

4. When a stump of a cut dominant tree from a dominant–suppressed union stayed alive, cambial growth of the suppressed donor tree was restricted. Reduction in competition was followed by increased growth of most of the residual trees whether they were grafted or not.

These experiments indicated that in root-grafted, suppressed trees some or all of the carbohydrates needed for their roots and lower stem were derived from the dominant trees to which they were grafted. This relationship can postpone the death of root-grafted suppressed trees growing in dense stands.

Translocation of Herbicides

A number of herbicides are readily translocated from one tree to another through root grafts. For example, in a 30-year-old eastern white pine plantation 43% of the untreated trees were killed by "backflash" or movement of ammonium sulfamate from treated to untreated trees through grafted roots (Bormann and Graham, 1960). About one-half the residual red pine trees also were killed by backflash in a similar situation (Stout, 1961). Recognizing the silvicultural implications of backflash, Eis (1972) emphasized that in species that graft freely, the use of silvicides in thinning and spacing treatments should be restricted to young stands before extensive root grafting occurs. Conversely, eliminating undesirable species could be aided by translocation of herbicides through root grafts.

Transmission of Disease and Decay Organisms

Causal agents of some of the most destructive tree diseases are translocated through root grafts. These include *Fomes pini* in Douglas-fir (Clark, 1949), *Armillaria mellea* in spruce (Wichmann, 1925), *Endothia gyrosa* in black oak (Weir, 1925), *Poria weirii* in Douglas-fir (Wallis and Buckland, 1955), *Ceratostomella ulmi* in elm (Verrall and Graham, 1935), and *Ceratocystis fagacearum* in oak (Kuntz and Riker, 1955). According to Eis (1972), grafted stumps were a source of infection with *Polyporus schweinitzii* of the carbohydrate donor tree. A relationship was found between the number of elm trees having Dutch elm disease and the spacing between trees (Himelick and Neely, 1962; Neely and Himelick, 1963). Because of the high incidence of infection through root grafts of trees spaced up to 8 m apart, Himelick and Neely (1962) recommended spacing of elms at least 9 m apart.

Ungrafted Plants

Transfer of various substances may also occur among closely spaced trees even when their roots are not grafted. For example, transfer of herbicides sometimes occurred between trees whose roots were not grafted together (Graham and Bormann, 1966). Radioactive isotopes injected into stumps of one species were later found in other species to which they were not connected by root grafts (Woods and Brock, 1964). Smith (1976) suggests that root exudates play a role in mineral cycling. Such observations provide strong evidence for the importance of root exudation and subsequent uptake of minerals by other trees, as well as transfer of such substances by mycorrhiza-forming fungi and rhizospheric organisms.

A number of allelopathic chemicals—released from trees and other plants by leaching, volatilization, excretion, exudation, and decay either directly or by activity or microorganisms—often inhibit seed germination and growth of adjacent plants. For example, in California deserts creosote bush seedlings die in the vicinity of adult plants of the same species, apparently because of the toxic action of chemicals excreted by roots of the adult plants (Went and Westergaard, 1949). For a further discussion of allelopathy the reader is referred to Chapter 17, this volume, and to Rice (1974).

MECHANISMS OF PHLOEM TRANSLOCATION

One of the most controversial and unsettled problems in plant physiology is the mechanism by which translocation of solutes in the phloem is brought about. Wardlaw (1974) entitled his review of translocation, "Phloem Transport: Physical Chemical or Impossible." The problem is complex because of the large amount of solute translocation that occurs. The problem is further complicated because solutes move either upward or downward through the phloem and a variety of substances such as minerals, growth regulators, vitamins, and viruses move along with sugars.

This section will briefly discuss those aspects of the anatomy of phloem tissues that are important to understanding translocation mechanisms. Various hypotheses that have been advanced to explain long-distance transport of solutes in the phloem will also be discussed.

Sieve Tubes of Angiosperms

In angiosperms, a number of conducting elements of the phloem, the sieve tube members, are joined end-to-end to form long sieve tubes. The term "sieve" refers to the end walls that are pierced by clusters of pores through which the protoplasts of adjacent sieve tube members are interconnected. Sieve plates, parts of the wall bearing sieve areas with large pores, generally occur on the end walls of sieve tube members (Fig. 11.8).

Protoplasts of young sieve tube members have all the cellular contents that normally occur in living plant cells. During final stages of differentiation, however, sieve tube members lose many of their cellular components, including the tonoplast, microtubules, ribosomes, and dictyosomes. In some species the nucleus disappears completely during differentiation; in others remnants of the degenerate nucleus persist for a long time (Evert, 1977). The sieve tube members of many species contain a proteinaceous substance called P-protein or slime (Fig. 11.9), which may occur as filaments distributed throughout the entire cell lumen, or occupy an entirely parietal position.

Small amounts, if any, of callose are present in sieve areas of mature conducting sieve tubes. As sieve tubes begin to senesce the amount of callose increases, and when

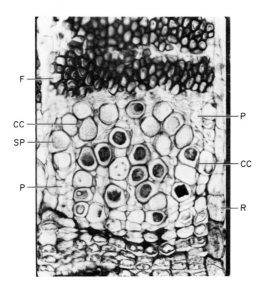

Fig. 11.8. Cross-section of secondary phloem of black locust. Some of the sieve tube members are sectioned in or near the plane of the sieve plate. The dense bodies in some sieve tube members are slime (P-protein) plugs, × 375; P: parenchyma cell; R: ray; CC: companion cell; F: fibers; SP: sieve plate. Photo courtesy of R. F. Evert.

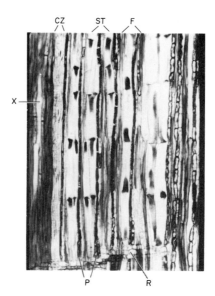

Fig. 11.9. Radial section showing portion of secondary xylem, cambial zone, and secondary phloem of American elm. Note the numerous slime (P-protein) plugs lodged against the sieve plates of the individual sieve tube members. The vertical series of sieve tube members constitute the sieve tubes, × 138; CZ: cambial zone; F: phloem fibers; P: phloem parenchyma cells; R: ray; ST: sieve tubes; X: xylem.

sieve tubes finally die and become inactive, their sieve plate areas may have very large amounts of callose. However, it eventually disappears from old, inactive cells. The walls of sieve tube members are commonly regarded as primary. Sieve tube members are almost invariably accompanied by parenchymatous cells, the companion cells, with which the sieve tubes are structurally and functionally related.

Sieve Cells of Gymnosperms

The conducting elements of gymnosperm phloem, called sieve cells, are similar in shape and size to tracheids. During differentiation the sieve cells become disorganized and lose many of their cells contents. Sieve cells lack P-protein and have only primary walls, except in the Pinaceae where secondary walls also are present. In gymnosperms, the counterparts of the companion cells of angiosperms are the albuminous cells (also called Strasburger cells).

Longevity of Conducting Elements

In most species of angiosperms the sieve elements are short lived and function in translocation only during the season in which they are formed. In a few genera, however, they remain alive and functional for more than 1 year. For example, the sieve tubes of grape and yellow-poplar remain functional for at least two seasons, the first summer of activity being followed by an inactive period during the winter. The sieve tubes of basswood may remain functional for 5 to 10 years. The dormant, inactive sieve tubes have heavy masses of callose on the sieve plates and sieve areas. When the sieve tubes become active in the spring the callose gradually dissolves. Phloem reactivation begins first near the cambium. The reactivating phloem can be distinguished from dormant phloem by the thin callose masses and conspicuous P-protein in the reactivating phloem (Esau, 1965). When sieve elements die, their associated companions cells or albuminous cells also die, emphasizing a close relationship between them.

In a number of species of angiosperms and gymnosperms translocation of carbohydrates can occur very early in the year because the first functional sieve elements are those that formed last during the previous growing season and overwintered as undifferentiated derivatives. These reach maturity early in the spring and are capable of translocating carbohydrates before the cambium is reactivated. Such overwintering sieve elements do not become inactive in translocation until after the newly formed, functional sieve tubes are present. In various evergreen dicotyledons and in gymnosperms, some of the phloem remains active in carbohydrate transport for parts of two seasons (Esau, 1965). In some angiosperms, such as boxelder and black locust, inactive sieve elements and associated cells collapse, but in others such as walnut, yellow-poplar, and basswood they remain unchanged in structure (Tucker and Evert, 1969). The sieve tubes of woody monocots must remain functional for the lifetime of the plants.

Driving Forces in Translocation

The most important compounds, such as sucrose and possibly some other sugars, accumulate in the phloem in concentrations exceeding that of the surrounding tissues. This is explained by "phloem-loading" or the secretion by active transport of solutes into the phloem by means of the expenditure of metabolic energy (Evert, 1977).

Several hypotheses have been proposed to explain the driving force causing movement of solutes after they enter the sieve tubes. These generally depend on one of two opposing concepts: (1) that solute molecules are translocated by a metabolic force, independently of the water; or (2) that solute molecules move with water as a flowing solution. The more important hypotheses will be discussed separately. More detailed discussions can be found in Zimmermann and Milburn (1975).

Diffusion

Movement of gases and even movement of solutes over distances of a few millimeters can be explained by diffusion, but this process cannot account for movement of solutes over distances of many meters. A number of experiments show that gradients of sucrose concentration exist in the phloem, that phloem near sources contains more sucrose than phloem near sinks, and that translocation of sucrose occurs along the concentration gradient. However, these gradients are much too small to account for known rates of sucrose translocation by diffusion.

Protoplasmic Streaming

De Vries (1885) suggested that protoplasmic streaming might be involved in solute translocation. Curtis (1935) favored such a theory on the grounds that it provided for simultaneous translocation of various substances in different directions and also accounted for the requirement of living cells. The major objection to a protoplasmic streaming mechanism is that it is quantitatively inadequate and cannot account for known rates of long-distance transport. Furthermore, protoplasmic streaming of the type that occurs in some cells has not been verified in mature sieve elements (Canny, 1973).

Electroosmosis

Electroosmotic flow often has been thought to be the driving force for solution flow. Spanner (1958), for example, advanced a theory that involved metabolically driven movement of potassium ions. A requirement is that an appreciable number of sieve plates in a file of conducting elements have their pores occluded with P-protein and that the sieve plates constitute a "membrane" well adapted for development of electroosmotic forces. Presumably the difference of electrical potential across the sieve plate is maintained by active uptake of potassium ions across the sieve tube membrane above the plate, and a loss below it. The movement is presumably energized by high-energy compounds, such as ATP, which is provided by companion cells.

A number of objections have been raised to the theory of electroosmotic flow. Among the most important of these are that: (1) it cannot provide for transport of both anions and cations, both of which are known to move in the phloem; (2) the circulating current of K^+ is too great; and (3) the system requires too much energy for recirculation of the potassium. For example, in trees or fruits more than all of the energy available to the phloem as a whole would be needed to recirculate the required amount of potassium (MacRobbie, 1971).

Transcellular Strands and Cytoplasmic Pumping

Thaine (1962) reported that strands of protoplasm were stretched throughout the length of sieve elements. He also reported seeing particles moving in both directions in sieve elements and through sieve pores into adjacent sieve elements. In 1969 he proposed that a strand (with a diameter of approximately 5 μm) enclosed several tubules with diameters of about 1 μm, with the remaining space made up of fluid containing mobile particles. He visualized that protein filaments in the wall of the strand underwent rhythmic contraction and expansion, thereby moving the contents of the tubules by a peristaltic pumping.

There has been much vigorous debate about the existence of transcellular strands. According to Evert (1977), P-protein does not normally exist in the form of transcellular strands. Evert et al. (1969) concluded that P-protein strands of a fibrillar network were artifacts caused by injury to cells. The lack of developmental evidence to support the normal presence of transcellular strands in sieve tube members argues strongly against Thaine's theory.

Pressure Flow

Münch (1930) proposed that there is a flow of solutes through the phloem from the supplying end (source) to the receiving end (sink). This theory requires that, (a) sieve tubes must possess differentially permeable membranes and function as osmotic systems, (b) that they must permit longitudinal flow, (c) that there be a loading mechanism for solutes at the source end and an unloading mechanism at the sink end, and (d) there must be a gradient of decreasing turgor pressure from source to sink to act as a driving force. A current form of the theory assumes that the phloem parenchyma cells in leaves accumulate sugar from the mesophyll cells and transport it into the sieve tubes. This "phloem loading" requires metabolic energy. The high concentration of sugar lowers the osmotic potential in the sieve tubes, causing water to enter them from adjacent tissue and producing a high turgor pressure. Removal of sugar (phloem unloading) at various sinks such as meristems and storage tissues lowers the osmotic potential in the sieve tubes, resulting in the outflow of water and causing mass flow of solution through the sieve tubes from source to sink. Thus the actual movement from source to sink is not dependent on metabolic energy, but the loading and unloading process are, making translocation sensitive to temperature and respiration inhibitors. Milburn (1975) discusses the uncertainties of the pressure flow theory in detail and suggests that it really applies only to individual sieve tubes. However, when strong sinks exist they operate in unison as a common system.

Among the objections offered to this theory are the rapid plugging of sieve plates with slime or callose in cut tissue, the difficulty of explaining bidirectional movement, and the difficulty of operating such a mechanism in water-stressed plants; also questions concerning the existence of a gradient in turgor pressure in the phloem. It is now believed that the plugging of sieve plates is an artifact caused by cutting the phloem. Obviously this theory does not permit simultaneous movement in two directions in a sieve tube but it permits flow in two directions in different bundles and perhaps different sieve tubes. The problem of bidirectional flow is discussed in Zimmermann and Milburn (1975, Chap. 10). It also permits reversal of direction of movement. For example a very young leaf functions as a sink, because it is using sugar but later it begins to function as a source because it is producing sugar. Storage tissues can function as sinks toward the end of the growing season, but become sources for root, bud, and cambium growth early in the spring before photosynthate is available.

Water stress reduces the rate of translocation, but some translocation is said to occur even in plants with wilted leaves, so long as "sinks" for organic substances exist, i.e. as long as growth is occurring. It appears that mass flow can occur as long as the osmotic potential of the phloem sap is lower than the water potential of the xylem (Wardlaw, 1974). There have also been questions concerning the existence of a turgor pressure gradient in the sieve tubes. However, there is no doubt that sap exudes from incisions made in the phloem of various herbaceous and woody species. Also, many liters of sap per day often flow from the stems of palms and agaves when their inflorescences are removed (Zimmermann and Milburn, 1975, Chap. 8). The behavior of aphids also indicates the existence of phloem pressure. Some species of aphids insert their stylets into sieve tubes and feed on the phloem sap which is forced into and through their bodies from which it exudes as "honey dew". If the aphid is severed from its stylet the latter functions as a tube through which phloem sap often continues to flow for days (Evert et al, 1968), unlike incisions which often are quickly plugged. The use of aphids to study translocation and phloem sap is described in Zimmermann and Milburn (1975, Chapters 6 and 7). These various lines of evidence leave little doubt that mass flow of solution occurs through the phloem, although many questions exist concerning some of the important details.

CONTROL OF PHLOEM TRANSPORT

Although it is important to understand the mechanism of phloem transport it is even more important to understand what controls the partitioning of metabolites. In other words, what controls the amount of food delivered to the various competing organs and tissues and brings about the necessary changes at various stages of development?

In germinating seeds food is translocated from the storage tissues to the various growing regions, including the developing leaves, until the latter begin to carry on photosynthesis. Then the direction of transport is reversed and photosynthate is translocated out of the leaves to the root and stem tips. In mature deciduous woody plants in the spring food is first moved from storage tissues of the stem and branches to stem tips. Then, as new leaves enlarge they export food to still newer leaves, to the cambium, and to the roots. If fruits and seeds begin to develop they become strong sinks to which food is transported at the expense of vegetative growth. Eventually, as growth ceases and fruits and seeds mature, food begins to accumulate in storage organs. During the height of the growing season, the relative strengths of the various sinks often are as follows: fruits and seeds > young leaves and stem tips > mature leaves > cambia > roots > storage.

The crucial question is, what determines the relative strength of the various sinks and thus controls the partitioning of food among the competing organs and tissues? It appears that the phloem has considerable excess transport capacity, because part of it can be removed with little or no permanent effect on growth. Also, the transport process seems to operate effectively over a considerable range of temperature and water stress.

Partitioning of food seems to be controlled first of all by the size of the food supply and the relative sizes of the various sinks, large sinks being stronger or more effective in obtaining food than small ones (Evans, in Wardlaw and Passioura, 1976). Relative distance from source to sink also is important, sinks usually being supplied from the nearest source. Thus young leaves have an advantage over the cambium of the bole and less food is delivered to the lower part of the bole than to the part in the crown. Roots are at an increasing disadvantage as the photosynthetic surface moves upward with increasing tree height. It should be remembered, however, that roots may be the strongest sinks when other parts of trees are not growing. For example, roots begin growing in the spring before shoots and stems do. Hence, for a while early in the season the roots are the strongest sinks and large amounts of currently produced carbohydrates are channeled to them (see Fig. 11.3). Roots of temperate zone trees also continue to grow later in the season than shoots and stems (see Chapter 3). Hence, roots are stronger sinks than shoots and stems in the late summer and early autumn and again in the early spring.

It is generally agreed that growth regulators or hormones play a role in determining the strength of sinks. For example, translocation of metabolites is usually increased by application of cytokinin or gibberellin to a particular region. Chalmers and van den Ende (1977) report that a hormone produced in developing peach seeds stimulates ethylene production in the young mesocarp and this in turn brings about translocation of food to the developing seed. In this instance the seed is said to be a weaker sink than the mesocarp because of the geometry of the conducting system, which leaves the seed at the end of the vascular system.

It is not clear whether hormones operate directly, for example, by expediting sieve tube loading or unloading, or indirectly by affecting relative strengths of sources and sinks. In some instances development of fruit seems to increase the rate of photosynthesis, but it is not clear whether the increase is caused by use of food in developing fruits or by a hormonal stimulus from the fruit. Perhaps they operate both ways. At any rate it is clear that some kind of control system exists that results in responses to changes in relative sizes of sources and sinks. A notable example is the increase in rate of photosynthesis of fruiting apple trees (Avery, 1977). Readers are referred to a series of papers in Wardlaw and Passioura (1976) for a more detailed discussion of this important problem.

GENERAL REFERENCES

Aronoff, S., Dainty, J., Gorham, P. R., Srivastava, L. M., and Swanson, C. A., eds. (1975). "Phloem Transport." Plenum, New York.

Canny, J. J. (1973). "Phloem Translocation." Cambridge Univ. Press, London and New York.

Crafts, A. S., and Crisp, C. E. (1971). "Phloem Transport in Plants." Freeman, San Francisco, California.

Esau, K. (1973). "Viruses in Plant Hosts: Form, Distribution and Pathologic Effects." Univ. of Wisconsin Press, Madison.

MacRobbie, E. A. C. (1971). Phloem translocation: Facts and mechanisms: A comparative survey. *Biol. Rev. Cambridge Philos. Soc.* **46,** 429–481.

Peel, A. J. (1974). "Transport of Nutrients in Plants." Butterworth, London.

Wardlaw, I. F., and Passioura, J. B., eds. (1976). "Transport and Transfer Processes in Plants." Academic Press, New York.

Zimmermann, M. H., and Milburn, J. A., eds. (1975). "Transport in Plants I. Phloem Transport," Encycl. Plant Physiol., New Ser., Vol. 1. Springer-Verlag, Berlin and New York.

12

The Importance of Water and the Process of Transpiration

INTRODUCTION

Over that part of the earth's surface where temperatures permit plant growth the occurrence of trees is controlled chiefly by the water supply. Most grasslands and deserts could support forests if the quantity and seasonal distribution of precipitation were favorable. Other large areas support only sparse stands of trees because of limited water. The ecological importance of water arises from its physiological importance. An adequate supply of water is just as essential to the successful growth of plants as photosynthesis and the other biochemical processes involved in the synthesis of food and its transformation into new tissues. The essential factor in plant water relations is maintenance of a sufficiently high water content and turgor to permit normal functioning of the physiological and biochemical processes involved in growth. This is controlled by the relative rates of water absorption and water loss, as we will see.

The Importance of Water

The importance of an adequate water supply for the growth of woody plants is well documented by Zahner (1968), who has an excellent review of the literature. He reported that up to 80% of the variation in diameter growth of trees in humid areas (and up to 90% in arid areas) can be attributed to variations in rainfall and water stress. Bassett (1964) found a very high correlation between wood production and available soil moisture in a pine stand in Arkansas over a 21-year period. In fact, prediction of past climatic conditions from tree ring width is well established as "dendrochronology" for certain dry regions (Fritts, 1976) and sometimes is possible in humid regions (Cook and Jacoby, 1977). These relationships will be discussed in more detail in Chapters 13 and 16.

The importance of water in the life of trees can be shown by listing its more important functions. These can be grouped under four headings:

1. Water is an essential constituent of protoplasm and forms 80 to 90% of the fresh weight of actively growing tissue.

2. Water is the solvent in which gases, salts, and other solvents move in and out of cells and from organ to organ.

3. Water is a reagent in photosynthesis and in a number of hydrolytic processes.

4. Water is essential for the maintenance of turgidity.

A certain degree of turgidity is essential for cell enlargement, stomatal opening, and the maintenance of the form of young leaves and other slightly lignified structures.

Complete understanding of plant water relations requires consideration of both soil and atmospheric moisture conditions. However, we will first concentrate on two interrelated aspects of plant water relations. One deals with the water relations of cells and tissues within the plant; the other deals with the water relations of the plant as a whole. Plant water relations involve the loss of water by transpiration, absorption of water, ascent of sap, and the internal water balance of the tree. On warm, sunny days transpiration often exceeds absorption, producing water deficits, loss of turgor, and competition among the various parts of a tree for water. The resulting redistribution of water is controlled by the water potential of the cells and tissues.

Cell Water Relations

The water relations of plants are controlled primarily by cell water relations; hence, consideration must be given to cell structure and functioning in relation to water movement.

Cell Structure

Living cells of plants consist of protoplasts surrounded by more or less rigid walls which severely limit changes in volume, particularly in older tissue where the walls are lignified. In mature cells the protoplasts consist of large central vacuoles enclosed in thin layers of cytoplasm pressed against the walls, in which are imbedded a nucleus and various other organelles such as plastids and mitochondria (see Fig. 12.1). Electron microscopy also reveals various other structures in the cytoplasm such as ribosomes, peroxisomes, dictyosomes, microtubules, and the complex system of membranes known as the endoplasmic reticulum. In active cells large amounts of water are bound to the protein framework, and the surface membranes of the protoplasts (plasmalemma and tonoplast) are permeable to water but relatively impermeable to solutes. As a result ions and organic solutes are accumulated in the vacuoles, producing osmotic potentials in the range of -5 to -50 bars. Often the protoplasts of adjacent cells are connected by strands of cytoplasm called plasmodesmata, forming a continuous system called the "symplast." The structure of plasmodesmata and their role in transport are reviewed by Gunning and Robards (1976). Vacuoles vary in size from tiny rod-shaped or spherical structures in meristematic tissue to the large central vacuoles of mature parenchyma cells that occupy more than 50% of the cell volume. They are filled with water in which a wide variety of ions and organic molecules are dissolved. Cell structure in relation to water is discussed in Chapter 1 of Kramer (1969) and Chapter 6 of Slatyer (1967) and in more detail in Bonner and Varner (1976).

Water Movement

Water movement occurs along gradients of decreasing free energy or molecular activity, often expressed as differences in water potential. If the difference in free energy or potential is produced by some external agent, such as pressure or gravity, the movement is termed mass flow. Examples are the flow of water in pipes under pressure, flow of water in streams caused by gravity, and the ascent of sap in plants, caused by evaporation from the shoots. If movement results from random motion of molecules caused by their own kinetic energy, as in evaporation, the process is called diffusion. Osmosis is an example of diffusion caused by a difference in potential of water on two

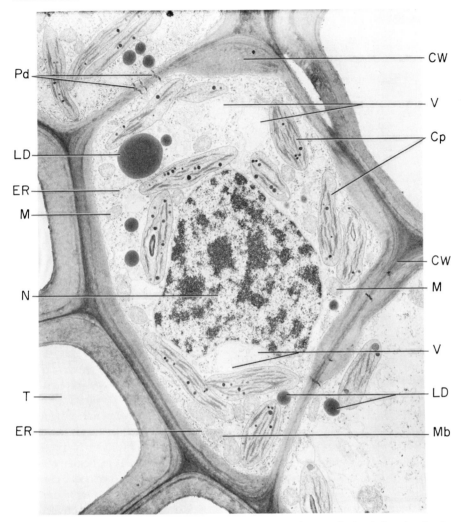

Fig. 12.1. An electron micrograph of a xylem ray parenchyma cell of red pine showing its principal structures (× 8000). CW, cell wall; Cp, chloroplast; LD, lipid droplet; ER, endoplasmic reticulum; Mb, microbody; N, nucleus; V, vacuole; T, tracheid; Pd, plasmodesmata; M, mitochondrion. Photo courtesy of D. Neuberger.

sides of a membrane, usually caused by differences in concentration across the membrane.

Terminology

The free energy of a system or a component of a system refers to its capacity to do work. It is difficult to measure the absolute free energy of water, but it is fairly easy to measure the difference in free energy between pure water and water in a solution such as the cell sap. This difference, which was formerly termed the suction force or diffusion pressure deficit, is now generally termed the water potential. Its derivation is discussed by Kramer (1969, pp. 18–20), Kramer *et al*. (1966), and Slayter (1967, pp. 17–21). Its relationship to the terminology used in the past can be shown as follows:

Suction force = Osmotic pressure − Turgor pressure

Diffusion
pressure   = Osmotic pressure − Turgor pressure
deficit

Water
potential   = Osmotic potential + Pressure potential

$$\psi_w \qquad = \psi_s + \psi_p \qquad\qquad (12.1)$$

Water potential usually is represented by the Greek letter Ψ, as in the above equation, where Ψ_w is the potential of the water in a cell, Ψ_s (sometimes written, Ψ_π) the osmotic potential, and Ψ_p the pressure potential. Sometimes the term Ψ_m (also written, Ψ_τ) for matric potential is added to account for the forces with which water is bound by solids. The values of Ψ_s and Ψ_m are negative, but Ψ_p is positive except in the rare instances of a negative wall pressure or in xylem sap under tension. The sum of the numbers on the right hand side is negative, except in fully turgid cells when it becomes zero. The situation in cells of varying turgor can be shown as follows, the numbers referring to bars:

$$
\begin{array}{lrcl}
 & \psi_w &=& \psi_s + \psi_p \\
\text{Turgid} & 0 &=& -18 + (+18) \\
\text{Partly turgid} & -10 &=& -19 + (+\ 9) \\
\text{Flaccid} & -20 &=& -20 + (0)
\end{array}
\qquad (12.2)
$$

The increase in osmotic potential (Ψ_s) from −20 to −18 bars with increasing turgor is caused by dilution of cell sap because the cell volume increases as turgor increases. Although water movement is controlled by water potential, the osmotic and pressure potentials also are important. Pressure potential or turgor pressure is particularly important with respect to cell enlargement and a decrease in osmotic potential can partly compensate for a decrease in water potential (see Chapter 13). Readers are referred to Kramer (1969), Slatyer (1967), and Meyer *et al*. (1973, Chapter 5) for more detailed discussions of cell water relations.

General Concepts in Plant Water Relations

One of the important contributions to plant water relations is the treatment of water movement through the soil, into roots, through the plant, and out into the air as a series of closely interrelated processes. This is sometimes called the soil–plant–atmosphere continuum concept (Philip, 1966) and it is useful in emphasizing the necessity of considering all aspects of water relations in studying the water balance of plants. This concept leads to the treatment of water movement in the soil-plant-atmosphere system as analogous to the flow of electricity in a conducting system and it therefore can be described by an analog of Ohm's Law where:

$$\text{Flow} = \frac{\text{difference in water potential}}{\text{resistance}} \qquad (12.3)$$

This concept can be applied to steady state flow through a plant as follows:

$$\text{Flow} = \frac{\psi_{\text{soil}} - \psi_{\text{root surfaces}}}{r_{\text{soil}}} = \frac{\psi_{\text{root surface}} - \psi_{\text{xylem}}}{r_{\text{root}}}$$

$$= \frac{\psi_{\text{xylem}} - \psi_{\text{leaf cells}}}{r_{\text{xylem}}} = \frac{\psi_{\text{leaf}} - \psi_{\text{air}}}{r_{\text{leaf}} + r_{\text{air}}} \qquad (12.4)$$

The continuum concept provides a useful, unifying theory in which water movement through soil, roots, stems, and leaves, and its evaporation into the air, can be studied in terms of the driving forces and resistances operating at each stage. The concept also is useful in analyzing the manner in which various plant and environmental factors affect water movement by influencing either the driving forces or the resistances, or sometimes both. For example, drying soil causes both an increase in resistance to water flow toward roots and a decrease in driving force or water potential; deficient aeration increases the resistance to water flow through roots; an increase in leaf and air temperature increases transpiration because it increases the vapor pressure gradient or driving

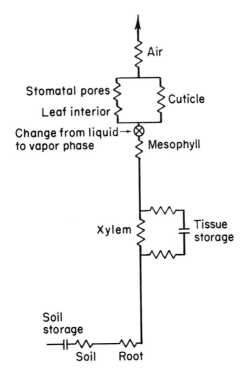

Fig. 12.2. A simplified diagram showing water flow through the soil–plant–air system as analogous to the flow of electricity through a series of resistances and capacitances. A more detailed diagram is given by Cowan (1965).

force from leaf to air (see Table 12.1). Closure of stomata increases the resistance to diffusion of water vapor out of leaves. The continuum concept is discussed by Weatherley (1976).

The continuum concept also facilitates modeling of water movement, as in the example shown in Fig. 12.2. Models vary from those for individual stomata (DeMichele and Sharpe, 1973) to those for whole stands of trees (Waggoner and Reifsnyder, 1968). Model builders hope eventually to be able to predict plant behavior over a wide range of environmental conditions, but much more information will be needed before this is possible.

Readers are warned that the continuum concept is an oversimplification because it assumes steady state conditions which seldom exist in plants. Also, complications occur because water movement in the liquid phase is proportional to the difference in water potential, while movement in the vapor phase is proportional to the gradient in water vapor pressure. More important, strict application of the Ohm's Law analogy to water flow in plants indicates that resistance to flow must change with rate of flow, which seems rather unlikely (Fiscus and Kramer, 1975). This problem is discussed in Chapter 13 in connection with water absorption.

TRANSPIRATION

Transpiration is the loss of water from plants in the form of vapor and is basically an evaporation process. However, it is partly controlled by plant structure and stomatal behavior, operating together with the physical factors that control evaporation from a free water surface. Transpiration is the dominant factor in the water relations of plants because evaporation of water produces the energy gradient that causes movement of water through plants. It therefore controls the rate of absorption and the ascent of sap and causes almost daily leaf water deficits. A single isolated tree may lose 200 to 400 liters per day and a hardwood forest at Coweeta in the humid southern Appalachians loses 42 to 55 cm of water per year (Hoover, 1944). Several hundred kilograms of water are used by plants for every kilogram of dry matter produced and about 95% of this simply passes through and is lost by transpiration.

It is sometimes argued that transpiration is beneficial because it cools leaves, causes the ascent of sap, and increases absorption and translocation of minerals. Gates (1965), for example, attaches great importance to the cooling effects of transpiration. All of this is partly true, but the role of transpiration is not critical for survival. Leaves developed in full sun are seldom injured by the rise in temperature that occurs when transpiration is reduced by wilting, and the use of water in growing tissues would cause a slow ascent of sap even if there were no transpiration. Water moves to the tops of tall trees as they grow upward and transpiration merely increases the speed and quantity moved. Absorption and translocation of salt probably are increased by transpiration, but many plants thrive in shaded, humid habitats where transpiration is very low.

On the other hand, rapidly transpiring plants lose so much water on sunny days that the cells of young twigs and leaves lose turgor and wilt, stomata close reducing photosynthesis, and growth is reduced or stopped. The harmful effects of water stress will be discussed further in Chapters 13 and 16. We regard transpiration as an unavoidable evil, unavoidable because of the structure of leaves and evil because it often produces water deficits and causes injury and death by desiccation.

The Process of Transpiration

Because of the great importance of transpiration in the overall water economy of plants, the nature of the process and the factors affecting it deserve careful attention. Transpiration is basically the physical process of evaporation which is controlled by physical factors. However, transpiration is also a physiological process, and as such it is affected by plant factors such as leaf structure and exposure and the behavior of stomata. It usually occurs in two stages, evaporation of water from cell walls into intercellular spaces and the diffusion of water vapor into the outside air.

Transpiration as a Physical Process

The rate of evaporation of water from any surface depends on the energy supply available to vaporize water, the vapor pressure or vapor concentration gradient that constitutes the driving force, and the resistances in the diffusion pathway. Most water vapor escapes through the stomata, some passes out through the epidermis of leaves and its cuticular covering, and some escapes from the lenticels in the bark of branches and twigs of woody species.

Evaporation can be described by a simple equation.

$$E = \frac{c_{water} - c_{air}}{r_{air}} \quad \text{or} \quad \frac{e_{water} - e_{air}}{r_{air}} \tag{12.5}$$

E is the evaporation in $g/cm^2/sec$; c_{water} and c_{air} are the concentrations of water vapor at the water surface and in the bulk air, respectively, in g/cm^3; e_{water} and e_{air} are the corresponding water vapor pressures in millimeters of mercury or millibars; and r_{air} is the boundary layer resistance encountered by diffusing molecules in sec/cm. Because transpiration is controlled to a considerable degree by leaf resistance additional terms must be added to describe it.

$$T = \frac{c_{leaf} - c_{air}}{r_{leaf} + r_{air}} \quad \text{or} \quad \frac{e_{leaf} - e_{air}}{r_{leaf} + r_{air}} \tag{12.6}$$

In this equation c_{leaf} and e_{leaf} are the water vapor concentration and pressure, respectively, at the evaporating surfaces within the leaf, and r_{leaf} is the additional resistance to diffusion in the leaf. This equation states that the rate of transpiration in grams of water per square centimeter of transpiring surface is proportional to c, the difference in concentration of water vapor, or e, the difference in vapor pressure, between the evaporating surfaces in the leaf and the bulk air outside, divided by the sum of the resistances to diffusion ($r_{leaf} + r_{air}$) in sec/cm. The situation with respect to resistances is indicated in Fig. 12.3. The components of Eq. (12.5) will be discussed after a brief review of the energy balance.

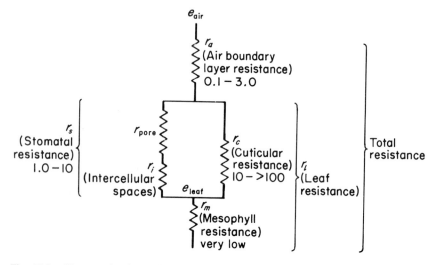

Fig. 12.3. Diagram showing resistances to the diffusion of water vapor from a leaf. The rate of transpiration is proportional to the steepness of the gradient in water vapor pressure, e_{leaf} to e_{air}, and is inversely proportional to the resistances measured in seconds per centimeter. Stomatal and cuticular resistances are given in seconds per centimeter. They vary widely among species and with degree of hydration and can be considerably higher than indicated here.

Energy Use in Transpiration

The energy input to a stand of plants or individual leaves comes from direct solar radiation, radiation reflected and reradiated from the soil and surrounding vegetation, and advective flow of sensible heat from the surroundings. The energy load is dissipated by three mechanisms: reradiation, convection of sensible heat, and dissipation of latent heat by evaporation of water (transpiration). The energy load on a leaf is partitioned as follows:

$$\underbrace{S + G - rS - R}_{\text{Net radiation}} \pm H \pm E + A = 0 \tag{12.7}$$

Net radiation is the actual radiation available to leaves. It consists of S, the total solar radiation, plus G, the long-wave radiation from the environment, minus rS, the radiation reflected from leaves, and R, that reradiated from leaves. $H =$ the sensible heat exchange with the environment by convection and advection, E the latent heat lost by transpiration, and A the energy used in metabolic processes, especially photosynthesis. The latter is only 2 or 3% of the total and usually can be neglected. Since all of the terms can vary considerably, the energy relations of individual leaves are rather complex. When leaf and air temperature are equal, reradiation and transpiration dissipate the entire heat load. If stomatal closure stops transpiration, the heat load must be dissipated by reradiation and sensible heat transfer, but usually there is a dynamic equilibrium in which all three mechanisms operate. According to Idso and Baker (1967) more heat is lost from individual leaves and plants by reradiation than by convection or transpiration, but loss by transpiration is most important for stands of plants. Occasionally, advective energy transfer from the surroundings to a small, isolated mass of vegetation results in a rate of transpiration exceeding that explainable in terms of incident radiation; this is the so-called oasis effect. At night leaves often are cooled by radiation to the sky, resulting in flow of sensible and latent heat toward them and the deposition of dew. This complex topic is discussed in more detail by Gates (1976) and Nobel (1974).

Vapor Pressure Gradient from Leaf to Air

As was mentioned earlier, the driving force for movement of water vapor out of plants is the difference in vapor pressure or vapor concentration between plant tissue and air, $c_{leaf} - c_{air}$ or $e_{leaf} - e_{air}$. This difference depends on two variables, the vapor pressure or concentration at the evaporating surfaces and that of the surrounding bulk air.

The vapor pressure of the evaporating surfaces of cells is influenced chiefly by the temperature and the water potential at the surfaces. If the water potential at the cell surfaces is taken as zero (cells turgid) the vapor pressure can be taken as the saturation vapor pressure at that temperature. The effect of temperature on the vapor pressure of water is shown in Tables 12.1 and 12.2, and Fig. 12.4, where it can be seen that increasing the temperature from 10° to 30°C more than triples the vapor pressure. Thus even small changes in leaf temperature can produce considerable changes in rate of transpiration, when r_{air} and r_{leaf} remain constant.

The effect of a reduction in Ψ_{leaf} on vapor pressure is quite small, a decrease in leaf Ψ_w to -40 bars reducing the vapor pressure gradient only about 5% at 50% relative humidity and 30°C. Thus moderate changes in leaf water potential or osmotic potential are unimportant compared to other factors affecting Δe and have little effect on transpiration.

TABLE 12.1 Effect of Increasing Temperature on the Vapor Pressure of Water in Leaves and on the Vapor Pressure Gradient from Leaf to Air at an Assumed Constant Relative Humidity of 60% [a,b]

Temperature (°C)	Vapor pressure of tissue (mb)	Vapor pressure of air at 60% relative humidity (mb)	Vapor pressure gradient (mb)
10	12.27	7.36	4.91
20	23.37	14.02	9.35
30	42.43	25.45	16.98

[a] The vapor pressure of the leaf tissue is assumed to be the saturation vapor pressure of water, because the lowering caused by cell solutes is only about 3% at an osmotic potential of -40 bars.

[b] Also refer to Fig. 12.4.

TABLE 12.2   Effect of Increasing Temperature of Leaf and Air with No Change in Absolute Humidity on Vapor Pressure Gradient from Leaf to Air

Leaf and air temperature (°C)	10	20	30
Relative humidity of air assuming no change in absolute humidity (%)	80	44	25
Vapor pressure at evaporating surface of leaf (mb)	12.27	23.37	42.43
Vapor pressure in air at indicated temperatures	9.81	10.10	10.50
Vapor pressure gradient from leaf to air	2.46	13.22	31.93

Although we generally assume the water potential at the mesophyll cell surfaces to be similar to that of the bulk tissue, this apparently is not always true. Several investigators have reported humidities in the intercellular spaces of rapidly transpiring plants equivalent to a Ψ_W of -100 bars or lower (Shimshi, 1963; Whiteman and Koller, 1964).

The vapor pressure of the bulk air surrounding plants depends on the temperature and the humidity, as shown in Tables 12.1 and 12.2. The actual amount of water present in the atmosphere is known as the "absolute humidity" and often is expressed

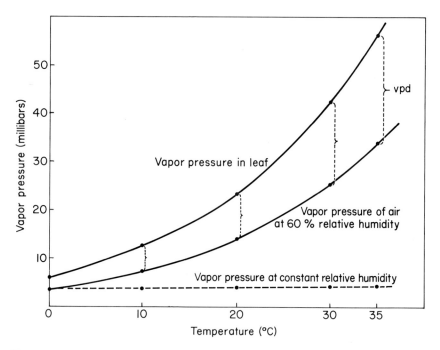

Fig. 12.4.   Effect of increasing temperature on vapor pressure difference (vpd) between leaf and air if air in leaf is assumed to be saturated and external air is at 60% relative humidity at each temperature. The dashed line shows vapor pressure of air if absolute humidity is kept the same at all temperatures.

in milligrams of water per liter of air. More often the moisture content of the air is expressed in terms of "relative humidity" which is the percentage of saturation at the existing temperature. Relative humidity is an unsatisfactory measure of atmospheric moisture conditions with respect to evaporation or transpiration because the relative humidity decreases when the temperature of an air mass is increased, but the vapor pressure increases. As seen in Table 12.1, the rate of evaporation from a moist surface would be more than three times as rapid at 30°C and 60% relative humidity as at 10°C and 60% relative humidity. The reason evaporation and transpiration increase with increasing temperature is because the vapor pressure of the water in leaves increases more rapidly than the vapor pressure of water in the unsaturated air, not as is often erroneously supposed because the relative humidity decreases. It is clearly more accurate if atmospheric moisture conditions in environments such as growth chambers are evaluated in terms of their vapor pressure deficits, that is, the difference between the existing atmospheric vapor pressure and the saturation vapor pressure at the prevailing temperature.

Resistances in the Water Vapor Pathway

Small amounts of water vapor escape through the bark, chiefly through lenticels. Some escapes through the epidermis, but about 90% escapes through the stomata because the resistance to diffusion through stomata is much lower when they are open than resistance to diffusion through the epidermis. There are two kinds of resistances to the diffusion of water vapor, the resistances associated with the leaf and the external boundary layer resistance in the air adjacent to the leaf surface. Nobel (1974) discussed resistances to gas exchange in detail.

Leaf Resistances

The outer epidermal surfaces are usually covered by a layer of cutin which is relatively impermeable to water. It differs greatly in thickness and permeability among leaves of different species and those developed in different environmental conditions. The cuticle often is covered by a deposit of wax which apparently is extruded through the wall and the cuticle (Hall, 1967) and accumulates on the outer surface, as was shown in Chapter 8. The role of wax in the cuticle was discussed in Chapter 8. Cuticular resistance varies widely and usually increases materially as leaves become dehydrated. The resistances to diffusion of water vapor through the stomata and the cuticle of several species are shown in Table 12.3 and differences in cuticular and stomatal transpiration among several species are shown in Table 12.4.

When the stomata are open the stomatal resistance, r_s, is so much lower than the cuticular resistance that most of the water escapes through the stomata. The principal factor affecting stomatal resistance is stomatal aperture, which is controlled largely by light intensity and leaf water potential, and to a lesser extent by the humidity of the air and CO_2 concentration. Wuenscher and Kozlowski (1971) reported that increasing temperature in the range of 20° to 40°C also increased stomatal resistance in trees of several species. It also is possible to distinguish resistances to water vapor diffusion in

TABLE 12.3   Resistances to Movement of Water Vapor and Carbon Dioxide through the Boundary Layer, r_a, the Cuticle, r_c, the Stomata (Open), r_s, and the Mesophyll Resistance for CO_2, r_m [a]

	Resistances in sec/cm				
	Water vapor			CO$_2$	
Species	r_a	r_s	r_c	r_s	r_m
Betula verrucosa	0.80	0.92	83	1.56	5.8
Quercus robur	0.69	6.70	380	11.30	9.6
Acer platanoides	0.69	4.70	85	8.00	7.3
Helianthus annuus	0.55	0.38	—	0.65	2.4

[a] From Holmgren et al. (1965).

the intercellular spaces and the mesophyll cells. The resistance in the intercellular spaces, as measured with a diffusion porometer, appears to be significant when the stomata are wide open (Jarvis and Slatyer, 1970). The importance of the mesophyll resistance has been debated for several decades. It was reported early in this century (Livingston and Brown, 1912) that the rate of transpiration often decreased with no apparent change in stomatal aperture. Livingston attributed this to retreat of menisci into the walls during periods of rapid transpiration and called it incipient drying. The existence of an increase in mesophyll resistance was denied by some workers, but has been reported more recently by Shimshi (1963) and Whiteman and Koller (1964). Jarvis and Slatyer (1970) attribute this to the reduced hydraulic conductivity caused by

TABLE 12.4   Total and Cuticular Transpiration of Leaves of Various Kinds of Plants under Standard Evaporating Conditions [a,b]

Species	Transpiration with open stomata	Cuticular transpiration with closed stomata	Cuticular transpiration as % of total
Woody plants			
Betula pendula	780	95	12.0
Fagus sylvatica	420	90	21.0
Picea abies	480	15	3.0
Pinus sylvestris	540	13	2.5
Rhododendron ferrugineum	600	60	10.0
Herbaceous plants			
Coronilla varia	2,000	190	9.5
Stachys recta	1,800	180	10.0
Oxytropis pilosa	1,700	100	6.0

[a] Rates are given in mg H_2O/dm^2/hr; the surface area includes both sides of the leaves.
[b] From Larcher (1975, p. 152).

the layer of cuticle that covers the outer surface of the mesophyll cell walls (Lewis, 1945; Scott, 1950). Farquhar and Raschke (1978) found no mesophyll cell wall resistance in several herbaceous species and concluded that the water vapor pressure at the evaporating surfaces is equal to its saturation vapor pressure. More details of this interesting problem are given by Kramer (1969, p. 306). Because the stomatal and cuticular resistances are in parallel they can be described as follows:

$$\frac{1}{r_1} = \frac{1}{r_c} + \frac{1}{r_s} \text{ and } r_s = r_m + r_i + r_p \tag{12.8}$$

The total leaf resistance is r_1, r_c is the cuticular resistance, r_s stomatal resistance, r_m the resistance in the mesophyll walls, r_i resistance in the intercellular spaces, and r_p the resistance of the stomatal pores. A more complicated equation is used by Milthorpe (1959). A diagram of the various resistances in a leaf was shown in Fig. 12.3.

External Resistances

The external resistance depends largely on leaf size and shape and on wind speed. The leaves are discussed in the section on plant factors affecting transpiration.

Increasing air movement acts directly to increase transpiration by removing the boundary layer of water vapor surrounding leaves in quiet air and reducing r_{air} in Eq. (12.6). Wind also acts indirectly to decrease transpiration by cooling leaves and decreasing the e_{leaf} of Eq. (12.6). Most of the effect occurs at low velocities, as is shown in Fig. 12.5. Knoerr (1967) pointed out that, although a breeze should increase transpiration of leaves exposed to low levels of radiation, at higher levels when they tend to be warmer than the air a breeze might decrease transpiration, by cooling the leaves as is shown in Fig. 12.6. However, the actual behavior of plants seems rather variable. Davies *et al.* (1974) reported significant differences in the reaction of seedlings of

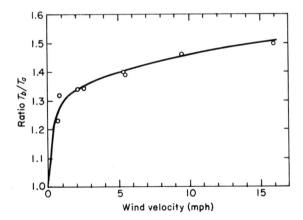

Fig. 12.5. Effect of increasing velocity of air movement on transpiration rate of potted sunflowers growing in a sunny greenhouse. The ordinate is the ratio of the rate of plants exposed to wind, T_b, to control plants in quiet air, T_a. Most of the effect occurs at a very low velocity. A velocity of 1 mph equals 44.7 cm/sec. From Martin and Clements (1935).

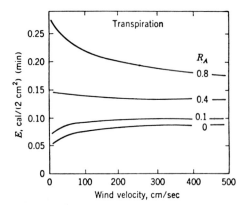

Fig. 12.6. Curves showing theoretical latent heat (*E*) exchange of a single leaf by transpiration at various wind speeds and net radiations (R_A). At high levels of radiation wind may decrease transpiration by cooling leaves, at low levels it might increase transpiration by supplying energy. From Knoerr (1967).

three species in a wind tunnel under artificial illumination of 28,700 to 35,500 lux and air speeds of 5.8 to 26 m/sec. The overall transpiration rates in both wind and quiet air were white ash > sugar maple > red pine. Wind increased transpiration of ash seedlings at all speeds, decreased transpiration of maple, and had no significant effect on pine. The stomata of maple leaves closed promptly when subjected to wind, but those of ash did not close until considerable dehydration had occurred.

Tranquillini (1969) also reported differences among species of the Austrian timberline zone. The transpiration of European larch and Mountain alder was higher at all air velocities up to 20 m/sec than in quiet air, but the rates of Norway spruce, Swiss stone pine, and *Rhododendron ferrugineum* were moderately to greatly decreased at 10 m/sec (see Fig. 12.7). Tranquillini attributed the decreases in transpiration to stomatal closure caused by local desiccation of the leaf surfaces rather than to general dehydration of the plants, which were subjected to only small reductions in water saturation deficits during the experiments. The species differences reported here seem generally to be related to differences in behavior of stomata and the amount of cuticular transpiration. However, Caldwell (1970) reported that, although exposure to wind causes immediate closure of stomata of *R. ferrugineum*, it has little effect on stomatal aperture of stone pine and any reduction of photosynthesis of the latter must be caused by change in needle exposure.

PLANT FACTORS AFFECTING TRANSPIRATION

Although the rate of transpiration is basically controlled by physical factors, it is influenced by several plant factors that affect both driving forces and resistances.

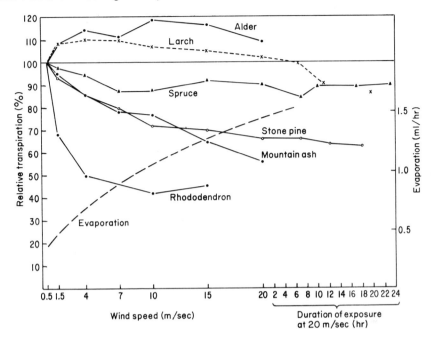

Fig. 12.7. Effect of increasing wind speed on transpiration of young potted subalpine plants in a wind tunnel at an air temperature of 20° C, soil temperature of 15° C, and light intensity of 30,000 lux. Evaporation is from a green Piche atmometer under the same conditions. Evaporation increases steadily with increasing wind speed, but transpiration of most species decreases. Alder is *Alnus viridis*; larch is *Larix decidua*; spruce, *Picea abies*; stone pine, *P. cembra*; mountain ash, *Sorbus aucuparia*; rhododendron, *Rhododendron ferrugineum*. From Tranquillini (1969).

Leaf Area

The total leaf area has significant effects on water loss of individual plants, plants with large leaf areas usually transpiring more than those with small leaf areas. However, removal of one-half of the leaves from a tree will not necessarily reduce its transpiration rate proportionally. Miller (1938, p. 454) cites several experiments in which removal of part of the leaves resulted in decreased transpiration per tree but increased transpiration per unit of leaf surface. The increase results from increased air movement and better exposure of the remaining leaves, and also from a higher ratio of root surface to leaf surface. Some woody species such as creosote bush shed most of their leaves when subjected to water stress, greatly reducing the transpiring surface. This also occurs in some mesophytic species such as buckeye and even in yellow-poplar. Curling and rolling of wilting leaves also reduces the exposed surface and increases resistance to diffusion of water vapor, especially if most of the stomata are on the inner surface of the curved leaf. Seasonal and developmental changes in the transpiring surface of a number of species are discussed by Killian and Lemée (1956).

TABLE 12.5   Transpiration Rates per Unit of Leaf Surface and per Seedling of Loblolly Pine and Hardwood Seedlings for the Period of August 22 to September 2 [a]

	Loblolly pine	Yellow-poplar	Northern red oak
Transpiration (g/day/dm²)	5.08	9.76	12.45
Transpiration (g/day/dm²)	106.70	59.10	77.00
Average leaf area per tree (dm²)	21.00	6.06	6.18
Average height of trees (cm)	34.00	34.00	20.00

[a] Average of six seedlings of each species.

Some species shed their leaves earlier than others, and it seems likely that such species remove less water from the soil during the early autumn than species, such as oaks, that retain their leaves much longer. If significant differences really exist it might be worthwhile to convert watershed cover to species with a minimum rate of transpiration in the autumn and thereby increase stream flow at that season. Some consideration has also been given to the feasibility of defoliating trees on watersheds in late summer to reduce transpiration and increase water yield. Growth might be reduced, but this would not be important where water yield is more important than timber production. Removal of the laurel and rhododendron understory on a watershed at Coweeta, North Carolina, greatly increased stream flow, but the yield declined in subsequent years because of regrowth of vegetation (Johnson and Kovner, 1956).

As shown in Table 12.5, there are wide variations in transpiration per unit of leaf area among species. However, such variations can be misleading because the differences in total leaf area may compensate for differences in rate per unit of leaf area. For example, as shown in Table 12.5, the transpiration rate per unit of leaf area is lower for loblolly pine than for certain deciduous species, but the total leaf area per pine seedling is so much greater that the water loss per seedling also is greater. Thus a loblolly pine tree may lose as much water per day as a hardwood tree with a crown of similar size.

Root/Shoot Ratio

The ratio of roots to shoots, or more accurately of absorbing surface to transpiring surface, is more important than leaf surface alone, because if absorption lags behind transpiration a water deficit develops, the stomata close and transpiration is reduced. Parker (1949) found that the rate of transpiration per unit of leaf area of northern red oak and loblolly pine seedlings growing in moist soil increased as the ratio of root to leaf surface increased (Fig. 12.8). Pereira and Kozlowski (1977a) found that sugar maple seedlings with a large leaf area developed more severe water stress than partly defoliated seedlings. Trees with extensive, much-branched root systems survive droughts much better than those with shallow or sparsely branched root systems.

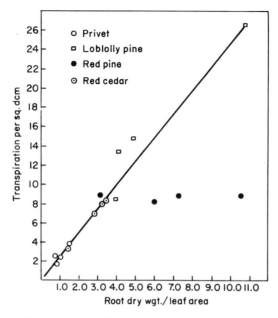

Fig. 12.8. Effect of increasing ratio of roots to shoots on transpiration rate of tree seedlings. The data are plotted as grams of water lost per square decimeter of leaf area over weight of roots divided by leaf area in square decimeters. Privet showed no change in transpiration with increasing root–shoot ratio, presumably because the amount of roots was never reduced enough to affect transpiration. From Parker (1949).

Loss of roots during lifting of seedlings is a serious problem because the most common cause of death of transplanted seedlings is desiccation caused by lack of an effective absorbing surface. Undercutting and "wrenching" of seedlings in seed beds is intended to produce compact, profusely branched root systems which can be lifted with minimum injury. Lopushinsky and Beebe (1976) reported that survival of out-planted Douglas-fir and ponderosa pine seedlings in a region with dry summers was improved by large root systems and large root–shoot ratios. Allen (1955) found that clipping the needles of longleaf pine planting stock back to 12.5 cm in length reduced mortality after planting. It is common practice to prune back the tops of transplanted trees and shrubs to compensate for loss of roots during the transplanting process. However, reduction in transpiring surface also reduces the photosynthetic surface, which is undesirable except for those times when conservation of water content is more important than loss of photosynthetic capacity. Other treatments are discussed in the section on control of transpiration.

Leaf Size and Shape

The size and shape of leaves affect the rate of transpiration per unit of surface. Slatyer (1967) reported that the air resistance, r_a, is about three times greater for a leaf

10 cm wide than for one only 1 cm wide. Also small, deeply dissected leaves and compound leaves with small leaflets tend to be cooler than large leaves because their thinner boundary layers permit more rapid sensible heat transfer. Tibbals *et al.* (1964) found that in quiet air broad leaves are considerably warmer than pine needles exposed to the same incident radiation. Nobel (1976) found that the large shade leaves of *Hyptis emoryi* become much warmer than the small sun leaves and this should increase transpiration. However, the thin boundary layer and lower r_{air} of small leaves also is more favorable to water vapor loss so the two effects tend to compensate with respect to latent heat transfer and transpiration if stomatal resistance is similar (Raschke, 1976). The energy relations of leaves are discussed by Gates (1965, 1976), Knoerr (1967), Nobel (1974), and Slatyer (1967, pp. 237–247).

Leaf Orientation

Most leaves grow in such a manner as to be more or less perpendicular to the brightest light that strikes them. This is noticeable on vines covering walls and on isolated trees where there is a complete mosaic of leaves on the outer surface neatly arranged so they intercept as much light as possible. On the other hand, the leaves of a few species such as *Silphium* and turkey oak are oriented vertically, and the leaves of longleaf pine seedlings in the grass stage grow upright. Such an orientation obviously decreases energy absorption and tends to decrease the midday leaf temperature, which may in turn decrease water loss, but it has never been demonstrated that this unusual orientation really has significant survival value. Needles of most pines occur in fascicles and shade one another. This decreases photosynthesis (Kramer and Clark, 1947) and presumably also decreases transpiration. The dropping and rolling characteristic of wilted leaves also decreases the amount of radiation received. It is an indication of water stress, but it probably causes sufficient decrease in further water loss to prolong life. Caldwell (1970) reported that wind changes the leaf orientation of stone pine enough to reduce photosynthesis.

Leaf Surfaces

We already have mentioned the importance of cuticle and wax in increasing resistance to water loss through the epidermis. The net effect of the thick coat of hairs found on some kinds of leaves is less certain. Pubescence would be expected to increase the boundary layer resistance, r_a, thereby decreasing both heat loss and the escape of water vapor in moving air. However, it was recently reported that conductance of CO_2 into the pubescent leaves of *Encelia farinosa* is not reduced (Ehleringer *et al.*, 1976) as compared with the nonpubescent leaves of *E. californica*. If r_a is not increased for CO_2 it presumably would not be increased for water vapor. Living hairs might increase transpiration by increasing the evaporating surface.

The albedo or reflective characteristics of leaf surfaces materially affects leaf temperature. Vegetation usually reflects 15 to 25% of the incident radiation and Billings and Morris (1951) reported that leaves of desert plants usually reflect more light than leaves of plants from less exposed habitats. The white, densely pubescent leaves of the desert shrub, *Encelia farinosa*, reflect about twice as much radiation as the green, nonpubescent leaves of *E. californica* native to the moist coastal region. In fact, so much light is reflected that net photosynthesis of *E. farinosa* is reduced (Ehleringer *et al.*, 1976). The reduction in transpiration reported to occur after the application of Bordeaux mixture (Miller, 1938) probably results from the lower leaf temperature caused by the white coating it produces on leaves.

Leaf Anatomy

Leaf structure can be greatly modified by the environment in which the leaves develop (Stålfelt, 1956). Sun leaves, as compared with shade leaves, usually have smaller cells, smaller surface and interveinal areas, thicker cutin, and are thicker, due to extra layers of palisade cells (see Fig. 12.9). The upper leaves of trees are said usually to be more xeromorphic in structure than the lower leaves. In general, leaves from dry habitats resemble sun leaves (xeromorphic type) and those from moist habitats resemble shade leaves (mesomorphic types). Examples of the two types are shown in Fig. 12.10.

It has often been assumed that water loss from mesomorphic types of leaves with thin cutin and large intercellular spaces such as those of yellow poplar, red oak, or maple is greater than from the thicker, more heavily cutinized xeromorphic types such as those of magnolia or holly. Maximov (1929) pointed out that this is not necessarily true for well-watered plants, and this is further illustrated by the data in Table 12.6. Both *Ilex glabra* and *Gordonia lasianthus* have thick, heavily cutinized leaves, yet their transpiration rates when well watered are higher per unit of leaf surface than those

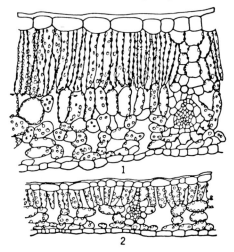

Fig. 12.9. Cross sections of (1) leaf from the southern edge and (2) from the center of the crown of an isolated sugar maple. From Weaver and Clements (1938). Copyright 1938; used with permission of McGraw-Hill Book Company.

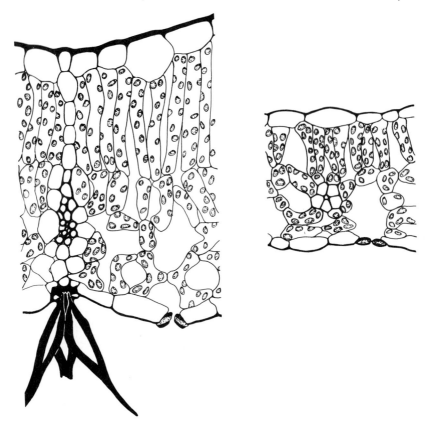

Fig. 12.10. Cross sections through leaves of post oak (*leaf*) and beech (*right*). Post oak leaves are representative of the xeromorphic type, with thick cutin, double layer of palisade cells, bundle sheath extension, and a high ratio of internal to external surface. Beech leaves are of the mesomorphic type. They are thinner, with thin cutin and a single layer of palisade cells and less internal surface exposed to intercellular spaces. (Courtesy of J. Philpott.) From Kramer and Kozlowski (1960).

of the oaks, maples, or yellow-poplar. Swanson (1943) reported that American holly transpired more rapidly than lilac, coleus, or tobacco on a sunny day, but on a cloudy day the transpiration rate of holly was lower than that of lilac.

These differences are at least partly related to the large ratio of internal to external surface in xeromorphic and sun leaves, caused by the larger amounts of palisade tissue in sun leaves than in shade and mesomorphic leaves (Turrell, 1936, 1944). Swanson (1943) found ratios of internal to external leaf surface of 12.9, 7.1, and 4.6, respectively, in American holly, tobacco, and coleus. A large ratio of internal to external surface provides more evaporating surface per unit of external leaf surface, and if well supplied with water it probably keeps the intercellular spaces nearly saturated. However, when drying soil produces a water deficit and the stomata close, the transpiration

TABLE 12.6 Midsummer Transpiration Rates of Various Species of Trees[a,b]

Species	Location	Season	Duration (days)	Number of plants	Average transpiration (g/dm²/day)
Liriodendron tulipifera[c]	Columbus, Ohio	August	1	7	10.11
Liriodendron tulipifera[d]	Durham, N.C.	August	3	4	11.78
Quercus alba[d]	Durham, N.C.	August	3	4	14.21
Quercus rubra[d]	Durham, N.C.	August	3	4	12.02
Quercus rubra[e]	Fayette, Mo.	July	14	6	8.1
Acer saccharum[e]	Fayette, Mo.	July	14	6	12.2
Acer negundo[e]	Fayette, Mo.	July	14	6	6.4
Platanus occidentalis[e]	Fayette, Mo.	July	14	6	8.8
Pinus taeda[d]	Durham, N.C.	August	3	4	4.65
Clethra alnifolia[d]	Durham, N.C.	August	3	4	9.73
Ilex glabra[d]	Durham, N.C.	August	3	4	16.10
Myrica cerifera[d]	Durham, N.C.	August	3	4	10.80
Gordonia lasianthus[d]	Durham, N.C.	July	23	4	17.77
Liriodendron tulipifera[f]	Durham, N.C.	August 26– September 2	12	6	9.76
Quercus rubra[f]	Durham, N.C.	August 26– September 2	12	6	12.45
Pinus taeda[f]	Durham, N.C.	August 26– September 2	12	6	5.08

[a] Expressed as grams of water lost per square decimeter of leaf surface per day.
[b] All seedlings were growing in soil near field capacity.
[c] From Meyer (1932).
[d] From Caughey (1945).
[e] From Biswell (1935).
[f] From Kramer (unpublished).

of xeromorphic leaves generally is lower than that of mesomorphic types because the cuticular transpiration of the former is very low. Stålfelt (1956) reported that the internal air space varies from 20 to 70% of the total leaf volume, the percentage being lowest in sun leaves and highest in shade leaves.

The foregoing discussion is based on the assumption that most of the internal evaporation occurs from the walls of the mesophyll cells. Recently it has been suggested by Meidner (1975, 1976) that considerable evaporation occurs from the inner surfaces of the epidermal cells, especially in the immediate vicinity of the stomata. This suggestion also neglects the possibility that the inner surfaces of epidermal cells may be cutinized, as reported for the lower epidermis of pear by Norris and Bukovac (1968). There is increasing evidence that the turgor of the guard cells can vary independently of that of the mesophyll. However, it seems improbable that enough of the inner surface of the epidermis is exposed to the air spaces within the leaf for it to be a major evaporating surface. Apparently, however, the relative importance of the various evaporating surfaces in leaves requires further investigation.

STOMATA

Most of the water lost from plants escapes through the stomata of the leaves (see Fig. 2.3) and most of the carbon dioxide used in photosynthesis enters by the same pathway. Although the stomatal pores usually occupy no more than 1% of the leaf surface, diffusion of water vapor through stomata often amounts to 50% of the rate of evaporation from a free water surface. This is because their size and spacing result in their functioning as very efficient pathways for diffusion of gases. Further information on stomata can be found in Chapter 2.

The size of stomatal pores is controlled by the turgor of the guard cells, increasing with increased turgor and decreasing with decreased turgor. In general, stomata open in light or in response to a low carbon dioxide concentration in the intercellular spaces and close in darkness. They also close if dehydration causes loss of turgor. There is still some uncertainty concerning the mechanism by which changes in light intensity or carbon dioxide concentration produce changes in guard cell turgor and stomatal aperture. However, the idea that changes in guard cell turgor result from changes in the proportions of starch and sugar has been supplanted by the idea that turgor changes are caused by gain or loss of ions, chiefly potassium. The stomatal mechanism is discussed by Hsiao (1973), Raschke (1975), Zelitch (1969), and Allaway and Milthorpe (1976).

In recent years it has been shown that exposure of the epidermis to dry air causes closure of stomata in turgid leaves of several species (Schulze *et al.*, 1972). Thus stomatal closure can be caused either by dehydration of the leaves or dehydration of the guard cells, and presumably the adjoining epidermal cells. Furthermore, Lawlor and Milford (1975) reported that the stomata of sugar beet leaves can be kept open by exposure to humid air even when a water deficit exists in the mesophyll. Tranquillini (1969) suggested that stomatal closure in several woody species subjected to wind was caused by desiccation of the leaf surfaces rather than by dehydration of the entire tissue. The data of Hall and Kaufmann (1975) and Kaufmann (1976) also indicate that low humidity causes stomatal closure, but the effect is decreased by low CO_2 concentration and high temperature.

Cyclic opening and closing of stomata of water-stressed herbaceous plants with periods of 15 to 120 min have been observed (Barrs, 1971), and Levy and Kaufmann (1976) reported that stomatal cycling occurs in citrus trees in orchards. The physiological significance of such cycling is uncertain, but Cowan (1972) proposed that it optimizes the conflicting requirements for uptake of carbon dioxide and control of water loss.

Further complications have been introduced by observations that stomatal behavior is affected by growth regulators, especially abscisic acid. It has been suggested that stomatal closure in water stressed plants is caused by a decrease in cytokinins and an increase in abscisic acid (Livne and Vaadia, 1972) and Davies and Kozlowski (1975a,b) reported that application of abscisic acid to the foliage of white ash, sugar maple, and Calamondin orange reduced transpiration. However, it seems likely that water stress will have caused stomatal closure by loss of guard cell turgor before it can have brought about sufficient change in the concentration of growth regulators to be effective. The role of abscisic acid and other factors in stomatal opening is discussed in more detail by Raschke (1975, 1976).

The responsiveness of stomata varies with age and environmental conditions. It is well known that stomata are responsive to light intensity, CO_2 concentration, and water stress, but their response is affected by their past history. As leaves age their stomata become less responsive and the midday stomatal resistance may increase severalfold because they do not open fully (Slatyer and Bierhuizen, 1964a). This behavior is very notable in some grasses (Brown and Pratt, 1965). It also is reported that the stomata on plants grown in greenhouses (Jordan and Ritchie, 1971) and growth chambers (Millar *et al.*, 1971) close at a lower level of water stress (higher leaf water potential) than stomata on plants grown in the field. These experiments were all performed on herbaceous plants and we know of no such experiments on woody plants. It is said that the stomata of most herbaceous species growing under favorable conditions can be grouped into three types (Miller, 1938, pp. 435–436): (1) the alfalfa type, which opens in the morning and closes in the evening; (2) the potato type, which is always open except for a few hours after sunset; and (3) the barley type, including many grasses, which begin to close soon after they open. We know of no attempt to classify the stomatal behavior of trees in this manner, but such a study might be worthwhile.

The data summarized by Lopushinsky (1969) indicated that considerable differences in sensitivity of stomata to water stress exist among conifer species, the stomata of pine generally being more sensitive to water stress than those of other conifers. In experiments with 2-year-old seedlings Lopushinsky found that stomatal closure occurred at lower water stress (higher Ψ_w) in ponderosa and lodgepole pine and Engelmann spruce than in Douglas-fir and grand fir seedlings (see Table 12.7). Running (1976) also reported differences among conifers with respect to the relationship between leaf water

TABLE 12.7 Water Content and Relative Water Content and Water Potential at Stomatal Closure in Several Western Conifers [a]

Species	Water content (% dry weight)	Relative water content (%)	Water potential (bars)
Ponderosa pine	31.3	84.4	−16.5
Lodgepole pine	29.4	81.6	−14.6
Grand fir	17.9	82.2	−25.1
Douglas-fir	21.4	85.0	−19.0
Engelmann spruce	32.8	86.1	−16.0

[a] From Lopushinsky (1969), University of Chicago Press.

stress and stomatal opening. Federer (1977) reported that stomatal closure occurred at -15 bars in birch, -17 bars in poplar, -21 bars in oak, and -23 bars in cherry. He regarded the differences among genera as more important than the differences caused by site or tree size. Hinckley (1978) reported that during a dry summer stomata of sugar maple were closed 50% of the time, those of white and black oak about 20%, and those of northern red oak nearly 30%. It is often difficult to evaluate the importance of prompt closure of stomata in water-stressed plants because the benefit of water conservation may be offset by decreased photosynthesis.

Stomatal Control of Transpiration

Earlier in this century much effort was expended attempting to determine the effect of partial closure of stomata on the rate of transpiration. Workers were influenced by the experiments of Brown and Escombe (1900) which were conducted in quiet air where the boundary layer resistance (r_a) was as high as the stomatal resistance (r_s). Their results indicated that large changes in stomatal aperture should have little effect on the rate of transpiration. However, it has been shown repeatedly that in moving air where r_a is low there is a strong relationship between stomatal aperture and transpiration (Stålfelt, 1932; Bange, 1953). It is now agreed that although partial closure has little effect on transpiration in quiet air it greatly reduces the rate in moving air, as is shown in Fig. 12.11. This subject was discussed in detail by Slatyer (1967, pp. 260–269), who emphasized that the effect of stomatal closure varies with the relative values of r_s and r_a.

Measurement of Stomatal Aperture

The realization that stomatal aperture has important effects on both loss of water vapor and uptake of CO_2 has stimulated interest in the measurement of stomatal opening. A number of methods have been used, including direct observation with a microscope, stripping off bits of epidermis and fixing them in absolute alcohol, and preparing impressions of the epidermis on collodion (Clements and Long, 1934) or silicone rubber films (Zelitch, 1961). Another method involves observation of the time required for infiltration of fluids of various viscosities, such as benzene, paraffin oil, and kerosene. Fry and Walker (1967) described a pressure infiltration method for use on conifer needles. This indicates whether stomata are open or closed but does not permit calculation of leaf resistance (Lassoie *et al.*, 1977).

In 1911 Darwin and Pertz introduced gas flow porometers which measured gas flow through leaves under a slight pressure. Numerous modifications have been described, including models suitable for use in the field. However, gas flow porometers measure what is basically a diffusion process by pressure flow, and if the pressure is too high it may cause stomatal closure (Raschke, 1975). This led to the development of diffusion porometers which measure diffusion of gas through leaves (Heath, 1959). Slatyer and Jarvis (1966) described a diffusion porometer using nitrous oxide, which permits continuous recording of stomatal resistance.

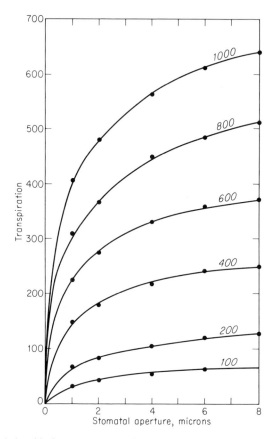

Fig. 12.11. Relationship between stomatal aperture and rate of transpiration at various potential rates of transpiration. The numbers on the curves indicate rates of evaporation from blotting paper atmometers expressed in milligrams of water per hour per 25 cm² of evaporating surface. Transpiration also is expressed in milligrams of water per 25 cm² of leaf surface. At low rates of evaporation and potential transpiration stomatal aperture has much less control over the rate of transpiration than at potentially high rates. From Stålfelt (1932).

Many measurements are now being made with various modifications of an instrument described by Kanemasu *et al.* (1969) that uses a humidity sensor connected to an electronic circuit and meter to measure changes in humidity in a cup placed over a leaf for a few seconds. These instruments are now commercially available and can be equipped with an electronic timer that increases the accuracy of measurement. An example of a simple type of porometer is shown in Fig. 12.12. Gas flow porometers can not be used satisfactorily on leaves with stomata on only one surface and veins that prevent lateral diffusion of gas (heterobaric type) (see Heath, 1959). Meidner and Mansfield (1968) reviewed the history of porometry and it is also discussed by Slavik (1974).

Fig. 12.12. A porometer for measuring the diffusion resistance of leaves. Photo courtesy of Lambda Instruments Corporation.

INTERACTION OF FACTORS AFFECTING TRANSPIRATION

In summary, the important environmental factors affecting transpiration are light intensity, vapor pressure deficit of the air, temperature, wind, and water supply to the roots. Plant factors include leaf area, leaf exposure and structure, stomatal behavior, and the effectiveness of the roots as absorbing surfaces. There are complex interactions among the various factors that can be summarized in terms of their effects on various terms of Eq. (12.6).

For example, changes in light intensity affect r_{leaf} by affecting stomatal aperture and e_{leaf} by effects on leaf temperature. Atmospheric temperature affects both e_{leaf} and e_{air} or Δe. Readers are reminded that although increasing the temperature of a given air mass from 20° to 30°C will decrease the relative humidity it will significantly increase the water vapor pressure of the air (see Table 12.2). An increase in temperature therefore causes an increase in transpiration because it increases the vapor pressure gradient, Δe, from leaf to air, *not* because it is accompanied by a decrease in relative humidity of the air. Likewise, at a constant temperature, change in atmospheric humidity affects transpiration by changing e_{air} and Δe from leaf to air. Martin (1943) found a very close relationship between transpiration of plants in darkness at a constant temperature and the vapor pressure of the atmosphere. Cole and Decker (1973) also found that transpiration is a linear function of Δe.

It was mentioned earlier that wind increases transpiration by sweeping away the water vapor in the boundary layer and reducing r_{air} and that it acts indirectly to decrease transpiration by cooling the leaves and reducing e_{leaf}. Other effects of wind such as increased ventilation of the intercellular spaces by flexing of leaves and increasing the passage of air through amphistomatous leaves (leaves with stomata on both surfaces) probably are of minor importance (Woolley, 1961). However, Shive and Brown (1978) found that flexing of cottonwood leaves causes significant bulk flow of gas through them and decreases total resistance by about 25%.

Leaf arrangement affects exposure to the sun and leaf temperature that in turn affect e_{leaf}. Upright leaves receive less energy at the hottest time of day than horizontal leaves, and clustered leaves such as fascicles of pine needles receive less than those arranged separately. Variations in internal geometry and volume of intercellular spaces may affect the resistance in the intercellular spaces r_i, thickness of cutin affects r_c, and extent of stomatal opening affects r_s, as was indicated in Fig. 12.3.

It should be emphasized that a change in one of the factors affecting transpiration does not necessarily produce a proportional change in transpiration, because the rate is not controlled by any single factor. An example is the fact that a breeze tends to

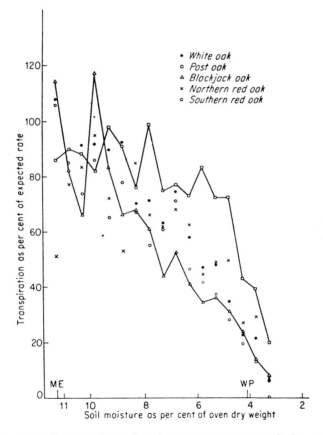

Fig. 12.13. Effect of decreasing soil moisture content on transpiration rates of oak seedlings. From Bourdeau (1954).

increase transpiration by lowering r_{air} but decreases it if the leaf is cooled enough to lower e_{leaf}. Likewise, as was shown in Fig. 12.11, partial closure of stomata has less effect in quiet air, where r_{air} is high (2.0) compared to r_s, than in moving air, where r_{air} is low (0.1). In general, the effects of various factors on the rate of transpiration can be explained in terms of their effects on the differences in vapor pressure between leaf and air ($\Delta e = e_{leaf} - e_{air}$) and the resistances in leaf and air pathways ($r_{leaf} + r_{air}$).

The supply of water to the roots also affects transpiration because a deficient water supply causes dehydration and stomatal closure. In soil near field capacity, movement of water into roots is rapid and the rate of transpiration is controlled largely by atmospheric factors, except for the occasional midday wilting of rapidly transpiring plants caused by high root resistance. However, as the soil water content decreases the supply of water to the roots becomes a limiting factor and the rate of transpiration decreases. It has been shown by various investigators from Hartig and von Höhnel in the 19th century to Kozlowski (1949), Bourdeau (1954), Lemée (1956), Slatyer (1956) and Jackson *et al*. (1973) that decreasing soil moisture causes decrease in the transpiration of trees (see Fig. 12.13). Lopushinsky and Klock (1974) found that the transpiration rate of several kinds of conifers began to decrease at a soil moisture potential of -1 or -2 bars, but the decrease at -10 bars was much greater in ponderosa and lodgepole pine than in Douglas-fir or grand fir (Fig. 12.14). According to Ringoet (1952), low soil moisture reduced the transpiration of oil palms so much that the trees transpired more during the rainy season than during the dry season, although atmospheric factors were more favorable for transpiration during the dry season. It has been shown that change in ratio of roots to leaf surface affects transpiration of sparsely rooted tree seedlings (Parker, 1949), but the effect is negligible in species with dense root systems (Andrews and Newman, 1968). Cold soil and high salt content also decrease water absorption. These problems are discussed in more detail in Chapter 13.

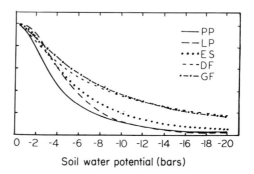

Soil water potential (bars)

Fig. 12.14. Effect of decreasing soil water potential on transpiration rates of seedlings of ponderosa pine (PP), lodgepole pine (LP), Engelmann spruce (ES), Douglas-fir (DF), and grand fir (GF). The more rapid reduction in transpiration of the pines occurs because their stomata begin closing at a higher leaf water potential than the stomata of grand fir and Douglas-fir, as shown in Table 12.6. From Lopushinsky and Klock (1974).

MEASUREMENT OF TRANSPIRATION

The first quantitative measurements of water loss from plants appear to have been made by Stephen Hales, prior to 1727. He measured water loss by weighing potted grapevines, apple and lemon trees, and various herbaceous plants. Several studies were made during the second half of the 19th century of which the best known are those by von Höhnel, published in 1881 and 1884. The early work on transpiration of trees was summarized by Raber (1937), and Miller (1938) discussed methods of measuring transpiration. Slatyer (1967), Kramer (1969), and Slavik (1974) present discussions of various methods and their advantages and disadvantages.

There has been an important change in viewpoint in recent years concerning what constitute useful measurements of transpiration. Originally, most efforts were concentrated on making measurements of water loss from single plants or individual leaves or twigs, but now there is increasing interest in estimating water loss from stands of plants or plant communities. Measurements of water loss from detached leaves or branches have important uses in physiological studies but they cannot be reliably extrapolated to estimate the water loss of whole plants or stands of plants. Nevertheless, these methods will be discussed because they are often the only ones available.

Gravimetric Methods

From the time of Hales (1727) to the present, investigators have grown plants in containers and measured water loss by weighing the container at regular intervals. It is necessary to enclose the soil mass in which the plant is growing in a waterproof container and to replenish soil moisture frequently so water supply does not become a limiting factor. The size of plants studied depends on the size of the container which can be weighed. Veihmeyer (1927) measured the transpiration of small trees growing in tanks of soil weighing about 450 kg. Nutman (1941) used a balance with a capacity of over 225 kg and a sensitivity of 25 gm to measure water loss from coffee trees. However, in many of the early studies the containers appear to have been too small for best results (Raber, 1937).

Data obtained by this method are useful for physiological studies such as comparing water loss from individual trees, but the extent to which the results can be applied to trees growing in their normal environment is debatable. The plants usually are grown in soil kept near field capacity instead of being subjected to the cycles of drying and rewetting characteristic of the field and they also usually are subjected to abnormal atmospheric conditions. One way to approximate natural conditions is to set the containers in pits with the tops level with the soil surface in the habitat where the plants normally grow, as was done by Biswell (1935) and Holch (1931) in their studies of the transpiration of tree seedlings in sun and shade in Nebraska. The logical development of this method is the use of lysimeters. These are devices containing large masses of soil in which vegetation can be grown, arranged so that changes in water content can be measured accurately. Several types are described by Tanner (1967). The ultimate in lysimeters with respect to trees probably was constructed by Fritschen *et al.* (1973) to contain a block of soil 3.7 × 3.7 × 1.2 m in which was rooted a Douglas-fir tree 28 m in height standing in the forest where it grew. The container, soil, and tree weighed 28,900 kg and the measuring apparatus had a sensitivity of 630 g.

The Cut-Shoot Method

Because of the limitations in size and the time and expense required to make measurements on potted plants, many workers have measured the water loss from detached leaves or twigs. Usually the measurements are made for only a few minutes after cutting because the rate tends to decline, although a temporary increase some-times occurs several minutes after cutting (the Ivanov effect). This method has been used by scores of investigators. Slavik discussed this method in detail (1974, pp. 253–257) and Franco and Magalhaes (1965) discussed its limitations. Ringoet (1952) made an extensive comparison of the transpiration of detached shoots and potted seedlings and found the rates obtained by measuring water loss from leaves and leaflets for 2-min intervals were higher than the rates measured with potted seedlings. The differences were greater for sun plants such as oil palm than for shade plants. Ringoet concluded that, in general, weighing detached plant parts measured the physical factors affecting evaporation while weighing intact potted plants resulted in data that repre-sented the interaction of the plant and environmental factors affecting transpiration. Halevy (1956) found that on mild autumn days the rates of transpiration of orange were similar for detached leaves and potted plants, but on hot, dry days rates of the latter were 25 to 50% lower than the rates of detached leaves. The errors in measurements on

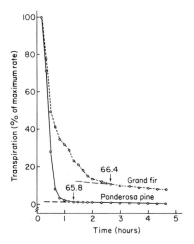

Fig. 12.15. Difference in transpiration rates of detached branches of ponderosa pine and grand fir. The numbers on the curves are the relative water contents (relative turgidities) at point of complete stomatal closure. The stomata of ponderosa pine close more rapidly under stress than those of grand fir and the pine needles have a lower rate of cuticular transpiration than those of grand fir. From Lopushinsky (1969).

detached leaves are increased by the large variations in rates found among individual leaves from the same plant and leaves from different plants of the same species (Hölzl, 1955). In spite of its inherent errors this method has been used to measure differences in transpiration rate of various heights and on the north and south sides of trees, and for comparisons among species (see Table 12.9). Hygen and others have used variations of this method to measure water loss from detached leaves and to determine when stomatal transpiration ceases and water loss occurs chiefly through the cuticle (see Slavik, 1974, pp. 284–285). An example of this type of study is shown in Fig. 12.15.

Volumetric Methods

Another method for studying water loss is to measure water uptake by a detached leaf or branch. Unfortunately, the rate of transpiration of a detached branch is likely to be quite different from the rate while it was attached because the attached branch is in competition with all other branches and its water supply is also dependent on the rate of absorption through the roots. Furthermore, water uptake by detached leaves and branches often is reduced by plugging of the conducting system with air and debris. More reliable results can be obtained with potometers in which entire root systems can be enclosed, provided that the root systems were grown in water culture. Sudden immersion in water of root systems grown in soil is likely to be followed by reduced water absorption, water deficit, and stomatal closure. Roberts (1977) made useful measurements of transpiration of Scotch pine trees up to 16 m in height by placing the cut bases of the trunks in containers of water and supporting the tops in their original position in the canopy.

Measurement of Water Vapor Loss

Many measurements of transpiration have been made by monitoring the change in water content of an air stream passed through a container enclosing the material under study. The containers usually are made of plastic and vary in size from cuvettes holding a single leaf (Bierhuizen and Slatyer, 1964) to plastic tents large enough to enclose small trees (Decker *et al.*, 1962; see Fig. 12.16). In open systems the difference in water content entering and leaving the container is measured, but in closed systems the increase in water content is measured.

Many methods have been used to measure changes in water content of the air passing over plant parts, including absorption in some hygroscopic substance, use of wet and dry bulb thermometers or thermocouples, the corona hygrometer, the microwave hygrometer, electrical resistance hygrometers, and infrared gas analyzers sensitive to water vapor. Most of these methods are discussed briefly by Kramer (1969) and in detail by Slavik (1974).

This method eliminates the errors caused by detaching leaves or branches, but it imposes a somewhat artificial environment on the leaf or plant enclosed in the container. The changes in leaf and air temperature, wind speed, and humidity can cause important differences between transpiration rates measured by these methods and those

Fig. 12.16. An Aleppo pine 7.2 m in height enclosed in a plastic tent for measurement of transpiration. The enclosure was ventilated with a blower, air entering near the bottom and leaving through apertures near the top. Transpiration rates were calculated from the air flow and the differences in humidity of the air as it entered and left the enclosure (Decker and Skau, 1964). Photograph courtesy of J. P. Decker.

of fully exposed plants. One way to control the environment in enclosures is to provide continuous compensation for changes in humidity and CO_2 concentration, as was done by Koller and Samish (1964), and Moss (1963). Apparatus for control of the environment and continuous, simultaneous measurement of water vapor and CO_2 exchange and stomatal resistance of leaves was described by Jarvis and Slatyer (1966).

Short period measurements of water loss eliminate some of the errors caused by prolonged enclosure of leaves. Grieve and Went (1965) described the use of a standard lithium chloride humidity sensor to measure the change in humidity in a container enclosing a single leaf. Ehrler and van Bavel (1968) found good agreement between rates of transpiration measured by weighing and by use of the form of this instrument described by van Bavel *et al.* (1965). Measurements of transpiration requiring less than 1 min can also be made with the differential psychrometer described by Slatyer and Bierhuizen (1964a). The cobalt chloride method measures the escape of water vapor by the time required to produce a standard change in color in a piece of paper impregnated with cobalt chloride and pressed against the leaf. However, rates measured by this method do not agree with rates obtained by gravimetric methods because it replaces the normal atmosphere with an abnormal one for a considerable period of time (Milthorpe, 1955).

Velocity of Sap Flow

Several investigators have attempted to estimate the rate of transpiration from measurements of the rate of sap flow through tree stems, using some form of the heat pulse method described by Huber and Schmidt (1937). Ladefoged (1963) used a diathermy machine as a source of heat and reported prompt responses to the passage of clouds and gusts of wind, and good indications of seasonal trends. He measured the water absorption of tree trunks cut off and placed in containers of water and extrapolated from the correlation between absorption and velocity in these trees to estimate the transpiration rates of intact trees. Decker and Skau (1964) found a good correlation between simultaneous measurements of sap velocity and transpiration rates (see Fig. 12.17). Swanson and Lee (1966) discussed the advantages and disadvantages of this and other methods of estimating transpiration. They concluded that although it is difficult to estimate transpiration from sap velocity measurements they are useful indicators of such things as when transpiration starts in the morning, how rapidly it increases, and how it is affected by changes in atmospheric conditions. Some of their data indicated a measurable lag in decrease in sap flow near the base of a tree trunk after a rain reduced transpiration. There is a similar lag in the morning when transpiration increases rapidly in the tree top, presumably because of the water storage capacity of tree trunks (Lassoie, 1973). Leyton (1970) summarized the information on the heat pulse method.

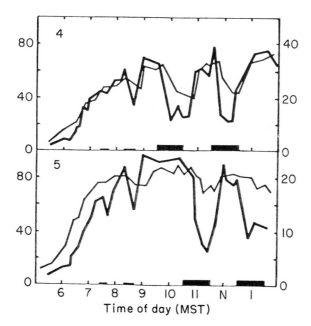

Fig. 12.17. The time course of transpiration (*heavy line*) in g/ min on the left ordinate and sap velocity (*light line*) in cm/hr on right ordinate. Data for an Aleppo pine in Tempe, Arizona. From Decker and Skau (1964).

TRANSPIRATION RATES

Numerous measurements have been made of the transpiration rates of trees and shrubs of various species and ages under a wide range of conditions. Some of the earlier results were summarized by Raber (1937) and many others occur in a series of papers by Pisek and his co-workers, cited by Larcher (1975). Only a few examples will be given here. In general, the range of variability in rates is similar to that for herbaceous plants. There are wide differences among individuals and among leaves of different ages and locations on the same individual. Some representative data on midsummer transpiration rates of tree seedlings are given in Table 12.6. The rate per unit of leaf surface is lower for loblolly pine than for the broadleaf species and the rates for holly and Gordonia, which have coriaceous leaves, are as high as the rates of trees such as yellow-poplar and red oak with mesomorphic leaves. Transpiration data for seedlings of two deciduous hardwoods and loblolly pine in Table 12.5 show that although the hardwoods transpired about twice as rapidly as pine per unit of leaf surface, the transpiration per seedling of similar size was greater for the pine because of its greater leaf surface. Long ago Groom (1910) found that the transpiration rate per unit of surface was lower in conifers, but the rate per tree was as high as in deciduous trees of similar size.

Seasonal cycles of transpiration for a deciduous and an evergreen species are shown in Fig. 12.18. In this experiment the average winter transpiration of loblolly pine was about 10% of the midsummer rate. In another experiment Kozlowski (1943) measured transpiration of evergreen and deciduous species in late December and early January (see Table 12.8) and the transpiration rate of loblolly pine was lower than that of the bare branches of the deciduous species. Both sets of measurements were made at Durham, North Carolina, but the weather may have been unusually cold during Kozlowski's measurements. Weaver and Mogensen (1919) in Nebraska and Ivanov (1924) at Leningrad reported that the winter transpiration rate of conifers was less than 1% of the summer rate. However, their winter temperatures were probably much lower than those usually occurring in North Carolina where warm sunny days are common.

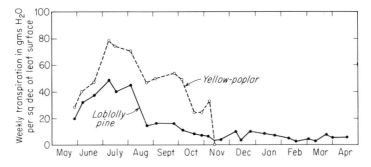

Fig. 12.18. Seasonal course of transpiration of potted seedlings of an evergreen and a deciduous tree species at Durham, North Carolina.

TABLE 12.8 Winter Transpiration Rates per Unit of Surface for Coniferous and Broadleaf Seedlings[a,b]

Seedling type	Transpiration rate (g/dm²/day)
Prunus laurocerasus[c]	1.65
Pinus taeda[c]	0.40
Acer saccharum[d]	0.26
Liriodendron tulipifera[d]	0.76
Quercus alba[d]	0.84

[a] Data for December 22 to January 5.
[b] From Kozlowski (1943).
[c] Per unit of leaf surface.
[d] Per unit of twig and stem surface.

Exposure to low temperature is said to greatly reduce transpiration of conifers (Christersson, 1972). Even in some parts of the tropics seasonal cycles in transpiration occur because of variations in rainfall, humidity, and soil moisture. Ringoet (1952), for example, found large seasonal differences in transpiration of oil palms growing in the Belgian Congo.

In view of the errors inherent in measurements of transpiration, readers may question the usefulness of presenting any actual rates. However, some of the data are more reliable than might have been expected. For example, summer transpiration rates of potted seedlings of yellow-poplar averaged 10.1 g/dm²/day at Columbus, Ohio, and 11.7 g/dm²/day at Durham, North Carolina. Comparison of the transpiration of six species of trees by two methods and four different investigators, shown in Table

TABLE 12.9 Relative Transpiration Rates of Various Tree Species[a]

	Investigator			
Species	Eidmann[b]	Huber[c]	Pisek and Cartellieri[c]	Polster[c]
Birch	618		541	740
Oak	282	468 (377–559)	512	460
Beech	268	379 (218–541)	137	372
Douglas-fir	130			94
Spruce	100	100 (64–136)	100	100
Pine	181	134 (118–150)	133	139
Larch	310	409 (341–476)	212	212

[a] From Huber (1953).
[b] Data taken from potted plants.
[c] Data taken from rapid weighing of cut branches.

12.9, all indicated that birch had the highest rate and spruce the lowest rate. Huber (1953) also commented on the surprisingly good agreement concerning relative rates of transpiration of various species measured in different ways. The principal difficulty arises when attempts are made to extrapolate from measurements made on seedlings or leaves to entire stands of trees.

WATER LOSS FROM PLANT STANDS

Foresters, horticulturists, and agriculturists are more interested in the amount of water lost from stands of plants than in the loss from individual plants. The loss from a forest, orchard, field, or grassland includes both transpiration from the vegetation and evaporation from the soil surface and the combined losses are usually termed evapotranspiration.

Methods of Measurement

Early attempts were made to estimate water loss from forests from the average daily transpiration rates per unit of leaf surface and the leaf surface per unit of soil surface. Using this method, Polster (1950) calculated the transpiration rates of German forests to range from 5.3 mm/day for Douglas-fir and 4.7 mm for birch to 2.3 mm for Scotch pine. By the middle of this century foresters and ecologists were turning to other methods (Huber, 1953). Four general methods often used to measure water loss from land surfaces are: (1) use of the water balance equation, (2) use of the energy balance equation, (3) the aerodynamic or vapor flow method, and (4) estimation by empirical formulas from meteorological data or rates of pan evaporation (Tanner, 1968). Useful data have also been obtained from lysimeters such as those in Holland and at San Dimas, California, and from controlled watersheds such as those in Africa, Switzerland, Colorado, North Carolina, and West Virginia.

Kramer (1969) discussed these methods briefly and Slatyer (1967) in more detail. Tanner (1967) discussed their advantages and disadvantages, and in a later paper dealt with their applications to forestry (Tanner, 1968). Rutter (1968) has an interesting discussion of evapotranspiration in relation to forestry and Horton (1973) compiled a useful collection of abstracts of papers dealing with water loss from forests.

Factors Controlling Evapotranspiration

Evaporation from soil and transpiration from plants may be regarded as alternative pathways for water movement into the bulk air. As mentioned earlier, evaporation depends on the supply of energy required to vaporize water, the difference in vapor pressure between the evaporating surface and the bulk air, and the resistances in the pathway. Escape of water vapor from vegetation (transpiration) is complicated by plant control over internal resistance and the variable nature of the evaporating surfaces. However, evapotranspiration can be described by a slight modification of Eq. (12.6):

$$E = \frac{C_{int} - C_{air}}{r_{int} + r_{air}} = \frac{e_{int} - e_{air}}{r_{int} + r_{air}} \tag{12.9}$$

The subscript int refers to the internal part of the pathway between the evaporating surface and the soil or plant surface. In wet soils r_{int} is negligible and C_{int} is the soil surface, but as the soil dries the evaporating surface retreats into the soil mass, r_{int} becomes important and the rate of evaporation decreases. When leaf surfaces are dry the evaporating surfaces are within them, but in stands of plants the surface of the stand is sometimes treated as the evaporating surface. However, this is an oversimplification because both air and leaf conditions vary from bottom to top of a crop canopy. Waggoner and Reifsnyder (1968) developed a model to deal with the interaction of factors which affect evaporation within a canopy if the incident radiation and resistances and leaf areas at various levels are known. The complex problems involved in the water relations of plants stands were discussed by Slatyer (1967, Chapter 2) and by Waggoner and Turner (1971), and will be dealt with only briefly.

The amount of water evaporated from a unit area of the earth's surface depends first of all on the energy available. Since on a bright summer day 320 to 380 gm cal/cm² are available to evaporate water and 570 calories are required to evaporate 1 gm of water, the maximum possible amount of evaporation is approximately 6 mm/day. However, incident energy sometimes is supplemented by advection (horizontal flow) of energy from the surroundings, as in the case of exposed trees or cultivated fields surrounded by desert—the so-called "oasis effect." Although the leaf area of stands of plants is commonly four to six times that of the soil on which they are growing the rate of water loss cannot exceed that from moist soil or a water surface receiving the same amount of energy.

Effects of Changes in Plant Cover

Foresters, hydrologists, and agriculturists are concerned with the effects of changes in composition, height, and density of vegetation in stands on the rate of water loss. It is often stated that the rate of water loss from closed stands of all sorts, including grass, cultivated crops, and forests, is similar as long as the soil is moist. However, as Rider (1957) warned, this statement should be viewed with caution because the albedo and the internal resistance differ among different types of vegetation. A light-colored canopy presumably would lose less water. According to Rutter (1968, p. 66) the stomatal resistance in forest stands probably is somewhat higher than in stands of herbaceous plants. However, the surfaces of forest canopies often are more irregular than those of low-growing crops and this should result in greater turbulence, reducing r_{int} as compared with crops having a very uniform surface. Nevertheless, most studies show small differences among tree species and between forests and grasslands so long as water supply is not limiting, water loss from grassland being about 80% or more of that from forests. When soil water deficits develop, evapotranspiration from grassland decreases more than that from forests, perhaps partly because of shallower roots. The data from a number of studies are presented by Rutter (1968, pp. 45–57) and summarized in Table 12.10.

TABLE 12.10   Comparison of Annual Evaporation from Forest and Adjacent Grasslands Growing in Moist Soil[a,b]

Forest type	Forest	Adjacent grass	Grass/forest
Picea sitchensis	800	416	0.52
Picea abies	579	521	0.90
Mixed conifer–deciduous	861	696	0.81
Mixed deciduous	—	—	0.8–1.0
Eucalyptus niphophila	—	—	1.0

[a] From Rutter (1968, p. 51).
[b] Evaporation given in millimeters.

Thinning

The thinning of forest stands may or may not decrease evapotranspiration. Knoerr (1965) studied soil water depletion under stands of California red fir varying from 50 to 100% cover and found maximum water uptake by stands with 70 to 80% cover. Hewlett and Hibbert (1961) found that increase in water yield from a watershed at Coweeta, North Carolina, was approximately proportional to the reduction in basal area, but part of the increase may have been caused by decreased interception in the thinned stands. Removal of understory vegetation also appears to reduce water loss (Rutter, 1968, p. 43). The effects on water yield of thinning forest stands appear to be variable (Rutter, 1968, pp. 42–44), although Hibbert (1967) reported that the results of 30 studies indicated that, in general, reduction in forest cover increased water yield and reforestation was accompanied by decreased water yield.

Changes in Species

The effects of changing the species composition of a forest stand on water yield are complicated by the effects on interception of precipitation, and by differences in depth of rooting and length of the transpiring season. Most of the experiments cited by Rutter (1968, pp. 45–50) show little difference among species, at least in the summer. Measurements made in Denmark and Holland indicate that, as might be expected, water loss from conifers over a year exceeds that from deciduous species. In an experiment at Coweeta, North Carolina, 15 years after two experimental watersheds had been converted from mature, deciduous hardwood forest to eastern white pine, annual stream flow was reduced 20% (Swank and Douglass, 1974). Reduction occurred during every month, but the largest reductions were in the dormant and early growing season when the leaf area index was 9.9 for pine, but less than 1 for hardwoods, resulting in greater interception and subsequent evaporation from the pine than from the bare hardwoods. The stream flow data indicate that combined interception and transpiration losses also are greater for pine during the growing season.

Relative Losses by Evaporation and Transpiration

Where water yield is important there is much interest in the relative amounts of water lost by evaporation and transpiration. Over the whole United States about one-fourth of the total precipitation escapes as stream flow and three-fourths is returned to the atmosphere by evapotranspiration (Ackerman and Loff, 1959, Chapter 3). It was stated in the preceding sections that there appear to be no large differences in water loss from different types of vegetation growing in moist soil. However, as the soil dries differences in depth of rooting and plant control of transpiration may become important. It is claimed that both in the Central Valley of California (Biswell and Schultz, 1957) and in southern California (Pillsbury *et al.*, 1961) conversion of chaparral to grass greatly increases water runoff.

Clear-cutting lodgepole pine in Colorado increased stream flow about 30% (Wilm and Dunford, 1948) and removal of all woody vegetation from a watershed at Coweeta, North Carolina, increased stream flow more than 70% the first year. The increase was greater on north-facing slopes. The effects of removing forest cover on stream flow varied with the amount and seasonal distribution of precipitation and the amount per storm (Hewlett and Hibbert, 1967), hence it was not an accurate indicator of the rate of transpiration. The actual loss by transpiration from the Coweeta forests probably was considerably greater than the amount indicated by the increase in runoff after clear-cutting. Patric *et al.* (1965) measured soil water depletion under stands of trees growing in soil covered with plastic to prevent loss by evaporation and estimated transpiration from April through October to be 41 cm for a 21-year-old loblolly pine stand and 37.2 cm for a stand of oak and hickory. Stålfelt (1963) reported that evaporation of water from the surface soil under an open stand of Norway spruce made up 20% of the total water loss, but Rutter reported only 8% lost by evaporation under a stand of Scotch pine. Baumgartner (1967), using an energy balance method, calculated evaporation from the soil under forests, meadows, and cultivated crops to be 10, 25, and 45% of the total water loss. Experiments with corn plots at Urbana, Illinois, suggest that about 50% of the total evapotranspiration was by evaporation from the soil surface. Higher evaporation losses are to be expected from crops where the soil is much more exposed early in the growing season than in forests.

It is fairly common for evapotranspiration to exceed precipitation during the growing season, as in the Illinois corn field where total evapotranspiration from the control plants exceeded rainfall during the growing season by 9.7 to 13.7 cm in a 3-year experiment. Trees can sometimes be established in areas of limited rainfall but they die when the moisture reserve in the soil is exhausted. Bunger and Thomson (1938) observed this situation in the panhandle of Oklahoma. Wiggans (1936, 1937) reported that in a 20-year-old apple orchard in eastern Nebraska evapotranspiration was removing 28 to 38 cm more water per year than was replaced by precipitation. He predicted the imminent death of these trees, which were already removing water to a depth of about 10 m. Unfortunately, a severe autumn freeze killed them before the soil water reserve was exhausted. Many plantations of forest trees were established in the prairie and plains states in the 1880's and 1890's. Most of these trees grew well for a number of years, but eventually began to die because they had exhausted all of the reserve soil water and could not survive on the current rainfall during dry cycles.

Methods for Reducing Transpiration

In view of the damage caused by excessive transpiration there has been much interest in finding ways to reduce the rate of water loss. Efforts have been centered on three problems. Reduction of transpiration following transplanting would enable plants to maintain turgor until their root systems are reestablished. Reduction during droughts would enable plants to survive with minimal injury, and reduction of transpiration of the plant cover on watersheds would increase the water yield usable for other purposes. The methods used consist basically either of the application of waterproof coatings or of materials which cause closure of stomata. Substances intended to reduce transpiration are often termed antitranspirants.

Some early studies involved dipping or spraying the tops of seedlings with various substances such as latex emulsion, polyvinyl, polyethylene, and vinyl acrylate compounds. Some reduction in transpiration and some increase in survival were observed, but Allen (1955) suggested that further study of such coatings should be made before recommending their use. Lee and Kozlowski (1974) and Davies and Kozlowski (1975a) discussed problems encountered in the use of antitranspirant coatings on tree seedlings. Their effectiveness seems to depend on the species, stage of development, and atmospheric conditions during the test period (Gale and Hagan, 1966). According to Turner and DeRoo (1974), antitranspirants do not reduce injury to evergreen trees when the air temperature is below freezing, but may be effective in the spring when air temperatures rise but the soil remains cold or frozen.

Films have limited usefulness on growing plants because repeated applications are necessary on plants with increasing leaf surfaces and because substances impermeable to water vapor also are quite impermeable to carbon dioxide and reduce the rate of photosynthesis. At this time films seem useful only where reduction of transpiration is more important than a high rate of photosynthesis. An example might be their use on fruit trees to increase the size of ripening fruit and improve its keeping qualities after picking (Uriu *et al.*, 1975).

Application of substances that bring about closure of stomata appears to be more promising because partial closure of stomata should reduce transpiration more than it reduces photosynthesis. This claim is based on the observation of Gaastra (1959) that the mesophyll resistance for entrance of carbon dioxide is considerably higher than the resistances affecting the exit of water vapor. Thus, a large increase in r_s should have a smaller effect on carbon dioxide uptake than on water loss. Slatyer and Bierhuizen (1964b) reported that they reduced transpiration more than photosynthesis by closing stomata with phenylmercuric acetate. On the other hand, it is reported that photosynthesis and transpiration were decreased to the same extent by stomatal closure in cotton, tomato, and loblolly pine (Barrs, 1968; Brix, 1962).

One of the more promising compounds for causing stomatal closure was phenylmercuric acetate, which was reported by Waggoner and Bravdo (1967) to significantly reduce transpiration of an entire pine stand. Unfortunately, it would be undesirable to add more mercury compounds to our already polluted environment. Furthermore, Waisel *et al.* (1969) reported that phenylmercuric acetate injured leaves of birch. Keller (1966) noted that both phenylmercuric acetate and a film-forming polyvinyl compound reduced photosynthesis and root growth of spruce seedlings and the phenylmercuric acetate injured the needles. Phenylmercuric acetate also is said to reduce vegetative growth of tea (Nagarajah and Ratnasooriya, 1977). After the discovery that abscisic acid inhibits stomatal opening it was tried as an antitranspirant (Jones and Mansfield, 1972). Davies and Kozlowski (1975a) found that it reduced transpiration of sugar maple, white ash, and Calamondin orange seedlings as much as 60%, and some reduction persisted up to 21 days after treatment. No toxic effects were observed. In another series of experiments a silicone coating was more effective than abscisic acid in reducing the transpiration of white ash and red pine seedlings (Davies and Kozlowski, 1975b). However, it was concluded that film-forming antitranspirants may be unsatisfactory for use on some gymnosperms because they reduced photosynthesis by 95% for at least 12 days. It appears that more research will be necessary to develop satisfactory methods of controlling transpiration. The effect of antitranspirants on photosynthesis was discussed in Chapter 5.

Transpiration Ratio

There is considerable interest in the amount of water required to produce a unit of dry matter, sometimes termed the transpiration ratio. Miller (1938) summarized the large amount of data accumulated on the transpiration ratio of crop plants, which ranges from 200 to 1,100 grams of water per gram of dry weight for various kinds of plants. The lowest ratio reported is about 50 for pineapple (Ekern, 1965). Slatyer (1967) pointed out that it might be as high as 5,000 for semideserts where plants are widely separated and relatively little energy is intercepted by leaves. Few data are available for trees, but Polster (1950) estimated that in Germany the amount of water required to produce 1 g of dry matter varied from 170 in beech and Douglas-fir to 300 g in Scotch pine, 317 in birch, and 344 in English oak. Koch (1957) claims that the ratio of photosynthesis to transpiration is more favorable in somewhat cloudy weather than in bright sunny weather because transpiration is reduced more than photosynthesis. Tranquillini (1969) made interesting calculations of what he termed the productivity of transpiration, described by the ratio of photosynthesis to transpiration at various wind speeds. The relationship was similar at all wind speeds for larch and spruce. Water loss decreased more than photosynthesis at first for Swiss stone pine, mountain ash and *Rhododendron*, but at higher wind speeds the rate of photosynthesis of *Rhododendron* decreased more rapidly than transpiration. Photosynthesis of green alder began to decrease more rapidly than water loss at the lowest wind speeds used.

Water Use Efficiency

The term water use efficiency, sometimes abbreviated as WUE, is increasingly employed to describe the relationship between plant production and water consumption. It is defined by Begg and Turner (1976) as the ratio of dry matter produced to water used in evapotranspiration. Because it includes water used by both transpiration and evaporation it is a more realistic description of conditions in the field and forest than the transpiration ratio.

As pointed out earlier, little can be done to modify the rate of evapotranspiration because this is controlled chiefly by the incident energy available to evaporate water. However, in agriculture the efficiency of water use can be increased by increasing the density of plant cover so that little radiation reaches the soil and evaporation is kept to a minimum. Under these conditions the largest possible fraction of the incident energy should be used in photosynthesis and the most dry matter produced per unit of water evaporated. However, maximum production of dry matter sometimes is less important in forest management than other considerations such as water yield from forested watersheds. As mentioned in an earlier section, stream flow often is increased by thinning, or even removing all trees. This is largely because deep-rooted trees remove water from much greater depths than does more shallow-rooted herbaceous vegetation. In spite of extensive research, questions still exist concerning the best kind of plant cover to use on specific watersheds to minimize erosion and maximize long-term water yield.

GENERAL REFERENCES

Allaway, W. G., and Milthorpe, F. G. (1976). Structure and functioning of stomata. *In* "Water Deficits and Plant Growth" (T. T. Kozlowski, ed.), Vol. 4, pp. 57–102. Academic Press, New York.

Fritts, H. C. (1977). "Tree Rings and Climate." Academic Press, New York.

Hinckley, T. M., Lassoie, J. P., and Running, S. W. (1978). Temporal and spatial variations in the water status of forest trees. *For. Sci. Monogr.* **20.**

Kozlowski, T. T., ed. (1968–1978). "Water Deficits and Plant Growth," Vols. 1–5. Academic Press, New York.

Kramer, P. J. (1969). "Plant and Soil Water Relationships: A Modern Synthesis." McGraw-Hill, New York.

Lange, O. L., Kappen, L., and Schulze, E. D., eds. (1976). "Water and Plant Life." Springer-Verlag, Berlin and New York.

Maximov, N. A. (1929). "The Plant in Relation to Water." Allen & Unwin, London.

Meidner, H., and Mansfield, T. A. (1968). "Physiology of Stomata." McGraw-Hill, New York.

Slatyer, R. O. (1967). "Plant Water Relationships." Academic Press, New York.

Slavik, B. (1974). "Methods of Studying Plant Water Relations." Czech. Acad. Sci. Publ. House, Prague.

Zahner, R. (1968). Water deficits and growth of trees. *In* "Water Deficits and Plant Growth" (T. T. Kozlowski, ed.), Vol. 2, pp. 191–254. Academic Press, New York.

13

Absorption of Water, Ascent of Sap, and Water Balance

In the preceding chapter it was stated that transpiration is the dominant process in plant water relations because it largely controls the rate of water absorption and movement through plants and causes water deficits. Continuous absorption of sufficient water to replace that lost by transpiration is essential for the growth and even the survival of plants. This chapter deals with three major areas of water relations: water absorption and related processes such as root and stem pressures, ascent of sap, and the water balance of plants.

THE ABSORPTION OF WATER

Most of the water absorbed by plants enters as liquid through their roots, but a small amount is absorbed through leaves and even through twigs.

Absorption through Leaves and Stems

Although the quantity of water absorbed through leaves and stems is very small, it has received considerable attention. The early literature, reviewed by Miller (1938, pp. 188–190), indicated that significant amounts of water can enter the leaves of many kinds of plants. The fact that the cuticle, when wetted, is moderately permeable permits foliar fertilization, which was discussed in Chapter 10. There also is some absorption of mineral nutrients and presumably of water through lenticels and other gaps in the bark, and even through leaf scars. The amount of dew absorbed and its importance to the water economy of plants was discussed by Stone (1957) and little has been added since. Stone and Fowells (1955) showed that in greenhouse experiments dew increased the survival of seedlings of ponderosa pine. However, there is a strong difference in opinion concerning its importance under field conditions, exemplified by the views of Gindel and Monteith. The latter argued that true dew, that is, atmospheric moisture condensed on leaves, is of little practical importance because of the small quantity of water supplied by this process. Monteith (1963) estimated that the maximum possible amount of dew deposited in one night is less than 0.5 mm and reports of larger deposits involve errors in measurement, such as inclusion of water vapor evaporated from the soil. On the other hand Duvdevani (1957, 1964) and Gindel (1973) in Israel claim that dew is important not only for survival but even for growth of both herbs and woody plants. Gindel (1966, 1973) even claims that Aleppo pine absorbs moisture from the air and transmits it to the roots where it moves out and brings about a measurable increase in soil water content in the root zone (1966, 1973). However, this increase in water content may occur because the cooler shaded soil under trees may function as a "sink" for water vapor.

Absorption of water by pine seedlings from a saturated atmosphere was demonstrated by Stone *et al.* (1950), and Slatyer (1956) also observed absorption of water from saturated air by either roots or shoots of pine seedlings and transport through the seedlings when a strong gradient in water potential was imposed. Breazeale and Crider (1934) reported that water was absorbed from the air, transported through plants, and escaped into the soil. It is claimed by F. Sudzuki that *Prosopis tamarugo,* growing in the Atacama Desert of Northern Chile where rainfall is negligible, depends on water vapor absorbed through its leaves for water (Went, 1975). Some of these situations deserve more study.

The converse of absorption through leaves is the leaching of minerals out of leaves by rain or sprinkler irrigation (Tukey *et al.,* 1965). Dew and fog drip also cause leaching. According to Madgwick and Ovington (1959) deciduous species lose more nutrients than conifers by leaching during the summer, but leaching from conifer leaves continues during the winter. Obviously if solutes can be leached out intake of water and solutes can also occur when liquid is present on leaf surfaces and the gradient in water potential is favorable.

Absorption through Roots

Root systems of woody perennial plants consist of roots in all stages of development from delicate, newly formed, unsuberized tips less than 1 mm in diameter to old woody roots covered with a thick layer of bark and having a diameter of many centimeters. Furthermore, roots are often modified by the presence of mycorrhizal fungi. As a result there are wide variations in permeability to water and salt, as is shown in Table 13.1. Figure 13.1 shows the tissues through which water must pass in order to enter young roots of yellow-poplar. The walls of the epidermal and cortical cells are composed largely of cellulose at this stage, but the walls of the endodermal cells already are beginning to thicken. Strips of suberized tissue, the Casparian strips, develop on the radial walls and are generally assumed to decrease their permeability to water and solutes. However, recent research suggests that the endodermis does not always form an impermeable barrier to water and solutes. For example, as young roots develop in the pericycle and push out through the endodermis, gaps are produced through which water and solutes can enter freely until the endodermis of the branch and parent roots is connected (Dumbroff and Peirson, 1971; Queen, 1967). Clarkson *et al.* (1971) suggest that water and solute movement may occur through plasmodesmata in the endodermal cell walls. Whatever the details, it seems certain that significant quantities of water and ions cross the endodermis many centimeters behind the tip in herbaceous roots and probably also in woody roots.

As roots grow older, the epidermis, roots hairs, and part of the cortex are destroyed by a cork cambium that develops in the outer part of the cortex (Fig. 13.2). Eventually

TABLE 13.1 Relative Permeabilities of Grape Roots of Various Ages to Water and ^{32}P[a,b]

	Relative permeabilities	
Zone and condition of roots	Water	^{32}P
Roots of Current Season		
(Growing)		
A Terminal 8 cm, elongating, unbranched, unsuberized	1	1
B Unsuberized, bearing elongating branches	155	75
(Dormant)		
B Main axis and branches dormant and partially suberized		
before elongation completed	545	320
C Main axis and branches dormant and partially suberized	65	35
Roots of Preceding Seasons		
(Segments bearing branches)		
E Heavily suberized main axis with many short suberized		
branches	0.2	0.04
(Segments unbranched)		
G Heavily suberized, thick bark, and relatively small xylem		
cylinder		
Intact	0.2	0.02
Decorticated	290.0	140.00

[a] From Queen (1967).
[b] Measurements taken under a pressure gradient of 660 mb.

even the endodermis is lost as a result of cambial activity and the root consists of xylem, cambium, phloem, and a suberized layer in the outer surface of the phloem.

It formerly was assumed that water and solutes move from cell to cell across the vacuoles of the cells lying between the root surface and the xylem, but the experiments of Strugger (1949) suggested that considerable movement of water may occur in the cell walls. There has been increasing support for this view in recent years. It is supported by evidence that the resistance to water flow through unsuberized cell walls is much lower than the resistance to flow across the protoplasts (Kramer, 1969, pp. 117–118 and 154), although this view is questioned by Newman (1976) who argues that most water movement probably occurs in the symplast. Presumably the Casparian strips block water movement through the walls of endodermal cells, but as stated earlier there probably is considerable mass flow through gaps in the endodermis and the endodermis is not always a complete barrier.

There is increasing evidence that considerable absorption occurs through the older suberized roots of woody plants. Newly planted tree seedlings bear few or no unsuberized roots and some survive for many months without producing new roots (Lopushinsky and Beebe, 1976). Citrus in California and pines in the Southeastern United States possess practically no growing roots in the winter, yet they must absorb large quantities of water on sunny days to replace losses by transpiration. Kramer and

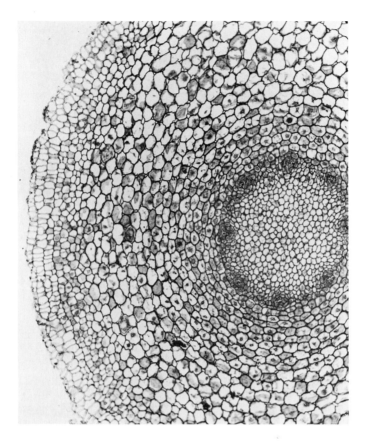

Fig. 13.1. Cross section of a young root of yellow-poplar ($\times$ ~80) about 0.6 mm behind the apex. Note the thick layer of cortical parenchyma surrounding the stele. From Popham (1952). By permission of the author.

Bullock (1966) found that during the summer less than one percent of the root surface under stands of yellow-poplar and loblolly pine was unsuberized and Head (1967) found a marked reduction in production of new roots on apple and plum during the summer. All three authors concluded that considerable amounts of water and salt must be absorbed through suberized roots. Direct measurements also indicate considerable absorption of water and solutes through suberized roots (Table 13.1; Queen 1967; Kramer and Bullock, 1966; Chung and Kramer, 1975). More information on root systems is presented in Chapter 2.

Root Resistance. In addition to the changes in resistance to water flow caused by maturation of roots there are puzzling changes in apparent root resistance related to rate of transpiration and water flow through roots. Some investigators report that apparent

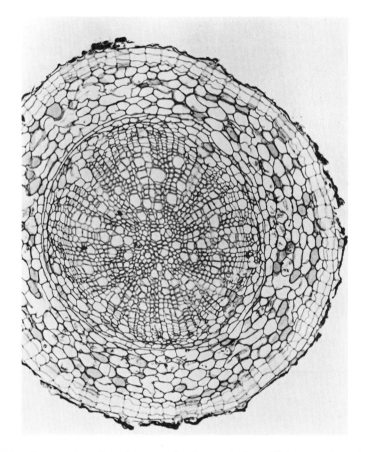

Fig. 13.2. Cross section of an older root of yellow-poplar ($\times$ ~60) from which most of the outer parenchyma has sloughed off. A layer of suberized tissue is developing at the outer surface. From Popham (1952). By permission of the author.

root resistance decreases as transpiration and water flow increase, but others do not (see Weatherley, 1976, for references). Fiscus attempted to explain the contradictory evidence as resulting from the varying contributions of osmotic and mass or hydraulic flow to total water flow as the rate of flow increases (Fiscus and Kramer, 1975). Diurnal changes in apparent root resistance also have been reported with a minimum at midday and a maximum near midnight (Parsons and Kramer, 1974). These cycles seem to be related to signals from the shoots because the cycles could be reset by changing the light-dark cycle to which the shoots were exposed. Research by Bunce (1978) on herbaceous plants also indicates that apparent root resistance is affected by the treatment of the shoot. Thus experimental conditions may materially influence measurements of apparent root resistance.

WATER ABSORPTION MECHANISMS

Following the terminology of Renner (1915), water absorption occurs by two mechanisms, active absorption which is common in slowly transpiring plants and passive absorption which predominates in actively transpiring plants and is responsible for most of the water absorption by woody plants. It should be emphasized that all water absorption occurs along gradients in water potential, from the medium in which the roots are growing, to the xylem. The difference between active and passive absorption is in the manner in which these gradients are produced.

Active Absorption

The roots of plants growing in warm, well-aerated, moist soil function as osmometers when the plants are transpiring slowly, because accumulation of salt in the xylem sap lowers the osmotic potential and consequently the water potential below the water potential of the soil. The resulting inward diffusion of water produces the "root pressure" that is responsible for guttation and the exudation from wounds observed in some plants such as birch trees and grape vines. Attempts have been made to explain root pressure as caused by active secretion of water or by electroosmosis, but a simple osmotic theory seems to provide an adequate explanation. There is no evidence that active transport of water even occurs in plants and electroosmosis probably could not move the volume of water that exudes from detopped root systems.

The principal problems are to explain how ions are concentrated in the xylem and what constitutes the ion barrier within which they are accumulated. It seems possible that the parenchyma cells bordering the xylem vessels actually secrete ions into the nonliving vessels (Läuchli *et al.*, 1971), but some writers have suggested that part of the solutes comes from the protoplasts of cells that are differentiating into xylem elements. Most of the literature on this topic was discussed by Kramer (1969, pp. 155–159). The endodermis usually is described as the ion barrier or differentially permeable membrane in roots, but Atkins (1916) proposed that the entire cortex might function as a multicellular, differentially permeable membrane. There is still a need to explain the diurnal variations in root pressure that have been reported for over a century and are shown in Fig. 13.3 (Vaadia, 1960; Parsons and Kramer, 1974). Also there is no fully adequate explanation for the fact that some species, including most conifers, seldom or never develop root pressure, although the observations of O'Leary (1965) suggest a possible reason. O'Leary obtained no exudation from stumps of healthy loblolly pine, white spruce, or sugar maple seedlings although stumps of red maple, birch, yellow-poplar, and grape exuded sap freely. However, he found that apical root segments of the three species that showed no exudation from the stumps produced measurable exudation and the sap contained considerable salt. Thus failure to exhibit root pressure did not result from failure to accumulate salt in the xylem sap. However, it is possible that the high internal resistance to longitudinal movement of water in the roots, combined with a tendency for sap to leak out of older regions of roots under

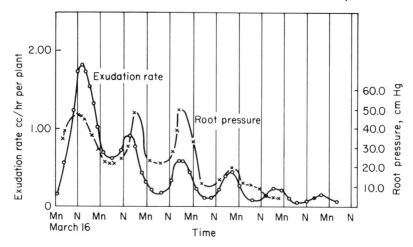

Fig. 13.3. Diurnal fluctuation in rate of exudation and root pressure of sunflower root systems kept at constant temperature for 6 days. Plants were in half-strength Hoagland solution during the experiment. From Vaadia (1960).

pressure, prevents transmission to the shoot of any pressure developed in the apical areas of roots. White *et al.* (1958) and Dimbleby (1952) also reported exudation from severed roots of conifers. Queen (1967) found that root pressure developed in dormant grapes even when no growing roots were present.

Passive Absorption

As the rate of transpiration increases and tension develops in the xylem sap, mass inflow of water begins to occur. This sweeps out the salt accumulated in the root xylem sap (Lopushinsky, 1964) and decreases the amount of osmotic movement. The roots become passive absorbing surfaces through which water is pulled in by mass flow generated in the transpiring shoots. It seems likely that practically all of the water absorption by transpiring plants, both woody and herbaceous, occurs passively. Writers such as Rufelt (1956) and Brouwer (1965), who claim that active and passive absorption act in parallel, even in rapidly transpiring plants, overlook the fact that rapid flow of water through the roots dilutes salt in the root xylem and destroys the osmotic gradient on which active absorption depends.

ROOT AND STEM PRESSURES

From very early days men have observed the exudation of sap from injured plants. In the Far East sap has been obtained from palms to make sugar and wine from before the beginning of recorded history. According to Evelyn (1670) birches had long been tapped in England and on the Continent and the sap was used for various purposes, including fermenting beer. Renewed interest in the use of birch sap has developed in the Ukraine, according to Sendak (1978). The first Europeans to visit Canada and New England found the Indians tapping maple trees and boiling down the sap to make sugar, and in Mexico the Spanish conquistadors found the natives collecting the sugar sap from agave and fermenting it into pulque. Unfortunately, early writers indiscriminately grouped together all examples of "bleeding" or "weeping" without regard to their origin. Wieler (1893) listed nearly 200 species belonging to many genera, but his list included examples of true root pressure, sap flow from wounds, guttation, and even secretion from glandular hairs. It is necessary to distinguish between sap flow caused by root pressure, as in grape and birch, and that caused by stem pressure, as in maple, or by wounding, as in palms.

Root Pressure

Root pressure is not common among trees of the Temperate Zone and occurs chiefly in the spring before leaves develop and transpiration is rapid. However, Parker (1964) reported copious exudation from black birch in New England in October and November, after leaf fall. There was no exudation following a dry summer. The daily course of root pressure is shown in Fig. 13.3. Clark (1874) tested over 60 species of woody plants in Massachusetts and found exudation from only a few species, including maple, birch, walnut, hophornbean, and grape. Hales (1727) made the first published measurements of root pressure and reported a pressure of 1 bar in grape while Clark (1874) and Merwin and Lyon (1909) reported pressures of 2 or 3 bars in birch. Stem and root pressures in maple and birch are shown in Fig. 13.4. According to Clark (1874) a paper birch 37.5 cm in diameter produced 28 liters of sap in one day and 675 liters during the spring, and Johnson (1944) reported yields of 20 to 100 liters in a season from paper birch trees 20 to 38.5 cm in diameter. Yield was not proportional to diameter, some small trees producing more sap than larger ones. Sap flow ceases as leaves develop and increasing transpiration produces negative pressure or tension in the xylem sap. The sugar content of birch sap is about 1.5%, lower than that of maple sap, and consists chiefly of reducing sugar.

Bollard (1960) reviewed the extensive literature on the composition of xylem sap and pointed out that it plays an important role in the translocation of minerals and organic nitrogen compounds synthesized in the roots. The xylem sap of some woody plants also contains cytokinins and gibberellins, and further study will probably reveal that these substances are generally present. The mineral content of xylem sap varies with the supply of salt available to the roots and with the season (see Figs. 10.12 and 13.5; also Bennett *et al.,* 1927; Carter and Larsen, 1965). Some investigators have attempted to use the composition of xylem sap as a guide to the mineral nutrient needs of plants. However, more useful information can be obtained by foliar analysis.

Guttation

In herbaceous plants the most common evidence of root pressure is the exudation of droplets of liquid from the margins and tips of leaves. The quantity of liquid exuded

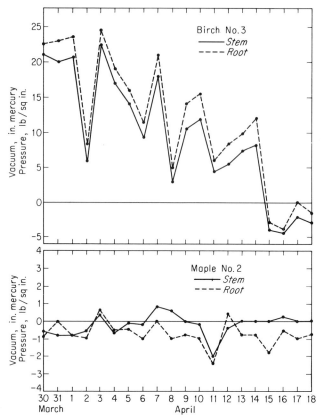

Fig. 13.4. Simultaneous measurements of root and stem pressure in river birch and red maple. Root pressures in birch exceed stem pressures and the two change almost simultaneously. Root pressure is usually absent in maple, even when positive pressure exists in the stems.

varies from a few drops to many milliliters, and the composition varies from almost pure water to a dilute solution of organic and inorganic substances. Guttation usually occurs through stomatalike openings in the epidermis called hydathodes, which are located near the ends of veins. In tropical rain forests guttation is common at night, but it is uncommon in woody plants of the Temperate Zone because the necessary combination of warm, moist soil and humid air is less common than in the tropics. A few instances of guttation from the twigs of trees have been reported (Büsgen and Münch, 1931). Raber (1937) observed sap flow from leaf scars of deciduous trees in Louisiana after leaf fall, and Friesner (1940) reported exudation from stump sprouts of red maple in February in Indiana. Exudation of liquid from roots and root hairs of woody plants also has been reported (Head, 1964), and, since this probably is caused by root pressure, it may be termed root guttation. No guttation has ever been reported in conifers, as would be expected because of the absence of root pressure, but artificial

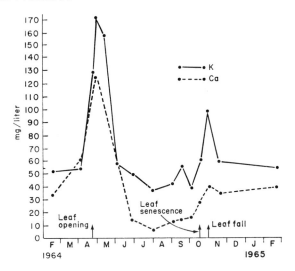

Fig. 13.5. Seasonal changes in concentration of calcium and potassium in xylem sap of hazel growing in Belgium. From Denaeyer-DeSmet (1967).

guttation can be caused by subjecting the root system to pressure (Klepper and Kaufmann, 1966).

Guttation is of negligible importance to plants. Occasionally injury to leaf margins is caused by deposits of salt left by evaporation of guttated water and it is claimed that the guttated liquid provides a pathway for the entrance of pathogenic organisms. In general, however, guttation can be regarded as simply an incidental result of the development of hydrostatic pressure in slowly transpiring plants.

Maple Sap Flow

Maple sap flow deserves special attention both because it forms the basis of an important industry in the northeastern United States and because it is interesting physiologically. There are several reasons for believing that it occurs quite independently of root pressure, including the fact that pressure gauges attached to roots of maple often show negative pressure when stems show positive pressure (see Fig. 13.4). More convincing is the fact that segments of trunks and branches removed from maple trees show sap flow if supplied with water and subjected to temperatures that rise above and fall below freezing (Stevens and Eggert, 1945; Marvin and Greene, 1951). The extensive observations on maple sap flow made by Clark (1874, 1875) over a century ago are still applicable. In Massachusetts, maple sap flow can occur any time from October to April if freezing nights are followed by warm days. Sap flow ceases if temperatures are continuously above or below freezing; it ceases in the spring when night temperatures no longer fall below freezing and it usually ceases in the afternoon and does not start again until the temperature rises above freezing the next morning.

Failure to understand that sap pressure in the stems of trees often undergoes daily variations from positive to negative has led to unfortunate errors in the interpretation of experimental data (Kramer, 1940). In contrast to the situation in maple, the root-pressure-generated flow of birch and grape sap increases as the soil warms until increased transpiration caused by opening of leaves brings an end to root pressure.

Sap flow usually starts first on the south side of trees, but it also occurs later from holes drilled in the north side of tree trunks. The sap comes from the sapwood and in Vermont over 60% of the flow occurs between 9:00 A.M. and noon (Jones et al., 1903). Because of its dependence on weather, sap flow usually is intermittent and 2 or 3 to 10 or 12 "runs" may occur in a single spring. Some producers of maple syrup are now using vacuums to increase the sap flow (Koelling et al., 1968). Sometimes the yield for a season can be more than tripled because sap can be obtained with vacuums on days when little or no flow would normally occur. According to Bryan et al. (1937), the average yield without vacuum is from 38 to 75 liters/tree in a season but occasional trees yield 150 liters. The sugar content varies from 0.5 to 7.0 or even 10.0%, but it usually is 2.0 or 3.0%, much lower than the sugar content of palm sap. Taylor (1956) made an extensive study which indicates that significant differences exist in the sugar content of sap from different trees and stands of trees. This indicates that selection of trees for high yields of sugar might be possible. Morselli, et al. (1978) reported that high yielding maple trees have more and larger rays than low yielding trees. The sugar concentration is typically low early in the season, rises quickly to a maximum, then gradually decreases later in the season. In addition to sucrose and a small amount of glucose, maple sap contains small amounts of inorganic salts, nitrogenous compounds such as peptides and amino acids, amylases, and unidentified organic constituents (Taylor, 1956). The characteristic taste is attributed to certain amino acids and is developed by heating (Pollard and Sproston, 1954). The sugar comes from starch accumulated during the preceding summer which is converted into sucrose in the late autumn and early winter. The activity of the enzymes involved in this conversion seems to be increased by low temperatures. According to Sauter et al. (1973) the sucrose is secreted into the xylem, causing a high concentration of sugar in the xylem sap. Apparently the loss of sugar by tapping is not injurious because many trees have been tapped for decades without apparent injury. More recently, trees have been tapped under vacuum for over 10 years without injury. Jones et al. (1903) estimated that tapping maples removes less than 10% of the total sugar, a loss too small to be important unless conditions were very unfavorable for photosynthesis the following summer. Trees on infertile or dry soil will yield less than those growing on fertile, moist soil. Sugar yield is obviously related to photosynthesis and large, well-exposed crowns are advantageous. Fertilization is also said to increase the yield. Trees grown for sap production should be more widely spaced than those grown for timber, and roadside trees are said to produce large quantities of sap. Jones et al. (1903) reported that defoliation during the summer greatly reduced syrup yield the next spring.

The flow of maple sap seems to be caused by stem pressure produced by rising temperatures following low but not necessarily freezing temperatures. One of the more recent explanations was developed by Sauter (1971) and his colleagues while working at the Harvard Forest. According to his explanation carbon dioxide accumulates in the intercellular spaces during the day and the resulting pressure forces sap out of wounds. At night the CO_2 is absorbed, reducing the pressure and causing upward movement of water from the roots which refills the xylem vessels.

Other Examples of Stem Pressure

Two other plants that yield commercial quantities of sap are palms and agaves. In the tropical regions of India and Asia palm sap probably was used as a source of sugar before sugar cane was cultivated. It also is fermented to make palm wine. Production was recently reported to be over 150,000 metric tons of sugar per year, obtained chiefly from coconut, date, and Palmyra palms. According to Molisch (1902), who studied the process in Java, sap flow usually is caused by cutting out the inflorescence and it can be maintained for weeks or even months by repeatedly cutting and pounding the stem. Sap is also obtained from the Palmyra palms by making incisions into the bark, and this process can be repeated year after year. When the central bud is cut out of date palms, sap flow ceases after several weeks and the palm dies (Corner, 1966). Davis (1961) thought root pressure was important in palms, but he later reported that it is rare and probably plays no part in palm sap flow (Milburn and Davis, 1973). The sap apparently originates from the phloem and the sugar probably was mobilized for use in the developing inflorescence or stem tips. Sap flow from agaves and palms is discussed in more detail by Van Die and Tammes in Zimmermann and Milburn (1975).

Many accounts of high pressures developed in stems of trees probably are the result of wounding (Molisch, 1902). MacDougal (1926) reported exudation pressures in holes bored in stems of large cacti, Monterey pine, English walnut, and oak, but attributed them to effects of wounding rather than to root pressure. Occasionally, flow of sap occurs from cracks and other wounds in trees and it is fermented by yeasts and bacteria, causing "slime flux." According to Carter (1945), in elms slime flux is associated with a water-soaked condition of the heartwood, called wetwood, caused by bacterial activity. Stem pressures high enough to blow cores out of increment borers have been reported in trees with decaying heartwood (Abell and Hursh, 1931). In some instances the gas escaping from the holes burns when ignited, presumably because it contains methane produced by the organisms causing decay. The production of methane in trees is discussed by Zeikus and Ward (1974).

Oleoresin Flow

One of the most important examples of exudation caused by wounding is the flow from pines of oleoresin, which forms the basis of the naval stores industry. However, oleoresins come from specialized resin ducts and the flow is not related to the sap flows discussed in this chapter. The flow of latex from wounded stems of rubber trees is another important example of exudation, which was discussed in Chapter 8.

FACTORS AFFECTING WATER ABSORPTION

In moist soil the rate of water absorption is controlled primarily by two factors—the rate of transpiration, because it largely controls the water potential in the root xylem, and the efficiency of root systems as absorbing surfaces. As soil dries the availability of water begins to be limited by decreasing water potential and hydraulic conductivity. Soil aeration, soil temperature, and the concentration and composition of the soil solution also sometimes limit the absorption of water.

Soil Moisture

In general the rate of water absorption depends on the steepness of the gradient in water potential from soil to roots. As the soil dries, water becomes progressively less available because its potential decreases and resistance to movement toward roots increases. The relationship between soil water potential and moisture content is shown in Fig. 13.6. The readily available water is often described as that lying between field capacity and the permanent wilting percentage. Field capacity is the water content a few days after the soil has been wetted, and downward movement has become very slow, while the permanent wilting percentage is the water content at which plants remain wilted unless the soil is rewetted. It is obvious from Fig. 13.6 that there is much more readily available water in fine-textured than in coarse-textured soils. Neither field capacity nor permanent wilting percentage are physical constants, but merely convenient regions on the water potential–water content curve. The permanent wilting percentage is usually said to occur at about −15 bars, but this is because sunflowers or similar mesophytes are used to determine it (Slatyer, 1957). Slatyer found the water potential of severely wilted privet to be as low as −70 bars, and values much lower than −15 bars have been reported for other plants.

At one time it was argued that soil water either was or was not available to plants (Veihmeyer and Hendrickson, 1950), but that view has been abandoned as both theoretically and practically untenable. Many research projects on tree seedlings in containers have shown that water becomes progressively less available as the soil water potential decreases (Fig. 12.13, for example).

One area of uncertainty concerns the relative resistance to water flow through soil and roots (r_{soil} versus r_{root}) in drying soil. It is well known that the resistance to water flow through soil increases rapidly as soil dries because of decrease in cross section available to flow as the films of water decrease in thickness and discontinuities develop. It also appears that as the soil dries shrinkage of soil and roots sometimes occurs, causing decreased movement of water from soil to roots (Huck, Klepper, and Taylor, 1970; Weatherley, 1976). Gardner (1960) and Cowan (1965) estimated that resistance to water movement through the soil would exceed root resistance at a soil water potential of −1 or −2 bars and soil resistance would dominate water movement toward roots. However, Newman (1969) found that actual root densities usually are considerably greater than those assumed by Gardner and Cowan. If root densities are greater water need not move as far or as fast through the soil as previously assumed and

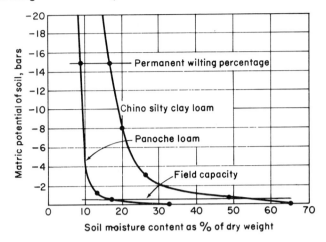

Fig. 13.6. The matric potentials of a sandy loam and a clay loam soil plotted over soil water content. The curve for Panoche loam is from Wadleigh *et al.* (1946) and that for Chino loam is from data of Richards and Weaver (1944).

soil resistance probably does not become a limiting factor for water absorption until the soil water potential approaches the permanent wilting percentage. This conclusion is also supported by the work of Lawlor (1972), although it is questioned by Caldwell (1976). It therefore seems that the availability of soil water ordinarily depends more on the steepness of the water potential gradient from soil to root (ψ_{root}-ψ_{soil}) than on the soil resistance (r_{soil}).

Concentration and Composition of Soil Solution

The soil water potential is controlled by the surface forces that bind water in capillaries and on surfaces (matric potential, ψ_m) and the osmotic forces produced by dissolved solutes (osmotic potential, ψ_s). If the osmotic potential is lower than -2 or -3 bars, plant growth is likely to be retarded even in soils with a water content near field capacity. However, excessive salinity is common only in arid regions where evapotranspiration greatly exceeds rainfall, and it is seldom a problem in forested areas. It sometimes is a problem for fruit trees in dry areas where the irrigation water often contains excessive amounts of salts. Also, there is some interest in identifying woody plants suitable for use in coastal areas where salt spray causes injury.

Soil Aeration

The growth and physiological activity of roots often are reduced by a deficiency of oxygen. While this is most severe in flooded soil, a chronic but moderate deficiency often exists in heavy clay soils which limits root penetration and possibly the uptake of mineral nutrients. It has even been suggested that poor aeration limited invasion of

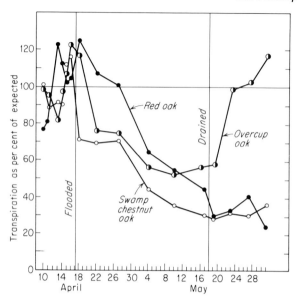

Fig. 13.7. Effects of flooding soil on water absorption as indicated by changes in rate of transpiration. Seedlings lost most of their leaves as a result of water stress caused by reduced water absorption, but the overcup oak was leafing out again when the soil was drained and recovered rapidly. From Parker (1950).

prairies by trees (McComb and Loomis, 1944). Flooding soil with water usually drastically reduces water absorption (Fig. 13.7) because it increases the resistance to water flow into roots. However, there are wide differences among species in flooding tolerance. Baldcypress and tupelo-gum grow indefinitely in flooded soil, willows thrive in saturated soil, many species survive annual periods of flooding, but some species such as dogwood and yellow-poplar are quickly killed in saturated soil.

Inadequate aeration not only reduces water and salt absorption but it reduces the synthetic activities of roots. There is evidence that the roots of at least some species synthesize cytokinins and gibberellins and it is well established that organic nitrogen compounds such as amides and amino acids are synthesized in the roots of many woody plants, including apple and other Rosaceous species (Bollard, 1958). Thus it is possible that deficient aeration and cold soil may reduce shoot growth by reducing the supply of growth regulators and organic nitrogen compounds, as well as by reducing water and salt absorption. Pereira and Kozlowski (1977b) discussed the numerous effects of flooding and the differences in response among tree species.

Soil Temperature

Many writers regard cold soil as an important ecological factor and the decreased availability of water in the cold soil at high altitudes may affect the vegetation (Whitfield, 1932; Clements and Martin, 1934) and the location of the timberline (Michaelis,

1934). Poorly drained soils are slow to warm up in the spring, and Firbas (1931) and Döring (1935) stated that the cold soils of European high moors limit plant growth. Cameron (1941) reported that orange trees often wilt during the winter in California because of slow absorption of water from cold soil. There are considerable differences among species with respect to the effects of low temperature on water absorption. Kozlowski (1943) found that absorption was reduced more in loblolly pine than in eastern white pine as the soil temperature was reduced from 15° to 5°C. In general, species from warm climates show greater reduction than species from cold climates, as is shown in Fig. 13.8. Citrus trees generally suffer more from cold soil than tree species from colder climates, but differences among varieties and species probably would be found if they were studied carefully.

Cold soil reduces water uptake in two ways—directly, by decreasing the permeability of the roots to water, and indirectly, by increasing the viscosity of water, which slows its movement through both soil and roots. The combined effect is an approximate doubling of the resistance to water flow through roots as the temperature decreases from 25° to 5°C. The reduced permeability at low temperatures is attributed by some writers to a transition from the liquid to the solid state of membrane lipids. For example, blocking of unsaturated fatty acid synthesis in cotton roots reduced water absorption in cold soil (St. John and Christiansen, 1976). The importance of the phase transition temperature of fatty acids also is discussed in Chapter 8.

Few data are available concerning the effects of high soil temperatures on water absorption, but Bialoglowski (1936) and Haas (1936) reported that temperatures above 30°C reduce water absorption of lemons, grapefruit, and Valencia oranges.

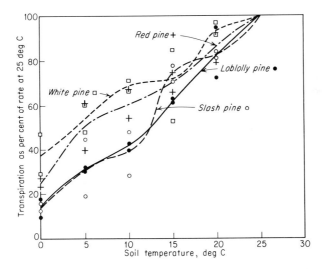

Fig. 13.8. Effect of cooling soil on water absorption of two southern and two northern species of pine, as measured by the rate of transpiration. Absorption from cold soil was reduced more in the southern species, slash and loblolly pine, than in the northern species, eastern white and red pine. From Kramer (1942).

There are secondary effects of temperature, such as decreased root extension and changes in root metabolism, but these are believed to be much less important than the direct effects on resistance to water flow.

Extent and Efficiency of Root Systems

The success of all kinds of plants with respect to water and mineral absorption depends on the extent and permeability of roots. These problems are dealt with in detail by Kramer (1969, Chapter 6) and by Caldwell (1976). As was mentioned in Chapter 2, most trees have root systems that extend beyond the spread of the branches and as deeply into the soil as aeration and soil physical structure permit. In closed stands of trees the soil is completely occupied by roots to a depth varying from 25 or 30 cm to several meters. On a deep, sandy loam soil at Davis, California, Proebsting (1943) found the maximum concentration of roots at 0.6 to 1.5 m, with many roots penetrating 5 m or more. According to Wiggans (1936), 18-year-old apple trees on a well-aerated loess soil in Nebraska were absorbing water from a depth of over 10 m. In contrast, pears on a poorly drained adobe soil in Oregon had nearly 90% of their roots in the upper meter of soil, and Coile (1937b) found that 90% of the roots were in the top 12.5 cm under pine and oak forests of the North Carolina Piedmont. The heavy concentration of small roots near the surface in North Carolina forests probably is partly caused by the poor aeration in deeper soil horizons and partly by the frequent wetting of a shallow surface layer by summer showers. In spite of the relatively small number of roots found deep in the soil under forest stands the soil is often dried to the permanent wilting percentage (Hoover *et al.,* 1953; Zahner, 1955). Russell (1973, Chapter 22) provides an interesting discussion of root development in relation to mineral and water absorption.

The efficiency of roots depends on the amount of surface in contact with the soil and on the permeability of the surface. Obviously, root systems bearing numerous small branches should be more efficient than systems consisting of fewer large, sparsely branched roots. Mycorrhizae presumably increase the efficiency of mineral absorption, chiefly because the hyphae extend out into the soil and thereby increase the absorbing surface. They also maintain an active absorption system on the older roots long after they have become suberized (Bowen, 1973). The effects of mycorrhizal roots on water absorption are more difficult to evaluate. Bowen (1973) stated that several investigators have reported that the presence of mycorrhizae increases drought resistance of tree seedlings. Also, resistance to water movement through soybean roots is decreased by the presence of mycorrhizae (Safir *et al.,* 1972). As stated earlier in this chapter, considerable absorption of water and minerals occurs through suberized roots in spite of their relatively low permeability.

THE ASCENT OF SAP

The existence of tall land plants became possible only after a vascular system evolved that permitted the rapid movement of water to the transpiring shoots. It is difficult for terrestrial plants more than 20 or 30 cm in height to exist in any except the most humid habitats without a vascular system, because water movement from cell to cell by diffusion is much too slow to keep the tops of transpiring plants from being dehydrated. The magnitude of the problem in trees is indicated by the fact that on a hot summer day 200 liters or more of water may move from the roots to the evaporating surfaces in the leaves 20, 30, or even 100 m above. Hales (1727) made careful observations on the absorption and loss of water and wrote, "The last three experiments all show that the capillary sap vessels imbibe moisture plentifully; but they have little power to protrude it farther without the assistance of the perspiring leaves, which do promote its progress." Hales' explanation foreshadowed our current explanation, although he did not understand how transpiration could "promote its progress." Toward the end of the 19th century, Boehm, Sachs, and Strasburger concluded that loss of water produces the pull causing the ascent of sap, but they also lacked an essential fact for a complete explanation. The final step was supplied by Askenasy (1895) and by Dixon and Joly (1895) who pointed out that water confined in small tubes such as the xylem elements has a very high cohesive force and can be subjected to tension. The history of study of the ascent of sap can be found in Miller (1938, pp. 855–872) and the ascent of sap is discussed in detail in Zimmermann and Brown (1971).

Although the cohesion theory of the ascent of sap has existed since the end of the 19th century, it has been rather reluctantly accepted and textbook writers still feel it necessary to defend it. Reluctance to accept the theory probably springs partly from an almost instinctive difficulty in believing that water can be subjected to tension, but it also arises from doubts about the possibility of maintaining a fragile, stressed system in a swaying tree trunk. The cohesion theory is based on the following premises:

1. Water has high internal cohesive forces and, when confined in small tubes with wettable walls, such as the xylem elements, it can sustain a tension of 30 to possibly 300 bars.

2. The water in a plant forms a continuous system in the water-saturated cell walls from the evaporating surfaces of the leaves to the absorbing surfaces of the roots.

3. When water evaporates from any part of the system, but chiefly from the leaves, the reduction in water potential at the evaporating surfaces causes movement of water out of the xylem to the evaporating surfaces.

4. Because of the cohesive attraction among water molecules, the loss of water produces tension in the xylem sap that is transmitted through the continuous water columns to the roots, where it reduces the water potential and causes inflow of water from the soil. Thus, as mentioned earlier, in the section, "Passive Absorption," in transpiring plants water absorption is controlled directly by the rate of transpiration.

There seems to be adequate evidence that water can sustain the tension necessary to pull sap to the top of tall trees. The theoretical intermolecular attractive forces in water are extremely large, and Ursprung (1915) measured a tension of 315 bars in annulus cells of fern sporangia while Briggs (1949) demonstrated a tension of 223 bars in water subjected to centrifugal force. Greenidge (1954) suggested that the highest tensions in trees would average only about 30 bars. However, measurements of xylem sap potential made with Scholander's pressure chamber indicate the existence of tensions up to 80 bars and a tension of only about 20 bars should suffice to overcome both gravity and the resistance to flow required to move water to the top of a tree 100 m in height (Dixon, 1914). It is true that many water columns break and Milburn and Johnson (1966) reported that by using an amplifying apparatus they could detect "clicks" as water columns broke in stems under stress. However, the bubbles formed by cavitation are composed of water vapor and usually are easily reabsorbed when the tension decreases. Data of Clark and Gibbs (1957) indicate that up to nearly 50% of the water in trunks of some trees may be replaced by gas during the summer (Fig. 13.9). However, the air that penetrates occupies only the larger vessels and does not block the entire conducting system. It has been demonstrated frequently that horizontal cuts made into a stem from opposite sides as close as 15 cm apart do not prevent the ascent of sap, because continuity of water columns is preserved in the shorter xylem elements and radial flow occurs around the cuts (Scholander *et al.,* 1957; Postlethwaite and Rogers, 1958; Mackay and Weatherley, 1973). However, the resistance to flow is increased.

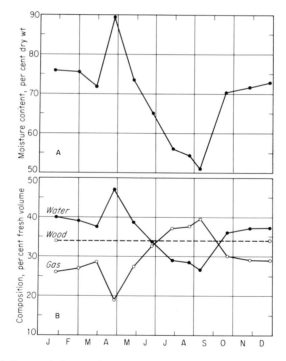

Fig. 13.9. (A) Seasonal changes in water content of yellow birch tree trunks determined from disks cut from the base, middle, and top of the trunks. (B) Seasonal changes in water and gas content of yellow birch tree trunks calculated as percentages of fresh volume. Note the midsummer decrease in water content and increase in gas content during the period of rapid transpiration, also the autumn increase after leaf fall. From Clark and Gibbs (1957).

Another difficulty with the cohesion theory is the possibility that freezing forces dissolved gases out of solution, forming bubbles that might block most or all of the xylem elements. However, Hammel (1967) reported that freezing stem segments and twigs of hemlock did not increase resistance to water flow after they were thawed, although it did produce an increase in resistance to flow in angiosperms. He suggested that in gymnosperms the sap is isolated in tracheids under pressure and the tiny gas bubbles are redissolved after thawing, but this does not occur in large vessels of ring-porous angiosperms. Zimmermann (1964b) suggested that in ring-porous trees such as oak and ash the old vessels remain filled with air, but new ones are formed each spring before the leaves are fully expanded. Diffuse-porous species probably behave like gymnosperms and the xylem is never blocked by gas bubbles. In a few species, such as birch and grape, root pressure may aid in dissolving the gas and refilling the vessels with sap. It seems probable that in many ring-porous trees, although the larger vessels are never refilled, the smaller ones in the latewood are never blocked and continue to function in water transport. Kozlowski (1961) and Zimmermann and Brown (1971, pp. 210–211) discussed this problem in some detail. It should also be kept in mind that most stems have a large surplus of conducting capacity and can lose a considerable fraction without serious injury, as will be discussed later in this chapter.

To move water upward against gravity a pull of −0.1 bar per meter, plus whatever pull is required to overcome frictional resistance to upward flow in the xylem. Connor *et al.* (1977) mention measurements where the water potential gradient in the stem appeared to be less than the required minimum. However, their extensive measurements on eucalypts 45 and 75 m in height gave gradients in water potential considerably less than the theoretical value of −0.1 bar/m, except when the foliage was wet. There also was a vertical profile in osmotic potential of about 0.1 bar/m in the early afternoon, but no significant vertical profile in stomatal resistance. The difference in hydrostatic pressure between the trees of two heights results in the leaves of the 75-m trees being subjected to at least −7.5 bars of stress, those of the 45-m trees to −4.5 bars. There is said to be a decrease in leaf size and increase in thickness of cuticle with increasing height of eucalypt trees.

It seems that the inherent problems of the cohesion theory of the ascent of sap have been overemphasized. In any event, as Renner (1912) pointed out long ago, the cohesion theory is the only one that explains how absorption and transpiration are effectively coupled together. The continuous water columns extending from leaves to roots provide the feedback mechanism by which changes in rates of water loss and absorption control one another. This mechanism is essential for the survival of transpiring plants, although its importance has been neglected by some critics of the cohesion theory.

THE WATER CONDUCTING SYSTEM

Essentially all the water moves from roots to leaves in the specialized conducting tissue called the xylem because it provides the path of lowest resistance. However, as mentioned earlier, water must cross several layers of living cells to enter the root xylem, and in the leaves it again passes through several cells before reaching the evaporating surfaces. In the xylem it moves through dead elements. The xylem consists of wood and ray parenchyma cells, fibers, tracheids, and, in angiosperms, vessels, but water movement occurs principally in the tracheids of conifers and in the vessels of angiosperms because they offer the least resistance to flow. The tracheids are single cells up to 5 mm in length and 30 microns in diameter and water must pass through thousands of cell walls as it moves up the stems. Although such movement is facilitated by the numerous pits in the tracheid walls, there is considerably more resistance to water movement through the tracheids of conifers and the short vessels of diffuse-porous wood than there is through the long vessels of ring-porous species. The vessels of angiosperms are complex, tubular structures formed by the dissolution of the end walls and protoplasts of large numbers of cells located end to end, resulting in the formation of tubes 20 to 700 or 800 microns in diameter, and several centimeters to many meters in length.

Complexity of the Conducting System

It would be a gross oversimplification to regard the xylem as a mere assemblage of tubes. Actually, as pointed out by Kozlowski and Winget (1963), it often forms a surprisingly complicated system in which sap follows unexpected pathways. For example, the xylem commonly grows in such a manner that conduction follows a spiral pathway more often than a vertical pathway. An example of the complicated spiral path

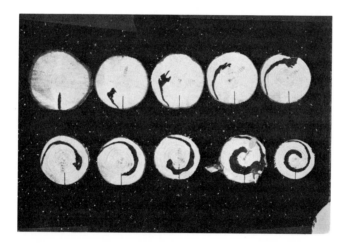

Fig. 13.10. Spiral path of ascent of sap in red pine tree. Acid fuchsin dye was injected into the stem base and rose in a spiral pattern. The vertical line is above the point of injection. The sections were cut at intervals of 60 cm, the lowest section being at the upper left. From Kozlowski and Winget (1963), University of Chicago Press.

followed by injected dye is shown in Fig. 13.10. In some gymnosperms there is more spiral in the ascending sap stream than can be accounted for by the structural spiral of the xylem. This probably is caused by the manner in which the bordered pits are arranged in the tracheids (Kozlowski *et al.,* 1966, 1967a). Thomas (1967) reported that dye moves spirally around as much as 90° of the circumference per meter of ascent in dogwood. Rudinsky and Vité (1959) claim that a spiral pattern of sap ascent provides more effective distribution of water to all parts of the crown than direct vertical ascent. This seems to be related to the observation that white oak, in which sap moves nearly vertically upward, suffers less injury from oak-wilt than pin oak, in which the transpiration stream spirals and spreads out in the top. The pathway is of considerable interest in connection with the injection of chemicals for protection from insects and fungi.

Vessel Length and Wood Structure

Numerous studies of vessel length have been made by observing the distance to which mercury, suspensions of starch, or India ink can be forced through stems. In general, vessels are a few centimeters in length in diffuse-porous species, but may be several meters long in ring-porous species. In fact in at least some ring-porous trees continuous vessels are differentiated from top to bottom in the spring and this is supported by data of Greenidge (1952) in Table 13.2. The vessels of most vines are large in diameter and very long, forming extremely effective conducting systems. The long vessels of ring-porous trees tend to become blocked by gas bubbles, tyloses, and other stoppages, so the effective vessel length usually decreases as the growing season

TABLE 13.2 Apparent Length of Vessels in Trunks of Various Hardwood Trees[a]

Species	Apparent vessel length[b]		
	Minimum	Maximum	Average
Diffuse-porous species			
Acer saccharum	81	94	88
Betula lutea	86	142	119
Fagus grandifolia	488	556	302
Populus tremuloides	101	132	122
Alnus rugosa	86	122	105
Ring-porous species			
Quercus rubra	853	1524	94.8[c]
Fraxinus americana	772	1829	97.1[c]
Ulmus americana	518	853	94.6[c]

[a] From Greenidge (1952).
[b] Measured in centimeters.
[c] Average percentage of height of tree through which air passed.

progresses and they generally cease to function in sap conduction after one or two seasons.

It might seem that the lower resistance to water movement through the large vessels of ring-porous species would be of considerable advantage, but some of the tallest trees in the world are conifers in which water movement occurs through tracheids at most only a few millimeters in length. Actually each type of wood structure has advantages and disadvantages. The diffuse-porous structure provides better protection against extensive blockage of transport because gas bubbles cannot spread easily, but it also produces a higher resistance to water flow. The low resistance to flow of the ring-porous structure is particularly important in long slender vines, but the large diameter of the vessels makes vines more vulnerable to blockage by cavitation when placed under tension. Huber (1935) considered the significance of the two types of conducting systems in detail and concluded that the ring-porous type of xylem is as successful biologically as the diffuse-porous structure in deciduous species where new vessels are formed each spring before leaves develop. However, he doubted if the ring-porous structure could succeed in evergreens because it loses so much conducting capacity by the end of each growing season. In support of this view he pointed out that the evergreen oaks of the Mediterranean region are diffuse porous, although deciduous oaks are ring porous. Much information on xylem structure in relation to function was presented by Carlquist (1975).

Efficiency of Water Conduction

According to Huber there are two ways to express the efficiency of the water conducting system. The first is the *specific conductivity,* which refers to the volume of water moved per unit of time under a given pressure through a stem segment of given length and cross section (meters per hour, per square centimeters of cross section, per bar of pressure, per meter of length). The other measure is in terms of *relative conducting surface,* which is the ratio of conducting surface (cross section of xylem elements) to transpiring surface.

Farmer (1918) reported that the specific conductivity of conifer stems is much lower than that of angiosperms, and Huber (1956) gave specific conductivities of 20 for conifers, 65 to 128 for deciduous broadleaf trees, 236 to 1,273 for vines, and even higher values in roots. It was reported that the specific conductivity of branches and twigs is lower than that of the trunk and that the specific conductivity of the trunk decreases from bottom to top. This decrease is compensated for by a considerable increase in relative conducting surface from base to top of trunk. The relative conducting surface, expressed as square millimeters of xylem per gram of leaf fresh weight, increases from 0.02 in an aquatic plant to about 0.5 in trees and 3.4 in nonsucculent desert plants (Huber, 1956). An example of change in relative conducting surface with height is seen in Fig. 13.11 Huber concluded that water movement through healthy plants is not limited by the resistance in the xylem but by that encountered in crossing the living cells of roots and leaves, a conclusion with which the authors agree. Roberts (1977) estimated that half of the resistance is in the soil–root component.

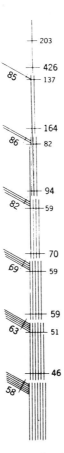

Fig. 13.11. Differences in relative amounts of water-conducting surface compared to leaf surface along main stem and in the branches of a 6-year-old white fir tree, expressed as hundredths of square millimeters of xylem cross section per gram of needle fresh weight. The relative conductivity increases from base to apex, but it is lower at the point where branch whorls are attached (numbers in light-face type) than between nodes (numbers in boldface type). After Huber (1928).

Although resistance to radial water movement from soil to xylem is high in roots, the resistance to longitudinal flow in the xylem is lower in woody roots than in stems. Stone and Stone (1975a) found that the conductivity of red pine roots was up to 50 times greater than that of stems, and that conductivity increased with distance from the base of the stem. No spiral movement was observed in roots, although it is common in stems. The low resistance to longitudinal flow through tree roots is in contrast to the high resistance reported in roots of some grasses (Passioura, 1972). It is reported that there is a constricted region in the xylem supplying the leaves of some trees, caused by reduction in number and diameter of vessels (Larson and Isebrands, 1978), that increases resistance to water flow into leaves.

Velocity of Sap Movement

The differences in specific conductivity between ring- and diffuse-porous species are brought out by the measurements of the velocity of sap flow shown in Table 13.3. Some of the measurements were made by injecting dyes such as acid fuchsin (Greenidge, 1958), or radioactive tracers (Fraser and Mawson, 1953; Moreland, 1950; Kuntz and Riker, 1955). Injection of dyes requires destruction of the stems to determine the distance they have moved, and measurements with dyes and radioactive tracers suffer from the possibility that the rate of movement in opened xylem is different from that in undisturbed xylem. The most satisfactory measurements of sap velocity seem to be those made by the thermoelectric or heat pulse method developed by Huber and his colleagues (Huber and Schmidt, 1937). Although it may underestimate the velocity of sap flow (Marshall, 1958), the method has been used on trees by a number of investigators including Ladefoged (1960), Skau and Swanson (1963), and Kurtzman (1966) to monitor diurnal variations in velocity of sap flow. With this method, heat is applied to the ascending sap stream by a small electric heating unit inserted under the bark or into the sapwood and the time required for the heated sap to reach a thermocouple or thermistor placed in the wood above the heating unit is measured. Daum (1967) increased the sensitivity by placing the heating unit under the bark. The general arrangement of the apparatus is shown in Fig. 13.12. Some examples of midday velocities were shown in Table 13.3 and the distribution of velocities in a tree is shown in Fig. 13.13. The velocity in coniferous and diffuse-porous species is

TABLE 13.3 Rates of Water Movement in Xylem as Determined by Various Methods

Investigator	Method	Material	Rate
Greenidge (1958)	Acid fuchsin	*Acer saccharum*	1.5–4.5 m/hr
	Acid fuchsin	*Fagus grandifolia*	3.6–4.2 m/hr
	Acid fuchsin	*Ulmus americana*	4.3–15.5 m/hr
Huber and Schmidt (1937)	Heat pulse	*Quercus pedunculata*	43.6 m/hr (maximum)
	Heat pulse	*Fraxinus excelsior*	25.7 m/hr (maximum)
	Heat pulse	*Ulmus effusa*	6.0 m/hr (maximum)
	Heat pulse	*Juglans cinerea*	3.79 m/hr (maximum)
	Heat pulse	*Liriodendron tulipifera*	2.62 m/hr (maximum)
	Heat pulse	Conifers	Less than 0.5 m/hr
Kuntz and Riker (1955)	[131]I	*Quercus ellipsoidalis*	27.5–60 m/hr (maximum)
	[86]Rb	*Quercus macrocarpa*	27.5–60 m/hr (maximum)
Decker and Skau (1964)	Heat pulse	*Juniperus osteosperma*	0.25 m/hr (maximum)
Owston *et al.* (1972)	[32]P	*Pinus contorta*	0.1 to 0.8 m/hr
Moreland (1950)	[32]P	*Pinus taeda*	1.2 m/hr (maximum)

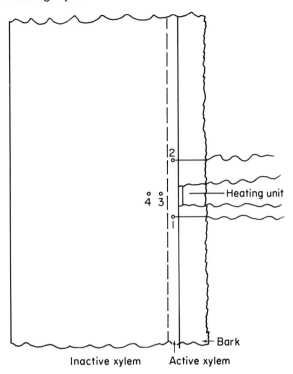

Fig. 13.12. A heat pulse installation. The heating unit is installed under the bark, against the cambium, or in a hole drilled in the outer xylem. Points 1 and 2 are thermocouples or thermistors used to measure temperature of the sap stream. Points 2 and 3 were used by Daum (1967) to determine the depth to which water conduction occurs. Details of the instrumentation are given by Swanson (1962).

low because water moves through a number of annual rings, while in ring-porous species it moves rapidly through only one or two annual rings. Figure 13.14 shows the daily change in rate of sap flow in three tree species. Because this method is nondestructive it can be used for long series of measurements. The problems encountered in its use were discussed by Leyton (1970).

Direction of Sap Flow

We have thus far assumed that water movement is always upward. This usually is true because water moves toward regions of lower water potential, which usually are in the transpiring leaves. However, water can move downward if a reverse gradient in water potential is produced, as was demonstrated by John Ray in 1669, Stephen Hales in 1727, and other early investigators. The reverse flow produced in pine seedlings by Slatyer (1956) and in other plants by various investigators indicates that there is little or no additional resistance to water flow in the reverse of the normal upward and down-

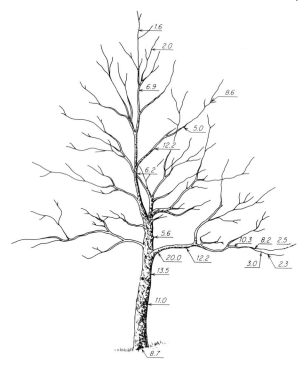

Fig. 13.13. Rate of water flow in meters per hour in various parts of an oak tree at midday, measured by the heat pulse method. The rate of flow decreases toward the top because the relative conductivity (ratio of xylem cross section to leaf area) increases, as was shown in Figure 13.11. In birch the rate increases toward the top because the relative conductivity decreases. From Huber (1956), after Huber and Schmidt (1937).

ward flow. Daum (1967) demonstrated downward flow of sap in one branch accompanied by upward flow in the other, more exposed branch, of a bifurcated ash tree.

Cross Section of Stems Involved in Ascent of Sap

The amount of the total cross section of tree trunks involved in water conduction varies widely. In most species the central portion is transformed into heartwood and becomes physiologically inactive. Not even all of the sapwood is involved in sap conduction, although there is considerable difference of opinion as to how much is involved. In at least some species of ring-porous trees, including chestnut, ash, and red oak, it appears that most of the water moves in the outermost annual ring, although some movement may occur in the latewood of the preceding year (Rumbold, 1920). According to Chaney and Kozlowski (1975), in white ash seedlings water movement occurs in the large earlywood vessels of the current annual ring, but in sugar maple seedlings it occurs in the large vessels of the current annual ring and two-thirds of the annual ring of the preceding year. Studies by Kozlowski and Winget (1963) also

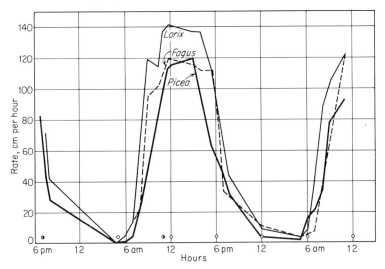

Fig. 13.14. Diurnal variations in the rate of ascent of sap in beech, larch, and spruce, measured by the heat pulse method. From Schubert (1939).

indicate that water movement is restricted to the outermost one or two annual rings in red pine, white oak, and bur oak. MacDougal *et al.,* (1929) reported upward movement of dye in concentric columns of the latewood in several species, but this was questioned by Baker and James (1933). The pattern of sap movement seems more complex in conifers and diffuse-porous trees because a considerable number of annual rings usually are involved. In dormant conifer seedlings up to 4 years of age, water movement occurred in all annual rings, but less movement occurred through the outermost annual ring than through the second ring. More water movement also occurred through the larger tracheids of the earlywood than through the smaller tracheids of the latewood (Kozlowski *et al.,* 1966). In older conifers there seems to be considerable variation in the width of the conducting sapwood; some data on the number of rings included in the sapwood were presented in Table 2.3. Swanson (1967) reported that in lodgepole pine and Engelmann spruce most rapid conduction of water occurs 15 to 20 mm within the wood and little upward movement occurs in the outer 5 mm of the wood. This is surprising because one would expect most rapid conduction in the outermost one or two annual rings, which presumably are most directly connected to the transpiring leaves. The anatomy of the conducting system apparently needs more study.

Tolerance of Injury

Trees seem to have a large safety factor in their water conducting system and can survive the destruction of a large part of the cross section. Jemison (1944) observed that oak trees in which 50% of the circumference had been killed by fire grew as much

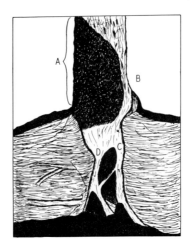

Fig. 13.15. Reorientation of xylem and phloem bypassing a fire wound. A: burned area; C and D: roots connected by new conducting tissue to surviving tissue, B. After Jemison (1944).

during the next 10 years as nearby uninjured trees. He also observed that injured trees quickly formed new xylem oriented to produce an efficient pathway around wounds (Fig. 13.15). This tendency to reorient the xylem and phloem around wounds is often observed when trees are girdled spirally. Mackay and Weatherley (1973) reported that a horizontal cut extending more than halfway through a tree trunk produces no measurable water deficit in the leaves, but two overlapping cuts in a tree trunk do produce a water deficit in the top. The effects of overlapping cuts are shown in Fig. 13.16.

Certain so-called vascular or wilt diseases such as oak and mimosa wilt, verticillium wilt of elm and maple, and Dutch elm disease occur because pathogenic organisms block the passage of water through the xylem. It is unlikely that the mycelium actually blocks the xylem itself. It is more likely that the pathogens produce toxins that injure the living cells adjoining the xylem elements and cause the formation of gum and tyloses that block the xylem and cause injury by dehydration (Kozlowski, 1962; Kuntz and Riker, 1955; Van Alten and Turner, 1975). Talboys (1968) points out that injuries from so-called vascular or wilt diseases are complex and are not all due to a single cause. Boring insects also cause injury to the xylem, perhaps partly because their burrows cause dehydration. In some instances the insects also introduce fungi that cause additional injury to the conducting system.

THE WATER BALANCE

The growth of both woody and herbaceous plants is reduced more often by water deficits than by any other single factor. The extensive evidence summarized by Zahner (1968), showing correlations between both height and diameter growth and available water, indicates that 70 to 80% of the variation in the width of annual rings in humid

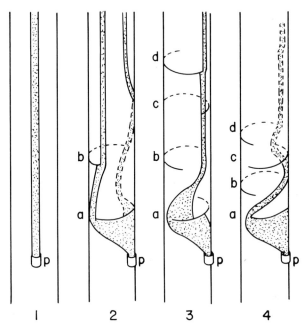

Fig. 13.16. Diagrams showing effects of horizontal cuts in a trunk of a pine tree on upward movement of sap labeled with [23]P. The cuts are designated as a, b, c, and d and extended halfway through the trunk. [32]P was supplied at point p and the stippled areas indicate its path. From Postlethwait and Rogers (1958).

regions and 90% in arid regions can be attributed to differences in water stress. The degree of water stress in plants is controlled by the relative rates of water absorption and water loss, and water deficits therefore can be caused either by too slow absorption, too rapid water loss, or most often by a combination of the two. Thus the study of factors affecting water absorption and transpiration is important because it contributes to an understanding of the internal water balance, which in turn affects the physiological processes and conditions controlling the quantity and quality of growth.

By plant water stress is meant a condition in which the cells are less than fully turgid and the water potential is substantially less than zero. The first visible effects of water stress are closure of stomata, wilting of leaves and young stems, and cessation of growth, but there are many important invisible effects which will be discussed later. The degree of water stress is often described quantitatively in terms of the saturation deficit, relative water content, or preferably the water potential. The causes, effects, and measurement of water stress will be discussed in some detail.

Causes of Water Stress

Use of such terms as "water balance" and "water economy" emphasizes the fact that the internal water relations of plants may be regarded as resembling a budget in

which water content or water balance is controlled by the relative rates of water
absorption (income) and water loss (expenditures).

The Absorption Lag

It is well established that there are often marked decreases in the water content of
leaves and stems of plants near midday in sunny weather. This is demonstrated by the
decrease in water content of leaves shown in Fig. 13.17 and in stem diameter reported
by MacDougal (1938), Kozlowski and Winget (1964b), Braekke and Kozlowski
(1975a) and others, and shown in Fig. 13.18. Gibbs (1935a) made a careful study of
diurnal changes in water content of the wood in birch tree trunks and some of his data
are summarized in Table 13.4. He found that the maximum water content occurred
near sunrise, decreased during the morning and midday and rose in the afternoon and
evening. This behavior seems to be characteristic of many kinds of plants in warm,
sunny weather and indicates that tree trunks act as a storage place for water which is
withdrawn when transpiration exceeds absorption and is replaced when the reverse
situation occurs.

The cause of this fluctuation in water content is the fact that the resistance to
withdrawal of water from turgid plant tissue is lower than the resistance to intake
through the roots (Fig. 13.19). Thus as transpiration increases in the morning absorption does not begin to increase until the decreasing leaf water potential produces
sufficient tension in the xylem sap to overcome the resistance to water flow through the
xylem and the even larger resistance to radial movement from the soil into the root
xylem. In the meantime water is removed from tissue offering low resistance to flow,
such as the parenchyma cells of leaves and stems, producing deficits that sometimes
are severe enough to cause temporary wilting of leaves. Hellkvist et al. (1974) reported
leaf water potentials of −12 to −15 bars and reduction in turgor to 40% of the
maximum in Sitka spruce growing in moist soil in Scotland.

That the removal of water from a tree trunk lags behind loss from the leaves is

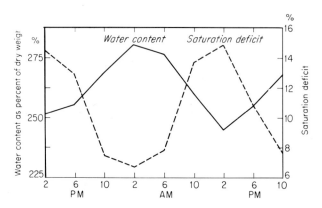

Fig. 13.17. Diurnal variation in water content and saturation deficit of pear leaves. From
Ackley (1954).

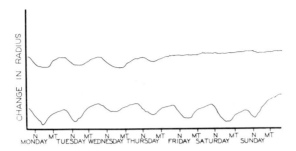

Fig. 13.18. Dendrograph traces showing shrinkage of red pine stems in the afternoon followed by swelling at night. The upper trace is for the week of July 10–17 in Wisconsin and the lower trace for August 21–28. The upper trace shows no daily shrinkage and swelling of the stem during the latter part of the week when cloudy and rainy weather prevailed. From Kozlowski (1968a).

shown by the observation of Waggoner and Turner (1971) that stem shrinkage at breast height in pine trees lags about two hours behind decrease in leaf water potential. Zaerr (1971) observed a similar lag in Douglas-fir. This lag indicates the presence of a significant resistance to water flow through the stem and branches and into the evaporating surfaces of the leaves. Late in the day as the temperature decreases and stomata close transpiration is rapidly reduced, but absorption continues until the water potential in the plant increases to approximately that in the soil. This may require all night, and as the soil dries there is less recovery on succeeding nights until permanent wilting occurs. If prolonged this severe water deficit causes death by desiccation.

Midday water deficits and temporary wilting are caused by transpiration temporarily exceeding absorption even for plants growing in soil at field capacity. However, permanent wilting occurs because reduced absorption, caused by drying soil or occasionally by low temperature or inadequate aeration, prevents replacement of the water lost by transpiration. As the plant water stress increases the stomata close, decreasing water loss, and trees with heavily cutinized leaves, such as olive and loblolly pine, can endure prolonged periods of water stress with a minimum of injury.

TABLE 13.4 Diurnal Variations in Water Content of Wood in Birch Trunks[a]

Variable	August 24			August 25		
Time	5:00 AM	1:00 PM	7:00 PM	5:00 AM	1:00 PM	7:00 PM
Weather	Clear	Clear, hot	Clear	Clear	Slightly overcast	Clear
Water content as percent dry weight	65	54	58	59	50	53

[a] From Gibbs, (1935a, Table 13).

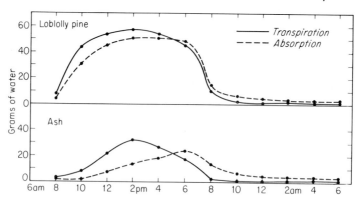

Fig. 13.19. The relationship between water absorption and transpiration of white ash and loblolly pine. The seedlings were grown in autoirrigated pots that permitted the measurement of water absorption. Rates were measured at 2-hr intervals. From Kramer (1937a).

Internal Competition for Water

During the growing season the various parts of trees and large herbaceous plants are often in competition for water. Because of differences in shading and in concentration of solutes, various parts of the shoots lose water at different rates and different levels of water deficits and water potential develop. This is especially important in drying soil when those regions in plants that develop the lowest water potentials obtain water at the expense of older tissue. Although young leaves may wilt first they usually are the last to die on plants suffering from water stress. Water stress hastens senescence, possibly in part because it reduces the supply of cytokinins and changes the balance of growth regulators in the leaves (Livne and Vaadia, 1972). Lower, shaded leaves also suffer because they produce less carbohydrate than upper, better exposed leaves, and they may be less able to compete osmotically for water. Thus, dehydration may be a factor in the death of the lower, shaded branches of trees. According to Chalmers and Wilson (1978) the demand of developing peach fruits for carbohydrates and the increased water stress reduce branch growth of fruiting peach trees.

The competition between leaves and fruits is well documented, fruits generally showing reduced growth or even shrinkage at midday when water deficits develop in the trees as a whole. An example is shown in Fig. 13.20. This shrinkage has been shown for lemons (Bartholomew, 1926), oranges (Rokach, 1953) pears (Hendrickson and Veihmeyer, 1941), cherries (Chaney and Kozlowski, 1969a), and other fruits as well as cones of gymnosperms (Chaney and Kozlowski, 1969b). However, Rokach (1953) found that young oranges, less than 35 mm in diameter, do not lose water during periods of stress. This agrees with the observation of Anderson and Kerr (1943) that leaves were unable to remove water from young cotton bolls, but older bolls showed daily midday shrinkage. This is in accord with the general concept that younger plant parts obtain or retain water at the expense of older parts, as was mentioned earlier in this section.

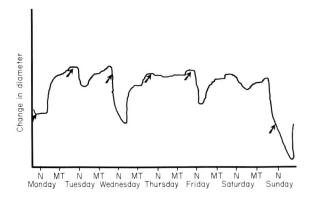

Fig. 13.20. Midday decreases in the diameters of cherry fruits followed by expansion at night when water stress disappears. Arrows indicate time of irrigation. After Kozlowski (1968c).

The variations in water content and water potential found in various parts of transpiring plants and even in different parts of large leaves create important problems in sampling for the measurement of these values, which will be discussed later.

Long-Term Variations in Water Content

Over 50% of the total fresh weight of a tree consists of water, but the water concentration varies widely in different parts of a tree and with species, age, site, and season. The water content of well-developed heartwood is usually much lower than that of the sapwood. Some data are shown in Fig. 13.21. Hickory is an exception because its heartwood consistently contains more water than the sapwood at all sea-

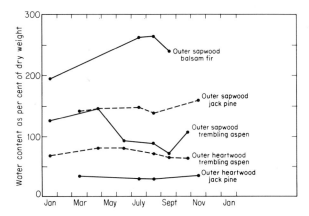

Fig. 13.21. Seasonal changes in water content of wood of coniferous and deciduous species in eastern Canada. In general the water content of conifer wood undergoes smaller variations than wood of deciduous species (see Fig. 13.9).

sons (Smith and Goebel, 1952). Attempts to reduce the water content by leaving the leafy top attached for some days after felling were unsuccessful in hickory, although it produced a large reduction in the water content of birch tree trunks (Gibbs, 1935a). Because of the unusual distribution of water, hickory timber is difficult to dry without splitting. According to Gibbs (1939), although the heartwood of jack pine and white spruce is very dry that of balsam fir and hemlock often contains wet areas that show daily or seasonal changes in water content. Parker (1954) reported that the water content of the heartwood of Douglas-fir and redcedar was lower than that of ponderosa pine or grand fir.

According to Ovington (1956) the water content usually increases from the base to the top of trees, but Ito (1955) reported that in *Castanea crenata* the water content decreases from the base upward. Luxford (1930) reported that the water content of the heartwood of redwood is greatest at the base and lower toward the top, but the situation in the sapwood is reversed, being lowest at the base and highest toward the top.

Seasonal Variations in Water Content

Large seasonal variations occur in the water content of the trunks of trees of some, but not all, species. These variations are not only interesting physiologically, but also have practical economic importance because they affect the rate of drying, flotation of logs, and cost of transport. In eastern Canada logs of birch and poplar have such a high density in late May and early June that they cannot float, but by September the density is reduced to 60 to 75% because some of the water is replaced by air. The water content and density of sapwood and wet heartwood of balsam fir remain high all summer (Gibbs, 1935a). Some data are summarized in Table 13.5. Although the largest seasonal variations in water content usually occur in hardwoods, Ito (1955) reported that in Japan there are larger seasonal variations in the water content of the wood of Japanese red pine than in Japanese chestnut, the minimum occurring in August in both species. According to Gibbs, R. Hartig and E. Münch reported that in Europe conifers show significant seasonal variations in water content, but Gibbs found rather small variations in conifers in eastern Canada (see Fig. 13.21).

The typical seasonal pattern of change in water content for a diffuse porous species, birch, was shown in Figure 13.9. Generally, in eastern Canada tree trunks of birches, cottonwoods, and some aspens and willows attain their greatest water content in the spring just before the leaves open. The water content decreases during the summer to a minimum just before leaf fall, then increases during the autumn after leaf fall reduces transpiration, but before the soil becomes cold enough to hinder water absorption. Some species show another decrease during the late winter, presumably because cold soil hinders water absorption, followed by an increase in water content to the maximum after the soil thaws, but before the leaves open. Among the variants from this pattern, white ash and American elm show no autumn increase, silver maple and beech attain maximum water content in the autumn, and beech is unique among the species studied by showing no spring increase in water content. Those interested in more details should consult the papers by Gibbs (1935a, 1939, 1953) and Clark and Gibbs (1957). Few

TABLE 13.5 Water and Gas Content of Tree Trunks of Several Species at Various Seasons[a]

Species	Season	Part of tree	Water (percent dry weight)	Percent fresh volume occupied by			Density of fresh wood[b]
				Water	Wood	Gas	
Birch	May–June	Outer rings	>120	>59	33	<8	>1.10
		Whole tree	97	47	33	20	0.98
	July–August	Outer rings	50	24	33	43	0.76
		Whole tree	54	26	33	41	0.77
Poplar	May	Whole tree	125	53	27	20	0.95
	September	Whole tree	66	27	27	46	0.69
Jack pine	All	Sapwood	170	65	25	10	1.04
		Heartwood	35	13	23	64	0.49
Balsam	All	Sapwood and wet patches of heartwood	200–250	62–80	20	0–18	0.93 1.11

[a] From Gibbs (1935b).
[b] Water = 1.0.

data are available for milder climates, but the winter decrease is less likely to occur where the soil does not freeze.

Methods of Expressing Water Content

It seems appropriate at this point to discuss methods of expressing the water content. It usually is expressed either as a percentage of fresh or dry weight, but both methods have some disadvantages. The fresh weight basis is unsatisfactory because the fresh weight of succulent tissue such as leaves and young stems can vary widely from day to day and even from hour to hour. Furthermore, large changes in the water content per unit of tissue result in deceptively small changes in percentage of fresh weight. Curtis and Clark (1950, p. 259) noted that when the water content of the leaves of the desert shrub *Nicotiana glauca* decreased from 85 to 80% on a fresh weight basis, they lost 25 g water per original 100 g of fresh weight, or 29.4% of the original water content. On a dry weight basis the leaf water content decreased from 566 to 400%, assuming no change in dry weight. Unfortunately, the dry weight is not a stable basis either, because photosynthesis, respiration, and translocation can produce rapid changes in dry weight, and over longer periods large increases in dry weight occur because of increasing thickness of cell walls. For example, Ackley (1954) found that the dry weight of pear leaves increased about 150% from June to August, while the water content remained unchanged (Fig. 13.22), resulting in a large decrease in water content per unit of dry weight.

Similar results were found for leaves of northern pin oak by Kozlowski and Clausen (1965). An early season increase in percentage water content of white spruce and tamarack cones was largely the result of an increase in water uptake. Later in the season, the percentage water content of cones decreased primarily because the dry weight of cones increased rapidly while the amount of water in them changed little (Clausen and Kozlowski, 1965b). Thus changes in percentage water content reflect changes in both dry matter and water content.

Mason and Maskell (1928) and Denny (1932) attempted to obtain a more suitable base for calculating changes in water and other constituents by extracting the leaves in dilute HCl to remove the easy hydrolyzable materials, leaving only the cell walls and other resistant constituents. This decreases hour-to-hour variations caused by photosynthesis, respiration, and translocation, but Weatherley (1950) pointed out that it does not eliminate long-term changes caused by increase in cell wall thickness. Investigators should be aware of the errors inherent in whatever method they use.

Effects of Water Stress

Water deficits affect every aspect of plant growth, modifying anatomy, morphology, physiology, and biochemistry. Trees are smaller on dry sites, their leaves usually are smaller, thicker, and more heavily cutinized, vessel diameter of earlywood is often smaller and the cell walls are usually thicker and more lignified. An extreme example of reduced growth on a dry site is the bristlecone pines on the White Mountains of California (Schulman, 1958). As mentioned at the beginning of this

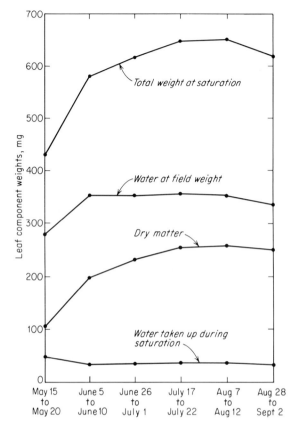

Fig. 13.22. Seasonal changes in dry weight, water content, and water absorbed to attain saturation by pear leaves. From Ackley (1954).

section, the amount of growth made by trees is closely correlated with the availability of water. In general, cell division is reduced less by water stress than cell enlargement, and plant size is reduced by lack of water primarily because some minimum degree of turgor is necessary for cell expansion (Hsiao, 1973). Turgor also is important in relation to the degree of opening of stomata, the expansion of leaves and flowers, and movements of plant parts, such as the nyctinastic folding of leaflets of mimosa. Another important effect of reduced turgor is the reduction in photosynthesis caused by closure of stomata, internal effects on the photosynthetic process, and reduction in leaf area. This was discussed in Chapter 5.

Research, chiefly on herbaceous plants, has shown that water stress affects many enzyme-mediated processes, including respiration, the dark reactions of photosynthesis, the formation of chlorophyll (Alberte *et al.*, 1975), carbohydrate and nitrogen metabolism (see Chapters 7 and 9), organelles such as mitochondria and ribosomes, and membrane structure (Vieira da Silva *et al.*, 1974; Giles *et al.*, 1976). The balance of growth regulators also is affected, the cytokinin content of shoots being reduced and abscisic acid and auxin content increased (Livne and Vaadia, 1972). The synthesis of gibberellin in roots may also be reduced (Skene, 1967). Most of this research was done on herbaceous plants but the results are probably equally applicable to woody plants.

Water Stress in Relation to Insect and Disease Resistance

There is considerable evidence that attacks on trees by boring insects that live in the inner bark and outer wood are more severe in dry years than in years when little water stress develops. Vité (1961) states that infestation of ponderosa pine by beetles is much more severe in water-stressed trees than in well watered trees. It also is reported that the extent and duration of water stress have an important effect on the susceptibility of loblolly pine to attack by the southern pine beetle. Apparently the high oleoresin pressures existing in unstressed trees discourage invasion by borers. A similar situation exists in white fir where engraver beetles establish themselves at a water stress of -20 bars, but not at -15 bars because of greater resin flow in the less stressed trees (Ferrell, 1978).

There also is some evidence that water stress favors invasion by certain fungi. Bier (1959) reported that the fungus causing bark cankers in willow invades the bark only when its relative water content is below 80% and he found a similar relationship for bark canker of poplar. A. F. Parker (1961) reviewed the literature on water content and disease and concluded that development of bark cankers usually is correlated with low water content. Damage by *Fomes annosus* also is said to be increased by water stress. Some leaf infesting fungi such as the powdery mildews are more troublesome in dry weather, but the spread of many fungi is increased by wet weather because leaf surfaces must remain wet for many hours to permit germination of spores of fungi such as that causing apple scab. The relationship of water stress to plant disease is discussed in detail by Ayres and by Schoeneweiss in Kozlowski, "Water Deficits and Plant Growth," Vol. 5 (1978).

The effects of water stress on vegetative and reproductive growth are discussed in more detail in Chapter 16. For more details readers are referred to the five volumes of "Water Deficits and Plant Growth" edited by Kozlowski (1968–1978), the review by Hsiao (1973), and Chapter 10 in Kramer (1969).

Beneficial Effects of Water Stress

Under some conditions moderate water stress can improve the quality of plant products even though it reduces vegetative growth. This is true of guayule which shows a large increase in rubber content under moderate water stress, even though the fresh weight per plant is reduced (Wadleigh *et al.,* 1946). Richards and Wadleigh (1952) stated that the quality of apples, pears, peaches, and plums is improved by water stress, and the oil content of olives is said to be increased (Evenari, 1960) although it is probable that the total yield is decreased. It is claimed that the alkaloid content of several drug plants is increased by water stress (Evenari, 1960) but Loustalot et al. (1947) reported that the alkaloid content of *Cinchona ledgeriana* is decreased. It might also be argued that the increased amount of thick walled xylem elements produced in trees subjected to water stress is sometimes beneficial (Zahner, 1968) because it results in wood of higher density. More research on the effects of water stress on wood quality would be worthwhile.

DROUGHT TOLERANCE

For many years the term "drought resistance" has been used in reference to the capacity of plants to survive drought. However, it is an unsatisfactory term because discussions of socalled drought resistance often confuse the environmental factor, drought, with the reactions of plants to lack of water, best described as water deficit or water stress. We prefer the term drought tolerance because it more accurately describes the reaction of plants to drought. It should be emphasized that drought is a meteorological occurrence, usually described as a period without rainfall of sufficient duration to cause depletion of soil moisture and reduction in plant growth. Drought may be permanent, as in arid regions; seasonal, as in areas with well-defined wet and dry seasons; or random, as in most humid areas. The length of the period without rainfall required to produce drought conditions depends chiefly on the water storage capacity of the soil and the rate of evapotranspiration, and to a lesser degree on the kind of vegetation. Even in such humid regions as Western Europe and the Southeastern United States injurious droughts are common (van Bavel and Verlinden, 1956).

Drought is an environmental factor that produces water deficit or water stress in plants. In engineering and the physical sciences stress produces strain, and the effect in the plant should be termed "water strain," rather than water stress (Levitt, 1972). However, in plant physiology the term "water stress" is used with reference to both the environmental water deficit and the plant water deficit. Plant water stress or water deficit is beginning to develop at a leaf water potential of -2 or -3 bars or when cell turgor begins to fall appreciably below its maximum value.

Plant water deficits and stress always accompany droughts, but also occur at other times either because of excessive transpiration or when absorption is hindered by cold soil, an excess of salt in the soil solution, or damage to root systems. Most plants are subjected to transient water deficits and stress at midday in hot sunny weather, even when growing in soil near field capacity or in a dilute nutrient solution. For example, Hellkvist *et al.* (1974) found appreciable water deficits in the upper branches of Sitka spruce growing in moist soil in the mild climate of Scotland. The upper, more exposed parts of tree crowns are usually subjected to greater stress than the lower parts.

The effects of water deficits produced by drought or other causes are just as important to the growth of forest, fruit, and ornamental trees as for annual herbaceous crop plants. Capacity to survive drought depends on a variety of phenological, morphological, and physiological factors. Farmers and foresters as well as ecologists and physiologists know that trees of some species survive drought with less injury than those of other species. For example, ponderosa pine survives better than grand fir; post oak and blackjack oak grow on sites too dry for red and white oak, and shortleaf pine grows on drier sites than loblolly pine. Some species from semiarid regions such as

Larrea, Laurus, olive, and some acacias survive severe dehydration during long droughts, but *Cornus florida* is severely injured by drought. Some races of loblolly pine survive water stress better than others and inland races of Douglas-fir survive dehydration better than coastal strains (Pharis and Ferrell, 1966). Other differences among populations from different habitats have been reported. For example, Ladiges (1974) found that seedlings of *Eucalyptus viminalis* from areas of low rainfall were more resistant to injury from desiccation than those from regions with high rainfall. It also appears that Monterey, loblolly, and shortleaf pines are most tolerant of desiccation in atmospheric conditions resembling their native environments (Heth and Kramer, 1975). Larcher (1975, pp. 168–175) collected data on drought tolerance of a wide variety of woody and herbaceous plants.

Causes of Drought Tolerance

Plants survive in regions of inadequate rainfall either because they avoid drought, because they possess morphological or physiological modifications which enable them to avoid or postpone desiccation, or because they can tolerate desiccation.

Drought Avoidance

Drought avoiding plants occur in regions with well defined dry seasons. They include the desert ephemerals with such short life cycles that they are completed in a few weeks after winter rains, and plants that mature early in the summer before the soil dries. The ephemerals include chiefly annual plants, although drought avoidance may be important to some perennial plants in Mediterranean climates.

Desiccation Avoidance or Postponement

The occurrence of an injurious degree of desiccation when the water supply to the roots is reduced can be postponed in several ways. The most obvious method is by the storage of a large volume of water in fleshy roots or in stems, but the usefulness of this is limited to a few species such as cacti which have a large storage capacity and good control of the transpiration rate. Although considerable water is stored in tree trunks the volume is small in comparison to the loss by transpiration from woody plants (Roberts, 1976).

Many plants native to arid regions and regions with long summer droughts have heavily cutinized leaves and very low transpiration rates after the stomata close. Oppenheimer (1951) reported that in Israel plants such as carob, laurel, olive, Aleppo pine, and *Arbutus andrachne* have very low transpiration rates when soil moisture is depleted, but almond and fig have poor control of transpiration. Kaul and Kramer (1965) found that the stomata of holly (*Ilex cornuta,* var *Burfordii*) closed at a much lower leaf water deficit than those of azalea (*Rhododendron poukhanensis*) and transpiration from cut branches initially was more rapid in azalea, suggesting better control of both cuticular and stomatal transpiration in holly. Transpiration is often reduced in stressed plants by leaf abscission but this also reduces photosynthesis. Leaf abscission is discussed by Parker (1968) and by Kozlowski (1976b).

Root Systems

Most observers agree that deep, wide-spreading root systems are important in postponing desiccation injury. Oppenheimer (1951) found this important in Israel and extensive root proliferation is said to be the chief cause of the greater desiccation avoidance of some strains of loblolly pine in Texas, with regulation of transpiration a secondary factor (van Buijtenen *et al.,* 1976). Large root systems were found to be important for the establishment of outplanted Douglas-fir and ponderosa pine seedlings in the Pacific Northwest (Lopushinsky and Beebe, 1976). Satoo (1956a) observed that the extent of root systems is an important factor in survival of conifer seedlings in Japan and Fowells and Kirk (1945) concluded that reduction of the absorbing system by injury during lifting and planting is an important cause of failure of ponderosa pine transplants. The importance of producing planting stock with vigorous root systems capable of resuming growth promptly after transplanting cannot be overemphasized.

Foresters and horticulturists are generally aware of the importance of deep rooting and the former have given considerable attention to differences in initial root habit of tree seedlings as a cause of differences in survival (Haig, 1936; Holch, 1931; Toumey, 1929). For example, baldcypress and yellow birch become established only in moist soil because their shallow roots do not enable them to survive summer droughts, whereas most upland species have relatively deep root systems. The failure of pine seedlings to survive under forest stands where hardwood seedlings become established can be attributed at least in part to the shallower root systems developed in the shade which makes them more susceptible to injury during summer droughts.

Desiccation Tolerance

Desiccation tolerance is at the other extreme, referring to the capacity of protoplasm to undergo extreme dehydration without irreversible injury. The outstanding examples occur among mosses and lichens, but a few flowering plants also can be dehydrated to air dryness (Gaff, 1971). Some woody plants from arid regions such as creosote bush, sagebrush, acacias, and shrubs of the Mediterranean maquis and California chaparral have considerable protoplasmic tolerance of dehydration. Bourdeau (1954) concluded that post and blackjack oak have more protoplasmic tolerance than white or red oak because they survive a degree of desiccation fatal to the other oaks, yet do not have more extensive root systems or better control of transpiration. It is worthy of note that the roots of these oaks seem more resistant to dehydration than the shoots, resulting in sprouting from the roots after the shoots have been killed by desiccation. This is in contrast to the observations of Brix (1960) and Leshem (1965) that pine roots are killed before the shoots. Pharis and Ferrell (1966) concluded that Douglas-fir seedlings from the interior were more resistant to dehydration than coastal seedlings and Parker (1968) considers desiccation tolerance to be an important factor in trees.

Bases of Desiccation Tolerance

Eventually the water content falls to a critical level where survival depends on the degree of dehydration which the protoplasm can endure without suffering irreversible injury. There seem to be wide differences among species in this respect. Oppenheimer (1932) reported that leaves of almond could be dried to a saturation deficit of 70% before injury occurred, olive to 60%, but fig to only 25%. Seasonal differences also exist. The leaves of creosote bush produced during moist weather are large and easily injured by water deficit, but the small leaves produced during dry weather can be dried to a saturation deficit of 50% (Runyon, 1936). Pisek and Larcher (1954) found that in several species tolerance to dehydration increases in the winter along with cold tolerance, then decreases in the spring. Examples are shown in Fig. 13.23.

Bound water was at one time regarded as an important factor in desiccation and cold tolerance, but most of the water is bound in the walls and is of little physiological importance (Kramer, 1955). High osmotic pressure also has been regarded as an important adaptation to water stress and the beneficial effects of osmotic adjustment to water stress are again being emphasized in crop plants (Begg and Turner, 1976, p. 186) and may be important in some woody plants. For example, Osonubi and Davies (1978) reported that solute accumulation was responsible for maintenance of turgor in water-stressed English oak, but not in birch.

European and Russian investigators have emphasized the importance of protoplasmic and biochemical changes which increase desiccation tolerance and some of this work is discussed by Parker (1968) and by Lee-Stadelmann and Stadelmann (1976).

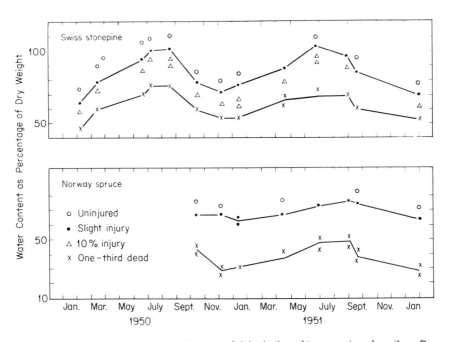

Fig. 13.23. Seasonal changes in tolerance of dehydration of two species of conifers. Dehydration tolerance increased during the winter and decreased during the growing season. Spruce can be dehydrated to a lower water content than pine without injury. From Pisek and Larcher (1954).

Levitt (1972) regarded the formation of $-SH$ groups as important and Stocker and Ross (1956) attached great importance to changes in protoplasmic structure. Stadelmann (1971) discussed methods of measuring protoplasmic permeability and viscosity in relation to desiccation tolerance. Today the emphasis seems to have shifted toward the resistance of fine structure to injury by dehydration, as indicated by the work of Giles *et al.* (1976) on maize and sorghum, Vieira da Silva on cotton (Vieira da Silva *et al.*, 1974; 1976), and Mooney *et al.* (1977) and Armond *et al.* (1978) on creosote bush.

In summary, as Parker (1956, 1968), Begg and Turner (1976), and Kozlowski (1976b) stated, there are several causes of drought tolerance. These include characteristics which postpone dehydration such as deep root systems, thick cutin, and good stomatal control of transpiration, as well as the capacity of protoplasm to endure desiccation. Levitt (1972) discussed these factors in great detail and concluded that capacity to avoid or postpone desiccation is more important than the capacity to endure or tolerate it (pp. 417–424). Although the capacity to tolerate and survive dehydration is often important in the establishment of seedlings and in the survival of natural vegetation neither modern forestry nor horticulture is likely to be profitable where prolonged and severe droughts occur, unless irrigation is feasible.

Drought Hardening

It is well known that plants which have previously been subjected to water stress suffer less injury from drought than plants not previously stressed. For example, when potted plants are suddenly transferred from a shaded, humid environment to full sun their leaves often suffer injury even though the plants are well watered. This is generally attributed to less cutinization and larger interveinal areas of shade-grown leaves, and a lower root-shoot ratio. Rook (1973) found that seedlings of Monterey pine watered daily had higher rates of stomatal and cuticular transpiration than those watered less frequently, but there was no difference in their root-shoot ratios. The seedlings watered daily suffered more severe water stress and made less root growth after transplanting than those watered less frequently, probably because the latter had better control of transpiration.

Growers of both herbaceous and woody plants for transplanting to the field commonly ''harden'' their seedlings to improve survival. Often this is done simply by exposing the seedlings to full sun and decreasing the frequency of watering. Forest nursery operators often prune the roots by undercutting and root wrenching their seedlings to produce compact, profusely branched root systems. These treatments also produce temporary water stress.

There likewise is evidence that protoplasmic changes are produced which are favorable to survival under water stress. For example, the work of Mooney *et al.* (1977) indicates that the photosynthetic apparatus of creosote bush produced in a dry habitat is more tolerant of water stress than that of plants produced in a moist habitat. This may be analogous to the temperature acclimation of chloroplast membranes of creosote bush reported by Mooney *et al.* (1977) and Armond *et al.* (1978).

MEASUREMENT OF WATER STRESS

It was realized early in this century by ecologists and physiologists that quantitative measurements of plant water stress were needed, but suitable methods were unavailable. Numerous measurements of osmotic pressure were made (Korstian, 1924; Harris, 1934), but after the advantages of measuring the water potential (then termed suction force or diffusion pressure deficit) were appreciated there was no satisfactory method of measuring it. As a result, much of the early research on water relations was inconclusive because no quantitative measurements were made of the degree of stress to which the plants were subjected. Fortunately, in the past two decades several practical methods have been developed and there is no longer any excuse for failing to measure plant water stress in experiments where the water status of plants is important.

Sampling Problems

Whatever method is used, the collection of representative and comparable samples is very important. Leaves are sensitive indicators of water stress, but their water status varies widely with age, time of day, degree of exposure, and location on the plant. Large errors can be introduced by comparing samples of different ages or those collected at different times of day. Care also must be taken to prevent changes in water status during the interval between collection and measurement.

Direct Measurement of Water Status

The errors inherent in measurement and calculation of water content on a fresh or a dry weight basis have already been mentioned and are discussed in detail by Barrs (1968, pp. 239–241). This has led some investigators to express tissue water content as a percentage of the fully turgid water content. Stocker, who introduced this method, termed the result calculated by the following equation the water deficit, but it is often termed the water saturation deficit or WSD:

$$\text{Water deficit} = \frac{\text{fully turgid wt} - \text{fresh wt}}{\text{fully turgid wt} - \text{oven-dry wt}} \times 100$$

Weatherley calculated what he termed the relative turgidity by a rearrangement of Stocker's equation:

$$\begin{matrix}\text{Relative turgidity}\\ \text{or}\\ \text{Relative water content}\end{matrix} = \frac{\text{fresh wt} - \text{oven-dry wt}}{\text{turgid wt} - \text{oven-dry wt}} \times 100$$

Relative turgidity is now often and preferably termed relative water content or RWC. The two terms are complementary, RWC = 100 − WSD. The exact procedure likely to give the most reliable results varies with the species. Weatherley introduced the use of disks of leaf tissue, but Clausen and Kozlowski (1965b) and Harms and McGregor (1962) found the use of entire needles satisfactory for several species of conifers and

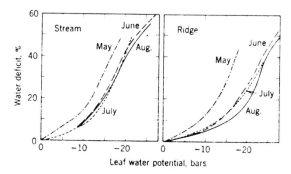

Fig. 13.24. Comparison of the relationship between water deficit and water potential of dogwood leaves of increasing age from two habitats. There was more change with age in leaves from the ridge than in leaves from the better-watered trees beside a stream. From Knipling (1967).

Hewlett and Kramer (1963) found entire leaves more satisfactory than disks for some woody species.

Use of the water saturation deficit or relative water content permits following changes in water content with a minimum of apparatus. Unfortunately, a given water deficit does not represent the same water potential in leaves of different ages, species, or habitats (Fig. 13.24). Neither can plant water stress measured in percentage be compared with soil water stress. The use of these methods is discussed critically by Barrs (1968).

Measurement of Water Potential

Probably the most satisfactory single measurement of plant and soil water status is measurement of water potential, because water movement from soil to plant and within the plant is controlled by its potential. This can be done either by the use of liquid equilibration methods, thermocouple psychrometers, or the Scholander pressure chamber. All of these methods are discussed in detail by Barrs (1968) and Slavik (1974).

The dye method requires no expensive equipment and can be used in the field, but some species show large errors (Brix, 1966; Knipling and Kramer, 1967). The pressure chamber method popularized by Scholander and his colleagues also is useful for field measurements (Waring and Cleary, 1967). It really measures the xylem water potential, but it is generally assumed that this is approximately equal to the water potential of leaf cells. Boyer (1967) found that measurements of the water potentials of yew and sunflower in a pressure chamber agreed with those made by the psychrometer method, but measurements on rhododendron did not. Kaufmann (1968b) also found a better agreement between the two methods for some species than for others. Use of the pressure chamber was discussed in detail by Ritchie and Hinckley (1975).

For many purposes, measurements made by thermocouple psychrometers are most useful because this instrument measures the free energy status of water in the system.

Also, after killing the sample the osmotic potential can be measured and the turgor pressure calculated. Unfortunately, the presence of salt on the leaf surfaces produces errors and the pressure chamber method probably is more accurate for leaves that secrete salt. The equipment for thermocouple psychrometers is expensive and difficult to use in the field. However, psychrometers are now available for measurements of the water potential of attached leaves, roots, and the soil *in situ,* as well as for detached plant parts and soil samples. The use of thermocouple psychrometers was discussed by Barrs (1968), by Wiebe *et al.* (1971), in a monograph edited by Brown and Van Haveren (1974), and by Slavik (1974).

Water potential is a measure of the free energy status of water in plants and soil. It controls water movement and probably is the best simple indicator of the water status of plants. However, cell enlargement is controlled by cell turgor or pressure potential and osmotic potentials may also be important (Hsiao *et al.,* 1976). Thus, when studying growth and cell enlargement it may be desirable or even necessary to measure both water potential and osmotic potential in order to estimate the turgor or pressure potential. The pressure volume method of Tyree and Hammel (1972) was used by Roberts and Knoerr (1977) to estimate the values of the various components of water potential in trees of several species. A consistent increase in the ratio of turgor pressure to water potential from summer to autumn was observed in the five species studied.

Indirect Estimates of Water Status

For various reasons many attempts have been made to characterize the water status of plants indirectly. Probably the oldest method is to observe wilting and describe it as slight, moderate, or severe, but this overlooks the fact the leaves of some plants wilt after losing very little water while others do not wilt even when severely dehydrated. Premature closure of stomata is a fairly reliable indicator of developing water stress in many, but not all, species, and the availability of diffusion porometers makes measurement easy, but it does not provide any quantitative measure of water stress. Decrease in the thickness of leaves and the diameter of stems and fruits also indicates the development of water stress. The development of beta gauges to measure changes in leaf mass permits monitoring rapid changes in water content, and the use of strain gauges permits accurate and rapid measurement of changes in dimensions of stems and fruits. Several investigators have shown a correlation between oleoresin exudation pressure and water stress in pines (Lorio and Hodges, 1968), and it appears that the latex pressure also is an indicator of water stress (Buttery and Boatman, 1966). However, none of these methods permit the quantitative measurements of the water status of plants that is absolutely necessary in all research involving the effects of water on plant processes and plant growth.

In conclusion, it should be reemphasized that plant water status or water balance is governed by complex interactions involving soil, plant, and atmosphere. Also, because water stress affects essentially every physiological process, drought is the environmental factor that most often limits tree growth. Thus study of plant water relations should emphasize a better understanding of how water stress reduces growth and how such reductions can be minimized.

GENERAL REFERENCES

Brown, R. W., and Van Haveren, B. P., eds. (1972). "Psychrometry in Water Relations Research." Utah Agric. Exp. Stn., Logan.

Dixon, H. H. (1974). "Transpiration and the Ascent of Sap in Plants." Macmillan, New York.

Eckardt, F. E., ed. (1965). "Methodology of Plant Eco-Physiology," Arid Zone Res. 25. UNESCO, Paris.

Esau, K. (1977). "Plant Anatomy," 3rd ed. Wiley, New York.

Hagan, R. W., Haise, H. R., and Edminster, T. W., eds. (1967). "Irrigation of Agricultural Lands," Agronomy 11. Am. Soc. Agron., Madison, Wisconsin.

Hsiao, T. C. (1973). Plant responses to water stress. *Annu. Rev. Plant Physiol.* **24,** 519–570.

Kozlowski, T. T., ed. (1968–1978). "Water Deficits and Plant Growth," Vols. 1–5. Academic Press, New York.

Kramer, P. J. (1969). "Plant and Soil Water Relationships. A Modern Synthesis." McGraw-Hill, New York.

Levitt, J. (1972). "Responses of Plants to Environmental Stresses." Academic Press, New York.

Slatyer, R. O. (1967). "Plant Water Relationships." Academic Press, New York.

Slavik, B. (1974). "Methods of Studying Plant Water Relations." Czech. Acad. Sci. Publ. House, Prague.

Zimmermann, M. H., and Brown, C. L. (1971). "Trees: Structure and Function." Springer-Verlag, Berlin and New York.

Also see references at end of Chapter 12.

Physiology of Seeds and Seedlings

INTRODUCTION

Growth of a woody plant usually begins with germination of its most important propagule, the seed. The essential structure in a seed is the living embryo and most of our concern in handling and storing seeds is with providing conditions that will keep the embryo alive and ready to resume growth when the seed is planted.

The resumption of growth of the embryo and its development into a new, independent seedling involves most of the important processes included in the realm of plant physiology such as absorption of water, digestion of foods, synthesis of enzymes and hormones, nitrogen, and phosphorus metabolism, translocation, and assimilation.

SEED STRUCTURE AND COMPOSITION

Seeds of woody plants vary widely in size, shape, color, and structure. They range in size from those that are barely visible, such as those of sourwood and rhododendron, to those of the coconut which may have a fresh weight of 9 kg. Surfaces of seed coats vary from highly polished to roughened. Seed appendages include wings, arils, caruncles, spines, tubercles, and hairs.

A true seed is a fertilized mature ovule that has an embryo, stored food material (rarely missing), and a protective coat or coats. However, in practice the term "seed" is not always restricted to this definition. Rather, seed is often used in a functional sense for a unit of dissemination, a disseminule. In this sense the term seed is applied to dry, one-seeded or rarely two- to several-seeded fruits as well as true seeds. For example, dry one-seeded fruits such as the samaras of elm and the nut and cupule of beech are generally, although incorrectly, referred to as seeds.

The embryo is a miniature plant comprised of one or more cotyledons (first leaves), a plumule (embryonic bud), hypocotyl (stem portion), and radicle (rudimentary root) (Fig. 14.1). The size of the embryo varies greatly in seeds of different species. In some species it is a rudimentary structure whereas in others it almost fills the seed (Fig. 14.2). The embryos of bamboo and palm seeds have only one cotyledon and therefore are classified as monocotyledons. Embryos of most woody angiosperms are dicotyledonous, having two cotyledons, while gymnosperms have from two to as many as 18 cotyledons, depending on the species.

The food supply in seeds may be stored either in the cotyledons or in tissue surrounding the embryo, which in angiosperms is endosperm. True endosperm is triploid in chromosome number, having been formed after union of the diploid fusion nucleus and a sperm, and is the principal food storage tissue of seeds of many dicotyledonous species. In seeds of some plants, such as ailanthus, some food is stored in the endosperm and some in the cotyledons. In gymnosperm seeds food is stored primarily in the megagametophyte (female gametophyte) that encloses the embryo. The megagametophyte is haploid in chromosome number and quite different in origin from the endosperm, although it serves the same function.

The seed coats, which protect the embryo from desiccation or attacks by pests, usually consist of an outer hard coat, the testa, and a thin, membranous inner coat. However, considerable variation occurs in seed coat characteristics. For example, in poplar and willow the testa is very soft, whereas in hawthorn, holly, and most legumes

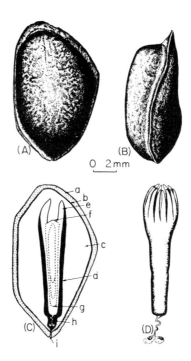

Fig. 14.1.   Structure of mature seed of sugar pine (A). (B) Exterior view of two planes. (C) Longitudinal section: a: seed coat; b: nucellus; c: endosperm; d: embryo cavity; e: cotyledons; f: plumule; g: radicle; h: suspensor; i: micropyle. (D) Embryo. From Anonymous (1948).

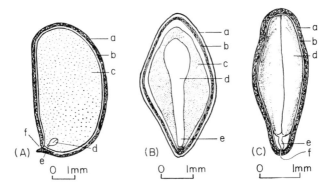

Fig. 14.2.   Variations in seed structure. (A) Aralia, with large endosperm and small embryo; (B) hemlock, with large embryo surrounded by endosperm; (C) shadbush, with no endosperm and embryo almost filling the seed cavity: a: outer seed coat; b: inner seed coat; c: endosperm; d: cotyledon; e: radicle; f: micropyle. From Anonymous (1948).

it is very hard. In elm both the inner and outer seed coats are membranous. The simple seed coats of gymnosperms vary from hard in pine to soft in fir.

Seeds contain variable quantities of foods in the form of carbohydrates, fats, and proteins. Seed starches are usually stored as granules; lipids occur in fat bodies. About 80% of the seed proteins are in storage organelles; the remaining 20% is distributed in nuclei, mitochondria, proplastids, microsomes, and cytosol (Ching, 1972). The proportions of carbohydrates, fats, and proteins vary greatly among seeds of different species, with carbohydrates or lipids usually predominating. Seeds of white oak and sugar maple are noteworthy for their high carbohydrate content, while those of pines and tung have high fat contents (Table 14.1). Sometimes there is wide variation in the seed composition of different species in the same genus. For example, seeds of sugar maple have very high carbohydrate contents, but in seeds of box elder lipids and proteins predominate. Although some seed proteins, such as enzyme proteins and nucleoproteins, are metabolically active, a large proportion is inactive. In addition to proteins, the nitrogenous material in seeds includes free amino acids and amides. The amides usually are glutamine and asparagine. Other seed constituents include variable quantities of minerals, phosphorus-containing compounds (phosphates, nucleotides. phospholipids, nucleoproteins), nucleic acids, alkaloids, organic acids, phytosterols, pigments, phenolic compounds, vitamins, and hormonal growth regulators. The complex metabolism of seed development was reviewed by Dure (1975).

Although the chemical composition of seeds is determined genetically, the relative amounts of various seed constituents often are appreciably influenced by the environmental regime at the seed source and by the nutrition of the parent tree. Durzan and Chalupa (1968) showed considerable variation in chemical composition of the embryos and megagametophytes of jack pine seeds collected from different geographical sources (Table 14.2). Climate at the seed source affected the degree to which

TABLE 14.1 Relative Carbohydrate, Fat, and Protein Contents of Tree Seeds[a]

Species	Percentage of air-dried seeds		
	Carbohydrates	Fats	Proteins
Silver maple	62.0	4.0	27.5
Horsechestnut	68.0	5.0	7.0
Chestnut	42.0	3.0	4.0
Pedunculate oak	47.0	3.0	3.0
White oak	58.4	6.8	7.4
Red oak	34.5	22.5	—
Tung	5.0	21.0	62.0
Eastern white pine	4.8	35.4	30.2
Longleaf pine	4.5	31.7	35.2

[a] From Mayer and Poljakoff-Mayber (1963) and Woody Plant Seed Manual (Anonymous, 1948).

TABLE 14.2 Variations in Chemical Composition of Megagametophytes and Embryos of Jack Pine Seed Collected from Various Geographical Sources[a]

	Neils Harbor, Nova Scotia	Smoky hills, Ontario	Wisconsin Dells, Wisconsin	Marl Lake, Michigan	Reindeer Lake, Saskatchewan
Gametophyte					
Dry weight, mg/100 gametophytes	200.80	152.30	255.40	224.40	178.40
Moisture, percent fresh weight	5.51	6.25	6.41	4.92	5.88
Soluble sugar, percent dry weight	3.36	3.93	3.21	3.13	4.14
Stachyose, percent dry weight	1.88	2.08	1.83	1.84	2.39
Raffinose, percent dry weight	0.53	0.96	0.51	0.50	0.90
Sucrose, percent dry weight	0.95	0.89	0.87	0.79	1.12
Soluble protein, μg/mg powder	17.80	19.60	16.60	17.20	19.20
Embryo					
Dry weight, mg/100 embryos	33.40	22.30	41.70	39.90	22.60
Moisture, percent fresh weight	4.39	4.09	4.37	4.33	4.18
Soluble sugar, percent dry weight	8.95	9.58	7.87	8.86	12.56
Stachyose, percent dry weight	4.08	4.57	3.75	4.58	5.61
Raffinose, percent dry weight	2.13	2.61	1.84	1.88	3.14
Sucrose, percent dry weight	2.74	2.40	2.28	2.40	3.81
Soluble protein, μg/mg powder	36.00	39.10	35.60	36.60	38.90
Embryo length, mm	2.83	2.48	2.98	3.04	2.37

[a] From Durzan and Chalupa (1968).

metabolism of carbon and nitrogen compounds proceeded before and during incipient germination.

SEED LONGEVITY

One of the most interesting characteristics of seeds is their wide variability in length of life, varying from a few days to several decades or even centuries. It was reported, for example, that seeds of the arctic tundra lupine that had been buried for at least 10,000 years in frozen silt germinated readily in the laboratory (Porsild *et al.*, 1967).

Short-lived seeds of woody plants include those high in water content such as those of yew, poplar, elm, willow, oak, hickory, birch, and buckeye. Seeds of many tropical species deteriorate rapidly. Tropical genera whose seeds characteristically have a short life span include *Theobroma, Coffea, Cinchona, Erythroxylon, Litchii, Montezuma, Macadamia, Hevea, Thea,* and *Cocos.* However, by temperature and humidity adjustments during storage, the life of many tropical seeds can be prolonged from a few weeks or months to at least a year. For detailed information on the storage conditions needed to prolong the life of seeds of many woody plants the reader is referred to the chapter by Harrington in Volume III of *Seed Biology* (Kozlowski, 1972c).

Seeds age progressively and grade imperceptibly from one stage of deterioration to the next. Initial symptoms of seed aging include a decrease in capacity to germinate as well as an increase in susceptibility to attacks by microorganisms. As seed deterioration continues the emerging radicles are short and cotyledons do not emerge from the seed coat. Finally the seed dies.

The rate of seed aging is controlled principally by relative humidity, which influences seed moisture content, and temperature, which affects biochemical processes. Harrington (1972) cited two useful rules, that have general validity and apply independently, on the relation of seed moisture in dry seeds and temperature to seed aging:

1. For each 1% increase in seed moisture content over the range from 5 to 14% the life of a seed is reduced by one-half. At seed moisture contents below 5%, seed aging often accelerates because of lipid autoxidation. At seed moisture contents above 14%, seed germination often is reduced by activities of fungi.

2. For each 5°C increase in temperature the life of a seed is reduced by one-half. This rule is generally applicable over a range of at least 0° to 50°C.

SEED TESTING

Concern with the longevity of seeds naturally leads to a consideration of the methods of testing their viability and quality. Knowledge concerning the percentage of seeds capable of germinating is essential, not only in studies of storage conditions, but also in nursery work in order to determine the rate of seeding.

Because the results obtained in germination tests depend on the environmental conditions and equipment used, seed testing has evolved into a highly regulated procedure involving prescribed and uniform methods. When properly applied by trained personnel, the methods used should provide results with a high degree of accuracy and reproducibility wherever the tests are made. At present, rules of the Association of Official Seed Analysts provide for the following tests: (1) purity test for dividing seed samples into pure seeds, other crop seeds, weed seeds, and inert matter; (2) examination for noxious weed seeds; and (3) germination test. Rules of the International Seed Testing Association provide for the three tests mentioned above as well as several seed quality tests, including seed health conditions such as seed-borne organisms, genuineness of species and cultivar, moisture content, provenance or locality of harvest, unit weight of seeds, and homogeneity of seed lots.

Direct tests of germination often require long periods of time. Attempts have been made to determine seed viability with such vital stains as indigo carmine and salts of selenium and tellurium. Other tests include use of x-ray photography and those based on greater exudation of sugar from dead than from viable seeds (MacKay, 1972). These methods have been largely abandoned and at present only two viability tests have been officially accepted by regulatory agencies. These will be discussed briefly.

Tetrazolium Test

The most generally employed test is one described by Lakon (1949, 1954) in Germany in which living cells are made visible by reduction of a colorless tetrazolium salt. Several different tetrazolium salts have been used but 2,3,4-triphenyltetrazolium chloride is used most. The colorless tetrazolium is reduced in living cells to insoluble pink or red formazan in the presence of dehydrogenases.

Over the years there have been several problems with the tetrazolium method, including (1) difficulty in staining some seeds; (2) the necessity of cutting seeds to observe color changes; (3) poor agreement with germination tests of certain seeds, especially those with low germination capacity; (4) lack of uniformity in interpreting staining; and (5) increase in labor over that required for standard germination tests. Some of these problems have been overcome (Grabe, 1970). Nevertheless, the tetrazolium test has been approved only for dormant seeds that do not germinate by conventional methods. The Association of Official Seed Analysts has approved the test for dormant seeds of *Fraxinus* spp., *Malus* spp., *Primus* spp., *Pyrus* spp., and *Pinus cembra*. The International Seed Testing Association has sanctioned the tetrazolium test for seeds of Atlantic white-cedar, baldcypress, nine species of pines, and all species of 17 other genera (Justice, 1972).

Embryo Excision Test

In this method embryos are excised from seeds, placed on wet filter paper in petri dishes, and tested for germination at ordinary light intensity and room temperature (not exceeding 24°C). Viable embryos generally germinate within 2 weeks. This test has been approved by the Association of Official Seed Analysts for seeds of eight species of pines, three other species, and all species of five genera. For more details on seed testing, the reader is referred to Justice (1972).

PATTERNS OF SEED GERMINATION

Seed germination may be considered to be the resumption of embryo growth resulting in seed coat rupture and emergence of the young plant. Growth of the embryo requires both cell division and elongation, cell division occurring first in some species and cell elongation in others. For example, cell division precedes cell elongation in embryo growth in *Pinus thunbergii* seeds (Goo, 1952). In cherry laurel, however, cell division and cell elongation begin more or less simultaneously in embryonic organs (Pollock and Olney, 1959). Reserve foods in the seed sustain the growing embryo until

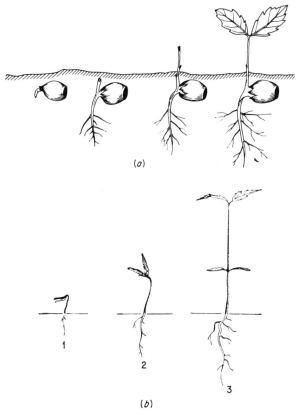

Fig. 14.3. Stages in germination of seeds. (a) Germination of white oak acorns in which cotyledons remain below ground (hypogeous). (b) Germination of red maple in which cotyledons are pushed out of the ground (epigeous). (Redrawn from various sources).

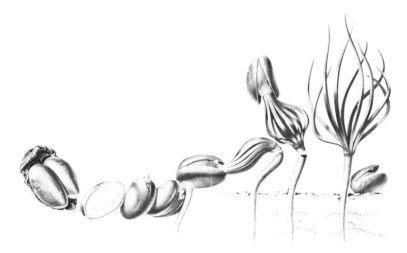

Fig. 14.4. Epigeous germination of pine seed. (Photo courtesy of St. Regis Paper Co.).

leaves expand to provide a photosynthetic system and roots develop to absorb water and minerals, thereby making the young plant physiologically self-sufficient.

As the embryo resumes growth during seed germination, the radicle elongates and penetrates the soil. In some woody plants—including most gymnosperms, beech, dogwood, black locust, ash, and most species of maple—the cotyledons are pushed out of the ground by the elongating hypocotyl (epigeous germination). In other species—including oak, walnut, and buckeye—the cotyledons remain underground while the epicotyl grows upward and develops foliage leaves (hypogeous germination) (Figs. 14.3 and 14.4).

Whereas all embryo cells divide during early seed germination, as seedlings develop the division of cells becomes localized in shoot and root apices. Important events following seed germination include the sequential formation of leaves, nodes, and internodes from apical meristems. Shoots may originate from apical meristems in leaf axils, providing the young plant with a system of branches. The root apical meristem forms a taproot or primary root. Often branch roots or secondary roots originate at new apical meristems in the pericycle of the taproot.

ENVIRONMENTAL CONTROL OF SEED GERMINATION

Rapid germination of seeds is very desirable because the shorter the time required the less opportunity there is for injury by insects, fungi, or unfavorable weather conditions or for seeds to be eaten by birds or rodents. Among the most important environmental factors controlling seed germination are water, temperature, light, oxygen, and various chemicals. These will be discussed separately.

Water

Nondormant seeds must imbibe a certain amount of water before they resume the physiological processes involved in germination. For example, seed respiration increases greatly with an increase in hydration above some critical level (Kozlowski and Gentile, 1959). The absolute amounts of water required to initiate germination are relatively small, usually not more than two to three times the weight of the seed (Koller, 1972). Following germination, however, a sustained supply of a large amount of water is needed by growing seedlings and this requirement becomes greater as transpiration increases.

Practically all viable seeds, except those with impermeable seed coats, can absorb enough water for germination from the soil at field capacity. In progressively drier soil both the rate of germination and final germination percentage decrease. For example, Kaufmann (1969) found that soil water deficits of -2.3 and -4.7 bars greatly inhibited germination of citrus seeds. After 31 days 88% of the seeds germinated when there was no water deficit (0 bar treatment) whereas at -2.3 and -4.7 bars only 23 and 3%, respectively, had germinated.

There is considerable variation among species in the effects of soil moisture availability on seed germination. As soil dried from field capacity, seed germination of Japanese red pine and Hinoki cypress decreased, with Hinoki cypress seeds being the more sensitive to drying. For example, seed germination of Hinoki cypress decreased by about 6% for each 1-bar decrease in soil water potential. The corresponding decrease was about 2.5% for Japanese red pine (Satoo, 1966).

The influence of soil moisture stress on germination often depends on the prevailing temperature. For example, at temperatures near 38°C, moisture stress was critical early in germination of mesquite seeds. However, at 29°C embryo growth was largely influenced by temperature, and soil moisture stress was not a limiting factor until later in the germination process (Scifres and Brock, 1969).

Temperature

After seed dormancy is broken by low temperatures, much higher temperatures are needed to induce rapid germination. Nondormant seeds can also germinate at low temperatures but much longer times are required.

Germination of any lot of nondormant seeds can occur over a temperature range within which there is an optimum at which the highest percent of germination is obtained in the shortest time. Minimum, optimum, and maximum temperatures for seed germination vary widely among seeds of different species and generally are lower for temperate zones species than for tropical species. Germination temperatures also vary considerably with seed source. Germination temperatures between 24° and 30°C were best for ponderosa pine seed sources east of the Rocky Mountains, whereas temperatures of 35°C or higher were optimal for Pacific Northwest sources (Callaham, 1964). Optimal germination temperatures often are different for seeds obtained from different plants of the same species.

Seeds of many species will germinate equally well over a rather wide temperature range. Seeds of lodgepole pine germinated at about the same rate at 20° as at 30°C (Critchfield, 1957), and germination of jack pine seed did not vary appreciably at 15°, 21°, or 27°C under continuous light (Ackerman and Farrar, 1965). Kaufmann and Eckard (1977) found that total emergence of seedlings of Englemann spruce and lodgepole pine was similar at 16° and 25°C, but reduced at 35°C. However, spruce seedlings emerged two days sooner than pine seedlings at 16°C. Other species have a rather narrow temperature range that may vary somewhat with preconditioning of seeds. For example, Norway maple seeds germinated best between 5° and 10°C. Box elder seeds had 67% germination as temperature alternated between 10° and 25°C, but only 12% when temperatures were alternated between 20° and 25°C (Roe, 1941).

Although seeds of many species will germinate at constant temperature, germination of most species requires or is increased by diurnal temperature fluctuations (Hatano and Asakawa, 1964). If seeds of Manchurian ash were first exposed to moist, low-temperature treatment and then placed in a constant temperature of 25°C, only a few germinated, and at a constant temperature of 8°C seed germination was greatly delayed. By comparison, alternating temperature between 8°C for 20 hr and 25°C for 4 hr each day greatly accelerated germination. Germination of Japanese red pine seeds also was accelerated by diurnal thermoperiodicity.

Radiation

Most seeds appear to be insensitive to light and germinate as well in the dark as in the light (Heit, 1968). However, seeds of some species require light for germination. These species will germinate at very low illuminance, those of spruce requiring only 0.08 lux; birch, 1 lux; and pine, 5 lux. Seeds of a few species require up to 100 lux for germination (Jones, 1961). Whereas light intensity has relatively minor effects on germination, both day length and wavelength often have pronounced effects. The promotive action of light on germination operates by increasing the growth potential of the embryo.

Day Length

For seeds of the majority of light-sensitive species of woody plants the most rapid and greatest total germination occur in daily light periods of 8 to 12 hr. Interrupting the dark period with a short light flash or increasing temperature usually has the same effect as extending the duration of exposure to light. A few examples of variation in photoperiodic requirements among species will be given. In eastern hemlock 8- or 12-hr days produced maximum seed germination, with no added response by increasing day length to 14 or 20 hr (Olson et al., 1959). Eucalyptus seeds germinated well in 8-hr days and those of birch in 20-hr days. Seeds of Douglas-fir, however, germinated in continuous light or 16-hr days, but not in 8-hr days (Jones, 1961).

Wavelength

Germination of seeds of a number of species of herbaceous and woody plants is sensitive to wavelength. Woody angiosperms showing such sensitivity include *Alnus inokuma, Artemisia monosperma, Betula pubescens, Fraxinus mandshurica,* and *Ulmus americana.* Sensitive gymnosperms include species of *Abies, Picea,* and *Pinus* (*P. thunbergii, P. strobus, P. palustris, P. sylvestris, P. taeda,* and *P. virginiana*) (Hatano and Asakawa, 1964; Koller, 1972).

The germination response to wavelength is controlled by the red and far-red phytochrome pigment system. Red light promotes germination and far-red light inhibits it. If red (650 nm) and far-red light (730 nm) are given successively, the capacity of seeds to germinate depends on the irradiation that is given last, the influence of red light in promoting germination being nullified if it is followed by far-red light. If, however, far-red light is followed by red light, then germination is stimulated (Table 14.3).

The red-light requirement for promoting germination often varies with temperature or duration of water uptake. Toole *et al.* (1961) noted, for example, that germination of Virginia pine seeds occurred faster for seeds promoted with red light after a 20-day period of imbibition of water at 5°C, than in seeds given a 1-day period of imbibition. Greater germination of seeds was promoted by red light when they had previously absorbed water at 5°C rather than at 25°C.

Both metabolic activity and mitosis in embryos are stimulated by red light and inhibited by far-red light in light-sensitive seeds. This was shown by Nyman (1961) by alternating red and far-red treatments of Scotch pine seeds and observing their effects on respiration, mitosis, and germination (Fig. 14.5). The time of response varied with the process measured. Significant increases in respiration were induced by red light after imbibition for 24 hr, whereas mitotic activity was stimulated after 36 hr of imbibition. Radicles did not emerge until after more than 48 hr of imbibition.

Phytochrome is a light-receptive, protein pigment complex that is widely distributed in low concentrations in green plants. It usually is most abundant in meristematic tissues. Light acts on phytochrome (P) to change it from an inactive form, with maximum absorption in the red part of the spectrum (660 nm), to the active form, with maximum absorption in the far red (730 nm). In mature seeds some P730 often is present, but during imbibition it changes to the inactive P660 form. Seeds conditioned to germinate through the activity of red light can revert to a nongerminating state by

TABLE 14.3 Influence of Alternating Red and Far-Red Irradiation on Germination of Virginia Pine Seeds[a]

Character of irradiation[b]	Percent germination
Dark control	4
R	92
R + FR	4
R + FR + R	94
R + FR + R + FR	3
R + FR + R + FR + R	93

[a] From Toole *et al.* (1961).
[b] R = red, FR = far red.

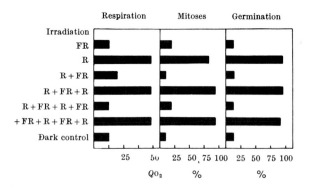

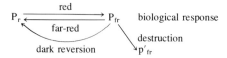

Fig. 14.5. Reversible effects of red (R) and far-red (FR) irradiation on respiration rate, occurrence of mitoses in embryos, and percent germination in seeds of Scotch pine. (From Nyman, 1961.)

exposure to far-red radiation, which changes P730 back to P660 (Taylorson and Hendricks, 1976). The transformations of phytochrome may be summarized as follows:

$$P_r \underset{\text{far-red}}{\overset{\text{red}}{\rightleftarrows}} P_{fr} \quad \text{biological response}$$
$$\searrow \text{destruction}$$
$$\text{dark reversion} \qquad p'_{fr}$$

In addition to affecting seed germination, phytochrome is also involved in flowering, stem elongation, phototropism, "sleep movements" of leaves (nyctinasty), and the orientation of chloroplasts in cells.

Oxygen

As stimulation of respiration is an essential early phase of seed germination, it is not surprising that oxygen supply affects germination. Seeds usually require higher oxygen concentrations for germination than seedlings require for subsequent growth. The relatively high oxygen requirements of seeds of some species are the result of their seed coats acting as barriers to diffusion of oxygen into seeds. Removal of coats of red pine seeds or exposure of intact seeds to high oxygen concentrations greatly accelerates the rate of oxygen uptake. Removal of seed coats, followed by exposure of the decoated seeds to high oxygen concentrations, accelerates respiration even more (Kozlowski and Gentile, 1959).

Oxygen plays a primary role as the electron acceptor in respiration. In some species it may also be involved in inactivation of one or more inhibitors. Germination of isolated embryos of European white birch and European silver birch was prevented by aqueous extracts of seeds, but such inhibition could be decreased by exposure to light (Black and Wareing, 1959). It appeared that the intact seed coat prevented germination in the dark by reducing the oxygen supply below a critical level. Nevertheless, embryos without seed coats germinated in low concentrations of oxygen, hence the embryo appeared to have a high oxygen requirement only when the seed coat was present.

Soaking seeds for a few hours hastens germination, but prolonged soaking induces injury and loss in viability of many seeds, presumably because of the reduced concentration and availability of dissolved oxygen in comparison with that of the air. However, the effects of soaking on germination vary widely among seeds of different species. Soaking seeds of several upland species for 3 to 5 days did not decrease germination, but soaking for 10 days reduced germination considerably and soaking for 30 days killed the seeds (Toumey and Durland, 1923). By comparison, seeds of bottomland species, such as tupelo-gum and baldcypress, have low oxygen requirements and can endure prolonged inundation without loss of viability. Hosner (1957) did not find any appreciable effect on germination of six bottomland species from soaking seeds for as long as 32 days.

Seedbeds

Because of wide differences in physical characteristics, temperatures, and availability of water and mineral nutrients, establishment of plants varies greatly in different natural seedbeds (Winget and Kozlowski, 1965a). Mineral soil is a good seedbed because of its high infiltration capacity, adequate aeration, and close contact between soil particles and seeds. Litter and duff often are less suitable than mineral soil because they warm slowly, inhibit root penetration, prevent seeds from contacting the mineral soil, dry rapidly, and shade small seedlings. Because of its high water-holding capacity, sphagnum moss often is a suitable seedbed for germination but it may subsequently smother young seedlings. Decayed wood also is an excellent natural seedbed for seeds of forest trees, probably because of its capacity for water retention (Place, 1955).

Chemicals

Several applied chemicals, including insecticides, fungicides, herbicides, and fertilizers sometimes check plant establishment by direct suppression of seed germination, toxicity to young seedlings, or both (Kozlowski and Sasaki, 1970). Such widely used chemicals as benzene hexachloride and the fungicide, N-[(trichloromethyl)]thio-4-cyclohexane-1,2-dicarboximide (captan), have been shown to injure roots and inhibit growth of young tree seedlings (Simkover and Shenefelt, 1952; Denne and Atkinson, 1973).

Triazine herbicides, such as 2-chloro-4-(ethylamino)-6-(isopropylamino)-s-triazine (atrazine) and 2-chloro-4,6-bis(ethylamino)-s-triazine (simazine), did not affect seed germination but were toxic to recently emerged seedlings. Other herbicides at comparable dosages, i.e., N-1-naphthylphthalamic acid (naptalam), 2-chlorallyl diethyl-dithiocarbamate (CDEC), s-ethyl dipropylthiocarbamate (EPTC), N,N-diallyl-2-chloracetamide (CDAA), and 2,4-dichlorophenoxyacetic acid (2,4-D) variously inhibited both seed germination and early seedling growth. Both 2,4-D and CDAA greatly suppressed seed germination (Sasaki *et al.*, 1968).

While some herbicides kill seedlings, others cause abnormal developmental changes such as curling, shriveling, or fusion of cotyledons (Fig. 14.6), and chlorosis, distortion, and growth inhibition of various foliar appendages. Wu *et al.* (1971) found that cotyledons, primary needles, and secondary needles of red pine were especially susceptible to damage. The primary mechanisms by which herbicides produce toxicity are diverse and involve interference with vital processes as well as direct injury to cells and tissues.

Herbicide toxicity varies greatly with methods of application because of differences in herbicide uptake among seedlings (Kozlowski and Torrie, 1965). Toxicity of a given

Fig. 14.6. Effect of herbicides on red pine seedlings in the cotyledon stage of development. Untreated control seedlings are shown on the left and herbicide-treated seedlings on the right. Upper photo: distortion of cotyledons of 20-day-old seedlings by Tordon (4-amino-3,5,6-trichloropicolinic acid). Lower photo: fusion of cotyledons and suppression of their development by CDEC (2 chloroallyldiethyldithiocarbamate).

herbicide that is applied to the soil surface often is low, intermediate if it is incorporated in the soil, and greatest if the herbicide is maintained in direct contact, in solution, or in suspension with plant tissues. The high absolute toxicity of many herbicides is variously masked in soil cultures because soil-applied herbicides are lost by evaporation, leaching, microbial or chemical decomposition, and irreversible adsorption in the soil (Kozlowski *et al.*, 1967a,b).

Seed germination and growth of young seedlings are inhibited not only by applied chemicals but also by a variety of naturally occurring compounds in plants that are released to the soil. Such allelopathic chemicals are released from roots and aerial tissues as well.

Naturally occurring compounds that have inhibitory effects on the seed germination and growth of neighboring plants include phenolic acids, coumarins and quinones, terpenes, essential oils, alkaloids, and organic cyanides. Allelopathic chemicals are ecologically important because they influence succession, dominance, vegetation dynamics, species diversity, structure of plant communities, and productivity (Whittaker, 1970). Effects of allelopathic chemicals are discussed further in Chapter 17 of this volume and in Rice (1974).

PHYSIOLOGY OF SEED GERMINATION

The essential event in seed germination is resumption of growth by the embryo and its development into an independent seedling. Many changes are set in motion as germination begins including: (1) seed hydration, (2) increased respiration, (3) enzyme turnover, (4) increase in adenosine phosphate, (5) increase in nucleic acids, (6) digestion of stored foods and transport of the soluble products to the embryo where cellular components are synthesized, (7) increase in cell division and enlargement, and (8) differentiation of cells into tissues and organs. The exact order of the early changes is not clear and there is considerable overlap but, with few exceptions, absorption of water is a necessary first step. Increase in hydration is associated with cell enlargement and cell division in the growing points as well as release of hormones that stimulate enzyme formation and activity. Although an increase in fresh weight of the seed accompanies imbibition, there is an early loss in dry weight due to oxidation of substrates and to some leakage. After the root emerges and begins to absorb minerals and the cotyledons or leaves become photosynthetically active, the dry weight of the seedling begins to increase until it regains and then surpasses the original seed weight.

Hydration

Water must be imbibed by seeds to increase protoplasmic hydration and set in motion the chain of metabolic events associated with germination. Imbibition of water softens hard seed coats and the swelling of the imbibing embryo bursts the seed coat, permitting emergence of the radicle.

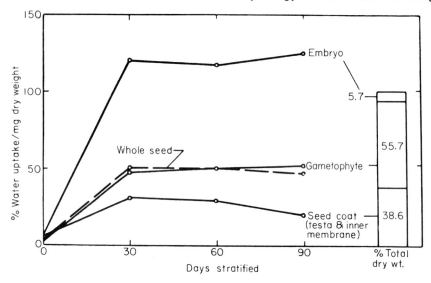

Fig. 14.7. Water uptake of various parts of sugar pine seeds during stratification. From Stanley (1958).

Considering that starch grains, reserve proteins, and fats are water insoluble, water probably is absorbed very early by metabolically functional organelles and outer membranes of storage organelles (Ching, 1972). Absorption of water by seeds often stops for several hours or days at the end of the initial imbibition period. It is then resumed and is rapid at the time of radicle emergence.

The amount of water absorbed by various parts of the seed during germination varies greatly. In sugar pine, the embryo, which was the smallest seed component, absorbed the most water as a percentage of its dry weight. The megagametophyte absorbed less water and the seed coat the least (Fig. 14.7). The rate and pattern of water uptake by embryos are influenced by dormancy-breaking treatments. For example, in embryos of sugar pine seeds, water uptake increased as stratification time under moist conditions was increased. The rate and amount of water imbibed by seeds also vary with the nature of the seed coat, size and chemical composition of seed, and water temperature.

Respiration

Oxygen uptake of dry seeds is extremely low but it increases greatly as water is imbibed and generally is correlated with the rate of water uptake. Following an increase in respiratory activity of the whole seed, embryo, or gametophyte, a plateau of oxygen uptake is achieved that may be maintained for a few days. Thereafter the rate of respiration increases greatly (Stanley, 1958).

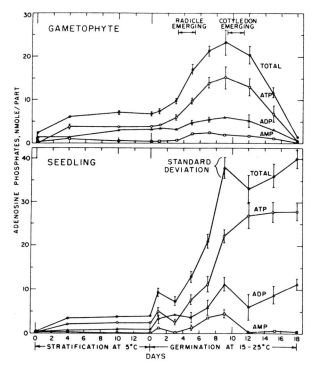

Fig. 14.8. Changes in adenosine monophosphate (AMP), adenosine diphosphate (ADP), adenosine triphosphate (ATP), and total adenosine phosphate in gametophyte and embryo or seedling of ponderosa pine during stratification and germination. From Ching and Ching (1972).

Respiration involves the oxidative breakdown of organic seed constituents—primarily starches, sugars, fatty acids, and triglycerides—providing the large amounts of energy in the form of ATP required for synthesizing the enzymes involved in the degradation of reserve foods in storage tissues of seeds and for subsequently building up cellular constituents in the seedling (see also Chapter 6).

Living cells of seeds contain mitochondria that produce ATP and contain enzyme systems for synthesizing ADP. During low-temperature stratification of ponderosa pine seeds, total adenosine phosphates (AP) increased seven times in the embryo and six times in the gametophyte. During germination, total adenosine phosphate increased to a 20-fold peak (Fig. 14.8). In sugar maple seeds, ATP levels were relatively low in embryo axes taken from dry, dormant seeds but they increased rapidly during the first 10 days of stratification at 5°C and subsequently at a lower rate (Table 14.4).

A high energy charge (EC) is important for termination of seed dormancy because of the role of ATP in respiration (see Chapter 6). The energy charge is the sum of the mole fraction of ATP plus one-half the mole fraction of ADP divided by the sum of the mole fractions of ATP, ADP, and AMP, as shown by the following equation:

TABLE 14.4   Effect of Stratification at 5°C on ATP, ADP, AMP, and Energy Charge in Sugar Maple Seeds[a]

Stratification period	Adenylates[b]			Energy charge[c]
	ATP	ADP	AMP	
Days				
0	46.9 ± 12.6	180.2 ± 34.6	690.8 ± 31.1	0.15
1	137.9 ± 13.4	163.3 ± 24.7	194.9 ± 15.0	0.44
5	238.9 ± 27.9	119.4 ± 14.1	57.3 ± 14.1	0.72
10	327.2 ± 31.7	98.1 ± 17.0	60.2 ± 14.0	0.78
20	354.3 ± 63.2	99.8 ± 21.0	63.6 ± 18.3	0.78
40	416.3 ± 48.8	92.1 ± 11.5	63.2 ± 12.2	0.80
75	456.3 ± 70.7	91.4 ± 29.3	56.8 ± 11.8	0.83

[a] From Simmonds and Dumbroff (1974).
[b] Measurements in nmoles/g dry weight.
[c] Energy charge = ATP + ½ ADP/ATP + ADP + AMP.

$$\text{Energy charge} = \frac{[ATP] + \frac{1}{2}[ADP]}{[ATP] + [ADP] + [AMP]}$$

Simmonds and Dumbroff (1974) showed that the energy charge increased greatly during stratification of sugar maple seeds (Table 14.4) and that, even at high ATP levels, embryonic axes elongated in response to gibberellic acid and kinetin only when the energy charge was near 0.8 or greater.

Enzyme Turnover

Even though some enzymes are active in dormant seeds, there generally is a marked increase in enzyme synthesis and activity after germination processes are set in motion. The increased activity of some enzymes is the result of their conversion from an inactive to an active form. However, many new enzymes are also synthesized after imbibition of water. Concurrently, existing enzymes are destroyed; hence, enzyme turnover is very great. Although the types of enzymes vary greatly among seeds and are related to the types of substrates present, they include those involved in digestion of accumulated foods and those that hydrolyze cell wall constituents.

As mentioned previously, hormones play an important role in controlling enzyme synthesis in seeds. For example gibberellin, which stimulates synthesis of amylase, occurs in starchy seeds, lipase in cotton seeds (Black and Altschul, 1965), and isocitrate lyase and RNA polymerase in hazel seeds (Pinfield, 1968a; Jarvis *et al.*, 1968). Such observations emphasize the importance of release of hormones as a first step after imbibition of water or after stratification.

Phosphorus Metabolism

Phosphorus-containing compounds in seeds include nucleotides, nucleic acids, phospholipids, phospate esters of sugars, and phytin. There is considerable interest in the phosphate metabolism of germinating seeds because of the relationship between phosphorus and energy transfer in metabolism. When cherry embryos were chilled to break dormancy, phosphate was translocated from the cotyledons and appeared in the embryo axis as sugar phosphates, high-energy nucleotides, and nucleic acids. In unchilled embryos, however, inorganic phosphates accumulated in cells (Olney and Pollock, 1960). Such experiments have been interpreted as showing that the breaking of dormancy is accompanied by phosphate metabolism and an increase in available energy to the embryo, as mentioned in Chapter 6.

Nucleic Acids

Growth of the seedling requires protein synthesis. Nucleic acids play an important role in the storage and readout of genetic information in cell nuclei as well as in the use of such information in protein synthesis. In general, nucleic acids decrease in storage tissues and increase in embryos during germination. Patterns of nucleic acid metabolism and protein synthesis vary somewhat among seeds and even among groups of the same species.

During germination of red pine seeds, the amounts of nucleic acids increased greatly in embryos whereas there was little change in the megagametophyte (Sasaki and Brown, 1969). The breaking of seed dormancy by chilling or by gibberellin is accompanied by increased synthesis of nucleic acids and the enzyme systems involved (Jarvis *et al.*, 1968; Villiers, 1972). The addition of abscisic acid, a hormone that appears to induce dormancy, inhibits production of nucleic acids (Villiers, 1975).

In Douglas-fir seeds the DNA content of the embryo increased slightly during stratification, doubled during the radicle emergence stage, and increased by 450% toward the end of germination. Synthesis of RNA also increased in seedlings, whereas it decreased in the megagametophyte. Changes in soluble nucleotides were similar to those in RNA. The changes in DNA, RNA, and soluble nucleotides indicated that nucleic acids were being synthesized (see Fig. 14.11).

Digestion, Translocation, and Utilization of Food Reserves

Germination of seeds involves a drastic reversal of metabolic processes in the food storage tissues. Cells that initially synthesized insoluble starch, protein, and lipids during seed development suddenly begin to hydrolyze these materials. During seed development there is transport into the storage tissues, but during germination the soluble products of hydrolysis are translocated out to the meristematic regions of the seedling. This must involve considerable activation and deactivation of enzymes and conversion of ''sinks'' into ''sources'' (Dure, 1975). This reduces the dry weight of storage tissues. For example, the dry weight of the megagametophyte of ponderosa

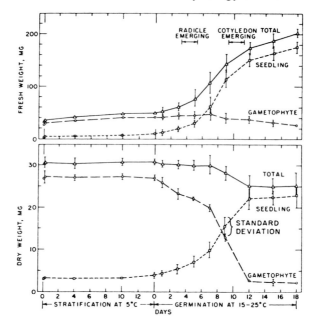

Fig. 14.9. Changes in fresh and dry weight in megagametophyte and embryo of ponderosa pine seedlings during stratification and germination. From Ching and Ching (1972).

pine seeds decreased greatly as it was depleted of reserves during germination (Fig. 14.9).

Carbohydrates

During the initial stages of germination, insoluble starch and reserve sugars are converted into soluble sugars, and the activity of amylases and phosphorylases increases. The soluble sugars are translocated from endosperm to cotyledon tissues to growing parts of the embryo. Cells of cotyledon tissues from dormant black oak acorns contain many starch granules, whereas cotyledons of germinating acorns contain few starch granules (Fig. 14.10).

Lipids

Reserve fats in seeds are first hydrolyzed to glycerol and fatty acids by the action of lipases. Some of the hydrolyzed fatty acids are reused in the synthesis of phospholipids and glycolipids that are needed as constituents of organelles and membranes. However, most of the fatty acids are converted to acetyl coenzyme A and then to sugar by reversal of the glycolytic pathway, as shown in Fig. 6.20. In seeds of jojoba wax esters play the role of food reserves during germination (Moreau and Huang, 1977). Compositional changes of Douglas-fir seed during germination are shown in Fig. 14.11. Lipids, the major food reserves, originally made up 48 and 55% of the dry weight of the gametophyte and embryo, respectively. During early germination the

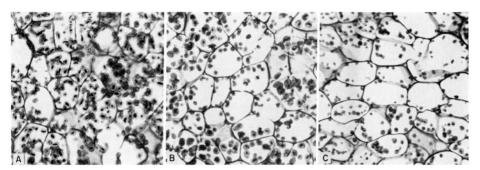

Fig. 14.10. Starch distribution in cotyledon of black oak acorns: (A) cells of dormant acorns, (B) cells of stratified acorns, (C) cells of germinated acorns. From Vozzo and Young (1975), University of Chicago Press.

lipids in the gametophyte decreased greatly and were used for embryo development. The dry weight of the embryo increased by 600% and that of the megagametophyte decreased by 70%.

Proteins

Reserve proteins in seeds are frequently broken down by proteolytic enzymes during germination to soluble nitrogen compounds which are then used by various parts of the seedling. Decrease in reserve proteins is associated with increases in amino acids and amides and is followed by synthesis of new protein in the growing part of the embryo (Durzan *et al.*, 1971; Mayer and Poljakoff-Mayber, 1975). Little nitrogen accumulates at storage sites because the rapid synthesis of new proteins in the developing embryo consumes the available nitrogen compounds.

Some of the proteins and peptidases are present in dry seeds and others appear during germination. Generally the enzymes with proteolytic activity that develop in the cotyledons or endosperm are similar to those found in other plant tissues.

SEED DORMANCY

Mature seeds of many species of woody plants will germinate immediately if planted under favorable environmental conditions, but seeds of most species exhibit some degree of dormancy. This means that they will not germinate promptly even when placed under the most favorable environmental conditions.

Seed dormancy may be advantageous or disadvantageous. The prolonged chilling requirement for breaking dormancy of seeds of many temperate zone plants prevents germination until spring. This tends to insure plant survival because earlier germination would subject the young plants to danger of injury by freezing. The seeds of some wild plants may remain dormant in the soil for many years and the period of germination of such seeds may be spread over years. Such dormancy provides for the establishment and survival of a species, even though the earliest emerging seedlings or even all of

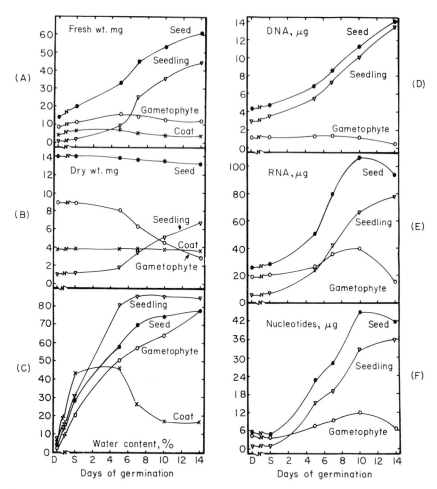

Fig. 14.11. A–R. Changes in weight and composition of embryo, megagametophyte, and whole seed of Douglas-fir during germination. D = air-dried seed, S = stratified seed. From Ching (1966).

those in a given year are killed by drought or frost. Another advantage of seed dormancy involves the restriction of seed germination in hot and dry regions to the short, wet period of the year. In seeds of some desert plants, inhibitors in the seed coat prevent germination. However, the inhibitors are leached out by sufficient rain to wet the soil thoroughly, insuring that the seeds germinate only when there is enough soil moisture for establishment (Wareing, 1963). In contrast, seed dormancy often is a nuisance to nursery operators who wish to have large quantities of seeds germinate

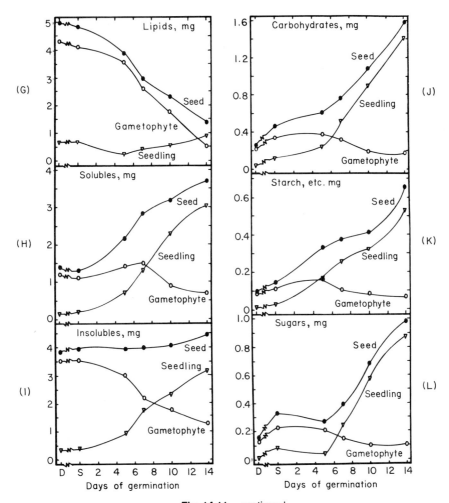

Fig. 14.11. continued

promptly in order to produce large and uniform crops of seedlings. The causes of seed dormancy and methods of breaking it are therefore of both physiological and practical importance.

Causes of Dormancy

Knowledge of the causes of seed dormancy often makes it possible to intelligently apply appropriate treatments to overcome the dormant condition of individual seed lots. Seed dormancy results from a number of causes, including: (1) immaturity of the embryo, (2) impermeability of seed coats, (3) mechanical resistance of seed coats to

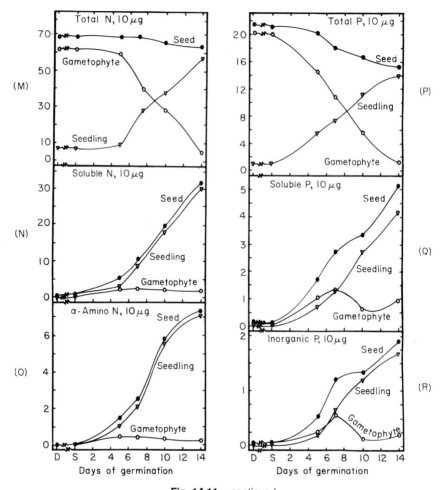

Fig. 14.11. continued

growth of the embryo, (4) metabolic blocks within the embryo, (5) a combination of
(1) to (4), or (6) secondary dormancy (Villiers, 1972).

Seed Coat Dormancy

A common cause of dormancy is the impermeability of seed coats to water or
oxygen. Seed coat dormancy is especially common in the seeds of Leguminosae,
which includes black locust, honey locust, and redbud. Redcedar, basswood, eastern
white pine, and apple seeds also have seed coat problems. The nature of seed coat
impermeability varies somewhat among species. In honey locust and black locust the
seed coat is a barrier both to imbibition of water and to oxygen uptake. However, in

eastern white pine and green ash the seed coat is permeable to water but restricts gas exchange. In apple seeds, the seed coats impede oxygen uptake, thereby making the supply inadequate for the high respiration rate necessary for germination of the embryo (Visser, 1954).

Seed coats of some species are said to be mechanically resistant, preventing the embryo from further development once it becomes fully grown in the seed. However, Villiers (1972) states that many such reported cases are probably caused by other factors such as physiological dormancy of the embryo.

Embryo Dormancy

Sometimes the embryo is immature and requires a period of "afterripening" (storage under favorable conditions) to reach a certain stage of development before germination occurs. Examples are the seeds of viburnum, holly, and ginkgo. However, the most common type of seed dormancy is one in which morphologically mature embryos are unable to resume growth and germinate. This type of physiological embryo dormancy is common in species of apple, lilac, oak, chestnut, dogwood, hickory, pear, and sycamore, among the angiosperms. Gymnosperms that show physiological embryo dormancy include some pines, baldcypress, Douglas-fir, hemlock, juniper, larch, spruce, and fir.

A state of physiological embryo dormancy, like bud dormancy, appears to develop in two stages in which mild and reversible dormancy passes progressively into deep-seated dormancy, which cannot be reversed by the same environmental conditions that induced it. Seeds of some species of *Fraxinus,* which normally become dormant, will germinate at once if they are harvested and planted before going through a drying phase.

Sometimes the failure of seeds to germinate is traceable to more than one specific type of dormancy. In some species of *Rosa,* seed germination is prevented by the mechanical restriction of a thick pericarp on embryo expansion, as well as by dormancy resulting from growth inhibitors in the achene (Jackson and Blundell, 1963). Such "double dormancy" has also been reported in seeds of hawthorn, junipers, yew, basswood, dogwood, osage-orange, yellowwood, witch-hazel, digger pine, Swiss stone pine, and whitebark pine. Dormancy in holly seed has been traced to both immature embryos and hard seed coats. Some idea of the complexity of the seed dormancy mechanism in certain species may be gained from Villiers' (1975) analysis of seed dormancy of European ash (Fig. 14.12). This species produces dry, single-seeded, dormant fruits, germination being normally postponed until at least the second season after the fruit is dispersed. The embryo is morphologically complete but it must grow to about twice its original size on reimbibition of water before germination will occur. However, expansion of the immature embryo is inhibited by the fruit coat, which interferes with oxygen uptake. Hence, growth of the embryo is further inhibited until the outer layers of the seed coat begin to decay. Even the fully grown embryo is dormant and cannot emerge from the seed until it is chilled for several months. Therefore, the need for embryo development as well as restriction of gas exchange

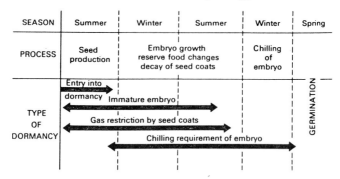

Fig. 14.12. Complexity of dormancy mechanisms of seeds of European ash. From Villiers (1975).

inhibit germination in the first spring. The chilling requirement is met in the second winter and germination finally occurs in the second spring after the seed is produced. Germination can be delayed even longer by slow decomposition of the fruit coat and inadequate chilling during the second winter.

Hormones and Seed Dormancy

Presumably all physiological dormancy is controlled by growth regulators. The onset of embryo dormancy often is associated with accumulation of growth inhibitors, and the breaking of dormancy with a shift in balance of growth promoters that overcome the effects of inhibitors (Wareing *et al.,* 1973; Taylorson and Hendricks, 1977). The similarity of embryo dormancy of seeds and of bud dormancy is emphasized by the similar appearance of physiologically dwarfed seedlings produced from unchilled embryos and the rosette growth of branches of fruit trees following a mild winter. Also, both embryo dormancy and bud dormancy can be broken by chilling, exogenous growth promoters, and/or long days.

Inhibitors

Various seed germination inhibitors occur in many species of woody plants in all parts of seeds and fruits, including the embryo, nucellus, testa, and pericarp. Abscisic acid (ABA) is perhaps the best known and most inhibitory substance of the inhibitor complex and is prevalent in seeds of peach, white ash, and apple (Lipe and Crane, 1966; Sondheimer *et al.,* 1968; Rudnicki, 1969). In some species, such as white ash, ABA decreases during the chilling of seeds. In other species, the inhibitor is not removed by chilling but its inhibitory effect may be overcome by an increase in growth promoters such as gibberellins or cytokinins. For example, chilling, which accelerated seed germination of European ash, did not reduce the activity of ABA in the embryo or endosperm but it did stimulate a germination promoter some time before germination occurred (Villiers and Wareing, 1965). Other naturally occurring germination inhibitors include such compounds as ethylene, ammonia, coumarin, and hydrogen cyanide.

Growth Promoters

The importance of growth promoters in overcoming seed dormancy is shown by several lines of evidence. For example, as mentioned earlier, during normal afterripening or after artificial chilling of some seeds, growth promoter levels increase although levels of inhibitors do not always decrease. Leaching of seeds, which might be expected to stimulate germination by removing inhibitors, often causes development of dwarf seedlings, possibly by removing growth-promoting substances. Also, seed germination in many species with dormant seeds can be increased by exogenous applications of growth promoters. For example, applied gibberellin induced enzymatic activity and growth of the embryo of hazel (Pinfield, 1968b). In sycamore maple, cytokinins but not gibberellins broke seed dormancy (Webb and Wareing, 1972; Webb *et al.*, 1973). In still other species, such as peach and sugar maple, both applied gibberellins and cytokinins can overcome seed dormancy (Khan and Heit, 1969; Webb and Dumbroff, 1969). These experiments emphasize the complexity and variability of specific hormonal controls of embryo dormancy in different species. Khan (1975) stressed the importance of hormonal interactions in seed dormancy and presented a useful model in which gibberellins were considered to play a primary role in bringing about germination, while the roles of inhibitors and cytokinins were visualized as secondary and essentially preventive and permissive.

Breaking of Dormancy

In many species, seed dormancy can be broken by treatments directed toward altering the growth inhibitor–promoter balance and increasing the permeability of seed coats or reducing their mechanical resistance to embryo growth. The efficiency of treatments varies greatly with the degree and kind of seed dormancy. In some species seed dormancy can be easily broken by any of several treatments, whereas seeds of other species respond only to a single, specific treatment. Seed dormancy of certain species sometimes cannot be broken by any of the methods commonly used.

Treatments used to break embryo dormancy generally operate by shifting the growth inhibitor–growth promoter balance in favor of the latter. This may be accomplished by decreasing the levels of endogenous inhibitors or by increasing the levels of growth promoters. For example, chilling of peach and white ash seeds greatly decreased inhibitor (ABA) levels (Lipe and Crane, 1966; Sondheimer *et al.*, 1968). However, a decrease in inhibitor levels does not always explain the breaking of seed dormancy in seeds that have a chilling requirement. Bradbeer (1958) found that chilling broke the dormancy of hazel seeds by inducing gibberellin synthesis. Hamilton and Carpenter (1975) found that the activity of a growth inhibitor in eleagnus seeds did not decrease when seeds were chilled but growth promoters, which appeared to counteract the effect of the inhibitor, were produced in the embryo during low-temperature afterripening.

Afterripening

For seeds having only a moderate degree of embryo dormancy a period of afterripening in dry storage is all that is necessary. During afterripening the tolerance of seeds to environmental conditions increases. The temperature range for germination, which for freshly harvested seeds may have been narrow and restricted to very low or very high temperature, gradually widens. Specific requirements for alternating temperatures or specific light regimes are gradually dissipated.

The rate of afterripening varies from hours to years in seeds of different species. Even in a genetically uniform population of seeds that afterripen in the same environmental regime, the individual seeds are not in the same afterripening stage.

A number of physical and chemical changes occur in some kinds of seeds during dry storage. At least some of these result from changes in seed coats that alter their tensile strength or increase their permeability to water and gases. In other cases changes occur in the embryo or surrounding tissues. For seeds with immature embryos, further morphological changes occur. In some species of ash, the morphologically complete embryos must increase in size before germination can occur. Biochemical changes during afterripening include decreases in amount of stored lipids, carbohydrates, and proteins; increases in metabolic activity; and changes in hormonal balance to favor growth promoters over inhibitors.

Stratification

Embryo dormancy is commonly broken by storing seeds at low temperatures, usually between 1° and 5°C, with abundant aeration and moisture, for periods varying from 30 to 120 days. Such treatments are attempts to simulate natural outdoor winter conditions to which seeds are exposed. The term "stratification" implies placing seeds in layers of moisture-retaining media such as peat moss, sawdust, or sand. However, low temperature and moisture are the essential features of layering. Seeds are considered to be "stratified" when they are moistened, put in plastic bags, and stored at low temperatures. After such treatment they can be planted, but if allowed to desiccate they may lapse into a very deep state of secondary dormancy.

Chemicals

Embryo dormancy of seeds has often been broken by various chemicals, such as gibberellic acid and the cytokinins. In species with relatively mild embryo dormancy (e.g., loblolly pine, slash pine, Japanese red pine, subalpine larch, and western larch) oxidizing agents such as hydrogen peroxide stimulate respiration and accelerate germination (Kozlowski, 1971a). However, hydrogen peroxide has been shown to have practical limitations in inducing germination of some seeds with embryo dormancy. For example, Kozlowski and Torrie (1964) found that exposure of eastern white pine seeds to strong hydrogen peroxide stimulated germination of some seeds but killed others, with the result that final germination percentages of various seed lots were reduced.

Scarification

Dormancy of seeds with impermeable seed coats can be broken by soaking seeds in concentrated H_2SO_4 for periods of 15 to 60 min. Permeability of seed coats in such seeds can also be increased by puncturing the seed coats or scratching the seeds with abrasives. For further details on breaking the dormancy of seeds of various species of woody plants the reader is referred to Schopmeyer (1974).

PHYSIOLOGY OF YOUNG SEEDLINGS

In both gymnosperm and angiosperm seedlings the cotyledons play a paramount physiological role in growth of seedlings. Cotyledons of hypogeously germinating plants (walnut, oak) serve primarily as storage organs. Epigeous cotyledons of some woody plants also store appreciable carbohydrates. Those of other species, for example, pines and dogwood, accumulate only small amounts of carbohydrates but they become photosynthetically active shortly after they emerge from the ground. Species with seeds that lack endosperm (exalbuminous seeds) have cotyledons adapted for both storage and photosynthesis; examples are beech and black locust. Cotyledons of species with endosperm act not only as storage organs but also as transfer organs in absorbing reserves from the endosperm and transferring them to growing axes. Endosperm was not essential for limited early growth of green ash seedlings. However, cotyledons in contact with the endosperm exhibited higher rates of elongation and dry weight increase as well as slower depletion of proteins and lipids than cotyledons separated from the endosperm. The rate of growth of intact seedlings was much greater than in seedlings grown from excised embryos (Table 14.5).

During their development, the cotyledons of some epigeous species progress sequentially through storage, transition, photosynthetic, and senescent stages. This requires drastic changes in enzyme activity, as mentioned earlier. In the storage phase cotyledons are filled with reserves (carbohydrates, proteins, lipids) that are depleted during germination and used for early seedling growth. The kinds of reserves stored by cotyledons vary among species. For example, boxelder cotyledons store primarily proteins, whereas those of tree of heaven store large amounts of lipids. Embryonic cotyledons of boxelder and black locust contain appreciable stored carbohydrates and those of tree of heaven and green ash only small amounts (Fig. 14.13).

Cotyledons also store mineral elements in varying amounts. Embryonic cotyledons from exalbuminous seeds of red maple and black locust store large amounts of nutrients that are translocated to rapidly developing axes during early seedling growth. In contrast, the small, thin cotyledons of green ash store small amounts of nutrient reserves (Marshall and Kozlowski, 1975).

The transition stage of cotyledon development is characterized by cotyledon expansion, depletion and utilization of cotyledon reserves by meristematic regions, differentiation of guard cells, emergence of cotyledons from seed coats, and synthesis of chlorophyll. The cotyledons emerge earlier from seed coats in species with exalbuminous seeds than in species with cotyledons imbedded in endosperm (Marshall and Kozlowski, 1977). The very important photosynthetic stage begins with the appearance of net photosynthesis and ends with cotyledon senescence. Several investigators have demonstrated an important relationship between photosynthesis of epigeous cotyledons and early seedling growth of both gymnosperms and angiosperms. Following seed

TABLE 14.5 Growth and Compositional Changes of 10-Day-Old Green Ash Cotyledons and Seedlings with Endosperm Removed at 2-Day Intervals[a]

Seedling age (days)	Endosperm	Cotyledon length (cm)	Cotyledon dry wt (mg/cotyledon)	Intact seedling dry wt (mg)	Cotyledon protein (mg/cotyledon)	Cotyledon lipids (mg/cotyledon)	Cotyledon total nonstructural carbohydrates (mg/cotyledon)	Cotyledon chlorophyll (mg/cotyledon)
0	±	0.60	1.1	3.2	0.40	0.45	0.05	0.0
2	+	0.90 NS[b]	1.4[c]	4.5 NS	0.31	0.42 NS	0.16 NS	0.5 NS
2	−	0.85	1.1	3.4	0.19[d]	0.42	0.13	0.5
4	+	1.25 NS	2.2[d]	6.9	0.24	0.60[c]	0.34 NS	2.5
4	−	1.15	1.1	3.5[c]	0.13[d]	0.35	0.28	4.8[c]
6	+	1.90	2.3	8.0	0.20	0.70	0.54	18.5
6	−	1.45[c]	1.1[d]	3.7[d]	0.14[c]	0.24[d]	0.25[a]	7.8[d]
8	+	2.10	2.5	8.9	0.28	0.50	0.62	22.0
8	−	1.50[d]	1.2[d]	4.0[d]	0.17[d]	0.14[d]	0.31[a]	9.2[d]
10	+	2.20	2.7	10.3	0.22	0.53	0.69	21.0
10	−	1.50[d]	1.4[d]	5.1[d]	0.14[c]	0.20[d]	0.42[a]	10.5[d]

[a] From Marshall and Kozlowski (1976b).
[b] NS = not significantly different.
[c] Significant at P ≤ 0.05.
[d] Significant at P ≤ 0.01.

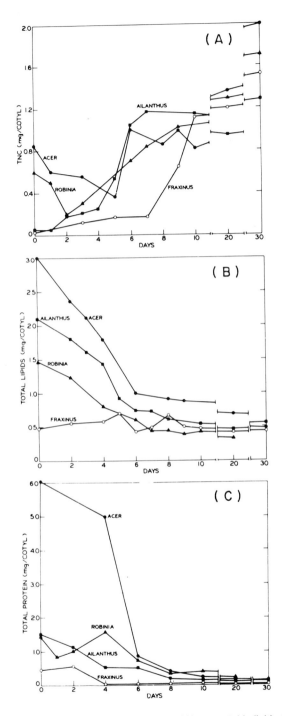

Fig. 14.13. Changes in amounts of carbohydrates (A), extractable lipids (B), and total protein (C) per cotyledon during early seedling growth of four species of woody angiosperms. From Marshall and Kozlowski (1976c).

TABLE 14.6 Effect of Temperature on Development of Cotyledons and Primary Needles of Red Pine[a,b]

	Temperature (°C)				
	10	15	20	25	30
Average number of cotyledons per plant	6.54 ± 0.09	6.52 ± 0.09	6.46 ± 0.08	6.60 ± 0.09	6.36 ± 0.07
Average number of primary needles per plant	2.74 ± 0.38	9.06 ± 0.44	16.74 ± 0.39	16.62 ± 0.50	17.58 ± 0.66
Average length of cotyledons per plant (mm)	16.14 ± 0.35	16.76 ± 0.44	18.22 ± 0.41	18.08 ± 0.43	17.46 ± 0.49
Average length of primary needles per plant (mm)	2.57 ± 0.41	7.34 ± 0.45	21.10 ± 0.77	23.46 ± 0.96	21.02 ± 0.98
Average dry weight of cotyledons per plant (mg)	4.11	4.00	4.07	2.62	2.76
Average dry weight of primary needles per plant (mg)	0.34	2.13	9.01	7.10	8.21
Average dry weight of cotyledons plus primary needles (mg)	4.45	6.13	13.08	9.72	10.97

[a] From Kozlowski and Borger (1971).
[b] Values shown, means ± s.e.m. ($n = 50$). Seedlings were grown from seed for 32 days at 23°–25°C and a light intensity of 750 lux (1.6×10^3 ergs/cm^2/sec); they were subsequently grown for 44 days at indicated temperatures and a light intensity of 13,000 lux (2.6×10^4 ergs/cm^2/sec). At 10°C, 27 plants out of 50 had expanded primary needles; at 15°C, 48 plants out of 50 had expanded primary needles.

germination, a pine seedling is a system of competing carbohydrate sinks. Seedling development is an integrated continuum, with the site of synthesis of carbohydrates shifting during ontogeny from cotyledons to primary needles to secondary needles. There is a close dependency of growth of one class of foliar appendages on the capacity of the preceding class to synthesize growth requirements. Hence, development of primary needles depends on contributions from cotyledons, and development of secondary needles depends on contributions from primary needles. The young seedling in the cotyledon stage appears to be operating at threshold levels of growth requirements and is especially sensitive to environmental stress. There is a strong influence of shoot environment early in ontogeny on initiation of all but the early-formed primary needle primordia and on expansion of all primary needles, including those formed early (Sasaki and Kozlowski, 1968a, 1969, 1970). Initiation of a few primary needles depends on the availability of current photosynthate of cotyledons. Low temperature or low light intensities during the cotyledon stage prevent initiation of most of the normal complement of primary needles of red pine (Tables 14.6 and 14.7). However, when seedlings are placed in a favorable environment, following prolonged exposure to low temperature or low light intensity, primordia of primary needles form readily and subsequently expand (Fig. 14.14).

Normal growth and development of angiosperm seedlings in the cotyledon stage are also drastically inhibited by environmental stresses, with the effects mediated through substances required for growth and supplied by the cotyledons. Most of the carbohydrates used in growth by some epigeous woody angiosperms are supplied by cotyledons until foliage leaves are fairly well expanded. Marshall and Kozlowski (1974a) found that cotyledonary photosynthates were exported to expanding leaf tissues. Fully expanded foliage leaves then became increasingly important until eventually more photosynthetic products were exported by them than by the cotyledons. The importance of healthy, photosynthetically active cotyledons to seedling development

TABLE 14.7   Effect of Light Intensity on Initiation and Expansion of Primary Needles of Red Pine[a,b]

Treatment	Average number of visible primary needles after:				
	32 days	39 days	46 days	53 days	60 days
Dark, 25°C	0	0	0	0	0
750 lux (1.6 × 10³ ergs/ cm²/sec), 23–25°C	0	0	0	0	0
6480 lux (1.3 × 10⁴ ergs/ cm²/sec), 25°C	3.9 ± 0.24	7.6 ± 0.24	12.3 ± 0.30	17.3 ± 0.39	21.7 ± 0.48
13,000 lux (2.6 × 10⁴ ergs/ cm²/sec), 25°C	7.4 ± 0.14	11.8 ± 0.32	16.3 ± 0.38	21.8 ± 0.43	25.3 ± 0.52

[a] From Kozlowski and Borger (1971).
[b] Values shown, means ± s.e.m. Time intervals indicate number of days after sowing.

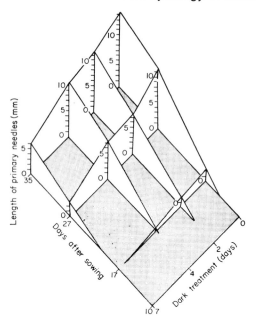

Fig. 14.14. Effects of reexposure of red pine seedlings to light, after various periods of dark treatment, on elongation of primary needles. From Sasaki and Kozlowski (1970).

has been shown by the inhibition of seedling growth following shading or removal of cotyledons, or the application of inhibitors of photosynthesis to cotyledons. At various times after seed germination, epigeous cotyledons of boxelder, tree of heaven, green ash, black locust, and American elm were excised or treated with DCMU [3-(3,4-dichlorophenyl)-1, 1-dimethylurea] to inhibit cotyledon photosynthesis. In all species, removal of cotyledons during the first 10 days after radicle emergence inhibited the growth of roots, hypocotyls, and leaves (Table 14.8). Since removal or covering of the cotyledons inhibited seedling growth similarly, cotyledon photosynthesis appeared to be important in seedling development (Marshall and Kozlowski, 1974a,b, 1976a).

Both the rate of cotyledon photosynthesis and the duration of the photosynthetic stage vary widely among angiosperm species. For example, the rate of photosynthesis of cotyledons is much lower in elm than in black locust, tree of heaven, or green ash. High rates of cotyledon photosynthesis are maintained for a longer time in tree of heaven and in green ash than in elm or black locust (Fig. 14.15). In cacao the epigeous cotyledons play an important role in storing fats, amino acids, and carbohydrates. These reserves sustain the growing seedling until foliage leaves emerge and begin to export carbohydrates. The cotyledons are relatively unimportant photosynthetic organs in cacao (Olofinboba, 1975).

The beginning of the senescent stage is characterized by yellowing of the cotyledons and continues until their abscission. The functional life span of cotyledons varies greatly among species. For example, epigeous cotyledons are relatively short lived in honey

TABLE 14.8   Dry Weights (mg) of Various Parts from Black Locust Seedlings with Cotyledons Removed at Different Seedling Ages[a]

Plant part	Seedling age (days)	2	4	6	8	10	Control
				Seedling age at decotylization, days			
Roots	14	2.1	2.2	3.2	4.4	7.1	22.7
	21	5.6	9.8	7.8	8.7	14.2	45.4
	28	18.5	19.4	12.1	20.6	27.7	59.5
Hypocotyls	14	1.0	1.4	1.7	1.8	1.9	3.0
	21	1.8	1.9	2.1	2.1	2.9	4.9
	28	2.6	3.2	2.3	2.8	3.2	7.6
Foliage	14	2.6	2.9	4.2	5.0	4.4	11.4
	21	8.0	11.0	9.7	8.6	14.0	22.6
	28	16.0	18.0	14.6	24.8	23.7	71.2

[a] From Marshall and Kozlowski (1976a).

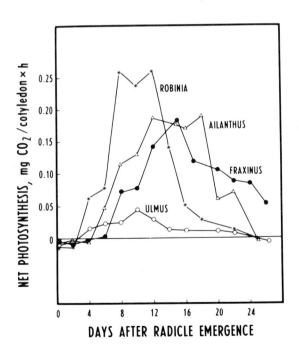

Fig. 14.15.   Photosynthesis in cotyledons of ailanthus, green ash, black locust, and American elm at various times after germination. From Marshall and Kozlowski (1976a).

locust, mulberry, and black willow (about 1 month); longer lived in cottonwood, hop-hornbeam, and sycamore (about 2 months); still longer lived in hercules-club, hackberry, and blue beech (3 months); and unusually long lived in American ash and magnolia (6 months or more) (Maisenhelder, 1969). It is difficult to establish the life span of cotyledons precisely for different species because cotyledon longevity is strongly influenced by environmental stresses. For example, drought can induce rapid senescence and abscission of mature cotyledons.

Most of the topics covered in this chapter are discussed in considerably more detail in the three volumes on *Seed Biology* (Kozlowski, 1972c).

GENERAL REFERENCES

Black, M. (1972). ''Control Processes in Germination and Dormancy.'' Oxford Univ. Press (Clarendon), London and New York.
Heydecker, W., ed. (1973). ''Seed Ecology.'' Butterworth, London.
Kozlowski, T. T., ed. (1972). ''Seed Biology.'' Vols. 1–3. Academic Press, New York.
Mayer, A. M., and Poljakoff-Mayber, A. (1975). ''The Germination of Seeds.'' Pergamon, Oxford.
Rice, E. (1974). ''Allelopathy.'' Academic Press, New York.
Roberts, E. H., ed. (1972). ''Viability of Seeds.'' Chapman & Hall, London.
Schopmeyer, C. S., ed. (1974). ''Seeds of Woody Plants in the United States,'' Agric. Handb. No. 450. U. S. For. Serv., Washington, D. C.
Taylorson, R. B., and Hendricks, S. B. (1977). Dormancy in seeds. *Annu. Rev. Plant Physiol.* **28,** 331–354.
Villiers, T. A. (1975). ''Dormancy and the Survival of Plants.'' Arnold, London.

15

Growth Regulators

INTRODUCTION

The structure of trees and other woody plants was described in Chapter 2 and their growth in Chapters 3 and 4. This chapter deals with hormones, specific substances that regulate or control growth and development in plants. Growth in simple terms refers to increase in size by cell division and enlargement, and development refers to the differentiation of cells into the various tissues and organs that finally produce a mature plant. These processes are relatively easy to observe in growing plants, beginning with germinating seeds. The first step in growth is the imbibition of water and the swelling of seeds, followed by the release of existing enzymes and synthesis of new ones, the hydrolysis of stored food, its translocation to growing points, and the synthesis of new metabolites and tissue (see Chapter 14). Cell division, enlargement, and differentiation into the various structures of the seedling produce a plant that eventually grows to maturity with a characteristic form and produces flowers, fruits, and seeds. All of this is easy to observe, but difficult to understand. The problem is to explain how the numerous physical and biochemical processes included in the growth and development of a plant are controlled and programmed so they occur in the proper sequences and quantities to produce a well-proportioned, efficiently functioning organism. The origin and development of form in living organisms has come to be known as morphogenesis. The broad problem of development is discussed in more detail by Torrey (1967), Wareing and Phillips (1970), and Wetmore and Steeves (1971).

GENERAL CONTROLS

Scope of the Problem

It has been mentioned previously that growth and development are controlled by both external and internal factors. The external factors include temperature, light, water, oxygen, carbon dioxide, and mineral nutrition. Some of these factors have been discussed in the chapters on photosynthesis, mineral nutrition, and water relations, or will be discussed more specifically in Chapter 17. As was pointed out in Chapter 1, external environmental factors affect growth by modifying internal physiological processes and conditions. For example, the reduction in turgor caused by a water deficit reduces cell enlargement and decreases plant size, but it also causes stomatal closure, reducing the amount of CO_2 available for photosynthesis, and the reduced supply of carbohydrates also affects growth and development. Light intensity, duration, and quality likewise are important for photosynthesis, but they also affect growth and flowering in more subtle ways through effects on phytochrome, hormones, and light-regulated enzymes. This raises the question as to how an environmental factor such as photoperiod can cause certain cells to make the appropriate response, in this instance for meristems to begin producing flower primordia. The same question arises with respect to the action of internal growth regulators such as auxin.

This chapter is concerned chiefly with the internal factors that control growth and development. These operate at two levels, within the cells and among them. The intracellular control is the genetic mechanism or genome contained largely in the DNA of the chromosomes, which controls through messenger RNA the kinds of proteins and enzymes synthesized, which in turn control cell structure and behavior. The problem of the control of growth and development is complicated by the fact that all cells in a plant are totipotent, e.g., each contains all the genetic information required to produce a complete plant. It is true that during maturation most cells lose the ability to use some of this information because they are subjected to gradients of nutrients and hormones. However, cells in tissue culture often regain the ability to produce new plants and a bit of Douglas-fir cotyledon is capable of producing callus tissue from which new plants can be produced (Cheng and Voqui, 1977). For a plant to be developed from a fertilized egg or from a single cell in culture requires a complex control system that can turn on various genes at the proper times to produce the messenger RNA needed to provide the enzymes required to synthesize the various kinds of materials used to build the different kinds of cells and tissues that constitute a plant, and then turn them off when no longer needed. The regulation of gene action usually is explained in terms of the scheme of Jacob and Monod, based on work with microorganisms (see Bidwell, 1974, pp. 327–329, for example). However, the intracellular control system of multicellular organisms such as trees is much more complex than that of unicellular organisms and not as well understood.

The extracellular control system operates to coordinate the activities of individual cells so that the various tissues and organs of the plant develop. It constitutes the internal environment in which cells develop and includes the supply of organic and inorganic nutrients, hormones, water status, and location. The location of cells is an important factor in determining how they differentiate. For example, cells divided off from the inside of the cambium differentiate into xylem, those on the outside into phloem, and some cells in a leaf primordium differentiate into epidermis, some into mesophyll, and others into the various tissues of the vascular bundles.

Two Kinds of Coordinating Systems

There are two major groups of extracellular coordinating factors in plants—the supply of metabolites and the kinds and amounts of plant hormones present. The chief metabolites are carbohydrates and nitrogen-containing compounds. One of the interesting problems in connection with crop yields is the extent to which the production of carbohydrates by photosynthesis controls growth and to what extent the use of carbohydrates in growth controls the rate of photosynthesis (Evans, 1975a; Wareing, 1970, pp. 15–19). Growth is often limited by the supply of nitrogen, and about 1920 much emphasis was placed on the carbohydrate/nitrogen ratio as a controlling factor in plant development. Some of the work on fruit trees was summarized by Gourley and Howlett (1941) and by Miller (1938, pp. 699–701). A deficiency of nitrogen produces small, woody plants, often but not always with few flowers, while an excess of nitrogen produces lush vegetative growth, and in some species reduces fruitfulness. Alternate year bearing of fruit trees is attributed to the depletion of food reserves by a heavy fruit crop at the time when buds for the following year are being initiated. Reduction of carbohydrate translocation out of the tops by stem and branch girdling sometimes causes earlier flower bud production and increases bearing in young trees. For many years the role of nutrients has been overshadowed by the emphasis on hormones as the controlling factors in growth and development. However, recently there has been renewed interest in the role of nutrients, but with the realization that their distribution may be influenced by hormones. Thus both the food supply and hormones play essential roles in growth and development (Phillips, 1975).

NATURALLY OCCURRING HORMONES

Much of the internal coordination of growth processes is attributed to hormones, so we will discuss the principal groups of plant hormones and consider some examples of their activities. The term ''hormone'' was first used by the animal physiologists Bayliss and Starling in 1904, and it is now generally applied to organic compounds produced by plants or animals, which in low concentrations (10^{-3} to $10^{-6}\,M$ or lower) affect various physiological processes, often at a distance from their point of origin. In the 19th century Sachs proposed the existence of root-, stem-, and leaf-forming substances and the Darwins and Boysen-Jensen suggested that a stimulus moving down from the tip causes phototropic curvature of oat coleoptiles. Went in 1928 showed that the stimulus is a specific substance now known as auxin and developed a bioassay for it. After World War II there was great activity in hormone research, resulting eventually in the identification of five families of plant growth regulators or hormones: auxins, cytokinins, gibberellins, ethylene, and the growth inhibitors of which abscisic acid is best known. The development of our knowledge of plant hormones was reviewed in detail by Thimann in 1972 and more briefly in 1974.

This chapter deals with the nature and general functions of plant hormones. Their roles in processes such as dormancy, shoot elongation, cambial activity, and the internal correlation of plant growth are discussed in detail in Chapter 16.

Auxins

The first plant hormones to be identified were the auxins, and for many years they were the only ones known to exist. The discovery of auxin developed from early research on the cause of phototropic bending of plant stems and petioles which started with the Darwins (1880) and continued until indole-3-acetic acid (IAA) was isolated from fungi in 1934 and from flowering plants in 1946. Auxins usually are defined as substances which in low concentrations (10^{-5} M) stimulate elongation of decapitated oat coleoptiles or segments of pea epicotyl. While some other naturally occurring indole compounds show a small amount of growth-promoting activity, IAA seems to be the major naturally occurring auxin. Its formula is shown below.

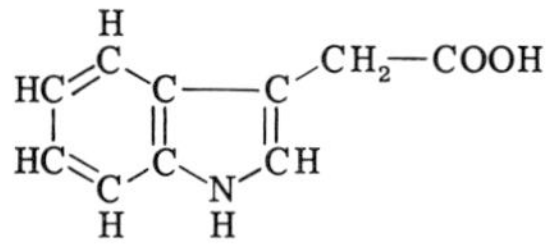

Indole-3-acetic acid

It is believed to be derived from the amino acid tryptophan through decarboxylation and deamination reactions to indole-3-acetaldehyde, which is then oxidized to IAA. This occurs chiefly in young, growing tissue such as stem tips, young leaves, flowers, embryos, and root tips. Auxin transport is strongly polar, and the auxin moves downward from stem tips and young leaves, producing a gradient of decreasing concentration from stem tips to roots. The subject of auxin transport was reviewed by Goldsmith (1977). Auxin is readily converted into other compounds, such as indoleacetyl aspartate or glucoside conjugates, and it also is rapidly oxidized by IAA oxidase and peroxidases. Thus the concentration of free auxin usually is quite low in plant tissue. Auxin also may be bound on proteins in the cytoplasm, making it difficult to demonstrate a clear correlation between growth and auxin content.

A number of synthetic compounds produce effects on plants similar to those produced by naturally occurring auxin. Among them are indolebutyric acid (IBA), α-naphthaleneacetic acid (NAA), 2,4,6-trichlorobenzoic acid, dichlorophenoxyacetic acid, (2,4-D), and trichlorophenoxyacetic acid (2,4,5-T). The latter two compounds are potent herbicides in high concentrations, but in low concentrations their effects can resemble those of indoleacetic acid.

Roles of Auxin

Auxin has a confusing variety of functions in plants. A concentration of 10^{-5} M promotes stem elongation, but the same concentration inhibits root elongation (Fig. 15.1). It causes apical dominance by inhibiting the development of axillary shoot buds, and relatively high concentrations cause root initiation on stems. Synthetic auxins such as IBA and NAA are therefore used extensively in horticulture and forestry to stimulate the rooting of cuttings. Auxin is involved in phototropism, the bending of stems and petioles toward light. The concentration becomes higher on the shaded side of the stem, resulting in greater cell elongation on that side and consequent bending toward the light. It also is involved in geotropism, the growth of stems upward and of roots downward in response to gravity. This response likewise appears to result from differential accumulation, the higher concentration on the lower side inhibiting cell elongation in roots and causing downward growth. An unsymmetrical distribution of gibberellic acid also has been reported in roots and there may be interaction between the two hormones. It is not certain why there is a differential accumulation of auxin or other growth regulators in roots and stems displaced from a vertical plane. The statolith theory, which attributes it to settlement of starch grains or other organelles to the lower side of cells, is still controversial but seems most plausible (Juniper, 1976).

Auxin induces flowering in a few plants, and NAA is used commercially to stimulate flowering of pineapple, although the effect may be indirect. It is now thought that auxin induces production of ethylene, which is the direct cause of flowering. Auxin also induces parthenocarpy, the production of fruits without seeds, if applied to stigmas of flowers of some kinds of plants. It can also be used on some plants to cause embryo

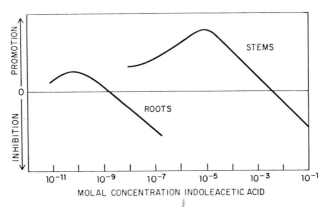

Fig. 15.1. Difference in response of roots and shoots to various concentrations of auxin. These differences may explain the positive geotropism of stems and negative geotropism of roots. Adapted from Leopold and Thimann (1949).

abortion after fertilization, causing flower drop. Synthetic auxin is sometimes used to thin fruit, but in other instances natural fruit drop is associated with a low level of auxin and can be prevented by spraying with an auxin. Auxin also appears to be involved in the abscission of leaves and other plant parts and in the initiation of cambial activity. For example, in trees auxin produced by the opening buds stimulates cell division in the cambium, but it now appears that gibberellins (Wareing *et al.*, 1964) and in some species cytokinins (Weaver, 1972) also play a role. In fact, since the identification of gibberellins, cytokinins, and ethylene as growth regulators, it is clear that they often interact to produce effects formerly attributed solely to auxin. This will be discussed later.

Auxins as Herbicides

It was soon found that concentrations of auxin higher than those normally found in plant tissues inhibit elongation; cause abnormal growth such as tumor formation, curling of petioles, and distortion of leaf blades; and that still higher concentrations cause death. Observations of these phenomena led to the idea of using auxins as herbicides and silvicides. Indoleacetic acid is not very useful because it breaks down too rapidly, but related synthetic compounds such as 2,4-D and 2,4,5-T are very effective in killing vegetation. Some compounds are highly selective. For example, at the proper concentration 2,4-D kills most broad-leaved plants, but does not injure grasses and cereals; and 2,4,5-T is more effective on some weeds and on most woody plants than 2,4-D.

Because conifers are usually more resistant to 2,4,5-T than broad-leaved plants it often can be used to removed competing brush from stands of young conifers with little damage to the latter. However, the susceptibility to injury varies considerably at various stages of growth, as is shown in Fig. 15.2.

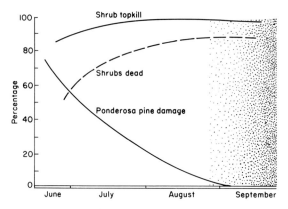

Fig. 15.2. Differences in susceptibility to 2,4,5-T between ponderosa pine and competing shrubs such as Pacific madrone, varnish leaf, deerbrush Ceanothus, and willows. Ponderosa pine becomes much more resistant in late summer than the competing shrubs. After Gratkowski (1977).

Gibberellins

Gibberellins were discovered in Japan before World War II, but did not become known in the West until after the war. They were discovered by scientists searching for the cause of the "foolish seedling" disease of rice that is characterized by abnormal height growth. It was found that the affected plants were infected with the fungus *Gibberella fujikuroi* (known in the imperfect stage as *Fusarium moniliforme*) and that an extract from this fungus causes abnormal elongation of rice stems. The active material isolated from the extract was termed "gibberellin." Research after World War II revealed that gibberellins occur commonly in seed plants and over 50 have been identified, of which gibberellin A_3, often termed GA_3 for gibberellic acid, is best known. Its formula is shown below.

GA_3

The chemical and regulatory characteristics of gibberellins were discussed by Paleg and West (1972), Leopold and Kriedemann (1975), and in a book edited by Krishnamoorthy (1975). According to Crozier *et al.* (1970) the different gibberellins vary considerably in activity. They are oxygenated diterpenes (see Chapter 8) and are synthesized in most plant organs, but especially in the leaf primordia of stem tips and in root tips. Gibberellins have nearly as many effects as auxins on plants. In fact, if gibberellins had been discovered first they might occupy the dominant position in the literature now occupied by auxin.

Physiological Roles

Gibberellins are usually identified through bioassay by their ability to cause elongation of the leaf sheaths of monocots or the internodes of dwarf dicots. In fact, the most conspicuous characteristic of the gibberellins is their ability to cause stem elongation, especially in dwarf plants, including many genetic dwarfs, as well as aster and corn plants stunted by a virus. Both cell elongation and division are stimulated by gibberellins. Although auxin affects stem elongation of intact plants, gibberellins have a much greater effect. In contrast, auxin has more effect than gibberellin on the elongation of excised sections of stems, coleoptiles, and hypocotyls. A combination of the two has a synergistic effect on some tissues, producing more elongation than either alone. Auxin usually is only translocated downward, but gibberellins supplied externally will move both upward and downward, indicating that they are translocated in both the xylem and phloem. Significant amounts of GA have been reported in grape root exudate (Skene, 1967) and in the xylem sap of apple and pear (Jones and Lacey, 1968).

Many herbaceous long-day plants can be caused to flower under short days by treatment with gibberellin. The application of gibberellin can also bring about "bolting" or premature flowering in herbaceous biennials that normally required a period of low temperature before they will flower. The use of gibberellins to promote flowering of conifers was reviewed by Pharis (1976) and Pharis and Kuo (1977). Gibberellin A_3 is often used to produce earlier, larger, and longer-lasting flowers on camellias and it increases the stem length of roses. However, GA appears to inhibit flower initiation in woody dicots. In some kinds of fruits gibberellin, like auxin, causes parthenocarpy, but it also causes parthenocarpy in peaches, apricots, and varieties of apples where auxin is ineffective. It is effective on Delaware grapes but not on other varieties, although it reduces berry shrivel in some grape varieties (Weaver, 1972). Gibberellin can replace the requirement for light in breaking the dormancy of light-sensitive seeds and in causing leaf expansion. The physiological and biochemical effects of gibberellins in conifers were reviewed by Kamienska *et al.* (1974), Pharis and Kuo (1977), and in herbaceous species by Jones (1973).

There has been considerable interest in the possibility of using gibberellins to increase the height of tree seedlings in nurseries. Treatment with gibberellins also breaks dormancy in a number of woody plants that normally require a period of low temperature before they will flower. Gibberellins may play a role in the initiation of shoot growth by dormant plants in the spring. For example, Lavender *et al.* (1973) found that for field-grown Douglas-fir there was a simultaneous increase in soil temperature, bud activity, and the GA content of the xylem sap. Also, when GA was applied to shoots of Douglas-fir seedlings growing in cold soil they resumed shoot growth as soon as seedlings growing in warm soil. This led the authors to speculate that when root systems are in cold soil resumption of shoot growth is delayed by reduced export of a growth regulator, probably GA, from the roots. On the other hand, Dumbroff and Brown (1976) cited failure to observe gibberellins in buds of sugar maple prior to resumption of growth and suggested that the appearance of gibberellins accompanies the breaking of dormancy rather than causes it. More research obviously is needed, with careful attention being paid to the assay techniques.

Mode of Action

It is as difficult to explain the diverse effects of gibberellins as it is to explain the effects of auxin. The problem is complicated by the difficulty of deciding whether externally supplied GA produces the same effects as endogenous GA, and also whether all the gibberellins extracted from plant tissue are physiologically active. In germinating seeds of barley and other cereals GA brings about the release of existing enzymes, particularly α-amylase, and the synthesis of α-amylase and several other hydrolytic enzymes. Enzyme release presumably occurs because of changes in the permeability of cell membranes; enzyme synthesis seems to indicate the synthesis of new RNA, including messenger RNA. Jones (1973) cited some interesting research on hazel seeds in which exogenously applied GA broke secondary dormancy and stimulated DNA and RNA metabolism.

The mode of action of gibberellins in whole plants is more difficult to analyze. Some of the effects of gibberellins on growth processes have been attributed to an increase in auxin, either because gibberellin stimulates auxin formation or inhibits its destruction (Paleg and West, 1972), but this is questionable. Leopold and Kriedemann (1975) think the experimental evidence indicates that auxin and gibberellin operate on different parts of the growth process. It is not yet clear how much of the effect of gibberellin on growing plants can be explained in terms of cell enlargement and how much results from its effects on cell division (Jones, 1973). Obviously much more research must be done before the role of gibberellin is fully understood.

Cytokinins

Cytokinins are basically substances that stimulate cell division, but they also are involved in other processes such as cell enlargement, tissue differentiation, flowering and fruit development, and senescence. Cytokinin activity is usually measured by its effect on the increase in fresh weight of soybean callus tissue, or by its action in delaying senescence, as indicated by the chlorophyll content of leaves or leaf discs (Kuhnle *et al.,* 1977). Cytokinins occur in all kinds of plant tissue, but are especially abundant in the milky endosperm tissue of seeds, in root tips, and in the xylem exudate of a number of plants.

Chemically, cytokinins are derived from the purine, adenine. The first natural cytokinin to be identified in plants was zeatin, extracted from maize seeds, and a number of other compounds with cytokinin activity are known. The structures for zeatin and a synthetic cytokinin, benzylaminopurine (benzyladenine) are given below.

Zeatin   Benzylaminopurine

At least five different cytokinins have been found in the xylem sap of grape (Weaver, 1972) and there probably are several in other woody species. Thus far the chief use of cytokinins has been in the laboratory to stimulate, in combination with auxin, the initiation of buds and leafy shoots in plant tissue cultures (Murashige, 1974). They also can break the dormancy of light-sensitive seeds, overcome apical dominance in axillary buds of apple and apricot, and stimulate tuber formation on potato stolons. A synthetic cytokinin induces parthenocarpy in Calimyrna figs, and cytokinins have been effective in causing the flowering of some plants under unfavorable photoperiods.

Taylor and Dumbroff (1975) and Dumbroff and Brown (1976) reported a large increase in cytokinin activity in sugar maple when root growth began in late February, but this was not directly related to breaking of dormancy (Fig. 15.3). The concentration in the xylem sap is decreased when roots are subjected to unfavorable environmental conditions, and this may have a significant effect on shoot development (Leopold and Kriedemann, 1975). The rapid senescence of older leaves on water-stressed or flooded plants may be caused as much by the decreased supply of cytokinins from the roots as by direct effects of water stress. Skene (1975) discussed the role of cytokinins produced in roots with respect to processes in shoots.

The ability of exogenously applied cytokinins to delay the senescence of leaves and leaf discs is well known and forms the basis for a bioassay. Senescence apparently is delayed by decreased synthesis of hydrolytic enzymes and increased transport of nutrients to the point of application (Bidwell, 1974). Perhaps cytokinins play a general role in controlling translocation. This would be consistent with their action in inhibiting

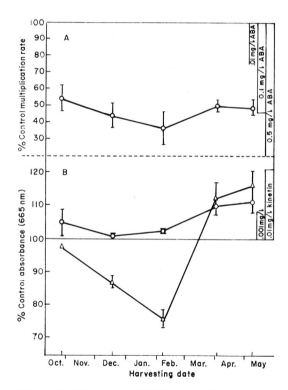

Fig. 15.3. Cytokinin and inhibitor activity (ABA) in buds of sugar maple during the winter. There was no significant decrease in ABA during the period in which dormancy was decreasing. The increase in cytokinins in late February and March occurred after bud dormancy was decreasing and probably was related to increasing root growth rather than bud activity. From Taylor and Dumbroff (1975).

apical dominance in axillary buds and promoting tuber formation. They also seem to play a role in nitrogen metabolism, as indicated by their action in delaying senescence, but it is not clear how much of this is caused by delay of protein hydrolysis and how much by increased protein synthesis. However, cytokinins seem to increase both RNA and protein synthesis. The site of action of cytokinins is unknown. Although cytokinin is a constituent of transfer RNA, it is doubtful if that fraction has any hormonal activity.

Ethylene

It has been known for several decades that ethylene gas ($CH_2=CH_2$) has important physiological effects on plants, including breaking dormancy in potatoes, hastening ripening of fruits, causing epinasty, and inducing abscission of leaves. The early observations are reviewed by Pratt and Goeschl (1969) and Abeles (1973). The auxin-induced flowering of pineapple appears to be caused by increased ethylene production in treated plants. Ethylene originally was of interest chiefly to physiologists studying the ripening and storage of fruit because it is produced by ripening fruits and hastens the ripening of bananas, citrus, persimmons, and some other fruits (Pratt and Goeschl, 1969). The ethylene concentration must be kept low in cold storage rooms to prevent hastening the ripening of apples and defoliation of nursery stock. The problem of ethylene accumulation in relation to the storage of plant materials is discussed in Dewey (1977).

Development of a rapid and accurate method for measuring ethylene concentration by gas chromatography caused a great increase in research. As a result, much has been learned about its role in plants and it is now accepted as a plant growth regulator, unique because it is a gas. Although considerable research has been done on the biosynthesis of ethylene, there is no general agreement about its origin. Methionine is a probable precursor, fatty acids another possibility, and nonenzymatic systems also have been proposed. It is produced in all kinds of tissue and its production is affected by environmental factors such as light and temperature, by water stress, by mechanical injury, and by fungal invasion. Some fungi produce large amounts of ethylene, as does the invaded tissue. Bruising or cutting plant tissue, especially some kinds of fruits, often increases ethylene production. Water stress is said to increase ethylene production and stimulate leaf abscission of cotton when it is rewatered. The epinasty observed in leaves of both herbaceous and woody plants when the soil is flooded with water may be caused by ethylene produced in the roots (Kawase, 1974, 1976; Clemens and Pearson, 1977). Normally this would escape into the soil, but ethylene is not very soluble in water so the concentration builds up in roots in saturated soil and diffuses to the shoots, producing an unusually high concentration. Ethylene diffuses about as rapidly as carbon dioxide and it therefore moves readily through air spaces in plant tissues. It is soluble in lipids and therefore may be concentrated in the lipid fraction of cell membranes where it might affect membrane permeability.

As indicated earlier ethylene has many functions. It tends to inhibit elongation growth, but sometimes stimulates cell enlargement and localized swelling in stems of pea seedlings. It also inhibits lateral bud growth in peas, and this and other observations led to the suggestion that auxin inhibition functions at least in part through increased synthesis of ethylene. However, the effects of ethylene and auxin on roots are different. Ethylene neutralizes the normal geotropic response of stems of a few kinds of plants, so that they grow horizontally instead of vertically. It is used to defoliate horticultural planting stock so it can be dug earlier, but it can produce disastrous defoliation of evergreens. Jerie and Chalmers (1976) claim that ethylene increases food movement into enlarging peach fruits. Hastening of ripening of fruits and of leaf abscission presumably is caused by increase in enzyme activity, but the exact mode of action of ethylene is unknown. Three theories have been suggested: (1) that ethylene becomes attached to a metal–protein that has a regulatory function, (2) that it becomes attached to membranes and alters their functioning, or (3) that it affects RNA and RNA-controlled protein synthesis. Perhaps all of these modes of action exist. Many effects of ethylene are inhibited by CO_2. There is no known system in plants to control the concentration of ethylene. Perhaps because it is a gas and diffuses readily through intercellular spaces it ordinarily escapes rapidly enough to prevent accumulation to undesirable levels.

Abscisic Acid

While working on dormancy in trees, Wareing and his colleagues in England isolated a substance from leaves of sycamore maple which, when placed on stem tips, stopped elongation and caused bud scales to develop (Eagles and Wareing, 1963). The active agent was isolated and called dormin. In the United States, Addicott and his colleagues, while investigating leaf abscission, isolated two substances that caused abscission and called them abscisin I and abscisin II. When purified, abscisin II proved to be identical with dormin and it is now known as abscisic acid or ABA (Addicott and Lyon, 1969). It is a sesquiterpene, possibly derived from a carotenoid or, more likely, from mevalonic acid. Its formula is shown below.

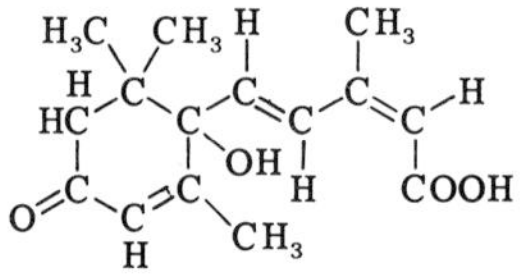

Abscisic acid

Abscisic acid probably occurs in all seed plants and apparently is synthesized in all plant organs. Unlike other hormones it is basically a growth inhibitor. It accumulates in at least some kinds of woody plants under short photoperiods, and application of ABA to some perennials causes dormancy, although this is not proof of a regulatory role on bud dormancy by endogenous ABA. Taylor and Dumbroff (1975) reported that although ABA occurs in both roots and stems of sugar maple seedlings, changes in concentration are not correlated with the breaking of dormancy. Although the decreasing photoperiod of late summer is accompanied by an increase in ABA and cessation of bud elongation, the correlation does not prove that accumulation of ABA is the cause of dormancy.

Application of ABA can delay the germination of seeds and maintain the dormancy of buds of potato tubers. It generally retards stem elongation and the growth of other organs, but in some instances it promotes root formation. Exogenous ABA also hastens senescence of excised leaves, causing the breakdown of chlorophyll in spite of the addition of cytokinin. Thus it is possible that some of the degenerative changes occurring during senescence are caused by the action of ABA. However, Milborrow (1974) regards these effects as probably indirect. Abscisic acid hastens leaf abscission, at least in some herbaceous species. It also seems to oppose some of the effects of GA and cytokinin in a number of processes, including the GA-mediated synthesis of α-amylase in the seeds of cereals. Milborrow (1974) wrote an extensive review of the chemistry and physiology of ABA, but was unable to identify specific sites of action.

Another interesting observation is that ABA can cause stomatal closure. As there is a marked increase in ABA in the leaves of plants suffering from water deficits caused by dry soil, waterlogging, or excess salt, it is suggested that this causes the closure of stomata observed in such circumstances. The ABA concentration usually returns to normal within a day or two after water stress is relieved. According to Loveys (1977) the ABA in leaves is synthesized in the chloroplasts; this relationship was discussed more extensively in Chapter 13. It has been claimed that decreases in cytokinin and perhaps GA interact with an increase in ABA in controlling stomatal behavior in water-stressed plants (Livne and Vaadia, 1972; Ahavoni *et al.,* 1977), but this was questioned by Hsiao (1973, p. 527). The suggestion that the accumulation of ABA in water-stressed leaves is involved in leaf abscission of cotton was found to be unlikely by Davenport *et al.* (1977).

Other Growth Inhibitors

There are other substances in addition to abscisic acid that function as inhibitors in plants. The most important are phenolic compounds, such as cinnamic acid, that inhibit auxin activity. Exogenously applied monophenols increase indoleacetic acid oxidase activity and the destruction of auxin, but di- and polyphenols inhibit the destruction of indoleacetic acid. There also are some rather confusing data indicating that phenolics are involved in the responses of seedlings to light (Leopold and Kriedemann, 1975). The flavonoids may have some role in the response of leaves to light (Thimann, 1972), and some unsaturated lactones such as coumarin also have been identified as growth inhibitors. Coumarin and protoanemonin are best known. Coumarin occurs in grasses and is responsible for the characteristic odor of newly mown grass. It inhibits lettuce seed germination and elongation of roots. Jacobson and Corcoran (1977) suggest that tannins are important antagonists and regulators of the gibberellins. Thimann (1972) and Leopold and Kriedemann (1975, Chapter 8) discuss some of these compounds, and others probably will be identified.

INTERACTIONS OF HORMONES

At one time it was expected that some major specific function might be performed by each family of hormones, but the reader has by now discovered that more than one type of hormone may be involved in controlling the same process and that there are important interactions among the various hormones. Thus the flowering of pineapple, originally attributed to auxin, appears to be caused by the increased ethylene production produced by applying auxin. There are important synergistic actions between auxin and cytokinins in the growth and differentiation of tissue cultures and probably also in bud development. A similar situation may exist for auxin and gibberellins in stem elongation. There also may be antagonistic actions, such as the effect of exogenous ABA in counterbalancing the effect of exogenous IAA on the abscission of leaves and fruits. Thus, in broad terms growth and development processes often appear to be controlled by the relative concentrations of various hormones that act in different ways.

Some specific roles of growth regulators in controlling growth processes such as dormancy, cambial activity, floral initiation, and correlations such as apical dominance and root–shoot balance are discussed in Chapter 16. Since many attempts to relate hormone levels to these phenomena have shown poor correlations and sometimes have involved questionable assays, we must depend largely on observational research in which a hormone is applied or withheld and the effects described. The validity of such experiments depends on the sometimes doubtful assumption that an exogenously applied hormone has the same effects as an endogenous hormone. There is far too little information concerning the operation of hormones at the molecular level, beyond the probability that they affect genes that control synthesis of RNA or act at one or more levels on preexisting RNA and thus affect the levels of various enzymes that are involved in essential metabolic processes. In some instances there may be more direct effects on membrane permeability. There obviously is need for more biochemical research on plant hormone action, but the difficulties of working with woody plants seem to discourage most investigators.

GROWTH REGULATORS AND DISEASE

It has often been suggested that certain symptoms that appear in plants attacked by pathogenic organisms may be caused by excessive hormone activity. The deformation of peach leaves caused by *Taphrina deformans,* the hypertrophy of crown gall, the root deformation called clubroot, and the galls produced on trees by *Cronartium* rust all suggest reactions to a high concentration of auxin and possibly to other growth regulators. An often-cited example is the abnormal growth of rice infected with *Gibberella fujikuroi* caused by an excess of gibberellin. On the other hand, it has been suggested that certain pathogens reduce growth by reducing the concentration of auxin or gibberellins. Another symptom, known as "green island" formation, caused by the retention of chlorophyll at infection sites on leaves, resembles greening in areas of senescing leaves where drops of cytokinin are applied (Dekhuijzen, 1976).

Many kinds of pathogenic and nonpathogenic bacteria and fungi produce auxin and other growth regulators, and the concentration of these substances is often higher in diseased than in healthy tissue. Thus it is tempting to ascribe abnormal growth to an excess of growth regulators, including ethylene, produced by the invading organism. However, it is uncertain how much of the increase is produced by the pathogen and how much by host cells. Dekhuijzen (1976) concludes that much of the increase results from changes in host cell metabolism rather than from synthesis by the pathogens.

A variety of symptoms associated with insect attacks also suggest hormone stimulation. Examples are the root galls associated with nematode invasion and the insect galls formed on leaves, all of which are caused by abnormal cell development. Green islands sometimes form in birch leaves attacked by leaf miners (Dekhuijzen, 1976) and their cytokinin content is high, but the origin of the elevated cytokinin concentration is not clear.

The role of growth regulators in both healthy and diseased tissue is discussed in considerable detail in the volume edited by Heitefuss and Williams (1976) and in the review by Sequiera (1973). However, it appears that much more research is needed to establish the cause-and-effect relationships between growth regulator concentrations and diseased plants.

GENERAL REFERENCES

Abeles, F. B. (1973). "Ethylene in Plant Biology." Academic Press, New York.

Audus, L. J. (1972). "Plant Growth Substances, Vol. 1. Chemistry and Physiology." Leonard Hill, London.

Audus, L. J., ed. (1976). "Herbicides," 2 vols. Academic Press, New York.

Bidwell, R. G. S. (1974). "Plant Physiology." Macmillan, New York.

Bieleski, R. L., Ferguson, A. R., and Creswell, M. M., eds. (1974). "Mechanics of Regulation of Plant Growth." Bull. No. 12 R. Soc., New Zealand.

Jones, R. L. (1973). Gibberellins: Their physiological role. *Annu. Rev. Plant Physiol.* **21,** 537–570.

Krishnamoorthy, H. N., ed. (1975). "Gibberellins and Plant Growth." Wiley, New York.

Leopold, A. C., and Kriedemann, P. E. (1975). "Plant Growth and Development." McGraw-Hill, New York.

Luckwill, L. C., and Cutting, C. V., eds. (1970). "Physiology of Tree Crops." Academic Press, New York.

Phillips, I. D. J. (1971). "The Biochemistry and Physiology of Plant Growth Hormones." McGraw-Hill, New York.

Thimann, K. V. (1972). The natural plant hormones. *In* "Plant Physiology: A Treatise" (F. C. Steward, ed.), Vol. 6. Academic Press, New York.

Thimann, K. V. (1974). Fifty years of plant hormone research. *Plant Physiol.* **54,** 450–453.

Thimann, K. V. (1978). "Hormone Action in the Whole Life of Plants." University of Massachusetts Press, Amherst.

Torrey, J. G. (1967). "Development in Flowering Plants." Macmillan, New York.

Wareing, P. F., and Phillips, I. D. J. (1970). "The Control of Growth and Differentiation in Plants." Pergamon, Oxford.

Weaver, R. J. (1972). "Plant Growth Substances in Agriculture." Freeman, San Francisco.

Wilkins, M. B., ed. (1969). "Physiology of Plant Growth and Development." McGraw-Hill, New York.

16
Internal Factors Affecting Growth

INTRODUCTION

In preceding chapters some of the most important processes were discussed individually and their reactions to environmental factors were described. Two important aspects of plant growth remain to be discussed—effects of environmental and cultural factors on vegetative and reproductive growth and the interactions of various internal growth requirements and processes on growth. The effects of environmental factors and cultural practices will be discussed in the next chapter. This chapter will discuss the internal environment or internal conditions that influence the quantity and quality of growth.

The various physiological processes do not operate independently of one another. Just as a woody plant is morphologically more than a collection of cells and organs, so it is more than an assemblage of unrelated processes. Its success as a multicellular organism results from the correlation of sequential processes involving synthesis of foods, their translocation, partitioning among various organs, and conversion to new tissues. Especially important are the correlations among organs to provide an efficient ratio of roots to shoots and of rates of physiological processes so the plant has a proper balance of water absorption to transpiration and of photosynthesis to respiration. The interactions among various physiological processes change during the normal course of plant development, even under optimal environmental conditions, and also in response to a variety of environmental stresses.

In addition to requiring foods and hormones, the growth of plants depends on an adequate supply of minerals, water, and vitamins. Food requirements are particularly high in meristematic regions where new tissues are being formed. Large amounts of nitrogenous compounds such as amides and amino acids are used in the formation of new protoplasm in the region of cell division. During cell enlargement and maturation, carbohydrates are used in the formation of new cell walls and as substrate for respiration. Most or perhaps all of the essential mineral elements, along with hormones and vitamins, are required in the growing regions. Some hormones, such as auxin, are mainly formed in growing regions; the rest must be supplied from other parts of the plant. Sufficient water is required to maintain turgidity, and water deficit is one of the most common factors limiting growth.

INTERNAL CONTROL OF VEGETATIVE GROWTH

The importance of mineral nutrients in vegetative growth was discussed in Chapter 10. Carbohydrates were discussed in considerable detail in Chapters 5, 6, 7, and 11 and will be considered only briefly here. Nitrogen metabolism was discussed in Chapter 9. Most of this chapter will concentrate on the role of plant water balance and hormone balance on the regulation of vegetative and reproductive growth.

Carbohydrates

Although growth requires large amounts of available carbohydrates, several lines of evidence indicate that cessation of growth of woody plants seldom is due primarily to carbohydrate deficiency. For instance, when the annual shoot growth of perennial plants slows down, a substantial carbohydrate reserve usually is still present. Priestley (1962a,b) showed, for example, that only about one-third of the extractable carbohydrate supply was depleted during the growth of apple trees. Shoot growth of many species is greatly increased with long photoperiods even when the added light is of such low intensity that it does not materially increase the amount of photosynthate. Furthermore, cambial growth can be rapidly checked by late-summer droughts when trees have large carbohydrate reserves. Hence, carbohydrate supplies in plants often appear to be adequate, but growth is inhibited by inadequate transport of substrates to growth centers and by internal blocks to the utilization and conversion of food into new tissues.

A deficiency of hormonal growth regulators, which may direct the transport of substrates, as well as internal water stress, undoubtedly play paramount roles in growth inhibition.

Because of quantitative correlations between the degree of defoliation by forest pests and the amount of cambial growth, there often has been a tendency to automatically attribute growth reduction to deficiency in carbohydrates. However, inhibition of cambial growth following defoliation undoubtedly is more complicated than a mere starvation response. Although carbohydrate supply and translocation to the lower stem are reduced by defoliation, the supply of hormonal growth regulators also is reduced. Isolation of the lower stem of trembling aspen and sugar maple trees by phloem blocks during the dormant season virtually prevented xylem differentiation during the next growing season. Cambial growth did not appear to be affected directly by the availability of substrate, because axial and ray parenchyma cells contained considerable starch before and after resumption of seasonal cambial activity and throughout the period of phloem and xylem differentiation (Evert and Kozlowski, 1967; Evert *et al.*, 1972).

Water Deficits

Growth often is inhibited by too little and occasionally by too much water. The paramount importance of water supply to tree growth is emphasized by Zahner's (1968) conclusion that 80 to 90% of the variation in tree growth can be attributed to water stress. This section will discuss the effects of plant water stress on shoot growth, cambial growth, and root growth.

Shoot Growth

The growth of shoots is suppressed by internal water deficits, the amount of inhibition varying among plant species and varieties; severity and time of drought; shoot location on the plant; and with different aspects of shoot growth such as bud formation, internode elongation, leaf expansion, and leaf abscission. In addition to modifying internode and leaf expansion, water deficits also affect leaf anatomy. For example, the leaves of several woody species were thicker and intervascular intervals were smaller in a year of severe drought than in a normal year (Turrell and Turrell, 1943).

Bud Formation and Internode Elongation

Shoot growth is decreased by the inhibitory effects of water deficits on both bud formation and bud elongation. In many temperate zone species that have a fully preformed shoot in the winter bud, potential shoot growth is governed to a large degree by the number of anatomical stem units present in the unopened bud (Lanner, 1971). Therefore, in such species environmental conditions during the year of bud formation control shoot length to a greater degree than do the environmental conditions during the year of bud expansion into a shoot. For example, Clements (1970) showed that irrigation of young red pine trees in late summer in Ontario, Canada, caused formation of large buds that produced long shoots in the subsequent year. Late-summer droughts resulted in formation of small buds that, in turn, expanded into short shoots. Irrigation in the spring of the year following bud formation did not appreciably influence shoot length, emphasizing the great influence of shoot predetermination in the unopened bud.

The importance of water deficits during bud formation on shoot growth in the subsequent year is also shown by the high correlations between shoot growth and the amount of rain during the previous year. For example, low rainfall in May to November of 1940 and 1944 was associated with little height growth of red pine trees in 1941 and 1945. By comparison, May to November of 1945 had more than twice as

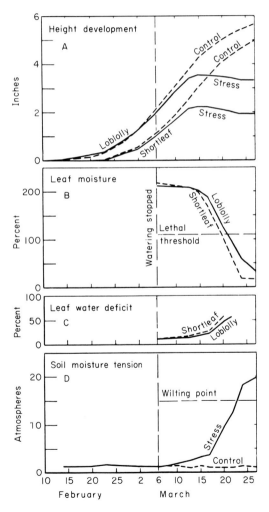

Fig. 16.1. Effect of drought on height growth, leaf water deficit, and soil water tension in loblolly pine and shortleaf pine trees. From Stransky and Wilson (1964).

much rain as the same period in 1944. This was reflected by more than doubling of shoot elongation in 1946 over that in 1945 (Motley, 1949).

Summer droughts often greatly reduce current shoot elongation in species that exhibit free growth or recurrent flushing. As was discussed in Chapter 3, these two groups usually continue to expand their shoots during much of the summer. Shoot extension of the yellow-poplar (which exhibits free growth) was greatly inhibited by internal water deficits that were induced by reducing the relative humidity of the air or by soil drying (Doley, 1970). Stransky and Wilson (1964) showed that shoot elongation of seedlings of the recurrently flushing loblolly and shortleaf pines was decreased when moisture tension in drying soil reached 2.5 bars. When soil moisture tension reached 3.5 bars, all plants stopped growing (Fig. 16.1). By the time soil moisture tension increased to 15 bars all the experimental seedlings died. It should be remembered that in recurrently flushing species, shoots variously located on the stem exhibit different numbers of seasonal growth flushes (see Chapter 3). Therefore shoots on the lower stem, which flush only once or not at all during a season, may not be affected by late-season droughts to the same degree as those in the upper stem, which flush several times.

In recurrently flushing species a drought in midsummer cannot inhibit the first seasonal growth flush that preceded the drought, but it may decrease the number of primordia that are forming in the new bud and will expand in a late-season flush of shoot growth. Therefore, the second seasonal flush of shoot expansion may be greatly limited by the reduced number of primordia, and if the drought continues into the period of the second growth flush, the expansion of these primordia may also be inhibited.

Differences among species in height growth response to water deficits are shown by comparing the studies of Zahner (1962) on loblolly pine and of Lotan and Zahner (1963) on red pine. Whereas height growth of loblolly pine, which occurs in several growth flushes in the same growing season and continues for much of the summer, was greatly inhibited by late-summer drought, that of red pine, which does not flush recurrently but completes height growth early in the summer, was little inhibited.

Leaf Expansion

Although the internode elongation of species with shoots wholly preformed in the winter bud often is not greatly influenced by water deficits during the year of bud expansion into a shoot, such deficits often inhibit leaf expansion. In general, cell enlargement is more sensitive to water stress than is cell division. For example, Sands and Rutter (1959) found that needle elongation of Scotch pine seedlings was decreased by soil moisture tensions as low as 0.5 bars (Table 16.1). Lister et al. (1967) maintained potted eastern white pine seedlings under moisture stress for much of the growing season and found that water deficits caused only a slight reduction of internode elongation but a very significant inhibition of needle expansion. It should be remembered that needle expansion of eastern white pine lasts about twice as long as internode elongation.

TABLE 16.1 Effect of Soil Moisture Tension on Needle Elongation of Scotch Pine[a]

Duration of treatment	Mean needle length (cm) at maximum soil moisture tension (bars)			
	0.1	0.5	1.5	5.0
June 7–Sept. 4	—	5.85	4.80	3.75
April 14–Sept. 4	5.05	4.25	4.20	3.40
June 1–Sept. 4	4.95	4.35	4.25	3.75
June 1–July 24	5.00	4.50	4.80	4.00
Mean	5.00	4.35	4.40	3.70

[a] From Sands and Rutter (1959).

Garrett and Zahner (1973) showed that shoot length and number of needle fascicles of 23-year-old red pine trees were controlled to a large extent by water supply during the middle of the previous growing season, whereas elongation of needles was much more responsive to current-year water supply. Length of terminal buds in the autumn of 1962 was a good indicator of the growth potential of shoots in 1963. Trees subjected to drought during June and July of the 1962 season had smaller buds by at least 30% than trees receiving water during this period. Water supply during April–May or August–September of 1962 did not affect the size of terminal buds. Needles continued to elongate well into August (1963), but the elongation rate of the middle period set the pattern for the season. Needles of trees subjected to drought during June and July of 1963 were 20% shorter than those on trees watered during this period.

Leaf Senescence and Abscission

Premature senescence and shedding of leaves can be induced by plant water deficits. In some species, the loss of leaves during drought involves true abscission; in other species the leaves merely wither and die (Kozlowski, 1976a). Yellow-poplar is notorious for shedding many leaves during summer droughts, sycamore sheds some leaves, and California buckeye sheds all of its leaves as the normal summer water deficit develops. On the other hand, leaves of dogwood or azalea usually wilt and die rather than abscise. When water deficits induce true abscission, they are associated with various hormonal changes. This is discussed in the section of this chapter on Control of Abscission.

Sometimes leaf shedding does not occur until after rehydration following drought damage, making the damage not immediately obvious. The leaves then drop rapidly, suggesting that stress-induced abscission requires adequate water, probably to begin the active cell division needed to form the abscission layer. For example, McMichael *et al.* (1973) found that abscission of cotton leaves did not occur during a period of water stress but followed rehydration of the abscission zone. Abscission occurred rapidly, with the oldest leaves shed first. Abscission layers of leaves at the first and second nodes generally formed within 12 hr after rewatering, whereas several days were needed for the formation of abscission layers of upper, more juvenile leaves. When citrus and almond trees in arid climates undergo enough desiccation to induce leaf abscission, the leaves do not drop as long as irrigation water is withheld. However, when the trees are watered the leaves are promptly shed.

Addicott and Lyon (1973) divided woody plants showing summer leaf fall into summer deciduous species and species that shed only part of their leaves during a drought. Summer deciduous species include many temperate zone plants. Species that shed only part of their leaves during summer droughts include some broad-leaved evergreens such as *Eucalyptus* spp., *Citrus* spp., and many tropical and subtropical evergreens. Although many tropical trees are classified as summer deciduous, some of them tend to shed their leaves during dry periods whether these occur during the actual summer months or not.

Often leaf shedding is associated with hot, dry winds such as the "Santa Anas" or "Northers" of southern California. Santa Anas in California induced two types of injury, "windburn" and "scorch" (Reed and Bartholomew, 1930). Citrus leaves killed by windburn first wilt and they dry out rapidly. If the wind stops after a few hours the leaves sometimes recover. However, if severe desiccation occurs they do not recover and are shed in a few days. Blades of scorched leaves turn brown and become brittle within a few hours, without an intermediate wilting stage. The scorched leaves remain attached for several weeks (Reed and Bartholomew, 1930).

In relatively dry tropical areas such as the "caatinga" and "cerrado" of Brazil many trees lose their leaves at the height of the dry season (Kozlowski, 1976a). Some species lose all their leaves; others shed only some of them before new ones grow. In many species new leaves emerge before the rainy season starts. Many trees of tropical rain forests quickly lose all their leaves in response to very mild droughts.

Stem Shrinkage

The cambial zone is under some degree of water stress during much of the growing season. Both the diurnal and seasonal shrinkage of stems indicate that water deficits occur in the cambial zone because most of the shrinkage is localized there. Daily water deficits first develop in leaves and are then transmitted through increased tension in the xylem sap to the cambial sheath. Such water deficits may recur daily because water is lost more rapidly in transpiration during the day than it is replaced by absorption through the roots (see Chapter 13). During the night both absorption and transpiration are low, but the rate of absorption exceeds the rate of transpiration (see Fig. 13.19). As plants tend to refill with water at night, the internal water deficits are eliminated, only to be induced again on the following day. Even plants growing in well-watered soils undergo diurnal stem shrinkage and water deficits on hot days when transpiration is rapid.

Transmission of water deficits from the leaves to the lower stem occurs quite rapidly. For example, the daily lag of minimum stem diameter behind maximum leaf

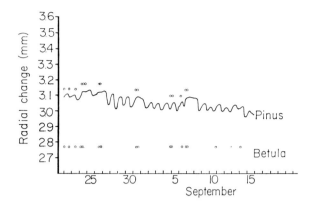

Fig. 16.2 Shrinkage of red pine stem during August and September. Diurnal stem shrinkage and expansion are superimposed on the progressive seasonal trend of shrinkage. From Braekke and Kozlowski (1975b).

water deficit was 1 to 2 hr for sugar maple and white birch and 3 to 4 hr for red pine and balsam fir (Pereira and Kozlowski, 1976, 1978).

Both diurnal and seasonal stem shrinkage of woody plants, indicating water deficits in the cambial zone, have been well documented (Kozlowski, 1958, 1964b, 1967a, 1972a) and only a few examples will be given here. In Wisconsin there was little diurnal stem shrinkage of red pine, trembling aspen, and northern pin oak trees early in the growing season when soil moisture was plentiful and the leaves were not fully expanded. Later in the season, as leaves expanded and transpiration increased, the amount of diurnal stem shrinkage increased. In late summer, when the soil dried and tree stems became severely dehydrated, the daily amplitude of stem shrinkage declined again (Kozlowski and Winget, 1964b).

During prolonged droughts the cambial sheath undergoes continuous water stress, as indicated by stem shrinkage for several days, weeks, or even months (Kozlowski, 1968a,b, 1972b). This has been demonstrated for many species of the temperate zone and tropics. Bormann and Kozlowski (1962) recorded stem shrinkage of mature eastern white pine trees for long periods during the growing season, and Braekke and Kozlowski (1975b) reported similar responses in red pine in Wisconsin (Fig. 16.2). In Uganda stems of rain forest trees shrink appreciably, often over a 2- to 3-month period (Dawkins, 1956). As may be seen in Fig. 16.3, stems of Douglas-fir trees in southwestern Colorado dehydrated and shrank progressively for more than 3 months during a rainless summer (Fritts *et al.*, 1965).

Cambial Growth

Cambial growth of woody plants is exceedingly sensitive to and inhibited by water deficits. The number of xylem cells produced, the seasonal duration of cambial

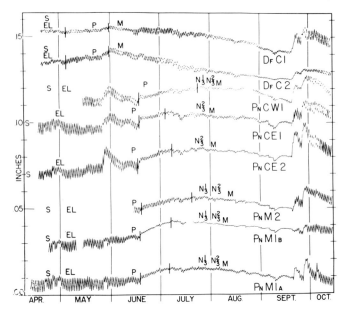

Fig. 16.3. Daily maximum and minimum stem sizes recorded by dendrographs. DꜰC 1 and DꜰC 2 are two Douglas-fir trees from Navajo Canyon. PɴCW 1 is a pinyon pine on a west-facing slope. PɴCE 1 and PɴCE 2 are pinyon pines on an east-facing slope. PɴM 2 is a pinyon pine on the mesa top. PɴM 1A and PɴM 1B represent a twin pinyon pine on the mesa top with a dendrograph mounted on each stem. Other symbols: S, buds swelling; EL, bud elongation; P, pollen shed; N⅓, needles one-third mature size; N⅔, needles two-thirds mature size; M, needles full size. Two vertical bars designate interval of 90% radial increase. From Fritts *et al.* (1965). Reproduced by permission of the Society for American Archaeology from *American Antiquity,* Vol. 31.

growth, the proportion of xylem to phloem increment, and earlywood–latewood relations are responsive to water deficits.

Water deficits affect cambial growth both directly and indirectly. Cambial growth is reduced indirectly by inhibition of synthesis and downward translocation of hormonal growth regulators from the crown. The influence of growth hormones on cambial growth is discussed in the section on Hormonal Growth Regulators.

Internal water deficits have direct inhibitory effects on cambial activity because high turgor is required for cell enlargement and cell wall deposition even in the presence of hormones such as auxin. Decreasing water potential from -3.1 to -5.8 bars decreased incorporation of glucose units into the cell walls of differentiating secondary xylem of Scotch pine by one-third. A further decrease in water potential to -28.1 bars reduced glucose incorporation by more than one-half (Whitmore and Zahner, 1967). Some idea of the complexity of growth control and the interactions of water deficits and hormonal growth regulators on cambial growth can be gained from the work of Doley and Leyton (1968). As may be seen in Figs. 16.4 and 16.5, water potential as well as IAA, GA, and their interactions had marked effects on both the production and enlargement of

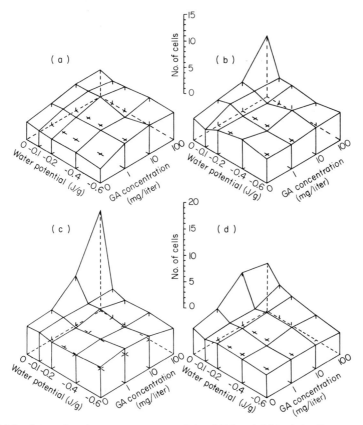

Fig. 16.4. Interactions between water potential and IAA and GA in their effects on production of cambial derivatives in *Fraxinus excelsior*. (a) Zero IAA; (b) 1 mg/liter IAA; (c) 10 mg/liter IAA; (d) 100 mg/liter IAA. From Doley and Leyton (1968).

cambial derivatives. The effect of decreasing the water potential (increasing water deficits) was to depress the effect of growth hormones. However, the greatest influence on cambial growth was exerted by water deficits, with even small deficits inhibiting cell division and expansion.

Wood Production. Internal water deficits do not appear to play an important role in the initiation of seasonal cambial growth, probably because water stress is rare in the spring. However, once seasonal cambial growth has begun, water deficits play a major role in subsequent control. As water deficits increase, xylem increment slows or ceases, and whenever these internal water deficits are decreased by rain or irrigation the xylem increment accelerates or resumes. Such periodic growth often produces multiple rings of wood in the same annual increment. During dry years cambial activity ceases early in the growing season and only a thin sheath of xylem is produced (Fig. 16.6). The close relationship between year-to-year variations in available water and

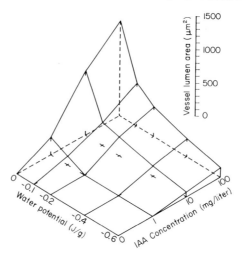

Fig. 16.5. Interaction between IAA concentration and water potential in their effects on cross-sectional areas of lumens in vessels of *Fraxinus excelsior*. From Doley and Leyton (1968).

width of the xylem ring is the basis of the science of dendrochronology, which is discussed in detail by Fritts (1976).

Zahner (1958) found that during a dry summer in Arkansas diameter growth of loblolly pine essentially ceased by August. However, it resumed during September, which was unusually rainy, and continued through October. That year approximately one-third of the total annual xylem increment was laid down during September and October. Bassett (1966) also showed that the seasonal duration of cambial growth of loblolly pine trees was greatly influenced by water stress. Diameter growth at breast height of dominant trees increased during 96% of the growing season during a wet year but during only 58% of the season in a dry year. Suppressed trees increased in diameter during 49% of the season in a wet year and only 8% of the season in a dry year (Table 16.2). In northern Wisconsin, diameter growth was greater and continued longer into the summer for red pine trees located on the lower part of a slope than for those on the upper part. The early inhibition of cambial growth of the upper-slope trees was attributed to their greater water deficits (Braekke and Kozlowski, 1975a).

The effects of water deficits on wood formation may be expected to vary somewhat among species. Whereas summer water deficits affect cell size in the whole annual ring of diffuse-porous angiosperms and the latewood portion of ring-porous angiosperms, they usually have little effect on the size of earlywood vessels of ring-porous angiosperms. This is because the latter expand and differentiate so rapidly (they generally are mature water-conducting elements even before leaves expand) that their expansion is not likely to be influenced by summer drought (Zahner, 1968).

Within a species the incidence of missing xylem rings increases as environmental stresses become more intense. Fritts *et al.* (1965) studied tree ring characteristics along a transect from the forest interior to a semidesert forest border. As moisture deficits

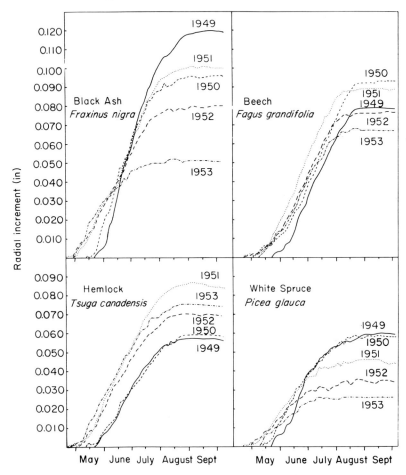

Fig. 16.6. Variations of cambial growth initiation, rate of growth, and duration of growth of four species of trees during five successive growing seasons in Ontario, Canada. Note the differences in duration and amount of cambial growth during a typically wet year (1949) and a dry year (1953). From Fraser (1956).

became greater toward the semiarid forest border, the percentage of absent xylem rings increased sharply.

Water deficits often inhibit cambial growth during the current year as well as the subsequent year. Important in this lag response is the effect of water balance in directly or indirectly influencing the number of leaf primordia that overwinter in buds and expand during the subsequent season. Hence, the amounts of carbohydrates and hormonal growth regulators produced by the leaves during a given year are affected by water deficits of the previous year. Zahner and Stage (1966) showed that water deficits in the summer of both the current and previous year inhibited cambial growth of western white pine in Idaho. Similar results were obtained by Zahner and Donnelly

TABLE 16.2 Variations in the Specific Gravity of
Earlywood and Latewood in Four Species of Young
Pines of the Southern United States[a]

	Specific gravity	
Species	Earlywood	Latewood
Longleaf pine	0.280	0.690
Loblolly pine	0.310	0.625
Shortleaf pine	0.265	0.600
Slash pine	0.275	0.570

[a] From Paul and Smith (1950).

(1967) for red pine, with 68% of the growth variation associated with current-season moisture conditions and 14% with moisture conditions of the previous season.

Earlywood–Latewood Relations.   Much interest has been shown in the control of earlywood and latewood formation. Both density and specific gravity of wood are functions of the proportion of earlywood to latewood in the annual ring. Latewood, having a larger proportion of cell wall substance per unit of volume than the earlywood in the same ring, has a high specific gravity. In gymnosperms the average specific gravity of latewood usually is about two to three times as high as that of earlywood (Table 16.3).

In addition to controlling width of the annual xylem ring, water supply affects the time of latewood initiation, the length of time during which latewood is produced, and the transition between earlywood and latewood. Water deficits trigger early formation of latewood, and sustained drought thereafter shortens the period of latewood formation. Several studies showed that water deficits cause latewood formation to start early in the growing season. For example, in 1954 depletion of soil moisture in Michigan began on June 21 and latewood formation in red pine began at the end of June. During the next year, depletion of soil moisture began earlier and the earlywood–latewood transition also was induced earlier (Kraus and Spurr, 1961). Zahner and Oliver (1962) demonstrated that red pine trees released by thinning began forming latewood about 2

TABLE 16.3 Average Number of Black and White Mycorrhizae per
Seedling on Virginia Pine Grown under Four Soil Moisture Levels[a]

Watering period	White	Black	Percent black
Every day	72.4	10.5	11.9
Every second day	18.4	8.3	59.9
Every third day	0.08	8.6	98.6
Every fourth day	0	2.4	100

[a] From Worley and Hacskaylo (1959).

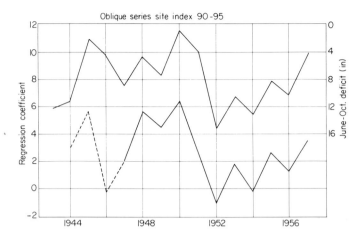

Fig. 16.7. Relation between latewood formation and summer water deficit. Upper curve represents soil water deficits, and the lower curve represents regression coefficients for latewood percentage on internodes from apex. From Smith and Wilsie (1961).

weeks later than trees in unthinned control stands. The longer duration of earlywood formation in the released trees was ascribed to less severe water deficits.

Much evidence indicates that mild water deficits late in the season decrease the total width of the latewood band. Barrow (1951) observed that Douglas-fir trees near a river had wider latewood bands than those some distance away. Smith and Wilsie (1961) found that large amounts of latewood were formed in loblolly pine during years of low water deficits (Fig. 16.7). The sharpness of the transition between earlywood and latewood is influenced by the water supply toward the end of the period of earlywood production. Harris (1955), for example, found that a severe drought at that time produced a sharp boundary between earlywood and latewood.

Root Growth

Water deficits in root meristems inhibit elongation, branching, and cambial growth in roots. The roots of trees are far from the source of photosynthates and shoot-produced hormones. Hence, roots undoubtedly are subjected to frequent deficiencies when water deficits in shoots reduce synthesis and phloem transport of these substances. Root growth may also be decreased by a reduction in turgor.

In dry regions root penetration is limited by the depth to which the soil is wetted. Not only is root elongation stopped in dry soil, but roots also tend to become suberized to their tips, thus reducing their capacity for absorbing water and minerals. Plants subjected to severe droughts may not regain their full capacity to absorb water for several days after the soil is rewetted (Kramer, 1969). At least some of the decreased growth of roots in dry soil is due to the physical resistance of the soil to root penetration.

Water stress in the summer often causes slowing of root growth, and during prolonged mid-season droughts, when recovery of turgor does not occur during the night, roots may stop growing completely. If the soil is subsequently recharged with water, root elongation resumes in many species even though seasonal shoot extension has been completed and bud formation initiated.

Kozlowski (1949) showed that large root systems developed in tree seedlings growing in well-watered soils and small, relatively unbranched root systems developed in trees growing in soil undergoing periodic drying cycles. Cessation of root growth during drought, and its resumption after rain, have been described for many species, including citrus (Cossmann, 1939), Monterey pine (Fielding, 1955), and Aleppo pine (Leshem, 1965). Kaufmann (1968a) found that when soil water potential declined to -6 or -7 bars, the rate of root growth of loblolly and white pine seedlings decreased to about one-fourth that of roots of plants in soil maintained near field capacity. When the soil was subjected to several drying cycles, less root growth occurred during the second and third cycle than during the first one. Root growth was reduced more by water stress than shoot growth.

Water Deficits and Mycorrhizae

Both the amount and type of mycorrhizae formed are affected by water supply. When several species of fungi invade a single host, they often show variable sensitivity to soil moisture stress. Worley and Hacskaylo (1959) studied the effects of four soil moisture levels on mycorrhizal associations of Virginia pine. A white fungus, the major mycorrhiza former when soil moisture content was high, was absent under drought conditions. A black fungus, *Cenococcum graniforme*, comprised only about one-tenth of the mycorrhizae formed under a high moisture content but became dominant as the moisture deficit increased (Table 16.3). Apparently the black fungus was more vigorous at high moisture deficits, while the white fungus was less vigorous. Mikola and Laiho (1962) noted that the drought-resistant *Cenococcum graniforme* predominated in soil levels that were subjected to periodic droughts.

Water Excess

A deficiency of oxygen in flooded soil often causes cessation of root growth, followed by injury or death of the root systems. Root injury usually is followed by yellowing and death of leaves, reduced stem growth, and, in severe cases, death of the trees. The extent of injury to roots by flooding varies with species, soil factors, timing and duration of flooding, and physicochemical conditions of the floodwater (Rowe and Beardsell, 1973).

An early response to flooding is the formation of adventitious roots in some species (Fig. 16.8). Another response to poor soil aeration is the increased susceptibility of roots to attacks by fungi and other organisms. A number of pathogenic species of organisms grew well in poorly aerated soil, and this combined with reduced root growth results in injury to the root systems of many species.

Excess moisture can destroy the mycorrhizal flora of soils rich in fungal symbionts. For example, roots in submerged layers of peat and in abandoned beaver ponds had no mycorrhiza-forming fungi (Wilde, 1954).

TABLE 16.4   Effect of Water Deficits on Various Aspects of Reproductive Growth in Cox's Orange Pippin Apple Trees[a]

		Treatment		
	Date	Droughted	Control	Irrigated
Flowers per tree	May 12	3228	3431	2464
Fruitlets per tree	June 9	275	540	591
Fruit set as percent of flower number	June 9	8.5	15.7	24.0
Fruit clusters per tree	June 9	144	252	219

[a] From Powell (1974).

Hormonal Growth Regulators

Balances among various endogenous growth promoters and inhibitors play a central role in regulating the vegetative growth of woody plants. Changes in amounts and balances of hormones frequently reflect environmental regimes and changes. A few examples will be given.

Some species of birch and pine grow slowly but steadily on infertile sandy soils, whereas others, such as sycamore maple and Sitka spruce, grow poorly. However, when tissues of both groups of species grown under low mineral nutrient regimes were analyzed, the mineral contents did not vary greatly. Wareing (1974) suggested that a nutrient deficiency may inhibit growth primarily by inhibiting hormone synthesis.

The effects of water supply may influence some aspects of growth directly as well as indirectly or synergistically with growth hormones. For example, both drought and waterlogging of soils induce formation of endogenous ethylene, which affects plant growth. Increased production of ethylene when water-stressed plants were rewatered

Fig. 16.8. Adventitious roots and hypertrophied lenticels induced on stem of cottonwood seedling by flooding. From Pereira and Kozlowski (1977b).

was important in causing the abscission of cotton leaves (Jordan *et al.*, 1972). Treating plants with ethylene reduced the plant water deficit required to induce leaf abscission from -17 to -7 bars, implying that water deficits may cause abscission-zone tissues to become predisposed to ethylene action. On the other hand, Kawase (1974, 1976) claims that ethylene also causes much of the injury observed in plants growing in flooded soil.

Plant responses to day length also are mediated through changes in endogenous hormones. Higher levels of endogenous growth promoters have been reported under long than under short days, and sometimes such differences are related to changes in growth. Increased shoot growth of birch seedlings under long days appeared to be related to increased amounts of gibberellins. Shoot growth was stopped by short days but application of GA_3 induced growth again (Wareing, 1974). As was discussed in Chapter 14, winter chilling also promotes a favorable balance of growth promoters over inhibitors in some seeds, thereby allowing seed germination to proceed in the spring.

Bud Dormancy

Buds of temperate zone woody plants alternate from active growth during the warm season to a dormant state during the cold season. When seasonal shoot growth ceases, the plants first enter a reversible phase of inactivity called "prerest," "quiescence," or "predormancy" (Romberger, 1963). Plants in this condition still have the capacity for growth, but the range of environmental conditions in which they can grow becomes narrower with the passage of time after predormancy has developed. The state of dormancy continues to deepen until true dormancy is attained, and shoot apices cannot elongate even under the most favorable environmental conditions. Eventually, true dormancy is terminated and a transition to postdormancy occurs. The tissues can again resume growth, at first under very narrow environmental limits, and later under much wider ones. Finally the tissues are completely released from dormancy (Vegis, 1964). These relations may be summarized as follows:

Active growth	Predormancy	True dormancy	Post-dormancy	Active growth
Occurs under a wide range of conditions	Range of conditions under which growth occurs narrows: reversible	No growth even under the most favorable conditions	Range of conditions under which growth occurs widens	Occurs under a wide range of conditions

Although dormant buds do not elongate, there often is appreciable meristematic and metabolic activity during the various phases of dormancy. For example, Perry and Simons (1967) found some growth of bud scales and leaves in several species of woody angiosperms during each month of the year in Raleigh, North Carolina. In California, mitotic figures were found in the apical meristems of *Araucaria* throughout the year, although from November to March cell elongation and mitotic activity were greatly reduced (Griffith, 1952).

Metabolic activity continues in dormant buds at a relatively low rate. Although respiration of dormant buds is low, Gäumann (1935) found that the dry weight of beech buds decreased by 6% and carbohydrate content decreased by 10% from the middle of October to mid-December. Later, appreciable amounts of fats stored in buds also disappeared. Such activity reflects changes in the kinds, amounts, and forms of enzymes as winter chilling progresses (Perry, 1971).

Control of Bud Dormancy. Dormancy can be induced in most plants by altering temperature, day length, light quality, mineral availability, or water supply. The effects of all of these on dormancy are mediated through internal physiological changes. However, the specific environmental factors that induce dormancy in nature often vary for different species. Dormancy can be experimentally induced in many woody plants by low temperatures or short days. It should not be assumed, however, that dormancy of all species in the field is brought on by the shortening days of autumn or by cold. Shoots of many woody plants stop growing before seasonal temperatures are low enough to stop growth and when days are still too long to promote dormancy. Species with shoots fully preformed in the bud stop elongating by midsummer when the days are long. By comparison, shoot growth of species exhibiting free growth and recurrently flushing species continues until the short days of autumn. Hence, factors such as water deficits and low nutrient availability may induce early promotion of quiescent buds in some species, and these buds are subsequently transformed into fully dormant buds under the influence of short days (Wareing and Saunders, 1971).

Over the years a number of theories on the internal control of bud dormancy have been advanced. Early theories emphasized the importance of blocking oxygen uptake by bud scales. These theories have been largely discarded because it now appears that bud dormancy is regulated by interactions between endogenous growth promoters and inhibitors. At least three major and several minor phases of bud development are recognized, each controlled by balances of growth hormones (Fig. 16.9). Michniewicz (1967) considered bud dormancy to involve an interaction of the influence of substances inhibitory to growth and the promotive influence of gibberellins. Abscisic acid

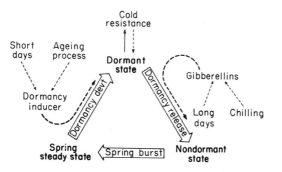

Fig. 16.9. The relationship of the dormancy phases of bud development to the annual cycle. The three steady states are shown in heavy lettering and the transitional phases in enclosed arrows. The possible mediation of environmental and endogenous factors by postulated substances is represented by broken arrows. From Smith and Kefford (1964).

may participate as a gibberellin antagonist since exogenous ABA will substitute for bud scales in promoting leaf growth and can act to inhibit GA_3-induced leaf growth (De Maggio and Freeberg, 1969). There is considerable evidence, however, that other plant hormones, such as cytokinins and ethylene, also are involved.

Development of Dormancy.   It is well known that growth inhibitors accumulate in bud scales, bud axes, and leaves within buds (Tinklin and Schwabe, 1970). At least three lines of evidence emphasize the importance of endogenous inhibitors in the development of bud dormancy: (1) under short-day conditions the leaves inhibit growth of the shoot tip; (2) generally more inhibitors are found in leaves and buds under short-day than under long-day conditions; and (3) when growth inhibitors such as ABA are extracted from leaves of a dormant woody plant and reapplied to plants of the same species, that were not dormant prior to application of the inhibitor, shoot elongation stops and sequential development toward the dormant state is initiated (Wareing, 1965).

In sycamore maple the greatest amounts of various inhibitors were found in the buds and leaves during the time of year when tissues were dormant, and the lowest amounts were found when the apex was actively growing. The increase in inhibitors in leaves up to August 20 was accompanied by an increase in inhibitors in the stem apex. The amount of inhibitors did not increase after August 20, and it decreased only after leafless plants were exposed to winter chilling. These observations suggested that growth inhibitors were produced in the leaves and translocated to the apex (Phillips and Wareing, 1958).

An important growth inhibitor may be ABA (see Chapter 15). Eagles and Wareing (1963, 1964) induced apparent dormancy in European silver birch seedlings by the application of ABA that had been extracted from dormant buds of the same species. Application of GA_3 to ABA-arrested buds caused them to grow again, emphasizing that the failure of bud growth was not caused by toxicity. The formation of resting buds by applying ABA has also been achieved in black currant (El-Antably *et al.*, 1967).

Release from Dormancy.   The release from bud dormancy is associated with an increase in growth promoters, a decrease in inhibitors, or both. Eagles and Wareing (1963, 1964) postulated that dormancy release involves the activity of gibberellins, which increase in response to chilling. Emergence from dormancy of sycamore maple buds was correlated more with an increase in gibberellin content of buds than with changes in levels of growth inhibitors. Browning (1973) found that gibberellin levels in coffee flower buds increased and ABA levels did not change when bud dormancy was released by rain or irrigation. Hence, emphasis was placed on gibberellin levels as the major stimulus for dormancy release in this species.

Growth promoters other than gibberellins also appear to play a role in release from bud dormancy. For example, kinetinlike activity was absent in dormant buds of white birch and balsam poplar. After bud dormancy was broken, kinetinlike activity increased progressively until shortly after buds opened, and it decreased thereafter (Domanski and Kozlowski, 1968). Cytokinins increased in both xylem sap and buds during chilling and bud burst of *Populus* × *robusta*. Such increases occurred in plants exposed both to natural chilling in the field and to artificial chilling. The levels of cytokinins often decreased in the xylem sap during bud swelling. However, this may have been due to dilution of the sap after transpiration became rapid (Hewett and Wareing, 1973a,b). Taylor and Dumbroff (1975) showed increases in cytokinin activity, but no significant changes in inhibitors during dormancy release in sugar maple buds.

Release from bud dormancy can be promoted by exogenous cytokinins. The effect varies with the specific type of cytokinin, its concentration, and the number of applications. A certain amount of cytokinin must penetrate to the site of action before bud dormancy can be broken. A single application of a high concentration of cytokinin is as effective as several applications of a lower concentration (Broome and Zimmerman, 1976).

Decreases in inhibitors during development of bud dormancy have been found for several tree species, including sycamore maple (Phillips and Wareing, 1958), persimmon, American elm, apple, and peach (Kawase, 1966).

Noting an increase in gibberellin activity in apricot buds shortly before the end of dormancy and a decline in activity of growth inhibitors at the time dormancy was probably broken, Ramsay and Martin (1970) suggested that release from bud dormancy was regulated by a delicate balance between growth promoters and inhibitors.

Bachelard and Wightman (1974) developed a useful model of dormancy release in balsam poplar buds that involved changes in favor of growth promoters over inhibitors and coordination of growth in the whole plant. They divided dormancy release into three sequential stages with the following important features: Phase I, increase in the gibberellin–inhibitor ratio, enhancement of metabolic activity, mobilization of food reserves, and beginning of shoot elongation; Phase II, translocation of metabolites including hormones to roots, initiation of root activity and stimulation of kinetin production by roots, translocation of cytokinins and gibberellins from roots to buds; and Phase III, activation by cytokinin of cell division in the apical meristem and development of the shoot by cell division and cell expansion.

Shoot Elongation

If specific growth regulators play an important role in shoot elongation, they should show a relation to the seasonal timing of growth and ample evidence exists of such a relation. For example, auxin yields were proportional to shoot growth of peach (Shalucha, 1946). Hatcher (1959) found an increase in auxin content in apple shoots in the spring as shoots began to expand. Auxin levels declined during the growing season and the decrease was followed by a slowing of shoot growth. In ginkgo the production of long shoots was correlated with high auxin production, first at the apex and later in lower internodes (Gunckel and Thimann, 1949). The auxin content of Norway spruce shoots was highly correlated with their rate of elongation (Dunberg, 1976). Such correlations have often tempted postulating direct control of shoot growth by auxin alone. However, in ginkgo maximum amounts of auxin occurred in internodes that had already passed their maximum growth rate. Furthermore, the shoots of most species have a changing complement of various growth regulators.

There is considerable evidence that gibberellins play a dominant role in the hormonal complex regulating shoot elongation. Evidence for this comes from an increase in shoot elongation following applications of gibberellins, the counteracting effects of applied gibberellins on those of endogenous growth inhibitors or applied growth retardants, and the correlation of shoot extension with endogenous gibberellin levels.

A number of investigators have shown that exogenous gibberellins increased height growth and internode elongation in a variety of woody angiosperms and gymnosperms. The effects of exogenous GA vary in detail and depend on the concentration, frequency, and method of application, and on the species and age of the trees. A few examples will be given below.

Gibberellins may be synthesized in partially expanded leaves as well as in other organs. The inhibition of internode extension following removal of the young leaves of apple was partially or entirely eliminated by exogenous GA_3 (Powell, 1972). The removal of the young leaf, just as it was unfolding, not only inhibited elongation of the internode below it but also that of two internodes above it. Applied GA_3 completely replaced the leaf with regard to expansion of the internode below, but only partially substituted for the leaf in controlling growth of internodes above it. This suggested that the leaf supplied growth-controlling factors in addition to gibberellins (Powell, 1972). Bachelard (1969a) showed that the effects of GA_3 on internode extension of *Eucalyptus camaldulensis* seedlings also varied with internode position. The relatively limited expansion of lower internodes was the result of cell elongation, whereas the proportionally greater expansion of upper internodes resulted primarily from cell division. Robitaille and Carlson (1976) found that GA_3 overcame ABA-induced inhibition of shoot elongation. Interstem-dwarfed apple trees stopped seasonal shoot growth earlier than shoots on vigorous trees. Abscisic acidlike activity was higher in stems from dwarfed trees. Injection experiments showed that increasing ABA concentrations decreased shoot elongation. The ABA-induced inhibition of shoot growth was reduced in proportion to the concentration of GA_3 in the injected solution.

In contrast to the stimulation of shoot growth in angiosperms by short-term treatments with GA, early experiments showed negligible or only slightly stimulatory effects of gibberellins on the shoot growth of conifers. However, in these early studies the lack of stimulation of shoot growth following exogenous gibberellin application may have been due to insufficient amounts of GA, application of the inappropriate GA, poor absorption, or overriding inhibitory factors (Pharis, 1976b).

Several lines of evidence now show that endogenous gibberellins are very important in regulating the shoot growth of conifers. Exogenous applications of gibberellins induce shoot elongation. For example, spray treatments of GA applied monthly for 9 months produced increases in height growth (observed for 18 months) of loblolly pine seedlings (Roberts *et al.,* 1963). Both soil drenches (applied several times weekly) and foliar sprays (applied weekly for 3 months) of GA_3 increased height growth and elongation of lateral shoots of balsam fir seedlings, the effect being associated with a change in the distribution of photosynthate rather than in the rate of photosynthesis (Little and Loach, 1975). Exogenous gibberellins have now been shown to increase shoot elongation in many species of conifers, including 13 species of Pinaceae (Pharis and Kuo, 1977).

Shoot elongation of gymnosperms has been shown to be inhibited in proportion to the amount by which endogenous GA production is decreased by certain applied growth retardants. For example, treatment of young seedlings of Norway spruce and Arizona cypress with GA_3 counteracted the effect of the growth retardant AMO-1618 (4-hydroxy-5-isopropyl (-2-methylphenyl)- trimethylammonium chloride 1-piperidine carboxylate) (Dunberg and Eliasson, 1972; Kuo and Pharis, 1975). Furthermore, apical dominance of intact plants, or the capacity of lateral buds or shoots to replace the missing terminal bud of decapitated seedlings, was decreased by the growth retardants AMO-1618 or B-995 (*N*-dimethylaminosuccinamic acid), and their action could be reversed by addition of GA_3 (Pharis *et al.*, 1967). Whereas AMO-1618 apparently interferes with GA biosynthesis, B-995 may act by increasing the interconversion of biologically active gibberellins to other gibberellins (or conjugates), these latter compounds perhaps being less active than their precursors (Kuo and Pharis, 1975).

Endogenous levels of gibberellinlike compounds are positively correlated with shoot elongation. In Pinaceae, gibberellinlike substances either are not detectable in dormant buds or they exist in very small amounts. As buds open and shoots elongate, however, gibberellin levels increase and qualitative changes in gibberellins also occur (Lavender *et al.*, 1973; Pharis, 1976b). Norway spruce shoots contain a number of gibberellinlike substances that appear to be necessary for normal shoot elongation (Dunberg, 1974). In this species there is a very rapid and large increase in gibberellinlike substances during the short period of most rapid shoot elongation. Shortly after shoots stop expanding, only very small amounts of gibberellinlike substances are present (Dunberg, 1976).

Leaf Senescence and Abscission

Leaves and various reproductive structures are shed by abscission, by mechanical factors, or by a combination of the two. In true abscission, physiological changes occur that lead to formation of a discrete abscission layer at which separation occurs. In simple leaves abscission occurs at or near the base of the petiole. In compound leaves, separate abscission zones form at the bases of individual leaflets as well as at the base of the petiole of the whole leaf.

Leaves of most deciduous trees of the temperate zone form an abscission layer during the season in which they expand and are shed in the autumn of the same year. However, some marcescent species such as oaks retain some of their leaves through the winter and shed them the following spring. In pin oak and scarlet oak abscission layers of leaves did not form by the end of the summer, but were first found in early winter. Leaf shedding began the following March (Hoshaw and Guard, 1949). In black oak some leaves form well-developed abscission layers and abscise in the autumn, but many remain attached until the following spring. In both instances, separation occurs from mechanical breakage through the thin walls of the recently divided cells of the separation layer (Marvin, 1964). Closely related marcescent species often shed their leaves at different times. For example, leaves of red oak, with large vascular strands having heavy cell walls, are shed later than those of scarlet oak, with small vascular strands (Berkley, 1931).

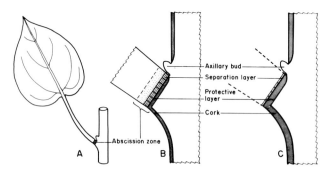

Fig. 16.10. Abscission zone of a leaf. A: Leaf with the abscission zone located at the base of the petiole; B: layers of the abscission zone shortly before leaf abscission; C: layers of the abscission zone after leaf abscission has occurred. From Addicott (1970); with permission of McGraw-Hill.

The abscission zone is made up of short and compact cells without intercellular spaces. The parenchyma cells of the abscission zone have thin, unlignified walls. In the vascular tissue lignification may occur only in the tracheary elements. As the time for abscission approaches, several important changes occur, including increased metabolic activity, development of tyloses and blocking of vessels, increase in density of protoplasm, and starch deposition in the abscission zone. The cell walls swell and digestion of pectin and cellulosic materials takes place. Actual separation of leaves occurs between rows of cells, usually leaving a smooth scar. Shortly before or after separation occurs, a protective layer begins to form through deposition of various substances such as suberin, wound gum, and lignin (Fig. 16.10).

Separation of leaves may result from dissolution of one or more layers of cells or cell parts. Three types of dissolution have been reported: (1) the middle lamella between two layers of cells dissolves, but the primary wall remains intact, (2) both the middle lamella and primary cell walls between two layers of cells dissolve, or (3) entire cells of one or more layers dissolve.

Control of Abscission. Osborne (1973) proposed an attractive model for the regulation of abscission that involved three sequential stages: stimulus, signal, and response (Fig. 16.11). According to this model, adverse environmental conditions such as temperature changes and short days provide the stimulus for leaf senescence. Because leaf senescence always precedes natural leaf abscission, it is considered to be the necessary signal. Senescence of leaves is associated with color changes, loss of chlorophyll, a decrease in some enzymes (e.g., pectin methylesterase), and an increase in hydrolytic enzymes such as proteases and nucleases. A decreased capacity of cells to synthesize RNA and protein appears to be a crucial malfunction that promotes senescence. Development of senescence also is usually accompanied by the export of carbohydrates, nitrogenous compounds, and minerals from leaves.

Internally, leaf senescence and abscission are under strong hormonal control. Current evidence indicates that primary roles are played by auxins, which prevent abscission, and ethylene, which triggers it. Leopold and Kriedemann (1975) succinctly sum-

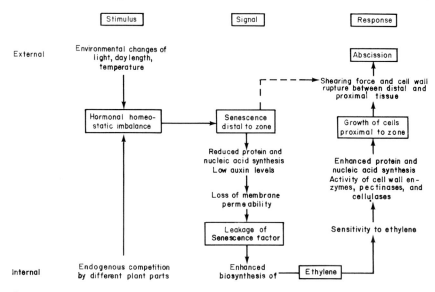

Fig. 16.11. The model for stimulus, signal, and response for leaf abscission. From Osborne (1973).

marized abscission as a correlative effect in which the leaf blade provides auxin as long as the leaf is healthy and growing, thereby suppressing abscission. As a leaf ages, auxin flow across the abscission zone diminishes and ethylene, which now increases in amount, can exert its effect in initiating abscission. The flow of auxin can also be inhibited by injury to the leaf blade, thus stimulating abscission. There is considerable evidence that other hormones—including cytokinins, gibberellins—and inhibitors also play a part in abscission. For example, regions high in cytokinins, together with auxins and gibberellins, are strong sinks to which nutrients move from other equally senescent regions. When the supply of nutrients is limited, the tendency of the plant to concentrate them in young leaves high in cytokinins, gibberellins, and auxin, leads to rapid senescence and abscission of old leaves (Addicott, 1970). However, Osborne (1973) suggested that various growth promoters and inhibitors act to a considerable degree by modulating the basic auxin–ethylene control system. Abscisic acid, for example, promotes ethylene production.

Numerous examples show that application of either auxin or gibberellin to leaves that are still green in the autumn will retard their senescence. For example, autumn coloration of the leaves of many species of deciduous trees in England was delayed by spraying them with GA_3 in the early autumn (Brian *et al.*, 1959). Treated leaves of European ash, sweet cherry, and sycamore maple remained green and did not abscise by November 21, whereas all untreated leaves had fallen by that date. Osborne and Hallaway (1960) obtained similar results by treating leaves of *Prunus senriko serrulata* with auxins. The treated leaves not only retained their green color but also maintained high rates of photosynthesis as well as high protein levels.

Evidence that ethylene initiates leaf abscission is impressive. A concentration as low as 0.1 μl/liter in the air can induce leaf abscission. The oldest leaves are shed first, indicating their greater sensitivity to ethylene. Abscission of both leaves and fruits can be stimulated by applications of Ethrel (2-chloroethylphosphonic acid), also called ethephon. Most Ethrel that is applied to plants eventually is converted to ethylene, which sets in motion the processes of abscission (Abeles, 1973). For further discussion of factors controlling abscission the reader is referred to the book on *Shedding of Plant Parts,* edited by Kozlowski (1973).

Cambial Growth

Several growth hormones play a major role in regulating the various phases of cambial growth, including cell division, increase in size of cambial derivatives, thickening of cell walls, the earlywood–latewood transition, formation of reaction wood, and seasonal cessation of cambial growth. Although auxins play a dominant role, normal cambial growth appears to be the end result of interactions among auxins and gibberellins produced in apical tissues, of cytokinins produced in the roots, as well as growth inhibitors and some nonhormonal substances.

Evidence for a dominant regulatory role of apically produced growth hormones on cambial growth comes from the correlation between bud growth in the spring and initiation of xylem production below buds, basipetal migration of the cambial growth wave, arrested cambial activity in defoliated or disbudded trees or below phloem-blocking stem girdles, and initiation of cambial growth with exogenous hormones.

Although some growth promoters such as auxin are produced by the cambium itself after it is activated by an apical stimulus (Sheldrake, 1971), normal development of xylem and phloem depends on a continuous supply of growth-regulating hormones from the shoots. Evert and Kozlowski (1967) and Evert *et al.* (1972) showed that severing the phloem of trembling aspen and sugar maple trees during the dormant season or at various times during the growing season affected subsequent production and differentiation of xylem and phloem below the phloem block. When the phloem was interrupted during the dormant season, xylem differentiation did not occur below the blockage during the next growing season. If the phloem was severed shortly after seasonal cambial activity began, relatively few xylem elements were produced during the same season, and these were short and without normally thickened walls. The most conspicuous effect of phloem interruption was the curtailment of secondary wall formation in both the xylem and phloem. When phloem blocks were applied in midseason, the first part of the annual xylem increment had cells of normal length and wall thickening. Wilson (1968) reported an increase in the number of xylem and phloem cells above phloem-severing stem girdles of eastern white pine trees, apparently because of a higher than normal mitotic index (percentage of cambial zone cells in mitosis) and because of the longer duration of mitotic activity. Below the phloem blockage, cell division and expansion stopped within a few weeks after trees were girdled, and cell wall thickening continued at a very low rate. Wodzicki and Wodzicki (1973) found severe reduction in both auxin content and cambial growth below phloem blockages in Scotch pine trees. In the following year, both auxin levels and cambial activity were negligible below the phloem block. Such experiments emphasize the dependence of cambial growth on basipetally translocated growth hormones. Neither the roots nor stem tissues near the base of the stem can supply enough hormones to sustain normal cambial growth.

Initiation of Cambial Growth. It is well known that growth-promoting hormones from active buds move down the branches and stem to provide the stimulus for the initiation of seasonal cambial growth. Whereas the cambium in the part of a pruned branch above the uppermost bud remains inactive, xylem and phloem are produced below the same bud. Also, disbudding of shoots during the dormant season greatly impedes cambial growth in the same shoots. However, application of auxin to cut surfaces of disbudded stems induces cambial activity.

There is considerable evidence that both IAA and GA are needed for cambial division and that they act synergistically (Thimann, 1972). Cambial response to auxin often is not precisely correlated with the amount of auxin present. In Scotch pine, cambial activity was more responsive to auxin in the early spring than later, and it was more responsive in the upper than in the lower stem (Zajaczkowski, 1973). This might indicate (1) that inhibitors accumulated during the dormant period and had to be removed before auxin could exert an effect on cambial activity; or (2) that levels of other growth promoters, such as gibberellins and cytokinins, which act synergistically with auxin, were too low for the added auxin to exert its effect (Brown, 1970). Furthermore, applications of GA stimulated xylem production in shoots of apricot (Bradley and Crane, 1957) and *Eucalyptus camaldulensis* (Waisel *et al.,* 1966), suggesting the involvement of hormones other than auxin.

Differentiation of Cambial Derivatives. Several growth hormones are involved in controlling differentiation of cambial derivatives, with auxins and gibberellins particularly important. Auxin plays a dominant role in regulating cell expansion and the thickening of cell walls.

Digby and Wareing (1966) found that exogenously applied auxin increased vessel diameter in black locust. They applied IAA and GA in various proportions to disbudded shoots of poplar. When GA_3 alone was applied, some xylem subsequently formed but no differentiated xylem was produced in the absence of IAA. Fully differentiated xylem occurred at low GA_3 and high IAA concentrations. By comparison, phloem production was promoted by high GA_3 and low IAA concentrations. No new phloem was produced with IAA alone, but a considerable amount formed with GA_3 alone. IAA also promoted elongation of fibers and vessels. GA_3 influenced elongation of fibers, but only in the presence of IAA (Fig. 16.12).

Hejnowicz and Tomaszewski (1969) applied various growth regulators, singly and in combinations, to disbudded Scotch pine shoots. Whereas IAA or NAA initiated cambial growth, GA or cytokinins did not. However, auxin alone did not substitute wholly for the cambial growth stimulus provided by the growing apex. Normal wood was produced only by combined applications of IAA (or NAA) plus GA and cytokinins. Both GA and cytokinins increased the rate of basipetal transport of auxins.

There is also evidence of the involvement of inhibitors in control of cambial growth. For example, high concentrations of inhibitors extracted from European larch tissues

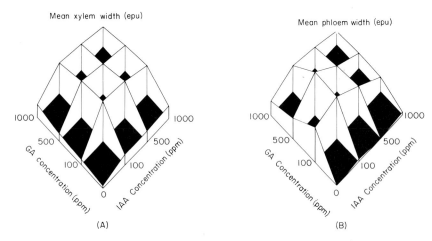

Fig. 16.12. Synergistic effects of gibberellin (GA) and indoleacetic acid (IAA) on development of xylem (A) and phloem (B) in *Populus*. The growth regulator concentrations shown were those in lanolin and do not indicate concentration in the tissues. Xylem width and phloem width are given in eye-piece units (epu). From Wareing *et al.* (1964).

reduced the effect of auxin on xylem differentiation of larch. A slight synergistic action was demonstrated between IAA and inhibitors at low concentrations of both substances (Wodzicki, 1965). Cronshaw and Morey (1965) also demonstrated that exogenously applied growth inhibitors modified the auxin stimulation of cambial activity and xylem differentiation.

Substances other than growth hormones apparently also influence vascular differentiation. For example, a high sucrose to auxin ratio leads to phloem differentiation, whereas other combinations of these stimulate xylem differentiation (Wetmore and Rier, 1963). Robards *et al.* (1969) applied IAA, NAA, 2,4-D, GA, FAP (6-furfurylaminopurine), myoinositol, and sucrose singly and in mixtures to the apical ends of disbudded willow stems. Each of these substances had some effect on xylem differentiation. Production and differentiation of xylem cells were increased most when IAA, GA, and FAP were applied together, but the response was greater when the mixture was augmented by inositol or sucrose. Wodzicki and Zajaczkowski (1974) applied auxins, together with various vitamins and substances known to regulate cell metabolism, to decapitated stems of young Scotch pine trees. Several substances, particularly inositol, vitamin A, and pyridoxine, acted synergistically with auxin in regulating the differentiation of cambial derivatives.

Earlywood–Latewood Relations. In gymnosperms earlywood tracheids form when internal control mechanisms favor radial expansion over secondary wall thickening. In red pine, radial expansion of tracheids usually occurs along the entire stem during the period of shoot growth as long as the needles are elongating. Later in the season, reduction in tracheid diameter resulting in latewood production begins at the base of the stem and subsequently occurs upward in the stem and outward in the growth ring (Fig. 16.13).

Larson (1962a,b, 1963c, 1964) emphasized the importance of hormones produced in the crown in earlywood–latewood relations. In red pine trees, large-diameter earlywood tracheids formed during the period of shoot elongation and high auxin synthesis, while narrow diameter latewood cells formed after shoot elongation stopped and auxin synthesis was reduced.

When Larson (1962a) subjected red pine trees to short days, growth of needles was first reduced and later stopped, and this change was followed by a decrease in tracheid diameter. In trees exposed to long days, the needles continued to elongate and large-diameter earlywood cells were produced. Eventually, however, both needle growth and the production of large-diameter cells stopped.

The variation in distribution of auxin across the cambial zone may influence the formation of latewood. As may be seen in Fig. 16.14, the concentration of ^{14}C-labeled IAA was very high in the cambial zone during the growing season and it declined greatly toward the maturing xylem of shortleaf pine stems. This distribution of auxin varied seasonally in relation to the transition of latewood formation (Nix and Wodzicki, 1974).

Several investigators have questioned the importance of auxin alone in regulating earlywood–latewood relations. In *Larix polonica,* thick-walled tracheids formed during active shoot growth under long-day conditions (Zelawski, 1957). Wodzicki (1965) concluded that changes in inhibitor content, rather than in auxins, were the primary factors controlling cell wall thickening in the tracheids of European larch. However, he also recognized an influence of growth promoters. Wodzicki did not find auxinlike

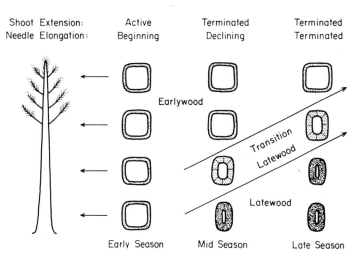

Fig. 16.13. Seasonal variation in formation of earlywood, transition latewood, and latewood at different stem heights in red pine. From Larson (1969b).

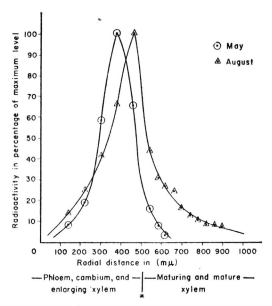

Fig. 16.14. Distribution across the cambial zone of radioactivity derived from applied ^{14}C-IAA in tissues of decapitated shortleaf pine stems. From Nix and Wodzicki (1974).

substances in larch as much as 60 days before latewood began to form. At the end of the season inhibitors were present in cortical tissues. These presumably were similar to those that accumulated under short-day conditions. The increase in inhibitors in cortical tissues was preceded by their accumulation in fully grown needles and shoot apices. Decapitation of shoots under short-day conditions caused growth inhibitors to accumulate. Wodzicki suggested that the inhibitors formed in the fully expanded needles in late summer and were translocated to growth apices and cortical tissues. The accumulation of inhibitors in cortical tissues in late summer was followed by formation of thick-walled tracheids. Wodzicki's data emphasized the importance of interactions between growth promoters and inhibitors, with high concentrations of inhibitors reducing the growth-promoting effects of auxins. The importance of inhibitors in earlywood–latewood relations was also emphasized by Jenkins (1974) who applied both ABA and IAA to stems of Monterey pine seedlings. IAA did not change cell diameters but it did increase cell wall deposition, whereas ABA reduced cell radial diameter as well as cell production. In addition, as mentioned earlier in this chapter in the section on Water Deficits, water stress also favors the formation of latewood.

Reaction Wood. A consequence of leaning of trees is a redistribution of the amount and nature of cambial growth on the upper and lower sides of the stem and of formation of abnormal ''reaction'' wood. Induction of reaction wood formation requires very little deflection of stems, about 2°, from the vertical (Timell, 1973). Reaction wood, which is called ''compression wood'' in gymnosperms because it occurs on the lower side and ''tension wood'' in angiosperms, where it occurs on the upper side of leaning stems, has several commercially undesirable characteristics such as a tendency toward shrinking, warping, weakness, and brittleness which affect its utilization.

In gymnosperms the compression wood forms preferentially on the lower side of inclined stems and branches, but it may sometimes form in various amounts on opposite sides of stems (Figs. 16.15 and 16.16). Formation of compression wood usually involves increased xylem production on the lower side of leaning stems and growth inhibition on the upper side. Compression wood functions in the righting of inclined stems and branches, apparently by expanding during and after cell differentiation. As soon as vertical orientation is attained, compression wood stops forming (Westing, 1965, 1968; Scurfield, 1973).

The structure of compression wood differs greatly from that of normal wood, having tracheids that are more nearly rounded in cross section and large intercellular spaces (Fig. 16.17). Compression wood tracheids are very thick walled, so no ready distinction can be made between earlywood and latewood. The inner layer (S_3) of the secondary wall of compression wood tracheids usually does not form or it develops poorly. The inner layer (the middle S_2 layer in normal wood) of compression wood is very thick. Because of more anticlinal divisions in compression wood, the tracheids generally are much shorter than in normal wood. The anatomy of ray cells is essentially the same in normal and compression wood. Sometimes a higher frequency and larger size of ray cells are noted in compression wood, reflecting a higher overall rate of growth. Timell (1973) did not find significant ultrastructual differences between tracheids of normal

Fig. 16.15. Eccentric cambial growth and compression wood in ponderosa pine. Photo courtesy of U.S. Forest Service, Forest Products Laboratory.

Fig. 16.16. Compression wood forming in bands around an entire spruce stem. Photo courtesy of U.S. Forest Service, Forest Products Laboratory.

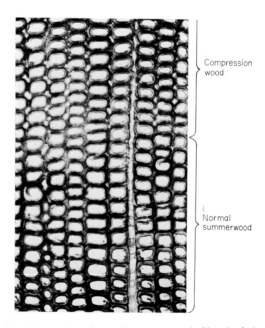

Fig. 16.17. Compression wood and normal summerwood of longleaf pine. Photo courtesy of U.S. Forest Service, Forest Products Laboratory.

wood and compression wood. Tracheids in compression wood have more cellulose and lignin than those in normal wood. Also, the cellulose of compression wood is less crystalline than that of normal wood.

The type of reaction wood called tension wood forms characteristically on the upper side of leaning angiosperm trees. Often, but not always, formation of tension wood is associated with eccentric cambial growth. Some leaning trees of paulownia and catalpa do not show cambial growth eccentricity (Hughes, 1965). When both increased xylem production and tension wood occur, their locations usually coincide, but sometimes they occur on opposite sides of branches or leaning stems. In S-shaped or recurved stems the eccentric growth may occur on different sides at various heights. In deciduous angiosperms, tension wood is most developed in earlywood and does not extend through all the latewood. In some evergreen angiosperms, such as *Eucalyptus* spp., however, tension wood often extends throughout both the earlywood and latewood (Wardrop and Dadswell, 1955). A characteristic feature of tension wood is the preponderance of gelatinous fibers, which can be identified microscopically by the gelatinous appearance of their secondary walls (Fig. 16.18).

Tension wood is not as easily identifiable (except microscopically) as compression wood. It has fewer and smaller vessels than normal wood and proportionally more thick-walled fibers. Ray and axial parenchyma cells are unchanged. Vessels of tension wood usually are well lignified, but sometimes they show reduced lignification. Re-

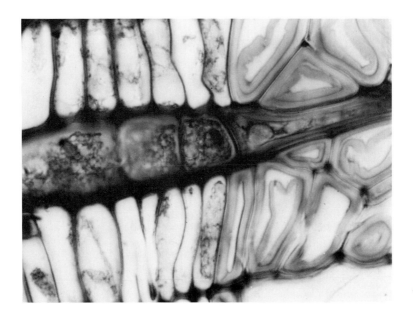

Fig. 16.18. Transverse section of the cambium showing subjacent gelatinous fibers of cottonwood. From Berlyn (1961).

duced lignification of the G layer (see below) is a common feature, and Dadswell and Wardrop (1956) stated that the sparse lignification is a more important feature of tension wood than are the associated anatomical changes.

The cell wall layer designated as S_2 or S_3 in normal wood is replaced in tension wood by an unlignified, often convoluted layer, designated as the G layer. When the S_2 layer is thus replaced, the new designation is $S_2(G)$. Sometimes the G layer is produced in addition to the S_1, S_2, and S_3 layers of normal xylem (Fig. 16.19). As the G layer consists almost wholly of cellulose, it has a highly ordered parallel molecular orientation. Both the thickness and form of the G layer vary conspicuously among species as well as among trees within a species. In some genera, such as *Acacia,* the G layer is convoluted, and in *Eucalyptus gigantea* it may almost fill the cell lumen (Wardrop, 1961).

Formation of reaction wood is a geotropic phenomenon that involves the internal redistribution of hormonal growth regulators. For example, compression wood forms toward the focus of gravitational attraction under conditions of a reversed gravitational field. If trees are grown upside down, compression wood forms on the morphologically upper sides of branches, which physically are the lower sides (Wershing and Bailey, 1942). When trees are grown on a revolving table the reaction wood forms on the outer side of the stem.

Much evidence shows that compression wood forms on the lower side of leaning gymnosperm stems because of a high auxin gradient, that causes mobilization of food. Onaka (1940) induced compression wood to form in a variety of gymnosperms with bud applications as well as with stem injections of IAA. Such experiments have been repeated for many species. Compression wood that was induced by applied IAA could not be separated physically from naturally occurring compression wood (Larson, 1969b).

The formation of tension wood is most probably a developmental response to auxin deficiency. This is shown by low auxin levels in the upper sides of tilted or bent stems (Leach and Wareing, 1967), inhibition of tension wood formation by applying auxins

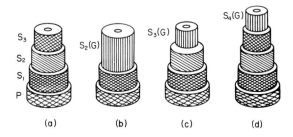

Fig. 16.19. Organization of cell walls in normal wood fibers and tension wood fibers. (a) Normal wood fiber of structure $P + S_1 + S_2 + S_3$; (b) tension wood fiber of structure $P + S_1 + S_2 (G)$; (c) tension wood fiber of structure $P + S_1 + S_2 + S_3 (G)$; (d) tension wood fiber of structure $P + S_1 + S_2 + S_3 + S_4 (G)$. P, primary wall; S_1, outer layer of secondary wall; S_2, middle layer of secondary wall; S_3, inner layer of secondary wall; S_4, gelatinous layer. From Wardrop (1964).

to the upper side of tilted stems (Morey, 1973), or induction of tension wood formation with applied auxin antagonists such as TIBA (2,3,5,-triiodobenzoic acid) or DNP (2,4-dinitrophenol) (Morey, 1973).

There is some evidence that auxin may stimulate cambial growth during the formation of reaction wood by increasing ethylene production. Imposition of stress on branches of eastern white pine and peach by tying them in knots increased ethylene levels (Leopold *et al.*, 1972). When a paste of ethephon in lanolin was applied to eastern white pine branches, ethylene production was increased and cambial growth was stimulated (Brown and Leopold, 1973). As mentioned earlier, the lower sides of horizontal branches contain more auxin than the upper sides. Hence, some auxin effects may be mediated through ethylene regulation because increases in auxin generally enhance ethylene production (Abeles, 1973).

The fact that gelatinous fibers sometimes are produced on the side opposite that of maximum xylem production indicates that there may be more than a single pathway to the gravitational stimulus. Robards (1965) suggested that a growth hormone could be the starting point of two separate pathways, one leading to the development of gelatinous fibers and the other to variations in cell division.

Root Growth

Both the primary and the secondary growth of roots depend to a large degree on a continuous supply of hormonal growth regulators. Defoliation, stem girdling, and insect or fungus injury to leaves decrease the downward flow of growth-promoting hormones and inhibit root growth, even when carbohydrates are plentiful (Fig. 16.20).

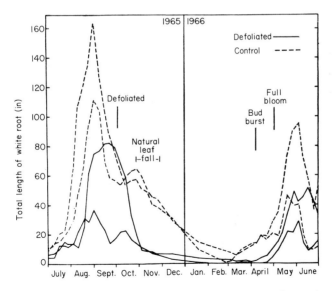

Fig. 16.20. Effects of defoliation on root development of Worcester Pearmain apple trees from July, 1965, to June, 1966. From Head (1969).

For example, Wilson and Bachelard (1975) showed that following defoliation or de-topping of *Eucalyptus regnans* seedlings, root elongation stopped within 2 to 4 days. Only a few leaves plus a continuous phloem connection between the roots and shoots were required for survival. Cambial growth of roots appears to be initiated and sustained by auxin moving down from the stem if cytokinins and gibberellins are present (Wilson, 1975).

Rooting of Cuttings

In addition to the factors controlling the formation of adventitious roots that were mentioned in Chapter 4, basipetally translocated hormones play a very prominent role in regulating the rooting of cuttings. The initiation of roots by cuttings can be blocked by the removal of leaves or buds. Conversely, initiation of roots is stimulated by chilling cuttings, but only if buds are not previously removed, indicating the necessity of a phloem-translocated hormone.

Voluminous evidence points to the importance of natural or artificially applied auxins in rooting. Formation of root initials apparently requires an auxin synergist as well as auxin. When both are present, RNA synthesis, which is involved in the formation of root primordia, is induced (Haissig, 1971).

The young leaves in terminal buds of growing shoots or expanding buds in spring contain abundant auxin. When a cutting is severed from a tree, the predominantly downward moving auxin accumulates at the base of the cutting. When an appropriate threshold level is reached, root initiation is triggered. The stimulating effect of the endogenous auxin can be enhanced by applying additional auxins such as IAA, IBA, or NAA to the stem base. By comparison, gibberellins and cytokinins applied to the bases of cuttings often suppress rooting. However, the effects of specific exogenous growth regulators vary greatly with histological events in root initiation. For example, IBA is required for both the preinitiative and postinitiative phases in root development of Monterey pine cuttings. Kinetin has a strong inhibitory effect during the preinitiative phase, but not after meristemoids are established. Whereas GA_3 is inhibitory during the preinitiative phase, it greatly stimulates rooting if applied at the first observable stage of root initiation. If GA_3 is applied after the establishment of meristemoids, it inhibits root formation (Smith and Thorpe, 1975). Application of root-inducing hormones is a common practice among plant propagators. For techniques the reader is referred to books by Weaver (1972) and Hartman and Kester (1975).

As the season progresses there is a pronounced decline in rooting response that cannot be overcome by applying synthetic auxins. This suggests that the control of rooting of cuttings involves other endogenous substances in addition to auxins. It appears that a balance of substances is involved and includes, in addition to auxins, carbohydrates, nitrogenous substances, and cofactors capable of acting synergistically with auxin. In a given system any one of these internal requirements may play a controlling role in root initiation.

The evidence for the essentiality of carbohydrates for rooting comes from several sources. Hess and Snyder (1956) found that rooting capacity is positively correlated with carbohydrate availability. Wounding the bases of cuttings by splitting and pro-

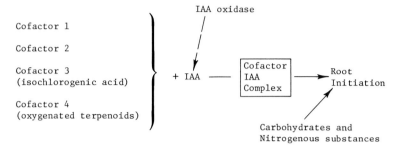

Fig. 16.21. Internal factors controlling initiation of adventitious roots. From Hess (1969).

longed soaking in a sucrose solution often improves rooting responses. However, cuttings with high carbohydrate reserves sometimes root poorly because of deficiencies of other internal requirements. Nanda *et al.* (1971) found that *Hibiscus rosa-sinensis* cuttings rooted best in June, when starch reserves in cuttings were lower than in other months.

High rooting capacity is associated with high levels of cofactors that act synergistically with auxin. Plants that are easy to root have higher levels of cofactors than those difficult to root. Girouard (1969) extracted four rooting cofactors from juvenile and mature English ivy cuttings. Domanski *et al.* (1969) demonstrated marked influences of temperature, exogenous hormones, and temperature–hormone interactions on root itiation in basket willow cuttings. Root formation was stimulated by NAA and its effects were enhanced by increasing the temperature from 22° to 25°C. In contrast to NAA, both GA and cytokinins inhibited root initiation. These experiments suggested regulation of rooting by the interactions of hormones and possible cofactors. As the temperature increased toward an optimum for root intiation, the balances of endogenous growth regulators and cofactors may have changed to bring out the stimulating effects of auxins over the inhibitory effects of gibberellins and cytokinins.

Hess (1969) presented an attractive model for internal control of the formation of adventitious roots (Fig. 16.21), which postulates that cuttings that are easy to root have all four rooting cofactors and enough IAA for cell division. Adventitious roots will form in such cuttings in the presence of adequate carbohydrates and nitrogenous substances. Variations in rooting capacity may be traceable to differences in the balances of auxins, nutritive substances, and cofactors. In addition to the downward translocated requirements for rooting, there also appear to be nonmobile or fixed cell components in the complex system controlling root initiation.

INTERNAL CONTROL OF REPRODUCTIVE GROWTH

The development of reproductive structures of both angiosperms and gymnosperms was discussed in Chapter 4. The internal requirements for growth of reproductive tissues are similar to those for vegetative growth and include carbohydrates, water, hormones, and minerals. The role of carbohydrates in reproductive growth was discussed in Chapters 5, 7, and 11; the role of minerals in Chapter 10. The use of mineral fertilizers in stimulating reproductive growth will be discussed in Chapter 17. The following sections will emphasize the importance of water and hormonal growth regulators in the control of reproductive growth.

Water Balance

It is more difficult to generalize about the effects of plant water deficits on reproductive growth than on vegetative growth. One reason for this is that the timing of the reproductive growth cycle varies greatly among species, with the time required to initiate and mature fruits varying from a few months to several years. In a mixed forest, for example, a drought may affect one species when it is initiating flowers, another species in full bloom, and yet another when it is maturing fruits. Furthermore, several stages of reproductive growth often occur on a plant at the same time. Another problem is that a given amount of water stress may inhibit one phase of reproductive growth and benefit another. For example, a heavy rain during the flowering period affects reproductive growth adversely by limiting pollen dispersal, whereas the same amount of rain later in the season will increase fruit enlargement. The effect of water balance on reproductive growth is also influenced by the plant's capacity for alternate bearing and by various other internal growth requirements, such as mineral supply and hormone balance.

Severe internal water deficits may inhibit each of the phases of reproductive growth. For example, floral initiation is suppressed by severe water deficits. In many angiosperms, the effect of water deficit on floral initiation may not be obvious until the subsequent year when flower buds open. In some pines the life of a seed cone extends over three growing seasons (see Chapter 4). Hence, the lag response of lessened cone production due to water deficits occurring at the time of cone initiation may be very long (Eis, 1976). Additional water deficits that occur after cone initiation further decrease cone production. Rehfeldt *et al.* (1971) reported that water deficits during late summer in the year preceding emergence of western white pine cones were detrimental to cone development.

As shown in Table 16.4, water deficits after floral initiation decreased fruit set in apple. In addition, trees undergoing drought retained fewer fruits than those with low water deficits (Powell, 1974). Short periods of water deficit at different stages of floral development of the olive inhibited fruit set almost as much as droughts during the entire period. In fact, severe water deficits in olive trees at any stage between the appearance of floral primordia and full bloom decreased the number of inflorescences (Hartmann and Panetsos, 1961).

Both the size and quality of fruits are affected by water deficits before and during the period of fruit enlargement. Crop yield following irrigation usually results chiefly from an increase in the number of fruits, but fruit size is also increased, as has been shown for cherries, grapes, peaches, pecans, and apples (Uriu and Magness, 1967; Goode and Ingram, 1971). Increase in the size of coffee beans depends greatly on water supply at

TABLE 16.5 Effect of Aging on Dry Weight Production and Photosynthetic
Efficiency of Even-Aged Stands of Beech and Scotch Pine[a]

Species and age (years)	Current annual dry weight production		Photosynthetic efficiency (%)
	(g/acre)	(cal/acre)	
Beech			
8	3.0×10^6	12.1×10^6	1.4
25	5.4×10^6	21.8×10^6	2.5
46	5.4×10^6	21.8×10^6	2.5
85	4.6×10^6	18.5×10^6	2.1
Scotch pine			
12	4.0×10^6	16.0×10^6	1.0
22	8.1×10^6	32.4×10^6	2.0
28	8.8×10^6	35.2×10^6	2.2
33	8.1×10^6	32.4×10^6	2.0
41	6.1×10^6	24.4×10^6	1.5
50	4.0×10^6	16.0×10^6	1.0

[a] From Hellmers and Bonner (1960). Data are based on yield data of Möller *et al.* (1954a,b) and Ovington (1957).

10 to 17 weeks after blooming, when the fruits have the capacity for rapid expansion. Water supply before and after this period has little effect on final bean size (Cannell, 1975).

Water deficits also affect fruit quality. Severe drought for several weeks before harvest produces peaches of tough, leathery texture. Extended drought not only reduces the size of grapes but also results in a darker wine (Veihmeyer and Hendrickson, 1952). Irrigated pear trees produce fruits with a smoother texture, higher sugar content, and lower acid content that unirrigated trees (Ryall and Aldrich, 1944), but the color of apples and keeping qualities of apples and pears usually are improved by moderate water stress (Richards and Wadleigh, 1952).

Beneficial Effects of Water Deficits

Sometimes a short period of water stress at a critical time in the reproductive cycle increases the initiation of flower buds. For example, drought conditions preceding and during the floral initiation period inhibited vegetative growth but stimulated flower bud formation in *Litchi chinensis* (Nakata and Suehisa, 1969). A period of water stress just before flower initiation is said to increase the flower crop of loblolly pine (Dewers and Moehring, 1970). Short periods of water stress may also break the dormancy of coffee flower buds. For example, when coffee trees were irrigated weekly the flower buds failed to open (Alvim, 1960). However, when the soil was allowed to dry to near the wilting percentage and then irrigated, flower buds opened readily. Alvim (1960) suggested that the water stress requirement for breaking dormancy in coffee buds did what was accomplished by chilling in other species. Other beneficial effects of water stress were mentioned in Chapter 13.

Hormonal Growth Regulators

Reproductive growth of woody plants is regulated by a series of hormonal signals that control differentiation, growth, and maturation of flowers, fruits, and seeds (Fig. 16.22). The complexity of control of the sequential processes involved may be illustrated by the growth of an ovary into a fruit. First, the ovary receives a hormonal signal to grow as the flower develops until bloom. Then a signal causes the slowing or stopping of growth until pollination occurs. At that time a hormonal signal stimulates another surge of growth that continues until the time of embryo growth (e.g., in stone fruits), at which time growth may again slow down or cease. Following embryo enlargement, fruit growth is again stimulated until maturity when yet another signal terminates growth (Leopold, 1962). This generalized model is reinforced by studies of specific growth hormones during reproduction. For example, auxin, which stimulates growth of the flower and floral stalk, may come from the ovary of the flower, the base of the inflorescence, and the flower stalk itself. Pollination of the ovary brings additional auxin to the reproductive structure. Pollen contains auxin, and growth of the pollen tubes promotes synthesis of even more auxin. Fruit growth may also require auxin that is synthesized in the seed region of the fruit. It should not be inferred, however, that auxin alone regulates reproductive growth, because voluminous evidence indicates that this growth is controlled by the complex interactive influences of several growth promoters and inhibitors.

Floral Initiation

The induction of floral primordia has long been thought to have a hormonal basis. Sachs suggested as early as 1887 that floral induction is caused by a chemical substance produced in the leaves. Chailakhyan enunciated the concept of a specific flowering hormone and called it "florigen" nearly 40 years ago (Chailakhyan, 1975), and extensive research has been conducted to isolate this hormone. Most attempts at isolating

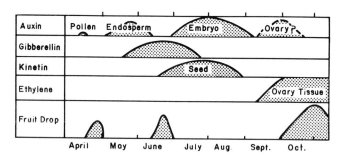

Fig. 16.22. Appearance and disappearance of various hormones during growth of a pomaceous fruit. From Thimann (1965).

florigen have involved direct extraction of leaves and apices by organic solvents. These generally have produced negative results or positive results that were subsequently questioned because of low reproducibility. Investigators have usually assumed that florigen is a single, organic, specific substance of low molecular weight. The inability to isolate and characterize florigen may indicate that it really is a complex of substances and that flowering is induced by several substances in proper balance. Although there is considerable evidence that flowering is induced by hormonal factors, their specific nature remains on enigma. Zeevart (1976) suggests that failure to identify a flowering hormone may result from lack of a reliable bioassay.

In some gymnosperms, the application of gibberellins induces precocious flowering. In species that normally require at least 10 years to begin flowering, exogenous gibberellins can induce flowering when plants are only a few months old. The treatments must be continued periodically for a long time, and if they are discontinued floral initiation ceases and the flowers already induced abort. For example, by applications of GA_3 Kato *et al.* (1958) induced flowering in both juvenile and adult *Cryptomeria japonica* trees. Subsequently, flowering was similarly induced in several other species of the Cupressaceae and Taxodiaceae. Because more GA_3 is required to induce flowering in juvenile than in adult plants, Pharis and Morf (1968) suggested that the juvenile stage was one in which endogenous GA had not yet reached the minimum concentrations required to cause flowering.

Except for Japanese larch, GA_3 did not induce flowering in species of the Pinaceae. Pharis and his colleagues postulated that flowering in Pinaceae may require a gibberellin other than GA_3, since the spectrum of GA-like substances found in conifers in which flowering was stimulated by cultural practices such as water stress and application of nitrate fertilizers (Pharis, 1976, 1977) showed both qualitative and quantitative changes with treatment. Thus, by treating plants with less oxidized (less polar) gibberellins, such as GA_4, GA_5, GA_7, and GA_9 they induced flowering in very young seedlings and nonflowering grafts of the Pinaceae, including Sitka spruce, white spruce, Norway spruce, Douglas-fir, lodgepole pine, and loblolly pine (see the review by Pharis and Kuo, 1977). The less oxidized gibberellins were most effective in combination with each other and with a low level of NAA (Fig. 16.23). Applications of GA_3 were generally ineffective (an exception being a modest promotion for loblolly pine, or where GA_3 was given in combination with a less polar GA).

Various growth-promoting hormones induce fruit set. In certain species fruit set is stimulated by auxin present in the pollen, and further growth depends on auxins and other hormones produced by the growing seeds. The effects of the pollen and seeds can be enhanced by exogenous hormones. For example, fruits of fig, grape, avocado, apple, apricot, and pear can be set by applying auxins. However, most species of woody plants do not set fruits following the application of auxin. For example, auxin causes fruit set in apricot but not in other stone fruits such as cherry, peach, and plum.

Fruits of some species of woody plants that can be set with auxin (citrus, fig, pear, apple) can be set as well or better with exogenous gibberellins. Fruit set of some species of *Rosa* responds to applied gibberellin, but *Rosa rugosa* also responds to auxin whereas *Rosa arvensis* does not. Maximum growth of the seedless fruits occurs

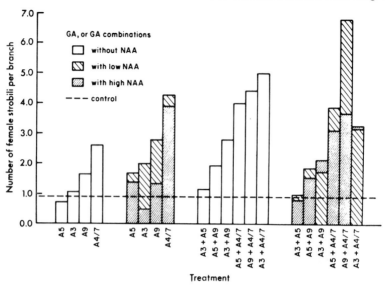

Fig. 16.23. Effects of different gibberellins and their combinations on stimulation of flowering in 6-year-old Douglas-fir seedlings. The gibberellins were applied at 2-week intervals in 80% ethanol (10 μl) at 200 μg each application over a 3-month period from April to June. Some treatments received NAA at 5 μg (low) or 25 μg (high) on each application date. From Pharis (1975).

when a mixture of both hormones is applied. In Bing cherry neither auxin nor gibberellin alone produces seedless fruits, whereas a mixture of the two is effective. Seedless apples of Cox's Orange Pippin cannot be produced by sprays of auxin or gibberellin alone, but they can be induced to form by a mixture of auxins, gibberellin, and cytokinin. It is unlikely that the fundamental physiology of various fruit types differs among species and cultivars. Fruit set probably requires adequate amounts of more than one hormone. It appears that the extent to which an applied hormone induces fruit set depends on variations among species and cultivars in deficiencies of specific hormones in unpollinated flowers. It should not be inferred, however, that the specific exogenous hormone that induces fruit set is the limiting one. An alternative explanation may be, for example, that applied gibberellin induces auxin production.

Fruit Enlargement

Increase in the size of fruits is highly correlated with supplies of hormones, particularly of auxins and gibberellins. The importance of auxin is supported by evidence of a high correlation between fruit size and seed development (seeds are rich sources of auxins) as well as the increase in fruit size in response to exogenous auxin. For example, application of auxins to apricot, blackberry, grape, and orange stimulates enlargement of fruits.

The presence of seeds is important in fruit growth because they produce a sequence of different hormones during their development in the fruit. As Crane and van Overbeek (1965) suggested, a major function of the fertilized ovule or seed in fruit growth is to synthesize hormones that initiate and maintain a metabolic gradient, along which foods and hormones are translocated from other parts of the plant.

The size and shape of some fruits, including grape, pear, apple, and blueberry, are highly correlated with seed number. Apples with few seeds often fail to achieve normal size and tend to abscise early. When seeds are unevenly distributed within a fruit it usually grows irregularly and becomes misshapen.

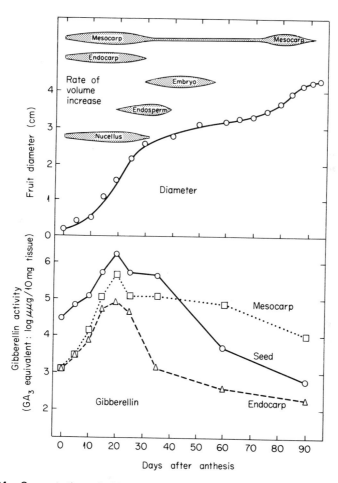

Fig. 16.24. Concentrations of gibberellinlike substances in methanol extracts of seed, endocarp, and mesocarp of apricots compared with their rate of growth during development. From Jackson and Coombe (1966). Copyright 1966 by the American Association for the Advancement of Science.

Fruit enlargement is not controlled by auxin alone. In apple, grape, and peach the variations in total seed auxins are not well correlated with growth curves of the fruits. This may be because in early studies the physiologically "bound" auxins were largely ignored and methods of both auxin extraction and auxin assay had limitations (Crane, 1964). The current view is that the role of auxins in fruit growth was overemphasized and that other hormonal substances, particularly gibberellins, are also importantly involved in fruit enlargement.

Extracts of young seeds of almond, apricot, and plum show gibberellinlike activity. Gibberellins in peach fruits regulate cell division and enlargement of the mesocarp (Crane, 1964). Gibberellin activity in the seed endocarp and mesocarp of apricot fruits was well correlated with growth rates in these tissues for the first 60 days after anthesis (Fig. 16.24). Gibberellin activity increased following anthesis and reached a maximum 20 days after anthesis. Most of the gibberellin activity was in the seed and least in the endocarp. Thereafter, the concentration of gibberellins declined in all three tissues, with the most rapid decrease occurring in the endocarp and the slowest in the mesocarp (Jackson and Coombe, 1966).

The importance of cytokinins in fruit growth is also well documented. Cytokinins, which are present in immature seeds and fruitlets, together with auxins, regulate cell division in fruits. The presence of cytokinins has been shown indirectly by stimulation of cell division in tissue explants following application of extracts of seeds and fruits of apple, plum, peach, pear, and quince. Natural cytokinins can be replaced by synthetic cytokinins. In this way tissues of various edible fruits have been subcultured successfully for many years. Very dramatic increases in the size of grapes have been obtained by dipping flower clusters into solutions of cytokinins (Weaver et al., 1966).

Fruit Ripening

All major categories of plant hormones are variously involved in regulating fruit ripening, with ethylene playing a dominant role. Whereas ethylene and ABA induce ripening, auxins, gibberellins, and cytokinins wholly or partly retard senescence and the ripening of fruits.

The volatile emanations of ethylene from some fruits trigger ripening in other fruits. For example, ethylene produced by orange fruits causes premature ripening of bananas. Ethylene in smoke produced by kerosene stoves has long been used in railroad cars and packing houses to induce ripening of orange fruits. In immature climacteric fruits, ethylene treatment shortens the time of occurrence of the climacteric and ripening without materially changing the pattern or magnitude of respiration. In nonclimacteric fruits, however, the rate of respiration increases as a function of ethylene concentration, at least up to 100 ppm (McGlasson, 1970).

Because ripening induced by ethylene treatment is similar biochemically to natural ripening, and because endogenous ethylene increases prior to natural ripening, it appears that ethylene is a natural ripening factor. Ethylene is produced in small amounts throughout the life of fruits. The rate of ethylene production varies widely among different fruits, but the endogenous level needed to induce ripening (0.1 to 1 ppm) is about the same in all fruits. Ethylene apparently induces ripening in all fruits as long as they are in a receptive state. As fruits grow their sensitivity to ethylene progressively increases. Hence the concentration of ethylene and the duration of exposure required to induce ripening decrease as fruit maturation progresses.

ABA induces ripening in both climacteric and nonclimacteric fruits. In citrus fruits an increase in ABA precedes other senescence phenomena. The importance of ABA in inducing ripening is shown by three lines of evidence: (1) endogenous ABA increases before or during fruit ripening, (2) treatments that accelerate senescence cause an increase in endogenous ABA, and (3) exogenous ABA accelerates fruit ripening (Sacher, 1973).

Studies with a variety of fruits, including bananas, pears, and grapes, show that auxin pretreatments delay ethylene-induced ripening. Endogenous auxin appears to be a ripening resistance factor that must be depleted to a critical level before ethylene can trigger the ripening process. However, under certain conditions applied auxins have been shown to actually enhance fruit ripening by increasing ethylene production.

Gibberellins delay ripening and block the ability of ethylene to act. For example, gibberellins retard the loss of chlorophyll, induce regreening, and delay rind softening of oranges. They also retard color changes in other fruits.

Cytokinins also act as senescence retardants in fruits. In mature green oranges the effect of benzyladenine in delaying color changes in oranges was associated with the maintenance of high levels of endogenous gibberellins and prevention of an increase in ABA (Sacher, 1973).

Storage of Harvested Fruits

Successful storage of harvested fruits is related to slowing down the rate of metabolism and senescence. Hence much research has been done on methods of controlling the environment to reduce respiration and undesirable biochemical changes so as to prolong the storage life and edibility of fruits. The beneficial effects of low temperature on fruit storage often can be supplemented by an atmosphere high in CO_2 and low in O_2. Such atmospheres are effective because low O_2 levels decrease ethylene production and fruit metabolism and CO_2 counteracts the action of ethylene. The life of fruits during shipping or storage can also be increased by removing ethylene by means of chemicals such as potassium permanganate or ozone. Another useful technique is to accelerate the escape of the ethylene produced by fruits by reducing the atmospheric pressure around them. For further details and references on the principles and techniques of fruit storage the reader is referred to the book by Abeles (1973) and the report edited by Dewey (1977).

INTERNAL CORRELATIONS

A number of correlative phenomena such as polarity, root–shoot balance, reciprocal relations between vegetative and reproductive growth, maturation and aging, and control of tree form influence the development of woody plants. These will be discussed separately.

Polarity

A basic feature of the growth of woody plants is their morphological and physiological polarity. As soon as a fertilized egg begins to divide and form an embryo, it begins to exhibit polarity. One end begins to develop differently from the other, and an embryo in a seed soon possesses apical and basal regions. Development of an embryo results in differentiation of the radicle, hypoctyl, epicotyl, and cotyledons, and finally in the roots, shoots, and other organs of mature plants.

Polarity is particularly important in the regeneration of woody plants. Cuttings form roots only at their basal ends and shoots only at their apical ends no matter how they are oriented while rooting. Polarity is also important in grafting. For example, when buds are grafted to a stem they must be properly oriented for a good union to occur. Polarity is also shown by the failure to form good graft unions between the two basal ends of different shoots. Another expression of polarity is the direction of growth. A number of morphologically polar responses of plants are associated with polar transport of hormones. Auxin, for example, shows a well-defined tendency to move downward in stems, and its distribution is an important factor in morphological polarity, as in the polarity of rooting of cuttings.

Root-Shoot Balance

The internal control of growth involves close interdependency between roots and shoots as sources of growth requirements. Roots depend on leaves for photosynthetic products and hormonal growth regulators such as auxins and gibberellins. Shoots, in turn, depend on roots for supplying water, minerals, and certain hormones such as cytokinins (Skene, 1975), and gibberellins. In addition, in many tree species, roots play an essential role in nitrogen metabolism. In apple trees, for example, nitrate reduction occurs primarily in the fine roots. Nitrogen compounds, mostly amides and ureides, formed in roots are translocated to shoots where they are used in protein synthesis. Because the shoots lack nitrate reductase, they cannot utilize nitrates. Similarly, shoot growth in peach trees depends on organic nitrogen compounds supplied by the roots (Luckwill, 1959).

The size of the root system relative to that of the shoot system is an important factor in its growth. A small root system inhibits the growth of aerial tissues by limiting the supply of water, minerals, and certain hormones to the crown, while reduction in the shoot system limits the growth of roots by curtailing their supply of carbohydrates and apically produced hormonal growth regulators. In a given species the root–shoot ratio decreases progressively with plant age and size. Nevertheless, plants of various species have characteristic root–shoot ratios, indicating a rather constant ratio between annual increments of roots and stems.

Unfortunately, the most efficient root–shoot ratio often is disturbed by unfavorable environmental factors or cultural treatments. For example, shading, pruning, defoliation, flowering, and fruiting all reduce root growth either by reducing photosynthesis or by diverting hormones and carbohydrates to fruit and seed production. Heavy applications of nitrogen usually stimulate shoot growth more than root growth; hence, although the amount of roots may be increased, the ratio of roots to shoots is decreased. An excess of soil water and very compact soil also reduce root growth.

If the root–shoot ratio is drastically altered by injury to either the roots or the shoots, physiological changes occur that lead to compensatory growth and tend to slowly bring the root–shoot ratio back into its characteristic balance. For example, partial defoliation of European white birch trees led to compensatory growth in which the shoots grew at a much higher relative rate than the roots. This was the result of greatly stimulated photosynthesis of the remaining leaves and was associated with higher levels of carboxylating enzymes (Wareing *et al.*, 1968). Pruning of both newly planted and mature tea plants stimulated rapid shoot growth and caused roots to stop growing for several months (Fordham, 1972). Compensatory growth also occurs when the root–shoot ratio is drastically altered by injury to the root system. Severe root pruning is followed by the preferential translocation of large amounts of hormones and carbohydrates to the roots, leading to rapid root proliferation.

Reproductive and Vegetative Growth

Reproductive growth and vegetative growth usually are negatively correlated, although occasionally the relationship is positive. For example, when both reproductive and vegetative growth are stimulated by fertilizers the correlation between them often is high and positive (Proebsting, 1958). Rapidly growing reproductive tissues are strong sinks that monopolize the available nutrients and thereby inhibit shoot growth, cambial growth, and root growth. The inhibitory effect of heavy fruiting on vegetative growth often occurs both during the current year and during the subsequent year or years.

The relationship between reproductive and vegetative growth may be considered to be linear over a considerable range, but this may not be true when fruit or seed crops are abnormally high or low, as is shown in Fig. 16.25. The vegetative–reproductive growth relationship of peach trees is more likely to be represented by the curve A–A' rather than B–B'. In the range of very low fruit production the physiological efficiency

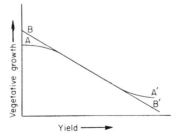

Fig. 16.25. Relations between vegetative growth and reproductive growth under extremes of cropping. For explanation see text. From Proebsting (1958).

of the tree appears to be lowered by some internal factor. Conversely, in the range of very high fruit production the physiological efficiency of the tree is increased.

There are many examples of the suppression of shoot growth and cambial growth by reproductive growth of woody plants. A few examples will be given below.

Balsam fir trees produced heavy seed crops and showed reduced shoot growth in alternate years (Morris, 1951). In another study, shoots of flowering balsam fir trees were only about one-half as long as those on nonflowering trees. Branches of flowering trees had almost twice as many buds per unit length of branches as nonflowering trees. Up to one-half of the vegetative buds on heavily flowering trees failed to develop and the shoots that grew had poorly developed needles (Blais, 1952). Powell (1977) suggested that a large crop of cones reduces the crop the succeeding year because the heavy use of carbohydrates by the developing cones inhibits lateral bud initiation and branch growth.

In 1967 yellow birch and white birch trees developed unusually large seed crops. Leaves were small or missing in heavily seeded parts of tree crowns. Buds failed to develop at tips of most branches. Shoot elongation and cambial growth were substantially reduced in 1967, and shoot growth was reduced in 1968. Both shoot elongation and bud production were inversely related to the amount of seed produced (Fig. 16.26).

Inhibition of vegetative growth by fruit growth has been dramatically demonstrated in biennially bearing fruit trees. Singh (1948), for example, showed that the physiological condition of the tree at the beginning of an "off" or nonbearing year was different from that of an "on" or bearing year. Leaf area per spur of off-year trees was nearly twice as great as that of on-year trees during the critical period of fruit bud formation. Maggs (1963) removed blossoms from apple trees at the time of flowering or removed fruits on May 30. After blossoms were removed, the dry weight increment and leaf size were greater than in fruiting trees (Fig. 16.27). Barlow (1966) showed that fruiting in apple trees decreased the number of long shoots and their proportion of all shoots on the tree. Severe competition between fruit and shoot meristems began only when the fruitlets began to develop actively.

During good seed years xylem increment was decreased in Douglas-fir, grand fir, and western white pine (Eis et al., 1965). In beech the width of annual rings in good seed years was only about one-half of that in years of low seed production. Heavy seed production reduced xylem increment for 2 years thereafter (Holmsgaard, 1962).

Maturation and Aging

During development, woody plants undergo various complex physiological changes as they progress from a juvenile to a mature condition and finally to a senescent state. This discussion will retain the distinction made by Wareing (1964) between maturation or phase change and the aging of woody plants. Maturation, which occurs during a restricted early period in the life of a woody plant, is considered to encompass the relatively abrupt and predictable changes characteristic of the transition from juvenility to maturity. Aging, which follows maturation, involves gradual reduction in growth

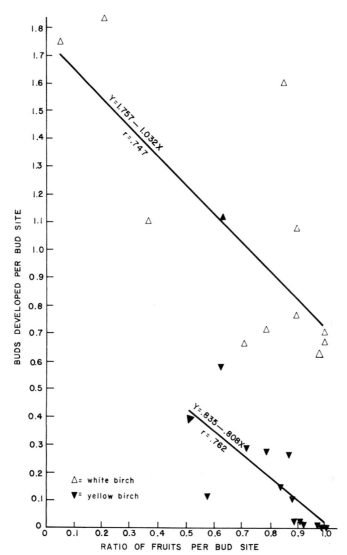

Fig. 16.26. Relation between production of buds and fruits in white birch and yellow birch. From Gross (1972).

and metabolism as woody plants increase in size and complexity. Hence, aging is characterized by orderly and progressive degradative changes.

Maturation and Phase Change

After seeds germinate, the young woody plants usually remain for several years in a juvenile condition during which they normally do not flower. While in the juvenile

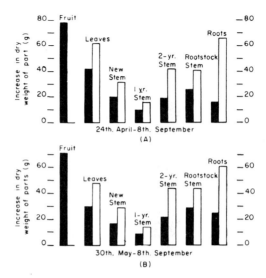

Fig. 16.27. Dry weight increment of parts of cropping apple trees (black bars) and noncropping trees (open bars). (A) From deblossoming on April 24 to September 12; (B) from defruiting on May 30 to September 12. From Maggs (1963).

stage, plants tend to exhibit an exponential increase in growth rate. The juvenile stage may also differ from the adult stage in leaf shape and structure (Fig. 16.28), phyllotaxy, ease of rooting of cuttings, leaf retention, stem anatomy, thorniness, and production of anthocyanin pigments.

A classic case of a plant that expresses a number of aspects of juvenility is the English ivy. The juvenile form is a vigorously growing, nonflowering, prostrate or climbing plant bearing lobed leaves and producing anthocyanins and aerial roots. The adult, fruiting phase is a slow-growing shrub with entire leaves that lack the capacity for anthocyanin production or aerial roots. In contrast to English ivy, some species express juvenility in only one or two characteristics.

Both juvenile and adult phases may occur on the same plant. For example, both needlelike juvenile and scalelike adult leaves may be found on the same branch of eastern redcedar (Fig. 16.29). The lower part of the tree may remain juvenile after the upper part has attained maturity as, for example, in mature black locust trees, where the basal branches are juvenile, bear thorns, and lack capacity to flower. In contrast, the thornless apical branches represent the adult phase, as is shown by their capacity to produce flowers and fruits (Trippi, 1963). The tendency of lower branches of beech and oak trees to retain their withered leaves during the winter is a juvenile characteristic.

Duration of juvenility varies greatly among species, some gymnosperms remaining in the juvenile stage for less than 1 year, while others retain juvenility for life. For example, the ornamental Retinosporas are actually juvenile forms of *Chamaecyparis*

Fig. 16.28. Variations in leaf form of juvenile, transitional, and adult leaves of English ivy. Photo courtesy of V. T. Stoutmeyer.

Fig. 16.29. Juvenile and adult leaves on eastern redcedar. (A) Needlelike juvenile leaves on proximal parts of the branch and scalelike, adult leaves on distal portions; (B) phase reversal in a single branch. Adult leaves on proximal parts are scalelike and appressed; leaves most recently produced are needlelike and represent a reversion to the juvenile condition. From Brink (1962).

and *Thuja,* but because their appearance differs so much from the adult form these plants were erroneously classified in the genus *Retinospora.*

The age of first flowering shows wide variability among different species and cultivars (see Chapter 4). Once the capacity for flowering is achieved, it is usually retained. However, an important distinction should be made between the capacity for flowering and the annual initiation of flower primordia. Many adult woody plants capable of flowering do not do so every year. Environmental and internal factors can control the initiation of flower primordia after the adult stage has been achieved.

Control of Phase Change. The possibility of effectively controlling phase change has enormous practical significance. Tree breeders find it desirable to accelerate phase change and to rapidly induce the adult condition so as to hasten the production of flower, fruit, and seed crops. At other times, it is more important to retain the juvenile condition for a long time, or to induce reversion of the adult to the juvenile condition, in order to retain desirable characteristics such as the capability of rooting cuttings.

Several investigators have shortened the juvenile stage of woody plants and induced flowering by controlling environmental conditions. Wareing and Robinson (1963) grew seedlings of several species of woody plants continuously under long days in a warm greenhouse. By so doing, they induced flowering in Japanese larch within 4 years, whereas normally this species remains juvenile for 10 to 15 years. For promotion of flowering they advocated that seedlings be grown to a critical minimum size as rapidly as possible and then subjected to additional treatments favorable to flowering that depended on the species. For example, long days were required for birch, short days for black currant, and horizontal training of branches for Japanese larch.

The juvenile phase sometimes can be shortened by use of appropriate rootstocks. The juvenile phase of apple seedlings was shortened by budding them on Malling IX rootstocks (Visser, 1964). Apple seedlings grafted on apomictic seedling rootstocks from *Malus sikkimensis* had a shorter juvenile phase than when worked on Malling IX rootstocks (Campbell, 1961). Precocious flowering can be induced in certain gymnosperms by the application of gibberellins.

Reversion of adult plants to juvenile forms has been accomplished by heavy pruning, grafting adult scions on juvenile stages, and treating adult material with gibberellins.

Doorenbos (1954) produced reversions of English ivy to the juvenile form by grafting the adult fruiting form on 2- and 3-year-old seedlings or on plants grown from cuttings. Reversion to juvenility of adult tissues grafted on juvenile forms was influenced by temperature and by the amount of mature tissues initially present in the graft combinations. Juvenility can also be enhanced by pruning, which not only forces out lower, more juvenile buds, but also enhances the degree of juvenility expressed in growth.

There is considerable evidence that physiologically active gibberellins play an important role in maintaining the juvenile state. Juvenile apices contain more gibberellins (particularly GA_3) than do mature apices (Frydman and Wareing, 1973). Furthermore, reversion of the adult to the juvenile condition can be accomplished by applications of gibberellins. Rogler and Hackett (1975a) developed a sensitive and reproducible method to obtain gibberellin-induced reversion of adult English ivy plants to the juvenile state. Other growth regulators, including IAA, kinetin, ABA, and Ethrel, were not effective. Several gibberellins, alone and in mixtures, stimulated reversion to juvenility, indicating that the response was specific for gibberellins as a class of hormones, but not specific for a particular form of gibberellin. Rogler and Hackett (1975b) also prevented gibberellin-induced reversion to the juvenile form by supplying ABA together with GA_3. Hence the adult form could be stabilized by regulating gibberellin levels either by inhibiting gibberellin action or the biosynthesis of gibberellin.

Aging

Some woody plants are by far the oldest living organisms, but there are wide variations in the life span of different species. Tundra shrubs frequently live from 30 to 50 years. Longevity of desert shrubs varies from 20 years, for *Calliandra eriophylla* and *Encelia farinosa,* to 60 years, for *Fouquieria splendens,* and 100 years, for *Larrea tridentata* (Harper and White, 1974).

The life span of trees varies greatly. For example, peach trees are old at 20 years, grey birch at 50 years, but some oaks continue to grow vigorously when 10 times that age. With very few exceptions, the life span of angiosperm trees as a group does not exceed 1,000 years and for most of them it is much less, but a number of gymnosperms live for several thousand years. However, if clonal reproduction occurs, great age may

Fig. 16.30. Very old, multiple-stemmed and branched bristlecone pine tree in California. Only one side of the tree is alive. Photo courtesy of U.S. Forest Service.

also be achieved in some angiosperms. For example, *Populus tremuloides* var. *aurea* may be 8,000 years old (Cottam, 1954).

The oldest living plants appear to be bristlecone pines in California (Fig. 16.30). Some of these are more than 5,000 years old. Redwoods achieve an age greater than 3,000 years. Other gymnosperms noted for their longevity include Douglas-fir, cedar of Lebanon, and Montezuma baldcypress.

Although various species of trees age at different rates, they show several common symptoms of aging. As a tree increases in size and builds up a complex branch system, it shows a decrease in metabolism, gradual reduction in growth of vegetative and reproductive tissues, loss of apical dominance, increase in dead branches, slow wound healing, heartwood formation, increased susceptibility to injury from certain insects and diseases and from unfavorable environmental conditions (see Chapter 17), and loss of geotropic responses. There also is a decrease in the proportion of photosynthetic to nonphotosynthetic tissue.

Shoot Growth.   In young trees the amount of annual shoot growth increases for a number of years but it attains a maximum rate relatively early in the life of the tree and gradually declines thereafter (Fig. 16.31).

The seasonal duration of shoot elongation often varies markedly with tree age. For example, Wareing (1956) reported that shoots of black locust seedlings grew into autumn in England, whereas those of mature trees stopped growing by the end of July. In the 2- and 3-year-old seedlings of loblolly pine studied by Kramer (1943) in North Carolina, shoot elongation began at about the same time but continued later than in the 13-year-old trees of Young and Kramer (1952). Shoot elongation of mature tung trees in the southern United States often is completed before July, but young orchard trees may continue shoot growth until August, and vigorous seedlings in the nursery until September or October. Hence, results vary among species, and the greater amounts of shoot growth of young relative to old trees appear to be traceable to differences in both the rate and the duration of growth. In many tropical species young trees exhibit far more continuous shoot growth than older ones (see Chapter 3).

Cambial Growth.   As trees age the rate of cambial growth follows a definite trend that varies with species and environment. As may be seen in Fig. 16.32, cambial growth accelerates annually for a number of years, attains a maximum, and then declines, at first rapidly and then more gradually (Mikola, 1950, 1951). Each successive xylem ring is narrower than the previous one, unless the pattern is altered materially by environmental influences. After maximum ring width is attained, the narrowing of annual rings as an aging phenomenon often amounts to less than 1% annually, but sometimes it is much greater. For example, on good forest soils in south Finland, xylem rings narrowed annually by 4 to 5% as trees aged (Mikola, 1950). The curve of basal area change with tree age differs from that of ring width, because each successive ring has a greater radius than the preceding one. As trees senesce they tend to have more discontinuous rings and often do not produce any xylem in the lower stem.

Root Growth.   Many investigators have reported variations in the root growth of trees during aging. In North Carolina, the number of roots up to 0.25 cm in diameter on loblolly pine and shortleaf pine trees increased rapidly until stands reached 20 years of

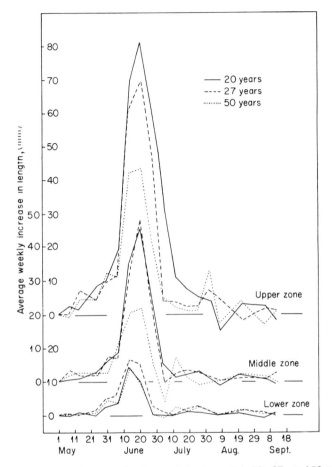

Fig. 16.31. Amounts and seasonal patterns of shoot growth in 20-, 27-, and 50-year-old red pine trees. Data are given for different locations on the tree. From Forward and Nolan (1964).

age, after which increase was slower. By the time the stands were 30 years old the amount of absorbing roots had reached a near-constant value (Scholtes, 1953). Thereafter, production of new roots was approximately balanced by loss of old roots.

Adventitious Rooting. The capacity of both intact trees and cuttings for producing adventitious roots is correlated with their age. After some critical tree age is reached, rooting capacity declines rapidly. For example, in intact spruce, birch, and poplar trees the maximum capacity for adventitious rooting was demonstrated by trees varying in age from 25 to 30 years (Kosceev, 1953). Norway spruce formed adventitious roots up to an age of 45 years, and inability of older trees to produce such roots probably accounted for their dieback on waterlogged soils (Kosceev, 1952).

Dry Weight Increment. The total dry matter increment of communities of trees and of individual trees, as well as distribution of the increment within trees, are altered

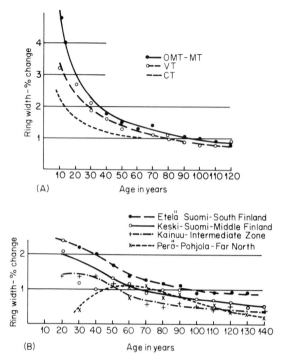

Fig. 16.32. Effect of aging on cambial growth of: (A) Scotch pine in three locations in south Finland; (B) Norway spruce in four locations in Finland. From Mikola (1950).

predictably as trees age. When a plantation is first established, annual dry weight increment per unit area of land is small. By the time the canopy is closed and the soil is thoroughly occupied by roots, a maximum level of productivity is attained. Thereafter, the annual increment decreases as a stand approaches maturity (Ovington, 1958). In European silver birch and Scotch pine, dry weight increase at first was logarithmic, but when the trees were sufficiently large to provide a complete leaf cover so the maximum amount of light was absorbed under prevailing conditions, the annual increase in dry weight reached a maximum value (Ovington and Pearsall, 1956). As may be seen in Table 16.5, dry weight production of 8-year-old stands of beech was low. It was higher and relatively constant in stands 25 to 46 years of age. Thereafter, a decline associated with aging ultimately occurred until 85-year-old trees produced dry matter at about 80% of the maximum value. In Scotch pine dry weight production of young stands increased with age to a maximum at about 20 years. At approximately age 30, a slow decline in the dry weight increment was evident. The decrease was accelerated after age 40, with 50-year-old trees producing only one-half as much dry matter as 33-year-old trees.

Although it sometimes is assumed that dry matter is lost from trees primarily through leaf abscission, appreciable losses from shedding of other tissues such as fruits also occur. In addition, significant losses in dry matter also result from the death of

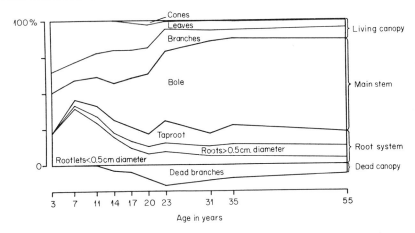

Fig. 16.33. Changes in distribution of dry weight of various plant parts as Scotch pine trees age. From Ovington (1957).

many fine roots each year, from the sloughing off of dead outer bark tissues, and from the loss of branches by abscission and natural pruning.

The relative proportions of crown, stem, and root system vary with age of trees (Fig. 16.33). In old trees more of the dry weight is in the main stem and proportionally less in the crown and root system. Whereas roots of young Scotch pine trees accounted for almost one-half the total weight of the plant, in old trees the proportion was much lower (Ovington, 1957). Ovington and Madgwick (1959) found striking changes in proportions of leaf, branch, and bole material of European silver birch trees as they became older. As the trees became larger the canopy and particularly the leaves formed a smaller percentage of total shoot weight. In mature trees the leaves represented only 1 or 2% of the total shoot weight, and the living branches accounted for about 18%. The weight of leaves, unlike that of boles or branches, did not continue to increase with age in older strands.

Anatomical Changes during Aging. After the adult stage is reached, external alterations of aging trees are accompanied by various internal structural changes in tree stems that influence wood quality (Dadswell, (1957). For example, the average length of xylem elements at any stem height in both angiosperms and gymnosperms increases from the pith outward for a number of years and then becomes more or less constant. Such changes in length of xylem elements parallel those in the size of cambial initials. The fibril angle is large in short cells and small in long cells. Hence, the increase in cell length from the pith outward is accompanied by a decrease in fibril (micellar) angle. Correlated with these changes is a decrease in longitudinal shrinkage and an increase in tangential shrinkage from the pith outward. Also, with increasing age the percentage of latewood increases for a number of years, and this change is accompanied by an increase in specific gravity and strength. In addition, with increasing age the durability of heartwood increases. In over-mature trees, however, the specific gravity of wood often declines and little or no latewood is produced. This was illustrated by Hale and

Clermont (1963), who compared wood formed by a Douglas-fir tree when it was 50 years old and when it was 300 years old. When 50 years old the tree was vigorous and producing about 30 rings of xylem per radial inch, with each annual xylem increment showing the normal progressive transition from large-diameter, earlywood cells to small diameter, latewood cells with thick walls. However, by the time the tree was 300 years old, the narrow xylem rings were composed primarily of thin-walled cells of very low specific gravity and little or no latewood. This over-mature wood had a higher lignin and lower α-cellulose content than wood formed when the tree was 50 years old.

Heartwood Formation.   The wood of young trees consists entirely of sapwood, with contains 5 to 40% living cells, mostly axial parenchyma and transversely oriented ray cells. Sapwood is physiologically important because it serves as the principal avenue for translocation of water and minerals; while the living cells carry on metabolic processes and store foods. In contrast, the dead heartwood is physiologically inactive (see Chapter 2).

The amount and rate of heartwood formation vary greatly with species, tree age, rate of growth, environment, and silvicultural practice. As may be seen in Table 16.6, crown class often influences the width of the sapwood band, with dominant trees having wider sapwood than lower crown classes (Wellwood, 1955). The age at which heartwood formation begins varies greatly among species. Eucalyptus heartwood usually begins to form at about 5 years. It forms at 15 to 20 years in several species of pine, at 60 to 70 years in European ash, and at 80 to 100 years in beech (Dadswell and Hillis, 1962). In a few species (e.g., *Alstonia scholaris*) heartwood may never form.

Cross sections of many trees show a distinct transition or intermediate zone, usually less than 1 cm wide, surrounding the heartwood. The transition zone usually is lighter in color than the heartwood and drier than either the heartwood or sapwood. In some species the transition zone is not readily recognized or does not exist. The outline of the heartwood core is irregular and often includes only part of some annual rings.

The most critical change during transformation of sapwood into heartwood is the death of ray and axial parenchyma cells. Other changes accompanying heartwood formation include a decrease in metabolic rates and in enzymatic activity, starch depletion, darkening of xylem associated with deposition of extractives, changes in wood density, anatomical changes such as increase in pit aspiration in gymnosperms

TABLE 16.6   Variations among Crown Classes in Width of Sapwood at Different Stem Heights of Douglas-Fir[a]

Crown class	Average diameter at breast height (cm)	Mean width of sapwood (cm)		
		Top	Middle	Base
Dominant	29.0	3.81	3.12	4.39
Codominant	20.3	2.51	2.18	2.69
Intermediate	18.3	1.85	1.75	2.16

[a] From Wellwood (1955).

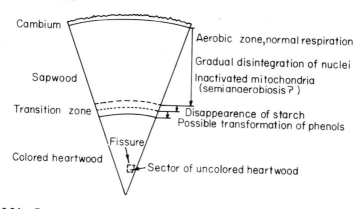

Fig. 16.34. Part of cross section of a tree stem showing cytological and physiological characteristics of different zones between the cambium and pith. From Frey-Wyssling and Bosshard (1959).

and formation of tyloses in angiosperms, and decrease in moisture content. Some of these changes will be discussed separately.

Some of the physiological changes in trees that lead to the formation of heartwood as postulated by Frey-Wyssling and Bosshard (1959) are shown in Fig. 16.34. A gradient of diminishing mitochondrial activity occurs along a ray from sapwood to heartwood and ceases short of the heartwood boundary. Some enzymes show increased activity in the intermediate zone between sapwood and heartwood, whereas others show progressively decreased activity from the outside of the stem inward. In pine and larch, peroxidase activity increased markedly in the stem area adjacent to the heartwood (Lairand, 1963). Similarly, the activity of enzymes that hydrolyzed sucrose and oxidized catechol was greatest in the intermediate zone and decreased progressively in the sapwood, heartwood, and controls of sterilized wood (Kondo, 1964). In contrast, phenylalanine deaminase, which might be associated with the biosynthesis of heartwood phenols, showed greatest activity in the cambial region of *Cryptomeria* and *Chamaecyparis,* but its activity decreased progressively inward until none was found in the heartwood (Higuchi and Fukazawa, 1966). The high activity in the cambial region was related primarily to production of a lignin precursor. However, in the sapwood and intermediate zone, where cells were completely differentiated and lignified, the phenylalanine deaminase was mostly responsible for the synthesis of heartwood phenols.

Deposition of Extractives. During heartwood formation, a wide variety of extractive substances, including tannins, assorted dyestuffs, oils, gums, resins, and salts of organic acids, accumulate in cell lumens and cell walls resulting in a dark-colored wood (Figs. 16.35 and 16.36). Some of these substances also occur in the sapwood, but usually in smaller amounts. Extractives in heartwood sometimes exceed 30% of the total weight and increase the color, density, and durability of the wood. Extractives are formed primarily in ray parenchyma cells but they may also form in axial parenchyma.

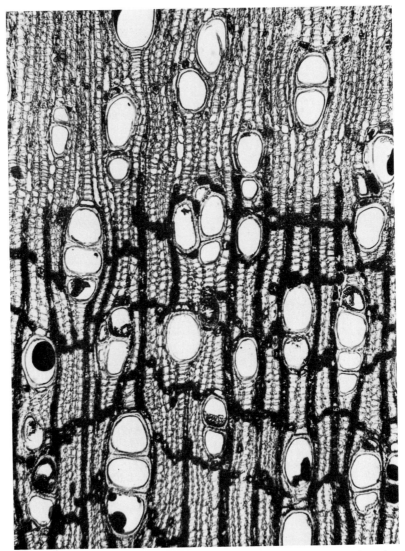

Fig. 16.35. Cross section of stem of *Excoecaria parvifolia* showing formation of poly-phenols at the sapwood–heartwood boundary. Photo courtesy of R. K. Bamber.

Among the most important of the heartwood extractives are the polyphenols. These are aromatic compounds with one or more phenolic hydroxyl groups. Usually, most phenolic substances obtained from tissues with living cells occur as glycosides or esters, while polyphenols obtained from heartwood are almost exclusively found as aglycones (organic compounds, usually a phenol or alcohol, combined with the sugar portion of a glycoside). The important chemical pathways leading to formation of

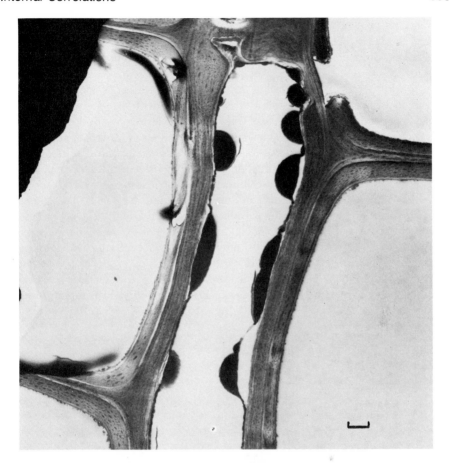

Fig. 16.36.   Cross section of ray cell in heartwood of eastern hemlock. Cell contents line the lumen on the ray cell and also occlude the half-bordered pit pair between the ray cell and longitudinal tracheid. From Krahmer and Coté (1963).

extractives are summarized by Hillis (1968). Factors influencing formation of phenolic compounds are discussed by Hillis *et al.* (1962).

In certain species, crystals of characteristic form are found in heartwood. Chattaway (1953) found yellowish-brown crystals in heartwood ray cells where a ray adjoined a vessel. Crystals also appeared in adjacent cells to form large patches in the wood. In every species examined the crystals were present in the proximity of the sapwood–heartwood boundary at various heights in the stem.

Pit Aspiration.   Pits apparently aspirate (see Chapter 2) where a tracheid wall is located between a tracheid containing water and another tracheid containing gas (see Fig. 2.16). In Monterey pine the percentage of pits aspirated increased rather gradually from a low value in the outermost annual ring to the border of the dry wood (transition) zone where approximately 50% of the pits were aspirated. There was an increase in aspirated pits within the dry wood zone to over 90%, and this increased slightly through the heartwood. Harris (1954) concluded that when more than 50% of the bordered pits of Monterey pine were aspirated, water transport through the system was blocked.

Formation of Tyloses.   Saclike structures called tyloses develop when turgor pressure causes part of the protoplast of parenchyma cells to balloon out through pit pairs into the lumens of adjoining cells (Fig. 16.37). Tyloses may also form as a result of growth of the pit membranes. Tyloses are common in xylem vessels of many genera of angiosperms, including *Populus, Rhus, Robinia, Morus, Sassafras, Catalpa, Juglans,* and *Quercus,* but they never occur in many other genera (Strelis and Green, 1962). Tyloses sometimes occur also in tracheids of gymnosperms.

Tyloses vary greatly in structure and may have a thin wall or a thick, lignified secondary wall. Sometimes, analogous structures called tylosoids develop because of growth of the walls of living cells into adjacent space. For example, tylosoids sometimes form in gymnosperms through the growth of epithelial cells that tend to fill resin canals.

Tyloses may be found in normal sapwood or in response to wounding, invasion by fungus pathogens, or virus infection (Beckman *et al.,* 1953). In many angiosperm

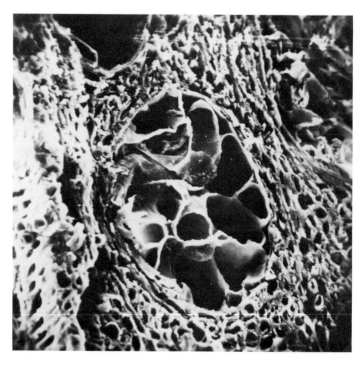

Fig. 16.37. Cross section of portion of white oak showing a large vessel occluded by tyloses. Photo courtesy of J. E. Kuntz.

genera the formation of tyloses is an important feature of the changeover of sapwood to heartwood. Hence, species that normally produce tyloses in the sapwood have more of them in the heartwood. A critical minimum size of the pit aperture between vessels and ray cells appears to be necessary for tyloses to form. When the pit aperture exceeded approximately 10 microns in diameter, a gumlike material was secreted into the vessels (Chattaway, 1949). During heartwood formation both tyloses and gums originate almost exclusively in the ray cells rather than in axial parenchyma cells. Hence, the ray cells play the predominant role in heartwood formation while axial parenchyma appears to be primarily a storage tissue.

Changes in Moisture Content. The water content, and therefore the weight of the sapwood, usually is considerably higher than that of heartwood in most species where the latter is well differentiated. The basic density of sapwood is lower, however, because heartwood is impregnated with various extractives, as was mentioned earlier. Some idea of the variations in moisture contents of sapwood and heartwood of gymnosperms is given in Table 16.7. There often is a rather steep moisture gradient even within the sapwood. The sharp decrease in moisture content along a radius may occur very abruptly, as over one or two annual rings.

Many deviations from the patterns cited above have been noted. It should be remembered that the moisture content of the sapwood of a species varies greatly with site and environmental conditions. It is not surprising, therefore, that many investigators recorded higher moisture contents in heartwood than in sapwood (e.g., in hickory, ash, elm, oak, gum, walnut, poplar, mulberry, and eucalyptus) (Hillis, 1965). In some species (e.g., *Fraxinus mandshurica* and *Ulmus davidiana*) the heartwood is wetter than the sapwood during all seasons of the year (Yazawa and Ishida, 1965).

Causes of Heartwood Formation. Although many of the changes occurring when sapwood turns into heartwood have been described, the triggering mechanism is not completely understood. It is generally accepted that the change of sapwood to heartwood is a DNA-coded effect of aging that can be modified by environment. A few

TABLE 16.7 Variations in Moisture Contents of Sapwood and Heartwood in Various Species

Species	Moisture content (percent dry weight)		Reference
	Sapwood	Heartwood	
Lodgepole pine	85–165	30–40	Reid (1961)
Ponderosa pine	124	110	Parker (1954)
Western redcedar	194	30	Parker (1954)
Douglas-fir	118	38	Parker (1954)
Monterey pine	92–111	38–44	Fielding (1952)
Northern white-cedar	236–262	31–38	Clark and Gibbs (1957)
White spruce	136–162	47–48	Clark and Gibbs (1957)
Red spruce	93–142	33–42	Clark and Gibbs (1957)
Balsam fir	138–186	57–75	Clark and Gibbs (1957)

of the theories of the triggering mechanism of heartwood formation that have been advanced over the years will be discussed briefly, and more details can be found in the reviews of Hillis (1968) and Shigo and Hillis (1973).

Many investigators have observed development of a central core of discoloration in tree stems of a variety of species following wounding by insects, squirrels, logging, increment borings, or dying of branches. Wound-induced discolorations result from cellular changes and may or may not be associated with organisms (see Chapter 3). Such discolorations, which may be superimposed on normal heartwood, have been variously classified as heartwood, "pathological heartwood," "false heartwood," "wound heartwood," "redheart," and "blackheart." Some investigators considered that because of similarity in color, wound-induced discolorations were an extension of normal heartwood into the sapwood. Despite the similarity in color, there appear to be some important differences between normal heartwood, formed from internal stimuli associated with aging, and the discoloration of sapwood induced by wounding.

As mentioned earlier, once normal heartwood formation is initiated it continues to increase in diameter throughout the life of the tree. In contrast, wound-initiated discoloration of wood of several species does not continue to increase in diameter but is limited to the diameter of the tree when it was wounded or the branch died (Fig. 16.38).

When branches die or wounds occur at approximately the same time, the discolored core that subsequently forms is contained within tissues bordered by the same growth ring. However, when dying of branches and wounding of stems occur at different times, the areas of discoloration caused by these wounds coalesce to form columns with rather uneven margins.

There also are important differences in the chemical composition of normal heartwood and discolored sapwood. Normal heartwood has a similar color throughout the stem cross section and a chemical composition that usually is constant in a given species. By comparison, in injured and discolored wood the amount of extractives is higher than in the sapwood, amounts of deposited substances that cause darkening substances are higher than in heartwood, and the extractable materials in these often differ qualitatively. Discolored woods of the same species, presumably resulting from the same cause, may have different ratios of components (Shigo and Hillis, 1973). J. H. Hart (1968) found that normal heartwood and discolored sapwood in the vicinity of wounds differed significantly in color, water content, frequency of amorphous deposits, percent of material soluble in water or 1% NaOH, ash content, and pH. These differences further emphasize that when living cells die as a result of injury of a type that results in discolored tissue, this tissue should not be considered an example of precocious development of normal heartwood.

Frey-Wyssling and Bosshard (1959) suggested that heartwood formation is related to semiaerobic respiration in inner parts of stems. Their theory is that starch hydrolysis occurs in the transition zone, and when starch disappears, the enzymes of sapwood parenchyma no longer control the ray cells (see Fig. 16.37).

J. H. Priestley (1932) postulated that heartwood formed because of accumulation of air in closed vessels, with consequent effects on permanent water content of the wood,

Fig. 16.38. Wood discoloration initiated at a branch stub of red oak advancing downward through the true heartwood. The very dark central column is discoloration initiated at the branch stub and is superimposed on the lighter, true heartwood. Tissues from the bark inward are sapwood, heartwood, discolored heartwood (these tissues were sapwood when the branch died), heartwood, and the central column of discolored heartwood. Photo courtesy of U.S. Forest Service.

which in turn caused changes in secretions from the living parenchyma cells. According to Erdtman (1955), the secondary constituents formed in the cambium are translocated along the vascular rays to the dead portions of the tree, heartwood, and bark, where they accumulate and sometimes exert a protective function. Stewart (1966) extended this proposal and considered these materials to be "excretory substances" formed during cell differentiation, respiration, synthesis, and degradation of starch. He believed that extractives are translocated in nontoxic concentrations along the rays toward the pith where they accumulate to lethal levels. As a result, the innermost parenchyma cells die and form the outer heartwood cylinder. The earlier-formed heartwood impedes further inward translocation, and the continued accumulation of toxic components at the sapwood heartwood boundary causes the death of cells and increases the width of the heartwood core. Bamber (1976) suggested that heartwood development is controlled by a centripetally translocated but unidentified "growth-active substance."

These proposals are challenged by an impressive body of evidence indicating that heartwood extractives are formed at the heartwood periphery or in the transition zone during the dormant season, from translocated or stored carbohydrates. As Hillis and Carle (1962) emphasized, if translocation of polyphenols occurred readily there should be marked biochemical relationships of the polyphenols of various tissues along the translocation path. However, sapwood polyphenols can be absent from the heartwood or the heartwood may have components that do not occur in the sapwood (Hillis, 1968; Hillis and Carle, 1962). Furthermore, the composition of polyphenols is different in heartwood, damaged sapwood, sapwood affected by the wood boring insect *Sirex,* and knotwood of Monterey pine, indicating that polyphenols are formed *in situ.* This view has also been supported by tracer studies showing that labeled sugar moves from the phloem through the sapwood to the sapwood–heartwood boundary (Hasegawa and Shiroya, 1967). Hillis *et al.* (1962) showed that the inner sapwood of *Angophora costata* trees had a starch content that was too low to account for the quantity of polyphenols present in the heartwood, indicating that a major part of the heartwood pholyphenols was formed at the sapwood–heartwood boundary from translocated carbohydrates that had not been utilized in growth. This conclusion is consistent with the observation that rapid growth and efficient utilization of available carbohydrates often are associated with a low amount of heartwood phenols (Hillis, 1968). Wardrop and Cronshaw (1962) also provided evidence of the origin of phenolic substances within cells. A relationship was found between the loss of reserve starch and processes leading to the formation of phenolic substances. Cells rich in phenolic substances had few or no starch grains.

Shigo and Hillis (1973) summarized persuasive evidence that ethylene has an important role in formation of the extractives that cause darkening of heartwood. Ethylene is produced by the transitional zone surrounding the heartwood of Monterey pine, and in greater amounts than in the sapwood. An increase in respiration of the transition zone, relative to that of the surrounding sapwood, is correlated with an increase in ethylene content. Ethylene stimulates both the activity and synthesis of a number of enzymes, including phenylalanine ammonia lyase, polyphenol oxidase, α-amylase, cellulase, and especially peroxidase. Both peroxidase, whose activity increases at the heartwood periphery, as well as phenol oxidases in the heartwood, can induce darkening of tissues after exposure to air.

In summary, the triggering mechanism of heartwood formation in many species has not been satisfactorily explained. More research is needed on this interesting problem.

Mechanisms of Aging.   The question of what causes aging in trees and controls the variations in longevity among species has intrigued plant physiologists for a long time. Many investigators have assigned a causal role to reproductive growth in influencing a senescent state. It is well known, for example, that removal of flowers and fruits from some kinds of annual plants delays senescence. A classic example of the effect of flowering on senescence is that of bamboo which flowers once and then promptly dies. Molisch (1938) suggested that developing fruits monopolized nutrients to such an extent that senescence of vegetative tissues inevitably resulted. Although it is clear that flowering and fruiting cause the movement of various compounds away from vegetative tissues, the relationship of such mobilization to the actual senescence-inducing mechanism is not fully understood.

The mechanisms of aging of woody plants are complex and undoubtedly involve changes in the availability of various metabolites to growing tissues. As trees age, changes in food, water, mineral, and hormone relations occur that may contribute variously to an increasingly unfavorable balance of anabolism to catabolism, leading to a deteriorative condition. Jacobs (1955) pointed out that during the life of a tree the proportion of stem to crown gradually increases with age and size, and the sheath of new xylem becomes progressively thinner. The gradually decreasing ratio of photosynthetic surface to nonphotosynthetic surface of aging trees results in a diminished ratio of food produced to that used in respiration. The leaf area of aging trees remains fairly constant, but its total photosynthetic output declines slightly while respiratory consumption of food increases appreciably (see Chapter 6).

There is much evidence of increasing difficulty in the translocation of food, water, minerals, and hormones as the distance from roots to shoots increases. In pruned apple trees the length of shoots was correlated with their distance from the base of the stem, and the decreasing growth of shoots in aging trees appeared to be a consequence of distance from roots rather than of age (Maggs, 1964a). In Scotch pine an important factor in aging is the competition for available nutrients among the increasingly larger number of buds as the branch system increases in size and complexity (Moorby and Wareing, 1963). The importance of competition among branches is borne out by the higher ratio of short shoots to long shoots in old than in young trees. The decline in vigor of aging trees can be readily reversed by grafting scions from aged shoots to young seedling stocks. Hence, the reduced growth of shoots of old trees is associated with unfavorable nutrient conditions in the branch systems rather than with aging of the meristems themselves.

Went (1942) emphasized that translocation of water to the crown becomes progressively more difficult in aging trees and may cause sufficiently severe water deficits in some leaves and branches to cause their death. Many tall redwoods have dead branches in the tops, i.e., are "stag topped." Enzymatic activity decreases in aging trees as shown by overall diminished metabolic rate. Hormone supplies tend to become limiting for growth of the lower stem and roots as the leaf mass becomes inadequate to supply the whole tree.

In old trees there is increasing susceptibility to certain pathogenic agents, and the possibility of infection increases as a function of age (see Chapter 17). For example, pathogenic virus populations may build up and weaken the host tree. Fungal attacks occurring from the pith outward may weaken the stem sufficiently to subject the tree to windthrow. Long-lived trees have characteristically durable woods and they resist fungal attacks in the heartwood. As Westing (1964) emphasized, an important factor in the long life-span of redwoods and bristlecone pines is resistance to decay and fire. Decay resistance usually is increased by high contents of resins and phenolic compounds.

CROWN FORM

Many people are interested in tree form, which refers to the size, shape, and composition (number of branches, twigs, etc.) of the crown. Landscape architects and arborists depend on tree form to convey a desired emotional appeal. Columnar forms are used as ornamentals for contrast; vase-shaped forms branch high so there is usable ground space below; pyramidal crowns provide strong contrast to trees with rounded crowns; irregular forms are used to provide interest and contrast to architectural masses; weeping forms direct attention to the ground area and add a softening effect to the hard lines of architecture.

The interest of foresters in tree form extends beyond esthetic considerations, because crown form greatly affects the amount and quality of wood produced and also influences the taper of tree stems (see Chapter 17). More wood is produced by trees with large crowns than by those with small ones, but branches on the lower stem reduce the quality of lumber by causing knots. Horticulturists are interested in the effects of tree form and size on fruit production and harvesting.

Variations in Crown Form

Most forest trees of the temperate zone can be classified as either excurrent or decurrent (deliquescent), depending on differences in the rates of elongation of buds and branches. In gymnosperms such as pines, spruces, and firs the terminal leader grows more each year than the lateral branches below it, producing a single central stem and the conical crown of the excurrent tree. In most angiosperm trees, such as oaks and maples, the lateral branches grow almost as fast or faster than the terminal leader, resulting in the broad crown of the decurrent tree. The decurrent crown form of elms is traceable to loss of terminal buds and to branching and rebranching of lateral shoots, causing loss of identity of the main stem of the crown.

Open-grown decurrent trees tend to develop shapes characteristic for the genera or species (Fig. 16.39). The most common crown form is ovate to elongate, as in ash, beech, and oak. In some trees, such as apple, the crowns may be broader than high; and in still others, elm for example, they often are vase shaped.

Tropical forests are especially well known for their diversity of crown forms (Hallé and Oldeman, 1975; Brunig, 1976). The shapes of tree crowns differ greatly among species occupying the different layers of tropical forests, the tallest trees having the widest and flattest crowns (Fig. 16.40). In the second layer tree crowns are about as wide as they are high, while in the third layer the trees tend to have tapering and conical crowns. The shapes of crowns in the various layers of tropical forests also are influenced by angles of branching. In upper strata most major branches tend to be upwardly oriented, whereas in the third layer they are more horizontally oriented. The young plants of species that eventually occupy the upper levels of tropical forests and the shrub layers have diverse forms. Whereas most of the shrubs have a main stem and resemble dwarf trees, other shrubs (for example, members of the Rubiaceae) lack a main stem and branch profusely near ground level.

Fig. 16.39. Variations in form of open-grown trees. (A) Eastern white pine; (B) Douglas-fir; (C) longleaf pine; (D) eastern hemlock; (E) balsam fir; (F) ponderosa pine; (G) white spruce; (H) white oak; (I) sweetgum; (J) shagbark hickory; (K) yellow-poplar; (L) sugar maple. Photos courtesy St. Regis Paper Co.

Crown forms of tropical trees of the upper canopy change progressively during their development. When young they have the long, tapering crowns characteristic of trees of lower strata; when nearly adult their crowns assume a more globose form; and when fully mature their crowns become flattened and wide (Richards, 1966).

Crown forms of tropical trees are also greatly modified by site. Species adapted to mesic sites tend to be tall with broad crowns, while species on xeric sites usually are

Fig. 16.40. Variations in crown form of trees occupying different layers of a tropical forest. From Beard (1946).

short and small-leaved and have what is known as a xeromorphic form. Low soil fertility usually accentuates the sclerophyllous and xeromorphic characteristics associated with drought resistance, inducing thick cuticles and a decrease in leaf size. The degree of xeromorphy often can be decreased by adding phosphate or nitrogen fertilizers (Beadle, 1966, 1968).

Control of Crown Form

Tree form results from interactions between environmental influences—such as gravity, light intensity, photoperiod, temperature, and mineral nutrition—and the internal correlating effects of hormones and genetic potentialities. Such aspects of tree form as branch angle, amount of branching, amount and duration of shoot growth, and degree of apical dominance are under genetic control, but they can also be modified by the environment. For example, some species grow into large trees on moist, fertile soil, but remain shrubs on hot, dry sites or near the timber line. Some of the factors that regulate tree form will now be discussed.

Apical Dominance

Differential elongation of buds and branches is an important factor in determining the form of woody plants. In many species of trees, crown form is controlled through the inhibition of lateral buds by active, terminal meristems. The excurrent growth form is widely considered to be an expression of strong apical dominance, and the deliquescent or decurrent form an expression of weak apical dominance. The existence of strong apical dominance in intact trees can be inferred from its cancellation by removal of terminal buds or injury to apical shoots. For example, apical dominance of eastern white pine trees often is temporarily destroyed when grubs of the white pine weevil (*Pissodes strobi*) kill the leading shoot. Eventually one of the lateral branches of the terminal whorl turns upward, assumes dominance, and suppresses growth of the other shoots in the same whorl.

Apical dominance of some species having shoots fully preformed in the winter bud reflects variations in bud size and in the rate and seasonal duration of the expansion of variously located shoots. In many gymnosperms, the terminal leaders with large buds often expand faster and for a longer time than do leading shoots of lateral branches. This causes a corresponding decrease in shoot growth from the top of the tree downward. In red pine, for example, both bud size and length of shoots produced from them decreased progressively from upper to lower whorls (Table 16.8; Fig. 16.41).

Apical dominance in recurrently flushing pines is correlated with differences in seasonal duration of internode elongation and in the number of growth flushes among variously located shoots. Shoots in the upper crown generally show more annual growth flushes than those in the lower crown. Some buds of lowermost branches may not open at all (Table 16.9). In a study of loblolly pine seedlings and saplings by Boyer (1970), the number of annual growth flushes and average shoot length all declined with increasing distance from the tree top. All seedling terminal shoots had three growth flushes and one-half of them had four. Forty percent of seedling lateral shoots had three growth flushes, 55% had two, and 5% had one. The number of buds failing to develop into shoots was low during the first seasonal growth flush, but was much higher for the third and fourth growth flushes of the terminal leader and the second and third flushes of lateral shoots.

The mechanism of inhibition of lateral shoots by terminal meristems has been widely investigated and debated. The overall control of apical dominance is very complex and appears to involve both hormonal and nutritional factors that influence differences in bud development, bud opening, and rate and duration of shoot expansion (Kozlowski, 1971a).

TABLE 16.8   Effect of Bud Size on Shoot Growth of 8-Year-Old Red Pine Trees[a,b]

	Bud diameter (mm)	Bud length (mm)	Shoot length (mm)
Terminal leader	8.2 ± 0.7	38.0 ± 2.8	742.0 ± 26.7
Whorl 1 shoots	5.9 ± 0.1	27.3 ± 0.7	484.8 ± 11.0
Whorl 2 shoots	5.5 ± 0.1	22.9 ± 0.8	403.2 ± 13.0
Whorl 3 shoots	4.5 ± 0.2	16.6 ± 0.9	271.4 ± 19.1
Whorl 4 shoots	3.8 ± 0.3	12.5 ± 1.0	132.1 ± 20.6
Whorl 5 shoots	3.7 ± 0.3	9.9 ± 0.8	65.2 ± 16.0
Whorl 6 shoots	3.3 ± 0.4	8.6 ± 1.4	74.4 ± 31.5

[a] From Kozlowski et al. (1973).

[b] Data are means and standard errors of bud diameters and lengths before initiation of shoot expansion (March 20, 1970) and final shoot lengths (August 19, 1970) at different stem locations.

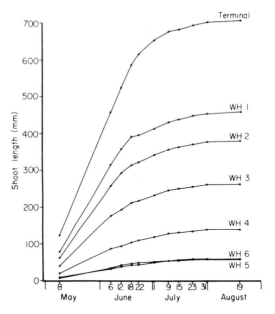

Fig. 16.41. Seasonal patterns of shoot elongation in the terminal leader and whorls 1 to 6 of 8-year-old red pine trees. From Kozlowski *et al.* (1973).

TABLE 16.9 Number of Shoot Growth Flushes at Different Heights in Loblolly Pine[a,b,c]

	Number of growth flushes			
Whorl location	0	1	2	3
Topmost		5	6	5
Second		3	8	4
Third		3	10	2
Third above middle		6	2	
Second above middle		2	3	
First above middle		15	3	
First above middle		12	2	
Second above middle		6		
Fourth from bottom		9		
Third from bottom	2	8		
Second from bottom	4	10		
Lowest	4	5		

[a] The trees were 10 to 15 ft tall and grew in Covington, Louisiana.
[b] The numbers indicate how many shoots elongated in each category.
[c] From Eggler (1961).

Most investigators stress the importance of a correlative inhibitory signal originating in the apical part of the shoot. For example, removal of the growing apical bud is followed by outgrowth of previously inhibited lateral buds. Stem girdling (phloem blockage) also releases buds below the girdle while at the same time the upper portions of the shoot continue to grow and consume nutrients and water. Phillips (1975) reasoned that lateral buds are inhibited by a downward movement of apically produced hormones rather than by a lack of nutrients or water. He cited failure to eliminate or reduce inhibition of one bud by another by direct applications of nutrients to buds as an argument against a purely nutritional basis of correlative growth inhibition.

Auxin derived from growing leaves at the stem apex undoubtedly is an important hormonal correlative signal in inhibition of lateral buds. For example, application of exogenous IAA can substitute for the apical bud in maintaining apical dominance in many species. A major role of auxin is also shown by reduction or abolition of apical dominance in plants treated with inhibitors of auxin transport, such as TIBA (2,3,5-triiodobenzoic acid). Nevertheless, it is unlikely that auxin alone can wholly account for apical dominance. Camus (1949) showed that apical buds checked growth of lateral buds even though the auxin contents of apical and lateral buds were not significantly different. Thimann (1964) placed great emphasis on the importance of auxin in apical dominance but also suggested that the mechanism involved interactions between auxin and a cytokinin. Wickson and Thimann (1958) found that exogenous auxin inhibited growth, but that the inhibition could be cancelled by adding kinetin. It appeared that inhibited lateral buds of intact plants could not synthesize the cytokinins necessary for their growth, and that release from auxin inhibition permitted cytokinin synthesis. Brown *et al.* (1967) also concluded that a balance of growth hormones, rather than auxin alone, exerts control over inhibition of lateral buds.

Pharis (1976b) summarized evidence showing that gibberellins play an important role in influencing crown form by controlling apical dominance of conifers in the Cupressaceae, Taxodiaceae, and Pinaceae. Exogenous applications of GA_3 enhanced the negatively geotropic growth of a lateral branch following excision of the terminal shoot of Arizona cypress (Pharis *et al.*, 1965). Endogenous gibberellins were thought to be responsible for this negatively geotropic response and also for the inhibition of development of lateral buds of Sequoia plants treated with growth retardants. McGraw (1973) showed that in decapitated Arizona cypress trees the speed with which a lateral branch turns upward and assumes dominance is increased by GA_3 applied as a soil drench. He also found increased localization of radioactivity on the lower side of the upturning branch after injecting radioactive gibberellins into seedlings.

When Arizona cypress trees are grown under short photoperiods, both the lateral branches and the apical shoot are induced to grow downward in a positively geotropic manner. This abnormal effect of gravity is counteracted by exogenous GA_3 (Pharis *et al.*, 1972). Thus, reduced amounts of endogenous GA_3 prevent normal plagiotropic or slightly negatively geotropic growth of laterals and also induce positive geotropic growth of all shoots, including the terminals.

Interactions of gibberellins and auxins in controlling bud growth of conifers also have been demonstrated. For example, application of GA_3 plus IAA delayed the release of interfascicular buds in decapitated Scotch pine plants (Tomaszewski, 1970). Pharis (1976b) suggested that in intact plants auxin from the terminal shoot may control geotropic growth of the lateral branches of conifers by affecting the distribution or metabolism of GA in lateral branches. However, when differential, negatively geotropic growth of a lateral shoot occurs after injury to or removal of the terminal shoot, such growth appears to be largely controlled by endogenous gibberellins.

A growing body of evidence shows that, in addition to hormones, the nutritional status of a plant plays an important role in apical dominance. As Wareing (1974) pointed out, some trees exhibit much stronger apical dominance under conditions of low soil fertility and low light intensity than under more favorable conditions. Gregory and Veale (1957) demonstrated that lateral buds of herbaceous plants were inhibited under conditions of nitrogen and carbohydrate deficiency. At low nitrogen levels growth activity could be maintained in only one meristem. Basal buds might begin growing, but later they competed with opening buds below the apex as well as with the apical bud, and growth was inhibited. At high nitrogen levels all buds tended to remain active and apical dominance was expressed poorly, if at all. Gregory and Veale (1957) visualized auxin as having an indirect role in apical dominance by controlling the development of vascular traces to axillary buds. They believed that high auxin content might inhibit formation of provascular strands to axillary buds, thereby impeding translocation of nutrients into them and inhibiting growth.

Wareing and Nasr (1958, 1961) also emphasized nutritional factors in apical dominance. When the uppermost lateral shoots of woody plants were trained horizontally and the lower ones vertically, the usual apical dominance relations were reversed. Attributing the reduced growth of leading shoots to large auxin supplies from the laterals would require acropetal auxin transport. Their results suggested an indirect role of auxin in correlative growth inhibition by control of transport of nutrients. They found that lateral buds grew at the point nearest the root at which the shoot was turned from the vertical. A mechanism of apical dominance was postulated in which nutrients were diverted to the highest upwardly directed meristem. Booth et al. (1962) showed that ^{14}C sucrose moved into decapitated internodes or mature leaves to which auxin was applied. Kozlowski and Winget (1964a) noted that a supply of reserves from the old needles of red pine was necessary early in the growing season to maintain dominance of the terminal leader over lateral branches. Such data suggested that hormone-directed translocation might redistribute nutrients from storage tissues to young, growing tissues and exert a role in the correlative inhibition of lateral buds.

Pruning and ^{32}P injection experiments by Moorby and Wareing (1963) suggested that a rapid increase in the number of growing shoots as the branches increased in complexity resulted in competition among them for available nutrients. In intact Scotch pine trees more minerals were obtained by leading shoots than by laterals. When distal parts of a branch were removed by pruning, increased growth of the laterals followed. Pruning also was followed by an increased availability of minerals to the remaining lateral branches. These experiments showed the disadvantage of the laterals in competing for nutrients with leading shoots in intact plants. Experiments by Little (1970) showed that eastern white pine shoots in a new whorl competed for nutrients translocated from the preceding whorl. The amount of nutrients mobilized by a shoot, and its growth, depended on the capacity of the shoot to produce hormonal growth regulators. Little (1970) emphasized that the degree of dominance of various whorls of eastern white pine depends on the supply of nutrients available at the time bud primordia are produced in the developing winter bud. The size of the buds borne in the current whorl of the shoot arising from the winter bud depends on the amount of nutrients available during the period of current shoot development. When these buds elongate during the following year, differences in shoot size, which reflect differences in bud size, depend on the minimum level of nutrition during the period of shoot elongation. These several observations indicate that apical dominance is the final expression of several sequential physiological events in shoot growth and appears to involve within-tree variations in the hormonally directed transport of plant nutrients and metabolites.

Aging and Tree Form

In aging trees a change in crown form is associated with a progressive inhibition of shoot growth and a loss of apical dominance. Wareing (1958) and Moorby and Wareing (1963) showed, that as a branch of Scotch pine or Japanese larch aged, the leader of the branch continued to growth rapidly for several years, while growth of many-branched laterals arising from proximal parts of the branch was impeded. The senescent condition gradually spread up the tree until finally the terminal leader lost its dominance and the tree formed a flat-topped crown. Also, as the branches become

TABLE 16.10 Shoot Development on Young Ginkgo Trees[a]

A. Development of long and short shoots from terminal and lateral buds in ginkgo seedlings grown from seed germinated in 1934.

	Development of terminal buds				
	1942	1943	1944	1945	1946
Number of short shoots	0	0	3	2	8
Number of long shoots	30	30	27	28	22
Percent long shoots	100	100	90	93.5	73.5

B. Development of long shoot laterals from short shoot laterals of the previous year on 8-year-old plants.

	1942	1943	1944	1945
Number of short shoot laterals	399	316	290	385
Number of long shoots from short shoot laterals	77	24	36	20
Percent long shoots	19.3	7.6	12.4	5.2

[a] From Gunckel et al. (1949).

older, they change their angle of growth from upright to a more nearly horizontal and finally a drooping one. Second-order laterals often grow vertically downwards. This change of growth pattern due to aging can be reversed by vegetatively propagating the old part. Hence, rooting or grafting of part of an old shoot on a seedling stock results in a revitalized shoot showing increased growth and strong apical dominance.

Several species of gymnosperms and a few angiosperms produce more short shoots when adult than when they are young. Table 16.10 shows this tendency for both terminal and lateral buds of ginkgo. Gunckel *et al.* (1949) found that practically all the terminal buds on a 15-year-old ginkgo tree produced long shoots, whereas a 100-year-old tree had approximately equal numbers of long- and short-shoot terminals. Young trees of this species have an excurrent form due to the predominance of long shoots. Old trees become globose in form as the terminal buds begin producing short shoots and lateral buds produce long ones. This change takes place when trees become reproductive at an age of 35 to 40 years. As may be seen in Table 16.11 the removal of a terminal long shoot in young plants causes one or more laterals to become long. With increasing age and decreasing vigor, however, the ability of laterals to form long shoots disappears.

In young plants of *Cercidiphyllum japonicum* long shoots predominate. When plants are 15 to 20 years old and adult, as indicated by flowering, the production of short shoots begins. Thereafter, proportionally more short shoots are produced as the tree ages until 90% or more of the buds of mature trees expand into short shoots (Titman and Wetmore, 1955).

European larch seedlings produce mostly long shoots. In trees 4 to 5 years old, the main axis grows vertically by monopodial growth and its axillary buds grow vigorously as long shoots. With increasing age, the growth of lower branches becomes suppressed and their terminal buds tend to develop into weak twigs that may wither at the top.

TABLE 16.11 Influence of Tree Age on Development of Lateral Long Shoots before and after Removal of Terminal Shoot[a]

	Age of plants (years)						
	3	4[b]	13[b]	14[b]	15	35	100
Percent of long shoot laterals on previous year's growth (intact plants)	27	0	0	0	—	—	—[c]
Percent of removals of terminals that cause one or more laterals to become long							
Same season	100	93	87	10	Rarely	Rarely	0
Following season	0	—	—	—	90	35	10

[a] From Gunckel *et al.* (1949).
[b] Greenhouse plants in pots.
[c] Five percent of all laterals on the tree, irrespective of age.

Most axillary buds of all branches then begin to form short shoots. In old trees small terminal buds of low branches also often produce short shoots. As trees age, vertical elongation continues, whereas lateral shoot growth is progressively decreased (Frampton, 1960).

Competition

Open-grown trees have large crowns, but those growing in stands tend to have small crowns. During the development of a community of trees, intense competition occurs for light, moisture, and minerals, resulting in stratification of trees into different crown classes. In a young, even-aged stand all trees may have more or less similar crown shapes. However, with increasing tree age, competition intensifies as the crowns begin to close. Some trees become suppressed and occupy low positions in the canopy, whereas others express dominance and become the largest and most vigorous trees.

Much interest has been shown in the crown sizes of forest trees because of their influence on wood production. In open-grown trees the crown covers most of the main stem, whereas in mature stands it is restricted to the upper part of the stem. After the crowns of forest trees close, the lower branches begin to die, causing a progressive decrease in the live-crown ratio (percent of total tree height occupied by functional branches). When the live-crown ratio decreases to a critical value, usually about 40% in many species, the rate of wood production decreases greatly. Ideally, competition among forest trees should be decreased at this stage by imposing thinning treatments to removed undesirable trees. This would result in increased wood production in the residual crop trees. Thereafter, thinning of the stand should be repeated often enough to maintain a relatively constant live-crown ratio. If the live-crown ratio is allowed to drop below 30 to 40% before a stand is thinned, the residual trees are unlikely to respond favorably in terms of increased diameter growth and they often are killed (Smith, 1962). The effects of stand thinning on cambial growth and stem form of forest trees are discussed in Chapter 17.

Shedding of Branches

The crown form of trees often is greatly modified by the shedding of lateral branches. For example, the crown of a 100-year-old oak tree often has only five or six orders of branches because it sheds branches readily. If it did not do so it would have 99 orders of branches. The shedding of branches also greatly influences lumber grades by influencing the size and type of knots. Early shedding of branches is desirable because it reduces the number and size of knots. When large dead branches are retained by trees, loose knots form that degrade lumber.

Shedding of lateral branches may occur by two separate mechanisms: (1) actual abscission of branches by a physiological process similar to that involved in leaf abscission, and (2) natural pruning by death of branches but without formation of an abscission zone.

Branch Abscission.   The shedding of branches by abscission, a process called cladoptosis, occurs through a well-defined abscission zone and is preceded by a weakening of tissues and by periderm formation. Cladoptosis occurs in response to several adverse environmental factors and to aging effects that result in a lack of branch vigor. Twig abscission does not occur in juvenile white oak trees, but is common in mature trees of this species (Millington and Chaney, 1973).

Cladoptosis is well known in a variety of shrubs and trees, both angiosperms and gymnosperms, of the temperate zone and tropics. Shedding of twigs in the temperate zone is particularly well known in poplars, willows, maples, walnut, ashes, and oaks (Fig. 16.42). Most of these shed twigs in the autumn, although maples do so largely in the spring and summer.

The loss of branches by abscission occurs very commonly in many tropical trees and shrubs, for example, in the following genera: *Antiaris, Albizzia, Canangia, Castilloa, Casuarina, Persea, Sonneratia,* and *Xylopia.* Van der Pijl (1952) described a specimen of *Casuarina sumatrana* from which 99% of the small twigs on the main axis had abscised. The strong tendency for tropical trees to shed branches is generally shown by their low number of branch orders. For example, a majority of tropical rain forest species have only about three orders of branches, whereas many species of the temperate zone have from five to as many as eight (Richards, 1966). Branch abscission also occurs in several temperate and tropical lianas. Examples are *Ampelopsis cordata, Parthenocissus quinquefolia, Vitis* spp., and climbing species of *Piper.*

Natural Pruning.   The first step in the natural pruning of trees undergoing competition involves the sequential physiological senescence and death of branches low on the stem. The dead branches are attacked by saprophytic fungi and insects that cause their decay, weakening, and breakage by wind, snow, or other elements of the environment. When a branch dies it is usually sealed off from the tree stem by deposits of resins in gymnosperms and gums or tyloses in angiosperms. The activity of fungi, which is influenced by temperature and moisture, often determines the rate of branch

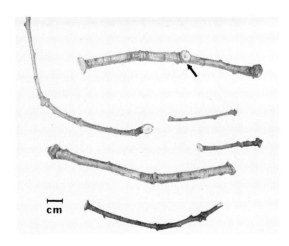

Fig. 16.42.   Twigs abscised from a mature white oak tree showing enlarged bases and a branch scar (*arrow*). From Chaney and Leopold (1972).

TABLE 16.12   Variations in Natural Pruning of Lateral Branches of Various Species of Trees Growing in Dense Stands

Good natural pruners		Poor natural pruners	
Angiosperms	Gymnosperms	Angiosperms	Gymnosperms
Betula lenta	Abies procera	Celtis laevigata	Abies balsamea
Fagus grandifolia	Larix laricina	Juglans nigra	Juniperus occidentalis
Fraxinus americana	Picea mariana	Quercus nigra	Juniperus virginiana
Populus balsamifera	Picea rubens	Quercus phellos	Larix occidentalis
Populus tremuloides	Pinus elliottii	Sequoia gigantea	Libocedrus decurrens
Populus trichocarpa	Pinus palustris		Picea engelmannii
Prunus serotina	Pinus resinosa		Pinus contorta
Quercus alba	Taxodium distichum		Pinus coulteri
Quercus rubra			Pinus monticola
Salix nigra			Pinus radiata
			Pinus strobus
			Pinus virginiana
			Tsuga canadensis

pruning. The degree of natural pruning in response to the low light intensities of dense tree stands also varies greatly among species (Table 16.12). For example, longleaf pine shows good natural pruning; Virginia pine does not (Fig. 16.43). For a good discussion of the shedding of branches the reader is referred to Millington and Chaney (1973).

Branch Angle

The angle of divergence of branches from the main stem greatly modifies tree form. The direction in which a branch grows depends on the angle it makes with the tree axis and the extent to which the branch will bend. Forest geneticists are interested in the effects of branch angles of trees on wood quality. Conifers with narrow or acute branch angles tend to prune less readily and have larger knots than those with wide branch angles.

Branch angles are genetically controlled and vary among species, cultivars, and within the same tree in predictable patterns. Differences in the crown forms of sugar maple, sycamore, and white oak are associated with variations in branch angles. Fastigiate forms of trees, with all branches oriented at acute angles to the vertical axis, are highly prized as ornamental specimen trees. Such fastigiate forms usually show weak apical dominance. For example, fastigiate forms of Monterey pine lack a main stem and have several competing, vertically oriented branches. Since the terminal buds lack strong apical control over the fascicle buds at the ends of vertical shoots, the latter elongate into long branches (Fielding, 1960).

In general, branch angles are less acute in excurrent species than in decurrent ones. Zimmermann and Brown (1971) attribute the more horizontal orientation of lateral branches in excurrent trees to strong apical control, whereby the terminal leader exerts a marked epinastic response that opposes the negative geotropic response of a branch.

Fig. 16.43. Natural pruning of conifers. (A) Good natural pruning of longleaf pine (Photo courtesy of U.S. Forest Service); (B) Poor natural pruning of Virginia pine (From Fenton and Bond, 1964).

In decurrent trees, in which the terminal leader is suppressed, a strong epinastic effect is lacking; hence, lateral branches tend to grow upward at more acute angles.

The initial angle of divergence of branches from the main stem varies at different stem heights. The usual pattern is one in which young branches in the upper crown tend to be more vertically oriented than those in the mid-crown, and the weak branches in the lower crown may actually droop. In profusely branched decurrent trees, many of the upper branches tend to be vertically oriented across the top of the crown.

The orientation of branches of many species changes appreciably during their development. Often branches that at first have an acute orientation with the main stem bend downward as they elongate. Subsequently the tips of these branches respond progressively to both gravity and light and turn upward. Such changes in branch orientation are particularly well known in many pines.

Gravimorphism

It has long been known that the tilting of stems from a vertical position has very dramatic effects on tree form because of the redistribution of hormones in response to gravity. For example, arching or horizontal training of branches of trees reduces vegetative growth and stimulates reproductive growth. Apical dominance is also affected. Another example of gravimorphism is the tendency for inclined stems to form reaction wood that tends to realign stem growth so as to eventually regain a vertical position. Success in achieving vertical alignment depends on such factors as age of the stem and duration of its inclination from the vertical (Fig. 16.44).

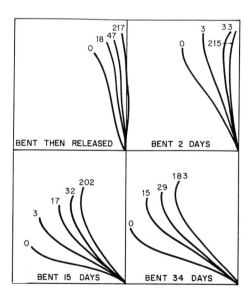

Fig. 16.44. Righting of stems of *Tristania conferta* seedlings that had been bent to a horizontal position for 0 to 34 days. The numbers indicate days after release from bending. From Scurfield (1973). Copyright 1973 by the American Association for the Advancement of Science.

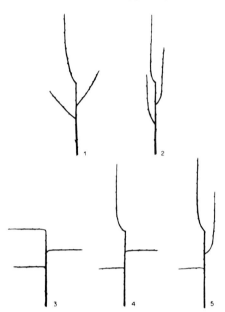

Fig 16.45. Effects of shoot orientation on growth and apical dominance of lateral shoots of apple. 1, The three shoots were left in their natural vertical "upswept" position. 2, The three shoots were trained vertically. 3, The three shoots were trained horizontally. 4, The first shoot (leader) was trained vertically and the other two shoots horizontally. 5, The first two shoots were trained vertically, and the third shoot was trained horizontally.

Wareing and Nasr (1961) studied growth of apple tree shoots that were trained vertically or horizontally in various combinations (Fig. 16.45). Elongation of lower laterals was accelerated by training them vertically, indicating that when laterals made a wide angle with the vertical axis their elongation growth was reduced by gravitational effects. When all three laterals were vertically oriented, the lowermost shoot grew least. However, when all three laterals were trained horizontally no differences occurred in elongation. These observations indicated that a leading shoot did not become dominant unless it was vertically oriented.

Jankiewicz (1971) showed that buds on the lower sides of horizontally oriented apple or poplar stems developed poorly as compared with buds on the upper sides. When trees were placed horizontally for only a few days at the time of bud opening, and then restored to a vertical position, the buds on the previously lower sides of stems produced weak shoots and those on the upper sides grew vigorously. Hence, even small differences in bud development that were induced during the short period of horizontal shoot orientation caused differences in shoot expansion (Jankiewicz and Stecki, 1976). The inhibition of buds on the undersides of horizontally placed shoots appears to be caused by movement under gravity of hormonal growth regulators from the upper to the lower side. When Mullins (1965) split shoot lengths of horizontal shoots of apple trees and separated them by a plastic barrier, long shoots grew from the lower as well as the upper side, indicating blocking of the gravitational inhibitory substance.

GENERAL REFERENCES

Abeles, F. B. (1973). "Ethylene in Plant Biology." Academic Press, New York.

Audus, L. J., ed. (1976). "Herbicides: Physiology, Biochemistry, Ecology," 2 vols. Academic Press, New York.

Bonner, J., and Varner, J. E., eds. (1976). "Plant Biochemistry," 3rd ed. Academic Press, New York.

Cannell, M. G. R., and Last, F. T., eds. (1976). "Tree Physiology and Yield Improvement." Academic Press, New York.

Hallé, F., Oldeman, R. A. A., and Tomlinson, P. B., eds. (1978). "Tropical Trees and Forests: An Architectural Analysis." Springer-Verlag, Berlin and New York.

Horn, H. S. (1971). "The Adaptive Geometry of Trees." Princeton Univ. Press, Princeton, New Jersey.

Kozlowski, T. T., ed. (1968–1978). "Water Deficits and Plant Growth," Vol. 1–5. Academic Press, New York.

Kozlowski, T. T., ed. (1973). "Shedding of Plant Parts." Academic Press, New York.

Kramer, P. J. (1969). "Plant and Soil Water Relationships. A Modern Synthesis." McGraw-Hill, New York.

Leopold, A. C., and Kriedemann, P. E. (1975). "Plant Growth and Development." McGraw-Hill, New York.

Sacher, J. A. (1973). Senescence and post harvest physiology. *Annu. Rev. Plant Physiol.* **24**, 197–224.

Scurfield, G. (1973). Reaction wood: Its structure and function. *Science* **79**, 647–655.

Thimann, K. V. (1972). The natural plant hormones. *In* "Plant Physiology: A Treatise" (F. C. Steward, ed.), Vol. 6B, Academic Press, New York.

Thimann, K. V. (1978). "Hormone Action in the Whole Life of Plants." University of Massachusetts Press, Amherst.

Tomlinson, P. B., and Zimmermann, M. H., eds. (1978). "Tropical Trees as Living Systems." Cambridge University Press, London and New York.

Wareing, P. F., and Phillips, I. D. J. (1970). "The Control of Growth and Differentiation in Plants." Pergamon, Oxford.

Wareing, P. F., and Saunders, P. F. (1971). Hormones and dormancy. *Annu. Rev. Plant Physiol.* **22**, 261–288.

Westing, A. H. (1965). Formation and function of compression wood in gymnosperms. *Bot. Rev.* **31**, 381–480.

Westing, A. H. (1968). Formation and function of compression wood in gymnosperms. II. *Bot. Rev.* **34**, 51–78.

17

Environmental and Cultural Factors Affecting Growth

INTRODUCTION

It was pointed out in Chapter 1 that the quantity and quality of growth made by plants depend on interactions between their hereditary potentialities and the environment in which they are growing. Many of the important problems facing ecologists, foresters, and horticulturists require evaluation of the relative importance of various factors of the environment and identification of the physiological processes through which they affect growth. It sometimes is questioned whether a single factor can be identified as controlling growth in a particular situation. It certainly is not as simple as Liebig (1843) supposed when he formulated the law of the minimum, later modified by Blackman (1905) and Mitscherlich (1909). The principle of limiting factors, as proposed by Blackman, stated that if a process is affected by a number of separate factors, its rate is limited by the factor present in the smallest amount relative to its minimum require-ment. The importance of the interaction among factors sometimes is recognized by referring to the most significant factor, indicating that although several factors may be affecting growth, one is more important than the others at a given time. Perhaps the view of Billings (1952) that limiting factors operate within an environmental complex, as is shown in Fig. 17.1, best describes the situation.

The principal environmental requirements for plant growth are sufficient light, water, oxygen, carbon dioxide, and mineral nutrients, and temperatures suitable for the essential physiological processes. These apparently simple requirements involve the interaction of numerous factors of varying importance.

COMPLEXITY OF ENVIRONMENTAL CONTROL OF GROWTH

The basic problem with respect to the physiological effects of environmental factors is to explain how or by what means a stimulus such as a change in a temperature, photoperiod, or water content is sensed and converted to metabolic processes which in turn modify the quantity and quality of growth. It is relatively easier to explain the effects of water and temperature, because they directly affect every cell in a plant. For example, temperature affects rates of enzyme-mediated processes, membrane permea-bility, and the viscosity of water and protoplasm. Water deficits not only affect cell

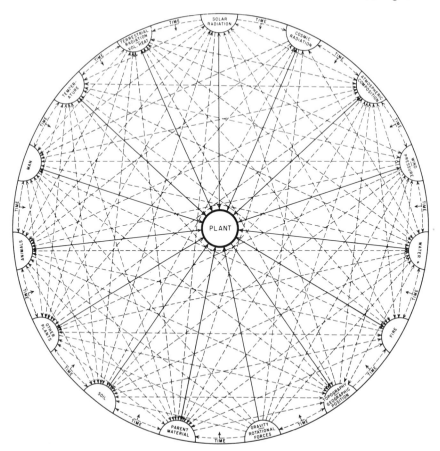

Fig. 17.1. Diagrammatic representation of the interrelationships among environmental factors and plants. Relations among factors are shown by dashed lines; relations between factors and plants are shown by solid lines. From Billings (1952).

turgor, which controls cell enlargement and stomatal aperture, but they also affect enzyme-mediated processes and RNA by mechanisms that are not yet fully understood.

The photomorphogenic effects of light are more difficult to explain because the stimulus is often sensed in one organ, but the response occurs at a distance. For example, the flowering response to photoperiod depends in many plants on reception of a light stimulus in the leaves by phytochrome. This apparently causes synthesis of a florigen that is transmitted to stem tips, which then begin to produce flower primordia. Presumably this occurs because phytochrome in the active form (Pfr or far-red absorbing form) causes certain genes to become active (derepressed) and produce messenger RNA, which instructs ribosomes to produce certain enzymes that in turn produce a florigen. The florigen then acts on the genomes of cells at the stem apex, repressing some genes and activating others, resulting in the cessation of vegetative growth and the initiation of flower primordia.

A problem in studying environmental effects on growth is that the relative importance of an environmental factor can change during the growing season. A given amount of precipitation early in the growing season, when the soil is fully charged with water, will have little effect on cambial growth, whereas one-half that amount later in the season will affect cambial growth markedly. In Wisconsin, the correlation of cambial growth of northern pin oak with temperature declined in late summer as soil moisture was depleted and growth was limited by water deficits (Kozlowski *et al.*, 1962).

The growth responses of trees often lag considerably behind environmental changes. For example, shoot growth and cambial growth are variously influenced by current-year weather as well as by the weather of the previous year or years. Another problem is that environmental preconditioning modifies the effect of the current environment on growth. When white spruce seedlings were brought to the same uniform environment, those grown the previous season under cool nights opened their buds later than seedlings that had been grown under warm nights (Rowe, 1964).

An abrupt change in environment does not alter growth similarly in all trees of the same species in a stand. This may be the result of differences among trees in exposure, crown size, depth of rooting, inherent growth characteristics, physiological preconditioning of trees, and other causes, including microenvironmental heterogeneity. Furthermore, the influence of a drastic environmental change often affects growth markedly in some parts of a tree and not in others.

Caution should be used in attributing cause-and-effect relationships to correlation analyses of growth and various environmental factors. A high degree of correlation may be taken as evidence that a certain factor is influencing growth when in fact it is merely associated with some other factor that is really effective, but is not even included in the analysis. For example, a prolonged drought often is accompanied by the death of trees which is attributed to dehydration. However, more careful study might reveal that they are dying from other causes. While recognizing the difficulties of evaluating the relative importance of various external factors in controlling growth, this chapter will discuss some of the influences of the important environmental factors on vegetative and reproductive growth.

ENVIRONMENTAL CONTROL OF VEGETATIVE GROWTH

Radiation

The term "light" refers to that portion of radiant energy visible to the human eye, and is only a small part of the total spectrum of radiation to which vegetation is exposed, as is shown in Fig. 17.2. At the short wavelength end of the spectrum is ultraviolet radiation and at the long wavelength end is infrared radiation, or heat. Radiation in the regions from approximately 400 to 700 nm is used in photosynthesis

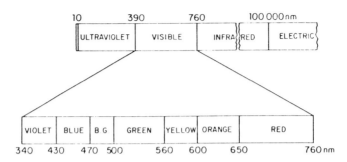

Fig. 17.2.   The spectrum of radiant energy.

and the region from 660 to 730 nm has important qualitative, photomorphogenic effects on growth. Physiologically, the effects of radiation on plants can be grouped in two categories—the high-energy ($>$1,000 lux) photochemical effects operating through the process of photosynthesis, and the low energy ($<$100 lux) effects. The latter include such photomorphogenic effects as etiolation and responses to photoperiod and the directive effects on stem and leaf orientation termed phototropism. Physically, the effects of light on plant growth can be treated as depending on irradiance or intensity, wavelength or quality, and photoperiod or duration of illumination.

Light Quality or Wavelength

Light reaching tree crowns is transmitted, reflected, and absorbed (Table 17.1). The wavelengths at which maxima and minima of absorption occur are nearly the same for all green leaves, indicating that they contain similar pigments. As sunlight filters through tree crowns, its spectral distribution is altered because of selective spectral absorption by leaves.

Federer and Tanner (1966) showed that spectral distribution of shade light between 400 and 700 nm is different under broad-leaved and gymnosperm trees and between clear and cloudy days. There is an energy maximum at 550 nm, a minimum at 670 to 680 nm, and a very high maximum in the near-infrared under all species. The increase in the infrared results from decreased leaf absorption and some reradiation and is higher under broad-leaved species than under pines. There is relatively more blue light under the gymnosperms than under the angiosperms, but on cloudy days this difference decreases, making the light within the stand whiter.

There has been much interest in light quality because of its effects on growth. The greatest increase in plant dry weight usually occurs in the full spectrum of sunlight. Expansion of leaf blades is prevented by darkness, retarded in green light, intermediate in blue, and greatest in white light.

Under natural conditions, growth is influenced less by changes in light quality than by changes in light intensity or photoperiod. Daubenmire (1974) stated that the influence of wavelength differed so much among species that generalization was difficult, and variations in light quality in natural communities usually were too small to be critical. On the other hand, light quality is very important for the growth of plants

TABLE 17.1   Reflectivity, Transmissivity, and Absorptivity as a Function of Wavelength for a Green Leaf and for Light of Normal Incidence (Percent)[a]

	Wavelength (nm)						
	400	450	500	550	670–680	740–750	1,000
Reflectivity	10	8	9	21	9	49	40
Transmissivity	3	3	6	17	4	47	40
Absorptivity	87	89	85	62	87	4	20

[a] From Federer and Tanner (1966).

under artificial illumination. Excessive stem elongation tends to occur under incandescent lamps, but stem elongation of some species is below normal under cool white or daylight-type fluorescent lamps. A few incandescent lamps added to banks of fluorescent tubes provide the far-red wavelengths missing from fluorescent lights, and this combination usually produces more satisfactory growth.

Light Intensity

Light intensity is the most important variable in nature because of its role in controlling photosynthesis and because very low light intensities cause etiolation of leaves. As was pointed out in Chapter 5, photosynthesis of many trees and canopies is limited by light intensities lower than one-third or one-fourth of full sun, and many require full sunlight for maximum photosynthesis in the entire crown. The light intensity to which trees are exposed varies with the season and with climatic conditions. Light intensity also varies with the age, composition, and density of stands, and it varies in different parts of the crown of an individual tree. Light transmission to the forest floor decreases rapidly as the density of tree crowns increases up to about 35%, but with further increase in crown density light transmission decreases more slowly. Under open, even-aged pine stands of the temperate zone, illumination at the forest floor may be 10 to 15%, and in temperate zone hardwoods 1 to 5%, of that in the open. Following leaf fall the light intensity in deciduous forests often approximates one-half that in the open. Under tropical rain forests relative illumination is very low, often less than 0.5% (Spurr, 1964).

There is a great deal of mutual shading within the crowns of individual trees (see Chapter 5). For example, light intensity in the interior of crowns of citrus trees varies from 0.5 to 2% of full sunlight. Light intensities within tree crowns also differ greatly among citrus varieties; those having dense crowns, such as Marsh seedless grapefruit and Clementine mandarin, are much darker than those of Shamouti orange (Monselise, 1951). It is difficult to assess the long-term physiological effects of such comparisons because of recurrent sunflecks that influence the light regime within tree crowns and on the forest floor. For example, the very deep shade of the forest floor is interrupted by sunflecks that temporarily increase relative illumination to values as high as 50 to 60%

of that in the open. In Nigerian forests sunflecks occupy 20–25% of the surface of the forest floor, where they account for 80% of the incident radiation in the middle of the day (Evans, 1956). Sunflecks appear to play an important role by temporarily increasing photosynthesis and offsetting respiratory losses of carbohydrates, thereby maintaining certain shade-adapted trees that otherwise might not survive (Leopold and Kriedemann, 1975).

Shade Tolerance.   Trees and shrubs vary widely in their capacity to grow in the shade and this often becomes a decisive factor in their success. In fact, climax communities are usually composed of shade-tolerant species because their seedlings are able to become established in the shade. This is why pine is replaced by hardwoods in natural succession in the southeastern United States.

Forest trees often are assigned tolerance ratings in several classes representing various degrees of capacity to endure shade (Table 17.2). Shade tolerance varies with the age of trees and with environmental conditions. Trees tend to show the greatest shade tolerance in their youth, and those on good sites and in the southern parts of their range are more tolerant to shade than those on poor sites or in the northern part of their range (Baker, 1950).

The extensive efforts made to identify the factors responsible for shade tolerance have been only partially successful. It has been reported that the stomata of shade-tolerant species open more rapidly in sunflecks than those of intolerant species (Woods and Turner, 1971; Davies and Kozlowski, 1974a), allowing the former to carry on photosynthesis during short periods of illumination. However, Pereira and Kozlowski (1976) found that variations in stomatal responses of five species were poorly correlated with shade tolerance. The difficulty of correlating shade tolerance with stomatal response to light intensity is complicated by the fact that the tolerance rating for a given species is more or less stable, although it may vary somewhat with site, whereas stomatal responses to changes in light intensity are greatly modified by a variety of factors, including light and water stress preconditioning, temperature, and mineral deficiency (Davies and Kozlowski, 1974a). Several factors in addition to stomatal control influence species shade tolerance. Important among these are genetic control of anatomical changes in leaves (Jackson, 1967), changes in chlorophyll–protein ratios, activity of enzymes involved in chemical processes in chloroplasts (Holmgren *et al.*, 1965; Bjorkman, 1973), respiration rates (Loach, 1967), photosynthetic rates (Kozlowski and Keller, 1966), and various metabolic changes (Durzan, 1971) in competitive situations.

The photosynthetic mechanism of shade tolerant plants usually is more efficient at low light intensities than that of intolerant species. For example, shade-grown leaves of beech take up four or five times as much CO_2 as sun leaves at a light intensity of 500 to 1000 lux. This was attributed to their lower chlorophyll content by Tranquillini (1956), but this seems unlikely because, as pointed out in Chapter 5, sun leaves usually contain more chlorophyll per unit of leaf area because they are thicker. According to Alberte *et al.* (1976) shade-grown leaves are more efficient than sun leaves at low light intensities because they contain a higher proportion of the light-harvesting chlorophyll a/b protein complex. This increases photosynthetic efficiency at low light intensities, but also

TABLE 17.2 Relative Shade Tolerance of Forest Trees[a]

Gymnosperms	Angiosperms
Very tolerant	
Eastern hemlock	American beech
Balsam fir	Sugar maple
Western hemlock	Flowering dogwood
Western redcedar	American holly
Alpine fir	American hophornbeam
Tolerant	
Red spruce	Red maple
Black spruce	Silver maple
White spruce	Basswood
Sitka spruce	Buckeye
White fir	Tanoak
Redwood	Bigleaf maple
Intermediate	
Eastern white pine	Yellow birch
Slash pine	White oak
Western white pine	Red oak
Sugar pine	Black oak
Douglas-fir	White ash
Giant sequoia	American elm
Intolerant	
Red pine	Yellow-poplar
Shortleaf pine	Paper birch
Loblolly pine	Sweetgum
Ponderosa pine	Black cherry
Lodgepole pine	Hickories
Noble fir	Black walnut
Very intolerant	
Longleaf pine	Quaking aspen
Jack pine	Gray birch
Tamarack	Willows
Digger pine	Cottonwood
Western larch	Black locust
Whitebark pine	

[b] Adapted from Baker (1950).

results in light saturation at a low light intensity. Alberte *et al.* (1976) suggested that the increased efficiency in low light might have adaptive value for photosynthesis in the winter and in the fog belt of the Pacific United States.

Shade-grown leaves of the intolerant yellow birch are light saturated at 10,000 lux compared to 40,000 lux to saturate sun leaves (Logan, 1970). They therefore do not benefit from sun flecks. Loach (1967) suggested that differences in adaptation of respiration may be important to the relative success of tolerant versus intolerant species in competitive situations. He compared photosynthetic and respiratory adaptation of species ranging from very tolerant to very intolerant. These included beech, red maple, red oak, yellow-poplar, and trembling aspen. There was some degree of adaptation to shade with respect to photosynthesis in all species, but not with respect to respiration. Leaves of the more tolerant beech, maple, and oak showed reduced respiration in the shade, but not those of the intolerant yellow-poplar and trembling aspen. Durzan (1971) found better metabolic adaptation to shade in shade tolerant species with respect to nitrogen metabolism and suggested that there may be greater metabolic stress in the intolerant jack pine than in the more tolerant white spruce. The photosynthetic capacity of leaves may be influenced by their mineral nutrition because stomatal opening and closing are slow in mineral deficient trees (Davies and Kozlowski, 1974a).

Shoot Growth.   Light intensity influences bud formation as well as expansion of internodes and leaves. These plant responses involve effects of light intensity on various processes such as chlorophyll synthesis, photosynthesis, hormone synthesis, stomatal opening, and transpiration. The specific effects of changes in light intensity are not easily assessed because increases in light intensity often are accompanied by higher temperatures which, in turn, influence each of the physiological processes already mentioned, and respiration as well.

As was discussed in Chapter 3, the ultimate length of shoots in many species is correlated with the size of the bud and the number of shoot primordia that are present in the dormant bud. The low light intensities received by the lower and inner branches of trees adversely influence physiological processes, especially food and hormone synthesis, sufficiently to inhibit bud development and thereby impose a limitation on shoot development. In understory striped maple trees, the development of buds is controlled by the light intensity reaching the leaves. All buds contain a pair of preformed early leaves as well as a pair of rudimentary leaf primordia. At low light intensities these rudimentary primordia form bud scales; at higher light intensities they form leaves (Wilson and Fischer, 1977). After buds form, the expansion of shoots is also influenced by light intensity. For example, shading of tamarack shoots at various times during the growing season inhibits their elongation (Clausen and Kozlowski, 1967b).

In addition to influencing the formation and extension of shoot primordia, natural shading often induces death of lower branches on tree stems. The degree of such natural pruning in response to the low light intensities within dense tree stands varies among species, as was discussed in Chapter 16. A common response to opening of stands by thinning or by pruning branches and suddenly exposing tree trunks to increased light intensities is stimulation of epicormic shoots (see Chapter 3).

Species vary greatly in shoot growth response to light intensity. Logan (1965, 1966a,b) compared the shoot growth of seedlings of several species of angiosperms and gymnosperms in full light and in shelters admitting 45, 25, or 13% of full sun. In general, heavy shading reduced shoot growth of the gymnosperms more than that of the angiosperms (Tables 17.3 and 17.4). Height growth of white birch, yellow birch, silver maple, and sugar maple was not reduced until the light intensity fell below 45% of maximum. Shoot growth of sugar maple was affected least by low light intensity.

TABLE 17.3 Effect of Shading for 5 Years on Shoot Growth Characteristics of Angiosperm Seedlings[a,b]

	Height (cm) at light intensity of				Dry weight of shoots (gm) at light intensity of				Dry weight of foliage (gm) at light intensity of			
	13%	25%	45%	100%	13%	25%	45%	100%	13%	25%	45%	100%
White birch	180.3	203.2	226.1	152.4	90.7	156.7	318.5	243.4	39.1	54.9	97.2	96.6
Yellow birch	152.4	195.6	213.4	149.9	88.1	154.8	237.6	236.2	36.5	51.1	72.3	95.0
Silver maple	111.8	121.9	119.4	76.2	34.2	44.2	54.5	50.7	18.5	27.5	34.0	50.4
Sugar maple	149.9	144.8	182.9	139.7	56.4	76.6	171.2	235.0	32.7	43.3	77.7	154.6

[a] From Logan (1965).
[b] Lines connect treatments in which a species showed no significant differences.

TABLE 17.4 Effect of Shading for 5 Years on Shoot Growth Characteristics of Gymnosperm Seedlings[a,b]

	Height (cm) at light intensity of				Dry weights of shoots (gm) at light intensity of[c]				Dry weight of foliage (gm) at light intensity of			
	13%	25%	45%	100%	13%	25%	45%	100%	13%	25%	45%	100%
Tamarack	76.2	111.8	172.7	170.2	4.2	10.2	30.3	40.7	—	—	—	—
Jack pine	40.6	73.7	99.1	111.8	2.7	16.2	32.1	52.7	—	—	—	—
White pine	27.9	38.1	55.9	55.9	2.6	5.4	17.3	22.7	5.4	13.6	28.4	31.3
Red pine	15.2	30.5	38.1	40.6	1.4	4.4	12.1	23.5	1.7	10.1	22.3	38.5

[a] From Logan (1966a).
[b] Lines connect treatments in which species showed no significant differences.
[c] Data on dry weight of shoots are given after 4 years.

Maximum height growth of this species occurred over a wide range, from 45% to 13% of full light. In contrast to the shoot weight of other species of angiosperms, that of sugar maple was not reduced by a decrease from full light to 25% of full light (Logan, 1965).

Reduction in light intensity also had only a limited effect on shoot elongation of basswood seedlings, dry weights of the main stem and leaf area not being influenced appreciably by a decrease in light intensity from full light to 25%. By comparison, American elm seedlings showed an increase in height and stem weight as light intensity was increased up to 45% of full light (Logan, 1966b).

Low light intensities greatly decreased shoot growth of tamarack, jack pine, eastern white pine, and red pine seedlings. By the fourth year the seedlings of all four species at the two lowest light intensities (13 and 25% of full light) were smaller than those in 45% or 100% of full light. Five-year-old jack pine plants required full light for maximum height growth, but height growth of the other species was not greatly different at the two highest light intensities. Nevertheless, shoot dry weight of each of the four species was reduced by each shading treatment. Shading depressed shoot growth more in red pine than in eastern white pine (Logan, 1966a).

Jackson and Palmer (1977a,b) exposed Cox's Orange Pippin apple trees to 100, 37, 25, or 11% of full daylight, in 1970 or 1971, or both years. Shading affected shoot growth in both years. In 1970 it reduced the number and weight of new shoots, diameter increase, leaf thickness, and leaf weight per unit area. Residual effects included a reduction in the number of shoots, and increases in shoot diameter and in leaf dry weight per unit area. The residual effects were attributed to greatly reduced competition for assimilates because of a large reduction in the number of fruits borne by shaded plants.

Sun and Shade Leaves.　There is considerable difference in structure between leaves produced in the sun and those produced in the shade. This applies to the shaded leaves produced within a tree crown compared to those on the periphery of the same crown, as well as to leaves of entire plants growing either in shade or full sun.

In general, shade leaves from the interior of tree crowns are smaller, thinner, less deeply lobed (Fig. 17.3), and contain less palisade tissue and less conducting tissue than sun leaves (Wylie, 1951). Shade leaves also usually have fewer stomata per unit of leaf area and larger interveinal areas and the ratio of internal to external surface usually is much less than in sun leaves. Similar differences also occur between sun and shade needles of conifers (McLaughlin and Madgwick, 1968). Important anatomical and physiological changes can occur even in fully expanded leaves, when exposed to high or low light intensity (Bunce *et al.*, 1977).

Cambial Growth.　The effects of light intensity on cambial growth are complicated and mediated chiefly through export from leaves of carbohydrates and hormonal growth regulators. As was mentioned previously, light and water conditions during one year influence the formation of leaf primordia and the number of leaves produced during the subsequent year. Thus, a lag effect of light conditions on cambial growth may be expected. In addition, light regimes influence the expansion and anatomy of

Fig. 17.3. Sun leaves *(left)* and shade leaves *(right)* of black oak. From Talbert and Holch (1957).

leaves and thereby control their potential production of assimilates and hormonal growth regulators.

The increased diameter growth of dominant over suppressed trees, and of residual trees following thinning of a stand, is an integrated response to an overall improved environmental regime that includes greater availability of water and minerals as well as better illumination. Perhaps cambial growth in variously shaded branches of a tree is a more direct indicator than growth in the main stem of the importance of light to cambial growth.

Cambial Growth Patterns in Branches

During their development the branches of many trees, especially gymnosperms, undergo successive suppression. Many pines, for example, annually produce a whorl of branches at the bases of the terminal and each branch leader. Consequently, each whorl from the apex downward is progressively more shaded after each flush of growth, and the growth characteristics change as its environment is altered.

Forward and Nolan (1961) studied the pattern of xylem increment at nodes of branches of different ages in 25- to 30-year-old red pine trees. In a wide range of environments annual xylem production increased for some distance from the branch apex downward and then it decreased. This pattern, which could be modified quantitatively, was a constant feature of all upper branches. In trees that had been grown in the open, suppressed, or suppressed and later released, the upper branches and parts of lower ones that were formed while near the tree apex showed a pattern of cambial growth similar to that of the main stem. As a branch was progressively suppressed during aging, there was a redistribution of its cambial increment, and growth of the xylem sheath was restricted in the lowermost whorls at all internodes. Hence, even in open-grown trees the lower branches were suppressed.

The lower, suppressed branches of many trees may fail to form annual rings for several years before the branches die. For example, in 35- to 77-year-old Douglas-fir trees Reukema (1959) noted that there often were 9 to 10 fewer xylem rings in the base of the branch than in the main stem at the point of attachment. Labyak and Schumacher (1954) observed that a branch of loblolly pine in the lower one-half of the crown with fewer than three branchlets, or one in the lower one-fourth of the crown with fewer than five branchlets, did not contribute to development of the main stem. Such observations indicate that suppressed lower branches often are unable to supply foods and growth hormones for growth of the main stem. Obviously the pruning of such lower "negative" branches will not detract from diameter increment of the main stem. Fig. 6.5 showed the volume contributed to growth of the main stem by branches at various heights.

Photoperiod

At the equator, days are of equal length during the entire year, but in temperate regions large seasonal differences occur in the length of the daylight period. For example, in arctic regions daylight is practically continuous at midsummer; Boston, Massachusetts, has about 15 hr of daylight on the longest day of the year and about 9 hr on the shortest day; and at Key West, Florida, the longest days are less than 14 hr long and the shortest days last about 10.6 hr. In equatorial regions there are about 12 hr of daylight during the entire year. It has been recognized ever since the classic research of Garner and Allard (1920) that changes in the duration of exposure to light (photoperiod) influence both vegetative and reproductive phases of plant growth. In various woody plants day length can affect shoot growth, diameter growth, leaf abscission, frost resistance, and seed germination.

Shoot Growth.   Short days stop shoot expansion of many woody species of the temperate zone and cause development of a dormant state, whereas long days delay or prevent dormancy. As shoot elongation slows under short-day conditions, successively shorter internodes are produced until growth eventually ceases (Figs. 17.4 and 17.5). Some species of the tropics also are responsive to day length. Experiments in controlled environments showed that shoot growth is greatly increased by days longer than normal in many tropical species, including *Terminalia superba, Chlorophora excelsa, Ceiba pentandra, Bombax buonopozense, Hilgardia barteri, Theobroma cacao, Coffea arabica,* and *Pinus caribaea* var. *hondurensis* (Longman and Jenik, 1974). *Terminalia superba* seedlings were so sensitive that significant effects of day length on shoot growth could be detected after only 3 days of treatment.

Exposure to short days by shading or by use of growth chambers is used extensively to experimentally induce cessation of shoot growth and cause dormancy. However, it cannot be assumed that short days are the primary factor causing dormancy in all species, because shoot growth ceases in many species of the temperate zone before the days begin to shorten. This is particularly true for species that show only a single period of shoot elongation that is completed very early in the frost-free season. On the other hand, shoot growth of heterophyllous and recurrently flushing species continues late into the growing season (see Chapter 3) and therefore is more likely to be influ-

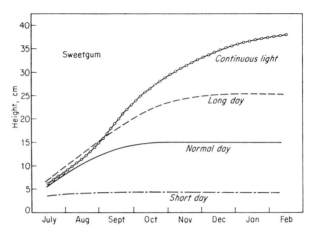

Fig. 17.4. Effects of varying day lengths on shoot growth of potted seedlings of sweetgum grown in a greenhouse. From Kramer (1936).

Fig. 17.5. Height growth of slash pine after 15 months on 12-, 14-, and 16-hr day lengths. From Downs (1962).

enced by the shortening days of late summer. In some species photoperiod may also influence growth of late-season lammas shoots (Heide, 1974).

Cessation of vegetative growth by short days can be brought about in different ways. For example, in poplar and dogwood grown under short days, the leaf primordia develop into scales instead of leaves, and in sumac and lilac the terminal meristem dies and abscises (Nitsch, 1957). Generally, the induction of dormancy by short days leads to formation of a terminal resting bud in monopodial species, and to abscission of the shoot apex in sympodial ones. Some species, such as yellow-poplar, redgum, beech, and some pines which are induced to a dormant state under short days, will resume growth if placed under long-day conditions. That these are true photoperiodic responses is shown by shoot expansion of even leafless dormant trees of these species when exposed to long days, whereas they are maintained in a dormant state under short days.

Species vary widely in their photoperiodic sensitivity. Yellow-poplar and black locust can be induced to grow continuously for at least 13 months under long days. In other species growth eventually stops, even under continuous illumination. For example, Scotch pine and sycamore maple enter dormancy even when illuminated continuously (Wareing, 1956).

Shoots of seedlings of species that normally tend to grow in flushes, such as some oaks, respond to long days by elongating in several additional recurrent flushes rather than by growing continuously. Some species of pines, which normally exhibit a single growth flush, also sometimes respond to long days or to continuous illumination by expanding in a series of flushes. Still other species, such as mountain ash, lilac, and some species of ash, appear to have little or no photoperiodic sensitivity (Wareing, 1956).

Site of Photoperiodic Perception. The locus of photoperiodic sensitivity varies among species and may be in very young leaf primordia, resting buds, partially expanded leaves, or mature leaves. The light-sensing pigment is phytochrome, which can convert differences in photoperiod into metabolic reactions that control growth (Schopfer, 1977).

In beech the photoperiodic perception arises in young leaf primordia in the buds. When dormant buds were covered and twigs exposed to continuous illumination dormancy was not broken. In contrast, continuous illumination of buds promoted their growth, even in the absence of bud scales, emphasizing a direct effect of light on the primordial tissue. Approximately 0.7% of the incident light was transmitted through the bud scales of leaf primordia and that was enough for photoperiodic response (Wareing, 1953). By comparison, the primary site of photoperiodic perception in sycamore maple and black locust was in the mature leaves.

Breaking of Dormancy. Species vary greatly in their capacity to break bud dormancy under continuous illumination. For example, bud dormancy of beech seedlings can be broken at any time by continuous light, and this can be accomplished whether the plants have leaves or not. In other species dormancy can be broken by photoperiod only if the buds are in a relatively mild state of dormancy. Scotch pine buds in a state of quiescence or summer dormancy, which normally would not have expanded until the following spring, opened prematurely after exposure to continuous illumination. However, when the buds were in the state of deep winter dormancy, continuous illumination was ineffective in inducing shoot growth (Wareing, 1956). Similarly, long-day treatments often induce shoot growth in oaks as long as buds are in a mild state of summer dormancy but not when they are in a truly dormant winter condition.

In some species long days generally are ineffective in breaking dormancy. For example, when dormancy was induced by short days in buds of sycamore maple and black locust, they subsequently could not be induced to grow even after 8 to 10 weeks of continuous light (Wareing, 1954).

Interactions of Chilling and Photoperiod. There are various interactions of chilling and photoperiod on the breaking of bud dormancy. Buds of beech do not break dormancy in a short photoperiod after chilling because their photoperiodic requirements are not altered by prolonged exposure to low temperatures (Wareing, 1953). In contrast, buds of European white birch readily respond to cold and, after chilling, break dormancy readily even under short days (Wareing, 1956). Even in species such as black locust and sycamore maple, which do not break dormancy in response to photoperiod when unchilled, bud break often occurs faster under long than under short days (Wareing, 1956).

Cambial Growth. Both the amount and nature of the cambial growth increment are responsive to day length. In many species of trees the continuation of cambial growth is linked to continued shoot expansion and ceases soon after shoot elongation stops. This relationship appears to be the result of stimulation of cell division in the cambium by hormones produced by actively growing shoots. Hence, in some species the effect of photoperiod on shoot growth will also influence the duration of cambial growth. There are many species, however, that have a very short period of shoot expansion and a much longer duration of cambial growth. Day length also influences cambial activity in the latter group. For example, duration of cambial activity in Scotch pine, which has a short period of shoot elongation, was greater under 15-hr than under 10-hr photoperiods. Cambial growth in this species could be prolonged in the autumn by supplementing the natural photoperiod with artificial light (Wareing, 1951). Wareing and Roberts (1956) showed that photoperiod also had an important effect in controlling the cambial growth of black locust seedlings. Plants were first exposed to short-day conditions in order to cause shoot extension to cease. If they were further exposed to short days for several additional weeks, cambial growth ceased. If, however, they were exposed to long days after shoot extension stopped, cambial activity usually was resumed. Girdling experiments demonstrated that the cambial stimulus, which originated in the leaves when they were exposed to long days, moved only downward in the stem.

In addition to controlling the duration of cambial growth, the photoperiod greatly influences the specific gravity of wood by controlling the proportion of large-diameter to small-diameter cells in the annual xylem ring. Larson (1962a) concluded that the influence of photoperiod on tracheid diameter was largely indirect and was associated with auxin production and distribution in terminal meristems (see Chapter 16). Waisel and Fahn (1965) found that photoperiod affected cambial growth of black locust, the types of derivatives formed being influenced more than the width of the xylem increment.

Photoperiodic Adaptation.   In many instances, adaptations of trees to local environments include the photoperiod, with both the beginning and cessation of shoot growth genetically fixed in relation to the local photoperiod. Such mechanisms probably evolved in response to a specific length of growing season. For example, when Pauley and Perry (1954) collected poplar clones from a wide latitudinal range and grew them in the intermediate day length of Weston, Massachusetts, the clones from high latitudes and longer days ceased growth earlier in the season than those from lower latitudes with shorter days. Vaartaja (1959) also showed that photoperiodic ecotypes (ecological variants adapted to local conditions) occur very commonly in species with wide north-to-south ranges in the northern hemisphere. Such ecotypic variations have great practical significance and should not be overlooked when considering sources of seeds for planting in given areas. Seed from northern long-day races should not be planted in southern latitudes with short summer days because the trees developing from such seed are likely to stop growing early and will be small. However, such seeds might be selected for sites with short growing seasons at high elevations in southern latitudes. Ecotypes with long growing seasons in a particular latitude should be avoided as seed sources for habitats with short seasons at the same latitude, because the trees that develop from these seeds may be subject to frost damage. For the same reason, such seeds should not be moved northward and planted in a long-day environment.

Photoperiod and Ornamental Plantings.   The increase in photoperiod caused by the expansion of street lighting and increased use of artificial lighting in parking lots and other public areas and around homes is beginning to disturb the normal development of both herbaceous and woody plants. Prolonged shoot growth and leaf retention by woody plants growing near street lights have been mentioned by several investigators. For example, those plants of an *Abelia* hedge growing near street lights continued to grow far into the autumn until the new growth was killed by freezing temperatures (Kramer, 1937b). Cathey and Campbell (1975) suggest that more care should be taken in the choice of plants, avoiding such trees as birch and sycamore that are sensitive to photoperiod in favor of less sensitive ones such as maple, holly, and pine. Use of light sources such as metal halide lamps, which have less radiation in the wavelengths causing the photoperiodic response than high-pressure sodium lamps, also is desirable in the vicinity of vegetation.

Temperature

Most plant processes are temperature dependent. When temperatures are low, molecular activity is slow and the available energy often is inadequate for maintenance of the essential biochemical processes involved in growth. Low temperatures also decrease the permeability of membranes and increase protoplasmic viscosity. When temperatures become excessively high, molecular activity may become so rapid that enzymes controlling metabolic processes are denatured or inactivated. The decrease in growth at high temperatures may also be associated with excessive transpiration (see Chapter 12) and high rates of respiration, which cause unnecessary depletion of carbohydrates (see Chapter 6).

Went (1953) emphasized the importance of day versus night temperatures under the term "thermoperiodism." For example, it appeared that growth of loblolly pine seedlings was more closely related to the difference between day and night temperatures than to the actual day or night temperature and that the least growth occurred when nights were as warm as days (Kramer, 1957, 1958). Perry (1962) found that the best day and night temperatures for growth of red maple seedlings from different geographic sources varied with the source. Plants from northern provenances tended to become dormant with night temperature above 23°C and below 10°C and with low light intensity. Seedlings from a Florida source were more tolerant of low light intensity and warm nights.

The concept of thermoperiod may have less importance than was originally supposed. For example, redwood thrives with little or no difference between day and night temperatures (Hellmers, 1966), and growth of Engelmann spruce seedlings is controlled almost entirely by night temperature (Hellmers et al., 1970). Height and total dry weight increased with increasing night temperature from 3° to 23°C. In contrast, the rapid growth of Monterey pine in New Zealand is partly because growth is increased by night temperature below 10°C (Hellmers and Rook, 1973).

Soil temperature also is important in influencing growth. Hellmers (1963), for example, found that root temperature affected the growth of Sequoia seedlings with uniform shoot temperatures. Cool soil and warm air conditions stimulated root growth. Roots grew best in 18°C soil under both high and low air temperature conditions.

Numerous attempts have been made to predict the effects of temperature on growth by use of various formulas. In 1898 Merriam proposed the use of heat sums to correlate plant growth with air temperature. One way to use this concept is to obtain the sum of all temperatures above some base or threshold temperature such as 5°C and see how this correlates with growth, flowering, and yield. In some instances separate indices are calculated for the day and the night. For example, Cleary and Waring (1969) studied Douglas-fir seedling growth under various day and night temperature regimes and developed a heat sum index that related the effects of field temperature to the distribution of Douglas-fir. Under controlled laboratory conditions of day and night soil and air temperatures, they then studied potential seedling growth during each day of the growing season. Finally, by summations they calculated a physiological index that related effects of field temperature conditions to plant distribution. However, they recognized that this procedure did not account for important interactions of temperature with other variables such as light and water.

Cardinal Temperature

The cardinal temperatures include the minimum below which a physiological process is not measurable, the maximum above which it is not measurable, and the optimum at which it proceeds most rapidly. In general, the rates of various physiological processes, including growth, increase as temperature is raised from near 0°C and attain a maximum in the range of 20° to 35°C depending on species. With further increase in temperature, the rates of processes decrease rapidly. This pattern closely follows the activity of enzymes at different temperatures.

Various plant processes have different optimal temperatures and various organs also have different cardinal temperatures for a given process. Growth of roots, for example, occurs at lower minimal temperatures than growth of shoots. Cardinal temperatures also vary with age of tissue, duration of temperature regimes, and other environmental factors.

Energy Exchange

Plants react with their environment through the exchange of energy (Fig. 17.6). When a plant receives more energy than it consumes it becomes warmer; if it loses more than it gains it becomes cooler. The energy input to plant leaves comes from direct solar radiation, radiation reflected and reradiated from soil and vegetation surfaces, and from advective (lateral) flow of sensible heat from its surroundings. The total amount of energy absorbed by plants depends on their structure; leaf color; orientation of leaves to the sun; and their capacity to absorb, reflect, or transmit solar energy.

If a plant continually absorbed heat energy its temperature would increase to a lethal point. This rarely happens because plants lose large amounts of heat energy by reradiation, convection (transfer of energy by movement of the air mass, usually vertically), and loss of latent heat as water vapor. Convective losses are greatest when there are large differences between leaf and air temperatures.

Leaf temperatures sometimes equal air temperatures, but they generally are higher or lower. Temperatures of leaves that are exposed to full sun often are a few degrees higher (although in extreme cases they may be as much as 20°C higher) than those of the surrounding air. Shaded leaves have temperatures that approximate air temperatures or are a few degrees lower, and temperatures of different leaves on the same plant often vary widely.

Large diurnal variations in leaf temperatures often occur. More heat is absorbed than is lost by plants during the day, hence, temperatures of many leaves exceed air temperatures. At night, heat is radiated faster from a plant than it is absorbed and exposed leaves generally are cooler than the surrounding air. The energy relations of plants are discussed in detail by Gates (1973, 1976) and Nobel (1974).

Shoot Growth

Temperature influences shoot growth through its effects on bud formation, bud dormancy, and the initiation and seasonal distribution of bud expansion into a shoot. The amount of shoot growth is influenced by the temperature of the year of bud formation as well as the temperature of the year of bud expansion into a shoot.

Bud Formation. Heide (1974) emphasized that if late-summer temperatures were low the period for complete bud differentiation of Norway spruce was too short and this was reflected in the production of short internodes in the following year. Pollard and Logan (1977) subjected young black spruce and white spruce seedlings to

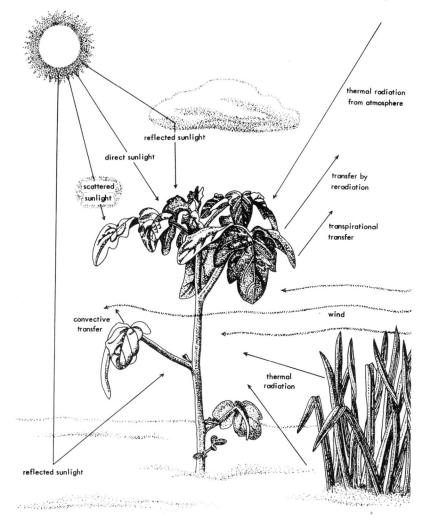

Fig. 17.6. Energy flow between a plant and the environment. From Gates (1965).

different environmental regimes during bud formation and then counted the numbers of needle primordia formed when bud morphogenesis was complete. Ambient temperature had a particularly noticeable effect on needle initiation. The optimum temperature was 25°C, and needle initiation was greatly inhibited by lower temperatures. These observations reinforce studies showing that, in species with fully preformed shoots in the winter buds, there often is better correlation between the amount of shoot growth and the temperature regime of the year of bud formation than with temperature during the period of bud expansion into a shoot. Mikola (1962), for example, concluded that the annual height growth of Scotch pine in Finland was determined mainly by temperature of the previous summer, and MacHattie and Horton (1963) found a similar relation for eastern white pine in Canada.

Breaking of Bud Dormancy. Bud dormancy of woody plants in the temperate zone is usually broken by winter cold and the southward extension of many northern species is limited by lack of enough low temperature to break dormancy. For example, most deciduous fruit trees cannot be grown successfully in subtropical climates, and occasionally the peach crop fails in the southern part of the United States because the winter is too mild to break dormancy (Weinberger, 1950). Lack of sufficient cold weather also is a problem with deciduous fruits in California.

Temperatures near 5°C are effective in breaking dormancy and freezing temperatures are not required. The amount of chilling required to break bud dormancy varies with the species, genotype, location of the buds on the tree, and possibly the weather of the preceding summer. About 1,000 hr of chilling are required to break the dormancy of Scotch pine (Nagata, 1967); 1,200 to 1,600 hr for sweetgum (Farmer, 1968); and over 2,000 hr for sugar maple in southern Canada. Sugar maple from Canada requires much more chilling than that from the United States (Kriebel and Wang, 1962; Taylor and Dumbroff, 1975), and red maple from the southern part of its range requires little or no chilling (Perry and Wang, 1960). One thousand hours of temperatures below 7°C will usually break dormancy in most peach varieties, but the requirement varies from 750 to over 1,200 hrs. In some instances it has been found that a fluctuating temperature is more effective than a constant one. For example, 900 hr of exposure at temperatures ranging from 0° to 5°C were required to break dormancy in *Tilia platyphyllos,* but 1,250 hr were required at a constant temperature of 3°C (Lyr *et al.,* 1970). However, if plants are exposed to low temperatures for a short time and then returned to high temperatures the effects of chilling are lost.

Another problem in specifying chilling requirements is the fact that different kinds of buds on a tree may have different temperature requirements. For example, Eggert (1951) found that flower buds of apple required less chilling than vegetative buds, and terminal buds less than lateral buds. The flower buds of some peach varieties also require less chilling than the vegetative buds, resulting in a lack of foliage to support the fruit set after a mild winter (Weinberger, 1950).

Phenology and Shoot Expansion. After buds of temperate zone trees are exposed to sufficient chilling to break dormancy, they need exposure to warm temperatures for a critical period before normal growth will occur. Following the breaking of bud dormancy by chilling, elm trees in Illinois required exposure to about 310 hr at 25°C for normal growth. Exposures to temperatures below 10°C and above 30°C were not effective (Perry, 1971). After the bud dormancy of sugar maple seedlings was broken by chilling, at least 140 to 190 hr of warm temperatures and long days were required for growth to begin (Taylor and Dumbroff, 1975).

Temperature probably is the most important environmental factor influencing the time of bud opening. For example, the date of initiation of shoot growth of sycamore in the same location varied in different years by as much as 21 days because of temperature variations (Kaszkurewicz and Fogg, 1967). Büsgen and Münch (1931) cited differences of 36 days in time of bud opening in different years for beech and 24 days for oak. The importance of temperature on bud opening is also shown by variations in the time of growth initiation of the same species at different latitudes. For example, eastern white pine and red pine trees began shoot growth in North Carolina in the latter part of March, but did not start growing in New Hampshire until the first day of May (Kramer, 1943).

There apparently are wide differences among species in critical temperatures for initiation of shoot growth. For example, red maple began to grow only after temperatures reached at least 15.6°C, whereas black ash, green ash, balsam fir, and eastern white pine began shoot growth only after the maximum temperature reached at least 21°C. Bud opening of basswood, bur oak, bigtooth aspen, and sugar maple appeared to be unrelated to specific temperatures (Ahlgren, 1957).

Early opening of buds, caused by unseasonably warm weather, results in much injury to forest and fruit trees in the temperate zone. There is wide interest among fruit growers in finding methods for delaying bud opening in the spring in order to reduce frost injury. If bud opening could be delayed 2 weeks, frost injury would be almost eliminated (Wolfe *et al.*, 1976). Evaporative cooling by overhead sprinkling or misting with water has proven effective in delaying flowering of apples, pears, and peaches and is being used extensively. However, it may also have undesirable effects such as decreased fruit yield and increased injury of pears by fire blight. Attention is being given to the possibility that blooming can be delayed by application of chemicals and there also is interest in finding rootstocks that will delay flowering and increase the cold hardiness of the tops.

In addition to influencing the time of bud opening, temperature regimes may influence shoot growth by regulating the rate and duration of shoot expansion. European larch seedlings of uniform mountain provenance that had been grown at an elevation of 1,000 m were transported in pots to three nurseries at different altitudes (700, 1,300, and 1,950 m) where annual shoot growth was studied. At 1,300 m the needles started to grow 29 days later, and at 1,950 m 80 to 90 days later than at 700 m. The total height growth of seedlings was greatly decreased as elevation increased and temperature regimes lowered. Height growth at 1,300 m was 60%, and at 1,950 m only 17%, of height growth at 700 m (Tranquillini and Unterholzer, 1968).

Cambial Growth

Temperature often influences the amount of xylem increment through its effects on time of initiation of cambial growth as well as on its rate and duration. Like shoot growth, cambial growth usually begins only after some critical minimum temperature is attained. Thereafter, the rate usually increases with increasing temperature to some critical level above which the rate begins to decline. However, it often is difficult to separate the direct effect of high temperature from the effects of water stress, which tends to develop at high temperatures. Heavy crops of seed or fruit also tend to reduce radial growth, complicating efforts to relate growth to environmental factors.

The effects of temperature on cambial activity are particularly noticeable in subarctic regions and at the alpine tree line where temperature is more likely to be limiting than water (Siren, 1963). Several investigators agree that cambial growth of trees in northern Europe is controlled by temperature. For example, Hustich (1948) and Mikola (1962) reported that the decreased tree growth in northern Finland in the early 1900's and the increase in rate in later years were closely correlated with mean July temperatures. On the east coast of Hudson Bay, cambial growth of Norway spruce lasts for less than 2 months (Marr, 1948), but further south at Chalk River, Ontario, it continues for about 3 months (Fraser, 1962).

Effects of Low Temperatures

The northern limit of the range of many species of woody plants is determined by the lowest temperature that they can survive. Thus the northward extension of species is limited by the occasional severe winter rather than by the average minimum temperature. For example, the severe freeze of 1894–1895 eliminated oranges from northern Florida. Much injury to plants in mild climates is caused by low temperatures following a period of mild weather that permitted growth to start and caused loss of cold resistance. In addition to exhibiting freezing injury, tropical and subtropical plants and a few temperate zone plants are susceptible to "chilling injury," which occurs when they are exposed to temperatures a few degrees above freezing. Such chilling injury is important to a number of tropical and subtropical crops when moved to cooler climates.

Freezing

Most cold-hardy plants survive low temperatures in a frozen condition (Levitt, 1972; Weiser, 1970) but a few avoid freezing by extreme undercooling (George and Burke, 1977). For example, George *et al.* (1974) found 25 woody species in which freezing occurred at −40°C or lower. The floral primordia in overwintering flower buds of several species of *Prunus* and a species of azalea *(Azalea kosterianum)* remain unfrozen at temperatures at which the stem axis and bud scales are frozen (George and Burke, 1977).

Freezing injury can be caused by intracellular freezing of the cell contents or indirectly by dehydration of tissues resulting from extracellular freezing. Plants usually are killed by formation of ice crystals within the cells, but formation of ice crystals in the intercellular spaces between cells is not necessarily fatal. If frost-hardened plants are cooled slowly, ice initially forms in the intercellular spaces, and as the temperature decreases water moves out of the cells to these ice nuclei. As a result the concentration of the cell sap is increased and its freezing point is lowered. If cold-hardened plants are cooled rapidly they often are injured, possibly because water does not move out of cells rapidly enough and intracellular freezing suddenly occurs. Killing by intracellular freezing is often attributed to mechanical disruption of the protoplasm. However, Levitt (1972) concluded that most freezing injury in seed plants is caused by dehydration, and freezing tolerance depends on the ability of the protoplasm to survive such dehydration.

Weiser (1970) summarized the complex sequence of events involved in slow freezing as follows:

Supercooling → Extracellular freezing of water between cells and in non-living xylem elements → Rapid propagation of ice throughout the stem resulting in: A substantial release of heat of fusion (an exotherm) which raises the tissue temperature from the supercooling point ($-2°$ to $-8°$C) to a plateau at the freezing point of the free water in the stem ($-0.3°$ to $-1°$C) $\rightarrow$ Further cooling after the readily available water is frozen $\rightarrow$ Migration of protoplasmic water out of cells to extracellular ice nuclei in response to the extracellular, aqueous, vapor-pressure deficit $\rightarrow$ A second distinct isotherm followed by decreasing tissue temperature and a continuous slow movement of cellular water out to extracellular ice nuclei $\rightarrow$ Shrinkage of the protoplasts, plasmolysis, and concentration of solutes in the cell $\rightarrow$ Continued slow movement of cellular water out of extracellular ice as the temperature decreases $\rightarrow$ A calorimetric lag indicating that freezing or water movement out of the cell is arrested $\rightarrow$ a third exotherm $\rightarrow$ granulation of the protoplasm $\rightarrow$ death.

Widely recognized forms of freezing injury include killing back of shoots, formation of frost rings, injury to stems, injury to roots, and frost heaving. These will be discussed separately.

Injury to Shoots.   Growing or only partially hardened shoots are often injured by early autumn frosts. Late application of fertilizers and irrigation sometimes prolong shoot growth and result in frost injury because the late growth does not have time to develop cold hardiness before frosts occur. Sudden killing of leaves by frost prevents the formation of abscission layers, and such leaves often remain attached all winter. Frost damage to white spruce needles is shown in Fig. 17.7. Spring frosts often cause severe injury to trees and shrubs that have resumed growth. Some branches often are injured more than others because of variations in the degree to which various buds have lost their cold hardiness. Of course, various parts of the tree may also be exposed to different temperatures and one sometimes sees all of the new leaves up to a certain height killed while those higher on the trees are uninjured.

Frost Rings.   Frost during the growing season often injures the cambium, causing abnormal ''frost rings'' to form. Such rings consist of an inner part comprised of cells killed by the frost (usually xylem mother cells and differentiating cambial derivatives) and an outer part of abnormal xylem cells produced after the frost. The frost rings of gymnosperms have underlignified, abnormal tracheids, collapsed cells, and traumatic parenchyma cells (Fig. 17.8). Usually the rays are laterally displaced and expanded.

The structure of frost rings varies somewhat among species as well as with the severity of the frost and activity of the cambium. The location of a frost ring often dates the frost, early spring frosts causing the abnormal cells to be localized in the early-formed portion of the annual growth increment. Frost rings occur more frequently in thin-barked trees than in those with a thick bark. Within the same tree small twigs are injured more than large branches, and the latter are injured more than the main stem (Peace, 1962).

Stem Injury.   Frost cracks (Fig. 17.9) and winter sunscald (sunscorch) lesions up to 1 m or more in length sometimes develop on stems of thin-barked trees when alternating freezing and thawing occur during the winter and early spring. The lesions can be recognized by dead bark patches, which sometimes peel and expose the wood, or by sunken cankers, which become sites for fungus and insect attacks (Fig. 17.10). Since the lesions damage the phloem, downward translocation of organic solutes is impeded. According to Gardner *et al.* (1952), rapid freezing of stems after sundown is largely responsible for winter sunscald lesions. The bark on the south side of a tree trunk may be 20°C warmer at midday than on the north side (Peace, 1962), suggesting

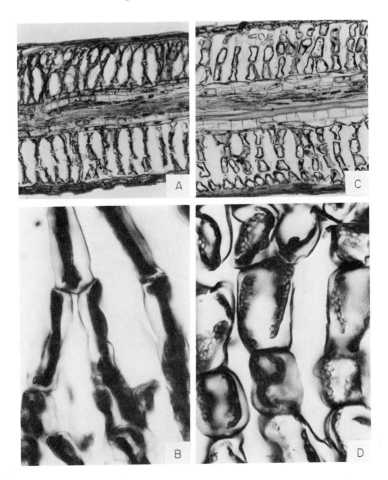

Fig. 17.7. Frost damage to white spruce needles. (A) Longitudinal section through a frost-damaged needle; mesophyll cells are collapsed and cytoplasm is coagulated, ×100; (B) longitudinal section through frost-damaged needles showing a few damaged mesophyll cells, ×425; (C) longitudinal section through normal needle; (D) longitudinal section through a normal needle, showing arrangement of a few mesophyll cells; note cell turgidity, ×550. From Glerum and Farrar (1965).

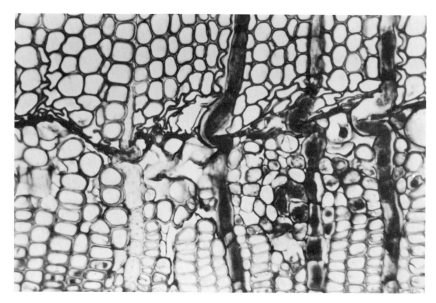

Fig. 17.8. Frost ring in a conifer. The cambium is near the bottom of the figure. The effects of frost are indicated by collapsed tracheids, displacement of rays, and excessive production of parenchyma tissue. Photo courtesy of U.S. Forest Service.

Fig. 17.9. Frost cracks *(arrows)* on stems of 13-year-old Golden Delicious apple trees on East Malling VII rootstock. Extreme splitting from the main scaffold branches to the stock–scion union *(left)*. Tree that has recovered from previous injury *(right)*. From Simons (1970).

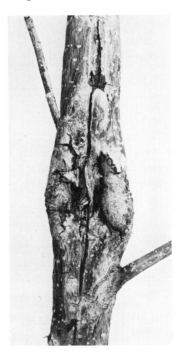

Fig. 17.10. Frost canker of *Populus*. From Zalasky (1976).

that the south side undergoes violent temperature fluctuations. Heating of the south sides of tree stems may initiate changes that decrease the cold hardiness of the cambium and make it very susceptible to frost injury. Attempts are sometimes made to avoid sunscald by painting tree trunks white or by wrapping them in white paper or tape. A more extensive discussion of sunscald is presented in the section on the effects of high temperature on vegetative growth.

Root Injury. Stem tissues are much hardier than roots, but roots are injured less in winter because the soil and snow cover protect them from exposure to freezing air temperatures. Nevertheless, when the soil freezes roots are often killed, especially the small, physiologically important ones. For example, Bode (1959) found that more than 90% of the absorbing roots of black walnut were lost during the winter.

Various investigators have found that roots develop frost resistance only to temperatures ranging from about −2° to −10°C. There are some exceptions, however. Tumanov and Khvalin (1967) reported that roots of some varieties of apple trees were hardy down to −15° to −18°C, whereas shoots survived down to −40°C. Roots show only small seasonal changes in cold hardiness (Parker, 1965).

The frost hardiness of roots varies with species and rootstocks. Cold injury to roots appears to be greater in sandy than in clay soils. Injury also appears to be greater in drier soils. Root injury by freezing can be controlled by deep planting and mulching, use of hardy rootstocks, pruning back the tops of injured trees, and careful handling of nursery stock in cold weather (Gardner *et al.*, 1952).

Recurrent lifting of tree seedlings from the soil by winter frosts often causes serious losses of trees in nurseries and young plantations. Such frost heaving occurs when roots become frozen in a mass of ice and then additional layers of ice form below. Some of the deeper, fine roots are broken as lifting occurs. The larger plants, with deeper and stronger roots, may be less affected because the frozen surface soil layer slides upward along their stems and down again on thawing. By comparison, smaller seedlings tend to remain lifted on thawing because their lower roots are more likely to be on a frozen layer. During subsequent freezing the already partially lifted plants tend to be pushed out even more. Injury or death usually follows if roots are broken or the shoots and exposed roots become desiccated.

Frost heaving is most common in heavy soils. It is also affected by soil water content, because during formation of ice near the soil surface, water moves upward by capillary action from the soil below. Hence, the amount of heaving is affected by soil water availability in both surface and deep layers (Schramm, 1958). Frost heaving is decreased by snow cover, ground cover, mulching, brush, and cultural practices such as use of fertilizers, irrigation, early seeding, and careful planting, which result in rapid production of large and deep-rooted plants (Peace, 1962).

Desiccation Injury

Much winter injury to conifers is the result of shoot desiccation rather than direct thermal injury. Such injury is well known in ornamental woody plants and forest trees. When the injury is severe, all the leaves and buds and even the trees are killed. More commonly, however, the leaves are killed but the buds are not and the trees survive.

Winter desiccation injury occurs when the absorption of water cannot keep up with transpirational losses. In many parts of the temperate zone appreciable transpiration occurs as the air temperatures rises above freezing during sunny winter or spring days and increases the vapor pressure gradient between the leaves and surrounding air. Since the soil is cold or frozen, water cannot be absorbed through the roots rapidly enough to replace transpirational losses (see Chapter 13) and the shoots become desiccated. Furthermore, when stems are chilled a few degrees below 0°C the water in the xylem elements freezes, thereby preventing water movement to the leaves even though part of the roots are in unfrozen soils (Zimmermann, 1964b; Havis, 1971). Thus the rates of water absorption and movement to leaves are greatly reduced by soil temperatures just above freezing.

Injury to conifers from winter desiccation is common throughout the northern hemisphere. Occasionally, the trees on whole mountain sides become discolored, some appearing as though scorched by fire. Damage is usually most severe on the south and southwest sides of trees and there is considerable difference among species. In the Adirondack Mountains of New York, the order of injury was red spruce > hemlock > eastern white pine > balsam fir, and little injury was observed on black or white spruce or red pine (Curry and Church, 1952). Similar discoloration has been reported near the timberline in the Rocky Mountains, and it is common on exposed windswept mountain slopes in Japan where the soil freezes (Okonoue and Sasaki, 1960; Sakai, 1970). Turner and DeRoo (1974) suggest that reduction in the water content of tissues continuously below freezing must be caused chiefly by extracellular freezing, because the rate of transpiration is quite low at subfreezing temperatures.

Chilling-sensitive species undergo irreversible injury to vegetative and reproductive tissues at temperatures between $+10°$ and $0°C$. For example, leaves of coffee and orange trees often are injured by exposure to temperatures near $3°C$ for a few hours. Chilling injury in vegetative tissues is commonly expressed in necrotic lesions, increased susceptibility to decay organisms, growth cessation, and ultimately death (Lyons, 1973). Symptoms of chilling injury vary among species, cultivars, and the tissue involved. If cotton seeds are chilled at the time of hydration, the radicle tip subsequently aborts, whereas chilling during early seedling growth results in damage to the root cortex (Christiansen, 1963). In general, chilling injury increases as temperature is lowered or as the duration of exposure to a chilling temperature is increased. Chilling injury is discussed further in the section on Environmental Control of Reproductive Growth.

Cold Hardiness

Low temperature often plays a leading role in limiting plant distribution because plants native to warm regions usually cannot be moved to cold regions. They do not develop enough hardiness to cold, do not harden fast enough to survive early cold weather, deharden too rapidly, and are killed by subfreezing temperatures.

Sakai and Weiser (1973) found much variation in freezing resistance of twigs of species collected in midwinter from various parts of North America (Table 17.5). Four northern species—trembling aspen, balsam poplar, white birch, and tamarack—resisted freezing to $-80°C$, and some survived temperatures of $-196°C$ following prefreezing to $-15°C$. Most of the northern Rocky and western Mountain conifers (ponderosa pine, western white pine, lodgepole pine, Jeffrey pine, blue spruce, Engelmann spruce, alpine fir, white fir, western larch) survived freezing between $-60°$ and $-80°C$. By comparison, species from the warmer southeastern coastal regions (slash pine, longleaf pine, live oak, southern magnolia) survived temperatures only down to $-15°C$.

There is much interest in within-species differences in freezing resistance. As a result of natural selection, climatic races have become adapted to particular environments and those of mild climates often are not sufficiently cold hardy when moved northward. The practical implications of lack of adequate cold hardiness of southern seed sources are of great interest to foresters, horticulturists, and arborists. Several investigators have demonstrated that plants from northern provenances are much more resistant than southern ones to freezing. Such differences have been reported for sugar maple (Kriebel, 1957), ponderosa pine (Squillace and Silen, 1962), sweetgum (Williams and McMillan, 1971), and northern red oak (Flint, 1972).

Acclimation to cold of various provenances of the same species often is closely related to phenology, seed sources that set buds early being less susceptible to injury from early frosts. For example, southern sources of Douglas-fir generally set buds later

TABLE 17.5 Variations in Freezing Resistance of North American Tree Species and Minimum Temperatures at Northern Limits of Natural Ranges or Artificial Plantings[a]

Relative hardiness classification	Representative species	Average minimum temperatures at northern limits of growth (°C)		Observed freezing resistance (°C)
		Natural range	Artificial plantings	
Tender evergreen species	Quercus virginiana	−3.9 to −6.7	−9 to −12	−7 to −8
Hardy evergreen species	Magnolia grandiflora	−9 to −12	−18 to −20	−15 to −20
Hardy deciduous species	Liquidambar styraciflua	−18 to −20	−26 to −29	−25 to −30
Very hardy deciduous species	Ulmus americana	−37 to −46	−40 to −43	−40 to −50
Extremely hardy deciduous species	Betula papyrifera	below −46	below −46	below −80
	Populus deltoides	−32 to −34	−37 to −45	below −80
	Salix nigra	−32 to −34	−37 to −45	below −80

[a] From Sakai and Weiser (1973).

than northern sources when both were grown at Corvallis, Oregon. For each additional week by which bud set preceded frost, the proportion of frost-damaged seedlings decreased by approximately 25%. For provenances that set buds in the same week, southern sources were more sensitive than northern sources, with the proportion damaged increasing by 4% for each degree of latitude (Campbell and Sorensen, 1973).

It should not be assumed that provenance variations in cold hardiness exist in all species. For example, Sakai and Weiser (1973) found that eastern cottonwood and black willow from locations with temperate or moderate winter climates survived freezing down to at least −50°C, regardless of their native habitats. Low winter temperature did not appear to be the principal factor governing the distribution of these species. Mohn and Pauley (1969), however, reported greater winter injury to southern sources of eastern cottonwood than to northern ones. This probably was the result of a late onset of cold hardening in the southern sources rather than to variations in their inherent capacity to become cold hardened. Smithberg and Weiser (1968) studied variations in timing of cold hardening of red-osier dogwood clones from 21 geographic locations when grown in St. Paul, Minnesota. Northern clones hardened earlier than southern clones, which showed injury in late autumn and early winter. However, there were no inherent differences among clones in their capacity to develop hardiness and all of them withstood −90°C by early December.

Hardiness of Different Organs and Tissues.   Studies of cold resistance are complicated. Different species and genetic materials vary in their capacity to resist freezing and the resistance of a given plant changes markedly during the year (Fig. 17.11). A plant that is killed at temperatures slightly below freezing in the summer may survive temperatures as low as −200°C in the winter (Weiser, 1970). Still another

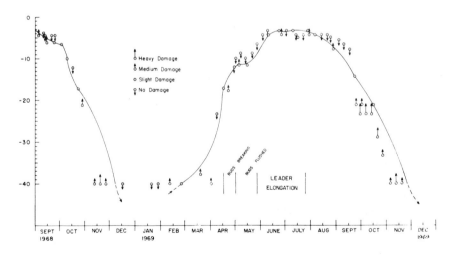

Fig. 17.11 Seasonal variation in frost hardiness of tamarack in Ontario, Canada. Frost hardiness increased from last August until maximum hardiness (−40°C) was attained in December. In April the rate of dehardening was rapid. From Glerum (1976).

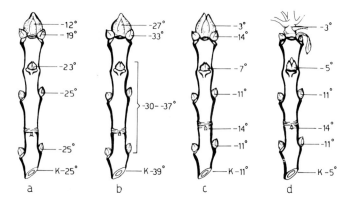

Fig. 17.12. Variations in cold resistance of terminal and lateral buds of *Fraxinus ornus* at various times during the year. (A) At end of November before severe frosts; (B) during a winter period of frost; (C) at initiation of bud swelling in April; (D) at time of bud opening in mid-April. The temperatures are those at which the buds can withstand freezing. The values with the symbol K are critical temperatures for frost hardiness of the cambium. From Mair (1968).

complication is that different organs vary in frost resistance. Roots normally are the most sensitive part of a tree to cold in winter and they do not harden more than a few degrees Celsius. Leaves of deciduous trees also do not harden to cold. Vegetative buds that begin to open in the spring are very tender and are especially susceptible to frost injury, but unopened buds may also be killed when large and sudden temperature drops occur. The susceptibility of buds to frost injury is correlated with the degree of bud advancement in the spring; the more developed the bud the greater are its chances of being killed by spring frosts. Mair (1968) found that terminal buds of *Fraxinus ornus* twigs were more frost resistant during the winter, and lost their frost resistance earlier in the spring, than the less-developed lateral buds that opened later in the spring (Fig. 17.12). Severe winters often are disastrous to a fruit or seed crop because of the high susceptibility of flower buds and young conelets to frost injury (Parker, 1965; Zasada, 1971). In Douglas-fir female buds were more susceptible than male buds or vegetative buds to frost injury (Timmis, 1977). In stems, the living xylem parenchyma and pith cells develop less frost resistance than bark cells, including those of the cambium, phloem, cortex, and epidermis (Potter, 1939). It is possible to cold harden one branch of a tree independently of the others, although there is evidence that the warm branches supply a factor to the chilled branch which prevents complete hardening (Timmis and Worrall, 1974).

Development of Cold Hardiness. According to Weiser (1970), cold-hardy woody plants typically undergo three sequential stages of acclimation to cold. The first stage, which is already underway in the autumn before the first frost occurs (Fig. 17.13), involves the cessation of growth and metabolic changes that condition the plant to respond to low temperature during the next phase of acclimation. The actual increase in frost resistance during the first phase is relatively minor. It is set in motion by

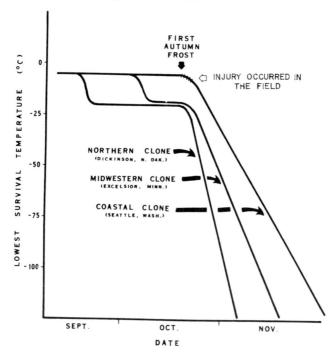

Fig. 17.13. Comparison of seasonal patterns of cold resistance in the living bark of three climatic races of red-osier dogwood that were grown in the field in Minnesota. From Weiser (1970). Copyright 1970 by the American Association for the Advancement of Science.

decreasing day length stopping growth and possibly by formation of a translocatable hardiness-promoting factor (Weiser, 1970).

The second state of acclimation to cold is induced by freezing or near-freezing temperatures, and neither photoperiod nor translocatable factors are involved. During this stage changes occur in sugars, proteins, amino acids, nucleic acids, and organic acids, and the plants develop resistance to freezing.

The third stage of acclimation is triggered by very low temperatures (in the range of −30° to −50°C). Some plants in this stage can sometimes withstand temperatures as low as −200°C. However, the capacity to withstand such low temperatures is easily lost by only a few hours of thawing. This final phase of acclimation appears to be largely a physical process involving the binding of water. According to Weiser (1970), the water in cells in this final phase is bound so strongly that it resists dehydration and reduces the amount of water available for destructive crystallization.

The overall patterns of development of frost hardiness are similar for climatic races of the same species grown in the same location, but differences occur among them in the timing of acclimation (see Fig. 17.13).

Cold Hardiness in Relation to Dormancy.   There is some question whether the attainment of deep dormancy in plants is a prerequisite to the development of frost hardiness. However, Weiser (1970) concluded that the major factor in the induction of frost hardiness appeared to be the cessation of growth rather than the development of dormancy, because low temperatures can stop growth and promote hardiness without necessarily inducing dormancy. Furthermore, some species of southern pines develop dormancy but do not tolerate very low temperatures.

Most temperate zone species enter winter dormancy before they become cold hardy. For example, eastern white pine in southern Canada was dormant by September and the dormant condition could only be broken by prolonged chilling. During chilling, cold hardiness increased to a maximum by early December, at which time the chilling requirement also was satisfied (Glerum, 1976). Some species, including the southern pines, become dormant but never acquire tolerance to low temperatures. On the other hand, Glerum (1976) suggested that a distinction should be made between species that must become winter dormant in order to attain maximum cold hardiness and those that lack this requirement. Sometimes there is evidence that growth processes begin before cold hardiness is entirely lost.

Physiological Changes during Development of Cold Hardiness.   During acclimation of plant tissues to cold, changes occur in the concentrations of sugars, proteins, amino acids, nucleic acids, and lipids. Hydration of tissues is reduced and permeability of membranes increases. Some of these changes, alone or in combination, have been causally related to frost hardiness by some investigators (Weiser, 1970).

There is evidence that sugars play an important role in the mechanism of frost hardiness. In most species sugars normally increase in the autumn as plants become frost hardy and they decrease in the spring as hardiness is lost. To a large extent the increase in sugars is correlated with starch digestion (see Chapter 7). In some plants, any treatment that increases the sugar content also increases frost hardiness (Yoshida and Sakai, 1967). The kinds of sugars that accumulate during the development of frost hardiness vary among species, but an increase in sucrose is most common. Sakai (1960) found wide variations in the specific sugars that increased during frost hardiness of 18 species of woody plants, and frost hardening was not consistently correlated with any one sugar. Sugars may increase frost hardiness: (1) by depressing the freezing point; (2) by accumulating in vacuoles and decreasing the amount of ice formed, thereby also decreasing freeze-induced cell dehydration; and (3) by being metabolized in the protoplasm, producing various protective changes that are not fully understood (Levitt, 1972).

Correlation between development of frost hardiness and an increase in sugar content has been demonstrated for a wide variety of orchard trees, forest trees, and ornamental woody plants. Sakai (1962) showed that if the chilling of parenchyma cells was not accompanied by an increase in sucrose concentration, they could not be hardened further by chilling. He concluded that low temperature itself, although it induced hardiness, had no direct effect on increase in hardiness, the accompanying increase in sugars in cells being the primary factor in frost hardiness. However, other investigators reported that the frost hardiness of some species was not strongly correlated with sugar content. For example, frost hardiness of poplar, English ivy, and Mediterranean evergreens was negligibly or not at all correlated with an increase in sugars (Sakai and

Yoshida, 1968; Steponkus and Lanphear, 1968; Pellett and White, 1969; Larcher, 1954).

Various investigators have demonstrated a strong correlation between cold hardiness and soluble protein content. Changes in soluble proteins may involve an increase in water-binding proteins that could decrease free cellular water. This would render the formation of intracellular ice during late stages of acclimation to cold less likely (Brown and Bixby, 1975).

Siminovitch and Briggs (1949, 1953) found that the amount of water-soluble proteins of black locust bark increased in the autumn, with the development of hardiness, and declined in the spring, when hardiness was lost. Similarly, Pomeroy *et al.* (1970) found a close relation in both needles and bark of eastern white pine between rapid changes in hardiness and seasonal fluctuation in protein nitrogen. Brown and Bixby (1975) followed soluble and insoluble protein concentrations during induction of freezing tolerance in black locust stem tissues. The concentration of soluble protein remained rather constant during the early stages of acclimation, but it increased significantly during later stages. The concentration of insoluble protein did not change materially during the induction of frost hardiness.

According to Levitt (1972), the initial stages of frost hardening, down to killing temperatures of about $-30°C$, may take place without an appreciable increase in soluble proteins. However, for an increase in frost hardiness at temperatures below $-30°C$, an increase in soluble proteins may be required. Some investigators (e.g., Sakai, 1962; Pellett and White, 1969) did not find the development of cold hardiness to be correlated with soluble proteins. Levitt (1972) believes that the discrepancies often were due to artifacts associated with different methods used in extracting proteins and places emphasis on the formation of proteins with hydrophilic bonds.

The concentration of amino acids often changes during frost hardening and dehardening. However, such changes generally are poorly correlated with frost hardening, in part because amino acids are rapidly converted to proteins. Parker (1963) did not find a consistent seasonal variation in the amino acids and amides of eastern white pine bark. Li *et al.* (1965) noted that certain amino acids (aspartate, glutamate, alanine, valine, and glycine) decreased during frost hardening of red-osier dogwood; others (glutamine, α-aminobutyrate, phenylalanine, leucine, and isoleucine) increased; and still others (serine, threonine, asparagine, β-alanine, and cystine) fluctuated in amount. In contrast to other amino acids, proline accumulates rather consistently during development of frost hardiness.

Substantial increases in RNA were found before or during development of cold hardiness in black locust and red-osier dogwood (Siminovitch, 1963; Li and Weiser, 1969). There was, however, no corresponding increase in DNA. Li and Weiser (1969) suggested that increases in nucleic acids represented an initial step in the anabolism of carbohydrates, amino acids, proteins, lipids, and phosphate compounds that induced frost hardiness.

A number of early investigators reported an autumn increase and spring decrease in plant lipids. Some of these reports were erroneous because they were based on the use of stains that accumulated in phenolic compounds as well as in fats and oils (Parker,

1963). However, subsequent studies with improved methodology also indicate that plants accumulate lipids during frost hardening. In black locust the increase is confined to phospholipids (Siminovitch et al., 1968). The degree of unsaturation of fatty acids also increases with acclimation to frost (Levitt, 1972). Some investigators have attributed chilling injury at temperatures above 0°C to phase changes in the lipid components of cell membranes that affect their permeability (Alden and Hermann, 1971; Lyons, 1973).

Effects of High Temperature

Exposure to relatively high temperatures often causes reduced growth and injury in trees. Heat injury may be direct or indirect. Direct injury is induced by very brief exposure to heat, with the plant responding during actual heating or immediately thereafter. Injury may also progress for as much as 1 day or even longer following the period of heat stress. By comparison, indirect injury by high temperature occurs slowly and may not be apparent for many hours or even days after exposure to high temperature. Indirect injury may also result from unfavorable effects of high temperature on physiological processes such as photosynthesis and respiration.

Levitt (1972) stated that the mechanism of heat injury usually depends on the temperature range in which it occurs, injury induced by the 15°–40°C range being indirect; but that in the 45°–60°C range being direct. At temperatures higher than 60°C injury occurs because of the breakdown of proteins.

Direct Effects of High Temperature.

Direct heat injury is relatively rare compared to the large amount of direct low-temperature or frost injury. Perhaps the greatest danger of heat injury occurs to seedlings growing in soil exposed to the sun, because the surface layer of exposed soil may reach temperatures well in excess of 60°C. Excessive heating of stems near the soil surface sometimes causes stem lesions that are known as stem girdle or heat canker. Hartley (1918) described sunken stem lesions in young conifer seedlings in a Nebraska nursery, which he termed "white spot." This type of injury is most prevalent on the south side of stems and resembles damping-off injury except that the spots are lighter in color and restricted to above-ground tissues.

Another type of lesion caused by drying out of the cambium and inner bark is known as sunscald or "bark scorch." Sunscald usually is found on south and southwest sides of stems of smooth-barked, older trees that have been transplanted or exposed by thinning. The large lesions may extend for several feet up the stem. Often long, dead strips of bark peel off and expose the sapwood. Sunscald degrades logs and provides an entrance for insects and fungi, which cause further deterioration. Daubenmire (1974) believes that sunscald is caused primarily by large temperature fluctuations rather than by high temperatures alone. As a precaution against sunscald, arborists often wrap stems of transplanted trees with paper tape or burlap or spray them with latex or wax. Sunscald of fruits also occurs and is of serious concern to horticulturists.

The thermal death point of most active plant cells varies from 50° to 60°C. However, lethal temperatures vary with species, age of tissue, and especially with the length of exposure to high temperatures. Lorenz (1939) found that the cortical parenchyma cells of seedlings of several species of angiosperms and gymnosperms were killed within 30 min when exposed to temperatures between 57° and 59°C, but only 1 min of exposure at 65° to 69°C was necessary to kill cells. Shirley (1936) concluded that resistance to heat increased with increasing age and size of the seedlings. He also reported that tops were more resistant than roots. Differences in resistance to fire injury probably are related more to differences in the insulating effects of bark than to differences in the heat tolerance of protoplasm. Protein denaturation appears to be the most important cause of heat injury, and thermostability of proteins is the basis of heat tolerance (Levitt, 1972).

Indirect Effect of High Temperature. High temperatures are unfavorable for the growth of many species because apparent photosynthesis begins to decline rapidly after a critical high temperature is reached, although respiration usually continues to increase above that temperature (see Fig. 5.18). Exposure of plants to a high temperature may, therefore, result in depletion of carbohydrate reserves and sometimes death. Indirect injury may also be associated with formation of toxic compounds, production of biochemical lesions, and breakdown of protoplasmic proteins (Levitt, 1972).

High temperatures also injure and often kill trees by desiccation resulting from high transpiration rates. A rapid increase in transpiration with rising temperature may be expected because of the direct effect of temperature on the diffusion constant of water and because of an increase in the vapor pressure gradient between the leaf and air. Such indirect high temperature injury is promoted by prolonged droughts or hot, dry winds (Kozlowski, 1976a). In California, hot winds cause two types of injury to citrus, called "windburn" and "scorch" (Reed and Bartholomew, 1930). Leaves killed by windburn first wilt, then dry out rapidly and become brittle within 1 day. If the wind stops within a few hours, the wilted leaves sometimes regain turgor, but if desiccated to a critical level they do not recover. Scorch, the more common type of injury, does not involve a wilting stage. The leaves turn brown, become brittle within a few hours, and may remain attached to twigs for several weeks.

Wind

Wind is an omnipresent part of the environment and has both beneficial and harmful effects on plants and especially on trees, which, because of their height, are particularly exposed to its effects. In fact, a writer in the British journal, *Forestry* (Anonymous, 1967) stated that in many areas wind is the most important single factor in the success of forest plantations in Great Britain. Its effects are especially noticeable on windy coast lines and near the timber line in mountains. Trees exposed to steady winds from one direction tend to have one-sided crowns and sometimes even the stems are flattened because most of the cambial activity occurs on the leeward side of the trunk. Normally erect trees often become prostrate clumps near the timber line because exposed buds are killed by desiccation, damaged by ice particles, or broken off. Sometimes wind-borne ice or sand actually erodes away the bark on the windward side. Wind-borne salt spray also causes injury along sea coasts.

High winds and hurricanes often cause severe damage to forests by uprooting trees or breaking them off if they are too firmly rooted to be overturned. Uprooting is particularly prevalent in forests on shallow soils, in bogs where root penetration is limited by deficient aeration (Sanderson and Armstrong, 1978), or when the soil has been softened by rain prior to high wind.

Trunks of trees grown in dense stands lack the mechanical strength of those grown in the open, and trees left isolated by cutting are often damaged by wind. Probably the enlarged base or butt swell of many tree trunks is at least partly caused by swaying in the wind. It has been shown by various investigators that tree trunks fastened so they cannot sway in the wind grow less in diameter and are weaker than those allowed to sway. It also has been found that the stems of nursery-grown trees that are kept firmly staked grow taller, but produce less diameter growth and are less able to support themselves than stems allowed to sway in the wind. In fact, even shaking the stems of sweetgum seedlings for 30 sec daily produces seedlings with shorter, but stronger stems than are found on seedlings not shaken nor allowed to sway in the winds (Neel and Harris, 1971, 1972). The shaken trees also became dormant sooner than unshaken controls. The physiological basis for this response has not been established, but it may result from increased production of ethylene in swaying stems.

Air movement increases transpiration by decreasing the boundary layer resistance around leaves, but at the same time it increases the CO_2 supply for photosynthesis and lowers the leaf temperature. Often a breeze increases transpiration enough to cause a water deficit and stomatal closure; but the net result of these interacting effects sometimes is difficult to predict. The majority of the important tree species of the temperate zone have their pollen and seed distributed by wind. The numerous effects of wind on plants are discussed by Daubenmire (1974) and in more detail by Grace (1977).

Windbreaks and Shelterbelts

The use of belts of trees as windbreaks is an ancient custom in Europe and a more recent one in North America. The benefits on the leeward side of shelterbelts include decrease in soil erosion and dust storms, reduction in mechanical damage to plants, increase in crop yields, control of snowdrifting, improved cover and increased food supply for wildlife, and protection of livestock (Stoeckeler, 1962). Windbreaks have often been useful in preventing wind damage and wind-throw of forest trees and in protecting young trees in plantations and forest nurseries (Gloyne, 1976). Heisler and Herrington (1976) emphasized the benefits of using groups or belts of trees to modify microclimates in metropolitan areas so as to improve human comfort and reduce energy consumption in homes. Tree barriers are also useful in reducing vehicular noise in cities (Reethof and Heisler, 1976).

Wind speed decreases to a minimum at some distance behind a shelterbelt depending on species, height of the shelterbelt, and the extent of its penetrability to wind. A belt of trees that allows wind to go through it at a reduced velocity provides a lower degree of shelter beyond the belt than an impenetrable belt does, but the effect of a permeable belt extends over a greater distance. Usually a shelterbelt that is moderately permeable to wind provides the best shelter.

Microclimate

Because wind velocity and turbulence are reduced by shelterbelts the microclimate is greatly modified in the protected zone. Evaporation on the leeward side is appreciably decreased, often as much as 20 to 30%. The decrease in evaporation varies seasonally and is maximal in the summer and autumn, intermediate in spring, and least in winter. Radiation balance is not altered greatly by shelterbelts, except very close to the belt. Air temperatures usually are slightly higher on the leeward side during the day because transport of sensible heat is reduced, night temperatures are lower because temperature inversions are less likely to be disrupted by air turbulence. The danger of night frosts is somewhat higher in sheltered than in unsheltered regions. This danger is decreased if shelterbelts are partially penetrable to wind. Both the absolute and relative humidity of the climate near the ground are lowered on the lee side of shelterbelts. However, the effects on lowering of humidity are local and relatively small (about 0.5 to 1 mm absolute humidity and 2 to 3% relative humidity (Caborn, 1957)).

Shelterbelts significantly alter the local distribution of rain and snow. Inasmuch as rain is usually accompanied by wind a shelterbelt in a relatively exposed area intercepts rain so that more of it falls over the trees than at some distance from them. Hence, a "rain shadow" develops on the leeward side for a distance that varies with wind velocity. Despite increased rainfall near the tree belt less soil moisture is available to crops near the belt than beyond it because of rapid absorption of water by the extensive root systems of the closely spaced trees.

Shelterbelts trap drifting snow and the trapped snow adds to soil moisture recharge as the snowpack melts. Dense, wide shelterbelts tend to accumulate snow very close to the belt; narrow and permeable belts distribute snow much more uniformly on the leeward side. For example, shelterbelts with one or more rows of densely growing shrubs about 3 m high trapped almost all the snow in drifts 1.5 to 3 m deep within 10 to 25 m on the leeward side. By comparison, narrow belts of trees that had been pruned below and were permeable to wind distributed snow uniformly in a layer about ⅓ to ⅔ m deep for a distance of 200 to 400 m (Stoeckeler and Dortignac, 1941). In North America the trapping of snow by shelterbelts is important for crop growth from Nebraska northward.

Crop Yields

Shelterbelts usually increase crop yields on the leeward side. This is largely the result of increased soil moisture and lowered plant water stress because of reduced evaporation, higher humidity, and the added water of snowmelt. The large areas of trapped snow result in more extensive areas of unfrozen soil than in unprotected areas. This soil condition provides for better infiltration and decreases water loss by runoff in the spring.

The amount by which shelterbelts increase average crop yields varies greatly with the crop, region, the age and composition of the shelterbelt, and other factors. The increase in crop yield varies with distance from the belt. Crop yields are reduced in a narrow zone bordering the shelterbelt because of depletion of soil moisture and by shading of crops by the shelterbelt trees. This unproductive strip usually is not wider than approximately half the height of the shelterbelt. The harmful effects of competition for soil moisture adjacent to a shelterbelt can be counteracted by using tree species that root deeply, root pruning of established trees, cultivating deeply near the shelterbelt to prevent growth of lateral roots, and using only species that do not develop root suckers (Daubenmire, 1974).

Caborn (1957) summarized the voluminous literature showing that shelterbelts increased yields of a wide variety of crops in Europe and America from a few to several hundred percent. The beneficial effects of shelterbelts on crop yields decrease greatly during droughts. For example, in the Great Plains of the United States water stress was lower in plants protected by windbreaks only when soil moisture contents were relatively high. During droughts windbreaks increased water stress in crops (Frank *et al.*, 1977). More detailed discussions of the effects of shelterbelts on microclimate and yield of a variety of crops are available in the papers by Caborn (1957) and Stoeckeler (1962). Read (1964) has an excellent discussion of factors influencing selection of tree species as well as planting, spacing, and management of shelterbelt trees.

Competition

A young forest stand may contain several thousand trees per hectare, but less than 300 will remain in a mature forest, the others having succumbed to competition. To a considerable extent this reduction occurs as a result of competition for light above ground and for water and minerals below ground. As trees increase in size they require more space to accommodate their increasing photosynthetic surface and a larger volume of soil to supply the increasing need for water and minerals. Hence a given area of land can support fewer and fewer trees as they grow larger. The survivors are those that are most efficient physiologically and therefore grow most rapidly; or those that arrived first in the case of naturally seeded stands. Thus differences in the reaction of physiological processes to environmental changes produced by crowding are very important in determining success in competition.

In young, even-aged stands the trees are relatively evenly spaced and have crowns that are more or less similar in size and shape. However, as the trees grow larger the lower branches of all trees and the entire crowns of slower growing trees begin to be shaded. The resulting decrease in photosynthesis of the slower-growing trees reduces the supply of carbohydrates and possibly of hormones, causing a reduction in cambial activity and root growth. The reduction in root growth causes a reduction in the absorption of water and minerals, which further reduces synthetic processes and growth. Eventually the slower-growing, suppressed trees die from the combined effects of a deficiency in internal growth requirements including carbohydrates, hormones, water, and minerals.

In dominant trees the annual ring is quite narrow in the uppermost internode of stems (Fig. 17.14). Annual ring width then increases toward the base and becomes thickest at the stem height where there is maximum leaf volume. The annual ring narrows below the crown and thickens again near the stem base. In suppressed trees the entire annual ring is thinner than in dominant trees, with the point of maximum ring

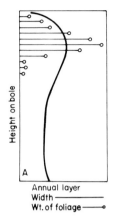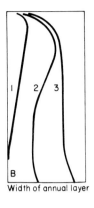

Annual layer
Width ————————
Wt. of foliage ————————○

Fig. 17.14. (A) Variations in the thickness of the annual ring at various stem heights. (B) Variations in thickness of the annual ring at various stem heights in suppressed (1), dominant (2), and open-grown (3) trees. From Farrar (1961).

thickness at a greater relative stem height. Below the point of maximum thickness the annual ring narrows rapidly. Often, very suppressed trees do not show any xylem increment at the base of the stem. In contrast to dominant and suppressed trees, open-grown trees usually develop a progressive increase in thickness of the annual ring from the height of maximum foliage down to the base of the stem. In competitive situations, the reduction in diameter growth and change in its distribution along the

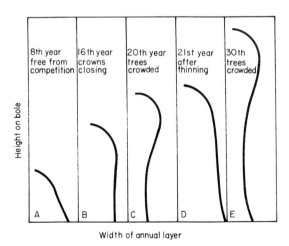

Width of annual layer

Fig. 17.15. Variations in thickness of the annual ring at various stem heights in plantation-grown conifers of varying age. (A) At 8 years, when crowns extend to the base of the tree; (B) crowns closing; (C) lower branches are dead; (D) shortly after thinning when crowns have been exposed to full light; (E) competition is again severe and crowns have closed. The horizontal scale is greatly exaggerated. From Farrar (1961).

stem are caused by late initiation and early cessation of cambial activity, as well as by a decrease in the growth rate (Kozlowski and Peterson, 1962; Winget and Kozlowski, 1965b). During the development of managed (periodically thinned) plantations of forest trees, predictable changes occur in the amount and distribution of cambial growth, as is shown in Fig. 17.15.

Diameter growth is much more sensitive than height growth to competition (Bormann, 1965) and especially to the relation of crown size to the length of stem that is devoid of branches. Bassett (1966) determined the amounts and duration of diameter growth of various crown classes of 30-year-old loblolly pine trees at breast height during each of five successive growing seasons in the southern United States. Whereas dominant and codominant trees continued cambial growth into October and a few into November, suppressed trees stopped growing by late July. On the average, dominant and codominant trees grew during 80 and 70%, respectively, of each of five seasons. Diameter increase of large-crowned trees occurred continuously from early March through June, and then recurrently during two-thirds of the rest of the growing season. Intermediate and suppressed trees increased in diameter during only 53 and 28%, respectively, of the growing period.

Allelopathy

In addition to competing for light, water, and minerals, plants inhibit seed germination and growth of neighboring plants by releasing a variety of toxic chemicals, sometimes called allelochems. The direct or indirect deleterious effect of one plant on another through the production of allelochems is called allelopathy.

The allelochems include a wide variety of compounds such as organic acids, lactones, quinones, terpenoids, steroids, phenolic compounds, cinnamic acid and its derivatives, flavonoids, tannins, and alkaloids. Allelochems are released by the following mechanisms (Rice, 1974):

1. Volatilization: Examples are *Artemisia* spp., which produce essential oils that inhibit seed germination and seedling growth of many species, and *Eucalyptus* spp., which produce volatile terpenes.

2. Leaching: Growth inhibitors are leached out of living or dead leaves of many species. Perhaps the best known allelochem is juglone in *Juglans*. It is washed into the soil from leaves, fruits, and roots and inhibits the growth of a variety of herbaceous and woody plants (Brooks, 1951). Release of allelochems by leaching from leaves has also been demonstrated in *Encelia farinosa, Eucalpytus globulus, Platanus occidentalis,* and *Rhus copallina.*

3. Exudation from Roots: Various toxic compounds are released from roots and can be absorbed by adjacent plants. Species known to release such compounds include *Araucaria cunninghamia, Pinus elliottii* and *Flindersia australis* (Bevage, 1968).

4. Decay of Plant Tissues: Release of allelochems during the decay of plant residues, either directly or by activity of microorganisms, has been demonstrated for such

species as *Artemisia absinthium, Rhus glabra, Platanus occidentalis,* and *Celtis laevigata.*

Although allelopathic effects sometimes are important under natural conditions, considerable caution should be exercised in interpreting the ecological significance of such toxins on the basis of laboratory experiments. Lerner and Evenari (1961), for example, found in laboratory experiments that leaf extracts of *Eucalyptus rostrata* contained substances that inhibited seed germination. However, tests of soil from beneath *Eucalyptus* trees showed that the allelopathic chemicals did not accumulate in the field to inhibitory levels. Under field conditions accumulation of allelochems is modified by such factors as soil moisture and soil type, and they often are destroyed by soil microflora. For a good discussion of allelopathy the reader is referred to the book by Rice (1974).

The Replant Problem

The difficulties encountered in replanting orchards and vineyards with trees of the same species are sometimes attributed to allelopathic reactions. For example, hundreds of thousands of peach replants have died prematurely in the southeastern United States and this has been attributed to toxic products of peach root decay and to substances released by injured roots (Proebsting and Gilmore, 1941; Israel *et al.,* 1973). However, tree survival can be increased by deep plowing or subsoiling before planting to improve aeration, and by soil fumigation, which destroys nematodes and fungi.

The replant problem has been observed in many kinds of fruits, including apple, peach, other stone fruits, citrus, and grapes. The causes probably are various and, in addition to effects of allelochems, include attacks by nematodes, fungi—such as *Phytopthora, Clitocybe,* and *Armillaria*—and poor drainage and soil aeration. In California and Florida, nematodes and *Phytopthora* are often associated with decline and death of citrus trees, and soil fumigation usually is beneficial (Ducharme, 1977). Soil fumigation improves the growth of replants in old vineyards and peach orchards and is beginning to be used for apples. In these cases it appears the nematodes and fungi are more important than allelochems in causing replant difficulties.

Thus far, little attention has been given to the replant problem in forestry, although attacks by *Armillaria* in plantations have been reported all over the northern hemisphere. It is likely that modern forestry practices, in which cutover land is immediately replanted to the same or similar species, will soon encounter replant problems. In fact there already are reports that the second crop of Monterey pine is not growing as rapidly as the first crop on land in southern Australia.

Plant Succession

The disturbance or elimination of a stable plant community by natural or artificial means is followed by plant succession that leads toward progressive restoration of a mature and stable climax ecosystem (Odum, 1971). For example, *Andropogon* grass is dominant on abandoned fields in the Piedmont Plateau of the southeastern United

States. This grass stage may be overtopped by either loblolly or shortleaf pine by the fifth year. In 10 to 15 years closed stands of pine are common. The understory of young pine stands is invariably composed of broad-leaved trees, and pine is naturally thinned out as it reaches overmaturity in 70 to 80 years. The climax community of broad-leaved trees will undergo major change only if there are significant environmental changes.

Plant succession is characterized by an orderly and gradual replacement of species, an increase in biomass, and the accumulation of organic matter. As the ecosystem continues to develop, its capacity to hold mineral nutrients in the biomass increases.

In early successional stages the rate of total photosynthesis exceeds the rate of community respiration, but in mature ecosystems the ratio of photosynthesis to respiration approaches 1. Hence, with increasing age the energy fixed by a stand tends toward an equilibrium, with the energy being used for maintenance rather than for increased dry weight production.

In the past much emphasis was given to the importance of competition for light, water, and minerals in causing the replacement of species during plant succession. However, considerable evidence is accumulating that allelopathy is also involved to various degrees in succession.

In the California chaparral, the competitive effects of shrubs plus the chemical inhibitions exerted by them prevent the germination of seeds and development of herbs. Fires also release the allelopathic effects of shrubs by eliminating sources of toxins and destroying toxins in the soil and litter (Rice, 1974).

Many forest trees are variously involved in allelopathic interactions during succession. For example, heather *(Calluna vulgaris)* impedes the establishment of Norway spruce by inhibiting formation of mycorrhizae (Handley, 1963), and leachable allelochems from dead bracken fern prevent the establishment of Douglas-fir (Stewart, 1975). In California the annual vegetation adjacent to naturalized stands of *Eucalpytus camaldulensis* is greatly inhibited by allelochems in the litter (Del Moral and Muller, 1970). Some forest trees, such as ailanthus and sassafras, remain in pure stands for a long time as a result of the action of the allelochems they produce (Voigt and Mergen, 1962; Gant and Clebsch, 1975).

CULTURAL PRACTICES AND VEGETATIVE GROWTH

Cultural practices generally attempt to improve the environment for tree growth, and they are effective only if they increase the overall efficiency of the physiological processes that control vegetative and reproductive growth. For example, irrigation helps maintain the turgid tissues necessary for growth, resulting in increased leaf area. Applications of fertilizers provide the minerals required in building new tissues and in various biochemical processes (see Chapter 10). When a stand of trees is thinned, the amount of growing space for both the roots and the crowns of residual trees is increased. The rate of growth is increased or maintained after thinning primarily because the greater availability of light, water, and minerals to remaining trees favors increased rates of photosynthesis as well as production of hormonal growth regulators. A less immediate but very important effect is the greater rate of photosynthesis that results from an increased photosynthetic surface as the crown increases in size.

Thinning of Forest Stands

After thinning a stand, the released trees respond to the more favorable environmental conditions by increasing crown width and leaf growth, and by increasing branch survival and size. The greater leaf area is accompanied by increased photosynthesis and general physiological activity of the crown, which in turn is followed by an increase in cambial growth and the redistribution of xylem increment along the stem. However, height growth usually is not greatly affected over a wide range of thinning.

Thinning produces a more tapered tree trunk because it is accompanied by a greater increase in cambial activity and radial growth toward the base of the tree than in the crown (Fig. 17.16). This redistribution of growth may be misleading because the increase in diameter growth at breast height after thinning may give an erroneous impression concerning the actual increase in total volume (Farrar, 1961). Later, as the crowns and root systems expand, the rate of increase of total volume accelerates as

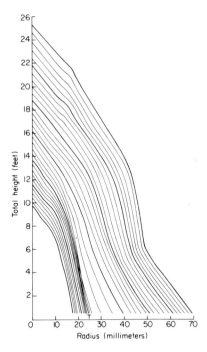

Fig. 17.16. Effect of thinning closely grown ponderosa pine trees on cambial growth of residual trees. Before thinning the annual increment was greatest in the upper stem. After thinning the annual increment became greater in the lower stem. From Myers (1963).

more xylem is formed along the entire bole. Still later, as competition again develops, maximum radial growth again becomes greatest near the base of the crown. In general, the size of the crown strongly affects stem taper, with stems of open-grown, large-crowned trees being more tapered than those of trees with small crowns in closed stands.

Strongly suppressed trees have small crowns and nearly cylindrical stems (Larson, 1963b). If trees are spaced too far apart in plantations they tend to have too much taper as well as too many knots, caused by the retention of lower branches. Thinning should occur before growth is greatly suppressed, and large increases in the diameter growth of the trees left after thinning generally indicate that the stand should have been thinned earlier.

Pruning

Pruning of woody plants has been practiced for centuries and was even recorded in the Bible. Foresters, arborists, and horticulturists prune trees routinely, but with somewhat different objectives. Foresters prune trees primarily to produce knot-free lumber. This is particularly desirable for gymnosperms such as spruces, eastern white pine, and Douglas-fir, because they do not prune naturally and may retain lower branches for many years. Arborists often remove branches to provide better landscape effects; to prevent crowding; to avoid street wires; and to eliminate diseased, mechanically injured, or insect-infested branches. Orchardists prune to control tree size and form and to open up the crown, allowing the penetration of light and facilitating spraying and fruit picking, all of which are intended to improve fruit production.

The removal of live branches of forest trees decreases the amount of photosynthetic surface, but it also decreases the amount of respiring tissue. Many suppressed basal branches with only a few leaves consume in respiration all the carbohydrates produced in photosynthesis and do not contribute carbohydrates for stem growth (Kozlowski, 1971b). Removal of such branches is obviously desirable because it will not lessen stem growth and it will produce knot-free lumber. Removal of dead branches does not affect growth but it reduces knots and decreases attacks by fungi. Height growth proceeds at the expense of carbohydrates and hormones produced in the upper crown, and a large part of the crown can be removed by pruning from below without appreciably inhibiting height growth. As may be seen in Fig. 17.17, removal of 30 to 70% of the live crown had little effect on the height growth of red pine, and this is also true for loblolly pine.

The influence of removal of live branches on xylem increment and stem form is the reverse of the effect of thinning. Thinning a stand stimulates radial growth at the base of residual trees, but pruning tends to inhibit cambial growth at the stem base, because the accretion of xylem following branch removal becomes concentrated in the upper stem. Pruning, therefore, tends to reduce stem taper, but the degree of reduction depends on pruning severity and timing as well as on the crown characteristics of the tree prior to pruning, the effect being greater on open-grown trees than those in closed stands. The more branches that are removed, the greater is the decrease in xylem

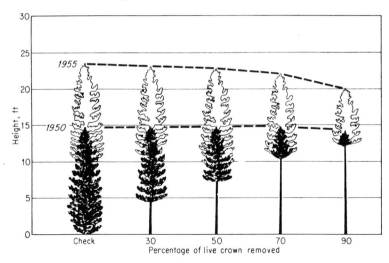

Fig. 17.17. The effect of removal of various percentages of live crown on height growth of red pine. From Slabaugh (1957).

production and the upward displacement of growth increment leading to a decrease in taper (Larson, 1963a). The correction of stem form by branch pruning of strongly tapered trees is also modified by the age of trees, stems of old trees being less susceptible than those of young ones to such modification. The failure of pruning experiments to alter stem form often has been traced to the removel of too few branches or to an excessive delay before pruning. As was emphasized by Larson (1963a,b), tree stems become more cylindrical with increasing age and with greater stand density. Thus, either a delay in pruning or removal of only a few branches from trees in closed stands may not be followed by noticeable changes in stem form.

Pruning experiments on loblolly pine in which the remaining crown was 50, 35, or 20% of the tree height demonstrated that the crown size of pruned trees had a marked effect on the amount of diameter growth below the crown but a relatively minor effect on growth within the crown (Fig. 17.18). Experiments by Labyak and Schumacher (1954) indicated that a crown occupying one-third of the tree height supports normal stem growth in loblolly pine. In addition to altering the amount of xylem production, pruning also tends to alter wood quality. In heavily pruned trees with smaller crowns there is a more abrupt latewood transition down the stem, and an increase in the percentage of latewood in the lower stem (Larson, 1969b).

Modern orchard practice is moving from the use of large, isolated trees to the use of smaller trees planted at a much greater density per hectare in "hedgerows." Such trees can be pruned by large machines that mow off the projecting branches along the sides and on top, followed by some hand pruning. Late-summer pruning of peaches is being investigated because it results in less vigorous vegetative growth. Some day, the use of chemical growth retardants may partly replace mechanical pruning. Readers are referred to the section on chemical growth retardants later in this chapter for more details.

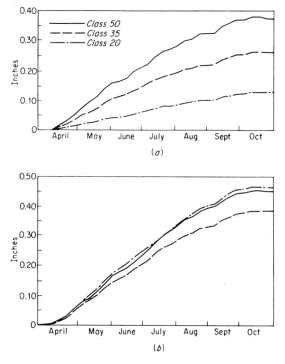

Fig. 17.18. Effect on diameter growth of pruning loblolly pine trees to various percentages of their height. (A) Diameter growth at breast height (135 cm). (B) Diameter growth at 80% of tree height. Class 50 trees were pruned to 50% of their height, class 35 trees to 35% of their height, and class 20 trees to 20% of their height. Reducing crown size decreased diameter growth much more at breast height than at 80% of height. From Young and Kramer (1952).

INSECTS AND DISEASES

Many insects and diseases adversely affect growth of woody plants by altering the rates and balances of physiological processes. Insects affect plant processes by chewing, sucking fluids from tissues, causing galls to form, and by pollinating flowers. They also affect growth and physiological processes by acting as vectors of some of the most important fungal, bacterial, and viral diseases of trees. Disease symptoms vary widely and may be expressed as color changes, necrosis, vein clearing, wilting, and leaf spots on leaves; atrophy, hypertrophy, and rotting of tissues; and dieback or abscission of plant parts. Malformations such as cankers, galls, intumescences, witches'-brooms, rosettes, fasciation, and leaf crinkling or rolling commonly indicate a diseased condition.

An initial insect or fungus attack often sets in motion or accelerates a sequential and very complicated series of metabolic disturbances, rather than a simple change in only one process, such as photosynthesis, as is sometimes supposed. For example, insect defoliation results in depression of photosynthesis and a decrease in transport of carbo-hydrates and hormonal growth regulators to the lower stem and roots. These changes adversely affect cambial growth and, sequentially, root growth. Root disease at first may decrease the absorption of water and minerals. Decreased water absorption sub-sequently leads to stomatal closure, then to reduced carbohydrate production and translocation, and a reduced supply of hormonal growth regulators. This sequence of events eventually further decreases root growth and the related physiological processes and can lead to death of the tree. It is important to reemphasize that the physiological impact of a localized attack in one part of a tree by a forest pest usually is transmitted to distant organs and tissues, often in a complex manner that eventually affects the whole tree. The effects of insect attacks or fungus disease may or may not be drastic, depending on the extent to which various processes are disturbed and on the physiolog-ical well-being of plants at the time of attack (Kozlowski, 1969).

Insects

It often has been stated that the growth reduction and mortality of trees are propor-tional to the amount of foliage removed by insects (Church, 1949). This statement should be viewed with caution because both the growth responses and mortality of defoliated trees also depend on other factors such as species, time of defoliation, tree vigor, site, soil moisture, and climatic conditions.

Defoliation of woody plants by insects usually inhibits growth much more than does removal of an equivalent amount of foliage by branch pruning. This is because pruning selectively removes only the physiologically inefficient lower branches, whereas many insects remove foliage in the upper crown, which is more important in synthesizing carbohydrates and hormonal growth regulators. Furthermore, some insects preferen-tially defoliate trees that are lacking in vigor and have small carbohydrate reserves (Kozlowski, 1973).

Marked differences exist among species in response to insect defoliation. Angio-sperms usually withstand defoliation better than gymnosperms. Angiosperms and de-ciduous gymnosperms usually survive a single severe defoliation, probably because the destroyed foliage is rapidly replaced by new, leaf-bearing shoots. Two severe defolia-tions in the same year may kill angiosperms, but many can survive a single annual defoliation repeated for many years. Evergreen gymnosperms often are killed by one complete defoliation, especially if it occurs late in the growing season. However, evergreen gymnosperms of the temperate zone generally can survive one complete removal of old needles prior to the beginning of the growing season (Kulman, 1971). There are, however, differences in the growth responses of pines, with recurrently flushing pines such as loblolly withstanding severe defoliation much better than red and other pines, which usually produce only one annual flush of shoot growth.

Partial defoliation may inhibit cambial growth in the same season, or there may be a lag in response, depending on the plant species, severity of defoliation, time of its occurrence, and other factors. According to Belyea (1952), defoliation of current-year foliage in gymnosperms must occur for more than one season before growth is severely decreased, but growth reduction in deciduous trees often occurs shortly after they are defoliated.

Once beyond the sapling stage, trees apparently acquire some resistance to attacks by certain insects. However, as trees become overmature their physiological activity is reduced and they again become subject to widespread attack by some insects. It cannot be stressed too strongly that a physiological change in a tree commonly is a prerequisite to insect attack. The age at which trees are most likely to be attacked reflects very specific conditions that predispose them to invasion. Such predisposing characteristics vary widely among species and many involve threshold levels of flowering, cambial activity, resin flow, critical sapwood moisture content, and products of physiologically altered tissues. For example, increasing water stress and decreased resin exudation pressure seems to be favorable to attacks by bark beetles (Lorio and Hodges, 1968; Vité, 1961).

There are many examples in the literature of the increasing susceptibility of trees, as they grow older, to attack by certain insects, and only a few examples will be given here. Most bark beetles favor mature or overmature trees. Some species of bark beetles may show individual preferences for trees of specific age groups. For example, *Dendroctonus brevicomis* attacks old trees of low vigor, *Dendroctonus monticolae* attacks much younger trees, and *Ips confusus* prefers relatively young trees or the tops of old ones (Rudinsky, 1962). The bronze birch borer *(Agrilus anxius)* prefers mature yellow birch, white birch, and gray birch trees. Epidemics of spruce budworm *(Choristoneura fumiferana)* usually are associated with mature stands of balsam fir. In this species, frequent and abundant production of staminate flowers, a characteristic of old age, appears to favor population increases of the spruce budworm.

Diseases

Whereas some disease fungi are found only in very young trees, others favor old trees and those lacking in vigor. However, the relations of fungus pathogens to host susceptibility often are very complex and many diseases, such as rusts, are even favored by vigorous growth of the host. According to Hart (1949), physiological vigor in trees, which often decreases with increasing age, usually increases susceptibility to obligate parasites and decreases susceptibility to facultative parasites. Disease incidence can in some cases be related to more specific physiological processes of the host than the several involved in the term "vigor." For example, both nitrogen and carohydrate metabolism of trees affect resistance of wood to decay. Many decay and staining fungi develop preferentially in tissues with high nitrogen contents. Changes in the reserve food contents of parenchyma cells during aging also affect susceptibility of sapwood to certain fungi.

The invasion of forest trees by fungi is complicated and may involve aggressiveness of the parasite, availability of nutrients at the infection site, and the presence of inhibitors of toxic substances produced by the host or parasite (Hare, 1966). The specific nature of disease resistance may involve morphological exclusion of the parasite, restriction of growth after entry, or destruction after entry. Many trees produce a variety of antifungal and antibacterial compounds which endow them with various degrees of disease resistance. For example, toxic extractable substances deposited during the formation of heartwood make some trees, or parts of trees, quite resistant to certain fungi. The phenols appear to be most important, but specific inhibitory compounds vary greatly among species. For example, tannins, pinosylvins, and chlorogenic acid occur in temperate zone trees, while in tropical trees various alkaloids, rotenoids, and saponins may contribute to disease resistance. Some compounds, which individually do not offer much disease resistance, may act synergistically and together provide resistance.

Some well-known fungal diseases are associated with definite ages of trees. "Damping-off," or death of plants caused by fungal infection of stems at the soil surface, is mostly confined to seedlings. Susceptibility decreases rapidly with increasing age, as tissues harden during periods of days to weeks. Needle rusts of gymnosperms rarely cause damage to old trees. The *Cronartium* stem rusts generally do the most damage to trees in seedling, sapling, and small-pole size classes (Patton, 1962). However, in a few instances, as in sweetfern rust, the actual damage to trees is greatest when the trees approach maturity. Hence a clear distinction should be made between the age of the host when susceptibility is greatest and the age when the greatest damage finally occurs.

Although cankers are most obvious on old trees, infection usually occurs before trees are 20 years old. Butt heart rots are most common in trunks of old and large trees, because the inner heartwood is less resistant to decay than the outer heartwood.

POLLUTION

Because of the increasing population and industrialization, plants are affected by a wide array of growth-inhibiting substances that contaminate the air, water, and soil. These substances include gases, acids, particulates, and radioactive materials.

Air pollutants appear to be relatively nonspecific agents that have many sites of action. They inhibit many enzyme systems and metabolic processes. The effect of a pollutant depends on its concentration in cells, as well as on cell metabolism. Most air pollutants decrease the photosynthetic process directly or indirectly, by causing loss of photosynthetic tissues (e.g., leaf abscission, chlorosis, necrosis) and by affecting stomatal aperture. Several investigators have confirmed the inhibitory effects of air pollutants on photosynthesis (see Kozlowski and Keller, 1966, for references). Exposure of trees to SO_2 in the morning is more injurious than exposure in the afternoon, suggesting that leaf turgor and stomatal aperture (greater in the morning) are important factors controlling SO_2 uptake.

The major air pollutants are sulfur dioxide; ozone; fluoride; peroxyacyl nitrates (PAN); oxides of nitrogen; and particulates such as cement kiln dusts, lead particles, soot, magnesium oxide, iron oxide, foundry dusts, and sulfuric acid aerosols (Mudd and Kozlowski, 1975). Air pollutants are often classified as primary or secondary. Primary pollutants are those originating at the source in a toxic form. Examples are sulfur dioxide and hydrogen fluoride. Secondary pollutants are those formed by chemical or photochemical reactions subsequent to their release from the source. Examples include such photochemical pollutants as peroxyacetyl nitrate (PAN) and ozone (O_3) which are formed by photochemical reactions in sunlight.

Effects of Air Pollution

The adverse effects of pollution on woody plants are extremely variable and range from subtle internal physiological changes to growth inhibition, visible injury, and death of the plants. The accumulation of toxic substances often causes marked changes in the structure and function of natural ecosystems (Woodwell, 1970). In addition to affecting ecosystems directly, atmospheric pollutants have some long-term effects on

Fig. 17.19.   Sulfur dioxide injury on pear leaves *(upper)* and Scotch pine needles *(lower).* Photos courtesy of T. C. Weidensaul.

plants by influencing CO_2 content, light intensity, temperature, and precipitation (Wenger *et al.*, 1971).

Pollution injury is commonly classed as acute, chronic, or hidden. Acute injury, which involves the death of tissue, occurs after a short-term, high level of pollution or when a plant is unusually sensitive. Chronic symptoms occur after exposure to low levels of pollution for a long time. Sometimes the physiological activity of affected plants is impaired before any external symptoms are visible. For this reason many investigators referred to "hidden," "invisible," or "physiological" injury of pollutants. As early as 1899 Sorauer and Ramann established three criteria for such invisible injury: (1) it involved a disturbance of the life of the plant that was eventually expressed as an effect on growth, (2) the disturbance was not evident to the naked eye, and (3) it was present where plants underwent prolonged exposure to concentrations of pollutants that did not produce visible markings. Changes in ultrastructure, such as alterations of the plasmalemma or chloroplast membranes, or both, precede visible symptoms. No standardized definition of hidden injury has been widely accepted. Rather, a wide variety of concepts and terms have been used.

The nature of pollution injury varies with the polluting substance. For example, SO_2 injury on broad-leaved trees is characterized by areas of injured tissues between the veins which stay green (Fig. 17.19), while classical ozone symptoms appear as flecking or stippling caused by dead tissue on the upper surface of the leaf. Usually only the palisade cells are affected. In gymnosperms, acute SO_2 injury involves reddish-brown discoloration of needle tips (Fig. 17.19). With continued fumigation the discoloration progresses toward the base of the needle. Acute ozone injury usually is characterized by death of the needle tip or the whole needle. Mild injury appears as chlorotic mottling of needles.

Effects of Combinations of Pollutants

Under natural conditions plants often are simultaneously exposed to more than one polluting substance. The effects of pollutant combinations can be less than, greater than, or equal to the additive effects of the single pollutants. When plants are injured by a combination of pollutants it usually is difficult to identify the pollutants involved. For example, injury from exposure to SO_2–NO_2 combinations often resembles that caused by ozone. The same environmental and plant factors that influence plant response to single pollutants also influence the response to pollutant combinations. Three additional variables affect plant response to pollutant combinations. These include (1) the concentration of each gas in the combination exposures with respect to the injury thresholds of the individual pollutants, (2) the ratio of the concentration of each gas to the other, and (3) whether there is simultaneous or intermittent application of the combined pollutant stress (Reinert *et al.*, 1975).

Several investigators have attributed injury of woody plants to pollutant combinations. For example, both ozone and sulfur dioxide were responsible for the physiogenic disorder of eastern white pine, known as "chlorotic dwarf" (Dochinger and Heck, 1969). Ozone and PAN act synergistically in causing foliar injury of *Populus maximowizcii* × *trichocarpa* exposed sequentially, the injury being greater than the additive injury from separate exposures (Kress, 1972). Houston (1974) reported a marked synergistic effect of sulfur dioxide and ozone on eastern white pine.

Species and Genetic Materials

Information on the susceptibility of various species to air pollutants has been obtained in the field by studying the damage done to plants at various distances from sources of pollution, and from controlled experiments in which plants were subjected to various pollutant concentrations and duration of exposure. Scheffer and Hedgecock (1955) rated gymnosperms in the field in the following order of decreasing susceptibility to sulfur dioxide: alpine fir, lodgepole pine, Engelmann spruce, ponderosa pine, and limber pine. Several investigators have shown that species vary appreciably in sensitivity to pollutants and rates of uptake of pollutants (Tables 17.6 to 17.8). Rates of SO_2 absorption were high in bigtooth aspen, a sensitive species, and low in sugar maple, an SO_2-tolerant species (Jensen and Kozlowski, 1975).

TABLE 17.6   Relative Susceptibility of Trees to Sulfur Dioxide[a]

Sensitive	Intermediate	Tolerant
Acer negundo var. *interius*	*Abies balsamea*	*Abies amabilis*
Amelanchier alnifolia	*Abies grandis*	*Abies concolor*
Betula alleghaniensis	*Acer glabrum*	*Acer platanoides*
Betula papyrifera	*Acer negundo*	*Acer saccharinum*
Betula pendula	*Acer rubrum*	*Acer saccharum*
Betula populifolia	*Alnus tenuifolia*	*Crataegus douglasii*
Fraxinus pennsylvanica	*Betula occidentalis*	*Ginkgo biloba*
Larix occidentalis	*Picea engelmannii*	*Juniperus occidentalis*
Pinus banksiana	*Picea glauca*	*Juniperus osteosperma*
Pinus resinosa	*Pinus contorta*	*Juniperus scopulorum*
Pinus strobus	*Pinus monticola*	*Picea pungens*
Populus grandidentata	*Pinus nigra*	*Pinus edulis*
Populus nigra "Italica"	*Pinus ponderosa*	*Pinus flexilis*
Populus tremuloides	*Populus angustifolia*	*Platanus* × *acerifolia*
Rhus typhina	*Populus balsamifera*	*Populus* × *canadensis*
Salix nigra	*Populus deltoides*	*Quercus gambelii*
Sorbus sitchensis	*Populus trichocarpa*	*Quercus palustris*
Ulmus parvifolia	*Prunus armeniaca*	*Quercus rubra*
	Prunus virginiana	*Rhus glabra*
	Pseudotsuga menziesii	*Thuja occidentalis*
	Quercus alba	*Thuja plicata*
	Sorbus aucuparia	*Tilia cordata*
	Syringa vulgaris	
	Tilia americana	
	Tsuga heterophylla	
	Ulmus americana	

[a] From Davis and Gerhold (1976).

TABLE 17.7 Relative Susceptibility of Trees to Ozone[a]

Sensitive	Intermediate	Resistant
Ailanthus altissima	*Acer negundo*	*Abies balsamea*
Amelanchier alnifolia	*Cercis canadensis*	*Abies concolor*
Fraxinus americana	*Larix leptolepis*	*Acer grandidentatum*
Fraxinus pennsylvanica	*Libocedrus decurrens*	*Acer platanoides*
Gleditsia triacanthos	*Liquidambar styraciflua*	*Acer rubrum*
Juglans regia	*Pinus attenuata*	*Acer saccharum*
Larix decidua	*Pinus contorta*	*Betula pendula*
Liriodendron tulipifera	*Pinus echinata*	*Cornus florida*
Pinus banksiana	*Pinus elliottii*	*Fagus sylvatica*
Pinus coulteri	*Pinus lambertiana*	*Ilex opaca*
Pinus jeffreyi	*Pinus rigida*	*Juglans nigra*
Pinus nigra	*Pinus strobus*	*Juniperus occidentalis*
Pinus ponderosa	*Pinus sylvestris*	*Nyssa sylvatica*
Pinus radiata	*Pinus torreyana*	*Persea americana*
Pinus taeda	*Quercus coccinea*	*Picea abies*
Pinus virginiana	*Quercus palustris*	*Picea glauca*
Platanus occidentalis	*Quercus velutina*	*Picea pungens*
Populus maximowiczii ×	*Syringa vulgaris*	*Pinus resinosa*
trichocarpa		
Populus tremuloides	*Ulmus parvifolia*	*Pinus sabiniana*
Quercus alba		*Pseudotsuga menziesii*
Quercus gambelii		*Pyrus communis*
Sorbus aucuparia		*Quercus macrocarpa*
Syringa × *chinensis*		*Quercus robur*
		Quercus rubra
		Robinia pseudoacacia
		Sequoia sempervirens
		Sequoiadendron giganteum
		Thuja occidentalis
		Tilia americana
		Tilia cordata
		Tsuga canadensis

[a] From Davis and Gerhold (1976).

Marked genetic variations in response to pollution have been demonstrated in poplar (Dochinger *et al.,* 1972), eastern white pine (Houston, 1974), and red maple (Townsend and Dochinger, 1974). Berry (1973) selected eastern white pine clones for tolerance and susceptibility to sulfur dioxide, fluorides, and ozone, in an attempt to identify plant materials that can be used in the development of pollution-tolerant trees.

Effects of Leaf Age

In broad-leaved plants neither very young nor very old leaves usually show pollution injury. Ting and Dugger (1971) found that the susceptibility of leaves to ozone was greatest after maximum leaf expansion occurred, when there was a maximum amount

TABLE 17.8   Rates of Ozone Uptake per Unit of Leaf Surface and Leaf Dry Weight of Seven Species from an Atmosphere Containing 0.20 ppm Ozone[a]

	Uptake rate	
Species	mg $O_3/dm^2/hr$	mg $O_3/g/hr$
Quercus alba	0.635	1.318
Betula papyrifera	0.536	2.347
Acer saccharum	0.371	0.863
Aesculus glabra	0.362	0.927
Liquidambar styraciflua	0.278	0.854
Acer rubrum	0.272	0.555
Fraxinus americana	0.239	0.562

[a] From Townsend (1974).

of intercellular space in the palisade layer. Lesser amounts of intercellular space before and after this period coincided with reduced sensitivity to ozone. By contrast, the relative amount of intercellular space in the spongy mesophyll layer increased gradually as leaves expanded. Hence, maximum ozone sensitivity was well correlated only with maximum palisade intercellular spaces.

Seedlings are particularly sensitive to air pollutants. For example, no white spruce, black spruce, or trembling aspen seedlings were found within 25 km of a sulfur-emitting plant in Ontario, Canada (Gordon and Gorham, 1963). Extreme sensitivity to air pollution of pine seedlings in the cotyledon stage may adversely influence seedling development and regeneration of pine stands. Fumigation of red pine seedlings with SO_2 at 0.5 to 4 ppm for as little as 15 min induced chlorosis in both cotyledons and primary needles, slowed the expansion of primary needles, inhibited dry weight increment of both cotyledons and primary needles, and induced tip necrosis in cotyledons (Constantinidou et al., 1976).

Mechanisms of Pollution Injury

A complication in evaluating the physiological mechanism of pollution injury is produced by the fact that such factors as light, water, temperature, and mineral nutrition affect the response of plants to pollutants. Still another complication is that, as was mentioned previously, often more than one pollutant is responsible for injury. Despite these difficulties, some useful information on the mechanism of injury has accumulated for specific pollutants (Mudd and Kozlowsi, 1975).

Ozone appears to cause damage to plants in at least three ways: by (1) interfering with mitochondrial activity, (2) by destroying membrane permeability, and (3) by inhibiting photosynthesis. The manner in which peroxyacetyl nitrate affects plants is less clear but its effects may be similar to those of ozone. Sulfur dioxide enters leaves through the stomata. It reacts with the wet surfaces of spongy mesophyll and palisade cells to form the very toxic sulfite (SO_2^{2-}) which in high concentrations, rapidly kills cells. At low levels sulfite is converted to sulfate (SO_4^{2-}) which is much less toxic than sulfite. Fluoride is absorbed from the air and translocated to leaf tips and margins where its high concentration rapidly kills cells.

Acid Rain

For a long time it was believed that most polluting substances were removed from the atmosphere relatively close to the site of emission. In recent years, however, much evidence has accumulated showing that atmospheric pollutants and their reaction products are dispersed by meteorological processes and often are deposited far from the source of emission.

Rain water in equilibrium with atmospheric CO_2 would be expected to be only slightly acid, with a pH of about 5.8. However, investigations in the United States and several European countries have reported areas having rains that are extremely acid. For example, at the Hubbard Brook Experimental Forest in New Hampshire the average pH of rain water during 1965 to 1971 varied from 4.03 to 4.19. Individual rain storms with pH values between 2.1 and 3 have also been reported in some locations in northeastern United States (Likens *et al.,* 1972; Likens and Bormann, 1974).

Much of the sulfur deposited by rain in an area comes from distant sources. For example, it has been estimated that more than 75% of the sulfur in rain deposited in Norway and Sweden originates in industrialized regions of England and Central Europe. The dispersion of sulfur compounds in rain is caused primarily by wind (Dochinger and Seliga, 1975, 1976).

Acid rains have harmful effects on both aquatic and terrestrial ecosystems. The influences on aquatic ecosystems lead to the extinction of fish. The effects on soils and plants are less clear. However, simulated acid rains have been reported to inhibit seed germination, injure foliage, accelerate the leaching of nutrients from foliage, and decrease the growth of trees. In forests most of the acid rain impinges on the foliage where ion exchange occurs. As a result the rain that reaches the soil is much less acid than that reaching the leaves. In addition to concern about direct effects, there is much interest in the potentially indirect effects of acid rains, including the leaching of nutrients from the soil and the erosion of plant cuticles, which would accelerate leaching from leaves and provide access to pathogens, biocides, and insects. Much more research is needed on the effects, distribution, and control of acid rains.

FIRE

The effects of fire on woody plants are complex and range from catastrophic to beneficial. Fire influences plants by interfering with physiological processes, by affecting site quality, and by destroying plants.

Responses of plants to fire vary greatly and depend on the type and severity of the fire as well as on the species. Much more damage is caused to trees by crown fires than by ground fires. The most serious cause of injury by crown fires is the reduction in photosynthetic surface by defoliation. This is especially serious in young forest stands, which are more likely to be completely defoliated than older, taller trees. Ground fires often kill areas of bark and cambium at the bases of trees, producing girdles. It often has been assumed that such injury interferes with phloem translocation and reduces growth. However, Jemison (1944) found that partial girdling of the bases of stems of deciduous trees by fire seldom reduced translocation or cambial growth in subsequent years. New xylem and phloem were laid down in newly oriented paths during the next growing season, quickly providing new translocation paths around wounds.

It should be remembered that even though growth may not be reduced by ground fires, timber quality often is greatly lowered by fire scars. Fire scars provide entry points for *Fomes* spp., which cause heart rot of aspen. In some areas, such as the Kentucky upland oak stands, almost all timber decay is traceable to fire injury (Berry, 1969). Fire may also stimulate the growth of host plants and thereby spread disease. An example is powdery mildew *(Rhizina undulata)* on blueberry. Germination of the ascospores is enhanced by fire, thereby spreading *Rhizina* root rot in postfire plantations of Scotch pine. On the other hand, fires reduce or control brown needle spot of longleaf pine, leafspot of blueberry, and Nectria cankers (Ahlgren, 1974).

Fire and Species Composition

Except for rain forests, most forested areas have been burned frequently. As a result, succession to a climatic climax stage is arrested in many regions and vegetation almost indefinitely maintained in a subfinal ''fire climax'' stage. For example in the Coastal Plain of the southeastern United States, subclimax forests of longleaf pine are maintained by recurring fires, which the pines survive and broad-leaved trees do not. In the northeastern United States, the occurrence of temporary species such as trembling aspen, white birch, red pine, jack pine, and pitch pine, is largely controlled by the frequent occurrence of fire. Other example of species that are dominant over vast acreages because of fire are Douglas-fir in northwestern United States and several species of *Eucalyptus* in Australia.

Adaptations to Fire

Some species are much more likely than others to survive fires. The insulating properties of bark often determine the extent of injury to the living phloem and cambium. Whereas species with thin bark, such as red oak, eastern white pine, and lodgepole pine often are killed by ground fires, those with thick bark, such as bur oak, longleaf pine, western larch, and ponderosa pine often escape fire injury.

Another adaptation to fire is the production of serotinous (late-to-open) cones. In such species as jack pine, pitch pine, lodgepole pine, sand pine, and black spruce, cones containing viable seed remain on the tree for years. When the resinous material on these serotinous cones is destroyed by fire, the cone scales open to release seeds.

Hence, where fires are common, the release of a large amount of seed from serotinous cones is likely to determine the dominant species, as in the case of lodgepole pine.

Some species (e.g., pitch pine) produce shoots from dormant buds even after crown fires. Others, such as various oaks, regenerate by root sprouts that were not killed by fire. In still other fire-adapted species, such as trembling aspen, the killing of shoots stimulates the growth of root suckers that arise from adventitious buds on the roots (Kozlowski, 1971a).

Fire and Site Quality

Fire influences site quality largely by the burning of organic matter and by heating surface soil layers, with the former effect being much more important. When organic matter is burned, CO_2 and nitrogen gas are released and minerals are concentrated in the ash. Hence, fire increases the amount of available minerals but decreases soil acidity. Although some nitrogen is lost, the gain from increased mineralization after fire may outweigh the loss (Viro, 1974). If the highly soluble minerals in the ash are leached into the soil and absorbed by roots, site quality is temporarily improved. But if these minerals leach below the root zone or are washed off the surface, site quality is reduced. Improvement of site quality by fire is characteristic of sandy to loamy soils on level ground. Site deterioration by loss of minerals is more likely to occur on very coarse sands or heavy soils (Spurr, 1964).

Fire is likely to degrade sites where the soil is almost wholly composed of organic matter. For example, when peat bogs are burned after extended droughts the soil is often destroyed. Another example is the exposure of erodable soil on steep slopes by the burning of organic matter. In contrast, in cold climates where low temperatures and high humidity prevent decomposition of organic matter and heavy mats of acid raw humus exist, fires generally improve the site quality for forest species.

Prescribed Burning

In recent years there has been recognition of the benefits of controlled or prescribed burning (Kayll, 1974). It is now widely recognized that fire is a normal component of many ecosystems and that complete exclusion of fire in many areas has caused dangerous fuel accumulation which may be expected to result in catastrophic fires. There are various reasons for prescribed burning, including the removal of fuels that accumulate naturally or from logging slash, control of insects and diseases, stimulation of seed production or opening of cones of serotinous species, and preparation of seedbeds for seeding. Silviculturists often use prescribed burning techniques to regulate factors that control regeneration of forest stands. Prescribed burning techniques have been especially well developed in Scandinavian countries, where one of the most serious obstacles to regeneration is a thick layer of raw humus. For further discussion of the diverse effects of natural fires and prescribed burning of various ecosystems, the reader is referred to the book by Kozlowski and Ahlgren (1974).

ENVIRONMENTAL CONTROL OF REPRODUCTIVE GROWTH

A variety of environmental factors interact to influence reproductive growth both indirectly, by altering physiological processes (especially carbohydrate and hormone relations), and directly, as by thermal injury. Because of interrelationships between vegetative growth and reproductive growth, any external factor that influences shoot growth, cambial growth, or root growth may eventually modify reproductive growth. Among the most important of these are light, temperature, water (see Chapter 16), and mineral supply. Light and temperature effects will be discussed briefly in this section and water and mineral supply in the section on cultural practices.

Light Intensity

Knowledge of the effects of light intensity on reproductive growth is essential to orchard managers in making decisions on pruning to control tree form, choosing rootstocks to control tree size, and spacing trees in orchard establishment; and to foresters in pruning and thinning practices, especially in seed orchards.

As was already mentioned, because of mutual shading within tree crowns various fruits on the same tree are exposed to many different microclimates and, therefore, vary in characteristics determined by the light intensity reaching the fruit surface. Red coloration of apples, for example, is determined by incident light and genotype. Furthermore, fruit development is influenced by the local light climate because the carbohydrates needed and mobilized by expanding fruits come from leaves relatively nearby (see Chapter 11).

Shading experiments have shown that fruit crop yield is reduced by low light intensity as a result of the inhibition of floral initiation, of fruit set, and of increase in size of fruits. For example, shading of trees reduced flower bud initiation in apple (Table 17.9), apricot, and grape. Shading after completion of blossoming (therefore not influencing the number of flowers or their pollination and fertilization) also de-

TABLE 17.9   Effect of Artificial Shading of Apple Trees in 1970 on Number of Flower Buds per Tree in 1971 [a]

Light intensity of outer crown [b]	Number of flower buds
100	159
37	96
25	69
11	33

[a] From Pereira (1975).
[b] As percentage of full sunlight.

creases the number of fruits at harvest (Pereira, 1975). Jackson and Palmer (1977a,b) shaded Cox's Orange Pippin apple trees during the postblossom growing season in 1970 and 1971. Shading reduced the retention of fruitlets, fruit size, and percentage of dry matter in the year of shading. It also reduced flower bud formation and decreased the percentage of flowers that set fruits in the following year. Jackson *et al.* (1977) also showed that shading reduced the size of apple fruits through reduction of cell size and the number of cells per fruit. Fruits grown under shade also had less dry matter and starch per unit fresh weight. Concentrations of N, P, K, Ca, and Mg were similar in fruits of the same size produced in shade or in full light, but smaller fruits had higher concentrations of Ca, N, and P than did larger ones.

A quantitative requirement for light in floral initiation has also been shown in forest trees, including pines (Fowells and Schubert, 1956) and *Cupressus* (Pharis *et al.*, (1970b). The influence of light intensity on floral initiation in forest trees is discussed further in the section on cultural practices.

Photoperiod

As was mentioned earlier, the cessation of shoot growth of some temperate zone woody plants is induced by short days and prolonged by long days, and because duration of shoot growth is closely related to time of flower initiation, Goo (1968) implicated day length in flower initiation in pines. Nevertheless, floral initiation in most woody plants is much less sensitive to day length than it is in many herbaceous plants. An exception is *Cupressus,* which showed a photoperiodic response, but only when flowering was induced by gibberellins (Pharis *et al.*, 1970b).

Temperature

Temperature influences many aspects of reproductive growth, including floral initiation, release of bud dormancy, anthesis, fruit set, and growth of fruits. In addition, flowers and fruits are commonly injured by extremely low or high temperatures.

The flower buds of many trees of the temperate zone resemble vegetative buds in that they require exposure to several hundred hours of low temperature to break their dormancy (see the section on bud dormancy, Chapter 16). As a result, flower buds of trees and shrubs planted toward the southern limits of their range sometimes fail to open properly after unusually mild winters. This has caused the failure of fruit crops from more northern latitudes in southern California, northern Florida, and in tropical and subtropical South America.

After bud dormancy is broken by low temperatures, higher temperatures are needed to induce flowering. The effect of temperature also is shown by comparing flowering dates of species over a wide geographical range. Flowering dogwood, for example, blooms near Jacksonville, Florida, in mid-February; in St. Louis, Missouri, in early April; and in Columbus, Ohio, in early May (Wyman, 1950). The time of flowering of the same species in a given location also varies from year to year because of temperature differences. At East Malling, England, about 75% of the year-to-year variability in time of "full bloom" of apple, as defined as the date when 50% of the flowers are open, was accounted for by a linear regression on the accumulated day degrees above 5.5°C from February 1 to April 15 (Jackson, 1975). Over a 43-year period the date of full bloom of Cox's Orange Pippin apple trees at East Malling, England, varied from April 15 to May 23rd (Tydeman, 1964). Elevation and latitude, through effects on temperature, also have a strong effect on flowering dates in pines. Bingham and Squillace (1957) noted that most pines showed a delay in flowering of about 5 days for each degree of latitude northward. There also was a 5-day delay in flowering of western white pine for each 300 m of elevation.

Pereira (1975) concluded that the yield and quality of apple crops in England were determined by temperature at three critical phases of reproductive growth. Most important was the absence of late spring frosts. Secondly, the temperature at pollination had to be adequate. The third critical period was in the month following full bloom. Warm, bright weather in the first one-half generally increased crop yield, whereas, in the second half it often decreased it.

Freezing Injury

Direct freezing injury of reproductive tissues is very common. Such injury includes midwinter killing of dormant flower buds as well as spring and autumn damage to flowers and fruits. Early destruction of reproductive structures in fruit trees may alter the bearing sequence. For example, when early frost damage destroys the fruit crop of a biennial bearing species, the normally bearing year becomes a vegetative one. The subsequent year, however, is one of heavy fruiting and the biennial habit is continued (Davis, 1957).

Probably the most common type of winter injury is the killing of flower buds. The critical temperatures at which buds are killed depends on many factors, including plant species, age and vigor of trees, stage of bud development, rate and time of occurrence of the temperature drop, and duration of the low-temperature regime. Apical and median buds usually begin growing earlier than basal buds; hence the latter are less likely to be injured. Flower buds often are killed while leaf buds are not. In general the more advanced the bloom the greater is the injury from a given low temperature. Apricots bloom before peaches, which, in turn, bloom before apples, and spring frost injury to bloom is therefore likely to be greatest in apricot and least in apple. There also is considerable variability among cultivars in susceptibility to spring frosts. For example, in peach the cultivars Elberta, Sunhigh, Redskin, and Golden Jubilee are injured more than Veteran, Vedette, Early Red Free, and Sunrise (Teskey and Shoemaker, 1972).

In some years spring freezing is a major cause of mortality and abortion of gymnosperm conelets. Usually only part of the conelet crop is killed by freezing. Susceptibility to frost varies with the stage of conelet development, and injury is greater in ovulate than in staminate conelets. Ovulate conelets at the stage of maximum pollen receptivity are very vulnerable to frost damage, whereas they are generally resistant to the post-pollination stages. In shortleaf pine ovulate conelets that were still covered with bud scales were only slightly damaged by frost or not at all, whereas those that had emerged from the bud scales were severely injured or killed. Staminate conelets were uninjured (Hutchinson and Bramlett, 1964). Variations in temperature within a tree crown or stand may also account for the mortality of only part of the conelet crop. In addition to killing first-year conelets, freezing temperatures often reduce the number of sound seeds in the cones that survive. Some ovules are killed, although the cone is not destroyed, or pollen is rendered sterile, thus inducing subsequent ovule abortion.

When frost injury to flowers or young fruits occurs, the mature fruits often are of low quality and abnormal in structure. Frost injury at blooming time in apples causes browning and dropping of petals. Injury extends throughout the maturation of the fruit. Damage to the fruit is extensive and consists of scattered areas to complete bands of discoloration on the fruit surface (Simons, 1959). A frost about 1 month after apple bloom resulted in abnormally shaped fruits with large areas of dead cells that persisted to maturity (Simons and Lott, 1963).

Chilling Injury

There is much concern about injury to tropical and some temperate zone fruits at low but above freezing temperatures. Chilling injury is of particular interest because many fruits are routinely shipped and stored at low temperatures to extend their life. Low temperatures above freezing also injure some fruits under field conditions. For example, in subtropical banana plantations night temperatures of 10–13°C often occur and injure growing bananas.

External symptoms of chilling injury in fruits include various degrees of surface pitting, necrotic lesions, and discoloration. Injured fruits are readily infected by decay organisms and their storage life is greatly reduced. Some fruits show rather specific responses. With severe chilling the green peel of banana shows subepidermal browning or blackening, and the peel often blackens completely on ripening. With less severe chilling green bananas may not show any effect but when they ripen the color of the peel is abnormal and varies from dull yellow to greyish-yellow or grey. Chilling in the field often causes brown epidermal streaks and softening of the banana pulp during ripening as well as predisposing the fruits to storage rots and blemishes (Tai, 1977). Symptoms of chilling injury in citrus fruits vary somewhat with species. Oranges develop small sunken spots in the rind as well as uniform browning over relatively extensive areas. Grapefruits typically develop brown areas, 2–10 mm in diameter, surrounded by a ring of small spots. In oranges and grapefruit both the rind and flesh may soften to produce a condition called "watery breakdown." Although lemons generally do not show external symptoms of chilling injury they undergo watery breakdown and darkening of membranes or carpellary walls between segments, sometimes affecting the central core tissues and inner rind tissues. In mango symptoms include pitting and grey discoloration of the skin, abnormal color development, and poor flavor. Apples typically exhibit "scald," a brown discoloration that gives the skin a cooked appearance. In apples low temperature breakdown in the cortex is a common response. In some varieties the injured zone is about 2–5 mm below the skin; in others it extends through most of the flesh. Peaches and plums develop a mealy texture as well as discoloration of the flesh.

After chilling, green fruits do not undergo normal ripening. For example, avocado fruits that are stored at chilling temperature do not ripen normally or show the climacteric increase in respiration that is associated with normal ripening. Abnormal patterns in both CO_2 and ethylene production have been demonstrated for chilled bananas, grapefruits, and oranges, after transfer to warm temperatures (Lyons, 1973).

In many tropical plants the critical low temperature at which chilling injury to fruits occurs is near 10 to 12°C, but species susceptibility varies appreciably with the region of origin. The lower temperature limit for injury is near 12°C for many varieties of banana; between 8 and 12°C for citrus, avocado, and mango; and 0 to 4°C for temperate zone fruits such as apples. There also are varietal differences in response to chilling. The critical temperature for the Lacatan variety of banana is exceptionally high, 14.4°C; for Gros Michel banana it is 11.6°C. Some banana varieties can tolerate temperatures of 10–11°C for up to 2 weeks and others are injured after only a few hours of exposure. Most bananas are transported at temperatures between 11 and 13°C, which keep chilling injury to a minimum.

Chilling injury is also influenced by duration of exposure to a given temperature. For example, exposure of many varieties of banana for a few hours at temperatures between -1 and 7°C lowers the quality of the fruit, but 12 hours of exposure injures the fruit so severely that it is no longer marketable. Fruits that are chilled for short periods of time may appear to be uninjured when removed from low temperatures. However, symptoms of chilling injury may become evident in a few days at warmer temperatures. The effects of chilling are cumulative and low temperatures in the field before harvest and during transport of the harvested fruit add to the effects of chilling in storage.

Susceptibility to low temperature injury is also influenced by maturity and chemical composition of fruits. For example, bananas are most sensitive to chilling injury at the stage at which they normally are harvested. Maximum low temperature breakdown occurs when apples are exposed to chilling temperatures at the peak of their respiratory climacteric. Conditions that favor low mineral contents in fruit result in extensive low temperature breakdown in apples (Fidler, 1968).

Mechanism of Chilling Injury.   Levitt (1972) divides chilling injury into a rapid, direct response called "cold shock" and a much slower indirect response. Slow chilling injury is much more common than cold shock and may require days or weeks at the chilling temperature to induce injury. Levitt explained cold shock by sudden increase in permeability of the plasmalemma resulting in loss of cell contents and death of cells. He associated indirect chilling injury with starvation caused by faster breakdown than synthesis of carbohydrates, and disturbance of biochemical processes such as respiration and protein metabolism, which might result in accumulation of toxic substances. All of these changes are associated with alterations in membrane permeability. According to Lyons (1973), the common early response in all chilling injuries is a phase transition in cell membranes. As the temperature is lowered, membrane lipids of chilling-sensitive species undergo a phase change from a liquid-crystalline to a gel state at a critical temperature. The change in state induces contraction that causes cracks or channels in membranes thereby increasing their permeability. This is followed by an upset in ion balance, leakage of ions from some tissues, metabolic changes, and accumulation of toxins.

CULTURAL PRACTICES AND REPRODUCTIVE GROWTH

A number of methods have been used to stimulate floral induction and the subsequent growth of flowers and fruits. Flowering often can be induced in young trees by manipulating the environment to make them grow as rapidly as possible until they achieve the adult stage and the critical size necessary for flowering (see Chapter 16). To promote flowering thereafter, rapid growth should be stimulated because there is a close correlation between the vigor of adult trees and their flowering capacity. However, this generalization should be viewed with caution because in individual adult trees, reproductive growth can also be triggered by treatments that retard vegetative growth at critical stages of reproductive growth (see Chapter 16). Among the most successful treatments for stimulating flowering and fruiting in adult trees are grafting, fertilizing, irrigating, and releasing trees from competition. Combinations of fertilizers and irrigation have often been more effective than either treatment alone. Applications of hormones also induce flowering in some species (see Chapters 15 and 16). Matthews (1963) suggested that fertilizers and irrigation be used routinely to insure regularity of large flower, seed, and fruit crops in high-value trees, such as those in seed orchards. Flowering can also be induced by several emergency treatments such as girdling, root pruning, and bending and knotting of stems and branches. However, some of these emergency measures may be harmful over a period of years and are not advisable for general use.

Grafting

Precocious flowering can be encouraged by grafting or dwarfing rootstocks, grafting on related species, grafting mature scions into seedlings, or grafting or budding in crowns of mature fruiting trees. When scions from adult trees are grafted to seedling rootstocks in the juvenile, nonflowering state, they usually soon flower. For good discussions of various grafting techniques, the reader is referred to Hartmann and Kester (1975) and Wright (1976).

Dwarfing Rootstocks

Perhaps the most widely used cultural technique for increasing early flowering in apple and pear is the grafting of a scion variety directly to a dwarfing rootstock. Shoot elongation of the compound tree ceases early and abruptly, leading to early and prolific formation of fruit buds. For example, some varieties of apple worked on East Malling

IX (M9) rootstocks may grow to only about one-third of normal size and begin to produce fruit in the second or third year.

On dwarfing rootstocks a larger proportion of the assimilates is directed toward reproductive tissues. For example, on the dwarfing apple stock M9 about 70% of the assimilates were directed to the fruit, largely at the expense of the stem and branches but also of the roots and leaves. By comparison only 40 to 50% of the assimilates were directed to the fruit of later-bearing trees on the vigorous rootstock M16 (Avery, 1969, 1970).

Because trees on dwarfing rootstocks are small and can be closely spaced, the yield of fruit per hectare often is high. Some rootstocks may even cause certain varieties of fruit trees to bear heavily at an early age without materially impeding vegetative growth. Weak rootstocks also tend to increase the size of fruit, probably by decreasing vegetative growth, and they may hasten fruit ripening. Although the growth rate of the compound tree is intermediate between the rates of rootstock and scion, the influence of the rootstock generally is greater than that of the scion (Tubbs, 1973a,b). Vegetative growth of some fruit trees can also be inhibited and flowering stimulated by inserting a dwarfing stem piece (interstock) between a vigorous root and a vigorous scion variety (Dana *et al.*, 1963). For further information on the types of dwarfing rootstocks used with various fruit trees and the reciprocal influences between rootstocks and scions, the reader is referred to Teskey and Shoemaker (1972) and Tubbs (1973a,b).

Fertilizers

Mineral requirements of reproductive tissues are high (see Chapter 9). For example, about one-third of the nitrogen absorbed per apple tree per year is used in fruit growth. In years of heavy fruiting very little nitrogen is stored in trees and reserves may become depleted.

Fruit Trees

There is a rich literature on the important role of fertilizers in the initiation of floral primordia, fruit set, and growth of fruit. A few examples will be given here.

Floral Initiation.   The initiation of flower primordia is strongly influenced by adding fertilizers, especially those high in nitrogen. For example, floral initiation in apple is stimulated by nitrogen fertilizers and the added nitrogen also reduces the tendency toward alternation of flowering. It appears that a deficiency of nitrogen in unfertilized trees limits the growth of leaf tissues sufficiently to prevent maximum floral induction (Bradford, 1924). Nitrogen fertilizers also stimulate floral induction in citrus and tung (Cameron *et al.*, 1952; Shear, 1966).

Fruit Set.   Mineral deficiency often inhibits fruit set. This is shown by the increase in fruit set after addition at the appropriate time of a fertilizer containing the deficient element. Although fruit set is most commonly inhibited by deficiencies of macronutrients, especially nitrogen, deficiency of minor elements is also sometimes involved (Batjer and Thompson, 1949).

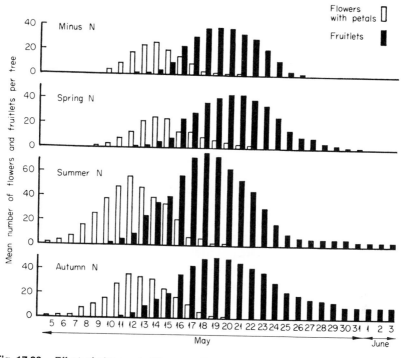

Fig. 17.20. Effect of nitrogen fertilizers applied at various times on flowering and fruitlet abscission of Lord Lambourne apple trees. From Hill-Cottingham and Williams (1967).

Although nitrogen fertilizers have been traditionally applied to fruit trees in the spring, there often are advantages to applying additional nitrogen later in the season. For example, summer applications of nitrogen fertilizers to some varieties of fruit trees induce more vigorous flowers the following spring, which are more likely to set fruit than those receiving fertilizer only in the spring. Hill-Cottingham and Williams (1967) found that there was practically no fruit set the following spring in control apple trees or those given nitrogen fertilizer in the preceding spring. By comparison, trees given nitrogen in the summer showed appreciable fruit set and those given nitrogen in the autumn a heavy fruit set the next spring (Fig. 17.20). According to Delap (1967), the increase in fruit set by summer and autumn applications of nitrogen over spring applications is associated with greater longevity of ovules and a longer receptive period of stigmas.

Growth Rate and Size of Fruits. Both the rate of fruit growth and fruit size at harvest are affected by the number of fruits per unit of leaf surface. Adding nitrogen fertilizers may decrease the average size of the harvested fruit if floral initiation and fruit set are increased proportionally more than leaf growth. However, if added nitrogen does not greatly increase floral initiation and fruit set, it often increases the size of the mature fruit (Fisher *et al.*, 1948). Addition of nitrogen sometimes increases the rate of photosynthesis per unit of leaf area as well as the duration of photosynthesis and this may increase fruit size. For a comprehensive review of the effects of fertilizers on stimulation of fruit yield the reader is referred to Childers (1966a,b).

Forest Trees

Addition of fertilizers often stimulates both the flowering and the seed production of forest trees. When fertilizers are used with a combination of crown release or irrigation, the results often are better than when fertilizers are used alone (Figs. 17.21, 17.22). Flowering of clones that tend to flower profusely can be influenced most by fertilization. Male and female flowering of some species often are affected differently by fertilizers. For example, nitrogen fertilizer promoted female flowering in pine, larch, and several angiosperms, but in pine the effect on initiation of male flowers was negligible or negative (Sweet and Will, 1965; Giertych and Forward, 1966). By comparison, in Douglas-fir, nitrogen fertilizer increased production of both male and female flowers (Smith *et al.*, 1968; Griffith, 1968). In some species the form of nitrogen applied is important to flowering. In Douglas-fir nitrate nitrogen promoted flowering whereas ammonium nitrogen did not (Ebell, 1972). The effects of form of nitrogen applied vary with soil conditions as well as species.

For stimulation of flower bud formation in forest trees of the temperate zone, fertilizers usually are applied in the early spring before new flower buds are differentiated. The time when fertilizers most effectively influence seed production varies among species because of differences in the time required to ripen seed. For example, in pines that require 2 years to mature seed, the influence of fertilizer applications in

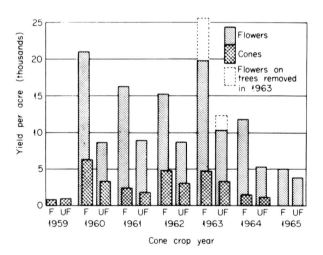

Fig. 17.21. Stimulation of reproductive growth with fertilizers. Flowers and cones of longleaf pine on cultivated and heavily thinned plants that were unfertilized (UF) or given annually 1,000 lbs/acre of 15–25–10 fertilizer in one application (F). From Shoulders (1968).

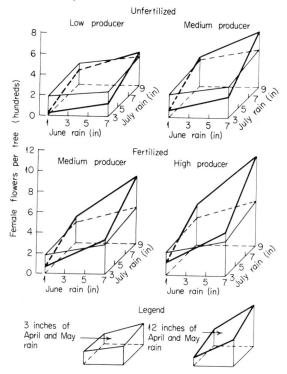

Fig. 17.22. Effect of fertilizers and rain on estimated flower production of longleaf pine. The data are for low-, medium-, and high-producing trees, with different rates of fertilization and rainfall in the spring and summer preceding flower bud formation. Average flower yields were assumed to be 150 per tree for low, 235 for medium, and 320 for high producers. Flower production 2 years earlier was 60, 90, and 120 flowers, respectively. From Shoulders (1967).

the spring will be shown in flowering in the spring of the subsequent year and in the ripened seeds during the autumn of the second year. As some gymnosperms and angiosperms ripen seeds in one growing season, fertilizers applied in the spring of one year will affect both the flowers and seed crop during the next year. The greatest effect of fertilizers generally is exerted on a single seed crop. Therefore, continuous high production of seeds requires repeated fertilizer applications (Matthews, 1963).

Irrigation

Irrigation has often been useful in stimulating reproductive growth in dry areas. However, the effects of irrigation are complicated and vary with the amount and distribution of rainfall, degree of plant water deficits at critical stages of reproductive growth, soil type, species, and the timing and amount of irrigation. Often there is an appreciable lag response of crop yield to irrigation. For example, Veihmeyer (1972) did not find decisive differences in the crop yield of irrigated and unirrigated fruit trees until about 5 years after irrigation treatments were started. In some species, such as coffee and litchi, short periods of water deficits between irrigations increase flowering (see Chapter 16).

Fruit Trees

The effects of irrigation on reproductive growth vary from negligible to very beneficial. In the coastal region of California, in years of normal rainfall, pear and apple trees on medium- or fine-textured soils do not reduce soil moisture content to the permanent wilting percentage until late in the season. In contrast, pear orchards in the interior valley of California reduce soil moisture to a critical level by late June (Hendrickson and Veihmeyer, 1942), emphasizing that the effects of irrigation depend on conditions affecting plant water deficits.

Beneficial effects of irrigation have been reported for both yield and quality of many edible fruits including apple, pears, peaches, plums, and almonds in California (Uriu and Magness, 1967). Even in humid England, frequent, intermediate, and infrequent irrigation during the summer increased the crop yield of Laxton's Superb apple trees by 40, 46, and 25%, respectively (Table 17.10). Medium watering provided the largest total and marketable crops but infrequent watering provided the largest increase in marketable crop per unit of water applied. Similar results were obtained with Cox's Orange Pippin apple trees in Kent, England (Goode and Ingram, 1971).

Although the irrigation of tropical fruit trees may not be necessary in humid zones, except during droughts, it is essential in arid regions. Hilgeman and Reuther (1967) described irrigation needs and practices for citrus, avocado, date palm, and olive trees. They pointed out that irrigation increases fruit yield primarily by maintaining the available water in the entire root zone during the period of fruit set. Irrigation after fruit set is much less important.

Forest Trees

Effects of irrigation on reproductive growth of forest trees are variable. Irrigation has often been used successfully in seed orchards but individual areas vary greatly in the amount of supplemental water needed. Seed production has sometimes been increased in loblolly pine seed orchards of the southeastern United States. For example, Bergman (1968) demonstrated increased cone production of loblolly pine clones after irrigating a seed orchard. In contrast, irrigation during the first five years after establishment of pine seed orchards on deep sands of northern Florida did not appreciably stimulate cone production (Bengston, 1969). In some seed orchards supplemental watering is useful in orchard establishment, stimulation of rapid early growth of trees, and early seed production but does not increase seed yields greatly in later years (Wright, 1976).

The beneficial effects of applied water on reproductive growth of forest trees appear to be closely related to the timing of irrigation. Although a short period of water stress just before flower initiation in pines promotes a better than average flower crop, greater availability of water is required prior to flower initiation and thereafter for seed development. Hence, many seed orchards are irrigated after flower initiation has occurred

TABLE 17.10 Effect of Irrigation during 1953–1960 on Yield of Apples during Bearing Years[a,b]

| Year | Treatment[c] | | | |
	Frequent irrigation	Medium irrigation	Infrequent irrigation	Control
1954	54.4	71.7	68.6	58.8
1956	169.2	169.1	126.7	135.8
1958	251.5	252.0	218.9	174.2
1960	380.2	407.8	366.4	271.2
Total	855.3	900.6	780.6	640.0

[a] From Goode and Hyrycz (1964).

[b] Yield measured in pounds per tree.

[c] Soil recharged with water to a depth of 1 m when soil moisture tension at ⅓ m was 10 cm (frequent irrigation), 20 cm (medium irrigation), and 50 cm (infrequent irrigation). Control was unwatered.

(Sweet, 1975). The importance of timing of irrigation to reproductive growth can also be inferred from studies of distribution of rainfall and flowering in pines. For example, abundant rainfall in April, May, June and July of the year preceding flowering greatly stimulated flowering of longleaf pine (Shoulders, 1967). Trees receiving fertilizers as well as unfertilized trees produced fewest flowers when high rainfall in April and May was followed by low rainfall in June and July (Fig. 17.22).

Thinning of Forest Stands

Vigorous, dominant trees produce more seed than intermediate or suppressed trees and, when competition is severe, suppressed trees often fail to produce any seed. Fowells and Schubert (1956) noted that almost all the cones were produced by dominant sugar pine trees in California and very few by intermediate and suppressed trees in the same stand. Within a tree crown the vigor of branches also influences fruit and cone development. For example, in red pine larger cones are produced on the more vigorous branches in the upper and middle thirds of the crowns than on the less vigorous lower branches, and the large cones contain more and better seeds than small cones (Dickmann and Kozlowski, 1971).

Further support for the importance of tree vigor to flowering and fruiting comes from observations of increased flower and seed crops in residual trees following thinning of forest stands. Wenger (1954) thinned a loblolly pine stand during the winter of 1946–1947. Flowering of the residual trees was almost immediately affected as an increased number of flower buds was formed during the first growing season after cutting. In 1949, the first year that release could affect mature cone production (although a very poor seed year), each released tree produced an average of 51 cones, whereas unreleased control trees produced only five cones. The effect of thinning carried over into 1950 and 1951, with released trees producing 107 and 132 cones per tree, and control trees bearing only 16 and 48 cones, during the same 2 years. Crown release of pine trees often is followed by an increase in pollen production, which results in an increase in the number of viable seeds per cone (Matthews, 1963).

The fundamental physiological question of why intermediate and suppressed trees do not produce seeds is enormously important, but it has not been adequately answered. Much research is urgently needed on the physiology of reproductive growth of trees subjected to competition in forest stands.

Chemical Growth Retardants

Rather spectacular effects on fruiting have been shown following applications of chemicals that retard vegetative growth. Among the most effective of these chemicals are *N*-dimethylaminosuccinamic acid (B9 or Alar) and 2-chloroethyl trimethyl ammonium chloride (Cycocel or Chlormequat). Trees treated with these chemicals exhibit many of the characteristics of those grafted on dwarfing rootstocks—short internodes, early cessation of shoot growth, and early and prolific formation of fruit buds. B9 and Cycocel do not act identically. For example, apical dominance is affected more by Cycocel than by B9. Also, B9 affects fruit color and Cycocel does not. Responses to both chemicals also vary among species and cultivars of a given species.

There is contradictory evidence as to whether the effects of growth retardants on vegetative growth and reproductive growth are independent. For example, chemicals that increased flower bud induction and fruit set of Eureka lemon also stimulated shoot growth (Monselise *et al.*, 1966). However, Batjer *et al.* (1964) increased the production of fruit buds over an entire tree by spraying only the lower part of the tree with B9, although vegetative growth was reduced only in the sprayed branches. The investigators suggested that this response may have been caused by translocation of the growth-retarding chemical from the treated branches to the roots, where it influenced production of a xylem-translocated hormone that subsequently stimulated flower initiation throughout the tree. Skene (1975) demonstrated that application of Cycocel to grape roots increased the concentration of cytokinin in the xylem sap.

Girdling

Cutting through the bark often stimulates reproductive growth because it impedes the basipetal translocation of carbohydrates and growth regulators in the phloem. When downward transport of organic solutes is blocked, they tend to diffuse into the xylem and are translocated upward in the transpiration stream and concentrate in the leaves and tissues involved in reproduction. Stephens (1964) stimulated production of seed cones by stem girdling in 22-year-old eastern white pine trees, but not in 3- to 14-year-old trees. Girdling also increased cone production on individually treated branches. Treatment in the summer of the year before flowering increased the yield of cones which otherwise would have been low. However, girdling did not stimulate reproductive growth in years when production of cones was high. Partial girdling of Douglas-fir stems late in August of 1957 or mid-May of 1958 greatly stimulated seed

TABLE 17.11 Effect of Stem Girdling on the Number of Seed Cones of Double-Stemmed 20-Year-Old Douglas-Fir Trees[a]

Year	August, 1957		May, 1958	
	Girdled	Control	Girdled	Control
1959	305	62	267	43
1960	0	0	0	0
1961	39	16	88	49
1962	62	50	9	6
Total	388	126	384	98

[a] From Ebell (1971).

cone production in 1959 (Table 17.11). No cones were produced in 1960, the second season after girdling, when cone production in ungirdled trees also failed. The girdling treatment continued to stimulate cone production for several years (Ebell, 1971). Severe girdling treatments, e.g., completely girdling the stem, sometimes causes severe damage to trees. Therefore, only partial girdles with knife cuts or pruning saws are recommended for stimulating reproductive growth.

Root Pruning

Flowering of woody plants sometimes has been stimulated by root pruning alone or in combination with other treatments. For example, root pruning induced formation of seed cones on 14- and 22-year-old eastern white pine trees. A combination of girdling of branches and root pruning was more effective than root pruning alone (Stephens, 1964).

Complexity of Effects of Cultural Practices on Growth

There are a number of puzzling effects of different cultural practices on vegetative and reproductive growth. For example, growth retarding chemicals, dwarfing rootstocks, and root pruning all reduce vegetative growth while they stimulate flowering and fruiting. On the other hand, the suppression of vegetative growth by plant competition is accompanied by marked inhibition of reproductive growth. Thus it appears that under some conditions reduction of vegetative growth is causally related to stimulation of reproductive growth, possibly by making greater amounts of metabolites and/or growth regulators available for the sequential phases of the reproductive process. Under severe competition, however, there appears to be a deficiency of substances required for both vegetative and reproductive growth. These contradictions indicate that more research is needed on the physiological basis of control of both vegetative and reproductive growth under different cultural practices.

GENERAL REFERENCES

Alvim, P. de T., and Kozlowski, T. T., eds. (1977). "Ecophysiology of Tropical Crops." Academic Press, New York.

Cannell, M. G. R., and Last, F. T., eds. (1976). "Tree Physiology and Yield Improvement." Academic Press, New York.

Daubenmire, R. F. (1974). "Plants and Environment: A Textbook of Plant Autecology." Wiley,New York.

Fowells, H. (1965). Silvics of forest trees. *U.S., For. Serv., Agric. Hand.* **271.**

Fritts, H. C. (1976). "Tree Rings and Climate." Academic Press, New York.

Gates, D. M., and Papian, L. E. (1971). "Atlas of Energy Budgets of Plant Leaves." Academic Press, New York.

Grace, J. (1977). "Plant Responses to Wind." Academic Press, New York.

Kozlowski, T. T., and Ahlgren, C. E., eds. (1974). "Fire and Ecosystems." Academic Press, New York.

Larcher, W. (1975). "Physiological Plant Ecology." Springer-Verlag, Berlin and New York.

Larson, P. R. (1963). Stem form development in forest trees. *For. Sci. Monogr.* **5.**

Leopold, A. C., and Kriedemann, P. E. (1975). "Plant Growth and Development." McGraw-Hill, New York.

Levitt, J. (1972). "Responses of Plants to Environmental Stresses." Academic Press, New York.

Li, P. H., and Sakai, A., eds. (1978). "Plant Cold Hardiness and Freezing Stress: Mechanisms and Crop Implications." Academic Press, New York.

Mudd, J. B., and Kozlowski, T. T., eds. (1975). "Responses of Plants to Air Pollution." Academic Press, New York.

Odum, E. P. (1971). "Fundamentals of Ecology." Saunders, Philadelphia.

Peace, T. R. (1962). "Pathology of Trees and Shrubs." Oxford Univ. Press (Clarendon), London and New York.

Pirone, P. O. (1978). "Tree Maintenance." Oxford Univ. Press, London and New York.

Precht, H., Christophersen, J., Hensel, H., and Larcher, W., eds. (1973). "Temperature and Life." Springer-Verlag, Berlin and New York.

Rice, E. L. (1974). "Allelopathy." Academic Press, New York.

Smith, D. M. (1962). "The Practice of Silviculture." Wiley, New York.

Tattar, T. A. (1978). "Diseases of Shade Trees." Academic Press, New York.

Teskey, J. E., and Shoemaker, J. S. (1972). "Tree Fruit Production." Avi Publ. Co., Westport, Connecticut.

Treshow, M. (1970). "Environment and Plant Response." McGraw-Hill, New York.

Scientific and Common Names of Woody Plants

Scientific Name	Common Name
Abelia grandiflora Rehd.	Glossy abelia
Abies alba Miller (*A. pectinata* (DC.))	European silver fir
Abies amabilis Forbes.	Pacific silver fir
Abies balsamea Mill.	Balsam fir
Abies concolor Lindl. & Gord.	White fir
Abies grandis Lindl.	Grand fir, Lowland white fir
Abies lasiocarpa (Hook.) Nutt.	Alpine fir, Subalpine fir
Abies magnifica A. Murr.	California red fir
Abies procera Rehd. (*A. nobilis* (Dougl.) Lindl.	Noble fir
Acacia catechu (L.F.) Willd.	Black cutch, Catechu
Acacia senegal (L.) Willd.	Sudan gum arabic
Acer buergerianum Mig.	Trident maple
Acer campestre L.	Hedge maple
Acer caudatum Wallich.	Kitamura (Nepal)
Acer ginnala Maxim.	Amur maple
Acer glabrum Torr.	Rocky Mountain maple
Acer grandidentatum Nutt.	Bigtooth maple
Acer macrophyllum Pursh	Bigleaf maple
Acer monspessulanum L.	Montpelier maple
Acer negundo L.	Boxelder
Acer negundo var *interius* (Britt.) Sarg.	Inland boxelder
Acer nigrum Michx. f.	Black maple
Acer pensylvanicum L.	Striped maple
Acer platanoides L.	Norway maple
Acer pseudoplatanus L.	Sycamore maple
Acer orientale L.	Cretan maple
Acer rubrum L.	Red maple
Acer rufinerve Sieb. & Zucc.	Redvein maple
Acer saccharinum L.	Silver maple
Acer saccharum Marsh.	Sugar maple
Acer spicatum Lam.	Mountain maple
Acer tataricum Lam.	Tatarian maple
Achras zapota L.	Sapodilla
Acrocarpus fraxinifolius Wight	Mundani
Adenostoma fasciculatum H. & A.	Greasewood chamise
Aesculus californica (Spach) Nutt.	California buckeye

Aesculus glabra Willd.	Ohio buckeye
Aesculus hippocastanum L.	Horsechestnut
Agathis australis Salisb.	New Zealand Kauri
Agave spp.	Agave
Ailanthus altissima (Mill.) Swingle	Ailanthus, Tree of heaven
Albizia spp.	Albizia
Aleurites fordii Hemsl.	Tung
Aleurites moluccana (L.) Willd.	Candle nut
Alnus glutinosa (L.) Gaertn.	Black alder, European alder
Alnus inokumai Murai & Kusaka	
Alnus oregoni Nutt.	Red alder
Alnus rugosa (DuRoi) Spreng.	Speckled alder
Alnus tenuifolia Nutt.	Thinleaf alder
Alnus viridis (Chaix) DC.	European green alder
Alstonia scholaris R. Br.	Pulai, White cheesewood
Amelanchier alnifolia (Nutt.) Nutt.	Saskatoon serviceberry
Amelanchier arborea (Michx. f.) Fern	Downy serviceberry, Shadbush
Amelanchier florida Lindl.	Pacific serviceberry, Western serviceberry
Amoora spp.	Amoora
Ampelopsis cordata Michx.	Heartleaf ampelopsis
Angophora costata (Gaertn.) Britt.	Smooth-barked-apple
Antiaris africana Engl.	Chenchen
Aralia spinosa L.	Devils-walkingstick, Hercules-club
Araucaria cunninghamii Ait.	Hoop-pine
Araucaria excelsa, see A. heterophylla	
Araucaria heterophylla (Salisb.) Franco	Norfolk Island pine
Arbutus andrachne L.	Greek strawberry tree
Arbutus menziesii Pursh	Pacific madrone
Arceuthobium spp.	Dwarf mistletoe
Ardisia spp.	Ardisia
Artemisia absinthium L.	Wormwood
Artemisia monosperma Delile	
Artemisia tridentata Nutt.	Big sagebrush
Asimina triloba (L.) Dunal	Pawpaw
Astragalus spp.	Astragalus
Atriplex spp.	Saltbush
Attalea excelsa Mart.	Attalea palm
Avicennia marina (Forsk.) Vierh.	
Avicennia nitida Jacq.	Black-mangrove
Avicennia resinifera Forst. f.	
Azalea spp.	Azalea
Bambusa spp.	Bamboo
Berberis spp.	Barberry
Bertholettia excelsa Humb. & Bonpl.	Brazil nut
Betula alleghaniensis Britt.	Yellow birch
Betula lenta L.	Sweet birch
Betula lutea, see Betula alleghaniensis	
Betula nigra L.	River birch
Betula occidentalis Hook.	Water birch
Betula papyrifera Marsh.	Paper birch, White birch
Betula pendula Roth	European white birch
Betula populifolia Marsh.	Gray birch

Betula pubescens Ehrh.	Hairy birch
Betula verrucosa Ehrh., *see Betula pendula*	
Bombax buonopozense Beauv.	Bombax
Bombax ceiba L. (*B. malabaricum*)	Silk cotton tree
Borassus flabellifer L.	Palmyra palm
Bosqueia angolensis Ficalho	Okure
Bougainvillea spp.	Bougainvillea
Broussonetia papyrifera (L.) Vent	Paper mulberry
Brownea spp.	Brownea
Bruguiera spp.	
Calliandra eriophylla Benth.	False mesquite calliandra
Callocedrus decurrens (Torr.) Florin	Incense-cedar
Calluna vulgaris (L.) Hull.	Heather
Camellia sinensis (L.) Ktze.	Tea
Camellia thea, see Camellia sinensis	
Canangia spp.	
Carica papaya L.	Papaya
Carapa spp.	Carapa
Carpinus caroliniana Walt.	American hornbeam, Blue beech
Carya glabra (Mill.) Sweet	Pignut hickory
Carya illinoensis (Wangenh.) K. Koch	Pecan
Carya ovata (Mill.) K. Koch	Shagbark hickory
Cassia fistula L.	Golden shower, Pudding-pipe-tree
Cassia splendida Vogel.	Golden-wonder
Castanea crenata Sieb. & Zucc.	Japanese chestnut
Castanea dentata (Marsh:) Borkh.	American chestnut
Castanea sativa (Mill.)	Spanish chestnut
Castanea vesca, see Castanea sativa	
Castilloa spp.	
Casuarina spp.	Casuarina, Beefwood
Casuarina sumatrana Jungh.	Sempilau
Catalpa bignonioides Walt.	Southern catalpa
Catalpa speciosa Warder	Northern catalpa
Ceanothus integerrimus Hook & Arn.	Deerbrush
Cedrus deodar Roxb. G. Don	Deodar
Cedrus libani A. Rich.	Cedar of Lebanon
Ceiba pentandra (L.) Gaertn.	Kapok
Celtis laevigata Willd.	Texas sugarberry
Celtis mildbraedii Engl.	Esa
Celtis occidentalis L.	Hackberry
Cephalotaxus spp.	Cephalotaxus
Ceratonia siliqua L.	Carob
Cercidiphyllum japonicum Sieb. & Zucc.	Katsura tree
Cercidium floridum Benth.	Blue paloverde
Cercis canadensis L.	Eastern redbud
Cercis siliquastrum L.	Judas tree
Ceriops spp.	
Ceroxylon andicola H. & B.	Wax palm
Chamaecyparis nootkatensis (D. Don) Spach	Alaska cedar
Chamaecyparis obtusa (Sieb. & Zucc.) Endl.	Hinoki cypress
Chamaecyparis thyoides (L.) B.S.P.	Atlantic white-cedar, Southern white-cedar
Chlorophora excelsa (Welw.) Benth.	Iroko

Cinchona ledgeriana Moens. ex Trimen	Cinchona bark tree
Citrus limon (L.) Burm. f.	Lemon
Citrus paradisi Macf.	Grapefruit
Citrus sinensis Osbeck	Sweet orange
Citrus reticulata ᵧ	Tangerine
Cladrastis lutea (Michx.f.) K. Koch	Yellowwood
Clematis spp.	Clematis, Virgin's bower
Clerodendrum incisum Klotzsch	
Clethra alnifolia L.	Sweet pepperbush
Clusia spp.	Clusia
Cocos nucifera L.	Coconut palm
Coffea arabica L.	Arabian coffee
Combretum spp.	Combretum
Comptonia peregrina (L.) J. Coult.	Sweet fern
Copernicia cerifera (Arr.) Mart.	Carnauba palm
Coriaria spp.	
Cornus canadensis L.	Dwarf cornus, Bunchberry
Cornus florida L.	Flowering dogwood
Cornus racemosa Lam.	Panicled dogwood
Cornus stolonifora Michx.	Red-osier dogwood
Corylus avellana L.	Filbert
Corylus cornuta Marsh. (*C. rostrata* Ait.)	Beaked hazel
Corylus cornuta var. *Californica*	California hazel
Crataegus spp.	Hawthorn
Crataegus douglasii Lindl.	Black hawthorn
Cryptomeria japonica (L.f.) D. Don.	Sugi, Japanese cedar
Cunninghamia spp.	China fir
Cupressus arizonica Greene	Arizona cypress
Cupressus macrocarpa Hartw.	Monterey cypress
Cycas spp.	Cycas, Bread palm
Cydonia oblonga Mill. (*C. vulgaris* Pers.)	Quince
Cytisus spp. L.	Broom
Dacrydium spp.	Dacrydium
Dillenia indica L.	Elephant-apple
Dillenia subfruticosa (Griff.) Mart.	Simpoh ayer
Diospyros virginiana L.	Persimmon
Dodonaea spp.	Varnish-leaves
Duabanga spp.	
Elaeocarpus spp.	
Elaeagnus spp.	Oleaster
Encelia californica Nutt.	California encelia
Encelia farinosa Gray.	Brittle bush, Incienso
Entandophragma angolense (Welw.) C. DC.	Tiama
Ephedra spp.	Ephedra, Joint fir
Erythroxylum spp.	Coca
Eucalyptus camaldulensis Dehnh. (*E. rostrata*)	Red gum
Eucalyptus gigantea Hook. f.	Alpine ash
Eucalyptus globulus Labill. (*E. delegatensis* R.T. Baker)	Blue gum
Eucalyptus gunnii var. *acervula* Hook.f.	Manna eucalyptus
Eucalyptus macarthurii H. Deane & Maiden.	Camden woolybutt
Eucalyptus marginata Sm.	Jarrah
Eucalyptus niphophila Maiden and Blakely	Snow gum
Eucalyptus regnans F. Muell.	Mountain ash
Eugenia spp.	

Euonymus alata Sieb.	Winged euonymus
Euphorbia spp.	
Excoecaria parvifolia Muell.	
Fagus grandifolia Ehr.	American beech
Fagus sylvatica L.	European beech
Ficus carica L.	Fig
Ficus ceriflua Jungh. (*E. variegata*)	Gondang
Ficus elastica Roxbg.	India rubber
Flindersia australis R. Br.	Flindose, Rasp-pad
Forsythia spp.	Forsythia
Fouquieria splendens Engelm.	Coach-whip
Fragaria spp.	Strawberry
Fraxinus americana L.	White ash
Fraxinus excelsior L.	European ash
Fraxinus mandshurica Rupr.	Manchurian ash
Fraxinus nigra Marsh.	Black ash
Fraxinus ornus L.	Manna ash
Fraxinus pennsylvanica Marsh.	Green ash
Ginkgo biloba L.	Ginkgo, Maidenhair tree
Gleditsia triacanthos L.	Honey locust
Gordonia lasianthus Ell.	Loblolly bay
Gnetum spp.	Gnetum
Gossypium hirsutum L.	Cotton
Gunnera spp.	
Hamamelis mollis Oliv.	Chinese witch-hazel
Hamamelis virginiana L.	Witch-hazel
Hedera helix L.	English ivy
Heimerliodendron brunonianum (Endl.) Skottsb.	
Heritiera spp.	Heritiera
Hevea brasiliensis (Willd. ex A. Juss) Mull-Arg.	Brazilian rubber tree
Hibiscus rosa-sinensis L.	Chinese hibiscus
Hildegardia barteri (M.T. Mast.) Kostern.	
Hippophaë spp.	Sea-buckthorn
Hopea spp.	
Hyptis emoryi Torr.	Desert lavender
Ilex coriacea (Pursh) Chapman	Gallberry
Ilex cornuta var. *burfordii* Lindl. & Paxt.	Chinese holly
Ilex glabra (L.) Gray	Inkberry, Bitter gallberry
Ilex opaca Ait.	American holly
Juglans cinerea L.	Butternut
Juglans nigra L.	Black walnut
Juglans regia	English walnut
Juniperus occidentalis Hook.	Western juniper
Juniperus osteosperma (Torr.) Little	Utah juniper
Juniperus scopulorum Sarg.	Rocky mountain juniper
Juniperus virginiana L.	Eastern redcedar
Kalmia latifolia L.	Mountain-laurel
Kalmia polifolia Wang.	Bog laurel
Kigelia africana Benth.	Sausage tree
Lagerstroemia flos-reginae Retz.	Queen crepe myrtle
Larix decidua Mill.	European larch
Larix laricina (DuRoi) K. Koch	Tamarack
Larix leptolepis (Sieb. & Zucc.) Gord.	Japanese larch
Larix lyallii Parl.	Subalpine larch

Larix occidentalis Nutt.	Western larch
Larix polonica Raciborski	Polish larch
Larrea divaricata Cav.	Creosote bush
Larrea tridentata (D.C.) Coville	Coville creosote bush
Laurus spp.	Laurel
Libocedrus decurrens, see Calocedrus decurrens	
Ligustrum spp.	Privet, Ligustrum
Liquidambar styraciflua L.	Sweetgum, Redgum
Liriodendron tulipifera L.	Yellow-poplar, Tulip tree
Litchi chinensis Sonn.	Litchi
Lithocarpus densiflorus (Hook. & Arn.) Rehd.	Tanoak
Lonicera spp.	Honeysuckle
Macadamia spp.	Macademia
Maclura pomifera (Raf.) Schneid.	Osage-orange
Magnolia acumunata L.	Cucumbertree
Magnolia grandiflora L.	Southern magnolia
Malus hupehensis (Pamp.) Rehd.	Tea crabapple
Malus sikkimensis (Wenz.) Kochne ex C.K. Schneid.	
Malus pumila Mill. (=*M. domestica*)	Common apple
Mangifera indica L.	Mango
Metasequoia glyptostroboides Hu & Cheng	Dawn redwood, Metasequoia
Michelia champaca L.	Champac
Mimosa pudica L.	Mimosa
Mitragyna stipulosa Kuntze.	Abura
Monodora tenuifolia Benth.	Dubiri
Montezuma speciosissima Sesse & Moc. ex DC.	Maga
Morus alba L.	White mulberry
Musa sapientum L.	Banana
Musanga cercopioides R. Br.	Umbrella tree
Myrica carolinensis Gray	Bayberry
Myrica cerifera L.	Wax myrtle, Southern bayberry
Myrica gale L. (=*Gale palustris* (Lam.) Chev.	Sweet gale, Meadow fern
Myrica pennsylvanica Loisel.	Northern bayberry
Nicotiana glauca Graham	Tree tobacco
Nothofagus spp.	Nothofagus
Nyssa aquatica L.	Tupelo-gum, Water tupelo
Nyssa sylvatica Marsh.	Blackgum, Black tupelo
Ochroma lagopus Sw.	Balsa
Olea europaea L.	Olive
Oreopanax spp.	Oreopanax
Ostrya virginiana (Mill.) K. Koch	Eastern hophornbeam
Oxytropis pilosa DC.	
Palaquium gutta (Hook.) Burck.	Gutta-percha
Pandanus spp.	Screw-pine
Parthenium argentatum A. Gray	Guayule
Parthenocissus quinquefolia (L.) Planch.	Virginia creeper, Woodbine
Paulownia tomentosa (Thunb.) Sieb. & Zucc.	Royal paulownia
Pavetta spp.	
Peganum harmala L.	Harmala shrub
Persea americana Mill.	Avocado
Phoenix dactylifera L.	Date palm
Phoradendron spp.	Green mistletoe
Phyllocladus spp.	Phyllocladus

Picea abies (L.) Karst.	Norway spruce
Picea engelmannii Parry	Engelmann spruce
Picea excelsa Link, *see Picea abies*	
Picea glauca (Moench) Voss	White spruce
Picea mariana (Mill.) B.S.P.	Black spruce
Picea pungens Engelm.	Blue spruce
Picea rubens Sarg.	Red spruce
Picea sitchensis (Bong.) Carr.	Sitka spruce
Pinus albicaulis Engelm.	Whitebark pine
Pinus aristata Engelm.	Rocky mountain bristlecone pine
Pinus attenuata Lemm.	Knobcone pine
Pinus banksiana Lamb.	Jack pine
Pinus canariensis Sweet ex K. Spreng.	Canary Islands pine
Pinus caribaea Morelet	Caribbean pine
Pinus cembra L.	Swiss stone pine
Pinus cembroides Zucc.	Mexican nut pine
Pinus contorta Dougl.	Lodgepole pine
Pinus coulteri D. Don	Coulter pine
Pinus densiflora Sieb. & Zucc.	Japanese red pine
Pinus echinata Mill.	Shortleaf pine
Pinus edulis Engelm.	Pinyon pine
Pinus elliottii Engelm.	Slash pine
Pinus flexilis James	Limber pine
Pinus halepensis Mill.	Aleppo pine
Pinus jeffreyi Grev. & Balf.	Jeffrey pine
Pinus insularis, see Pinus kesiya	
Pinus kesiya Royal ex Gordon	Benguet pine
Pinus lambertiana Dougl.	Sugar pine
Pinus longaeva D.K. Bailey	Great basin bristlecone pine
Pinus merkusii Jungh & de Vriese	Tenasserim pine
Pinus monticola D. Don	Western white pine
Pinus mugo Turra	Mugo or Swiss mountain pine
Pinus nigra Arnold.	Austrian pine or black pine
Pinus nigra var. *calabrica* (Loud.) Schneider	Corsican pine
Pinus oocarpa Schiede.	Ocote pine
Pinus palustris Mill.	Longleaf pine
Pinus pinea L.	Italian stone pine
Pinus ponderosa Laws.	Ponderosa pine
Pinus radiata D. Don	Monterey pine
Pinus resinosa Ait.	Red or Norway pine
Pinus rigida Mill.	Pitch pine
Pinus sabiniana Dougl.	Digger pine
Pinus serotina Michx.	Pond pine
Pinus strobus L.	Eastern white pine
Pinus sylvestris L.	Scotch pine, Scots pine
Pinus taeda L.	Loblolly pine
Pinus thunbergii Parl.	Japanese black pine
Pinus thunbergiana Franco, *see Pinus thunbergii*	
Pinus torreyana Carr.	Torrey pine
Pinus tropicalis Morelet	Tropical red pine
Pinus virginiana Mill.	Virginia pine
Piper spp.	
Platanus x *acerifolia* Ait. Willd.	London plane

Platanus occidentalis L.	American sycamore
Podocarpus spp.	Podocarpus
Populus angustifolia James	Narrowleaf cottonwood
Populus balsamifera L.	Balsam poplar
Populus deltoides Bartr.	Eastern cottonwood
Populus euroamericana marilandica	
Populus grandidentata Michx.	Bigtooth aspen
Populus maximowiczii x *trichocarpa* Schreiner & Stout	Japanese poplar
Populus nigra L. 'Italica'	Lombardy poplar
Populus x *robusta*	
Populus tacamahaca Mill., see *Populus balsamifera*	
Populus tremula L.	European aspen
Populus tremuloides Michx.	Quaking aspen
Populus trichocarpa T. & G.	Black cottonwood, Balsam cottonwood
Prosopis tamarugo F. Phil.	Tamarugo
Prunus amygdalus Batsch	Almond
Prunus armeniaca L.	Apricot
Prunus avium L.	Sweet cherry, Mazzard, Bing cherry
Prunus cerasus L.	Sour cherry
Prunus domestica L.	Garden plum
Prunus laurocerasus L.	Cherry laurel
Prunus nigra Ait.	Red plum
Prunus persica Batsch	Peach
Prunus senriko Lindl.	Japanese cherry
Prunus serotina Ehrh.	Black cherry
Prunus virginiana L.	Choke cherry
Pseudotsuga menziesii (Mirb.) Franco	Douglas-fir
Psychotria spp.	Wild coffee
Pterocarpus indicus Willd.	Narra
Pterygota horsefieldii Kost.	White tulip-oak
Purshia spp.	Antelope bush
Pyrus communis L.	Common pear
Quercus alba L.	White oak
Quercus agrifolia Née	California live oak
Quercus coccinea Muench.	Scarlet oak
Quercus ellipsoidalis E.J. Hill	Northern pin oak
Quercus falcata var. *falcata*	Southern red oak (typical)
Quercus gambelii Nutt.	Gambel oak
Quercus kelloggii Newb.	California black oak
Quercus laevis Walt. (*Q. catesbaei* Walt.)	Turkey oak
Quercus lyrata Walt.	Overcup oak
Quercus macrocarpa Michx.	Bur oak
Quercus marilandica Muench.	Blackjack oak
Quercus palustris Muench.	Pin oak
Quercus pedunculata J.F. Ehrh.	Pedunculate oak (European)
Quercus phellos L.	Willow oak
Quercus prinus L.	Chestnut oak
Quercus robur L.	English oak
Quercus rubra L.	Northern red or Eastern red oak
Quercus stellata Wang.	Post oak
Quercus suber L.	Cork oak
Quercus velutina Lam.	Black oak
Quercus virginiana Mill.	Live oak

Raphia pedunculata Beauv.	Madagascar or raffia palm
Remijia pendunculata Triana	Cuprea
Retinospora spp.	
Rhagodia baccata Moq.	
Rhamnus spp.	Buckthorn, Cascara
Rhizophora mangle L.	American mangrove
Rhododendron ferrugineum L.	Alpine rose
Rhododendron poukhanense Lev.	Korean azalea
Rhus copallina L.	Winged sumac, Shining sumac
Rhus glabra L.	Smooth sumac
Rhus typhina L.	Staghorn sumac
Ribes spp.	Gooseberry, Currant
Ribes nigrum L.	Black currant
Robinia pseudoacacia L.	Black locust
Rosa arvensis Huds.	Ayrshire rose
Rosa rugosa Thunb.	Turkestan rose, Japanese rose
Rubus spp.	Blackberry, Raspberry
Salix fragilis L.	Crack willow
Salix nigra Marsh.	Black willow
Salix viminalis L.	Basket willow
Sambucus canadensis L.	American elder
Sambucus nigra L.	European elder
Santalum album L.	White sandalwood
Sassafras albidum (Nutt.) Nees	Sassafras
Sassafras officinale, see Sassafras albidum	
Schizolobium excelsum, see Schizolobium parahybum	
Schizolobium parahybum (Vell.) Blake	Quamwood, Tambar
Schornia spp.	
Sciadopitys verticillata (Thumb.) Sieb. & Zucc.	Umbrella-pine
Sequoia sempervirens (D. Don) Endl.	Redwood
Sequoiadendron giganteum (Lindl.) Buchh.	Giant sequoia, Big tree
Shepherdia spp.	Buffaloberry
Shorea robusta Gaertn. f.	Sal
Silphium spp.	Rosin weed
Simmondsia chinensis (Link) C.K. Schneid.	Jojoba
Sonneratia spp.	
Sorbus aucuparia L.	European mountain ash
Sorbus sitchensis M.J. Roem.	Western mountain ash
Spathodea campanulata Beauv.	African tulip tree
Strychnos spp.	
Swietenia mahogani L.	West Indies mahogany
Syringa chinensis Willd.	Chinese laurel
Syringa vulgaris L.	Common lilac
Tabebuia serratifolia (Vahl.) Nichols.	Yellow poui
Taxodium distichum (L.) Rich	Baldcypress
Taxodium mucronatum Ten.	Montezuma baldcypress
Taxus spp.	Yew
Terminalia catappa L.	Indian almond
Terminalia ivorensis A. Chev.	Idigbo, Emeri
Terminalia superba Engl. & Diels.	Afara, Limba
Thea sinensis, see Camellia sinensis	
Theobroma cacao L.	Cacao
Thespasia spp.	

Thuja occidentalis L.	Northern white-cedar, Eastern arborvitae
Thuja plicata Donn	Western redcedar
Tilia americana L.	Basswood
Tilia cordata Mill.	Little leaf linden
Tilia platyphyllos Scop.	Large leaf linden
Torreya spp.	Torreya
Tovomita spp.	
Trema guineensis (Schumach & Thonn.) Ficalho	Afefe
Trema orientalis (L.) Bl.	Anabiong
Tsuga canadensis Carr.	Eastern hemlock
Tsuga caroliniana Engelm.	Carolina hemlock
Tsuga heterophylla Sarg.	Western hemlock
Ulmus alata Michx.	Winged elm
Ulmus americana L.	American elm
Ulmus Davidiana Planchon	Harunire
Ulmus effusa Willd., *see Ulmus laevis*	
Ulmus laevis Pall.	European white elm
Ulmus parvifolia Jacq.	Chinese elm
Ulmus pumila L.	Siberian elm
Ulmus rubra L.	Slippery elm
Vaccinium angustifolium Ait.	Lowbush blueberry
Vaccinium corymbosum L.	Highbush blueberry
Viburnum pubescens Pursh, *see Viburnum rafinesquianum*	
Viburnum rafinesquianum Schultes	Downy viburnum
Vitis vinifera L.	Wine grape
Welwitschia mirabilis Hook.	Welwitschia
Xylopia spp.	
Zilla spinosa Prantl	
Zygophyllum dumosum Boiss.	

Bibliography

Asen, S. (1977). Flavonoid chemical markers as an adjunct for the identification of cultivars. *Hortscience* **12,** 410.

Abeles, F. B. (1973). "Ethylene in Plant Biology." Academic Press, New York.

Abell, C. A., and Hursh, C. R. (1931). Positive gas and water pressures in oaks. *Science* **73,** 449.

Ackerman, E., and Loff, G. (1959). "Technology in American Water Development." Johns Hopkins Press, Baltimore, Maryland.

Ackerman, R. F., and Farrar, J. L. (1965). The effect of light and temperature on the germination of jack pine and lodgepole pine seeds. *Univ. Toronto, Fac. For., Tech. Rep.* **5.**

Ackley, W. B. (1954). Seasonal and diurnal changes in the water contents and water deficits of Bartlett pear leaves. *Plant Physiol.* **29,** 445–448.

Adams, M. S., and Strain, B. R. (1969). Seasonal photosynthetic rates in stems of *Cercidium floridum* Benth. *Photosynthetica* **3,** 55–62.

Addicott, F. T. (1970). Plant hormones in the control of abscission. *Biol. Rev. Cambridge Philos. Soc.* **45,** 485–524.

Addicott, F. T., and Lyon, J. L. (1969). Physiology of abscisic acid and related substances. *Annu. Rev. Plant Physiol.* **20,** 139–164.

Addicott, F. T., and Lyon, J. L. (1973). The physiological ecology of abscission. *In* "Shedding of Plant Parts" (T. T. Kozlowski, ed.), pp. 475–524. Academic Press, New York.

Addoms, R. M. (1937). Nutritional studies on loblolly pine. *Plant Physiol.* **12,** 199–205.

Ahavoni, N., Blumenfeld, A., and Richmond, A. E. (1977). Hormonal activity in detached leaves as affected by leaf water content. *Plant Physiol.* **59,** 1169–1173.

Ahlgren, C. E. (1957). Phenological observations of nineteen native tree species. *Ecology* **38,** 622–628.

Ahlgren, I. (1974). The effect of fire on soil organisms. *In* "Fire and Ecosystems" (T. T. Kozlowski and C. E. Ahlgren, eds.), pp. 47–72. Academic Press, New York.

Al-Ani, H. A., Strain, B. R., and Mooney, H. A. (1972). The physiological ecology of diverse populations of the desert shrub *Simmondsia chinensis*. *J. Ecol.* **60,** 41–57.

Albersheim, P. (1965). The substructure and function of the cell wall. *In* "Plant Biochemistry" (J. Bonner and J. E. Varner, eds.), 2nd ed., pp. 151–186. Academic Press, New York.

Albersheim, P., and Anderson-Prouty, A. J. (1975). Carbohydrates, proteins, cell surfaces, and the biochemistry of pathogenesis. *Annu. Rev. Plant Physiol.* **26,** 31–52.

Alberte, R. S., Fiscus, E. L., and Naylor, A. W. (1975). The effects of water stress on the development of the photosynthetic apparatus in greening leaves. *Plant Physiol.* **55,** 317–321.

Alberte, R. S., McClure, P. R., and Thornber, J. P. (1976). Photosynthesis in trees. Organization of chlorophyll and photosynthetic unit size in isolated gymnosperm chloroplasts. *Plant Physiol.* **58,** 341–344.

Alberte, R. S., Thornber, J. P., and Fiscus, E. L. (1977). Water stress effects on the content and organization of chlorophyll in mesophyll and bundle sheath chloroplasts of maize. *Plant Physiol.* **59,** 351–353.

Alden, J., and Hermann, R. K. (1971). Aspects of the cold-hardiness mechanism in plants. *Bot. Rev.* **37,** 37–142.

Aldrich-Blake, R. N. (1930). The root system of the Corsican pine. *Oxford For. Mem.* **12,** 1–64.

Alfieri, F. J., and Evert, R. F. (1968). Seasonal development of the secondary phloem in *Pinus*. *Am. J. Bot.* **55,** 518–528.

Alfieri, F. J., and Evert, R. F. (1973). Structure and seasonal development of the secondary phloem in the Pinaceae. *Bot. Gaz. (Chicago)* **134,** 17–25.

Allaway, W. G., and Milthorpe, F. L. (1976). Structure and functioning in stomata. *In* "Water Deficits and Plant Growth" (T. T. Kozlowski, ed.), Vol. 4, pp. 57–152. Academic Press, New York.

Allen, E. K., and Allen, O. N. (1958). Biological aspects of symbiotic nitrogen fixation. *Encyl. Plant Physiol.,* **8,** 48–118.

Allen, G. S., and Owens, J. N. (1972). "The Life History of Douglas Fir." Can. For. Serv., Ottawa.

Allen, R. M. (1955). Foliage treatments improve survival of longleaf pine plantings. *J. For.* **53,** 724–727.

Allen, R. M., and Scarbrough, N. M. (1969). Development of a year's height growth in longleaf pine saplings. *U.S. For. Serv., Res. Pap. SO* **45.**

Allmendinger, D. F., Kenworthy, A. O., and Overholser, E. L. (1943). The carbon dioxide intake of apple leaves as affected by reducing the available soil water to different levels. *Proc. Am. Soc. Hortic. Sci.* **42,** 133–140.

Allsopp, A., and Misra, P. (1940). The constitution of the cambium, the new wood, and mature sapwood of the common ash, the common elm and the Scotch pine. *Biochem. J.* **34,** 1078–1084.

Alvim, P. de T. (1960). Moisture stress as a requirement for flowering of coffee. *Science* **132,** 354.

Alvim, P. de T. (1964). Tree growth perodicity in tropical climates. *In* "The Formation of Wood in Forest Trees" (M. H. Zimmermann, ed.), pp. 479–496. Academic Press, New York.

Alvim, P. de T., and Kozlowski, T. T., eds. (1977). "Ecophysiology of Tropical Crops." Academic Press, New York.

Alway, F. J., Kittredge, J., and Methley, W. J. (1933). Components of the forest floor layers under different forest trees on the same soil type. *Soil Sci.* **36,** 387–398.

Anderson, D. B., and Kerr, T. (1943). A note on the growth behavior of cotton bolls. *Plant Physiol.* **18,** 261–269.

Anderson, M. G. (1967). Photon flux, chlorophyll content, and photosynthesis under natural conditions. *Ecology* **48,** 1050–1053.

Anderson, N. F., and Guard, A. T. (1964). A comparative study of the vegetative, transitional and floral apex of *Acer pseudoplatanus* L. *Phytomorphology* **14,** 500–508.

Anderson, W. P. (1976). Transport through roots. *Encycl. Plant Physiol., New Ser.* **2B,** 129–156.

Anderssen, F. G. (1929). Some seasonal changes in the tracheal sap of pear and apricot trees. *Plant Physiol.* **4,** 459–476.

Anderssen, F. G. (1932). Chlorosis of deciduous fruit trees due to a copper deficiency. *J. Pomol.* **10,** 130–146.

Andersson, E. (1963). Seed stands and seed orchards in the breeding of conifers. *Proc. World Consult. For. Genet. For. Tree Improve., 2nd,* 1963, FAO/FORGEN 63C8/1/, pp. 1–18.

Andrews, R. E., and Newman, E. I. (1968). The influence of root pruning on the growth and transpiration of wheat under different soil moisture conditions. *New Phytol.* **67,** 617–630.

Anonymous (1948). Woody plant seed manual. *U.S., Dep. Agric., Misc. Publ.* **654.**

Anonymous (1967). Wind. *Forestry* **40,** 111–113.

Anonymous (1968). "Forest Fertilization: Theory and Practice," Symposium on Forest Fertilization, Gainesville, Florida, 1967. Tenn. Valley Auth., Muscle Shoals, Alabama.

Antonovics, A., Bradshaw, A. D., and Turner, R. G. (1971). Heavy metal tolerance in plants. *Adv. Ecol. Res.* **7,** 1–85.

Armond, P. A., Schreiber, U., and Björkman, O. (1978). Photosynthetic acclimation to temperature in *Larrea divaricata:* light harvesting efficiency and capacity of photosynthetic electron transport reactions. II. Light harvesting efficiency and electron transport. *Plant Physiol.* **61,** 411–415.

Arrhenius, O. (1942). Fettmängdens variation hos vára träd. *Sven. Bot. Tidskr.* **36,** 95–99.

Artschwager, E. (1950). The time factor in the differentiation of secondary xylem and phloem in pecan. *Am. J. Bot.* **37,** 15–24.

Ashton, F. M., and Crafts, A. S. (1973). "Mode of Action of Herbicides." Wiley, New York.

Askenasy, E. (1895). Über das Saftsteigen. *Bot. Zentralbl.* **62,** 237–238.

Atkins, W. R. G. (1916). "Some Recent Researches in Plant Physiology." Whitaker and Co., London.

Avery, D. J. (1969). Comparisons of fruiting and deblossomed maiden apple trees, and of nonfruiting trees on a dwarfing and an invigorating root stock. *New Phytol.* **68,** 323–336.

Avery, D. J. (1970). Effects of fruiting on the growth of apple trees on four rootstock varieties. *New Phytol.* **69,** 19–30.

Avery, D. J. (1977). Maximum photosynthetic rate—a case study in apple. *New Phytol.* **78,** 55–63.

Ayers, J. C., and Barden, J. A. (1975). Net photosynthesis and dark respiration of apple leaves as affected by pesticides. *J. Am. Soc. Hortic. Sci.* **100,** 24–28.

Babalola, O., Boersma, L., and Youngberg, C. T. (1968). Photosynthesis and transpiration of Monterey pine seedlings as a function of soil water suction and soil temperature. *Plant Physiol.* **43,** 515–521.

Bachelard, E. P. (1969a). Effects of gibberellic acid on internode growth and starch contents of *Eucalyptus camaldulensis* seedlings. *New Phytol.* **68,** 1017–1022.

Bachelard, E. P. (1969b). Studies on the formation of epicormic shoots on Eucalypt stem segments. *Aust. J. Biol. Sci.* **22,** 1291–1296.

Bachelard, E. P., and Wightman, F. (1974). Biochemical and physiological studies on dormancy release in tree buds. III. Changes in endogenous growth substances and a possible mechanism of dormancy release in overwintering vegetative buds of *Populus balsamifera*. *Can. J. Bot.* **51,** 2315–2326.

Baes, C. F., Jr., Goeller, H. E., Olson, J. S., and Rotty, R. M. (1977). Carbon dioxide and the climate: The uncontrolled experiment. *Am. Sci.* **66,** 310–320.

Bagda, H. (1948). Morphologische und physiologische Untersuchungen über Valonia Eichen (*Quercus macrolepis* Ky.) in Haci-Kadin-Tal Bei Ankara. *Univ. Ankara Fac. Sci. Commun.* **1,** 89–125.

Bagda, H. (1952). Untersuchungen über den weiblichen Gametophyten der Valonia Eichen (*Quercus macrolepis* Ky.). *Rev. Fac. Sci. Univ. Istanbul* **17,** 77–94.

Bailey, I. W. (1920). The cambium and its derivative tissues. II. Size variations of cambium initials in gymnosperms and angiosperms. *Am. J. Bot.* **7,** 355–367.

Baker, F. S. (1950). "Principles of Silviculture." McGraw-Hill, New York.

Baker, H., and James, W. O. (1933). The behaviour of dyes in the transpiration stream of sycamore (*Acer pseudoplatanus*). *New Phytol.* **32,** 245–260.

Bamber, R. K. (1976). Heartwood, its function and formation. *Wood Sci. Technol.* **10,** 1–8.

Bange, G. G. J. (1953). On the quantitative explanation of stomatal transpiration. *Acta Bot. Neerl.* **2,** 255–269.

Bannan, M. W. (1955). The vascular cambium and radial growth of *Thuja occidentalis* L. *Can. J. Bot.* **33,** 113–138.

Bannan, M. W. (1957). The structure and growth of the cambium. *Tappi* **40,** 220–225.

Bannan, M. W. (1960). Ontogenetic trends in conifer cambium with respect to frequency of anticlinal division and cell length. *Can. J. Bot.* **40,** 795–802.

Bannan, M. W. (1962). The vascular cambium and tree-ring development. *In* "Tree Growth" (T. T. Kozlowski, ed.), pp. 3–21. Ronald, New York.

Bannan, M. W. (1964). Tracheid size and anticlinal divisions in the cambium of *Pseudotsuga*. *Can. J. Bot.* **42,** 603–631.

Bannan, M. W. (1967). Anticlinal divisions and cell length in conifer cambium. *For. Prod. J.* **17,** 63–69.

Bannan, M. W. (1968). Polarity in the survival and elongation of fusiform initials in conifer cambium. *Can. J. Bot.* **46,** 1005–1008.

Barber, S. A. (1962). A diffusion and mass-flow concept of soil nutrient availability. *Soil Sci.* **93,** 39–49.

Barbour, M. G. (1973). Desert dogma reexamined: root:shoot productivity and plant spacing. *Am. Midl. Nat.* **89,** 41–57.

Barden, J. A. (1971). Factors determining the determination of net photosynthesis of apple leaves. *HortScience* **6,** 448–451.

Barlow, H. W. B. (1966). The effect of cropping on the numbers and kinds of shoots on four apple varieties. *Annu. Rep., East Malling Res. Stn.* 1965, 120–124.

Barner, J. (1961). Wirkungen von organischen und anorganischen Fungiziden auf die innere Blattstruktur and Stoffproduction der Pflanzen. *Mitt. Biol. Bundesanst. Land- Forstwirtsch., Berlin-Dahlem* **104,** 178–183.

Barnes, R. L. (1958). Studies on physiology of isolated pine roots and root callus cultures. Ph.D. Dissertation, Duke University, Durham, North Carolina.

Barnes, R. L. (1963a). Nitrogen transport in the xylem of trees. *J. For.* **61**, 50–51.

Barnes, R. L. (1963b). Organic nitrogen compounds in tree xylem sap. *For. Sci.* **9**, 98–102.

Barnes, R. L. (1972). Effects of chronic exposure to ozone on photosynthesis and respiration of pines. *Environ. Pollut.* **3**, 133–138.

Barney, C. W. (1951). Effects of soil temperature and light intensity on root growth of loblolly pine seedlings. *Plant Physiol.* **26**, 146–163.

Barrow, G. P. (1951). Loss of weight of three Douglas-fir poles. *Q. J. For.* **45**, 235–236.

Barrs, H. D. (1968). Effect of cyclic variations in gas exchange under constant environmental conditions on the ratio of transpiration to net photosynthesis. *Physiol. Plant.* **21**, 918–929.

Barrs, H. D. (1971). Cyclic variations in stomatal aperture, transpiration, and leaf water potential under constant environmental conditions. *Annu. Rev. Plant Physiol.* **22**, 223–236.

Bartholomew, E. T. (1926). Internal decline of lemons. III. Water deficit in lemon fruits caused by excessive leaf evaporation. *Am. J. Bot.* **13**, 102–117.

Bassett, J. R. (1964). Tree growth as affected by soil moisture availability. *Soil. Sci. Soc. Am., Proc.* **28**, 436–438.

Bassett, J. R. (1966). Seasonal diameter growth of loblolly pines. *J. For.* **64**, 674–676.

Bassham, J. A. (1977). Increasing crop production through more controlled photosynthesis. *Science* **197**, 630–638.

Batjer, L. P., and Degman, E. S. (1940). Effect of various amounts of nitrogen, potassium and phosphorous on growth and assimilation in young apple trees. *J. Agric. Res.* **60**, 101–116.

Batjer, L. P., and Thompson, A. H. (1949). Effect of boric acid sprays applied during bloom upon the set of pear fruits. *Proc. Am. Soc. Hortic. Sci.* **53**, 141–142.

Batjer, L. P., Williams, M. W., and Martin, G. C. (1964). Effects of N-di-methylamine succinamic acid (B.9) on vegetative and fruit characteristics of apples, pears, and sweet cherries. *Proc. Am. Soc. Hortic. Sci.* **85**, 11–19.

Bauch, J., Liese, W., and Schultze, R. (1972). The morphological variability of the bordered pit membranes in gymnosperms. *Wood Sci. Technol.* **6**, 165–184.

Bauer, H. (1972). CO_2-gaswecheel nach Hitzestress bei *Abies alba* Mill. und *Acer pseudoplatanus* L. *Photosynthetica* **6**, 424–434.

Baumgartner, A. (1967). Energetic bases for differential vaporization from forest and agricultural lands. *In* "Forest Hydrology" (W. E. Sopper and H. W. Lull, eds.), pp. 381–389. Pergamon, Oxford.

Baxter, D. V. (1943). "Pathology in Forest Practice." Wiley, New York.

Beadle, C. L., and Jarvis, P. G. (1977). The effects of shoot water status on some photosynthetic partial processes in Sitka spruce. *Physiol. Plant.* **41**, 7–13.

Beadle, N. C. W. (1966). Soil phosphate and its role in molding segments of the Australian flora and vegetation, with special reference to xeromorphy and sclerophylly. *Ecology* **47**, 992–1007.

Beadle, N. C. W. (1968). Some aspects of the ecology and physiology of Australian xeromorphic plants. *Aust. J. Sci.* **30**, 348–354.

Bear, F. E. (1942). "Soils and Fertilizers." Wiley, New York.

Beard, J. S. (1946). The natural vegetation of Trinidad. *Oxford For. Mem.* **20**.

Becking, J. H. (1972). Enige gegevens en Kanttekeningen over de betekenis van de zwarte els voor de houtteelt in Nederland. *Ned. Bosbouw-Tijdschr.* **44**, 128–131.

Becking, J. H. (1975). Root nodules in nonlegumes. *In* "The Development and Function of Roots" (J. G. Torrey and D. T. Clarkson, eds.), pp. 508–566. Academic Press, New York.

Beckman, C. H., Kuntz, J. E., Riker, A. J., and Berbee, J. G. (1953). Host responses associated with the development of oak wilt. *Phytopathology* **43**, 448–454.

Beckman, C. H., Brun, W. A., and Buddenhagen, I. W. (1962). Water relations in banana plants infected with *Pseudomonas solanacearum*. *Phytopathology* **52**, 1144–1148.

Beeson, K. C., Lazar, V. A., and Boyce, S. G. (1955). Some plant accumulators of the micronutrient elements. *Ecology* **36**, 155–156.

Beevers, H., and Hageman, R. H. (1969). Nitrate reduction in green plants, *Annu. Rev. Plant Physiol.* **20**, 495–522.

Begg, J. E., and Turner, N. C. (1976). Crop water deficits. *Adv. Agron.* **28**, 161–217.

Belyea, R. M. (1952). Death and deterioration of balsam fir weakened by spruce budworm defoliation in Ontario. *J. For.* **50**, 729–738.

Bengtson, G. W. (1968). Progress and needs in forest fertilization research in the South. *In* "Forest Fertilization: Theory and Practice," Anonymous, pp. 234–241. Tenn. Valley Auth., Muscle Shoals, Alabama.

Bennett, C. W. (1956). Biological relations of plant viruses. *Annu. Rev. Plant Physiol.* **7**, 143–170.

Bennett, J. P., Anderssen, F. G., and Milad, Y. (1927). Methods of obtaining tracheal sap from woody plants. *New Phytol.* **26**, 316–323.

Benzian, B., and Warren, R. G. (1957). Copper deficiency in Sitka spruce seedlings. *Nature (London)* **178**, 864–865.

Berbee, J. G., Omuemu, J. O., Martin, R. R., and Castello, J. P. (1976). Detection and elimination of viruses in poplars. *U.S., For. Serv., Gen. Tech. Rep. NC* **21**, 85–91.

Berg, T. M. (1964). Studies on poplar mosaic virus and its relation to the host. *Meded. Landbouwhogesch. Wageningen* **64**, 1–59.

Berkley, E. E. (1931). Marcescent leaves of certain species of *Quercus. Bot. Gaz. (Chicago)* **92**, 85–93.

Berlyn, G. P. (1961). Recent advances in wood anatomy. The cell wall in secondary xylem. *For. Prod. J.* **14**, 467–476.

Berlyn, G. P. (1962). Developmental patterns in pine polyembryony. *Am. J. Bot.* **49**, 327–333.

Berlyn, G. P. (1967). The structure of germination in *Pinus lambertiana. Yale Univ. Sch. For. Bull.* **71**.

Berry, C. R. (1973). The differential sensitivity of eastern white pine to three types of air pollution. *Can. J. For. Res.* **3**, 543–547.

Berry, F. H. (1969). Decay in the upland oak stands of Kentucky. *U.S., For. Serv., Res. Pap. NE* **126**, 1–16.

Bevage, D. I. (1968). Inhibition of seedling hoop pine (*Araucaria cunninghamii* Ait.) on forest soils by phytotoxic substances from the root zone of *Pinus, Araucaria,* and *Flindersia. Plant Soil* **29**, 263–273.

Biale, J. B. (1950). Postharvest physiology and biochemistry of fruits. *Annu. Rev Plant Physiol.* **1**, 183–206.

Biale, J. B. (1954). The ripening of fruit. *Sci. Am.* **190**, 40–44.

Biale, J. B. (1960). The postharvest biochemistry of tropical and subtropical fruits. *Adv. Food Res.* **10**, 293–354.

Bialoglowski, J. (1936). Effect of extent and temperature of roots on transpiration of rooted lemon cuttings. *Proc. Am. Soc. Hortic. Sci.* **34**, 96–102.

Bidwell, R. G. S. (1974). "Plant Physiology." Macmillan, New York.

Bier, J. E. (1959). The relation of bark moisture to the development of canker diseases caused by native, facultative parasites. I. Cryptodiaporthe canker on willow. *Can. J. Bot.* **37**, 229–238.

Bierhuizen, J. F., and Slatyer, R. O. (1964). Photosynthesis of cotton leaves under a range of environmental conditions in relation to internal and external diffusive resistances. *Aust. J. Biol. Sci.* **17**, 348–359.

Bilan, M. V. (1960). Root development of loblolly pine seedlings in modified environments. *Austin State Coll. Dep. For., Bull.* **4**.

Billings, W. D. (1952). The environmental complex in relation to plant growth and distribution. *Q. Rev. Biol.* **27**, 251–265.

Billings, W. D., and Morris, R. J. (1951). Reflection of visible and infrared radiation from leaves of different ecological groups. *Am. J. Bot.* **38**, 327–331.

Bingham, R. T., and Squillace, A. E. (1957). Phenology and other features of flowering of pines, with special reference to *Pinus monticola,* Dougl. *North Region Intermount. For. Range Exp. Stn., Res. Pap.* **53**.

Biswell, H. H. (1935). Effect of the environment upon the root habits of certain deciduous forest trees. *Bot. Gaz. (Chicago)* **96**, 676–708.

Biswell, H. H., and Schultz, A. M. (1957). Spring flow affected by brush. *Calif. Agric.* **11**, 3–4.

Björkman, O. (1973). Comparative studies on photosynthesis in higher plants. *Photophysiology* **8,** 1–63.

Bjurman, B. (1959). The photosynthesis in diploid and tetraploid *Ribes satigrum. Physiol. Plant.* **12,** 183–187.

Black, H. S., and Altschul, A. M. (1965). Gibberellic acid induced lipase and α-amylase formation and their inhibition by aflatoxin. *Biochem. Biophys. Res. Commun.* **19,** 661–664.

Black, M., and Wareing, P. F. (1959). The role of germination inhibitors and oxygen in the dormancy of the light-sensitive seed of *Betula* spp. *J. Exp. Bot.* **10,** 134–145.

Blackman, F. F. (1905). Optima and limiting factors. *Ann. Bot., (London)* **19,** 281–295.

Blais, J. R. (1952). The relationship of the spruce budworm (*Choristoneura fumiferana* Clem.) to the flowering condition of balsam fir (*Abies balsamea* (L.) Mill.). *Can. J. Zool.* **30,** 1–29.

Blum, B. M. (1963). Excessive exposure stimulates epicormic branching in young northern hardwoods. *U.S., For. Serv., Res. Note NE* **NE-9.**

Boardman, N. K. (1977). Comparative photosynthesis of sun and shade plants. *Annu. Rev. Plant Physiol.* **28,** 355–377.

Bode, H. R. (1959). Über den Zusammenhang zwischen Blattenfaltung und Neubildung der Saugwurzeln bei *Juglans. Ber. Dtsch. Bot. Ges.* **72,** 93–98.

Bogar, G. D., and Smith, F. H. (1965). Anatomy of seedling roots of *Pseudotsuga menziesii. Am. J. Bot.* **52,** 720–729.

Böhning, R. H. (1949). Time course of photosynthesis in apple leaves exposed to continuous illumination. *Plant Physiol.* **24,** 222–240.

Bollard, E. G. (1953). The use of tracheal sap in the study of apple tree nutrition. *J. Exp. Bot.* **4,** 363–368.

Bollard, E. G. (1955). Trace element deficiencies of fruit crops in New Zealand. *N. Z. Dep. Sci. Ind. Res., Bull.* **115.**

Bollard, E. G. (1957a). Nitrogenous compounds in tracheal sap of woody members of the family Rosaceae. *Aust. J. Biol. Sci.* **10,** 288–291.

Bollard, E. G. (1957b). Translocation of organic nitrogen in the xylem. *Aust. J. Biol. Sci.* **10,** 292–301.

Bollard, E. G. (1957c). Effect of a permanent grass cover on apple-tree yield in the first years after grassing. *N. Z. J. Sci. Technol., Sect. A* **38,** 527–532.

Bollard, E. G. (1958). Nitrogenous compounds in tree xylem sap. *In* "The Physiology of Forest Trees" (K. V. Thimann, ed.), pp. 83–93. Ronald, New York.

Bollard, E. G. (1960). Transport in the xylem. *Annu. Rev. Plant Physiol.* **11,** 141–166.

Bollard, E. G. (1970). The physiology and nutrition of developing fruits. *In* "The Biochemistry of Fruits and Their Products" (A. C. Hulme, ed.), pp. 387–425. Academic Press, New York.

Bollard, E. G., and Butler, G. W. (1966). Mineral nutrition of plants. *Annu. Rev. Plant Physiol.* **17,** 77–112.

Bond, G. (1956). Evidence for fixation of nitrogen by root nodules of alder (*Alnus*) under field conditions. *New Phytol.* **55,** 147–153.

Bond, G. (1967). Fixation of nitrogen by higher plants other than legumes. *Annu. Rev. Plant Physiol.* **18,** 107–126.

Bond, G. (1976). The results of the IBP survey of root-nodule formation in non-leguminous angiosperms. *In* "Symbiotic Nitrogen Fixation in Plants" (P. S. Nutman, ed.), pp. 443–474. Cambridge Univ. Press, London and New York.

Bond, G., and Gardner, L. C. (1957). Nitrogen fixation in non-legume root nodule plants. *Nature (London)* **179,** 680–681.

Bonner, J., ed. (1950). "Plant Biochemistry," 1st ed. Academic Press, New York.

Bonner, J. (1965). Isoprenoids. *In* "Plant Biochemistry" (J. Bonner and J. E. Varner, eds.), 2nd ed., pp. 665–692. Academic Press, New York.

Bonner, J., and Varner, J. E., eds. (1976). "Plant Biochemistry," 3rd ed. Academic Press, New York.

Bonner, W. D., Jr. (1973). Mitochondria and plant respiration. *Phytochemistry* **3,** 221–261.

Booth, A., Moorby, J., Davies, C. R., Jones, H., and Wareing, P. F. (1962). Effects of indolyl-3-acetic acid on the movement of nutrients within plants. *Nature (London)* **194,** 204–205.

Borchert, R. (1969). Unusual shoot growth patterns in a tropical tree, *Oreopanax* (Araliaceae). *Am. J. Bot.* **56,** 1033–1041.

Borger, G. A. (1973). Development and shedding of bark. *In* "Shedding of Plant Parts" (T. T. Kozlowski, ed.), pp. 205–236. Academic Press, New York.

Borger, G. A., and Kozlowski, T. T. (1972a). Early periderm ontogeny in *Fraxinus pennsylvanica, Ailanthus altissima, Robinia pseudoacacia,* and *Pinus resinosa* seedlings. *Can. J. For. Res.* **2,** 135–143.

Borger, G. A., and Kozlowski, T. T. (1972b). Effects of water deficits on first periderm and xylem development in *Fraxinus pennsylvanica. Can. J. For. Res.* **2,** 144–151.

Borger, G. A., and Kozlowski, T. T. (1972c). Effects of light intensity on first periderm and xylem development in *Pinus resinosa, Fraxinus pennsylvanica,* and *Robinia pseudoacacia. Can. J. For. Res.* **2,** 190–197.

Borger, G. A., and Kozlowski, T. T. (1972d). Effect of temperature on first periderm and xylem development in *Fraxinus pennsylvanica, Robinia pseudoacacia,* and *Ailanthus altissima. Can. J. For. Res.* **2,** 198–205.

Borger, G. A., and Kozlowski, T. T. (1972e). Effects of cotyledons, leaves, and stem apex on early periderm development in *Fraximus pennsylvanica* seedlings. *New Phytol.* **71,** 691–702.

Borger, G. A., and Kozlowski, T. T. (1972f). Effects of photoperiod on early periderm and xylem development in *Fraxinus pennsylvanica, Robinia pseudoacacia,* and *Ailanthus altissima* seedlings. *New Phytol.* **71,** 703–708.

Borger, G. A., and Kozlowski, T. T. (1972g). Effect of growth regulators and herbicides on normal and wound periderm ontogeny in *Fraxinus pennsylvanica* seedlings. *Weed Res.* **12,** 190–194.

Bormann, F. H. (1953). Factors determining the role of loblolly pine and sweetgum in early old-field succession in the Piedmont of North Carolina. *Ecol. Monogr.* **23,** 339–358.

Bormann, F. H. (1956). Ecological implications of changes in the photosynthetic response of *Pinus taeda* seedlings during ontogeny. *Ecology* **37,** 70–75.

Bormann, F. H. (1965). Changes in the growth pattern of white pine trees undergoing suppression. *Ecology* **46,** 269–277.

Bormann, F. H., and Graham, B. F., Jr. (1960). Translocation of silvicides through root grafts. *J. For.* **58,** 402–403.

Bormann, F. H., and Kozlowski, T. T. (1962). Measurements of tree ring growth with dial gage dendrometers and vernier tree ring bands. *Ecology* **43,** 289–294.

Bormann, F. H., Likens, G. E., and Melillo, J. M. (1977). Nitrogen budget for an aggrading northern hardwood forest ecosystem. *Science* **196,** 981–983.

Börtitz, S. (1964). Physiologische und biochemische Beiträge zur Rauchschadenforschung. I. Untersuchungen über die individuell unterschiedliche Wirkung von SO_2 auf Assimilation und einige Inhaltstoffe der Nadeln von Fichte (*Picea abies* L. Karst.) durch Küvettenbegasung einzelner Zweige im Freilandversuch. *Biol. Zentralbl.* **83,** 501–513.

Bosian G., Paetzholdt, M., and Ensgraber, A. (1960). Ueber die Beeinflussung der CO_2 - Assimilation der Rebe durch Pflanzenschutzmittel. *Proc. Int. Congr. Crop. Prot., 4th, 1957.* pp. 1517–1522.

Botkin, D. B., Smith, W. H., and Carlson, R. W. (1971). Ozone suppression of white pine net photosynthesis. *J. Air Pollut. Control Assoc.* **21,** 778–780.

Botkin, D. B., Smith, W. H., Carlson, R. W., and Smith, J. L. (1972). Effects of ozone on white pine saplings: Variation in inhibition and recovery of net photosynthesis. *Environ. Pollut.* **3,** 273–289.

Bourdeau, P. F. (1954). Oak seedling ecology determining segregation of species in Piedmont oak-hickory forests. *Ecol. Monogr.* **24,** 297–320.

Bourdeau, P. F., and Laverick, M. L. (1958). Tolerance and photosynthetic adaptability to light intensity in white pine, red pine, hemlock, and ailanthus seedlings. *For. Sci.* **4,** 196–207.

Bourdeau, P. F., and Schopmeyer, C. S. (1958). Oleoresin exudation pressure in slash pine: Its measurement, heritability and relation to oleoresin yield. *In* "The Physiology of Forest Trees" (K. V. Thimann, ed.), pp. 313–319. Ronald, New York.

Bourdeau, P. F., and Woodwell, G. M. (1964). Field measurements of carbon dioxide exchange by *Pinus rigida* trees exposed to chronic gamma irradiation. *Ecology* **45,** 403–406.

Bourque, D. P., and Naylor, A. W. (1971). Large effects of small water deficits on chlorophyll accumulation and ribonucleic acid synthesis in etiolated leaves of jack bean (*Canavalia ensiformis* (L.) D. C.). *Plant Physiol.* **47,** 591–594.

Bowen, G. D. (1973). Mineral nutrition of ectomycorrhizae. *In* "Ectomycorrhizae" (G. C. Marks and T. T. Kozlowski, eds.), pp. 151–205. Academic Press, New York.

Boyce, J. S. (1948). "Forest Pathology." McGraw-Hill, New York.

Boyer, J. S. (1967). Leaf water potentials measured with a pressure chamber. *Plant Physiol.* **42,** 133–137.

Boyer, J. S. (1976a). Water deficits and photosynthesis. *In* "Water Deficits and Plant Growth" (T. T. Kozlowski, ed.), Vol. 4, pp. 154–190. Academic Press, New York.

Boyer, J. S. (1976b). Photosynthesis at low water potentials. *Phil. Trans. Roy. Soc. London* **B273,** 501–522.

Boyer, W. D. (1970). Shoot growth patterns of young loblolly pine. *For. Sci.* **16,** 472–482.

Boyle, J. R. (1976). A system for evaluating potential impacts of whole-tree harvesting on site quality. *Tappi* **59**(7) 79–80.

Bradbeer, C. (1958). Incorporation of carbon-14 dioxide into sugars by darkened cotyledons from etiolated sunflower seedlings. *Nature (London)* **182,** 1429–1430.

Bradbury, I. K., and Malcolm, D. C. (1978). Dry matter accumulation by *Picea sitchensis* seedlings during winter. *Can. J. For. Res.* **8,** 207–213.

Bradford, F. C. (1924). Nitrogen-carrying fertilizers and the bearing habits of mature apple trees. *Mich., Agric. Exp. Stn., Spec. Bull.* **127.**

Bradley, M. V., and Crane, J. C. (1957). Gibberellin-stimulated cambial activity in stems of apricot spur shoots. *Science* **126,** 972–973.

Braekke, F. H., and Kozlowski, T. T. (1975a). Effect of climatic and edaphic factors on radial stem growth of *Pinus resinosa* and *Betula papyrifera* in northern Wisconsin. *Adv. Front. Plant Sci.* **30,** 201–221.

Braekke, F. H., and Kozlowski, T. T. (1975b). Shrinking and swelling of stems of *Pinus resinosa* and *Betula papyrifera* in northern Wisconsin. *Plant Soil* **43,** 387–410.

Braun, E. L. (1950). "Deciduous Forests of Eastern North America." McGraw-Hill, New York.

Bray, J. R., and Gorham, E. (1964). Litter production in forests of the world *Adv. Ecol. Res.* **2,** 101–157.

Bray, R. H. (1954). A nutrient mobility concept of soil-plant relationships. *Soil Sci.* **78,** 9–22.

Breazeale, J. F., and Crider, F. J. (1934). Plant association and survival, and the build-up of moisture in semi-arid soils. *Ariz., Agric. Exp. Stn., Tech. Bull.* **53.**

Brian, P. W., Petty, J. H. P., and Richmond, P. T. (1959). Effects of gibberellic acid on development of autumn color and leaf-fall of deciduous woody plants. *Nature (London)* **183,** 58–59.

Briggs, L. J. (1949). A new method of measuring the limiting negative pressure in liquids. *Science* **109,** 440.

Brink, R. A. (1962). Phase change in higher plants and somatic cell heredity. *Q. J. Biol.* **37,** 1–22.

Brix, H. (1960). Determination of viability of loblolly pine seedlings after wilting. *Bot. Gaz. (Chicago)* **121,** 200–223.

Brix, H. (1962). The effect of water stress on the rates of photosynthesis and respiration in tomato plants and loblolly pine seedlings. *Physiol. Plant.* **15,** 10–20.

Brix, H. (1966). Errors in measurement of leaf water potential of some woody plants with the Schardakov dye method. *Can., For. Branch, Dep. Publ.* **1164.**

Brix, H. (1967). An analysis of dry matter production of Douglas-fir seedlings in relation to temperature and light intensity. *Can. J. Bot.* **45,** 2063–2072.

Brix, H. (1971). Effects of nitrogen fertilization on photosynthesis and respiration in Douglas-fir. *For. Sci.* **17,** 407–414.

Brix, H. (1972). Nitrogen fertilization and water effects on photosynthesis and earlywood-latewood production in Douglas-fir. *Can. J. For. Res.* **2,** 467–478.

Brooks, M. G. (1951). Effect of black walnut trees and their products on other vegetation. *W. Va., Agric. Exp. Stn., Bull.* **347.**

Broome, O. C., and Zimmerman, R. H. (1976). Breaking bud dormancy in tea crabapple (*Malus hupehensis* (Pamp.) Rehd.) with cytokinins. *J. Am. Soc. Hortic. Sci.* **101,** 28–30.

Brouwer, R. (1965). Water movement across the root. *Symp. Soc. Exp. Biol.* **19,** 131–149.

Brown, C. L. (1970). Physiology of wood formation in conifers. *Wood Sci.* **3,** 8–22.

Brown, C. L. (1976). Forests as energy sources in the year 2000: What man can imagine, man can do. *J. For.* **74,** 7–12.

Brown, C. L., McAlpine, R. G., and Kormanik, P. P. (1967). Apical dominance and form in woody plants: A reappraisal. *Am. J. Bot.* **54**, 153–162.

Brown, G. N., and Bixby, J. A. (1975). Soluble and insoluble protein patterns during induction of freezing tolerance in black locust seedlings. *Physiol. Plant.* **34**, 187–191.

Brown, H. T., and Escombe, F. (1900). Static diffusion of gases and liquids in relation to the assimilation of carbon and translocation of plants. *Philos. Trans. R. Soc. London, Ser. B* **193**, 223–291.

Brown, J. C. (1956). Iron chlorosis. *Annu. Rev. Plant Physiol.* **7**, 171–190.

Brown, J. W., Wadleigh, C. H., and Hayward, H. E. (1953). Foliar analysis of stone fruit and almond trees on saline substrates. *Proc. Am. Soc. Hortic. Sci.* **61**, 49–55.

Brown, K. M., and Leopold, A. C. (1973). Ethylene and the regulation of growth in pine. *Can. J. For. Res.* **3**, 143–145.

Brown, R. W., and Van Haveren, B. P., eds. (1972). "Psychrometry in Water Relations Research." Utah Agric. Exp. Stn., Logan.

Brown, W. V., and Pratt, G. A. (1965). Stomatal inactivity in grasses. *Southwest. Nat.* **10**, 48–56.

Browning, G. (1973). Flower bud dormancy in *Coffea arabica* L. II. Relation of cytokinins in xylem sap and flower buds to dormancy-release. *J. Hortic. Sci.* **48**, 297–310.

Broyer, T. C., Carlton, A. B., Johnson, C. M., and Stout, P. R. (1954). Chlorine: A micronutrient element for higher plants. *Plant Physiol.* **29**, 526–532.

Brunig, E. F. (1976). Tree forms in relation to environmental conditions: An ecological viewpoint. *In* "Tree Physiology and Yield Improvement" (M. G. R. Cannell and F. T. Last, eds.), pp. 139–156. Academic Press, New York.

Bryan, A. H., Hubbard, W. F., and Sherwood, S. F. (1937). Production of maple syrup and sugar. *U.S., Dep. Agric., Farmers' Bull.* **1366.**

Bubrjak, I. I. (1961). Concerning the flowering and fruiting of tea in Transcarpathia. *Agrobiologiya* (Russ.) **2**, 301–303.

Bukovac, M. J., and Wittwer, S. H. (1957). Absorption and mobility of foliar applied nutrients. *Plant Physiol.* **32**, 428–435.

Bunce, J. A. (1978). Effects of shoot environment on apparent resistance to water flow in whole soybean and cotton plants. *J. Expt. Bot.* **29**, 595–601.

Bunce, J. A., and Miller, L. N. (1976). Differential effects of water stress on respiration in the light in woody plants from wet and dry habitats. *Can. J. Bot.* **54**, 2457–2464.

Bunce, J. A., Patterson, D. T., Peet, M. M., and Alberte, R. S. (1977). Light acclimation during and after leaf expansion in soybean. *Plant Physiol.* **60**, 255–258.

Bunger, M. T., and Thomson, H. J. (1938). Root development as a factor in the success or failure of windbreak trees in the Southern High Plains. *J. For.* **36**, 790–803.

Burris, R. H. (1976). Nitrogen fixation. *In* "Plant Biochemistry" (J. Bonner and J. E. Varner, eds.), 3rd ed., pp. 887–908. Academic Press, New York.

Büsgen, M., and Münch, E. (1931). "The Structure and Life of Forest Trees" (transl. by T. Thomson), 3rd ed. Wiley, New York.

Buttery, B. R., and Boatman, S. G. (1966). Manometric measurement of turgor pressures in laticiferous phloem tissues. *J. Exp. Bot.* **17**, 283–296.

Buttery, B. R., and Boatman, S. G. (1976). Water deficits and flow of latex. *In* "Water Deficits and Plant Growth" (T. T. Kozlowski, ed.), Vol. 4, pp. 233–289. Academic Press, New York.

Byram, G. M., and Doolittle, W. T. (1950). A year of growth for a shortleaf pine. *Ecology* **31**, 27–35.

Caborn, J. M. (1957). Shelterbelts and microclimates. *Forestry Comm. Bull. No. 29.* London.

Caldwell, M. M. (1970). Plant gas exchange at high wind speeds. *Plant Physiol.* **46**, 535–537.

Caldwell, M. M. (1976). Root extension and water absorption. *In* "Water and Plant Life" (O. L. Lange, L. Kappen, and E.-D. Schulze, eds.), pp. 63–85. Springer-Verlag, Berlin and New York.

Callaham, R. Z. (1964). *Pinus ponderosa:* Geographic variation in germination response to temperature. *Proc. Int. Bot. Congr., 9th, 1959* Vol. 2, pp. 57–58.

Cameron, S. H. (1941). The influence of soil temperature on the rate of transpiration of young orange trees. *Proc. Am. Soc. Hortic. Sci.* **38**, 75–79.

Cameron, S. H., and Appleman, D. (1933). The distribution of total nitrogen in the orange tree. *Proc. Am. Soc. Hortic. Sci.* **30**, 341–348.

Cameron, S. H., and Borst, G. (1938). Starch in the avocado tree. *Proc. Am. Soc. Hortic. Sci.* **36**, 255–258.

Cameron, S. H., and Compton, O. C. (1945). Nitrogen in bearing orange trees. *Proc. Am. Soc. Hortic. Sci.* **46**, 60–68.

Cameron, S. H., and Schroeder, C. A. (1945). Cambial activity and starch cycle in bearing orange trees. *Proc. Am. Soc. Hortic. Sci.* **46**, 55–59.

Cameron, S. H., Mueller, R. T., Wallace, A., and Sartori, E. (1952). Influence of age of leaf, season of growth, and fruit production on the size and inorganic composition of Valencia orange leaves. *Proc. Am. Soc. Hortic. Sci.* **60**, 42–50.

Campbell, A. I. (1961). Shortening the juvenile phase of apple seedlings. *Nature (London)* **191**, 517.

Campbell, R. K., and Rediske, J. H. (1966). Genetic variability of photosynthetic efficiency and dry-matter accumulation in seedling Douglas-fir. *Silvae Genet.* **15**, 65–72.

Campbell, R. K., and Sorenson, F. C. (1973). Cold-acclimation in seedling Douglas-fir related to phenology and provenance. *Ecology* **54**, 1148–1151.

Campbell, W. A., and Copeland, O. L. (1954). Little leaf disease of shortleaf and loblolly pines. *U.S., Dep. Agric., Circ.* **940.**

Camus, G. (1949). Recherches sur le rôle des bourgeons dans les phénomènes de morphogénèse. *Rev. Cytol. Biol. Veg.* **11**, 1–199.

Cannell, M. G. R. (1975). Crop physiological aspects of coffee bean yield: A review. *J. Coffee Res.* **5**, 7–20.

Cannell, M. G. R., and Last, F. T., eds. (1976). ''Tree Physiology and Yield Improvement.'' Academic Press, New York.

Cannell, M. G. R., and Willett, S. C. (1975). Rates and times at which needles are initiated in buds on differing provenances of *Pinus contorta* and *Picea sitchensis* in Scotland. *Can. J. For. Res.* **5**, 367–380.

Canning, R. E., and Kramer, P. J. (1958). Salt absorption and accumulation in various regions of roots. *Am. J. Bot.* **45**, 378–382.

Cannon, H. L. (1960). Botanical prospecting for ore deposits. *Science* **132**, 591–598.

Cannon, W. A. (1932). Absorption of oxygen by roots when the shoot is in darkness or in light. *Plant Physiol.* **7**, 673–684.

Canny, J .J. (1973). ''Phloem Translocation''. Cambridge Univ. Press, London and New York.

Carlquist, S. (1975). ''Ecological Strategies of Xylem Evolution.'' Univ. of California Press, Berkeley.

Carlson, M. C. (1938). The formation of nodal adventitious roots in *Salix cordata. Am. J. Bot.* **25**, 721–725.

Carlson, M. C. (1950). Nodal adventitious roots in willow stems of different ages. *Am. J. Bot.* **37**, 555–556.

Carter, J. C. (1945). Wetwood of elms. *Ill. Nat. Hist. Surv., Circ.* **23**, 401–448.

Carter, M. C. (1972). Net photosynthesis in trees. *In* ''Net Carbon Dioxide Assimilation in Higher Plants'' (C. Black, ed.), pp. 54–74. Am. Soc. Plant Physiol., Atlanta, Georgia.

Carter, M. C., and Larsen, H. S. (1965). Soil nutrients and loblolly pine xylem sap composition. *For. Sci.* **11**, 216–220.

Cathey, H. M., and Campbell, L. E. (1975). Effectiveness of five fission-lighting sources on photo-regulation of 22 species of ornamental plants. *J. Am. Soc. Hortic. Sci.* **100**, 65–71.

Caughey, M. G. (1945). Water relations of pocosins or bog shrubs. *Plant Physiol.* **20**, 671–689.

Chabot, B. F., and Lewis, A. R. (1976). Thermal acclimation of photosynthesis in northern red oak. *Photosynthetica* **10**, 130–135.

Chailakhyan, M. K. (1975). Forty years of research on the hormonal basis of flowering—some personal reflections. *Bot. Rev.* **41**, 1–29.

Chalk, L. (1937). A note on the meaning of the terms earlywood and latewood. *Leeds Philos. Soc. Proc.* **3**, 324–325.

Chalmers, D. J., and van den Ende, B. (1975). Productivity of peach trees: Factors affecting dry-weight distribution during tree growth. *Ann. Bot. (London)* **39**, 423–432.

Chalmers, D. J., and van den Ende, B. (1977). The relation between seed and fruit development in the peach (*Prunus persica* L.). *Ann. Bot. (London)* **41**, 707–714.

Chalmers, D. J., and Wilson, I. B. (1978). Productivity of peach trees: tree growth and water stress in relation to fruit growth and assimilate demand. *Ann. Bot. (London)* **42**, 285–294.

Chambers, T. C., Ritchie, I. M., and Booth, M. A. (1976). Chemical models for plant wax morphogenesis. *New Phytol.* **77**, 43–49.

Chandler, R. F. (1938). The influence of nitrogenous fertilizer applications on the growth and seed production of certain deciduous forest trees. *J. For.* **36**, 761–766.

Chandler, R. F. (1944). The amount and mineral nutrient content of freshly fallen needle litter of some northeastern conifers. *Soil Sci. Soc. Am., Proc.* **8**, 409–411.

Chandler, R. F., Jr. (1941). The amount and mineral nutrient content of freshly fallen leaf litter in the hardwood forests of central New York. *J. Am. Soc. Agron.* **33**, 859–871.

Chandler, W. H. (1957). "Deciduous Orchards." Lea & Febiger, Philadelphia.

Chaney, W. R., and Kozlowski, T. T. (1969a). Seasonal and diurnal expansion and contraction of leaves and fruits of English Morello cherry. *Ann. Bot. (London)* [N.S.] **33**, 691–699.

Chaney, W. R., and Kozlowski, T. T. (1969b). Seasonal and diurnal changes in water balance of fruits, cones, and leaves of forest trees. *Can. J. Bot.* **47**, 1407–1417.

Chaney, W. R., and Kozlowski, T. T. (1969c). Seasonal and diurnal expansion and contraction of *Pinus banksiana* and *Picea glauca* cones. *New Phytol.* **68**, 873–882.

Chaney, W. R., and Kozlowski, T. T. (1977). Patterns of water movement in intact and excised stems of *Fraxinus americana* and *Acer saccharum* seedlings. *Ann. Bot. (London)* **41**, 1093–1100.

Chaney, W. R., and Leopold, A. C. (1972). Enhancement of twig abscission in white oak by ethephon. *Can. J. For. Res.* **2**, 492–495.

Chapman, A. G. (1935). The effects of black locust on associated species with special reference to forest trees. *Ecol. Monogr.* **5**, 37–60.

Chapman, A. G., and Lane, R. D. (1951). Effects of some cover types on interplanted forest tree species. *U.S., For. Serv., Cent. States For. Exp. Stn., Tech. Pap.* **125.**

Chase, W. W. (1934). The composition, quantity and physiological significance of gases in tree stems. *Minn., Agric. Exp. Stn., Tech. Bull.* **99.**

Chattaway, M. M. (1949). The development of tyloses and secretion of gum in heartwood formation. *Aust. J. Sci. Res., Ser. B* **2**, 227–240.

Chattaway, M. M. (1953). The occurrence of heartwood crystals in certain timbers. *Aust. J. Bot.* **1**, 27–38.

Cheng, T. Y., and Voqui, T. H. (1977). Regeneration of Douglas-fir plantlets through tissue culture. *Science* **198**, 306–307.

Cheyney, E. G. (1942). "American Silvics and Silviculture." Univ. of Minnesota Press, Minneapolis.

Childers, N. F. (1937). The influence of certain nutrients on the photosynthetic activity of apple leaves. *Proc. Am. Soc. Hortic. Sci.* **35**, 253–254.

Childers, N. F., ed. (1966a). "Fruit Nutrition," Hortic. Publ. Rutgers University, New Brunswick, New Jersey.

Childers, N. F. (1966b). "Nutrition of Fruit Crops," Hortic. Publ. Rutgers University, New Brunswick, New Jersey.

Childers, N. F., and Cowart, F. F. (1935). The photosynthesis, transpiration, and stomata of apple leaves as affected by certain nutrient deficiencies. *Proc. Am. Soc. Hortic. Sci.* **33**, 160–163.

Childers, N. F., and White, D. G. (1942). Influence of submersion of the roots on transpiration, apparent photosynthesis, and respiration of young apple trees. *Plant Physiol.* **17**, 603–618.

Chilvers, G. A., and Pryor, L. D. (1965). The structure of Eucalypt mycorrhizas. *Aust. J. Bot.* **13**, 245–249.

Ching, T. M. (1966). Compositional changes of Douglas-fir seeds during germination. *Plant Physiol.* **41**, 1313–1319.

Ching, T. M. (1972). Metabolism of germinating seeds. *In* "Seed Biology" (T. T. Kozlowski, ed.), Vol. 2, pp. 103–218. Academic Press, New York.

Ching, T. M., and Ching, K. K. (1962). Physical and physiological changes in maturing Douglas-fir cones and seeds. *For. Sci.* **8**, 21–31.

Ching, T. M., and Ching, K. K. (1972). Content of adenosine phosphates and adenylate energy charge in germinating ponderosa pine seeds. *Plant Physiol.* **50**, 536–540.

Chowdhury, K. (1939). The formation of growth rings in Indian trees. I. *Indian For. Rec., Util.* **2**, 1–39.

Christensen, N. L. (1973). Fire and the nitrogen cycle in California chaparral. *Science* **181,** 66–68.

Christersson, L. (1972). The transpiration rate of unhardened, hardened, and dehardened seedlings of spruce and pine. *Physiol. Plant.* **26,** 258–263.

Christiansen, M. N. (1963). Influence of chilling upon seedling development of cotton. *Plant Physiol.* **38,** 520–522.

Chung, H. H., and Barnes, R. L. (1977). Photosynthate allocation in *Pinus taeda*. I. Substrate requirements for synthesis of shoot biomass. *Can. J. For. Res.* **7,** 106–111.

Chung, H. H., and Kramer, P. J. (1975). Absorption of water and ³²P through suberized and unsuberized roots of loblolly pine. *Can. J. For. Res.* **5,** 229–235.

Church, T. W. (1949). Effects of defoliation on growth of certain conifers. *U.S., For. Serv., Northeast. For. Exp. Stn. Pap.* **22.**

Clark, F. B., and Liming, F. G. (1953). Sprouting of blackjack oak in the Missouri Ozarks. *U.S., For. Serv., Cent. States For. Exp. Stn., Tech. Pap.* **137.**

Clark, J. (1961). Photosynthesis and respiration in white spruce and balsam fir. *N.Y. State Univ. Coll. For. Syracuse Univ., Tech. Bull.* **85.**

Clark, J., and Gibbs, R. D. (1957). Studies in tree physiology. IV. Further investigations of seasonal changes in moisture content of certain Canadian forest trees. *Can. J. Bot.* **35,** 219–253.

Clark, J. W. (1949). Infections of *Fomes pini* through root grafts of Douglas-fir. M.S. Thesis, University of Washington, Seattle.

Clark, W. S. (1874). The circulation of sap in plants. *Mass. State Board Agric., Annu. Rep.* **21,** 159–204.

Clark, W. S. (1875). Observations upon the phenomena of plant life. *Mass. State Board Agric. Annu. Rep.* **22,** 204–312.

Clarkson, D. T., and Sanderson, J. (1974). The endodermis and its development in barley roots as related to radial migration of ions and water. *In* "Structure and Function of Primary Root Tissues" (J. Kolek, ed.), pp. 87–100. Slovak Acad. Sci. Bratislava.

Clarkson, D. T., Robards, A. W., and Sanderson, J. (1971). The tertiary endodermis in barley roots: fine structure in relation to radial transport of ions and water. *Planta* **96,** 292–305.

Clausen, J. J., and Kozlowski, T. T. (1965a). Seasonal changes in moisture contents of gymnosperm cones. *Nature (London)* **206,** 112–113.

Clausen, J. J., and Kozlowski, T. T. (1965b). Use of the relative turgidity technique for measurement of water stresses in gymnosperm leaves. *Can. J. Bot.* **43,** 305–316.

Clausen, J. J., and Kozlowski, T. T. (1967a). Food sources for growth of *Pinus resinosa* shoots. *Adv. Front. Plant Sci.* **18,** 23–32.

Clausen, J. J., and Kozlowski, T. T. (1967b). Seasonal growth characteristics of long and short shoots of tamarack. *Can. J. Bot.* **45,** 1643–1651.

Clausen, J. J., and Kozlowski, T. T. (1970). Observations on growth of long shoots of *Larix laricina*. *Can. J. Bot.* **48,** 1045–1048.

Cleary, B. D., and Waring, R. H. (1969). Temperature: Collection of data and its analysis for the interpretation of plant growth and distribution. *Can. J. Bot.* **47,** 167–173.

Clemens, J., and Pearson, C. J. (1977). The effect of waterlogging on the growth and ethylene content of *Eucalyptus robusta* Sm. (swamp mahogany). *Oecologia* **29,** 249–255.

Clements, F. E., and Long, F. L. (1934). The method of collodion films for stomata. *Am. J. Bot.* **21,** 7–17.

Clements, F. E., and Martin, E. V. (1934). Effect of soil temperature on transpiration in *Helianthus annuus*. *Plant Physiol.* **9,** 619–630.

Clements, J. R. (1970). Shoot responses of young red pine to watering applied over two seasons. *Can. J. Bot.* **48,** 75–80.

Clowes, F. A. L. (1950). Root apical meristems of *Fagus sylvatica*. *New Phytol.* **49,** 249–268.

Coile, T. S. (1937a). Composition of leaf litter of forest trees. *Soil Sci.* **43,** 349–355.

Coile, T. S. (1937b). Distribution of forest tree roots in North Carolina Piedmont soils. *J. For.* **35,** 247–257.

Cole, F. D., and Decker, J. P. (1973). Relation of transpiration to atmospheric vapor pressure. *J. Ariz. Acad. Sci.* **8,** 74–75.

Connor, D. J., Begge, N.J., and Turner, N.C. (1977). Water relations of mountain ash (*Eucalyptus regnans* F. Muell.) forests. *Aust. J. Plant Physiol.* **4,** 753–762.

Constantinidou, H. C., Kozlowski, T. T., and Jensen, K. (1976). Effect of sulfur dioxide on *Pinus resinosa* seedlings in the cotyledon stage. *J. Environ. Qual.* **5**, 141–144.

Cook, E. R., and Jacoby, G. C., Jr. (1977). Tree-ring drought relationships in the Hudson Valley, New York. *Science* **198**, 399–401.

Coombe, B. G. (1976). The development of fleshy fruits. *Annu. Rev. Plant Physiol.* **27**, 507–528.

Copeland, O. L. (1962). Relation of forest diseases to soils and soil management. *Proc. World For. Congr., 5th, 1960* Vol. 1, pp. 518–523.

Copes, D. L. (1969). Graft union formation in Douglas-fir. *Am. J. Bot.* **56**, 285–289.

Copes, D. L. (1970). Initiation and development of graft incompatibility symptoms. *Silvae Genet.* **19**, 101–107.

Copes, D. L. (1973). Inheritance of graft incompatibility in Douglas-fir. *Bot. Gaz. (Chicago)* **134**, 49–52.

Copes, D. L. (1974). Genetics of graft rejection in Douglas-fir. *Can. J. For. Res.* **4**, 186–192.

Corner, E. J. H. (1966). "The Natural History of Palms." Univ. of California Press, Berkeley.

Cossmann, K. F. (1939). Citrus roots: Their anatomy, osmotic pressure, and periodicity of growth. *Palest. J. Bot.* **3**, 3–41.

Coté, W. A. (1963). Structural factors affecting the permeability of wood. *J. Polym. Sci., Part C* **72**, 231–242.

Coté, W. A. (1967). "Wood Ultrastructure." Univ. of Washington Press, Seattle.

Cottam, W. P. (1954). Prevernal leafing of aspen in Utah Mountains. *J. Arnold Arbor., Harv. Univ.* **35**, 239–250.

Cowan, I. R. (1965). Transport of water in the soil-plant-atmosphere system. *J. Appl. Ecol.* **2**, 221–239.

Cowan, I. R. (1972). Oscillations in stomatal conductance and plant functioning associated with stomatal conductance: Observations and a model. *Planta* **106**, 185–219.

Crafts, A. S. (1961). "Translocation in Plants." Holt, New York.

Crafts, A. S., and Crisp, C. E. (1971). "Phloem Transport in Plants." Freeman, San Francisco.

Crafts, A. S., and Yamaguchi, S. (1964). The autoradiography of plant materials. *Calif., Agric. Exp. Stn., Ext. Serv. Man.* **35**.

Crane, J. C. (1964). Growth substances in fruit setting and development. *Annu. Rev. Plant Physiol.* **15**, 303–326.

Crane, J. C., and van Overbeek, J. (1965). Kinin-induced parthenocarpy in the fig, *Ficus carica* L. *Science* **147**, 1468–1469.

Crawford, R. M. M. (1967). Alcohol dehydrogenase activity in relation to flooding tolerance in roots. *J. Exp. Bot.* **18**, 458–464.

Cremer, K. W. (1976). Daily patterns of shoot elongation in *Pinus radiata* and *Eucalyptus regnans*. *New Phytol.* **76**, 459–468.

Critchfield, W. B. (1957). Geographic variation in *Pinus contorta*. *Maria Moors Cabot Found., Publ.* **3**.

Critchfield, W. B. (1960). Leaf dimorphism in *Populus trichocarpa*. *Am. J. Bot.* **47**, 699–711.

Critchfield, W. B. (1971). Shoot growth and heterophylly in *Acer*. *J. Arnold Arbor., Harv. Univ.* **52**, 240–266.

Crocker, R. L., and Major, J. (1955). Soil development in relation to vegetation and surface age at Glacier Bay, Alaska. *J. Ecol.* **43**, 427–448.

Cromack, K., Jr., and Monk, C. D. (1975). Litter production, decomposition, and nutrient cycling in a mixed hardwood watershed and a white pine watershed. *In* "Mineral Cycling in Southeastern Ecosystems" (F. G. Howell, J. B. Gentry, and M. H. Smith, eds.), ERDA Symp. Ser. (Conf. 740513), pp. 609–624. Natl. Tech. Inf. Serv., Springfield, Virginia.

Cronshaw, J., and Morey, P. R. (1965). Induction of tension wood by 2,3,5-triiodobenzoic acid. *Nature (London)* **205**, 816–818.

Crozier, A., Kuo, R., Durley, R. C., and Pharis, R. P. (1970). The biological activities of 26 gibberellins in nine plant bioassays. *Can. J. Bot.* **48**, 867–877.

Curlin, J. W. (1970). Nutrient cycling as a factor in site productivity and forest fertilization. *In* "Tree Growth and Forest Soils" (C. T. Youngberg and C. B. Davey, eds.), pp. 313–325. Oregon State Univ. Press, Corvallis.

Curry, J. R., and Church, T. W. (1952). Observations on winter drying of conifers in the Adirondacks. *J. For.* **50**, 114–116.

Curtis, J., and Blondeau, R. (1946). Influence of time of day on latex flow from *Cryptostegia grandiflora. Am. J. Bot.* **33**, 264–270.

Curtis, O. F. (1935). "The Translocation of Solutes in Plants. A Critical Consideration of Evidence Bearing upon Solute Movement." McGraw-Hill, New York.

Curtis, O. F., and Clark, D. G. (1950). "An Introduction to Plant Physiology." McGraw-Hill, New York.

Czaja, A. T. (1966). Über die Einwirkung von Stauben speziell von Zementofenstaub auf Pflanzen. *Angew. Bot.* **40**, 106–120.

Dadswell, H. E. (1957). Tree growth characteristics and their influence on wood structure and properties. *Br. Commonw. For. Conf., 7th,* CSIRO Melbourne, pp. 1–19.

Dadswell, H. E., and Hillis, W. E. (1962). Wood. *In* "Wood Extractives and Their Significance to the Pulp and Paper Industries" (W. E. Hillis, ed.), pp. 3–55. Academic Press, New York.

Dadswell, H. E., and Wardrop, A. B. (1956). Structure and properties of tension wood. *Holzforschung* **4**, 97–104.

Daly, J. M. (1976). The carbon balance of diseased plants: Changes in respiration, photosynthesis and translocation. *Encycl. Plant Physiol., New Ser.* **4**, 450–479.

Dana, M. N., Lantz, H. L., and Loomis, W. E. (1962). Effects of interstock grafts on growth of Golden Delicious apples. *Proc. Am. Soc. Hortic. Sci.* **81**, 1–11.

Darwin, F., and Pertz, D. F. M. (1911). On a new method of estimating the aperture of stomata. *Proc. R. Soc. London, Ser. B* **84**, 136–154.

Daubenmire, R. F. (1974). "Plants and Environment" A Textbook of Autecology." Wiley, New York.

Daum, C. R. (1967). A method for determining water transport in trees. *Ecology* **48**, 425–431.

Davenport, D. C., Fisher, M. A., and Hagan, R. M. (1971). Retarded stomatal closure by phenylmercuric acetate. *Physiol. Plant.* **24**, 330–336.

Davenport, T. L., Jordan, W. R., and Morgan, P. W. (1977). Movement and endogenous levels of abscisic acid during water-stress-induced abscission in cotton seedlings. *Plant Physiol.* **59**, 1165–1168.

Davies, J. D., and Evert, R. F. (1965). Phloem development in *Populus tremuloides. Am. J. Bot.* **52**, 627.

Davies, W. J., and Kozlowski, T. T. (1974a). Stomatal responses of five woody angiosperms to light intensity and humidity. *Can. J. Bot.* **52**, 1525–1534.

Davies, W. J., and Kozlowski, T. T. (1974b). Short- and long-term effects of antitranspirants on water relations and photosynthesis of woody plants. *J. Am. Soc. Hortic. Sci.* **99**, 297–304.

Davies, W. J., and Kozlowski, T. T. (1975a). Effects of applied abscisic acid and plant water stress on transpiration of woody angiosperms. *For. Sci.* **22**, 191–195.

Davies, W. J., and Kozlowski, T. T. (1975b). Effect of applied abscisic acid and silicone on water relations and photosynthesis of woody plants. *Can. J. For. Res.* **5**, 90–96.

Davies, W. J., Kozlowski, T. T., Chaney, W. R., and Lee, K. J. (1973). Effects of transplanting on physiological responses and growth of shade trees. *Proc. Int. Shade Tree Conf., 48th, 1972* pp. 22–30.

Davies, W. J., Kozlowski, T. T., and Lee, K. J. (1974). Stomatal characteristics of *Pinus resinosa* and *Pinus strobus* in relation to transpiration and antitranspirant efficiency. *Can. J. For. Res.* **4**, 571–574.

Davies, W. J., Kozlowski, T. T., and Pereira, J. (1974). Effect of wind on transpiration and stomatal aperture of woody plants. *In* "Mechanisms of Regulation of Plant Growth" (R. L. Bieleski, A. R. Ferguson, and M. M. Creswell, eds.), Bull. No. 12, pp. 433–438. R. Soc. N.Z., Wellington.

Davis, D. D., and Gerhold, H. (1976). Selection of trees for tolerance of air pollutants. *U.S. For. Serv., Gen. Tech. Rep. NE* **22**, 61–66.

Davis, D. E. (1949). Some effects of calcium deficiency on the anatomy of *Pinus taeda. Am. J. Bot.* **36**, 276–282.

Davis, J. T., and Sparks, D. (1974). Assimilation and translocation patterns of carbon-14 in the shoot of fruiting pecan trees. *J. Am. Soc. Hortic. Sci.* **99**, 468–480.

Davis, L. D. (1957). Flowering and alternate bearing. *Proc. Am. Soc. Hortic. Sci.* **70**, 545–556.

Davis, T. A. (1961). High root-pressures in palms. *Nature (London)* **192**, 227–278.

Dawkins, H. C. (1956). Rapid detection of aberrant girth increment of rain-forest trees. *Emp. For. Rev.* **35**, 448–454.

Decker, J. P. (1944). Effect of temperature on photosynthesis and respiration in red and loblolly pines. *Plant Physiol.* **19**, 679–688.

Decker, J. P. (1947). The effect of air supply on apparent photosynthesis. *Plant Physiol.* **22**, 561–571.

Decker, J. P. (1955a). The uncommon denominator in photosynthesis as related to tolerance. *For. Sci.* **1**, 88–89.

Decker, J. P. (1955b). A rapid postillumination deceleration of respiration in green leaves. *Plant Physiol.* **30**, 82–84.

Decker, J. P. (1959). Comparative responses of carbon dioxide outburst and uptake in tobacco. *Plant Physiol.* **34**, 103–106.

Decker, J. P., and Skau, C. M. (1964). Simultaneous studies of transpiration rate and sap velocity in trees. *Plant Physiol.* **39**, 213–215.

Decker, J. P., and Tio, M. A. (1958). Photosynthesis of papaya as affected by leaf mosaic. *Univ. P. R. J. Agric.* **42**, 145–150.

Decker, J. P., and Wien, J. D. (1958). Carbon dioxide surges in green leaves. *J. Sol. Energy Sci. Eng.* **2**, 39–41.

Decker, J. P., Gaylor, W. G., and Cole, F. D. (1962). Measuring transpiration of undisturbed tamarisk shrubs. *Plant Physiol.* **37**, 393–397.

Dekhuijzen, H. M. (1976). Endogenous cytokinins in healthy and diseased plants. *Encycl. Plant Physiol. New Ser.* **4**, 526–559.

Delap, A. V. (1967). The effect of supplying nitrate at different seasons on the growth, blossoming and nitrogen content of young apple trees in sand culture. *J. Hortic. Sci.* **42**, 149–167.

Del Moral, R., and Muller, C. (1970). The allelopathic effects of *Eucalyptus camaldulensis*. *Am. Midl. Nat.* **83**, 254–282.

De Maggio, A. E., and Freeberg, J. A. (1969). Dormancy regulation: Hormonal interaction in maple (*Acer platanoides*). *Can. J. Bot.* **47**, 1165–1169.

DeMichele, D. W., and Sharpe, P. J. H. (1973). An analysis of the mechanics of guard cell motion. *J. Theor. Biol.* **41**, 77–96.

Denaeyer-DeSmet, S. (1967). Contribution à l'étude chimique de la sève du bois de *Corylus avellana* L. *Bull. Soc. R. Bot. Belg.* **100**, 353–371.

Denne, M. P., and Atkinson, L. D. (1973). A phytotoxic effect of captan on the growth of conifer seedlings. *Forestry* **46**, 49–53.

Denny, F. E. (1932). Changes in leaves during the night. *Contrib. Boyce Thompson Inst.* **4**, 65–83.

Derr, W. F., and Evert, R. F. (1967). The cambium and seasonal development of the phloem in *Robinia pseudoacacia*. *Am. J. Bot.* **54**, 147–153.

Deshpande, B. P. (1967). Initiation of cambial activity and its relation to primary growth in *Tilia americana* L. Ph.D. Dissertation, University of Wisconsin, Madison.

Deuel, H. J. (1951). "The Lipids: Their Chemistry and Biochemistry." Wiley (Interscience), New York.

de Vries, H. (1885). Uber die Bedeutung der Circulation und der Rotation des Protoplasma für den Stofftransport in der Pflanze. *Bot. Ztg.* **43**, 1–6, 17–26.

Dewey, D. H., ed. (1977). "Controlled Atmospheres for the Storage and Transport of Perishable Agricultural Commodities," Hortic. Rep. No. 28. Michigan State University, East Lansing.

Dickmann, D. I., and Kozlowski, T. T. (1968). Mobilization by *Pinus resinosa* cones and shoots of C^{14}-photosynthate from needles of different ages. *Am. J. Bot.* **55**, 900–906.

Dickmann, D. I., and Kozlowski, T. T. (1969a). Seasonal growth patterns of ovulate strobili of *Pinus resinosa* in central Wisconsin. *Can. J. Bot.* **47**, 839–848.

Dickmann, D. I., and Kozlowski, T. T. (1969b). Seasonal variations in reserve and structural components of *Pinus resinosa* Ait. cones. *Am. J. Bot.* **56**, 515–521.

Dickmann, D. I., and Kozlowski, T. T. (1969c). Seasonal changes in the macro and micronutrient composition of ovulate strobili and seeds of *Pinus resinosa* Ait. *Can. J. Bot.* **47**, 1547–1554.

Dickmann, D. I., and Kozlowski, T. T. (1970a). Mobilization and incorporation of photoassimilated ^{14}C by growing vegetative and reproductive tissues of adult *Pinus resinosa* Ait. trees. *Plant Physiol.* **45**, 284–288.

Dickmann, D. I., and Kozlowski, T. T. (1970b). Photosynthesis by rapidly expanding green strobili of *Pinus resinosa*. *Life Sci.* **9,** Part 2, 549–552.

Dickmann, D. I., and Kozlowski, T. T. (1971). Cone size and seed yield in red pine. *Am. Midl. Nat.* **85,** 431–436.

Dickmann, D. I., and Kozlowski, T. T. (1973). "Water, Nutrient and Carbohydrate Relations in Growth of *Pinus resinosa* Ovulate Strobili," pp. 195–209. Novosibirsk, USSR.

Dickmann, D. I., Gjerstad, D. H., and Gordon, J. C. (1975). Developmental patterns of CO_2 exchange, diffusion resistance and protein synthesis in leaves of *Populus* x *euramericana*. *In* "Environmental and Biological Control of Photosynthesis" (R. Marcelle, ed.), pp. 171–181. Junk Publ., The Hague.

Dickson, R. E., and Larson, P. R. (1977). Muka from poplar leaves: A high energy feed supplement for livestock. *TAPPI For. Biol. Wood Chem. Conf.* [*Conf. Pap.*], *1977* pp. 95–99.

Dietrichs, H. H., and Schaich, E. (1965). Type, proportion and distribution of low molecular carbohydrates in *Fagus sylvatica*. *For. Abstr.* **26,** No. 1699.

Digby, J., and Wareing, P. F. (1966). The effect of applied growth hormones on cambial division and the differentiation of the cambial derivatives. *Ann. Bot. (London)* [N.S.] **30,** 539–548.

Dimbleby, G. W. (1952). The root sap of birch on a podzol. *Plant Soil* **4,** 141–153.

Dixon, H. H. (1914). "Transpiration and the Ascent of Sap in Plants." Macmillan, New York.

Dixon, H. H., and Joly, J. (1895). The path of the transpiration current. *Ann. Bot. (London)* **9,** 416–419.

Dochinger, L. S., and Heck, W. W. (1969). An ozone-sulfur dioxide synergism produces symptoms of chlorotic dwarf of eastern white pine. *Phytopathology* **59,** 399.

Dochinger, L. S., and Seliga, T. A. (1975). Acid precipitation and the forest ecosystem. *J. Air Pollut. Control Assoc* **25,** 1103–1105.

Dochinger, L. S., and Seliga, T. A. (1976). Acid precipitation and the forest ecosystem. *BioScience* **26,** 564–565.

Dochinger, L. S., Townsend, A. M., Seegrist, D. W., and Bender, F. W. (1972). Responses of hybrid poplar trees to sulfur dioxide fumigation. *J. Air Pollut. Control Assoc.* **22,** 369–371.

Doley, D. (1970). Effects of simulated drought on shoot development in *Liriodendron* seedlings. *New Phytol.* **69,** 655–673.

Doley, D. (1974). Alternatives to the assessment of earlywood and latewood in dicotyledonous trees: A study of structural variation in growth rings of apple (*Malus pumila* Mill.). *New Phytol.* **73,** 157–171.

Doley, D., and Leyton, L. (1968). Effects of growth regulating substances and water potential on the development of secondary xylem in *Fraxinus*. *New Phytol.* **67,** 579–594.

Domanski, R., and Kozlowski, T. T. (1968). Variations in kinetin-like activity in buds of *Betula* and *Populus* during release from dormancy. *Can. J. Bot.* **46,** 397–403.

Domanski, R., Kozlowski, T. T., and Sasaki, S. (1969). Interactions of applied growth regulators and temperature on root initiation in *Salix* cuttings. *J. Am. Soc. Hortic. Sci.* **94,** 39–41.

Doorenbos, J. (1954). "Rejuvenation" of *Hedera helix* in graft combinations. *Proc. K. Ned. Akad. Wet., Ser. C.* **57,** 99–102.

Döring, B. (1935). Die Temperaturabhängigkeit der Wasseraufnahme und ihre ökologische Bedeutung. *Z. Bot.* **28,** 305–383.

Downs, R. J. (1962). Photocontrol of growth and dormancy in woody plants. *In* "Tree Growth" (T. T. Kozlowski, ed.), pp. 133–148. Ronald, New York.

Downs, R. J., and Hellmers. H. (1975). "Environment and the Experimental Control of Plant Growth." Academic Press, New York.

Doyle, J. (1938). On the supposed accumulation of fat in conifer leaves in winter. *New Phytol.* **37,** 375–376.

Doyle, J. (1945). Developmental lines in pollination mechanisms in the Coniferales. *Sci. Proc. R. Dublin Soc.* **24,** 43–62.

Drosdoff, M., Sell, H. M., and Winter, S. G. (1947). Some effects of potassium deficiency on the nitrogen metabolism and oil synthesis in the tung tree (*Aleurites fordii*). *Plant Physiol.* **22,** 538–547.

Ducharme, E. P. (1977). Citrus tree decline and physiology of root-soil microbial interaction. *In* "Physiology of Root-Microorganisms Associations" (H. M. Vines, ed.), pp. 26–46. Am. Soc. Plant Physiol., Atlanta, Georgia.

Duff, G. H., and Nolan, N. J. (1958). Growth and morphogenesis in the Canadian forest species. III. The time scale of morphogenesis at the stem apex of *Pinus resinosa* Ait. *Can. J. Bot.* **36**, 687–706.

Dumbroff, E. B., and Brown, D. C. W. (1976). Cytokinin and inhibitor activity in roots and stems of sugar maple seedlings through the dormant season. *Can. J. Bot.* **54**, 191–197.

Dumbroff, E. B., and Peirson, D. R. (1971). Probable sites for passive movement of ions across the endodermis. *Can. J. Bot.* **49**, 35–38.

Dunberg, A. (1974). Occurrence of gibberellin-like substances in Norway Spruce (*Picea abies* (L.) Karst.) and their possible relation to growth and flowering. *Stud. For. Suec.* **111**, 1–62.

Dunberg, A. (1976). Changes in gibberellin-like substances and indole-3-acetic acid in *Picea abies* during the period of shoot elongation. *Physiol. Plant.* **38**, 186–190.

Dunberg, A., and Eliasson, L. (1972). Effects of growth retardants on Norway spruce (*Picea abies*). *Physiol. Plant.* **26**, 302–305.

Dure, L. S., III (1975). Seed formation. *Annu. Rev. Plant Physiol.* **26**, 259–278.

Durzan, D. J. (1971). Free amino acids as affected by light intensity and the relation of responses to the shade tolerance of white spruce and shade intolerance of jack pine. *Can. J. For. Res.* **1**, 131–140.

Durzan, D. J., and Campbell, R. A. (1974). Prospects for the mass production of improved stock of forest trees by cell and tissue culture. *Can. J. For. Res.* **4**, 151–174.

Durzan, D. J., and Chalupa, V. (1968). Free sugars, amino acids, and soluble proteins in the embryo and female gametophyte of jack pine as related to climate at the seed source. *Can. J. Bot.* **46**, 417–428.

Durzan, D. J., Mia, A. J., and Ramaiah, P. K. (1971). The metabolism and subcellular organization of the jack pine embryo (*Pinus banksiana*) during germination. *Can. J. Bot.* **49**, 927–938.

du Sablon, L. (1896). Sur la formation des reserves non azotées de la noix et de l'amande. *C. R. Hebd. Seances Acad. Sci.* **123**, 1084–1086.

Duvdevani, A. (1957). Dew research for arid agriculture. *Discovery* **18**, 330–334.

Duvdevani, A. (1964). Dew in Israel and its effect on plants. *Soil Sci.* **98**, 14–21.

Duvigneaud, P., and Denaeyer-DeSmet, S. (1970). Biological cycling of minerals in temperate deciduous forests. *In* "Analysis of Temperate Deciduous Forest Ecosystems" (D. Reichle, ed.), Vol. I, pp. 199–225. Springer-Verlag, Berlin and New York.

Eagles, C. F., and Wareing, P. F. (1963). Dormancy regulators in woody plants. Experimental induction of dormancy in *Betula pubescens. Nature (London)* **199**, 874–875.

Eagles, C. F., and Wareing, P. F. (1964). The role of growth substances in the regulation of bud dormancy. *Physiol. Plant.* **17**, 697–709.

Eames, A. J. (1961). "Morphology of the Angiosperms." McGraw-Hill, New York.

Eames, A. J., and MacDaniels, L. H. (1947). "An Introduction to Plant Anatomy." McGraw-Hill, New York.

Ebell, L. F. (1971). Girdling: Its effect on carbohydrate status and on reproductive bud and cone development of Douglas-fir. *Can. J. Bot.* **49**, 453–466.

Ebell, L. F. (1972). Cone induction response of Douglas-fir to form of nitrogen and time of treatment. *Can. J. For. Res.* **2**, 317–326.

Eggert, F. P. (1951). A study of rest in several varieties of apple and in other fruit species grown in New York State. *Proc. Am. Soc. Hortic. Sci.* **57**, 169–178.

Eggler, W. A. (1961). Stem elongation and time of cone initiation in southern pines. *For. Sci.* **7**, 149–158.

Eglinton, G., and Hamilton, R. J. (1967). Leaf epicuticular waxes. *Science* **156**, 1322–1335.

Ehleringer, J., Bjorkman, O., and Mooney, H. A. (1976). Leaf pubescence: Effects on absorptance and photosynthesis in a desert shrub. *Science* **192**, 376–377.

Ehlig, C. F. (1960). Effect of salinity on four varieties of table grapes grown in sand culture. *Proc. Am. Soc. Hortic. Sci.* **76**, 323–335.

Ehrler, W. L., and van Bavel, C. H. M. (1968). Leaf diffusion resistance, illuminance, and transpiration. *Plant Physiol.* **43**, 208–214.

Eichenberger, W., and Grob, E. C. (1962). The biochemistry of plant plastids. 1. A study of autumn coloring. *Helv. Chim. Acta* **45**, 974–981.

Eis, S. (1972). Root grafts and their silvicultural implications. *Can. J. For. Res.* **2**, 111–120.

Eis, S. (1976). Association of western white pine cone crops with weather variables. *Can. J. For. Res.* **6**, 6–12.

Eis, S., Garman, E. H., and Ebell, L. F. (1965). Relation between cone production and diameter increment of Douglas-fir (*Pseudotsuga menziesii* (Mirb.) Franco), grand fir (*Abies grandis* (Dougl.) Lindl.), and western white pine (*Pinus monticola* Dougl.). *Can. J. Bot.* **43**, 1553–1559.

Ekern, P. C. (1965). Evapotranspiration of pineapple in Hawaii. *Plant Physiol.* **40**, 736–739.

El-Antably, H. M. M., Wareing, P. F., and Hillman, J. (1967). Some physiological responses to d,1 abscisin (dormin). *Planta* **73**, 74–90.

Embleton, T. W., Jones, W. W., and Platt, R. G. (1975). Plant nutrition and citrus fruit crop quality and yield. *HortScience* **10**, 48–50.

Epstein, E. (1972). "Mineral Nutrition of Plants: Principles and Perspectives." Wiley, New York.

Erdtman, H. (1955). The chemistry of heartwood constituents of conifers and their taxonomic importance. *Experientia, Suppl.* **2**, 156–180.

Erdtman, H. (1973). Molecular taxonomy. *Phytochemistry* **3**, 327–350.

Erickson, L. C., and Brannaman, B. L. (1960). Abscission of reproductive structures and leaves of orange trees. *Proc. Am. Soc. Hortic. Sci.* **75**, 222–229.

Ersov, M. F. (1957). O fotosinteze cistyh i zaplenny listev lipy melkolistnoj i vjaza melkolistnogo. *Dokl. Akad. Nauk SSSR* **112**, 1136–1138.

Esau, K. (1965). "Plant Anatomy." Wiley, New York.

Esau, K. (1972). "Anatomy of Seed Plants." Wiley, New York.

Esau, K., and Cheadle, V. I. (1969). Secondary growth in *Bougainvillea. Ann. Bot. (London)* [N.S.] **33**, 807–818.

Evans, G. C. (1956). An area survey method of investigating the distribution of light intensity on woodlands with particular reference to sunflecks. *J. Ecol.* **44**, 391–428.

Evans, G. C. (1972). "The Quantitative Analysis of Plant Growth." Univ. of California Press, Berkeley.

Evans, H. J. (1956). Role of molybdenum in plant nutrition. *Soil Sci.* **81**, 199–208.

Evans, L. T. (1975a). Beyond photosynthesis—the role of respiration, translocation, and growth potential in determining productivity. *In* "Photosynthesis and Productivity in Different Environments" (J. P. Cooper, ed.) IBP, Vol. 3, pp. 501–507. Cambridge Univ. Press, London and New York.

Evans, L. T., ed. (1975b). "Crop Physiology." Cambridge Univ. Press, London and New York.

Evelyn, J. (1670). "Sylva." J. Martyn and J. Allestry, London.

Evenari, M. (1960). Plant physiology and arid zone research. *Arid Zone Res.* **18**, 175–195.

Evert, R. F. (1960). Phloem structure in *Pyrus communis* L. and its seasonal changes. *Univ. Calif., Berkeley, Publ. Bot.* **32**, 127–194.

Evert, R. F. (1961). Some aspects of cambial development in *Pyrus communis. Am. J. Bot.* **48**, 479–488.

Evert, R. F. (1963). The cambium and seasonal development of the phloem in *Pyrus malus. Am. J. Bot.* **50**, 149–159.

Evert, R. F. (1977). Phloem structure and histochemistry. *Annu. Rev. Plant Physiol.* **28**, 199–222.

Evert, R. F., and Kozlowski, T. T. (1967). Effect of isolation of bark on cambial activity and development of xylem and phloem in trembling aspen. *Am. J. Bot.* **54**, 1045–1055.

Evert, R. F., Eschrich, W., Medler, J. T., and Alfieri, F. J. (1968). Observations on penetration of linden branches by stylets of upland *Longistigma caryae. Am. J. Bot.* **55**, 860–874.

Evert, R. F. Tucker, C. M., Davis, J. D., and Deshpande, B. P. (1969). Light microscope investigation of sieve element ontogeny and structure in *Ulmus americana. Am. J. Bot.* **56**, 999–1017.

Evert, R. F., Kozlowski, T. T., and Davis, J. D. (1972). Influence of phloem blockage on cambial growth of *Acer saccharum. Am. J. Bot.* **49**, 632–641.

Faegri, K., and Iverson, J. (1975). "Textbook of Pollen Analysis." Hafner, New York.

Fahn, A. (1967). "Plant Anatomy." Pergamon, Oxford.

Fairbrothers, D. E., Mabry, T. J., Scogin, R. L., and Turner, B. L. (1975). The basis of angiosperm phylogeny: Chemotaxonomy. *Ann. Missouri Bot. Gard.* **62**, 765–800.

Farmer, J. B. (1918). On the quantitative differences in the water conductivity of the wood in trees and shrubs. II. The deciduous plants. *Proc. R. Soc. London, Ser. B* **90**, 232–250.

Farmer, R. E., Jr. (1968). Sweetgum dormancy release: Effects of chilling, photoperiod, and genotype. *Physiol. Plant.* **21,** 1241–1248.

Farmer, R. E., Jr. (1976). Relationships between genetic differences in yield of deciduous tree species and variation in canopy size, structure and duration. *In* "Tree Physiology and Yield Improvement" (M. G. R. Cannell and F. T. Last, eds.), pp. 119–137. Academic Press, New York.

Farquhar, G. D. and Raschke, K. (1978). On the resistance to transpiration of the sites of evaporation within the leaf. *Plant Physiol.* **61,** 1000–1005.

Farrar, J. L. (1961). Longitudinal variations in the thickness of the annual ring. *For. Chron.* **37,** 323–331.

Fayle, D. C. F. (1968). Radial growth in tree roots. *Univ. Toronto, Fac. For. Tech. Rep.* **9.**

Federer, C. A. (1977). Leaf resistance and xylem potential differ among broadleaved species. *For. Sci.* **23,** 411–419.

Federer, C. A., and Tanner, C. B. (1966). Spectral distribution of light in the forest. *Ecology* **47,** 555–560.

Fenton, R. H. and Bond, A. R. (1964). The silvics and silviculture of Virginia pine in southern Maryland. *U.S. For. Serv. N.E. Exp. Sta. Res. Paper,* **NE-27.**

Fernandez, O. A., and Caldwell, M. M. (1975). Phenology and dynamics of root growth of three cool semi-desert shrubs under field conditions. *J. Ecol.* **63,** 703–714.

Ferrell, G. T. (1978). Moisture stress threshold of susceptibility to fir engraver beetles in pole-size white fir. *For. Sci.* 24, 85–94.

Fidler, J. C. (1968). Low temperature injury to fruits and vegetables. *In* "Low Temperature Biology of Foodstuffs " (J. Hawthorn and E. J. Rolfe, eds.), pp. 271–283. Pergamon Press, London.

Fielding, J. M. (1952). The moisture content of the trunks of Monterey pine trees. *Aust. For.* **16,** 3–21.

Fielding, J. M. (1955). The seasonal and daily elongation of shoots of Monterey pine and the daily elongation of roots. *For. Timber Bur. Aust., Leafl.* **75.**

Fielding, J. M. (1960). Branching and flowering characteristics of Monterey pine. *For. Timber Bur. Aust., Bull.* **37.**

Firbas, R. (1931). Untersuchungen über den Wasserhaushalt der Hochmoorpflanzen. *Jahrb. Wiss. Bot.* **74,** 457–696.

Fischer, A. (1891). Beiträge zur Physiologie der Holzgewächse. *Jahrb. Wiss. Bot.* **22,** 73–160.

Fiscus, E. L., and Kramer, P. J. (1975). General model for osmotic and pressure-induced flow in plant roots. *Proc. Natl. Acad. Sci. U.S.A.* **72,** 3114–3118.

Fisher, E., Boynton, D., and Skodvin, K. (1948). Nitrogen fertilization of the McIntosh apple with leaf sprays of urea. *Proc. Am. Soc. Hortic. Sci.* **51,** 23–30.

Flake, R. H., von Rudloff, E., and Turner, B. L. (1969). Quantitative study of clinal variation in *Juniperus virginiana* using terpenoid data. *Proc. Natl. Acad. Sci. U.S.A.* **64,** 487–494.

Flint, H. L. (1972). Cold hardiness of twigs of *Quercus rubra* L. as a function of geographic origin. *Ecology* **53,** 1163–1170.

Foote, K. C., and Schaedle, M. (1976). Diurnal and seasonal patterns of photosynthesis and respiration by stems of *Populus tremuloides* Michx. *Plant Physiol.* **58,** 651–655.

Fordham, R. (1972). Observations on the growth of roots and shoots of tea (*Camellia sinensis* L.) in southern Malawi. *J. Hortic. Sci.* **47,** 221–229.

Forward, D. F., and Nolan, N. J. (1961). Growth and morphogenesis in the Canadian forest species. IV. Further studies of wood growth in branches and main axis of *Pinus resinosa* Ait. under conditions of open growth, suppression, and release. *Can. J. Bot.* **39,** 411–436.

Forward, D. F., and Nolan, N. J. (1964). Growth and morphogenesis in the Canadian forest species. VII. Progress and control of longitudinal growth of branches in *Pinus resinosa* Ait. *Can. J. Bot.* **42,** 932–950.

Foster, A. A. (1968). Damage to forests by fungi and insects as affected by fertilizers. *In* "Forest Fertilization: Theory and Practice," pp. 42–46. Tenn. Valley Auth., Muscle Shoals, Alabama.

Fowells, H. A., and Kirk, B. M. (1945). Availability of soil moisture to ponderosa pine. *J. For.* **43,** 601–604.

Fowells, H. A., and Schubert, G. H. (1956). Seed crops of forest trees in the pine region of California. *U.S. Dep. Agric., Tech. Bull.* **1150.**

Frampton, C. V. (1960). Some aspects of the development anatomy of the 'long shoot' in *Larix decidua* Mill. with particular reference to seasonal periodicity. *New Phytol.* **59,** 175–191.

Franco, C. M., and Magalhães, A. C. (1965). Techniques for the measurement of transpiration of individual plants. *Arid Zone Res.* **25,** 211–224.

Frank, A. B., Harris, D. G., and Willis, W. O. (1977). Plant water relationships of spring wheat as influenced by shelter and soil water. *Agron. J.* **69,** 906–910.

Franklin, E. C. (1976). Within-tree variation of monoterpene composition and yield in slash pine clones and families. *For. Sci.* **22,** 185–192.

Fraser, D. A. (1956). Ecological studies of forest trees at Chalk River, Ontario, Canada. II. Ecological conditions and radial increment. *Ecology* **37,** 777–789.

Fraser, D. A. (1962). Apical and radial growth of white spruce (*Picea glauca* (Moench) Voss) at Chalk River, Ontario, Canada. *Can. J. Bot.* **40,** 659–668.

Fraser, D. A., and Mawson, C. A. (1953). Movement of radioactive isotopes in yellow birch and white pine as detected with a portable scintillation counter. *Can. J. Bot.* **31,** 324–333.

Freeland, R. O. (1952). Effect of age of leaves upon the rate of photosynthesis in some conifers. *Plant Physiol.* **27,** 685–690.

Fretz, T. A. (1977). Identification of *Juniperus horizontalis* Moench cultivars by foliage monoterpenes. *Scientiae Horticulturae* **6,** 143–148.

Frey-Wyssling, A., and Bosshard, H. H. (1959). Cytology of the ray cells in sapwood and heartwood. *Holzforschung* **13,** 129–137.

Fried, M., and Broeshart, H. (1967). "The Soil-Plant System in Relation to Inorganic Nutrition." Academic Press, New York.

Friedrich, G. (1962). Ueber das assimilatorische Verhalten der Obstgehölze. *Tagungsber., Dtsch. Akad. Landwirtschaftswiss. Berlin* **35,** 217–227.

Friedrich, G., and Schmidt, G. (1959). Untersuchungen über das assimilatorische Verhalten von Apfel, Berne, Kirsche und Pflaume unter Verwendung einer neu entwickelten Apparatur. *Arch. Gartenbau* **7,** 321–346.

Friesner, R. C. (1940). An observation on the effectiveness of root pressure in the ascent of sap. *Butler Univ. Bot. Stud.* **4,** 226–227.

Fritschen, L. J., Cox, L., and Kinerson, R. (1973). A 28-meter Douglas-fir in a weighing lysimeter. *For. Sci.* **19,** 256–261.

Fritts, H. C. (1976). "Tree Rings and Climate." Academic Press, New York.

Fritts, H. C., and Fritts, E. C. (1955). A new dendrograph for recording radial changes of a tree. *For. Sci.* **1,** 271–276.

Fritts, H. C., Smith, D. G., and Stokes, M. A. (1965). The biological model for paleoclimatic interpretation of Mesa Verde tree-ring series. *Am. Antiq.* **31,** 101–121.

Fröhlich, H. J. (1961). "Jungwuchspflege und Läuterung mit synthetischen Wuchsstoffen," Mitt. Hess Staatsforstverw. 3 Sauerländer Verlag, Frankfurt a. Main.

Fry, D. J., and Phillips, I. D. J. (1977). Photosynthesis of conifers in relation to annual growth cycles. II. Seasonal photosynthetic capacity and mesophyll ultrastructure in *Abies grandis, Picea sitchensis, Tsuga heterophylla* and *Larix leptolepis* growing in S.W. England. *Physiol. Plant.* **40,** 300–306.

Fry, K. E., and Walker, R. B. (1967). A pressure-infiltration method for estimating stomatal opening in conifers. *Ecology* **48,** 155–157.

Frydman, V. M., and Wareing, P. F. (1973). Phase changes in *Hedera helix* L. I. Gibberellin-like substances in the two growth phases. *J. Exp. Bot.* **24,** 1131–1138.

Fryer, J. H., and Ledig, F. T. (1972). Microevolution of the photosynthetic temperature optimum in relation to the elevational complex gradient. *Can. J. Bot.* **50,** 1231–1235.

Funsch, R. W., Mattson, R. H., and Mowry, G. W. (1970). CO_2-supplemented atmosphere increases growth of *Pinus strobus* seedlings. *For. Sci.* **16,** 459–460.

Furr, J. R., Cooper, W. C., and Reece, P. C. (1947). An investigation of flower formation in adult and juvenile citrus trees. *Am. J. Bot.* **34,** 1–8.

Gaastra, P. (1959). Photosynthesis of crop plants as influenced by light, carbon dioxide, temperature, and stomatal diffusion resistances. *Meded. Landbouwhogesch. Wageningen* **59,** 1–68.

Gabriel, W. J. (1968). Dichogamy in *Acer saccharum*. *Bot. Gaz. (Chicago)* **129**, 334–338.

Gaff, D. F. (1971). Desiccation-tolerant flowering plants of Southern Africa. *Science* **174**, 1033–1034.

Gale, J., and Hagan, R. M. (1966). Plant antitranspirants. *Annu. Rev. Plant Physiol.* **17**, 269–282.

Galil, J., and Neeman, G. (1977). Pollen transfer and pollination in the common fig (*Ficus carica* L.). *New Phytol.* **79**, 163–171.

Galliard, T., and Mercer, E. I., eds. (1975). ''Recent Advances in the Chemistry and Biochemistry of Plant Lipids.'' Academic Press, New York.

Gant, R. E., and Clebsch, E. E. C. (1975). The allelopathic influences of *Sassafras albidum* in old-field succession in Tennessee. *Ecology* **56**, 604–615.

Gardner, V. R., Bradford, F. C., and Hooker, H. C. (1952). ''Fundamentals of Fruit Production.'' McGraw-Hill, New York.

Gardner, W. R. (1960). Dynamic aspects of water availability to plants. *Soil Sci.* **89**, 63–73.

Garner, R. J. (1967). ''The Grafter's Handbook,'' 2nd ed. Faber & Faber, London.

Garner, W. W., and Allard, H. A. (1920). Effect of relative length of day and night and other factors of the environment on growth and reproduction in plants. *J. Agric. Res.* **18**, 553–606.

Garratt, G. A. (1922). Poisonous woods. *J. For.* **20**, 479–487.

Garrett, P. W., and Zahner, R. (1973). Fascicle density and needle growth responses of red pine to water supply over two seasons. *Ecology* **54**, 1328–1334.

Gates, D. M. (1965). Energy, plants, and ecology. *Ecology* **46**, 1–13.

Gates, D. M. (1976). Energy exchange and transpiration. *In* ''Water and Plant Life'' (O. L. Lange, L. Kappen, and E. D. Schulze, eds.), pp. 137–147. Springer-Verlag, Berlin and New York.

Gatherum, G. E. (1964). Photosynthesis, respiration, and growth of forest tree seedlings in relation to seed source and environment. *Proc. Cent. States For. Tree Improvement Conf. 4th*, pp. 10–18.

Gatherum, G. E., Gordon, J. C., and Broerman, B. F. S. (1967). Effects of clone and light intensity on photosynthesis, respiration and growth of aspen-poplar hybrids. *Silvae Genet.* **16**, 128–132.

Gauch, H. G. (1972). ''Inorganic Plant Nutrition.'' Dowden, Hutchinson & Ross, Stroudsburg, Pennsylvania.

Gäumann, E. (1935). Der Stoffhaushalt der Büche (*Fagus sylvatica* L.) im Laufe eines Jahres. Ber. Dtsch. *Bot. Ges.* **53**, 366–377.

George, M. F., and Burke, M. J. (1977). Cold hardiness and deep supercooling in xylem of shagbark hickory. *Plant Physiol.* **59**, 319–325.

George, M. F., Burke, M. J., Pellett, H. M., and Johnson, A. G. (1974). Low temperature exotherms and woody plant distribution. *HortScience* **9**, 519–522.

Gerhold, H. D., Schreiner, E. J., McDermott, R. E., and Winieski, J. A., eds. (1966). ''Breeding Pest-Resistant Trees.'' Pergamon, Oxford.

Gerloff, G. C. (1963). Comparative mineral nutrition of plants. *Annu. Rev. Plant Physiol.* **14**, 107–124.

Gerloff, G. C., Moore, D. G., and Curtis, J. T. (1966). Selective absorption of mineral elements by native plants in Wisconsin. *Plant Soil* **25**, 393–405.

Geurten, I. (1950). Untersuchungen über den Gaswechsel von Baumrinden. *Forstwiss. Centralbl.* **69**, 704–743.

Gibbs, R. D. (1935a). Studies of wood. II. The water content of certain Canadian trees, and changes in the water-gas system during seasoning and flotation. *Can. J. Res.* **12**, 727–760.

Gibbs, R. D. (1935b). Studies of wood. III. On the physiology of the tree, with special reference to the ascent of sap and the movement of water before and after death. *Can. J. Res.* **12**, 761–787.

Gibbs, R. D. (1939). Studies in tree physiology. I. General introduction: Water contents of certain Canadian trees. *Can. J. Res., Sect.* C **17**, 460–482.

Gibbs, R. D. (1953). Seasonal changes in water contents of trees. *Proc. Int. Bot. Congr., 7th, 1950* pp. 230–231.

Gibbs, R. D. (1958). The Mäule reaction, lignins, and the relationships between woody plants. *In* ''The Physiology of Forest Trees'' (K. V. Thimann, ed.), pp. 269–312. Ronald, New York.

Gibbs, R. D. (1974). ''Chemotaxonomy of Flowering Plants.'' McGill, Univ. Press, Montreal, Canada.

Giertych, M. M., and Forward, D. F. (1966). Growth regulator changes in relation to growth and development of *Pinus resinosa* Ait. *Can. J. Bot.* **44**, 718–738.

Gifford, K. M. (1974). A comparison of potential photosynthesis, productivity and yield of plant species with differing photosynthetic metabolism. *Aust. J. Plant Physiol.* **1**, 107–117.

Giles, K. L., Cohen, D., and Beardsell, M. F. (1976). Effects of water stress on the ultrastructure of leaf cells of *Sorghum bicolor*. *Plant Physiol.* **57**, 11–14.

Gindel, I. (1966). Attraction of atmospheric moisture by woody xerophytes in arid climates. *Common. For. Rev.* **45**, 297–321.

Gindel, I. (1973). "A New Ecophysiological Approach to Forest-Water Relationships in Arid Climates." Junk Publ., The Hague.

Ginzburg, C. (1963). Some anatomic features of splitting of desert shrubs. *Phytomorphology* **13**, 92–97.

Girouard, R. M. (1967a). Initiation and development of adventitious roots in stem cuttings of *Hedera helix*. Anatomical studies of the juvenile growth phase. *Can. J. Bot.* **45**, 1877–1881.

Girouard, R. M. (1967b). Initiation and development of adventitious roots in stem cuttings of *Hedera helix*. Anatomical studies of the mature growth phase. *Can. J. Bot.* **45**, 1883–1886.

Girouard, R. M. (1969). Physiological and biochemical studies of adventitious root formation. Extractible rooting cofactors from *Hedera helix*. *Can. J. Bot.* **47**, 687–699.

Glerum, C. (1976). Frost hardiness of forest trees. *In* "Tree Physiology and Yield Improvement" (M. G. R. Cannell and F. T. Last, eds.), pp. 403–420. Academic Press, New York.

Glerum, C., and Farrar, J. L. (1965). A note on internal frost damage in white spruce needles. *Can. J. Bot.* **43**, 1590–1591.

Glock, W. S., Agerter, Ş. R., and Studhalter, R. A. (1964). Tip growth in trees of west Texas and Maryland. *Adv. Front. Plant Sci.* **9**, 15–106.

Glock, W. S., Studhalter, R. A., and Agerter, S. R. (1960). Classification and multiplicity of growth layers in the branches of trees at the extreme lower border. *Smithson. Misc. Collect.* **4421.**

Gloyne, R. W. (1976). Shelter in agriculture, forestry, and horticulture—a review. A.D.A.S. Quart. Rev. **21**, 197–207.

Godwin, H. (1935). The effect of handling on the respiration of cherry laurel leaves. *New Phytol.* **34**, 403–406.

Goldsmith, M. H. M. (1977). The polar transport of auxin. *Annu. Rev. Plant Physiol.* **28**, 439–478.

Goo, M. (1952). When cell division begins in germinating seeds of *Pinus thunbergii*. *J. Jpn. For. Soc.* **34**, 3.

Goo, M. (1968). Photoperiod and flowering of *Pinus densiflora* seedlings. *Tokyo Univ., For. Misc. Inf. Ser.* **17**, 101–104.

Goode, J. E., and Hyrycz, K. J. (1964). The response of Laxton's Superb apple trees to different soil moisture conditions. *J. Hortic. Sci.* **39**, 254–276.

Goode, J. E., and Ingram, J. (1971). The effect of irrigation on the growth, cropping, and nutrition of Cox's Orange Pippin apple trees. *J. Hortic. Sci.* **46**, 195–208.

Goodwin, R. H., and Goddard, D. R. (1940). The oxygen consumption of isolated woody tissues. *Am. J. Bot.* **27**, 234–237.

Goodwin, T. W. (1958). Studies in carotenogenesis, 24. The changes in carotenoid and chlorophyll pigments in the leaves of deciduous trees during autumn necrosis. *Biochem. J.* **68**, 503–511.

Goodwin, T. W., and Mercer, E. I. (1972). "Introduction to Plant Biochemistry." Pergamon, Oxford.

Gordon, A. G., and Gorham, E. (1963). Ecological aspects of air pollution from an iron sintering plant at Wawa, Ontario. *Can. J. Bot.* **41**, 1063–1078.

Gordon, J. C., and Gatherum, G. E. ((1968). Photosynthesis and growth of selected Scotch pine seed sources. *U.S., For. Serv., Rev. Pap. NC* **NC-23.**

Gordon, J. C., and Larson, P. R. (1968). Seasonal course of photosynthesis, respiration and distribution of ^{14}C in young *Pinus resinosa* trees as related to wood formation. *Plant Physiol.* **43**, 1617–1621.

Gordon, J. C., and Larson, P. R. (1970). Redistribution of ^{14}C - labeled reserve food in young red pines during shoot elongation. *For. Sci.* **16**, 14–20.

Gourley, J. H., and Howlett, F. S. (1941). "Modern Fruit Production." Macmillan, New York.

Govindjee (1975). "Bioenergetics of Photosynthesis". Academic Press, New York.

Govindjee and Govindjee, R. (1975). Introduction to photosynthesis. *In* "Bioenergetics of Photosynthesis" (Govindjee, ed.), pp. 1–50. Academic Press, New York.

Grabe, D. F. (1970). Tetrazolium testing handbook for agricultural seeds. *Assoc. Off. Seed. Anal. Handb. Contrib.* No. 29.

Grace, J. (1977). "Plant Response to Wind." Academic Press, New York.

Graham, B. F. Jr. (1957). Labelling pollen of woody plants with radioactive isotopes. *Ecology* **38**, 156–158.

Graham, B. F., Jr., and Bormann, F. H. (1966). Natural root grafts. *Bot. Rev.* **32**, 255–292.

Gratkowski, H. J. (1977). Seasonal effects of phenoxy herbicides on ponderosa pine and associated brush species. *For. Sci.* **23**, 2–12.

Green, K. and Wright, R. (1977). Field response of photosynthesis to CO_2 enhancement in ponderosa pine. *Ecology* **58**, 687–692.

Greenidge, K. N. H. (1952). An approach to the study of vessel length in hardwood species. *Am. J. Bot.* **39**, 570–574.

Greenidge, K. N. H. (1954). Studies in the physiology of forest trees. I. Physical factors affecting the movement of moisture. *Am. J. Bot.* **41**, 807–811.

Greenidge, K. N. H. (1958). A note on the rates of upward travel of moisture in trees under differing experimental conditions. *Can. J. Bot.* **36**, 357–361.

Greenland, D. J., and Kowal, J. M. L. (1960). Nutrient content of a moist tropical forest of Ghana. *Plant Soil* **12**, 154–174.

Gregory, F. G., and Veale, J. A. (1957). A reassessment of the problem of apical dominance. *Symp. Soc. Exp. Biol.* **11**, 2–20.

Gregory, R. P. F. (1977). "Biochemistry of Photosynthesis." Wiley, New York.

Grieve, B. J., and Went, F. W. (1965). An electric hygrometer apparatus for measuring water vapour loss from plants in the field. *Arid Zone Res.* **25**, 247–256.

Griffith, B. G. (1968). Phenology, growth, and flower and cone production on 154 Douglas-fir trees on the University Research Forest as influenced by climates and fertilizer. 1957–1967. *Univ. B. C. Fac. For. Bull.* **6**, 1–70.

Griffith, M. M. (1952). The structure and growth of the shoot apex in *Araucaria*. *Am. J. Bot.* **39**, 253–263.

Grigal, D. F., Ohmann, L. F., and Brander, R. B. (1976). Seasonal dynamics of tall shrubs in northeastern Minnesota: Biomass and nutrient element changes. *For. Sci.* **22**, 195–208.

Grillos, S. J., and Smith, F. H. (1959). The secondary phloem of Douglas-fir. *For. Sci.* **5**, 377–388.

Grochowska, M. J. (1973). Comparative studies on physiological and morphological features of bearing and non-bearing spurs of the apple tree. I. Changes in starch content during growth. *J. Hortic. Sci.* **48**, 347–356.

Groom, P. (1910). Remarks on the ecology of Coniferae. *Ann. Bot. (London)* **24**, 241–269.

Groom, P., and Wilson, S. E. (1925). On the pneumatophores of paludah species of *Amoora, Carapa,* and *Heritiera. Ann. Bot. (London)* **39**, 9–24.

Grosenbaugh, L. R. (1963). Optical dendrometers for out-of-reach diameters: A conspectus and some new theory. *For. Sci. Monogr.* **4**.

Gross, H. L. (1972). Crown deterioration and reduced growth associated with excessive seed production in birch. *Can. J. Bot.* **50**, 2431–2437.

Guest, P. L., and Chapman, H. D. (1944). Some effects of pH on growth of citrus in sand and solution cultures. *Soil Sci.* **58**, 455–465.

Gunckel, J. E., and Thimann, K. V. (1949). Studies of development in long shoots and short shoots of *Ginkga biloba* L. III. Auxin production in shoot growth. *Am. J. Bot.* **36**, 145–151.

Gunckel, J. E., Thimann, K. V., and Wetmore, R. H. (1949). Study of development in long shoots and short shoots of *Ginkgo biloba* L. IV. Growth, habit, shoot expansion, and the mechanism of its control. *Am. J. Bot.* **36**, 309–318.

Gunning, B. E. S., and Robards, A. W. (1976). Plasmodesmata and symplastic transport. *In* "Transport and Transfer Processes in Plants" (I. F. Wardlaw and J. B. Passioura, eds.), pp. 15–41. Academic Press, New York.

Haaglund, E. (1951). "Chemistry of Wood." Academic Press, New York.

Haas, A. R. C. (1936). Growth and water losses in citrus affected by soil temperature. *Calif. Citrogr.* **21**, 467–469.

Hacskaylo, E. (1973). Carbohydrate physiology of ectomycorrhizae. *In* "Ectomycorrhizae" (G. C. Marks and T. T. Kozlowski, eds.), pp. 207–230. Academic Press, New York.

Hacskaylo, J., Finn, R. F., and Vimmersteadt, J. P. (1969). Deficiency symptoms of some forest trees. *Ohio, Agric. Res. Dev. Cent., Res. Bull.* **1015.**

Hadley, E. B., and Woodwell, G. M. (1966). Effects of ionizing radiation on rates of CO_2 exchange of pine seedlings. *Radiat. Res.* **24,** 650–666.

Hagem, O. (1962). Additional observations on the dry matter increase of coniferous seedlings in winter. *Medd. Nor. Inst. Skogforsk.* **37,** 5.

Hagerup, O. (1942). The morphology and biology of the *Corylus* fruit. *K. Dan. Vidensk. Selsk.* **17,** 1–32.

Haig, I. T. (1936). Factors controlling initial establishment of western white pine and associated species. *Yale Univ. Sch. For. Bull.* **41.**

Haissig, B. E. (1971). Influence of indole-3-acetic acid on incorporation of ^{14}C-uridine by adventitious root primordia in brittle willow. *Bot. Gaz. (Chicago)* **132,** 263–267.

Haissig, B. E. (1974). Origins of adventitious roots. *N. Z. J. For. Sci.* **4,** 299–310.

Hale, C. R., and Weaver, R. J. (1962). The effect of developmental stage on direction of translocation of photosynthate in *Vitis vinifera*. *Hilgardia* **33,** 89–131.

Hale, J. D., and Clermont, L. P. (1963). Influence of prosenchyma cell-wall morphology on basic physical and chemical characteristics of wood. *J. Polym. Sci., Part C* **2,** 253–261.

Hales, S. (1727). "Vegetable Staticks." W. & J. Innys and T. Woodward, London.

Halevy, A. (1956). Orange leaf transpiration under orchard conditions. V. Influence of leaf age and changing exposure to light on transpiration, on normal and dry summer days. *Bull. Res. Counc. Isr., Sect. D.* **5,** 165–175.

Hall, A. E., and Kaufmann, M. R. (1975). Stomatal response to environment with *Sesamum indicum* L. *Plant Physiol.* **55,** 455–459.

Hall, D. M. (1967). Wax microchannels in the epidermis of white clover. *Science* **158,** 505–506.

Hallé, and Oldeman, R. A. A. (1975). "An Essay on the Architecture and Dynamics of Growth of Tropical Trees" (transl. from the French by B. C. Stone). Penerbit University Malaya, Kuala Lumpur, Malaysia.

Hamilton, D. F., and Carpenter, P. L. (1975). Regulation of seed dormancy in *Eleagnus umbellata* by endogenous growth substances. *Can. J. Bot.* **53,** 2303–2311.

Hammel, H. T. (1967). Freezing of xylem sap without cavitation. *Plant Physiol.* **42,** 55–66.

Handley, W. R. C. (1963). Mycorrhizal associations and *Calluna* heathland afforestation. *G. B. For. Comm., Bull.* No. 36.

Hansen, P. (1967a). ^{14}C-studies on apple trees. I. The effect of the fruit on the translocation and distribution of photosynthates. *Physiol. Plant.* **20,** 382–391.

Hansen, P. (1967b). ^{14}C-studies on apple trees. II. Distribution of photosynthates from top and base leaves from extension shoots. *Physiol. Plant.* **20,** 720–725.

Hansen, P. (1967c). ^{14}C-studies on apple trees. III. The influence of season on storage and mobilization of labelled compounds. *Physiol. Plant.* **20,** 1103–1111.

Hansen, P. (1971). ^{14}C-studies on apple trees. VII. The early seasonal growth in leaves, flowers and shoots as dependent upon current photosynthates and existing reserves. *Physiol. Plant.* **25,** 469–473.

Hansen, P., and Grauslund, J. (1973). ^{14}C-studies on apple trees. VIII. The seasonal variation and nature of reserves. *Physiol. Plant.* **28,** 24–32.

Hardy, R. W. F., and Havelka, U. D. (1976). Photosynthate as a major factor limiting nitrogen fixation by field-grown legumes with emphasis on soybeans. *In* "Symbiotic Nitrogen Fixation in Plants" (P. S. Nutman, ed.), pp. 421–439. Cambridge Univ. Press, London and New York.

Hare, R. C. (1966). Physiology of resistance to fungal diseases in plants. *Bot. Rev.* **32,** 95–137.

Harley, J. L. (1956). The mycorrhiza of forest trees. *Endeavour* **15,** 43–48.

Harley, J. L. (1969). "The Biology of Mycorrhiza." Leonard Hill, London.

Harley, J. L. (1970). Mycorrhiza and nutrient uptake in forest trees. *In* "Physiology of Tree Crops" (C. V. Cutting and L. C. Luckwill, eds.), pp. 163–178. Academic Press, New York.

Harley, J. L. (1971). Fungi in ecosystems. *J. Ecol.* **59,** 653–668.

Harley, J. L., and Lewis, D. H. (1969). The physiology of mycorrhizas. *Adv. Microb. Physiol.* **3,** 53–78.

Harlow, W. M., Coté, W. A., Jr., and Day, A. C. (1964). The opening mechanism of pine cone scales. *J. For.* **62**, 538–540.

Harms, W. R., and McGregor, W. H. D. (1962). A method for measuring the water balance of pine needles. *Ecology* **43**, 531–532.

Harper, J. L., and White, J. (1974). The demography of plants. *Annu. Rev. Ecol. Syst.* **5**, 419–463.

Harrington, J. F. (1972). Seed storage and longevity. *In* "Seed Biology" (T. T. Kozlowski, ed.), Vol. 3, pp. 145–245. Academic Press, New York.

Harris, F. H. (1955). The effect of rainfall on the latewood of Scots pine and other conifers in East Anglia. *Forestry* **28**, 136–140.

Harris, J. A. (1934). "The Physico-Chemical Properties of Plant Saps in Relation to Phytogeography." Univ. of Minnesota Press, Minneapolis.

Harris, J. M. (1954). Heartwood formation in *Pinus radiata* (D. Don.). *New Phytol.* **53**, 517–524.

Hart, H. (1949). Nature and variability of disease resistance in plants. *Annu. Rev. Microbiol.* **3**, 289–316.

Hart, J. H. (1968). Morphological and chemical differences between sapwood, discolored sapwood, and heartwood in black locust and osage orange. *For. Sci.* **14**, 334–338.

Hartley, C. (1918). Stem lesions caused by excessive heat. *J. Agric. Res.* **14**, 595–604.

Hartmann, H. T., and Kester, D. E. (1975). "Plant Propagation: Principles and Practices." Prentice-Hall, Englewood Cliffs, New Jersey.

Hartmann, H. T., and Panetsos, C. (1961). Effects of soil moisture deficiency during floral development on fruitfulness in the olive. *Proc. Am. Soc. Hortic. Sci.* **78**, 209–217.

Hasegawa, M., and Shiroya, M. (1967). Translocation and transformation of sucrose in the wood of *Prunus yedoensis*. *IUFRO Meet., 1967* Sect. 41.

Hashizume, H. (1962). Initiation and development of flower buds in *Cryptomeria japonica*. *J. Jpn. For. Soc.* **44**, 312–319.

Hassid, W. Z. (1969). Biosynthesis of oligosaccharides and polysaccharides in plants. *Science* **165**, 137–144.

Hatano, K., and Asakawa, S. (1964). Physiological processes in forest tree seeds during maturation, storage, and germination. *Int. Rev. For. Res.* **1**, 279–323.

Hatcher, E. S. J. (1959). Auxin relations of the woody shoot. *Ann. Bot. (London)* [N.S.] **23**, 409–423.

Hauck, R. D. (1968). Nitrogen source requirements in different soil-plant systems. *In* "Forest Fertilization: Theory and Practice," pp. 47–57. Tenn. Valley Auth., Muscle Shoals, Ala.

Havis, J. R. (1971). Water movement in stems during freezing. *Cryobiology* **8**, 581–585.

Hawksworth, F. G., and Wiens, D. (1972). Biology and classification of dwarf mistletoes (*Arceuthobium*). *U.S., Dep. Agric., Agric. Handb.* **401**.

Hayward, H. E., and Long, E. M. (1942). The anatomy of the seedling and roots of the Valencia orange. *U.S., Dep. Agric., Tech. Bull.* **786**.

Hayward, H. E., Blair, W. M., and Skaling, P. E. (1942). Device for measuring entry of water into roots. *Bot. Gaz. (Chicago)* **104**, 152–160.

Hayward, H. E., Long, E. M., and Uhvits, R. (1946). Effects of chloride and sulfate salts on the growth and development of the Elberta peach on Shalil and Lovell rootstocks. *U.S., Dep. Agric., Tech. Bull.* **922**.

Head, G. C. (1964). A study of 'exudation' from the root hairs of apple roots by time-lapse cine-photomicrography. *Ann. Bot. (London)* [N.S.] **28**, 495–498.

Head, G. C. (1965). Studies of diurnal changes in cherry root growth and nutational movements of apple root tips by time-lapse cinematography. *Ann. Bot. (London)* [N.S.] **29**, 219–224.

Head, G. C. (1966a). Estimating seasonal changes in the quantity of white unsuberized root on fruit trees. *J. Hortic. Sci.* **41**, 197–206.

Head, G. C. (1966b). Studies on growth and development of roots of fruit plants in relation to environment, season and growth of the aerial parts. Ph.D. Thesis, University of London.

Head, G. C. (1967). Effects of seasonal changes in shoot growth on the amount of unsuberized root on apple and plum trees. *J. Hortic. Sci.* **42**, 169–180.

Head, G. C. (1968). Seasonal changes in the diameter of secondarily thickened roots of fruit trees in relation to growth of other parts of the tree. *J. Hortic. Sci.* **43**, 275–282.

Head, G. C. (1969). The effects of fruiting and defoliation on seasonal trends in new root production on apple trees. *J. Hortic. Sci.* **42**, 169–180.

Head, G. C. (1973). Shedding of roots. *In* "Shedding of Plant Parts" (T. T. Kozlowski, ed.), pp. 237–293. Academic Press, New York.

Heaman, J. C., and Owens, J. N. (1972). Callus formation and root initiation in stem cuttings of Douglas-fir (*Pseudotsuga menziesii* (Mirb.) Franco). *Can. J. For. Res.* **2**, 121–134.

Heath, O. V. S. (1959). The water relations of stomatal cells and the mechanisms of stomatal movement. *Plant Physiol.* **2**, 193–250.

Heiberg, S. O., and White, D. P. (1951). Potassium deficiency of reforested pine and spruce stands in northern New York. *Soil Sci. Soc. Am., Proc.* **15**, 369–376.

Heide, O. M. (1974). Growth and dormancy in Norway spruce ecotypes (*Picea abies*). I. Interaction of photoperiod and temperature. *Physiol. Plant* **30**, 1–12.

Heinicke, A. J. (1934). Photosynthesis in apple leaves during late fall and its significance in annual bearing. *Proc. Am. Soc. Hortic. Sci.* **32**, 77–80.

Heinicke, A. J. (1937a). How lime sulphur spray affects the photosynthesis of an entire ten year old apple tree. *Proc. Am. Soc. Hortic. Sci.* **35**, 256–259.

Heinicke, A. J. (1937b). Some cultural conditions influencing the manufacture of carbohydrates by apple leaves. *Proc. N.Y. State Hortic. Soc.*, pp. 149–156.

Heinicke, A. J., and Childers, N. F. (1937). The daily rate of photosynthesis during the growing season of 1935, of a young apple tree of bearing age. *N.Y., Agric. Exp. Stn., Ithaca, Mem.* **201.**

Heinicke, A. J., and Hoffman, M. B. (1933). The rate of photosynthesis of apple leaves under natural conditions. I. *N.Y., Agric. Exp. Stn., Ithaca, Bull.* **577.**

Heinicke, D. R. (1966). The effect of natural shade on photosynthesis and light intensity in Red Delicious apple trees. *Proc. Am. Soc. Hortic. Sci.* **88**, 1–8.

Heisler, G. M., and Herrington, L. P. (1976). Selection of trees for modifying metropolitan climates. *In* "Better Trees for Metropolitan Landscapes" (F. S. Santamour, H. D. Gerhold, and S. Little, eds.), pp. 31–37. U.S. Forest Service. Gen. Tech. Rept. NE-22.

Heit, C. E. (1968). Thirty-five years of testing tree and shrub seed. *J. For.* **66**, 632–634.

Heitefuss, R., and Williams, P. H., eds. (1976). "Physiological Plant Pathology," Encycl. Plant Physiol., New Ser., Vol. 4. Springer-Verlag, Berlin and New York.

Hejnowicz, A., and Tomaszewski, M. (1969). Growth regulators and wood formation in *Pinus silvestris*. *Physiol. Plant.* **22**, 984–992.

Hellkvist, J., Richards, G. P., and Jarvis, P. G. (1974). Vertical gradients of water potential and tissue water relations in Sitka spruce trees measured with the pressure chamber. *J. Appl. Ecol.* **7**, 637–667.

Hellmers, H. (1963). Effect of soil and air temperatures on growth of redwood seedlings. *Bot. Gaz.* **124**, 172–177.

Hellmers, H. (1966). Growth response of redwood seedlings to thermoperiodism. *For. Sci.* **12**, 276–283.

Hellmers, H., and Bonner, J. (1960). Photosynthetic limits of forest tree yields. *Proc. Soc. Am. For., 1959* pp. 32–35.

Hellmers, H., and Rook, D. A. (1973). Air temperature and growth of radiata pine seedlings. *N. Z. J. For. Sci.* **3**, 217–285.

Hellmers, H., Genthe, M. K., and Ronco, F. (1970). Temperature affects growth and development of Engelmann spruce. *For. Sci.* **16**, 447–452.

Hellmuth, E. O. (1968). Ecophysiological studies on plants in arid and semi arid regions in Western Australia. I. Autecology of *Rhagodia baccata* (Labill.) Moq. *J. Ecol.* **56**, 319–341.

Helms, J. A. (1964). Apparent photosynthesis of Douglas-fir in relation to silvicultural treatment. *For. Sci.* **10**, 432–442.

Helms, J. A. (1976). Factors influencing net photosynthesis in trees: An ecological viewpoint. *In* "Tree Physiology and Yield Improvement" (M. G. R. Cannell and F. T. Last, eds.), pp. 55–78. Academic Press, New York.

Hendrickson, A. H., and Veihmeyer, F. J. (1941). Some factors affecting the growth rate of pears. *Proc. Am. Soc. Hortic. Sci.* **39**, 1–7.

Hendrickson, A. H., and Veihmeyer, F. J. (1942). Readily available soil moisture and the sizes of fruit. *Proc. Am. Soc. Hortic. Sci.* **40,** 13–18.

Hepting, G. H. (1945). Reserve food storage in shortleaf pine in relation to little-leaf disease. *Phytopathology* **35,** 106–119.

Herrero, J. (1956). Incompatibilidad entre patron e injerto. III. Comparacion de sintomas producidas por incompatibilidad y por el anillado del tronco. *An. Aula Dei* **4,** 262–265.

Hess, C. E. (1969). Internal and external factors regulating root initiation. *In* "Root Growth" (W. J. Whittingham, ed.), pp. 42–53. Butterworth, London.

Hess, C. E., and Snyder, W. E. (1956). A physiological comparison of the use of mist with other propagation procedures used in rooting cuttings. *Int. Hortic. Congr., Rep., 14th,* Vol. II, p. 1133.

Heth, D., and Kramer, P. J. (1975). Drought tolerance of pine seedlings under various climatic conditions. *For. Sci.* **21,** 72–82.

Hewett, E. W., and Wareing, P. F. (1973a). Cytokinins in *Populus* x *robusta:* Changes during chilling and bud burst. *Physiol. Plant* **28,** 393–399.

Hewett, E. W., and Wareing, P. F. (1973b). Cytokinins in *Populus* x *robusta:* Qualitative changes during development. *Physiol. Plant.* **29,** 386–389.

Hewitt, E. J., and Cutting, C. V., eds. (1968). "Recent Aspects of Nitrogen Metabolism in Plants" Academic Press, New York.

Hewitt, E. J., and Smith, T. A. (1975). "Plant Mineral Nutrition." Wiley, New York.

Hewlett, J. D., and Hibbert, A. R. (1961). Increases in water yield after several types of forest cutting. *Int. Assoc. Sci. Hydrol., Bull.* **6,** 5–17.

Hewlett, J. D., and Hibbert, A. R. (1967). Factors affecting the response of small watersheds to precipitation in humid areas. *In* "Forest Hydrology" (W. E. Sopper and H. W. Lull, eds.), pp. 275–290. Pergamon, Oxford.

Hewlett, J. D., and Kramer, P. J. (1963). The measurement of water deficits in broadleaf plants. *Protoplasma* **57,** 381–391.

Hibbert, A. R. (1967). Forest treatment effects on water yield. *In* "Forest Hydrology" (W. E. Sopper and H. W. Lull, eds.), pp. 527–543. Pergamon, Oxford.

Higuchi, T., and Fukazawa, K. (1966). Study on the mechanism of heartwood formation. III. On the role of phenylalanine deaminase. *J. Jpn. Wood Res. Soc.* **12,** 135–139.

Hilgeman, R. H., and Reuther, W. (1967). Evergreen tree fruits. *Am. Soc. Agron., Monogr.* **11,** 704–718.

Hilgeman, R. H., Dunlap, J. A., and Sharples, G. C. (1967). Effect of time of harvest on Valencia oranges, leaf carbohydrate content, and subsequent set of fruit. *Proc. Am. Soc. Hortic. Sci.* **90,** 110–115.

Hill-Cottingham, D. G., and Williams, R. R. (1967). Effect of time of application of fertilizer nitrogen on the growth, flower development, and fruit set of maiden apple trees. var. Lord Lambourne, and on the distribution of total nitrogen within the trees. *J. Hortic. Sci.* **42,** 319–338.

Hillis, W. E. (1965). Biological aspects of heartwood formation. *IUFRO Meet., 1965* Sect. 41.

Hillis, W. E. (1968). Chemical aspects of heartwood formation. *Wood Sci. Technol.* **2,** 241–259.

Hillis, W. E., and Carle, A. (1962). The origin of the wood and bark polyphenols of Eucalyptus species. *Biochem. J.* **82,** 435–439.

Hillis, W. E., Humphreys, F. H., Bamber, R. K., and Carle, A. (1962). Factors influencing the formation of phloem and heartwood phenols. *Holzforschung* **16,** 114–121.

Hillman, W. S. (1963). "The Physiology of Flowering." Holt, New York.

Himelick, E. B., and Neely, D. (1962). Root grafting of city-planted American elms. *Plant Dis. Rep.* **46,** 86–87.

Hinkle, P. C. and McCarty, R. E. (1978). How cells make ATP. *Sci. Am.* **238**(3), 104–123.

Hinckley, T. M. (1978). Leaf conductance and photosynthesis in four species of the oak-hickory forest type. *For. Sci.* **24,** 73–84.

Hitchcock, C. (1975). Structure and distribution of plant acyl lipids. *In* "Recent Advances in the Chemistry and Biochemistry of Plant Lipids" (T. Galliard and E. I. Mercer, eds.), pp. 1–19. Academic Press, New York.

Hitchcock, C., and Nichols, B. W. (1971). "Plant Lipid Biochemistry." Academic Press, New York.

Hobbs, C. H. (1944). Studies on mineral deficiency in pine. *Plant Physiol.* **19**, 590–602.

Hodges, J. D. (1967). Patterns of photosynthesis under natural environmental conditions. *Ecology* **48**, 234–242.

Hoffmann, G. (1966). Verlauf der Tiefendurchwurzelung und Feinwurzelbildung bei einigen Baumarten. *Arch. Forstwes.* **15**, 825–826.

Hofmeyer, J. O. J., and Oberholzer, P. C. V. (1948). Genetic aspects associated with the propagation of citrus. *Farming S. Afr.* **23**, 201–208.

Holch, A. E. (1931). Development of roots and shoots of certain deciduous tree seedlings in different forest sites. *Ecology* **12**, 259–298.

Holdheide, W. (1951). Anatomie mitteleuropaischer Gehölzrinden. *In* "Handbuch der Mikroskopie in der Technik" (H. Freund, ed.), Vol. 5, pp. 195–367. Umsachen-Verlag, Frankfurt.

Holmes, J. W., and Shim, S. Y. (1968). Diurnal changes in stem diameter of Canary Island pine trees (*Pinus canariensis,* C. Smith) caused by soil water stress and microclimate. *J. Exp. Bot.* **19**, 219–232.

Holmgren, P., Jarvis, P. G., and Jarvis, M. S. (1965). Resistances to carbon dioxide and water vapour transfer in leaves of different plant species. *Physiol. Plant.* **18**, 557–573.

Holmsgaard, E. (1962). Influence of weather on growth and reproduction of beech. *Commun. Inst. For. Fenn.* **55**, 1–5.

Holmsgaard, E., and Scharff, O. (1963). Levende stødi rødgrandsevoks-ninger. *Forstl. Forsoegsvaes. Dan.* **30**, 1–17.

Holttum, R. E. (1953). Evolutionary trends in an equatorial climate. *Symp. Soc. Exp. Biol.* **7**, 159–173.

Hölzl, J. (1955). Über Streuung der Transpirations werte bei verschiedenen Blättern einer Pflanze und bei artgleichen Pflanzen eines Bestandes. *Sitzungsber. Oesterr. Akad. Wiss. Math-Naturwiss. Kl., Pt. I* **164**, 659–721.

Hook, D. D. and Brown, C. L. (1973). Root adaptations and relative flood tolerance of five hardwood species. *For. Sci.* **19**, 225–229.

Hoover, M. D. (1944). Effect of removal of forest vegetation upon water yields. *Trans. Am. Geophys. Union* **25**, 969–977.

Hoover, M. D., Olson, D. F., and Greene, G. E. (1953). Soil moisture under a young loblolly pine plantation. *Soil Sci. Soc. Am., Proc.* **17**, 147–150.

Horton, J. S. (1973). Evapotranspiration and water research as related to riparian and phreatophyte management. *U.S. For. Serv., Misc. Publ.* **1234.**

Hoshaw, R. W., and Guard, A. T. (1949). Abscission of marcescent leaves of *Quercus palustris* and *Q. coccinea. Bot. Gaz. (Chicago)* **110**, 587–593.

Hosner, J. (1957). Effects of water upon the seed germination of bottomland trees. *For. Sci.* **3**, 67–70.

Houston, D. B. (1974). Response of selected *Pinus strobus* L. clones to fumigations with sulfur dioxide and ozone. *Can. J. For. Res.* **4**, 65–68.

Howell, F. G., Gentry, J. B., and Smith, M. H., eds. (1975). "Mineral Cycling in Southeastern Ecosystems," ERDA Symp. Ser. (Conf. 740513). Natl. Tech. Inf. Serv., Springfield, Virginia.

Howell, J. (1932). Relation of western yellow pine seedlings to the reaction of the culture solution. *Plant Physiol.* **7**, 657–671.

Howes, F. N. (1949). "Vegetable Gums and Resins." Chronica Botanica, Waltham, Massachusetts.

Hsiao, T. C. (1973). Plant responses to water stress. *Annu. Rev. Plant Physiol.* **24**, 519–570.

Huber, B. (1928). Weitere quantitative Untersuchungen über das Wasserleitungssystem der Pflanzen. *Jahrb. Wiss. Bot.* **67**, 877–959.

Huber, B. (1935). Die physiologische Bedeutung der Ring- und Zerstreutporigkeit. *Ber. Dtsch. Bot. Ges.* **53**, 711–719.

Huber, B. (1937). Wasserumsatz und Stoffbewegungen. *Forstchr. Bot.* **7**, 197–207.

Huber, B. (1939). Das Siebröhrensystem unserer Bäume und seine jahreszeitlichen Veränderungen. *Jahrb. Wiss. Bot.* **88**, 176–242.

Huber, B. (1953). Was wissen wir vom Wasserverbrauch des Waldes? *Forstwiss. Centralbl.* **72**, 257–264.

Huber, B. (1956). Die Gefassleitung. *Encycl. Plant Physiol.* **3**, 541–582.

Huber, B. (1958). Recording gaseous changes under field conditions. *In* "The Physiology of Forest Trees" (K. V. Thimann, ed.), pp. 187–195. Ronald, New York.

Huber, B., and Polster, H. (1955). Zur Frage der physiologischen Ursachen der unterschiedlichen Stoffer-zeugung von Pappelklonen. *Biol. Zentrabl.* **74,** 370–420.

Huber, B., and Schmidt, E. (1937). Eine Kompensationsmethode zur thermoelektrischen Messung langsamer Saftströme. *Ber. Dtsch. Bot. Ges.* **50,** 514–529.

Huck, M. G., Klepper, B., and Taylor, H. M. (1970). Diurnal variations in root diameter. *Plant Physiol.* **45,** 529–530.

Hughes, J. F. (1965). Tension wood: A review of literature. *For. Abstr.* **26,** 1–16.

Hull, R. J., and Leonard, O. A. (1964a). Physiological aspects of parasitism in mistletoes (*Arceuthobium* and *Phoradendron*). I. The carbohydrate nutrition of mistletoe. *Plant Physiol.* **39,** 996–1007.

Hull, R. J., and Leonard, O. A. (1964b). Physiological aspects of parasitism in mistletoes (*Arceuthobium* and *Phoradendron*). II. The photosynthetic capacity of mistletoe. *Plant Physiol.* **39,** 1008–1017.

Hulme, A. C. ed. (1970–71). "The Biochemistry of Fruits and their Products. 2 vols. Academic Press, London.

Humphries, E. C. (1947). Wilt of cacao fruits (*Theobroma cacao*). IV. Seasonal variation in the carbohy-drate reserves of the bark and wood of the cacao tree. *Ann. Bot. (London)* [N.S.] **11,** 219–244.

Humphries, E. C., and Wheeler, A. W. (1963). The physiology of leaf growth. *Annu. Rev. Plant Physiol.* **14,** 385–410.

Husch, B., Miller, C. I., and Beers, T. W. (1972). "Forest Mensuration." Ronald, New York.

Hustich, I. (1948). The Scotch pine in northernmost Finland and its dependence on the climate in the last decades. *Acta Bot. Fenn.* **42,** 4–75.

Hutchinson, J. G., and Bramlett, D. L. (1964). Frost damage to shortleaf pine flowers. *J. For.* **62,** 343.

Huxley, P. A., and Van Eck, W. A. (1974). Seasonal changes in growth and development of some woody perennials near Kampala, Uganda. *J. Ecol.* **62,** 579–592.

Hyre, R. A. (1939). The effect of sulfur fungicides on the photosynthesis and transpiration of apple leaves. *N.Y., Agric. Exp. Stn., Ithaca, Mem.* **222.**

Idso, S. B., and Baker, D. G. (1967). Relative importance of reradiation, convection, and transpiration in heat transfer from plants. *Plant Physiol.* **42,** 631–640.

Ikuma, H. (1972). Electron transport in plant respiration. *Annu. Rev. Plant Physiol.* **23,** 419–436.

Iljin, W. S. (1951). Metabolism of plants affected with lime-induced chlorosis (calciose). I. Nitrogen metabolism. *Plant Soil* **3,** 239–256.

Ingestad, T. (1957). Studies on the nutrition of forest tree seedlings. I. Mineral nutrition of birch. *Physiol. Plant.* **10,** 418–439.

Isebrands, J. G., Promnitz, L. C., and Dawson, D. H. (1977). Leaf area development in short rotation intensive cultured *Populus* plots. *TAPPI For. Biol. Wood Chem. Conf.* [*Conf. Pap.*], *1977* pp. 201–210.

Ishibe, O. (1935). The seasonal changes in starch and fat reserves of some woody plants. *Kyoto Imp. Univ., Bot. Inst. Publ.* **42.**

Israel, D. W., Giddens, J. E., and Powell, W. W. (1973). The toxicity of peach tree roots. *Plant Soil* **39,** 103–112.

Ito, M. (1955). On the water amount and distribution in the stems of Akamatsu (*Pinus densiflora* S. and Z.) and Kuri (*Castanea crenata* S. and Z.) grown at Kurokawa district in Gifu Prefecture. *Fac. Arts Sci., Sci. Rep., Gifu Univ.* **3,** 299–307.

Ivanov, L. A. (1924). Über die Transpiration der Holzgewächse im Winter. *Ber. Dtsch. Bot. Ges.* **42,** 44–49.

Jackson, C. H. (1975). Date of blossoming of Bramley's seedling apple in relation to temperature. *Common. Agric. Bur. Res. Rev.* **5,** 47–50.

Jackson, D. I., and Coombe, B. G. (1966). Gibberellin-like substances in developing apricot fruit. *Science* **154,** 277–278.

Jackson, D. I., and Sweet, G. B. (1972). Flower determination in temperate woody plants. *Hortic. Abstr.* **42,** 9–24.

Jackson, D. S., Gifford, H. H. and Hobbs, I. W. (1973). Daily transpiration rates of radiata pine. *N. Z. J. For. Sci.* **3**(1), 70–81.

Jackson, G. A. D., and Blundell, J. B. (1963). Germination in *Rosa. J. Hortic. Sci.* **38,** 310–320.

Jackson, J. E., and Palmer, J. W. (1977a). Effects of shade on the growth and cropping of apple trees. I. Experimental details and effects on vegetative growth. *J. Hortic. Sci.* **52**, 245–252.

Jackson, J. E., and Palmer, J. W. (1977b). Effects of shade on the growth and cropping of apple trees. II. Effects on components of yield. *J. Hortic. Sci.* **52**, 253–256.

Jackson, J. E., Palmer, J. W., Penning, M. A., and Sharples, R. O. (1977). Effects of shade on the growth and cropping of apple trees. III. Effects on fruit growth, chemical composition and quality at harvest and after storage. *J. Hortic. Sci.* **52**, 267–282.

Jackson, L. W. R. (1967). Effect of shade on leaf structure of deciduous tree species. *Ecology* **48**, 498–499.

Jacobs, M. R. (1955). Growth habits of the eucalypts. *For. Timber Bur., Aust.* pp. 1–262.

Jacobson, A., and Corcoran, M. R. (1977). Tannins as gibberellin antagonists in the synthesis of α-amylase and acid phosphatase by barley seeds. *Plant Physiol.* **59**, 129–133.

Jacoby, B. (1964). Function of the root and stems in sodium retention. *Plant Physiol.* **39**, 445–449.

Jankiewicz, L. S. (1971). Gravimorphism in higher plants. *In* "Gravity and the Organism" (S. A. Gordon and M. J. Cohen, eds.), pp. 317–331. Univ. of Chicago Press, Chicago, Illinois.

Jankiewicz, L. S., and Stecki, Z. J. (1976). Some mechanisms responsible for differences in tree growth. *In* "Tree Physiology and Yield Improvement" (M. G. R. Cannell and F. T. Last, eds.), pp. 157–172. Academic Press, New York.

Jarvis, B. C., Frankland, B., and Cherry, J. H. (1968). Increased nucleic acid synthesis in relation to the breaking of dormancy of hazel seed by gibberellic acid. *Planta* **83**, 257–266.

Jarvis, P. G., and Slatyer, R. O. (1966). A controlled environment chamber for studies of gas exchange by each surface of a leaf. *CSIRO Div. Land Res., Tech. Pap.* **29**.

Jarvis, P. G., and Slatyer, R. O. (1970). The role of the mesophyll cell wall in leaf transpiration. *Planta* **90**, 303–322.

Jemison, G. M. (1944). The effect of basal wounding by forest fires on the diameter growth of some southern Appalachian hardwoods. *Duke [Univ] Sch. For. Bull.* **9**.

Jenkins, P. A. (1974). Influence of applied indoleacetic acid and abscisic acid on xylem cell dimensions in *Pinus radiata* D. Don. *In* "Mechanisms of Regulation of Plant Growth" (R. L. Bieleski, A. R. Ferguson, and M. M. Creswell, eds.), Bull. 12, pp. 737–742. R. Soc. N.Z., Wellington.

Jensen, K. F., and Kozlowski, T. T. (1974). Effect of SO_2 on photosynthesis of quaking aspen and white ash seedlings. *In* "Proceedings of the Third North American Forest Biology Workshop" (C. P. P. Reid and G. H. Fechner, eds.), p. 359. Colorado State University, Fort Collins.

Jensen, K. F., and Kozlowski, T. T. (1975). Absorption and translocation of sulfur dioxide by seedlings of four forest tree species. *J. Environ. Qual.* **4**, 379–382.

Jeremias, K. (1964). Über die jahrperiodisch bedingten Veränderungen der Ablagerungs form der Kohlenhydrate in Vegetativen Pflanzenteilen. *Bot. Stud.* **15**.

Jerie, P. H., and Chalmers, D. J. (1976). Ethylene as a growth hormone in peach fruit. *Aust. J. Plant Physiol.* **3**, 429–434.

Johansson, N. (1933). The relation between the tree-stem's respiration and its growth. *J. Swed. For. Soc.* **31**, 53–133.

Johnson, E. A., and Kovner, J. L. (1956). Effect on streamflow of cutting a forest understory. *For. Sci.* **2**, 82–91.

Johnson, L. P. V. (1944). Sugar production by white and yellow birches. *Can. J. Res., Sect. C* **22**, 1–6.

Johnson, N. E. (1976). Biological opportunities and risks associated with fast-growing plantations in the tropics. *J. For.* **74**, 206–211.

Jones, C. G., Edson, A. W., and Morse, W. J. (1903). The maple sap flow. *Vt., Agric. Exp. Stn., Bull.* **103**.

Jones, C. H., and Bradlee, J. L. (1933). The carbohydrate content of the maple tree. *Vt., Agric. Exp. Stn., Bull.* **358**.

Jones, H. C., III, and Curlin, J. W. (1968). The role of fertilizers in improving the hardwoods of the Tennessee Valley. *In* "Forest Fertilization: Theory and Practice," pp. 185–196. Tenn. Valley Auth., Muscle Shoals, Ala.

Jones, K. (1970). Nitrogen fixation in the phyllosphere of Douglas-fir. *Ann. Bot. (London) [N.S.]* **34**, 239–244.

Jones, L. (1961). Effect of light on germination of forest tree seeds. *Proc. Int. Seed Test. Assoc.* **26**, 437–452.

Jones, O. P., and Lacey, H. J. (1968). Gibberellin-like substances in the transpiration stream of apple and pear trees. *J. Exp. Bot.* **19**, 526–531.

Jones, R. J., and Mansfield, T. A. (1972). Effects of abscisic acid and its esters on stomatal aperture and the transpiration ratio. *Physiol. Plant.* **26**, 321–327.

Jones, R. L. (1973). Gibberellins: Their physiological role. *Annu. Rev. Plant Physiol.* **24**, 571–598.

Jones, W. W., and Cree, C. B. (1954). Effect of time of harvest on yield, size and grade of Valencia oranges. *Proc. Am. Soc. Hortic. Sci.* **64**, 139–145.

Jones, W. W., and Embleton, T. W. (1969). Development and current status of citrus leaf analysis as a guide to fertilization in California. *Proc. Int. Citrus Symp., 1st, 1968* Vol. 3, pp. 1669–1671.

Jones, W. W., and Parker, E. R. (1951). Seasonal trends in mineral composition of Valencia orange leaves. *Proc. Am. Soc. Hortic. Sci.* **57**, 101–103.

Jones, W. W., Embleton, T. W., Steinacker, M. L., and Cree, C. B. (1964). The effect of time of fruit harvest on fruiting and carbohydrate supply in the Valencia orange. *Proc. Am. Soc. Hortic. Sci.* **84**, 152–157.

Jordan, W. R., and Ritchie, J. T. (1971). Influence of soil water stress on evaporation, root absorption, and internal water status of cotton. *Plant Physiol.* **48**, 783–788.

Jordan, W. R., Morgan, P. W., and Davenport, T. L. (1972). Water stress enhances ethylene-mediated leaf abscission in cotton. *Plant Physiol.* **50**, 756–758.

Jump, J. A. (1938). A study of forking in red pine. *Phytopathology* **28**, 798–811.

Juniper, B. E. (1976). Geotropism. *Annu. Rev. Plant. Physiol.* **27**, 385–406.

Justice, O. L. (1972). Essentials of seed testing. *In* "Seed Biology" (T. T. Kozlowski, ed.), Vol. 3, pp. 301–370. Academic Press, New York.

Kahdr, A. H., Wallace, A., and Romney, E. M. (1965). Mineral nutritional problems of trifoliate orange rootstock. *Calif. Agric.* **6**(9). 12–13.

Kamienska, A., Pharis, R. P., Wample, R. L., Kuo, C. C., and Durley, R. C. (1974). Occurrence and metabolism of gibberellins in conifers. *In* "Plant Growth Substances" (S. Tamura, ed.), pp. 305–313. Hirokawa Publ. Co., Tokyo.

Kanemasu, E. T., Thurtell, G. W., and Tanner, C. B. (1969). Design, calibration and field use of a stomatal diffusion porometer. *Plant Physiol.* **44**, 881–885.

Kaszkurewicz, A., and Fogg, P. J. (1967). Growing seasons of cottonwood and sycamore as related to geographic and environmental factors. *Ecology* **48**, 785–793.

Kato, Y., Miyake, I., and Mishikawa, H. (1958). Initiation of flower bud by gibberellin in *Cryptomeria japonica*. *J. Jpn. For. Soc.* **40**, 35–36.

Kaufmann, M. R. (1968a). Water relations of pine seedlings in relation to root and shoot growth. *Plant Physiol.* **43**, 281–288.

Kaufmann, M. R. (1968b). Evaluation of the pressure chamber technique for estimating plant water potential of forest tree species. *For. Sci.* **14**, 369–374.

Kaufman, M. R. (1969). Effects of water potential on germination of lettuce, sunflower, and citrus seeds. *Can. J. Bot.* **47**, 1761–1764.

Kaufmann, M. R. (1976). Stomatal response of Engelmann spruce to humidity, light, and water stress. *Plant Physiol.* **57**, 898–901.

Kaufmann, M. R. and Eckard, A. N. (1977). Water potential and temperature effects on germination of Engelmann spruce and lodgepole pine seeds. *For. Sci.* **23**, 27–33.

Kaul, O. N., and Kramer, P. J. (1965). Comparative drought resistance of two woody species. *Indian For.* **91**, 462–469.

Kawase, M. (1966). Growth-inhibiting substance and bud dormancy in woody plants. *Proc. Am. Soc. Hortic. Sci.* **89**, 752–757.

Kawase, M. (1974). Role of ethylene in induction of flooding damage in sunflower. *Physiol. Plant.* **31**, 29–38.

Kawase, M. (1976). Ethylene accumulation in flooded plants. *Physiol. Plant.* **36**, 236–241.

Kayll, A. J. (1974). Use of fire in land management. *In* "Fire and Ecosystems" (T. T. Kozlowski and C. E. Ahlgren, eds.), pp. 483–511. Academic Press, New York.

Keller, T. (1964). Beeinflussen insektizide die Photosynthese und Transpiration van Pappelblättern? *Sond. Anz. Schäedlingskd.* **6,** 87–89.

Keller, T. (1966). Über den Einfluss von transpirationshemmenden Chemikalien (Antitranspirantien) auf Transpiration, CO_2-Aufnahme und Wurzelwachstum van Jungfichten. *Forstwiss. Centralbl.* **85,** 65–79.

Keller, T. (1973). On the phytotoxicity of dust-like fluoride compounds. *Staub—Reinhalt. Luft* **33,** 379–381 (in English).

Keller, T., and Koch, W. (1962a). Der Einfluss der Mineralstofferernährung auf CO_2-Gaswechsel und Blattpigmentgehalt der Papel. I. Stickstoff. *Mitt. Schweiz. Anst. Forstl. Versuchswes.* **38,** 253–282.

Keller, T., and Koch, W. (1962b). Der Einfluss der Mineralstofferernährung auf CO_2-Gaswechsel und Blattpigmentgehalt der Pappel. II. Eisen. *Mitt., Schweiz. Anst. Forstl. Versuchswes.* **38,** 283–318.

Keller, T., and Koch, W. (1964). The effect of iron chelate fertilization of poplar upon CO_2 uptake, leaf size, and content of leaf pigments and iron. *Plant Soil* **20,** 116–126.

Keller, T., and Wehrmann, J. (1963). CO_2-Assimilation, Wurzelatmung und Ertrag von Fichten- und Kiefernsämlingen bei unterschiedlicher Mineralstofferernährung. *Mitt., Schweiz. Anst. Forstl. Versuchswes.* **39,** 217–242.

Kelly, G. J., Latzko, E. and Gibbs, M. (1976). Regulatory aspects of photosynthetic carbon metabolism. *Annu. Rev. Plant Physiol.* **27,** 181–205.

Kessel, S. N., and Stoate, T. N. (1938). Pine nutrition. *West. Aust., For. Dep., Bull.* **50.**

Khan, A. A. (1975). Primary, preventive, and permissive roles of hormones in plant systems. *Bot. Rev.* **41,** 391–420.

Khan, A. A., and Heit, C. E. (1969). Selective effects of hormones on nucleic acid metabolism during germination of pear embryos. *Biochem. J.* **113,** 707–712.

Kienholz, R. (1932). Fasciation in red pine. *Bot. Gaz. (Chicago)* **94,** 404–410.

Kienholz, R. (1941). Seasonal course of height growth in some hardwoods in Connecticut. *Ecology* **22,** 249–258.

Killian, C., and Lemée, G. (1956). Les xerophytes: Leur économie d'eau. *Encycl. Plant Physiol.,* **3,** 787–824.

Kimmins, J. P. (1977). Evaluation of the consequences for future tree productivity of the loss of nutrients in whole tree harvesting. *For. Ecol. Manage.* **1,** 169–183.

Kinerson, R. S. (1975). Relationships between plant surface area and respiration in loblolly pine. *J. Appl. Ecol.* **12,** 965–971.

Kinerson, R. S., Ralston, C., and Wells, C. (1977). Carbon cycling in a loblolly pine plantation. *Oecologia* **29,** 1–10.

King, R. W. (1976). Implications for plant growth of the transport of regulatory compounds in phloem and xylem. *In* "Transport and Transfer Processes in Plants" (I. F. Wardlaw and J. B. Passioura, eds.), pp. 415–431. Academic Press, New York.

Kira, T. (1975). Primary productivity of forests. *In* "Photosynthesis and Productivity in Different Environments" (J. P. Cooper, ed.), IBP, Vol. 3, pp. 5–40. Cambridge Univ. Press, London and New York.

Klebs, G. (1913). Über das Verhaltniss der Aussenwelt zur Entwicklung der Pflanzen. *Sitzungsber. Heidelb. Akad. Wiss., Abt. B* **5,** 1–47.

Klebs, G. (1914). Über das Treiben der einheimischen Bäume, speziell der Buche. *Sitzungsber. Heidelb. Akad. Wiss., Abh. Math.-Naturwiss. Kl.* **3,** reviewed in *Plant World* **18,** 19 (1915).

Klepper, B., and Kaufmann, M. R. (1966). Removal of salt from xylem sap by leaves and stems of guttating plants. *Plant Physiol.* **41,** 1743–1747.

Knipling, E. B. (1967). Effect of leaf aging on water deficit-water potential relationship of dogwood leaves growing in two environments. *Physiol. Plant.* **20,** 65–72.

Knipling, E. B., and Kramer, P. J. (1967). Comparison of the dye method with the thermocouple psychrometer for measuring leaf water potentials. *Plant Physiol.* **42,** 1315–1320.

Knoerr, K. R. (1965). Partitioning of the radiant heat load by forest stands. *Proc. Soc. Am. For., 1964* pp. 105–109.

Knoerr, K. R. (1967). Contrasts in energy balances between individual leaves and vegetated surfaces. *In* "Forest Hydrology" (W. E. Sopper and H. W. Lull, eds.), pp. 391–401. Pergamon, Oxford.

Koch, W. (1957). Der Tagesgang der "Produktivität der Transpiration." *Planta* **48,** 418–452.

Koch, W. (1963). Die Kohlensäure als Standortsfaktor. *Allg. Forst. Jagdzg.* **134,** 54–57.

Kodenko, A. N., and Erygina, N. P. (1953). The effect of side dressings on photosynthetic activity and yield of vines. *Vinodel. Vinograd. SSSR* **8,** 41–42.

Koelling, M. R., Blum, B. M., and Gibbs, C. B. (1968). A summary and evaluation of research on the use of plastic tubing in maple sap production. *U.S. For. Serv., Res. Pap. NE* **NE 116.**

Kolattukudy, P. E. (1975). Biochemistry of cutin, suberin and waxes, the lipid barriers on plants. *In* "Recent Advances in the Chemistry and Biochemistry of Plant Lipids" (T. Galliard and E. I. Mercer, eds.), pp. 203–246. Academic Press, New York.

Kolesnikov, V. A. (1966). "Fruit Biology." Mir Publishers, Moscow.

Koller, D. (1972). Environmental control of seed germination. *In* "Seed Biology" (T. T. Kozlowski, ed.), Vol. 2, pp. 1–101. Academic Press, New York.

Koller, D., and Samish, Y. (1964). A nullpoint compensating system for simultaneous and continuous measurement of net photosynthesis and transpiration by controlled gas-stream analysis. *Bot. Gaz. (Chicago)* **125,** 81–88.

Konar, R. N., and Oberoi, Y. P. (1969). Recent work on reproductive structures of living conifers and taxads-a review. *Bot. Rev.* **35,** 89–116.

Kondo, T. (1964). On the wood enzyme. *J. Jpn. Wood Res. Soc.* **10,** 43–48.

Koriba, K. (1958). On the periodicity of tree growth in the tropics, with reference to the mode of branching, the leaf fall, and the formation of the resting bud. *Gardens' Bull.* **17,** 11–81.

Kormanik, P. P., and Brown, C. L. (1967). Root buds and the development of root suckers in sweetgum. *For. Sci.* **13,** 338–345.

Korstian, C. F. (1924). Density of cell sap in relation to environmental conditions in the Wasatch Mountains of Utah. *J. Agric. Res.* **28,** 845–909.

Kosceev, A. L. (1952). Lesovodstvennoe znacenie pridatocnyh kornei drevesnyh porod. *Lesn. Khoz.* **5,** 48–50; *For. Abstr.* **16,** 3886 (1955).

Kosceev, A. L. (1953). The silvicultural significance of adventitious roots on tree species in waterlogged clear-felled areas. Dep. For., Ottawa; transl. from *Tr. Inst. Les.* No. 13, pp. 116–129.

Kozlowski, T. T. (1943). Transpiration rates of some forest tree species during the dormant season. *Plant Physiol.* **18,** 252–260.

Kozlowski, T. T. (1949). Light and water in relation to growth and competition of Piedmont forest tree species. *Ecol. Monogr.* **19,** 207–231.

Kozlowski, T. T. (1957). Effect of continuous high light intensity on photosynthesis of forest tree seedlings. *For. Sci.* **3,** 220–224.

Kozlowski, T. T. (1958). Water relations and growth of trees. *J. For.* **56,** 498–502.

Kozlowski, T. T. (1961). The movement of water in trees. *For. Sci.* **7,** 177–192.

Kozlowski, T. T. (1962). Water transport in trees. *J. Int. Soc. Trop. Ecol.* **3,** 84–100.

Kozlowski, T. T. (1963). Characteristics and improvement of forest growth. *Adv. Front. Plant Sci.* **2,** 73–136.

Kozlowski, T. T. (1964a). Shoot growth in woody plants. *Bot. Rev.* **30,** 335–392.

Kozlowski, T. T. (1964b). "Water Metabolism in Plants." Harper, New York.

Kozlowski, T. T. (1967a). Diurnal variation in stem diameters of small trees. *Bot. Gaz. (Chicago)* **128,** 60–68.

Kozlowski, T. T. (1967b). Continuous recording of diameter changes in seedlings. *For. Sci.* **13,** 100–101.

Kozlowski, T. T., ed. (1968–1978). "Water Deficits and Plant Growth," Vols. 1–5. Academic Press, New York.

Kozlowski, T. T. (1968a). Water balance in shade trees. *Proc. Int. Shade Tree Conf., 44th, 1968* pp. 29–42.

Kozlowski, T. T. (1968b). Soil water and tree growth. *In* "The Ecology of Southern Forests" (N. E. Linnartz, ed.), pp. 30–57. Louisiana State Univ. Press, Baton Rouge.

Kozlowski, T. T. (1968c). Diurnal changes in diameters of fruits and stems of Montmorency cherry. *J. Hortic. Sci.* **43,** 1–15.

Kozlowski, T. T. (1969). Tree physiology and forest pests. *J. For.* **69,** 118–122.

Kozlowski, T. T., ed. (1971a). "Growth and Development of Trees," Vol. 1. Academic Press, New York.

Kozlowski, T. T., ed. (1971b). "Growth and Development of Trees," Vol. 2. Academic Press, New York.

Kozlowski, T. T. (1972a). Shrinking and swelling of plant tissues. *In* "Water Deficits and Plant Growth" (T. T. Kozlowski, ed.), Vol. 3, pp. 1–64. Academic Press, New York.

Kozlowski, T. T. (1972b). Physiology of water stress. *U.S., Dep. Agric., For. Serv., Gen. Tech. Rep. INT-1,* 229–244.

Kozlowski, T. T., ed. (1972c). "Seed Biology," Vol. 1–3. Academic Press, New York.

Kozlowski, T. T., ed. (1973). "Shedding of Plant Parts." Academic Press, New York.

Kozlowski, T. T. (1976a). Water supply and leaf shedding. *In* "Water Deficits and Plant Growth" (T. T. Kozlowski, ed.), Vol. 4, pp. 191–231. Academic Press, New York.

Kozlowski, T. T. (1976b). Water relations and tree improvement. *In* "Tree Physiology and Yield Improvement" (M. G. R. Cannell and F. T. Last, eds.), pp. 307–327. Academic Press, New York.

Kozlowski, T. T., and Ahlgren, C. E., eds. (1974). "Fire and Ecosystems." Academic Press, New York.

Kozlowski, T. T., and Borger, G. A. (1971). Effect of temperature and light intensity early in ontogeny in growth of *Pinus resinosa* seedlings. *Can. J. For. Res.* **1,** 57–65.

Kozlowski, T. T., and Clausen, J. J. (1965). Changes in moisture contents and dry weights of buds and leaves of forest trees. *Bot. Gaz. (Chicago)* **126,** 20–26.

Kozlowski, T. T., and Clausen, J. J. (1966). Shoot growth characteristics of heterophyllous woody plants. *Can. J. Bot.* **44,** 827–843.

Kozlowski, T. T., and Clausen, J. J. (1970). Effect of decenylsuccinic acid on needle moisture content and shoot growth of *Pinus resinosa*. *Can. J. Plant Sci.* **50,** 355–356.

Kozlowski, T. T., and Cooley, J. C. (1961). Root grafting in northern Wisconsin. *J. For.* **59,** 105–107.

Kozlowski, T. T., and Gentile, A. C. (1958). Respiration of white pine buds in relation to oxygen availability and moisture content. *For. Sci.* **4,** 147–152.

Kozlowski, T. T., and Gentile, A. C. (1959). Influence of the seed coat on germination, water absorption, and oxygen uptake of eastern white pine seed. *For. Sci.* **5,** 389–395.

Kozlowski, T. T., and Greathouse, T. E. (1970). Shoot growth characteristics of tropical pines. *Unasylva* **24,** 1–10.

Kozlowski, T. T., and Keller, T. (1966). Food relations of woody plants. *Bot. Rev.* **32,** 293–382.

Kozlowski, T. T., and Peterson, T. A. (1962). Seasonal growth of dominant, intermediate, and suppressed red pine trees. *Bot. Gaz. (Chicago)* **124,** 146–154.

Kozlowski, T. T., and Sasaki, S. (1970). Effects of herbicides on seed germination and development of young pine seedlings. *Proc. Int. Symp Seed Physiol. Woody Plants, 1968* pp. 19–24.

Kozlowski, T. T., and Scholtes, W. H. (1948). Growth of roots and root hairs of pine and hardwood seedlings in the Piedmont. *J. For.* **46,** 750–754.

Kozlowski, T. T., and Torrie, J. H. (1964). Effects of hydrogen peroxide on germination of eastern white pine seed. *Adv. Front. Plant Sci.* **9,** 131–144.

Kozlowski, T. T., and Torrie, J. H. (1965). Effect of soil incorporation of herbicides on seed germination and growth of pine seedlings. *Soil Sci.* **100,** 139–146.

Kozlowski, T. T., and Ward, R. C. (1961). Shoot elongation characteristics of forest trees. *For. Sci.* **7,** 357–368.

Kozlowski, T. T., and Winget, C. H. (1963). Patterns of water movement in forest trees. *Bot Gaz. (Chicago)* **124,** 301–311.

Kozlowski, T. T., and Winget, C. H. (1964a). The role of reserves in leaves, branches, stems, and roots on shoot growth of red pine. *Am. J. Bot.* **51,** 522–529.

Kozlowski, T. T., and Winget, C. H. (1964b). Diurnal and seasonal variation in radii of tree stems. *Ecology* **45,** 149–155.

Kozlowski, T. T., Winget, C. H., and Torrie, J. H. (1962). Daily radial growth of oak in relation to maximum and minimum temperature. *Bot. Gaz. (Chicago)* **124,** 9–17.

Kozlowski, T. T., Hughes, J. F., and Leyton, L. (1966). Patterns of water movement in dormant gymnosperm seedlings. *Biorheology* **3,** 77–85.

Kozlowski, T. T., Sasaki, S., and Torrie, J. H. (1967a). Influence of temperature on phytotoxicity of triazine herbicides to pine seedlings. *Am. J. Bot.* **54**, 790–796.

Kozlowski, T. T., Sasaki, S., and Torrie, J. H. (1967b). Effects of temperature on phytotoxicity of monuron, picloram, CDEC, EPTC, CDAA, and sesone to young pine seedlings. *Silva Fenn,* **32**, 13–28.

Kozlowski, T. T., Hughes, J. F., and Leyton, L. (1967). Dye movement in gymnosperms in relation to tracheid alignment. *Forestry* **40**, 209–227.

Kozlowski, T. T., Torrie, J. H., and Marshall, P. E. (1973). Predictability of shoot length from bud size in *Pinus resinosa* Ait. *Can. J. For. Res.* **3**, 34–38.

Kozlowski, T. T., Davies, W. J., and Carlson, S. D. (1974). Transpiration rates of *Fraxinus americana* and *Acer saccharum* leaves. *Can. J. For. Res.* **4**, 259–267.

Krahmer, R. L., and Coté, W. A., Jr. (1963). Changes in coniferous wood cells associated with heartwood formation. *Tappi* **46**, 42–49.

Kramer, P. J. (1936). Effect of variation in length of day on growth and dormancy of trees. *Plant Physiol.* **11**, 127–137.

Kramer, P. J. (1937a). The relation between rate of transpiration and rate of absorption of water in plants. *Am. J. Bot.* **24**, 10–15.

Kramer, P. J. (1937b). Photoperiodic stimulation of growth by artificial light as a cause of winterkilling. *Plant Physiol.* **12**, 881–883.

Kramer, P. J. (1940). Sap pressure and exudation. *Am. J. Bot.* **27**, 929–931.

Kramer, P. J. (1942). Species differences with respect to water absorption at low soil temperature. *Am. J. Bot.* **29**, 828–832.

Kramer, P. J. (1943). Amount and duration of growth of various species of tree seedlings. *Plant Physiol.* **18**, 239–251.

Kramer, P. J. (1946). Absorption of water through suberized roots of trees. *Plant Physiol.* **21**, 37–41.

Kramer, P. J. (1949). "Plant and Soil Water Relationships." McGraw-Hill, New York.

Kramer, P. J. (1951). Effects of respiration inhibitors on accumulation of radioactive phosphorus by roots of loblolly pine. *Plant Physiol.* **26**, 30–36.

Kramer, P. J. (1955). Bound water. *In* "Encyclopedia of Plant Physiology." Vol. 1, 223–242.

Kramer, P. J. (1957). Some effects of various combinations of day and night temperatures and photoperiod on the height growth of loblolly pine seedlings. *For. Sci.* **3**, 45–55.

Kramer, P. J. (1958). Thermoperiodism in trees. *In* "The Physiology of Forest Trees" (K. V. Thimann, ed.), pp. 573–580. Ronald, New York.

Kramer, P. J. (1969). "Plant and Soil Water Relationships: A Modern Synthesis." McGraw-Hill, New York.

Kramer, P. J., and Bullock, H. C. (1966). Seasonal variations in the proportions of suberized and unsuberized roots of trees in relation to the absorption of water. *Am. J. Bot.* **53**, 200–204.

Kramer, P. J., and Clark, W. S. (1947). A comparison of photosynthesis in individual pine needles and entire seedlings at various light intensities. *Plant Physiol.* **22**, 51–57.

Kramer, P. J., and Decker, J. P. (1944). Relation between light intensity and rate of photosynthesis of loblolly pine and certain hardwoods. *Plant Physiol.* **19**, 350–358.

Kramer, P. J., and Kozlowski, T. T. (1960). "Physiology of Trees." McGraw-Hill, New York.

Kramer, P. J., Riley, W. S., and Bannister, T. T. (1952). Gas exchange of cypress (*Taxodium distichum*) knees. *Ecology* **33**, 117–121.

Kramer, P. J., Knipling, E. B., and Miller, L. N. (1966). Terminology of cell-water relations. *Science* **153**, 889–890.

Kraus, J. F., and Spurr, S. H. (1961). Relationship of soil moisture to the springwood-summerwood transition in southern Michigan red pine. *J. For.* **50**, 510–511.

Krawczyszyn, J. (1977). The transition from nonstoried to storied cambium in *Fraxinus excelsior*. I. The occurrence of radial anticlinal divisions. *Can. J. Bot.* **55**, 3034–3041.

Kress, L. W. (1972). "Response of Hybrid Poplar to Sequential Exposures to Ozone and PAN," Publ. No. 250. Cent. Air Environ. Stud., Pennsylvania State University, University Park.

Kriebel, H. B. (1957). Patterns of genetic variation in sugar maple. *Ohio, Agric. Exp. Stn., Res. Bull.* **791**, 1–56.

Kriebel, H. B., and Wang, C. (1962). The interaction between provenance and degree of chilling in bud-break of sugar maple. Silvae Genet. **11**, 125–130.

Kriedemann, P. E. (1968a). ¹⁴C translocation patterns in peach and apricot shoots. *Aust. J. Agric. Res.* **19**, 775–780.

Kriedemann, P. E. (1968b). Some photosynthetic characteristics of citrus leaves. *Aust. J. Biol. Sci.* **21**, 895–905.

Kriedemann, P. E. (1969). ¹⁴C translocation in orange plants. *Aust. J. Agric. Res.* **20**, 291–300.

Kriedemann, P. E. (1971). Photosynthesis and transpiration as a function of gaseous diffusive resistances in orange leaves. *Physiol. Plant.* **24**, 218–225.

Kriedemann, P. E., and Canterford, R. L. (1971). The photosynthetic activity of pear leaves (*Pyrus communis* L.). *Aust. J. Biol. Sci.* **24**, 197–205.

Kriedemann, P. E., and Smart, R. E. (1971). Effects of irradiance, temperature, and leaf water potential on photosynthesis of vine leaves. *Photosynthetica* **5**, 6–15.

Kriedemann, P. E., Kliewer, W. M., and Harris, J. M. (1970). Leaf age and photosynthesis in *Vitis vinifera* L. *Vitis* **9**, 97–104.

Krishnamoorthy, H. N., ed. (1975). "Gibberellins and Plant Growth." Wiley, New York.

Krotkov, G. (1941). The respiratory metabolism of McIntosh apples during ontogeny as determined at 22°C. *Plant Physiol.* **16**, 799–812.

Krueger, K. W. (1967). Nitrogen, phosphorus and carbohydrate in expanding and year-old Douglas-fir shoots. *For. Sci.* **13**, 352–356.

Krueger, K. W., and Ferrell, W. K. (1965). Comparative photosynthetic and respiratory responses to temperature and light by *Pseudotsuga menziesii* var. *menziesii* and var. *glauca* seedlings. *Ecology* **46**, 794–801.

Krugman, S. L., Stein, W. I., and Schmitt, D. M. (1974). Seed biology. *U.S. For. Serv., Agric. Handb.* **450**, 5–40.

Kruse, P. F., Jr., and Patterson, M. K., eds. (1973). "Tissue Culture: Methods and Application." Academic Press, New York.

Kuhnle, J. A., Fuller, G., Corse, J., and Mackey, B. E. (1977). Antisenescent activity of cytokinins. *Physiol. Plant.* **41**, 14–21.

Kuhns, L. J. and Fretz, T. A. (1978). A study of the potential use of electrophoresis in distinguishing rose cultivars. *Ohio Agr. Res. Dev. Center Res. Bull.* 1094.

Kulman, H. M. (1971). Effects of insect defoliation on growth and mortality of trees. *Annu. Rev. Entomol.* **16**, 289–324.

Kummerow, J., Krause, D., and Jow, W. (1977). Root systems of chaparral shrubs. *Oecologia* **29**, 163–177.

Kummerow, J., Alexander, J. V., Neel, J. W., and Fishbeck, K. (1978). Symbiotic nitrogen fixation in Ceanothus roots. *Am. J. Bot.* **65**, 63–69.

Kuntz, J. E., and Riker, A. J. (1955). The use of radioactive isotopes to ascertain the role of root grafting in the translocation of water, nutrients, and disease-inducing organisms. *Proc. Int. Conf. Peaceful Uses At. Energy 1st, 1955* Vol. 12, pp. 144–148.

Kuo, C. G., and Pharis, R. P. (1975). Effects of AMO-1618 and B-995 on growth and endogenous gibberellin content of *Cupressus arizonica* seedlings. *Physiol. Plant.* **34**, 288–292.

Kurtzman, R. H., Jr. (1966). Xylem sap flow as affected by metabolic inhibitors and girdling. *Plant Physiol.* **41**, 641–646.

Kurz, H., and Demaree, D. (1934). Cypress buttresses and knees in relation to water and air. *Ecology* **15**, 36–41.

Kvet, J., Ondok, J. P., Nečas, J., and Jarvis, P. G. (1971). Methods of growth analysis. *In* "Plant Photosynthetic Production" (Z. Sestak, J. Čatsky, and P. G. Jarvis, eds.), pp. 343–391. Junk Publ., The Hague.

Labanauskas, C. K., and Handy, M. F. (1972). Nutrient removal by Valencia orange fruit from citrus orchards in California. *Calif. Agric.* **26**, 3–4.

Labyak, L. F., and Schumacher, F. X. (1954). The contribution of its branches to the main stem growth of loblolly pine. *J. For.* **52,** 333–337.

Ladefoged, K. (1952). The periodicity of wood formation. *Dan. Biol. Skr.* **7,** 1–98.

Ladefoged, K. (1960). A method for measuring the water consumption of larger intact trees. *Physiol. Plant.* **13,** 648–658.

Ladefoged, K. (1963). Transpiration of forest trees. *Physiol. Plant.* **16,** 378–414.

Laing, E. V. (1932). Studies on tree roots. *Bull. For. Comm., London* No. 13, pp. 1–72.

Lairand, D. E. (1963). About the cytochemistry of wood elements. *Drev. Vysk.* **1,** 1–11.

Lakon, G. (1949). The topographical tetrazolium method for determining the germinating capacity of seeds. *Plant Physiol.* **24,** 389–394.

Lakon, G. (1954). Neuere Beiträge zur topographischen Tetrazolium-Methode. *Ber. Dtsch. Bot. Ges.* **67,** 146–157.

Lanner, R. M. (1964). Temperature and the diurnal rhythm of height growth in pines. *J. For.* **62,** 493–495.

Lanner, R. M. (1966a). The phenology and growth habits of pines in Hawaii. *U.S., For. Serv., Res. Pap. PSW 29.*

Lanner, R. M. (1966b). Needed: A new approach to the study of pollen dispersion. *Silvae Genet.* **15,** 50–52.

Lanner, R. M. (1971). Shoot growth patterns of loblolly pine. *For. Sci.* **17,** 486–487.

Lanner, R. M. (1976). Patterns of shoot development in *Pinus* and their relationship to growth potential. *In* "Tree Physiology and Yield Improvement" (M. G. R. Cannell and F. T. Last, eds.), pp. 223–243. Academic Press, New York.

Larcher, W. (1954). Die Kälteresistenz mediterraner Immergrüner und ihre Beeinflussbarkeit. *Planta* **44,** 607–635.

Larcher, W. (1961). Zur Assimilationsökologie der immergrünen *Quercus pubescens* im nördlichen Gardaseegebiet. *Planta* **56,** 607–617.

Larcher, W. (1969). The effect of environmental and physiological variables on the carbon dioxide gas exchange of trees. *Photosynthetica* **3,** 167–198.

Larcher, W. (1975). "Physiological Plant Ecology." Springer-Verlag, Berlin and New York.

Larsen, A. L. (1969). Isoenzymes and varietal identification. *Seed World* **104,** 5.

Larson, P. R. (1962a). The indirect effect of photoperiod on tracheid diameter in red pine. *Am. J. Bot.* **49,** 132–137.

Larson, P. R. (1962b). Auxin gradients and the regulation of cambial activity. *In* "Tree Growth" (T. T. Kozlowski, ed.), pp. 97–117. Ronald, New York.

Larson, P. R. (1963a). Stem form and silviculture. *Proc. Soc. Am. For.* pp. 103–107.

Larson, P. R. (1963b). Stem form development in forest trees. *For. Sci. Monogr.* **5.**

Larson, P. R. (1963c). The indirect effect of drought on tracheid diameter in red pine. *For. Sci.* **9,** 52–62.

Larson, P. R. (1964). Some indirect effects of environment on wood formation. *In* "The Formation of Wood in Forest Trees" (M. H. Zimmermann, ed.), pp. 345–365. Academic Press, New York.

Larson, P. R. (1969a). Incorporation of ^{14}C in the developing walls of *Pinus resinosa* tracheids (earlywood and latewood). *Holzforschung* **23,** 17–26.

Larson, P. R. (1969b). Wood formation and the concept of wood quality. *Yale Sch. For. Bull.* **74.**

Larson, P. R., and Gordon, J. C. (1969a). Leaf development, photosynthesis and ^{14}C distribution in *Populus deltoides* seedlings. *Am. J. Bot.* **56,** 1058–1066.

Larson, P. R., and Gordon, J. C. (1969b). Photosynthesis and wood yield. *Agric. Sci. Rev.* **7,** 7–14.

Larson, P. R., and J. G. Isebrands (1978). Functional significance of the nodal constricted zone in *Populus deltoides* Bartr. *Can. J. Bot.* **56,** 801–804.

Lassoie, J. P. (1973). Diurnal dimensional fluctuations in a Douglas-fir stem in response to tree water status. *For. Sci.* **19,** 251–255.

Lassoie, J. P., Fetcher, N., and Salo, D. J. (1977). Stomatal infiltration pressure versus diffusion porometer measurements of needle resistance in Douglas-fir and lodgepole pine foliage. *Can. J. For. Res.* **7,** 192–196.

Laüchli, A., Spurr, A. R., and Epstein, E. (1971). Lateral transport of ions into the xylem of corn roots. II. Evaluation of a stelar pump. *Plant Physiol.* **48,** 118–124.

Lavender, D. P., Sweet, G. B., Zaerr, J. B., and Hermann, R. K. (1973). Spring shoot growth in Douglas-fir may be initiated by gibberellins exported from the roots. *Science* **182**, 838–839.

Lawlor, D. W. (1972). Growth and water use of *Lolium perenne*. I. Water transport. *J. Appl. Ecol.* **9**, 79–98.

Lawlor, D. W., and Milford, G. F. J. (1975). The control of water and carbon dioxide flux in water-stressed sugar beet. *J. Exp. Bot.* **26**, 657–665.

Leach, R. W. A., and Wareing, P. F. (1967). Distribution of auxin in horizontal woody stems in relation to gravimorphism. *Nature (London)* **214**, 1025–1027.

Ledig, F. T. (1969). A growth model for tree seedlings based on the rate of photosynthesis and the distribution of photosynthate. *Photosynthetica* **3**, 263–275.

Ledig, F. T. (1976). Physiological genetics, photosynthesis and growth models. *In* "Tree Physiology and Yield Improvement." (M. G. R. Cannell and F. T. Last, eds.), pp. 21–54. Academic Press, New York.

Ledig, F. T. and Perry, T. O. (1967). Variation in photosynthesis and respiration among loblolly pine progenies. *Ninth Sou. Conf. For. Tree Improvement*. Knoxville, Tenn., pp. 120–128.

Lee, K. J., and Kozlowski, T. T. (1974). Effects of silicone antitranspirant on woody plants. *Plant Soil* **40**, 493–510.

Lee-Stadelman, O. Y. and Stadelman, E. J. (1976). Cell permeability and water stress. *In* "Water and Plant Life" (O. B. Lange, L. Kappen, and E.-D. Schulze, eds, pp. 268–280. Springer-Verlag, Berlin.

Lehninger, A. L. (1971). "Bioenergetics." Benjamin, Menlo Park, California.

Lemée, G. (1956). Recherches eco-physiologiques sur le cacaoyer. *Rev. Gen. Bot.* **63**, 41–95.

Lenz, F. (1977). Einfluss der Frucht auf Photosynthese und Atmung. *Z. Pflanzenernaehr. Bodenkd.* **140**, 51–61.

Leopold, A. C. (1962). The roles of growth substances in flowers and fruits. *Can. J. Bot.* **40**, 745–755.

Leopold, A. C., and Kriedemann, P. E. (1975). "Plant Growth and Development." McGraw-Hill, New York.

Leopold, A. C., and Thimann, K. V. (1949). The effect of auxin on flower initiation. *Am. J. Bot.* **36**, 342–347.

Leopold, A. C., Brown, K. M., and Emerson, F. H. (1972). Ethylene in the wood of stressed trees. *HortScience* **7**, 175.

Lerner, R. H., and Evenari, M. (1961). The nature of the germination inhibitor present in leaves of *Eucalyptus rostrata*. *Physiol. Plant.* **14**, 221–229.

Leshem, B. (1965). The annual activity of intermediary roots of the Aleppo pine. *For. Sci.* **11**, 291–298.

Levi, M. P., and Cowling, E. B. (1968). Role of nitrogen in wood deterioration. V. Change in decay susceptibility of oak sapwood with season of cutting. *Phytopathology* **58**, 246–249.

Levitt, J. (1972). "Responses of Plants to Environmental Stresses." Academic Press, New York.

Levy, Y., and Kaufmann, M. R. (1976). Cycling of leaf conductance in citrus exposed to natural and controlled environments. *Can. J. Bot.* **54**, 2215–2218.

Lewandowska, M., and Jarvis, P. G. (1978). Quantum requirements of photosynthetic electron transport in Sitka spruce from different environments. *Physiol. Plant.* **42**, 277–282.

Lewis, F. J. (1945). Physical condition of the surface of the mesophyll cell walls of the leaf. *Nature (London)* **156**, 407–490.

Lewis, F. J., and Tuttle, G. M. (1920). Osmotic properties of some plant cells at low temperatures. *Ann. Bot. (London)* **34**, 405–416.

Lewis, F. J., and Tuttle, G. M. (1923). On the phenomena attending seasonal changes in the organization in leaf cells of *Picea canadensis* (Mill.) BSP. *New Phytol.* **22**, 225–232.

Lewis, L. N., Coggins, C. W., Jr., and Hield, H. Z. (1964). The effect of biennial bearing and NAA on the carbohydrate and nitrogen composition of Wilking Mandarin leaves. *Proc. Am. Soc. Hortic. Sci.* **84**, 147–151.

Leyton, L. (1952). The effect of pH and form of nitrogen on the growth of Sitka spruce seedlings. *Forestry* **25**, 32–40.

Leyton, L. (1954). The growth and mineral nutrition of spruce and pine in heathland plantations. *Pap., Imp. For. Inst., Oxford* **31**.

Leyton, L. (1970). Problems and techniques in measuring transpiration from trees. *In* "Physiology of Tree Crops" (L. C. Luckwill and C. V. Cutting, eds.), pp. 101–112. Academic Press, London.

Leyton, L., and Rousseau, L. Z. (1958). Root growth of tree seedlings in relation to aeration. *In* "Physiology of Forest Trees" (K. V. Thimann, ed.), pp. 467–475. Ronald, New York.

Li, P. H., and Weiser, C. (1969). Metabolism of nucleic acids in one year old apple twigs during cold dehardening and hardening. *Plant Cell Physiol.* **10,** 21–30.

Li, P. H., Weiser, C. J., and Van Huystee, R. B. (1965). Changes in metabolites of red-osier dogwood during cold acclimation. *Proc. Am. Soc. Hortic. Sci.* **86,** 723–730.

Liebig, J. (1843). "Chemistry and Its Application to Agriculture and Physiology," 3rd ed. Peterson, Philadelphia, Pennsylvania.

Lieth, H. (1972). Über die Primärproduktion der Pflanzendecke der Erde. *Angew. Bot.* **46,** 1–34.

Lieth, H. (1975). Primary productivity of the major vegetation units of the world. *In* "Primary Productivity of the Biosphere" (H. Lieth and R. H. Whittaker, eds.), pp. 203–215. Springer-Verlag, Berlin and New York.

Likens, G. E., and Bormann, F. H. (1974). Acid rain: A serious regional environmental problem. *Science* **184,** 1176–1179.

Likens, G. E., Bormann, F. H., Johnson, N. M., Fisher, D. W., and Pierce, R. S. (1970). Effects of forest cutting and herbicide treatment on nutrient budgets in the Hubbard Brook watershed ecosystem. *Ecol. Monogr.* **40,** 23–47.

Likens, G. E., Bormann, F. H., and Johnson, N. M. (1972). Acid rain. *Environment* **14,** 33–40.

Likens, G. E., Bormann, F. H., Pierce, R. S., Eaton, J. S., and Johnson, N. M. (1977). "Biogeochemistry of a Forested Ecosystem." Springer-Verlag, Berlin and New York.

Lilleland, O., Uriu, K., Murdoka, T., and Pearson, J. (1962). The relationship of potassium in the peach leaf to fruit growth and size at harvest. *Proc. Am. Soc. Hortic. Sci.* **81,** 162–167.

Liming, F. G. (1946). A sectional pole for measuring tree height. *J. For.* **44,** 512–514.

Liming, F. G. (1957). Homemade dendrometers. *J. For.* **55,** 575–577.

Lipe, W. N., and Crane, J. C. (1966). Dormancy regulation in peach seeds. *Science* **153,** 541–542.

Lister, G. R., Slankis, V., Krotkov, G., and Nelson, C. D. (1967). Physiology of *Pinus strobus* L. seedlings grown under high or low soil moisture conditions. *Ann. Bot. (London)* [N.S.] **31,** 121–132.

Little, C. H. A. (1970). Apical dominance in long shoots of white pine (*Pinus strobus*). *Can J. Bot.* **48,** 239–253.

Little, C. H. A., and Loach, K. (1975). Effect of gibberellic acid on growth and photosynthesis in *Abies balsamea*. *Can. J. Bot.* **53,** 1805–1810.

Little, E. L. (1944). Layering after a heavy snow storm in Maryland. *Ecology* **25,** 112–113.

Little, S. (1938). Relationships between vigor of resprouting and intensity of cutting in coppice stands. *J. For.* **36,** 1216–1223.

Little, S., and Somes, H. A. (1956). Buds enable pitch and shortleaf pine to recover from injury. *U.S., For. Serv., Northeast. For. Exp. Stn., Stn. Pap.* **81.**

Livingston, B. E., and Brown, W. H. (1912). Relation of the daily march of transpiration to variations in the water content of foliage leaves. *Bot. Gaz. (Chicago)* **53,** 309–330.

Livingston, G. G., and Ching, K. K. (1967). The longevity and fertility of freeze-dried Douglas-fir pollen. *Silvae Genet.* **16,** 98–101.

Livne, A., and Vaadia, Y. (1972). Water deficits and hormone relations. *In* "Water Deficits and Plant Growth" (T. T. Kozlowski, ed.), Vol. 3, pp. 255–275. Academic Press, New York.

Lloyd, F. E. (1914). Morphological instability, especially in *Pinus radiata*. *Bot. Gaz. (Chicago)* **57,** 314–319.

Loach, K. (1967). Shade tolerance in tree seedlings. I. Leaf photosynthesis and respiration in plants raised under artificial shade. *New Phytol.* **66,** 607–621.

Loach, K., and Little, C. H. A. (1972). Production, storage, and use of photosynthate during shoot elongation in balsam fir (*Abies balsamea*). *Can. J. Bot.* **51,** 1161–1168.

Lodewick, J. E. (1931). Some effects of irrigation and fertilization on the size of longleaf pine needles. *For. Worker U.S.* **7,** 12–13.

Logan, K. T. (1965). Growth of tree seedlings as affected by light intensity. I. White birch, yellow birch, sugar maple, and silver maple. *Can., For. Branch, Dep. Publ.* **1121.**

Logan, K. T. (1966a). Growth of tree seedlings as affected by light intensity. II. Red pine, white pine, jack pine, and eastern larch. *Can., For. Branch, Dep. Publ.* **1160.**

Logan, K. T. (1966b). Growth of tree seedlings as affected by light intensity. III. Basswood and white elm. *Can., For. Branch, Dep. Publ.* **1176.**

Logan, K. T. (1970). Adaptations of the photosynthetic apparatus of sun- and shade-grown yellow birch (*Betula alleghaniensis* Britt.). *Can. J. Bot.* **48,** 1681–1688.

Logan, K. T. (1971). Monthly variations in photosynthetic rate of jack pine provenances in relation to their height. *Can. J. For. Res.* **1,** 256–261.

Logan, K. T., and Krotkov, G. (1969). Adaptations of the photosynthetic mechanism of sugar maple (*Acer saccharum*) seedlings grown in various light intensities. *Physiol. Plant.* **22,** 104–116.

Loneragan, J. F., Snowball, K., and Robson, A. D. (1976). Remobilization of nutrients and its significance in plant nutrition. *In* "Transport and Transfer Processes in Plants" (I. F. Wardlaw and J. B. Passioura, eds.), pp. 463–469. Academic Press, New York.

Longman, K. A., and Jenik, J. (1974). "Tropical Forest and its Environment." Longmans, Green, New York.

Lopushinsky, W. (1964). Effect of water movement on ion movement into the xylem of tomato roots. *Plant Physiol.* **39,** 494–501.

Lopushinsky, W. (1969). Stomatal closure in conifer seedlings in response to leaf moisture stress. *Bot. Gaz. (Chicago)* **130,** 258–263.

Lopushinsky, W., and Beebe, T. (1976). Relationship of shoot-root ratio to survival and growth of outplanted Douglas-fir and ponderosa pine seedlings. *U.S., For. Serv., Res. Note PNW* **274.**

Lopushinsky, W., and Klock, G. O. (1974). Transpiration of conifer seedlings in relation to soil water potential. *For. Sci.* **20,** 181–186.

Lorenz, R. W. (1939). High temperature tolerance of forest trees. *Minn., Agric. Exp. Stn., Tech. Bull.* **141.**

Lorio, P. L., and Hodges, J. D. (1968). Oleoresin exudation pressure and relative water content of inner bark as indicators of moisture stress in loblolly pines. *For. Sci.* **14,** 392–398.

Lotan, J. E., and Zahner, R. (1963). Shoot and needle responses of 20-year-old red pine to current soil moisture regimes. *For. Sci.* **9,** 497–506.

Lotocki, A., and Zelawski, W. (1973). Effect of ammonium and nitrate source of nitrogen on productivity of photosynthesis in Scots pine (*Pinus silvestris* L.) seedlings. *Acta Soc. Bot. Pol.* **42,** 599–605.

Lott, R. V., and Simons, R. K. (1964). Floral tube and style abscission in the peach and their use as physiological reference points. *Proc. Am. Soc. Hortic. Sci.* **85,** 141–153.

Lott, R. V., and Simons, R. K. (1966). Sequential development of floral-tube and style abscission in the Montmorency cherry (*Prunus cerasus* L.). *Proc. Am. Soc. Hortic. Sci.* **88,** 208–218.

Lott, R. V., and Simons, R. K. (1968a). The developmental morphology and anatomy of floral-tube and style abscission in the 'Wilson Delicious' apricot (*Prunus armeniaca* L.). *Hortic. Res.* **8,** 67–73.

Lott, R. V., and Simons, R. K. (1968b). The morphology and anatomy of floral tube and style abscission and of associated floral organs in the 'Starking Hardy Giant' cherry(*Prunus avium* L.). *Hortic. Res.* **8,** 74–82.

Loustalot, A. J. (1943). Effect of ringing the stem on photosynthesis, transpiration, and respiration of pecan leaves. *Proc. Am. Soc. Hortic. Sci.* **42,** 127–142.

Loustalot, A. J. (1945). Influence of soil moisture conditions on apparent photosynthesis and transpiration of pecan leaves. *J. Agric. Res.* **71,** 519–532.

Loustalot, A. J., and Hamilton, J. (1941). The effect of downy spot on photosynthesis and transpiration of pecan leaves in the fall. *Proc. Am. Soc. Hortic. Sci.* **39,** 80–84.

Loustalot, A. J., Burrows, F. W., Gilbert, S. G., and Nason, A. (1945). Effect of copper and zinc deficiencies on the photosynthetic activity of the foliage of young tung trees. *Plant Physiol.* **20,** 283–288.

Loustalot, A. J., Gilbert, S. G., and Drosdoff, A. M. (1950). The effect of nitrogen and potassium levels in tung seedlings on growth, apparent photosynthesis, and carbohydrate composition. *Plant Physiol.* **25,** 394–412.

Loustalot, A. J., Winters, H. F., and Childers, N. F. (1947). Influence of high, medium, and low soil moisture on growth and alkaloid content of *Cinchona ledgeriana*. *Plant Physiol.* **22**, 613–619.

Loveys, B. R. (1977). The intracellular location of abscisic acid in stressed and non-stressed leaf tissue. *Physiol. Plant.* **40**, 6–10.

Luckwill, L.C. (1959). The physiological relationships of root and shoot. *Sci. Hortic.* **14**, 22–26.

Lundegardh, H. (1931). "Environment and Plant Development." Arnold, London.

Lunderstädt, J. (1976). Isolation and analysis of plant phenolics from foliage in relation to species characterization and to resistance against insects and pathogens. *In* "Modern Methods in Forest Genetics" (J. P. Miksche, ed.), pp. 158–164. Springer-Verlag, Berlin and New York.

Lüttge, U., and Pitman, M. G., eds. (1976). "Transport in Plants," Vol. IIB. Springer-Verlag, Berlin and New York.

Lutz, H. J. (1939). Layering in eastern white pine. *Bot. Gaz. (Chicago)* **101**, 505–507.

Lutz, H. J., and Chandler, R. F. (1946). "Forest Soils." Wiley, New York.

Luukkanen, O., and Kozlowski, T. T. (1972). Gas exchange in six *Populus* clones. *Silvae Genet.* **21**, 220–229.

Luxford, R. F. (1930). Distribution and amount of moisture in virgin redwood trees. *J. For.* **28**, 770–772.

Lyford, W. H. (1975). Rhizography of the non-woody roots of trees in the forest floor. *In* "The Development and Function of Roots" (J. G. Torrey and D. T. Clarkson, eds.), pp. 179–196. Academic Press, London.

Lyford, W. H., and Wilson, B. F. (1964). Development of the root system of *Acer rubrum* L. *Harv. For. Pap.* **10**.

Lyons, A. (1956). The seed production capacity and efficiency of red pine cones (*Pinus resinosa* Ait.). *Can. J. Bot.* **34**, 27–36.

Lyons, J. M. (1973). Chilling injury in plants. *Annu. Rev. Plant Physiol.* **24**, 445–466.

Lyr, H., and Hoffmann, G. (1967). Growth rates and growth periodicity of tree roots. *Int. Rev. For. Res.* **2**, 181–206.

Lyr, H., Hoffmann, G., and Richter, R. (1970). On the chilling requirement of dormant buds of *Tilia platyphyllos* Scop. *Biochem. Physiol. Pflanz.* **161**, 133–141.

McCarthy, J. (1962). The form and development of knee roots in *Mitragyna stipulosa*. *Phytomorphology* **12**, 20–30.

McComb, A. O., and Loomis, W. E. (1944). Subclimax prairie. *Bull. Torrey Bot. Club* **71**, 46–76.

McCusker, T. (1971). Knee roots in *Avicennia marina* (Forsk.) Vierh. *Ann. Bot. (London)* [N.S.] **35**, 707–712.

MacDaniels, L. H. (1953). Anatomical basis of so called adventitious buds in apple. *N. Y., Agric. Exp. Stn., Ithaca, Mem.* **325**.

MacDaniels, L. H., and Cowart, F. F. (1940). The development and structure of the apple leaf. *N.Y., Agric. Exp. Stn., Ithaca, Mem.* **258**.

MacDougal, D. T. (1921). Growth in trees. *Carnegie Inst. Washington Publ.* **307**.

MacDougal, D. T. (1926). The hydrostatic system of trees. *Carnegie Inst. Washington Publ.* **373**.

MacDougal, D. T. (1938). "Tree Growth." Chronica Botanica, Waltham, Massachusetts.

MacDougal, D. T., and Working, E. B. (1933). The pneumatic system of plants especially trees. *Carnegie Inst. Washington Publ.* **441**.

MacDougal, D. T., Overton, J. B., and Smith, G. M. (1929). The hydrostatic-pneumatic system of certain trees: Movements of liquids and gases. *Carnegie Inst. Washington Publ.* **397**.

McGlasson, W. B. (1970). The ethylene factor. *In* "The Biochemistry of Fruits and Their Products" (A. C. Hulme, ed.), Vol. 1, pp. 475–519. Academic Press, New York.

McGlasson, W. B., and Raison, J. K. (1973). Occurrence of a temperature-induced phase transition in mitochondria isolated from apple fruit. *Plant Physiol.* **52**, 390–392.

McGraw, D. (1973). An investigation into the role of gibberellins in apical dominance in the Cupressaceae. M.S. Thesis, University of Calgary, Canada.

McGregor, W. H. D., and Kramer, P. J. (1963). Seasonal trends in rates of photosynthesis and respiration of loblolly pine. *Am. J. Bot.* **50**, 760–765.

McGregor, W. H. D., Allen, R. M., and Kramer, P. J. (1961). The effect of photoperiod on growth, photosynthesis, and respiration of loblolly pine seedlings from two geographic sources. *For. Sci.* **7,** 342–348.

MacHattie, L. B., and Horton, K. W. (1963). Influence of microclimates on mortality and growth of planted white spruce, jack pine and white pine. *For. Chron.* **39,** 301–312.

MacKay, D. B. (1972). The measurement of viability. *In* "Viability of Seeds" (E. H. Roberts, ed.), pp. 172–208. Chapman & Hall, London.

Mackay, J. F. G., and Weatherley, P. E. (1973). The effects of transverse cuts through the stems of transpiring woody plants on water transport and stress in the leaves. *J. Exp. Bot.* **24,** 15–28.

McLaughlin, S. B., and Madgwick, H. A. I. (1968). The effects of position in crown on the morphology of needles of loblolly pine (*Pinus taeda* L.). *Am. Midl. Nat.* **80,** 547–550.

McClenahan, F. M. (1909). The development of fat in the black walnut. *J. Am. Chem. Soc.* **31,** 1093–1098.

McMichael, B. L., Jordan, W. R., and Powell, R. D. (1973). Abscission processes in cotton: Induction by plant water deficit. *Agron. J.* **65,** 202–204.

MacRobbie, E. A. C. (1971). Phloem translocation: Facts and mechanisms: A comparative survey. *Biol. Rev. Cambridge Philos. Soc.* **46,** 429–481.

McWilliam, J. R. (1958). The role of the micropyle in the pollination of *Pinus. Bot. Gaz. (Chicago)* **120,** 109–117.

McWilliam, J. R., Phillips, P. J., and Parkes, R. R. (1973). Measurement of photosynthetic rate using labelled carbon dioxide. *CSIRO, Aust., Div. Plant Ind., Tech. Pap.* **31.**

Madgwick, H. A. I. (1970). The nutrient content of old-field *Pinus virginia* stands. *Tree Growth For. Soils, Proc. North Am. For. Soils Conf., 3rd, 1968* pp. 275–282.

Madgwick, H. A. I., and Ovington, J. D. (1959). The chemical composition of precipitation in adjacent forest and open plots. *Forestry* **32,** 14–22.

Maggs, D. H. (1963). The reduction in growth of apple trees brought about by fruiting. *J. Hortic. Sci.* **38,** 119–128.

Maggs, D. H. (1964a). The distance from tree base to shoot origin as a factor in shoot and tree growth. *J. Hortic. Sci.* **39,** 298–307.

Maggs, D. H. (1964b). Growth rates in relation to assimilate supply and demand. I. Leaves and roots as limiting regions. *J. Exp. Bot.* **15,** 574–583.

Maggs, D. H. (1965). Growth rates in relation to assimilate supply and demand. II. The effect of particular leaves and growing regions in determining dry matter distribution in young apple leaves. *J. Exp. Bot.* **16,** 387–404.

Magness, J. R., and Regeimbal, L. O. (1938). The nitrogen requirement of the apple. *Proc. Am. Soc. Hortic. Sci.* **36,** 51–55.

Magness, J. R., Degman, E. S., and Furr, J. R. (1935). Soil moisture and irrigation investigations in eastern apple orchards. *U.S., Dep. Agric., Tech. Bull.* **491.**

Maheshwari, P. (1950). "An Introduction to the Embryology of Angiosperms." McGraw-Hill, New York.

Maheshwari, P., and Rangaswamy, N. S. (1965). Embryology in relation to physiology and genetics. *Adv. Bot. Res.* **2,** 219–321.

Maheshwari, P., and Sachar, R. C. (1963). Polyembryony. *In* "Recent Advances in the Embryology of Angiosperms" (P. Maheshwari, ed.), pp. 265–296, Catholic Press, Ranchi, India.

Mair, B. (1968). Frosthärtegradienten entlang der Knospenfolge auf Eschentrieben. *Planta* **82,** 164–169.

Maisenhelder, L. C. (1969). Identifying juvenile seedlings in southern hardwood forests. *U.S., For. Serv., Res. Pap. SO* **47.**

Majid, A. (1954). Root systems of ash and sycamore (*Acer pseudoplatanus*) seedlings. *J. Oxford Univ. For. Soc., Ser. 4* No. 2, pp. 18–21.

Marcelle, R. ed. (1975). "Environmental and Biological Control of Photosynthesis." W. Junk, The Hague.

Mark, W. R., and Reid, C. P. P. (1971). Lodgepole pine - dwarf mistletoe xylem water potentials. *For. Sci.* **17,** 470–471.

Marks, G. C., and Kozlowski, T. T., eds. (1973). "Ectomycorrhizae." Academic Press, New York.

Marr, J. W. (1948). Ecology of the forest-tundra ecotone on the east coast of Hudson Bay. *Ecol. Monogr.* **18,** 117–144.

Marshall, D. C. (1958). Measurement of sap flow in conifers by heat transport. *Plant Physiol.* **21,** 95–101.

Marshall, P. E., and Kozlowski, T. T. (1974a). Photosynthetic activity of cotyledons and foliage leaves of young angiosperm seedlings. *Can. J. Bot.* **52**, 2023–2032.

Marshall, P. E., and Kozlowski, T. T. (1974b). The role of cotyledons in growth and development of woody angiosperms. *Can. J. Bot.* **52**, 239–245.

Marshall, P. E., and Kozlowski, T. T. (1975). Changes in mineral contents of cotyledons and young seedlings of woody angiosperms. *Can. J. Bot.* **53**, 2026–2031.

Marshall, P. E., and Kozlowski, T. T. (1976a). Importance of photosynthetic cotyledons for early growth of woody angiosperms. *Physiol. Plant.* **37**, 336–340.

Marshall, P. E., and Kozlowski, T. T. (1976b). Importance of endosperm for nutrition of *Fraxinus pennsylvanica* seedlings. *J. Exp. Bot.* **27**, 572–574.

Marshall, P. E., and Kozlowski, T. T. (1976c). Compositional changes in cotyledons of woody angiosperms. *Can. J. Bot.* **54**, 2473–2477.

Marshall, P. E., and Kozlowski, T. T. (1977). Changes in structure and function of epigeous cotyledons of woody angiosperms during early seedling growth. *Can. J. Bot.* **55**, 208–215.

Martin, E. V. (1943). Studies of evaporation and transpiration under controlled conditions. *Carnegie Inst. Washington Publ.* **550**.

Martin, E. V., and Clements, F. E. (1935). Studies of the effect of artificial wind on growth and transpiration in *Helianthus annuus*. *Plant Physiol.* **10**, 613–636.

Martin, J. T. (1966). The cuticles of plants. *NAAS Q. Rev.* **72**, 139–144.

Marvin, C. O. (1964). Abscission of marcescent leaves in *Quercus velutina* Lam. M.S. Thesis, University of Wisconsin, Madison.

Marvin, J. W., and Greene, M. T. (1951). Temperature-induced sap flow in excised stem of *Acer*. *Plant Physiol.* **26**, 565–580.

Marx, D. H. (1969). The influence of ectotrophic mycorrhizal fungi on the resistance of pine roots to pathogenic infection. II. Production, identification, and biological activity of antibiotics produced by *Leucopaxillus cerealus* var. *piceina*. *Phytopathology* **59**, 411–417.

Marx, D. H. (1973). Mycorrhizae and feeder root diseases. *In* "Ectomycorrhizae" (G. C. Marks and T. T. Kozlowski, eds.), pp. 351–377. Academic Press, New York.

Mason, G. F., Bhar, D. S., and Hilton, R. J. (1970). Root growth studies on Mugho pine. *Can. J. Bot.* **48**, 43–47.

Mason, T. G., and Maskell, E. J. (1928). Studies on the transport of carbohydrates in the cotton plant. I. A study of diurnal variation in the carbohydrates of leaf, bark, and wood, and the effects of ringing. *Ann. Bot. (London)* **42**, 189–253.

Matthews, J. D. (1963). Factors affecting the production of seed by forest trees. *For. Abstr.* **24**, 1–13.

Matthews, J. D. (1970). Flowering and seed production in conifers. *In* "Physiology of Tree Crops" (L. C. Luckwill and C. V. Cutting, eds.), pp. 45–53. Academic Press, London.

Maximov, N. A. (1929). "The Plant in Relation to Water." Allen & Unwin, London.

Mayer, A. M., and Poljakoff-Mayber, A. (1963). "The Germination of Seeds." Macmillan, New York.

Mayer, A. M., and Poljakoff-Mayber, A. (1975). "The Germination of Seeds." Macmillan, New York.

Mazliak, P. (1973). Lipid metabolism in plants. *Annu. Rev. Plant Physiol.* **24**, 287–310.

Meidner, H. (1975). Water supply, evaporation, and vapour diffusion in leaves. *J. Exp. Bot.* **26**, 666–674.

Meidner, H. (1976). Vapour loss through stomatal pores with the mesophyll tissue excluded. *J. Exp. Bot.* **27**, 172–174.

Meidner, H., and Mansfield, T. A. (1968). "Physiology of Stomata." McGraw-Hill, New York.

Melin, E., and Nilsson, H. (1950). Transfer of radioactive phosphorus to pine seedlings by means of mycorrhizal fungi. *Physiol. Plant.* **3**, 88–92.

Melin, E., and Nilsson, H. (1955). Ca^{45} used as an indicator of transport of cations to pine seedlings by means of mycorrhizal mycelium. *Sven. Bot. Tidskr.* **49**, 119–122.

Melin, E., and Nilsson, H. (1957). Transport of C^{14} - labelled photosynthate to the fungal associate of pine mycorrhizae. *Sven. Bot. Tidskr.* **51**, 166–186.

Mendes, A. J. T. (1941). Cytological observations in *Coffea*. VI. Embryo and endosperm development in *Coffea arabica* L. *Am. J. Bot.* **28**, 784–789.

Mergen, F. (1955). Grafting slash pine in the field and in the greenhouse. *J. For.* **53**, 836–842.

Mergen, F., and Koerting, L. E. (1957). Initiation and development of flower primordia in slash pine. *For. Sci.* **3**, 145–155.

Merriam, C. H. (1898). Life zones and crop zones of the United States. *U.S. Dep. Agric. Biol. Survey Bull.* **10**.

Merrill, W., and Cowling, E. B. (1966). Role of nitrogen in wood deterioration. Amounts and distribution of nitrogen in tree stems. *Can. J. Bot.* **44**, 1555–1580.

Merwin, H. E., and Lyon, H. (1909). Sap pressure in the birch stem. *Bot. Gaz. (Chicago)* **48**, 442–458.

Metz, L. J. (1952). Weight and nitrogen and calcium content of the annual litter fall of forests in the South Carolina Piedmont. *Soil. Sci. Soc. Am., Proc.* **16**, 38–41.

Meyer, B. S. (1932). The daily periodicity of transpiration in the tulip poplar, *Liriodendron tulipifera* L. *Ohio J. Sci.* **32**, 104–114.

Meyer, B. S., Anderson, D. B., Bohning, R. H., and Fratianne, D. G. (1973). "Introduction to Plant Physiology." Van Nostrand-Reinhold, Princeton, New Jersey.

Meyer, F. H. (1966). Mycorrhiza and other plant symbioses. *In* "Symbiosis" (S. M. Henry, ed.), Vol. 1, pp. 171–255. Academic Press, New York.

Meyer, F. H. (1974). Physiology of mycorrhiza. *Annu. Rev. Plant Physiol.* **25**, 567–586.

Michaelis, P. (1934). Ökologische Studien an der alpinen Baumgrenze. IV. Zur Kenntnis des winterlichen Wasserhaushaltes. *Jahrb. Wiss. Bot.* **80**, 169–247.

Michniewicz, M. (1967). The dynamics of gibberellin-like substances and growth inhibitors in ontogeny of conifers. *Wiss. Z. Univ. Rostock, Math.-Naturwiss. Riche* **16**, 577–583.

Mika, A., and Antoszewski, R. (1972). Effect of leaf position and tree shape on the rate of photosynthesis in the apple tree. *Photosynthetica* **6**, 381–386.

Mikola, P. (1950). Puiden kasvun vaihteluista ja niden merkityksesta kasvututkimuksissa. *Commun. Inst. For. Fenn.* **385**, 1–131.

Mikola, P. (1951). Kasvun luonnollinen kehitys. Eripainos Metsät. *Aikakauslehdestä* **2**, 1–4.

Mikola, P. (1962). Temperature and tree growth near the northern timber line. *In* "Tree Growth" (T. T. Kozlowski, ed.), pp. 265–274. Ronald, New York.

Mikola, P., and Laiho, O. (1962). Mycorrhizal relations in the raw humus layer of northern spruce forests. *Commun. Inst. For. Fenn.* **55**, 1–13.

Milborrow, B. V. (1974). The chemistry and physiology of abscisic acid. *Annu. Rev. Plant Physiol.* **25**, 259–307.

Milburn, J. A. (1975). Pressure flow. *In* "Transport in Plants" (M. H. Zimmermann and J. A. Milburn, eds.), pp. 328–353. Springer-Verlag, Berlin and New York.

Milburn, J. A., and Davis, T. A. (1973). Role of pressure in xylem transport of coconut and other palms. *Physiol. Plant.* **29**, 415–420.

Milburn, J. A., and Johnson, R. P. C. (1966). The conduction of sap. II. Detection of vibrations produced by sap cavitation in *Ricinus* xylem. *Planta* **69**, 43–52.

Miliszewski, D., and Levanty, Z. (1972). Effect of oxygen concentration on the incorporation of ^{14}C into products of photosynthesis of balsam fir. *Z. Pflanzenphysiol.* **67**, 305–310.

Millar, A. A., Gardner, W. R., and Goltz, S. M. (1971). Internal water status and water transport in seed onion plants. *Agron. J.* **63**, 779–784.

Miller, E. C. (1938). "Plant Physiology." McGraw-Hill, New York.

Miller, J. R., and Tocher, R. D. (1975). Photosynthesis and respiration of *Arceuthobium tsugense* (Loranthaceae). *Am. J. Bot.* **62**, 765–769.

Miller, L. N. (1965). Changes in radiosensitivity of pine seedlings subjected to water stress during chronic gamma irradiation. *Health Phys.* **11**, 1653–1662.

Miller, P. R. (1973). Oxidant-induced community change in a mixed conifer forest. *Adv. Chem. Ser.* **122**, 101–117.

Miller, P. R., Parmeter, J. R., Jr., Flick, B. H., and Martinez, C. W. (1969). Ozone dosage response of ponderosa pine seedlings. *J. Air. Pollut. Control Assoc.* **19**, 435–438.

Miller, R., and Rüsch, J. (1960). Zur Frage der Kohlensäureversorgung des Waldes. *Fortstwiss. Centralbl.* **79**, 42–62.

Millington, W. F. (1963). Shoot tip abortion in *Ulmus americana*. *Am. J. Bot.* **50**, 371–378.

Millington, W. F., and Chaney, W. R. (1973). Shedding of shoots and branches. *In* "Shedding of Plant Parts" (T. T. Kozlowski, ed.), pp. 149–204. Academic Press, New York.

Milthorpe, F. L. (1955). The significance of the measurement made by the cobalt paper method. *J. Exp. Bot.* **6,** 17–19.

Milthorpe, F. L. (1959). Transpiration from crop plants. *Field Crop Abstr.* **12,** 1–9.

Minckler, L. S. (1976). Directions of forest research in America. *J. For.* **74,** 212–216.

Minckler, L. S., and Woerheide, J. D. (1968). Weekly height growth of cottonwood. *For. Sci.* **14,** 212–222.

Mirov, N. T. (1954). Chemical composition of gum turpentines of pines of the United States and Canada. *J. For. Prod. Res. Soc.* **4,** 1–7.

Mirov, N. T. (1961). Composition of gum turpentines of pines. *U.S., Dep. Agric., Tech. Bull.* **1239.**

Mirov, N. T. (1967). "The Genus *Pinus.*" Ronald, New York.

Mitchell, H. L. (1936). Trends in the nitrogen, phosphorus, potassium, and calcium content of the leaves of some forest trees during the growing season. *Black Rock For. Bull.* **9.**

Mitchell, H. L., and Chandler, R. F., Jr. (1939). The nitrogen nutrition and growth of certain deciduous trees of northeastern United States. *Black Rock For. Bull.* **11.**

Mitchell, J. E., Waide, J. B., and Todd, R. L. (1975). A preliminary compartment model of the nitrogen cycle in a deciduous forest ecosystem. *In* "Mineral Cycling in Southeastern Ecosystems" (F. G. Howell, J. B. Gentry, and M. H. Smith, eds.), ERDA Symp. Ser. (Conf. 740513), pp. 41–57. Natl. Tech. Inf. Center, Springfield, Virginia.

Mitscherlich, E. A. (1909). Des Gesetz des Minimums und das Gesetz des abnehmenden Bodenertrags. *Landwirtsch. Jahrb.* **38,** 537–552.

Mochizuki, T. (1962). Studies on the elucidation of factors affecting the decline in tree vigor in apples as induced by fruit load. *Bull. Fac Agric., Hirosaki Univ.* **8,** 40–124.

Mochizuki, T., and Hanada, S. (1957). The anisophylly on the lateral shoots of apple trees and the effect of soil moisture. *Bull. Fac. Agric., Hirosaki Univ.* **3,** 1–8.

Mohn, C. A., and Pauley, S. (1969). Early performance of cottonwood and seed sources in Minnesota. *Minn. For. Res. Notes* **207,** 1–4.

Molisch, H. (1902). Über localen Blutungsdruck und seine Ursachen. *Bot. Zg.* **60,** 45–63.

Molisch, H. (1938). "The Longevity of Plants." Science Press, Lancaster, Pennsylvania.

Möller, C. M. (1946). Untersuchungen über Laubmenge, Stoffverlust und Stoffproduktion des Waldes. *Forstl. Forsoegsvaes. Dan.* **17,** 1–287.

Möller, C. M., Müller, D., and Nielsen, J. (1954). Graphic presentation of dry matter production of European beech. *Forstl. Forsoegsvaes. Dan.* **21,** 327–335. (see also Schweiz. *Bot. Ges.* **64,** 487, 1954).

Monselise, S. P. (1951). Light distribution in citrus trees. *Bull. Res. Counc. Isr.* **1,** 36–53.

Monselise, S. P., Goren, R., and Halevy, A. H. (1966). Effects of B.9, Cycocel and benzothiazole oxyacetate on flower bud induction of lemon trees. *Proc. Am. Soc. Hortic. Sci.* **89,** 195–200.

Monteith, J. L. (1963). Dew: Facts and fallacies. *In* "The Water Relations of Plants" (A. J. Rutter and F. H. Whitehead, eds.), pp. 37–56. Wiley, New York.

Mooney, H. A., and Hays, R. I. (1973). Carbohydrate storage cycles in two Californian Mediterranean - climate trees. *Flora (Jena)* **162,** 295–304.

Mooney, H. A., Björkman, O., and Collatz, G. J. (1977). Photosynthetic acclimation to temperature and water stress in the desert shrub *Larrea divaricata.* Carnegie Inst. *Yrbk* **76,** 328–335.

Moorby, J., and Wareing, P. F. (1963). Aging in woody plants. *Ann. Bot. (London)* [N.S.] **27,** 291–308.

Moore, P. D. (1974). Misunderstandings over C_4 carbon fixation. *Nature (London)* **252,** 438–439.

Moreau, R. A., and Huang, A. H. C. (1977). Gluconeogenesis from storage wax in the cotyledens of jojoba seedlings. *Plant Physiol.* **60,** 329–333.

Moreland, D. E. (1950). A study of translocation of radioactive phosphorous in loblolly pine (*Pinus taeda* L.). *J. Elisha Mitchell Sci. Soc.* **66,** 175–181.

Morey, P. R. (1973). "How Trees Grow." Arnold, London.

Mork, E. (1928). Die Qualtität des Fichtenholzes unter besonderer Rücksichtnahme auf Schleif-und Papierholz. *Pap.-Fabrik.* **26,** 741–747.

Morris, R. F. (1951). The effects of flowering on the foliage production and growth of balsam fir. *For. Chron.* **27,** 40–57.

Morselli, M. F., Marvin, J. W., and Laing, F. M. (1978). Image-analyzing computer in plant science: more and larger vascular rays in sugar maples of high sap and sugar yield. *Can. J. Bot.* **56,** 983–986.

Moss, D. N. (1963). The effect of environment on gas exchange of leaves. *Conn., Agric. Exp. Stn., New Haven, Bull.* **664,** 86–101.

Mosse, B. (1962). Graft-incompatability in fruit trees with particular reference to its underlying causes. *Tech. Commun. Bur. Hortic. Plant. Crops, East Malling* **28.**

Mothes, K., and Engelbrecht, L. (1952). Über Allantoinsäure und Allantoin. I. Ihre Rolle als Wanderform des Stickstoffs und ihre Beziehungen zum Eiweisstoffwechsel des Alhorns. *Flora (Jena)* **139,** 586–597.

Motley, J. A. (1949). Correlation of elongation in white and red pine with rainfall. *Butler Univ. Bot. Stud.* **9,** 1–8.

Mounts, B. T. (1932). The development of foliage leaves. *Stud. Nat. Hist. Univ. Iowa* **14,** 1–19.

Mudd, J. B., and Kozlowski, T. T., eds. (1975). "Responses of Plants to Air Pollution." Academic Press, New York.

Mulay, A. S. (1931). Seasonal changes in total soluble protein, non-protein and insoluble nitrogen in current year's shoots of Bartlett pear. *Plant Physiol.* **6,** 519–529.

Mulder, E. G. (1975). Physiology and ecology of free-living nitrogen-fixing bacteria. *In* "Nitrogen Fixation by Free-Living Micro-Organisms" (W. D. P. Stewart, ed.), pp. 3–28. Cambridge Univ. Press, London and New York.

Müller, D. (1949). The physiological basis for the deficiency symptoms of plants. *Physiol. Plant.* **2,** 11–23.

Mullins, M. G. (1965). Lateral shoot growth in horizontal apple stems. *Ann. Bot. (London)* [N.S.] **29,** 73–78.

Münch, E. (1930). "Die Stoffbewegungen in der Pflanze." Fischer, Jena.

Murashige, T. (1974). Plant propagation through tissue cultures. *Annu. Rev. Plant Physiol.* **25,** 135–166.

Murata, N., Troughton, J. H., and Fork, D. C. (1975). Relationships between the transition of the physical phase of membrane lipids and photosynthetic parameters of *Anacystis nidulans* and lettuce and spinach chloroplasts. *Plant Physiol.* **56,** 508–517.

Murmanis, L., and Evert, R. F. (1967). Parenchyma cells of secondary phloem in *Pinus strobus. Planta* **73,** 301–318.

Murneek, A. E. (1930). Quantitative distribution and seasonal fluctuation of nitrogen in apple trees. *Proc. Am. Soc. Hortic. Sci.* **27,** 228–231.

Murneek, A. E. (1933). Carbohydrate storage in apple trees. *Proc. Am. Soc. Hortic. Sci.* **30,** 319–321.

Murneek, A. E. (1942). Quantitative distribution of nitrogen and carbohydrates in apple trees. *Mo., Agric. Exp. Stn., Res. Bull.* **348.**

Myers, C. A. (1963). Vertical distribution of annual increment in thinned ponderosa pine. *For. Sci.* **9,** 394–404.

Nagarajah, S., and Ratnasooriya, G. B. (1977). Studies with antitranspirants on tea (*Camellia sinensis* L.). *Plant Soil* **48,** 185–197.

Nagata, H. (1967). Studies on the photoperiodism in the dormant bud of *Pinus densiflora* Sieb. et Zucc. II. Effects of temperature and photoperiod on the breaking of winter dormancy of first-year seedlings. *J. Jpn. For. Soc.* **49,** 415–420.

Nakata, S., and Suehisa, R. (1969). Growth and development of *Litchi chinensis* as affected by soil-moisture stress. *Am. J. Bot.* **56,** 1121–1126.

Namken, L. N., Bartholic, J. F., and Runkles, J. R. (1969). Monitoring cotton plant stem radius as an indication of water stress. *Agron. J.* **61,** 891–893.

Nanda, K. K., Anand, V. K., Kochhov, V. K., and Jain, M. (1971). Studies on the physiology of rooting of stem cuttings. *Indian Agric.* **15,** 49–57.

Neales, T. F., and Incoll, L. D. (1968). The control of leaf photosynthesis rate by the level of assimilate concentration in the leaf: A review of the hypothesis. *Bot. Rev.* **34,** 107–125.

Neel, P. L., and Harris, R. W. (1971). Motion-induced inhibition of elongation and induction of dormancy in *Liquidambar. Science* **173,** 58–59.

Neel, P. L., and Harris, R. W. (1972). Tree seedling growth: Effects of shaking. *Science* **175,** 918–919.

Neely, D. E. (1970). Healing of wounds on trees. *J. Am. Soc. Hortic. Sci.* **95,** 536–540.

Neely, D. E., and Himelick, E. B. (1963). Root graft transmission of Dutch elm disease in municipalities. *Plant Dis. Rep.* **47**, 83–85.

Neely, D. E., Himelick, E. B., and Crowley, W. R., Jr. (1970). Fertilization of established trees. *Ill. Nat. Hist. Surv., Bull.* **30**, 235–266.

Negisi, K., and Satoo, T. (1954a). The effect of drying of soil on apparent photosynthesis, transpiration, carbohydrate reserves and growth of seedlings of Akamatu (*Pinus densiflora* Sieb. et Zucc.). *J. Jpn. For. Soc.* **36**, 66–71.

Negisi, K., and Satoo, T. (1954b). Influence of soil moisture on photosynthesis and respiration of seedlings of akamatu (*Pinus densiflora* Sieb. et Zucc.) and sugi (*Cryptomeria japonica* D. Don.). *J. Jpn. For. Soc.* **36**, 113–118.

Nelson, C. D. (1964). The production and translocation of photosynthate - C_{14} in conifers. *In* "The Formation of Wood in Forest Trees" (M. H. Zimmermann, ed.), pp. 243–257. Academic Press, New York.

Nelson, L. E., Switzer, G. L., and Smith, W. H. (1970). Dry matter and nutrient accumulation in young loblolly pine (*Pinus taeda* L.). *Tree Growth For. Soils, Proc. North Am. For. Soils Conf., 3rd, 1968* pp. 261–273.

Nemec, A., and Kvapil, K. (1927). Über den Einfluss verschiedener Waldbestände auf den Gehalt und die Bildung von Nitraten in Waldböden. *Z. Forst.- Jagdwes.* **59**, 321–352.

Neuwirth, G., and Fritzsche, K. H. (1964). Untersuchungen über den Einfluss verschiedener Düngergaben auf das gasstoffwechselökologische Verhalten einjähriger Pappel-Steckholzaufwüchse. *Arch. Forstwes.* **13**, 233–246.

Newman, E. I. (1969). Resistance to water flow in soil and plant. I. Soil resistance in relation to amounts of root: Theoretical estimates. *J. Appl. Ecol.* **6**, 1–12.

Newman, E. I. (1976). Water movement through root systems. *Phil. Trans. Roy. Soc. London* **B273**, 463–478.

Newman, E. I., and Andrews, R. E. (1973). Uptake of phosphorus and potassium in relation to root growth and root density. *Plant Soil* **38**, 49–69.

Nissen, P. (1974). Uptake mechanisms: Inorganic and organic. *Annu. Rev. Plant Physiol.* **25**, 53–79.

Nitsch, J. P. (1953). The physiology of fruit growth. *Annu. Rev. Plant Physiol.* **4**, 199–236.

Nitsch, J. P. (1957). Photoperiodism in woody plants. *Proc. Am. Soc. Hortic. Sci.* **70**, 526–544.

Nix, L. E., and Wodzicki, T. J. (1974). The radial distribution and metabolism of IAA$-^{14}$C in *Pinus echinata* stems in relation to wood formation. *Can. J. Bot.* **52**, 1349–1355.

Nixon, R. W., and Wedding, R. T. (1956). Age of date leaves in relation to efficiency of photosynthesis. *Proc. Am. Soc. Hortic. Sci.* **67**, 265–269.

Njoku, E. (1963). Seasonal periodicity in the growth and development of some forest trees in Nigeria. *J. Ecol.* **59**, 617–624.

Njoku, E. (1964). Seasonal periodicity in the growth and development of some forest trees in Nigeria. II. Observations on seedlings. *J. Ecol.* **52**, 19–26.

Nobel, P. S. (1974). "Introduction to Biophysical Plant Physiology." Freeman, San Francisco.

Nobel, P. S. (1976). Photosynthetic rates of sun versus shade leaves of *Hyptis emoryi* Torr. *Plant Physiol.* **58**, 218–223.

Noel, A. R. A. (1968). Callus formation and differentiation at an exposed cambial surface. *Ann. Bot. (London)* [N.S.] **32**, 347–359.

Noelle, W. (1910). Studien zur vergleichenden Anatomie und Morphologie der Konifernwurzeln mit Ruchsicht auf die Systematik. *Bot. Ztg.* **68**, 169–266.

Norris, R. F., and Bukovac, M. J. (1968). Structure of the pear leaf cuticle with special reference to cuticular penetration. *Am. J. Bot.* **55**, 975–983.

Nutman, F. J. (1941). Studies of the physiology of *Coffea arabica*. III. Transpiration rates of whole trees in relation to natural environmental conditions. *Ann. Bot. (London)* **5**, 59–82.

Nutman, P. S., ed. (1976). "Symbiotic Nitrogen Fixation in Plants." Cambridge Univ. Press, London and New York.

Nyman, B. (1961). Effect of red and far red irradiation on the germination process in seeds of *Pinus sylvestris* L. *Nature (London)* **191**, 1219–1220.

Obaton, M. (1960). Les lianes ligneuses, a structure anormale des fôrets denses d'Afrique occidentale. *Ann. Sci. Nat., Bot. Biol. Veg.* [12] **1**, 1–220.

Odum, E. P. (1971). "Fundamentals of Ecology." Saunders, Philadelphia.

Oechel, W. C., Strain, B. R., and Odening, W. R. (1972). Tissue water potential, photosynthesis, ^{14}C-labeled photosynthate utilization and growth in the desert shrub *Larrea divaricata* Cav. *Ecol. Monogr.* **42**, 127–141.

Okonoue, M., and Sasaki, O. (1960). Depth of frozen ground on slope with no snow cover in winter. *J. Jpn. For. Soc.* **42**, 339–342.

Oland, K. (1963). Changes in the content of dry matter and major nutrient elements of apple foliage during senescence and abscission. *Physiol. Plant.* **16**, 682–694.

O'Leary, J. W. (1965). Root-pressure exudation in woody plants. *Bot. Gaz. (Chicago)* **126**, 108–115.

O'Leary, J. W., and Kramer, P. J. (1964). Root pressure in conifers. *Science* **145**, 284–285.

Oliver, D. J., and Zelitch, I. (1977). Increasing photosynthesis by inhibiting photorespiration with glyoxylate. *Science* **196**, 1450–1451.

Olney, H. O., and Pollock, B. M. (1960). Studies of rest period. II. Nitrogen and phosphorus changes in embryonic organs of after-ripening cherry seed. *Plant Physiol.* **35**, 970–975.

Olofinboba, M. O. (1969). Seasonal variations in the carbohydrates in the xylem of *Antiaris africana*. *Ann. Bot. (London)* [N.S.] **33**, 339–349.

Olofinboba, M. O. (1975). Studies on seedlings of *Theobroma cacao* L., variety F_3 Amazon. I. Role of cotyledons in seedling development. *Turrialba* **25**, 121–127.

Olofinboba, M. O., and Kozlowski, T. T. (1973). Accumulation and utilization of carbohydrate reserves in shoot growth of *Pinus resinosa*. *Can. J. For. Res.* **3**, 346–353.

Olofinboba, M. O., Kozlowski, T. T., and Marshall, P. E. (1974). Effects of antitranspirants on distribution and utilization of photosynthate in *Pinus resinosa* seedlings. *Plant Soil* **40**, 619–635.

Olsen, S. R., and Kemper, W. D. (1968). Movement of nutrients to plant roots. *Adv. Agron.* **20**, 91–151.

Olson, J. S., Stearns, F., and Nienstaedt, H. (1959). Eastern hemlock seeds and seedlings. Response to photoperiod and temperature. *Conn., Agric. Exp. Stn., New Haven, Bull.* **620**.

Onaka, F. (1940). On the influence of auxin on radial growth, particularly regarding compression wood formation in trees. *J. Jpn. For. Soc.* **22**, 573–580.

Oppenheimer, H. R. (1932). Zur Kenntnis der hochsomerlichen Wasserbilanz mediterranean Gehölze. *Ber. Dtsch. Bot. Ges.* **50**, 185–243.

Oppenheimer, H. R. (1951). Summer drought and water balance of plants growing in the Near East. *J. Ecol.* **39**, 356–362.

Orlov, A. J. (1960). Rost i vozrastnye izmenenija sosuscih kornej eli *Picea excelsa* Link. *Bot. Ztg.* **45**, 888–896.

Orr-Ewing, A. L. (1957). Possible occurrence of viable unfertilized seeds in Douglas-fir. *For. Sci.* **3**, 243–248.

Osborne, D. J. (1973). Internal factors regulating abscission. *In* "Shedding of Plant Parts" (T. T. Kozlowski, ed.), pp. 125–147. Academic Press, New York.

Osborne, D. J., and Hallaway, M. (1960). The role of auxins in the control of leaf senescence. Some effects of local applications of 2,4-dichlorophenoxyacetic acid on carbon and nitrogen metabolism. *In* "Plant Growth Regulation" (W. Klein, ed.), pp. 329–340. Iowa State Univ. Press, Ames.

Osonubi, O. and Davies, W. J. (1978). Solute accumulation in leaves and roots of woody plants subjected to water stress. *Oecologia* **32**, 323–332.

Ovington, J. D. (1956). The form, weights, and productivity of tree species grown in close stands. *New Phytol.* **55**, 289–388.

Ovington, J. D. (1957). Dry matter production by *Pinus sylvestris* L. *Ann. Bot. (London)* [N.S.] **21**, 287–314.

Ovington, J. D. (1958). Some biological considerations of forest production. *In* "The Biological Production of Britain," (W. B. Yapp and D. J. Watson, eds.), pp. 1–18. Inst. Biol., London.

Ovington, J. D. (1965). Organic production, turnover and mineral cycling in woodlands. *Biol. Rev. Cambridge Philos. Soc.* **40**, 295–336.

Ovington, J. D., and Madgwick, H. A. I. (1959). The growth and composition of mature stands of birch. I. Dry matter production. *Plant Soil* **10**, 271–283.

Ovington, J. D., and Pearsall, W. H. (1956). Production ecology. 2. Estimates of average production by trees. *Oikos* **7**, 202–205.

Owens, J. N. (1968). Initiation and development of leaves in Douglas-fir. *Can. J. Bot.* **46**, 271–278.

Owens, J. N. (1969). The relative importance of initiation and early development on cone production in Douglas-fir. *Can. J. Bot.* **47**, 1039–1049.

Owens, J. N., and Molder, M. (1973). Bud development in western hemlock. I. Annual growth cycle of vegetative buds. *Can. J. Bot.* **51**, 2223–2231.

Owens, J. N., and Molder, M. (1974). Bud development in western hemlock. II. Initiation and early development of pollen cones and seed cones. *Can. J. Bot.* **52**, 238–294.

Owens, J. N., and Pharis, R. P. (1971). Initiation and development of western red cedar cones in response to gibberellin induction and under natural conditions. *Can. J. Bot.* **49**, 1165–1175.

Owens, J. N., and Smith, F. H. (1964). The initiation and early development of the seed cone of Douglas-fir. *Can. J. Bot.* **42**, 1031–1047.

Owens, J. N., and Smith, F. H. (1965). Development of the seed cone of Douglas-fir following dormancy. *Can. J. Bot.* **43**, 317–332.

Owston, P. W., Smith, J. L., and Halverson, H. G. (1972). Seasonal water movement in tree stems. *For. Sci.* **18**, 266–272.

Paleg, L. G., and West, G. A. (1972). The gibberellins. *In* "Plant Physiology" (F. C. Steward, ed.), pp. 146–181. Academic Press, New York.

Park, R. B. (1976). The chloroplast. *In* "Plant Biochemistry" (J. Bonner and J. E. Varner, eds.), 3rd ed., pp. 115–145. Academic Press, New York.

Parker, A. F. (1961). Bark moisture relations in disease development: Present status and future needs. *Recent Adv. Bot.* **2**, 1535–1537.

Parker, J. (1949). Effects of variations in the root-leaf ratio on transpiration rate. *Plant Physiol.* **24**, 739–743.

Parker, J. (1950). The effects of flooding on the transpiration and survival of some southeastern forest tree species. *Plant Physiol.* **25**, 453–460.

Parker, J. (1952). Desiccation in conifer leaves: Anatomical changes and determination of the lethal level. *Bot. Gaz. (Chicago)* **114**, 189–198.

Parker, J. (1953). Photosynthesis of *Picea excelsa* in winter. *Ecology* **34**, 605–609.

Parker, J. (1954). Available water in stems of some Rocky mountain conifers. *Bot. Gaz. (Chicago)* **115**, 380–385.

Parker, J. (1956). Variations in copper, boron, and manganese in leaves of *Pinus ponderosa*. *For. Sci.* **2**, 190–198.

Parker, J. (1958). Changes in sugars and nitrogenous compounds of tree barks from summer to winter. *Naturwissenschaften* **45**, 139.

Parker, J. (1963). Cold resistance in woody plants. *Bot. Rev.* **29**, 123–201.

Parker, J. (1964). Autumn exudation from black birch. *Sci. Tree Top.* **2**, 9–11.

Parker, J. (1965). Physiological diseases of trees and shrubs. *Adv. Front. Plant Sci.* **12**, 97–248.

Parker, J. (1968). Drought-resistance mechanisms. *In* "Water Deficits and Plant Growth" (T. T. Kozlowski, ed.), Vol. 1, pp. 195–234. Academic Press, New York.

Parker, J., and Philpott, D. E. (1963). Seasonal continuity of chloroplasts in white pine and rhododendron. *Protoplasma* **56**, 355–361.

Parker, K. G., Tyler, L. J., Welch, D. S., and Pope, S. (1947). Nutrition of the trees and development of Dutch elm disease. *Phytopathology* **37**, 215–224.

Parr, J. F. (1968). The soil microbiological equilibrium: Nature and duration of changes induced by cultural practices. *In* "Forest Fertilization: Theory and Practice," pp. 28–37. Tenn. Valley Auth., Muscle Shoals, Alabama.

Parsons, L. R., and Kramer, P. J. (1974). Diurnal cycling in root resistance to water movement. *Physiol. Plant.* **30**, 19–23.

Passioura, J. B. (1972). The effect of root geometry on the yield of wheat growing on stored water. *Aust. J. Agric. Res.* **23,** 745–752.

Passioura, J. B. (1976). The control of water movement through plants. *In* "Transport and Transfer Processes in Plants." (I. F. Wardlaw and J. B. Passioura, eds.), pp. 373–380. Academic Press, New York.

Patric, J. H., Douglass, J. E., and Hewlett, J. D. (1965). Soil water absorption by mountain and Piedmont forests. *Soil Sci. Soc. Am., Proc.* **29,** 303–308.

Patterson, D. T. (1975a). Photosynthetic acclimation to irradiance in *Celastrus orbiculatus* Thunb. *Photosynthetica* **9,** 140–144.

Patterson, D. T. (1975b). Nutrient return in the stem flow and throughfall of individual trees in the piedmont deciduous forest. *In* "Mineral Cycling in Southeastern Ecosystems" (F. G. Howell, J. B. Gentry, and M. H. Smith, eds.), ERDA Symp. Ser. (Conf. 740513), pp. 800–812. Natl. Tech. Inf. Serv., Springfield, Virginia.

Patterson, D. T., Bunce, J. A., Alberte, R. S., and Van Volkenburgh, E. (1977). Photosynthesis in relation to leaf characteristics of cotton from controlled and field environments. *Plant Physiol.* **59,** 384–387.

Patton, R. F. (1962). Prospect of disease problems in plantations. *Proc. Soc. Am. For., 1961* pp. 27–33.

Paul, B. H., and Smith, D. M. (1950). Summary on growth in relation to quality of southern yellow pine. *U.S., For. Prod. Lab., Rep.* **D1751.**

Pauley, S. S., and Perry, T. O. (1954). Ecotypic variation of the photoperiodic response in *Populus. J. Arnold Arbor. Harv. Univ.* **35,** 167–188.

Peace, T. R. (1962). "Pathology of Trees and Shrubs." Oxford Univ. Press (Clarendon), London and New York.

Pearcy, R. W. (1977). Acclimation of photosynthetic and respiratory carbon dioxide exchange to growth temperature in *Atriplex lentiformis* (Torr.) Wats. *Plant Physiol.* **59,** 795–799.

Pellett, N. E., and White, D. B. (1969). Relationship of seasonal tissue changes to cold acclimation of *Juniperus chinensis* Hetzi. *J. Am. Soc. Hortic. Sci.* **94,** 460–462.

Penfound, W. T. (1934). Comparative structure of the wood in the "knees," swollen bases, and normal trunks of the tupelo gum (*Nyssa aquatica* L.). *Am. J. Bot.* **21,** 623–631.

Penning de Vries, F. W. T., Murphy, C. E., Jr., Wells, C. G., and Jorgensen, J. R. (1975). Simulation of nitrogen distribution and its effect on productivity in even-aged loblolly pine plantations. *In* "Mineral Cycling in Southeastern Ecosystems" (F. G. Howell, J. B. Gentry, and M. H. Smith, eds.), ERDA Symp. Ser. (Conf. 740513), pp. 70–83. Natl. Tech. Inf. Center, Springfield, Virginia.

Pereira, H. C. (1975). Climate and the orchard. *Commonw. Bur. Hortic. Plant. Crops (G. B.), Res. Rev.* **5.**

Pereira, J. S., and Kozlowski, T. T. (1976). Diurnal and seasonal changes in water balance of *Abies balsamea* and *Pinus resinosa. Oecol. Plant.* **11,** 397–412.

Pereira, J. S., and Kozlowski, T. T. (1977a). Influence of light intensity, temperature, and leaf area on stomatal aperture and water potential of woody plants. *Can. J. For. Res.* **7,** 145–153.

Pereira, J. S., and Kozlowski, T. T. (1977b). Variations among woody angiosperms in response to flooding. *Physiol. Plant.* **41,** 184–192.

Pereira, J. S., and Kozlowski, T. T. (1978). Diurnal and seasonal water deficits of *Acer saccharum* and *Betula papyrifera. Physiol. Plant.* **43,** 19–30.

Perry, T. O. (1962). Racial variation in the day and night requirements of red maple and loblolly pine. *For. Sci.* **8,** 336–344.

Perry, T. O. (1971). Dormancy of trees in winter. *Science* **171,** 29–36.

Perry, T. O., and Baldwin, G. W. (1966). Winter breakdown of the photosynthetic apparatus of evergreen species. *For. Sci.* **12,** 298–300.

Perry, T. O., and Simons, R. W. (1967). Growth of bud scales and leaves during the winter. *For. Sci.* **13,** 400–401.

Perry, T. O., and Wang, C. W. (1960). Genetic variation in the winter chilling requirement for date of dormancy break for *Acer rubrum. Ecology* **41,** 785–790.

Pessin, L. J. (1937). The effect of nutrient deficiency on the growth of longleaf pine seedlings. *Occas. Pap., Southeast For. Exp. Stn.,* **65.**

Petritschek, K. (1953). Über die Beziehungen zwischen Geschwindigkeit und Elektrolytgehalt des aufsteigenden Saftstromes. *Flora (Jena)* **140**, 345–385.

Pharis, R. P. (1975). Promotion of flowering in conifers by gibberellins. *For. Chron.* **51**, 244–248.

Pharis, R. P. (1976). Manipulation of flowering in conifers through the use of plant hormones. *In* "Modern Methods in Forest Genetics" (J. P. Miksche, ed.), pp. 265–282. Springer-Verlag, Berlin and New York.

Pharis, R. P. (1977). Probable roles of plant hormones in regulating shoot elongation, diameter growth, and crown form of forest trees. *In* "Tree Physiology and Yield Improvement" (M. G. R. Cannell and F. T Last, eds.), pp. 291–306. Academic Press, New York.

Pharis, R. P., and Ferrell, W. K. (1966). Differences in drought resistance between coastal and inland sources of Douglas-fir. *Can. J. Bot.* **44**, 1651–1659.

Pharis, R. P., and Kuo, C. G. (1977). Physiology of gibberellins in conifers. *Can. J. For. Res.* **7**, 299–325.

Pharis, R. P., and Morf, W. (1968). Physiology of gibberellin-induced flowering in conifers. *Biochem. Physiol. Plant Growth Subst., Proc. Int. Conf. Plant Growth Subst., 6th, 1967* pp. 1341–1356.

Pharis, R. P., Barnes, R. L., and Naylor, A. W. (1964). Effects of nitrogen level, calcium level and nitrogen source upon the growth and composition of *Pinus taeda* L. *Physiol. Plant.* **17**, 560–572.

Pharis, R. P., Ruddat, M., Phillips, C. C., and Heftmann, E. (1965). Gibberellin, growth retardants and apical dominance in Arizona cypress. *Naturwissenschaften* **52**, 88–89.

Pharis, R. P., Ruddat, M., Phillips, C. C., and Heftmann, E. (1967). Response of conifers to growth retardants. *Bot. Gaz (Chicago)* **128**, 105–109.

Pharis, R. P., Hellmers, H., and Schuurmans, E. (1970a). Effects of subfreezing temperatures on photosynthesis of evergreen conifers under controlled conditions. *Photosynthetica* **4**, 273–279.

Pharis, R. P., Ruddat, M. D. E., Glenn, J. L., and Morf, W. (1970b). A quantitative requirement for long day in the induction of staminate strobili by gibberellin in the conifer *Cupressus arizonica*. *Can. J. Bot.* **48**, 653–658.

Pharis, R. P., Kuo, C. C., and Glenn, J. L. (1972). Gibberellin, a primary determinant in the expression of apical dominance, apical control and geotropic movement of conifer shoots. *Proc. Int. Conf. Plant Growth Subst., 7th, 1970* pp. 441–448.

Philip, J. R. (1966). Plant water relations: Some physical aspects. *Annu. Rev. Plant Physiol.* **17**, 245–268.

Phillips, I. D. J. (1975). Apical dominance. *Annu. Rev. Plant Physiol.* **26**, 341–367.

Phillips, I. D. J., and Wareing, P. F. (1958). Studies in the dormancy of sycamore. I. Seasonal changes in growth substance content of the shoot. *J. Exp. Bot.* **9**, 350–364.

Phipps, R. L., and Gilbert, G. E. (1960). An electric dendrograph. *Ecology* **41**, 389–390.

Pillsbury, A. F., Pelishek, R. E., Osborn, J. F., and Szuszkiewicz, T. E. (1961). Chaparral to grass conversion doubles watershed runoff. *Calif. Agric.* **15**, 12–13.

Pinfield, N. J. (1968a). The promotion of isocitrate lyase activity in hazel cotyledons by exogenous gibberellin. *Planta* **82**, 337–341.

Pinfield, N. J. (1968b). The effects of gibberellin on the metabolism of ethanol-soluble constituent in the cotyledons of hazel seeds (*Corylus avellana* L.). *J. Exp. Bot.* **19**, 452–459.

Pirie, N. W., ed. (1975). "Food Protein Sources." Cambridge Univ. Press, London and New York.

Pirone, P. O. (1972). "Tree Maintenance." Oxford Univ. Press, London and New York.

Pirson, A. (1958). Mineralstoffe and photosynthese. *Encycl. Plant Physiol.* **4**, 355–381.

Pisek, A., and Larcher, W. (1954). Zusammenhang zwischen Austrocknungsresistenz und Frosthärte bei Immergrünen. *Protoplasma* **44**, 30–46.

Pisek, A., and Tranquillini, W. (1954). Assimilation und Kohlenstoffhaushalt in der Krone von Fichten- (*Picea excelsa* Link) und Rotbuchenbäumen (*Fagus silvatica* L.). *Flora (Jena)* **141**, 237–270.

Pisek, A., and Winkler, E. (1958). Assimilationsvermögen und Respiration der Fichte (*Picea excelsa* L.) in verschiedener Höhenlage und der Zirbe (*Pinus cembra* L.) an der alpinen Waldgrenze. *Planta* **51**, 518–543.

Place, I. C. M. (1955). The influence of seed-bed conditions on the regeneration of spruce and fir. *Can., For. Branch, Bull.* **117**.

Pollard, D. F. W. (1970). Leaf area development on different shoot types in a young aspen stand and its effect upon production. *Can. J. Bot.* **48**, 1801–1804.

Pollard, D. F. W. (1973). Provenance variation in phenology of needle initiation in white spruce. *Can. J. For. Res.* **3**, 589–593.

Pollard, D. F. W., and Logan, K. T. (1974). The role of tree growth in the differentiation of provenances of black spruce *Picea mariana* (Mill.) B.S.P. *Can. J. For. Res.* **4**, 308–311.

Pollard, D. F. W., and Logan, K. T. (1976). Inherent variation in "free growth" in relation to numbers of needles produced by provenances of *Picea mariana. In* "Tree Physiology and Yield Improvement " (M. G. R. Cannell and F. T. Last, eds.), pp. 245–251. Academic Press, New York.

Pollard, D. F. W., and Logan, K. T. (1977). The effects of light intensity, photoperiod, soil moisture potential, and temperature on bud morphogenesis in *Picea* species. *Can. J. For. Res.* **7**, 415–421.

Pollard, D. F. W., and Wareing, P. F. (1968). Rates of dry matter production in forest tree seedlings. *Ann. Bot. (London)* [N.S.] **32**, 573–591.

Pollard, J. K., and Sproston, T. (1954). Nitrogenous constituents of sap exuded from the sapwood of *Acer saccharum. Plant Physiol.* **29**, 360–364.

Pollock, B. M. (1953). The respiration of *Acer* buds in relation to the inception and termination of the winter rest. *Physiol. Plant.* **6**, 47–64.

Pollock, B. M., and Olney, H. O. (1959). Studies of the rest period. I. Growth, translocation, and respiratory changes in the embryonic organs of the after-ripening cherry seed. *Plant Physiol.* **34**, 131–142.

Polster, H. (1950). "Die Physiologischen Grundlagen der Stofferzeugung im Walde." Bayerischer Lanwirtschaftsverlag, Munich.

Polster, H. (1955). Vergleichende Untersuchungen über die Kohlendioxdassimilation und Atmung der Douglasie, Fichte und Weymouthskiefer. *Arch. Forstwes.* **4**, 689–714.

Polster, H., and Weise, G. (1962). Vergleichende Assimilationsuntersuchungen an Klonen verschiedener Larchenherkunfte (*Larix decidua* und *L. leptolepis*) unter Frieland und Klimaraumbedingungen. *Züchter* **32**, 103–110.

Pomeroy, M. K., Simonovitch, D., and Wightman, F. (1970). Seasonal biochemical changes in the living bark and needles of red pine (*Pinus resinosa*) in relation to adaptation to freezing. *Can. J. Bot.* **48**, 953–967.

Popham, R. A. (1952). "Developmental Plant Anatomy." Long's College Book Co., Columbus, Ohio.

Porsild, A. E., Harrington, C. R., and Mulligan, G. A., (1967). *Lupinus arcticus* Wats. grown from seeds of pleistocene age. *Science* **158**, 114–115.

Possingham, J. V. (1970). Aspects of the physiology of grape vines. *In* "Physiology of Tree Crops" (L. C. Luckwill and C. V. Cutting, eds.), pp. 335–349. Academic Press, London.

Postlethwait, S. N., and Rogers, B. (1958). Tracing the path of the transpiration stream in trees by the use of radioactive isotopes. *Am. J. Bot.* **45**, 753–757.

Potter, G. F. (1939). Low temperature effects on woody plants. *Proc. Am. Soc. Hortic. Sci.* **36**, 185–195.

Powell, D. B. B. (1974). Some effects of water stress in late spring on apple trees. *J. Hortic. Sci.* **49**, 257–272.

Powell, G. R. (1977). Biennial strobilus production in balsam fir: a review of its morphogenesis and a discussion of its apparent physiological basis. *Can. J. For. Res.* **7**, 547–555.

Powell, L. E. (1972). Naturally occurring plant growth regulators and their physiological roles in fruit trees. *Acta Hortic.* **34**, 33–39.

Pratt, H. K., and Goeschl, J. D. (1969). Physiological roles of ethylene in plants. *Annu. Rev. Plant Physiol.* **29**, 541–584.

Preston, J. F., and Phillips, F. J. (1911). Seasonal variation in the food reserve of trees. *For. Q.* **9**, 232–243.

Priestley, C. A. (1962a). Carbohydrate resources within the perennial plant. *Commonw. Bur. Hortic. Plant. Crops (G.B.), Tech Commun.* **27**.

Priestley, C. A. (1962b). The location of carbohydrate resources within the apple tree. *Proc. Int. Hortic. Congr., 16th,* pp. 319–327.

Priestley, J. H. (1932). The growing tree. *Forestry* **6**, 105–112.

Pritchett, W. L. (1968). Progress in the development of techniques and standards for soil and foliar diagnosis of phosphorus deficiency in slash pine *In* "Forest Fertilization: Theory and Practice," pp. 81–87. Tenn. Valley Auth., Muscle Shoals, Alabama.

Proebsting, E. L. (1943). Root distribution of some deciduous fruit trees in a California orchard. *Proc. Am. Soc. Hortic. Sci.* **43**, 1–4.

Proebsting, E. L. (1958). A quantitative evaluation of the effect of fruiting on growth of Elberta peach trees. *Proc. Am. Soc. Hortic. Sci.* **71**, 103–109.

Proebsting, E. L., and Gilmore, A. E., (1941). The relation of peach root toxicity to re-establishment of peach orchards. *Proc. Am. Soc. Hortic. Sci.* **38**, 21–26.

Queen, W. H. (1967). Radial movement of water and ^{32}P through suberized and unsuberized roots of grape. Ph.D. Dissertation, Duke University, Durham, North Carolina.

Quinlan, J. D. (1965). The pattern of distribution of ^{14}C in a potted rootstock following assimilation of ^{14}CO$_2$ by a single leaf. *Annu. Rep. East Malling Res. Stn., Kent*, 117–118.

Quinlan, J. D. (1969). Mobilization of ^{14}C in the spring following autumn assimilation of ^{14}CO$_2$ by apple rootstock. *J. Hortic. Sci.* **44**, 107–110.

Quinlan, J. D., and Weaver, R. J. (1970). Modification of patterns of the photosynthate movement within and between shoots of *Vitis vinifera* L. *Plant Physiol.* **46**, 527–530.

Quispel, A., ed. (1974). "The Biology of Nitrogen Fixation." Am. Elsevier, New York.

Raber, O. (1937). Water utilization by trees, with special reference to the economic forest species of the north temperate zone. *U.S., Dep. Agric., Misc. Publ.* **257**.

Radmer, R., and Kok, B. (1977). Photosynthesis: Limited yields, unlimited dreams. *BioScience* **27**, 599–605.

Ralston, C. W., and Prince, A. B. (1965). Accumulation of dry matter and nutrients by pine and hardwood forests in the lower Piedmont of North Carolina. *In* "Forest-Soil Relationships in North America" (C. T. Youngberg, ed.), pp. 77–94. Oregon State Univ. Press, Corvallis.

Ramsay, J., and Martin, G. C. (1970). Seasonal changes in growth promoters and inhibitors in buds of apricot. *J. Am. Soc. Hortic. Sci.* **95**, 569–570.

Rangenekar, P. V., and Forward, D. F. (1969). Foliar nutrition and growth in red pine: The fate of photoassimilated carbon in a seedling tree. *Can. J. Bot.* **47**, 897–906.

Rangenekar, P. V., Forward, D. F., and Nolan, N. J. (1969). Foliar nutrition and wood growth in red pine: The distribution of radiocarbon photoassimilated by individual branches of young trees. *Can. J. Bot.* **47**, 1701–1711.

Raschke, K. (1975). Stomatal action. *Annu. Rev. Plant Physiol.* **26**, 309–340.

Raschke, K. (1976). How stomata resolve the problem of opposing priorities. *Phil. Trans. Roy. Soc. London* **B273**, 551–560.

Rasmussen, R. A., and Went, F. W. (1965). Volatile organic matter of plant origin in the atmosphere. *Proc. Natl. Acad. Sci. U.S.A.* **53**, 215–220.

Read, R. A. (1964). Tree windbreaks for the central Great Plains. U.S.D.A. Agr. Handbook No. 250.

Reader, R. J. (1978). Contribution of overwintering leaves to the growth of three broad-leaved evergreen shrubs belonging to the Ericaceae family. *Can. J. Bot.* **56**, 1248–1261.

Reed, H. S. (1938). Cytology of leaves affected with little-leaf. *Am. J. Bot.* **25**, 174–186.

Reed, H. S., and Bartholomew, E. T. (1930). The effects of desiccating winds on citrus trees. *Calif., Agric. Exp. Stn., Bull.* **484**, 1–59.

Reed, H. S., and Dufrenoy, J. (1935). The effects of zinc and iron salt on the cell structure of mottled orange leaves. *Hilgardia* **9**, 113–137.

Reed, J. F. (1939). Root and shoot growth of shortleaf and loblolly pines in relation to certain environmental conditions. *Duke Univ. Sch. For., Bull.* **4**.

Rees, A. R. (1964a). Some observations on the flowering behavior of *Coffea rupestris* in southern Nigeria. *J. Ecol.* **52**, 1–7.

Rees, A. R. (1964b). The flowering behavior of *Clerodendron incisum* in southern Nigeria. *J. Ecol.* **52**, 9–17.

Reethof, G., and Heisler, G. M. (1976). Trees and forests for noise abatement and visual screening. *In* "Better Trees for Metropolitan Landscape" (F. S. Santamour, H. D. Gerhold, and S. Little, eds.), pp. 39–48. U.S. Forest Service. Gen. Tech. Rept. NE-22.

Rehfeldt, G. E., Stage, A. E., and Bingham, R. T. (1971). Strobili development in western white pine: Periodicity, prediction, and association with weather. *For. Sci.* **17**, 454–461.

Reid, C. P. P., and Fechner, G. H., eds. (1974). "Proceedings of the Third North American Forest Biology Workshop." Colorado State University, Fort Collins.

Reid, R. W. (1961). Moisture changes in lodgepole pine before and after attack by the mountain pine beetle. *For. Chron.* **37**, 368–375.

Reinert, R. A., Heagle, A. S., and Heck, W. W. (1975). Plant responses to pollutant combinations. *In* "Responses of Plants to Air Pollution" (J. B. Mudd and T. T. Kozlowski, eds.), pp. 159–177. Academic Press, New York.

Reinken, G. (1963). Wachstum, Assimilation und Transpiration von Apfelbäumen und ihre Beeinflussung durch Phosphor. *Phosphorsaure* **23**, 91–108.

Reisenauer, H. M., ed. (1976). "Soil and Plant-Tissue Testing in California," No. 1879. Div. Agric. Sci., University of California, Davis.

Renner, O. (1912). Versuche zur Mechanik der Wasserversorgung. 2. Über Wurzeltätigkeit. *Ber. Dtsch. Bot. Ges.* **30**, 576–580 and 642–648.

Renner, O. (1915). Die Wasserversorgung der Pflanzen. *Handworterbuch Naturwiss.* **10**,538–557.

Reukema, D. L. (1959). Missing annual rings in branches of young Douglas-fir. *Ecology* **40**, 480–482.

Reuther, W., and Burrows, F. W. (1942). The effect of manganese sulfate on the photosynthetic activity of frenched tung foliage. *Proc. Am. Soc. Hortic. Sci.* **40**, 73–76.

Rhoads, W. A., and Wedding, R. T. (1953). The photosynthetic and respiratory rates of citrus leaves of four different ages. *Citrus Leaves* **33**, 10–11.

Rice, E. L. (1974). "Allelopathy." Academic Press, New York.

Richards, L. A., and Wadleigh, C. H. (1952). Soil water and plant growth. *In* "Soil Physical Conditions and Plant Growth" (B. T. Shaw, ed.), pp. 73–251. Academic Press, New York.

Richards, L. A., and Weaver, L. R. (1944). Moisture retention by some irrigated soils as related to soil-moisture tension. *J. Agric. Res.* **69**, 215–235.

Richards, P. W. (1966). "Tropical Rain Forest." Cambridge Univ. Press, London and New York.

Richardson, C. J., and Lund, J. A. (1975). Effects of clear-cutting on nutrient losses in aspen forests on three soil types in Michigan. *In* "Mineral Cycling in Southeastern Ecosystems" (F. G. Howell, J. B. Gentry, and N. H. Smith, eds.), ERDA Symp. Ser. (Conf. 740513), pp. 673–686. Natl. Tech. Inf. Serv., Springfield, Virginia.

Richardson, S. D. (1953a). A note on some differences in root-hair formation between seedlings of sycamore and American oak. *New Phytol.* **52**, 80–82.

Richardson, S. D. (1953b). Root growth of *Acer pseudoplatanus* L. in relation to grass cover and nitrogen deficiency. *Meded. Landbouwhogesch. Wageningen* **53**, 75–97.

Rider, N. E. (1957). Water losses from various land surfaces. *Q. J. R. Meteorol. Soc.* **83**, 181–193.

Ringoet, A. (1952). Recherches sur la transpiration et le bilan d'eau de quelques plantes tropicales. *Publ. Inst. Natl. Etude Agron. Congo Belge, Ser. Sci.* **56**.

Ritchie, G. A. and Hinckley, T. M. (1975). The pressure chamber as an instrument for ecological research. *Adv. Ecol. Res.* **9**, 165–254.

Robards, A. W. (1965). Tension wood and eccentric growth in crack willow (*Salix fragilis* L.). *Ann. Bot. (London)* [N.S.] **29**, 419–431.

Robards, A. W., Davison, E., and Kidwai, P. (1969). Short-term effects of some chemicals on cambial activity. *J. Exp. Bot.* **20**, 912–921.

Roberds, J. H., Namkoong, G., and Davey, C. B. (1976). Family variation in growth response of loblolly pine to fertilizing with urea. *For. Sci.* **22**, 291–299.

Roberts, B. R. (1972). Net photosynthesis, growth, and transpiration in American elm seedlings as influenced by Dutch elm disease and plant-water stress. *Phytopathology* **62**, 457–459.

Roberts, B. R., Kramer, P. J., and Karl, C. M., Jr. (1963). Long-term effects of gibberellin on the growth of loblolly pine seedlings. *For. Sci.* **9**, 202–205.

Roberts, D. R., and Peters, W. J. (1977). Chemically inducing lightwood formation in southern pines. *For. Prod. J.* **27**, 28–30.

Roberts, D. R., Joye, N. M., Jr., Proveaux, A. T., Peters, W. J., and Lawrence, R. V. (1973). A new and more efficient method of naval stores production. *Nav. Stores Rev.* **83**, 4–5.

Roberts, J. (1976). An examination of the quantity of water stored in mature *Pinus sylvestris* L. trees. *J. Exp. Bot.* **27**, 473–479.

Roberts, J. (1977). The use of tree-cutting techniques in the study of water relations of mature *Pinus sylvestris* L. *J. Exp. Bot.* **28**, 751–767.

Roberts, S. W., and Knoerr, K. R. (1977). Components of water potential estimated from xylem pressure measurements in five tree species. *Oecologia* **28**, 191–202.

Robitaille, H. A., and Carlson, R. F. (1976). Gibberellic and abscisic acid-like substances and the regulation of apple shoot extension. *J. Am. Soc. Hortic. Sci.* **101**, 388–392.

Roe, E. I. (1941). Effect of temperature in seed germination. *J. For.* **39**, 413–414.

Rogers, W. S., and Booth, G. A. (1959–1960). The roots of fruit trees. *Sci. Hortic.* **14**, 27–34.

Rogers, W. S., and Head, G. C. (1969). Factors affecting the distribution of roots in perennial woody plants. *In* "Root Growth " (W. J. Whittington, ed.), pp. 280–295. Butterworths, London.

Rogler, C. E., and Hackett, W. P. (1975a). Phase change in *Hedera helix:* Induction of the mature to juvenile phase change by gibberellin A₃. *Physiol. Plant.* **34**, 141–147.

Rogler, C. E., and Hackett, W. P. (1975b). Phase change in *Hedera helix:* Stabilization of the mature form with abscisic acid and growth retardants. *Physiol. Plant.* **34**, 148–152.

Rokach, A. (1953). Water transfer from fruits to leaves in the Shamouti orange tree and related topics. *Palest. J. Bot.* **8**, 146–151.

Rook, D. A. (1973). Conditioning radiata pine seedlings to transplanting by restricted watering. *N. Z. J. For. Sci.* **3**, 54–59.

Romberger, J. A. (1963). Meristems, growth and development in woody plants. *U.S., Dep. Agric., Tech. Bull.* **1293.**

Ronco, F. (1970). Influence of high light intensity on survival of planted Engelmann spruce. *For. Sci.* **16**, 331–339.

Rowe, J. S. (1964). Environmental preconditioning with special reference to forestry. *Ecology* **45**, 399–403.

Rowe, J. W., Conner, A. H., Diehl, M. A., and Wroblewska, H. (1976). Effects of treating northern and western conifers with paraquat. *Lightwood Coord. Counc. Annu. Meet., 1976* pp. 66–76.

Rowe, R. N., and Beardsell, D. V. (1973). Waterlogging of fruit trees. *Hortic. Abstr.* **43**, 534–548.

Rudinsky, J. A. (1962). Ecology of Scolytidae. *Annu. Rev. Entomol.* **7**, 327–348.

Rudinsky, J. A., and Vité, J. P. (1959). Certain ecological and phylogenetic aspects of the pattern of water conduction in conifers. *For. Sci.* **5**, 259–266.

Rudnicki, R. (1969). Studies on abscisic acid in apple seeds. *Planta* **86**, 63–68.

Rudolph, T. D. (1964). Lammas growth and prolepsis in jack pine in the Lake States. *For. Sci. Monogr.* **6.**

Rufelt, H. (1956). Influence of the root pressure on the transpiration of wheat plants. *Physiol. Plant.* **9**, 154–164.

Ruinen, J. (1965). The phyllosphere. III. Nitrogen fixation in the phyllosphere. *Plant Soil* **22**, 375–394.

Rumbold, C. (1920). The injection of chemicals into chestnut trees. *Am. J. Bot.* **7**, 45–57.

Running, S. W. (1976). Environmental control of leaf water conductance in conifers. *Can. J. For. Res,* **6**, 104–112.

Runyon, E. H. (1936). Ratio of water content to dry weight in leaves of the creosote bush. *Bot. Gaz. (Chicago)* **97**, 518–553.

Russell, C. E., and Berryman, A. A. (1976). Host resistance to the fir engraver beetle. I. Monoterpene composition of *Abies grandis* pitch blisters and fungus-infected wounds. *Can. J. Bot.* **54**, 14–18.

Russell, E. W. (1973). "Soil Conditions and Plant Growth," 10th ed. Longmans, Green, New York.

Russell, R. S., and Sanderson, J. (1967). Nutrient uptake by different parts of the intact roots of plants. *J. Exp. Bot.* **18**, 491–508.

Rutter, A. J. (1957). Studies in the growth of young plants of *Pinus sylvestris* L. I. The annual cycle of assimilation and growth. *Ann. Bot. (London)* [N.S.] **21**, 399–426.

Rutter, A. J. (1968). Water consumption by forests. *In* "Water Deficits and Plant Growth" (T. T. Kozlowski, ed.), Vol. 2, pp. 23–84. Academic Press, New York.

Ryall, A. L., and Aldrich, W. W. (1944). The effects of water deficits in the tree upon maturity, composition, and storage quality of Bosc pears. *J. Agric. Res.* **68**, 121–133.

Ryugo, K., and Davis, L. D. (1959). The effect of the time of ripening on the starch content of bearing peach branches. *Proc. Am. Soc. Hortic. Sci.* **74**, 130–133.

Sacher, J. A. (1973). Senescence and post harvest physiology. *Annu. Rev. Plant Physiol.* **24**, 197–224.

Saeki, T., and Nomoto, N. (1958). On the seasonal change of photosynthetic activity of some deciduous and evergreen broadleaf trees. *Bot. Mag. (Tokyo)* **71**, 235–241.

Safir, G. R., Boyer, J. S., and Gerdemann, J. W. (1972). Nutrient status and mycorrhizal enhancement of water transport in soybean. *Plant Physiol.* **49**, 700–703.

St. John, J. B., and Christiansen, M. N. (1976). Inhibition of linolenic acid synthesis and modification of chilling resistance in cotton seedlings. *Plant Physiol.* **57**, 257–259.

Sakai, A. (1960). The frost hardening process of woody plants. VII. Seasonal variations in sugars. *Contrib. Inst. Low Temp Sci., Hokkaido Univ., Ser. B* **18**, 1–14.

Sakai, A. (1962). Studies on the frost hardiness of woody plants. I. The causal relation between sugar content and frost hardiness. *Contrib. Inst. Low Temp. Sci., Hokkaido Univ., Ser. B* **11**, 1–40.

Sakai, A. (1970). Mechanism of desiccation damage of conifers wintering in soil-frozen areas. *Ecology* **51**, 657–664.

Sakai, A., and Weiser, C. J. (1973). Freezing resistance of trees in North America with reference to tree regions. *Ecology* **54**, 118–126.

Sakai, A., and Yoshida, S. (1968). The role of sugar and related compounds in variations of freezing resistance. *Cryobiology* **5**, 160–174.

Sampson, A. W., and Samisch, R. (1935). Growth and seasonal changes in composition of oak leaves. *Plant Physiol.* **10**, 739–751.

Sanchez, P. A. (1973). A review of soils research in tropical Latin America. *N. C., Agric. Exp. Stn., Tech. Bull.* **219**.

Sanderson, P. L. and Armstrong, W. (1978). Soil waterlogging, root rot and conifer windthrow: oxygen deficiency or phytotoxicity? *Plant and Soil* **49**, 185–190.

Sands, K., and Rutter, A. J. (1959). Studies in the growth of young plants of *Pinus sylvestris* L. II. The relation of growth to soil moisture tension. *Ann. Bot. (London)* [N.S.] **23**, 269–284.

Sargent, C. S. (1926). "Manual of the Trees of North America." Houghton, Boston.

Sarvas, R. (1955a). Investigations into the flowering and seed quality of forest trees. *Commun. Inst. For. Fenn.* **45**.

Sarvas, R. (1955b). Ein Beitrag zur Fernverbreitung des Blütenstaubes einiger Waldbäume. 2. *Forstgenet. Forstpflanz.* **4**, 137–142.

Sarvas, R. (1962). Investigations on the flowering and seed crop of *Pinus silvestris. Commun. Inst. For. Fenn.* **53**, 1–198.

Sasaki, S., and Brown, G. N. (1969). Changes in nucleic acid fractions of seed components of red pine (*Pinus resinosa* Ait.). *Plant Physiol.* **44**, 1729–1733.

Sasaki, S., and Kozlowski, T. T. (1968a). The role of cotyledons in early development of pine seedlings. *Can. J. Bot.* **46**, 1173–1183.

Sasaki, S., and Kozlowski, T. T. (1968b). Effects of herbicides on respiration of red pine (*Pinus resinosa* Ait.) seedlings. I. S-triazine and chlorophenoxy acid herbicides. *Adv. Front. Plant Sci.* **22**, 187–202.

Sasaki, S., and Kozlowski, T. T. (1968c). Effects of herbicides on respiration of red pine (*Pinus resinosa* Ait.) seedlings. II. Monuron, diuron, DCPA, Dalapon, CDEC, CDAA, EPTC, and NPA. *Bot. Gaz. (Chicago)* **129**, 286–293.

Sasaki, S., and Kozlowski, T. T. (1969). Utilization of seed reserves and currently produced photosynthates of embryonic tissues of pine seedlings. *Ann. Bot. (London)* [N.S.] **33**, 472–482.

Sasaki, S., and Kozlowski, T. T. (1970). Effects of cotyledons and hypocotyl photosynthesis on growth of young pine seedlings. *New Phytol.* **69**, 493–500.

Satoo, T. (1956a). Drought resistance of some conifers at the first summer after their emergence. *Bull. Tokyo Univ. For.* **51**, 1–108.

Satoo, T. (1956b). Anatomical studies on the rooting of cuttings in conifer species. *Bull. Tokyo Univ. For,* **51**, 111–157.

Satoo, T. (1966). Variation in response of conifer seed germination to soil moisture conditions. *Tokyo Univ. For., Misc. Inf.* **16**, 17–20.

Sauter, J. J. (1971). Physiology of sugar maple. *Harv. For. Annu. Rep., 1970–1971* pp. 10–11.

Sauter, J. J. (1972). Respiratory and phosphatase activities in contact cells of wood rays and their possible role in sugar secretion. *Z. Pflanzenphysiol.* **67**, 135–145.

Sauter, J. J., Iten, W., and Zimmermann, M. H. (1973). Studies on the release of sugar into the vessels of sugar maple (*Acer saccharum*). *Can. J. Bot.* **51**, 1–8.

Scandalios, J. G. (1974). Isozymes in development and differentiation. *Annu. Rev. Plant Physiol.* **25**, 225–258.

Schaedle, M. (1975). Tree photosynthesis. *Annu. Rev. Plant Physiol.* **26**, 101–115.

Scheffer, T. C., and Hedgecock, G. G. (1955). Injury to northwestern forest trees by sulfur dioxide from smelters. *U.S., For. Serv., Tech. Bull.* **1117**, 1–49.

Schier, G. A. (1970). Seasonal pathways of ^{14}C-photosynthate in red pine labeled in May, July, and October. *For. Sci.* **16**, 2–13.

Schier, G. A., and Zasada, J. C. (1973). Role of carbohydrate reserves in the development of root suckers in *Populus tremuloides*. *Can. J. For. Res.* **3**, 243–250.

Schimper, F. W. (1903). "Plant Geography upon a Physiological Basis" (Engl. transl.). Oxford Univ. Press (Clarendon), London and New York.

Schmidtling, R. C. (1973). Intensive culture increases growth without affecting wood quality of young southern pines. *Can. J. For. Res.* **3**, 565–573.

Schneider, G. W., and Childers, N. F. (1941). Influence of soil moisture on photosynthesis, respiration, and transpiration of apple leaves. *Plant Physiol.* **16**, 565–583.

Scholander, P. F., Love, W. E., and Kanwisher, J. W. (1955). The rise of sap in tall grapevines. *Plant Physiol.* **30**, 93–104.

Scholander, P. F., Ruud, B., and Leivestad, H. (1957). The rise of sap in a tropical liana. *Plant Physiol.* **41**, 529–532.

Scholander, P. F., Hammel, H. T., Bradsheet, E. D., and Hemmingsen, E. A. (1965). Sap pressure in vascular plants. *Science* **148**, 339–346.

Scholander, P. F., van Dam, L., and Scholander, S. I. (1955). Gas exchange in the roots of mangroves. *Am. J. Bot.* **42**, 92–98.

Scholtes, W. H. (1953). The concentration of forest tree roots in the surface zone of some Piedmont soils. *Proc. Iowa Acad. Sci.* **60**, 243–259.

Schönherr, J. (1976). Water permeability of isolated cuticular membranes: The effect of cuticular waxes on diffusion of water. *Planta* **131**, 159–164.

Schopfer, P. (1977). Phytochrome control of enzymes. *Annu. Rev. Plant Physiol.* **28**, 223–252.

Schopmeyer, C. S. (1974). Seeds of woody plants in the United States. *U.S., Dep. Agric., Agric. Handb.* **450**.

Schramm, J. R. (1958). The mechanism of frost heaving of tree seedlings. *Proc. Am. Philos. Soc.* **102**, 333–350.

Schreiber, J. D., Duffy, P. D., and McClurkin, D. C. (1976). Dissolved nutrient losses in storm runoff from five southern pine watersheds. *J. Environ. Qual.* **5**, 201–205.

Schubert, A. (1939). Untersuchungen über den Transpirationstrom der Nadelhölzer und den Wasserbedarf von Fichte und Lärche. *Tharandter Forstl. Jahrb.* **90**, 821–883.

Schulman, E. (1958). Bristlecone pine, oldest known living thing. *Natl. Geogr. Mag.* **113**, 355–372.

Schultz, R. P., and Woods, F. W. (1967). The frequency and implication of intraspecific root-grafting in loblolly pine. *For. Sci.* **13**, 226–239.

Schulz, J. P. (1960). "Ecological Studies on Rain Forest in Northern Surinam." North-Holland Publ., Amsterdam.

Schulze, E. D., Lange, O. L., Buschbom, U., Kappen, L., and Evenari, M. (1972). Stomatal responses to changes in humidity in plants growing in the desert. *Planta* **108**, 259–270.

Scifres, C. J., and Brock, J. H. (1969). Moisture-temperature interrelations in germination and early seedling development of mesquite. *J. Range Manage.* **22**, 334–337.

Scott, F. M. (1950). Internal suberization of tissues. *Bot. Gaz. (Chicago)* **110**, 492–495.

Scott, F. M. (1963). Root hair zone of soil-grown plants. *Nature (London)* **199**, 1009–1010.

Scott, F. M. (1964). Lipid deposition in intercellular space. *Nature (London)* **203**, 164–165.

Scott, F. M., Schroeder, M. R., and Turrell, F. M. (1948). Development, cell shape, suberization of internal surface, and abscission in the leaf of the Valencia orange, *Citrus sinensis*. *Bot. Gaz. (Chicago)* **109**, 381–411.

Scurfield, G. (1973). Reaction wood: Its structure and function. *Science* **179**, 647–655.

Sell, H. M., Best, A. H., Reuther, W., and Drosdoff, M. (1948). Changes in chemical composition and biological activity of developing tung fruit with references to oil synthesis. *Plant Physiol.* **23**, 359–372.

Sendak, P. E. (1978). Birch sap utilization in the Ukraine. *J. For.* **76**, 120–121.

Senser, N., Schotz, F., and Beck, E. (1975). Seasonal changes in structure and function of spruce chloroplasts. *Planta* **126**, 1–10.

Sequiera, L. (1973). Hormone metabolism in diseased plants. *Annu. Rev. Plant Physiol.* **24**, 353–380.

Servaites, J. C., and Ogren, W. L. (1977). Chemical inhibition of the glycolate pathway in soybean leaf cells. *Plant Physiol.* **60**, 461–466.

Sestak, Z., Catsky, J., and Jarvis, P. G., eds. (1971). ''Plant Photosynthetic Production: Manual of Methods.'' Junk Publ., The Hague.

Shain, L., and Hillis, W. E. (1973). Ethylene production in xylem of *Pinus radiata* in relation to heartwood formation. *Can. J. Bot.* **51**, 1331–1385.

Shalucha, B. (1946). Auxin and nitrogen content of developing peach shoots. *Am. J. Bot.* **33**, 838.

Shaner, D. L., and Boyer, J. S. (1976). Nitrate reductase activity in maize (*Zea mays* L.) leaves. I. Regulation by nitrate flux. *Plant Physiol.* **58**, 499–504.

Shannon, L. M. (1954). Internal bark necrosis of the Delicious apple. *Proc. Am. Soc. Hortic. Sci.* **64**, 165–174.

Shapiro, S. (1958). The role of light in the growth of root primordia in the stem of Lombardy Poplar. *In* ''The Physiology of Forest Trees'' (K. V. Thimann, ed.), pp. 445–465. Ronald, New York.

Sharon, F. M. (1974). An altered pattern of enzyme activity in tissues associated with wounds in *Acer saccharum*. *Physiol. Plant Pathol.* **4**, 307–312.

Sharp, W. M., and Chisman, H. H. (1961). Flowering and fruiting in the white oaks. I. Staminate flowering through pollen dispersal. *Ecology* **42**, 365–372.

Sharples, A., and Gunnery, H. (1933). Callus formation in *Hibiscus rosa-sinensis* L. and *Hevea brasiliensis* Müll. Arg. *Ann. Bot. (London)* **47**, 827–840.

Sharples, G. C., and Burkhart, L. (1954). Seasonal changes in carbohydrates in the Marsh grapefruit tree in Arizona. *Proc. Am. Soc. Hortic. Sci.* **63**, 74–80.

Shear, C. B. (1966). Tung nutrition. *In* ''Fruit Nutrition'' (N. F. Childers, ed.), Hortic. Publ., pp. 549–568. Rutgers University, New Brunswick, New Jersey.

Sheldrake, A. R. (1971). Auxin in the cambium and its differentiating derivatives. *J. Exp. Bot.* **22**, 735–740.

Shigo, A. L. (1975). Biology of decay and wood quality. *In* ''Biological Transformation of Wood by Microorganisms'' (W. Liese, ed.), pp. 1–15. Springer-Verlag, Berlin and New York.

Shigo, A. L., and Hillis, W. E. (1973). Heartwood, discolored wood, and microorganisms in living trees. *Annu. Rev. Phytopathol.* **11**, 197–222.

Shigo, A. L., and Wilson, C. L. (1977). Wound dressings on red maple and American elm; effectiveness after five years. *J. Arboricult.* **3**, 81–87.

Shimshi, D. (1963). Effect of soil moisture and phenylmercuric acetate upon stomatal aperture, transpiration, and photosynthesis. *Plant Physiol.* **38**, 713–721.

Shirley, H. L. (1936). Lethal high temperatures for conifers and the cooling effects of transpiration. *J. Agric. Res.* **53**, 239–258.

Shiroya, T., Slankis, V., Krotkov, G., and Nelson, C. D. (1962a). The nature of photosynthate in *Pinus strobus* seedlings. *Can. J. Bot.* **40**, 669–676.

Shiroya, T., Lister, G., Slankis, V., Krotkov, G., and Nelson, C. D. (1962b). Translocation of the products of photosynthesis to roots of pine seedlings. *Can. J. Bot.* **40**, 1125–1135.

Shive, J. B. Jr., and Brown, K. W. (1978). Quaking and gas exchange in leaves of cottonwood (*Populus deltoides* Marsh). *Plant Physiol.* **61**, 331–333.

Shoulders, E. (1967). Fertilizer application, inherent fruitfulness, and rainfall affect flowering of longleaf pine. *For. Sci.* **13**, 376–383.

Shoulders, E. (1968). Fertilization increases longleaf and slash pine flower and cone crops in Louisiana. *J. For.* **66**, 192–197.

Siminovitch, D. (1963). Evidence from increase in ribonucleic acid and protein synthesis in autumn for increase in protoplasm during the frost-hardening of black locust bark cells. *Can. J. Bot.* **41**, 1301–1308.

Siminovitch, D., and Briggs, D. R. (1949). The chemistry of the living bark of the black locust tree in relation to frost hardiness. I. Seasonal variations in protein content. *Arch. Biochem.* **23**, 8–17.

Siminovitch, D., and Briggs, D. R. (1953). Studies on the chemistry of the living bark of the black locust tree in relation to frost hardiness. IV. Effects of ringing on translocation, protein synthesis and the development of hardiness. *Plant Physiol.* **28**, 177–200.

Siminovitch, D., Wilson, C. M., and Briggs, D. R. (1953). Studies on the chemistry of the living bark of the black locust in relation to frost hardiness. V. Seasonal transformations and variations in the carbohydrates: Starch-sucrose interconversions. *Plant Physiol.* **28**, 383–400.

Siminovitch, D., Rheaume, B., Pomeroy, K., and Lepage, M. (1968). Phospholipid, protein, and nucleic acid increases in protoplasm and membrane structures associated with development of extreme freezing resistance in black locust tree cells. *Cryobiology* **5**, 202–225.

Simkover, H. G., and Shenefelt, R. D. (1952). Phytotoxicity of some insecticides to coniferous seedlings with particular reference to benzene hexachloride. *J. Econ. Entomol.* **45**, 11–15.

Simmonds, J. A., and Dumbroff, E. B. (1974). High energy charge as a requirement for axis elongation in response to gibberellic acid and kinetin during stratification of *Acer saccharum* seeds. *Plant Physiol.* **53**, 91–95.

Simons, R. K. (1959). Anatomical and morphological responses of four varieties of apples to frost injury. *Proc. Am. Soc. Hortic. Sci.* **74**, 10–24.

Simons, R. K. (1970). Phloem tissue development response to freeze injury to trunks of apple trees. *J. Am. Soc. Hortic. Sci.* **95**, 182–190.

Simons, R. K., and Lott, R. V. (1963). The morphological and anatomical development of apple injured by late spring frost. *Proc. Am. Soc. Hortic. Sci.* **83**, 88–100.

Singh, D., and Smalley, E. B. (1969a). Nitrogenous compounds in the xylem sap of American elms with Dutch elm disease. *Can. J. Bot.* **47**, 1061–1065.

Singh, D., and Smalley, E. B. (1969b). Nitrogenous compounds in the xylem sap of *Ulmus americana:* Seasonal variation in relation to Dutch elm disease susceptibility. *For. Sci.* **15**, 299–304.

Singh, H., and Johri, B. M. (1972). Development of gymnosperm seeds. *In* "Seed Biology" (T. T. Kozlowski, ed.), Vol. 1, pp. 21–75. Academic Press, New York.

Singh, L. B. (1948). Studies in biennial bearing. III. Growth studies in the "on" and "off" year trees. *J. Hortic. Sci.* **24**, 123–148.

Sinnott, E. W. (1918). Factors determining character and distribution of food reserve in woody plants. *Bot. Gaz. (Chicago)* **66**, 162–175.

Siren, G. (1963). Tree rings and climatic forecasts. *New Sci.* **346**, 18–20.

Siwecki, R., and Kozlowski, T. T. (1973). Leaf anatomy and water relations of excised leaves of six *Populus* clones. *Arbor. Kornikie* **8**, 83–105.

Skau, C. M., and Swanson, R. H. (1963). An improved heat pulse velocity meter as an indicator of sap speed and transpiration. *J. Geophys. Res.* **68**, 4743–4749.

Skene, D. S. (1969). The period of time taken by cambial derivatives to grow and differentiate into tracheids in *Pinus radiata*. D. Don. *Ann. Bot. (London)* [N.S.] **33**, 253–262.

Skene, D. S. (1972). The kinetics of tracheid development in *Tsuga canadensis* Carr. and its relation to tree vigor. *Ann. Bot. (London)* [N.S.] **36**, 179–187.

Skene, K. G. M. (1967). Gibberellin-like substances in root exudate of *Vitis vinifera*. *Planta* **74**, 250–262.

Skene, K. G. M. (1975). Cytokinin production by roots as a factor in the control of plant growth. *In* "The Development and Function of Roots" (J. G. Torrey and D. T. Clarkson, eds.), pp. 365–396. Academic Press, New York.

Slabaugh, P. E. (1957). Effects of live crown removal on the growth of red pine. *J. For.* **55**, 904–906.

Slatyer, R. O. (1956). Absorption of water from atmospheres of different humidity and its transport through plants. *Aust. J. Biol. Sci.* **9**, 552–558.

Stone, E. L. (1968). Microelement nutrition of forest trees: A review. *In* "Forest Fertilization: Theory and Practice," pp. 132–175. Tenn. Valley Auth. Muscle Shoals, Alabama.

Slatyer, R. O. (1957). The significance of the permanent wilting percentage in studies of plant and soil water relations. *Bot. Rev.* **23**, 585–636.

Slatyer, R. O. (1967). "Plant-Water Relationships." Academic Press, New York.

Slatyer, R. O., and Bierhuizen, J. F. (1964a). Transpiration from cotton leaves under a range of environmental conditions in relation to internal and external diffusive resistances. *Aust. J. Biol. Sci.* **17**, 115–130.

Slatyer, R. O., and Bierhuizen, J. F. (1964b). The influence of several transpiration suppressants on transpiration, photosynthesis, and water-use efficiency of cotton leaves. *Aust. J. Biol. Sci.* **17**, 131–146.

Slatyer, R. O., and Jarvis, P. G. (1966). A gaseous-diffusion porometer for continuous measurement of diffusive resistance of leaves. *Science* **151**, 574–576.

Slavik, B. (1974). "Methods of Studying Plant Water Relations." Academia, Prague.

Smith, A. P. (1972). Buttressing of tropical trees: A descriptive model and a new hypothesis. *Am. Nat.* **106**, 32–46.

Smith, D. M. (1962). "The Practice of Silviculture." Wiley, New York.

Smith, D. M., and Johnson, E. W. (1977). Silviculture: Highly energy efficient. *J. For.* **75**, 208–210.

Smith, D. M., and Wilsie, M. C. (1961). Some anatomical responses of loblolly pine to soil-water deficiencies. *Tappi* **44**, 179–185.

Smith, D. R., and Thorpe, T. A. (1975). Root initiation in cuttings of *Pinus radiata* seedlings. II. Growth regulator interactions. *J. Exp. Bot.* **26**, 193–202.

Smith, H., and Kefford, N. P. (1964). The chemical regulation of the dormancy phases of bud development. *Am. J. Bot.* **51**, 1002–1012.

Smith, H. C. (1966). Epicormic branching on eight species of Appalachian hardwoods. *U.S., For. Serv., Res. Note* **NE-53**.

Smith, J. H. G., Walters, J., and Kozak, A. (1968). Influences of fertilizers on cone production and growth of young Douglas-fir, western hemlock, and western red cedar on U. B. C. research forest. *U. B. C. Fac. For., Bull.* **5**.

Smith, M. E. (1943). Micronutrients essential for the growth of *Pinus radiata*. *Aust. For.* **7**, 22–85.

Smith, M. E., and Bayliss, N. S. (1942). The necessity of zinc for *Pinus radiata*. *Plant Physiol.* **17**, 303–310.

Smith, P. F., Reuther, W., and Specht, A. W. (1952). Seasonal changes in Valencia orange leaves. II. Changes in micro-elements, sodium, and carbohydrates in leaves. *Proc. Am. Soc. Hortic. Sci.* **59**, 31–35.

Smith, W. H. (1976). Character and significance of forest tree root exudates. *Ecology* **57**, 324–331.

Smith, W. R., and Goebel, N. B. (1952). The moisture content of green hickory. *J. For.* **50**, 616–618.

Smithberg, M. H., and Weiser, C. J. (1968). Patterns of variation among climatic races of red osier dogwood. *Ecology* **49**, 495–505.

Soe, K. (1959). Anatomical studies of bark regeneration following scarring. *J. Arnold Arbor., Harv. Univ.* **40**, 260–267.

Solomis, T. (1977). Cyanide-resistant respiration in higher plants. *Annu. Rev. Plant Physiol.* **28**, 279–297.

Sondheimer, E., Tzou, D. S., and Galson, E. C. (1968). Abscisic acid levels and seed dormancy. *Plant Physiol.* **43**, 1443–1447.

Sorauer, P., and Ramann, F. (1899). Sogenannte unsichtbare Rauchbeschädigungen. *Bot. Zentralbl.* **80**, 50–56, 106–116, 156–158, 205–216, and 251–262.

Southwick, F. W., and Childers, N. F. (1941). Influence of Bordeaux mixture and its component parts on transpiration and apparent photosynthesis of apple leaves. *Plant Physiol.* **16**, 721–754.

Spanner, D. C. (1958). The translocation of sugar in sieve tubes. *J. Exp. Bot.* **9**, 332–342.

Splinter, W. E. (1970). An electronic micrometer for monitoring plant growth. *Pap.–Am. Soc. Agric. Eng.* **67-111**.

Splittstoesser, W. E., and Meyer, M. M., Jr. (1971). Evergreen foliage contributions to the spring growth of *Taxus*. *Physiol. Plant.* **24**, 528–533.

Sprague, H. B., ed. (1964). "Hunger Signs in Crops" 3rd ed. Am. Soc. Agric. and Nat. Fertilizer Assoc. McKay, New York.

Sprent, J. I. (1976). Water deficits and nitrogen-fixing root nodules. *In* "Water Deficits and Plant Growth" (T. T. Kozlowski, ed.), Vol. 4, pp. 291–315. Academic Press, New York.

Spurr, S. H. (1960). "Photogrammetry and Photointerpretation." Ronald, New York.

Spurr, S. H. (1964). "Forest Ecology." Ronald, New York.

Squillace, A. E. (1971). Inheritance of monoterpene composition in cortical oleoresin of slash pine. *For. Sci.* **17**, 381–387.

Squillace, A .E. (1976). Analyses of monoterpenes by gas-liquid chromatography. *In* "Modern Methods of Forest Genetics" (J. P. Miksche, ed.), pp. 120–157. Springer-Verlag, Berlin and New York.

Squillace, A. E., and Silen, R. R. (1962). Racial variation in ponderosa pine. *For. Sci. Monogr.* **2**.

Srivastava, L. M. (1963). Secondary phloem in the Pinaceae. *Univ. Calif., Berkeley, Publ. Bot.* **36**, 1–142.

Srivastava, L. M. (1964). Anatomy, chemistry, and physiology of bark. *Int. Rev. For. Res.* **1**, 204–274.

Stålfelt, M. G. (1932). Der stomatäre Regulator in der pflanzlichen Transpiration. *Planta* **17**, 22–85.

Stadelman, E J. 1971. The protoplasmic basis for drought-resistance. A quantitative approach for measuring protoplasmic properties. *In* "Food, Fiber, and the Arid Lands" (W. G. McGinnies, B. J. Goldman, and P. Paylore, eds.), pp. 337–352. Univ. Arizona Press, Tucson.

Stålfelt, M. G. (1956). Morphologie und Anatomie des Blattes als Transpirations-organen. *Encycl. Plant Physiol.* **3**, 324–341.

Stålfelt, M. G. (1963). On the distribution of the precipitation in a spruce stand. *In* "The Water Relations of Plants" (A. J. Rutter and F. H. Whitehead, eds.), pp. 116–126. Blackwell, Oxford.

Stanley, R. G. (1958). Gross respiratory and water uptake patterns in germinating sugar pine seed. *Physiol. Plant.* **11**, 503–515.

Stanley, R. G. (1964). Physiology of pollen and pistil. *Sci. Prog.* **52**, 122–132.

Stark, N. M. (1977). Fire and nutrient cycling in a Douglas-fir/larch forest. *Ecology* **58**, 16–30.

Steinberg, R. A. (1951). Correlations between protein-carbohydrate metabolism and mineral deficiencies in plants. *In* "Mineral Nutrition of Plants" (E. Truog, ed.), pp. 359–386. Univ. of Wisconsin Press, Madison.

Stephens, G. R., Jr. (1964). Stimulation of flowering in eastern white pine. *For. Sci.* **10**, 28–34.

Steponkus, P. L., and Lanphear, F. O. (1968). The relationship of carbohydrates to cold acclimation of *Hedera helix* L.v. Thorndale. *Physiol. Plant.* **2**, 778–791.

Stevens, C. L., and Eggert, R. L. (1945). Observations on the causes of the flow of sap in red maple. *Plant Physiol.* **20**, 636–648.

Stewart, C. M. (1966). The chemistry of secondary growth in trees. *CSIRO Div. For. Prod., Tech. Pap.* **43**.

Stewart, R. E. (1975). Allelopathic potential of western bracken. *J. Chem. Ecol.* **1**, 161–169.

Stewart, W. D. P., ed. (1975). "Nitrogen Fixation by Free-Living Microorganisms." Cambridge Univ. Press, London and New York.

Stoate, T. N. (1950). Nutrition of the pine. *Bull. For. Bur., Aust.* **30**, 1–61.

Stocker, O. (1935). III. Ein Beitrag zur Transpirationsgrösse im javanischer Regenwald. *Jahrb. Wiss. Bot.* **81**, 464–496.

Stocker, O., and Ross, H. (1956). Reaktions und Restitutionsphase der Plasmaviskosität bei Dürre- und Schüttelreizen. *Naturwissenschaften* **43**, 283–284.

Stoeckeler, J. H. (1962). Shelterbelt influence on Great Plains field environment and crops. U.S.D.A. Prod. Res. Rept. **62**.

Stoeckeler, J. H., and Dortignac, E. J. (1941). Snowdrifts as a factor in growth and longevity of shelterbelts in the Great Plains. *Ecology* **22**, 117–124.

Stoeckeler, J. H., and Mason, J. W. (1956). Regeneration of aspen cutover areas in northern Wisconsin. *J. For.* **54**, 13–16.

Stone, E. C. (1957). Dew as an ecological factor. I. A review of the literature. *Ecology* **38**, 407–413.

Stone, E. C., and Fowells, H. A. (1955). The survival value of dew as determined under laboratory conditions. I. *Pinus ponderosa. For. Sci.* **1**, 183–188.

Stone, E. C., Went, F. W., and Young, C. L. (1950). Water absorption from the atmosphere by plants growing in dry soil. *Science* **111**, 546–548.

Stone, E. L. (1953). Magnesium deficiency of some northeastern pines. *Soil Sci. Soc. Am., Proc.* **17**, 297–300.

Stone, E. L. (1974). The communal root system of red pine: Growth of girdled trees. *For. Sci.* **20,** 294–305.

Stone, E. L. (1975). Effects of species on nutrient cycles and soil change. *Philos. Trans. R. Soc. London, Ser. B* **271,** 149–162.

Stone, E. L., and Kszystyniak, R. (1977). Conservation of potassium in the *Pinus resinosa* ecosystem. *Science* **198,** 192–194.

Stone, E. L., Jr., and Stone, M. H. (1954). Root collar sprouts in pine. *J. For.* **52,** 487–491.

Stone, J. E., and Stone, E. L. (1975a). Water conduction in lateral roots of red pine. *For. Sci.* **21,** 53–60.

Stone, J. E., and Stone, E. L. (1975b). The communal root system of red pine: Water conduction through root grafts. *For. Sci.* **22,** 255–262.

Stösser, R., Rasmussen, H. P., and Bukovac, M. J. (1969). A histological study of abscission layer formation in cherry fruits during maturation. *J. Am. Soc. Hortic. Sci.* **94,** 239–243.

Stout, B. B. (1961). Season influences the amount of backflash in a red pine plantation. *J. For.* **59,** 897–898.

Stout, P. R., and Hoagland, D. R. (1939). Upward and lateral movement of salt in certain plants as indicated by radioactive isotopes of potassium, sodium and phosphorus absorbed by roots. *Am. J. Bot.* **26,** 320–324.

Stover, E. L. (1944). Varying structure of conifer leaves in different habitats. *Bot. Gaz. (Chicago)* **106,** 12–25.

Strain, B. R. (1975). Field measurements of carbon dioxide exchange in some woody perennials. *In* "Perspectives in Biophysical Ecology" (D. M. Gates and R. B. Schmerl, eds.), pp. 145–158. Springer-Verlag, Berlin and New York.

Strain, B. R., Higginbotham, K. O., and Mulroy, J. C. (1976). Temperature preconditioning and photosynthetic capacity of *Pinus taeda* L. *Photosynthetica* **10,** 47–52.

Strain, H. H., and Svec, W. A. (1966). Extraction, separation and isolation of chlorophylls. *In* "Chlorophylls" (L. P. Vernon and G. R. Seely, eds.), pp. 21–66. Academic Press, New York.

Stransky, J. J., and Wilson, D. R. (1964). Terminal elongation of loblolly and shortleaf pine seedlings under soil moisture stress. *Soil Sci. Soc. Am., Proc.* **28,** 439–440.

Street, H. E., ed. (1973). "Plant Tissue and Cell Culture," Bot. Monogr. 2. Univ. of California Press, Berkeley.

Strelis, I., and Green, H. V. (1962). Tyloses and their detection. *Pulp & Pap. Mag. Can.* **63,** 307–310 and 330.

Strobel, G. A. (1974). Phytotoxins produced by plant parasites. *Annu. Rev. Plant Physiol.* **25,** 541–566.

Strugger, S. (1949). "Prakticum der Zell-und Gewebephysiologie der Pflanzen." Springer-Verlag, Berlin and New York.

Studholm, W. P., and Philipson, W. R. (1966). A comparison of the cambium in two woods with included phloem: *Heimerliriodendron brunonianum* and *Avicennia resinifera. N. Z. J. Bot.* **4,** 355–365.

Stumpf, P. K. (1976). Lipid metabolism. *In* "Plant Biochemistry" (J. Bonner and J. E. Varner, eds.), 3rd ed., pp. 428–463. Academic Press, New York.

Sutcliffe, J. F. (1976). Regulation in the whole plant. *In* "Transport in Plants." Encyclopedia of Plant Physiol. New series II B 394–417. Springer-Verlag, Berlin.

Sutton, R. F. (1969). Form and development of conifer root systems. *Commonw. For. Bur. Oxford, Engl. Tech. Commun.* **7.**

Swank, W. T., and Douglass, J. E. (1974). Streamflow greatly reduced by converting deciduous hardwood stands to pine. *Science* **185,** 857–859.

Swanson, C. A. (1943). Transpiration in American holly in relation to leaf structure. *Ohio J. Sci.* **43,** 43–46.

Swanson, R. H. (1962). An instrument for detecting sap movement in woody plants. *U.S. For. Serv., Rocky Mount. For. Range Exp. Stn., Pap.* **68.**

Swanson, R. H. (1967). Seasonal course of transpiration of lodgepole pine and Engelmann spruce. *In* "Forest Hydrology" (W. E. Sopper and H. W. Lull, eds.), pp. 419–433. Pergamon, Oxford.

Swanson, R. H., and Lee, R. (1966). Measurement of water movement from and through shrubs and trees. *J. For.* **64,** 187–190.

Sweet, G. B. (1975). Flowering and seed production. *In* "Seed Orchards" (R. Faulkner, ed.), pp. 72–82. British For. Comm. Bull. 54, London.

Sweet, G. B. and Thulin, I. J. (1973). Graft incompatibility in radiata pine in New Zealand. *N. Z. F. For. Sci.* **3,** 82–90.

Sweet, G. B., and Wareing, P. F. (1966). Role of plant growth in regulating photosynthesis. *Nature (London)* **210,** 77–79.

Sweet, G. B., and Wareing, P. F. (1968). A comparison of the rates of growth and photosynthesis in first-year seedlings of four provenances of *Pinus contorta.* Dougl. *Ann. Bot. (London)* [N.S.] **32,** 735–751.

Sweet, G. B., and Will, G. M. (1965). Precocious male cone production associated with low nutrient status in clones of *Pinus radiata. Nature (London)* **206,** 739.

Switzer, G. L., and Nelson, L. E. (1972). Nutrient accumulation and cycling in loblolly pine (*Pinus taeda* L.) plantation ecosystems: The first twenty years. *Soil Sci. Soc. Am., Proc.* **36,** 143–147.

Switzer, G. L., Nelson, L. E., and Smith, W. H. (1968). The mineral cycle in forest stands. *In* "Forest Fertilization: Theory and Practice," pp. 1–9. Tenn. Valley Auth., Muscle Shoals, Alabama.

Tai, E. A. (1977). Banana. *In* "Ecophysiology of Tropical Crops" (P. de T. Alvim and T. T. Kozlowski, eds.), pp. 441–460. Academic Press, New York.

Tainter, F. H., and French, D. W. (1973). The movement of dye solution to dwarf-mistletoe infected black spruce trees. *Can. J. For. Res.* **3,** 312–315.

Takahara, S. (1954). Influence of pruning on the growth of Sugi and Hinoki. *Bull. Tokyo Univ. For.* **46,** 1–95.

Talbert, C. M., and Holch, A. E. (1957). A study of the lobing of sun and shade leaves. *Ecology* **38,** 655–658.

Talboys, P. W. (1968). Water deficits in vascular disease. *In* "Water Deficits and Plant Growth" (T. T. Kozlowski, ed.), Vol. 2, pp. 255–311. Academic Press, New York.

Tamm, C. O. (1964). Determination of nutrient requirement of forest stands. *Int. Rev. For. Res.* **1,** 115–170.

Tamm, C. O. (1968). The evolution of forest fertilization in European silviculculture. *In* "Forest Fertilization: Theory and Practice," pp. 242–247. Tenn. Valley Auth., Muscle Shoals, Alabama.

Tanner, C. B. (1967). Measurement of evapotranspiration. *In* "Irrigation of Agricultural Lands" (R. M. Hagan, H. R. Haise, and T. R. Edminster, eds.), Monograph 11, pp. 534–574. Am. Soc. Agron. Madison, Wisconsin.

Tanner, C. B. (1968). Evaporation of water from plants and soil. *In* "Water Deficits and Plant Growth" (T. T. Kozlowski, ed.), Vol. 1, pp. 73–106. Academic Press, New York.

Taylor, B. K., and May, L. H. (1967). The nitrogen nutrition of the peach tree. II. Storage and mobilization of nitrogen in young trees. *Aust. J. Biol. Sci.* **20,** 389–411.

Taylor, F. H. (1956). Variation in sugar content of maple sap. *Vt., Agric. Exp. Stn., Bull.* **587,** 1–39.

Taylor, J. S., and Dumbroff, E. B. (1975). Bud, root, and growth-regulator activity in *Acer saccharum* during the dormant season. *Can. J. Bot.* **53,** 321–331.

Taylorson, R. B., and Hendricks, S. B. (1976). Aspects of dormancy in vascular plants. *BioScience* **26,** 95–101.

Taylorson, R. B., and Hendricks, S. B. (1977). Dormancy in seeds. *Annu. Rev. Plant Physiol.* **28,** 331–354.

Tepper, H. B. (1963). Leader growth of young pitch and shortleaf pines. *For. Sci.* **9,** 344–353.

Tepper, H. B., and Hollis, C. A. (1967). Mitotic reactivation of the terminal bud and cambium of white ash. *Science* **156,** 1635–1636.

Teskey, B. J. E., and Shoemaker, J. S. (1972). "Tree Fruit Production." Avi Publ. Co., Westport, Connecticut.

Tew, R. K. (1970). Root carbohydrate reserves in vegetative reproduction of aspen. *For. Sci.* **16,** 318–320.

Thaine, R. (1962). A translocation hypothesis based on the structure of plant cytoplasm. *J. Exp. Bot.* **13,** 152–160.

Thaine, R. (1969). Movement of sugars through plants by cytoplasmic pumping. *Nature (London)* **222,** 873–875.

Theologis, A., and Laties, G. (1978). Operation of the cyanide resistant path at various stages of ripening. *Plant Physiol.* **61**(4), suppl .p. 26.

Thielges, B. A. (1972). Intraspecific variation in foliage polyphenols of *Pinus* (subsection Sylvestres). *Silvae Genet.* **21**, 114–119.

Thimann, K. V. (1965). Toward an endocrinology of higher plants. *Recent Prog. Horm. Res.* **21**, 579–596.

Thimann, K. V. (1972). The natural plant hormones. *In* "Plant Physiology" Vol. 6B, (F. C. Steward, ed.), pp. 3–145. Academic Press, New York.

Thimann, K. V. (1974). Fifty years of plant hormone research. *Plant Physiol.* **54**, 450–453.

Thom, L. A. (1951). A study of the respiration of hardy pear buds in relation to rest period. Ph.D. Diss. Univ. of California, Berkeley.

Thomas. W. (1927). Nitrogenous metabolism of *Pyrus malus*. III. The partition of nitrogen in the leaves, one- and two-year branch growth and non-bearing spurs throughout a year's cycle. *Plant Physiol.* **2**, 109–137.

Thomas, W. A. (1967). Dye and calcium ascent in dogwood trees. *Plant Physiol.* **42**, 1800–1802.

Thor, C. J. B., and Smith, C. L. (1935). A physiological study of seasonal changes in the composition of the pecan fruit during development. *J. Agric. Res.* **50**, 97–121.

Thornber, J. P. (1975). Chlorophyll-proteins: Light harvesting and reaction center components of plants. *Annu. Rev. Plant Physiol.* **26**, 127–158.

Thornber, J. P., Alberte, R. S., Hunter, F. A., Shizowa, J. A., and Kan, K. S. (1977). The organization of chlorophyll in the plant photosynthetic unit. *Brookhaven Symp. Biol.* **28**, 132–148.

Thorne, J. H., and Koller, H. R. (1974). Influence of assimilate demand on photosynthesis, diffusive resistances, translocation and carbohydrate levels of soybean leaves. *Plant Physiol.* **54**, 201–207.

Tibbals, E. C., Carr, E. K., Gates, D. M., and Kreith, F. (1964). Radiation and convection in conifers. *Am. J. Bot.* **51**, 529–538.

Timell, T. E. (1973). Ultrastructure of the dormant and active cambial zones and the dormant phloem associated with formation of normal and compression woods in *Picea abies* (L.). Karst. *State Univ. Coll. Tech. Publ.* **96**. Environ. Sci. For. Syracuse Univ., New York.

Timmis, R. (1977). Critical forest temperatures for Douglas-fir cone buds. *Can. J. For. Res.* **7**, 19–22.

Timmis, R. and Worral, J. (1974). Translocation of dehardening and bud-break promoters in climatically "split" Douglas-fir. *Can. J. For. Res.* **4**, 229–237.

Ting, I. P., and Dugger, W. M., Jr. (1971). Ozone resistance in tobacco plants: Possible relationship to water balance. *Atmos. Environ.* **5**, 147–150.

Tingey, D. T., and Ratsch, H. C. (1978). Factors influencing isoprene emissions from live oak. *Plant Physiol.* **61**(4), Suppl: 86.

Tinklin, I. G., and Schwabe, W. W. (1970). Lateral bud dormancy in the black currant *Ribes nigrum* (L.). *Ann. Bot. (London)* [N.S.] **34**, 691–706.

Titman, P. W., and Wetmore, R. H. (1955). The growth of long and short shoots in *Cercidiphyllum. Am. J. Bot.* **42**, 364–372.

Tomaszewski, M. (1970). Auxin-gibberellin interactions in apical dominance. *Bull. Acad. Pol. Sci., Ser. Sci. Biol.* **18**, 361–366.

Tomlinson, P. B., and Gill, A. M. (1973). Growth habits of tropical trees: Some guiding principles. *In* "Tropical Forest Ecosystems in Africa and South America: A Comparative Review" (B. J. Eggers, E. S. Ayensu, and W. D. Duckworth, eds.), pp. 129–143. Smithson. Inst. Press, Washington, D.C.

Toole, V. K., Toole, E. H., Hendricks, S. B., Borthwick, H. S., and Snow, A. G., Jr. (1961). Responses of seeds of *Pinus virginiana* to light. *Plant Physiol.* **36**, 285–290.

Torrey, J. G. (1967). "Development in Flowering Plants." Macmillan, New York.

Torrey, J. G. (1976). Root hormones and plant growth. *Annu. Rev. Plant Physiol.* **27**, 435–459.

Torrey, J. G., Fosket, D. E., and Hepler, P. K. (1971). Xylem formation: A paradigm of cytodifferentiation in higher plants. *Am. Sci.* **59**, 338–352.

Toumey, J. W. (1929). Initial root habit in American trees and its bearing on regeneration. *Proc. Int. Bot. Congr. 4th, 1926* Vol. 1, pp. 713–728.

Toumey, J. W., and Durland, W. D. (1923). The effect of soaking certain tree seeds in water at greenhouse temperatures on viability and the time required for germination. *J. For.* **21**, 369–375.

Townsend, A. M. (1974). Sorption of ozone by nine shade tree species. *J. Am. Soc. Hortic. Sci.* **99**, 206–208.

Townsend, A. M., and Dochinger, L. S. (1974). Relationship of seed source and developmental stage to the ozone tolerance of *Acer rubrum* seedlings. *Atmos. Environ.* **8,** 957–961.

Tranquillini, W. (1955). Die Bedeutung des Lichtes und der Temperatur für die Kohlensäureassimilation von *Pinus cembra* Jungwuchs an einem hochalpinen Standort. *Planta* **46,** 154–178.

Tranquillini, W. (1956). Die Lichtabhängigkeit der Assimilation von Sonnen und Schattenblättern einer Buche unter ökologischen Bedingungen. *Congr. Int. Bot., Rapp. Commun., 8th, 1954* Sect. 13, pp. 100–102.

Tranquillini, W. (1957). Standortsklima, Wasserbilanz und CO_2-Gaswechsel junger Zirben (*Pinus cembra* L.) an der alpinen Waldgrenze. *Planta* **49,** 612–661.

Tranquillini, W. (1959). Die Stoffproduktion der Zirbe (*Pinus cembra* L.) an der Waldgrenze während eines Jahres. I. Standortsklima und CO_2-Assimilation. *Planta* **54,** 107–129.

Tranquillini, W. (1962). Beitrag zur Kausalanalyse des Wettbewerbs ökologisch verschiedener Holzarten. *Ber. Dtsch. Bot. Ges.* **75,** 353–364.

Tranquillini, W. (1969). Photosynthese und Transpiration einiger Holzarten bei verschieden starkem Wind. *Centralbl. Gesamte Forstwes.* **86,** 35–48.

Tranquillini, W., and Unterholzer, R. (1968). Das Wachstum zweijähriger Lärchen einheitlicher Herkunft in verschiedener Seehöhe. *Centralbl. Gesamte Forstwes.* **85,** 43–49.

Trimble, G. R., Jr., and Seegrist, D. W. (1973). Epicormic branching on hardwood trees bordering forest openings. *U.S., For. Serv., Res. Pap NE* **NE 261.**

Trip, P., Krotkov, G., and Nelson, C. D. (1963). Biosynthesis of mannitol-C^{14} from $C^{14}O_2$ by detached leaves of white ash and lilac. *Can. J. Bot.* **41,** 1005–1010.

Trippi, V. S. (1963). Studies on ontogeny and senility in plants. I. Changes in growth vigor during the juvenile and adult phases of ontogeny in *Tilia parviflora* and growth in juvenile and adult zones of *Tilia, Ilex aquifolium,* and *Robinia pseudoacacia. Phyton (Buenos Aires)* **20,** 137–145.

Tromp, J. (1970). Storage and mobilization of nitrogenous compounds in apple trees with special reference to arginine. *In* "Physiology of Tree Crops" (L. C. Luckwill and C. V. Cutting, eds.), pp. 143–159. Academic Press, London.

Troughton, J. H., and Slatyer, R. O. (1969). Plant water status, leaf temperature, and the calculated mesophyll resistance to carbon dioxide of cotton leaves. *Aust. J. Biol. Sci.* **22,** 815–827.

Tubbs, F. R. (1973a). Research fields in the interaction of rootstock and scions in woody perennials. Part I. *Hortic. Abstr.* **43,** 247–253.

Tubbs, F. R. (1973b). Research fields in the interaction of rootstock and scions in woody perennials. Part II. *Hortic. Abstr.* **43,** 325–335.

Tucker, C. M., and Evert, R. F. (1969). Seasonal development of the secondary phloem in *Acer negundo. Am. J. Bot.* **56,** 275–284.

Tukey, H. B. (1935). Growth of the embryo, seed, and pericarp of the sour cherry (*Prunus cerasus*) in relation to season of fruit ripening. *Proc. Am. Soc. Hortic. Sci.* **31,** 125–144.

Tukey, H. B., and Young, J. O. (1942). Gross morphology and histology of developing fruit of the apple. *Bot. Gaz. (Chicago)* **104,** 3–25.

Tukey, H. B., Ticknor, R. L., Hinsvark, O. N., and Wittwer, S. H. (1952). Absorption of nutrients by stems and branches of woody plants. *Science* **116,** 167–168.

Tukey, H. B., Jr. (1970). The leaching of substances from plants. *Annu. Rev. Plant Physiol.* **21,** 305–324.

Tukey, H. B., Jr., Mecklenburg, R. A., and Morgan, J. V. (1965). A mechanism for the leaching of metabolites from foliage. *In* "Isotopes and Radiation in Soil-Plant Nutrition Studies," pp. 371–385. IAEA, Vienna.

Tumanov, I. I., and Khvalin, N. N. (1967). Causes of poor cold resistance in roots of fruit trees. *Sov. Plant Physiol. (Engl. Transl.)* **14,** 763–770.

Turner, N. C., and DeRoo, H. C. (1974). Hydration of eastern hemlock as influenced by waxing and weather. *For. Sci.* **20,** 19–24.

Turrell, F. M. (1936). The area of the internal exposed surface of dicotyledon leaves. *Am. J. Bot.* **23,** 255–264.

Turrell, F. M. (1944). Correlation between internal surface and transpiration rate in mesomorphic and xeromorphic leaves grown under artificial light. *Bot. Gaz. (Chicago)* **105,** 413–425.

Turrell, F. M., and Turrell, M. E. (1943). The effect of the great drought of 1934 on the leaf structure of certain Iowa plants. *Proc. Iowa Acad. Sci.* **50,** 185–192.

Tydeman, H. M. (1964). The relation between time of leaf break and of flowering in seedling apples. *Annu. Rep., East Malling Res. Stn., Kent* 70–72.

Tyree, M. T., and Hammel, H. T. (1972). The measurement of the turgor pressure and the water relations of plants by the pressure-bomb technique. *J. Exp. Bot.* **23,** 267–282.

Uritani, I. (1976). Protein metabolism. *Encycl. Plant Physiol., New Ser.* **4,** 509–525.

Uriu, K., and Magness, J. R. (1967). Deciduous tree fruits and nuts. *In* "Irrigation of Agricultural Lands" (R. M. Hagan, H. R Haise, and T. W. Edminster, eds.), Monogr. 11, pp. 686–703. Am. Soc. Agron., Madison, Wisconsin.

Uriu, K., Davenport, D., and Hagan, R. M. (1975). Preharvest antitranspirant spray on cherries. I. Effect on fruit size. II. Postharvest fruit benefits. *Calif. Agric.* **29,** 7–11.

Ursino, D. J. (1973). The translocation of ^{14}C-photosynthate in single tree progeny of white spruce (*Picea glauca* (Moench) Voss). *Can. J. For. Res.* **3,** 315–318.

Ursino, D. J., Nelson, C. D., and Krotkov, G. (1968). Seasonal changes in the distribution of photoassimilated ^{14}C in young pine plants. *Plant Physiol.* **43,** 845–852.

Ursprung, A. (1915). Über die Kohäsion des Wassers im Farnanulus. *Ber. Dtsch. Bot. Ges.* **33,** 153–162.

Vaadia, Y. (1960). Autonomic diurnal fluctuations in rate of exudation and root pressure of decapitated sunflower plants. *Physiol. Plant.* **13,** 701–717.

Vaartaja, O. (1959). Evidence of photoperiodic ecotypes in trees. *Ecol. Monogr.* **29,** 91–111.

Van Alten, N. K., and Turner, N. C. (1975). Influence of a *Ceratocystis ulmi* toxin on water relations of elm (*Ulmus americana*). *Plant Physiol.* **55,** 312–316.

Van Bavel, C. H. M., and Verlinden, F. J. (1956). Agricultural drought in North Carolina. *N.C., Agric. Exp. Stn., Tech. Bull.* **122.**

Van Bavel, C. H. M., Nakayama, F. S., and Ehrler, W. L. (1965) Measuring transpiration resistance of leaves. *Plant Physiol.* **40,** 535–540.

Van Buitjtenen, J. P., Bilan, M. V., and Zimmerman, R. H. (1976). Morpho-physiological characteristics related to drought resistance in *Pinus taeda. In* "Tree Physiology and Yield Improvement" (M. G. R. Cannell and F. T. Last, eds.), pp. 348–359. Academic Press, New York.

van Die, J., and Willemse, P. C. M. (1975). Mineral and organic nutrients in sieve tube exudate and xylem vessel sap of *Quercus rubra* L. *Acta Bot. Neerl.* **24,** 237–239.

Van der Pijl, L. (1951). Absciss-joints in the stems and leaves of tropical plants. *Proc. K. Ned. Akad. Wet.* **42,** 574–586.

Van Steveninck, R. F. M. (1976). Effect of hormones and related substances on ion transport. *Encycl. Plant Physiol., New Ser.* **3,** 307–342. Springer-Verlag, Berlin.

Vegis, A. (1964). Dormancy in higher plants. *Annu. Rev. Plant Physiol.* **15,** 185–224.

Veihmeyer, F. J. (1927). Some factors affecting the irrigation requirements of deciduous orchards. *Hilgardia* **2,** 125–284.

Veihmeyer, F. J. (1972). The availability of soil moisture to plants: Results of empirical experiments with fruit trees. *Soil Sci.* **114,** 268–294.

Veihmeyer, F. J., and Hendrickson, A. H. (1950). Soil moisture in relation to plant growth. *Annu. Rev. Plant Physiol.* **1,** 285–304.

Veihmeyer, F. J., and Hendrickson, A. H. (1952). The effects of soil moisture on deciduous fruit trees. *Proc. Int. Hortic. Congr., 13th* Vol. 1, pp. 306–319.

Verrall, A. F., and Graham, T. W. (1935). The transmission of *Ceratostomella ulmi* through root grafts. *Phytopathology* **25,** 1039–1040.

Vieira da Silva, J. (1976) Water stress, ultrastructure and enzymatic activity. *In* "Water and Plant Life" (O. L. Lange, L. Kappen, and E.-D. Schulze, eds.), pp. 207–224. Springer-Verlag, Berlin.

Vieira da Silva, J., Naylor, A. W., and Kramer, P. J. (1974). Some ultrastructural and enzymatic effects of water stress in cotton (*Gossypium hirsutum* L.) leaves. *Proc. Natl. Acad. Sci. U.S.A.* **71,** 3243–3247.

Villiers, T. A. (1972). Seed dormancy. *In* "Seed Biology" (T. T. Kozlowski, ed.), Vol. 2, pp. 220–281. Academic Press, New York.

Villiers, T. A. (1975). "Dormancy and the Survival of Plants." Arnold, London.

Villiers, T. A., and Wareing, P. F. (1965). The possible role of low temperature in breaking the dormancy of seeds of *Fraxinus excelsior* L. *J. Exp. Bot.* **16,** 519–531.

Viro, P. J. (1974). Effects of fire on soil. *In* "Fire and Ecosystems" (T. T. Kozlcwski and C. E. Ahlgren, eds.), pp. 39–45. Academic Press, New York.

Virtanen, A. I. (1957). Investigations on nitrogen fixation by the alder. II. Associated culture of spruce and inoculated alder without combined nitrogen. *Physiol. Plant.* **10**, 164–169.

Visser, T. (1954). After-ripening and termination of apple seeds in relation to the seed coats. *Proc. K. Ned. Akad. Wet., Ser. C* **57**, 175–185.

Visser, T. (1964). Juvenile phase and growth of apple and pear seedlings. *Euphytica* **13**, 119–129.

Vité, J. P. (1961). The influence of water supply on oleoresin exudation pressure and resistance to bark beetle attack in *Pinus ponderosa. Contrib. Boyce Thompson Inst.* **21**, 37–66.

Vité, J. P., and Wood, D. L. (1961). A study of the applicability of the measurement of oleoresin exudation pressure in determining susceptibility of second growth ponderosa pine to bark beetle infestation. *Contrib. Boyce Thompson Inst.* **21**, 67–78.

Vogl, M. (1964). Physiologische und biochemische Beiträge zur Rauchschadenforschung. II. Vergleichende quantitative Messungen der SO_2und CO_2Absorption von Kiefernnadeln bei künstlicher Schwefeldioxydbegasung. *Biol. Zentralbl.* **83**, 587–594.

Vogl, M., Börtitz, S., and Polster, H. (1964). Physiologische und biochemische Beiträge zur Rauchschadenforschung. III. Der Einfluss stossartiger, starker SO_2 Begasung auf die CO_2-Absorption und einige Nadelinhaltstoffe von Fichte (*Picea Abies*) und Bergkiefer (*Pinus mugo* Turra) unter Laboratoriumsbedingungen. *Arch. Forstwes.* **13**, 1031–1043.

Voigt, G. K. (1968). Variation in nutrient uptake by trees. *In* "Forest Fertilization: Theory and Practice," pp. 20–27. Tenn. Valley Auth., Muscle Shoals, Ala.

Voigt, G. K., and Mergen, F. (1962). Seasonal variation in toxicity of *Ailanthus* leaves to pine seedlings. *Bot. Gaz. (Chicago)* **123**, 262–265.

Voigt, G. K., Richards, B. N., and Mannion, E. C. (1964). Nutrient utilization by young pitch pine. *Soil Sci. Soc. Am., Proc.* **28**, 707–709.

Voronkov, V. V. (1956). The dying off of the feeder root system in the tea plant. *Dokl. Vses. Akad. Seljsk. Nauk* **21**, 22–24; *Hortic. Abstr.* **27**, 2977 (1957).

Vozzo, J. A., and Young, R. W. (1975). Carbohydrate, lipid, and protein distribution in dormant, stratified, and germinated *Quercus nigra* embryos. *Bot. Gaz. (Chicago)* **136**, 306–311.

Wadleigh, C. H., Gauch, H. and G., Magistad, O. C. (1946). Growth and rubber accumulation in guayule as conditioned by soil salinity and irrigation regime. *U.S., Dep. Agric., Tech. Bull.* **925**.

Wakeley, P. C., and Marrero, J. (1958). Five-year intercept as site index in Southern pine plantations. *J. For.* **56**, 332–336.

Wallace, J. W., and Mansell, R. L., eds. (1975). "Biochemical Interactions Between Plants and Insects." Plenum, New York.

Wallis, G. W., and Buckland, D. B. (1955). The effect of trenching on the spread of yellow laminated root rot of Douglas-fir. *For. Chron.* **31**, 356–359.

Walter, H. (1962). "Die Vegetation der Erde in ökologischer Betrachtung." Fischer, Jena.

Ward, W. W. (1966). Epicormic branching of black and white oaks. *For. Sci.* **12**, 290–296.

Wardlaw, I. F., and Passioura, J. B., eds. (1976). "Transport and Transfer Processes in Plants." Academic Press, New York.

Waggoner, P. E., and Bravdo, B. (1967). Stomata and the hydrologic cycle. *Proc. Natl. Acad. Sci. U.S.A.* **57**, 1096–1102.

Waggoner, P. E., and Reifsnyder, W. E. (1968). Simulation of the temperature, humidity, and evaporation profiles in a leaf canopy. *J. Appl. Meterol.* **7**, 400–409.

Waggoner, P. E., and Turner, N. C. (1971). Transpiration and its control by stomata in a pine forest. *Conn., Agric. Exp. Stn., New Haven, Bull.* **726**.

Waisel, Y., and Fahn, A. (1965). The effect of environment on wood formation and cambial activity in *Robinia pseudoacacia* L. *New Phytol.* **64**, 436–442.

Waisel, Y., Noah, I., and Fahn, A. (1966). Cambial activity in *Eucalyptus camaldulensis* Dehn. II. The production of phloem and xylem elements. *New Phytol.* **65**, 319–324.

Waisel, Y., Borger, G. A., and Kozlowski, T. T. (1969). Effects of phenylmercuric acetate on stomatal movement and transpiration of excised *Betula papyrifera* Marsh. leaves. *Plant Physiol.* **44**, 685–690.

Wardrop, A. B. (1954). Observations on crossed lamellar structures in the cell walls of higher plants. *Aust. J. Bot.* **2**, 154–164.

Wardrop, A. B. (1961). The structure and organization of thickened cell walls. *Rep. For. Prod. Aust.* **476.**

Wardrop, A. B. (1962). Cell wall organization in higher plants. I. The primary wall. *Bot. Rev.* **28**, 241–285.

Wardrop, A. B. (1964). The reaction anatomy of arborescent angiosperms. *In* "The Formation of Wood in Forest Trees" (M. H. Zimmermann, ed.), pp. 405–456. Academic Press, New York.

Wardrop, A. B., and Cronshaw, J. (1962). Formation of phenolic substances in the ray parenchyma of angiosperms. *Nature (London)* **193**, 90–92.

Wardrop, A. B., and Dadswell, H. E. (1955). The nature of reaction wood. IV. Variations in cell wall organization of tension wood fibers. *Aust. J. Bot.* **3**, 177–189.

Wareing, P. F. (1951). Growth studies in woody species. III. Further photoperiodic effects in *Pinus silvestris. Physiol. Plant.* **4**, 546–562.

Wareing, P. F. (1953). Growth studies in woody species. V. Photoperiodism in dormant buds of *Fagus sylvatica* L. *Physiol. Plant.* **6**, 692–706.

Wareing, P. F. (1954). Growth studies in woody species. VI. The locus of photoperiodic perception in relation to dormancy. *Physiol. Plant.* **7**, 261–277.

Wareing, P. F. (1956). Photoperiodism in woody plants. *Annu. Rev. Plant Physiol.* **7**, 191–214.

Wareing, P. F. (1958). Reproductive development in *Pinus sylvestris. In* "The Physiology of Forest Trees" (K. V. Thimann, ed.), pp. 643–654. Ronald, New York.

Wareing, P. F. (1963). The germination of seeds. *Vistas Bot.* **3**, 195–227.

Wareing, P. F. (1964). Tree physiology in relation to genetics and breeding. *Unasylva* **18**, 1–10.

Wareing, P. F. (1965). Dormancy in plants. *Sci. Prog.* **53**, 529–537.

Wareing, P. F. (1970). Growth and its coordination in trees. *In* "Physiology of Tree Crops" (L. C. Luckwill and C. V. Cutting, eds.), pp. 1–21. Academic Press, New York.

Wareing, P. F. (1974). Plant hormones and crop growth. *J. R. Soc. Encour. Arts, Manuf. Commer.* November, 818–827.

Wareing, P. F., and Nasr, T. A. A. (1958). Gravimorphism in trees. Effects of gravity on growth, apical dominance, and flowering in fruit trees. *Nature (London)* **182**, 379–381.

Wareing, P. F., and Nasr, T. A. A. (1961). Gravimorphism in trees. Effects of gravity on growth and apical dominance in fruit trees. *Ann. Bot. (London)* [N.S.] **25**, 321–340.

Wareing, P. F., and Patrick, J. (1975). Source-sink relations and the partition of assimilates in the plant. *In* "Photosynthesis and Productivity in Different Environments" (J. P. Cooper, ed.), IBP, Vol. 3, pp. 481–499. Cambridge Univ. Press, London and New York.

Wareing, P. F., and Phillips, I. D. J. (1970). "The Control of Growth and Differentiation in Plants." Pergamon, Oxford.

Wareing, P. F., and Roberts, D. L. (1956). Photoperiodic control of cambial activity in *Robinia pseudoacacia* L. *New Phytol.* **55**, 356–366.

Wareing, P. F., and Robinson, L. W. (1963). Juvenility problems in woody plants. *Rep. For. Res.* 125–127.

Wareing, P. F., and Saunders, P. F. (1971). Hormones and dormancy. *Annu. Rev. Plant Physiol.* **22**, 261–288.

Wareing, P. F., Van Staden, V., and Webb. D. P. (1973). Endogenous hormones in the control of seed dormancy. *In* "Seed Ecology" (W. Heidecker, ed.), pp. 145–168. Pennsylvania State Univ. Press, University Park.

Wareing, P. F., Hanney, C. E. A., and Digby, J. (1964). The role of endogenous hormones in cambial activity and xylem differentiation. *In* "The Formation of Wood in Forest Trees" (M. H. Zimmermann, ed.), pp. 323–344. Academic Press, New York.

Wareing, P. F., Khalifa, M. M., and Treharne, K. J. (1968). Rate-limiting processes in photosynthesis at saturating light intensities. *Nature (London)* **220**, 453–457.

Wargo, P. M. (1976). Variation of starch content among and within roots of red and white oak trees. *For. Sci.* **22**, 468–471.

Waring, R. H., and Cleary, B. D. (1967). Plant moisture stress: Evaluation by pressure bomb. *Science* **155**, 1248 and 1253–1254.

Watson, D. J. (1952). The physiological basis of variation in yield. *Adv. Agron.* **4**, 101–145.

Weatherley, P. E. (1950). Studies in the water relations of the cotton plant. I. The field measurements of water deficits in leaves. *New Phytol.* **49**, 81–97.

Weatherley, P. E. (1976). Introduction: water movement through plants. *Phil. Trans. Roy. Soc. London,* **B273**, 435–444.

Weaver, J. E., and Clements, F. E. (1938). "Plant Ecology." McGraw-Hill, New York.

Weaver, J. E., and Mogensen, A. (1919). Relative transpiration of conifers and broadleaved trees in autumn and winter. *Bot. Gaz. (Chicago)* **68**, 393–424.

Weaver, R. J. (1972). "Plant Growth Substances in Agriculture." Freeman, San Francisco, California.

Weaver, R. J., Van Overbeek, J., and Pool, R. M. (1966). Effect of kinins on fruit set and development in *Vitis vinifera. Hilgardia* **37**, 181–201.

Webb, D. P., and Dumbroff, E. B. (1969). Factors influencing the stratification process in seeds of *Acer saccharum. Can. J. Bot.* **47**, 1555–1563.

Webb, D. P., and Wareing, P. F. (1972). Seed dormancy in *Acer*. Endogenous germination inhibitors and dormancy in *Acer pseudoplatanus* L. *Planta* **104**, 115–125.

Webb, D. P., Van Staden, J., and Wareing, P. F. (1973). Seed dormancy in *Acer*. Changes in endogenous germination inhibitors, cytokinins, and gibberellins during the breaking of dormancy in *Acer pseudoplatanus* L. *J. Exp. Bot.* **24**, 741–750.

Wedding, R. T., Riehl, L. A., and Rhoads, W. A. (1952). Effect of petroleum oil spray on photosynthesis and respiration in citrus leaves. *Plant Physiol.* **27**, 269–278.

Wedding, R. T., Erickson, L. C., and Brannaman, B. L. (1954). Effect of 2,4-dichlorophenoxyacetic acid on photosynthesis and respiration. *Plant Physiol.* **29**, 64–69.

Weide, H. (1962). Untersuchungen zur Assimilation, Atmung und Transpiration von *Sequoia glyptostroboides* (Hu et Cheng) Weide. *Arch. Forstwes.* **11**, 1209–1229.

Weinberger, J. H. (1950). Prolonged dormancy of peaches. *Proc. Am. Soc. Hortic. Sci.* **56**, 129–133.

Weiner, J., and Mirkes, K. (1972). "Forest Fertilization," Bibliogr. Ser. No. 258. Inst. Pap. Chem., Appleton, Wisconsin.

Weir, J. R. (1925). Notes on the parasitism of *Endothia gyrosa* (Schw.) Fr. *Phytopathology* **15**, 489–491.

Weiser, C. J. (1970). Cold resistance and injury in woody plants. *Science* **169**, 1269–1278.

Wells, C. G. (1968). Techniques and standards for foliar diagnosis of N deficiency in loblolly pine. *In* "Forest Fertilization: Theory and Practice," pp. 72-76. Tenn. Valley Auth., Muscle Shoals, Alabama.

Wells, C. G., Jorgensen, J. R., and Burnette, C. E. (1975). Biomass and mineral elements in a thinned loblolly pine plantation at age 16. *U.S. For. Serv., Res. Pap. SE* **126**.

Wells, C. G., Crutchfield, D. M., and Trew, I. F. (1976). Five-year volume increment from nitrogen fertilization in thinned plantations of pole-size loblolly pine. *For. Sci.* **22**, 85–100.

Wellwood, R. W. (1955). Sapwood-heartwood relationships in second growth Douglas-fir. *For. Prod. J.* **5**, 108–111.

Wenger, K. F. (1953a). The sprouting of sweetgum in relation to season of cutting and carbohydrate content. *Plant Physiol.* **28**, 35–49.

Wenger, K. F. (1953b). The effect of fertilization and injury on the cone and seed production of loblolly pine seed trees. *J. For.* **51**, 570–573.

Wenger, K. F. (1954). The stimulation of loblolly pine seed trees by preharvest release. *J. For.* **52**, 115–118.

Wenger, K. F., Ostrom, C. E., Larson, P. R., and Rudolph, T. D. (1971). Potential effects of global atmospheric conditions on forest ecosystems. *In* "Man's Impact on Terrestrial and Ocean Ecosystems" (W. M. Matthews, E. E. Smith, and E. D. Goldberg, eds.), pp. 192–202. MIT Press, Cambridge, Massachusetts.

Wenham, M. W., and Cusick, F. (1975). The growth of secondary wood fibers. *New Phytol.* **74**, 247–271.

Went, F. W. 1928. Wuchstoff und Wachstum. *Rec. Trav. Bot. Neer.* **25**, 1–116.

Went, F. W. (1942). Some physiological factors in the aging of a tree. *Proc. Natl. Shade Tree Conf., 18th, 1942* pp. 330–334.

Went, F. W. (1953). The effect of temperature on plant growth. *Annu. Rev. Plant Physiol.* **4**, 347–362.

Went, F. W. (1958). The physiology of photosynthesis in higher plants. *Preslia* **30**, 225–249.

Went, F. W. (1975). Water vapor absorption in *Prosopis*. *In* "Physiological Adaptation to the Environment" (F. J. Vernberg, ed.), pp. 67–75. Intext Educational Publications, New York.

Went, F. W., and Stark, N. (1968). The biological and mechanical role of soil fungi. *Proc. Natl. Acad. Sci. U.S.A.* **60**, 497–504.

Went, F. W., and Westergaard, M. (1949). Ecology of desert plants. III. Development of plants in the Death Valley Monument, California. *Ecology* **30**, 26–38.

Wershing, H. F., and Bailey, I. W. (1942). Seedlings as experimental material in the study of "redwood" in conifers. *J. For.* **40**, 411–414.

Westing, A. H. (1964). The longevity and aging of trees. *Gerontologist* **4**, 10–15.

Westing, A. H. (1965). Formation and function of compression wood in gymnosperms. *Bot. Rev.* **31**, 381–480.

Westing, A. H. (1968). Formation and function of compression wood in gymnosperms. II. *Bot. Rev.* **34**, 51–78.

Westwood, M. N., Batjer, L. P., and Billingsley, H. D. (1960). Effects of several organic spray materials on fruit growth and foliage efficiency of apple and pear. *Proc. Am. Soc. Hortic. Sci.* **76**, 59–67.

Wetmore, R. H., and Rier, J. P. (1963). Experimental induction of vascular tissue in callus of angiosperms. *Am. J. Bot.* **50**, 418–423.

Wetmore, R. H., and Steeves, T. A. (1971). Morphological introduction to growth and development. *In* "Plant Physiology" Vol. 6A (F. C. Steward, ed.), pp. 3–166. Academic Press, New York.

White, D. P., and Leaf, A. L. (1957). Forest fertilization. *State Univ. Coll. For., Syracuse Univ., Tech. Publ.* **81**.

White, P. R., Schuker, E., Kern, J. R., and Fuller, F. H. (1958). "Root-pressure" in gymnosperms. *Science* **128**, 308–309.

Whiteman, P. C., and Koller, D. (1964). Saturation deficit of the mesophyll evaporation surfaces in a desert halophyte. *Science* **146**, 1320–1321.

Whitfield, C. J. (1932). Ecological aspects of transpiration. II. Pikes Peak and Santa Barbara regions: Edaphic and climatic aspects. *Bot. Gaz. (Chicago)* **94**, 183–196.

Whitford, L. A. (1956). A theory on the formation of cypress knees. *J. Elisha Mitchell Sci. Soc.* **72**, 80–83.

Whitmore, F. W., and Zahner, R. (1966). Development of the xylem ring in stems of young red pine trees. *For. Sci.* **12**, 198–210.

Whitmore, F. W., and Zahner, R. (1967). Evidence for a direct effect of water stress in the metabolism of cell wall in *Pinus*. *For. Sci.* **13**, 397–400.

Whittaker, R. H. (1970). The biochemical ecology of higher plants. *In* "Chemical Ecology" (E. Sondheimer and J. B. Simeone, eds.), pp. 43–70. Academic Press, New York.

Whittingham, C. P. (1974). "The Mechanism of Photosynthesis." Arnold, London.

Wichmann, H. E. (1925). Wurzelwachsungen und Stockuberwallung bei Abietineen. *Zentralbl. Gesamte Forstwes.* **51**, 250–258.

Wickson, M., and Thimann, K. V. (1958). The antagonism of auxin and kinetin in apical dominance. *Physiol. Plant.* **11**, 62–74.

Wiebe, H. H., and Kramer, P. J. (1954). Translocation of radioactive isotopes from various regions of roots of barley seedlings. *Plant Physiol.* **29**, 342–348.

Wiebe, H. H., Campbell, G. S., Gardner, W. H., Rawlins, S. L., Cary, J. W., and Brown, R. W. (1971). Measurement of plant and soil water status. *Utah, Agric. Exp. Stn., Bull.* **484**.

Wieckowski, S. (1958). Studies on the autumnal breakdown of chlorophyll. *Acta Biol. Cracov., Ser. Bot.* **1**, 131–135.

Wieler, A. (1893). Das Bluten der Pflanzen. *Beitr. Biol. Pflanz.* **6**, 1–211.

Wiggans, C. C. (1936). The effect of orchard plants on subsoil moisture. *Proc. Am. Soc. Hortic. Sci.* **33**, 103–107.

Wiggans, C. C. (1937). Some further observations on the depletion of subsoil moisture by apple trees. *Proc. Am. Soc. Hortic. Sci.* **34**, 160–163.

Wilcox, H. (1940). The spectrographic analysis of white pine. M.S. Thesis, New York State College of Forestry, Syracuse, New York.

Wilcox, H. (1954). Primary organization of active and dormant roots of noble fir. *Abies procera. Am. J. Bot.* **41**, 818–821.

Wilcox, H. (1962a). Cambial growth characteristics. *In* "Tree Growth" (T. T. Kozlowski, ed.), pp. 57–88. Ronald, New York.

Wilcox, H. (1962b). Growth studies of the root of incense cedar, *Libocedrus decurrens*. II. Morphological features of the root system and growth behavior. *Am. J. Bot.* **49**, 237–245.

Wilcox, H. (1964). Xylem in roots of *Pinus resinosa* Ait. in relation to heterorhizy and growth activity. *In* "The Formation of Wood in Forest Trees" (M. H. Zimmermann, ed.), pp. 459–478. Academic Press, New York.

Wilcox, H. (1968). Morphological studies of the root of red pine, *Pinus resinosa*. I. Growth characteristics and patterns of branching. *Am. J. Bot.* **55**, 247–254.

Wilde, S. A. (1954). Mycorrhizal fungi: Their distribution and effect on tree growth. *Soil Sci.* **78**, 23–31.

Willemot, C. (1977). Simultaneous inhibition of linolenic acid synthesis in winter wheat roots and frost hardening by BASF 13-338, a derivative of pyridazine. *Plant Physiol.* **60**, 1–4.

Williams, R. F. (1955). Redistribution of mineral elements during development. *Annu. Rev. Plant Physiol.* **6**, 25–40.

Williamson, M. J. (1966). Premature abscissions and white oak acorn crops. *For. Sci.* **12**, 19–21.

Willis, C. P. (1917). Incidental results of a study of Douglas-fir seed in the Pacific Northwest. *J. For.* **15**, 991–1002.

Wilm, H. G., and Dunford, E. G. (1948). Effect of timber cutting on water available for stream flow from a lodgepole pine forest. *U.S., Dep. Agric., Tech. Bull.* **968.**

Wilson, B. F. (1963). Increase in cell wall surface area during enlargement of cambial derivatives in *Abies concolor. Am. J. Bot.* **50**, 95–102.

Wilson, B. F. (1964). Structure and growth of woody roots of *Acer rubrum* L. *Harvard For. Pap.* No. 11.

Wilson, B. F. (1966). Development of the shoot system of *Acer rubrum. Harvard For. Pap.* No. 14.

Wilson, B. F. (1967). Root growth around barriers. *Bot. Gaz. (Chicago)* **128**, 79–82.

Wilson, B. F. (1968a). Red maple stump sprouts. Development the first year. *Harvard For. Pap.* **18.**

Wilson, B. F. (1968b). Effect of girdling on cambial activity in white pine. *Can. J. Bot.* **46**, 141–146.

Wilson, B. F. (1975). Distribution of secondary thickening in tree root systems. *In* "The Development and Function of Roots" (J. G. Torrey and D. T. Clarkson, eds.), pp. 197–219. Academic Press, New York.

Wilson, B. F., and Bachelard, E. P. (1975). Effects of girdling and defoliation on root activity and survival of *Eucalyptus regnans* and *E. viminalis* seedlings. *Aust. J. Plant Physiol.* **2**, 197–206.

Wilson, B. F., and Fischer, B. C. (1977). Striped maple: Shoot growth and bud formation related to light intensity. *Can. J. For. Res.* **7**, 1–7.

Wilson, B. F., Wodzicki, T., and Zahner, R. (1966). Differentiation of cambial derivatives: Proposed terminology, *For. Sci.* **12**, 438–440.

Wilson, C. C. (1948). Fog and atmospheric carbon dioxide as related to apparent photosynthetic rate of some broadleaf evergreens. *Ecology* **29**, 507–508.

Winget, C. H., and Kozlowski, T. T. (1965a). Yellow birch germination and seedling growth. *For. Sci.* **11**, 386–392.

Winget, C. H., and Kozlowski, T. T. (1965b). Seasonal basal area growth as an expression of competition in northern hardwoods. *Ecology* **46**, 786–793.

Winkler, E. (1957). Klimaelemente für Innsbruck (582 m) und Patscherkofel (1909 m) im Zusammenhang mit der Assimilation von Fichten in Verschiedenen Hohenlagen. *Veröff. Mus. Ferdinandeum Innsbruck* **37**, 19–48.

Winton, L., and Huhtinen, O. (1976). Tissue culture of trees. *In* "Modern Methods in Forest Genetics" (J. Miksche, ed.), pp. 243–264. Springer-Verlag, Berlin and New York.

Wise, L. E., and Jahn, E. C. (1952). "Wood Chemistry," Vol. I. Van Nostrand. Reinhold, Princeton, New Jersey.

Wittwer, S. H., and Robb, W. (1964). Carbon dioxide enrichment of greenhouse atmospheres for food crop production. *Econ. Bot.* **18**, 34–56.

Wodzicki, T. J. (1965). Annual ring of wood formation and seasonal changes of natural growth-inhibitors in larch. *Acta Soc. Bot. Pol.* **34**, 117–151.

Wodzicki, T. J., and Brown, C. L. (1973a). Cellular differentiation of the cambium in the Pinaceae. *Bot. Gaz. (Chicago)* **134**, 139–146.

Wodzicki, T. J., and Brown, C. L. (1973b). Organization and breakdown of the protoplast during maturation of pine tracheids. *Am. J. Bot.* **60**, 631–640.

Wodzicki, T. J., and Wodzicki, A. B. (1973). Auxin stimulation of cambial activity in *Pinus silvestris*. II. Dependence upon basipetal transport. *Physiol. Plant.* **29**, 288–292.

Wodzicki, T. J., and Zajaczkowski, S. (1974). Effect of auxin on xylem tracheids differentiation in decapitated stems of *Pinus silvestris* L. and its interaction with some vitamins and growth regulators. *Acta Soc. Bot. Pol.* **43**, 129–148.

Wolf, F. T. (1956). Changes in chlorophylls A and B in autumn leaves. *Am. J. Bot.* **43**, 714–718.

Wolfe, J. W., Lombard, P. B., and Tabor, N. (1976). The effectiveness of a mist versus a low pressure sprinkler system for bloom delay. *Trans. ASAE* **19**, 510–513.

Wolff, I. A. (1966). Seed lipids. *Science* **154**, 1140–1149.

Wolter, K. E. (1977). Ethylene-potential alternative to bipyridilium herbicides for inducing lightwood in pine. *Proc. Lightwood Res. Coord. Counc., 1977,* pp. 90–99.

Woodman, J. N. (1971). Variation of net photosynthesis within the crown of a large forest-grown conifer. *Photosynthetica* **5**, 50–54.

Woods, D. B., and Turner, N. C. (1971). Stomatal response to changing light by four tree species of varying shade tolerance. *New Phytol.* **70**, 77–84.

Woods, F. W., and Brock, K. (1964). Interspecific transfer of Ca^{45} and P^{32} by root systems. *Ecology* **38**, 357–359.

Woodwell, G. M. (1970). Effects of pollution on the structure and physiology of ecosystems. *Science* **168**, 429–433.

Woolley, J. T. (1961). Mechanisms by which wind influences transpiration. *Plant Physiol.* **36**, 112–114.

Worley, C. L., Lesselbaum, H. R., and Mathews, T. M. (1941). Deficiency symptoms for the major elements in seedlings of three broad-leaved trees. *J. Tenn. Acad. Sci.* **6**, 239–247.

Worley, J. F., and Hacskaylo, E. (1959). The effect of available moisture on the mycorrhizal association of Virginia pine. *For. Sci.* **5**, 267–278.

Worral, J. (1973). Seasonal, daily, and hourly growth of height and radius in Norway spruce. *Can. J. For. Res.* **3**, 501–511.

Wright, J. W. (1952). Pollen dispersion of some forest trees. *U.S., For Serv., Northeast. For. Exp. Stn. Pap.* **46.**

Wright, J. W. (1953). Pollen dispersion studies; some practical applications. *J. For.* **51**, 114–118.

Wright, J. W. (1962). Genetics of forest tree improvement. *FAO For. For. Prod. Stud.* **16.**

Wright, J. W. (1976). "Introduction to Forest Genetics." Academic Press, New York.

Wu, C. C., Kozlowski, T. T., Evert, R. F., and Sasaki, S. (1971). Effects of direct contact on *Pinus resinosa* seeds and young seedlings with 2,4-D or picloram on seedling development. *Can. J. Bot.* **49**, 1737–1741.

Wuenscher, J. E., and Kozlowski, T. T. (1971a). Relationship of gas-exchange resistance to tree-seedling ecology. *Ecology* **52**, 1016–1029.

Wuenscher, J. E., and Kozlowski, T. T. (1971b). The response of transpiration resistance to leaf temperature as a desiccation resistance mechanism in trees. *Physiol. Plant.* **24**, 254–259.

Wylie, R. B. (1951). Principles of foliar organization shown by sun-shade leaves from ten species of deciduous dicotyledon trees. *Am. J. Bot.* **38**, 355–361.

Wyman, D. (1950). Order of bloom. *Arnoldia (Boston)* **10**, 41–56.

Yazawa, K., and Ishida, S. (1965). On the wet heartwood of some broadleaved trees grown in Japan. II. Seasonal moisture content of Yachi-damo and Haru-nire by months. *J. Fac. Agric., Hokkaido Univ.* **54**, Part 2, 123–136.

Yelenosky, G. (1964). The tolerance of trees to poor soil aeration. Ph.D. Dissertation, Duke University, Durham, North Carolina.

Yokoyama, H., Hayman, E. P., Hsu, W. J., Poling, S. M., and Baumann, A. J. (1977). Chemical bio-induction of rubber in guayule plant. *Science* **197**, 1076–1078.

Yoshida, S., and Sakai, A. (1967). The frost hardening process of woody plants. XIII. Relation between frost resistance and various substances in stem bark of black locust trees. *Contrib. Inst. Low Temp. Sci., Hokkaido Univ., Ser. B* **25**, 29–44.

Young, H. E. (1976). Muka: A good Russian idea. *J. For.* **74**, 160.

Young, H. E., and Kramer, P. J. (1952). The effect of pruning on the height and diameter growth of loblolly pine. *J. For.* **50**, 474–479.

Youngberg, C. T., and Davey, C. R., eds. (1970). "Tree Growth and Forest Soils." Oregon State Univ. Press, Corvallis.

Zaerr, J. B. (1971). Moisture stress and stem diameter in young douglas-fir. *For. Sci.* **17**, 466–469.

Zahner, R. (1955). Soil water depletion by pine and hardwood stands during a dry season. *For. Sci.* **1**, 258–264.

Zahner, R. (1958). September rains bring growth gains. *U.S. For. Serv., South. For. Exp. Stn., For. Note* **113.**

Zahner, R. (1962). Terminal growth and wood formation by juvenile loblolly pine under two soil moisture regimes. *For. Sci.* **8**, 345–352.

Zahner, R. (1968). Water deficits and growth of trees. *In* "Water Deficits and Plant Growth" (T. T. Kozlowski, ed.), Vol. 2, pp. 191–254. Academic Press, New York.

Zahner, R., and Donnelly, J. R. (1967). Refining correlations of water deficits and radial growth in red pine. *Ecology* **48**, 525–530.

Zahner, R., and Oliver, W. W. (1962). The influence of thinning and pruning on the date of summerwood initiation in red and jack pines. *For. Sci.* **8**, 51–63.

Zahner, R., and Stage, A. R. (1966). A procedure for calculating daily moisture stress and its utility in regressions of tree growth on weather. *Ecology* **47**, 64–74.

Zajaczkowska, J. (1974). Gas exchange and organic substance production of Scots pine (*Pinus silvestris* L.) seedlings grown in soil cultures with ammonium or nitrate form of nitrogen. *Acta Soc. Bot. Pol.* **43**, 103–116.

Zajaczkowski, S. (1973). Auxin stimulation of cambial activity in *Pinus silvestris*. I. The differential cambial response. *Physiol. Plant.* **29**, 281–287.

Zak, B. (1964). Role of mycorrhizae in root disease. *Annu. Rev. Phytopathol.* **2**, 377–392.

Zalasky, H. (1976). Frost damage in poplar on the prairies. *For. Chron.* **52**, 61–64.

Zasada, J. C. (1971). Frost damage to white spruce cones in interior Alaska. *U.S., For. Serv., Res. Note PNW* **149.**

Zasada, J. C., and Zahner, R. (1969). Vessel element development in the earlywood of red oak (*Quercus rubra*). *Can. J. Bot.* **47**, 1965–1971.

Zavitkovski, J., and Ferrell, W. K. (1970). Effect of drought upon rates of photosynthesis, respiration, and transpiration of seedlings of two ecotypes of Douglas-fir. II. Two-year-old seedlings. *Photosynthetica* **4**, 58–67.

Zavitkovski, J., Isebrands, J. G., and Crow, T. R. (1974). Application of growth analysis in forest biomass studies. *In* "Proceedings of the North American Biology Workshop, Third" (C. P. P. Reid and G. H. Fechner, eds.), pp. 196–226. Colorado State University, Fort Collins.

Zeevart, J. A. D. (1976). Physiology of flower formation. *Annu. Rev. Plant Physiol.* **27**, 321–348.

Zeikus, J. G., and Ward, J. C. (1974). Methane formation in living trees: A microbial origin. *Science* **184**, 1181–1183.

Zelawski, W. (1957). Dalsze badania reakcji fotoperiodycznej siewek modrzewia (*Larix europaea* D.C.). *Acta Soc. Bot. Pol.* **26**, 79–103.

Zelawski, W., and Goral, I. (1966). Seasonal changes in the photosynthetic rate of Scots pine seedlings grown from seed of varicus provenances. *Acta Soc. Bot. Pol.* **35**, 587–598.

Zelawski, W., and Walker, R. B. (1976). Photosynthesis, respiration, and dry matter production. *In* "Modern Methods in Forest Genetics" (J. P. Miksche, ed.), pp. 89–119. Springer-Verlag, Berlin and New York.

Zelitch, I. (1961). Biochemical control of stomatal opening in leaves. *Proc. Natl. Acad. Sci. U.S.A.* **47**, 1423–1433.

Zelitch, I. (1969). Stomatal control. *Annu. Rev. Plant Physiol.* **20**, 329–350.

Zelitch, I. (1971). "Photosynthesis, Photorespiration, and Plant Productivity." Academic Press, New York.

Zeller, O. (1955). Entwicklungsverlauf auf der Infloreszenknospen einiger Kernund Steinobstsorten. *Angew. Bot.* **29,** 69–89.

Ziegler, H. (1964). Storage, mobilization, and distribution of reserve material in trees. *In* "The Formation of Wood in Forest Trees" (M. H. Zimmermann, ed.), pp. 303–320. Academic Press. New York.

Ziegler, H. (1965). Use of isotopes in the study of translocation in rays. *In* "Isotopes and Radiation in Soil-Plant Nutrition Studies," pp. 361–370. IAEA, Vienna.

Ziegler, H. (1975). Nature of transported substances. *In* "Transport in Plants" (M. H. Zimmermann and J. A. Milburn, eds.), pp. 59–100. Springer-Verlag, Berlin and New York.

Zimmer, W. J., and Grose, R. J. (1958). Root systems and root-shoot ratios of seedlings of some Victorian Eucalypts. *Aust. For.* **22,** 13–18.

Zimmermann, M. H. (1957). Translocation of organic substances in trees. I. The nature of sugars in the sieve tube exudate of trees. *Plant Physiol.* **32,** 288–291.

Zimmermann, M. H. (1961). Movement of organic substances in trees. *Science* **133,** 73–79

Zimmermann, M. H. (1964). Effect of low temperature on ascent of sap in trees. *Plant Physiol.* **39,** 568–572.

Zimmermann, M. H., and Brown, C. L. (1971). "Trees: Structure and Function." Springer-Verlag, Berlin and New York.

Zimmermann, M. H., and Milburn, J. A., eds. (1975). "Transport in Plants I. Phloem Transport." Springer-Verlag, Berlin and New York.

Zimmerman, U. (1978). Physics of turgor and osmoregulation. *Annu. Rev. Plant Physiol* .**29,** 121–148.

Zobel, B. J. (1951). Oleoresin composition as a determinant of pine hybridity. *Bot. Gaz. (Chicago)* **113,** 221–227.

Index